Hoover's Handbook of

World Business 2016

HOOVERS™
A D&B COMPANY

Austin, Texas

HOOVERS™
A D&B COMPANY

10 9 8 7 6 5 4 3 2 1

Publishers Cataloging-in-Publication Data
Hoover's Handbook of World Business 2016

Includes indexes.

ISBN 978-1-63053-823-1

ISSN 1055-7199

1. Business enterprises — Directories. 2. Corporations — Directories.

HF3010 338.7

U.S. AND WORLD BOOK SALES

Mergent Inc.
580 Kingsley Park Drive
Fort Mill, SC
29715
Phone: 800-342-5647
e-mail: orders@mergent.com
Web: www.mergentbusinesspress.com

Mergent Inc.

CEO: Jonathan Worrall

Executive Managing Director: John Pedernales

Executive Vice President of Sales: Fred Jenkins

Managing Director of Relationship Management: Chris Henry

Managing Director of Print Products: Thomas Wecera

Production Research: Charlot Volny

MERGENT CUSTOMER SERVICE

Support and Fulfillment Manager: Melanie Horvat

ABOUT MERGENT, INC.

Mergent, Inc. is a leading provider of business and financial data on global publicly listed companies. Based in the U.S, the company maintains a strong global presence, with offices in New York, Charlotte, San Diego, London, Tokyo and Melbourne.

Founded in 1900, Mergent operates one of the longest continuously collected databases of: descriptive and fundamental information on domestic and international companies; pricing and terms and conditions data on fixed income and equity securities; and corporate action data.

In addition, Mergent's Indxis subsidiary develops and licenses equity and fixed income investment products based on its proprietary investment methodologies. Our licensed products have over $9 billion in assets under management and are offered by major investment management firms. The Indxis calculation platform is the chosen technology for some of the world's largest index companies. Its index calculation and pricing distribution protocols are used to administer index rules and distribute real-time pricing data.

Abbreviations

AB – Aktiebolag (Swedish)*
ADR – American Depositary Receipts
AG – Aktiengesellschaft (German)*
AFL-CIO – American Federation of Labor and Congress of Industrial Organizations
AMEX – American Stock Exchange
A/S – Aktieselskab (Danish)*
ASA – Allmenne Aksjeselskaper (Norwegian)*
ATM – asynchronous transfer mode; automated teller machine
CAD/CAM – computer-aided design/computer-aided manufacturing
CASE – computer-aided software engineering
CD-ROM – compact disc – read-only memory
CEO – chief executive officer
CFO – chief financial officer
CMOS – complementary metal-oxide semiconductor
COMECON – Council for Mutual Economic Assistance
COO – chief operating officer
DAT – digital audio tape
DOD – Department of Defense
DOE – Department of Energy
DOT – Department of Transportation
DRAM – dynamic random-access memory
DVD – digital versatile disc/digital video disc
EC – European Community
EPA – Environmental Protection Agency
EPS – earnings per share
EU – European Union
EVP – executive vice president
FCC – Federal Communications Commission
FDA – Food and Drug Administration
FDIC – Federal Deposit Insurance Corporation
FTC – Federal Trade Commission
GATT – General Agreement on Tariffs and Trade
GmbH – Gesellschaft mit beschränkter Haftung (German)*
GNP – gross national product
HDTV – high-definition television
HMO – health maintenance organization
HR – human resources
HTML – hypertext markup language
ICC – Interstate Commerce Commission
IMF – International Monetary Fund
IPO – initial public offering
IRS – Internal Revenue Service
KGaA – Kommanditgesellschaft auf Aktien (German)*
LAN – local-area network
LBO – leveraged buyout
LNG – liquefied natural gas
LP – limited partnership
Ltd. – Limited
MFN – Most Favored Nation
MITI – Ministry of International Trade and Industry (Japan)
NAFTA – North American Free Trade Agreement
Nasdaq – National Association of Securities Dealers Automated Quotations
NATO – North Atlantic Treaty Organization
NV – Naamlose Vennootschap (Dutch)*
NYSE – New York Stock Exchange
OAO – open joint stock company (Russian)
OAS – Organization of American States
OECD – Organization for Economic Cooperation and Development
OEM – original equipment manufacturer
OOO – limited liability company (Russian)
OPEC – Organization of Petroleum Exporting Countries
OS – operating system
OTC – over-the-counter
P/E – price-to-earnings ratio
PLC – public limited company (UK)*
RAM – random-access memory
R&D – research and development
RISC – reduced instruction set computer
ROA – return on assets
ROI – return on investment
SA – Société Anonyme (French)*; Sociedad(e) Anónima (Spanish and Portuguese)*
SA de CV – Sociedad Anónima de Capital Variable (Spanish)*
SEC – Securities and Exchange Commission
SEVP – senior executive vice president
SIC – Standard Industrial Classification
SpA – Società per Azioni (Italian)*
SPARC – scalable processor architecture
SVP – senior vice president
VAR – value-added reseller
VAT – value-added tax
VC – venture capitalist
VP – vice president
WAN – wide-area network
WWW – World Wide Web
ZAO – closed joint stock company (Russian)

* These abbreviations are used in companies' names to convey that the companies are limited liability enterprises; the meanings are usually the equivalent of *corporation* or *incorporated*.

Contents

List of Lists

HOOVER'S RANKINGS

Companies Profiled

Companies Profiled (continued)

About Hoover's Handbook of World Business 2016

This edition of *Hoover's Handbook of World Business* is focused on its mission of providing you with premier coverage of the global business scene. Featuring 300 of the world's most influential companies based outside of the United States, this book is one of the most complete sources of in-depth information on large, non-US-based business enterprises available anywhere.

Hoover's Handbook of World Business is one of our four-title series of handbooks that covers, literally, the world of business. The series is available as an indexed set, and also includes *Hoover's Handbook of American Business*, *Hoover's Handbook of Private Companies*, and *Hoover's Handbook of Emerging Companies*. This series brings you information on the biggest, fastest-growing, and most influential enterprises in the world.

HOOVER'S ONLINE FOR BUSINESS NEEDS

In addition to Hoover's widely used MasterList and Handbooks series, comprehensive coverage of more than 40,000 business enterprises is available in electronic format on our Web site at www.hoovers.com. Our goal is to provide our customers the fastest path to business with insight and actionable information about companies, industries, and key decision makers, along with the powerful tools to find and connect to the right people to get business done. Hoover's has partnered with other prestigious business information and service providers to bring you all the right business information, services, and links in one place.

We welcome the recognition we have received as the premier provider of high-quality company information — online, electronically, and in print — and continue to look for ways to make our products more available and more useful to you.

We believe that anyone who buys from, sells to, invests in, lends to, competes with, interviews with, or works for a company should know all there is to know about that enterprise. Taken together, this book and the other Hoover's products and resources represent the most complete source of basic corporate information readily available to the general public.

HOW TO USE THIS BOOK

This book has four sections:

1. "Using Hoover's Handbooks" describes the contents of our profiles and explains the ways in which we gather and compile our data.

2. "A List-Lover's Compendium" contains lists of the largest, fastest-growing, and most valuable companies of global importance.

3. The company profiles section makes up the largest and most important part of the book — 300 profiles of major business enterprises, arranged alphabetically.

4. Three indexes complete the book. The first sorts companies by industry groups, the second by headquarters location. The third index is a list of all the executives found in the Executives section of each company profile.

Using Hoover's Handbooks

SELECTION OF THE COMPANIES PROFILED

The 500 profiles in this book include a variety of international enterprises, ranging from some of the largest publicly traded companies in the world — Daimler AG, for example — to Malaysia's largest and oldest conglomerate, Sime Darby Berhad. It also includes many private businesses, such as Bertelsmann AG and LEGO, as well as a selection of government-owned entities, such as Mexico's Petróleos Mexicanos. The companies selected represent a cross-section of the largest, most influential, and most interesting companies based outside the United States.

In selecting these companies, we followed several basic criteria. We started with the global giants, including Toyota and Royal Dutch Shell, and then looked at companies with substantial activity in the US, such as Vivendi and Diageo. We also included companies that dominate their industries (e.g., AB Electrolux, the world's #1 producer of household appliances), as well as representative companies from around the world (an Indian conglomerate, Tata; two firms from Finland, Nokia and Stora Enso Oyj; and two companies from Russia, OAO Gazprom and OAO LUKOIL). Companies that weren't necessarily global powerhouses but that had a high profile with consumers (e.g., IKEA) or had interesting stories (Virgin Group) were included. Finally, because of their truly global reach, we added the Big Four accounting firms (even though they are headquartered or co-headquartered in the US).

ORGANIZATION

The profiles are presented in alphabetical order. You will find the commonly used name of the enterprise at the beginning of the profile; the full, legal name is found in the Locations section. For some companies, primarily Japanese, the commonly translated English name differs from the actual legal name of the company, so both are provided. (The legal name of Nippon Steel Corporation is Shin Nippon Seitetsu Kabushiki Kaisha.) If a company name starts with a person's first name (e.g., George Weston Limited), it is alphabetized under the first name. We've also tried to alphabetize companies where you would expect to find them — for example, Deutsche Lufthansa is in the L's and Grupo Televisa can be found under T.

The annual financial information contained in the profiles is current through fiscal year-ends occurring as late as December 2015. We have included certain nonfinancial developments, such as officer changes, through December 2015.

OVERVIEW

In the first section of the profile, we have tried to give a thumbnail description of the company and what it does. The description will usually include information on the company's strategy, reputation, and ownership. We recommend that you read this section first.

HISTORY

This extended section, which is present for most companies, reflects our belief that every enterprise is the sum of its history and that you have to know where you came from in order to know where you are going. While some companies have limited historical awareness, we think the vast majority of the enterprises in this book have colorful backgrounds. We have tried to focus on the people who made the enterprises what they are today. We have found these histories to be full of twists and ironies; they make fascinating reading.

EXECUTIVES

Here we list the names of the people who run the company, insofar as space allows. We have shown age and pay information where available, although most non-US companies are not required to report the level of detail revealed in the US.

Although companies are free to structure their management titles any way they please, most modern corporations follow standard practices. The ultimate power in any corporation lies with the shareholders, who elect a board of directors, usually including officers or "insiders," as well as individuals from outside the company. The chief officer, the person on whose desk the buck stops, is usually called the chief executive officer (CEO) in the US. In other countries, practices vary widely. In the UK, traditionally, the Managing Director performs the functions of the CEO without the title, although the use of the term

CEO is on the rise there. In Germany it is customary to have two boards of directors: a managing board populated by the top executives of the company and a higher-level supervisory board consisting of outsiders.

As corporate management has become more complex, it is common for the CEO to have a "right-hand person" who oversees the day-to-day operations of the company, allowing the CEO plenty of time to focus on strategy and long-term issues. This right-hand person is usually designated the chief operating officer (COO) and is often the president of the company. In other cases one person is both chairman and president.

We have tried to list each company's most important officers, including the chief financial officer (CFO) and the chief legal officer. For companies with US operations, we have included the names of the US CEO, CFO, and top human resources executive, where available.

The people named in the Executives section are indexed at the back of the book.

The Executives section also includes the name of the company's auditing (accounting) firm, where available.

LOCATIONS

Here we include the company's full legal name and its headquarters, street address, telephone and fax numbers, and Web site, as available. We also list the same information for the US office for each company, if one exists. Telephone numbers of foreign offices are shown using the standardized conventions of international dialing. The back of the book includes an index of companies by headquarters location.

In some cases we have also included information on the geographic distribution of the company's business, including sales and profit data. Note that these profit numbers, like those in the Products/Operations section below, are usually operating or pretax profits rather than net profits. Operating profits are generally those before financing costs (interest income and payments) and before taxes, which are considered costs attributable to the whole company rather than to one division or part of the world. For this reason the net income figures (in the Historical Financials section) are usually much lower, since they are after interest and taxes. Pretax profits are after interest but before taxes.

PRODUCTS/OPERATIONS

This section lists as many of the company's products, services, brand names, divisions, subsidiaries, and joint ventures as we could fit. We have tried to include all its major lines and all familiar brand names. The nature of this section varies by company and the amount of information available. If the company publishes sales and profit information by type of business, we have included it (in US dollars).

COMPETITORS

In this section we have listed enterprises that compete with the profiled company. This feature is included as a quick way to locate similar companies and compare them. Because of the difficulty in identifying companies that only compete in foreign markets, the list of competitors is still weighted to large international companies with a strong US presence.

HISTORICAL FINANCIALS

Here we have tried to present as much data about each enterprise's financial performance as we could compile in the allocated space. Financial data for all companies is presented in US dollars, using the appropriate exchange rate at fiscal year-end.

While the information presented varies somewhat from industry to industry, it is less complete in the case of private companies that do not release data (although we have always tried to provide annual sales and employment). The following information is generally present.

A five-year table, with relevant annualized compound growth rates, covers:

- Sales — fiscal year sales (year-end assets for most financial companies)
- Net income — fiscal year net income (before accounting changes)
- Net profit margin — fiscal year net income as a percent of sales (as a percent of assets for most financial firms)
- Employees — fiscal year-end or average number of employees
- Stock price — the fiscal year close
- P/E — high and low price/earnings ratio
- Earnings per share — fiscal year earnings per share (EPS)
- Dividends per share — fiscal year dividends per share

The information on the number of employees is intended to aid the reader interested in knowing whether a company has a long-term trend of increasing or decreasing employment. As far as we know, we are the only company that publishes this information in print format.

The numbers on the left in each row of the Historical Financials section give the month and the year in which the company's fiscal year actually ends. Thus, a company with a September 30, 2015, year-end is shown as 9/15.

In addition, we have provided in graph form a stock price history for companies that trade on the major US exchanges. The graphs, covering up to five years, show the range of trading between the high and the low price, as well as the closing price for each fiscal year. For public companies that trade on the OTC or Pink Sheets or that do not trade on US exchanges, we graph net income. Generally, for private companies, we have graphed net income, or, if that is unavailable, sales.

Key year-end statistics in this section generally show the financial strength of the enterprise, including:

- Debt ratio (long-term debt as a percent of shareholders' equity)
- Return on equity (net income divided by the average of beginning and ending common shareholders' equity)
- Cash and cash equivalents
- Current ratio (ratio of current assets to current liabilities)
- Total long-term debt (including capital lease obligations)
- Number of shares of common stock outstanding
- Dividend yield (fiscal year dividends per share divided by the fiscal year-end closing stock price)
- Dividend payout (fiscal year dividends divided by fiscal year EPS)
- Market value at fiscal year-end (fiscal year-end closing stock price multiplied by fiscal year-end number of shares outstanding)
- Fiscal year sales for financial institutions.

Per share data has been adjusted for stock splits. The data for public companies with sponsored American Depositary Receipts has been provided to us by Morningstar, Inc. Other public company information was compiled by Hoover's, which takes full responsibility for the content of this section.

In the case of private companies that do not publicly disclose financial information, we usually did not have access to such standardized data. We have gathered estimates of sales and other statistics from numerous sources.

Hoover's Handbook of

World Business

A List-Lover's Compendium

The 100 Largest Companies by Sales in Hoover's Handbook of World Business 2016

Rank	Company	Sales ($ bil)
1	Wal-Mart Stores, Inc.	$485,651
2	China Petroleum & Chemical C	$455,325
3	Royal Dutch Shell Plc	$431,344
4	Exxon Mobil Corp.	$411,939
5	PetroChina Co Ltd	$367,842
6	BP plc	$357,783
7	Oil and Natural Gas Corp. Lt	$266,779
8	Volkswagen A.G. (Germany, Fe	$246,089
9	Apple Inc	$233,715
10	Toyota Motor Corp	$226,993
11	Glencore PLC	$221,073
12	Total S.A.	$212,018
13	Chevron Corporation	$211,970
14	Berkshire Hathaway Inc.	$194,673
15	Samsung Electronics Co., Ltd	$188,470
16	McKesson Corp.	$179,045
17	Phillips 66	$164,093
18	Industrial and Commercial Ba	$162,342
19	Daimler AG	$157,860
20	UnitedHealth Group Inc	$157,107
21	CVS Health Corp	$153,290
22	General Motors Co.	$152,356
23	Ford Motor Co. (DE)	$149,558
24	General Electric Co	$148,589
25	PJSC Lukoil	$144,167
26	Petroleo Brasileiro S.A.	$143,657
27	AXA S.A.	$142,100
28	China Construction Bank Corp	$141,642
29	AmerisourceBergen Corp.	$135,962
30	E.ON SE	$135,942
31	ENI S.p.A.	$134,858
32	Hon Hai Precision Industry C	$133,056
33	AT&T Inc	$132,447
34	Valero Energy Corp.	$130,844

Rank	Company	Sales ($ bil)
35	Agricultural Bank of China	$129,107
36	Verizon Communications Inc	$127,079
37	Bank of China Ltd	$120,283
38	Allianz SE	$118,233
39	Fiat Chrysler Automobiles NV	$116,798
40	Fannie Mae	$116,461
41	Costco Wholesale Corp	$116,199
42	BNP Paribas (Suisse) SA (Swit	$114,611
43	BNP Paribas (France)	$114,611
44	Federal Reserve System	$114,299
45	Honda Motor Co., Ltd.	$111,087
46	Societe Generale	$108,728
47	Kroger Co (The)	$108,465
48	Amazon.com Inc.	$107,006
49	Assicurazioni Generali S.p.A	$105,191
50	P.T. Argo Pantes (Indonesia)	$104,819
51	Walgreens Boots Alliance Inc	$103,444
52	HP Inc	$103,355
53	China Mobile Limited	$103,353
54	Cardinal Health, Inc.	$102,531
55	JPMorgan Chase & Co	$102,102
56	Express Scripts Holding Co	$101,752
57	SAIC Motor Corp Ltd	$101,509
58	Marathon Petroleum Corp.	$98,102
59	Bayer Motoren WK	$97,728
60	Bayerische Motoren Werke AG	$97,728
61	HSBC Holdings Plc	$96,963
62	Boeing Co.	$96,114
63	Tesco PLC	$96,065
64	Banco Santander SA	$95,810
65	China Railway Construction C	$95,381
66	Bank of America Corp.	$95,181
67	China Railway Group Ltd	$95,090
68	Nissan Motor Co., Ltd.	$94,810

Rank	Company	Sales ($ bil)
69	PJSC Gazprom	$94,586
70	Prudential Plc	$94,331
71	Microsoft Corporation	$93,580
72	Rosneft Oil Co OJSC (Moscow)	$93,493
73	Nestle S.A.	$92,869
74	International Business Machi	$92,793
75	Carrefour S.A.	$92,765
76	Nippon Telegraph & Telephone	$92,477
77	Enel Societa Per Azioni	$92,124
78	Engie SA	$91,317
79	JX Holdings, Inc.	$90,703
80	Citigroup Inc	$90,572
81	BASF SE	$90,344
82	Electricite de France	$88,579
83	Wells Fargo & Co.	$88,372
84	PTT Public Co Ltd.	$86,214
85	Noble Group Ltd	$85,816
86	Siemens AG (Germany)	$84,800
87	Statoil ASA	$83,920
88	Home Depot Inc	$83,176
89	Hyundai Motor Co., Ltd.	$81,579
90	Hitachi, Ltd.	$81,472
91	Ping An Insurance (Group) Co	$81,268
92	Archer Daniels Midland Co.	$81,201
93	Legal & General Group PLC (U	$80,419
94	Philip Morris International	$80,106
95	ArcelorMittal SA	$79,282
96	Munich Re Group	$76,442
97	Procter & Gamble Co	$76,279
98	Deutsche Telekom AG	$76,161
99	Alphabet Inc	$74,989
100	Comcast Corp	$74,510

SOURCE: HOOVER'S, INC., DATABASE, OCTOBER 2015

The 100 Most Profitable Companies in Hoover's Handbook of World Business 2016

Rank	Company	Net Income ($ bil)
1	Apple Inc	$53,394
2	Industrial and Commercial Ba	$44,440
3	China Construction Bank Corp	$36,709
4	Exxon Mobil Corp.	$32,520
5	Oil and Natural Gas Corp. Lt	$29,313
6	Agricultural Bank of China	$28,916
7	Bank of China Ltd	$27,326
8	Wells Fargo & Co.	$23,057
9	JPMorgan Chase & Co	$21,762
10	Samsung Electronics Co., Ltd	$21,097
11	Berkshire Hathaway Inc.	$19,872
12	Chevron Corporation	$19,241
13	Toyota Motor Corp	$18,114
14	China Mobile Limited	$17,608
15	PetroChina Co Ltd	$17,268
16	Wal-Mart Stores, Inc.	$16,363
17	Alphabet Inc	$16,348
18	Johnson & Johnson	$16,323
19	General Electric Co	$15,233
20	Surgutneftegas OAO	$15,149
21	Royal Dutch Shell Plc	$14,874
22	Nestle S.A.	$14,614
23	Fannie Mae	$14,208
24	HSBC Holdings Plc	$13,688
25	Volkswagen A.G. (Germany, Fe	$13,185
26	Mitsubishi UFJ Financial Gro	$12,762
27	Microsoft Corporation	$12,193
28	Gilead Sciences, Inc.	$12,101
29	Norges Bank (Norway)	$12,071
30	International Business Machi	$12,022
31	Merck & Co., Inc	$11,920
32	Intel Corp	$11,420
33	Bank of Communications Co.,	$10,610
34	Novartis AG Basel	$10,210
35	Oracle Corp.	$9,938
36	Cnooc Ltd.	$9,700
37	General Motors Co.	$9,687
38	Verizon Communications Inc	$9,625
39	Roche Holding Ltd.	$9,434
40	Anheuser-Busch Inbev SA	$9,216
41	Pfizer Inc	$9,135
42	China Merchants Bank Co Ltd	$9,009
43	Cisco Systems, Inc.	$8,981
44	Vodafone Group Plc	$8,514
45	Goldman Sachs Group, Inc.	$8,477
46	Daimler AG	$8,462
47	Disney (Walt) Co. (The)	$8,382
48	Twenty-First Century Fox Inc	$8,306
49	Siemens AG (Germany)	$8,164
50	Comcast Corp	$8,163
51	Taiwan Semiconductor Manufac	$8,031
52	Power Assets Holdings Ltd.	$7,866
53	Freddie Mac	$7,690
54	Dow Chemical Co.	$7,685
55	United Technologies Corp	$7,608
56	Industrial Bank Co., Ltd.	$7,595
57	Allianz SE	$7,562
58	Royal Bank of Canada (Montre	$7,542
59	American International Group	$7,529
60	Yahoo! Inc.	$7,522
61	Philip Morris International	$7,493
62	China Petroleum & Chemical C	$7,487
63	Ford Motor Co. (DE)	$7,373
64	Citigroup Inc	$7,313
65	China Minsheng Banking Corp	$7,177
66	Coca-Cola Co (The)	$7,098
67	Banco Santander SA	$7,069
68	Bayer Motoren WK	$7,047
69	Bayerische Motoren Werke AG	$7,047
70	Procter & Gamble Co	$7,036
71	Commonwealth Bank of Austral	$6,965
72	Amgen Inc	$6,939
73	ConocoPhillips	$6,869
74	LVMH Moet Hennessy Louis Vui	$6,865
75	Hyundai Motor Co., Ltd.	$6,715
76	China Citic Bank Corp Ltd	$6,556
77	Investor AB	$6,553
78	Rio Tinto Ltd	$6,527
79	Itau Unibanco Holding S.A.	$6,499
80	Home Depot Inc	$6,345
81	Ping An Insurance (Group) Co	$6,329
82	Visa Inc	$6,328
83	MetLife Inc	$6,309
84	Unilever Plc (United Kingdom	$6,285
85	Unilever N.V.	$6,285
86	Sumitomo Mitsui Financial Gr	$6,281
87	BASF SE	$6,266
88	Central Bank of China	$6,251
89	China Shenhua Energy Co., Lt	$6,234
90	AT&T Inc	$6,224
91	AXA S.A.	$6,107
92	L'Oreal S.A.	$5,968
93	Toronto Dominion Bank	$5,937
94	Rosneft Oil Co OJSC (Moscow)	$5,912
95	American Express Co.	$5,885
96	U.S. Bancorp (DE)	$5,851
97	UnitedHealth Group Inc	$5,813
98	Vivendi	$5,766
99	Banco Bradesco S.A.	$5,763
100	Westpac Banking Corp	$5,631

SOURCE: HOOVER'S, INC., DATABASE, OCTOBER 2015

The 100 Largest Employers in Hoover's Handbook of World Business 2016

Rank	Company	Employees
1	Wal-Mart Stores, Inc.	2,200,000
2	G4S Plc	631,465
3	Randstad Holding N.V.	609,020
4	Volkswagen A.G. (Germany, Fe	592,586
5	Kelly Services, Inc.	563,300
6	PetroChina Co Ltd	534,652
7	Agricultural Bank of China	517,671
8	Compass Group PLC (United Ki	515,864
9	ISS A/S (Denmark)	510,968
10	Tesco PLC	506,984
11	Yum! Brands, Inc.	505,000
12	Deutsche Post RG	488,824
13	Deutsche Post AG	488,824
14	Industrial and Commercial Ba	462,282
15	United Parcel Service Inc	435,000
16	Jardine Matheson Holdings Ltd	430,000
17	Sodexo	422,844
18	McDonald's Corp	420,000
19	Pou Chen Corp	411,593
20	Yue Yuen Industrial (Holding	408,000
21	Kroger Co (The)	400,000
22	Hitachi, Ltd.	385,262
23	Carrefour S.A.	381,227
24	International Business Machi	379,592
25	China Construction Bank Corp	372,321
26	Home Depot Inc	371,000
27	Walgreens Boots Alliance Inc	360,000
28	China Petroleum & Chemical C	358,571
29	Accenture plc	358,000
30	Siemens AG (Germany)	348,000
31	Target Corp	347,000
32	Toyota Motor Corp	344,109
33	Fonciere Euris SA	340,060
34	Finatis SA	340,060
35	Nestle S.A.	339,000
36	Casino Guichard Perrachon S.	335,436
37	Berkshire Hathaway Inc.	316,000
38	Bank of China Ltd	308,128
39	General Electric Co	305,000
40	China Telecom Corp Ltd	300,960

Rank	Company	Employees
41	Deutsche Bahn AG	295,763
42	China Railway Group Ltd	293,592
43	Bosch (Robert) GmbH (Germany	290,183
44	HP Inc	287,000
45	China Unicom (Hong Kong) Ltd	281,420
46	Daimler AG	279,972
47	Securitas AB	277,438
48	HSBC Holdings Plc	266,000
49	Lowe's Companies Inc	266,000
50	Aramark	265,500
51	Wells Fargo & Co.	264,500
52	Pepsico Inc.	263,000
53	Panasonic Corp	254,084
54	AT&T Inc	253,000
55	China Resources Beer Holding	252,000
56	China Railway Construction C	249,624
57	Rosneft Oil Co OJSC (Moscow)	248,900
58	Societe Nationale des Chemins	245,763
59	Jardine Cycle & Carriage Ltd	245,000
60	CVS Health Corp	243,000
61	Nippon Telegraph & Telephone	241,600
62	China Mobile Limited	241,550
63	JPMorgan Chase & Co	241,359
64	Citigroup Inc	241,000
65	Sumitomo Electric Industries	240,798
66	Hewlett Packard Enterprise C	240,000
67	Starbucks Corp.	238,000
68	Ping An Insurance (Group) Co	235,999
69	Metro AG	233,962
70	Amazon.com Inc.	230,800
71	Fiat Chrysler Automobiles NV	228,690
72	Wal-Mart de Mexico S.A.B. de	228,063
73	Deutsche Telekom AG	227,811
74	Koninklijke Ahold NV (Nether	227,000
75	HCA Holdings Inc	225,000
76	Robert Half International In	225,000
77	Bank of America Corp.	224,000
78	ArcelorMittal SA	222,327
79	ACS Actividades de Construcc	217,908
80	Fomento Economico Mexicano,	216,740

Rank	Company	Employees
81	Rewe-Zentral AG (Germany, Fed	216,414
82	Fresenius SE & Co KGaA	216,275
83	JBS S.A.	216,000
84	General Motors Co.	215,000
85	Cognizant Technology Solutio	211,500
86	Magnit PJSC	207,853
87	Costco Wholesale Corp	205,000
88	Wesfarmers Ltd.	205,000
89	Honda Motor Co., Ltd.	204,730
90	UnitedHealth Group Inc	200,000
91	Ford Motor Co. (DE)	199,000
92	Toshiba Corp	198,741
93	TJX Companies, Inc.	198,000
94	United Technologies Corp	197,200
95	Yamato Holdings Co., Ltd.	197,056
96	Sears Holdings Corp	196,000
97	Loblaw Cos. Ltd.	195,000
98	Onex Corp.	192,000
99	Canon, Inc.	191,889
100	America Movil, S.A.B. de C.V	191,156

SOURCE: HOOVER'S, INC., DATABASE, OCTOBER 2015

Hoover's Handbook of

World Business

The Companies

77 Bank, Ltd. (The) (Japan)

Unlike 77 Sunset Strip 77 Bank's name doesn't denote its address but its order in the history of Japanese banking. 77 Bank was founded in 1878 as the 77th national bank in Japan. Operating more than 140 branches in the northern area of Japan's largest island Honshu 77 Bank provides the usual banking services of savings and lending as well some other operations such as temporary employment property appraisal and credit-document custody. 77 Bank also provides financial-related services that include leasing credit investigation computer-based contract services and a credit card.

EXECUTIVES

President, Teruhiko Ujiie
Auditors: Deloitte Touche Tohmatsu LLC

LOCATIONS

HQ: 77 Bank, Ltd. (The) (Japan)
3-3-20 Chuo, Aoba-ku, Sendai, Miyagi 980-8777
Phone: (81) 22 267 1111
Web: www.77bank.co.jp

COMPETITORS

Fukuoka Financial Group	Ito-Yokado
Gunma Bank	Japan Post
	Sumitomo Mitsui

HISTORICAL FINANCIALS

Company Type: Public

Income Statement FYE: March 31

	ASSETS ($ mil.)	NET INCOME ($ mil.)	INCOME AS % OF ASSETS	EMPLOYEES
03/15	71,582	142	0.2%	3,001
03/14	82,418	145	0.2%	3,002
03/13	87,798	132	0.2%	3,038
03/12	92,853	130	0.1%	3,128
03/11	75,086	(367)	—	3,149
Annual Growth	(1.2%)	—	—	(1.2%)

2015 Year-End Financials

Return on assets: 0.2%	Dividends
Return on equity: 4.0%	Yield: —
Long-term debt ($ mil.): —	Payout: —
No. of shares (mil.): 374	Market value ($ mil.): —
Sales ($ mil): 941	

Aareal Bank AG

Aareal Bank is engaged internationally in a variety of property-related banking and financial services for the public and private sectors. The company's business is organized into two primary segments. Structured property financing (its most profitable business) specializes in financing large-scale retail hotel and logistics industry properties. The consulting/services segment offers IT products that help users manage residential and commercial properties. Aareal Bank operates in more than 30 countries in Europe North America and the Asia/Pacific region. In fiscal 2014 the financial institution boosted its core business by acquiring Germany's Corealcredit Bank AG for 342 million.

EXECUTIVES

Member Management Board, Thomas Ortmanns, $300,000 total compensation
Chairman Supervisory Board, Marija G. Korsch, age 67
Chairman Management Board, Hermann J. Merkens, age 49
Auditors: PricewaterhouseCoopers Aktiengesellschaft Wirtschaftprufungsgesellschaft

LOCATIONS

HQ: Aareal Bank AG
Paulinenstrasse 15, Wiesbaden D-65189
Phone: (49) 611 348 3009 **Fax:** (49) 611 348 2637
Web: www.aareal-bank.com

PRODUCTS/OPERATIONS

2013 Sales

	% of total
Interest income	97
Commission income	2
Other operating income	1
Total	**100**

COMPETITORS

AWD	Landesbank Berlin
BayernLB	UBS
Commerzbank	UniCredit Bank AG
Deutsche Bank	Wstenrot & Wrttembergische
HSBC	

HISTORICAL FINANCIALS

Company Type: Public

Income Statement FYE: December 31

	ASSETS ($ mil.)	NET INCOME ($ mil.)	INCOME AS % OF ASSETS	EMPLOYEES
12/14	60,236	384	0.6%	2,548
12/13	59,173	161	0.3%	2,375
12/12	60,279	138	0.2%	2,289
12/11	54,084	147	0.3%	2,353
12/10	55,163	101	0.2%	2,407
Annual Growth	2.2%	39.4%	—	1.4%

2014 Year-End Financials

Return on assets: 0.6%	Dividends
Return on equity: 13.4%	Yield: —
Long-term debt ($ mil.): —	Payout: —
No. of shares (mil.): 59	Market value ($ mil.): 2,454
Sales ($ mil): 1,473	

	STOCK PRICE ($) FY Close	P/E High/Low		PER SHARE ($) Earnings	Dividends	Book Value
12/14	41.00	14	13	5.92	0.00	50.38
12/13	37.40	36	19	2.68	0.00	50.78
12/12	21.08	26	14	2.31	0.00	46.44
12/11	17.50	31	14	2.73	0.00	41.62
12/10	20.25	23	15	2.38	0.00	54.53
Annual Growth	19.3%	—	—	25.6%	—	(2.0%)

ABB Ltd

You could be forgiven for thinking that ABB is short for "A Bunch of Businesses" –though that bunch has evolved over some 130 years. ABB engineers power and automation technologies for a broad base of utility industrial and commercial customers. Its lines run from robots to light switches. Power products include transmission and distribution components as well as turnkey substation systems. Automation technologies are used to monitor and control equipment and processes in industrial plants and utilities. The company has established a presence in about 100 countries with its core businesses concentrated in power and automation markets.

Geographic Reach

ABB's operations extend to around 100 countries. A large portion of the company's production and development facilities reside in Canada China Finland Germany India Italy Norway Sweden Switzerland and the US.

Europe accounted for 36% of its total sales in 2012; the Americas and Asia each generated 27% while Africa and the Middle East brought in 10%.

Operations

ABB operates through five segments: Power Products Power Systems Discrete Automation and Motion Low Voltage Products and Process Automation. The Power Products and Power Systems segments are driven primarily by the capital expenditures of electrical utilities.

The Automation Products Process Automation and Low Voltage Products segments are impacted by the health of several industries including automotive consumer products metals and minerals paper and pulp and pharmaceuticals. A global presence and competitive cost base however have helped to buffer ABB's exposure to regional recessions and slow economies.

Major subsidiaries owned by ABB include ABB Inc. ABB Limited Baldor Electric Company Thomas & Betts Ventyx Tropos Networks ABB AG ABB Ltda. Power-One and ABB Contracting.

Sales and Marketing

ABB sells its products through direct sales and external channel partners like wholesalers distributors system integrators EPCs and OEMs.

Financial Performance

ABB generated $39.3 billion in revenues for 2012 a historic milestone for the company; this represented a 3% increase from the $37.8 billion it earned in 2011. The spike in revenues was mainly due to a solid order level as well as the favorable impact of its 2012 Thomas & Betts acquisition.

While ABB has enjoyed three straight years of revenue growth its profits slipped by 15% from $3.2 billion in 2011 to $2.7 billion in 2012 due to an increase in the cost of sales. This was the result of an unfavorable business mix coupled with higher prices involved with restructuring its segments.

Strategy

As the global economy moves away from the recession ABB has been making some milestone acquisitions to boost its product offerings operations and geographic reach. In mid-2013 it purchased Power-One a major provider of solar inverters technology used to convert the sun's energy into electricity. ABB made the $1 billion deal to boost its renewable energy business and expand its solar product portfolio.

In 2012 ABB bought Thomas & Betts (T&B) for about $3.9 billion. T&B sells electrical connectors HVAC equipment and transmission towers. The acquisition significantly added to ABB's North

American presence giving it access to T&B's network of more than 6000 distributor locations and wholesalers throughout the continent. Shortly after that transaction was made ABB snapped up Tropos Networks a California firm that makes wireless technologies and products for distribution area communication networks. The acquisition broadened ABB's communications systems portfolio and enabled it to better cater to North American clients in the power transportation and mining sectors.

In 2011 ABB acquired the Trasfor Group which advanced its portfolio of specialty dry-type transformers used in drives railway rolling stock offshore wind power and other renewable energy applications. Months earlier ABB swallowed up Baldor Electric for $3.1 billion. Baldor Electric a US industrial motors business strengthened ABB's energy efficient offerings most notably in North America.

Other completed acquisitions that year include ABB's takeover of Mincom an Australia-based software and services company with clients ranging from mining companies (Rio Tinto and Anglo American) to big manufacturing companies (Boeing and Caterpillar). Not only did the deal bring an estimated $200 million in revenues but it also expanded ABB's software capabilities.

HISTORY

Asea Brown Boveri (ABB) was formed in 1988 when two giants ASEA AB of Sweden and BBC Brown Boveri of Switzerland combined their electrical engineering and equipment businesses. Percy Barnevik head of ASEA became CEO.

ASEA was born in Stockholm in 1883 when Ludwig Fredholm founded Electriska Aktiebolaget to manufacture an electric dynamo created by engineer Jonas Wenstrom. In 1890 the company merged with Wenstrom's brother's firm to form Allmanna Svenska Electriska Aktiebolaget (ASEA) a pioneer in industrial electrification. Early in the 1900s ASEA began its first railway electrification project. By the 1920s it was providing locomotives and other equipment to Sweden's national railway and by the next decade ASEA was one of Sweden's largest electric equipment manufacturers. In 1962 it bought 20% of appliance maker Electrolux. ASEA created the nuclear power venture ASEA-ATOM with the Swedish government in 1968 and bought full control in 1982.

BBC Brown Boveri was formed in 1891 as the Brown Boveri and Company partnership between Charles Brown and Walter Boveri in Baden Switzerland. It made power generation equipment and produced the first steam turbines in Europe in 1900. BBC entered Germany (1893) France (1894) and Italy (1903) and diversified into nuclear power equipment after WWII.

By 1988 BBC the bigger company had a West German network that ASEA the more profitable company coveted. Both had US joint ventures. In an unusual merger ASEA (which became ABB AB) and BBC (later ABB AG) continued as separate entities sharing equal ownership of ABB. Barnevik crafted a unique decentralized management structure under which national subsidiaries were closely linked to their local customers and labor forces. In six years ABB took over more than 150 companies worldwide.

An ABB-led consortium built one of the world's largest hydroelectric plants in Iran in 1992 and in 1995 ABB merged its transportation segment into Adtranz (a joint venture with Daimler-Benz) to form the world's #1 maker of trains.

Tragedy struck in 1996. Robert Donovan CEO of ABB's US subsidiary died in a plane crash along with Commerce Secretary Ron Brown and other executives on a trade mission. Donovan's death hastened the US unit's restructuring.

In 1997 Barnevik gave up the title of CEO remaining as chairman and was succeeded by Goran Lindahl an engineer who worked his way up the ranks at ASEA. (Barnevik remained chairman until 2001.) After 1997 profits dipped drastically Lindahl scrapped Barnevik's vaunted regional matrix structure in favor of one organized by product areas under a strong central management. Though the Asian financial crisis slowed orders ABB still pulled in large contracts including one to build the world's largest cracker plant in Texas in 1998.

In 1999 ABB acquired Elsag Bailey a Dutch maker of industrial control systems for about $1.5 billion and sold its 50% stake in Adtranz to DaimlerChrysler for about $472 million. ABB and France's ALSTOM combined their power generation businesses to form the world's largest power plant equipment maker. That year ABB AB and ABB AG were at last united under a single stock through holding company ABB Ltd.

ABB scaled back its power plant-related activities in 2000. The company sold its nuclear power business to BNFL for $485 million and its 50% stake in ABB Alstom Power to ALSTOM for $1.2 billion. (Areva acquired ALSTOM's transmission and distribution business in 2004.) In 2001 Lindahl resigned and Jrgen Centerman head of the company's automation business replaced him. Centerman promptly reorganized ABB's industrial operations into four segments based on customer type and two based on product type.

Also in 2001 ABB acquired French company Entrelec a supplier of industrial automation and control products. With economic slowdowns occurring in the company's key markets ABB announced plans in 2001 to cut 12000 jobs over 18 months. Later that year amid rising numbers of asbestos claims against US subsidiary Combustion Engineering ABB took a $470 million fourth-quarter charge to cover asbestos liabilities. The claims charged asbestos exposures stemming from products supplied before the mid-1970s by Combustion Engineering which ABB acquired in 1990.

In 2002 ABB found itself embroiled in controversy after revealing not only a record loss but also payments of large pensions to former chairman Barnevik and former chief executive Lindahl. The former executives agreed that year to return a part (about $82 million) of their pension payouts to ABB. That year the company which faced $4.4 billion in debts after industry slumps affected its sales of power systems and equipment industrial automation and controls sold part of its financial services unit to GE Commercial Finance for $2.3 billion.

The day after the company sold its structured finances unit ABB's chief executive Jrgen Centerman resigned and was replaced by the chairman Jürgen Dormann. That year ABB sold its metering business to Germany-based Ruhrgas for $244 million.

In 2003 as part of its settlement with asbestos plaintiffs ABB placed Combustion Engineering into bankruptcy. Later that same year the company announced that it would sell its Sirius International reinsurance business to the Bermuda-based White Mountains; the deal was completed in 2004 for about $425 million. ABB also sold its upstream oil gas and petrochemicals unit to Candover Partners 3i and J.P. Morgan Partners for $925 million in 2004. (To clear the way for the sale ABB also agreed to pay US regulators $16 million in fines to settle bribery cases at US-based ABB Vetco Gray and Scotland-based ABB Vetco UK. The subsidiaries –part of the petroleum business that was sold –allegedly paid off government officials in Angola Kazakhstan and Nigeria in order to win oil contracts between 1998 and 2003.)

Sulzer CEO Fred Kindle succeeded Dormann as ABB's CEO in 2005. (Dormann remained chairman until his retirement in 2007.) The company made a number of small dispositions in 2005 including its Japanese control valves business its foundry business and several cable and power line businesses.

ABB ended years of litigation –and a major corporate headache –when it reached a settlement on an asbestos liability case related to US subsidiary Combustion Engineering in 2006. As part of the settlement ABB committed more than $1.4 billion to pay settled claims.

After consolidating its remaining businesses into the two areas power technologies and automation technologies ABB restructured its operations into five divisions in 2006: Power Products Power Systems Automation Products Process Automation and Robotics. It took further steps to streamline operations and position itself for growth for example by moving its main robotics operation from Detroit to Shanghai.

In 2006 ABB voluntarily disclosed to the US Department of Justice and the SEC that the company made payments in the Middle East that might have violated anti-bribery laws. The following year ABB disclosed similar suspect payments at subsidiaries in Asia Europe and South America.

Kindle left ABB in 2008 due to what the company called "irreconcilable differences" concerning the leadership of the company; former GE Healthcare CEO Joe Hogan became CEO of ABB later that year.

In 2008 the company dug deeper into its investment purse spending $653 million to complete 12 deals. Most notably ABB purchased Kuhlman Electric a US-based transformer manufacturer from The Carlyle Group for $513 million including assumed debt. Kuhlman Electric was integrated into ABB's Power Products division in North America and deepens ABB's geographic footprint and product offerings in the industrial and electric utility sectors.

ABB's bunch of businesses has been peeled back too. Several divestitures were completed in 2008 and 2007; ABB exited its 50% interest in South Africa's ABB Powertech Transformers to Powertech owned by the Altron Group for $11 million. In 2007 ABB sold subsidiary ABB Lummus Global to Chicago Bridge & Iron Co. for some $870 million in cash as well as its Building Systems business in Germany and power plant interests in India and Morocco to Abu Dhabi National Oil. Power Lines businesses in Brazil and Mexico were also put on the sale block for $20 million.

ABB plowed in $209 million in 2009 adding eight new operations. Among them the company acquired the assets of Sinai Engineering a designer and provider of services for electrical generation and transmission systems planning as well as construction management. The transaction completed through its US ABB Inc. expanded ABB's presence in western Canada. On the other side of the world ABB picked up South Africa's Westingcorp (Pty) Ltd. The move ramped up ABB's line of power capacitors (machines that add to a system's power quality and energy efficiency) and opened the door to local and global electric utilities and mining markets.

ABB in mid-2010 acquired K-TEK a maker of level detection technology used in the oil and gas industry as well as water and other industries. Its instrumentation and sensing technologies which number more than 350000 installations enhanced ABB's slate of measurement products part of its Process Automation division. The deal garnered K-TEK's facilities in the US the Netherlands China India and South Africa.

ABB picked up US software provider Insert Key Solutions in late 2010. Its combination with the earlier acquisition of Ventyx (valued at approximately $1 billion) from Vista Equity Partners created a comprehensive portfolio of software for managing asset-intensive businesses engaged in the utility energy and communications industries. Ventyx and Insert Key Solutions joined ABB's network management business.

EXECUTIVES

Region Manager North America, Greg Scheu, age 54
Region Manager India Middle East & Africa, Frank Duggan, age 56
Division Manager Power Products, Bernhard Jucker, age 61, $919,999 total compensation
Region Manager South Asia, Haider Rashid
EVP and CFO, Eric Elzvik, age 55
Region Manager South America, Enrique Santacana
CEO, Ulrich Spiesshofer, age 51, $730,004 total compensation
Division Manager Process Automation, Veli-Matti Reinikkala, age 58, $648,995 total compensation
Region Manager Central Europe, Peter Terwiesch
Managing Director Canadas, Nathalie Pilon
Division Manager Power Systems, Claudio Facchin
Division Manager Low Voltage Products, Tarak Mehta, age 49
Division Manager Discrete Automation and Motion, Pekka Tiitinen, age 49
Region Manager Northern Europe, Trevor Gregory
Region Manager Mediterranean, Matteo Marini
Region Manager North Asia, Chunyuan Gu
CTO, Bazmi Husain
Chairman, Hubertus von Gr nberg, age 73
Auditors: Ernst & Young AG

LOCATIONS

HQ: ABB Ltd
Affolternstrasse 44, Zurich CH-8050
Phone: (41) 43 317 7111 **Fax:** (41) 43 317 7992
Web: www.abb.com

2012 Sales

	$ mil.	% of total
Europe	14,073	36
Asia	10,750	27
Americas	10,699	27
Middle East & Africa	3,814	10
Total	**39,336**	**100**

PRODUCTS/OPERATIONS

2012 Sales

	$ mil.	% of total
Power Products	10,717	25
Discrete Automation & Motion	9,405	22
Process Automation	8,156	19
Power Systems	7,852	18
Low Voltage Products	6,638	16
Corporate & other	(3432)	
Total	**39,336**	**100**

Selected Mergers and Acquisitions

FY2013
Power-One Inc. ($1 billion; Camarillo California; maker of solar inverters)
FY2012
Thomas & Betts Corporation ($3.9 billion; Memphis Tennessee; electrical connectors HVAC equipment and transmission towers)
Tropos Networks Inc. (Silicon Valley California; wireless technologies and products for distribution area communication networks)
FY2011
Trasfor Group (Switzerland; specialty dry-type transformers)
Baldor Electric ($3.1 billion; Fort Smith Arkansas; industrial motors)

Selected Products

Automation Products
Breakers
Control products
DIN-rail components
Drives
Enclosures
Generators
Instrumentation
Low-voltage switchgear
Motors
Power electronics systems
Switches
Wiring accessories
Electrical Products
Boxes and covers (Bowers Commander Steel City)
Cable ties (Catamount Ty-Fast Ty-Rap)
Connectors (Blackburn Color-Keyed)
Lighting (Carlon Red Dot Lumacell)
Wire management systems (Carlon T&B)
HVAC
Evaporative cooling and energy recovery equipment (International Energy Saver)
Heaters (EK Campbell Reznor)
Heating mechanical and refrigeration supplies (T&B)
Power Products
Circuit breakers for all current and voltage levels
High- and medium-voltage switchgear and apparatus
Power and distribution transformers
Sensors
Power Systems
Power plant automation and electrification solutions
Transmission and distribution systems
Process Automation
Automation products and solutions
Controls
Industry-specific application knowledge and services
Plant optimization
Robotics
Industrial robots
Industrial software products
Robot contollers and software
Steel Structures
Power connectors and accessories (Elastimold)
Steel poles (Meyer)
Transmission towers (Lehigh)

COMPETITORS

ALSTOM
AREVA
Bharat Heavy Electricals
Cisco Systems
Crompton Greaves
Danaher
Drr
Eaton
Emerson Electric
Endress + Hauser
Ericsson
FANUC
GE
Hitachi
Honeywell International
Hyosung
Hyundai Corporation
KUKA
Kawasaki Heavy Industries
Larsen & Toubro
Legrand
Metso
Mitsubishi Heavy Industries
Nokia
Rittal Corp.
Rockwell Automation
SPX
Schneider Electric
Siemens AG
Toshiba
Voith
WEG Indstrias
Yaskawa Electric
Yokogawa Electric

HISTORICAL FINANCIALS

Company Type: Public

Income Statement FYE: December 31

	REVENUE ($ mil.)	NET INCOME ($ mil.)	NET PROFIT MARGIN	EMPLOYEES
12/14	39,830	2,594	6.5%	140,400
12/13	41,848	2,787	6.7%	147,700
12/12	39,336	2,704	6.9%	146,100
12/11	37,990	3,168	8.3%	133,600
12/10	31,589	2,561	8.1%	116,500
Annual Growth	6.0%	0.3%	—	4.8%

2014 Year-End Financials

Debt ratio: 17.1%
Return on equity: 14.8%
Cash ($ mil.): 6,768
Current ratio: 1.60
Long-term debt ($ mil.): 7,338
No. of shares (mil.): —
Dividends
Yield: 3.6%
Payout: 68.0%
Market value ($ mil.): —

	STOCK PRICE ($) FY Close	P/E High/Low		PER SHARE ($) Earnings	Dividends	Book Value
12/14	21.15	24	18	1.13	0.77	7.20
12/13	26.56	22	17	1.21	0.70	8.14
12/12	20.79	19	13	1.18	0.69	7.36
12/11	18.83	20	12	1.38	0.67	6.89
12/10	22.45	20	14	1.12	0.47	6.52
Annual Growth	(1.5%)	—	—	0.2%	12.9%	2.5%

Abbey National Treasury Services PLC (United Kingdom)

EXECUTIVES

Director, Jacques Ripoll
Auditors: Deloitte LLP

LOCATIONS

HQ: Abbey National Treasury Services PLC (United Kingdom)
2 Triton Square, Regent' s Place, London NW1 3AN
Phone: (44) 870 607 6000

HISTORICAL FINANCIALS

Company Type: Public

Income Statement FYE: December 31

	ASSETS ($ mil.)	NET INCOME ($ mil.)	INCOME AS % OF ASSETS	EMPLOYEES
12/14	167,761	188	0.1%	862
12/13	345,929	271	0.1%	764
12/12	351,245	425	0.1%	717
12/11	340,444	531	0.2%	817
12/10	393,221	714	0.2%	621
Annual Growth	(19.2%)	(28.3%)	—	8.5%

2014 Year-End Financials

Return on assets: 0.0%
Return on equity: 3.7%
Long-term debt ($ mil.): —
No. of shares (mil.): —
Sales ($ mil): 4,587
Dividends
Yield: —
Payout: —
Market value ($ mil.): —

Abu Dhabi Commercial Bank

LOCATIONS

HQ: Abu Dhabi Commercial Bank
P.O. Box 939, Abu Dhabi
Phone: (971) 2 696 2222
Web: www.adcb.com

HISTORICAL FINANCIALS

Company Type: Public

Income Statement FYE: December 31

	ASSETS ($ mil.)	NET INCOME ($ mil.)	INCOME AS % OF ASSETS	EMPLOYEES
12/14	55,548	1,102	2.0%	0
12/13	49,861	916	1.8%	0
12/12	49,218	744	1.5%	0
12/11	50,019	823	1.6%	0
12/10	48,534	103	0.2%	2,714
Annual Growth	3.4%	80.6%	—	—

2014 Year-End Financials

Return on assets: 2.0%
Return on equity: 16.0%
Long-term debt ($ mil.): —
No. of shares (mil.): —
Sales ($ mil): 2,520
Dividends
Yield: —
Payout: —
Market value ($ mil.): —

Accenture plc

For Accenture the accent is on helping businesses improve their performance. The world's largest consulting firm Accenture offers a well-balanced portfolio of management consulting technology and business process outsourcing (BPO) services to some of the top companies and government organizations in the world. Corporate clients span a broad spectrum of industries —from retail to communications —and include more than three-quarters of the FORTUNE 500. Clients use Accenture's services to enter new markets increase revenue in existing markets improve operational performance and deliver new products to market. Accenture is domiciled in Dublin but headquartered in New York.

Geographic Reach

Accenture serves clients in more than 200 cities spanning 120 countries. The majority of its revenue is balanced between the Americas and Europe Middle East and Africa (EMEA). The US is its largest individual market generating about one-third of total revenue. The remainder is made in the Asia/Pacific region.

Operations

Accenture's business is divided into five operating groups: Communications Media & Technology; Financial Services; Health & Public Service; Products; and Resources. Although revenue generated by these operating groups is well dispersed Products is the company's largest segment serving mainly consumer-oriented industries including automotive consumer goods life sciences retail transportation and travel services.

Accenture has a global network of innovation centers in the US Australia China Japan Singapore India France and South Africa.

Financial Performance

As the global economy has improved and the demand for its consulting and outsourcing services has increased Accenture recognized a 9% spike in revenue ($27.4 billion to $29.7 billion) and a 12 % rise in profits ($2.3 billion to $2.6 billion) from 2011 to 2012.

The recent growth was attributed to double digit growth across all its five operating groups. Accenture has also benefited from its growth strategy that is focused on further differentiating its products and services in the marketplace and improving its competitiveness. It has also been helped from a positive increase in the local currency.

Strategy

Accenture's strategy is focused on deepening and differentiating its industry and technology capabilities from competitors. It is doing so in part by investing in analytics cloud computing insight-driven health interactive and digital marketing mobility and smart grid. Acquisitions joint ventures and alliances are key means through which Accenture enhances and adds to its offerings. One such partnership is a five-year research collaboration with MIT announced in early 2013 to develop advanced analytics specifically how to harness the challenges of big data and develop new approaches to improve the science of decision-making. In late 2012 Accenture and GE Aviation formed a joint venture company called Taleris to provide global airlines and cargo carriers with intelligent operations services to improve efficiency.

From a geographic standpoint the company is focusing expansion efforts on certain emerging markets in particular such as Brazil China India Mexico Russia South Africa South Korea Turkey and certain countries in Southeast Asia and the Middle East.

Mergers and Acquisitions

To help its clients more effectively measure and monitor the progress of their change programs Accenture in 2013 acquired ChangeTrack Research an Australia-based provider of analytics-based tools and services for change management usage. The acquisition complemented Accenture's suite of tools and capabilities to help its clients achieve the goals of their most significant organizational transformations.

Adding to its footprint in Asia/Pacific Accenture acquired in 2012 Singapore-based Newspage Pte Ltd a provider of distributor management and mobility software that helps consumer goods companies improve their operations sales performance and data visibility.

Earlier in 2012 the company expanded its operations through the purchase of Octagon Research Solutions a provider of clinical and regulatory information management solutions and software for the pharmaceutical industry. The deal gives Accenture a means to provide clinical and regulatory services to pharmaceutical companies.

HISTORY

Accenture traces its history back to the storied accounting firm of Arthur Andersen & Co. Founded by Northwestern University professor and accounting legend Arthur Andersen in 1913 the firm's expanding scope of operations led it into forensic accounting and advising clients on financial reporting processes forming the basis for a management consulting arm. Arthur Andersen led the firm until his death in 1947. His successor Leonard Spacek split off the consulting operations as a separate unit in 1954.

The consulting business grew quickly during the 1970s and 1980s thanks in part to an orgy of US corporate re-engineering. By 1988 consulting accounted for 40% of Andersen's sales. Chafing at sharing profits with the auditors (who faced growing price pressures and a rising tide of legal action due to the accounting irregularities of their clients) the consultants sought more power within the firm. The result was a 1989 restructuring that established Andersen Worldwide (later Andersen) as the parent of two independent units Arthur Andersen and Andersen Consulting (AC). The growing revenue imbalance between the operations remained unresolved however and a year later Arthur Andersen poured gas on the flames by establishing its own business consultancy.

Meanwhile AC continued to expand during the 1990s by forming practices focused on manufacturing finance and government. It addressed the shift from mainframes to PCs by forming alliances with technology heavyweights Hewlett-Packard Sun Microsystems and Microsoft. In 1996 AC teamed up with Internet service provider BBN (acquired by GTE in 1997) to form ServiceNet a joint venture to develop Internet commerce and other systems.

The Andersen family feud took a turn for the worse in 1997 with the retirement of CEO Lawrence Weinbach. A deadlocked vote for a new leader led the board to appoint accounting partner Robert Grafton as CEO angering the consulting partners. Later that year AC asked the International Chamber of Commerce to negotiate a breakup of Andersen Worldwide. George Shaheen to whom many attributed the heightened tensions between the units resigned as CEO of AC in 1999 and was replaced by Joe Forehand.

While the separation dispute dragged on the consulting business grew and diversified amid increasing consolidation in the industry. In 1999 the company moved into e-commerce venture funding with the formation of Andersen Consulting Ventures and in 2000 it inked partnership deals with Microsoft (Microsoft system implementation services) Sun Microsystems (for B2B Internet office supply sales) and BT (Internet-based human resources services).

That year an international arbitrator finally approved AC's separation from its parent ruling that the consultancy must change its name and pay Andersen Worldwide $1 billion (far less than the $15 billion demanded by the accounting partners). Renamed Accenture the company went public in 2001. While the new name (a made-up word) might have struck some as a marketing challenge having an identity distinct from that of its former parent proved to be a stroke of luck for Accenture. Andersen broke apart in 2002 after becoming embroiled in the accounting scandals of energy giant Enron.

In 2004 Accenture successfully bid on a $10 billion 10-year contract to create a system to identify visitors and immigrants coming into the country. Dubbed US-VISIT (United States Visitor and Immigrant Status Indicator Technology) the system was to be employed by the Department of Homeland Security to prevent terrorists from entering the US. However Accenture's bid nearly ran afoul of congressional critics who tried to pass spending amendments barring firms headquartered outside the US from winning security-related business.

Forehand stepped down as CEO of Accenture in 2004 and was replaced by company veteran William Green. Forehand remained chairman until he retired in 2006 when Green was named to that post as well.

Accenture acquired Capgemini's North American health practice in 2005 for $175 million in order to strengthen its offerings to hospitals and health care systems. In 2006 the firm expanded its outsourcing operations by buying NaviSys a leading provider of software for the life insurance industry along with key assets of Kansas-based accountant Savista.

In mid-2008 Accenture swallowed up ATAN an industrial and automation services provider based in Brazil that caters to the mining energy and utilities sectors. It also obtained SOPIA a Tokyo-based consulting firm specializing in Oracle systems integration. During that year Accenture added to its transportation and travel services operations (located within its Products Division) when it bought AddVal Technology. AddVal provided software and technology used for freight order management and the deal enhanced Accenture's ability to integrate and simplify its clients' freight management services capabilities.

In late 2009 Accenture looked to solidify its position in a vital market when it obtained the Symbian professional services unit of Nokia. The unit offers engineering and support services for the Symbian operating system one of the world's most widely used operating systems for smart phones. The acquired operations provided a broad range of embedded software services for mobile devices and were rebranded Accenture Embedded Mobility Services.

Accenture obtained RiskControl a consulting firm based in Brazil in early 2010. Also that year Accenture bought Beijing Genesis Interactive Technology Company an embedded software firm providing mobile software outsourcing services to companies in China. The acquisitions furthered Accenture's penetration into the cutting-edge smart phone support services market.

Focusing on beefing up its Financial Services segment in 2011 Accenture acquired Duck Creek Technologies a provider of software and tools catering to the insurance and health care sectors. At the time of the transaction Duck Creek served about 60 clients throughout North America and the UK.

At the beginning of 2011 Pierre Nanterme the former head of the company's financial services operations was promoted to become the company's newest CEO. Green remains with Accenture as chairman.

EXECUTIVES

Group Chief Executive Financial Services, Richard A. Lumb, age 54, $972,812 total compensation
Chairman and CEO, Pierre Nanterme, age 56, $1,126,333 total compensation
SVP Finance, David P. Rowland, age 54, $1,082,750 total compensation
Group Chief Executive Growth Markets, Gianfranco Casati, age 56
COO, Johan G. (Jo) Deblaere, age 53
Group Chief Executive Accenture Operations, Michael J. (Mike) Salvino
Group Chief Executive Resources, Jean-Marc Ollagnier, age 54
Group Chief Executive Products, Alexander M. (Sander) van't Noordende, $1,292,769 total compensation
Group Chief Executive Communications Media and Technology, Robert E. (Bob) Sell
Group Chief Executive Health and Public Service, Daniel T. (Dan) London, age 50
CTO, Paul Daugherty
Group Chief Executive Accenture Technology Delivery, Bhaskar Ghosh
Group Chief Executive Accenture Digital, Michael R. (Mike) Sutcliff
Group CEO North America, Julie Spellman, age 47
Managing Director India, Anindya Basu
Chairman Accenture India, Rekha M. Menon
Auditors: KPMG LLP

LOCATIONS

HQ: Accenture plc
1 Grand Canal Square, Grand Canal Harbour, Dublin 2
Phone: (353) 1 646 2000
Web: www.accenture.com

2012 Sales

	% of total
Americas	45
Europe Middle East & Africa	40
Asia/Pacific	15
Total	**100**

PRODUCTS/OPERATIONS

2012 Sales

	% of total
Products	23
Communications media & tech	22
Financial services	22
Resources	18
Health & public service	15
Total	**100**

2012 Sales

	% of total
Consulting	56
Outsourcing	44
Total	**100**

Selected Mergers and Acquisitions

FY2013
- ChangeTrack Research Pty Ltd (Sydney Australia; analytics-based tools and services)

FY2012
- Octagon Research Solutions Inc. (clinical and regulatory information management services and software)

FY2011
- Duck Creek Technologies (software and tools for insurance and health care)
- CAS Computer Anwendungs- und Systemberatung (CRM and mobility software)

FY2010
- Beijing Genesis Interactive Technology Co. (embedded software services)
- Knowledge Rules (provider of business solutions utilizing BPM software)
- Acceria (technology and consulting business services)
- CadenceQuest (customer data and analytics)
- Risk Control (risk management)

Selected Practice Areas

Communications and high technology
- Communications
- Electronics and high technology
- Media and entertainment

Products
- Automotive
- Consumer goods and services
- Health and life sciences
- Industrial equipment
- Retail
- Transportation and travel services

Financial services
- Banking
- Capital markets
- Insurance

Resources
- Chemicals
- Energy
- Natural resources
- Utilities

Government

Selected Services

Business consulting
- Customer relationship management
- Finance and performance management
- Human performance
- Strategy
- Supply chain management

Outsourcing
- Application outsourcing
- Business process outsourcing (BPO)
- Customer contact
- Finance and accounting
- Human resources
- Learning
- Procurement
- Infrastructure outsourcing

Systems integration and technology
- Enterprise architecture
- Information management
- Infrastructure consulting
- Intellectual property
- Research and development

COMPETITORS

Bain & Company
Booz Allen
Boston Consulting
Capgemini
Capgemini North America
Charteris
Computer Sciences Corp.
Deloitte Consulting
HP Enterprise Services
IBM
McKinsey & Company
Unisys

HISTORICAL FINANCIALS

Company Type: Public

Income Statement FYE: August 31

	REVENUE ($ mil.)	NET INCOME ($ mil.)	NET PROFIT MARGIN	EMPLOYEES
08/15	32,914	3,053	9.3%	358,000
08/14	31,874	2,941	9.2%	305,000
08/13	30,394	3,281	10.8%	275,000
08/12	29,777	2,553	8.6%	257,000
08/11	27,352	2,277	8.3%	236,000
Annual Growth	4.7%	7.6%	—	11.0%

2015 Year-End Financials

Debt ratio: 0.1%
Return on equity: 51.4%
Cash ($ mil.): 4,360
Current ratio: 1.36
Long-term debt ($ mil.): 25
No. of shares (mil.): 650
Dividends
Yield: 2.1%
Payout: 43.5%
Market value ($ mil.): —

ACS Actividades de Construccion y Servicios, S.A.

Turning the rains (and the wind) on the plains of Spain into electricity provides the current for growth at ACS Actividades de Construcci&oa-cute;n y Servicios one of Spain's largest construction and infrastructure groups. ACS Group operates in three primary business areas: construction environment and industrial services. The company's activities include civil engineering installation and maintenance for energy facilities transport services and highway management. ACS has grown by investing in such firms as former construction rival Dragados and Germany-based infrastructure giant HOCHTIEF. The group is active in more than 70 countries mainly in Europe and Latin America.

Operations

Of ACS' four business segments (construction environment industrial services and corporate) the construction unit is the largest. Bringing in nearly three-fourths of the group's revenues in 2014 the unit includes subsidiaries Dragados Hochtief and Iridium which are engaged in the construction of civil works and residential and commercial buildings the management of concession activities and mining and real estate ventures. Typical construction projects include roads railways parking garages sports facilities and hospitals. ACS focuses on public-private partnership arrangements for jobs such as public protection housing developments.

Industrial services (including installing and maintaining industrial infrastructure projects in the energy communications and control systems sectors) represented nearly 20% of sales in 2014. ACS has invested in the segment's growth including making investments in renewable energies. The group develops such projects as wind farms and solar energy plants as well as traditional power stations and toll systems.

Environment the smallest segment provides services ranging from road cleaning and waste collection to urban landscaping and (through Clece) building maintenance; it contributed some 7% of sales in 2014.

Geographic Reach

ACS is active in more than 70 countries; its largest markets are the US (accounting for nearly 40% of all sales) Australia Spain Mexico and Germany.

Financial Performance

Note: Growth rates may differ after conversion to US dollars.

After seeing years of growth revenue declined 35% to 34.8 billion in 2014 as sales in the construction and industrial services segments fell; this was partially offset by growth in the environment segment. Overall the construction business was sluggish in Spain and industrial services slowed down in that country as the company completed a number of projects. Elsewhere the sale of Hochtief's services business negatively impacted ACS in the rest of Europe while the devaluation of the Australian dollar affected results in the Asia/Pacific region. Activity in Africa also dipped slightly.

Net income has recovered after taking a major loss in fiscal 2012. In 2014 it rose 2% to 707 million largely due to a decline in fixed asset depreciation costs and other operating results. Cash flow from operations fell 262 million to 824 million due to changes in working capital.

Strategy

To maintain growth the group plans to continue expanding in key markets including North America Europe the Asia/Pacific region and Latin America. It is also intent on investing in infrastructure development projects.

HISTORY

In war-torn Europe in 1942 the Spanish construction company Obras y Construcciones Industriales (Ocisa) was born. The company soon began a 50-year association with Spain's hydroelectric industry marked by the completion of the dam and reservoir project Presa de Bachimana in 1950. The company built nine more dam and reservoir projects in Spain (including Presa de la Llosa completed in 1997).

As the demand for public works projects decreased and competition increased Spanish constructors began working abroad especially in Latin America where Ocisa was contracted in 1975 to create an irrigation tunnel in Venezuela's Andes.

A six-year economic expansion measured by the success of Spain's "Big Seven" construction companies including #5 Ocisa reached its end in 1992 when the Spanish government the country's biggest builder was forced to cut spending on infrastructure. This triggered consolidation in Spain's construction industry including Ocisa's 1993 acquisition of Construcciones Padros in which Ocisa held a 25% stake. Adopting the new name OCP Construcciones it also absorbed the assets of its installation and assembly subsidiary Compania de la Distribucion de Electricidad (Grupo Cobra).

The slowdown in public works projects continued and companies sought additional pooling of resources and diversification of activities at home and abroad. In 1996 OCP bought a 40% stake in the state-owned construction firm Auxini increased to 100% a year later. Also in 1997 the OCP group led by its president Florentino Perez acquired Gines Navarro Construcciones controlled (79%) by the powerful investment group led by brothers Carlos and Juan March. The two companies combined to create Spain's third-largest construction group Actividades de Construcciones y Servicios or Grupo ACS.

EXECUTIVES

Chairman President and CEO, Florentino P ©ez Rodr guez, age 68

Chairman and CEO Industrial Services, Eugenio Llorente G mez

Chairman and CEO Turner Construction, Peter J. Davoren, age 60

Chairman and CEO Flatiron, John A. DiCiurcio, age 60

CEO Dragados, Ignacio Segura Suri ±ach

Corporate General Manager, Angel Manuel Garcia Altozano

Chairman and CEO Construction Environment & Logistics and Concesisons; Chairman and CEO Dragados, Marcelino Fern ¨ndez Verdes

General Manager Urbaser, Jos ©Mar a L pez-Pi ±ol

CEO HOCHTIEF Solutions, Nikolaus Graf von Matuschka, age 52

CEO Iridium, Juan Santamaria Cases

Vice Chairman, Pablo Vallbona Vadell

Executive Vice Chairman, Antonio Garc a Ferrer, age 70

Auditors: DELOITTE, S.L.

LOCATIONS

HQ: ACS Actividades de Construccion y Servicios, S.A.
Avda. Pio XII, 102, Madrid 28036

Phone: (34) 91 343 9200 **Fax:** (34) 91 343 9456

Web: www.grupoacs.com

2013 Sales

	% of total
Asia Pacific	39
Americas	34
Spain	14
Rest of Europe	12
Africa	1
Total	**100**

PRODUCTS/OPERATIONS

2013 Sales

	% of total
Construction	77
Industrial Services	18
Environment	5
Total	**100**

Selected Subsidiaries

Concessions
- Concesiones Viarias Chile S.A. (infrastructures)
- Iridium Concesiones de Infraestructuras S.A.

Construction
- Acainsa S.A. (real estate development)
- Ave Lalin
- Consorcio Tecdra S.A.
- Constructora Norte Sur S.A. (48% Chile)
- Desaladora Barcelona (28%)
- Guadarrama Iv (33%)
- Inmobiliaria Alabega S.A. (real estate development)
- Isla Verde Ute (35%)
- Soterram. Basurto Ute Tecsa-Necso (50%)
- Terminal Aeropuerto (70%)

Environment
- Consenur S.A. (management and treatment of hospital waste)
- Empordanesa de Neteja S.A. (urban solid waste management and street cleaning)
- Mapide S.A. (interior cleaning)
- Publimedia Sistemas Publicitarios S.L. (advertising services)
- RetraOil S.L. (treatment of oils and marpoles)
- Servicios Generales de Jaén S.A. (75% water)
- Somasur S.A. (intermediary company Morocco)
- Urbaser de Méjico S.A. (collection of urban solid waste and street cleaning)
- Urbaser Valencia C.A. (collection of urban solid waste and street cleaning)
- Ute Ecoparc V (20% USW treatment)
- Vertederos de Residuos S.A. (84% VERTRESA collection of urban solid waste and street cleaning)

Industrial Services
- ACS industrial Services LLC (energy production US)
- Actividades de Servicios e Instalaciones Cobra S.A. (auxiliary energy and communications distribution Guatemala)
- Andasol 1 S.A. (energy production)
- API Movilidad S.A. (road maintenance)
- BTOB Construccion Ventures S.L. (administrative management)
- Central Térmica de Mejillones S.A. (engineering supply and construction Chile)
- Cobra Ingeniería de Montajes S.A. (installations and assembly)
- Cobra Perú S.A. (auxiliary energy and communications distribution)
- Coinsal Instalaciones y Servicios S.A. de C.V. (installations and assembly El Salvador)
- Cymi Holding S.A. (securities holding company Brazil)
- Dragados Gulf Construction Ltd. (Saudi Arabia)
- Emurtel S.A. (50% electrical installations)
- Enq S.L. (electrical installations)
- Etra Catalu?a S.A. (electrical installations)
- Extresol-1 S.L. (energy production)
- Gerovitae La Guancha S.A. (senior social and health center operations)
- Humiclima Est S.A. (air conditioning)
- Incro S.A. (50% engineering)
- Infraest. Energéticas Medioambi. Extreme?as S.L. (services)
- Instalaciones y Servicios Codeven C.A. (air conditioning)
- Mantenimiento y Montajes Industriales S.A. (industrial maintenance and assemblies)
- Mexsemi S.A. de C.V. (99.7% assemblies Mexico)
- Opade Organizac. y Promoc de Actividades Deportivas S.A. (athletic activities organization and promotion)
- Parque Eólico Marmellar S.L. (70% energy production)
- Portumasa S.A. (manufacture and sale of electical equipment Portugal)
- Semi Maroc S.A. (99.7% assemblies)
- Serveis Catalans Serveica S.A. (electrical installations)
- SICE LLC. (design construction installation and maintenance of traffic and trade)
- Sistemas Radiantes F. Moyano S.A. (telecommunications)
- Tecnotel de Canarias S.A. (air conditioning)
- Ute C.T. Andasol 1 (80% fossil fuel plant)
- Venezolana de Limpiezas Indust. C.A. (83% VENELIN Venezuela)

Services
- Valdemingomez 2000 S.A. (34% Valdemingómez degasification)

COMPETITORS

Abengoa
Acciona
Aker Solutions
Andrade Gutierrez
Balfour Beatty
Bechtel
Bilfinger
Black & Veatch
Brisa
Cintra
DP World
FCC Barcelona
Ferrovial
Grupo San Jos©
Hyundai Engineering and Construction
Kellogg Brown & Root UK
OHL
Odebrecht
Salini Impregilo
Skanska
TECNOCOM
VINCI

HISTORICAL FINANCIALS

Company Type: Public

Income Statement FYE: December 31

	REVENUE ($ mil.)	NET INCOME ($ mil.)	NET PROFIT MARGIN	EMPLOYEES
12/14	43,201	871	2.0%	217,908
12/13	53,626	965	1.8%	164,750
12/12	51,173	(2,539)	—	164,342
12/11	37,520	1,244	3.3%	164,923
12/10	21,110	1,756	8.3%	138,542
Annual Growth	19.6%	(16.1%)	—	12.0%

2014 Year-End Financials

Debt ratio: 35.7%
Return on equity: 22.7%
Cash ($ mil.): 6,280
Current ratio: 1.02
Long-term debt ($ mil.): 7,144

No. of shares (mil.): 320
Dividends
Yield: —
Payout: —
Market value ($ mil.): —

Adecco S.A. (Switzerland)

Any way you stack it Adecco is the world's largest employment agency serving some 100000 clients from more than 5500 offices worldwide. The company primarily provides temporary staffing services but Adecco also offers permanent employee placement project assistance outsourcing and other human resources-related services. Besides its core industrial and office staffing services Adecco maintains six professional lines: Engineering & Technical; Finance & Legal; Human Capital Solutions; Information Technology; Medical & Scientific; and Sales Marketing & Events. Adecco traces its roots to 1957 and has a history of growing through mergers and acquisitions.

HISTORY

Swiss accountant Henri-Ferdinand Lavanchy founded Adia in 1957 when a client asked him to find someone to fill a job. The company expanded internationally in the 1960s with offices in Belgium and elsewhere in Europe and entered the US in 1972. When Adia went public in Switzerland in 1979 Lavanchy retired from active management. Martin Pestalozzi succeeded him. The US operation Adia Services went public in 1984.

Pestalozzi's management group was ousted when retailer Asko Deutsche Kaufhaus and Swiss investor Klaus Jacobs bought about 50% of Adia in 1991 after a scandal involving the sale of part of the company to Swiss financier (later fugitive) Werner Ray. Jacobs bought out Asko in 1993 as well as Adia's US investors bringing US operations under company ownership again.

Adia and Ecco SA one of the top French employment services companies merged in 1996 to form Adecco. (Adia chairman Jacobs and Ecco chairman Philippe Foriel-Destezet began a revolving chairmanship and former Adia executive John Bowmer became CEO.) After the merger Adecco bought ICON Recruitment (IT recruiting Australia; 1996) Seagate Associates (outplacement consulting New Jersey; 1997) and Massachusetts-based TAD Resources International the largest private staffing services company in the US in 1997. The company bought rival Olsten's staffing and IT business in 2000 to further solidify Adecco as the world's largest temporary staffing firm.

Adecco restructured around four divisions (Adecco Staffing Ajilon Staffing and Managed Services Career Services and e-Recruiting and Executive Search) in 2001. In 2002 Klaus retired from the company; Bowmer became chairman and 10-year company veteran J ©´me Caille took over as CEO. Adecco sold jobpilot an online job board to Monster Worldwide in 2004. In 2005 the company acquired French human resources firm Altedia. Caille left the company in 2005 and Jacobs came back on board as chairman and interim CEO. In 2006 Dieter Scheiff was named as the new CEO.

Adecco augmented its German operations in mid-2007 when it acquired German staffing company Tuja Holding GmbH for about $1 billion. Tuja's estimated revenue for 2007 was around $870 million.

After years of acquisitions (and a failed attempt to buy rival Michael Page International in 2008) the company appointed Patrick De Maeseneire as the new CEO effective June 2009. A former Adecco executive De Maeseneire had served as the CEO of chocolate maker Barry Callebaut since 2002. Adecco made a megadeal in January 2010 with the acquisition of rival MPS Group for $1.3 billion.

EXECUTIVES

Regional Head North America, Robert P. (Bob) Crouch, age 47
Regional Head Japan and Asia, Christophe Duchatellier, age 53
CEO, Alain Dehaze, age 51, $150,745 total compensation
Regional Head Germany and Austria, Andreas Dinges, age 57, $158,282 total compensation
Regional Head Italy and Eastern Europe, Federico Vione, age 44, $113,059 total compensation
Regional Head UK and Ireland, Peter Searle, $106,963 total compensation
Regional Head Iberia and South America, Enrique Sanchez, age 49, $161,296 total compensation
CIO, Frank Meyer
Regional Head Northern Europe, Martin Alonso, age 51
CFO, Hans P. van Amstel
Chairman, Rolf Dorig, age 58
Vice Chairman, Andreas Jacobs, age 52
Auditors: Ernst & Young Ltd.

LOCATIONS

HQ: Adecco S.A. (Switzerland)
Saegereistrasse 10, Glattbrugg 8152
Phone: (41) 44 878 88 88 **Fax:** (41) 44 829 88 88
Web: www.adecco.com

PRODUCTS/OPERATIONS

2014 Sales

	% of total
France	23
North America	19
UK & Ireland	10
Germany & Austria	8
Japan	5
Italy	5
Benelux	5
Nordics	4
Iberia	4
Australia & New Zealand	2
Switzerland	3
Emerging Markets	10
LHH	2
Total	**100**

2014 Sales

	% of total
General Staffing	75
Professional Staffing	23
Solutions	2
Total	**100**

COMPETITORS

Insperity
Kelly Services
ManpowerGroup
Randstad Holding
Robert Half
Synergie
Technical Aid Corporation
Volt Information

HISTORICAL FINANCIALS

Company Type: Public

Income Statement FYE: December 31

	REVENUE ($ mil.)	NET INCOME ($ mil.)	NET PROFIT MARGIN	EMPLOYEES
12/14	24,310	775	3.2%	31,576
12/13	26,850	766	2.9%	31,329
12/12	27,067	496	1.8%	32,987
12/11	26,573	671	2.5%	32,826
12/10	24,968	566	2.3%	31,279
Annual Growth	(0.7%)	8.2%	—	0.2%

2014 Year-End Financials

Debt ratio: 21.5%
Return on equity: 17.2%
Cash ($ mil.): 844
Current ratio: 1.25
Long-term debt ($ mil.): 1,925
No. of shares (mil.): 173
Dividends
Yield: 3.1%
Payout: 21.6%
Market value ($ mil.): 5,951

	STOCK PRICE ($) FY Close	P/E High/Low	PER SHARE ($) Earnings	Dividends	Book Value
12/14	34.31	11 8	4.39	1.08	26.88
12/13	39.83	13 9	4.24	0.94	27.46
12/12	26.45	13 10	2.64	0.95	26.39
12/11	20.86	12 7	3.52	0.54	28.90
12/10	32.62	15 11	2.90	0.19	27.31
Annual Growth	1.3%	— —	10.9%	54.6%	(0.4%)

AEGON N.V.

Not only has AEGON expanded across Europe it has also spread Transamerica. The Dutch life insurance giant is using its expertise in acquisition (US rival Transamerica was its largest catch) and consolidation to build a transnational collection of financial service businesses serving 40 million customers worldwide. Its subsidiaries operate primarily in the US the Netherlands and the UK offering personal and commercial life insurance pensions and annuities and accident and supplemental health insurance as well as retirement and savings advice and management services. AEGON has insurance operations in 25 countries in the Americas Europe and Asia as well as banking operations in the Netherlands.

Operations

The group operates in five segments: Aegon Americas (which includes business units in the US Canada Brazil and Mexico); Aegon the Netherlands; Aegon UK; New Markets (Central and Eastern Europe Asia Spain France as well as variable annuity activities in Europe and asset management); and Holding (financing employee relations and other administrative expenses).

Asset management operations include equity and fixed-income and cover Aegon's insurance subsidiaries as well as third-party clients and insurance-linked products.

Geographic Reach

Aegon's primary operations are in the Netherlands the US and the UK. In Central and Eastern Europe it operates in the Czech Republic Hungary Poland Romania Slovakia Turkey and the Ukraine. The group also operates in Hong Kong Ireland and Spain. Through a distribution agreement with Santander Aegon sells its products in Portugal.

The group also has joint ventures in Brazil China France India Japan and Mexico.

Sales and Marketing

Marketing arm Aegon Direct Affinity Marketings operates in Australia Indonesia Japan Singapore and Thailand. The group sells in the UK through retail advisor channels workplace channels and direct channels. In the Netherlands Aegon offers non-life insurance products through its intermediary channel and through the direct Aegon Online channel and partnerships.

Financial Performance

After seeing a dip in 2011 the group's revenues climbed for two years. In 2014 revenues again slipped 4% to 46.3 billion as financial transactions declined; these declines were partially offset by an increase in investment fee and commission income.

Following the decline in revenues net income fell 23% to 757 million.

Cash flow from operations rose to 4.1 billion (versus an outflow of 2 billion in 2013); this improvement was due to an increase in cash provided by sales of investments and derivatives.

Strategy

The company has established a strong growth pattern for existing and new international markets largely through strategic acquisitions. Aegon which derives about 60% of its revenues from life insurance premiums is focused on organic expansion in the high-growth regions of Asia Central and Eastern Europe and Latin America. To consolidate its market position in Spain Aegon in mid-2013 inked an exclusive 25-year strategic partnership with Santander. As part of the agreement AEGON acquired a 51% stake in the joint venture which consists of a life insurance company and a non-life insurance company. The venture distributes life and general insurance products through Santander's branch network while Aegon Spain provides back-office services.

Aegon's strategic priorities also include divesting or closing business that don't contribute to its long-term goals. It has divested units worth more than 3 billion since 2010 including its stake in France's La Mondiale Participations the UK's Guardian Assurance as well as its US reinsurance activities. It has placed its institutional markets division in run-off.

Other goals include improving customer service to increase client loyalty investing in new distribution channels and strengthening its brands. The group is also focused on growing its online presence and cutting operational costs.

HISTORY

AEGON traces its roots to 1844 when former civil servant and funeral society agent J. Oosterhoff founded Algemeene Friesche a burial society for low-income workers. The next year a similar organization Groot-Noordhollandsche was founded. These companies later became insurers and expanded nationwide. Meanwhile Olveh a civil servants' aid group was founded in 1877. The three companies merged in 1968 to form mutual insurer AGO.

AEGON's other operations came from different traditions. Vennootschap Nederland was founded in 1858 as a tontine (essentially a death pool with the survivors taking the pot) by Count A. Langrand-Dumonceau an ex-French Foreign Legionnaire from Belgium. In 1913 the company merged with Eerste Nederlandsche whose accident and health division had been previously spun off as Nieuwe Eerste Nederlandsche.

A year after Vennootschap was founded C. F. W. Wiggers van Kerchem founded a similar scheme Nillmij in the Dutch East Indies. The government promoted Nillmij to colonial civil servants and military people and for a while the company enjoyed a monopoly in the colony. Nillmij's Indonesian operations were nationalized after independence in 1957 but its Dutch subsidiaries continued to operate. All insurers were hit by fast-growing postwar government social programs. As a result industry consolidation came early to the Netherlands. In 1969 Eerste Nederlandsche Nieuwe Eerste Nederlandsche and Nillmij merged to form Ennia.

AGO demutualized in 1978 and became AGO Holding N.V. which was owned by Vereniging AGO. Meanwhile the shrinking Dutch insurance market forced companies to look overseas. AGO moved into the US in 1979 by buying Life Investors; by 1982 half of its sales came from outside the Netherlands. Ennia meanwhile expanded in Europe (it entered Spain in 1980) and the US (buying Arkansas-based National Old Line Insurance in 1981).

AGO and Ennia merged in 1983 to form AEGON. Vereniging AGO became Vereniging AEGON and received a 49% stake in the combined entity. (This stake was later reduced.) The company made more purchases at home and abroad and spent much of the rest of the decade assimilating operations.

AEGON's US units accounted for about 40% of sales in the mid-1980s and the firm increased that figure with acquisitions. In 1986 it bought Baltimore-based Monumental Corp. (life and health insurance) and expanded the company's US penetration.

This left AEGON underrepresented in Europe as deregulation paved the way for economic union and social service cutbacks spurred opportunities in private financial planning in the region. So in the 1990s AEGON began buying European companies including Regency Life (UK 1991) and Allami Biztosito (Hungary 1992). It formed an alliance with Mexico's Grupo Financiero Banamex in 1994. This reduced its reliance on US sales. It continued buying specialty operations in the US particularly asset management lines.

In 1997 AEGON began to concentrate on life insurance and financial services and shed its other operations. It bought the insurance business of Providian (now part of Washington Mutual) and sold noncore lines such as auto coverage. The next year it sold FGH Bank (mortgages) to Germany's Bayerische Vereinsbank (now Bayerische Hypotheken und Vereinsbank) and in 1999 sold auto insurer Worldwide Insurance.

That year AEGON expanded further in the US with the $9.7 billion purchase of Transamerica and bought the life and pensions businesses of the UK's Guardian Royal Exchange. In 2000 the company sold Labouchere N.V. a Dutch banking subsidiary to Dexia. Also in 2000 AEGON acquired UK-based third-party administrator HS Administrative Services.

Following the Transamerica acquisition the company divested several assets to focus on life insurance and pensions. In 2003 and 2004 diverse parts of Transamerica Finance (including its real estate tax unit and trailer leasing business) were sold to various companies including First American GE Commercial Finance and a joint venture held by Goldman Sachs and Cerberus Capital Management.

EXECUTIVES

CEO AEGON The Netherlands and Member Management Board, Marco Keim, age 54

CEO and Chairman of the Executive and Management Boards, Alexander R. (Alex) Wynaendts, age 54, $864,583 total compensation

CEO AmericasMember Management Board;, Mark W. Mullin, age 53

CFO and Member Executive and Management Boards, Darryl D. Button, age 46

CEO AEGON Central and Eastern Europe and Member Management Board, G ˇbor Kepecs

CEO Aegon UK Member Management Board Aegis N.V., Adrian Grace

CIO, Brenda Clancy

Chief Risk Officer, Allegra van H ¶ell-Patrizi, age 41

Vice Chairman, Irving W. Bailey, age 73

Chairman Supervisory Board., Robert J. Routs, age 69

Auditors: PricewaterhouseCoopers Accountants N.V.

LOCATIONS

HQ: AEGON N.V.
Aegonplein 50, P.O. Box 85, The Hague 2501 CB
Phone: (31) 70 3445458
Web: www.aegon.com

2014 Sales

	% of total
The Americas	42
UK	23
The Netherlands	24
Other regions	11
Total	**100**

PRODUCTS/OPERATIONS

2014 Revenue

	% of total
Life insurance	56
Investment income	27
Accident & health insurance	8
Fee and commission income	7
General insurance	2
Total	**100**

Selected Subsidiaries and Affiliates

The Americas
- AEGON USA LLC Cedar Rapids Iowa (US)
- Transamerica Advisors Life Insurance Company Little Rock Arkansas (US)
- Transamerica Advisors Life Insurance Company of New York New York New York (US)
- Transamerica Premier Life Insurance Company (formerly Monumental Life Insurance Company Cedar Rapids Iowa) (US)
- Stonebridge Casualty Insurance Company Columbus Ohio (US)
- Stonebridge Life Insurance Company Rutland Vermont (US)
- Transamerica Financial Life Insurance Company Inc. Purchase New York (US)
- Transamerica Life Insurance Company Cedar Rapids Iowa (US)
- Western Reserve Life Assurance Co. of Ohio Columbus Ohio (US)
- Transamerica Life Canada Toronto Ontario (Canada)

The Netherlands
- AEGON Bank NV Utrecht
- AEGON Levensverzekering NV The Hague
- AEGON Schadeverzekering NV The Hague
- OPTAS Pensioenen NV Rotterdam

The UK
- Scottish Equitable plc Edinburgh
- Origen Financial Services Ltd. London
- Positive Solutions (Financial Services) Ltd. Newcastle

Other regions
- AEGON Espa?a S.A. Madrid Spain (99.98%)
- AEGON Magyarország Általános Biztosító Zrt. Budapest Hungary
- AEGON Towarzystwo Ubezpieczeń na Życie Spółka Akcyjna. Warsaw Poland
- AEGON Asset Management Company Mumbai India (75%)

Selected Joint Ventures

AEGON Sony Life Insurance Cy (50%) life insurance Tokyo
AEGON-CNOOC Life Insurance Company Ltd (50%) life insurance Shanghai
AMVEST Vastgoed BV (50%) property management and development; Utrecht Netherlands
CAN Vida y Pensiones Sociedad Anónima de Seguros (50%) life insurance and pension; Pamplona Spain
Caixa Terrassa Vida y Pensiones Sociedad Anónima de Seguros (50%) life and accident insurance and pension; Terrassa Spain

COMPETITORS

AIG
AXA
Achmea
Allianz
Allstate
American General
Ameriprise

Aviva
Aviva Life Insurance India
BMO Financial Group
Canada Life
Delta Lloyd
Desjardins Financial Security
E-L Financial
FMR
Fidelity & Guaranty Life
Franklin Templeton
Generali Deutschland
ING
Industrial Alliance Insurance and Financial Servic
Jackson National Life
John Hancock Financial Services
Legal & General Group
Lincoln Financial Group
Lloyds Banking Group
Manulife Financial
MassMutual
MetLife
Munich Re Group
Mutual of Omaha
Nationwide
New York Life
Old Mutual
OppenheimerFunds
Power Corporation of Canada
Primerica
Principal Financial
Prudential
Prudential plc
Putnam
RBC Insurance
Rabobank Group
SNS REAAL
Standard Life
Sun Life
Swiss Life
Symetra
T. Rowe Price
The Hartford
The Vanguard Group
Western & Southern Financial
Zurich Insurance Group

HISTORICAL FINANCIALS

Company Type: Public

Income Statement

FYE: December 31

	ASSETS ($ mil.)	NET INCOME ($ mil.)	INCOME AS % OF ASSETS	EMPLOYEES
12/14	515,941	918	0.2%	26,981
12/13	487,013	1,346	0.3%	26,891
12/12	482,493	2,017	0.4%	24,407
12/11	446,987	1,124	0.3%	25,288
12/10	444,745	2,354	0.5%	27,474
Annual Growth	3.8%	(21.0%)	—	(0.5%)

2014 Year-End Financials

Return on assets: 0.1%
Return on equity: 2.8%
Long-term debt ($ mil.): —
No. of shares (mil.): —
Sales ($ mil): 49,226

Dividends
Yield: 3.9%
Payout: 75.9%
Market value ($ mil.): —

	STOCK PRICE ($) FY Close	P/E High/Low	PER SHARE ($) Earnings	Dividends	Book Value
12/14	7.50	29 24	0.35	0.30	12.62
12/13	9.48	26 17	0.50	0.29	16.52
12/12	6.44	10 6	0.88	0.23	20.11
12/11	4.02	— —	(0.08)	0.00	17.69
12/10	6.13	9 6	1.11	0.00	18.36
Annual Growth	5.2%	— —	(24.9%)	—	(8.9%)

Aeon Co. Ltd. (Japan)

Japanese giant AEON CO. has enough retail ventures to last for eons. The holding company has about 180 subsidiaries and 25 affiliated companies. It runs the Aeon and Jusco chains of general merchandise stores and Japan's #1 supermarket chain with 1300 stores under the MaxValu and other banners as well as 3500-plus MINISTOP convenience stores. AEON also operates specialty chains including The Body Shop and Laura Ashley stores in Japan. It has a joint venture in Japan with Sports Authority and also operates HapYcom a leading drugstore chain in Japan. Other operations include shopping center development and financial services. Facing slow growth at home AEON is expanding in China and other Asian economies.

To that end AEON's China-based subsidiary and its MaxValu supermarket chain in 2012 formed a joint venture to operate supermarkets in China.

Sales across the vast AEON group inched up less than 1% in fiscal 2011 (ends February) vs. the previous year. Sales in Japan rose 4% while sales in the rest of Asia fell.

AEON has adopted a holding company structure in a bid to increase its responsiveness to changing (mostly negative) retail trends in Japan where it rings up about 95% of its total sales. A prolonged economic slump aging and shrinking population and weakness in the supermarket and department store sectors have the Japanese retailer looking abroad for future growth. Important Asian markets for AEON include China Hong Kong Malaysia South Korea and Thailand. The company beat a hasty retreat from North America with the sale of its majority stake in ladies apparel chain The Talbots in 2010 to better focus on its retail and financial service operations in Asia.

To grow in China AEON established a subsidiary in Shenzhen and greatly increased its investment there. At the end of fiscal 2011 (ends February) AEON had about 80 stores in China including specialty and general merchandise stores and supermarkets. Also AEON operates two mall-style shopping centers located in Beijing and in Huizhou northeast of Shenzhen. The malls are populated by specialty shops including AEON-owned banners such as Jusco and The Body Shop.

To adapt to changing demographics in its home country AEON is focusing on the "senior market" by developing products especially for seniors and developing senior-friendly floor plans and stores as well as services. The company's My Basket chain of more than 220 small-size urban supermarkets was developed specifically to serve Japan's aging and increasingly urban population. In early 2012 the retailer spun off its My Basket division into a wholly-owned subsidiary with the aim of tripling its store count in the Tokyo metro area by the end of fiscal 2013.

Among Japanese retailers AEON is one of the most proactive in preparing to defend its business from foreign competitors including the world's #1 retailer Wal-Mart and Britain's Tesco. To compete it has cut prices and distribution costs adopted western sales techniques and has acquired smaller retailers. The company is upgrading its computer systems to rival those of US giant Wal-Mart. Also AEON beat out Wal-Mart to buy eight hypermarkets in Japan operated by France's Carrefour which abandoned the Japanese market. In mid-2012 AEON agreed to acquired a 50% stake in Tesco Japan a subsidiary of UK's largest retailer Tesco plc for just 1 yen. Tesco Japan operates about 120 small Tesco and Tsurukame supermarkets in and around Tokyo. AEON is expected to acquire the remainder of Tesco Japan in the future.

EXECUTIVES

President, Motoya Okada, age 63
EVP, Noriyuki Murakami
VP, Atsunobu Agata
SEVP, Yoshiki Mori
VP; President AEON Mall, Soichi Okazaki
EVP, Hiroshi Yokoo
EVP, Jerry Black
EVP, Shouhei Murai
EVP, Masaaki Toyoshima
VP; CEO ASEAN, Nagahisa Oyama
VP; CEO China, Haruyoshi Tsuji
Chairman, Naoki Hayashi
Auditors: Deloitte Touche Tohmatsu LLC

LOCATIONS

HQ: Aeon Co. Ltd. (Japan)
1-5-1 Nakase, Mihama-ku, Chiba 261-8515
Phone: (81) 43 212 6042 **Fax:** (81) 43 212 6849
Web: www.aeon.info

2015 Sales

	% of total
Japan	92
ASEAN	4
China	3
Other	1
Total	**100**

PRODUCTS/OPERATIONS

2015 Sales

	% of total
GMS	45
Supermarket DiscountStore and Small-sizedStore	29
SpecServices and Specialty Store	10
Financial Services	4
Shopping Center Development	3
ASEAN	3
China	2
Other	4
Adjustments	0
Total	**100**

Selected Store Names

Abilities Jusco (CDs DVDs and books)
Asbee (shoe stores)
Blue Grass (apparel for teenage girls)
Claire' s Nippon (women' s clothing)
Cox (family casual clothing)
HapYcom (drugstores)
Home Wide Corp. (home centers)
JUSCO (apparel food and household item superstores)
JUS-Photo (film developing)
Laura Ashley Japan (clothing and home furnishings)
Maxvalu (supermarkets)
Mega Sports (Sports Authority stores)
MINISTOP (convenience stores)
MYCAL Corporation (supermarkets)
My Basket (small-scale supermarkets)
Nustep (family footwear stores)
Petcity (pets & pet supplies)
Sports Authority (sporting goods)

COMPETITORS

A.S. Watson
Carrefour
Costco Wholesale
Dairy Farm International
Fast Retailing
Heiwado
Isetan Mitsukoshi
Ito-Yokado
METRO AG
Rakuten
Seiyu
Seven & i
Takashimaya
Tesco
The Gap
Uny

HISTORICAL FINANCIALS

Company Type: Public

Income Statement FYE: February 28

	REVENUE ($ mil.)	NET INCOME ($ mil.)	NET PROFIT MARGIN	EMPLOYEES
02/15	59,323	352	0.6%	126,440
02/14	62,775	447	0.7%	109,523
02/13	61,696	810	1.3%	91,646
02/12	64,736	830	1.3%	81,483
02/11	62,252	729	1.2%	74,465
Annual Growth	(1.2%)	(16.6%)	—	14.2%

2015 Year-End Financials

Debt ratio: 0.2%
Return on equity: 3.6%
Cash ($ mil.): 6,798
Current ratio: 0.98
Long-term debt ($ mil.): 10,531
No. of shares (mil.): 841
Dividends
Yield: —
Payout: —
Market value ($ mil.): 8,981

	STOCK PRICE ($) FY Close	P/E High/Low	PER SHARE ($) Earnings	Dividends	Book Value
02/15	10.67	— —	0.42	0.00	18.23
02/14	12.14	— —	0.49	0.25	19.55
02/13	11.27	— —	0.95	0.43	19.86
02/12	12.66	— —	0.95	0.26	20.72
02/11	12.54	— —	0.83	0.21	19.47
Annual Growth	(3.9%)	— —	(16.0%)	—	(1.6%)

Ageas NV

Auditors: KPMG Reviseurs d'Entreprises/Bedrijfsrevisren

LOCATIONS

HQ: Ageas NV
Rue du Marquis 1, Brussels 1000
Phone: (32) 2 557 57 11 **Fax:** (32) 2 557 57 50
Web: www.ageas.com

HISTORICAL FINANCIALS

Company Type: Public

Income Statement FYE: December 31

	ASSETS ($ mil.)	NET INCOME ($ mil.)	INCOME AS % OF ASSETS	EMPLOYEES
12/14	125,876	578	0.5%	12,204
12/13	131,802	784	0.6%	13,071
12/12	127,999	979	0.8%	13,335
12/11	117,189	(747)	—	12,557
12/10	132,721	298	0.2%	11,707
Annual Growth	(1.3%)	18.0%	—	1.0%

2014 Year-End Financials

Return on assets: 0.4%
Return on equity: 5.0%
Long-term debt ($ mil.): —
No. of shares (mil.): 219
Sales ($ mil): 17,282
Dividends
Yield: 7.9%
Payout: 48.7%
Market value ($ mil.): 7,780

	STOCK PRICE ($) FY Close	P/E High/Low	PER SHARE ($) Earnings	Dividends	Book Value
12/14	35.47	19 14	2.59	2.81	56.65
12/13	42.81	18 13	3.43	2.55	51.83
12/12	30.25	10 1	4.13	0.00	56.35
12/11	1.52	— —	(2.97)	0.00	41.71
12/10	2.25	5 2	1.20	0.00	42.73
Annual Growth	99.3%	— —	21.1%	—	7.3%

Agricultural Bank of China

Agricultural Bank of China (ABC) provides a veritable alphabet soup of products and services to customers across China. Boasting assets of $2.6 trillion and more than 23600 branches across China the commercial bank is its home country's (and the world's) third-largest bank. Beyond providing retail and commercial banking and lending services to agricultural industrial commercial and transportation enterprises in rural areas the bank also offers credit cards treasury management investment banking fund management private banking and life insurance products and services. Founded in 1951 ABC also operates around 10 overseas branches in locations including Hong Kong and Singapore and representative offices in London and Tokyo.

Operations

ABC divides its banking operations into three segments: Corporate Banking (54% of total operating income in 2014) Retail Banking (36%) and treasury (9%). By the end of 2014 ABC had 3.45 million corporate banking customers (up from 2.81 million in 2011) and 456 million retail customers (up from 395 million in 2011). About 64% of its loan assets were corporate loans in 2014 while retail loans and overseas loans made up 30% and 5% of its loan portfolio respectively. ABC's net interest income made up about 82% of ABC's total operating income in 2014 while 15% came from net fee and commission income including bank card fees (4%) settlement and clearing fees (4%) agency commissions (4%) consultancy and advisory fees (2%) electronic banking service fees (1%) custody and fiduciary service fees (less than 1%) and various other miscellaneous income sources.

Geographic Reach

Most of ABC's operating income in 2014 came from customers located in Western China (21%) the Yangtze River Delta (19%) and the Bohai Rim (16%). The bank's overseas operations brought in 2% of its operating income. Financial PerformanceNote: Growth rates may differ after conversion to US dollars. This analysis uses financials from the company's annual report. ABC's revenues and profits have been rising over the past several years mostly thanks to aggressive loan business growth (its loan assets grew 60% from 2009 through 2014) but also thanks to its expansion of fee-based business lines.The bank's revenue grew double digits to RMB$801.25 billion ($130.2 billion) mostly thanks to higher interest income as its loan assets grew by 9% to nearly RMB$8 trillion ($1.3 trillion); medium and long-term corporate loans and retail loan growth led most of the growth. The bank's loan yields also rose by eight basis points to 6.06% as it improved its mix of loan business also boosting interest income. Fee and commission income dipped by around 4% mostly as its consultancy and advisory fees (and other investment banking business) declined during the year. Higher revenue and a decrease in the bank's cost-to-income ratio drove ABC's net income up 8% to RMB$179.51 billion ($29.2 billion). The bank's operating cash levels also improved modestly to RMB$34.62 billion ($5.6 billion) with the higher cash earnings.

Strategy

ABC in late 2014 remained "committed to catering to the needs of Sannong and capitalizing on the synergy between the Urban and County areas across China." The company's business in urban areas has been growing and made up 62.2% of its operating income in 2014 up from 60% in 2013. The company also in 2014 continued to grow its higher-margin investment banking and private banking businesses. That year it established private banking departments in 30 branches and grew its private banking customer base of high net worth individuals to 57000 with some RMB$640 billion ($104 billion) in assets under custody.Beyond China it also looked to continue its international expansions plans and provide a variety of services "to become an international first-class large-scale commercial bank."

Company Background ABC completed one of the world's largest initial public offerings in 2010 raising more than $22 billion. Prior to the listing ABC was the only non-listed bank among the big four state-owned commercial banks in China. (The others are Bank of China China Construction Bank and Industrial and Commercial Bank of China.) The money raised in the IPO was used to strengthen the bank's capital base.

EXECUTIVES

Chairman, Liu Shiyu, age 55
EVP, Cai Huaxiang, age 55
Executive Director and EVP, Lou Wenlong, age 57
EVP and Secretary Party Discipline Committee, Gong Chao
EVP, Wang Wei
EVP, Li Zhenjiang
Auditors: PricewaterhouseCoopers Zhong Tian LLP

LOCATIONS

HQ: Agricultural Bank of China
No. 69, Jianguomen Nei Avenue, Dongcheng District, Beijing 100005
Phone: (86) 10 85109619 **Fax:** (86) 10 85108557
Web: www.abchina.com

2011 Sales

	% of total
Yangtze River Delta	22
Western China	21
Bohai Rim	15
Head Office	13
Pearl River Delta	13
Central China	12
Northeastern China	3
Overseas & other	1
Total	**100**

PRODUCTS/OPERATIONS

2011 Sales

	% of total
Corporate banking	58
Retail banking	36
Treasury operations	6
Total	**100**

COMPETITORS

Bank of China
China Construction Bank
China Development Bank

China Merchants Bank
Hua Xia Bank
Industrial and Commercial Bank of China
Shenzhen Development Bank

HISTORICAL FINANCIALS

Company Type: Public

Income Statement FYE: December 31

	ASSETS ($ mil.)	NET INCOME ($ mil.)	INCOME AS % OF ASSETS	EMPLOYEES
12/14	2,573,832	28,915	1.1%	517,671
12/13	2,405,410	27,472	1.1%	513,750
12/12	2,124,449	23,273	1.1%	501,762
12/11	1,855,232	19,370	1.0%	490,121
12/10	1,568,269	14,393	0.9%	485,800
Annual Growth	13.2%	19.1%		1.6%

2014 Year-End Financials

Return on assets: 1.1%
Return on equity: 19.1%
Long-term debt ($ mil.): —
No. of shares (mil.): —
Sales ($ mil): 129,106
Dividends
Yield: 4.7%
Payout: 675.7%
Market value ($ mil.): —

	STOCK PRICE ($) FY Close	P/E High/Low	PER SHARE ($) Earnings	Dividends	Book Value
12/14	12.62	23 18	0.09	0.60	0.51
12/13	12.33	29 19	0.08	0.52	0.43
12/12	12.60	29 20	0.07	0.42	0.37
12/11	10.63	43 20	0.06	0.17	0.32
Annual Growth	5.9%		10.1%	36.1%	12.6%

AIA Group Ltd.

What's decades old brand new named "American" but operates in Asia? American International Assurance –better known as AIA Group! The life insurance and wealth management company operates in 17 countries across Asia and the Pacific. It offers life insurance credit insurance employee benefits and pension services to its corporate clients. For individuals the company provides basic life insurance along with savings investment and retirement products. Founded in 1919 it was the original business that would later grow to become American International Group (AIG) and was a cornerstone of that company's Asia-based operations. However in 2010 AIG spun off the business through a public offering.

Operations

AIA's reportable segments are Hong Kong (including Macau) Thailand Singapore (including Brunei) Malaysia China Korea Other Markets and Group Corporate Centre. Except for the latter segment they all provide life accident and health insurance and distribute savings plans and related financial services. Through its extensive network of agents partners and employees across the region AIA serves more than 28 million individual policyholders and more than 16 million participating members of group insurance schemes.

Geographic Reach

The company has operations in 17 countries in the Asia/Pacific region with the notable exception of Japan. (AIG kept its Japanese holdings separate.) It owns branches and subsidiaries in Hong Kong Thailand Singapore Malaysia China Korea the Philippines Australia Indonesia Taiwan Vietnam New Zealand Macau Brunei Sri Lanka; it also owns a minority stake in an Indian joint venture and has a representative office in Myanmar.

Sales and Marketing

AIA markets its products through agents partners and employees throughout the region.

Financial Performance

In 2014 revenue increased 16% to $25.4 billion primarily on growth of new business. China and Hong Kong in particular performed well as did Malaysia Thailand and Singapore. Net income increased 22% to $3.4 billion that year driven by the higher revenue.

Cash flow from operations fell 30% to $744 million due to higher financial investments and an increase in taxes paid.

Strategy

While its roots are deep in China the company is looking to grow in markets with underdeveloped life insurance markets including India the Philippines and Vietnam. Its growth plans include selling its individual insurance products through banks. In 2013 it reached a bancassurance agreement with Citibank that encompasses 11 markets in the Asia/Pacific.

The company is also expanding the scope of its offerings to attract new customers. In 2014 AIA introduced a comprehensive critical illness product for families and a new disability income plan targeting the middle class.

EXECUTIVES

Executive Director and Group Chief Executive and President, Mark E. Tucker, age 57
Group CFO, Garth Jones
Regional Chief Executive, Gordon Watson
Regional Chief Executive, Ng Keng Hooi
Group COO, Simeon Preston
Group Chief Investment Officer, John Tai-Wo Chu
CEO AIA Singapore, Patrick Teow
Regional Chief Executive Malaysia Korea Sri Lanka India and Cambodia, William Lisle, age 50
Chairman, Edmund S.W. Tse, age 77
Auditors: PricewaterhouseCoopers

LOCATIONS

HQ: AIA Group Ltd.
35/F, AIA Central, No. 1 Connaught Road Central,
Phone: (852) 2832 1800 **Fax:** (852) 2834 1753
Web: www.aia.com

2014 Sales

	% of total
Hong Kong	24
Thailand	19
Singapore	16
Malaysia	11
China	10
Korea	9
Other markets	10
Group corporate	1
Total	**100**

PRODUCTS/OPERATIONS

2014 Sales

	% of total
Net premiums & fee income	67
Investment returns	32
Other operating revenue	1
Total	**100**

COMPETITORS

AXA Asia Pacific
Aviva
Cathay Life Insurance
China Insurance
China Life Insurance
China Pacific Insurance
Chubb Limited
MetLife
Ping An Insurance
Sun Life

HISTORICAL FINANCIALS

Company Type: Public

Income Statement FYE: November 30

	REVENUE ($ mil.)	NET INCOME ($ mil.)	NET PROFIT MARGIN	EMPLOYEES
11/14	25,433	3,450	13.6%	20,000
11/13	21,926	2,822	12.9%	26,000
11/12	20,387	3,019	14.8%	18,000
11/11	14,388	1,600	11.1%	20,000
11/10	18,394	2,701	14.7%	21,000
Annual Growth	8.4%	6.3%	—	(1.2%)

2014 Year-End Financials

Debt ratio: —
Return on equity: 12.4%
Cash ($ mil.): 1,835
Current ratio: —
Long-term debt ($ mil.): —
No. of shares (mil.): —
Dividends
Yield: 0.0%
Payout: 66.2%
Market value ($ mil.): —

	STOCK PRICE ($) FY Close	P/E High/Low	PER SHARE ($) Earnings	Dividends	Book Value
11/14	23.12	81 62	0.29	0.19	2.56
11/13	20.31	88 65	0.24	0.17	2.05
11/12	15.62	66 46	0.25	0.15	2.22
11/11	12.53	116 79	0.13	0.05	1.77
Annual Growth	22.7%	— —	22.2%	40.4%	9.6%

Air France-KLM

Air France and KLM represent years of French and Dutch airline tradition but Air France-KLM represents a first: a holding company made up of two national airlines. Together Air France-KLM is the second-largest airline in Europe after Deutsche Lufthansa and one of the largest in the world. Through its operating units the company serves more than 315 destinations in about 115 countries with a fleet of some 540 aircraft. Air France and KLM operate independently from hubs in Paris and Amsterdam but have coordinated their operations both as sister companies and as members of the SkyTeam alliance which also includes Alitalia Delta Air Lines and Korean Air Lines.

Geographic ReachThe Air France-KLM network is organized around its hubs at Paris-Charles de Gaulle and Amsterdam-Schiphol. With these two major hubs the company links Europe to the rest of the world spanning 316 destinations in 115 countries.

OperationsAir France-KLM offers passenger transportation cargo transportation and aircraft maintenance services and transported 87.4 million passengers and 1.3 million tons of cargo in 2015. It has a fleet of 546 aircraft in operation.

Financial Performance

The company's net sales decreased by 608 million from 2013 to 2014 due to decreased sales from its passenger and cargo businesses. The company also suffered net losses in 2013 and 2014 due to impairment charges and negative impacts from fuel hedges.

Strategy

Air France-KLM has identified three main growth areas: Asia where it plans to reinforce its existing partnerships and develop new ones with airlines which are similar to its own airlines in size; the European leisure market where it will accelerate Transavia's growth; and the maintenance market where it plans to continue to make acquisitions to supplement its organic growth.

EXECUTIVES

EVP Engineering & Maintenance; COO Air France, Alain Bassil, age 58
Chairman and CEO Air France, Fr @ @c Gagey, age 60
Chairman and CEO Air France-KLM, Alexandre de Juniac, age 53
EVP Cargo, Erik Varwijk, age 54
EVP Human Resources, Wim Kooijman, age 64
CFO, Pierre-Fran $is Riolacci, age 48
EVP Engineering and Maintenance, Franck Terner, age 55
EVP and Corporate Secretary, Jacques Le Pape
EVP Commercial Sales and Marketing, Patrick Alexandre, age 60
EVP Commercial Marketing, Pieter Bootsma, age 46
President and CEO KLM Royal Dutch Airlines, Pieter Elbers, age 45
EVP Strategy Passenger Business, Bram Gr ¤ber, age 50
EVP Information Technology, Jean-Christophe Lalanne
CEO Transavia France, Nathalie Stubler
Vice Chairman, Peter Hartman
Auditors: Deloitte et Associ ©

LOCATIONS

HQ: Air France-KLM
2, rue Robert Esnault-Pelterie, Paris 75007
Phone: (33) 1 41 56 78 00 **Fax:** (33) 1 41 56 56 00
Web: www.airfranceklm-finance.com

2014 Sales

	% of total
Metropolitan France Benelux	31
Africa	22
Europe	14
America	11
North	10
Middle-EasternGulfIndia	5
West Indies Caribbean Guyana Indian Ocean South America	5
AsiaPacific	2
Total	**100**

PRODUCTS/OPERATIONS

2014 Sales

	% of total
Passenger	78
Cargo	11
Maintenance	5
Other	6
Total	**100**

COMPETITORS

Aer Lingus
Air Berlin
American Airlines Group
Austrian Airlines
Brussels Airlines
IAG
Lufthansa
Ryanair
SAS
SNCF
United Continental
Virgin Atlantic Airways
easyJet

HISTORICAL FINANCIALS

Company Type: Public

Income Statement FYE: December 31

	REVENUE ($ mil.)	NET INCOME ($ mil.)	NET PROFIT MARGIN	EMPLOYEES
12/14	30,302	(240)	—	94,666
12/13	35,148	(2,515)	—	95,961
12/12	33,806	(1,571)	—	100,744
12/11*	24,672	(571)	—	102,277
03/11	33,607	872	2.6%	102,012
Annual Growth	(2.6%)	—	—	(1.9%)

*Fiscal year change

2014 Year-End Financials

Debt ratio: 52.9%
Return on equity: (-25.2%)
Cash ($ mil.): 3,839
Current ratio: 0.61
Long-term debt ($ mil.): 9,716
No. of shares (mil.): 296
Dividends
Yield: —
Payout: —
Market value ($ mil.): 2,803

	STOCK PRICE ($) FY Close	P/E High/Low	PER SHARE ($) Earnings	Dividends	Book Value
12/14	9.47	— —	(0.81)	0.00	(2.76)
12/13	10.47	— —	(8.49)	0.00	10.43
12/12	9.67	— —	(5.31)	0.00	21.92
12/11*	5.16	— —	(1.94)	0.00	26.52
03/11	16.80	10 6	2.42	0.00	32.97
Annual Growth	(13.4%)	— —	—	—	—

*Fiscal year change

Airbus Group SE

Airbus Group (formerly European Aeronautic Defence and Space Company or EADS) is busy in the commercial and military aerospace and related markets. Considered Europe's largest supplier it rivals Boeing in the competitive skies. The company's largest segment is Airbus; its commercial division ranks among the top two makers of large commercial aircraft (seats 100-plus passengers) while its military division manufactures transport tankers and mission aircraft. Other segments include Airbus Helicopters (civil/military helicopters); and Airbus Defence and Space (satellites and launcher systems combat aircraft missile systems radar defense electronics and unmanned aerial systems).

Geographic Reach

Airbus Group operates in more than 170 locations worldwide.

Operations

Airbus Group has three operating Divisions: Airbus Airbus Defence and Space and Airbus Helicopters.Airbus is one of the world's leading aircraft manufacturers offering the most modern and efficient passenger aircraft on the more than 100-seat market. The Airbus commercial product line comprises aircraft that range in size from the 107-seat single-aisle A318 aircraft to the 525-seat A380 widebody aircraft.Airbus Helicopters (formerly Eurocopter) is a global leader in the civil and military rotorcraft market. Its product range includes light single-engine light twin-engine medium and medium-heavy rotorcraft which are adaptable to all kinds of mission types based on customer needs. With more than 3000 operators in more 150 countries Airbus Helicopters supports some 12000 in-service rotorcraft.In 2014 the defense and space businesses of Airbus Military Astrium and Cassidian were combined into the new Airbus Defence and Space. This segment is Europe's number one defense and space enterprise and the world's second largest space business. Its core businesses are Space Military Aircraft Missiles and related systems and services.Other businesses include turboprop manufacturer ATR aerostructure and aircraft seat business Sogerma.

Financial Performance

Airbus Group's revenues have risen consistently since 2010.In 2014 net sales increased by 5% due to higher Airbus and Airbus Helicopters segment sales partially offset by decreased sales from Airbus Defence and Space.Airbus' revenues increased by 7% driven by the overall increase in deliveries to a more favorable delivery mix including 30 A380s (compared to only 25 in 2013); Airbus Helicopters sales increased thanks to government programs including the ramp-up in NH90 activity. By contrast Airbus Defence and Space's revenue decrease was driven by lower deliveries of military aircraft and fewer Ariane 5 launches.Airbus Group's net income has followed similar a trend that of its revenues.In 2014 net income increased by 58% due to higher sales lower selling expenses and administrative expenses partially offset by increased research and development expenses. Selling and administrative expenses decreased by 6% in 2014. Research and development expenses increased by 9% reflecting R&D activities at Airbus. The main contribution to the expenses comes from the A350 XWB program. Net cash provided by the operating activities increased by 35%.

Stategy

Airbus Group is seeking to dominate the commercial aeronautics military aircraft and space markets by driving innovation globalization services and value-chain optimization. As part of this strategy in 2014 the company pooled its scattered defense activities into a new unit Airbus Defence and Space. In 2015 Airbus launched its global aerospace business accelerator where start-ups and Airbus “intrapreneurs” (internal entrepreneurs) can work together to speed up the transformation of their innovative ideas into valuable businesses.

That year ATR and TAP M&E signed a dual partnership. On one hand TAP M&E joined the network of centers recommended by ATR for the maintenance of the airframes of its aircraft; on the other hand the aircraft manufacturer has also chosen TAP M&E as first spare parts repair center in Brazil for support of its maintenance contracts offered to ATR operators.

In 2014 the joint venture Airbus Safran Launchers was created after the approval of the development and production of a new Ariane 6 launcher at the ESA Ministerial Conference.

The company has also sold a number of assets as part of its streamlining process and to pay down debt. In 2014 Airbus Defence and Space sold its Test & Services activities to a consortium consisting of ACE Management S.A. and IRDI S.A. for 31 million. That year it also sold its 26.8% share in Patria Oyj to the Finnish defence security and aviation services provider for 133 million. It also sold Dassault Aviation shares for 794 million.

Mergers and Acquisitions

In 2014 Airbus Operations S.L.U. Getafe (Spain) acquired a additional 58.49% shares in Alestis Aerospace S.L. La Rinconada (Spain) for 28 million including 6 million due to the separate recognition of settlements of preexisting relationships. That year Airbus Group acquired Salzburg München Bank AG from Raiffeisenverband Salzburg allowing the aeronautics and space group to establish a company bank in order to provide additional financing options. All parts of Airbus Group should benefit from the increased financing flexibility that this bank will provide.

HISTORY

The growth of the European Aeronautic Defence and Space Company –EADS –is overshadowed by the long history of its components and by the obstacles overcome to cement the deal: The French and the Germans historically aren't overly fond of each other so how did it come to pass that Germany's DaimlerChrysler Aerospace AG (DASA) and France's Aerospatiale Matra put aside their differences to band together with Spain's Construcciones Aeronáuticas SA (CASA)?

The US aerospace sector in the 1990s saw many companies consolidate scrambling to make their way in the post-Cold War era. Boeing the largest aerospace company in the world got that way by acquiring a number of operations including Rockwell International's aerospace and defense operations (1995) and most importantly McDonnell Douglas in a $16 billion deal (1997). In the same era defense giant Lockheed merged with Martin Marietta (1995) and acquired Loral (1997). These US companies had it relatively easy –they all paid taxes to Uncle Sam but acquisition deals in Europe were stymied by concerns over national security and privatization because much of Europe's defense industry was government-owned.

Spurred into action by their US rivals DASA and British Aerospace (now BAE SYSTEMS) – partners in Airbus –began merger talks in 1997. Fearful of being left out in the cold France's government-owned Aerospatiale – another Airbus partner –began talks to merge with Matra a French defense company controlled by Lagardère. Weeks after the Aerospatiale-Matra deal was announced in 1998 the chairman of DASA's parent company Jürgen Schrempp met with Lagardère's CEO Jean-Luc Lagard & egrave;re and proposed a three-way deal. It never occurred and in 1999 the BAE SYSTEMS and DASA deal fell through as well.

Later that year Schrempp and Lagardère met again and laid the groundwork for a merger between DASA and Aerospatiale Matra. Less than three weeks after the Aerospatiale-Matra merger was completed Lagardère found itself pitching the DASA/Aerospatiale Matra merger idea to a stunned French government (which still held a 48% stake in Aerospatiale Matra). Marathon negotiations ensued. Late in the year Spain's Construcciones Aeronáuticas SA (CASA) agreed to become part of EADS.

In 2000 EADS went public and Airbus announced that it would abandon its consortium structure in favor of incorporation. The next year EADS began pushing for a consolidation of army and naval equipment manufacturing among EU countries similar to the aerospace consolidation that created EADS. For Airbus the long-sought switch from consortium to corporation finally occurred in July 2001 when Airbus S.A.S. was incorporated.

EADS bought out BAE SYSTEMS' 25% share in their Astrium joint venture in 2003. In October 2004 EADS agreed to acquire US defense electronics maker Racal Instruments as part of its plan to increase defense sales in the US. Rumors surfaced the next month that EADS was discussing a merger deal with French defense company Thales.

In December 2004 EADS and BAE SYSTEMS gave Airbus the green-light to build the superjumbo twin-deck A380 a plane that competes directly with Boeing's upcoming 787 Dreamliner. A few months later in early 2005 EADS was given preferred bidder status for the UK's Royal Air Force aerial refueling tanker contract. The program was valued at approximately $25 billion.

Claiming victory at last in 2006 Airbus beat Boeing on deliveries (434 vs. 398) but Boeing racked up a record 1004 plane orders while Airbus notched only 790. Moreover EADS' shares took a pounding in 2006 on Airbus' announcement that deliveries of the A380 would be delayed by six or seven months due to manufacturing glitches. A group of EADS shareholders cried foul and filed suit when it was revealed that co-CEO Noël Forgeard and five other EADS directors exercised stock options weeks before an internal investigation into the delays was launched. Two weeks later Forgeard fell on his sword and resigned. Louis Gallois former chairman of Socit Nationale des Chemins de Fer Français (SNCF) France's state railway company was named to replace him. The same fate befell Airbus boss Gustav Humbert who was replaced by Christian Streiff a former executive at French building materials concern Compagnie de Saint-Gobain.

The production logjams at Airbus also prompted some of the company's airline customers to seek compensation in lieu of taking their business elsewhere (Boeing). EADS forecast that the production delays at Airbus would be a $2.5 billion drain on profits over four years. In the wake of the additional delivery delays Airbus CEO Christian Streiff was sent packing after only three months on the job. EADS Co-CEO Louis Gallois was named as his replacement.

In 2006 Daimler announced plans to gradually reduce its stake in EADS from about 30% to half that amount. Later that year EADS acquired Sofrelog of France (a maker of maritime monitoring systems). Russian bank Vneshtorgbank (100% controlled by the Russian government) also purchased a 5% stake in EADS for about $1.17 billion. The stake did not entitle Vneshtorgbank to a board seat but the move was expected to strengthen cooperation between EADS and the re-emerging Russian aerospace industry.

After long negotiations EADS shifted in 2007 to a new management structure aimed at cutting down on the damaging political bickering between its German and French management and shareholder factions. Politicians like German Chancellor Angela Merkel and French President Nicolas Sarkozy touted the compromise as a success. Others namely labor forces were more skeptical –calling the latest management shake-up just another round of musical chairs that leaves the power struggles between Paris and Munich largely unresolved.

EADS continued to expand into emerging markets especially regions including Asia the Middle East and North and South America. Deliveries included the company's (long-delayed) A380 model launched with Singapore Airlines in late 2008. Adding to Airbus's standing the all-new A350-XWB (made for the most part of lighter-weight composite materials) sliced into about two-thirds of jet demand in the Middle East. It also forged alliances and won contracts in Brazil China Japan and North America.

Airbus launched a cost-cutting initiative in 2008 that slashed some 10000 jobs. Dubbed Power8 the plan marched out cost-saving measures that aimed to reduce development cycles by two years and boost overall productivity by 20%. Central to Power8 was the spinoff of some of Airbus's manufacturing facilities to new partners. Partner funding of planes like the A350-XWB (spurred by assurances of subcontract work) plus plant sales risked an ongoing row between Airbus and unions as well as factory owners –stakeholders who feared plant divestitures and more job cuts. That year EADS captured its first big US military contract when Airbus North America was given the opportunity to make US Army light utility helicopters.

The company was awarded a contract to replace outdated KC-135 refueling tankers in conjunction with Northrop Grumman for the US Air Force –an upset protested by rival bidder Boeing. Soon after the Government Accountability Office (GAO) announced its findings of flaws in the bidding process. EADS and Northrop Grumman dropped out of the bidding in early 2010 with EADS vowing not to submit a proposal unless it was assured that it had a fair chance to win. By late summer – after US president Obama assured French president Nicolas Sarkozy that the Pentagon tanker bidding process would be fair –EADS announced that it would consider once again to enter into the bidding war. The contract to build the US tanker valued at approximately $35 billion went to Boeing in early 2011.

In September 2012 EADS (now the Airbus Group) announced it was considering a merger with UK-based BAE Systems a global provider of sensors flight controls and aircraft. However the proposed $45 billion merger –which would have created the largest global aerospace and defense player on the planet both in total sales and market value –was called off weeks later after it failed to pass European governmental and regulatory hurdles.

Preparing to capitalize on demand Airbus Group hammered out its Vision 2020 goals under which it pursues the world's #1 position in air and space platforms systems and services. Services are targeted to achieve a 25% share of the business in less than 10 years. To this end Airbus Group has been scouting deals in the services sector. In August 2011 it agreed to purchase Vizada a global satellite-based mobile communication services provider from French private-equity Apax France. The whopping 673 million ($969 million) deal bolsters Airbus Group's subsidiary Astrium a top contractor of space-technology wares in Europe and furthers opportunities beyond Europe with maritime aerospace as well as land media and other commercial customers. Hard on its heels Airbus Group took over more than 98% of Canada-based Vector Aerospace for C$625 million (about $341 million). Vector joins Eurocopter as a standalone business adding a multi-platform aviation repair and overhaul business.

EXECUTIVES

EVP Space Systems; CEO Airbus Defence and Space France, Fran $is Auque, age 57
CEO, Thomas (Tom) Enders, age 54
CTO, Jean J. Botti, age 56
CEO Airbus Helicopters, Guillaume Faury, age 46
CFO Airbus Group and Airbus, Harald Wilhelm, age 47
EVP Military Aircraft Airbus Defence and Space, Domingo Urena-Raso, age 55
CEO Airbus, Fabrice Bregier, age 52
COO, Gunter Butschek, age 52
Chief Human Resources Officer Airbus Group and Airbus, Thierry Baril, age 48
CEO Airbus Defence and Space, Bernhard Gerwert, age 60
CEO Airbus Group North America, Allan McArtor, age 72
Vice Chairman, Josep Pique i Camps, age 60
Chairman, Denis Ranque, age 63
Auditors: Ernst & Young Accountants LLP

LOCATIONS

HQ: Airbus Group SE
Mendelweg 30, Leiden 2333 CS
Phone:
Web: www.airbus-group.com

2014 Sales

	% of total
Europe	33
Asia/Pacific	32
North America	16
Rest of the World	19
Total	**100**

PRODUCTS/OPERATIONS

2014 Sales

	% of total
Airbus	68
Airbus Defence and Space	21
Airbus Helicopters	11
Other HQ / Consolidation	0
Total	**100**

Selected Operations and Interests

Business aircraft (JV with Dassault Aviation 46%)
Commercial airplanes (Airbus)
- A320 (single-aisle aircraft)
- A330/A340
- A350 XWB (extra wide body)

Helicopters (Eurocopter SAS)
- EC135 (light twin engine)
- EC175 (multi-role)
- EC225 (Super Puma)
- EC725
- E225/ED725 (twin engine)
- NH90 (medium-weight multi-role)
- Tiger (medium-weight

Satellites (Astrium)
- Ariane 5 (heavy-lift satellite)
- Automated Transfer Vehicle (ATV)
- Eurostar 3000 (telecommunications satellite)

Security combat and missile systems (Cassidian)
- Cassidian Professional Mobile Radio (PMR)
- Eurofighter (aka "Typhoon")combat aircraft (JV with Dassault Aviation 46%)
- MBDA missile systems (JV with BAE systems and Finmeccanica)
- Radars
- Unmanned Aerial Systems (UAS; partnered with Northrop Grumman

Other businesses
- ATR (50- to 74-seat turboprop aircraft; JV with Alenia Aeronautica)
- EADS North America
- EADS UK

COMPETITORS

Aerojet Rocketdyne
AgustaWestland
BAE SYSTEMS
BAE Systems Inc.
Boeing
Bombardier
E' Prime Aerospace
Embraer
Lockheed Martin
Northrop Grumman
RUAG Holding
Raytheon
Textron

HISTORICAL FINANCIALS

Company Type: Public

Income Statement

FYE: December 31

	REVENUE ($ mil.)	NET INCOME ($ mil.)	NET PROFIT MARGIN	EMPLOYEES
12/14	73,796	2,847	3.9%	138,622
12/13	81,579	2,016	2.5%	144,061
12/12	74,443	1,618	2.2%	140,405
12/11	63,544	1,336	2.1%	140,405
12/10	61,233	740	1.2%	121,691
Annual Growth	4.8%	40.1%	—	3.3%

2014 Year-End Financials

Debt ratio: 9.3%
Return on equity: 25.9%
Cash ($ mil.): 8,837
Current ratio: 0.99
Long-term debt ($ mil.): 7,630
No. of shares (mil.): 784
Dividends
Yield: 1.5%
Payout: 25.0%
Market value ($ mil.): 9,679

	STOCK PRICE ($) FY Close	P/E High	P/E Low	PER SHARE ($) Earnings	Dividends	Book Value
12/14	12.34	6	4	3.63	0.20	10.94
12/13	19.15	37	9	2.53	0.83	19.43
12/12	39.71	28	21	1.98	0.59	16.69
12/11	31.40	26	18	1.64	0.28	14.05
12/10	23.45	39	26	0.91	0.00	14.59
Annual Growth	(14.8%)	—	—	41.4%	—	(6.9%)

Aisin Seiki Co., Ltd.

Nothing stops Aisin Seiki from making its line of brake systems and powertrain components for cars. Aisin's main automotive business offers automotive-related products such as transmissions brakes and engine and car navigation systems. Its Life and Amenity business offers items for more comfortable living with products that range from heating and cooling systems to toilets with jet sprays; well-care items include electric wheelchairs and reclining beds. The company has around 180 consolidated subsidiaries and companies worldwide. Separate business segments include Aisin AW Group Aisin Seiki Group Advics Group and Aisin Takaoka Group.

Operations

Aisin Seiki operates through nearly 180 subsidiaries that are spread throughout four main segments. Aisin AW Group is its largest segment (37% of total sales in 2015) and makes automatic transmissions and car navigation systems. Aisin Seiki Group (36%) sells its automotive parts as well as its life and energy products. Advics Group is responsible for making brake components (17%) while Aisin Takaoka Group (6%) manufacturers the cart-iron parts for engines and brakes.

Financial Performance

Aisin Seiki's revenues increased 5% from 2014 to 2015. The growth was due to increased sales from Aisin AW Group Aisin Seiki Group and Aisin Takaoka Group. The company's net income in 2015 declined mainly due to increased freight and packaging expenses coupled with a spike in selling general and administrative expenses.

Strategy

Aisin Seiki is looking to diversify its customer mix by expanding production overseas to achieve a 50% ratio in the years ahead. It established new subsidiaries in Indonesia in 2014 and began constructing a new facility in Brazil also that year.

Aisin Seiki continues to make automotive components and systems but it also focuses on increasing sales of main products such as transmissions car navigation systems and power sliding doors. The company's business segments have worked autonomously in the past; however Aisin Seiki is working to combine and link its individual businesses thus strengthening and maximizing the potential of the products and technologies that are cultivated by each company.

Company Background

Aisin Seiki traces its roots to 1943 when Tokai Hikoki was founded to produce airplane engines for the Japanese war effort. After the war the company switched to manufacturing sewing machines and auto parts. Aisin Seiki took its present name in 1965 after Tokai Hikoki merged with Shinkawa Kogyo.

HISTORY

Aisin Seiki traces its roots to 1943 when Tokai Hikoki was founded to produce airplane engines for the Japanese war effort. After the war the company switched to manufacturing sewing machines and auto parts. Aisin Seiki took its present name in 1965 after Tokai Hikoki merged with Shinkawa Kogyo.

The company's operations were limited to Japan until 1969 when it signed a technical agreement with a German company regarding steering gears. International expansion continued as Aisin Seiki formed Aisin USA (to import aftermarket parts for imported cars) in 1970 Aisin Europe in 1971 and Aisin (UK) and Aisin (Australia) Pty. in 1972. Other operations sprung up in Mexico (1973) Brazil (1974) Singapore (1977) and Germany (1978). In the late 1980s the company worked at expanding the sale of body components such as sunroofs and seats.

Although Aisin Seiki USA had been formed to import parts for imported cars by 1990 the unit imported more parts for domestic cars than it did for imports. In 1996 Aisin Seiki set up Tangshan Aisin Gear a joint venture with Tangshan Gear Works to produce manual transmissions in China. The next year the company's Kariya plant which produced brake and clutch parts used in many Toyotas burned down. The disruption forced Toyota — which accounted for about 80% of the Kariya plant's sales —to temporarily shut down its 20 Japanese auto plants. Also in 1997 Aisin Seiki formed Aisin GM Allison Co. a joint venture with General Motors to produce automatic transmissions in Japan and the Pacific Rim region. Aisin GM Allison was dissolved in 2007 as GM geared up to sell Allison Transmission.

In 1998 the company formed Aisin Europe Manufacturing in the UK its first manufacturing facility in Europe. Also that year it began work on subsidiary Aisin A W Co. to supply engine parts for the Toyota facility in West Virginia. Despite increasing sales Aisin Seiki announced in 2000 that it would post a loss due to a charge for retirement benefits.

EXECUTIVES

EVP, Toshikazu Nagura
EVP and Director, Fumio Fujimori
EVP, Naofumi Fujie
EVP, Makoto Mitsuya
EVP, Toshiyuki Mizushima
President, Kanshiro Toyoda, age 73
Auditors: PricewaterhouseCoopers Aarata

LOCATIONS

HQ: Aisin Seiki Co., Ltd.
2-1 Asahi-machi, Kariya, Aichi 448-8650
Phone: (81) 566 24 8265
Web: www.aisin.co.jp

PRODUCTS/OPERATIONS

2015 Sales

	% of total
Aisin AW Group	37
Aisin Seiki Group	36
Advics Group	17
Aisin Takaoka Group	6
Other	4
Total	100

Selected Products

Automotive
- Drivetrain products (transmission and clutch systems)
- Brake and chassis products (drum brakes master cylinders air suspension systems)
- Body products (door frames and locks sunroofs power seats)
- Engine products (water pumps pistons exhaust manifolds)
- Information and other products (navigation systems Intelligent Parking Assist)
- Aftermarket products

Energy System
- GHP
- Cogeneration system
- Cryopump
- Cryocooler
- Peltier modules

Life and Amenity
- Bed furniture and fabric (ASLEEP)
- Housing equipment
- House remodeling service (Livelan)
- Home-use sewing machine
- Embroidery machine
- Facility consulting service (CONTRACT)
- Business consulting service (TSS)
- Audio equipment

COMPETITORS

APM Automotive
BorgWarner
Calsonic Kansei
DENSO
DURA Automotive
Dana Holding
Delphi Automotive Systems
Faurecia
Haldex
Hitachi America
Lear Corp
Magna International
Meritor
Mitsubishi Electric
Modine Manufacturing
Panasonic Corp
Robert Bosch
Sumitomo Electric
Tenneco
Torotrak
Valeo
Visteon
ZF Friedrichshafen
ZF TRW Automotive

HISTORICAL FINANCIALS

Company Type: Public

Income Statement FYE: March 31

	REVENUE ($ mil.)	NET INCOME ($ mil.)	NET PROFIT MARGIN	EMPLOYEES
03/15	24,704	644	2.6%	94,748
03/14	27,341	872	3.2%	89,531
03/13	26,888	823	3.1%	83,378
03/12	28,089	676	2.4%	78,212
03/11	27,261	841	3.1%	74,671
Annual Growth	(2.4%)	(6.4%)	—	6.1%

2015 Year-End Financials

Debt ratio: 0.1%
Return on equity: 7.1%
Cash ($ mil.): 2,283
Current ratio: 1.46
Long-term debt ($ mil.): 2,676
No. of shares (mil.): 282
Dividends
Yield: 2.6%
Payout: —
Market value ($ mil.): 10,245

	STOCK PRICE ($) FY Close	P/E High/Low	PER SHARE ($) Earnings	Dividends	Book Value
03/15	36.25	— —	2.28	0.97	45.20
03/14	36.21	— —	3.09	0.87	45.62
03/13	30.60	— —	2.92	0.00	42.85
03/12	36.71	— —	2.40	0.00	41.94
03/11	24.25	— —	2.99	0.00	39.39
Annual Growth	10.6%	— —	(6.6%)	—	3.5%

AKBANK

The vaults at Akbank have enough room for Turkish lira and the euro. The bank provides banking services in Turkey through nearly 1000 branches about 4300 ATMs and more than 360000 point-of-sale terminals. Internationally Akbank operates branches in Germany and in Malta; it also has subsidiary banks in the Netherlands and in Dubai. Akbank which is Turkey's second-largest publicly traded bank after Is Bankasi also provides private bank and international trade finance services. Subsidiaries provide non-banking financial capital-market and investment services. The Sabanci family and its companies control 55% of Akbank.

OperationsAkbank operates five main business segments: Retail Banking which serves consumers; the Corporate Banking Commercial Banking and SME Banking division which provides financial and banking services to large medium and small corporate and commercial customers; The Treasury Unit which trades a variety of treasury bond foreign currency and derivative trading securities on behalf the bank; Private Banking which provides banking and investment management services for affluent individuals; and International Banking which provides foreign currency financing foreign currency and TL clearances and money transfers through agent financial institutions.Akbank generated 81% of its total revenue from interest income on loans in 2014 while 16% of the bank's revenue came from fee and commission income. Its loan portfolio was comprised of corporate loans (32% of loan assets) SME loans (37%) and consumer loans (31%). Akbank's overseas subsidiaries include its German bank Akbank AG; Akbank Dubai Limited while its non-banking subsidiaries include AkInvestment AKAsset Management and Aklease. Geographic ReachAkbank boasts more than 990 branches across Turkey and has an additional branch in Malta. It also operates overseas through subsidiary banks in Frankfurt Germany and in Dubai UAE.Sales and MarketingAkbank serves a wide variety of industries including the energy infrastructure petrochemicals real estate telecommunications and transportation industries. Financial PerformanceNote: Growth rates may differ after conversion to US dollars.Akbank has struggled to sustain revenue or profit growth in recent years though its business has remained stable. The bank had a breakout year in 2014 however with revenue jumping by 22% to TL$18.1 billion (around $7.7 billion). Most of the rise was driven by strong interest income growth from both the Retail Banking and the Corporate Banking Commercial banking and SME Banking divisions as the bank successfully grew its consumer loans (excluding credit card loans) by nearly 12% its general purpose loans by 21% and its mortgage loans by nearly 4% during the year. Akbank's fee and commission income also grew by 12% during the year further padding its top line.Higher revenue and foreign exchange gains in 2014 drove the bank's net income higher by 7% to TL$3.3 billion (roughly $1.4 billion). Akbank's operating cash however declined by 30% to TL$1.4 billion for the year as the bank collected less cash from deposits during the year.

Stategy

As the second-largest bank in Turkey Akbank reiterated in 2015 that it's mid to long-term growth plans include being the leader of the country's banking industry while also looking toward international growth in markets where its clients enjoy high business volumes. It's also been working to manage its costs effectively executing more than 60 effective cost management actions in 2014 alone for an estimated TL$26 million (about $11 million) in sustainable savings.Domestically Akbank has been moving toward digital banking channels that are quickly taking the industry by storm allowing the bank to slow expensive branch-expansion plans and cut operating costs significantly while giving customers faster access to banking services. In 2014 the bank launched new versions of its Akbank Direkt platform for mobile and internet banking differentiating user experiences for its variety of customer groups. Its Direkt Business was introduced for micro business segment customers while its Akbank Direkt Plus was unveiled for higher-income clients. Meanwhile its Mobile Banking platform was updated with iBeacon technology which allowed customers to make card-free cash withdrawal transactions from ATMs; while its cash management e-Invoice system allowed bank customers to send and receive e-invoices to and from business partners and suppliers.Toward gaining more international exposure in growing regions Akbank sometimes partners with prominent banks in based in other regions. In 2014 for example the bank secured a cooperation agreement with Barclays Africa Group to provide banking services for Turkish companies that do business or invest in sub-Saharan countries in Africa via Barclays Africa branches. The deal also included joint financing opportunities for Turkish companies looking to grow in Africa as well as cooperation in trade and letters of guarantee transactions between Turkey and African countries.

EXECUTIVES

EVP Treasury, Kerim Rota
EVP Information Technology, Turgut G ney
EVP Consumer Banking, A. Galip T ₰ge
CEO and Board Member, Hakan Binbasgil
EVP International Banking, H lya Kefeli
EVP Payment Systems and Corporate Communication, Mehmet Sindel
EVP Commercial Banking, Kaan G r
EVP Credits, Ahmet Fuat Ayla
EVP Corporate Banking, Alper Hakan Y ksel
EVP Direct Banking, Orkun Oguz
EVP SME Banking, B lent Oguz
EVP and CFO, K.Atil -zus
EVP Private Banking, Saltik Galatali
EVP Operation, -zlen Sanibelli
EVP Human Resources and Strategy, Burcu Civelek Y ce
Vice Chairman, Hayri Culhaci
Chairman, Suzan Sabanci Din ₰r
Auditors: Guney Bagimsiz Denetim ve Serbest Muhasebeci Mali Musavirlik A.S.

LOCATIONS

HQ: AKBANK
Sabanci Center 4, Istanbul, Levent 34330
Phone: (90) 212 385 55 55 **Fax:** (90) 212 319 52 52
Web: www.akbank.com

PRODUCTS/OPERATIONS

2014 Sales

	% of total
Interest income	81
Fee and commission received	16
Dividend income	
Other operating income	3
Total	100

Selected Businesses

AKAssetmanagement
AKLease
AKInvestment
AKbank AG
Akbank Dubai Limited

COMPETITORS

Citi Turkey
Finansbank
GarantiBank
Isbank
Ko§
Trk Ekonomi Bankasi
Yapi Kredi

HISTORICAL FINANCIALS

Company Type: Public

Income Statement FYE: December 31

	ASSETS ($ mil.)	NET INCOME ($ mil.)	INCOME AS % OF ASSETS	EMPLOYEES
12/14	93,246	1,480	1.6%	16,543
12/13	90,778	1,509	1.7%	16,473
12/12	90,693	1,721	1.9%	16,515
12/11	73,777	1,370	1.9%	15,548
12/10	77,517	1,948	2.5%	15,550
Annual Growth	4.7%	(6.6%)	—	1.6%

2014 Year-End Financials

Return on assets: 1.6%
Return on equity: 14.0%
Long-term debt ($ mil.): —
No. of shares (mil.): —
Sales ($ mil): 7,646
Dividends
Yield: 1.1%
Payout: 2,083.1%
Market value ($ mil.): —

	STOCK PRICE ($) FY Close	P/E High/Low	PER SHARE ($) Earnings	Dividends	Book Value
12/14	7.32	893557	0.00	0.08	0.03
12/13	6.25	1207720	0.00	0.12	0.03
12/12	10.05	1294762	0.00	0.09	0.03
12/11	6.28	1443905	0.00	0.11	0.02
12/10	11.25	18991189	0.00	0.18	0.03
Annual Growth	(10.2%)	—	—	(6.6%)	(18.1%) (0.6%)

Alecta pensionsforsakring, omsesidigt (Sweden)

EXECUTIVES

Ekonomichef, Katarina Thorslund
Auditors: Ernst & Young AB

LOCATIONS

HQ: Alecta pensionsforsakring, omsesidigt (Sweden)
Regeringsgatan 107, Stockholm SE-103 73
Phone: (46) 20 441 60 00 **Fax:** (46) 8 441 60 90
Web: www.alecta.se

HISTORICAL FINANCIALS

Company Type: Public

Income Statement FYE: December 31

	ASSETS ($ mil.)	NET INCOME ($ mil.)	INCOME AS % OF ASSETS	EMPLOYEES
12/14	90,621	2,356	2.6%	406
12/13	95,447	13,525	14.2%	424
12/12	85,837	10,446	12.2%	426
12/11	72,503	(13,343)	—	445
12/10	75,552	4,876	6.5%	459
Annual Growth	4.7%	(16.6%)	—	(3.0%)

2014 Year-End Financials

Return on assets: 2.7%
Return on equity: 7.2%
Long-term debt ($ mil.): —
No. of shares (mil.): —
Sales ($ mil): 14,477
Dividends
Yield: —
Payout: —
Market value ($ mil.): —

Alfresa Holdings Corp Tokyo

Alfresa Holdings primarily serves as a pharmaceutical wholesaler in the Japanese market. The company encompasses Alfresa Corp. which oversees the wholesale side of the business and Alfresa Pharma which takes care of development manufacturing and marketing of prescription pharmaceuticals and medical devices. The wholesale division which accounts for 99% of the company's revenues deals not only in prescription drugs but also OTC pharmaceuticals diagnostic reagents medical equipment health foods and beauty supplies. Customers include hospitals medical centers drugstores and pharmacies throughout Japan. Founded in 2003 Alfresa operates about 10 distribution centers and two manufacturing plants.

Operations

Alfresa's three operating segments are Ethical Pharmaceutical Wholesaling Self-Medication Products Wholesaling (general pharmaceuticals) and Manufacturing.

Financial Performance

Alfresa decreased revenues by 3% to some ¥2421 billion in fiscal 2015 (ended March) due to declines across all operating segments. In the ethical pharmaceuticals wholesaling business drug prices declined by an average of nearly 3% under new medical fee revisions made in 2014. Net income fell 10% to ¥22.9 billion due to an absence of settlement earnings received that year as well as corporate restructuring expenses.

Strategy

Alfresa is focused on growing its network of wholesaling businesses as well as on expanding the operations of its manufacturing division. Growth measures include organic build-up of its nationwide marketing network as well as expanding its services in the self-medication wholesale market.

In 2015 Alfresa merged subsidiaries Seiwa Sangyo and Tokiwa Yakuhin to form TS Alfresa Corporation. The unit provides ethical pharmaceuticals and devices from a wide range of manufacturers; it is focused on improving its own operating efficiencies and strengthening its marketing activities.

In manufacturing subsidiary Alfresa Fine Chemical Corporation is increasingly focused on making active pharmaceutical ingredients (APIs) for ethical pharmaceuticals; it is also working to release new products in point-of-care testing and other fields. In addition to launching new products it intends to increase market share for growth.

Mergers and Acquisitions

Alfresa expanded its business during 2015 through the acquisition of 51% of Nihon Apoch a pharmacy business serving Saitama Prefecture.

Company Background

Another example of merger and acquisition activity in the Japanese drug industry Alfresa was created in 2003 from the combination of wholesalers Azwell and Fukujin.

EXECUTIVES

Deputy President and Director, Shozo Hasebe
SVP Director and Executive Officer, Taizo Kubo
Deputy President and Director, Yasuo Takita
President and Representative Director, Denroku Ishiguro, age 64
Deputy President and Director, Hidetomi Takahashi
SVP Director and Executive Officer, Shunichi Miyake
Deputy President and Director, Hiroyuki Kanome
Deputy President and Director, Tsuneo Shinohara
Honorary Chairman and Director, Kunio Fukujin
Auditors: KPMG AZSA LLC

LOCATIONS

HQ: Alfresa Holdings Corp Tokyo
1-1-3 Otemachi, Chiyoda-ku, Tokyo 100-0004
Phone: (81) 3 5219 5100 **Fax:** (81) 3 5219 5103
Web: www.alfresa.com

COMPETITORS

Astellas
Daiichi Sankyo
Medipal
Shionogi & Co.
Sumitomo Chemical
Sumitomo Dainippon Pharma
Suzuken
Takeda Pharmaceutical
Toho Pharmaceutical

HISTORICAL FINANCIALS

Company Type: Public

Income Statement FYE: March 31

	REVENUE ($ mil.)	NET INCOME ($ mil.)	NET PROFIT MARGIN	EMPLOYEES
03/15	20,179	191	0.9%	11,366
03/14	24,263	247	1.0%	10,936
03/13	25,374	220	0.9%	10,939
03/12	28,443	80	0.3%	10,713
03/11	26,366	79	0.3%	10,956
Annual Growth	(6.5%)	24.5%	—	0.9%

2015 Year-End Financials

Debt ratio: 0.0%
Return on equity: 6.9%
Cash ($ mil.): 877
Current ratio: 1.16
Long-term debt ($ mil.): 35
No. of shares (mil.): 223
Dividends
Yield: —
Payout: —
Market value ($ mil.): —

Alimentation-Couche Tard, Inc.

Alimentation Couche-Tard sells fuel for you and your car on both sides of the US-Canada border. It's the second-largest convenience store operator in North America and the leader in Canada with some 6000 outlets: Couche-Tard in Qubec; Mac's in central and western Canada; and more than 4600-plus Circle K shops in more than 40 US states and a dozen countries. (It bought the Circle K chain in the US from ConocoPhillips in 2003.) Most of its sales are rung up in the US. Alimentation Couche-Tard French for "food for those who go to bed late" sells gas at more than three-quarters of its stores. The fast-growing chain is known for expanding at home and abroad through splashy acquisitions.

Operations

In Couche-Tard's global operations Statoil Couche-Tard Mac's and Circle K are its key brands. Fuel makes up a majority of sales in every geographic region but merchandise helps even out fuel volatility and delivers generally better profit margins.

Geographic Reach

Couche-Tard operates and licenses a total of about 13100 global locations with more than 6000 convenience stores in North America. The company divides the US market into nine geographic business units with the largest retail presence in the Great Lakes region and Arizona. Its European operations include about 2260 stores concentrated in Scandinavia and the Baltics with a growing presence in Poland. In Asia it licenses the Circle K brand to operators of more than 4600 stores in a dozen mostly Asian countries.

Financial Performance

Sales at Couche-Tard's convenience stores in fiscal 2014 (ends April) climbed to $38 billion an increase of 7% over the prior year due to higher sales driven by recovering economic conditions and new store acquisitions. Net earnings rose about 42% from $573 million to $812 million due to higher revenue and some non-recurring costs in 2013 that made 2014's books look good by comparison. Without the one-time events net earnings still would have grown 23% due to contributions from acquisitions higher fuel margins in Europe and Canada and growth in same-store merchandise sales. Cash from operations rose 23% from $1161 to $1429 based on the higher net earnings one-off events in 2013 and a better exchange rate for foreign currency.

Strategy

Acquisitions are a big part of Couche-Tard's growth strategy. Its purchase of The Pantry Inc. is the latest is the latest in a long chain of acquisitions that includes the 2012 purchase of Statoil its largest ever and the purchase of Circle K nearly a decade ago. The Circle K acquisition established the Canadian firm as a major player in the US market while Statoil moved it into Europe. The fragmented US convenience store market and trend by major oil companies to cast off their retail operations has afforded Couche-Tard (and rival 7-Eleven) ample opportunity to acquire small independently-operated chains and occasionally a big fish. With about 70% of its sales (even more in the US) coming from gas Couche-Tard is vulnerable to fluctuations in motor fuel prices. To protect itself from such volatility the retailer is focused on developing its in-store merchandise sales (especially fresh foods) which return higher margins and are less volatile.

Mergers and Acquisitions

Overall in fiscal 2014 the company acquired about 166 stores and built only 25. The big news came at the end of the calendar year with Couche-Tard said it would pay $860 million for The Pantry Inc. with more than 1500 Kangaroo Express stores in 13 US states; locations are concentrated in the southeast part of the country.

The $2.6-billion purchase of Statoil Fuel & Retail ASA with about 2300 locations in northern Europe mainly in Scandinavia closed in June 2012. Statoil is a Norway-based road transport fuel retailer and operates a network of retail stores across Scandinavia Poland the Baltic States and Russia. Statoil owns and operates a dozen key terminals as well as 38 depots in eight countries and a fleet of about 400 road tankers.

EXECUTIVES

CEO, Brian P. Hannasch, $286,000 total compensation
VP and CFO, Raymond Par ©
Group President European Operations, Jacob Schram
Group President Fuel Americas and Operations North-East, Jean Bernier
EVP Scandinavia, Hans-Olav H ̧idahl
EVP Central and Eastern Europe, Joern Madsen
SVP Special Products, Jonas Palm
Chairman, Alain Bouchard
Auditors: PricewaterhouseCoopers LLP

LOCATIONS

HQ: Alimentation-Couche Tard, Inc.
4204 Boulevard Industriel, Laval, Quebec H7L 0E3
Phone: 450 662-3272 **Fax:** 450 662-6633
Web: www.couche-tard.com

2015 Sales

	$ mil.	% of total
US	19,962	58
Europe	10,057	29
Canada	4,546	13
Total	**34,529**	**100**

PRODUCTS/OPERATIONS

2015 Sales

	$ mil.	% of total
Road transportation fuel	27,281	70
Merchandise & services	8,275	24
Other	1,972	6
Total	**34,529**	**100**

Selected Proprietary Brands

Beverages
- Froster (frozen)
- Sloche (flavored)
- Sunshine Joe (coffee)

Sandwiches
- Handfull
- La Maisonnée

COMPETITORS

7-Eleven
Casey' s General Stores
Chevron
Cumberland Farms
Exxon Mobil
Gate Petroleum
Kroger
Kum & Go
Loblaw
Marathon Oil
Pilot Flying J
Publix
QuikTrip
Racetrac Petroleum
Royal Dutch Shell
Sheetz
Shell Oil
Sobeys
The Pantry
TravelCenters of America

HISTORICAL FINANCIALS

Company Type: Public

Income Statement FYE: April 26

	REVENUE ($ mil.)	NET INCOME ($ mil.)	NET PROFIT MARGIN	EMPLOYEES
04/15	34,529	932	2.7%	0
04/14	37,956	811	2.1%	78,000
04/13	35,543	572	1.6%	78,500
04/12	22,997	457	2.0%	60,000
04/11	18,550	369	2.0%	53,000
Annual Growth	16.8%	26.1%	—	—

2015 Year-End Financials

Debt ratio: 28.3%
Return on equity: 23.8%
Cash ($ mil.): 575
Current ratio: 1.12
Long-term debt ($ mil.): 3,053
No. of shares (mil.): 567
Dividends
Yield: 0.0%
Payout: 9.3%
Market value ($ mil.): 22,575

	STOCK PRICE ($) FY Close	P/E High/Low	PER SHARE ($) Earnings	Dividends	Book Value
04/15	39.79	25 16	1.64	0.15	6.86
04/14	27.35	59 19	1.43	0.11	7.00
04/13	58.57	57 37	1.02	0.10	5.72
04/12	42.55	50 31	0.83	0.09	4.05
04/11	26.60	41 26	0.65	0.06	3.59
Annual Growth	10.6%	— —	25.9%	27.4%	17.5%

Allianz SE

One of the world's biggest insurers Allianz SE offers a range of insurance products and services —including life health and property/casualty coverage for individuals and businesses —through more than 1000 subsidiaries ventures and affiliates operating all over the globe (Allianz SE and its subsidiaries are collectively known as the Allianz Group). The company serves some 85 million customers in such key markets as France Germany Italy and the US. In addition to selling insurance Allianz provides retail and institutional asset management services through Allianz Global Investors private equity investment through Allianz Capital Partners and banking services through Allianz Bank.

Operations

On the insurance front Allianz gets more than half of its revenues from its life and health division which operates under the Allianz brand and serves individual and group accounts. The property/casualty operations account for 40% of revenues. Allianz offers specialty property/casualty and marine insurance under the Allianz Global Corporate and Specialty brand. The unit has offices in more than a dozen locations and is one of the world's largest providers of marine insurance.

Though it has restructured to focus on core insurance and asset management offerings Allianz still has banking operations in Germany and other global regions.

Its two primary investment management businesses PIMCO and AllianzGI operate under the Allianz Asset Management segment. The group has some 1801 billion total assets under management making it one of the largest active asset managers in the world. Some two-thirds of third-party assets are from institutional investors while the rest are from retail investors. Core markets include France Germany Italy the UK the US and the Asia/Pacific region.

Geographic Reach

Allianz operates in more than 70 countries with most of its operations in Europe. It also operates in the Asia/Pacific region and the Americas.

Sales and Marketing

Allianz markets its products through independent agents and brokers dedicated agents bank representatives and direct marketing channels. It has about 150000 sales force associates 1200 distribution partners and about 2000 agencies in its worldwide network.

Financials

Allianz reported a 2% increase in revenues to some 103.2 billion in 2014 due to a 4% increase in property/casualty premiums and 19% growth in life and health statutory premiums (largely driven by its fixed-index annuity business in the US). A rise in sales of unit-linked and savings products in Italy as well as increased single-premium sales in Germany also contributed to the improvement. However these rises were partially offset by lower asset management performance fees which declined after a very strong year in 2013. Banking operations remained flat.

Net income rose 4% to 6.6 billion in 2014 primarily as a result of the higher revenue as well as a decline in income tax provisions. Cash flow from operations increased 39% to 32.2 billion largely as a result of higher unearned premiums and reserves in the life and health segment.

Strategy

Allianz is focused on achieving sustainable growth in its property/casualty life and health and asset management operations. It also seeks to achieve operational synergies among its businesses through shared technology investments capital allocations and best practice sharing. The company's investment strategy is conservative with the goal of providing stable returns.

While the US and Europe are Allianz's largest markets the company is pursuing growth in emerging markets as well. It has established significant operations in select Asian countries and it is expanding its presence in Central and Eastern Europe and the Asia/Pacific region. Targeted markets include China India and Russia.

The group has been restructuring its North American business. In 2014 it absorbed the commercial lines of Fireman's Fund Insurance Company into its Allianz Global Corporate & Specialty industrial insurer; it plans to launch new financial lines including directors and officers coverage professional indemnity and errors and omissions insurance. The following year Allianz sold its Fireman's Fund Personal Insurance division to Chubb Limited for $365 million marking the end of the Fireman's Fund brand name.

Mergers and Acquisitions

Boosting its share of the Italian market Allianz acquired certain distribution activities (comprising a network of 725 agencies) of UnipolSai Assicurazioni's property/casualty business in 2014. It also purchased the property/casualty in-force portfolio managed by the acquired agencies.

The group also purchased the property/casualty business of Australia's Territory Insurance Office in late 2014; it additionally gained servicing responsibilities for the Government Motors Accidents Compensation program.

Ownership

Allianz is part of a web of interlocking German corporate ownership. It holds a stake in reinsurance giant Munich Re which in turn has a small stake in Allianz. Munich Re is also the company's principal external reinsurer though Allianz itself reinsures a significant amount of its insurance companies' risk. Allianz also serves as a reinsurer for third parties.

HISTORY

Carl Thieme founded Allianz in Germany in 1890. That year the company took part in the creation of the Calamity Association of Accident Insurance Companies a consortium of German Austrian Swiss and Russian firms to insure international commerce.

By 1898 Thieme had established offices in the UK Switzerland and the Netherlands. His successor Paul von der Nahmer expanded Allianz into the Balkans France Italy Scandinavia and the US. After a hiatus during WWI Allianz returned to foreign markets.

In WWII Allianz insured Auschwitz Dachau and other death camps. Company documents show Allianz wasn't worried about risk at the SS troop-guarded camps. After the German defeat the victors seized Allianz's foreign holdings except for a stake in Spain's Plus Ultra. In the 1950s Allianz repurchased confiscated holdings in Italian and Austrian companies.

Allianz saturated the German market and began a full-scale international drive in the late 1950s and 1960s. It became Europe's largest insurer through a series of acquisitions beginning in 1973. Allianz formed Los Angeles-based Allianz Insurance in 1977.

In 1981 Allianz launched a takeover (which turned hostile) of the UK's Eagle Star insurance company. After a 1983 bidding joust with Britain's B.A.T Industries (now part of Zurich Financial Services) Allianz withdrew.

The firm consoled itself by shopping. In 1984 it won control of Riunione Adriatica di Sicurtà (Ras) Italy's second-largest insurance company. Two years later the firm bought Cornhill (now Allianz Insurance plc) on its third try. As the Iron Curtain crumbled Allianz in 1989 acquired 49% of Hungaria Biztosito. Its drang nach Osten continued the next year after national reunification when it gained control of Deutsche Versicherungs AG East Germany's insurance monopoly. Allianz that year became the first German insurer licensed in Japan; it also bought the US's Fireman's Fund Insurance.

Natural disasters led to large claims and set the company back in 1992 the first time in 20 years it lost money from its German operations. Allianz restructured operations that year; profits surged in 1993 mostly from international business.

Allianz expanded in Mexico in 1995 forming a life and health insurance joint venture with Grupo Financiero BanCrecer (now owned by Grupo Financiero Banorte). The company set up an asset management arm in Hong Kong in 1996 with an eye to further Asian expansion getting a license in China the next year. In 1997 after Holocaust survivors sued Allianz and other insurers for failing to pay on life policies after WWII Allianz agreed to participate in a repayment fund.

In 1998 Allianz bought control of Assurances Gnrales de France; it was the white knight that prevented Assicurazioni Generali from taking the company. In 1999 Allianz said it would restructure some of its insurance operations including spinning off its marine and aviation lines to better compete in the multinational market. That year US subsidiary Allianz Life bought Life USA Holding. In 2000 Allianz bought 70% of PIMCO Advisors Holdings to strengthen its asset management operations. That year the company continued its push into Asia buying a 12% stake in Hana Bank of South Korea and planning to boost its ownership of Malaysia British Assurance Life. Also in 2000 Allianz acquired Dutch insurer Zwolsche Algemeene.

Allianz remained acquisitive in 2001 buying US investment manager Nicholas-Applegate and taking a majority stake in ROSNO one of Russia's largest insurers. Also that year it bought a nearly 96% stake in German banking giant Dresdner and acquired the remainder the following year.

Allianz paid out claims of some $1.3 billion relating to the terrorist attacks on the World Trade Center. The company set up a terrorism insurance unit offering coverage primarily for companies within the European Union.

EXECUTIVES

CEO Allianz Worldwide Care, Ida Luka-Lognon ©
age 53
Member Management Board and Chairman and CEO, Oliver B ¤te, age 50, $700,000 total compensation
Management Board Member and COO, Christof Mascher, age 55, $216,000 total compensation
Management Board Member and CFO, Dieter Wemmer, age 59
Management Board Member Investments, Maximilian Zimmerer, age 57
Management Board Member Global Insurance Lines and Anglo Markets, Axel Theis, age 58
CEO TIO, Daryl Madden
Chief Market Manager, Paul Kernaghan
Vice Chairman, Wulf H. Bernotat, age 67
Auditors: KPMG AG Wirtschaftsprufungsgesellschaft

LOCATIONS

HQ: Allianz SE
Koeniginstrasse 28, Munich D-80802
Phone: (49) 89 38 00 0 **Fax:** (49) 89 38 00 3425
Web: www.allianz.com

PRODUCTS/OPERATIONS

2014 Sales

	% of total
Life & health insurance	55
Property/casualty insurance	40
Asset management	5
Corporate & other	-
Total	**100**

Selected Operations and Brands

Allianz
Allianz Global Corporate and Specialty
Allianz Global Investors
Allianz Worldwide Care
Euler Hermes
PIMCO

COMPETITORS

AEGON
AXA
Allstate
Aviva
Munich Re Group
New York Life
Nippon Life Insurance
Old Mutual
Berkshire Hathaway
CNP Assurances
Citigroup
ERGO
Generali
Generali Deutschland
Groupama
ING
Legal & General Group
MetLife
Prudential
Prudential plc
RSA Insurance
State Farm
Swiss Re
Talanx
The Hartford
Victoria Versicherung
Zurich Insurance Group
ageas SA/NV

HISTORICAL FINANCIALS

Company Type: Public

Income Statement FYE: December 31

	ASSETS ($ mil.)	NET INCOME ($ mil.)	INCOME AS % OF ASSETS	EMPLOYEES
12/14	979,438	7,561	0.8%	147,425
12/13	979,588	8,254	0.8%	147,627
12/12	915,544	6,813	0.7%	144,094
12/11	829,713	3,291	0.4%	141,938
12/10	836,409	6,762	0.8%	151,338
Annual Growth	4.0%	2.8%	—	(0.7%)

2014 Year-End Financials

Return on assets: 0.8%
Return on equity: 11.2%
Long-term debt ($ mil.): —
No. of shares (mil.): 454
Sales ($ mil): 118,233
Dividends
Yield: 3.2%
Payout: —
Market value ($ mil.): 7,527

	STOCK PRICE ($) FY Close	P/E High/Low		PER SHARE ($) Earnings	Dividends	Book Value
12/14	16.57	1	1	16.58	0.54	162.55
12/13	18.13	1	1	17.97	0.44	151.97
12/12	13.82	1	1	14.95	0.43	155.76
12/11	9.47	3	1	7.09	0.00	128.40
12/10	11.87	1	1	14.88	0.38	131.87
Annual Growth	8.7%	—	—	2.7%	9.0%	5.4%

Allied Irish Banks Plc

Allied Irish Banks (AIB) one of Ireland's largest banks and private employers is looking beyond the Emerald Isle for its proverbial pot o' gold. The company offers retail and commercial accounts and loans life insurance financing leasing pension and trust services through a network of 200 branches 74 EBS Limited offices 10 business centers and 755 ATMs. The company's capital markets division offers commercial treasury services corporate finance and investment banking services. In the US AIB specializes in financial services for the not-for-profit sector.

Operations

Over the years AIB has reorganized into a more simplified structure in which its divisions were integrated and its AIB and First Trust operations were more closely aligned. To attract additional customers the bank also introduced mobile banking services to its offerings.

HISTORY

Allied Irish Banks was formed in 1966 by the "trinity" of Provincial Bank (founded 1825) The Royal Bank (founded 1836) and Munster and Leinster (founded 1885 but with origins back to the late 1600s). Both AIB and its then-larger rival Bank of Ireland had to consolidate in order to compete with North American banks entering Ireland. From its start AIB sought to expand overseas and by 1968 it had an alliance with Canada's Toronto-Dominion Bank.

In the 1970s AIB expanded its branch network to England and Scotland. The 1980s saw AIB boost its presence in the US market (it had already debuted AIB branches) with the acquisition of First Maryland Bancorp.

The Irish Parliament's Finance Act of 1986 instituted a withholding tax known as the Deposit Interest Retention Tax (DIRT) for Irish residents. Consequently (with a wink and a nod) AIB and other banks let customers create bogus non-resident accounts to avoid paying DIRT. An investigation indicated that at one point AIB's branch in Tralee had 14700 non-resident accounts on its rolls –more than half the local population. After tax authorities began probing many of the accounts in question were reclassified as "resident" and customers had to pay the taxes on them. In 1991 AIB was reprimanded but neither the bank nor its customers have paid the remaining $100 million tax bill.

Tom Mulcahy who integrated AIB's treasury investment and international banking activities became chief executive in 1994. Mulcahy a respected leader envisioned AIB as an international Ireland-based bank.

In 1995 AIB bought UK-based investment fund manager John Govett from London Pacific Group (now Berkeley Technology Limited). Mulcahy moved AIB the same year into Eastern Europe with a stake in Poland-based Wielkopolski Bank Kredytowy (or WBK).

AIB was busy in 1999. It gained a toehold in Asia by entering a cross-marketing agreement with Singapore's Keppel TatLee bank a survivor of the region's financial crisis. Liberalized Singapore banking laws allowed AIB the right to buy one-quarter of the bank by 2001. AIB also bought an 80% stake of Bank Zachodni in Poland in 1999.

That year AIB merged First Maryland Bancorp and its other US holdings into the renamed Allfirst Financial a sizable mid-Atlantic states bank.

To consolidate its power in Eastern Europe in 2001 AIB merged its Polish banks (Wielkopolski Bank Kredytowy and Bank Zachodni) into Bank Zachodni WBK. That year Mulcahy retired but was appointed by the Irish government to take over as chairman of troubled airline Aer Lingus.

AIB lost nearly $700 million from 1996 to 2002 apparently from bogus foreign exchange transactions made by rogue trader John Rusnak who pleaded guilty to bank fraud.

In 2003 AIB sold troubled Maryland-based bank Allfirst Financial to M&T Bank Corporation. As part of the deal AIB assumed ownership of more than 20% of M&T becoming the company's largest shareholder. Under AIB's direction Allfirst had grown into a major regional player with about 250 branches in Maryland Pennsylvania Virginia and Washington DC.

In the midst of the global financial crisis the Irish government injected 2 billion ($2.8 billion) into AIB in exchange for a 25% share in voting rights in 2008. Ireland also provided capital for Bank of Ireland and Irish Bank Resolution Corporation to help stabilize the plunging Irish financial system. AIB also sought capital from the private sector.

EXECUTIVES

Director Personal Business and Corporate Banking, Bernard Byrne, age 46
CFO and Director, Mark G. Bourke, age 48
CEO, David Duffy, age 53
COO, Stephen White
Chairman, Richard A. Pym, age 66
CFO and Director, Mark G. Bourke, age 48
Deputy Chairman, Michael Somers, age 73
Auditors: Deloitte & Touche

LOCATIONS

HQ: Allied Irish Banks Plc
Bankcentre, Ballsbridge, Dublin 4
Phone: (353) 1 6600311 **Fax:** 212 515-6710
Web: www.aibgroup.com

PRODUCTS/OPERATIONS

2013 Sales

	% of total
Interest and similar income	86
Fee and commission income	11
Others	3
Total	**100**

COMPETITORS

Bank Millennium	HSBC
Bank of America	Irish Bank Resolution
Bank of Ireland	Lloyds Banking Group
Barclays	Royal Bank of Scotland
Citigroup	Ulster Bank

HISTORICAL FINANCIALS
Company Type: Public

Income Statement
FYE: December 31

	ASSETS ($ mil.)	NET INCOME ($ mil.)	INCOME AS % OF ASSETS	EMPLOYEES
12/14	130,612	1,070	0.8%	11,047
12/13	162,088	(2,198)	—	12,648
12/12	161,482	(4,806)	—	14,708
12/11	176,751	(2,990)	—	16,716
12/10	194,361	(13,694)	—	23,208
Annual Growth	**(9.5%)**	—	—	**(16.9%)**

2014 Year-End Financials

Return on assets: 0.7%
Return on equity: 7.9%
Long-term debt ($ mil.): —
No. of shares (mil.): 2,093
Sales ($ mil.): 4,866

Dividends
Yield: —
Payout: —
Market value ($ mil.): —

Aluminum Corp of China Ltd.

Auditors: Ernst & Young Hua Ming LLP

LOCATIONS

HQ: Aluminum Corp of China Ltd.
No. 62, North Xizhimen Street, Haidian District, Beijing 100082
Phone: (86) 10 8229 8560 **Fax:** (86) 10 8229 8158
Web: www.chalco.com.cn

HISTORICAL FINANCIALS
Company Type: Public

Income Statement
FYE: December 31

	REVENUE ($ mil.)	NET INCOME ($ mil.)	NET PROFIT MARGIN	EMPLOYEES
12/14	22,843	(2,612)	—	75,749
12/13	27,987	161	0.6%	90,207
12/12	23,977	(1,320)	—	97,990
12/11	23,175	37	0.2%	101,259
12/10	18,355	118	0.6%	108,256
Annual Growth	**5.6%**	—	—	**(8.5%)**

2014 Year-End Financials

Debt ratio: 10.0%
Return on equity: (-44.6%)
Cash ($ mil.): 2,621
Current ratio: 0.61
Long-term debt ($ mil.): 7,213

No. of shares (mil.): —
Dividends
Yield: —
Payout: —
Market value ($ mil.): —

	STOCK PRICE ($) FY Close	P/E High/Low	PER SHARE ($) Earnings	Dividends	Book Value
12/14	11.52	— —	(0.19)	0.00	0.34
12/13	8.70	195107	0.01	0.00	0.54
12/12	11.91	— —	(0.10)	0.00	0.52
12/11	10.80	1348521	0.00	0.04	0.61
12/10	22.79	587316	0.01	0.00	0.58
Annual Growth (15.7%) (12.6%)		— —	—	—	—

America Movil, S.A.B. de C.V.

Amrica Móvil offers wireless phone service from the Rio Grande to Tierra del Fuego. The company is Latin America's top mobile carrier with more than 225 million subscribers in 18 countries. In Mexico the company enjoys a 70% market share with nearly 65 million subscribers to its Telcel brand which has 260+ retail stores. Its second largest market is Brazil which serves more than 50 million subscribers through Claro. Amrica Móvil also provides fixed-line service in Central America and the Caribbean with more than 5 million lines. TracFone Wireless is Amrica Móvil's US presence. Majority owner Carlos Slim Helú combined Amrica Móvil with his fixed-line businesses Telmex in 2010 as part of a broader restructuring effort.

The $21 billion dollar deal was structured so that Amrica Móvil acquired the minority stakes in Telmex that Helú did not already own through a stock transaction with their controlling holding company Carso Global Telecom. The plan combined Helú's wired and wireless telecom interests in hopes of holding ground against increasing competition from smaller telephone companies and cable television operators like Televisa which offer bundled phone TV and Internet services. The combined wired operations of Telmex and the wireless business of Amrica Móvil provides phone TV and Internet services. As one company the merger was slated to save about $700 million in administrative costs following the delisting of Telint and Carso Global.

In the US the company operates through subsidiary TracFone which is a leading provider of prepaid wireless services. TracFone products feature a pay-as-you-go prepaid mobile phone with no annual contracts or activation fees. Its services account for more than 5% of Amrica Móvil's total revenue. The company also owns more than 71% of Telvista a call center company with locations in the US and Mexico.

Amrica Móvil's operating revenues rose more than 8% in 2010 over 2009.

In 2012 Tracfone acquired Simple Mobile which is one of the largest mobile virtual network operators for T-Mobile. The previous year Amrica Móvil paid $75 million for a license to provide Costa Rica with satellite television wireless phone and Internet service under its Claro brand. Currently the only telecom provider in the country is the government-controlled Instituto Costarricense de Electricidad (Grupo ICE). Telef&oa-

cute;nica also plans to provide telecom services in Costa Rica.

Amrica Móvil is acquiring 100% control of Telmex by buying the 40+% of the company it doesn't already own. Telmex will be delisted from the exchanges it trades on when the acquisition is complete and it now operates as a brand that provides fixed-line service in Mexico and Columbia.

The family of Mexican billionaire Carlos Slim Helú (also the world's wealthiest person) controls more than 46% of Amrica Móvil; AT&T owns nearly one quarter of the company and operates as a competitor in some of its smaller markets.

HISTORY

The company was formed in 2000 as a result of a spinoff from Telmex which was at the time Mexico's largest local and long-distance phone service provider. In late 2006 Amrica Móvil acquired majority owner Amrica Telecom in a move to streamline the structure of the company and to free up assets for share buybacks or dividends.

The company expanded its presence in the Caribbean region in 2007 with the acquisition of Puerto Rico Telephone from Verizon Communications and a handful of other shareholders for nearly $2 billion. The next year it bought Jamaican wireless service provider Oceanic Digital Jamaica and became licenced to provide wireless services in Panama.

Also in 2008 the company rebranded its operations in Argentina Paraguay and Uruguay to its Claro brand which Amrica Móvil now uses for all of its operations in Central America and the Caribbean. That year it bought Estesa Holding a cable TV and data services provider in Nicaragua for $48 million. The acquisition of Estesa boosted Amrica Móvil's cable television and broadband offerings and gave the company greater access to the Nicaraguan market.

EXECUTIVES

Vicepresidente de Consejo, Patrick Slim Domit
Auditors: Mancera, S.C. (member of Ernst & Young Global)

LOCATIONS

HQ: America Movil, S.A.B. de C.V.
Lago Zurich 245, Plaza Carso/Edificio Telcel, Piso 16, Colonia Granada Ampliacion, Mexico, D.F. 11529
Phone: (52) 55 2581 4449 **Fax:** (52) 55 2581 4422
Web: www.americamovil.com

2014 Sales

	% of total
Brazil	24
Mexico wireless	23
Mexico fixed	12
United States	10
Colombia	9
Southern cone	7
Andean region	5
Europe	4
Central America	3
Caribbean	3
Total	**100**

PRODUCTS/OPERATIONS

2014 Sales

	% of total
Mobile voice services	30
Mobile data voice services	23
Fixed voice services	14
Fixed data services	11
Sales of equipment accessories and computer	11
Paid television	8
Other services	3
Total	**100**

Selected Operations

América Móvil Peru (8.3 million subscribers)
AM Wireless Uruguay (800000 subscribers)
AMX Argentina (17 million subscribers)
AMX Paraguay (500000 subscribers)
Claro Chile (3.6 million subscribers)
Claro Panama (100000 subscribers)
Codetel (Dominican Republic 4.8 million subscribers)
Comcel (Colombia 27.7 million subscribers)
Conecel (Ecuador 9.4 million subscribers)
CTE (El Salvador 800000 subscribers)
ENITEL (Nicaragua 2.2 million subscribers)
Oceanic (Jamaica 400000 subscribers)
Sercom Honduras (1.4 million subscribers)
TELPRI (Puerto Rico 1.6 million subscribers)
TracFone (US 14.4 million subscribers)
Telgua (Guatemala 1.2 million subscribers)

COMPETITORS

AT&T
Alfa SA
Axtel
Brasil Telecom
Cable & Wireless Communications
Iusacell
Millicom
NII Holdings
Portugal Telecom
Sprint Communications
TIM Participa$µes
Tele Norte Leste
Telecom Argentina
Telefnica
Telefnica de Argentina
Telef'nica Brasil
Telemig Celular
Vivo Participa$µes

HISTORICAL FINANCIALS

Company Type: Public

Income Statement

FYE: December 31

	REVENUE ($ mil.)	NET INCOME ($ mil.)	NET PROFIT MARGIN	EMPLOYEES
12/14	57,713	3,139	5.4%	191,156
12/13	60,030	5,698	9.5%	173,174
12/12	59,648	7,037	11.8%	158,719
12/11	47,627	5,931	12.5%	158,694
12/10	49,032	7,350	15.0%	150,079
Annual Growth	4.2%	(19.2%)	—	6.2%

2014 Year-End Financials

Debt ratio: 3.2%
Return on equity: 23.8%
Cash ($ mil.): 4,522
Current ratio: 0.76
Long-term debt ($ mil.): 37,144
No. of shares (mil.): —
Dividends
Yield: 1.6%
Payout: 713.9%
Market value ($ mil.): —

	STOCK PRICE ($) FY Close	P/E High/Low	PER SHARE ($) Earnings	Dividends	Book Value
12/14	22.18	35 25	0.05	0.36	0.18
12/13	23.37	24 17	0.08	0.34	0.22
12/12	23.14	24 19	0.09	0.30	0.31
12/11	22.60	49 18	0.08	0.26	0.27
12/10	57.34	51 39	0.09	0.25	0.31
Annual Growth	(21.1%)	— —	(16.3%)	9.1%	(12.1%)

AMP Ltd.

AMP is on top –down under. The company is one of Australia's largest insurance and investment management groups. Through its AMP Financial Services (AFS) division more than 2000 representatives sell the company's financial offerings which include life home vehicle travel and business insurance as well as retirement products financial planning and advice superannuation products (professionally managed retirement investment funds) and banking. AMP Capital Investors provides investment management to AFS and to other individual and institutional investors. AMP Limited also provides retail financial services under the Hillcross and Arrive Wealth Management brands.

HISTORY

AMP was conceived in Sydney in 1848 by W. S. Walsh (a clergyman) Thomas Mort (a businessman) and Thomas Holt (a wool trader) who convened with two others to discuss forming a mutual life insurance company in Australia. (Many of the UK's and US's largest mutuals were also founded about this time.) The next year Australian Mutual Provident Society was born; it opened for business with a staff of two: secretary William Perry and a small boy. In its first year the company sold only 42 policies. Luckily no one died in the first three years of operations and the company was able to build up some reserves. The company grew slowly over the next decade appointing just two agents – in Auckland New Zealand and Hobart Australia.

Sales took off with the 1860 appointment of the company's first full-time agent Benjamin Short who had the novel idea of actively recruiting customers and actually selling policies. The company opened an office in New Zealand in 1871; it opened a branch in the UK in 1908.

In the next few decades the company helped build the Australian economy through investment of its reserves. It funded industry and infrastructure including farming communities as part of the South Australian Land Development Scheme. The company grew free of foreign competition protected by regulations severely restricting the activities of foreign companies in the banking and financial industries in Australia. In 1958 the company formed AMP Fire and General Insurance (changed to AMP General in 1990).

In 1988 AMP moved abroad with the acquisition of London Life Assurance. The following year it made history with its acquisition of funds management group Pearl Assurance then the largest takeover of a British financial firm by a foreign company.

The company founded AMP Asset Management in 1991 to manage its overseas assets. In 1995 the company expanded its international presence through a joint venture with the financial services arm of UK-based Virgin Group. The company also began offering mortgage and banking products in Australia through a new unit Priority One.

After a careful inquiry in 1996 AMP's board recommended demutualization; policyholders approved in 1997 and the conversion was completed the next year with the company taking the name AMP Limited. Trading got off to a rocky start however as the company imposed an unusual pricing mechanism by which the official initial stock price was linked to pricing activity over the first five days of trading. This was done to protect individual policyholders from typical opening-day stock gyrations but institutional investors were unable to value their investments for several days (a technical breach of accounting rules).

AMP bought Citibank's New Zealand retail banking business and UK fund manager Henderson in 1998. The next year AMP battled to buy general insurer GIO Australia Holdings picking up 57% after resistance to its original low-ball offer; it also bought UK mutual insurer National Provident Institution (NPI).

The company streamlined all of its investment-management operations into a single unit in 1999 and expanded Asian operations with offices in Beijing and Tokyo. In 2000 the problems arising from the GIO takeover resulted in a board shakeup; chairman Ian Burgess resigned.

Local rival Suncorp-Metway bought AMP's domestic general insurance unit in 2001 and Churchill Insurance (a subsidiary of Credit Suisse) acquired its similar operations in the UK that year.

AMP split off its UK-based operations as HHG at the end of 2003 (retaining a 10% share). HHG eventually changed its name to Henderson Group plc in 2005. AMP sold its shares in Henderson later that year.

EXECUTIVES

CEO and Managing Director, Craig Meller, age 52
Managing Director AMP Capital, Stephen Dunne, $548,000 total compensation
Group Executive Operations and Director Melbourne, Wendy Thorpe
CIO, Lee Barnett
Group Executive Insurance and Superannuation, Pauline Blight-Johnston
Group Executive Advice and Banking, Rob Caprioli
CFO, Gordon Lefevre
CIO, Craig Ryman
Chairman, Simon McKeon
Auditors: Ernst & Young

LOCATIONS

HQ: AMP Ltd.
33 Alfred Street, Sydney, New South Wales 2000
Phone: (61) 2 9257 5000 **Fax:** (61) 2 9257 7178
Web: www.amp.com.au

PRODUCTS/OPERATIONS

2013 Sales

	% of total
Investment gains	75
Fee revenue	12
Life insurance premiums & related revenue	11
Other	2
Total	**100**

Selected Services

Business Banking
Insurance Products
Investment Products
Loans
Personal Banking
Retirement Products
Superannuation

COMPETITORS

AXA Asia Pacific
Australia and New Zealand Banking
Aviva
Commonwealth Bank of Australia
Macquarie Group
National Australia Bank
QBE
RSA Insurance
St. Andrew' s Australia
Suncorp-Metway
ageas SA/NV

HISTORICAL FINANCIALS

Company Type: Public

Income Statement

FYE: December 31

	ASSETS ($ mil.)	NET INCOME ($ mil.)	INCOME AS % OF ASSETS	EMPLOYEES
12/14	110,678	725	0.7%	5,400
12/13	119,111	600	0.5%	5,700
12/12	123,395	731	0.6%	5,829
12/11	112,176	699	0.6%	6,000
12/10	90,783	788	0.9%	3,700
Annual Growth	5.1%	(2.1%)	—	9.9%

2014 Year-End Financials

Return on assets: 0.6%
Return on equity: 10.8%
Long-term debt ($ mil.): —
No. of shares (mil.): —
Sales ($ mil): 14,444
Dividends
Yield: —
Payout: 240.0%
Market value ($ mil.): —

Anglo American Plc (United Kingdom)

Anglo American's name might be a little misleading —it has never been American. The UK-based company owns significant stakes in global producers of platinum (75% of Anglo Platinum) and diamonds (85% of De Beers S.A.). In addition Anglo American has interests in ferrous and base metals and industrial minerals. It ranks among the world's largest iron ore producers and is also a leading copper producer. Anglo is one of the world's largest coal miners and exporters of metallurgical coal a key raw material in steel production. It also produces thermal coal used to generate electricity. The founding Oppenheimer family no longer controls Anglo American.

Anglo American has been growing by strategic investments in long-life low-cost assets. It also has been increasing its organic growth by delivering projects ahead of or on schedule. For the past five years the company has been slimming down its operations setting strict targets and investing in strategic growth opportunities. It does not look to investments on the basis of short-term drivers but makes its decisions based on long-term investments that will be sound for the next decade or beyond. The company tries to look beyond current market volatility while making its investments.

It 2009 Anglo decided to continue investing in four major projects: Kolomela iron ore mine in South Africa Barro Alto (nickel) and Minas-Rio (iron ore) mines in Brazil and Los Bronces copper mine in Chile. By 2011 all but the Minas-Rio iron ore project had started production on or ahead of schedule. A discovery of caves at the Minas-Rio iron ore project caused a delay in the work schedule because of a need for specialized assessment.

In 2011 Anglo delivered a strong performance which was boosted by higher prices. The company achieved a record group operating profit that year of $11.1 billion up 14% from the prior year and driven in part by solid performances by its Kumba Iron Ore Metallurgical Coal and Thermal Coal divisions. However the company's net income dipped slightly from that in 2010 when the company posted larger gains on divestments.

Anglo also made acquisitions in 2011 that significantly increased its growth. Perhaps its most historic purchase in recent years was its agreement in late 2011 to acquire the Oppenheimer family's 40% stake in giant diamond company De Beers for $5.1 billion. The interest of the Oppenheimers —who had been in the diamond industry for more than a century —increased Anglo American's 45% stake to 85%. The government of Botswana holds the remaining 15%.

In addition to giving it majority control of the mining company Anglo American believes the acquisition will provide it with De Beers' expertise in administrative functions such as financial management supply chain and technical operations. The acquisition comes after a new 10-year sales agreement with the mining company's partner the government of Botswana. De Beers and Russia's ALROSA account for about half of the world's diamond production.

The company also stirred up controversy in 2011 by selling nearly 25% of its stake in Anglo American Sur copper mining subsidiary in Chile to Japan's Mitsubishi Corporation for $5.4 billion. The deal angered Chilean mining and government officials because Codelco Chile's state-owned resources company and the world's largest copper company wanted to exercise its option to buy a 49% stake in the company. Chile acted quickly to obtain a court injunction to block Anglo from selling any more of its shares of Anglo American Sur.

Although in 2012 a Chilean court rejected a bid by Codelco to have 49% of the dividends from Anglo American Sur frozen and held in escrow the dispute may drag on for years.

Anglo American and Lafarge SA agreed in 2011 to form a joint venture valued at $2.8 billion to combine their cement aggregates ready-mixed concrete asphalt and contracting businesses in the UK (Tarmac UK and Lafarge UK). The joint operations are expected to save a total of about $96 million a year through increased efficiency and improved logistics. The venture is designed to take advantage of an anticipated economic recovery. The UK's Competition Commission however ruled in 2012 that both Anglo and Lafarge would have to divest several operations including Lafarge's Hope cement plant in northern England —one of the largest in the UK.

The company also significantly expanded its metallurgical coal interests in 2011 with the acquisition of Peace River Coal Limited Partnership which holds exploration leases in British Columbia. Peace River Coal holds approximately 1 billion metric tons of high-quality coking coal.

In 2012 the company completed the final step of its $1.4 billion divestment of the Scaw Metals Group by selling Scaw South Africa an integrated steel maker to an investment consortium led by the Industrial Development Corporation of South Africa. The sale follows Anglo's disposal of Scaw's Moly-Cop and AltaSteel businesses to OneSteel in 2010.

HISTORY

In 1905 the Oppenheimers a German family with a major interest in the Premier Diamond Mining Company of South Africa began buying some of the region's richest gold-bearing land. The family formed Anglo American Corporation of South Africa in 1917 to raise money from J. P. Morgan and other US investors. The name was chosen to disguise the company's German background during WWI.

Under Ernest Oppenheimer the company bought diamond fields in German Southwest Africa (now Namibia) in 1920 breaking the De Beers hegemony in diamond production. Oppenheimer's 1928 negotiations with Hans Merensky the person credited with the discovery of South Africa's "platinum arc" led to Anglo American's interest in platinum.

The diamond monopoly resurfaced in 1929 when Anglo American won control of De Beers formed by Cecil Rhodes in 1888 with the help of England's powerful Rothschild family.

Anglo American and De Beers had become the largest gold producers in South Africa by the 1950s. They were also major world producers of coal uranium and copper. In the 1960s and 1970s Anglo American expanded through mergers and cross holdings in industrial and financial companies. It set up Luxembourg-based Minorco to own holdings outside South Africa and help the company avoid sanctions placed on firms doing business in the apartheid country.

Minorco sold its interest in Consolidated Gold Fields in 1989 and in 1990 it bought Freeport-McMoRan Gold Company (US). In 1993 Minorco bought Anglo American's and De Beers' South American European and Australian operations as part of a swap that put all of Anglo American's non-African assets except diamonds in Minorco's hands. Some analysts claimed the company had moved the assets to protect them from possible nationalization by the new black-controlled South African government. The company spun off insurer African Life to a group of black investors in 1994.

Anglo American bought a stake in UK-based conglomerate Lonrho (now Lonmin) in 1996. In 1997 Anglo American made mining acquisitions in Zambia Colombia and Tanzania and began reorganizing its gold and diamond operations. In 1998 the company's First National and Southern Life financial units merged with Rand Merchant Bank's Momentum Life Assurers to form FirstRand. (Anglo American has divested most of its interest in FirstRand.)

The company moved to the UK in 1999 and began trading on the London Stock Exchange in an effort to reach international investors. When it was based in South Africa Anglo American was unable to send its money overseas (the result of boycotts connected to that country's apartheid policies) so it bulked up on South African interests. Anglo American has evolved such that it can depend on product and geographic diversity to weather global economic turmoil. South African operations now make up less than half of the company's total sales and its base metals and platinum units each account for about a quarter of sales.

In 2000 the company bought UK building materials company Tarmac plc and later sold Tarmac America to Greece-based Titan Cement for $636 million. That year De Beers paid $590 million for Anglovaal Mining's stake in De Beers' flagship Venetia diamond mine and $900 million for Royal Dutch Shell's Australian coal mining business. On the disposal side Anglo American sold its 68% stake in LTA and its 14% stake in Li & Fung a Hong Kong trading company. Harry Oppenheimer died that year at the age of 92.

In a surprising move in early 2001 Anglo American announced that it had formed a consortium with Central Holding (the Oppenheimer family) and Debswana Diamond to acquire De Beers. In February De Beers agreed to be acquired in a deal worth about $17.6 billion. The deal –giving Anglo American and Central Holding 45% each and Debswana a 10% stake –was completed in June 2001.

In 2002 Anglo American and Japan-based conglomerate Mitsui pooled their Australian coal resources; Anglo American owns 51% of the joint venture. The company also completed a $1.3 billion deal that year for Chilean copper assets (two mines and a smelter) formerly owned by Exxon Mobil. In 2003 the company eyed the red hot iron ore market when it acquired a controlling stake in South Africa-based iron producer Kumba Resources.

Anglo American sold its 20% stake in Gold Fields to Norilsk Nickel in 2004 and reduced its stake in AngloGold Ashanti to 42% from its former 51% in 2006 then to below 20% the following year and finally entirely in 2009. In divesting its gold interests Anglo American seemed to capitulate to demands from the investor community and the idea that the gold industry is sufficiently different from the rest of the mining industry as to necessitate separate management.

The company set up new units in 2009 along product and geographical lines. The new divisions consisted of platinum (South Africa) copper (Chile) nickel (Brazil) metallurgical coal (Australia) thermal coal (South Africa) Kumba Iron Ore (of which Anglo American owned 65% South Africa) and Iron Ore Brazil. The change capped off several years of reorganization and divestment.

In 2009 the board of Anglo American rejected an offer to merge with rival Xstrata (renamed Glencore in 2014). Although Xstrata called the bid a "merger of equals" based on similar capitalization sizes Anglo American's board was not convinced of the benefits of the $68 billion all stock deal. Although Anglo American used to have a majority stake in AngloGold Ashanti it divested its remaining shares in 2009.

In 2010 Anglo American through its subsidiary Anglo Zinc completed the divestment of its zinc assets to Vedanta Resources subsidiary Sterlite Industries in a $1.3 billion deal. That year the company also sold Tarmac's aggregates businesses in France Germany Poland and the Czech Republic as well as its French and Belgian concrete products operations for $483 million.

Nicky Oppenheimer grandson of the founder retired from the board in 2011.

EXECUTIVES

CEO De Beers Group, Philippe Mellier, age 60
CEO Base Metals and Minerals, Duncan Wanblad, age 48
Group Director Strategy and Business Development, Bruce Cleaver, age 50
Chief Executive, Mark Cutifani, age 56, $891,000 total compensation
CEO Kumba Iron Ore, Norman B. Mbazima, age 57
CEO Platinum, Chris Griffith, age 50
Finance Director, Ren ©M ©dori, age 57, $765,000 total compensation
CEO Coal, Seamus French, age 52
CEO Marketing, Peter Whitcutt, age 49
Group Director Technical and Sustainability, Tony O 'Neill, age 57
Executive Head of Strategy and Corporate Affairs, Gareth Mostyn
Chairman, John Parker, age 73
Auditors: Deloitte LLP

LOCATIONS

HQ: Anglo American Plc (United Kingdom)
20 Carlton House Terrace, London SW1Y 5AN
Phone: (44) 20 7968 8888 **Fax:** (44) 20 7968 8500
Web: www.angloamerican.com

PRODUCTS/OPERATIONS

2014 Sales

	% of total
Iron ore & manganese	17
Platinum	17
Copper	16
coal	19
Niobium	1
Phosphate	2
Nickel	0
De Beer	22
Other mining & industrial	6
Total	**100**

Selected Subsidiaries

Platinum
- Anglo Platinum Corporation Limited (75% South Africa)

Base Metals
Anglo American Sur (75% copper mines Chile)
- Empresa Minera de Mantos Blancos SA (copper Chile)
- Minera Loma de Níquel CA (91% nickel Venezuela)
- Minera Quellaveco SA (80% copper Peru)
- Minera Sur Andes Limitada (copper Chile)

Coal
Anglo Coal (South Africa)
- Anglo Coal (Callide) Pty Limited (Australia)

Ferrous Metals and Industries
- Kumba Resources Limited (65%; coal iron ore heavy minerals; South Africa)

Industrial Minerals
- Copebras Limitada (phosphate products Brazil)

Diamonds
- De Beers S.A. (45%)

COMPETITORS

BHP Billiton	Pe±oles
Freeport-McMoRan	Rio Tinto Limited
Glencore	Teck
Impala Platinum	Vale
Norilsk Nickel	Vedanta Resources

HISTORICAL FINANCIALS

Company Type: Public

Income Statement

FYE: December 31

	REVENUE ($ mil.)	NET INCOME ($ mil.)	NET PROFIT MARGIN	EMPLOYEES
12/14	27,073	(2,513)	—	95,000
12/13	29,342	(961)	—	98,000
12/12	28,680	(1,470)	—	106,000
12/11	30,580	6,169	20.2%	100,000
12/10	27,960	6,544	23.4%	100,000
Annual Growth	(0.8%)	—	—	(1.3%)

2014 Year-End Financials

Debt ratio: 28.0%
Return on equity: (-8.6%)
Cash ($ mil.): 6,748
Current ratio: 2.13
Long-term debt ($ mil.): 16,917

No. of shares (mil.): 1,280
Dividends
Yield: —
Payout: —
Market value ($ mil.): —

Anheuser-Busch Inbev SA

Anheuser-Busch InBev (AB InBev) knows how to say "beer" in a lot of languages. The company operates more than 140 breweries across six geographic regions worldwide. It boasts a product list of 200-plus brands including global best-sellers Budweiser (brewed by Anheuser Busch) Stella Artois and Beck's. The Belgian brewer holds a slew of regional beers including Leffe and Hoegaarden as well as local favorites Michelob Skol and Brahma. AB InBev controls Mexico's largest brewer Grupo Modelo which produces Corona Extra Modelo Especial and Pacifico. AB InBev isn't just for grown ups - it also makes and distributes soft drinks mostly in Latin America. All told it operates in some 20 countries worldwide.

Operations

In addition to its beverage production AB InBev has nearly 40 global facilities making everything from malt syrup to hop pellets to labels bottles and cans. It also has hop farms in Germany and the US.

Non-beer operations include an exclusive license to bottle and distribute PepsiCo products (Pepsi 7UP and Gatorade) in Brazil through its Ambev subsidiary. The unit also handles PepsiCo products in other parts of Latin America and has a exclusive deal to distribute Monster Energy drinks in Brazil. Soft drinks account for about 10% of AB InBev revenue.

Geographic Reach

The company brews beer and soda at plants spread across its six geographic zones. Latin America North and Asia Pacific have the highest number of factories with about 35 each. Latin America South and North America come in next with around 20 each. Western Europe the original home of the InBev part of AB InBev has about 15 and the Central and Eastern Europe region has around 10. Most of the facilities produce beer but nearly 20 produce both beer and soda and about a dozen (mostly in Latin America) make only soda.

North America original home of the AB part of AB InBev accounts for the majority of sales for the company.

Sales and Marketing

The company distributes it products globally according to local regulations and agreements. Generally it pursues direct distribution where possible and indirect distribution elsewhere. When using indirect distribution it strives to secure exclusive agreements. In regions where AB InBev has no direct affiliates it often licenses local brewers to produce its key brands.

Though the company has a long list of brands its employs a "focus brands" marketing strategy wherein its concentrates money people and attention on the brands that account for about 70% of its beer sales by volume. Those include its three global brands Budweiser Beck's and Stella Artois; what it calls multi-country brands (Leffe and Hoegaarden); and its "local champions" including Bud Light Jupiler Sibirskaya Korona Skol Harbin and Quilmes.

Financial Performance

AB InBev saw a modest 7% increase in revenue (adjusted to account for acquisitions and disposals) mainly due to price increases in North and South America as well as increased sales volume in Asia. Acquisitions and disposals also positively impacted nearly all the company's expenses resulting in a modest $9 million profit for 2012.

Strategy

In both developed and developing markets which each account for about half the company's sales AB InBev focuses its efforts on it core brands while developing regional favorites as well. It uses large events and social media to stay connected with its customers and introduce new products to bring in new customers.

The company also keeps costs in check through strict financial discipline and improving manufacturing efficiencies.

In 2013 the company expects to invest in new capacity projects in China Brazil and Argentina to meet future demand expectations in these growing markets.

Mergers and Acquisitions

In 2013 AB InBev acquired almost all of Mexico's largest beer company Grupo Modelo (it had already owned 50%) for some $20 billion. Owner of the ubiquitous south of the US border brands Corona Extra Modelo Especial and Pacifico Modelo will help expand AB InBev's annual revenues to around $47 billion with operations in 24 countries. The deal allows AB InBev further exposure in emerging markets like Mexico an economy that grew by 4.6% in the first quarter of 2012. Part of the arrangement include selling Grupo Modelo's US business to rival brewer Constellation Brands for about $5 billion.

HISTORY

Monks at the Leffe Abbey in Belgium were brewing beer as early as 1240 and surviving records from 1366 mention Belgium's Den Horen brewery. Belgian master brewer Sebastien Artois (best known for his Stella Artois lager) took over Den Horen in 1717. In 1853 the Piedboeuf family founded a brewery at Liege and established the Jupiler lager. Albert Van Damme assumed management of that brewery in 1920.

Over the years the Artois and Piedboeuf families took over or established operations both in and outside Belgium. Direct descendants (the clans de Spoelberch Van Damme and de Mevius) of the two families were still managing the companies in 1987 when they decided the key to survival in the fragmented European beer market was to merge.

Artois-Piedboeuf-Interbrew acquired the Hoegaarden brewery in Belgium in 1989. The company changed its name to Interbrew three years later acquired another Belgian brewery (Belle-Vue) and bought stakes in breweries in Bulgaria Croatia and Hungary. In 1995 Dommelsche Bierbrouwerij bought Allied Breweries Nederland an Allied Domecq subsidiary and Interbrew acquired the Oranjeboom breweries in the Netherlands.

The company purchased John Labatt Ltd. for $2 billion in 1995. As a result of the deal Interbrew gained control of Latrobe Brewing (Rolling Rock beer US) 22% of Mexico's FEMSA Cerveza (increased to 30% in 1998) the Toronto Argonauts football team 90% of the Toronto Blue Jays (it sold an 80% stake in the baseball team to cable firm Rogers Communications in 2000) and various broadcast properties.

Interbrew sold many noncore assets including Lehigh Valley Dairies (US) and John Labatt Retail (pubs UK) in 1996. Also that year the company established joint ventures in the Dominican Republic and the US (to import Mexican beers through FEMSA).

In 1998 Interbrew paid $250 million for 50% of the Doosan Group's Oriental Brewery South Korea's second-largest brewer and bought a majority stake in Russian brewer Rosar. The next year Interbrew combined its Russian operations with Sun Brewing forming Russian brewer Sun-Interbrew. It then bought Korea's Jinro-Coors Brewery for about $378 million. Hugo Powell was later named CEO of Interbrew.

Interbrew bought Britain's third-largest brewer Whitbread Beer Company in 2000 for $590 million. Having gained a foothold in the UK market the company then bought Bass Brewers from Bass PLC in 2000 for more than $3 billion. Interbrew went public on the Euronext (Brussels) exchange in 2000.

In 2001 Baron Paul De Keersmaeker retired as chairman and was replaced by Pierre Jean Everaert. That year the company took an 80% stake in Germany's tenth-largest brewer Diebels. Interbrew also sold Carling which controls about 18% of the UK beer market to Coors for $1.7 billion after being ordered to remedy unfair competition advantages related to the Bass Brewers purchase.

John Brock former COO of Cadbury Schweppes became CEO of Interbrew in 2003. That year it sold a minority stake of its Namibian Breweries in southern Africa to Diageo and Heineken.

In 2004 Interbrew purchased a 70% stake in Chinese brewer Zhejiang Shiliang which gave Interbrew nearly a 50% market share in China's Zhejiang province.

InBev was created through a 2005 merger of Interbrew and AmBev. The merger resulted in a series of transactions between Interbrew subsidiary Labatt and Mexico's FEMSA. By creating InBev Interbrew gave up interest in distributing FEMSA beer brands in the US. In return Interbrew retained full control of the US division of Labatt. InBev merged Labatt U.S.A. with what was Beck's North America to create its US operations.

Exiting the Slovenian market InBev sold its stake in Pivovarna Union to Pivovarna Lasko in 2005. That year it also acquired Russian premium brewer Tinkoff and sold its stake in soft-drink company Bremer Erfrischungsgetr□nke to Coca-Cola. It sold its minority stake in Spanish brewer Damm as well. At year-end Carlos Brito formerly zone president for the company's North American operations succeeded John Brock as CEO of InBev.

Saying it intended to concentrate on import brands in the US market in 2006 the company sold subsidiary InBev USA's domestic beer brand Rolling Rock to Anheuser-Busch for $82 million. Later in the year InBev and A-B struck an additional deal for A-B to serve as the exclusive distributor for some of its European brands such as Beck's Bass and Stella Artois. In addition it paid some $1 billion to increase its stake in Quinsa an Argentine brewer to 90% from 57% that year.

Auditors: PwC Bedrijfsrevisoren Bcvba

LOCATIONS

HQ: Anheuser-Busch Inbev SA
Brouwerijplein 1, Leuven 3000
Phone: (32) 16 27 6111 **Fax:** (32) 16 50 6111
Web: www.ab-inbev.com

HISTORICAL FINANCIALS

Company Type: Public

Income Statement FYE: December 31

	REVENUE ($ mil.)	NET INCOME ($ mil.)	NET PROFIT MARGIN	EMPLOYEES
12/14	47,063	9,216	19.6%	154,029
12/13	43,195	14,394	33.3%	154,587
12/12	39,758	7,243	18.2%	117,632
12/11	39,046	5,855	15.0%	116,278
12/10	36,297	4,026	11.1%	114,313
Annual Growth	6.7%	23.0%	—	7.7%

2014 Year-End Financials

Debt ratio: 35.8%	No. of shares (mil.): 1,607
Return on equity: 18.3%	Dividends
Cash ($ mil.): 8,357	Yield: 2.8%
Current ratio: 0.68	Payout: 58.4%
Long-term debt ($ mil.): 43,630	Market value ($ mil.): 180,539

	STOCK PRICE ($) FY Close	P/E High/Low		PER SHARE ($) Earnings	Dividends	Book Value
12/14	112.32	21	17	5.54	3.24	31.09
12/13	106.46	12	9	8.72	3.03	31.36
12/12	87.41	20	13	4.45	1.56	25.68
12/11	60.99	17	14	3.63	1.18	23.46
12/10	57.09	25	18	2.50	0.49	22.13
Annual Growth	18.4%	—	—	22.0%	60.0%	8.9%

Aozora Bank, Ltd.

Aozora Bank hopes that the clouds have passed and blue skies are ahead. Aozora (which means blue sky in Japanese) was the second Japanese credit bank nationalized in the wake of Asia's financial crisis (after Shinsei Bank). Bad loans and Japan's "Big Bang" financial deregulation added to its troubles. Now a full-service commercial bank Aozora has some 20 branches in Japan and three offices overseas (New York Shanghai and Singapore). It provides a host of retail and business banking services as well as corporate banking services (loans and derivative products consulting and advisory) and specialty finance and financial markets offerings. Aozora is seeking to expand in Southeast Asia particularly Indonesia.

EXECUTIVES

Senior Managing Executive Officer Head of Investment Banking Group Acting Head of Corporate Banking Group and General Manager Capital Markets Division, Shinsuke Baba
Deputy President and Director, Masaki Tanabe
Senior Managing Executive Officer Director Chief Risk Officer and Chief Credit Risk Officer, Takeo Saito
Senior Managing Executive Officer, Masaki Yamagata
Managing Executive Officer, Clark D. Graninger
Managing Executive Officer, Katsuya Hosono
Managing Executive Officer, Masatatsu Ozeki
Managing Executive Officer, Kei Tanikawa

Chairman, Makoto Fukuda
Auditors: Deloitte Touche Tohmatsu LLC

LOCATIONS

HQ: Aozora Bank, Ltd.
1-3-1 Kudan-Minami, Chiyoda-ku, Tokyo 102-8660
Phone: (81) 3 3263 1111
Web: www.aozorabank.co.jp

PRODUCTS/OPERATIONS

2013 Sales

	% of total
Interest income	
Loans and discounts	31
Dividends on securities	11
Others	2
Other ordinary income	19
Fees and commissions	10
Trading income	8
Others	19
Total	**100**

2013 Sales

	% of total
Lending	42
Securities investment	34
Derivatives	7
Others	17
Total	**100**

Selected affiliates

Aozora Asia Pacific Finance Limited
Aozora GMAC Investment Limited
Aozora Investment Inc.
Aozora Investments LLC
Aozora Regional Consulting Co. Ltd.
AZB CLO1 Limited
AZB CLO2 Limited
AZB CLO3 Limited
AZB CLO4 Limited
AZB Funding
AZB Funding 2
AZB Funding 3
AZB Funding 4 Limited

COMPETITORS

Mitsubishi UFJ Financial Group
Mizuho Financial
Mizuho Trust & Banking Ltd
Norinchukin Bank
Resona
Shinsei Bank
Sumitomo Mitsui
Sumitomo Mitsui Trust Holdings
Tokyo Tomin Bank

HISTORICAL FINANCIALS

Company Type: Public

Income Statement — FYE: March 31

	ASSETS ($ mil.)	NET INCOME ($ mil.)	INCOME AS % OF ASSETS	EMPLOYEES
03/15	41,044	364	0.9%	1,794
03/14	46,555	410	0.9%	1,655
03/13	53,316	431	0.8%	1,615
03/12	62,140	564	0.9%	1,604
03/11	59,395	396	0.7%	1,626
Annual Growth	(8.8%)	(2.1%)	—	2.5%

2015 Year-End Financials

Return on assets: 0.9%
Return on equity: 8.0%
Long-term debt ($ mil.): —
No. of shares (mil.): 1,166
Sales ($ mil): 1,083
Dividends
Yield: —
Payout: —
Market value ($ mil.): 87,888

	STOCK PRICE ($) FY Close	P/E High/Low	PER SHARE ($) Earnings	Dividends	Book Value
03/15	75.35	— —	0.23	0.00	4.05
03/14	58.20	— —	0.26	0.00	4.29
03/13	58.40	— —	0.24	0.00	4.88
Annual Growth	13.6%	—	(0.6%)	—	(4.5%)

Arab National Bank

Arab National Bank offers banking services for primarily commercial but also growing retail segments of the Saudi Arabia market including Shariah (Islamic) services. Its 200-plus branches (51 are women-only) provide savings and checking accounts credit and debit cards loans and investment services. Its Corporate Banking Group segment serves mid-sized and large Saudi businesses while its treasury branch offers foreign exchange services international stock trading international bonds and margin trading accounts. Arab National Bank also owns and operates one branch located in the UK. Arab Bank owns a 40% stake in Arab National Bank which was formed in 1979.

EXECUTIVES

CEO, Bassam Al-Mubarak
Auditors: Ernst & Young

LOCATIONS

HQ: Arab National Bank
P.O. Box 56921, Riyadh 11564
Phone: (966) 1 402 9000 **Fax:** (966) 1 402 7747
Web: www.anb.com.sa

COMPETITORS

Ahli United Bank
Al Rajhi Banking
Arab Banking Corp.
Dallah Albaraka Group
Gulf International Bank
NBK
Saudi British Bank
Standard Chartered

HISTORICAL FINANCIALS

Company Type: Public

Income Statement — FYE: December 31

	ASSETS ($ mil.)	NET INCOME ($ mil.)	INCOME AS % OF ASSETS	EMPLOYEES
12/14	43,883	766	1.7%	4,554
12/13	36,776	672	1.8%	4,586
12/12	36,432	632	1.7%	4,627
12/11	31,353	578	1.8%	4,225
12/10	30,941	509	1.6%	3,495
Annual Growth	9.1%	10.7%	—	6.8%

2014 Year-End Financials

Return on assets: 1.9%
Return on equity: 14.4%
Long-term debt ($ mil.): —
No. of shares (mil.): 850
Sales ($ mil): 1,599
Dividends
Yield: —
Payout: —
Market value ($ mil.): —

ArcelorMittal SA

Few metal makers have the mettle of ArcelorMittal. The company is easily the largest steel-making entity in the world producing more than 90 million metric tons of crude steel annually about 6% of the world steel output. Operating in more than 60 countries ArcelorMittal manufactures the full range of steel products: slabs and coil coated steel and tinplate wire rod and rebar and billets and blooms as well as all manner of electrical steel products. It also has 15 mining operations and is one of the world's largest iron ore producers. In 2014 it produced 77 million metric tons of iron ore and 7.7 million metric tons of metallurgical coal. CEO and founder Lakshmi Mittal controls about 39% of ArcelorMittal.

Geographic Reach

The company has steel-making operations in 19 countries on four continents including 56 integrated and mini-mill steel-making facilities

ArcelorMittal operates through subsidiaries in Europe Africa Asia and the Americas (including ArcelorMittal Brasil). It's the largest producer of steel in North and South America and Africa the sixth-largest steel producer in the Commonwealth of Independent States region and has a growing presence in Asia including investments in China. It is also the largest steel producer in the European Union.

In addition many of ArcelorMittal's units have access to developing markets that are expected to experience significant future growth in steel consumption such as Central and Eastern Europe South America India Africa and Russia. Overall about 47% of its steel is produced in Europe 38% in the Americas and 15% in other countries such as Kazakhstan South Africa and Ukraine.

ArcelorMittal has steel-making operations in 19 countries on four continents including 56 integrated and mini-mill steel-making facilities.

Operations

In 2014 ArcelorMittal reorganized from six to five reportable segments: NAFTA; Europe; Brazil; ACIS (Africa and CIS); and Mining. NAFTA produces flat long and tubular products. Flat products include slabs hot-rolled coil cold-rolled coil coated steel products and plate. These products are sold primarily to customers in the following industries: distribution and processing; automotive; pipes and tubes; construction; packaging and appliances. In 2014 shipments from NAFTA totaled 23.1 million tons.Brazil makes flat (slabs hot-rolled coil cold-rolled coil and coated steel) long and tubular products.Europe produces flat long and tubular products. Flat products include hot-rolled coil cold-rolled coil coated products tinplate plate and slab. These products are sold primarily to customers in the automotive general industry and packaging industries. In 2014 shipments from Europe totaled 39.6 million tons. (Europe contributed about 47% of ArcelorMittal's revenues that year).ACIS manufactures flat long and tubular products at six flat and long production plants in three countries.Mining provides the company's steel operations with high quality and low-cost iron ore and coal reserves and also sells limited amounts of mineral products to third parties. The company has mines in North and South America Europe the CIS and Africa.

Sales and MarketingArcelorMittal produces a wide variety of products across all steel-consuming industries including the automotive appliance engineering construction energy and machinery markets. The company sells its products in local markets and through a centralized marketing organization in more than 170 countries. Its strategy depends on maintaining its size and scale in the global steel market vertical integration of its operations producing a diverse portfolio of products and continuously improving its quality.Financial PerformanceThe company's revenues have been declining in recent years.In 2014 ArcelorMittal's net sales decreased by 0.2% due to the reduced revenues from Asia Africa and Europe. That year the company's net loss decreased by 62% due to lower cost of sales and net income attributable to non-controlling interests. Cost of sales was positively affected by a decrease in depreciation following a change in assessment of certain property plant and equipment and a decline in raw material prices. Net income attributable to non-controlling interests was $112 million in 2014 as compared with net loss attributable to non-controlling interests of $30 million in 2013. Net income attributable to non-controlling interests increased in 2014 primarily as a result of income attributable to non-controlling interests in ArcelorMittal Mines Canada and Belgo Bekaert Arames partially offset by losses generated in ArcelorMittal South Africa which were however significantly lower than in 2013.In 2014 net cash provided by operating activities decreased by $426 million due to a change in inventories and trade accounts payable.

Stategy

ArcelorMittal's strategy is to leverage four distinctive attributes that will enable it to capture leading positions in the most attractive areas of the steel industry value chain from mining at one end to distribution and first-stage processing at the other. These are global scale and scope; unmatched technical capabilities; a diverse portfolio of steel and related businesses particularly mining; and financial capability.

In 2014 ArcelorMittal entered into an agreement to establish the joint venture in Turkey ArcelorMittal RZK Celik Servis Merkezi Sanayi ve Ticaret Anonim Sirketi (“AM RZK”).To raise cash that year ArcelorMittal and Gerdau completed the sale of their respective 50% interests in Gallatin Steel Company a flat rolled mini-mill located in Gallatin County Kentucky to Nucor for $770 million.In 2014 ArcelorMittal also sold its 78% stake in European port handling and logistics company ATIC Services for EUR 155.4 million; its interest in the Kuzbass coal mines in the Kemerovo region of Siberia Russia to Russia's National Fuel Company; and diluted its stake in Algeria's Tebessa mines in Ouenza and Boukhadra .

To focus on its core businesses and pay down debt in 2013 the company sold 15% of its ArcelorMittal Mines Canada subsidiary to Chinese and Korean steelmakers for $1.1 billion.

ArcelorMittal became a conglomerate through acquisitions and strategic partnerships. In 2013 it formed a joint venture with Nippon Steel & Sumitomo Metal to buy ThyssenKrupp Steel USA from ThyssenKrupp.

Mergers and Acquisitions

In 2014 the ArcelorMittal and Nippon Steel & Sumitomo Metal joint venture acquired ThyssenKrupp Steel USA and its steel processing plant in Calvert Alabama for $1.6 billion. The Calvert plant has a total capacity of 5.3 million tons including hot rolling cold rolling coating and finishing lines. The deal is expected to deliver $60 million in annual savings.In 2013 ArcelorMittal also acquired control of the joint operation DJ Galvanizing a hot dip galvanizing line located in Canada through the acquisition of the 50% interest held by the other joint operator.

HISTORY

ArcelorMittal is the product of decades of steelmaking by India's Mittal family. In 1967 patriarch Mohan Mittal unsuccessfully tried to open a steel mill in Egypt. He and his four younger brothers then set up a steel company in India but squabbles pushed Mohan to chart his own course eventually giving rise to an empire that flourished under the Ispat name. Mohan's son Lakshmi began working part-time at the family steel mill while in school; he started full-time at 21 after graduating in 1971.

Mohan set up an operation in Indonesia in 1975 (Ispat Indo) and put Lakshmi in charge. The next year fueled by ambitions and held back by government regulations in India Lakshmi formed Ispat International in Jakarta Indonesia to focus on expansion through acquisitions. He spent the next decade strengthening the Indonesian operations and perfecting the minimill process using direct-reduced iron (DRI).

Ispat took advantage of the recessionary late 1980s and early 1990s by making a string of acquisitions. In 1988 it took over the management of Trinidad and Tobago's state steel companies (bought in 1994; renamed Caribbean Ispat).

In 1992 Ispat bought Mexico's third-largest (albeit bankrupt) steel and DRI producer. Two years later it acquired Canada's Sidbec-Dosco steelmaker. Also that year Lakshmi took exclusive control of international operations leaving his brothers Pramod and Vinod to control the Indian divisions.

The mid-1990s brought more acquisitions: In 1995 Ispat bought Germany's Hamburger Stahlwerks and a mill in Kazakhstan. The next year it purchased Ireland's only steelmaker Irish Steel. Lakshmi moved to London in 1996 and purchased a home on Bishops Avenue known as "millionaire's row." (Saudi Arabia's King Fahd was a neighbor.)

In 1997 the company bought the long-product (wire rod) division of Germany's Thyssen AG (renamed Ispat Stahlwerk Ruhrort and Ispat Walzdraht Hochfeld). It also completed a $776 million IPO.

Ispat acquired Chicago-based Inland Steel in 1998 (and renamed it Ispat Inland) including the steel-finishing operations of I/N Tek (60% Inland-owned joint venture with Nippon Steel) and I/N Kote (50% Inland-owned joint venture with NSC).

In 1999 Ispat formed a joint venture with Mexican steelmaker Grupo Imsa to make flat-rolled steel to sell throughout most of the Americas. It also paid $96 million for France-based Usinor's Unimtal Trfileurope and Socit Mtallurgique de Rvigny subsidiaries which specialize in carbon long products. That year Ispat Inland became the target of a US federal criminal grand jury investigation and a related civil lawsuit for allegedly defrauding the Louisiana Highway Department. (The case was settled for $30 million with the cost split between Ispat Inland and Contech Construction Products Inc. of Ohio.)

In 2000 the company responded to a downturn in the steel industry by starting a Web-based joint venture with Commerce One to connect buyers and sellers in the worldwide metals market. It also offered to buy VSZ Slovakia's #1 steelworks but was outbid by U.S. Steel.

After struggling with heavy debt high labor and energy costs new environmental regulations and EU steel quotas in 2001 Ispat closed down its subsidiary Irish Ispat which accounted for about 2% of the parent company's steel production.

In 2002 the company's 51%-owned pipe making subsidiary Productura Mexicana de Tuberia sold almost all of its production assets.

The present ArcelorMittal was forged in 2004 when Ispat International (of which the Mittal family owned 70%) purchased LNM Holdings (wholly owned by the Mittals) for $13 billion. In 2006 the former Mittal Steel agreed to buy rival Arcelor for about $34 billion to create ArcelorMittal.

Mittal Steel had established its hold on the world steel market through its 2005 purchase of the US-based International Steel Group (ISG) for $4.5 billion. The purchase made the company the largest steel producer (ahead of U.S. Steel and Nucor) in the US a market that had long been a targeted area for expansion for CEO Mittal. Once the deal closed the company combined ISG's operations with those of subsidiary Ispat Inland to form a single North American entity Mittal Steel USA (now ArcelorMittal USA.

Also in 2005 Mittal Steel acquired a 93% stake in Ukrainian state-run steel company KryvorizhStal with the winning $4.84 billion bid in an auction held by the Ukrainian government. The price was high but Mittal was anxious to gain a stronger foothold in the region –and to keep its rivals away from KryvorizhStal. (This fact incidentally went a long way to convincing Mittal it needed to combine with Arcelor; the competition for acquisitions was driving prices dramatically upward.)

The company also began to broaden its portfolio outside the steel industry dipping its toe into the energy business. In mid-2005 Mittal formed two joint ventures with India's government-controlled Oil & Natural Gas Corporation: one to buy stakes in foreign oil and gas projects the other involved in oil and gas trading and shipping. The ventures began to look for business in places like Indonesia Kazakhstan Angola and Trinidad and Tobago.

After consolidating his family's various steel interests in the early part of this decade Mittal began work on the steel industry as a whole and was soon the world's largest steel producer.

By 2006 Mittal Steel no longer was content to be merely the world's largest steel producer; it wanted to dominate the market. The company announced an offer to the shareholders of Arcelor then the industry's #2 player to buy that company and in the process create the world's first 100-million-ton steel producer. Arcelor and seemingly half the governments of Western Europe initially fought the attempt.

Mittal improved its proposed price however and Arcelor's board finally approved the offer when Mittal also made ownership/corporate governance concessions. The combined company is 43% owned by the Mittal family. After a few months of a transitional management team arrangement Lakshmi Mittal took over as CEO of the combined company toward the end of 2006.

In 2009 ArcelorMittal completed its acquisition of the laser-welding steel activities of Noble International a leader in the niche industry. It also acquired Mexican steel producer Sicarsta for nearly $1.5 billion an acquisition that combined with its Lazaro Cardenas created Mexico's largest steel company.

In 2011 the company spun off its stainless and specialty steels steel operations into Aperam which immediately became the world's sixth-largest stainless steel producer. ArcelorMittal made the decision in 2010 to spin off its stainless steel units in Europe and Brazil after determining that they were underperforming and would better thrive as a separate business.After spinning its wheels in an escalating bidding war in 2011 ArcelorMittal joined rival Nunavut Iron Ore in making a joint acquisition of Canada-based Baffinland Iron Mines for $594 million. Both companies sought access to Baffinland's Mary River Project an undeveloped deposit of iron ore on sparsely populated North Baffin Island located inside the Arctic Circle as a source of raw materials. The venture faces stiff challenges including building an infrastructure around the mine's formidable location and shipping the ore out to Europe and other production sites.

Also that year the company bought a 40% stake in G Steel Public Company greatly expanding its presence in Asia. G Steel produces about 2.5 million ton of steel annually at its two slab-rolling plants in Thailand. The deal was part of ArcelorMittal's strategy of establishing a presence in emerging markets with with the potential for future growth.

In 2012 ArcelorMittal expanded its presence in China by increasing its stake in a joint venture with Valin Group known as Valin ArcelorMittal Automotive (VAMA) from 33% to 49%. VAMA is trying to enhance its position in China as a supplier of high-strength steels and products for the automotive market. The joint venture scheduled to become operational in 2014 will increase its planned capacity from 1.2 million tons to 1.5 million tons.

That year it sold New Jersey-based Skyline Steel a North American steel foundation and piling products distributor and specialty steel plate and bar producer Astralloy to US-based Nucor for $605 million.

EXECUTIVES

Chairman and CEO, Lakshmi N. Mittal, age 64
Director Finance and Mergers and Acquisitions and Director, Aditya Mittal, age 39
CEO ArcelorMittal Americas, Louis (Lou) Schorsch, age 66
CEO ArcelorMittal USA, John L. Brett
CEO ArcelorMittal USA, Andy Harshaw
VP Commercial Flat Carbon South America, Benjamin M. Baptista Filho
CEO AM/NS Calvert, Robrecht Himpe, age 57
VP Global Automotive and Commercial Coordination, Brian Aranha
CEO ArcelorMittal Mining, Simon Wandke
CEO ArcelorMittal Nafta Flat Rolled, Jim Baske
CEO ArcelorMittal Africa and CIS Algeria Kazakhstan South Africa and Ukraine, Davinder Chugh
CEO South America Long, Jefferson de Paula
Auditors: Deloitte Audit S. .r.l.

LOCATIONS

HQ: ArcelorMittal SA
24-26, Boulevard daAvranches, Luxembourg L-1160
Phone: (352) 4792 2484 **Fax:** (352) 4792 89 3937
Web: www.arcelormittal.com

2014 Sales

	$ mil.	% of total
Europe	36,283	46
Americas	32,297	41
Asia & Africa	10,702	13
Total	**79,282**	**100**

PRODUCTS/OPERATIONS

Segments and Selected Products

Flat Carbon Europe
- Coated products
- Coil
- Cold-rolled
- Hot-rolled
- Plate
- Slab
- Tin plate

Flat Carbon Americas
- Coated products
- Steel
- Plate
- Coil
- Cold-rolled
- Hot-rolled
- Slabs

Long Carbo
- Billets
- Blooms
- Rebar
- Sections
- Wire rod

Asia Africa & Comonwealth of Independent States
- Flat products
- Long products
- Pipes
- Tubes

ArcelorMittal Steel Solutions & Services (in-house trading and distribution arm)

COMPETITORS

AK Steel Holding Corporation
BHP Billiton
Baosteel
BlueScope Steel
China Steel
Essar Group
Evraz
Gerdau
JFE Holdings
Mechel OAO
Nippon Steel & Sumitomo Metal Corporation
Nucor
POSCO
Severstal
Shougang Corp.
Tata Steel
Tenaris
Ternium
ThyssenKrupp Steel
United States Steel

HISTORICAL FINANCIALS

Company Type: Public

Income Statement FYE: December 31

	REVENUE ($ mil.)	NET INCOME ($ mil.)	NET PROFIT MARGIN	EMPLOYEES
12/14	79,282	(1,086)	—	222,327
12/13	79,440	(2,545)	—	232,353
12/12	84,213	(3,726)	—	273,811
12/11	93,973	2,263	2.4%	260,523
12/10	78,025	2,916	3.7%	273,811
Annual Growth	0.4%	—	—	(5.1%)

2014 Year-End Financials

Debt ratio: 19.9%
Return on equity: (-2.3%)
Cash ($ mil.): 3,893
Current ratio: 1.33
Long-term debt ($ mil.): 17,275
No. of shares (mil.): 1,654
Dividends
Yield: 1.5%
Payout: —
Market value ($ mil.): 18,248

	STOCK PRICE ($) FY Close	P/E High/Low	PER SHARE ($) Earnings	Dividends	Book Value
12/14	11.03	— —	(1.00)	0.17	25.44
12/13	17.84	— —	(1.46)	0.49	30.11
12/12	17.47	— —	(2.41)	0.64	33.39
12/11	18.19	26 10	1.19	0.64	36.60
12/10	38.13	25 14	1.72	0.64	40.31
Annual Growth	(26.7%)	— —	—	(28.1%)	(10.9%)

Asea Brown Boveri AG (Austria)

Auditors: Ernst & Young AG

LOCATIONS

HQ: Asea Brown Boveri AG (Austria)
P.O. Box 8131, Zurich 8050
Phone: (41) 43 317 71 11 **Fax:** (41) 43 317 79 58
Web: www.abb.com

HISTORICAL FINANCIALS

Company Type: Public

Income Statement FYE: December 31

	REVENUE ($ mil.)	NET INCOME ($ mil.)	NET PROFIT MARGIN	EMPLOYEES
12/14	39,830	2,594	6.5%	140,400
12/13	41,848	2,787	6.7%	147,700
12/12	39,336	2,704	6.9%	0
12/10	37,990	3,168	8.3%	0
12/94	230	0	0.0%	1,609
Annual Growth	29.4%	70.9%	—	25.0%

2014 Year-End Financials

Debt ratio: 17.1%
Return on equity: 14.8%
Cash ($ mil.): 5,443
Current ratio: 1.60
Long-term debt ($ mil.): 7,338
No. of shares (mil.): —
Dividends
Yield: —
Payout: 67.7%
Market value ($ mil.): —

Assicurazioni Generali S.p.A.

Italy's largest insurance company (and one of the largest in Europe) Assicurazioni Generali writes insurance for risks as varied as pensions and car insurance. Present in more than 60 countries Generali's core businesses are involved in both life and property/casualty insurance (including accident health motor fire marine/aviation and reinsurance). Generali is noted for being a leading insurer of satellite and space missions which it has been covering since 1964. In more earthbound realms the company targets individuals and small to midsized businesses and has been in business since 1831.

Operations

Generali operates through about 500 companies throughout the world. Life insurance makes up the lion's share of its business with products that include savings and protection policies health business and supplementary pension policies. More than 70% of its written premiums are generated through its life insurance segment. Its non-life segment centers on retail markets.

Generali also promotes its financial services operations including Banca Generali which offer such services as wealth management and bank insurance products.

Geographic Reach

The company primarily operates in Western Europe especially in Italy Austria Germany France Spain and Switzerland. It also does business in Central and Eastern Europe. Generali also operates in Asia (including China Hong Kong India Indonesia Japan the Philippines Singapore Thailand Malaysia and Vietnam) Central and South America and the Middle East; it has offices in India and China.

Sales and Marketing

Generali serves some 65 million customers around the world. It sells through channels including its own global network of agents as well as financial advisors and brokers. It also sells by telephone and online.

Financial Performance

Generali's earnings were negatively impacted in 2011 by broadspread economic instabilities in the eurozone but revenues have been climbing back since then. In 2014 revenues rose 5% to 88.3 billion thanks to premium growth in Italy that was driven by rising sales of alternative products and hybrid lines. Other markets performed well too including France Austria Asia and the Middle East. The banking segment also reported higher earnings that year.

However net income fell 13% to 1.7 billion as the company paid out more in claims and reported unrealized and impairment losses. Cash flow from operations rose 49% to 19.7 billion as Generali changed its mathematical provisions and other provisions in its life segment.

Strategy

Generali's strategy for growth is based entering new market segments and countries. With its place firmly cemented in Western Europe it is looking to expand its presence in Eastern Europe Latin America and Asia through joint ventures and acquisitions. To that end Generali has targeted the fast-growing life insurance market of Vietnam.

Other strategic initiatives include improving its overall operating efficiencies including centralizing its IT operations into a single data center; optimizing its distribution networks and the developing proprietary networks; delivering innovative products; and diversifying its distribution methods. To reach younger customers it is particularly vested in providing direct channels via mobile applications and the web. The company leads in direct-to-consumers telephone and online channels in Italy Germany and France where it offers both life and property/casualty products.

The group has been disposing of certain units to both raise capital and to focus on its core insurance businesses. It had a stated goal of raising 4 billion by 2015. To those ends Generali sold its BSI private banking division in 2014. It also sold Fata Assicurazioni Danni for 194.7 million and in 2013 it sold its US reinsurance business.

Mergers and Acquisitions

In 2014 Generali entered the Malaysian market when it acquired a 49% stake in property/casualty insurer Multi-Purpose Insurance a subsidiary of Multi-Purpose Capital Holdings for 81.4 million.

The following year the group acquired the 24% of Generali PPF Holding it didn't already own for 1.3 billion. The unit which operates in Central and Eastern Europe was renamed Generali CEE Holding.

HISTORY

Assicurazioni Generali was founded as Assicurazioni Generali Austro-Italiche in 1831 by a group of merchants led by Giuseppe Morpurgo in the Austro-Hungarian port of Trieste. Formed to provide insurance to the city's bustling trade industry the company offered life marine fire flood and shipping coverage. That year Morpurgo established what he intended to be Generali's headquarters in Venice. (While the company maintained offices in both cities Trieste ultimately won out.)

By 1835 Generali had opened 25 offices in Central and Western Europe; it had also expelled Morpurgo. The firm moved into Africa and Asia in the 1880s. In 1900 Generali began selling injury and theft insurance. In 1907 Generali's Prague office provided the young experimental writer Franz Kafka his first job. (He found it disagreeable and quit after a few months.)

During WWI the firm's Venice office pledged allegiance to Italy while the office in Trieste (still part of Austria-Hungary) stayed loyal to the Hapsburgs. After the war Trieste was absorbed by the new Italian republic. Under Edgardo Morpurgo Generali expanded further in the 1920s managing 30 subsidiaries and operating in 17 countries. As fascist Italy aligned itself with Germany in the 1930s adoption of anti-Semitic laws caused Morpurgo and a number of other high-ranking Jewish employees to flee the country. In 1938 Generali moved its headquarters to Rome (but moved them back to Trieste after war's end).

The firm maintained steady business both before and during Nazi occupation in WWII; in 1945 however the Soviets seized all Italian properties in Eastern Europe including 14 Generali subsidiaries. In 1950 Generali invaded the US market offering shipping and fire insurance and reinsurance. Generali established a cooperative agreement with Aetna Life and Casualty (now Aetna Inc.) in 1966 further cementing its US connections.

In 1988 Generali tried to acquire French insurer Compagnie du Midi. Foreshadowing Generali's later dealings with Istituto Nazionale delle Assicurazioni (INA) Midi escaped Generali's grasp through a merger with AXA. As the Iron Curtain frayed in 1989 Generali formed AB Generali Budapest through a joint venture with a Hungarian insurer. In 1990 the firm opened an office in Tokyo through an agreement with Taisho Marine and Fire Insurance (which became Mitsui Marine & Fire Insurance and is now Mitsui Sumitomo Insurance). By 1993 Generali had become Italy's largest insurer.

In 1997 the firm was accused along with other major European insurers of not paying on policies of Holocaust victims. (It moved to settle claims in 1999.)

EXECUTIVES

CEO Italy, Philippe Donnet, age 55
Group Head Global Business Lines, Paolo Vagnone, age 52
Group Compliance Officer, Maurizio Basso
CEO Generali CEE Holding B.V., Luciano Cirin , age 51
CEO France, Eric Lombard
Group Chief Risk Officer, Sandro Panizza
Group CFO, Alberto Minali
Group COO, C. Schildknecht
Group Chief Investment Officer, Nikhil Srinivasan
CEO Germany, Giovanni Liverani
Group Head Information Systems, Bruce M. Hodges
Chairman and Acting Group CEO, Peter Hobbs
Group Insurance and Reinsurance, Valter Trevisani
Group Chief Data Officer, Elana Rasa
Regional Officer EMEA, Jaime Anch stegui
Regional Officer Americas, Antonio Cassio dos Santos
Regional Officer Asia, Jack Howell
Group Strategy and Business Development, Giovanni Giuliani
Vice Chairman, Francesco G. Caltagirone, age 72
Vice Chairman, Clemente Rebecchini, age 51
Auditors: Reconta Ernst & Young S.p.A.

LOCATIONS

HQ: Assicurazioni Generali S.p.A.
Piazza Duca degli Abruzzi 2, P.O. Box 538, Trieste 34132
Phone: (39) 40 6711 **Fax:** (39) 40 671 600
Web: www.generali.com

2014 Written Premiums by Location

	% of total
Europe	
Italy	30
Germany	21
France	13
Austria	3
Spain	3
Switzerland	2
Other Europe	23
Other regions	5
Total	**100**

PRODUCTS/OPERATIONS

2014 Net Earned Premiums

	% of total
Life insurance	69
Non-life earned premium	31
Total	**100**

2014 Written Premiums

	% of total
Life insurance	71
Property and casualty	29
Total	**100**

Mergers Acquisitions and Divestitures

COMPETITORS

AIG
AXA
Achmea
Allianz
Assurances G©n©rales de France
Camfin
ERGO
ING
Milano Assicurazioni
Swiss Re
Unipol
UnipolSai
Zurich Insurance Group
ageas SA/NV

HISTORICAL FINANCIALS

Company Type: Public

Income Statement FYE: December 31

	ASSETS ($ mil.)	NET INCOME ($ mil.)	INCOME AS % OF ASSETS	EMPLOYEES
12/14	609,354	2,029	0.3%	78,333
12/13	619,057	2,636	0.4%	77,185
12/12	582,241	118	0.0%	79,454
12/11	547,204	1,107	0.2%	81,997
12/10	565,381	2,277	0.4%	85,368
Annual Growth	1.9%	(2.8%)	—	(2.1%)

2014 Year-End Financials

Return on assets: 0.3%
Return on equity: 7.7%
Long-term debt ($ mil.): —
No. of shares (mil.): 1,556
Sales ($ mil): 105,191
Dividends
Yield: —
Payout: 42.4%
Market value ($ mil.): —

AstraZeneca Plc

AstraZeneca's products run the gamut from A (blood pressure drug Atacand) to Z (prostate and breast cancer drug Zoladex). One of the world's major pharmaceutical firms AstraZeneca specializes in drugs for cardiovascular metabolic neurological gastrointestinal respiratory oncology and infection therapy areas. The firm's biggest sellers include cholesterol reducer Crestor cardiovascular drug Brilinta acid reflux remedy Nexium and Symbicort for asthma. AstraZeneca also markets drugs that aim to treat high cholesterol diabetes pain viral diseases and various cancers. The company's products are sold in more than 100 countries.

Operations

In 2013 AstraZeneca sold its only non-pharma business Aptium Oncology which operates cancer treatment centers in the US. This came on the heels of selling its other non-core units Astra Tech (medical devices) and DENTSPLY (dental implant systems). The moves are part of the company's focus on streamlining its operations around core drug development and commercialization efforts in targeted therapeutic areas for the past few years as part of strategic restructuring efforts in the face of looming patent expirations and increasing generic competition.

Since 2010 the number of AstraZeneca's drugs with sales of more than $1 billion each dropped from 10 to seven: Crestor Atacand Nexium Seroquel IR Seroquel XR Zoladex and Symbicort. The firm has especially been feeling the effects of generic competition for some of its top sellers in the US (the company's largest market) where revenues were down due to patent losses and increased generic competition. Established markets Western Europe and Canada also saw double digit drops as Crestor lost patent protection in Canada and sales of Seroquel IR Nexium Arimidex and Meronem decreased.

AstraZeneca has had several successes in its R&D organization as it works to keep the bestsellers coming and sales of newer drugs such as Crestor and Symbicort have helped sustain overall revenues for the company. During 2014 it received a dozen approvals for new molecular entities or major life cycle management projects in major markets. With a pipeline of about 135 drugs in various development stages it also looks for acquisitions to boost its product development.

The company has been focusing efforts on respiratory inflammation and autoimmunity therapies where it has eight products in phase III or registration status. In 2015 it acquired rights to Almirall's respiratory business and it plans to buy Actavis' branded respiratory business in the US and Canada.

Geographic Reach

AstraZeneca has operations in Europe North America Central America South America the Middle East Africa and the Asia/Pacific region. It manufactures products in 16 countries.

Growth in China and other emerging markets (including Russia Africa India Indonesia Malaysia South Korea Vietnam Brazil Argentina and Chile) is key for AstraZeneca's as it sees sales dip in established markets due to patent expiration in its older medications.

The Americas accounted for about 50% of AstraZeneca's revenue in 2014. Sales in emerging markets were up 8% in 2013 and 12% in 2014 thanks to sales growth in China and Russia. China was really the bright spot with a 22% increase in sales on the strength of the company's cardio and respiratory drugs. As a result the firm is increasing investments in emerging markets; for instance it built a $200 million manufacturing plant to meet market needs in China.

Sales and Marketing

The company markets its products to physicians through sales and marketing teams who are active in more than 100 countries. It typically sells through local marketing companies which it owns as well as through distributors and local representative offices.

Financial Performance

AstraZeneca saw revenue declines in 2012 and 2013 as a result of patent losses. Despite these losses it has managed to stay one step ahead of the game through its balanced growth and cost-control efforts. In 2014 revenue increased by just over 1% to $26.1 billion; driving that growth were the successes of such products as Brilinta/Brilique its diabetes and respiratory franchises Farxiga/Forxiga and the Bydureon Pen (which was launched in the US). The company also grew in its emerging markets operations with China (its second-largest market) increasing 22% that year. Pricing pressures in the region put a bit of a damper on those increases though.

The US saw a 4% increase largely due to the firm's diabetes products as well as growth in the Symbicort and Brilinta lines. However this was offset by declines from sales of Nexium Seroquel IR and Synagis. European revenues also slipped in 2014 primarily as a result of dropping sales of Atacand and Seroquel XR both of which are contending with generics in the region.

Although revenue saw a modest rise in 2014 net income continued its downward trend that year falling 52% to $1.2 billion as a result of R&D expenses surrounding the company's late-stage pipeline. Other factors cutting into profits were selling general and administrative costs as AstraZeneca focuses on its growth platforms. Cash flow from operations fell 5% to $7.1 billion.

Strategy

After a number of strategic moves including workforce reductions exits from certain markets an overhaul of its IT organization and management changes AstraZeneca is on track to return to growth by 2017. The company introduced a sixth growth platform —oncology —adding to its focus on respiratory inflammation and autoimmunity; and cardiovascular and metabolic diseases.

The firm is making a concerted effort to strengthen its industry position ahead of patent expirations by overhauling its R&D organization including by building up its late-stage drug development pipeline through internal research and development acquisitions and collaborations. Through its MedImmune unit it is also building up its R&D programs for new biologic medicines which enjoy longer terms of patent protection. In 2014 its Lynparza was approved for ovarian cancer treatment in the US and Europe and its Movantik tablet (constipation) and Myalept (leptin deficiency) products were approved in the US. The company also launched Nexium Direct which delivers Nexium directly to the homes of eligible patients.

As the company faces losing exclusivity in the US for its cholesterol-lowering drug Crestor AstraZeneca is looking to boost its cardiovascular disease portfolio. It bought California-based biotech ZS Pharma for $2.7 billion in late 2015. That purchase adds ZS Pharma's ZS-9 candidate which is under review in the US for the treatment of hyperkalemia (high potassium levels in the blood).

At the same time AstraZeneca is streamlining the pipeline to concentrate on the most promising research areas by reducing the number of disease targets within its six core therapy areas (cardiovascular gastrointestinal infection neuroscience oncology and respiratory/inflammation). For example it announced plans to spin off its antibiotics division in early 2015. It also agreed to sell cancer drug Caprelsa to Sanofi for up to $300 million. These efforts have resulted in the consolidation of some R&D facilities.

In emerging markets primarily China Russia and Brazil AstraZeneca has concentrated on delivering new products and investing in marketing and sales. In 2014 the company's facility in Taizhou China delivered its first product while its facility in Vorsino Russia is nearing regulatory validation.

Mergers and Acquisitions

Along with discovering its own new drugs and collaborating with its pharmaceutical cohorts AstraZeneca also expands its R&D pipeline through occasional acquisitions. In 2016 it took a majority (55%) stake in Acerta Pharma gaining access to that firm's acalabrutinib candidate for the treatment of B-cell cancers. In late 2015 it acquired biotech firm ZS Pharma adding that firm's ZS-9 candidate for the treatment of hyperkalemia. The company acquired Amylin buying out the partnership in early 2014. Also that year it acquired the rights to Almirall's respiratory franchise and inhalation device subsidiary. It bought out Bristol-Myers Squibb's share of the companies' diabetes alliance gaining ownership of the intellectual property and global rights for the development manufacturing and marketing of the related products which include Onglyza Kombiglyze XR Farxiga and Byetta.

In 2013 AstraZeneca focused expansion efforts on the cardiovascular market. It purchased Alpha-Core a US-based private biotech firm; and purchased Omthera which is working to develop heart medicines based on omega-3 fatty acids for some $443 million.

HISTORY

AstraZeneca forerunner Imperial Chemical Industries (ICI) was created from the 1926 merger of four British chemical companies –Nobel Industries; Brunner Mond and Company; United Alkali; and British Dyestuffs –in reaction to the German amalgamation that created I. G. Farben. ICI plunged into research recruiting chemists engineers and managers and forming alliances with universities. Between 1933 and 1935 at least 87 new products were created including polyethylene.

Fortunes declined as competition increased after WWII. In 1980 ICI posted losses and cut its dividend for the first time. In 1982 turnaround artist John Harvey-Jones shifted ICI from bulk chemicals to high-margin specialty chemicals such as pharmaceuticals and pesticides. That business became Zeneca which ICI spun off in 1993.

The takeover specter loomed large over the company during its first year. Zeneca had several drugs in its pipeline but it also had expiring patents on others making them fair game for competitors. Bankrolled by its agrochemical business Zeneca forged alliances with other pharmaceutical firms. In 1994 it entered a marketing alliance with Amersham International (now Amersham) to sell Metastron a nuclear-medicine cancer agent. The next year Zeneca formed a joint venture with Chinese companies Advanced Chemicals and Tianli to make textile-coating chemicals.

In 1995 Glaxo was forced to sell a migraine drug candidate to complete its merger with Wellcome. Zeneca's gamble in buying the then-unproven drug (Zomig) paid off when the product gained US FDA approval two years later.

By 1997 Zeneca completed its gradual acquisition of Salick Health Care formed to create more humane cancer treatment programs. The purchase followed a trend of large drug firms moving into managed care which raised concerns that centers might be pressured to use their parent companies' drugs but Zeneca maintained that Salick would remain independent except to the extent that it offered an opportunity to evaluate treatments.

In 1998 Zeneca got the FDA's OK to sell its brand of tamoxifen (Nolvadex) to women at high risk of contracting breast cancer. In 1999 it sued Eli Lilly to protect Nolvadex against Lilly's marketing claim that its osteoporosis treatment Evista reduced breast cancer risk a use for which it was not approved.

In 1999 Zeneca completed its purchase of Sweden's Astra to form AstraZeneca. That year the firm sold its specialty chemicals unit Zeneca Specialties to Cinven Group and Investcorp. With its agricultural business stagnated due to crippled markets in Asia and Europe AstraZeneca announced plans to merge the unit with the agrochemicals business of Novartis and spun it off as Syngenta.

EXECUTIVES

EVP Global Operations and Information Services, David Smith

CEO, Pascal Soriot, age 54

EVP MedImmune, Bahija Jallal

EVP Global Medicines Development and Chief Medical Officer, Briggs Morrison

CFO, Marc Dunoyer

EVP International, Mark Mallon
EVP Innovative Medicines and Early Development, Menelas (Mene) Pangalos
EVP North America; President AstraZeneca US, Paul Hudson
EVP Europe, Ruud Dobber
EVP Human Resources and Corporate Affairs, Caroline Hempstead
EVP Global Portfolio and Product Strategy, Luke Miels
EVP and Human Resources, Fiona Cicconi
Chairman, Leif Johansson, age 64
Auditors: KPMG LLP

LOCATIONS

HQ: AstraZeneca Plc
2 Kingdom Street, London W2 6BD
Phone: (44) 20 7604 8000 **Fax:** (44) 20 7604 8151
Web: www.astrazeneca.com

2014 Sales

	$ mil.	% of total
Americas		
US	10,485	28
Canada & other Americas	4,094	10
Europe		
Continental Europe	10,520	28
UK	6,482	17
Asia Africa & Australia	6,397	17
Eliminations	(11883)	-
Total	**26,095**	**100**

PRODUCTS/OPERATIONS

2014 Sales

	$ mil.	% of total
Cardiovascular & Metabolic	9,802	38
Neuroscience Gastrointestinal Infection & other	8,203	31
Respiratory Inflammation & Autoimmunity	5,063	19
Oncology	3,027	12
Total	**26,095**	**100**

COMPETITORS

Abbott Labs
Amgen
Aptium Oncology
Bayer AG
Bristol-Myers Squibb
Eli Lilly
Gilead Sciences
GlaxoSmithKline
Johnson & Johnson
Memorial Sloan-Kettering
Merck
Novartis
Pfizer
Ranbaxy Laboratories
Roche Holding
Sanofi
Teva
US Oncology

HISTORICAL FINANCIALS

Company Type: Public

Income Statement FYE: December 31

	REVENUE ($ mil.)	NET INCOME ($ mil.)	NET PROFIT MARGIN	EMPLOYEES
12/14	26,095	1,233	4.7%	57,500
12/13	25,711	2,556	9.9%	51,500
12/12	27,973	6,297	22.5%	51,700
12/11	33,591	9,983	29.7%	57,200
12/10	33,269	8,053	24.2%	61,100
Annual Growth	(5.9%)	(37.4%)	—	(1.5%)

2014 Year-End Financials

Debt ratio: 18.5%	No. of shares (mil.): 1,263
Return on equity: 5.7%	Dividends
Cash ($ mil.): 6,360	Yield: 3.9%
Current ratio: 0.96	Payout: 142.8%
Long-term debt ($ mil.): 8,397	Market value ($ mil.): 88,900

	STOCK PRICE ($) FY Close	P/E High/Low	PER SHARE ($) Earnings	Dividends	Book Value
12/14	70.38	83 60	0.98	1.40	15.54
12/13	59.37	29 22	2.04	1.40	18.47
12/12	47.27	10 8	4.98	1.43	19.04
12/11	46.29	7 6	7.30	1.35	17.99
12/10	46.19	10 7	5.57	1.21	16.47
Annual Growth	11.1%	— —	(35.2%)	3.8%	(1.5%)

AUDI AG Vormals Audi-NSU Auto Union AG

Auditors: PricewaterhouseCoopers Aktiengesellschaft Wirtschaftspruefungsgesellschaft

LOCATIONS

HQ: AUDI AG Vormals Audi-NSU Auto Union AG
I/FF-12, P.O. Box 10 04 57, Ingolstadt 85045
Phone: (49) 841 89 0 **Fax:** (49) 841 89 325 24
Web: www.audi.com

HISTORICAL FINANCIALS

Company Type: Public

Income Statement FYE: December 31

	REVENUE ($ mil.)	NET INCOME ($ mil.)	NET PROFIT MARGIN	EMPLOYEES
12/14	65,378	5,308	8.1%	77,247
12/13	68,671	5,453	7.9%	71,781
12/12	64,282	5,646	8.8%	67,231
12/11	57,036	5,676	10.0%	62,806
12/10	47,433	3,461	7.3%	59,513
Annual Growth	8.4%	11.3%	—	6.7%

2014 Year-End Financials

Debt ratio: 18.7%	No. of shares (mil.): 43
Return on equity: 23.5%	Dividends
Cash ($ mil.): 13,845	Yield: —
Current ratio: 1.51	Payout: —
Long-term debt ($ mil.): 1,162	Market value ($ mil.): 33,794

	STOCK PRICE ($) FY Close	P/E High/Low	PER SHARE ($) Earnings	Dividends	Book Value
12/14	785.90	15 11	123.43	0.00	531.32
12/13	890.00	18 14	126.84	0.00	584.95
12/12	702.39	14 10	131.30	0.00	452.77
12/11	741.00	18 11	132.01	0.00	382.14
12/10	899.00	28 26	80.48	0.00	347.73
Annual Growth	(3.3%)	— —	11.3%	—	11.2%

Australia and New Zealand Banking Group Ltd

Australia and New Zealand Banking Group (ANZ) one of Australia's Big Four banks and one of New Zealand's top banks offers commercial and retail banking and financial services from about 1400 branches and offices primarily in Australia and New Zealand but also across the Asia/Pacific region. Offerings include standard deposit and lending services credit cards wealth management agribusiness finance and insurance and foreign exchange services for other financial institutions. Altogether the group serves 8 million customers in more than 30 countries including China Germany India the UK and the US. ANZ traces its roots to the 1835 founding of Bank of Australasia.

ANZ which generates about 95% of its revenues in Australia and New Zealand is focused on expansion in the Asia/Pacific region where it has opened new branches and acquired existing operations. In 2009 it bought the businesses of Royal Bank of Scotland (which had been selling noncore operations) in six Asian countries (Hong Kong Indonesia Philippines Singapore Taiwan and Vietnam) for $550 million. ANZ typically teams with other firms to enter new markets or accelerate growth; the bank has taken minority stakes or formed partnerships with among others Metrobank (Philippines) Bank of Tianjin (China) Sacombank (Vietnam) Panin Bank (Indonesia) and AmBank Group (Malaysia).

To further its strategy of becoming a superregional bank ANZ entered an agreement with wheat marketer AWB Limited allowing the bank to exclusively market its offerings to AWB's 100000 customers. In 2010 the company acquired the loan and deposit books of Landmark Financial Services a division of AWB's Landmark rural arm. Landmark Financial Services provides services to some 10000 agribusiness customers.

In a bid to catch up with its rivals in domestic fund management the company formed OnePath (formerly ING Australia) a wealth management joint venture with Dutch financial services giant ING Groep. The division offers investment retirement insurance and superannuation products. In late 2009 ANZ bought out ING's 51% stake in the venture and rebranded it OnePath. OnePath has about A$54 billion in funds under management.

HISTORY

Captain Cook claimed Australia for the crown in 1770. By 1800 convicts and free immigrants had built a thriving wool trade with the mother country but the land needed financial infrastructure. In 1835 the Bank of Australasia was founded and two years later Union Bank of Australia both backed by London investors. In 1838 the Union Bank moved into New Zealand.

Economic depression during the 1840s helped both the Bank of Australasia and the Union Bank pick off some of their competitors. In 1852 English Scottish and Australia Bank was founded. A gold rush revived the economy and led to several decades of growth during which much of the banks' profits were returned to London.

In 1951 Australasia and Union banks merged to form ANZ. For the next 20-some years Australia's banks developed a large branch network. ANZ formed a savings bank subsidiary Australia and New Zealand Savings Bank in 1955. For the next 15 years the combined bank made sporadic overtures to English Scottish and Australia Bank and in 1970 the marriage finally took place. ANZ became the third-largest bank in Australia.

The company moved its headquarters from London to Australia in 1976. Merger mania hit Australia in the early 1980s as the industry geared up for foreign competition after an open-door policy was instituted. ANZ began building operations inside and outside the country. It bought UK-based Grindlays Bank Group and its offices in 40 countries.

During the 1980s and 1990s ANZ built up its holdings overseas and broadened its offerings into insurance leasing asset management and securities often through acquisitions while trimming a variety of operating companies it had accumulated. In 1995 alone it sold about 75 companies.

Although ANZ still derived about 75% of sales from its home markets its foreign exposure brought pain when the Asian currency crisis spread to Russia and South America in 1998. ANZ realigned its business and liquidated noncore Asian operations. As part of this effort in 1999 the company sold its retail brokerage operations to Citigroup's Salomon Smith Barney and bought a stake in E*Trade's Australian operations.

Also in 1999 ANZ reaffirmed its commitment to Asia. The company's Indonesian subsidiary PT ANZ Panin Bank bought the credit card operations of PT Bank Papan Sejahtera from the Indonesian Bank Restructuring Agency.

ANZ sold its Grindlays subsidiaries in 2000 to Standard Chartered in order to simplify operations.

In 2003 ANZ bought the National Bank of New Zealand from Lloyds Banking Group. Although the Reserve Bank of New Zealand initially required that the two banks remain separate legal entities it eventually permitted them to merge with caveats. The new subsidiary known as ANZ National Bank must see itself as a New Zealand company first and foremost and it must establish facilities that will allow it to operate as a stand alone in the event any of its foreign service providers including its Australian owner fails to deliver.

A year later ANZ sold the majority of its London-headquartered project finance business to Standard Chartered for about $1.5 billion. The business operated in four regions: the UK the US the Middle East and South Asia (especially India).

ANZ then expanded in the Pacific region buying Bank of Hawaii's operations in Papua New Guinea Vanuatu and Fiji. ANZ started selling mutual funds in India but abandoned those plans for a pan-Asian Internet bank it developed with Oversea-Chinese Banking Corporation of Singapore.

Auditors: KPMG

LOCATIONS

HQ: Australia and New Zealand Banking Group Ltd
ANZ Centre Melbourne, Level 9, 833 Collins Street, Docklands, Melbourne, Victoria 3008
Phone: (61) 3 9273 5555 **Fax:** (61) 3 8542 5252
Web: www.anz.com

HISTORICAL FINANCIALS

Company Type: Public

Income Statement FYE: September 30

	ASSETS ($ mil.)	NET INCOME ($ mil.)	INCOME AS % OF ASSETS	EMPLOYEES
09/15	625,438	5,266	0.8%	50,152
09/14	672,786	6,335	0.9%	50,328
09/13	654,877	5,842	0.9%	47,512
09/12	670,134	5,907	0.9%	45,900
09/11	577,526	5,202	0.9%	50,439
Annual Growth	2.0%	0.3%	—	(0.1%)

2015 Year-End Financials

Return on assets: 0.9%
Return on equity: 14.0%
Long-term debt ($ mil.): —
No. of shares (mil.): —
Sales ($ mil): 26,697
Dividends
Yield: 4.3%
Payout: 37.9%
Market value ($ mil.): —

	STOCK PRICE ($) FY Close	P/E High/Low		PER SHARE ($) Earnings	Dividends	Book Value
09/15	19.05	10	7	1.81	0.83	13.92
09/14	27.07	11	9	2.24	1.57	15.63
09/13	28.59	13	9	2.09	1.47	15.56
09/12	25.69	12	9	2.15	1.45	15.90
09/11	18.58	12	8	1.93	1.39	14.08
Annual Growth	0.6%	—	—	(1.6%)	(12.0%)	(0.3%)

Aviva Plc (United Kingdom)

In the consolidating European insurance industry Aviva is a lively player. As the top insurance provider in the UK and a leading insurance firm worldwide Aviva offers both life and general insurance. Its long-term savings segment focuses on life insurance pensions unit trusts and other products while its general insurance segment includes the stuff which is called "non-life" or "property/casualty" elsewhere: home auto accident and fire coverage. Its Aviva Investors arm provides asset management globally. In the UK it also offers private medical insurance through employers. All of the company's businesses operate under the Aviva banner.OperationsAviva's long-term insurance segment includes life insurance pensions annuities bonds savings and other investment and protection products and accounts for about three-fourths of annual revenues. General insurance offerings include personal and commercial property/casualty coverage as well as health plans and account for nearly a quarter of sales.Geographic ReachAviva operates in about 20 countries. In addition to the UK which accounts for about a third of sales primary markets include Canada France Ireland Italy and Spain. The company also has operations in emerging markets such as China India Poland Turkey and Singapore.Sales and MarketingAviva distributes its products through many channels — including direct sales forces independent brokers partners and bank representatives —tailored to each market where it operates. In the UK it has exclusive distribution deals for the sale of protection products with such firms as Royal Bank of Scotland Barclays Santander and Tesco.The company operates across four primary market sectors: life insurance and savings general insurance health insurance and fund management. It serves some 31 million customers around the globe.Financial PerformanceRevenue has fluctuated for Aviva in recent years due to economic conditions and restructuring measures. In 2014 the company achieved 18% revenue growth (to some £43.5 billion) due to higher investment income levels. Increased revenue was especially seen in core markets including France and Italy as well as certain emerging markets including Poland.The company's net income fell 26% to £1.5 billion in 2014 due to higher unallocated divisible surplus expense primarily driven by France and Italy (which saw lower corporate and government bond yields during the year). After a couple of years of growth cash flow from operations took a huge dip. Aviva's net outflow of £544 million (versus an inflow of £5 billion in 2013) occurred for a number of reasons including lower premium income payments of claims and trades of operating assets including financial investments.

Stategy

Through restructuring measures in recent years Aviva has refocused on producing attractive financial returns in its narrowed business markets reducing capital volatility to build financial strength and improving revenue growth and profits.After taking a big hit in 2008 due to investment losses tied to the global recession Aviva has downsized its operations in subsequent years to try to repair the damage including the sale of non-core international operations. To further focus on priority markets where it has a strong presence the company sold subsidiaries in Turkey Russia and Malaysia in 2013. The following year it divested holdings in Spain's CSG Aviva Corporaracion Caixa Galicia de Seguros y Reaseguros US equity manager River Road Asset Management and South Korean unit Woori Aviva Life Insurance.To further simplify its business the company has combined the operations of a number of businesses especially in Europe to simplify its product range and shorten the time to launch new products. The company has also simplified its branding messages across its operations. Its global operations now operate as Aviva.Mergers and AcquisitionsBuilding up its domestic market position in 2015 Aviva bought rival Friends Life for £5.6 billion sealing its presence at the top of the UK's life insurance market.

HISTORY

When insurers hiked premiums after the 1861 Great Tooley Street Fire of London merchants formed Commercial Union Fire Insurance (CU). It opened offices throughout the UK and in foreign ports and soon added life (1862) and marine (1863) coverage.

Over the next 20 years CU's foreign business thrived. The firm had offices across the US by the 1880s. In the 1890s CU entered Australia India and Southeast Asia. Foreign business eventually accounted for some 75% of CU's sales.

CU went shopping in the 20th century adding accident insurer Palatine Insurance Co. of Manchester in 1900 and rescuing two companies ruined by San Francisco's 1906 earthquake and fire. CU recovered from the Depression with the help of a booming auto insurance market and spent most of the 1930s and WWII consolidating operations to cut costs.

Profits suffered in the 1950s as CU faced increased competition in the US. To boost sales it merged with both multiline rival North British and Mercantile and life insurer Northern and Employers Assurance in the early 1960s. While US business continued to lag in the 1970s the company's European business grew.

From 1982 to 1996 CU cut its operations in the US entered new markets (Poland 1992; South Africa and Vietnam 1996) and sold its New Zealand subsidiaries (1995). As competition in the UK increased the company in 1997 reorganized and merged with General Accident in 1998.

General Accident & Employers Liability Assurance Association (GA) was formed in 1885 in Perth Scotland to sell workers' compensation insurance. Within a few years GA had branches in London and Scotland. It diversified into insurance for train accidents (1887) autos (1896) and fire (1899); in 1906 its name changed to General Accident Fire and Life Assurance.

GA expanded into Australia Europe and Africa at the turn of the century. After WWI the company's auto insurance grew along with car ownership. During the 1930s the company entered the US auto insurance market. WWII put a stop to GA's growth.

The company expanded after the war forming Pennsylvania General Fire Insurance Association (1963) and acquiring the UK's Yorkshire Insurance Co. (1967). By the 1980s about one-third of its sales came from the US.

After 1986 GA acquired some 500 real estate brokerage agencies to cross-sell its home and life insurance. To increase presence in Asia and the Pacific the company in 1988 acquired NZI Corp. a New Zealand banking and insurance company whose failing operations cost GA millions. At the same time new US government regulations and a series of damaging storms hammered the company.

In response GA cut costs posting a profit by 1993. As the industry consolidated the company bought nonstandard auto insurer Sabre (1995) life insurer Provident Mutual (1996) and General Insurance Group Ltd. in Canada (1997). Unable to compete on its own GA merged with Commercial Union to form CGU in 1998.

After the merger CGU added personal pension plans and entered alliances to sell insurance in Italy and India. Merger costs and exceptional losses for 1998 hit operating profits hard. In 1999 CGU upped its stake in French bank Socit Gnrale to about 7% to help it fend off a hostile takeover attempt by Banque Nationale de Paris (now BNP Paribas).

In 2000 CGU merged with rival Norwich Union to form CGNU and made plans to exit the Canadian life and the US general insurance businesses. In 2001 CGNU sold its US property/casualty operations to White Mountains Insurance.

In an attempt to strengthen its brand name the company changed its name to Aviva in 2002. Following the name change the company merged and rebranded many of its subsidiaries. Aviva also made changes to its Asian operations in 2004 selling its general insurance business in Asia to Mitsui Sumitomo Insurance.

Back home Aviva acquired UK-based automotive service company RAC in 2005 (sold to The Carlyle Group in 2011) to gain access to its auto insurance and loan businesses. To get to the meaty middle Aviva stripped off RAC's non-core businesses including its fleet services which it sold to VT Group in 2006. At around the same time the company also divested its 50% ownership in Lex Vehicle Leasing to HBOS (which later merged with Lloyds TSB to become Lloyds Banking Group).

Looking to Asia for operational strategies Aviva moved more of its back-office operations to India and Sri Lanka but then reversed the trend in 2008 when it sold the business process outsourcing units to WNS.

Having entered Russia in March 2006 Aviva gained an 8% share of the Russian market by 2011 through a major push including the purchase of the Russian pension fund operations of ING in 2009. In 2010 the company re-entered the Singaporean insurance market after a five-year absence by offering direct online car insurance.

As part of an effort to focus on the Aviva brand the company changed the long-time UK brand name of Norwich Union to Aviva UK in 2009. It also changed brand names in Ireland and Poland in 2010.

The company expand its US investment management operations through the £83 million ($128 million) purchase of River Road Asset Management in 2010.

The company sold its Aviva Australia insurance and wealth management operations business to National Australia Bank in 2009 for $825 million. To loosen up a bit more cash Aviva then spun off about 40% of its Netherlands-based Delta Lloyd subsidiary in an initial public offering. It hoped to raise around $1.2 billion Euros but actually got $995 million. In 2011 the company reduced its stake in its Netherlands-based Delta Lloyd subsidiary to 43%. Aviva also exited its partnership in the United Arab Emirates that year.Aviva also sold its UK roadside assistance and insurance unit RAC to The Carlyle Group for £1 billion (about $1.6 billion) in 2011 to focus on its insurance and savings businesses.

EXECUTIVES

Chief Operations and Transformation Officer, Nick Amin, age 59
Chairman Global Health Insurance; CEO Aviva Europe, David H. McMillan, age 50
CEO Aviva Investors, Euan Munro, age 45
Group CEO, Mark A. Wilson, age 49
Chairman Global General Insurance; CEO Aviva UK and Ireland General Insurance, Maurice Tulloch, age 46
CFO, Thomas D. (Tom) Stoddard
CIO, Monique Shivanandan, age 52
Chairman Friends Provident International Limited (FPI), Chris Wei, age 48
Group Chief Risk Officer, John Lister, age 57
Chief Capital and Investments Officer, Jason Windsor
CEO UK and Ireland Life, Andy Briggs, age 49
Chief Executive Global Real Estate, Ed Casal
Chairman, Adrian A. Montague, age 67
Auditors: PricewaterhouseCoopers LLP

LOCATIONS

HQ: Aviva Plc (United Kingdom)
St. Helen' s, 1 Undershaft, London EC3P 3DQ
Phone: (44) 20 7662 8934
Web: www.aviva.com

2014 Revenues

	% of total
UK & Ireland	41
France	27
Canada	11
Poland	2
Italy Spain & other	16
Asia	3
Total	**100**

PRODUCTS/OPERATIONS

2014 Net Earned Premium

	% of total
Long-term (life) insurance	59
General insurance & health	41
Fund management	-
Total	**100**

COMPETITORS

AEGON
AXA
Ageas Insurance International
Allianz
Bank of Ireland
Canada Life
Generali
ING
Legal & General Group
Lloyds Banking Group
Prudential plc
QBE
RSA Insurance
Royal Bank of Scotland
Standard Life
Zurich Insurance Group

HISTORICAL FINANCIALS

Company Type: Public

Income Statement FYE: December 31

	ASSETS ($ mil.)	NET INCOME ($ mil.)	INCOME AS % OF ASSETS	EMPLOYEES
12/14	446,013	2,449	0.5%	26,364
12/13	460,864	3,318	0.7%	27,718
12/12	508,848	(5,186)	—	33,122
12/11	482,575	347	0.1%	36,562
12/10	574,642	2,271	0.4%	45,142
Annual Growth	(6.1%)	1.9%	—	(12.6%)

2014 Year-End Financials

Return on assets: 0.5%
Return on equity: 15.1%
Long-term debt ($ mil.): —
No. of shares (mil.): —
Sales ($ mil): 67,899
Dividends
Yield: 3.2%
Payout: 58.6%
Market value ($ mil.): —

	STOCK PRICE ($) FY Close	P/E High/Low	PER SHARE ($) Earnings	Dividends	Book Value
12/14	14.90	33 27	0.77	0.48	5.88
12/13	15.15	23 15	1.07	0.45	5.35
12/12	12.41	— —	(1.82)	0.82	5.35
12/11	9.25	259146	0.09	0.80	7.35
12/10	12.41	26 19	0.77	0.73	7.70
Annual Growth	4.7%	— —	0.1%	(10.2%)	(6.5%)

AXA S.A.

The insurance world revolves around this AXA. The company which started as a sleepy collection of mutual insurance companies is today one of the world's largest insurers and a financial management powerhouse. In addition to its strong presence in France AXA owns US-based AXA Financial which controls life insurance firm AXA Equitable and investment manager AllianceBernstein. The company also has major subsidiaries in the UK (AXA UK) Germany (AXA Konzern) Japan (AXA Life) and Belgium (AXA Belgium). The AXA companies offer life insurance personal and commercial property and casualty insurance financial services and asset management services. AXA has about 1 trillion (or $1.45 trillion) in assets under management.

Geographic Reach

Rather than trying to run a cross-border organization AXA instead buys and builds up businesses in each country rebranding them under the AXA name. The company serves more than 100 million customers in 60 countries primarily in Europe North America and Asia as well as in Africa Latin America and the Middle East. The central and eastern European market is the largest geographic segment accounting for about 30% of annual sales.

Operations

AXA's operations are divided into five segments with the largest business division –life and savings –accounting for about 60% of annual revenues. Life and savings products include savings retirement life insurance and health insurance offerings for groups and individuals; the division serves some 40 million customers in 30 countries around the globe. AXA's property/casualty segment accounting for about 30% of sales offers commercial and personal auto homeowners property and liability insurance primarily in Europe the Middle East and Latin America.

Meanwhile the asset management (investment fund management) international insurance (corporate solutions assurance offerings) and banking (retail banking savings and mortgage loans in Europe) segments together account for the remainder of revenues. The asset management business while small compared to AXA's two larger segments has a sizable presence in the investment market with assets under management of more than 1000 billion.

Sales and Marketing

AXA markets its products through independent agents and brokers as well as through direct and salaried sales forces. It also has distribution partnerships with entities including banks car dealerships and other retail locations.

AXA sells its products both to individuals and to corporate groups. Its commercial property/casualty unit primarily targets small to midsized companies. The asset management business targets institutional investors (including AXA's insurance subsidiaries) and individuals.

Financial Performance

AXA reported revenues of some 86 billion ($132 billion) in 2011 a decrease of about 19% from 2010 sales. A majority of the decline is due to the divestiture of operations in certain regions. However gains on asset sales caused AXA's net income to rise 46% to $4.5 billion.

Other factors impacting revenues included decreased insurance sales in regions including Latin America the Mediterranean Belgium France Japan and Central and Eastern Europe which was offset by growth in the US Switzerland Hong Kong and other Asian markets.

Strategy

AXA invests in a diverse spread of business to reduce risk and volatility across its operations and it focuses on building a solid business foundation and distribution network in each respective market where it operates.

To focus on core operations (life and savings property/casualty and asset management) as well as to free up capital and allow for expansion in emerging markets AXA is conducting some divestitures. For instance in 2013 the company sold the older books of life insurance policies issued by its MONY Life subsidiaries to Protective Life for some $1.1 billion to reduce its exposure to the underperforming North America market. AXA plans to focus on growth in the US in select markets where it has experienced momentum.

In addition in late 2011 the company sold its Canadian arm to Intact Financial for about $2.6 billion. Also in 2011 AXA exited its Australian and New Zealand joint venture operations through a complex transaction with Australian insurer AMP. (However AXA also expanded its Asian operations through the AMP deal.)

Mergers and Acquisitions

The transaction with AMP was one of the company's largest deals conducted in recent years. Through the transaction AXA took full control of the Asian operations of former majority-owned subsidiary AXA Asia Pacific (AXA APH) in 2011 for some A$9.8 billion ($9.4 billion) gaining full control of subsidiaries joint ventures and partnerships in China Hong Kong India Indonesia Malaysia the Philippines Singapore and Thailand. Former joint-venture partner AMP took full control of AXA APH's operations in Australia and New Zealand for some A$3.5 billion ($3.4 billion).

AXA further expanded its insurance operations in emerging markets in 2012 when it acquired the Asian (mainly Hong Kong and Singapore) and Latin American (Mexico) property/casualty operations of HSBC. The purchase also expanded AXA's bancassurance operations (where insurance is sold at partnering retail banks) in the regions.

Ownership

Mutuelles AXA (two mutuals) controls AXA through a more than 20% stake. In 2010 AXA voluntarily delisted its stock from the NYSE to focus on its larger-volume listing on the Euronext Paris exchange.

HISTORY

AXA dates to the 1817 formation of regional fire insurer Compagnie d'Assurances Mutuelles contre l'incendie in Rouen France (northwest of Paris). In 1881 France's first mutual life insurer was founded: Mutuelle Vie.

In 1946 these two operations and the younger Anciennes Mutuelles Accidents (founded 1922) were brought together by Sahut d'Izarn (general manager of Compagnie d'Assurances) as the Groupe Ancienne Mutuelle. Later members included Ancienne Mutuelle of Calvados (1946) Ancienne Mutuelle of Orleans (1950) Mutualit © G ⓖ ⓔale (1953) and Participation (1954).

A long-term thinker d'Izarn named not only his successor Lucien Aubert but also Aubert's successor: Claude B Ⓑ ⓐr a 23-year-old friend of d'Izarn's son. Never having held a job B Ⓑ ⓐr found the whole thing amusing and decided to try it.

Groupe Ancienne Mutuelle prospered during the 1960s thanks to d'Izarn's disciplined management but his technophobia kept the company from entering the computer age.

D'Izarn died in 1972. Aubert capitulated to worker demands during a series of strikes in the early 1970s; B Ⓑ ⓐr ended a 1974 strike by threatening to use force against an employee sit-in then ousted Aubert. B Ⓑ ⓐr spent the rest of the 1970s upgrading the firm's technology. During this period the company became known as Mutuelles Unies.

B Ⓑ ⓐr then began building the firm through a series of spectacular acquisitions. In 1982 Mutuelles Unies gained control of crisis-ridden stock insurer Drouot. Two years later the company's name became AXA (which has no meaning and was chosen because it is pronounced the same in most Western languages). When another old-line insurer Providence went on the market AXA went after it. Providence's management was entertaining another offer when AXA bought tiny inactive Bayas Tudjus which held the right to a seat on the Providence board. B Ⓑ ⓐr capitalized on small stockholders' dissatisfaction to spark a bidding war and used a new issue of Drouot stock in 1986 to buy Providence —France's first hostile takeover.

AXA bought lackluster US firm Equitable (later named AXA Financial) in 1991 infusing $1 billion into the firm in return for the right to own up to 50% of its stock upon demutualization in 1992. AXA moved into Asia with the purchase of Australia's National Mutual in 1995.

B Ⓑ ⓐr consolidated the operations into a global organization. In 1996 AXA bought the ailing Union des Assurances de Paris which had done poorly since its 1994 privatization. It bought the 52% of Belgian insurer Royale Belge SA it didn't already own as well as Belgian savings bank Anhyp in 1998.

B Ⓑ ⓐr raised hackles when he supported the Soci ©ⒸG ⓖ ⓔale-Paribas bank merger then supported BNP's hostile takeover attempt of both (which garnered only Paribas). In 1999 AXA bought Guardian Royal Exchange then sold the life and pensions business to Dutch insurer AEGON; B Ⓑ ⓐr announced his retirement in 1999. In 2000 he stepped down from the management board but took over as chairman of the supervisory board. Henri de Castries was placed in the top executive position as chairman of the management board.

That year AXA took control of Japan's Nippon Dantai Life Insurance. It also bought the remaining shares of AXA Financial and the 44% of AXA UK (formerly Sun Life and Provincial Holdings) it didn't already own. The next year AXA unloaded its debt-heavy subsidiary Banque Worms to Deutsche Bank.

In an attempt to strengthen its US retail insurance and annuity business AXA through subsidiary AXA Financial bought MONY Group for some $1.5 billion in 2004. The deal was opposed by some of MONY's shareholders but it ultimately gained approval. On the down side AXA discontinued its slumping US-based reinsurance operations (AXA Corporate Solutions Reinsurance and AXA Corporate Solutions Life Reinsurance).

Also in 2004 the company exited its operations in Uruguay thus exiting the South American market and sold its Dutch brokerage and health insurance subsidiaries and its German mortgage lending business.

AXA made a major coup in the insurance industry when it acquired the Winterthur Group from Credit Suisse Group for 7.9 billion ($11 billion) in 2006. Winterthur added subsidiaries in 17 countries with 13 million customers and especially strengthened AXA's European operations. The primary Swiss Winterthur division was renamed AXA Versicherungen. AXA also sold the assets of AXA Re that year.

In 2007 AXA sold noncore Dutch subsidiaries AXA Netherlands Winterthur Netherlands and DBV Netherlands. To expand its insurance operations in emerging markets AXA acquired South Korean car insurance provider Kyobo Auto (now Kyobo AXA General Insurance). In addition it formed a partnership with BNP Paribas to provide property/casualty insurance in the Ukraine.

That year the company's property fund division AXA Investment Managers announced plans to invest more than $15 billion in Asian real estate by 2013. In addition AXA established the AXA Research Fund in 2008 to invest $500 million in social science research institutions over five years.

After a long career at the center of AXA's operations B Ⓑ ⓐr retired as chairman of the supervisory board in 2008 but retained the title of honorary chairman of the company.

AXA bought out its Turkish joint venture partner pension fund Oyak for $525 million in 2008 to take full control of AXA Holding A.S. (formerly AXA Oyak) a provider of life and other insurance products in the fast-growing Turkish market. Later that year the company purchased #3 Mexican life insurance company ING Seguros (now AXA Seguros) for $1.5 billion from ING Groep. AXA also made an investment in the Russian property/casualty market.

To further expand in emerging markets by targeting the high-growth regions of Central and Eastern Europe in 2010 AXA entered the Romanian life insurance market with the buy of Omniasig Life. The deal followed AXA's buy of minority interests in Omniasig's Hungarian Czech and Polish subsidiaries from the European Bank for Reconstruction and Development in late 2009.

To focus on core operations in 2010 the company sold parts of its UK life insurance business (including traditional life and pension corporate pension and annuity operations) to acquisition vehicle Resolution Ltd. for 3.3 billion ($4.1 million). Resolution added the acquired operations to another insurance firm Friends Provident picked up in 2009; the former AXA operations are now known as Friends Life. The asset sale allowed AXA UK to focus its life operations on high-growth wealth management services including its specialist pension and direct protection businesses. AXA UK also retained its property/casualty health insurance and investment management operations.

AXA also simplified its management organization to reduce complexities and create a nimble leadership team to face future customer needs and economic challenges. In 2010 the company streamlined its governance structure by combining its supervisory board and its management board into a single board of directors led by Henri de Castries as chairman and CEO; Castries had previously been chairman of the management board.

AXA took full control of the Asian operations of former majority-owned subsidiary AXA Asia Pacific (AXA APH in which it previously owned a 54% stake) in 2011 to strengthen its operations in the fast-paced region. The firm completed a deal with Australian insurer AMP through which AMP acquired all of AXA APH for some A$13.3 billion ($12.8 billion); AMP then sold the Asian operations to AXA for some A$9.8 billion ($9.4 billion) while retaining AXA APH's operations in Australia and New Zealand. The deal was agreed upon in late 2010 after a year-long bidding war for control of AXA APH between AMP and rival National Australia Bank (NAB).

Also in 2011 it sold its roughly 16% stake in Taikang Life (China's fourth-largest life insurer) to a group of shareholders for $1.2 billion to meet regulatory conditions for the AXA APH asset acquisition. (AXA gained a stronger position in another joint venture in China with Industrial and Commercial Bank of China through the AXA APH deal.)

Auditors: Mazars

LOCATIONS

HQ: AXA S.A.
25, avenue Matignon, Paris 75008
Phone: (33) 1 40 75 57 00
Web: www.axa.com

HISTORICAL FINANCIALS

Company Type: Public

Income Statement

FYE: December 31

	ASSETS ($ mil.)	NET INCOME ($ mil.)	INCOME AS % OF ASSETS	EMPLOYEES
12/14	1,021,107	6,106	0.6%	96,279
12/13	1,042,385	6,170	0.6%	93,146
12/12	1,004,154	5,472	0.5%	94,364
12/11	944,329	5,592	0.6%	96,999
12/10	979,224	3,679	0.4%	102,957
Annual Growth	1.1%	13.5%	—	(1.7%)

2014 Year-End Financials

Return on assets: 0.6%
Return on equity: 8.5%
Long-term debt ($ mil.): —
No. of shares (mil.): —
Sales ($ mil): 142,099
Dividends
Yield: 4.9%
Payout: 41.7%
Market value ($ mil.): —

	STOCK PRICE ($) FY Close	P/E High	P/E Low	PER SHARE ($) Earnings	Dividends	Book Value
12/14	22.89	13	11	2.36	1.13	32.47
12/13	27.89	16	10	2.41	0.93	30.18
12/12	18.22	11	7	2.16	0.89	29.61
12/11	12.86	12	6	2.26	0.89	26.85
12/10	16.65	22	14	1.45	1.25	28.98
Annual Growth	8.3%	—	—	13.0%	(2.6%)	2.9%

BAE Systems Plc

BAE Systems helped win the Battle of Britain in 1940 with its Spitfire and Mosquito fighters; today it is a leading military contractor and major foreign player in the US defense market. BAE's main operating groups –cyber security financial crime communications intelligence and digital transformation –provide products and services that include electro-optical sensors flight controls commercial and financial security ship repair and modernization and aircraft. BAE's fighter aircraft include the Hawk Tornado and the next-generation Eurofighter Typhoon. North America is BAE's biggest market (maintained by BAE Systems Inc.) with the US Department of Defense (DoD) its largest single customer.

Geographic Reach

The company is based in the UK and has 40 offices serving clients across the UK and Europe the Americas Asia Pacific and the Middle East. The US contributed 39% of its net sales in 2014.

Sales and MarketingBAE's largest customers are governments but it also sells to large prime contractors and commercial businesses. About 45% of its sales are services-related contracts that are typically longer term.

Financial Performance

BAE's revenues decreased from 2013 to 2014 due to volume reductions within its land and armaments business. The company was also affected by unfavorable foreign exchange translations.

Its profits increased by £576 million from 2013 to 2014 due to a decrease in taxation expenses and a decline in the impairment of intangible assets due to performance issues in the US commercial shipbuilding market.

Strategy

Amid sharp reductions in defense spending in both of the company's biggest markets the US and UK BAE Systems has launched a strategy that besides focusing on electronics and cyber and intelligence includes developing more export business to support its platforms segments and expanding its operations internationally.

In regards to the US market in late 2014 BAE for $233 million acquired Perimeter Internetworking Corp. which trades as SilverSky a commercial cyber service provider. SilverSky is a commercial cyber services and compliance provider headquartered in New York with operations in the US and the Philippines.

HISTORY

Post-Wright brothers and pre-WWII a host of aviation companies sprang up to serve the British Empire –too many to survive after the war when the empire contracted. Parliament took steps in 1960 to save the industry by merging companies to form larger stronger entities –Hawker-Siddeley Aviation and British Aircraft Corporation (BAC).

Hawker-Siddeley made up of aircraft and missiles divisions was created by combining A.V. Roe Gloster Aircraft Hawker Aircraft Armstrong Whitworth and Folland Aircraft. It attained fame in the 1960s for developing the Harrier "jump jet."

BAC was formed from the merger of Bristol Aeroplane English Electric and Vicker-Armstrong. In 1962 it joined France's Aerospatiale to build the supersonic Concorde and became a partner in ventures to develop the Tornado and Jaguar fighters. The cost of these ventures plus the commercial failure of the Concorde was more than the company could bear. Realizing British aviation was again in trouble the British government nationalized BAC and Hawker-Siddeley in 1976 and merged them in 1977 with Scottish Aviation to form British Aerospace (BAe).

EXECUTIVES

Chairman BAE Systems India (Services) Private Limited, Deepak S. Parekh, age 69
COO, Charles Woodburn, age 43
CEO, Ian King, age 59, $850,000 total compensation
Group Managing Director International, Guy Griffiths
Group Finance Director, Peter Lynas
CEO Australia, Glynn Phillips
Chairman, Roger Carr
Auditors: KPMG LLP

LOCATIONS

HQ: BAE Systems Plc
6 Carlton Gardens, London SW1Y 5 AD
Phone: (44) 1252 373232
Web: www.baesystems.com

2014 Sales

		% in total
US		39
UK		23
Saudi Arabia		20
Rest of Europe		10
Australia		4
Other		4
Total	**0**	**100**

PRODUCTS/OPERATIONS

Selected Products and Services

Air
- Avionics
- Combat aircraft
- Commercial aircraft
- Controls (flight and engine)
- Jet trainers
- Maintenance repair and upgrades
- Missiles and counter measures
- Reconnaissance aircraft

Unmanned a

Homeland Security
- Border and coastal surveillance

Information Technology

Intelligen

Land
- Artillery
- Combat and tactical vehicles
- Munitions
- Radar
- Unmanned systems

Sea
- Amphibious and auxiliary ships
- Naval guns
- Submarines
- Underwater systems
- Warships

Systems In
- C4ISR (Command Control Communications Computers Intelligence Surveillance Reconnaissance)
- Communications

Electronic
- Imaging systems
- Intelligence systems
- Navigation systems
- Sensor systems

Technology and Innovation
Through-Life Support

2014 Sales

	% of total
Platforms & services	
Platforms & services (UK)	41
Platforms & services (US)	20
Platforms & services (international)	17
Electronic systems	15
Cyber & intelligence	7
Total	**100**

COMPETITORS

Aerojet Rocketdyne
Airbus Group
Astronautics
Boeing
ITT Corp.
L-3 Communications
Lockheed Martin
Meggitt-USA

Bombardier	Navistar International
DRS Technologies	Northrop Grumman
Fabbrica D' Armi Pietro Beretta	RUAG Holding
Finmeccanica	Rockwell Collins
General Dynamics	Sotera Defense
Honeywell International	Thales
Horstman Defence Systems	Ultra Electronics
	United Technologies

HISTORICAL FINANCIALS

Company Type: Public

Income Statement FYE: December 31

	REVENUE ($ mil.)	NET INCOME ($ mil.)	NET PROFIT MARGIN	EMPLOYEES
12/14	24,086	1,155	4.8%	76,000
12/13	27,869	277	1.0%	78,000
12/12	26,789	1,721	6.4%	81,000
12/11	27,452	1,915	7.0%	87,000
12/10	32,756	1,633	5.0%	92,000
Annual Growth	(7.4%)	(8.3%)	—	(4.7%)

2014 Year-End Financials

Debt ratio: 26.4%	No. of shares (mil.): —
Return on equity: 28.3%	Dividends
Cash ($ mil.): 3,602	Yield: 4.4%
Current ratio: 0.74	Payout: 334.1%
Long-term debt ($ mil.): 4,477	Market value ($ mil.): —

	STOCK PRICE ($) FY Close	P/E High/Low	PER SHARE ($) Earnings	Dividends	Book Value
12/14	29.16	129104	0.36	1.29	0.91
12/13	29.29	596419	0.09	1.20	1.74
12/12	22.28	72 53	0.53	1.15	1.84
12/11	17.66	61 41	0.57	1.06	2.02
12/10	20.85	80 60	0.47	0.95	2.43
Annual Growth	8.7%	—	(6.2%)	7.7%	(21.7%)

Baloise Holding AG

Founded in 1863 as a fire insurance company Bâloise-Holding today is a general insurer that sells such standardized products as group and individual life policies and accident property and auto insurance to small firms and individuals. The company is one of the leading insurers in Switzerland operating primarily there and in Germany; together the countries account for about 70% of its sales. Through subsidiaries it also operates in other nearby countries including Belgium and Luxembourg. Bâloise also provides banking pension plans and other financial services through its Bâloise Bank SoBa. The company uses its own sales force as well as partner distributors and independent brokers to sell its wares.

Operations

Bâloise operates through four segments: Non-Life Life Banking (including asset management) and Other Activities. Its Non-Life segment offers accident and health coverage as well as liability motor property and marine products which are primarily targeted towards retail clients. Life provides individuals and companies with endowment policies term insurance investment-linked products and private placement life insurance. Bâloise's Banking segment includes subsidiaries Bâloise Bank SoBa in Switzerland and Deutscher Ring Bausparkasse in Germany while the group's Other Activities segment comprises investment companies real estate companies and financing firms.

Geographic Reach

Switzerland accounts for about half of Bâloise's revenues. The group also has operations in Germany (including the regional branches of Basler Sachversicherungs and Basler Lebensversicherungs in the Czech Republic and Slovakia). In Luxembourg the company operates Bâloise Life Liechtenstein.

Sales and Marketing

The company sells its products through its own sales department as well as partners and outside brokers. It serves individuals small to midsized firms and selected industrial enterprises.

Financial Performance

Revenue increased 3% to CHF 9.3 billion (approximately $10.4 billion) in 2014 as a result of growth in Switzerland Belgium and Luxembourg. Swiss division Basler Switzerland saw growth in its unit-linked life insurance business as did Bâloise's operations in Belgium which established new banking partnerships during the year. Business in Luxembourg rose primarily as a result of the acquisition of P&V Assurances which boosted its conventional life insurance lines. The group also benefited from an increase in realized gains on investments.

Net income rose 57% (percentages may differ upon conversion to US currency) to CHF 710.7 million thanks to the increased revenue as well as the disposal of Bâloise's stake in Nationale Suisse and the sale of Basler Austria. Gains realized on equities and real estate also contributed to the rise in profits.

Cash flow from operations spiked more than 700% that year to CHF 609.7 million.

Strategy

Bâloise focuses on organic growth and market penetration to expand in its core geographic areas. The company also exits certain markets it feels are underperforming. In 2014 it sold its Croatian and Serbian subsidiaries to UNIQA Group for 75 million withdrawing from southeastern Europe. It also sold Basler Versicherungs-Aktiengesellschaft in Austria and National Suisse.

Mergers and Acquisitions

In Luxembourg Bâloise acquired P&V Assurances in 2014.

HISTORY

In 1863 15 business leaders in Basel Switzerland formed the Bâloise Fire Insurance Company. This was followed in 1864 by the formation of the Baloise transportation and life insurance companies.

Bâloise-Holding was created in 1962 as a holding company for the previously independent insurance entities. In 1971 it merged all of its non-life companies into the Baloise Insurance Group.

Under its then-new chairman and president Rolf Schäuble Bâloise-Holding began in 1993 to reorganize its operations as it implemented a new corporate strategy. Key components of the strategy included a focus on the company's core European markets and a pattern of discarding less-profitable businesses. In 1998 Bâloise-Holding sold off its US operations.

Strengthening its position as a full-fledged financial services company in 2000 Bâloise acquired Swiss bank Solothurner (now Bâloise Bank SoBa).

The same year it purchased Belgian bank HBK-Spaarbank Belgian insurer Amazon Insurance N.V. and Swiss regional bank Solothurner Bank SoBa.

EXECUTIVES

Head Asset Management, Martin Wenk, age 58
CFO, German Egloff, age 57
Head Corporate Center, Thomas Sieber
CEO Basler Germany, Jan De Meulder
CEO Basler Switzerland, Michael Mueller
Group CEO, Gert De Winter
Auditors: PricewaterhouseCoopers AG

LOCATIONS

HQ: Baloise Holding AG
Aeschengraben 21, Basel CH-4002
Phone: (41) 58 285 85 85 **Fax:** (41) 58 285 70 70
Web: www.baloise.com

2014 Sales

	% of total
Switzerland	48
Germany	18
Belgium	17
Luxembourg	16
Other	1
Total	**100**

PRODUCTS/OPERATIONS

2014 Sales

	% of total
Non-life insurance	47
Life	53
Total	**100**

Selected Subsidiaries

Austria
Basler Versicherungen (insurance and pension products for private and business clients)
Belgium
Mercator Verzekeringen (personal and property insurance for individuals and small to mid-sized businesses)
Germany
Basler Versicherungen (personal and property insurance for individuals small and mid-sized enterprises and selected industrial clients)
Deutscher Ring (insurance and pension products for individuals)
Luxembourg
Bâloise Assurances (life personal and property insurance for private and business clients)
Switzerland
Bâloise Bank SoBa (banking products and services)
Basler Versicherungen (insurance and pension products for individuals and small to mid-sized enterprises)

COMPETITORS

AEGON	Helvetia Group
AIG	ING
AXA	Itasa
AXA Versicherungen	Munich Re Group
Achmea	Prudential plc
Allianz	Swiss Life
Hannover Re	Zurich Insurance Group

HISTORICAL FINANCIALS

Company Type: Public

Income Statement FYE: December 31

	ASSETS ($ mil.)	NET INCOME ($ mil.)	INCOME AS % OF ASSETS	EMPLOYEES
12/14	80,209	1,438	1.8%	7,617
12/13	84,952	1,019	1.2%	8,613
12/12	80,208	958	1.2%	8,795
12/11	73,412	129	0.2%	9,141
12/10	69,878	929	1.3%	8,800
Annual Growth	3.5%	11.5%	—	(3.5%)

2014 Year-End Financials

Return on assets: 1.8%
Return on equity: 26.7%
Long-term debt ($ mil.): —
No. of shares (mil.): 46
Sales ($ mil): 10,418

Dividends
Yield: 0.0%
Payout: 2.4%
Market value ($ mil.): 613

	STOCK PRICE ($) FY Close	P/E High	P/E Low	PER SHARE ($) Earnings	Dividends	Book Value
12/14	13.05	1	1	14.79	0.36	124.69
12/13	12.42	2	1	10.53	0.33	116.02
12/12	7.89	1	1	9.91	0.34	112.25
12/11	9.71	11	9	1.37	0.37	87.76
12/10	9.15	1	1	9.50	0.25	92.83
Annual Growth	9.3%	—	—	11.7%	10.2%	7.7%

Banca CARIGE S.p.A.

Auditors: Reconta Ernst & Young S.p.A.

LOCATIONS

HQ: Banca CARIGE S.p.A.
Via Cassa Di Risparmio 15, Genoa 16123
Phone: (39) 10 5791 **Fax:** (39) 10 579 400000
Web: www.carige.it

HISTORICAL FINANCIALS

Company Type: Public

Income Statement

FYE: December 31

	ASSETS ($ mil.)	NET INCOME ($ mil.)	INCOME AS % OF ASSETS	EMPLOYEES
12/14	46,565	(660)	—	5,737
12/13	58,038	(2,425)	—	5,851
12/12	65,013	(83)	—	5,914
12/11	58,024	241	0.4%	5,974
12/10	53,548	237	0.4%	6,003
Annual Growth	(3.4%)	—	—	(1.1%)

2014 Year-End Financials

Return on assets: (-1.3%)
Return on equity: (-32.4%)
Long-term debt ($ mil.): —
No. of shares (mil.): —
Sales ($ mil): 1,473

Dividends
Yield: —
Payout: —
Market value ($ mil.): —

Banca Popolare di Milano

Founded in 1865 Banca Popolare di Milano (also known as Banca Pop Milano) is a cooperative bank with some 640 branches in Italy concentrated in and around Milan and in northern and central portions of the country. It also operates an online bank (Webank) and commercial banks Banca Popolare di Mantova and Banca Akros. In addition to standard retail services such as deposit accounts credit cards and loans the company offers corporate and investment banking insurance and wealth management. Banca Popolare di Milano serves about 1.4 million customers primarily individuals and small- and medium-sized businesses. It has historically grown by acquiring other banks.

OperationsNet interest income (mostly from loans) made up more than 49% of Banca Pop Milano's operating income in 2014. Another 39% of its operating income came from net fee and commission income with half of that coming from management trading and advisory services and the other half coming from traditional banking services such as guarantees collections and payment services management of current accounts and other services. The remaining 12% of its operating income came from trading gains.Nearly 50% of the banking group's loan portfolio was made up of mortgage loans in 2014. An additional 11% of the loan portfolio was made up of current account overdrafts while the rest of the portfolio was split among impaired assets (11% of the portfolio) credit card debt personal loans and salary-backed loans (2%) finance leases (less than 1%) repurchase agreements (less than 1%) and other loans (25%). Geographic ReachAll 636 of Banca Pop Milano's branches and all 25 of its corporate and private banking centers were located in Italy in 2014. About 62% of its branches were located in Lombardia (half of which were in the Province of Milan) while another 14% of branches were located in Piemonte and 10% were in Lazio. Other branches were located in the Emilia Romagna and Puglia regions.

Stategy

Banca Pop Milano is increasingly moving toward digital banking channels that are quickly taking the industry by storm allowing the bank to decrease its branch network and cut operating costs significantly while giving customers faster access to banking services at the same time. Indeed the bank shrunk its branch network by 9% during 2014 alone from 698 branches to 636 branches by the end of 2014. Meanwhile by the end of 2014 Banca Pop Milano saw its internet banking customer base jump by 6% to a total of 693000 customers (including 588000 individual customers and 105000 businesses clients); meaning half of its 1.4 million customers were banking over its internet channel. It's also been pushing its telephone banking service which served some 414000 of its customers (nearly one-third of its total customer base) at the end of 2014.Mergers and AcquisitionsIn November 2014 Banca Pop Milano acquired WeBank S.p.A to strengthen its digital banking expertise and expand its online customer base.

EXECUTIVES

Vice Presidente, UMBERTO BOCCHINO
Vice Presidente, GIUSEPPE COPPINI
Amministratore Delegato, PIERO LUIGI MONTANI
Auditors: Reconta Ernst & Young S.p.A.

LOCATIONS

HQ: Banca Popolare di Milano
Piazza F. Meda 4, Milan I-20121
Phone: (39) 02 77001 **Fax:** (39) 02 7700 2993
Web: www.gruppobpm.it

2013 Branch Locations

	No.
Lombardia	430
Piemonte	93
Lazio	71
Puglia	40
Emilia Romagna	31
Other regions	31
Total	**696**

PRODUCTS/OPERATIONS

2013 Sales

	% of total
Interest income	51
Non interest income	
Fee and commission income	34
Others	15
Total	**100**

Selected subsidiaries

Banca Akros SpA
Banca Popolare di Mantova SpA
Banca Popolare di Milano
ProFamily SpA
WeBank SpA

COMPETITORS

Banco Popolare
Deutsche Bank (Italy)
Intesa Sanpaolo
Mediobanca
Monte dei Paschi di Siena
UniCredit

HISTORICAL FINANCIALS

Company Type: Public

Income Statement

FYE: December 31

	ASSETS ($ mil.)	NET INCOME ($ mil.)	INCOME AS % OF ASSETS	EMPLOYEES
12/14	58,674	282	0.5%	7,759
12/13	67,946	40	0.1%	7,846
12/12	69,164	(566)	—	8,312
12/11	67,170	(794)	—	8,467
12/08	62,968	105	0.2%	8,786
Annual Growth	(1.2%)	17.9%	—	(2.1%)

2014 Year-End Financials

Return on assets: 0.4%
Return on equity: 5.6%
Long-term debt ($ mil.): —
No. of shares (mil.): —
Sales ($ mil): 2,773

Dividends
Yield: 0.1%
Payout: 1,101.8%
Market value ($ mil.): —

	STOCK PRICE ($) FY Close	P/E High	P/E Low	PER SHARE ($) Earnings	Dividends	Book Value
12/14	3.42	154	88	0.07	0.79	1.26
12/13	3.80	794	717	0.01	0.00	1.55
12/12	2.79	—	—	(0.18)	0.00	1.64
Annual Growth	10.7%	—	—	—	—	(4.3%)

Banco Bilbao Vizcaya Argentaria SA (BBVA)

It's not Cortez revisited but Banco Bilbao Vizcaya Argentaria (BBVA) –one of Spain's top banks –is conquering the New World. Although much of its business activity is in Spain (more than half of its loans) the company also operates in about 10 Latin American countries through subsidiaries including BBVA Bancomer in Mexico; Banco Bilbao Vizcaya Argentaria Chile; and BBVA Banco Franc ©in Argentina. With some 7400 offices in 30 countries the bank offers retail corporate and institutional banking; investment banking; asset management; insurance; and securities brokerage. BBVA also operates in other European countries and is expanding in China as well as in the US where it owns Compass Bank.

The company is focused on five geographic areas: Spain Mexico South America the US and Eurasia (which includes BBVA's Portugese and Turkish operations).

As one of Spain's largest banks (along with Santander) BBVA has been struggling with the worldwide financial downturn and the sovereign debt crisis. Unemployment in the country remains above 20% and the gross domestic product has been shrinking. More than a quarter of the bank's real estate loans are non-performing loans which has led to lower revenues. Another key market Mexico has seen some bright spots (mortgage activities have begun to rebound there) but is also still vulnerable to the troubled economic climate. Goodwill impairment in the US contributed to a loss in the market in 2011. That year BBVA's revenues grew 11% to $47.2 billion but net income fell 41% to $3.9 billion. A decrease in net interest income (due to an upturn in interest rates in the Eurozone) a decline in asset values slower customer activities and a reduction of earnings from portfolio sales all served to drag down the company's earnings.

As part of a larger restructuring of banks in Spain the company acquired Unnim Banc which had been taken over by the Bank of Spain for a symbolic 1 in 2012. BBVA also assumed 20% of Unnim's real estate losses amounting to some 300 million. The acquisition gives the bank more than 600 branches in Catalonia which has been a target market for BBVA. The deal also made BBVA Spain's largest bank by assets.

The company has worked to expand internationally to help diversify operations beyond its home market. BBVA has targeted Asia as a growth market forming an alliance with China's CITIC Group. In accordance the company owns a 30% stake in CITIC International Financial Holdings and a 15% stake in China Citic Bank.

BBVA is expanding in other markets too. In 2011 it acquired Credit Uruguay Banco from Credit Agricole to become one of Uruguay's largest financial institutions. The company also bought a 25% stake in Turkish bank Garanti which it jointly manages with Turkish conglomerate Dogus Group.

To better focus on its expansion in the US BBVA is selling its Puerto Rican operations to OFG Bancorp for $500 million. The sale represents less than 1% of BBVA's total assets. BBVA plans to sell other operations in Latin America including the Provida Bancomer and Horizonte Peru pension management companies.

HISTORY

Banco Bilbao Vizcaya Argentaria (BBVA) is the progeny of the 2000 merger of Banco Bilbao Vizcaya (BBV) and Argentaria Caja Postal y Banco Hipotecario. BBV formed when Banco de Bilbao and Banco de Vizcaya merged in 1988 while Argentaria Caja Postal y Banco Hipotecario coalesced from the 1991 merger of six government-owned banks.

In 1857 a group of Basque businessmen banded together to offer loans and other banking services to businesses. The bank –eventually Banco de Bilbao –helped fund the region's industrialization. Its first foray beyond the Basque region was Paris not Madrid in 1902. It later entered London Madrid and other major European cities.

Franco's rise to power and the isolation of WWII deterred industrial growth. In protectionist Spain Bilbao bought 16 banks between 1941 and 1943 and formed a unit to focus on US and Latin American partnerships.

In the 1960s Bilbao reorganized and formed a unit focused on industrial growth. It rolled with the punches as banking rules continued to change in the 1970s and 1980s. The bank expanded consumer services began issuing credit cards (1971) and bought banks that couldn't cope with changing regulations.

To compete in financially deregulated Europe Spain's overpopulated banking industry began to consolidate in the early 1990s. After #3 Bilbao failed to take over #2 Banco Espa ±ol de Cr ©dito it merged with regional rival Banco de Vizcaya.

Formed in 1901 by Basque merchants Banco de Vizcaya expanded through purchases and had some 200 branches by 1935 including offices in Europe's leading cities. During the post-WWII bust it bought weaker banks and invested in Spain's industrial complex.

In the 1960s and 1970s Vizcaya added industrial banking insurance personal investment management and leasing. The bank refocused on international growth opening branches in London Mexico City New York and other cities. It entered consumer banking and became another participant in the branch race; by 1980 Vizcaya had some 900 offices. Looking to be a strong player in deregulated Europe the bank merged with Bilbao in 1988; together the two banks had nearly 3400 branches.

The merger almost unraveled after Vizcaya chair Pedro Toledo (set to lead the new bank with Bilbao chair Jos © ngel S ˇnchez Asiain) died in 1989. The two banks fought over Toledo's replacement until the Bank of Spain suggested in 1990 Bilbao executive Emilio Ybarra y Churruca become the only chair.

Until 1992 government regulations and strong unions prevented BBV from cutting some 5000 jobs and 600 branches. After Europe's 1992 deregulation the company targeted Latin America buying banks in Mexico and Peru (1995); Argentina Colombia and Venezuela (1996); and Brazil and Chile (1997). The merger of rivals Banco Santander and Banco Central Hispanoamericano in 1999 prompted BBV to merge with Argentaria in 2000.

After the merger BBVA teamed with top Spanish telecom Telef nica to develop online banking services. The duo announced plans to merge BBVA's Uno-e online bank with First-e one of Europe's first Internet-only banks. The merger which would have created the largest Internet bank in the world collapsed as the dotcom crisis began and online banks experienced losses.

Also in 2000 BBVA bought 30% of Grupo Financiero Bancomer Mexico's #2 bank and merged it into its existing Mexican bank Grupo Financiero BBV-Probursa; the resulting Grupo Financiero BBVA-Bancomer is the country's largest bank. The bank completed the renaming of its subsidiaries to reflect their position as BBVA subsidiaries in 2002.

In 2004 BBVA bought the 40% of Mexico's BBVA Bancomer that it did not already own. To finance about half of the approximately $4 billion bid the company issued 195 million new shares.

The next year BBVA tried to buy the rest of Italian bank Banca Nazionale del Lavoro (BNL) (it already owned 15%). However Italian regulatory bodies nixed the deal and BNP Paribas bought BNL. BBVA later sold its stake in the Italian bank.

To break into the US market BBVA purchased Texas banks Laredo National Bancshares for $850 million in 2005 Texas Regional Bancshares for more than $2 billion in 2006 and State National Bancshares for $480 million in 2007. BBVA's strategy in the US was centered around capturing more of the lucrative business transacted between the US and Mexico and to access the exploding Spanish-speaking market in the states. BBVA expanded its US operations again when it bought Compass Bank in 2007.

Adding on to its US operations BBVA acquired the failed Guaranty Financial Group in 2009. The deal which was facilitated by the FDIC fit in with BBVA's strategy of expanding in the Sunbelt especially Texas. BBVA merged its previously acquired State National Bancshares Laredo National Bancshares and Texas Regional Bancshares into Compass.

Auditors: DELOITTE, S.L.

LOCATIONS

HQ: Banco Bilbao Vizcaya Argentaria SA (BBVA)
Plaza de San Nicolas, 4, Bilbao, Viscaya 48005
Phone: (34) 91 537 7000 **Fax:** (34) 91 537 6766
Web: www.bbva.com

HISTORICAL FINANCIALS

Company Type: Public

Income Statement FYE: December 31

	ASSETS ($ mil.)	NET INCOME ($ mil.)	INCOME AS % OF ASSETS	EMPLOYEES
12/14	768,128	3,182	0.4%	109,239
12/13	802,051	3,067	0.4%	112,589
12/12	840,632	2,209	0.3%	113,924
12/11	773,080	3,885	0.5%	109,694
12/10	739,769	6,164	0.8%	104,755
Annual Growth	0.9%	(15.2%)	—	1.1%

2014 Year-End Financials

Return on assets: 0.4%
Return on equity: 5.7%
Long-term debt ($ mil.): —
No. of shares (mil.): —
Sales ($ mil): 43,209

Dividends
Yield: 5.7%
Payout: 91.5%
Market value ($ mil.): —

	STOCK PRICE ($) FY Close	P/E High/Low	PER SHARE ($) Earnings	Dividends	Book Value
12/14	9.39	27 21	0.53	0.54	9.74
12/13	12.39	32 22	0.54	0.55	10.12
12/12	9.42	30 18	0.42	0.53	10.05
12/11	8.57	19 11	0.83	0.57	10.16
12/10	10.17	16 8	1.53	0.94	10.84
Annual Growth	(2.0%)	— —	(23.1%)	(12.8%)	(2.7%)

Banco BPI SA (Portugal)

Banco BPI is well aware of the color of Portuguese money. The bank is engaged in a wide range of investment banking and commercial banking activities. Investment-related services offered by the bank include corporate finance equities treasury and bonds asset management private banking and venture capital. Its commercial business includes banking for individuals companies and institutions and the usual array of lending leasing and mortgaging and credit services. Banco BPI serves about 1.5 million customers through more than 600 branches across Portugal as well as more than 30 investment centers and various other operations. The company has insurance partnerships in Portugal with Allianz and Cosec.

In 2009 the Portugese government made an offer to buy Companhia de Seguro de Creditos or Cosec a provider of credit and bond insurance services. Banco BPI joinly owns Cosec with France's Euler Hermes.

EXECUTIVES

President Board of Directors, Artur Silva
Board of Directors Vice President, Fernando Ulrich
Membro du Conselho de Administra § Ŀo, Luis Pi
Membro du Conselho de Administra § Ŀo, Carla Bambulo
Membro du Conselho de Administra § Ŀo, Alfredo Almeida
Membro du Conselho de Administra § Ŀo, Ant nio Xavier
Membro du Conselho de Administra § Ŀo, Ant nio Silva
Membro du Conselho de Administra § Ŀo, Ant nio Domingues
Membro du Conselho de Administra § Ŀo, Armando Pinho
Membro du Conselho de Administra § Ŀo, Carlos Silva
Membro du Conselho de Administra § Ŀo, Edgar Ferreira
Auditors: Deloitte & Associados, SROC S.A.

LOCATIONS

HQ: Banco BPI SA (Portugal)
Rua Tenente Valadim 284, 3 piso, Porto 4100-476
Phone: (351) 22 607 3337 **Fax:** (351) 22 607 4738
Web: www.bpi.pt

COMPETITORS

Banco Comercial Portugus
Caixa Geral de Depsitos
Espirito Santo Investment Bank
Esprito Santo

HISTORICAL FINANCIALS

Company Type: Public

Income Statement FYE: December 31

	ASSETS ($ mil.)	NET INCOME ($ mil.)	INCOME AS % OF ASSETS	EMPLOYEES
12/14	51,815	(198)	—	8,638
12/13	58,786	92	0.2%	8,864
12/12	58,738	328	0.6%	8,964
12/11	55,561	(368)	—	9,292
12/10	61,109	247	0.4%	9,494
Annual Growth	(4.0%)	—	—	(2.3%)

2014 Year-End Financials

Return on assets: (-0.3%)
Return on equity: (-8.0%)
Long-term debt ($ mil.): —
No. of shares (mil.): 1,450
Sales ($ mil): 2,153
Dividends
Yield: —
Payout: —
Market value ($ mil.): —

Banco Bradesco S.A.

Auditors: KPMG Auditores Independentes

LOCATIONS

HQ: Banco Bradesco S.A.
Cidade de Deus S/N, Vila Yara, Osasco, SP 06029-900
Phone: (55) 11 3684 3702 **Fax:** (55) 11 3684 3213
Web: www.bradesco.com.br

HISTORICAL FINANCIALS

Company Type: Public

Income Statement FYE: December 31

	ASSETS ($ mil.)	NET INCOME ($ mil.)	INCOME AS % OF ASSETS	EMPLOYEES
12/14	350,149	5,763	1.6%	95,520
12/13	354,881	5,247	1.5%	100,489
12/12	391,868	5,522	1.4%	103,385
12/11	387,177	5,875	1.5%	104,684
12/10	363,225	5,987	1.6%	95,248
Annual Growth	(0.9%)	(1.0%)	—	0.1%

2014 Year-End Financials

Return on assets: 1.7%
Return on equity: 19.8%
Long-term debt ($ mil.): —
No. of shares (mil.): —
Sales ($ mil): 46,394
Dividends
Yield: 3.7%
Payout: 29.9%
Market value ($ mil.): —

	STOCK PRICE ($) FY Close	P/E High	P/E Low	PER SHARE ($) Earnings	Dividends	Book Value
12/14	13.37	5	3	1.09	0.42	6.14
12/13	12.53	7	5	0.99	0.31	6.04
12/12	17.37	8	6	1.05	0.39	6.91
12/11	16.68	9	7	1.11	0.43	6.29
12/10	20.29	12	9	1.15	0.39	6.19
Annual Growth	(9.9%)	—	—	(1.3%)	1.6%	(0.2%)

Banco Comercial Portugues, S.A.

With its home country's history of exploration it's no surprise that Banco Comercial Portugu s (BCP) is charting a successful course through the world's financial markets. BCP offers a multitude of financial services for business and consumer customers under the Millennium bcp brand. It provides asset management through Millennium bcp fundos de investimento private banking through Millennium Banque Priv © and vehicle management through Millennium bcp renting. BCP also offers health insurance in Portugal through M ©dis. In addition to about 1510 branches the bank has on its home turf it also has operations in Africa Asia Europe (primarily Poland and Greece) and North America.

Geographic Reach

The company operates almost 775 branches in Portugal as well as roughly 680 branches internationally.

Company Background

Banco Comercial Portugu s (BCP) was formed in 1985 by a group of Portugal's leading industrialists; it was the first private commercial bank to open after civil unrest brought socialism to the country.

Auditors: KPMG & Associados - Sociedade de Revisores Oficiais de Contas, S.A.

LOCATIONS

HQ: Banco Comercial Portugues, S.A.
Praca D. Joao I, 28, Porto 4000-295
Phone: (351) 21 321 1081 **Fax:** (351) 21 321 1079
Web: www.millenniumbcp.pt

HISTORICAL FINANCIALS

Company Type: Public

Income Statement FYE: December 31

	ASSETS ($ mil.)	NET INCOME ($ mil.)	INCOME AS % OF ASSETS	EMPLOYEES
12/14	92,817	(275)	—	17,939
12/13	112,902	(1,019)	—	18,873
12/12	118,287	(1,606)	—	21,297
12/11	120,914	(1,097)	—	21,470
12/10	133,850	403	0.3%	21,774
Annual Growth	(8.7%)	—	—	(4.7%)

2014 Year-End Financials

Return on assets: (-0.2%)
Return on equity: (-6.6%)
Long-term debt ($ mil.): —
No. of shares (mil.): —
Sales ($ mil): 4,654
Dividends
Yield: 0.6%
Payout: —
Market value ($ mil.): —

	STOCK PRICE ($) FY Close	P/E High	P/E Low	PER SHARE ($) Earnings	Dividends	Book Value
12/14	9.19	—	—	(0.01)	9.38	0.09
12/13	1.00	—	—	(0.06)	0.00	0.18
Annual Growth	819.0%	—	—	—	—	(15.0%)

Banco de Chile

Banco de Chile proffers a place for pesos. Chile's second-largest bank after Banco Santander Chile it has some 300 branches and 1400 ATMs in its home country as well as operations in Argentina Brazil China Mexico and the US. In addition to corporate and retail banking the company offers (through subsidiaries) mutual funds brokerage insurance financial planning factoring and other services. The Luksic family through such entities as Quiñenco and Sociedad Matriz Banco de Chile controls a majority of the bank. In 2008 Citigroup bought a 10% stake in the bank (with an option to acquire more) from Quiñenco and merged its Chilean operations into Banco de Chile.

In 2010 Citigroup upped its interest in the bank to more than 40% as part of its option to acquire up to half of the company.

Banco de Chile was founded in 1893.

EXECUTIVES

Vicepresidente, Francisco Aristeguieta Silva
Vicepresidente, Andronico Luksic Craig
Presidente Junta Directiva, Pablo Granifo Lavin
Auditors: Ernst & Young Ltda.

LOCATIONS

HQ: Banco de Chile
Paseo Ahumada 251, Santiago
Phone: (56) 2 637 1111 **Fax:** (56) 2 653 5156
Web: www.bancochile.com

COMPETITORS

BBVA Chile
BBVA Provida
Banco Santander Chile
Banco de Cr©dito e Inversiones
CORPBANCA

HISTORICAL FINANCIALS

Company Type: Public

Income Statement FYE: December 31

	ASSETS ($ mil.)	NET INCOME ($ mil.)	INCOME AS % OF ASSETS	EMPLOYEES
12/14	45,540	983	2.2%	14,803
12/13	49,227	1,046	2.1%	14,723
12/12	48,274	994	2.1%	14,581
12/11	41,809	824	2.0%	14,129
12/10	39,013	808	2.1%	14,016
Annual Growth	3.9%	5.0%	—	1.4%

2014 Year-End Financials

Return on assets: 2.2%
Return on equity: 21.3%
Long-term debt ($ mil.): —
No. of shares (mil.): —
Sales ($ mil): 3,808

Dividends
Yield: 4.2%
Payout: 24,732.6%
Market value ($ mil.): —

	STOCK PRICE ($) FY Close	P/E High/Low	PER SHARE ($) Earnings	Dividends	Book Value
12/14	68.94	12 10	0.01	2.83	0.05
12/13	87.80	16 13	0.01	3.31	0.05
12/12	96.50	19 15	0.01	2.80	0.05
12/11	81.75	18 13	0.01	2.49	0.04
12/10	88.38	22 14	0.01	2.81	0.03
Annual Growth	(6.0%)	— —	3.0%	0.2%	10.4%

Banco De Sabadell SA

Banco de Sabadell (also known as BancoSabadell) is one of the top banking groups in Spain offering corporate commercial and private banking through more than 2400 branches mostly in Spain as well as in France Morocco the UK and the US. The company operates under five banking brands: SabadellAtlántico and SabadellHerrero for business banking; SabadellSolbank which specializes in providing banking services for tourists and the tourism industry; ActivoBank for online banking; and SabadellUrquijo for private banking. BancoSabadell also offers insurance products through bancassurance along with asset management and securities brokerage services.

OperationsBancoSabadell operates four main business segments: Commercial Banking; Corporate Banking and Global Businesses; Markets and Private Banking; and Asset Management.The Commercial Banking division generates more than 80% of BancoSabadell's total revenue and provides traditional banking products and services to large and medium-sized businesses SMEs retailers and sole proprietors mostly under its SabadellAtlántico brand in Spain as well as under a number of regional brand names. The division also operates bancassurance which provides insurance products. Corporate Banking and Global Businesses (10% of overall revenue) provides corporate banking structured and corporate finance development capital consumer finance and national trade services serving mostly large corporations and financial institutions in Spain and overseas. The Markets and Private Banking segment (4% of overall revenue) provides savings and investment management services including securities market trading wealth management and custody services. The division comprises the group's SabadellUrquijo Private Banking business; Investment Products and Research unit; Treasury and Capital Markets unit; and Securities Trading and Custody Services unit.The Asset Management division (3% of overall revenue) manages real estate as well as non-performing assets through real estate asset manager Solvia. Solvia boasts a retail sales unit and sales teams that specializes in consolidating portfolio assets for sale to institutional buyers. It also liquidates assets with special or unusual features.The bank's foreign country affiliates include BS America (in Florida); and BancSabadell d'Andorra (in the Principality of Andorra) in which Banco Sabadell holds a nearly 51% controlling stake.Geographic ReachMost of the bank's 2400-plus branches are located in Spain though it also has branches in France Morocco the UK and the US (in Miami Florida). Additionally it has representative offices in Algeri Brazil China Dominican Republic India Mexico Poland Singapore Turkey Venezuela United Arab Emirates and the US.Financial PerformanceNote: Growth rates may differ after conversion to US dollars.BancoSabadell's revenues and profits have been trending higher over the past few years thanks to growing fee income from the sale of managed investment products coupled with declining loan loss provisions as the bank has worked to de-risk its loan portfolio by selling off non-performing assets.The bank's net interest income jumped by 25% to 2.26 billion ($2.74 billion) in 2014 as the bank paid less in interest expense on deposits while net fee income and net trading income also grew by double-digits due to higher sales of managed investment products and services and higher capital gains respectively. Higher revenue in 2014 also pushed BancoSabadell's profit higher by a whopping 154% to 371.68 million ($451.77 million) for the year.

Stategy

Banco Sabadell reiterated in 2015 its strategy toward improving profitability domestically which included three main priorities: to grow its existing domestic business by cross-selling its wide variety of services to existing customers and by leveraging its large scale to boost profit margins; continue to de-risk its loan portfolio and strengthen its balance sheet; and increase overall productivity across its operations without sacrificing service quality. These initiatives the company insists will help support future plans to expand internationally.As part of its global expansion plans the bank announced in late 2015 that it would begin operations in Mexico for the first time and begin to introduce its business banking services before launching its banking services for individuals. Earlier during the year the bank acquired TSB Bank expanding its reach significantly in the UK market.Toward its long-term balance sheet transformation strategy which spanned from 2014 through 2016 Banco Sabadell regularly sells its non-performing loan assets to de-risk its loan portfolio. To this end in 2014 for example the company sold a fully-provisioned loan portfolio (worth 554 million or roughly $673 million) to international investor Aiqon Capital reducing the bank's exposure to non-strategic assets.The company is not opposed to selling off underperforming parts of its business either to free up resources. In mid-2014 it sold its unpaid debt management and collection business to Lindorff Spain for a capital gain amounting to 162 million (about $197 million). Mergers and AcquisitionsIn April 2014 the group purchased Britain-based TSB Banking Group plc from Lloyds Banking Group for £1.7 billion ($2.5 billion) as part of its global expansion plans. The deal meant that 22% of Sabadell's assets would be located outside of Spain compared with just 5% at present. In 2014 Banco Sabadell purchased JGB Bank from GNB Holdings for some $49.6 million. Following the acquisition JGB Bank was folded into Sabadell United Bank (SUB) the group's Florida-based subsidiary. In 2013 the bank purchased Lloyds Banking Group España from Lloyds TSB Bank Plc which included 28 branches and 1.71 million in assets as well as Spanish subsidiaries Lloyds Bank International S.A.U. and Lloyds Investment España.

Company Background

Previously BancoSabadell acquired Miami-based Mellon United National Bank (which it rebranded Sabadell United Bank) and its 15 branches from The Bank of New York Mellon in 2010. The following year it acquired the assets and branches of the failed Lydian Private Bank further adding to its operations in the region. In 2007 the company acquired TransAtlantic Bank and BBVA's private banking business also both based in Miami.

Closer to home BancoSabadell acquired smaller rival Banco Guipuzcoano in 2010. The following year it acquired savings bank Caja de Ahorros del Mediterraneo (CAM) which had been seized by the government for a symbolic 1. That deal brought some 5 million additional customers to the bank increased its assets by around 75% and upped its branch numbers by more than 900. CAM is now SabadellCAM.

EXECUTIVES

Managing Director, Jaime Guardiola Romojaro
General Manager, Tomas Varela Muina
General Manager, Miguel Montes Guell
Director-General Manager, Jose Luis Negro Rodriguez
Chairman, Jose Oliu Creus
Auditors: PricewaterhouseCoopers Auditores, S.L.

LOCATIONS

HQ: Banco De Sabadell SA
Plaza de Sant Roc, 20, Barcelona, Sabadell 08201
Phone: (34) 93 902 323 555 **Fax:** (34) 93 935 916 062
Web: www.bancsabadell.com

PRODUCTS/OPERATIONS

2013 Sales

	% of total
Net interest income	44
Income from trading and exchange differences	38
Fee and Commission income	18
Total	100

2014 Sales

		%
Commercial Banking		83
Corporate Banking		10
Sabadell Urquijo Banking		2
Investment Managment		2
Real Estate Asset Management		3
Total	0	100

COMPETITORS

BBVA
Banco Pastor
Banco Popular Espa±ol
Grupo Santander

HISTORICAL FINANCIALS

Company Type: Public

Income Statement FYE: December 31

	ASSETS ($ mil.)	NET INCOME ($ mil.)	INCOME AS % OF ASSETS	EMPLOYEES
12/14	198,547	6	0.0%	17,760
12/13	225,015	28	0.0%	16,427
12/12	212,927	18	0.0%	14,291
12/11	129,910	5	0.0%	10,675
12/10	129,954	3	0.0%	10,777
Annual Growth	11.2%	11.9%	—	13.3%

2014 Year-End Financials

Return on assets: 0.0% Dividends
Return on equity: 0.0% Yield: 0.0%
Long-term debt ($ mil.): — Payout: 14.5%
No. of shares (mil.): — Market value ($ mil.): —
Sales ($ mil): 9,228

	STOCK PRICE ($) FY Close	P/E High/Low	PER SHARE ($) Earnings	Dividends	Book Value
12/14	5.39	79 55	0.11	0.02	3.37
12/13	5.03	144 54	0.10	0.35	3.55
12/12	5.77	254140	0.04	0.72	3.92
12/11	8.68	52 44	0.19	0.19	5.40
12/10	7.90	39 25	0.37	0.16	5.71
Annual Growth	(9.1%)	— —	(26.3%)	(43.9%)	(12.3%)

Banco do Brasil S.A.

Auditors: KPMG Auditores Independentes

LOCATIONS

HQ: Banco do Brasil S.A.
SBS Q.1, BL C, Lote 32, ED. Sede III, 5 Andar, Asa Sul, Brasilia, DF 70073-901
Phone: (55) 61 3310 3752 **Fax:** (55) 61 3310 3735
Web: www.bb.com.br

HISTORICAL FINANCIALS

Company Type: Public

Income Statement FYE: December 31

	ASSETS ($ mil.)	NET INCOME ($ mil.)	INCOME AS % OF ASSETS	EMPLOYEES
12/14	480,990	4,460	0.9%	111,628
12/13	491,985	4,418	0.9%	112,216
12/12	555,632	5,500	1.0%	114,182
12/11	518,403	6,799	1.3%	113,810
12/10	483,626	6,804	1.4%	109,026
Annual Growth	(0.1%)	(10.0%)	—	0.6%

2014 Year-End Financials

Return on assets: 0.9% Dividends
Return on equity: 15.3% Yield: 6.3%
Long-term debt ($ mil.): — Payout: 30.7%
No. of shares (mil.): — Market value ($ mil.): —
Sales ($ mil): 62,214

	STOCK PRICE ($) FY Close	P/E High/Low	PER SHARE ($) Earnings	Dividends	Book Value
12/14	8.68	3 2	1.59	0.55	11.01
12/13	10.38	3 2	1.56	1.05	11.03
12/12	12.67	4 2	1.92	0.65	11.87
12/11	12.60	4 3	2.37	0.86	11.70
12/10	19.50	5 4	2.49	0.90	11.44
Annual Growth	(18.3%)	— —	(10.6%)	(11.5%)	(1.0%)

Banco Popular Espanol, S.A.

HISTORY

Things got rolling in 1926 for Banco Popular Espa ±ol then known as Banco Popular de los Previsores del Porvenir. Formed to provide "all the types of operations ... proper to credit companies" the bank endured the Spanish Civil War and WWII before adopting its present name in 1947.

Banco Popular grew rapidly in the 1960s as Spain's economy stabilized and banks grappled with a decree that they separate their commercial and investment operations. In 1962 Banco Popular implemented merchant banking services through Banco Europeo de Negocios or Eurobanco (Banco Popular acquired the rest of it in 1974.) Like most of its peers Banco Popular sidestepped the restrictive banking laws by launching specialized companies. In 1964 it joined forces with Heller Overseas (now a Fuji Bank subsidiary) to form Heller Factoring Espa ±ola in 1964; it created investment fund manager Sogeval in 1965 and leasing company Iberleasing in 1966.

Banking restrictions also led to Banco Popular's 1967 creation of five "'Popularinsa'" regional banking companies: Banco de Andaluc a Banco de Castilla Banco de Cr ©dito Balear Banco de Galicia and Banco de Vasconia. By the late 1970s legal changes allowed Banco Popular and the regional banks to act as one. In 1987 the "Popularinsa" banks were made subsidiaries. Two years later Javier Valls was tapped to join his elder brother Luis in the bank's chairmanship.

In 1991 the bank stuck a tentative toe in the international water forming Banco Popular Comercial in France. But while its peers scrambled furiously to become cross-border players the company's growth plan remained focused on domestic retail and commercial banking. Such dedication did not go unrewarded: Banco Popular has consistently been ranked as one of the world's most profitable banks.

To build on its products and services the bank allied with US-based Bankers Trust (now part of Deutsche Bank) in 1994 to offer investment services to its top-end customers in Spain. In 1996 it joined French credit company Cofinoga to issue private-label credit cards and on-the-spot credit in Spain; through agreements with foreign banks Banco Popular also moved into Canada Southeast Asia and Latin America that year.

German-based insurer Allianz bought into the bank in 1998 (its stake is now less than 10%). In 1999 the bank moved to cut costs by consolidating its fund management and private banking services. Banco Popular started Internet-based Bancopopular-e.com in 2000. Luis Valls resigned in 2004. Angel Ron then became co-chairman with Javier Valls who resigned in 2006 and left Ron as the sole chair. Luis Valls died in 2006.

The company sold Banco Popular France to Credit Mutuel in 2008.

Auditors: PricewaterhouseCoopers Auditores, S.L.

LOCATIONS

HQ: Banco Popular Espanol, S.A.
Velazquez 34, Madrid 28001
Phone: (34) 91 520 70 00 **Fax:** (34) 91 577 92 08
Web: www.bancopopular.es

HISTORICAL FINANCIALS

Company Type: Public

Income Statement FYE: December 31

	ASSETS ($ mil.)	NET INCOME ($ mil.)	INCOME AS % OF ASSETS	EMPLOYEES
12/14	196,251	401	0.2%	15,321
12/13	203,552	447	0.2%	16,027
12/12	207,748	(3,243)	—	16,501
12/11	169,346	620	0.4%	14,062
12/10	174,175	789	0.5%	14,252
Annual Growth	3.0%	(15.6%)	—	1.8%

2014 Year-End Financials

Return on assets: 0.2% Dividends
Return on equity: 2.7% Yield: —
Long-term debt ($ mil.): — Payout: —
No. of shares (mil.): 2,126 Market value ($ mil.): 45,307
Sales ($ mil): 7,549

	STOCK PRICE ($) FY Close	P/E High/Low	PER SHARE ($) Earnings	Dividends	Book Value
12/14	21.31	155132	0.19	0.00	7.23
Annual Growth	—	— —	—	—	—

Banco Santander Brasil SA

If you're looking for a place to park a "brazillion" dollars Banco Santander (Brasil) is there. The bank part of Spain's Banco Santander provides financial services through 3566 branches primarily in Brazil's south and southeast with a major presence in the states of São Paulo and Rio Grande do Sul. Santander Brasil also offers wholesale banking to large corporations. Additional services include asset management private banking and insurance. In 2013 it launched a new category of specialized financial services (61 Santander Select branches with 400 relationship managers). The company accounts for about a quarter of its parent's revenues. Banco Santander owns more than 80% of Santander Brasil.

Company Background

The parent company listed approximately 15% of its shares of its Brazilian unit on the New York Stock Exchange in a 2009 IPO. It turned out to be the world's largest IPO that year raising some R$13 billion ($8 billion). The proceeds from the offering have been used to drive growth by funding new branches and lending. It is also growing its insurance and credit card businesses; the company recently began offering its Santander-Ferrari credit card.In late 2010 Santander rebranded its Brazilian brands –Banco Real and Santander Brasil– under the same name and platform. (It completed similar restructuring efforts in the UK and Mexico.) The parent company has high hopes for its Latin American operations especially in the high-growth markets of Brazil and Mexico. As such Santander is committed to investing in those units as it solidifies its position as a leading global bank. Santander Brasil is the result of the 2006 merger of Banco Santander banks Banco Santander Brasil Banco Santander Meridional and Banco do Estado de São Paulo. The company added to its Brazilian bank empire when it acquired Banco Real in 2008. At the time Banco Real was the fourth largest non government-owned Brazilian bank. The acquisition boosted Santander Brasil into the top three of banks in Brazil (along with Banco Bradesco and Itaú Unibanco)Brazil is a promising region of the world for banking. The country was a resilient market during the economic downturn. Employment levels rose and a new middle class emerged. As the Brazilian economy expands Santander Brasil expects lending and overall demand for banking services to grow.

EXECUTIVES

VP Executive Officer, Juan Sebasti ˜n Moreno Blanco, age 51
SVP Executive Officer, Conrado Engel, age 58
SVP Executive Officer, Jos ©de Paiva Ferreira, age 56
VP Executive Officer, Angel Santodomingo Martell, age 50
Vice Chairman, Jes s Maria Zabalza Lotina, age 57
VP Executive Officer, Antonio Pardo de Santayana Montes, age 44
VP Executive Officer, Carlos Alberto L pez Gal ˜n, age 53
VP Executive Officer, Carlos Rey de Vicente, age 42
VP Executive Officer, Ign ˜cio Dominguez-Adame Bozzano, age 47
VP Executive Officer, Jo o Guilherme de Andrade S Consiglio, age 47
VP Executive Officer, Manoel Marcos Madureira, age 64
VP Executive Officer, Oscar Rodrigues Herrero, age 44
Chairman, Celso Clemente Giacometti, age 72
Auditors: Deloitte Touche Tohmatsu

LOCATIONS

HQ: Banco Santander Brasil SA
Avenida Presidente Juscelino Kubitschek, 2235 and 2041 a Bloco A, Sao Paulo 04543-011
Phone: (55) 11 3174 8589 **Fax:** (55) 11 3174 6751
Web: www.santander.com.br

PRODUCTS/OPERATIONS

2013 Sales

	% of total
Interest and similar income	82
Fee and commission income	17
Gains on financial transactons	1
Total	**100**

COMPETITORS

Banco Bradesco
Banco do Brasil
Caixa Econ´mica Federal
Credicorp
Ita Unibanco

HISTORICAL FINANCIALS

Company Type: Public

Income Statement FYE: December 31

	REVENUE ($ mil.)	NET INCOME ($ mil.)	NET PROFIT MARGIN	EMPLOYEES
12/14	26,207	2,118	8.1%	49,309
12/13	25,823	2,422	9.4%	49,621
12/12	30,184	2,664	8.8%	53,992
12/11	32,163	4,154	12.9%	54,602
12/10	30,314	4,447	14.7%	54,406
Annual Growth	(3.6%)	(16.9%)	—	(2.4%)

2014 Year-End Financials

Debt ratio: —
Return on equity: 7.0%
Cash ($ mil.): 21,037
Current ratio: —
Long-term debt ($ mil.): —
No. of shares (mil.): —
Dividends
Yield: 17.3%
Payout: 289.4%
Market value ($ mil.): —

	STOCK PRICE ($) FY Close	P/E High/Low		PER SHARE ($) Earnings	Dividends	Book Value
12/14	5.02	9	6	0.27	0.87	4.26
12/13	6.10	469382		0.01	0.21	4.77
12/12	7.28	0	0	351.60	0.30	5.50
12/11	8.14	0	0	547.05	0.41	5.78
12/10	13.60	0	0	585.45	0.46	11.42
Annual Growth	(22.1%)	—	—	(85.4%)	16.9%	(21.8%)

Banco Santander Chile

A majority-owned indirect subsidiary of Spanish financial services giant Grupo Santander Banco Santander Chile is the largest bank in its home country. From more than 460 branches throughout Chile (including about 100 Banafe bank locations catering to middle-income clients) the bank offers consumer banking residential mortgage financing credit cards auto loans and investment management services for approximately 2.3 million customers. The bank also has about 40 payment centers operating as Santander SuperCaja. Corporate banking services include commercial lending and leasing trade financing financial advisory services and cash management.

The bank is looking to attract more small and medium sized business customers which only make up about 15% of its client base. About 40% of Banco Santader Chile's customers are individuals –a segment that also has the opportunity for growth. Only one in four working people in Chile has a checking account and about 50% of the population has no relationship with a bank.

Banco Santander Chile also offers mutual fund management insurance and securities brokerage services. The company sold its Santiago Express consumer finance business to Chilean chain store Almacenes Paris in 2004.

EXECUTIVES

Presidente, Mauricio Larra n Garces
1er. Vicepresidente, Jesus Maria Zabalza Lotina
2do. Vicepresidente, Oscar Von Chrismar Carvajal
Auditors: Deloitte

LOCATIONS

HQ: Banco Santander Chile
Bandera 140, 19th Floor, Santiago
Phone: (11) 562 320 2000
Web: www.santander.cl

COMPETITORS

BBVA Chile
BBVA Provida
Banco de Chile
Banco de Cr©dito e Inversiones
Scotiabank

HISTORICAL FINANCIALS

Company Type: Public

Income Statement FYE: December 31

	ASSETS ($ mil.)	NET INCOME ($ mil.)	INCOME AS % OF ASSETS	EMPLOYEES
12/14	51,143	940	1.8%	11,478
12/13	51,602	841	1.6%	11,516
12/12	51,524	741	1.4%	11,713
12/11	47,440	772	1.6%	11,566
12/10	47,189	1,019	2.2%	11,001
Annual Growth	2.0%	(2.0%)	—	1.1%

2014 Year-End Financials

Return on assets: 1.9%
Return on equity: 22.8%
Long-term debt ($ mil.): —
No. of shares (mil.): —
Sales ($ mil): 3,896
Dividends
Yield: 3.8%
Payout: 13,992.1%
Market value ($ mil.): —

	STOCK PRICE ($) FY Close	P/E High/Low		PER SHARE ($) Earnings	Dividends	Book Value
12/14	19.72	8	6	0.00	0.77	0.02
12/13	23.57	12	9	0.00	0.81	0.02
12/12	28.49	47	14	0.00	0.89	0.02
12/11	75.70	41	29	0.00	0.77	0.02
12/10	93.47	42	27	0.01	0.80	0.02
Annual Growth	(32.2%)	—	—	(2.0%)	(1.0%)	2.7%

Banco Santander SA

Though it started as only a contender in the running of the banks in Spain Banco Santander has since expanded to become one of the largest banks in the world. Beyond Spain it offers retail banking and consumer finance in Portugal the UK and other parts of Europe as well as the US. Subsidiaries such as Banco Santander Chile Banco Santander (Brasil) Santander Río in Argentina and Grupo Financiero Santander make it a top banking group in Latin America (almost 40% of the group's attributable profit). Other units offer asset management private banking corporate and investment banking and insurance. All told the company has some 117 million customers and 12950 locations in more than 40 countries.

Operations

The global banking concern has operations in retail banking and consumer finance commercial and wholesale banking private banking asset management and insurance.

Geographic Reach

The bank operates in Europe Latin America and the US.

Financial Performance

Despite a tough global regulatory environment Santander saw its revenues (gross income) grow by almost 2% in 2014 and its attributable profit rise by 39.3% largely thanks to improvement in commercial activities customer growth and cost containment.

Strategy

Over the years Santander has expanded to become more geographically diverse –a key strategy for the company as it looks to reduce risk. The bank's strategy revolves around making acquisitions and boosting deposits in growth nations; it generates more than half of its profits in emerging markets. Santander has taken advantage of the economic downturn to snap up businesses and asset portfolios from struggling companies at bargain prices.

One target market for growth is Latin America where profits have been growing; the company hopes to further strengthen its presence in the region and in a number of European countries as well. In addition to Latin America and Europe Banco Santander is making its move in the US. The company's American holdings include northeastern regional bank Santander Holdings USA (formerly Sovereign Bancorp).

The Botín family has led Grupo Santander since its founding in 1857. Under the leadership of Ana Botín (chairman since 2014) Santander aims to boost its "loyal" global retail customer base (only 12.1 million in 2014) to 17 million by 2017 while complying with growing regulatory demands to lower risk and increase banking transparency.

HISTORY

In 1857 a group of Basque businessmen had formed Banco Santander to finance Latin American trade. The emergence of Cantabria as a leading province after WWI helped the bank expand first regionally and then nationally.

The Botín family has been closely identified with the bank for decades. Emilio Botín served first as a board member and then for a few years as chairman before his death in 1923. The post was held by his son Emilio Botín-Sanz de Sautuola from 1950 to 1986 when his son Emilio Botín Sanz de Sautuola y García de los Ríos (known as Don Emilio) took over.

Spanish banks were spared the worst of the Great Depression (thanks to their isolation and the country's shunning the gold standard) but Spain's civil war was draining. In the early 1940s Santander expanded into Madrid and other major Spanish cities and merged with a few rivals. In the 1950s and 1960s as interest rates were controlled and mergers halted banks competed by building branch networks and investing overseas particularly in Latin America. In 1965 Santander joined with Bank of America to form Bankinter (it divested most of its stake by the mid-1990s).

Tight economic controls were relaxed in the 1970s after Franco's death. Despite global recession Santander continued to invest in Latin America through the mid-1980s.

In the late 1980s Santander prepared to compete in a deregulated Spain and Europe forming alliances with Royal Bank of Scotland Kemper (now part of Zurich Financial Services) and Metropolitan Life Insurance. In 1989 the bank jump-started competition by introducing Spain's first high-interest account.

Santander focused on home in the 1990s. Spurned by Banco Hispano Americano (BHA) Santander acquired a 60% stake in the ailing Banco Español de Crdito (Banesto) which became wholly owned in 1998. The bank took a hit when Latin America plunged into an economic crisis that year. With profit margins falling the bank merged with BCH in 1999.

BCH was formed by the 1991 merger of Banco Central and BHA. BHA had been established in 1900 by investors in Latin America; Central had been founded in 1919. The mixed banks offered both commercial and investment banking; they funded industrialization and investment in Latin America and became two of Spain's largest banks before the civil war.

After the war BHA sold its Latin American assets when the currency dried up while Central used mergers and acquisitions to expand across Spain. Isolated from WWII by Franco the two banks used their dual strategies to fund overseas investment and domestic-branch growth.

After Franco's death the banks faced increased competition at home and abroad. Central bought BHA in 1991 to remain competitive as Spain entered the European Economic Community (now the EU) in 1992.

Following the merger BCH trimmed 20% of its branches fired some 10000 employees and sold unprofitable holdings. Focused on Latin America the bank took small stakes in small banks. Losing its edge BCH merged with Santander in 1999.

In 2000 the newly merged BSCH focused on expanding in Europe and Latin America. Among its European moves was its alliance with Socit Gnrale to buy investment-fund management firms particularly in the US. In Latin America the bank bought Brazil's Banco Meridional Banco do Estado de São Paulo (Banespa) and Grupo Financiero Serfin Mexico's #3 bank. Critics questioned the $5 billion price tag BSCH paid for Banespa charging that the formerly state-run bank was overvalued in 2001. Executive in-fighting saw ex-Santander chairman Emilio Botín triumph over ex-BCH chairman Jos María Amusátegui for control of BSCH's helm. Soon after the bank started doing business as simply Santander Central Hispano. The following year the bank sold off its shares of Germany's Commerzbank and France's Socit Gnrale.

In one of Europe's largest cross-border bank mergers ever Santander paid more than 12 billion ($15 billion) for British bank Abbey National in 2004. It solidified its UK operations through the approximately 1.25 billion ($2.6 billion) purchase of Alliance & Leicester. Abbey then acquired the retail deposit business of Bradford & Bingley after it was nationalized in 2008.

Another acquisition helped Santander grow in South America. In 2007 the company along with Royal Bank of Scotland and Fortis acquired the Netherlands-based ABN AMRO (the international retail banking giant with more than 4350 branches) for around 71 billion ($87 billion). As part of the bid Banco Santander took ABN AMRO's Brazilian operations doubling its market share in Brazil. Also a part of the ABN AMRO deal Santander became the largest non-government-owned bank in Uruguay.

In 2009 the Venezuelan government took over Banco Santander subsidiary Banco de Venezuela the third-largest bank in the country. The government paid some 755 million ($1 billion) to nationalize the bank.

Also that year Santander acquired the approximately three-quarters of Sovereign it didn't already own. Santander then purchased a more than 3 billion ($4 billion) US car loan portfolio and a loan servicing platform from HSBC.

In 2010 Santander took full control of its Mexico unit by acquiring Bank of America's 25% stake in Grupo Financiero Santander for 2 billion ($2.5 billion) as well as the rest of Puerto Rican unit Santander BanCorp it didn't already own. It then acquired GE Capital's $2 billion consumer mortgage business in Mexico for $162 million plus the assumption of debt. The company has also been opening new branches in the region. While the financial downturn and the European sovereign debt crisis has been rough for Spain and Portugal Mexico holds promise for growth. Hoping to cash in on some of that growth Banco Santander spun off nearly 25% of Grupo Financiero Santander in a public offering worth more than $4 billion.

Banco Santander also made a big move into Eastern Europe. In 2011 it paid 4 billion (nearly $6 billion) for Poland's Bank Zachodni. The acquisition may signal more acquisitions for Santander in neighboring Eastern European countries.

In 2010 Santander bought a 2.5 billion ($3 billion) auto loan portfolio from Citigroup.

Banco Santander also operates Santander UK the result of the 2010 merger of Abbey National Bradford & Bingley and the former Alliance & Leicester (all of which were acquired by Santander). Santander's acquisitions in the UK helped bump up profits from the region in 2009 and 2010 but in 2011 profits slipped as a result of remediation charges related to mis-sold payment protection insurance.

EXECUTIVES

CEO Banco Santander USA, Scott E. Powell, age 52
CEO, Jose Antonio Alvarez
CFO, Jose Garcia Cantera
Head Technology and Operations, Andreu Plaza Lopez
President Brazil, Sergio Rial
First Vice Chairman, Bruce N. Carnegie-Brown, age 56
Director, Rodrigo Echenique Gorillo
Chairman, Ana P. Bot n, age 55
Auditors: DELOITTE, S.L.

LOCATIONS

HQ: Banco Santander SA
28660 Boadilla del Monte, Madrid
Phone: (34) 91 289 0000 **Fax:** (34) 91 254 1038
Web: www.gruposantander.com

COMPETITORS

BBVA
Banco Comercial Portugus
Banco Popular Espa±ol
Banco do Brasil
Bank of America
Citigroup
Deutsche Bank
Esprito Santo
HSBC
JPMorgan Chase

HISTORICAL FINANCIALS

Company Type: Public

Income Statement FYE: December 31

	ASSETS ($ mil.)	NET INCOME ($ mil.)	INCOME AS % OF ASSETS	EMPLOYEES
12/14	1,539,188	7,069	0.5%	183,938
12/13	1,535,938	6,016	0.4%	186,373
12/12	1,673,432	2,906	0.2%	188,779
12/11	1,618,788	6,921	0.4%	187,233
12/10	1,629,469	10,949	0.7%	172,909
Annual Growth	(1.4%)	(10.4%)	—	1.6%

2014 Year-End Financials

Return on assets: 0.4%
Return on equity: 7.6%
Long-term debt ($ mil.): —
No. of shares (mil.): —
Sales ($ mil): 95,809
Dividends
Yield: 7.4%
Payout: 125.8%
Market value ($ mil.): —

	STOCK PRICE ($) FY Close	P/E High/Low		PER SHARE ($) Earnings	Dividends	Book Value
12/14	8.33	20	16	0.58	0.62	7.80
12/13	9.07	23	17	0.55	0.63	8.57
12/12	8.17	38	23	0.29	0.64	9.53
12/11	7.52	20	11	0.78	0.79	11.09
12/10	10.65	17	10	1.25	0.64	12.05
Annual Growth	(6.0%)	—	—	(17.4%)	(0.8%)	(10.3%)

BanColombia, S.A.

Bancolombia has a wealth of services for wealthy and average Colombians alike. Serving more than 6.4 million customers Bancolombia is the #1 bank in Colombia with more than 700 branches and some 2300 ATMs throughout the country. Its Banagrícola division has another 100 branches located in El Salvador. The bank provides traditional commercial and retail banking services including deposit accounts loans and mortgages credit and debit cards and cash management. It also offers asset management insurance investment banking and brokerage services. In addition to its core Colombia and El Salvador operations the bank is also present in the US Panama and Peru. Bancolombia traces its roots back to 1945.

EXECUTIVES

Presidente, CARLOS RAUL YEPES JIMENEZ
Auditors: PricewaterhouseCoopers Ltda.

LOCATIONS

HQ: BanColombia, S.A.
Carrera 48 # 26-85, Avenida Los Industriales, Medellin
Phone: (57) 4 404 1837 **Fax:** (57) 4 404 5146
Web: www.grupobancolombia.com

PRODUCTS/OPERATIONS

2013 Sales

	% of total
Interest income	
Loans	65
Financial leases	9
Investment sercurities	5
Fees and other service income	
Credit and debit card fees	7
Commissions from banking services	4
Collections and payment fees	3
Trust activities	2
Checking fees	1
Others	4
Total	**100**

Selected Subsidiaries

Banca de Inversion Bancolombia S.A. (investment banking)
Bancolombia (Panamá) S.A.
Bancolombia Puerto Rico
Factoring Bancolombia S.A. (99.97%)
Fiduciaria Bancolombia S.A. (trust services 98.8%)
Inversiones Financieras Banco Agricola S.A. (investments 98.4%)
Leasing Bancolombia S.A.
Patrimonio Autonomo CV Sufinanciamiento (loan management)
Valores Bancolombia S.A. (securities brokerage)

COMPETITORS

BBVA
Banco Latinoamericano de Comercio Exterior
Banco de Cr©dito e Inversiones
Bicsa Panama
Citigroup
Credicorp

HISTORICAL FINANCIALS

Company Type: Public

Income Statement FYE: December 31

	ASSETS ($ mil.)	NET INCOME ($ mil.)	INCOME AS % OF ASSETS	EMPLOYEES
12/14	62,202	785	1.3%	30,158
12/13	67,799	785	1.2%	28,759
12/12	55,180	959	1.7%	24,820
12/11	44,098	858	1.9%	24,126
12/10	34,232	722	2.1%	22,992
Annual Growth	16.1%	2.1%	—	7.0%

2014 Year-End Financials

Return on assets: 1.3%
Return on equity: 12.8%
Long-term debt ($ mil.): —
No. of shares (mil.): 509
Sales ($ mil): 5,418
Dividends
Yield: 3.2%
Payout: —
Market value ($ mil.): 24,405

	STOCK PRICE ($) FY Close	P/E High/Low		PER SHARE ($) Earnings	Dividends	Book Value
12/14	47.88	—	—	(0.00)	1.58	13.39
12/13	49.02	—	—	(0.00)	1.61	12.25
12/12	66.58	—	—	(0.00)	1.59	12.74
12/11	59.56	—	—	(0.00)	0.00	9.03
12/10	61.91	—	—	(0.00)	1.33	7.77
Annual Growth	(6.2%)	—	—	—	4.4%	14.6%

Bangkok Bank Public Co., Ltd. (Thailand)

Bangkok Bank wants to protect the baht you've got. One of the largest commercial banks in Thailand Bangkok Bank provides a variety of banking services to individual and commercial clients including checking and savings accounts loans Internet banking and treasury and investment banking services. It operates about 1200 branches serving 16 million customers throughout Thailand about a dozen other Southeast Asian countries the UK and the US. The bank was founded in 1944 in response to the difficulty Thai businessmen encountered in receiving credit facilities from foreign banks; it has since had a hand in developing its homeland's industry and agriculture.

EXECUTIVES

President, Chartsiri Sophonpanich
Chairman of the Board, Chatri Sophonpanich
Auditors: Deloitte Touche Tohmatsu Jaiyos Audit Co., Ltd.

LOCATIONS

HQ: Bangkok Bank Public Co., Ltd. (Thailand)
333 Silom Road, Bangkok 10500
Phone: (66) 0 2231 4333 **Fax:** 212 422-0728
Web: www.bangkokbank.com

COMPETITORS

Bank of Ayudhya
CIMB Group
DBS Group Holdings
KASIKORNBANK
Krung Thai
Siam Commercial
Standard Chartered
TMB Bank
Thanachart Capital
United Overseas Bank

HISTORICAL FINANCIALS

Company Type: Public

Income Statement FYE: December 31

	ASSETS ($ mil.)	NET INCOME ($ mil.)	INCOME AS % OF ASSETS	EMPLOYEES
12/14	83,937	1,104	1.3%	26,132
12/13	79,311	1,096	1.4%	24,096
12/12	79,046	1,079	1.4%	22,934
12/11	66,949	868	1.3%	21,503
12/10	64,913	818	1.3%	21,229
Annual Growth	6.6%	7.8%	—	5.3%

2014 Year-End Financials

Return on assets: 1.3%
Return on equity: 11.7%
Long-term debt ($ mil.): —
No. of shares (mil.): 1,908
Sales ($ mil): 4,524
Dividends
Yield: —
Payout: —
Market value ($ mil.): 11,453

	STOCK PRICE ($) FY Close	P/E High/Low		PER SHARE ($) Earnings	Dividends	Book Value
12/14	6.00	0	0	0.58	0.00	5.15
12/13	7.41	0	0	0.57	0.00	4.74
12/12	5.39	0	0	0.57	0.00	4.68
12/11	4.42	0	0	0.46	0.00	4.06
12/10	4.31	0	0	0.43	0.00	4.02
Annual Growth	8.6%	—	—	7.8%	—	6.4%

Bank Audi S.A.L

Commercial banks not chartered
Auditors: BDO, Semaan, Gholam & Co.

LOCATIONS

HQ: Bank Audi S.A.L
Banque Audi Plaza, Bab Idriss, Beirut 2021 8102
Phone: (961) 1 994000 **Fax:** (961) 1 990555
Web: www.bankaudigroup.com

HISTORICAL FINANCIALS

Company Type: Public

Income Statement FYE: December 31

	ASSETS ($ mil.)	NET INCOME ($ mil.)	INCOME AS % OF ASSETS	EMPLOYEES
12/14	41,836	339	0.8%	6,408
12/13	36,311	302	0.8%	5,894
12/12	31,343	375	1.2%	5,070
12/11	28,736	361	1.3%	5,051
12/10	28,774	338	1.2%	4,838
Annual Growth	9.8%	0.1%	—	7.3%

2014 Year-End Financials

Return on assets: 0.8%
Return on equity: 11.4%
Long-term debt ($ mil.): —
No. of shares (mil.): 283
Sales ($ mil): 2,797
Dividends
Yield: —
Payout: —
Market value ($ mil.): —

	STOCK PRICE ($) FY Close	P/E High/Low		PER SHARE ($) Earnings	Dividends	Book Value
12/14	0.00	—	—	0.86	0.00	11.63
12/13	0.00	—	—	0.80	0.00	10.77
12/12	6.35	—	—	1.01	0.00	10.56
Annual Growth	—	—	—	(4.1%)	—	2.4%

Bank Hapoalim B.M. (Israel)

The largest bank in Israel Bank Hapoalim caters to individual commercial and corporate clients at home and abroad. Within Israel the Bank Hapoalim Group has more than 270 full-service branches and business centers. Another 30 express branches are in the works. Overseas it has about 45 branches correspondent offices and financial subsidiaries in Asia Australia Europe Latin America and North America; its international focus is on private banking and the corporate sector. Bank Hapoalim provides investment banking services including the underwriting of and investment in companies; it also provides trust services to individuals and businesses.

Bank Hapoalim was founded in 1921. Shari Arison Israel's wealthiest person is the controlling shareholder.

The bank has undergone major shakeups in its leadership since Arison took control of the bank in 2007. Dan Dankner also came on board as chairman that year. In March 2009 Zvi Ziv resigned as CEO after clashing with Dankner; deputy CEO Zion Keinan was picked to replace him. Bank of Israel (the nation's central bank) then wrangled with Arison over Hapoalim's performance and leadership threatening to remove Dankner if significant changes weren't made. Dankner seemed to get the message and resigned in 2009. Yair Seroussi replaced him.

The company planned to acquire control of Ukraine bank OJSC Ukraininan Innovation Bank (Ukrinbank) but was blocked by Bank of Israel. As a result Bank Hapoalim has suspended its planned growth in Eastern Europe. However it is examining opportunities in other regions to add to such investments as Bank Pozitif in Turkey and DKB in Kazakhstan. Other international businesses include Hapoalim Switzerland The PAM Group and Bank Hapoalim (Cayman). Hapoalim Securities U.S.A. offers securities trading for customers in Israel and abroad.

Auditors: Ziv Haft

LOCATIONS

HQ: Bank Hapoalim B.M. (Israel)
50 Rothschild Blvd., Tel-Aviv 66883
Phone: (972) 3 567 3333 **Fax:** (972) 3 560 7028
Web: www.bankhapoalim.com

COMPETITORS

Bank Leumi le-Israel
First International Bank of Israel
Israel Discount Bank
Mizrahi Tefahot
UBS

HISTORICAL FINANCIALS

Company Type: Public

Income Statement FYE: December 31

	ASSETS ($ mil.)	NET INCOME ($ mil.)	INCOME AS % OF ASSETS	EMPLOYEES
12/14	104,943	705	0.7%	12,405
12/13	109,581	743	0.7%	12,891
12/12	100,980	682	0.7%	27,113
12/11	93,300	718	0.8%	13,408
12/10	90,552	628	0.7%	13,605
Annual Growth	3.8%	2.9%	—	(2.3%)

2014 Year-End Financials

Return on assets: 0.7%
Return on equity: 9.0%
Long-term debt ($ mil.): —
No. of shares (mil.): 1,323
Sales ($ mil): 4,358
Dividends
Yield: —
Payout: —
Market value ($ mil.): —

Bank Leumi Le-Israel B.M.

Bank Leumi le-Israel looms large as one of Israel's largest financial institutions. The company whose name translates as National Bank of Israel offers retail banking (for consumers and small businesses) commercial banking (middle-market businesses) corporate banking (large companies) and private banking (wealthy clients) through deposits mortgages and other loans credit cards trust services and investments. It has about 235 branches in Israel and more than 80 locations (including branches agencies and representative offices) in some 20 countries including the US. Subsidiary Leumi Partners provides corporate investment banking services and makes direct investments in nonbanking businesses.

Other subsidiaries include The Arab Israel Bank Leumi Mortgage Bank and retail and private banking units in the UK Switzerland Luxembourg and Romania. In 2011 Bank Leumi bought Geneva-based private bank Banque Safdi ©from the Safdi © family. It plans to merge the firm with Bank Leumi Switzerland. In a restructuring move that will cut costs Bank Leumi plans to absorb Leumi Mortgage Bank in 2012. The company will then provide mortgage services through a newly created mortgage division.

After the Israeli parliament passed a number of capital market reform laws in 2005 Bank Leumi was compelled to sell its mutual fund and investment portfolio management operations. It has since focused on providing investment and pension counseling to its clients.

The Israeli government owns more than 10% of Bank Leumi but has been selling off its stake in the company and intends to eventually divest its entire holding.

HISTORY

At the beginning of the 20th century a group of prominent Jewish men led by Austrian Zionist Theodor Herzl founded the Jewish Colonial Trust (which would later become known as Otzar Hityashvut Hayehudim or OHH). An advocate of the Jewish settlement of Palestine the trust recognized the need for a financial institution to promote colonization in the region which was then part of the Ottoman Empire. In 1902 it established the Anglo-Palestine Company the forerunner of Bank Leumi le-Israel. A year later the London-based company opened its first Palestinian office in Jaffa (now Tel Aviv).

As WWI began the company had half a dozen branches. The outbreak of hostilities between Great Britain and the Ottoman Empire forced the London-based bank to close its offices but it continued to operate from the Spanish Consulate in Jerusalem. By the mid-1920s the company was known as the Anglo-Palestine Bank and was playing a significant role in the development of local agriculture.

During the following decade Palestine saw an influx of refugees from Nazism in Europe. The bank assisted in transferring assets to Palestine and anchored the area's economy through WWII. When Israel gained independence in 1948 the Anglo-Palestine Bank became the nation's fiscal agency and printed monetary notes for the new government. It began to focus its efforts on international operations and in 1950 opened its first US office in New York City. But even though it was the national bank of the newly formed Israeli state the bank was still based in London. In 1951 a company named leumi Le'Israel was founded in Tel Aviv and assumed control of the bank which took the name Bank Leumi le-Israel (National Bank of Israel) in 1954. Also that year the government formed the Bank of Israel and Bank Leumi resumed its commercial banking activities.

Bank Leumi maintained its status as Israel's leading bank until the 1980s when triple-digit inflation hit the country. The bottom fell out in 1983 when investors pulled out of the stock market fearing devaluation of the shekel. As they had done for several years Bank Leumi and Israel's other major banking groups reacted by taking out massive loans to buy their own stock and shield against losses in share price. The artificially inflated bank stocks crashed and thousands of individual investors lost their savings. The Israeli government intervened paying some $7 billion to bail out the banks. Though the state now held most of Bank Leumi's stock the OHH maintained voting rights.

In 1986 following a government inquiry into the stock scandal chairman Ernst Japhet and the company's board were forced to resign prompting more contention. On their way out Japhet and his officers received millions of dollars in severance pay and monthly pensions. The ramifications of what became known as "Leumigate" resulted in the company's next two chairmen also being ousted over the next two years. Rival Bank Hapoalim wrested the mantle of Israel's #1 bank from Bank Leumi in 1987.

The government sold off 10% of its interest in the firm to a unit of Deutsche Bank in 1993 and in 1995 mandated that banks sell their nonfinancial holdings. That year Galia Maor became CEO as the first woman head of an Israeli bank and Eitan Raff became chairman (he announced his retirement in 2010).

Controvery continued however. In 1997 Bank Leumi sold a majority stake in Migdal Insurance to Assicurazioni Generali which amplified questions regarding the buyer's handling of life insurance policies of Jewish Holocaust victims. The inquiry spread to Bank Leumi which released information about dormant accounts the next year but nonetheless faced government scrutiny and lawsuits from descendants of Holocaust victims.

In 2006 an Israeli law established a company to collect restitution for property deemed abandoned by Holocaust victims who had made bank deposits and bought real estate and bank shares in Israel in anticipation of the establishment of a Jewish homeland in Palestine. After years of wrangling The Company for Restitution of Holocaust Victims Assets in mid-2009 filed suit against Bank Leumi considered to be the holder of the most Jewish Holocaust assets; the lawsuit asked for NIS 300 million ($75 million) in restitution for more than 3500 victims. Denying any financial culpability the bank later that year offered NIS 20 million ($5 million). In 2010 it agreed to arbitration.

Auditors: Kost Forer Gabbay & Kasierer

LOCATIONS

HQ: Bank Leumi Le-Israel B.M.
34 Yehuda Halevi Street, Tel-Aviv 65546
Phone: (972) 3 514 8111 **Fax:** (972) 3 566 1872
Web: www.bankleumi.com

COMPETITORS

Bank Hapoalim	HSBC
Bank of America	Israel Discount Bank
Citigroup	Mizrahi Tefahot
First International Bank of Israel	Standard Chartered
	UniCredit

HISTORICAL FINANCIALS

Company Type: Public

Income Statement FYE: December 31

	ASSETS ($ mil.)	NET INCOME ($ mil.)	INCOME AS % OF ASSETS	EMPLOYEES
12/14	101,942	386	0.4%	12,690
12/13	107,885	561	0.5%	13,004
12/12	100,919	249	0.2%	13,407
12/11	95,697	494	0.5%	13,633
12/10	92,610	671	0.7%	13,490
Annual Growth	2.4%	(12.9%)	—	(1.5%)

2014 Year-End Financials

Return on assets: 0.3%
Return on equity: 5.5%
Long-term debt ($ mil.): —
No. of shares (mil.): 1,473
Sales ($ mil): 3,907
Dividends
Yield: —
Payout: —
Market value ($ mil.): —

Bank of China Ltd

The Bank of China (BOC) has its sights set on global conquest –of the financial kind. One of the largest banks in the world's most populous country BOC is a financial giant. It has more than 10000 domestic branches as well as foreign offices in about 30 countries. Commercial banking (including corporate and retail banking and treasury operations) accounts for about 90% of its revenues. BOC International provides investment banking services in China the UK the US and Singapore. BOC Group Insurance sells general and life insurance products in China. The group provides aircraft leasing through BOC Aviation. China's government owns about 70% of BOC one of the nation's four state-owned commercial banks.

Despite the sluggish economic climate around the world BOC's operating income and profits both grew by 19% in 2011. Additionally its assets grew by 13% to RMB 11.8 trillion ($1.9 trillion). The solid performance was credited to an increase in both interest and noninterest earnings and the bank's relatively low portfolio of bad loans decreased even further that year. Loan demand remains healthy and the bank expects to grow its domestic lending by more than 10% in 2012.

It could be argued that BOC's goal of becoming a premier multinational banking group was achieved in late 2011 when the company was named to the list of Global Systematically Important Financial Institutions (firms that are considered too big to fail). It was China's only company to be named to the list. BOC's strategic development plan for further growth includes efforts to streamline its structure expand internationally (it was the first major Chinese bank to offer RMB products in the US) and invest in its technology and branch network. In 2011 BOC divested some of its riskier holdings in bonds issued by Ireland Italy Greece Portugal and Spain.

HISTORY

The Bank of China (BOC) has always had strong ties to the government of China. Established as a central bank in 1912 right after the establishment of the Provisional Government of the Republic of China BOC became a government-chartered international exchange bank in 1928. Their first overseas branch was opened in London in 1929 leading to a global network of 34 overseas branches over the next two decades.

After WWII the bank specialized in foreign exchange supporting foreign trade and the development of China's national economy. Between 1984 and 2001 BOC issued bonds in the international capital market 27 times. In 1993 when China initiated reform in its foreign exchange system BOC played a key role in the unification of exchange rates foreign exchange purchases and sales and the incorporation of foreign-funded enterprises into the foreign exchange sales system.

In 1994 BOC began to transform from a specialized bank to a wider-based state-owned commercial bank by issuing its first BOC Hong Kong dollar notes and then Macao pataca notes. The issue of both notes helped stabilize their respective markets.

BOC International Holdings a wholly owned subsidiary of BOC specializing in investment banking was incorporated in Hong Kong in 1998. Three years later the group restructured its Hong Kong operations by merging 10 of its member banks into Bank of China (Hong Kong) Limited a locally registered bank that successfully listed on the Hong Kong Stock Exchange in July 2003.

The bank was not free of scandal. A 2002 probe into BOC's New York branch by the US Office of the Comptroller of the Currency revealed that preferential treatment was given to certain customers who had personal relationships with some members of the bank's previous management. Regulators from the US and China fined BOC $20 million for "unsafe and unsound" business practices.

In 2005 the Royal Bank of Scotland (RBS) formed a consortium that bought a 10% stake in BOC. In exchange BOC agreed to distribute the Scottish bank's credit cards and other products. RBS sold its stake in 2009 and the banks ended their partnership agreement.

BOC went public in 2006. Its IPO was estimated to be the world's largest in six years. Foreign banks and investors scrambled for a piece of the action; Saudi investor Prince Alwaleed bin Talal invested $2 billion in the bank. The successful IPO was fraught with symbolism for the banking industry in China which had been struggling. China had had to bail out two of the country's top banks BOC and China Construction Bank three times within six years. And for decades money in China's state banks had been used to support failing state companies leaving the banks with a mountain of bad loans.

To increase its non-interest income BOC acquired Singapore Aircraft Leasing (since renamed BOC Aviation) for $965 million in late 2006. The BOC Aviation portfolio includes more than 75 aircraft in about 20 countries.

BOC announced plans in 2008 to acquire 20% of French private bank La Compagnie Financiere Edmond de Rothschild but dropped those plans in 2009 after failing to get approval from Chinese regulators.

In early 2009 BOC faced selloffs by major investors as several subprime-battered financial institutions lined up to divest their stakes in the bank. UBS sold its entire 1% stake and Bank of America dumped its 3% share. Royal Bank of Scotland also sold its 4% stake in BOC. The two banks then cut their strategic partnership ties.

Auditors: Ernst & Young Hua Ming LLP

LOCATIONS

HQ: Bank of China Ltd
No. 1 Fuxingmen Nei Dajie, Beijing 100818
Phone: (86) 10 6659 6688 **Fax:** (86) 10 6601 6871
Web: www.boc.cn

HISTORICAL FINANCIALS

Company Type: Public

Income Statement FYE: December 31

	ASSETS ($ mil.)	NET INCOME ($ mil.)	INCOME AS % OF ASSETS	EMPLOYEES
12/14	2,457,375	27,325	1.1%	308,128
12/13	2,291,797	25,919	1.1%	305,675
12/12	2,034,025	22,365	1.1%	302,016
12/11	1,879,458	19,728	1.0%	289,951
12/10	1,586,847	15,841	1.0%	279,301
Annual Growth	11.6%	14.6%	—	2.5%

2014 Year-End Financials

Return on assets: 1.1%
Return on equity: 16.4%
Long-term debt ($ mil.): —
No. of shares (mil.): —
Sales ($ mil): 120,283
Dividends
Yield: 44.0%
Payout: 34.2%
Market value ($ mil.): —

Bank of Communications Co., Ltd.

Bank of Communications (BoCom) is one of the largest commercial banks in China based on total assets. The company offers services in corporate banking personal banking and treasury operations. Its offerings include personal savings accounts personal loans corporate loans trade financing wealth management e-banking and credit card services. BoCom boasts 30 provincial branches and a network of more than 2600 outlets in some 180 cities –including overseas branches in New York Tokyo and Singapore and representative offices in London and Frankfurt. The bank is also one of China's oldest. HSBC Holdings holds close to a 20% interest in BoCom.

Geographic Reach

BoCom has a dozen overseas institutions that consist of branches located in Hong Kong New York Tokyo Singapore Seoul Frankfurt Macau Ho Chi Minh City Sydney and San Francisco. It also operates a representative office in Taipei and Bank of Communications (UK) Co. Ltd.

Operations

The bank organizes its operations into four segments. Its personal banking unit focuses on personal savings bank cards personal lending payment and settlement investment services insurance services and wealth management. BoComm's corporate banking segment comprises cash management supply chain financing investment banking financial institution banking and asset custody services. The company's international banking unit consists of foreign exchange wealth management document settlement remittance and bill services trade finance and offshore banking. BoComm's fourth segment e-banking provides personal online banking enterprise online banking telephone banking and self-help banking.

Strategy

The company has continued to expand its offerings by venturing into new lines of business. With its purchase of an 85% stake in Hubei International Trust and Investment Corporation BoComm entered the trust industry. Soon after it began to also cater to the insurance industry with the launch of BoCommLife Insurance a joint venture with the Commonwealth Bank of Australia. BoCom is among the nation's first commercial banks allowed to tap into the insurance industry.

Auditors: PricewaterhouseCoopers Zhong Tian LLP

LOCATIONS

HQ: Bank of Communications Co., Ltd.
No. 188 Yincheng Zhong Road, Pudong New District, Shanghai 200120
Phone: (86) 21 58766688 **Fax:** (86) 21 58798398
Web: www.bankcomm.com

HISTORICAL FINANCIALS

Company Type: Public

Income Statement FYE: December 31

	ASSETS ($ mil.)	NET INCOME ($ mil.)	INCOME AS % OF ASSETS	EMPLOYEES
12/14	1,009,978	10,610	1.1%	93,658
12/13	984,645	10,290	1.0%	99,919
12/12	845,872	9,363	1.1%	96,259
12/11	732,584	8,060	1.1%	90,149
12/10	599,489	5,922	1.0%	85,290
Annual Growth	13.9%	15.7%	—	2.4%

2014 Year-End Financials

Return on assets: 1.0%
Return on equity: 14.7%
Long-term debt ($ mil.): —
No. of shares (mil.): —
Sales ($ mil): 54,084
Dividends
Yield: 3.8%
Payout: 16.3%
Market value ($ mil.): —

	STOCK PRICE ($) FY Close	P/E High/Low		PER SHARE ($) Earnings	Dividends	Book Value
12/14	23.55	1	0	0.14	0.90	1.02
12/13	19.15	1	1	0.14	0.02	0.93
12/12	17.99	1	0	0.14	0.01	0.82
12/11	19.15	1	1	0.13	0.00	0.70
12/10	25.00	1	1	0.10	0.05	0.55
Annual Growth	(1.5%)	—	—	9.2%	109.5%	17.0%

Bank of East Asia Ltd.

Bank of East Asia provides retail and commercial banking services in Hong Kong and mainland China. Its offerings include deposit accounts consumer loans mortgages business loans credit cards private banking and investment management. Bank of East Asia has some 130 locations in Hong Kong and more than 60 in mainland China; internationally it has about 30 offices in the British Virgin Islands Malaysia Singapore the UK and Vietnam. The bank's subsidiaries include online securities and futures brokerage provider East Asia Securities Blue Cross (Asia-Pacific) Insurance and Tricor which performs outsourced business services.

Like many of its peers Bank of East Asia is seeking new revenue lines by branching into related industries. In 2009 it arranged to buy a minority stake in fund house Golden Eagle Asset Management allowing it to enter China's growing fund market. Bank of East Asia also launched a trust business in that country.

With an increased focus on Hong Kong and China the bank is also streamlining elsewhere. It sold a majority stake of its Canadian network (a half-dozen branches) to Industrial and Commercial Bank of China (ICBC) in 2010 and arranged to sell its US operations to that company the following year.

EXECUTIVES

Chairman and CEO, David K. P. Li, age 77
Chief Investment Officer, Samson K. C. Li, age 55
Deputy Chief Executive, Adrian David M. K. Li, age 42
Deputy Chief Executive, Brian David M. B. Li, age 41
COO, Tong Hon-shing, age 56
Deputy Chairman, Allan C. Y. Wong, age 64
Deputy Chairman, Arthur K. C. Li, age 70
Auditors: KPMG

LOCATIONS

HQ: Bank of East Asia Ltd.
10 Des Voeux Road Central,
Phone: (852) 3608 3608 **Fax:** (852) 3608 6000
Web: www.hkbea.com

PRODUCTS/OPERATIONS

2014 Sales

	% of total
Interest income	83
Non-interest income	17
Total	**100**

COMPETITORS

Bank of China (Hong Kong)
Bank of Communications
CITIC International Financial
China Development Bank
China Minsheng Banking
Chong Hing Bank
Dah Sing Banking
Dah Sing Financial Holdings Limited
Hang Seng Bank
Public Financial Holdings
Shanghai Pudong Development Bank

HISTORICAL FINANCIALS

Company Type: Public

Income Statement FYE: December 31

	ASSETS ($ mil.)	NET INCOME ($ mil.)	INCOME AS % OF ASSETS	EMPLOYEES
12/14	102,626	858	0.8%	13,103
12/13	97,236	852	0.9%	12,698
12/12	89,285	781	0.9%	12,441
12/11	78,707	561	0.7%	12,238
12/10	68,728	543	0.8%	11,412
Annual Growth	10.5%	12.1%	—	3.5%

2014 Year-End Financials

Return on assets: 0.8%
Return on equity: 10.0%
Long-term debt ($ mil.): —
No. of shares (mil.): —
Sales ($ mil): 4,542
Dividends
Yield: 3.1%
Payout: 35.7%
Market value ($ mil.): —

	STOCK PRICE ($) FY Close	P/E High/Low		PER SHARE ($) Earnings	Dividends	Book Value
12/14	3.95	2	1	0.35	0.13	3.78
12/13	4.14	2	1	0.36	0.12	3.59
12/12	3.86	2	1	0.35	0.11	3.31
12/11	3.70	2	1	0.25	0.11	2.95
12/10	4.15	2	2	0.25	0.10	2.79
Annual Growth	(1.2%)	—	—	9.2%	6.4%	7.9%

Bank of Ireland (Ireland)

HISTORY

Bank of Ireland opened for business in Dublin in 1783 at Mary's Abbey. The bank had 600000 19 employees and a desire to offer more consistent service than the unstable private banks traders and merchants active at the time.

In 1784 Bank of Ireland began to print notes. As the government's unofficial banker it received all funds owed to the Irish treasury and administered all loans to and from the state.

By 1790 the bank's original building at Mary's Abbey had expanded into four. The bank's growth continued to outpace its premises. In 1803 the bank acquired Parliament House in College Green; after five years of remodeling the building was opened to the public. (It remained the bank's headquarters until the 1960s.)

Over time the bank ventured out of Dublin to open branch offices. Expansion began in 1825 with the establishment of seven branches; by 1883 the number had risen to 58 and by 1920 there were 75.

In 1926 the bank bought National Land Bank and renamed it National City Bank. More acquisitions followed –Hibernian Bank in 1958 and National Bank in 1965.

Much like its counterparts in the US the company was impacted by declining real estate values and higher unemployment rates in its home country. In 2008 the Irish government injected 2 billion ($2.8 billion) into the bank in exchange for a 25% voting stake. Ireland also provided capital for Allied Irish Banks and Irish Bank Resolution to help stabilize the nation's financial system which plunged amid the global financial crisis and its own financial slump.

As part of the bailout the bank was compelled to sell off parts of itself. Bank of Ireland divested two units Iridian Asset Management and Guggenheim Alternative Investment Management in 2009. Other sales followed.

EXECUTIVES

Director, MICHAEL SWEENEY
Auditors: PricewaterhouseCoopers

LOCATIONS

HQ: Bank of Ireland (Ireland)
40 Mespil Road, Dublin 4
Phone:
Web: www.bankofireland.com

HISTORICAL FINANCIALS

Company Type: Public

Income Statement FYE: December 31

	ASSETS ($ mil.)	NET INCOME ($ mil.)	INCOME AS % OF ASSETS	EMPLOYEES
12/14	157,772	955	0.6%	11,086
12/13	181,917	(670)	—	11,255
12/12	195,263	(2,404)	—	12,016
12/11	200,329	58	0.0%	13,671
12/10	224,141	(821)	—	14,284
Annual Growth	(8.4%)	—	—	(6.1%)

2014 Year-End Financials

Return on assets: 0.6%
Return on equity: 9.4%
Long-term debt ($ mil.): —
No. of shares (mil.): —
Sales ($ mil): 7,970
Dividends
Yield: —
Payout: —
Market value ($ mil.): —

	STOCK PRICE ($) FY Close	P/E High/Low	PER SHARE ($) Earnings	Dividends	Book Value
12/14	15.22	952610	0.02	0.00	0.33
12/13	14.41	— —	(0.03)	0.00	0.34
12/12	6.50	— —	(0.09)	0.00	0.38
12/11	4.24	— —	(0.01)	0.00	0.44
12/10	2.65	— —	(0.29)	0.00	1.87
Annual Growth	54.8%	— —	—	—	(35.2%)

Bank of Kyoto, Ltd. (Japan)

For financial services in Kyoto proper protocol might involve a visit to The Bank of Kyoto. The regional bank serves Kyoto and neighboring prefectures through some 165 branch offices. The bank serves businesses particularly small and medium-sized local companies as well as individual consumers. In addition to traditional deposit banking and lending The Bank of Kyoto and its subsidiaries offer credit cards leasing stock brokerage and business consulting services. The bank has worked to expand its operations beyond its home base and has opened branches to the north in the Kinki Region. Founded in 1941 the bank has about $81 billion in assets and ranks as Kyoto Prefecture's largest retail bank.

Geographic Reach

The Bank of Kyoto operates 110 branches in Kyoto Prefecture 28 in Osaka Prefecture a dozen in Shiga eight in Hyogo and seven branches in Nara.

Strategy

The Bank of Kyoto is aggressively opening branches to expand its reach beyond Kyoto Prefecture. Since opening its first branch at Kusatsu in Shiga Prefecture in 2000 the bank has opened branches in five neighboring prefectures (Kyoto Osaka Shiga Nara and Hyogo).

EXECUTIVES

President, Nobuhiro Doi
Auditors: Deloitte Touche Tohmatsu LLC

LOCATIONS

HQ: Bank of Kyoto, Ltd. (Japan)
700 Yamashimae-cho, Karasuma-dori Matsubara-Agaru, Shimogyo-ku, Kyoto 600-8652
Phone: (81) 75 361 2211 **Fax:** (81) 75 343 1276
Web: www.kyotobank.co.jp

COMPETITORS

Mitsubishi UFJ Financial Group
Mizuho Financial
Resona
Sumitomo Mitsui

HISTORICAL FINANCIALS

Company Type: Public

Income Statement FYE: March 31

	ASSETS ($ mil.)	NET INCOME ($ mil.)	INCOME AS % OF ASSETS	EMPLOYEES
03/15	68,806	177	0.3%	3,569
03/14	76,476	162	0.2%	3,566
03/13	81,057	186	0.2%	3,570
03/12	89,714	189	0.2%	3,545
03/11	87,986	221	0.3%	3,485
Annual Growth	(6.0%)	(5.5%)	—	0.6%

2015 Year-End Financials

Return on assets: 0.2%
Return on equity: 3.4%
Long-term debt ($ mil.): —
No. of shares (mil.): 377
Sales ($ mil): 958
Dividends
Yield: —
Payout: —
Market value ($ mil.): —

	STOCK PRICE ($) FY Close	P/E High/Low	PER SHARE ($) Earnings	Dividends	Book Value
03/15	0.00	— —	0.47	0.00	15.35
03/14	0.00	— —	0.43	0.00	13.99
Annual Growth	—	— —	2.2%	—	2.3%

Bank of Montreal

Auditors: KPMG LLP

LOCATIONS

HQ: Bank of Montreal
129 rue Saint-Jacques, Montreal, Quebec H2Y 1L6
Phone: 416 867-6785 **Fax:** 416 867-6793
Web: www.bmo.com

HISTORICAL FINANCIALS

Company Type: Public

Income Statement FYE: October 31

	ASSETS ($ mil.)	NET INCOME ($ mil.)	INCOME AS % OF ASSETS	EMPLOYEES
10/15	487,793	3,320	0.7%	47,000
10/14	526,078	3,822	0.7%	47,000
10/13	513,702	3,999	0.8%	45,500
10/12	526,880	4,126	0.8%	46,000
10/11	502,570	3,053	0.6%	47,000
Annual Growth	(0.7%)	2.1%	—	0.0%

2015 Year-End Financials

Return on assets: 0.7%
Return on equity: 11.8%
Long-term debt ($ mil.): —
No. of shares (mil.): 642
Sales ($ mil): 18,074
Dividends
Yield: 0.0%
Payout: 49.3%
Market value ($ mil.): 37,328

	STOCK PRICE ($) FY Close	P/E High/Low	PER SHARE ($) Earnings	Dividends	Book Value
10/15	58.09	10 8	4.99	2.46	46.62
10/14	72.60	12 9	5.73	2.79	47.25
10/13	69.70	11 9	5.99	2.88	45.14
10/12	59.12	10 9	6.17	2.83	44.16
10/11	59.17	13 11	4.86	2.88	41.41
Annual Growth	(0.5%)	— —	0.7%	(3.8%)	3.0%

Bank of Nova Scotia Halifax

The last place to look for The Bank of Nova Scotia's headquarters is in Nova Scotia. Although the company (aka Scotiabank) was founded in that province in 1832 it moved to Toronto in 1900. One of Canada's Big Five banks (along with Royal Bank of Canada TD Bank Bank of Montreal and CIBC) Scotiabank provides retail corporate and investment banking services around the world. In addition to about 1000 domestic branches Scotiabank has approximately 1700 offices in more than 50 other countries mainly in the Caribbean and Central and South America. Services include deposit accounts loans insurance brokerage asset management mutual funds and trust services.

While its domestic competitors have been expanding in the US Scotiabank has been focused mainly on making inroads in the Caribbean Latin America and Asia. The bank plans growth in Mexico the Caribbean and South America in addition to its home market. As it looks outward for growth Scotiabank has benefitted from a strong Canadian dollar bolstered by the nation's natural resources sector. The company reported record net income for fiscal 2010.

In 2012 the company rebranded its Scotia Capital Scotia Waterous and ScotiaMocotta investment banking units as Scotiabank in an effort to solidify its brand. The firms became part of Scotiabank's Global Banking and Markets division which offers such services as securities underwriting and mergers and acquisitions advice to corporate clients.

Later that year Scotiabank acquired US-based Howard Weil a boutique investment bank focused on the energy sector. The company built its investment banking practice in South America through the 2010 acquisitions of Dresdner Bank Brazil from Germany's Commerzbank and Royal Bank of Scotland's wholesale banking operations in Colombia.

Domestically Scotiabank wants to be the dominant money manager. As part of its strategy it announced a consolidated wealth management arm in 2009: Scotia Asset Management which includes ScotiaFunds ScotiaMcLeod and Scotia Cassels Investment Counsel. The year before Scotiabank acquired a large minority stake of fund manager CI Financial from Sun Life Financial. In a similar move the company acquired Dundee Corporation's stake in DundeeWealth for some $2.3 billion in 2011. The acquisition gave Scotiabank control of another one of Canada's largest wealth managers.

In 2012 Scotiabank agreed to buy ING Bank of Canada from Dutch group ING for C$3.1 billion. ING Bank of Canada operating as ING Direct primarily serves its clients via the Internet and has marketed itself as an alternative to big banks. Scotiabank plans to continue to run ING Direct as a standalone bank. (ING Groep has been selling off parts of its business as it tries to gain capital strength.)

The company also expanded its wealth management segment with the 2010 acquisition of the money management operations of BNP Paribas in the Bahamas the Cayman Islands and Panama and an agreement to purchase The WaterStreet Group which caters to ultra-high-net-worth clients. Scotiabank is also growing its wealth management business by offering new investment products.

Increasing its focus on insurance as well Scotiabank in 2009 rebranded its ScotiaLife Financial business which offers credit travel life and health coverage. It has also built up its online brokerage capabilities acquiring TradeFreedom Securities in 2007 and E*TRADE Canada from E*TRADE in 2008. Other areas of focus for Scotiabank include mobile banking and global foreign exchange.

Beyond Canada the company owns interests in banks in Chile (Scotiabank Chile formerly Banco del Desarrollo) Mexico (Scotiabank Inverlat) and Central America (Scotiabank El Salvador and Groupo BNS de Costa Rica). In 2010 Scotiabank bought Royal Bank of Scotland's Chilean business and its wholesale banking operations in Colombia making it the only Canadian-owned institution with a presence in the latter country. More expansion in the Caribbean was achieved when Scotiabank acquired R&G Financial's troubled R-G Premier Bank of Puerto Rico. The transaction which was assisted by the FDIC added nearly 30 branches to Scotiabank's network on the island.

Scotiabank expanded in Peru one of South America's fastest-growing economies with its 2006 acquisition of some 80% of Banco Wiese Sudameris (now Scotiabank Peru) from Italian banking group Banca Intesa (now Intesa Sanpaolo) which held on to the rest. It also holds an interest in Peru-based pension-fund manager AFP ProFuturo. Scotiabank entered Uruguay for the first time in 2010 by buying controlling stakes in private bank Nuevo Banco Comercial and consumer lender Pronto. Further expanding in Latin America during 2011 the company acquired wholesale bank Dresdner Bank Brasil (now Scotiabank Brasil) and a majority stake in Colombia-based retail bank Banco Colpatria. In 2012 it announced plans to buy a majority of Colfondos a Colombian pension fund firm with more than $9 billion in assets under management.

Building its position in the Asia-Pacific region Scotiabank in 2009 increased its stake in Thailand's Thanachart Bank to 49% the Thai limit for foreign ownership. The next year Thanachart acquired Siam City Bank making it Thailand's fifth-largest bank. Scotiabank also upped its stake in China's Xi'an City Commercial Bank to almost 15% and arranged to acquire nearly 20% of the state-run Chinese institution Bank of Guangzhou.

EXECUTIVES

EVP General Counsel and Secretary, Deborah M. Alexander
President and CEO, Brian J. Porter, $450,000 total compensation
Group Head and CEO Global Banking and Markets, Dieter W. Jentsch
EVP and Chief Administration Officer Global Banking and Markets, Anne Marie O'Donovan
EVP Information Technology and Solutions, Kimberlee B. (Kim) McKenzie
EVP and CFO, Sean McGuckin
EVP Retail Products and Services Canadian Banking, Robin S. Hibberd
EVP Personal and Commercial Banking Canada, Anatol von Hahn
Chief Risk Officer, Stephen P. Hart
EVP and Group Treasurer, Jeffrey C. (Jeff) Heath
EVP and Chief Administrative Officer International Banking, Marianne Hasold-Schilter
EVP Retail Distribution Canadian Banking, James McPhedran
EVP Global Financial Institutions and Transaction Banking, Marian Lawson
EVP and Chief Market Risk Officer, Andrew Branion
EVP and Chief Credit Officer, Terry Fryett
EVP Global Wealth Management, James O'Sullivan
Group Head International Banking, Ignacio (Nacho) Deschamps
Auditors: KPMG LLP

LOCATIONS

HQ: Bank of Nova Scotia Halifax
1709 Hollis Street, Halifax, Nova Scotia B3J 1W1
Phone: 416 866-6161 **Fax:** 416 866-7767
Web: www.scotiabank.com

PRODUCTS/OPERATIONS

2013 Sales

	% of total
Interest	
Loans	58
Securities	3
Other	2
Noninterest	
Fee and Commission income	25
Trading revenues	4
Others	8
Total	**100**

Selected Canadian Subsidiaries

BNS Capital Trust
BNS Investment Inc.
Montreal Trust Company of Canada
Scotia Merchant Capital Corporation
Dundee Bank of Canada
Maple Trust Company
National Trustco Inc.
The Bank of Nova Scotia Trust Company
National Trust Company
RoyNat Inc.
Scotia Capital Inc.
1548489 Ontario Limited
Scotia iTrade Corp.
Scotia Asset Management L.P.
Scotia Capital Inc.
Scotia Dealer Advantage Inc.
Scotia Insurance Agency Inc.
Scotia Life Insurance Company
Scotia Mortgage Corporation
Scotia Securities Inc.
Scotiabank Capital Trust
Scotiabank Subordinated Notes Trust.
Scotiabank Tier 1 Trust

Selected International Subsidiaries

The Bank of Nova Scotia Berhad (Malaysia)
The Bank of Nova Scotia International Limited (Bahamas)
The Bank of Nova Scotia Asia Limited (Singapore)
The Bank of Nova Scotia Trust Company (Bahamas) Ltd.
Scotiabank & Trust (Cayman) Ltd. (Cayman Islands)
BNS (Colombia) Holdings Limited
Grupo BNS de Costa Rica S.A.
Scotia Insurance (Barbados) Limited
Scotiabank (Bahamas) Limited
Scotiabank (British Virgin Islands) Limited
Scotiabank Caribbean Treasury Limited (Bahamas)
Scotiabank (Hong Kong) Limited
Scotiabank (Ireland) Limited
Scotia Group Jamaica Limited (72%)
The Bank of Nova Scotia Jamaica Limited
Scotia DBG Investments Limited (77% Jamaica)
Grupo Financiero Scotiabank Inverlat S.A. de C.V. (97% Mexico)
Nova Scotia Inversiones Limitada (Chile)
Scotiabank Chile S.A.
Scotia Capital (USA) Inc.
Scotia Holdings (US) Inc.
The Bank of Nova Scotia Trust Company of New York
Scotiabanc Inc. (US)
Scotia International Limited (Bahamas)
Scotiabank Anguilla Limited
Scotiabank de Puerto Rico
Scotiabank El Salvador S.A.
Scotiabank Europe plc (UK)
Scotiabank Peru S.A.A.
Scotiabank Trinidad and Tobago Limited

COMPETITORS

BMO Financial Group
Banamex
Banco Santander Chile
Bank of America
Bicsa Panama
CIBC
Citigroup
HSBC Bank Canada
JPMorgan Chase
National Bank of Canada
RBC Financial Group
TD Bank

HISTORICAL FINANCIALS

Company Type: Public

Income Statement FYE: October 31

	ASSETS ($ mil.)	NET INCOME ($ mil.)	INCOME AS % OF ASSETS	EMPLOYEES
10/15	650,889	5,241	0.8%	89,000
10/14	720,015	6,180	0.9%	86,932
10/13	711,122	5,932	0.8%	83,000
10/12	669,863	6,039	0.9%	81,497
10/11	577,548	4,978	0.9%	75,362
Annual Growth	3.0%	1.3%	—	4.2%

2015 Year-End Financials

Return on assets: 0.8%
Return on equity: 13.8%
Long-term debt ($ mil.): —
No. of shares (mil.): 1,202
Sales ($ mil): 23,743
Dividends
Yield: 0.0%
Payout: 47.9%
Market value ($ mil.): 56,514

	STOCK PRICE ($) FY Close	P/E High/Low		PER SHARE ($) Earnings	Dividends	Book Value
10/15	46.98	9	7	4.31	2.07	32.86
10/14	61.30	12	9	5.06	2.35	35.19
10/13	60.77	12	10	4.92	2.34	35.32
10/12	54.38	11	9	5.23	2.18	33.56
10/11	52.61	13	11	4.64	2.06	30.20
Annual Growth	(2.8%)	—	—	(1.8%)	0.0%	2.1%

Bank of Yokohama, Ltd.

The Bank of Yokohama serves its native Kanagawa prefecture and southern portions of neighboring Tokyo. It offers standard retail banking services such as deposits housing loans credit cards securities brokerage and investment products and advice. The bank also provides small and medium-sized commercial financing including venture capital investment and boasts units that offer leasing and factoring. The Bank of Yokohama which was formed in 1920 and had total assets of ¥15 trillion (around $128 billion) in 2015 operates more than 610 Japanese branches. In late 2015 the bank agreed to merge with rival Higashi-Nippon Bank to create Japan's largest regional bank.

Change in Company TypeIn September 2015 Bank of Yokohama agreed to merge with smaller rival Higashi-Nippon Bank to create Japan's largest regional bank. With the deal scheduled to be completed by April 2016 the newly created Concordia Financial Group would have total assets of ¥17.3 trillion yen making it larger than

Fukuoka Financial Group Japan's current largest regional bank.OperationsThe Bank of Yokohama generated 41% of its revenue from interest on loans and other bills discounted in fiscal 2015 (ended March 31) while another 10% came from interest and dividends on securities interest on call loans and bills bought interest due from banks and other interest income. About 21% of its revenue came from fees and commission income while most of the rest came from gains on security trades and other kinds of trading income.Geographic ReachThe bank's 610 domestic branches are mainly in the cities of Kanagawa Tokyo Aichi Gunma and Osaka. It also has representative offices in Bangkok Hong Kong London New York and Shanghai.Financial PerformanceNote: Growth rates may differ after conversion to US dollars.The Bank of Yokohama has struggled to consistently grow its revenues in recent years due to shrinking interest margins on loans amidst the low-interest environment in Japan. Its profits however have been rising thanks to declining interest expenses and lower loan loss provisions as its loan portfolio's credit quality has improved with higher property valuations in the strengthened economy.The bank had a breakout year in fiscal 2015 (ended March 31) however as its revenue rose by nearly 7% to ¥318 billion ($2.66 billion) mostly thanks to larger gains on derivatives a bargain purchase (where an acquisition cost is lower than the net asset value) and other gains on investment sales and securities. Its interest on loans continued to decline though its fees and commissions income grew by more than 5% during the year.Higher revenue in FY2015 drove The Bank of Yokohama's net income higher by 26% to ¥76.3 billion ($640 million). The bank's operating cash levels more than doubled to ¥1331 billion ($11 billion) for the year mostly thanks to an increase in borrowed money (excluding subordinated borrowing) and an increase in call money and others.

Stategy

The Bank of Yokohama regularly partners with other financial corporations to expand its service offerings. During 2015 and 2014 its retail division strengthened its trust services in Japan after partnering with Asahi Trust in a move to cater to the country's aging population and asset succession needs. Capitalizing on similar opportunities The Bank of Yokohama also partnered with Sumitomo Mitsui Trust Bank in late 2014 to establish an asset management company; partnered with the Higashi-Nippon Bank to establish Concordia Financial Group; and made an equity investment in the Regional Health Care Industry Support Fund which supports businesses in Japan's medical and nursing sectors.The bank also has been pursuing overseas expansion through strategic partnerships and through broadening its service lines at its operations abroad. During 2015 for example it extended its financial service support to its customers in India through a strategic partnership with the State Bank of India. The Bank of Yokohama established a similar relationship with Metropolitan Bank and Trust Company (which owns Metrobank) to extend its financial service support to its customers in the Philippines. In late 2014 it strengthened its support capability in Asia by introducing RMB services at its Shanghai Branch and established a business alliance with the Joint Stock Commercial Bank for Investment and Development of Vietnam.

EXECUTIVES

Deputy President and Representative Director, Chiyuki Okubo
Managing Executive Officer and Director, Atsushi Mochizuki
President and Representative Director, Tatsumaro Terazawa
Managing Executive Officer and Representative Director, Kengo Takano
Managing Executive Officer and Director, Susumu Koshida
Managing Executive Officer, Shizumi Maesako
Managing Executive Officer, Yoshiyuki Hiranuma
Auditors: Deloitte Touche Tohmatsu LLC

LOCATIONS

HQ: Bank of Yokohama, Ltd.
3-1-1 Minatomirai, Nishi-ku, Yokohama, Kanagawa 220-8611
Phone: (81) 45 225 1111 **Fax:** (81) 45 225 1160
Web: www.boy.co.jp

PRODUCTS/OPERATIONS

2014 Sales

	% of total
Interest income	
Interest on loans & bills discounted	46
Interest & dividends on securities	8
Other interest income	2
Fees & commissions	21
Other operating income	18
Trading profits	1
Other income	4
Total	**100**

Selected Group Companies

BANKCARD Service Japan Co. Ltd.
Hamagin Business Operations Center Co. Ltd.
Hamagin Finance Co. Ltd.
Hamagin Mortgage Service Co. Ltd.
Hamagin Research Institute Ltd.
Hamagin Tokai Tokyo Securities Co. Ltd.
Yokohama Capital Co. Ltd.
Yokohama Guarantee Co. Ltd.
Yokohama Operation Service Co. Ltd.
Yokohama Staff Service Co. Ltd.

COMPETITORS

Mitsubishi UFJ Financial Group
Mizuho Financial
Norinchukin Bank
Sumitomo Mitsui
Suruga Bank
Tokyo Star Bank

HISTORICAL FINANCIALS

Company Type: Public

Income Statement

FYE: March 31

	ASSETS ($ mil.)	NET INCOME ($ mil.)	INCOME AS % OF ASSETS	EMPLOYEES
03/15	128,170	636	0.5%	4,815
03/14	134,006	587	0.4%	4,780
03/13	143,144	588	0.4%	4,751
03/12	156,066	624	0.4%	4,752
03/11	151,202	568	0.4%	4,768
Annual Growth	(4.0%)	2.8%	—	0.2%

2015 Year-End Financials

Return on assets: 0.5%
Return on equity: 8.3%
Long-term debt ($ mil.): —
No. of shares (mil.): 1,246
Sales ($ mil): 2,647
Dividends
Yield: 1.8%
Payout: —
Market value ($ mil.): 29,118

	STOCK PRICE ($) FY Close	P/E High/Low		PER SHARE ($) Earnings	Dividends	Book Value
03/15	23.37	—	—	0.50	0.44	6.76
03/14	19.90	—	—	0.45	0.45	6.97
03/13	23.18	—	—	0.44	0.00	7.27
03/12	19.90	—	—	0.46	0.00	7.54
03/11	47.80	—	—	0.42	0.46	6.99
Annual Growth	(16.4%)	—	—	4.8%	(1.0%)	(0.8%)

Bank Polska Kasa Opieki - Grupa Pekao S.A.

Bank Polska Kasa Opieki better known as Bank Pekao (from its initials P.K.O.) offers retail corporate and investment banking services primarily in Poland. It also provides leasing and asset management services. Branches can also be found in France and the Ukraine. In addition to traditional deposit products Bank Pekao offers loans leasing and factoring services custodial services currency exchange and foreign trade facilitation. Originally founded as a state-owned bank to provide banking services to Polish emigrants Bank Pekao is now controlled by Italian bank UniCredit which holds approximately 53% of its shares.

EXECUTIVES

Prezes Zarzadu, Luigi Lovaglio
Czlonek rady nadzorczej, Laura Penna
Czlonek rady nadzorczej, Doris Tomanek
Czlonek rady nadzorczej, Alessandro Decio
Auditors: Deloitte Polska Sp. z o.o.

LOCATIONS

HQ: Bank Polska Kasa Opieki - Grupa Pekao S.A.
53/57 Grzybowska Street, Warsaw 00-950
Phone: (48) 22 656 00 00 **Fax:** (48) 22 656 00 04
Web: www.pekao.com.pl

COMPETITORS

AIB
Bank BPH
Bank Millennium
Citi Handlowy
Nordea Bank
PKO Bank Polski SA
Provident Financial

HISTORICAL FINANCIALS

Company Type: Public

Income Statement

FYE: December 31

	ASSETS ($ mil.)	NET INCOME ($ mil.)	INCOME AS % OF ASSETS	EMPLOYEES
12/14	47,604	770	1.6%	18,765
12/13	52,578	923	1.8%	18,916
12/12	48,793	955	2.0%	19,816
12/11	42,541	841	2.0%	20,256
12/10	45,320	853	1.9%	20,783
Annual Growth	1.2%	(2.5%)	—	(2.5%)

2014 Year-End Financials

Return on assets: 1.6%
Return on equity: 11.4%
Long-term debt ($ mil.): —
No. of shares (mil.): 262
Sales ($ mil): 2,707
Dividends
Yield: —
Payout: 77.7%
Market value ($ mil.): —

	STOCK PRICE ($) FY Close	P/E High/Low		PER SHARE ($) Earnings	Dividends	Book Value
12/14	0.00	—	—	2.94	2.28	25.99
Annual Growth						

Bankinter, S.A.

Founded in 1965 as a joint venture between what is now Grupo Santander and Bank of America Bankinter is among the top six banks in Spain. The company offers a variety of consumer and business banking services through about 360 branch locations agents telephone services mobile banking and the Internet. A pioneer in Internet stock trading Bankinter conducts more than half of its transactions online. It serves corporations individuals and small enterprises. Bankinter provides mutual and pension funds mortgages leasing and securities brokerage focusing on convenient low-cost delivery and customer service. Investment firm Cartival S.A. owns about 23% of Bankinter.Although Bankinter has about 360 branches in Spain more than half of its transactions are conducted on the Internet. The bank has pioneered technologies to make its online services more accessible including making Web pages compatible with software used by the visually impaired.The bank is making a strong push to court the small and medium enterprise (SME) segment of the market. In recent years Bankinter launched dozens of new service centers catering to SMEs. The bank also continues to open other private banking and business management branches in fast-growing towns throughout the country.Bankinter announced in 2009 it will buy the 50% of auto insurer Linea Directa Aseguradora it already does not own from Royal Bank of Scotland. The proposed shift follows a change in control at Royal Bank which was taken over by the government in 2008.France's Credit Agricole owns about 20% of Bankinter. Through investment firm Cartival former Bankinter chairman Jaime Botín controls more than 15% of the bank's stock. The Botín family leads Grupo Santander which includes Spain's largest bank.

HISTORY

In 1962 Franco tried to end mixed banks in Spain with a decree that prevented banks from taking part in both commercial and investment operations. The banks circumvented this through cosmetic compliance spending the next decade nominally spinning off operations. In 1965 Banco Santander (now Grupo Santander) and Bank of America created Banco Intercontinental Espanol (Bankinter) in Madrid to specialize in industrial banking.

From 1970 to 1985 Bankinter evolved into a retail bank; it introduced credit cards personal loans and other services and offered financing to larger corporations. Bankinter was not consumed by the great branch race that defined banking-industry competition in Franco-era Spain; the bank had only 150 branches by 1985.

The bank became independent as both Bank of America (in 1987) and Santander (1994) reduced their stock holdings. Bankinter began diversifying its operations opening branches and gaining more clients. Bankinter's successful 1987 introduction of a high-interest special deposit account was dulled when other banks followed suit slowing growth. The bank took its current name in 1990 and in 1991 introduced some of Spain's first mutual funds. Within a recession-hammered economy Bankinter worked to cut costs through the introduction of telephone banking (1992) and other innovative conveniences.

Attracted by the low-cost liquidity of private banking Bankinter entered that segment in 1995. It took a step in the allfinanz direction that year creating an auto and home insurance alliance with Royal Bank of Scotland subsidiary Direct Line; the UK bank already had insurance ventures with Bankinter sibling Santander. Two years later Bankinter began BKNet Spain's first online stock-trading service.

In 1998 the bank opened a Mexican office to explore the possibility of transferring its high-tech operations into that country. As the financial industry's global consolidation continued the bank in 1999 said it was seeking a foreign ally possibly one that could help expand Bankinter's online technology.

The bank found willing partners later that year inking deals to form an Internet bank in Spain with a joint venture of US Web portal Lycos (now part of Terra Networks) and German media giant Bertelsmann as well as another Internet bank with Portugal's Banco Espirito Santo.

Although Bankinter recorded 2004 as a particularly profitable year with income up nearly 25% it also suffered the death of a deputy manager Jos Garcia in the March 11 terrorist attacks against Madrid.

In 2007 the bank sold 50% of its life insurance division to Spanish insurer Mapfre. The sale boosted Bankinter's capital.

In 2008 Credit Agricole increased its ownership in the bank to about 20%. It became the bank's largest shareholder edging out former chairman Jaime Botín.

EXECUTIVES

CEO, Maria Dolores Dancausa Trevino
Chairman, Pedro Guerrero Guerrero
Auditors: Deloitte, S.L. (member of Deloitte & Touche Tohmatsu)

LOCATIONS

HQ: Bankinter, S.A.
Paseo de la Castellana, 29, Madrid 28046
Phone: (34) 91 339 75 00 **Fax:** (34) 91 339 83 23
Web: www.bankinter.es

PRODUCTS/OPERATIONS

2014 Sales

	% of total
Interest and similar income	54
Fee and commission income	14
Other revenues	32
Total	**100**

Selected Subsidiaries

Aircraft S.A.
Bankinter Consultoria Asesoramiento y Atencion Telefonica S.A.
Bankinter Gestion de Seguros S.A.
Bankinter International B.V. (Netherlands)
Bankinter Seguros de Vida S.A.
Gesbankinter S.A.
Hispamarket S.A.
Intergestora S.A.
Intergestora Nuevas Tecnologias S.C.R. S.A.
Intermobiliaria S.A.

COMPETITORS

AEGON
BBVA
Banco Espa±ol de Cr©dito
Banco Popular Espa±ol
Banco de Sabadell
Deutsche Bank
Esprito Santo
Grupo Santander
La Caixa

HISTORICAL FINANCIALS

Company Type: Public

Income Statement

FYE: December 31

	ASSETS ($ mil.)	NET INCOME ($ mil.)	INCOME AS % OF ASSETS	EMPLOYEES
12/14	69,688	335	0.5%	3,953
12/13	75,907	296	0.4%	3,820
12/12	76,665	164	0.2%	3,853
12/11	76,949	234	0.3%	3,904
12/10	72,475	201	0.3%	4,740
Annual Growth	(1.0%)	13.5%	—	(4.4%)

2014 Year-End Financials

Return on assets: 0.4%
Return on equity: 7.8%
Long-term debt ($ mil.): —
No. of shares (mil.): 898
Sales ($ mil): 3,169
Dividends
Yield: 1.3%
Payout: 19.8%
Market value ($ mil.): 7,074

	STOCK PRICE ($) FY Close	P/E High/Low	PER SHARE ($) Earnings	Dividends	Book Value
12/14	7.87	29 19	0.38	0.11	4.93
12/13	6.50	34 12	0.37	0.08	5.23
12/12	4.35	30 12	0.30	0.14	7.55
12/11	6.01	19 12	0.45	0.12	8.37
12/10	5.30	31 17	0.43	0.26	7.29
Annual Growth	10.4%	—	—	(3.2%)	(20.0%) (9.3%)

Banque Cantonale Vaudoise

Banque Cantonale Vaudoise (BCV) provides a variety of financial services primarily to customers in the canton of Vaud in southwestern Switzerland. With about 70 retail locations it offers commercial corporate and private banking services as well as wealth management and securities brokerage. The bank is dedicated to the canton's development and in fact does business with some two-thirds of Vaud's small and midsized enterprises. The Vaud government owns more than half of BCV which was originally founded in 1845.

EXECUTIVES

ManagingDirector, Pascal Kiener
Chairman Of The Board, Olivier Steimer
Vice Chairman Of The Board, Stephan Bachmann
Board Member, Ingrid Deltenre
Board Member, Reto Donatsch
Board Member, Pierre Lamuni¨re
Board Member, Luc Recordon
Board Member, Paul Andr ©Sanglard
Auditors: PricewaterhouseCoopers Ltd

LOCATIONS

HQ: Banque Cantonale Vaudoise
Place Saint-Francois 14, P.O. Box 300, Lausanne 1001
Phone: (41) 21 212 10 10 **Fax:** (41) 21 212 12 22
Web: www.bcv.ch

COMPETITORS

Bank Sarasin
Credit Suisse
HSBC Private Bank
Merrill Lynch Bank (Suisse)
Swiss Post
UBS

HISTORICAL FINANCIALS

Company Type: Public

Income Statement FYE: December 31

	ASSETS ($ mil.)	NET INCOME ($ mil.)	INCOME AS % OF ASSETS	EMPLOYEES
12/14	42,527	299	0.7%	1,946
12/13	45,400	314	0.7%	1,987
12/12	43,416	339	0.8%	1,931
12/11	40,288	321	0.8%	2,042
12/10	38,026	334	0.9%	1,986
Annual Growth	2.8%	(2.8%)	—	(0.5%)

2014 Year-End Financials

Return on assets: 0.7%
Return on equity: 8.8%
Long-term debt ($ mil.): —
No. of shares (mil.): 8
Sales ($ mil): 1,273
Dividends
Yield: —
Payout: —
Market value ($ mil.): —

Banque Federative du Credit Mutuel (France)

National commercial banks nsk

EXECUTIVES

Pr ©sident Directeur G ©n ©ral, Etienne PFLIMLIN
Auditors: ERNST & YOUNG et Autres

LOCATIONS

HQ: Banque Federative du Credit Mutuel (France)
34 rue du Wacken, B.P. 412, Strasbourg, Cedex 67000
Phone: (33) 3 88 14 88 14 **Fax:** (33) 3 88 14 67 00
Web: www.bfcm.creditmutuel.fr

HISTORICAL FINANCIALS

Company Type: Public

Income Statement FYE: December 31

	REVENUE ($ mil.)	NET INCOME ($ mil.)	NET PROFIT MARGIN	EMPLOYEES
12/14	37,780	1,682	4.5%	42,366
12/13	40,123	1,667	4.2%	39,686
12/12	39,298	1,225	3.1%	40,258
12/11	34,870	1,056	3.0%	40,223
12/10	40,544	1,880	4.6%	37,707
Annual Growth	(1.7%)	(2.7%)	—	3.0%

2014 Year-End Financials

Debt ratio: —
Return on equity: 8.3%
Cash ($ mil.): 28,371
Current ratio: —
Long-term debt ($ mil.): —
No. of shares (mil.): 31
Dividends
Yield: —
Payout: —
Market value ($ mil.): —

Banque Nationale de Belgique (National Bank of Belgium)

No prizes for guessing the role of the Nationale Bank van Belgi «. NBB is indeed the national central bank for Belgium and a member of the European System of Central Banks (ESCB). Founded in 1850 the institution performs a variety of functions aimed at maintaining stability and liquidity for Belgium's banks and financial markets including arranging fund transfers between banks overseeing settlement activities for securities markets and issuing banknotes and coins. The bank's chief executive known as its governor is appointed by the Belgian monarch. NBB is also known by its names in French (Banque nationale de Belgique) English (National Bank of Belgium) and German (Belgische Nationalbank).

The bank carries out various other functions within Belgium's financial system. As the nation's lender of last resort NBB is also able to provide emergency funds when times of exceptional financial crisis. It did as much in 2008 with the cross-national bailout of Fortis. NBB has also printed currency notes (and distributed coins struck by Belgium's Royal Mint) since 1851.

EXECUTIVES

Manager Director, Fran $ise Masai
Manager Director, Norbert De Baetselier
Manager Director, peter Praet
Manager Director, Marcia De Wachter
Manager Director, Jean Hilgers
Auditors: Ernst & Young R ©iseurs dâ ™Entreprises sccrl/?Ernst &

LOCATIONS

HQ: Banque Nationale de Belgique (National Bank of Belgium)
Boulevard de Berlaimont 14, Brussels BE-1000
Phone: (32) 2 221 21 11 **Fax:** (32) 2 221 31 00
Web: www.nbb.be

COMPETITORS

Bank of England
Deutsche Bundesbank
Federal Reserve
Swiss National Bank

HISTORICAL FINANCIALS

Company Type: Public

Income Statement FYE: December 31

	ASSETS ($ mil.)	NET INCOME ($ mil.)	INCOME AS % OF ASSETS	EMPLOYEES
12/14	91,800	826	0.9%	2,265
12/13	107,110	1,303	1.2%	2,301
12/12	144,660	1,762	1.2%	2,103
12/11	165,193	1,162	0.7%	2,101
12/10	99,973	1,113	1.1%	2,065
Annual Growth	(2.1%)	(7.2%)	—	2.3%

	STOCK PRICE ($) FY Close	P/E High/Low	PER SHARE ($) Earnings	Dividends	Book Value
12/14	4,588.76	— —	(0.00)	0.00	16,908.51
12/13	3,857.57	— —	(0.00)	0.00	19,257.07
12/12	2,975.00	— —	(0.00)	0.00	18,613.61
12/11	2,600.00	— —	(0.00)	0.00	16,122.66
12/10	4,900.00	— —	(0.00)	0.00	15,756.78
Annual Growth	(1.6%)	—	—	—	1.8%

Baoshan Iron & Steel Co Ltd

Blast furnaces and steel mills nsk
Auditors: Deloitte Touche Tohmatsu Certified Public Accountants Limited

LOCATIONS

HQ: Baoshan Iron & Steel Co Ltd
Baosteel Command Center, No. 885, Fujin Road, Baoshan District, Shanghai 201900
Phone: (86) 21 26647000 **Fax:** (86) 21 26646999
Web: www.baosteel.com/plc/

HISTORICAL FINANCIALS

Company Type: Public

Income Statement FYE: December 31

	REVENUE ($ mil.)	NET INCOME ($ mil.)	NET PROFIT MARGIN	EMPLOYEES
12/14	30,257	933	3.1%	0
12/13	31,389	961	3.1%	0
12/12	30,719	1,666	5.4%	32,598
12/11	35,405	1,169	3.3%	41,919
12/10	30,707	1,955	6.4%	42,308
Annual Growth	(0.4%)	(16.9%)	—	—

2014 Year-End Financials

Debt ratio: 3.1%
Return on equity: 5.1%
Cash ($ mil.): 1,950
Current ratio: 0.83
Long-term debt ($ mil.): 2,088
No. of shares (mil.): —
Dividends
Yield: —
Payout: —
Market value ($ mil.): —

Barclays Africa Group Ltd

Can Absa help with your banking needs in Africa? Absa-lutely! Serving nearly 12 million consumers small businesses and commercial clients the company's Absa Bank is one of the largest retail banks and mortgage lenders in South Africa with about 700 branches and 9000 ATMs most of them in that country. The bank and other subsidiaries offer deposits loans credit cards insurance investments financial planning brokerage wealth management and investment banking services. British bank Barclays owns about 55% of Absa Group making it one of South Africa's largest foreign investors since apartheid ended in 1994.

Beyond South Africa Absa Group owns some 80% of Barclays Bank Mozambique and a majority of National Bank of Commerce in Tanzania. The company which also has representative offices in Namibia and Nigeria is taking steps to broaden its presence in its existing markets and the surrounding region. It acquired Global Alliance Seguros a Mozambique-based life and property/casualty insurer in 2011. Absa Group launched an insurance unit in Botswana that year as well.

In 2008 Absa Group acquired controlling interests in Meeg Bank and Woolworths Holdings' financial services operations further strengthening its presence in South Africa. The moves came after Absa Group canceled plans to buy Barclays' retail operations in Zimbabwe Zambia Kenya Botswana Ghana Tanzania the Seychelles and Mauritius. Additional acquisitions are expected.

The traditionally consumer-focused company is also making efforts to attract more commercial clients. During 2010 it established a corporate bank and invested in a transactional banking platform for commercial clients. Meanwhile the company is not ignoring consumers however as it retooled its retail franchise to focus more on value rather than volume. Absa Group has also used technology to simplify processes streamline customer service and improve access to banking.

Maria Ramos was named CEO of Absa Group in 2009 after former chief executive Steve Booysen retired after 20 years with the company.

EXECUTIVES

Group Chief Executive and Director, Maria Ramos, age 56
Finance Director and Board Member, David W. P. Hodnett, age 45
COO, N. Alfie Naidoo, age 47
Chief Executive Absa Capital, Stephen van Coller, age 49
Chief Executive Absa Africa, John Gachora
Auditors: PricewaterhouseCoopers Inc.

LOCATIONS

HQ: Barclays Africa Group Ltd
7th Floor, Absa Towers West, 15 Troye Street, Johannesburg 2001
Phone: (27) 11 350 4000
Web: www.barclaysafrica.com

PRODUCTS/OPERATIONS

2010 Sales

	% of total
Interest & similar income	68
Net fee & commission income	21
Net insurance premium income	6
Gains from banking & trading activities	3
Other	2
Total	**100**

COMPETITORS

FirstRand
Nedcor
Sanlam
Standard Bank Group
Standard Chartered

HISTORICAL FINANCIALS

Company Type: Public

Income Statement FYE: December 31

	ASSETS ($ mil.)	NET INCOME ($ mil.)	INCOME AS % OF ASSETS	EMPLOYEES
12/14	85,820	1,144	1.3%	41,644
12/13	91,102	1,137	1.2%	46,320
12/12	94,899	985	1.0%	0
12/11	97,146	1,194	1.2%	39,659
12/10	107,841	1,221	1.1%	43,239
Annual Growth	(5.6%)	(1.6%)	—	(0.9%)

2014 Year-End Financials

Return on assets: 1.3%
Return on equity: 16.5%
Long-term debt ($ mil.): —
No. of shares (mil.): 846
Sales ($ mil): 8,659
Dividends
Yield: —
Payout: 55.8%
Market value ($ mil.): —

Barclays Bank Plc

Barclays Bank is the flagship subsidiary of global financial group Barclays PLC. The bank is primarily active in the UK where it has some 1700 branches but also has significant retail and commercial operations in Europe Africa (it owns more than half of South African bank Absa Group) the Middle East and the US. Barclays Bank offers standard retail services such as deposit accounts and lending including Woolwich-brand mortgages. The bank also provides commercial money transfer services insurance products the Barclaycard line of credit cards and financial advisory services. Barclays Bank traces its roots to the late 17th century.

Barclays Bank has been building up its portfolio of global credit card accounts especially as other financial groups sell off noncore units during the economic recovery. In 2010 the company acquired the Italian credit card accounts of Citigroup in a deal that included some 197000 card accounts and approximately 234 million ($320 million) worth of assets. It previously bought Goldfish the struggling UK credit card unit of Discover Financial Services for some £46 million ($70 million). In 2011 Barclays acquired Egg UK's credit card portfolio which added more than 1 million accounts; it has agreed to buy more Citibank card accounts.

The bank has also been offloading some of its own holdings as part of an overall corporate restructuring. In 2010 Barclays sold its US subprime loan servicing business HomEq Servicing to Ocwen Financial. It also announced plans to abandon retail banking in certain international markets and instead focus on wholesale and commercial banking. In 2011 it shuttered its Indonesian retail unit Bank Akita which it had acquired only two years before. The company also sold its Russian retail and commercial operations to a group of investors citing difficulties competing in the market. Barclays will instead focus on its investment banking activities in the region.

In 2010 Barclays acquired Standard Life Bank from Standard Life for £226 million ($369 million). The deal added Standard Life's savings and mortgage books to the Barclays fold. Also as part of the deal Barclays and Standard Life entered into a partnership whereby Barclays markets pension products to its clients.

Despite challenges in the economy especially in regards to Europe's debt problems Barclays Bank's revenues grew 8% in 2011. Its Africa business performed relatively strongly with credit impairments improving as did Barclaycard thanks to the portfolio acquisitions which delivered profits. That year the bank closed nearly 150 European branches (largely located in Spain) the costs of which contributed to a 5% decline in net income.

EXECUTIVES

CEO Barclaycard, Valerie (Val) Soranno-Keating
CEO Retail and Business Banking, Ashok Vaswani
Co-Head of Corporate Banking Origination, Kevin Wall
CEO, John Winter
Co-Head of London region and Head of Retail and Wholesale, Richard Lowe
Head of Agribusiness, Tim Seeley
CEO Africa Regional Management, Mizinga Melu
Chief Risk Officer, Barry Cole
Head of International Business, Carole Machell
Co-Head of Corporate Banking Origination, Alan Turner
Co-Head of UK & Ireland and Head of South region, Gavin Isle
Co-Head of UK & Ireland and Head of Northern region, Tony Walsh
Co-Head of London Region, Michael (Mike) Daniels
Head of Northern Ireland, Adrian Doran
Head of Eastern Region, Jane Galvin
Head of Midlands and Wales, Ray O'Donoghue
Head of Scotland and Northern Ireland, Ally Scott
Head of Corporate Banking International and Financial Institutions Group, Matt Tuck
Head of Global Corporates, David Farrow
Managing Director and Head of Coverage Corporate Banking Iberia, Andr ©Baltar
Managing Director Head of Coverage Corporate & Investment Banking division Barclays Bank PLC India, Pushkaraj Gumaste
Managing Director Co-Head of Corporate Banking Origination Asia, Silas Lee
Managing Director Head of Corporate Banking Origination Americas and Co-Head of Global Corporates Americas, Keith Mackie
Managing Director Co-Head of Corporate Banking Origination Asia and Head of Financial Institutions Asia Pacific, Gwynne Master
Head of Corporate Banking UAE & GCC, Rezwan Mirza
Head of Corporate Banking Origination Italy, Federico Morvillo
Head of Corporate Banking Barclays Africa Group, Temi Ofong
Managing Director Head of Corporate Banking Origination Northern Europe, Jacques Sourbier
Head of Business Services, Nicki Thomson
Head of Banks Financial Institutions Group, David Scola
Head of Insurance & Financial Intermediaries, Carl Boulton
Head of Healthcare and Public Sector, Paul Birley
Head of Hospitality and Leisure, Mike Saul
Head of Manufacturing Transport and Logistics, Mike Rigby
Head of Natural Resources & UK Multinationals, Daniel Firth
Head of London Real Estate, Gregor Bamert
Head of Technology Media and Telecoms, Sean Duffy
Head of Cash Management, Michael Mueller
Head of Debt Finance, Karl Nolson
Head of Trade & Working Capital, Dan Roberts
Head of Risk Solutions and Group Products, Rhian-Mari Thomas
Head of Specialist Sectors, Dennis Watson
CEO Ireland, Sasha Wiggins
Chairman, David A. Walker, age 70
Deputy Chairman, Michael D. V. (Mike) Rake, age 67
Auditors: PricewaterhouseCoopers LLP

Barclays PLC

LOCATIONS

HQ: Barclays Bank Plc
1 Churchill Place, London E14 5HP
Phone: (44) 20 7116 1000
Web: www.barclays.com

2014 Sales

	% of total
UK	48
Americas	22
Africa & Middle East	16
Europe	11
Asia	3
Total	**100**

PRODUCTS/OPERATIONS

2014 Sales

	% of total
Barclays Core	
Personal and corporate banking	35
Investment banking	29
Barclaycard	17
Africa Banking	14
Head office	1
Barclays Non-Core	4
Total	**100**

2014 Sales

	% of total
Interest	53
Fees & commissions	30
Net trading income	10
Net investment income	4
Net insurance premiums & other	3
Total	**100**

COMPETITORS

Citibank
Credit Suisse
Deutsche Bank
HSBC
ING
Lloyds Banking Group
Nationwide Building Society
Royal Bank of Scotland
Standard Chartered

HISTORICAL FINANCIALS

Company Type: Public

Income Statement

FYE: December 31

	ASSETS ($ mil.)	NET INCOME ($ mil.)	INCOME AS % OF ASSETS	EMPLOYEES
12/14	2,120,950	824	0.0%	132,300
12/13	2,169,572	1,591	0.1%	139,600
12/12	2,402,885	(1,165)	—	139,200
12/11	2,415,227	5,586	0.2%	141,100
12/10	2,313,492	6,477	0.3%	147,500
Annual Growth	(2.1%)	(40.3%)	—	(2.7%)

2014 Year-End Financials

Return on assets: 0.0%
Return on equity: 0.8%
Long-term debt ($ mil.): —
No. of shares (mil.): —
Sales ($ mil): 50,378
Dividends
Yield: —
Payout: —
Market value ($ mil.): —

	STOCK PRICE ($) FY Close	P/E High/Low	PER SHARE ($) Earnings	Dividends	Book Value
12/14	31.51	— —	(0.00)	0.00	42.51
12/13	42.55	— —	(0.00)	0.00	43.04
12/12	31.81	— —	(0.00)	0.00	41.31
12/11	35.53	— —	(0.00)	0.00	40.95
12/10	37.61	— —	(0.00)	0.00	39.23
Annual Growth	(4.3%)	— —	—	—	2.0%

Raising the bar for global finance Barclays owns one of Europe's largest banks a top market-making investment bank the top UK credit card and an international wealth management firm. Its flagship Barclays Bank has some 1500 branches in the UK as well as operations throughout Europe Africa the Middle East and the Americas. In addition to holding one of the world's largest investment banks the company's Barclaycard arm has more than 20 million credit cards and provides consumer lending and payment processing services primarily in Europe. Altogether Barclays serves more than 48 million customers in more than 50 countries.

OperationsBarclays PLC is the holding company of Barclays Bank Plc. In May 2014 Barclays Bank reorganized its operations into four main core divisions. The company's Personal and Corporate Banking (PCB) business generates nearly 35% of Barclays' revenue and consists of the company's personal banking corporate banking and wealth and investment management businesses.Barclays' Investment Bank division brings in another 30% of revenue and offers financial advisory capital raising financing and risk management services to corporations and institutions as well as governments around the world. It also has a markets business within the segment which provides investment and risk management services as well as a research arm that provides economic and market research to its clients.The company's credit card and consumer-lending payments service provider business Barclaycard (which includes US division Barclays Bank Delaware) brings in nearly 20% of revenue. Barclays' Africa Banking division (which includes the South African bank Absa) makes up nearly 15% of revenue and includes the retail cards wealth corporate and investment banking operations in Africa. Geographic ReachThrough its network of 7000 branches worldwide the company serves some 48 million customers in more than 50 countries. Nearly 50% of revenue is generated in the UK while another more than 20% comes from the US. The Africa and Middle East account for more than 15% of revenue while Europe brings in more than 10%.Sales and MarketingBarclays targets its marketing toward individuals small and medium businesses and corporate and institutional clients. The company spent $558 million on marketing in 2014 down from $583 million in 2013 and $572 million in 2012.Financial PerformanceNote: Growth rates may differ after conversion to US dollars.Barclay Bank's revenue has generally trended downward in recent years. Revenue in 2014 fell by double digits to £32.71 billion (about $50.13 billion) mostly due to a decline in the Investment Bank division's debt underwriting fees and cash commission income as volumes declined. Geographically revenue fell mostly in the Asia and European markets (falling by 40% and 28% respectively) while revenue grew by 6% in the UK. Profit fell for a second year with after-tax profit falling by 35% to £845 million ($1.31 billion) in 2014 mostly due to losses from recently sold subsidiaries associates and joint ventures (related to the announced disposal of the bank's Spanish operations).Operations used $16.22 billion or less than half as much cash as in 2013 thanks to an inflow of cash from reverse repurchase agreements and other liabilities.

Stategy

Enduring years of declining revenues in recent years following the last market crash Barclays has been selling many of its non-core businesses cutting costs through branch closures and workforce reductions and restructuring its credit market exposures. In early 2015 Barclays sold its Spanish retail and corporate banking operations to CaixaBank as it worked on a major restructuring and shrinking some of its struggling European divisions.

The company's Barclaycard division has been growing in recent years as the global economy improves. In 2014 the division gained 3.6 million new customers and enjoyed £18.5 billion ($28.7 billion) worth of new and renewed lending to households in all regions. Barclaycard continues to focus on next-generation payment technology in the UK South Africa and in the US with the goal of helping its customers adopt new digital platforms to pay using "tap and go" cards contactless stickers and smart phones.

Legal troubles have caused headwinds for Barclays's bottom line in recent years. In mid-2012 the company admitted to manipulating the London Interbank Offered Rate (LIBOR) a benchmark for daily global short-term interest rates. The bank repeatedly manipulated the LIBOR in order to make its funding position look stronger than it actually was; the rigging also helped the bank make money on credit derivatives. Chairman Martin Agius and CEO Bob Diamond both resigned as a result of the developments and the company paid US and UK regulators some £290 million ($453 million) in settlement fines. Shortly after the LIBOR scandal the UK's Serious Fraud Office launched an inquiry into payments Barclays made to sovereign investor Qatar Holding in 2008. That same year investment fund Qatar Investment Authority became the bank's largest shareholder with a 5% stake. Investigations for both the bid-rigging and bribery allegations continue.

HISTORY

Barclays first spread its wings in 1736 when James Barclay united his family's goldsmithing and banking businesses. As other family members joined the London enterprise it became known as Barclays Bevan & Tritton (1782).

Banking first became regulated in the 19th century. To ward off takeovers 20 banks combined with Barclays in 1896. The new firm Barclay & Co. began preying on other banks. Within 20 years it bought 17 including the Colonial Bank chartered in 1836 to serve the West Indies and British Guiana (now Guyana). The company renamed Barclays Bank Ltd. in 1917 weathered the Depression as the UK's #2 bank.

Barclays began expanding again after WWII and by the late 1950s it had become the UK's top bank. It had a computer network by 1959 and in 1966 it introduced the Barclaycard in conjunction with Bank of America's BankAmericard (now Visa).

In 1968 the UK's Monopolies Commission barred Barclays' merger with two other big London banks but had no objections to a two-way merger so Barclays bought competitor Martins.

Barclays moved into the US consumer finance market in 1980 when it bought American Credit 138 former Beneficial Finance offices and Bankers Trust's branch network.

During the 1980s London banks faced competition from invading overseas banks local building societies and other financial firms. Banking reform in 1984 led to formation of a holding company for Barclays Bank PLC.

To prepare for British financial deregulation in 1986 Barclays formed Barclays de Zoete Wedd (BZW) by merging its merchant bank with two other London financial firms. Faced with sagging profits Barclays sold its California bank in 1988 and its US consumer finance business in 1989.

In 1990 Barclays bought private German bank Merck Finck & Co. and Paris bank L'Europenne de Banque. The company countered 1992's bad-loan-induced losses by accelerating a cost-cutting program begun in 1989. To appease stockholders chairman and CEO Andrew Buxton (a descendant of one of the bank's founding families) gave up his CEO title hiring Martin Taylor (previously CEO of textile firm Courtaulds) for the post.

The company sold its Australian retail banking business in 1994 then began trimming other operations including French corporate banking and US mortgage operations. However it bought the Wells Fargo Nikko Investment Company to boost Asian operations.

Barclays' piecemeal sale of BZW signaled its failure to become a global investment banking powerhouse. In 1997 it sold BZW's European investment banking business to Credit Suisse First Boston retaining the fixed-income and foreign exchange business. (Credit Suisse bought Barclays' Asian investment banking operations in 1998.)

Losses in Russia and a $250 million bailout of US hedge fund Long-Term Capital Management hit Barclays Capital in 1998. Taylor resigned that year in part because of his radical plans for the bank. Sir Peter Middleton stepped in as acting CEO; Barclays later tapped Canadian banker Matthew Barrett for the post. (Middleton also became chairman upon Buxton's retirement.)

Barclays in 1999 started a move toward online banking at the expense of traditional branches. The company announced free lifetime Internet access for new bank customers.

In 2000 the bank ruffled feathers when it announced the closure of about 170 mostly rural UK branches. Also in 2000 the company sold its Dial auto leasing unit to ABN AMRO and bought Woolwich plc. The following year Barclay's closed its own life insurance division opting instead to sell the life insurance and pension products of London-based Legal & General Group.

In 2004 chief executive Barrett was named Barclays' chairman succeeding Peter Middleton who became chairman of Centre for Effective Dispute Resolution (CEDR) and later chancellor of the University of Sheffield.

After exiting the South African market in 1987 over apartheid concerns Barclays returned in a big way in 2005 buying a majority stake (about 57%) in the Absa Group one of the country's largest retail banks. The deal also represented the largest-ever direct foreign investment there. The next year Barclays sold its South African businesses including corporate international retail and commercial operations to Absa.

The company entered the US credit card market when it bought Juniper Financial (now Barclays Bank Delaware) from Canadian Imperial Bank of Commerce (CIBC) in 2004. In a previous hook-up with CIBC Barclays merged its Caribbean banking business with CIBC's to create an 85-branch regional bank FirstCaribbean International Bank with each company owning 44%; Barclays sold its stake to CIBC in 2006.

In 2005 the bank sold its vendor finance businesses in the UK and Germany to CIT Group. Barclays said that the sale will allow it to focus on its commercial leasing business.

The bank moved to assimilate its Woolwich acquisition in 2006 when it closed 200 branches and consolidated Woolwich branches into existing Barclays locations. It retained the Woolwich mortgage brand but switched account holders to Barclays accounts.

The company and HSBC formed a joint venture that manages their cash handling operations in the UK. Named Vaultex the joint venture acquired Loomis Cash Management in 2007.

Marcus Agius succeeded the retiring Matthew Barrett as chairman in 2007.

Although the company withdrew its bid for Dutch banking giant ABN AMRO (narrowly escaping that troubled deal) in 2008 it bought Russian bank Expobank from Petropavlovsk Finance. Expobank was one of the largest ATM networks in Russia and part of the booming consumer banking industry there. Also that year Barclays sold noncore business Barclays Life and its portfolio of some 760000 life and pension policies to Swiss Re for £753 million ($1.5 billion).

The group chose not to participate in the UK's bank bailouts as the global financial crisis intensified in late 2008 but pursued its own capital-raising plan. Through the deal sovereign investment fund Qatar Investment Authority became the bank's largest shareholder with a 5% stake.

In 2009 it shut down US-based subprime mortgage lender EquiFirst which it had purchased from Regions Financial before it fell victim to the mortgage bust.

Later that year it sold a majority of Barclays Global Investors to American money manager BlackRock for £9.5 billion ($15 billion). In exchange it gained a 20% stake in the new BlackRock with some $3 trillion under management for institutional clients around the world. The deal provided the bank with much-needed cash and cleared the way for a commercial partnership with BlackRock.

Another major transaction was the £1 billion ($1.8 billion) acquisition of Lehman Brothers' North American operations a deal which made Barclays Capital one of the world's largest investment banks.

EXECUTIVES

Group CEO and Director, James E. (Jes) Staley, age 58
CEO Wealth and Investment Management, Akshaya Bhargava
CEO Investment Bank, Thomas (Tom) King
CEO Personal and Corporate Banking, Ashok Vaswani
Group Chief Risk Officer, Robert Le Blanc, age 58
Group Head of Compliance, Michael E. Roemer, age 53
Chief Operations and Technology Officer, Michael R. Harte
Chairman EMEA Banking, Makram Azar
CEO Barclays Africa Group, Maria Ramos, age 56
Interim CEO Barclaycard, Amer Sajed
Group Finance Director, Tushar Morzaria
Managing Director and Head Equity Sales Trading Hong Kong, Daniel Miller
Group General Counsel, Bob Hoyt
Group Human Resources Director, Irene McDermott Brown
Head of Banking Hong Kong; Chairman Global Finance Asia Pacific, John Pratt
CEO Barclays Germany, Alexander Doll
Head Global Finance and Risk Solutions, John Langley
Executive Chairman, John McFarlane, age 68
Auditors: PricewaterhouseCoopers LLP

LOCATIONS

HQ: Barclays PLC
1 Churchill Place, London E14 5HP
Phone: (44) 20 7116 1000
Web: www.barclays.com

2014 Sales

	% of total
UK	48
Americas	22
Africa & Middle East	16
Europe	11
Asia	3
Total	**100**

PRODUCTS/OPERATIONS

2014 Sales

	% of total
Interest income	53
Fee and Commission income	30
Net trading income	10
Net investment income	4
Net premiums from insurance contracts	2
Other income	1
Total	**100**

2014 Sales

	% of total
Barclays Core	
Personal and corporate banking	35
Investment banking	29
Barclaycard	17
Africa Banking	14
Head office	1
Barclays Non-Core	4
Total	**100**

COMPETITORS

AXA UK
Bank of New York Mellon
CIBC
Citigroup
Deutsche Bank
Grupo Santander
HSBC
Invesco
JPMorgan Chase
Lloyds Banking Group
Mitsubishi UFJ Financial Group
Mizuho Financial
RBC Financial Group
Royal Bank of Scotland
Standard Chartered
The Vanguard Group
UBS

HISTORICAL FINANCIALS

Company Type: Public

Income Statement

FYE: December 31

	ASSETS ($ mil.)	NET INCOME ($ mil.)	INCOME AS % OF ASSETS	EMPLOYEES
12/14	2,119,722	118	0.0%	132,300
12/13	2,168,625	892	0.0%	140,300
12/12	2,402,198	(1,677)	—	143,700
12/11	2,415,420	4,645	0.2%	141,100
12/10	2,312,882	5,533	0.2%	147,500
Annual Growth	(2.2%)	(61.7%)	—	(2.7%)

2014 Year-End Financials

Return on assets: 0.0%
Return on equity: 0.1%
Long-term debt ($ mil.): —
No. of shares (mil.): —
Sales ($ mil): 50,386
Dividends
Yield: 2.7%
Payout: —
Market value ($ mil.): —

	STOCK PRICE ($) FY Close	P/E High/Low	PER SHARE ($) Earnings	Dividends	Book Value
12/14	15.01	— —	(0.01)	0.42	5.64
12/13	18.13	572435	0.06	0.40	5.68
12/12	17.32	— —	(0.14)	0.38	7.06
12/11	10.99	83 34	0.37	0.34	7.04
12/10	16.52	78 53	0.44	0.27	6.48
Annual Growth	(2.4%)	— —	—	11.1%	(3.4%)

BASF SE

The world is BASF's ester. BASF is the world's largest chemical company ahead of Dow and DuPont. It has more than 370 manufacturing facilities and does business worldwide through six business segments: plastics (polymers and polyurethanes) performance products (including dispersions and pigments adhesives and sealants personal care and pharma additives paper chemicals and lubricant additives) chemicals (plasticizers and solvents) oil and gas exploration and production (through subsidiary Wintershall AG) functional solutions (catalysts coatings and construction chemicals) and agricultural products (fungicides herbicides insecticides). BASF has divested most of its fertilizer operations.

BASF uses what it calls Verbund strategy throughout its facilities –plants are both customers and suppliers of each other. While the company still gets more than half its sales from Europe it continues to expand overseas particularly in Asia. It saw early on that the chemicals market in Asia would be the equal of that in Europe and wanted a healthy piece of the action. With a new unit based in the US it has begun positioning itself to become a leading supplier of battery materials for automotive battery applications –including cathode materials used to produce advanced lithium-ion batteries for electric vehicles.

In 2011 several events affected the growth of the company including the nuclear diaster in Japan Germany's decision to exit nuclear energy the suspension of crude oil in Libya and the debt crisis in Europe. Weak demand and an increase in the cost of raw materals also plagued BASF's two top divisions plastics and chemicals.

However BASF managed to surpass the record levels it set in 2010 in sales and earnings. After cutting costs and raising prices the company posted $98.7 billion in sales in 2011 up nearly 17% over the previous year as well as a net income of $8.3 billion up nearly 38%. But most of the increase was due to the sale of its 10% stake in K+S AG which began its exit from the fertilizer business. By 2012 BASF had sold most of its fertilizer operations including production plants in Antwerp Belgium and its share of the PEC-Rhin joint venture in France to Russia's EuroChem in a deal worth about $1.1 billion.

The company initiated several projects in 2011 including the startup of the first leg of the Nord Stream offshore gas pipeline that will eventually extend from Russia to Germany. Wintershall is involved in constructing the Nord Stream and South Stream gas pipelines to connect gas from Russia to Europe.

It also strengthened its presence in Asia that year by beginning the second expansion of its petrochemical site in Nanjing China with 50-50 joint venture partner Sinopec. And it founded BASF Hock Mining Chemical (China) Company with JiNing Hock Mining & Engineering Equipment Company. BASF holds a 75% stake in BASF Hock which makes cavity-filling products for the coal mining industry.

Much of the company's expansion has targeted the US market as well. In early 2012 the company halted its cultivation and development of genetically modified (GM) plants in Europe. Heavy resistance from European consumers farmers and politicians resulted in the company moving its plant science division from Limburgerhof Germany to Raleigh North Carolina. Some of its products for the European market included its Amflora starch potato for industrial use developed to be resistant to blight disease.

That year the company also strengthened its global crop protection operations by buying US-based Becker Underwood for $1.02 billion. The Iowa-based company provides biological seed treatment worldwide from 10 production sites. The BASF Crop Protection division plans to create Functional Crop Care a global business unit that will merge existing R&D and marketing activities in seed treatment crop protection and plant health with those of Becker Underwood.

BASF has also been collaborating with US-based Monsanto in the research and development of crops that have higher yields and better resistance to disease. For its GM products BASF focuses on markets in the Americas and Asia. It has not completely closed the door on Europe; it is still seeking authorizations to sell its potato products there.

In early 2012 BASF began a new global business unit Battery Materials to integrate its battery materials activities within an operating unit of New Jersey-based subsidiary BASF Catalysts. In moves to become a global leader in the supply of battery materials the company has made a series of acquisitions and licensing agreements to broaden its coverage of technology materials and components to serve cell and battery manufacturers worldwide. It has been licensed by the Argonne National Laboratory in Illinois to commercialize some of its advanced cathode materials used in hybrid and full-electric vehicles.

Adding to its battery operations again in 2012 BASF acquired Cleveland-based Novolyte Technologies from private equity group Arsenal Capital Partners for an undisclosed price. Novolyte manufactures electrolyte formulations for lithium-ion batteries and other specialty chemicals. It operates sites in the US and China. BASF will continue Novolyte's joint venture with Korean company Foosung which produces lithium hexafluorophospate a high-purity specialty salt used in producing lithium-iron battery electrolytes. The electrolytes are key components in lithium-ion batteries for the automotive consumer and industrial markets.

To expand its leadership position in polyurethane systems the company acquired US-based ITWC in 2012. ITWC manufactures cast elastomer polyurethane systems and polyester polyols in facilities in Iowa and California. The acquisition extends BASF's North American polyurethanes operations. Cast elastomers known for their abrasion resistance are used in several applications including industrial tires recreational wheels transportation gears and pulleys and sealants and adhesives.

The company's venture capital unit also poured $18.2 million into US-based renewable specialty chemicals company Allylix in 2012. Allylix owns a technology platform for developing terpenes and other chemicals for flavor and fragrance food ingredients cosmetics and other markets.

To expand its Nutrition and Health division in 2012 BASF acquired Equatec a UK-based supplier of omega-3 fatty acids for the pharmaceutical industry for an undisclosed price. Equatec which has a production site on the Isle of Lewis in Scotland will become part of BASF's Pharma Ingredients and Services unit.

BASF acquired inge watertechnologies a Germany-based provider of ultrafiltration membrane technology used to treat drinking water process water wastewater and seawater in 2011. The deal improves BASF's position in the water treatment industry and fits within its growth strategy for its chemicals and membrane filtration business.

After shelving previous efforts to exit the business in 2011 BASF formed a styrenics joint venture with INEOS called Styrolution. The venture produces styrene monomers polystyrene acrylonitrile butadiene styrene styrene-butadiene block copolymers and other styrene-based copolymers and copolymer blends. Styrolution is projected to have annual sales of $6.6 billion.

HISTORY

Originally named Badische Anilin & Soda-Fabrik BASF AG was founded in Mannheim Germany by jeweler Frederick Englehorn in 1861. Unable to find enough land for expansion in Mannheim BASF moved to nearby Ludwigshafen in 1865. The company was a pioneer in coal tar dyes and it developed a synthetic indigo in 1897. Its synthetic dyes rapidly replaced more expensive organic dyes.

BASF scientist Fritz Haber synthesized ammonia in 1909 giving BASF access to the market for nitrogenous fertilizer (1913). Haber received a Nobel Prize in 1918 but was later charged with war crimes for his work with poison gases. Managed by Carl Bosch another Nobel Prize winner BASF joined the I.G. Farben cartel with Bayer Hoechst and others in 1925 to create a German chemical colossus. Within the cartel BASF developed polystyrene PVC and magnetic tape. Part of the Nazi war machine I.G. Farben made synthetic rubber and used labor from the Auschwitz concentration camp during WWII.

After the war I.G. Farben was dismantled. BASF regained its independence in 1952 and rebuilt its war-ravaged factories. Strong postwar domestic demand for basic chemicals aided its recovery and in 1958 BASF launched a US joint venture with Dow Chemical. (BASF bought out Dow's half in 1978.) The company moved into petrochemicals and became a leading manufacturer of plastic and synthetic fiber.

In the US the company purchased Wyandotte Chemicals (1969) Chemetron (1979) and Inmont (1985) among others. To expand its natural gas business in Europe in 1991 the company signed deals with Russia's Gazprom and France's Elf Aquitaine. BASF bought Mobil's polystyrene-resin business and gained almost 10% of the US market.

BASF bought Imperial Chemical's polypropylene business in 1994 and became Europe's second-largest producer of the plastic. The next year the company paid $1.4 billion for the pharmaceutical arm of UK retailer Boots.

In 1997 BASF formed a joint venture with PetroFina (now TOTAL); in 2001 the venture opened the world's largest liquid steam cracker in Port Arthur Texas.

BASF made seven major acquisitions in 1998 including the complexing business of Ciba Specialty Chemicals. It also made six divestitures which included its European buildings-paints operations sold to Nobel N.V.

In 1999 the US fined the company $225 million for its part in a worldwide vitamin price-fixing cartel (in 2001 the European Commission fined it another $260 million bringing the total expected cost of fines out-of-court settlements and legal expenses to about $800 million). BASF also faced a class-action suit as a result of the scheme. That year the company moved into oil and gas exploration in Russia through a partnership agreement with Russia's Gazprom. BASF also merged its textile operations into Bayer and Hoechst's DyStar joint venture forming a $1 billion company that is a world-leading dye maker.

BASF completed its acquisition of Rohm and Haas' industrial coatings business in 2000 and bought the Cyanamid division (herbicides fungicides and pesticides) of American Home Products (now Wyeth). That year BASF expanded its superabsorbents business by paying $656 million for US-based Amcol International's Chemdal International unit.

Rather than attempt to compete in the rapidly consolidating pharmaceutical industry in 2001 BASF sold its midsized Knoll Pharmaceutical unit to Abbott Laboratories for about $6.9 billion. It also announced that it was closing 10 plants and cutting about 4000 jobs (4% of its workforce).

BASF sold its fibers unit in 2003 to focus on core chemical operations which it added to throughout the next few years. For example it bought a portion of Bayer's agchem businesses for $1.3 billion when European antitrust regulators mandated the Bayer divestment following its acquisition of Aventis CropScience. BASF also acquired Honeywell Specialty Materials' engineering plastics business in exchange for its fibers division. BASF's acquisition later that year of MSA's Callery Chemical Division strengthened BASF's line of inorganics which it planned to focus on providing to the pharmaceutical industry. Other acquisitions included Ticona's nylon 66 business and Sunoco's plasticizers unit.

That year also brought chairman J rgen Hambrecht's announcement that the company would push forward with a restructuring of its North American business. The focus of the plan was to save more than $250 million over the next three years. Included among the steps were job cuts of approximately 1000 and the relocation of its North American headquarters (though remaining in New Jersey) in late 2004. (The move to smaller facilities was enabled by the sale of Knoll Pharmaceuticals in 2001 which reduced operations at the home base.)

BASF sold Basell its petrochemical JV with Shell in 2005. The two companies had announced in 2004 that they planned to exit the polyolefins business with the sale of Basell. The deal was finalized late the next year. Investment group Access Industries came in with the winning bid of about $5.7 billion. That company's name was changed to LyondellBasell after its 2007 acquisition of Lyondell Chemical Company.

The company opened two Verbund sites in Asia —one in Nanjing China and the other in Kuantan Malaysia. The Chinese site delivered its first product in early 2005 and began operating fully in the middle of that year. It's the centerpiece and primary operation of BASF-YPC a joint venture with Sinopec that was formed in 2000. BASF's goal is to achieve 70% of its sales in the region from local production by 2015; that figure hovered at about 60% in 2008.

The company also legally changed its name from BASF Aktiengesellschaft to BASF SE in 2008. The move made formal BASF's transition to a European company as opposed to one organized in Germany.

In 2009 BASF spent about $4 billion to acquire Swiss chemicals giant Ciba. Following a review phase of Ciba's operations and their fit within the structure of BASF the company began integrating Ciba into its performance products segment; this entailed the sale or closure of almost half of Ciba's 55 manufacturing facilities and the loss of about 3700 of its employees. As part of that strategy BASF SE sold the Regulatory and Safety Testing businesses of Ciba's Expert Services unit to London-based Intertek Group in 2010.

Also in 2010 BASF acquired specialty chemicals company Cognis GmbH in a $3.8 billion deal. Cognis gave BASF a boost in entering several high-margin business lines such as personal care and cosmetics.

EXECUTIVES

CFO, Hans-Ulrich Engel, age 57, $555 total compensation
Chairman, Kurt W. Bock, age 58, $1,200 total compensation
President Advanced Materials and Systems Research, Harald Lauke, age 56
President Care Chemicals division, Hans W. Reiners
Division Head Dispersions and Pigments Care Chemicals Nutrition and Health Paper Chemicals Performance Chemicals; Member Executive Board, Michael Heinz, age 52
President Market and Business Development North America, Teressa Szelest
President Bioscience Research, Peter Eckes
President Nutrition and Health Division, Saori Dubourg, age 44
President Paper Chemicals, Uwe Liebelt, age 49
General Manager BASF Shanghai Coatings Co. Ltd., Thierry Herning
Head BASF 's Animal Nutrition, Christopher Rieker
President Performance Chemicals division, Christian Fischer
President Intermediates Division Ludwigshafen, Stefan Blank
Head BASF New Business, Guido Voit
Head Greater China Asia Pacific ASEAN South and East Asia; Member Board of Executive Directors, Sanjeev Gandhi, age 49
Division Head Intermediates Monomers Petrochemicals and Process Research and Chemical Engineering, Wayne T. Smith, age 55
President Oil and Gas; Head of Wintershall, Mario Mehren
Vice Chairman, Michael Diekmann, age 61
Chairman, J rgen Hambrecht, age 69
Vice Chairman, Robert Oswald, age 60
Vice Chairman, Martin Brudermuller, age 54
Auditors: KPMG AG

LOCATIONS

HQ: BASF SE
Carl-Bosch-Strasse 38, Ludwigshafen D-67056
Phone: (49) 621 60 0 **Fax:** (49) 621 602525
Web: www.basf.com

2011 Sales by Region

	% of total
Europe	
Germany	39
Other countries	17
North America	20
Asia/Pacific	18
South America/Africa/Middle East	6
Total	**100**

PRODUCTS/OPERATIONS

2011 Sales

	% of total
Performance Products	21
Chemicals	18
Oil & Gas	16
Functional Solutions	15
Plastics	15
Agricultural Solutions	6
Other	9
Total	**100**

Selected Products

Oil and Gas
- Crude oil and natural gas exploration
- Natural gas distribution and trading

Chemicals
- Inorganics
- Ammonia
- Formaldehyde
- Melamine
- Sulfuric acid
- Urea
- Intermediates
- Performance chemicals
- Water-based resins
- Petrochemicals
- Feedstocks
- Industrial gases
- Plasticizers
- Specialty chemicals

Plastics
- Engineering plastics
- Foams
- Polyamides and intermediates
- Polyurethanes
- Styrenics

Functional Solutions
- Catalysts
- Battery materials
- Chemical catalysts
- Coatings
- Automotive coatings
- Decorative paints
- Industrial coatings
- Pigments
- Construction chemicals

Performance Products
- Automotive fluids
- Care chemicals
- Paper chemicals
- Pharma ingredients
- Textile chemicals

Agricultural Solutions
- Crop protection
- Fungicides
- Herbicides
- Insecticides

COMPETITORS

3M
Air Products
Akzo Nobel
Albemarle
Ashland Inc.
BP
Bayer AG
Cargill
DSM
Dow Chemical
DuPont
Eastman Chemical
Evonik Degussa
Exxon Mobil
FMC
Formosa Plastics
Henkel
LANXESS
LG Group
Monsanto Company
Royal Dutch Shell
SABIC
TOTAL
Taminco

HISTORICAL FINANCIALS

Company Type: Public

Income Statement

FYE: December 31

	REVENUE ($ mil.)	NET INCOME ($ mil.)	NET PROFIT MARGIN	EMPLOYEES
12/14	90,343	6,265	6.9%	113,292
12/13	101,841	6,666	6.5%	112,206
12/12	103,768	6,430	6.2%	113,262
12/11	95,064	8,003	8.4%	111,141
12/10	85,485	6,098	7.1%	109,140
Annual Growth	1.4%	0.7%	—	0.9%

2014 Year-End Financials

Debt ratio: 6.0%
Return on equity: 18.8%
Cash ($ mil.): 2,088
Current ratio: 1.73
Long-term debt ($ mil.): —
No. of shares (mil.): 918
Dividends
Yield: 3.2%
Payout: —
Market value ($ mil.): 76,592

	STOCK PRICE ($) FY Close	P/E High/Low	PER SHARE ($) Earnings	Dividends	Book Value
12/14	83.39	19 14	6.81	2.72	36.54
12/13	107.79	21 17	7.26	2.47	40.64
12/12	95.00	18 13	7.00	2.41	35.27
12/11	69.73	13 8	8.70	0.00	33.99
12/10	79.96	17 11	6.64	1.62	31.19
Annual Growth	1.1%	— —	0.6%	13.9%	4.0%

Bayer AG

You could get a headache trying to name all of Bayer's products. The company which created aspirin in 1897 makes pharmaceuticals OTC drugs and animal health care products through Bayer HealthCare plastics and high-performance specialty materials via Covestro and crop protection and home garden care items through Bayer Crop-

Science. Aside from Bayer Aspirin the company's best-known consumer brands include Aleve Alka-Seltzer and One-A-Day vitamins. Its top selling pharmaceuticals include multiple sclerosis treatment Betaseron and birth control pill YAZ. Also known as Bayer Group the firm has some 300 operating subsidiaries worldwide; it operates in the US through Bayer Corporation.

Operations

The global HealthCare segment comprises pharmaceuticals and consumer health. Pharmaceuticals focuses on prescription products especially for women's health care and cardiology and on specialty therapeutics in the area of oncology hematology and opthamology. The consumer health business includes consumer care medical care and animal health (both livestock and pets). Consumer health focuses primarily on non-prescription medicines supplements and dermatology products while medical care includes the radiology business unit. HealthCare accounted for about half of Bayer's revenue in 2014.

The CropScience segment does business in seeds crop protection and non-agricultural pest control. Its two segments crop protection/seeds and environmental science together accounted for 22% of revenue in 2014.

Covestro (formerly MaterialScience) develops makes and markets high-tech polymer materials and specialty chemicals; it also makes inorganic base chemicals. Its operating units are polyurethanes polycarbonates and coatings adhesives and specialties. It accounted for 30% of revenue in 2014.

Geographic Reach

The majority of Bayer's sales come from European countries (roughly 40% of revenues) and North America (about 25% of sales) and most of the company's core manufacturing facilities are in Germany and the US. The company also has operations Latin America Africa and the Middle East.

The Bayer Group comprises about 300 consolidated companies operating in 75 countries around the world.

Sales and Marketing

Bayer markets over 5000 products through a global sales and distribution network. Offerings from its largest division the HealthCare segment are distributed primarily through wholesalers hospitals and pharmacy chains while CropScience products are sold through wholesalers and regional distributors.

Financial Performance

The company has generally seen steady growth due to organic measures. Revenue increased 5% to 42.3 billion in 2014 due to growth across all segments. Pharmaceuticals grew 28% that year with the help of launches of products including Xarelto Eylea Stivarga Xofigo and Adempas. CropScience sales rose 11.2% due to increased sales of Crop Protection products.

Net income also rose in 2014 growing 7% to 3.4 billion thanks to the higher revenue. Higher profits led to a 12% increase in operating cash flow to 5.8 billion.

Strategy

Bayer is growing all three of its core businesses by enhancing its strong positions in key markets as well as by expanding into emerging geographic areas and investing in innovative technologies. Within its HealthCare division which accounts for just about half of its annual sales the company's growth strategy includes making targeted acquisitions entering into licensing and development deals with other pharmaceutical companies and performing in-house research and development. To counteract the effect of weakened sales in Europe and North America the HealthCare Pharmaceuticals segment is working to expand drug marketing efforts in China Brazil Mexico Russia and other high-growth markets.

The company received European approval for its Eylea solution to treat patients with visual impairments in 2014.

As revenue from the company's health care business has grown it has made moves to focus its efforts there. To that end in 2014 Bayer announced it would spin off Bayer MaterialScience (now operating as Covestro) in an IPO. It also sold the interventional device business to Boston Scientific and in 2013 sold its global powder polyester resins business Stepan Company for 45 million.

In early 2016 Bayer sold its diabetes devices unit to Panasonic Healthcare for about 1 billion; the sale marked its exit from the business which had been lagging due to aging products and price pressures.

Mergers and Acquisitions

Acquisitions in the health arena include the company's 2014 purchase of Merck's consumer care business which brought well-known brands including Claritin MiraLAX Coppertone and Dr. Scholl's under the Bayer umbrella. The company paid about $14.2 billion for the deal and moved into second place globally among OTC companies between a Novartis- GlaxoSmithKline joint venture and Johnson & Johnson.

Bayer also bought dermatology product specialist Dihon Pharmaceutical Group in China and former cancer drug Xofigo partner Algeta in Norway. CropScience purchases included Argentina's Biagro group (organic seed treatments and crop protection products) and the seed business of Paraguayan firm Granar. Altogether the company spent 13.5 billion on acquisitions during 2014.

HISTORY

Friedrich Bayer founded Bayer in Germany in 1863 to make synthetic dyes. Research led to such discoveries as Antinonin (synthetic pesticide 1892) aspirin (1897) and synthetic rubber (1915).

Under Carl Duisberg Bayer allegedly made the first poison gas used by Germany in WWI. During the war the US seized Bayer's US operations and trademark rights and sold them to Sterling Drug.

In 1925 Bayer BASF Hoechst and other German chemical concerns merged to form I.G. Farben Trust. Their photography businesses combined as Agfa also joined the trust. Between wars Bayer developed polyurethanes and the first sulfa drug Prontosil (1935).

During WWII the trust took over chemical plants of Nazi-occupied countries used slave labor and helped make Zyklon B gas used to kill people at Auschwitz. At war's end Bayer lost its 50% of Winthrop Laboratories (US) and Bayer of Canada (to Sterling Drug). The 1945 Potsdam Agreement called for the breakup of I.G. Farben and Bayer AG emerged in 1951 as an independent company with many of its original operations including Agfa.

After rebuilding in West Germany Bayer AG and Monsanto formed a joint venture (Mobay 1954); Bayer AG later bought Monsanto's share (1967). In the 1960s the company offered more dyes plastics and polyurethanes and added factories worldwide. Agfa merged with Gevaert (photography Belgium) in 1964; Bayer AG retained 60%. Over the next 25 years it acquired Miles Labs (Alka-Seltzer US 1978) the rest of Agfa-Gevaert (1981) Compugraphic (electronic imaging US 1989) and Nova's Polysar (rubber Canada 1990).

Bayer AG integrated its US holdings under the name Miles in 1992 (renamed Bayer Corporation in 1995). The next year it introduced its first genetically engineered product Kogenate hemophilia treatment. It regained US rights to the Bayer brand and logo in 1994 by paying SmithKline Beecham $1 billion for the North American business of Sterling Winthrop.

EXECUTIVES

Chairman Board of Management, Marijn E. Dekkers, age 58

Member Management Board Innovation Technology and Environment and Asia/Pacific, Wolfgang Plischke, age 64, $448,000 total compensation

CEO Bayer CropScience, Sandra E. Peterson, age 57

Member Management Board Strategy and Human Resources and Americas Africa and Middle East, Richard Pott, age 62, $448,000 total compensation

President and CEO Bayer MaterialScience LLC, Gregory S. (Greg) Babe, age 58

CEO Bayer MaterialScience, Patrick W. Thomas, age 58

CFO and Member Board of Management, Werner Baumann, age 53

Chairman Bayer Business Services, Daniel Hartert

CEO Bayer HealthCare, J ¶g Reinhardt, age 59

Managing Director Bayer Technology Services, Dirk Van Meirvenne, age 52

Head Pharmaceuticals Division, Dieter Weinand

Chairman Supervisory Board, Manfred Schneider, age 77

Vice Chairman Supervisory Board, Oliver Z hlke, age 47

Auditors: PricewaterhouseCoopers Aktiengesellschaft Wirtschaftspruefungsgesellschaft

LOCATIONS

HQ: Bayer AG
Kaiser-Wilhelm Allee, Leverkusen D-51368
Phone: (49) 214 30 1 **Fax:** (49) 214 30 71985
Web: www.bayer.com

2014 Sales

	% of total
Europe	37
North America	24
Asia/Pacific	22
Latin America/Africa/Middle East	17
Total	**100**

PRODUCTS/OPERATIONS

2014 Sales

	% of total
Health Care	
Pharmaceuticals	28
Consumer Health	19
MaterialScience	28
CropScience	22
Other	3
Total	**100**

Selected Operations and Products

HealthCare
- Animal health products
- Diabetes care products
- Consumer care products (over-the-counter drugs)
- Pharmaceuticals

MaterialScience
- Coatings
- Colorants
- Plastics
- Polyurethanes

CropScience
- BioScience (biotechnology and seeds)
- Crop protection (insecticides and herbicides)
- Environmental science (lawn care and non-agricultural pesticides)

Selected Brands

HealthCare
- Adalat (cardiovascular medication)
- Advantage (animal health)
- Aleve/Flanax (analgesic)
- Alka-Seltzer (analgesic and antacid)
- Aspirin (analgesic)

Aspirin Cardio (cardiovascular)
Avalox/Avelox (antibiotic)
Bepanthen/Bepanthol (skin care treatment)
Betaferon/Betaseron (multiple sclerosis medication)
Baytril (animal health infections)
Breeze/Contour (diabetes care glucose meters)
Canesten (antifungal)
Cipro/Ciprobay (antibiotic)
Glucobay (diabetes treatment)
Iopamiron (diagnostic imaging)
Kogenate (hematology/cardiology)
Levitra (impotence drug)
Magnevist (diagnostic imaging)
Mirena (contraceptive)
Nexavar (oncology)
One-A-Day (vitamins)
Supradyn (multivitamin)
Ultravist (diagnostic imaging)
Yasmin/Yasminelle/YAZ (contraceptive)

MaterialScience
Baydur/Bayflex/Bayblend (polyurethane)
Desmodur/Desmophen (isocyanates polyesters and polyols for polyurethanes)
Makrolon (polycarbonate resin)

CropScience
Betanal (herbicides)
Confidor/Gaucho/Admire/Merit (insecticides/seed treatment)
Decis (insecticides)
Flint/Stratego/Sphere/Nativo (fungicides)
Folicur/Raxil (fungicides/seed treatment)
Poncho (seed treatment)
Proline (fungicides)
Puma (herbicides)

COMPETITORS

3M
Abbott Labs
Akzo Nobel
Allergan plc
AstraZeneca
BASF SE
Baxter International
Boehringer Ingelheim
Boston Scientific
Bristol-Myers Squibb
Celanese
DSM
Dow Chemical
DuPont
Eastman Chemical
Eli Lilly
Evonik Degussa
GE Healthcare
GlaxoSmithKline
Johnson & Johnson
Merck
Merck KGaA
Mitsubishi Chemical Holdings
Monsanto Company
Novartis
Pfizer
Ranbaxy Laboratories
Rhodia
Roche Holding
Sanofi
Syngenta
Teva

HISTORICAL FINANCIALS

Company Type: Public

Income Statement FYE: December 31

	REVENUE ($ mil.)	NET INCOME ($ mil.)	NET PROFIT MARGIN	EMPLOYEES
12/14	51,341	4,164	8.1%	118,888
12/13	55,285	4,390	7.9%	113,200
12/12	52,405	3,223	6.2%	110,500
12/11	47,247	3,194	6.8%	111,800
12/10	46,960	1,741	3.7%	111,400
Annual Growth	2.3%	24.4%	—	1.6%

2014 Year-End Financials

Debt ratio: 5.8%
Return on equity: 16.7%
Cash ($ mil.): 2,252
Current ratio: 1.43
Long-term debt ($ mil.): —
No. of shares (mil.): 826
Dividends
Yield: 1.5%
Payout: 36.8%
Market value ($ mil.): 113,160

	STOCK PRICE ($) FY Close	P/E High/Low		PER SHARE ($) Earnings	Dividends	Book Value
12/14	136.84	35	27	5.03	2.11	29.55
12/13	142.00	37	25	5.31	1.80	34.49
12/12	95.92	32	22	3.90	1.56	29.44
12/11	63.80	25	16	3.87	1.42	30.05
12/10	73.36	50	37	2.10	1.34	30.48
Annual Growth	16.9%	—	—	24.4%	12.1%	(0.8%)

Bayer Motoren WK

Auditors: KPMG AG Wirtschaftspruefungsgesellschaft

LOCATIONS

HQ: Bayer Motoren WK
Petuelring 130, Munchen 80788
Phone: (49) 89 382 25387
Web: www.bmwgroup.com

HISTORICAL FINANCIALS

Company Type: Public

Income Statement FYE: December 31

	REVENUE ($ mil.)	NET INCOME ($ mil.)	NET PROFIT MARGIN	EMPLOYEES
12/14	97,727	7,047	7.2%	116,324
12/13	104,711	7,315	7.0%	110,351
12/12	101,289	6,702	6.6%	105,876
Annual Growth	(1.8%)	2.5%	—	4.8%

2014 Year-End Financials

Debt ratio: —
Return on equity: 15.9%
Cash ($ mil.): 9,344
Current ratio: 0.96
Long-term debt ($ mil.): —
No. of shares (mil.): 602
Dividends
Yield: —
Payout: —
Market value ($ mil.): —

	STOCK PRICE ($) FY Close	P/E High/Low		PER SHARE ($) Earnings	Dividends	Book Value
12/14	0.00	—	—	10.76	0.00	75.15
12/13	0.00	—	—	11.15	0.00	81.08
Annual Growth	—	—	—	(1.8%)	—	(3.7%)

Bayerische Motoren Werke AG

Bayerische Motoren Werke better known as BMW is among the top 10 automakers in the world. It manufactures premium brand cars and off-road vehicles under the BMW MINI and Rolls-Royce names as well as motorcycles under the BMW and Husqvarna names. Spare parts and accessories are also offered. Its vehicles and products are sold worldwide through company branches independent dealers subsidiaries and importers. BMW's financial services segment offers car leasing and credit financing for both retail and corporate fleet customers; dealer financing; insurance; and deposit banking.

Geographic Reach

BMW operates in more than 140 countries and operates 30 production and assembly facilities in 14 countries. It generates about half of its revenue in Europe while the remainder is well dispersed among the Americas (mainly the US) China and other parts of the world.

Operations

To support global markets BMW has 30 production facilities in 14 countries. It also has about 12 R&D centers in Austria Germany the US Japan and China. Some assembly is undertaken with external partners in emerging markets including India Malaysia Thailand and Russia.

Sales and Marketing

The company has a global sales network that spans more than 140 countries. BMW and MINI brand products are sold in Germany through the company's own branches and independent authorized dealers. Sales outside of Germany are carried out mainly by subsidiaries and in certain markets by independent importers. Rolls-Royce brand vehicles are sold in the US by a subsidiary and elsewhere by dealers. At year end 2014 BMW's car sales network was made up of 3250 BMW 1550 MINI and 130 Rolls-Royce dealerships cover 650 locations worldwide.

Financial Performance

(Note: growth rates differ after conversion to US dollar.) BMW in 2014 experienced a 6% rise in sales primarily by the continued upward trend in sales volumes across all segments. It also experienced an uptick in external revenues from the sale of BMW MINI and Rolls-Royce brand cars. Revenue from its Automotive segment grew by 6% Motorcycles by 12% and Financial Services by 4%.

In addition to revenue growth BMW posted a surge in profits from 2013 to 2014 due to the revenue increase coupled with improvement from other operating income and expenses. Its operating cash flow however decreased during 2014 primarily due to higher cash outflows for taxes.

Strategy

BMW is in the midst of what it call its Number ONE strategy an initiative begun in 2007 that continues today to boost profitability and enable expansion of its global production and sales networks. From 2007 to 2014 the company expanded from 23 production facilities to 30. More recent manufacturing plants have been opened in China through its BMW Brilliance joint venture with Brilliance China Automotive. BMW's goal is to sell more than 2 million BMW MINI and Rolls-Royce vehicles by 2016 –up from the 2.1 million cars it sold in fiscal 2014.

From an environmental perspective BMW's strategy is to invest in and develop technologies that support making its vehicle fleet more fuel efficient and reducing carbon dioxide emissions by 25% between 2008 and 2020. To this end it is increasing R&D expenditures in part to support continued development of a new fuel efficient engine family called Efficient Dynamics and improvement of a hybrid technology called ActiveHybrid. New vehicle models like the pure electric BMWi family were launched in late 2013.

In other areas of its business BMW is dealing with contracting motorcycle markets worldwide and is therefore changing strategic course. In early 2013 it sold its Husqvarna motorcycle business to Austrian company Pierer Industrie AG in order

HISTORY

BMW's logo speaks to its origin: a propeller in blue and white the colors of Bavaria. In 1913 Karl Rapp opened an aircraft-engine design shop near Munich. He named it Bayerische Motoren Werke (BMW) in 1917. The end of WWI brought German aircraft production to a halt and BMW shifted to making railway brakes until the 1930s. BMW debuted its first motorcycle the R32 in 1923 and the company began making automobiles in 1928 after buying small-car company Fahrzeugwerke Eisenach.

In 1933 BMW launched a line of larger cars. The company built aircraft engines for Hitler's Luftwaffe in the 1930s and stopped all auto and motorcycle production in 1941. BMW chief Josef Popp resisted and was ousted. Under the Nazis the company operated in occupied countries built rockets and developed the world's first production jet engine.

With its factories dismantled after WWII BMW survived by making kitchen and garden equipment. In 1948 it introduced a one-cylinder motorcycle which sold well as cheap transportation in postwar Germany. BMW autos in the 1950s were large and expensive and sold poorly. When motorcycle sales dropped the company escaped demise in the mid-1950s by launching the Isetta a seven-foot three-wheeled "bubble car."

In the 1970s BMW's European exports soared and the company set up a distribution subsidiary in the US. The company also produced larger cars that put BMW on par with Mercedes-Benz.

EXECUTIVES

Member Management Board Production, Norbert Reithofer, age 60, $840,000 total compensation
Member Management Board Sales and Marketing, Ian Robertson, age 58, $420,000 total compensation
Member Management Board Production, Harald Kr ger, age 51, $420,000 total compensation
Member Management Board Finance, Friedrich Eichiner, age 61, $420,000 total compensation
Member Management Board Purchasing and Supplier Network, Klaus Draeger, age 60, $430,000 total compensation
Head of Purchasing and Supplier Network, Herbert Diess, age 58, $420,000 total compensation
Deputy Chairman Supervisory Board, Manfred Schoch
Chairman Supervisory Board, Joachim Milberg, age 72
Member Supervisory Board, Karl-Ludwig Kley, age 64
Deputy Chairman Supervisory Board, Stefan Quandt
Deputy Chairman Supervisory Board, Stefan Schmid
Auditors: KPMG AG

LOCATIONS

HQ: Bayerische Motoren Werke AG
Petuelring 130, Munich 80788
Phone: (49) 89 3 82 0 **Fax:** (49) 89 3895 5858
Web: www.bmwgroup.com

2014 Sales

	% of total
Europe	
Germany	16
Rest of Europe	30
Americas	
US	17
Rest of Americas	4
Asia	
China	19
Other	14
Total	**100**

PRODUCTS/OPERATIONS

Selected Products

Automobiles
BMW
1 Series
3-door
5-door
Convertible
Coupe
3 Series
Convertible
Coupe
Sedan
Touring
5 Series
Gran Turismo
Sedan
Touring
6 Series
Convertible
Coupe
Gran Coupe
7 Series
Sedan
X3 X5 X6 sports utility vehicles
M Models
M3 Convertible
M3 Coupe
M3 Sedan
M6 Convertible
M6 Coupe
Z4
Coupe
Roadster
MINI
John Cooper Works (Hardtop Convertible Clubman)
MINI Cooper
MINI Cooper Clubman
MINI Cooper Convertible
MINI Cooper S
MINI Cooper S Clubman
MINI Cooper S Convertible
Rolls-Royce
Ghost
Phantom
Phantom Coupe
Motorcycles
BMW

2014 Sales

	% of total
Automobiles	93
Financial services	26
Motorcycles	2
Elimination (21)	
Total	**100**

COMPETITORS

Daimler	Mitsubishi Motors
Ducati	Nissan
FCA US	Porsche
Fiat Chrysler	Renault
Ford Motor	Suzuki Motor
General Motors	Toyota
Harley-Davidson	Ultra Motorcycle
Honda	Volkswagen
Kawasaki Heavy Industries	Yamaha
Mazda	Yamaha Motor

HISTORICAL FINANCIALS

Company Type: Public

Income Statement

FYE: December 31

	REVENUE ($ mil.)	NET INCOME ($ mil.)	NET PROFIT MARGIN	EMPLOYEES
12/14	97,727	7,047	7.2%	116,324
12/13	104,711	7,315	7.0%	110,351
12/12	101,289	6,716	6.6%	105,876
12/11	89,016	6,313	7.1%	100,306
12/10	80,940	4,306	5.3%	95,453
Annual Growth	4.8%	13.1%	—	5.1%

2014 Year-End Financials

Debt ratio: 63.3%
Return on equity: 15.9%
Cash ($ mil.): 9,344
Current ratio: 0.96
Long-term debt ($ mil.): 52,469
No. of shares (mil.): 602
Dividends
Yield: 2.3%
Payout: 6.8%
Market value ($ mil.): 21,443

	STOCK PRICE ($) FY Close	P/E High	P/E Low	PER SHARE ($) Earnings	Dividends	Book Value
12/14	35.62	4	4	10.73	0.83	75.15
12/13	39.43	5	4	11.15	0.74	81.08
12/12	32.60	4	3	10.24	0.67	66.33
12/11	22.23	4	3	9.64	0.37	58.09
12/10	26.09	6	3	6.57	0.08	51.30
Annual Growth	8.1%	—	—	13.0%	79.1%	10.0%

BDO Unibank Inc.

BDO could stand for "Big Darn Operation" but instead it's short for Banco de Oro Unibank the latest iteration of a merger that took place in 2007 between two Filipino entities Banco de Oro Universal Bank and Equitable PCI Bank. Since 1968 Banco de Oro has provided corporate commercial retail and investment banking services throughout the country. Established in 1938 Equitable PCI brings to the coupling its commercial banking small and middle market lending trust leasing and remittances expertise. Combined BDO operates a network of more than 680 branches and some 1200 ATMs in Metro Manila as well as the Luzon Mindanao and Visayas provinces.

BDO –the largest bank in the Philippines by assets –has utilized partnerships with other lenders to foster its own growth. In 2009 the company made a deal with GE Capital in which BDO acquired the local arm of GE Money Bank; GE Capital in turn took a 10% stake of BDO. Two years earlier the bank acquired the American Express Bank Philippines giving it the exclusive right to issue American Express credit cards in the Philippines.

SM Prime Holdings — one of the largest conglomerates in the Philippines with interests in shopping malls real estate development tourism entertainment and financial services —owns more than a third of BDO.

The firm strengthened its business franchise in 2008 with the consolidation of its wholly-owned subsidiaries thrift banks Equitable Savings Bank (ESB) and BDO Elite Savings Bank (BDO Elite) and investment house PCI Capital Corp. into BDO. The four-way merger optimizes BDO's capital structure and streamlines operations in the bank's network.

EXECUTIVES

President & Chief Executive Officer, Nestor Tan
Senior Executive Vice President, Antonio Cotoco
Senior Executive Vice President, Walter Wassamer
Senior Executive Vice President, Jaime Yu
Executive Vice President, Pedro Florescio
Senior Vice President & Treasurer, Marilyn Go
Executive Vice President, Ador Abrogena
Executive Vice President, Stella Cabalatungan
Executive Vice President, Anthony Chua
Executive Vice President, Julie Chua
Company Secretary, Edmundo Tan
Auditors: Punongbayan & Araullo

LOCATIONS

HQ: BDO Unibank Inc.
BDO Corporate Center, 7899 Makati Avenue, Makati City 0726
Phone: (63) 2 840 7000
Web: www.bdo.com.ph

COMPETITORS

Bank of the Philippine Islands
Citibank
Metropolitan Bank and Trust
Philippine National Bank

HISTORICAL FINANCIALS

Company Type: Public

Income Statement FYE: December 31

	ASSETS ($ mil.)	NET INCOME ($ mil.)	INCOME AS % OF ASSETS	EMPLOYEES
12/14	41,665	509	1.2%	24,779
12/13	37,666	509	1.4%	23,227
12/12	30,343	348	1.1%	21,746
12/11	25,065	240	1.0%	0
12/10	22,926	202	0.9%	20,053
Annual Growth	16.1%	26.0%	—	5.4%

2014 Year-End Financials

Return on assets: 1.2%
Return on equity: 13.3%
Long-term debt ($ mil.): —
No. of shares (mil.): —
Sales ($ mil): 2,080
Dividends
Yield: 0.0%
Payout: 33.4%
Market value ($ mil.): —

	STOCK PRICE ($) FY Close	P/E High/Low	PER SHARE ($) Earnings	Dividends	Book Value
12/14	25.04	4 4	0.14	0.05	1.12
Annual Growth	—	— —	—	—	—

Bertelsmann AG (Germany, Fed. Rep.)

This company is so big it takes up space on the bookshelf the magazine stand and on television. Bertelsmann is one of the world's leading media conglomerates with operations in publishing and TV. It owns about 90% of RTL Group Europe's #1 TV broadcaster with more than 40 channels operating in a dozen countries. Bertelsmann also owns Random House the world's top trade book publisher as well as 75% of magazine publisher Gruner + Jahr. In addition its arvato unit is a leading provider of distribution manufacturing and other business services to media companies. Carl Bertelsmann founded the company in 1835. His descendants the Mohn family control the business through the Bertelsmann Stiftung foundation.

One unique quality of Bertelsmann is that its divisions operate more like stand-alone businesses rather than being integrated with one another in a fashion similar to Time Warner or News Corporation. Within its home market of Germany Bertelsmann competes most directly with publisher Axel Springer and broadcaster ProSiebenSat.

Bertelsmann is certainly one of the largest but also one of the very few media conglomerates to dominate the European continent: While its TV and publishing businesses range across dozens of countries most of the company's nearest competitors restrict their activities to one or two countries.

But being a global powerhouse in publishing and broadcasting has made Bertelsmann vulnerable during the global recession. Advertising revenue has suffered steep declines in many markets while many of Gruner + Jahr's magazine titles struggle to hold on to readers in the age of digital distribution and expanding competition. Bertelsmann is also focused on managing its high level of debt in the face of declining revenue.

Bertelsmann is currently focused on exploiting new opportunities to turn its various businesses around. RTL Group is working to diversify away from commercial advertising by expanding its pay-TV and digital media operations. The broadcasting group is also buoyed by its FremantleMedia production unit responsible for spawning Pop Idol American Idol and all the other Idol competition programs around the world. Random House meanwhile is eyeing growth of electronic publishing thanks to popular reading devices such as the Kindle from Amazon.com and Apple's iPad tablet device.

Another growth area for the company is music publishing royalties. In 2008 Bertelsmann launched BMG Rights Management a joint venture with US-based private equity firm KKR which controls the rights to more than 75000 songs. BMG acquired US-based publisher Cherry Lane Music Publishing the following year. Bertelsmann had abandoned the music business earlier in 2008 when the company sold its 50% stake in Sony BMG Music Entertainment (now Sony Music Entertainment) to former joint venture partner Sony for $1.2 billion in cash. (The deal included $300 million from Sony Music's balance sheet.) In 2006 it sold BMG Music Publishing to Universal Music Group for $2.1 billion.

HISTORY

Carl Bertelsmann founded his publishing company C. Bertelsmann Verlag in G tersloh Germany in 1835. The company primarily published hymnals and religious materials expanding into newspapers during the 1860s. Heinrich Mohn a fourth-generation descendant took over the company in 1921 and expanded its operations to include popular fiction which helped Bertelsmann expand to more than 400 employees by 1939.

During WWII the company published books and propaganda material for the German army but was closed by the Nazi government in 1944 as it was not considered important to the war effort. (The company had maintained for decades it was closed because it produced religious materials but contrary evidence was uncovered in 2000 by historians working at the behest of the company.) After WWII Mohn's son Reinhard (who had been captured by the Allies and interned in a Kansas POW camp) returned to Germany determined to rebuild the company.

Bertelsmann boosted book sales by launching book clubs in Germany during the 1950s and bought Germany's UFA (TV and film production) in 1964. It took a minority interest in publisher Gruner + Jahr in 1969 taking a controlling stake in 1973. In the US Bertelsmann bought 51% of Bantam Books in 1977 (and the rest in 1981) and Arista Records in 1979. In 1986 it took control of Doubleday Publishing and bought RCA Records (forming Bertelsmann Music Group the next year). Mohn transferred substantial non-voting shares in the company to the Bertelsmann Foundation (Bertelsmann Stiftung) in 1993.

The company teamed up with AOL in 1995 to form AOL Europe and with Luxembourg broadcaster CLT it launched CLT-Ufa in 1997. Bertelsmann acquired book publisher Random House the next year. The company also took a 50% stake in online bookseller barnesandnoble.com (retaining nearly 40% after an IPO in 1999). In addition Thomas Middelhoff became chairman and CEO in 1998. The next year Bertelsmann acquired some 85% of scientific publisher Springer Verlag. Also in 1999 Reinhard Mohn transferred his controlling shares in the company to Bertelsmann Verwaltungsgesellschaft a firm controlled by Bertelsmann executives and the Mohn family.

In 2000 Bertelsmann announced that it would sell its half-interest in AOL Europe back to AOL by mid-2002; it also spun off Lycos Europe (retaining 27% now about 20%). It later merged CLT-Ufa with Pearson TV to form RTL Group. (Bertelsmann got a 37% stake.) That year Bertelsmann bought online music retailer CDNOW and began negotiating a merger between BMG and EMI Group. (Those talks fell apart in 2001.) Late in 2000 the company formed an alliance with online music service Napster loaning the company start-up cash and allowing it to use the BMG music catalog to develop a subscription-based service. (Bertelsmann later tried to acquire Napster but a bankruptcy court quashed the deal. Napster went out of business shortly after although its name was acquired by Roxio now Napster.)

Bertelsmann bought Groupe Bruxelles Lambert 's 30% stake in RTL Group in 2001. As part of the deal Bruxelles gained a 25% stake in Bertelsmann –with the understanding that it would be able to float its interest to the public in four years. Bertelsmann combined RTL's Ufa Sports unit with French sports-rights company Jean-Claude Darmon in exchange for a 40% stake in the combined company now called Sportfive. Later that year it sold its stake in online music venture GetMusic to Universal Music Group. Also that year it bought Pearson's 22% stake in RTL Group.

The company's board fired Middelhoff in 2002 citing disagreements over the direction of the company. He was replaced by Gunter Thielen chairman of Bertelsmann's arvato business unit. The following year Bertelsmann sold its science publishing subsidiary BertelsmannSpringer. Music subsidiary BMG Entertainment merged with Sony Music in 2004 to create Sony BMG Music Entertainment a joint venture with Sony Corporation.

After a contentious few months in 2006 when Groupe Bruxelles Lambert almost forced an IPO of the notoriously private media firm the Mohn family bought out Lambert's interest in the company for $5.7 billion (leaving the Mohns with a 23% interest in Bertelsmann and the Bertelsmann Foundation owning the rest). Later that year the company sold BMG Music Publishing (which was not part of the BMG-Sony Music merger) to Universal Music Group for $2.1 billion.

Thielen stepped down as CEO of Bertelsmann at the beginning of 2008 and was replaced by Hartmut Ostrowski. Later that year Bertelsmann sold its stake in Sony BMG Music Entertainment to Sony for $1.2 billion in cash and stock. (The music business then changed its name to Sony Music Entertainment.)

EXECUTIVES

Chairman and CEO Random House Group UK, Gail Rebuck, age 63
EVP Bertelsmann US (BInc.), Rob Sorrentino
CFO, Elmar Heggen, age 47

Executive Vice President Regional Operations & Business Development CEE and Asia, Andreas Rudas, age 62
President & CEO Random House of Canada, R. Bradley (Brad) Martin
Chief Executive Officer Penguin Random House, Markus Dohle, age 46
CEO Bertelsmann China Corporate Center; Managing Director Bertelsmann Asia Investments, Annabelle Yu Long
EVP Financial Reporting and Accounting, Martin Rembde
President Corporate Development and New Business, Thomas Hesse
Co-CEO RTL Group, Guillaume de Posch
Co-CEO RTL Group, Anke Sch ¤ferkordt
CEO Gruner + Jahr, Julia J ¤kel
CEO Be Printers Prinovis, Bertram Stausberg
CEO Arvato AG, Achim Berg
Auditors: PricewaterhouseCoopers Aktiengesellschaft Wirtschaftspruefungsgesellschaft

LOCATIONS

HQ: Bertelsmann AG (Germany, Fed. Rep.)
Carl-Bertelsmann-Strasse 270, Guetersloh D-33311
Phone: (49) 5241 80 0 **Fax:** (49) 5241 80 66 13
Web: www.bertelsmann.com

PRODUCTS/OPERATIONS

Selected Operations

arvato
DirectGroup
Gruner + J
Random House
RTL Group

COMPETITORS

21st Century Fox
Amazon.com
Axel Springer
Bauer Verlagsgruppe
CANAL+
Cinram
Disney
Hearst Corporation
ITV
Lagard□re
NBCUniversal
ProSiebenSat
Time Warner
Verlagsgruppe Georg von Holtzbrinck
Viacom

HISTORICAL FINANCIALS

Company Type: Public

Income Statement FYE: December 31

	REVENUE ($ mil.)	NET INCOME ($ mil.)	NET PROFIT MARGIN	EMPLOYEES
12/14	20,629	198	1.0%	112,037
12/13	22,830	685	3.0%	111,763
12/12	21,489	637	3.0%	104,286
12/11	20,038	601	3.0%	100,626
12/10	21,330	639	3.0%	97,528
Annual Growth	(0.8%)	(25.4%)	—	3.5%

2014 Year-End Financials

Debt ratio: 17.0%
Return on equity: 2.4%
Cash ($ mil.): 1,615
Current ratio: 1.10
Long-term debt ($ mil.): 2,873
No. of shares (mil.): 0
Dividends
Yield: —
Payout: —
Market value ($ mil.): —

Bharat Petroleum Corp Ltd. (India)

Although it carries the ancient Sanskrit name for India (Bharat) Bharat Petroleum Corporation Limited (BPCL) is a modern refining and distribution company. It vies with Hindustan Petroleum for the #2 slot behind Indian Oil. The company's refineries —in Mumbai Kochi and Numaligarh (62%-owned) –collectively process more than 24 million metric tons of crude oil per year. BPCL sells engine oils and gasolines liquefied petroleum gas (LPG) and kerosene. It has10000 gas stations a national network of kerosene dealers and more than 2450 LPG distributors. The company operates 50 LPG bottling plants and serves more than 30 million LPG customers across India.

With an eye to expanding BPCL's global hydrocarbon supply and lowering production costs BPCL's exploration and production unit Bharat PetroResources partners with major oil companies to develop oil and gas fields in India and abroad. In fiscal 2011 Bharat PetroResources reported five oil and gas discoveries in Brazil Indonesia and Mozambique.

BPCL is also modernizing and expanding its Indian refineries to handle increased demand. In fiscal 2011 it teamed up with Bharat Oman Refineries to develop a 6 million metric-ton-per-year refinery in Madya Pradesh to support BPCL's activities in the central and northern part of India. It also launched an expansion of its Kochi refinery to expand that plant's capacity from 7.5 million metric tons per year to 9.5 million metric tons per year.

It is also expanding its gas station network to meet growing domestic demand adding 600 retail outlets in fiscal 2011 with another 700 projected to be added in fiscal 2012. Depending on future growth BPCL may add up to 2500 gas stations by 2017.

Higher oil prices increased production and the expansion of its retail network helped to lift BPCL's revenues in fiscal 2011. Increased costs related to crude oil for resale and raw materials meant that net income was essentially flat for the year.

The Indian government owns 55% of the firm although it is considering eventually selling this stake as part of industrywide deregulation.
Auditors: Haribhakti & Co. LLP

LOCATIONS

HQ: Bharat Petroleum Corp Ltd. (India)
Bharat Bhavan, 4 & 6 Currimbhoy Road, Ballard Estate, Mumbai 400 001
Phone: (91) 22 2271 3000 **Fax:** (91) 22 2271 3688
Web: www.bharatpetroleum.in

HISTORICAL FINANCIALS

Company Type: Public

Income Statement FYE: March 31

	REVENUE ($ mil.)	NET INCOME ($ mil.)	NET PROFIT MARGIN	EMPLOYEES
03/15	39,127	768	2.0%	12,687
03/14	44,267	651	1.5%	13,214
03/13	44,894	346	0.8%	13,213
03/12	41,984	153	0.4%	13,429
03/11	34,835	366	1.1%	13,915
Annual Growth	2.9%	20.3%	—	(2.3%)

2015 Year-End Financials

Debt ratio: 0.3%
Return on equity: 22.8%
Cash ($ mil.): 551
Current ratio: 0.90
Long-term debt ($ mil.): 3,092
No. of shares (mil.): 723
Dividends
Yield: —
Payout: —
Market value ($ mil.): —

BHP Billiton Ltd.

Two heads (or headquarters) are better than one. Aussie minerals and oil company BHP Limited acquired UK miner Billiton plc in 2001. The result: a two-headquartered dual-listed company run as a single entity with the same board of directors and management. The Melbourne side is BHP Billiton Limited the London side is BHP Billiton Plc; collectively they are known as BHP Billiton. One of the largest diversified natural resources companies it ranks among the world's top producers of iron ore and coal (thermal and metallurgical). Other products include aluminum copper manganese nickel silver uranium and potash. BHP also has crude oil and natural gas holdings.

Geographic Reach

The company has far-flung operations. In Canada's Saskatchewan province BHP produces potash a primary raw material used to manufacture fertilizers and a top priority for the global titans of mining. In Australia it operates a coal-producing joint venture with Mitsubishi that has mining projects in Australia. Its Australian minerals businesses include not only iron ore coal and potash but also copper and uranium. Its Chilean operations include a 58% stake in the Escondida mine one of the world's largest and lowest-cost copper producers. BHP's oil and gas operations are worldwide ranging from its Shenzi deepwater oil and gas field in the Gulf of Mexico to onshore natural gas production in Pakistan.

Operations

The group operates four businesses aligned with the commodities it extracts and markets:

The Petroleum and Potash business headquartered in Houston is engaged unconventional and non-conventional oil and gas operations and a potash project based in Saskatchewan Canada. Headquartered in Santiago Chile BHP's Copper business is one of the world's leading producers of copper concentrate and cathode uranium oxide and a producer of zinc concentrate. It's portfolio of mining operations includes the Escondida mine in Chile a leading producer of copper and Olympic Dam in South Australia a major producer of copper and uranium oxide. The company's Coal Business headquartered in Brisbane is the world's largest supplier of seaborne metallurgical coal a key input in steel production. It is also a large supplier of seaborne energy coal (thermal or steaming coal) and a domestic energy coal supplier in the countries where its mines are located. BHP's Iron Ore Business based in Perth Australia is one of the world's leading iron ore producers. It sells lump and fine products produced in Australia and produces pellets from its operations in Brazil.

Sales and Marketing

Due to its proximity to customers in Asia the primary hub for BHP's marketing activities is Singapore while marketing of oil and gas is based in Houston. In addition it has marketing teams located close to customers in nine cities around the world. Financial Performance 2014 BHP's fiscal revenues have been restated due to the company's 2015 spin off of a selection of assets that included BHP's interests in its integrated aluminum business Energy Coal South Africa the Illawarra metallurgical coal the manganese business the Cerro Matoso nickel operation and the Cannington silver-lead-zinc mine. In fiscal 2015 the company's net sales decreased by 34% due to lower revenues across all businesses but mainly in the Iron Ore and Petroleum and Potash Businesses.

The slump in Iron Ore sales was primarily due to a 41% decline in the average realized price of iron ore which more than offset a 13% volume increase from its Western Australia Iron Ore operations as a result of continued improvement in the performance of integrated supply chain and the successful ramp-up of the Jimblebar mining hub. The decrease in Petroleum revenues was primarily driven by lower realized prices. In fiscal 2015 BHP's net income decreased by 86% due to a decline in revenues and loss from discontinued operations. The company's operating cash inflow decreased by 25% due to net loss and a change in working capital.

Strategy

BHP's strategy is to own and operate large long-life low-cost expandable upstream assets diversified by commodity geography and market. The company has created a diversified portfolio of tier one natural resources by investing in large high-quality low-cost assets. In addition to strategic acquisitions BHP seeks organic growth through investments in major projects for its segments. Its diversified portfolio of high-quality assets gives it resilience and flexibility to enhance value throughout the commodity cycle. In 2015 BHP spun off a selection of its aluminum coal manganese nickel and silver-lead-zinc assets to create an independent metals and mining company South32.

In late 2015 the Brazilian government demanded $5 billion in compensation from BHP and Vale over flooding from a dam collapse at joint venture Samarco's mine which resulted in one of the worst environmental disasters in Brazil's history.

HISTORY

In 1883 Charles Rasp a boundary rider for the Mt. Gipps sheep station believed valuable ore lay in the Broken Hill outcrop in New South Wales Australia. He gathered a few young speculators and The Broken Hill Proprietary Company (BHP) was incorporated in 1885. BHP immediately found a massive lode of silver lead and zinc. None of the founders knew how to run a mine so they recruited US engineers William Patton and Herman Schlapp. From the beginning labor and management clashed. The founding directors set up the head office in Melbourne far from the mine and gambled with gold sovereigns in the boardroom. But the miners worked in dangerous conditions. An 1892 labor strike was the first of BHP's bitter strikes.

In 1902 the new general manager Guillaume Delprat invented a flotation process that recovered valuable metals from iron ore waste. Delprat also foresaw a future in steel although Australia had no steel industry. BHP commissioned the Newcastle steelworks in 1915 and soon became the country's largest steel producer. BHP's 1935 purchase of Australian Iron and Steel its only competitor gave it a virtual steel monopoly while high tariffs protected it from outside competition. Its exhausted Broken Hill mine was closed that year.

In the 1960s BHP got into oil when it partnered with Esso Standard the Australian subsidiary of Standard Oil of New Jersey for offshore exploration. In 1967 the partners found oil in the Bass Strait which soon supplied 70% of Australia's petroleum. In the 1960s and 1970s BHP began expanding its iron ore manganese and coal interests. Meanwhile public opposition mounted to BHP's market power and labor practices and in 1972 the government took steps to limit BHP's power removing some subsidies and tax breaks.

The weak steel market of the 1970s and 1980s caused BHP to lay off almost a third of its steelworkers in 1983 but with government intervention BHP radically improved its steel productivity. In 1984 BHP bought Utah International's mining assets from General Electric (including Chile's rich Escondida copper mine). In 1986 corporate raider Robert Holmes à Court took a run at BHP; BHP decided to become an international mining company to prevent further raids. Its acquisitions in the late 1980s included ERG Inc. and Monsanto Oil (combined into BHP Americas) Aquila Steel and Pacific Refining in Hawaii.

A peace deal with Holmes à Court gave BHP about 37% of Foster's Brewing but in 1992 BHP took a $700 million write-down after Foster's stock declined. BHP also bought Arizona-based Magma Copper in 1996 but plunging world copper prices forced a $420 million write-down.

With new worries over Asia's economic troubles BHP soon was struggling. In 1997 BHP sold most of its stake in Foster's and three senior executives resigned. In 1998 the company unloaded Pacific Refining which was acquired by Tesoro Petroleum for about $275 million.

As BHP's woes continued CEO John Prescott resigned; Paul Anderson was recruited from Duke Energy to succeed Prescott. In 1999 D. R. Argus took over as chairman replacing Jeremy Ellis. In a restructuring move the company sold its engineering power insurance and information technology businesses in 1999 and 2000. BHP began to sell $2 billion worth of steel operations (including its long product unit OneSteel). In 2000 the company shortened its official name to BHP Limited.

BHP acquired Billiton in 2001 forming BHP Billiton Ltd. and BHP Billiton plc. The combined BHP Billiton had sales of almost $20 billion and a market capitalization approaching $30 billion. In addition BHP paid $436 million for Dia Met Minerals which owned 29% of Canada's only producing diamond mine Ekati.

Also in 2001 BHP Billiton and Alcoa combined their North American metals distribution businesses as joint venture Integris Metals (subsequently sold and integrated into Ryerson). In order to focus on its minerals and oil and gas operations in 2002 BHP Billiton spun off its steel business as BHP Steel (now called Bluescope Steel).

In 2005 BHP Billiton acquired metals and minerals company WMC Resources which had been the subject of much takeover speculation and the target of the Swiss mining heavyweight Xstrata (since renamed Glencore). Its offer of $7.3 billion surpassed Xstrata's and was accepted and endorsed by the WMC board which had turned down the two earlier proposals by Xstrata. The addition of WMC added significantly to BHP Billiton's copper nickel and uranium operations.

In 2008 BHP Billiton Mitsubishi Alliance (BMA) spent $2.4 billion to buy the Saraji East metallurgical coal project from New Hope Corporation. Each of BMA's owners paid $1.2 billion to New Hope for the project which lies adjacent to one of BMA's coal mines.

Though the global recession of 2008-2009 certainly pushed the company's fortunes down BHP Billiton experienced eyebrow-raising growth thanks in part to generally high commodity prices and the emerging Asian economies. China for example represented 20% of the company's total sales in 2007 doubling its share from just three years prior. The continent as a whole accounted for more than half of sales.

Due to the strong demand BHP Billiton increased production of iron ore coking coal and manganese. The shifting nature of the market though changed the company's highest-grossing segments. In 2009 high coal prices helped that business immensely while conversely the Base Metals business of copper lead zinc and precious metals mining suffered from low prices driving down the unit's revenues. On the petroleum side the company continued to acquire oil and gas exploration leases in the Gulf of Mexico.

Two failed deals by BHP Billiton occurred in 2010: a $39 billion takeover of Potash Corporation of Saskatchewan and a proposed joint venture with Rio Tinto Ltd. BHP Billiton's offer for Potash Corporation was first rejected by that company's board as inadequate and then by Canadian regulators who ruled the offer to be anticompetitive. After a $150 billion bid to buy Rio Tinto fell through due to the global economic meltdown the companies proposed a joint iron ore venture in Western Australia which also failed because of opposition from European regulatory authorities.

In 2010 BHP Billiton acquired Athabasca Potash Inc. (API) for about $320 million. API's projects are located in Saskatchewan close to BHP Billiton's own potash operations.

In 2011 BHP acquired Chesapeake Energy's Fayetteville shale gas holdings in Arkansas for $4.75 billion. That year it also acquired Petrohawk Energy another US-based gas producer with projects in the Eagle Ford and Haynesville shale plays for $15.1 billion. In 2012 natural gas prices began to plummet. Although the company defended the long-term growth outlook for the shale assets it did not rule out a possible writedown later that year for those investments.

Following the Petrohawk announcement in 2011 BHP acquired three subsidiaries of HWE Mining a company owned by Leighton Holdings for $735 million. The HWE Mining subsidiaries provide contract iron ore mining services in Western Australia to BHP and the acquisition allows the company to both own and operate the mines.

In 2012 it sold its 51% stake in the Chidliak diamond exploration project in Canada's Baffin Island to the project operator Peregrine Diamonds giving it full ownership. The sale follows BHP's review of its diamond businesses to determine whether they fit in its strategy. The company also owns an 80% stake in Canada's EKATI diamond mine which is still under review. The company could receive less than $500 million for the sale of the mine.

EXECUTIVES

CEO, Andrew Mackenzie
President Iron Ore, Jimmy Wilson
President Coal, Mike Henry
President Petroleum and Potash, Tim Cutt
President HSE Marketing and Technology, Dean Della Valle
President Copper, Daniel Malchuk
CFO, Peter Beaven
President Corporate Affairs, Tony Cudmore
Interim President Copper, Edgar Basto
President Human Resources, Mike Fraser
Chairman, Jacques A. (Jac) Nasser, age 66
Auditors: KPMG

LOCATIONS

HQ: BHP Billiton Ltd.
BHP Billiton Centre, 171 Collins Street, Melbourne, Victoria 3000
Phone: (61) 3 9609 3333 **Fax:** (61) 3 9609 3015
Web: www.bhpbilliton.com

2015 Sales

	% of total
Asia Pacific	
China	36
Japan	11
South Korea	6

Australia	5
India	4
Rest of Asia	11
Europe	
United Kingdom	1
Rest of Europe	5
North America	17
South America	3
Rest of the world	1
Total	**100**

PRODUCTS/OPERATIONS

2015 Sales

	% of total
Iron ore	33
Petroleum and Potash	26
Copper	26
Coal	13
Group and unallocated items	2
Total	**100**

Selected Divisions

- Coal
  - Metallurgical
  - Energy
- Iron ore
- Petroleum
  - Crude oil
  - Ethane
  - LPG
  - Natural gas
- Base metals
  - Copper
  - Gold
  - Lead
  - Silver
  - Zinc
- Aluminum
  - Alumina
  - Aluminum
  - Bauxite
- Manganese
- Stainless steel materials
  - Cobalt
  - Ferrochrome
  - Nickel
- Diamonds and specialty products
  - Diamonds
  - Potash
  - Titanium minerals

COMPETITORS

Alcoa
Anglo American
ArcelorMittal
BP
Chevron
Chinalco
Codelco
ConocoPhillips
Exxon Mobil
Fortescue Metals
Freeport-McMoRan
Koch Industries Inc.
Kumba Iron Ore
Marathon Oil
Newmont Mining
Nippon Steel & Sumitomo Metal Corporation
Norsk Hydro ASA
Repsol
Rio Tinto Limited
Royal Dutch Shell
TOTAL
Tata Europe
Teck
Vale

HISTORICAL FINANCIALS

Company Type: Public

Income Statement FYE: June 30

	REVENUE ($ mil.)	NET INCOME ($ mil.)	NET PROFIT MARGIN	EMPLOYEES
06/15	44,636	1,910	4.3%	29,670
06/14	67,206	13,832	20.6%	47,044
06/13	65,968	10,876	16.5%	49,496
06/12	72,226	15,417	21.3%	46,370
06/11	71,739	23,648	33.0%	40,757
Annual Growth	(11.2%)	(46.7%)	—	(7.6%)

2015 Year-End Financials

Debt ratio: 25.0%
Return on equity: 2.6%
Cash ($ mil.): 6,753
Current ratio: 1.27
Long-term debt ($ mil.): 27,969
No. of shares (mil.): —
Dividends
Yield: 6.0%
Payout: 692.7%
Market value ($ mil.): —

	STOCK PRICE ($) FY Close	P/E High/Low	PER SHARE ($) Earnings	Dividends	Book Value
06/15	40.71	205116	0.36	2.48	12.17
06/14	68.45	28 22	2.59	2.36	14.87
06/13	57.66	39 28	2.04	2.28	13.28
06/12	65.30	33 21	2.88	2.20	12.38
06/11	94.63	24 14	4.27	1.82	10.66
Annual Growth	(19.0%)	— —	(46.2%)	8.0%	3.4%

BHP Billiton Plc

BHP Billiton Plc is one half of a dual-listed mining giant. It is headquartered in London; the other part of the company BHP Billiton Limited is based in Australia. Although they maintain separate listings the companies are managed as a single entity and have the same management team and board of directors. One of the largest diversified natural resources companies it ranks among the world's top producers of iron ore and coal (thermal and metallurgical). Other products include aluminum copper manganese nickel silver uranium and potash. BHP also has crude oil and natural gas holdings. For detailed information on the company's operations and history refer to Hoover's BHP Billiton Limited profile.

HISTORY

After starting out on its own in 1860 Billiton was subsequently bought first by Royal Dutch Shell and then by Gencor only to end up on its own once again. In 1860 a group of Dutch shareholders formed Billiton NV. The company bought the rich tin deposits of Billiton island (now part of Indonesia) for which it was named. The business grew to include tin and lead smelting in the Netherlands. Billiton NV began mining bauxite in the 1940s but WWII caused a production slowdown.

While demand for petroleum products exploded in the 1950s and 1960s in 1970 the industry nosedived. Royal Dutch Shell (formed from the merger of Royal Dutch and Shell Transport and Trading) responded by diversifying buying Billiton NV which it renamed Billiton International. Shell had gotten its start in commodities in the 1880s selling Russian oil of the Rothschilds to the Far East. Royal Dutch formed in 1890 after buying the rights to drill for oil in the Dutch East Indies. The two companies merged in 1907.

The 1970 Billiton purchase helped Royal Dutch Shell make up for the 1970s oil shortage and rationing that had resulted from OPEC's crude oil price hikes. Slow worldwide economic growth a major recession and oil and chemicals overcapacity impacted the company in the late 1970s and early 1980s.

Royal Dutch Shell sold Billiton in 1994 to Gencor which had been formed in 1980 by the merger of General Mining and Finance Corporation and Union Corporation. General Mining began mining gold in South Africa in the 1890s and Gencor continued its predecessors' metals and manufacturing operations. Gencor however spent the early 1980s focused on manufacturing because it anticipated a downturn in base metals. But the recession inflation and high interest rates stifled Gencor's success and the company became known as an unfocused conglomerate. In 1986 a newly appointed chairman separated Gencor's manufacturing and mining interests.

By 1989 Gencor had cut its staff and reorganized. That year it bought 31% of South Africa's Richards Bay aluminum smelter. Within two years Gencor had become a holding company with a primary interest in mining. In 1993 the firm unbundled its non-mining activities. With the end of apartheid in 1994 Gencor was able to expand abroad. Its purchase of Billiton catapulted its presence into 13 countries but in 1996 the metals market spiraled downward.

Billiton was spun off by Gencor in 1997. It took over all of Gencor's nonprecious metal interests including its aluminum titanium ferroalloy and coal assets. That year Billiton combined its nickel interests with QNI of Australia. Making good on its plan to buy new base metals assets Billiton entered a joint venture in 1998 to explore for lead and zinc with Ireland's Ennex. Billiton also sold its metals brokerage subsidiary to Metallgesellschaft AG (Germany).

In 1999 Billiton announced that it would invest in smaller companies with promising properties and limit its own in-house exploration operations. It entered joint ventures with PT Taraco Mining to explore for coal in Indonesia and with Comet Resources to develop the Ravensthorpe Nickel Project in Western Australia.

Billiton's offer for a 21% stake in the Gove bauxite-alumina project in Australia was bested by Alcan in 2000. The company agreed to pay Alcoa about $1.5 billion for its majority stake in the Worsley alumina refinery in Australia. With Anglo American and Glencore International (now Glencore Xstrata) it acquired a 50% stake in Colombia's Cerrejon Zona Norte coal mine for $384 million; it then bought Canadian mining company Rio Algom (copper molybdenum uranium and coal) for $1.2 billion.

In 2001 Billiton closed the purchase of Alcoa's share of the Worsley smelter. The same year Billiton agreed to be acquired by Aussie natural resources company BHP Ltd. to form a dual-listed entity —known collectively as BHP Billiton —consisting of BHP Billiton Limited (run from Melbourne) and BHP Billiton plc (run from London). The deal closed in June 2001.

EXECUTIVES

CEO, Andrew Mackenzie, $1,120,620 total compensation
President Copper, Peter Beaven
CFO, Graham Kerr
President Iron Ore, Jimmy Wilson
President Marketing & Technology, Mike Henry
President Production BHP Billiton Petroleum, Tim Cutt
President Aluminium Manganese & Nickel, Daniel Malchuk

President Coal, Dean Della Valle
President Aluminium Manganese & Nickel, Daniel MalchukBE
Auditors: KPMG Audit Plc

LOCATIONS

HQ: BHP Billiton Plc
Neathouse Place, Victoria, London SW1V 1BH
Phone: (44) 20 7802 4000 **Fax:** (44) 20 7802 4111
Web: www.bhpbilliton.com

2015 Sales

	% of total
Australia	5
United Kingdom	1
Rest of Europe	5
China	36
Japan	11
Rest of Asia	11
North America	17
South America	3
Southern Africa	-
Rest of world	1
India	4
South Korea	6
Total	**100**

PRODUCTS/OPERATIONS

2015 Sales

	% of total
Iron Ore	33
Petroleum and Potash	26
Copper	26
Coal	13
Group and unallocated items	2
Total	**100**

COMPETITORS

Alcoa
Anglo American
BP
Chevron
Newmont Mining
Norilsk Nickel
Norsk Hydro ASA
Rio Tinto plc
Vale

HISTORICAL FINANCIALS

Company Type: Public

Income Statement

FYE: June 30

	REVENUE ($ mil.)	NET INCOME ($ mil.)	NET PROFIT MARGIN	EMPLOYEES
06/15	44,636	1,910	4.3%	29,670
06/14	67,206	13,832	20.6%	47,044
06/13	65,968	10,876	16.5%	49,496
06/12	72,226	15,417	21.3%	46,370
06/11	71,739	23,648	33.0%	40,757
Annual Growth	(11.2%)	(46.7%)	—	(7.6%)

2015 Year-End Financials

Debt ratio: 25.0%
Return on equity: 2.6%
Cash ($ mil.): 6,753
Current ratio: 1.27
Long-term debt ($ mil.): 27,969
No. of shares (mil.): —
Dividends
Yield: 6.2%
Payout: 692.7%
Market value ($ mil.): —

	STOCK PRICE ($) FY Close	P/E High/Low	PER SHARE ($) Earnings	Dividends	Book Value
06/15	39.56	198110	0.36	2.48	12.17
06/14	65.23	26 19	2.59	2.36	14.87
06/13	51.27	35 25	2.04	2.28	13.28
06/12	57.19	28 18	2.88	2.20	12.38
06/11	78.43	20 12	4.27	1.82	10.66
Annual Growth	(15.7%)	— —	(46.2%)	8.0%	3.4%

BNP Paribas (France)

One of Europe's largest banks BNP Paribas and its many subsidiaries specialize in retail banking corporate and investment banking and investment services across more than 75 countries mostly in Europe but also in North America Africa and Asia. BNP Paribas operates in Italy through BNL banca commerciale. The French banking giant also owns Belgium's BNP Paribas Fortis which operates more than 1000 branches in Europe and the US. In the western US the company owns BancWest (the parent of Bank of the West and First Hawaiian Bank). BNP Paribas earns over 75% of its revenue from customers in Europe (mainly in Belgium France Italy and Luxembourg).

Operations

BNP Paribas operates three core businesses: Retail Banking Investment Solutions (IS) and Corporate and Investment Banking (CIB). Retail banking operates more than 7000 branches in 49 countries and accounted for more than 60% of the bank's total revenue in 2014. The segment consists of its domestic retail banking operations in France Italy (BNL banca commerciale) Belgium and Luxembourg (BNP Paribas Fortis and BGL BNP Paribas) and its international retail banking operations which are outside the euro zone including the Europe Mediterranean and the US (including BancWest). The segment also operates the Personal Finance unit through BNP Paribas Personal Finance (PF) which is a consumer credit specialist and also holds a residential mortgage lending business (which it's winding down). The Corporate and Investment Banking segment (22% of revenue) includes its Advisory & Capital Markets (equities and equity derivatives fixed income and forex and corporate finance) and Corporate Banking (lending specialty financing as well as cash management and international trade services across Europe Asia Americas Middle East Africa) businesses.

BNP Paribas' Investment Solutions segment (17% of revenue) provides wealth management asset management securities services insurance and real estate services. Some of its subsidiaries include BNP Paribas Securities BNP Paribas Wealth Management and insurance firms BNP Paribas Cardif and Pinnacle Insurance (Cardif Pinnacle). Other holdings include private bank BNP Paribas Banque Prive consumer lender Cetelem online brokerage Consorsbank (formerly Cortal Consors) and BNP Paribas Asset Management.Broadly speaking about 51% of the bank's net operating income came from interest income (mostly from loans) in 2014. Another 19% came from commission income. The rest of its net operating income came from non-recurring sources such as net gains on financial instruments available for sale financial assets and other activities.

Geographic Reach

While it caters to more than 75 countries the Paris-based bank focuses mainly on four domestic markets: Belgium France Italy and Luxembourg. Europe is the bank's largest market accounting for more than 75% of revenue in 2014. North America contributed about 10% while the Asia-Pacific and Africa region and other countries each contributed more than 5%.

Financial Performance

Note: Growth rates may differ after conversion to US dollars. This analysis uses financials from the company's annual report.BNP Paribas has struggled to grow its revenue and profits over the past several years as the European economy has faced headwinds toward consistent growth.The bank's revenues (net of operating expenses) rose 2% to 39.2 billion ($47.6 billion) in 2014 thanks mostly to a 4% increase in net interest income as loan business grew 7% during the year. An 8% rise in commission income and a 21% jump in net gains on available-for-sale financial assets and other financial assets not measured at fair value also helped buoy the bank's top-line growth. All of the segments grew with Retail Banking growing by 2% (driving most of the firm's overall growth) Investment solutions up 3.7% and Corporate and Investment Banking up 2.1%.Despite revenue growth in 2014 BNP Paribas' net income plummeted 97% to 157 million ($190.8 million) mostly due to a 6 billion ($7.3 billion) settlement charge with US authorities related "to violations of certain US laws and regulations regarding economic sanctions against certain countries and related recordkeeping" according to BNP. The group's operating cash levels nearly doubled to 16.5 billion ($20 billion) in 2014 mostly thanks to a net increase in cash related to transactions with credit institutions.

Strategy

While retail banking has remained relatively strong BNP Paribas has seen declines in its corporate and investment banking unit due to poor market conditions and losses on sales of sovereign bond debt. As a result the bank is engaged in ongoing cost cutting and the implementation of 2014-2016 business development plan. The plan includes three fundamental programs: Simple & Efficient a reorganization and efficiency program now under way; the Asia Pacific plan intended to increase revenues at Corporate and Investment Banking and Investment Solutions; and Hello bank! aimed at developing the digital bank.Using its Simple & Efficient plan (which began in 2013) as a blueprint BNP Paribas has taken a number of cost-cutting and growth initiative measures in recent years to boost profits amidst an increasingly regulated industry. Indeed by late 2015 BNP reported that its transformation costs (investments in efficiency improvements) of around 620 million had led to savings of more than 2.514 billion per year in costs about 84% of what it aimed to save annually by the end of 2016 (and beyond).Since launching Hello bank! in 2013 and acquiring DAB Bank through its Consorbank subsidiary in late 2014 BNP Paribas has been moving toward digital banking channels that are quickly taking the industry by storm allowing the bank to slow expensive branch-expansion plans and cut operating costs significantly while giving customers faster access to banking services. In late 2015 in the German market for example the bank noted that between DAB Bank and Consorbank BNP Paribas was the country's 3rd-largest digital bank with some 1.5 million customers as well as the largest online broker in the country.

Mergers and Acquisitions

In November 2013 BNP acquired Belgium's 25% share in its local consumer-banking unit BNP Paribas Fortis for 3.25 billion euros ($4.37 billion) as the country works to cut public debt. It also acquired Poland's Bank BGZ from Rabobank Group in 2013.

HISTORY

Company BackgroundBNP Paribas Group's predecessor Banque Nationale de Paris (BNP) is the progeny of two state banks with parallel histories; each was set up to jump-start the economy after a revolution in 1848.

For a century Paris-based Comptoir National d'Escompte de Paris (CNEP) bounced between private and public status depending on government whim. It was the #3 bank in France from the late 19th century through the 1950s.

Banque National pour le Commerce et l'Industrie (BNCI) started in Alsace a region that was part of Germany from the Franco-Prussian War until WWI. BNCI served as an economic bridge between Germany and France which had to give the bank governmental resuscitation during the Depression. By the 1960s BNCI had passed CNEP in size.

French leader Charles de Gaulle expected banking to drive post-WWII reconstruction and in 1945 CNEP and BNCI were nationalized. In 1966 France's finance minister merged them and they became BNP. That year the company started an association with Dresdner Bank of Germany under which the two still operate joint ventures primarily in Eastern Europe.

By 1993 privatization was again in vogue and BNP was cut loose by the government. It expanded outside France to ameliorate the influences of the French economy and government. Even before it was privatized BNP was involved in such politically charged actions as the bailout of OPEC money repository Banque Arabe and the extension of credit to Algeria's state oil company Sonatrach.

The privatized BNP looked overseas in the late 1990s. In 1997 alone it won the right to operate in New Zealand bought Laurentian Bank and Trust of the Bahamas took control of its joint venture with Egypt's Banque du Caire and opened a subsidiary in Brazil.

BNP bought failed Peregrine Investment's Chinese operations in 1998. That year the bank also expanded in Peru opened an office in Algeria opened a representative office in Uzbekistan set up an investment banking subsidiary in India and bought Australian stock brokerage operations from Prudential.

After a decade of globe-trotting BNP brought it on home in 1999 and set off a year of tumult in French banking. As France's other two large banks (Socit Gnrale and Paribas) made plans to merge BNP decided it would absorb both banks as a means to get a bigger chunk of the to-be-privatized Crdit Lyonnais and to protect France from Euro-megabank penetration by creating the globe's largest bank.

Executives at Socit Gnrale (SG) had other ideas forming a cartel called "Action Against the BNP Raid." Meanwhile BNP tried to boost to controlling stakes its holdings in the two banks. (In Europe's cross-ownership tradition the target banks also owned part of BNP.) France's central bank tried unsuccessfully to negotiate a deal (the government supported the triumvirate merger). A war of words was played out in the media and finally shareholders had to vote on the proposals. In the end BNP won control of Paribas but not SG. As BNP prepared to integrate a reluctant Paribas into its operations regulators ordered BNP to relinquish its stake in SG. The newly merged company was dubbed BNP Paribas Group.

In 2000 BNP Paribas and Avis Group launched a fleet-management joint venture. BNP also bought 150 shopping centers from French retailer Carrefour and the 40% of merchant bank Cobepa that it didn't already own. In 2001 BNP Paribas took full control of US-based BancWest. The company bought United California Bank from UFJ Holdings (now part of Mitsubishi UFJ Financial Group) the following year.

The bank opened up a second "home market" when it bought Italy's Banca Nazionale del Lavoro (BNL) for $11 billion in 2006.

Two of the French bank's most transformative acquisitions included the deal to buy Italian bank Banca Nazionale del Lavoro in 2006 and the 75% purchase of Fortis Bank (which also included a 25% stake in Fortis Insurance). Both deals boosted BNP Paribas' retail banking business across Europe. Retail banking is now responsible for more than 60% of BNP Paribas' revenues.

In addition to the Fortis and BNL acquisitions BNP Paribas looked to grow in new markets. BNP Paribas acquired Sahara Bank in Libya and a 51% stake in UkrSibbank one of Ukraine's leading banks. In 2008 as the world's economies struggled to stay afloat the French government agreed to inject 10.5 billion ($14 billion) into the nation's top six banks including BNP Paribas. The government didn't receive shares in the banks it assisted; rather the capital injections were meant to help reenergize lending activities in France. A year after receiving the cash BNP Paribas announced plans to repay the government's aid.

In 2009 after a couple of false starts and a seven-month saga BNP Paribas acquired control of Fortis Banque (also known as Fortis Bank). Fortis' Dutch operations were excluded from the transaction. The deal further cemented BNP Paribas as a top European bank. Fortis Bank was nationalized in October 2008 to prevent its collapse and the takeover by BNP Paribas was delayed and revised to satisfy Fortis shareholders and other interested parties. Upon the closing of the deal BNP Paribas became the market leader in Belgium and Luxembourg. The Belgian government gained more than 10% of BNP Paribas in the transaction.

BNP Paribas complimented its 2009 acquisition of Fortis with the purchase of private bank Insinger de Beaufort.

In 2011 BNP Paribas continued its strategy of expanding in high growth markets and acquired a majority of South Africa's Cadiz Securities. BNP Paribas also owns Banque Internationale pour le Commerce et l'Industrie which is active in six African nations and a majority of Türk Ekonomi Bankasi in Turkey. BNP Paribas has been expanding in China Egypt Israel and Russia as well.

In 2012 the company sold the bulk of its controlling stake in real estate firm Klpierre to US mall owner Simon for some 1.5 billion (around $2 billion) to further raise its capital levels.

EXECUTIVES

Head Group Risk Management, Michel Konczaty
COO, Philippe Bordenave
CEO BNP Paribas Fortis, Maxime Jadot, age 59
Deputy Chief Operating Officer and Head of International Financial Services, Jacques d'Estais, age 56
Deputy Chief Operating Officer and General Manager North America, Alain Papiasse, age 56
Head of International Retail Banking, Stefaan Decraene, age 50
Head of Asia-Pacific Region, ric Raynaud
CEO BNP Paribas Leasing Solutions, Charlotte Dennery, age 50
Chief Executive Officer, Jean-Laurent Bonnaf ©
Head of French Retail Banking, Marie-Claire Capobianco
Head of Group Compliance and Internal Control Coordination, Eric Martin
Head of Corporate and Investment Banking, Yann G ©ardin
Head of Group Risk Management, Frank Roncey
Deputy COO and Head of Domestic Markets, Thierry Laborde
CEO BNP Paribas MF, Sharad Sharma
CEO BNP Paribas Malaysia, Philippe Aroyo
CEO Sydney and Head of Country Australia and New Zealand, James Gibson
CEO South Korea, Philippe Noirot
Country Head and CEO Vietnam; CEO Ho Chi Minh City BNP Bank Vietnam, Aymar Beaufort
Regional Head Southeast Asia; CEO BNP Bank Singapore, Pierre Veyres
CEO BNP Paribas Personal Finance, Laurent David
Managing Director and Chief Investment Officer, Prashant Bhayani
Chairman and CEO Asia, Mignonne Cheng
Chairman, Jean Lemierre, age 66
Auditors: Deloitte & Associ ©

LOCATIONS

HQ: BNP Paribas (France)
16, boulevard des Italiens, Paris 75009
Phone: (33) 1 40 14 45 46
Web: www.bnpparibas.com

2013 Revenue

	% of total
Europe	77
North America	10
Asia-Pacific & Africa	7
Other	6
Total	**100**

PRODUCTS/OPERATIONS

2013 Sales by Segment

	% of total
Retail banking	62
Corporate and investment banking	22
Investment solutions	16
Total	**100**

COMPETITORS

ABN AMRO Group
BBVA
Banco Popular Espa±ol
Bank of America
Barclays
Citigroup
Cr©dit Agricole
Deutsche Bank
HSBC
JPMorgan Chase
Natixis
Soci©t© G©n©rale
U.S. Bancorp
UBS
Wells Fargo

HISTORICAL FINANCIALS

Company Type: Public

Income Statement FYE: December 31

	ASSETS ($ mil.)	NET INCOME ($ mil.)	INCOME AS % OF ASSETS	EMPLOYEES
12/14	2,525,526	190	0.0%	187,903
12/13	2,478,315	6,652	0.3%	184,545
12/12	2,513,902	8,637	0.3%	188,551
12/11	2,541,999	7,825	0.3%	198,423
12/10	2,674,279	10,496	0.4%	205,348
Annual Growth	(1.4%)	(63.3%)	—	(2.2%)

2014 Year-End Financials

Return on assets: 0.0%
Return on equity: 0.1%
Long-term debt ($ mil.): —
No. of shares (mil.): 1,242
Sales ($ mil): 114,611
Dividends
Yield: 3.4%
Payout: —
Market value ($ mil.): 36,519

	STOCK PRICE ($) FY Close	P/E High	P/E Low	PER SHARE ($) Earnings	Dividends	Book Value
12/14	29.38	—	—	(0.09)	1.02	87.43
12/13	39.20	11	7	5.07	0.97	97.06
12/12	29.21	6	3	6.79	0.75	91.38
12/11	19.65	8	3	6.22	1.34	81.80
12/10	31.95	6	4	8.46	1.87	83.57
Annual Growth	(2.1%)	—	—	—	(14.0%)	1.1%

BNP Paribas (Suisse) SA (Switzerland)

EXECUTIVES

Chairman Of The Board, Jean-Marc Bazin
Auditors: Deloitte SA

LOCATIONS

HQ: BNP Paribas (Suisse) SA (Switzerland)
Place de Hollande 2, Geneva CH-1211
Phone: (41) 58 212 21 11 **Fax:** (41) 58 212 22 22
Web: www.bnpparibas.ch

HISTORICAL FINANCIALS

Company Type: Public

Income Statement FYE: December 31

	ASSETS ($ mil.)	NET INCOME ($ mil.)	INCOME AS % OF ASSETS	EMPLOYEES
12/14	2,525,526	190	0.0%	0
12/13	2,492,609	6,633	0.3%	1,631
12/12	32,926	362	1.1%	1,691
12/11	35,891	350	1.0%	1,818
12/10	46,828	336	0.7%	1,832
Annual Growth	171.0%	(13.2%)	—	—

2014 Year-End Financials

Return on assets: 0.0%
Return on equity: 0.1%
Long-term debt ($ mil.): —
No. of shares (mil.): 1,245
Sales ($ mil): 114,611

Dividends
Yield: —
Payout: —
Market value ($ mil.): —

Boc Hong Kong Holdings Ltd

BOC Hong Kong (Holdings) is the parent of Bank of China (Hong Kong) which has about 300 branches in Hong Kong as well as on mainland China. The bank serves local businesses and consumers providing loans deposit accounts and other standard services as well as securities brokerage wealth management and project financing and syndication. It also prints currency. In addition Bank of China (Hong Kong) owns Nanyang Commercial Bank and some 70% of Chiyu Banking Corporation (both are also based in Hong Kong) as well as BOC Credit Card (International). Bank of China which is controlled by the Chinese government owns about two-thirds of BOC Hong Kong.

The company wants to diversify its revenue mix by focusing on increasing its business in wealth management insurance and corporate finance. It is looking to China for growth and has plans to expand to other parts of Asia as well.

EXECUTIVES

Vice Chairman and CEO, Yue Yi, age 58
CFO, Sui Yang, age 40
COO, Zhong Xiangqun
Deputy Chief Executive Corporate Banking Financial Institutions and Product Management Corporate Credit Management Centre and China Business, Lin Jingzhen, age 50
Deputy Chief Executive Personal Banking and Product Management Channel Management Private Banking and BOCCC, Kung Yeung (Ann) Yun Chi, age 52
Vice Chairman, Chen Siqing, age 54
Chairman, Tian Guoli, age 53
Auditors: Ernst & Young

LOCATIONS

HQ: Boc Hong Kong Holdings Ltd
52nd Floor, Bank of China Tower, 1 Garden Road,
Phone: (852) 2846 2700 **Fax:** (852) 2810 5830
Web: www.bochk.com

PRODUCTS/OPERATIONS

2014 Sales

	% of total
Interest income	58
Fee and commission income	17
Gross earned premiums	20
Net trading gain	3
Others	2
Total	100

COMPETITORS

AXA Asia Pacific
Bank of Communications
Bank of East Asia
CITIC International Financial
Chong Hing Bank
Citigroup
Dah Sing Financial Holdings Limited
HSBC
Hang Seng Bank
Standard Chartered

HISTORICAL FINANCIALS

Company Type: Public

Income Statement FYE: December 31

	ASSETS ($ mil.)	NET INCOME ($ mil.)	INCOME AS % OF ASSETS	EMPLOYEES
12/14	282,309	3,169	1.1%	14,926
12/13	263,989	2,869	1.1%	14,647
12/12	236,174	2,700	1.1%	14,638
12/11	223,804	2,630	1.2%	14,475
12/10	213,705	2,083	1.0%	13,806
Annual Growth	7.2%	11.1%	—	2.0%

2014 Year-End Financials

Return on assets: 1.1%
Return on equity: 14.6%
Long-term debt ($ mil.): —
No. of shares (mil.): —
Sales ($ mil): 9,512

Dividends
Yield: 3.8%
Payout: 855.1%
Market value ($ mil.): —

	STOCK PRICE ($) FY Close	P/E High/Low		PER SHARE ($) Earnings	Dividends	Book Value
12/14	67.01	31	24	0.30	2.56	2.16
12/13	64.52	34	29	0.27	3.15	1.94
12/12	63.05	33	24	0.26	2.80	1.84
12/11	47.16	37	19	0.25	3.05	1.58
12/10	68.43	48	27	0.20	2.45	1.40
Annual Growth	(0.5%)	—	—	11.1%	1.1%	11.4%

Bombardier Inc.

Canada's Bombardier is the world's only manufacturer of both planes and trains (but no automobiles). The company's Aerospace division manufactures business (Learjet) commercial (CSeries) and amphibious military (Bombardier 415) aircraft while overseas its Germany-based Transportation division manufactures rail vehicles including monorails light rails metros commuter trains high-speed trains (including the very high speed ZEFIRO) and locomotives. Both are industry-leading businesses. A third division Flexjet offers fractional jet ownership and charter services. (In late 2013 Bombardier announced it was selling Flexjet.)

Strategy

Over the next decade industry forecasts show sustained growth in business and commercial aircraft markets. As a result Bombardier's Aerospace unit continues to invest in and develop new state-of-the art aircraft lines such as its CSeries commercial aircraft family which is aiming to be the world's greenest and most fuel efficient mainliner.

The Aerospace division made one of its largest business aircraft sales in its history in late 2012 when luxury aviation company VistaJet signed a deal for up to 142 Global family business jets for $7.8 billion if all options are exercised. Deliveries of these aircraft will begin in 2014. Prior to that in mid-2012 Bombardier Aerospace won another landmark business jet order from NetJets for a whopping $7.3 billion.

On the rail transportation side demand for sturdy and efficient trains continues to be driven by urban and suburban development worldwide as well as ongoing demand for reliable public transportation. In South America's largest metropolis Sao Paulo Brazil Bombardier's Transportation division is undertaking a notable project to build the world's largest largest mass transit monorail to deal with the city's congestion. The monorail is due to begin operating in early 2014. The project is part of a broader effort by Bombardier to gain a stronger foothold in emerging markets with high growth potential; others include China India and Russia.

Bombardier's Transportation division is actively involved in China's development of urban mass transit and advanced rail networks. Demand is strong there as the growing popularity of rail transportation is actually eating into the profits of regional aviation companies. Bombardier Transportation has three joint ventures in China as well as several wholly owned foreign enterprises and offices in Beijing Guangzhou Shanghai and Hong Kong. One of its key contracts is a $4 billion order from China's Ministry of Railways (MOR) to deliver of several different types of ZEFIRO very high speed trains.

Ownership

The company is controlled by the Bombardier family.

Company Background

Bombardier engineers and industrial designers spent two years designing the Vancouver 2010 Olympic torch. To ensure the flame would not extinguish in temperatures reaching minus 36 degrees Celsius (minus 96.8 degrees Fahrenheit) the company blended propane and isobutane a mixture that supports fire at extremely cold temperatures. It manufactured 12000 torches each with a side vent to allow the flame to unfurl like a flag.

HISTORY

Bombardier got its start in the 1920s when mechanic Joseph-Armand Bombardier began converting old cars into snowmobiles. He founded L'Auto-Neige Bombardier Limited in 1942 to make commercial snow vehicles. In 1959 Bombardier introduced the first personal snowmobile the Ski-Doo.

At age 27 Laurent Beaudoin became the company's president in 1966. Bombardier went public in 1969. When the bottom dropped out of the snowmobile business due to the energy crisis in 1973 Beaudoin diversified and in 1974 Bombardier won its first mass transit contract to build Montreal subway cars. Expanding further into mass transportation Bombardier merged with MLW-Worthington Limited a builder of diesel engines and diesel-electric locomotives. In 1978 the company became Bombardier Inc.

During the 1980s Bombardier continued to diversify. It expanded into military vehicles and became the leading supplier to the North American rail transit industry. The company entered the European railcar market in 1986 the same year it acquired Canadair Canada's largest aerospace company from the national government.

Founded in 1920 as the aircraft division of Canadian Vickers Canadair became a separate company producing military and civilian aircraft in 1944. Acquired by Electric Boat (which became part of General Dynamics) in 1947 it was nationalized by the Canadian government in 1976. In 1978 Canadair introduced its Challenger 600 business jet which became a major seller.

Bombardier began development of a commuter aircraft the Canadian Regional Jet (a 50-seat derivative of the Challenger) in 1989. In 1990 the company bought US-based Learjet and its service centers and two years later it acquired a stake in de Havilland a regional aircraft maker which it jointly owned with the Province of Ontario. The company bought German railroad equipment maker Waggonfabrik Talbot in 1995.

Amtrak selected an international consortium in 1996 headed by Bombardier to produce high-speed trains electric locomotives and train maintenance facilities. Also that year the Global Express business jet made its first flight.

Bombardier doubled the size of its European operations in 1998 by buying German railcar maker Deutsche Waggonbau. In 1999 Bombardier announced the launch of its all-new business jet the eight-passenger Continental.

The company sold its 50% stake in Shorts Missile Systems to Thomson-CSF (now Thales) in 2000. Also that year Bombardier landed an $817 million contract to supply Spanish carrier Air Nostrum with 44 planes. It also inked a $2 billion deal to make 94 regional jets for Delta Air Lines; the Delta order included options for an additional 406 aircraft through 2010.

Bombardier signed a deal with SkyWest in 2001 worth about $1.4 billion for 64 Canadair regional jets. It was also selected by a bankruptcy court as winning bidder for Outboard Marine's Evinrude and Johnson outboard marine engine assets. Completing an agreement made the year before Bombardier acquired DaimlerChrysler's Adtranz rail systems unit for about $725 million making it part of its Bombardier Transportation division. Later in the year the company announced that it would take a charge of about $600 million and lay off about 10% of its aerospace workforce (it also said that it would cut another 7% of that workforce if demand did not grow).

Bombardier sought about $870 million in damages in 2002 from DaimlerChrysler (now Daimler) over the Adtranz deal claiming that the level of equity in Adtranz was overstated and that the costs related to third-party contracts were higher than stated at the time of the deal. Later that year Bombardier temporarily suspended business jet production. Bombardier divested its Recreational Products unit (snowmobiles and personal watercraft) in 2003.

Bombardier announced in 2004 that it was considering building a family (CSeries) of 100- to 130-seat jets that would compete directly with Boeing and Airbus. The next year the company's board approved the larger CSeries planes but it deferred its final decision; in 2006 Bombardier announced that it would focus instead on 80- to 100-seat passenger planes. In 2007 the company announced the new project's official name —the CRJ1000. That same year Bombardier began a performance improvement project at its Transportation division. The project which aimed to improve performance by trimming costs —chiefly procurement costs — began to show signs of effectiveness in 2007. The company continued to seek the right mix of suppliers for parts including low-cost sources.

CEO Paul Tellier resigned in 2004 amid rumored boardroom differences with Laurent Beaudoin who assumed the CEO duties. A year later in 2005 the company sold its inventory finance division which provided equipment financing to GE Commercial Finance for $2.4 billion ($1.4 billion in cash and $1 billion in assumed liabilities).

Deliveries and orders were booming for Bombardier's line of business jets before the worldwide credit crisis and recession hit in 2008. The company had 232 deliveries for business jets in fiscal 2008 compared with 212 in 2007 and 197 in 2006.

Laurent Beaudoin maintained his role as chairman when in 2008 he handed over the president and CEO titles to his son Pierre.

The business and civil aircraft markets experienced their most turbulent conditions since the aftermath of September 11 due to the global recession and credit crisis in 2009. The perpetually dicey financial condition of the airline industry —due to fluctuating fuel prices and shifts in consumer spending —affected demand for commercial aircraft. Bombardier's limited number of customers many of which are government agencies or publicly held companies watched as their own revenues fell due to the recession.

Bombardier adapted by reducing its production of business jets and CRJ regional aircraft and reducing its workforce by 4700 (about 13%). The company also took the opportunity to build on its customer services opening a service center in Europe and a third service center in the US.

EXECUTIVES

President and CEO, Alain M. Bellemare, age 53
President Bombardier Commercial Aircraft, Fred S. Cromer
President Division Western Europe Middle East and Africa Transportation, Laurent Troger
President Bombardier Business Aircraft, David M. Coleal
President Bombardier Aerostructures & Engineering Services, Jean S ©uin
SVP and CFO, John DiBert
President Bombardier China, Jianwei Zhang
Vice Chairman, Jean-Louis Fontaine, age 76
Vice Chairman, J. R. Andr ©Bombardier, age 73
President and CEO, Pierre Beaudoin, age 53
Auditors: Ernst & Young LLP

LOCATIONS

HQ: Bombardier Inc.
800 Rene-Levesque Blvd. West, 29th Floor, Montreal, Quebec H3B 1Y8
Phone: 514 861-9481 **Fax:** 514 861-2629
Web: www.bombardier.com

2011 Aircraft Sales

	% of total
North America	
US	38
Europe	30
Asia/Pacific	17
Other regions	15
Total	**100**

2011 Transportation Sales

	% of total
Europe	65
Asia/Pacific	18
North America	13
Other regions	4
Total	**100**

PRODUCTS/OPERATIONS

2011 Sales by Segment

	% of total
Transportation	51
Aerospace	49
Total	**100**

2011 Sales by Industry

	% of total
Manufacturing	73
Services	16
Other	11
Total	**100**

2011 Aerospace Sales by Market

	% of total
Business aircraft	44
Commercial aircraft	25
Services	18
Other	13
Total	**100**

2011 Transportation Sales by Market

	% of total
Rolling stock	70
Services	15
System and signaling	15
Total	**100**

Selected Operations

Aerospace
- Amphibious aircraft
- 415
- 415 MP
- Business aircraft
- Challenger
- Global
- Learjet
- Commercial aircraft
- CRJ Series
- CSeries
- Q-Series
- Flying training
- Military aircraft technical service
- Specialized aircraft modified for special missions
- Training and aircraft services
- Maintenance
- Parts
- Technical support
- Training

Flexjet
- Fractional ownership
- Whole aircraft ownership and management

Transportation
- Customized transportation systems
- Propulsion and controls
- Rail control systems
- Rail vehicles
- Automated people movers
- Commuter/regional trains
- Intercity/high-speed trains
- Light rail vehicles
- Locomotives
- Metros
- Monorails
- Rapid transit
- Services
- Fleet maintenance
- Material management
- Operations and maintenance
- Vehicle refurbishment and modernization

COMPETITORS

ALSTOM
AeroCentury
Airbus
Airbus Group
Blue Star Jets
Boeing
COMAC
Dassault Aviation
Embraer
Finmeccanica
Flight Options
Gulfstream Aerospace
Kawasaki Rail Car
Mitsubishi Heavy Industries
NetJets
Piper Aircraft
Siemens AG
Thales
XOJET

HISTORICAL FINANCIALS

Company Type: Public

Income Statement FYE: December 31

	REVENUE ($ mil.)	NET INCOME ($ mil.)	NET PROFIT MARGIN	EMPLOYEES
12/14	20,111	(1,260)	—	74,000
12/13	18,151	564	3.1%	76,400
12/12	16,768	588	3.5%	71,500
12/11*	18,347	837	4.6%	70,000
01/11	17,712	755	4.3%	65,370
Annual Growth	3.2%	—	—	3.1%

*Fiscal year change

2014 Year-End Financials

Debt ratio: 27.6%
Return on equity: (-102.1%)
Cash ($ mil.): 2,489
Current ratio: 0.98
Long-term debt ($ mil.): 7,627
No. of shares (mil.): 1,739
Dividends
Yield: 0.0%
Payout: —
Market value ($ mil.): 6,245

	STOCK PRICE ($) FY Close	P/E High/Low		PER SHARE ($) Earnings	Dividends	Book Value
12/14	3.59	—	—	(0.74)	0.09	0.02
12/13	4.35	17	12	0.31	0.10	1.39
12/12	3.81	15	9	0.32	0.13	0.77
12/11*	3.95	16	7	0.47	0.10	0.37
01/11	5.75	15	10	0.42	0.10	2.48
Annual Growth	(11.1%) (68.6%)	—	—	—	(2.4%)	

*Fiscal year change

Bosch (Robert) GmbH (Germany Fed. Rep.)

Robert Bosch has spent more than a century establishing a name for really "boss" automobile and industrial equipment as well as consumer goods and building systems. Bosch operates via 440 subsidiaries in 60 countries; its core lines include mobility (auto) systems from diesel/hybrid drive to steering starter motors and generators electronics and brakes. Subsidiary Bosch Rexroth makes electric hydraulic and pneumatic machinery for industrial use. Bosch Security makes various protection systems. Bosch also makes photovoltaic and wind-turbine components heat pumps for buildings and home appliances through Bosch-Siemens Hausgerate. Charitable foundation Robert Bosch Stiftung controls the company.

Geographic Reach

The company has operations in 60 countries and plies its wares globally. Europe accounted for 53% of the revenue in 2014. The company also operates in Americas and Asia/Pacific. Bouncing back from the global recession which hit the automotive industry particularly hard Bosch has been expanding in the Asia Pacific region where recession effects were minimal or delayed.

Operations

Bosch divides its business into four main categories. The company's Mobility Solutions group is the world's largest independent auto parts supplier. The Industrial Technology segment includes Drive and Control Technology and Packaging Technology which supply the mechanical engineering and packaging and process engineering sectors respectively. Consumer Goods provides Power Tools and Household Appliances and the Energy and Building Technology segment offers HVAC solar energy and security systems products and services.

Sales and Marketing

Bosch is represented in about 150 countries.

Financial Performance

The company's revenues increased by 6% in 2014 due to an increase in Mobility Solutions' sales as the result of a strong demand for modern gasoline direct injection systems transmission control systems and continuously variable transmissions. In Europe and China Bosch's diesel technology business benefited from the ramp-up of new injection systems. Consumer Goods sales increased by 5% due to a growth in sales from the Power Tools division; Energy and Building Technology revenues increased by 2%. Bosch's net income increased by 111% as the result of higher revenues and the positive effects from changes in exchange rates and improved investment results.Operating cash flow decreased by 10% due to an increase in cash used in inventories receivables and other assets.

Strategy

Bosch's strategic focus is on energy efficiency. Drivers include the growing demand for energy ever tighter climate-protection regulations and the finite nature of fossil fuels. The company generates 40% of its sales from products that contribute to energy efficiency environmental protection and resource conservation. These products account for more than half of the company's current research and development expenditure.To deal with the economic woes of recent years and position itself for growth Bosch has been investing in Asia. By 2020 the company aims to double its sales in Asia/Pacific and the Americas compared with 2013 to grow faster than the market in Europe and to increase its annual sales in Africa to 2 billion euros.Streamlining its operations for future growth Bosch plans to set up a new division in 2016 Bosch Global Service Solutions to bring together all the internal and external services offered by the company. The division will emerge from the Service Solutions business unit which is run by Bosch Sicherheitssysteme GmbH.Global expansion is a key aspect of the company's strategy. Bosch is focusing on the growing African market and is continuing to expand its presence on that continent. In 2015 it opened a new sales and service company in Lagos Nigeria.

That year Bosch also laid the foundation stone for its new plant in Russia. In 2014 the company opened a new research and technology center opened in Bangalore (India) its first center for software development and engineering services in North America in Guadalajara (Mexico) and its second automotive technology manufacturing plant in Romania. Bosch is also expanding its presence in Turkey.

Bosch applied for some 4600 patents worldwide in 2014.

Mergers and Acquisitions

Broadening its portfolio in 2015 in the US Bosch acquired Climatec a provider of energy efficiency building automation security and life-safety solutions and Osgood Industries a filling and packaging machine specialist.In 2015 the company acquired ProSyst which specializes in the development of gateway software and middleware and planned to merge it with Bosch Software Innovations GmbH the software and systems unit of Bosch. Strengthening Bosch's consumer goods business in 2014 the company acquired 50/50 joint ventures BSH Bosch und Siemens Hausgeräte GmbH (for 3 billion) and ZF Lenksysteme GmbH.

The company in 2013 acquired software firm Bauer Optimierungstechnik. The company which is part of Bosch's Energy and Building Solutions group makes software-based air conditioning and ventilation control systems.

Ownership

Bosch is unique not only in that it is large (with ties to almost every automobile enterprise in the world) but that it is heavy influenced by a charitable foundation. Robert Bosch Stiftung holds 92% of shares in the company. (More than 90% of voting rights are held by Robert Bosch Industrietreuhand an industrial trust.) The remaining shares are held by the Bosch family and other investors.

HISTORY

Self-taught electrical engineer Robert Bosch opened a Stuttgart workshop in 1886 and the following year produced the world's first alternator for a stationary engine. In 1897 his company built the first automobile alternator. Later electrical automotive product launches included spark plugs (1902) starters (1912) and regulators (1913). Bosch believed in treating employees well and shortened their workday to eight hours (extraordinary for 1906).

US operations begun in 1909 were confiscated during WWI as part of a trade embargo against Germany. Bosch survived the German depression of the 1920s introduced power tools (1928) and appliances (1933) and bought Blaupunkt (car radios 1933). Industrial and military demand for the company's products continued from the 1930s until WWII. Bosch died in 1942 and left 90% of his company to charity.

Bosch suffered severe damage in WWII and its US operations were again confiscated. It rebuilt after the war and enjoyed growing demand for its appliances and automotive products as postwar incomes increased worldwide. In 1963 Hans Merkle took the helm. Believing fuel efficiency and pollution control would be important issues in the future Bosch invested heavily to develop automotive components that would raise gas mileage and lower emissions. The company made the world's first electronic fuel-injection (EFI) system in 1967. Also that year Bosch and Siemens (West Germany) formed Bosch-Siemens Hausgerate to make home appliances.

The oil crisis of the 1970s increased awareness of fuel efficiency and benefited sales of EFI systems. Buying a plant in Charleston South Carolina Bosch re-entered the US in 1974 to make fuel-injection systems. It introduced the first antilock braking system in 1978.

A 1984 strike against Bosch in Germany disrupted automobile production throughout Europe. In the late 1980s the company developed technology for multiplexing (employing one wire to replace many by using semiconductor controllers) in automobiles established it as an industry standard and licensed it to chip makers Intel (US) Philips (the Netherlands) and Motorola (US). Throughout the 1980s and into the 1990s Bosch acquired various telecommunications companies.

In 1993 Bosch's sales dropped for the first time since 1967. In response the company cut its workforce. In 1996 Bosch bought Emerson's half of joint venture S-B Power Tool Co. which makes

Bosch Dremel and Skil brand tools. Further consolidating its position as a world leader in braking systems Bosch also purchased AlliedSignal's struggling light-vehicle braking unit. The company sold its private mobile radio business to Motorola in 1997 and to speed its business for mobile phones bought Dancall Telecom (a maker of mobile-phone handsets) from UK-based Amstrad.

In 1998 the company's Bosch-Siemens Hausgerate joint venture opened a plant in the US and bought Masco's Thermador unit (cooktops ovens and ranges). In 1999 Bosch sold its US-based telecom unit to a joint venture of Motorola and Cisco Systems. The next year UK-based General Electric Company (now Marconi) bought the German operations of Bosch's telecom unit.

Early in 2000 the company sold its mobile-phone business to Siemens AG. That year the company's joint venture with Siemens bought Rexroth AG (Atecs Mannesmann AG's automation and packaging technology group) for about $9.2 billion. The new division was named Bosch Rexroth AG. In 2001 Bosch bought out Siemens' stake in Bosch Rexroth and consolidated its operations as a wholly owned subsidiary.

In 2006 Robert Bosch purchased Telex Communications for $420 million. Telex is a provider of audio wireless communications and safety equipment with applications in large public places including stadiums and airports.

Bosch along with the entire automotive industry was hard hit in the global economic crisis of 2008 and 2009. Bosch struggled to stay in the public's favor by avoiding cuts in headcount as it worked to shore up net earnings which waned more than 85% in 2008 from 2007 and plunged to a loss of 1214 ($1.6 billion) in 2009. In response Bosch shed weaker units. North American sales which declined more than 10% in 2009 from 2008 were partially offset by Bosch's hammering out a sale with Akebono Brake Industry. The Japanese manufacturer of brakes bought Bosch's North American foundation brake production. (Bosch's significant stake in Akebono gave the German auto parts maker a solid position.) The transaction included Bosch assets to manufacture corner modules drum brakes disc brakes and related parts at plants in Michigan Tennessee and South Carolina.

In late 2008 Bosch sold its "car infotainment" business branded Blaupunkt to Aurelius a German investment group. The deal comprised the trade name and portfolio of car radio hi-fi component and advanced navigation devices. Also that same year it bought a majority stake in ersol Solar Energy (renamed Bosch Solar Energy in 2009) a German manufacturer of wafer-based mono- and polycrystalline silicon solar cells and thin-film solar modules used to generate electricity from sunlight.

In 2012 the Bosch Automotive Aftermarket division spent about $120 million euros in a spark plug and brake pad manufacturing facility in Nanjing China. The facility which represents Bosch's largest investment anywhere houses testing and R&D operations. The move put Bosch in the center of fast growing Asia and positioned it close to many of its automotive OEM customers.

EXECUTIVES

Member Management Board, Uwe Raschke, age 57
Chairman and CTO, Volkmar Denner, age 59
President Gasoline Systems, Peter Tyroller, age 58
Member Management Board, Wolf-Henning Scheider
President Chassis Systems Modulation, Werner Struth
Deputy Chairman, Stefan Asenkerschbaumer, age 59
Member Management Board, Christoph Kuebel
Member Management Board, Stefan Hartung
Member Management Board, Dirk Hoheisel
Member Management Board, Rolf Bulander, age 57
Auditors: PricewaterhouseCoopers Aktiengesellschaft Wirtschaftprufungsgesellschaft

LOCATIONS

HQ: Bosch (Robert) GmbH (Germany Fed. Rep.)
Postfach 10 60 50, Stuttgart D-70049
Phone: (49) 711 811 0 **Fax:** (49) 711 811 6630
Web: www.bosch.com

2014 Sales

	% of total
Europe	53
Asia	25
Americas	20
Other region	2
Total	**100**

PRODUCTS/OPERATIONS

2014 Sales

	% of total
Mobility Solutions	68
Industrial technology	14
Energy and building technology	9
Consumer goods	9
Total	**100**

Selected Divisions and Products

Automotive Technology
- Car multimedia
- Chassis systems brakes
- Chassis systmes control
- Diesel systems
- Electrical drives
- Gasoline systems
- Starter motors and generators
- Steering systems

Consumer Goods and Building Technology
- Household appliances
- Power tools
- Security systems
- Thermotechnology (gas-fired hot water heating systems)

Industrial Technology
- Drive and control technology
- Packaging technology
- Solar energy

COMPETITORS

BorgWarner
DENSO
Dana Holding
Delphi Automotive Systems
Electrolux
Emerson Electric
Federal-Mogul
GE
Honeywell International
Ingersoll-Rand
Johnson Controls
Magna International
Pioneer Corporation
Prestolite Electric
Senior plc
Snap-on
Standard Motor Products
Stanley Black and Decker
Tenneco
Trane Inc.
Valeo
Visteon
Whirlpool

HISTORICAL FINANCIALS

Company Type: Public

Income Statement FYE: December 31

	REVENUE ($ mil.)	NET INCOME ($ mil.)	NET PROFIT MARGIN	EMPLOYEES
12/14	59,500	2,929	4.9%	290,183
12/13	63,423	1,508	2.4%	281,381
12/12	69,150	2,980	4.3%	305,877
12/11	66,605	2,258	3.4%	302,519
12/10	63,250	3,181	5.0%	283,507
Annual Growth	(1.5%)	(2.0%)	—	0.6%

2014 Year-End Financials

Debt ratio: 10.2%	No. of shares (mil.): 1,200
Return on equity: 8.7%	Dividends
Cash ($ mil.): 6,701	Yield: —
Current ratio: 2.10	Payout: —
Long-term debt ($ mil.): 6,111	Market value ($ mil.): —

Bouygues S.A.

If all roads lead to Bouygues that's because the company built them. Bouygues (pronounced "bweeg") operates in three primary business areas: construction; telecommunications; and media. Its road work buildings and property development contracting services account for about 80% of the group's sales and operate through road builder Colas (about 35% of sales) Bouygues Construction (35%) and Bouygues Immobilier (10%) which develops commercial and residential properties. The group also owns a 90% stake in Bouygues Telecom (France's #3 mobile phone carrier); more than 40% of TF1 (France's #1 TV channel); and 29% of industrial group ALSTOM.

Operations

Bouygues SA is a diversified industrial group with five main business segments: Construction through Bouygues Construction (building civil works energy and services); Property through Bouygues Immobilier (property); Roads through road builder Colas; Telecoms through Bouygues Telecom; and Media through TF1 (Tlvision Francaise 1 SA).

Subsidiary Bouygues Construction is a force in itself with several subsidiaries performing civil construction and electrical/maintenance work. The group focuses on public-private partnerships those lucrative partnerships that governments use to build roads prisons schools and other infrastructure. Bouygues has increasingly participated in sustainable development projects with investments in training research and resources.

The French conglomerate also has a 29% stake in Alstom (making it the largest shareholder) which builds rail cars ships and power plants.

Geographic Reach

Paris-based Bouygues SA's largest market is France which accounts for about 60% of its total sales. The European Union and the rest of Europe contributes about 15%. The firm is also active in North America Asia Africa the Middle East and Central and South America. Overall the group does business in about 80 countries worldwide.

Financial Performance

Note: Growth rates may differ after conversion to US dollars.Bouygues revenues have been steadily rising over the past few years thanks to strengthened demand for construction projects and property development. Profits however have been in decline due to impairment losses on the company's struggling Alstom business.The company's revenue was mostly flat in 2014 inching up by less than 1% to 33.12 million ($40.3 million) with growth overseas and declining business in France. Its construction business' sales grew by 2% mostly thanks to a higher volume of international construction projects through its Bouygues Construction division. Bouygues Immobilier grew by 11% as commercial property sales doubled over the prior years' results. Its Colas business shrank by 3% as its project sales in France slipped by double digits while its TF1 subsidiary and Bouygues Telecom shrank by 9% and 5% respectively.Bouygues' net income rebounded sharply to 807 million ($980.9 million) from a $1 billion loss in 2013 mostly due to the absence of a non-recurring 1.4 billion ($1.7 billion) impairment loss on its Alstom business that it incurred in 2013 and because of non-recurring gains on the sale of the company's equity interests in Cofi route and Eurosport International. Not counting these non-recurring items Bouygues' net income would have declined by 158 million during the year.The company's operating cash fell by 13% to 1.9 billion for the year as it collected less from its share of profits from its joint ventures and associates.

Strategy

Bouygues completed a strong collection of high-value projects in 2014. Bouygues Construction completed the Tuen Mun-Chek Lap Kok tunnel in Hong Kong Zagreb Airport in Croatia and the L2 bypass in Marseille. Meanwhile Colas put the final touches on the Tangier-Kenitra high-speed rail link in Morocco the Santiago metro in Chile and a roads maintenance contract in London. In late 2014 Bouygues Construction began its first civil works contract in Azerbaijan; its Bouygues Travaux Publics subsidiary secured a 147 million contract to design and build the "28 May" station of the capital Baku's metro line; and its Dragages Hong Kong and Bouygues Travex Publics subsidiaries won a 490 million-contract with MTR Corporation to build two twin-tube tunnels on the 6-km extension of the Shatin to Central Link metro line.To reduce its dependence on its home country and Europe the French firm is expanding in international markets especially Asia and the Middle East. As of 2015 Bouygues Construction generated 46% of its sales outside of France while Colas generates 43% in international markets.Mergers and AcquisitionsIn December 2014 Bouygues Immobilier acquired Loticis to to expand its urban-planning-subdivision business in the Paris region. Also in 2014 subsidiary Bouygues Energies et Services bought an 85% equity stake in Toronto-based Plan Group.OwnershipBouygues SA is controlled by the founding Bouygues family and led by billionaire Martin Bouygues. Holding company SCDM owned a 20.9% stake in the company at the end of 2014. Company Background Looking to grow its telecoms business Bouygues in 2014 bid 10.5 billion ($14.4 billion) in cash to acquire the telecoms arm of Vivendi SFR and 46% of the new company in a planned spin-off. It lost out to French cable operator Numericable. A tie-up between SFR and Bouygues would have created Europe's seventh-biggest telecoms group by sales and in France would rank ahead of market leader Orange in market share.

HISTORY

Company BackgroundWith the equivalent of $1700 in borrowed money Francis Bouygues son of a Paris engineer started Entreprise Francis Bouygues in 1952 as an industrial works and construction firm in the Paris region of France. Within four years his firm had expanded into property development.

By the mid-1960s Bouygues had entered the civil engineering and public works sectors and developed regional construction units across France. In 1970 it was listed on the Paris stock exchange. Four years later the company established Bouygues Offshore to build oil platforms.

In 1978 the firm built Terminal 2 of Paris' Charles de Gaulle airport. Three years later it won the contract to construct the University of Riyadh in Saudi Arabia (then the world's largest building project at 3.2 million sq. ft.) which was completed in 1984. That year Bouygues acquired France's #3 water supply company Saur and power transmission and supply firm ETDE.

Expansion continued in 1986 with the purchase of the Screg Group which included Colas France's top highway contractor. The next year the company led a consortium to buy 50% of newly privatized network Socit Tlvision Française 1 (TF1). Bouygues became the largest shareholder with a 25% stake (increased to 40% by 1999). In 1988 the company began building the Channel Tunnel (completed 1994) and moved into its new ultramodern headquarters dubbed Challenger in Saint-Quentin-en-Yvelines outside Paris.

After rumors of failing health Francis Bouygues resigned as chairman in 1989. His son Martin took over as chairman and CEO although the patriarch called France's "Emperor of Concrete" remained on the board until his death in 1993.

Despite fears that the group would suffer without its founder's leadership Bouygues continued to grow with the 1989 acquisition of a majority interest in Grands Moulins de Paris France's largest flour milling firm (sold 1998). In 1990 it purchased Swiss construction group Losinger.

The company entered the telecom industry in 1993 with a national paging network and added a mobile phone license a year later. In 1996 the group listed 40% of Bouygues Offshore's shares on the New York and Paris stock exchanges. Also that year it launched mobile phone operator Bouygues Telecom and entered a partnership with Telecom Italia.

By 1999 Bouygues Telecom had reached 2 million customers and Bouygues bought back a 20% share held by the UK's Cable and Wireless to increase its stake to nearly 54%. That year Bouygues Offshore bought Norwegian engineering firm Kvaerner and the group spun off its construction sector creating Bouygues Construction.

After word circulated that Deutsche Telekom wanted to acquire the group's telecom unit Bouygues became the target of takeover rumors. Francois Pinault France's richest businessman became Bouygues' largest non-family shareholder when he increased his stake to 14% (later reduced to about 2%). Pinault's biggest rival Bernard Arnault upped his stake to more than 9% of the group fueling speculation of a battle over control of the board.

In 2001 the company pulled out of France's auction for a third-generation wireless license and remained the only European incumbent mobile carrier without a major domestic investment in 3G technology (until 2009). The next year the company agreed to buy Telecom Italia's stake in Bouygues Telecom increasing Bouygues' ownership in the mobile operator from 54% to more than 65%. In 2002 the company sold its 51% stake in oil field platform construction unit Bouygues Offshore to Italian oil services group Saipem which announced plans to bid for the remaining shares.

However talks with German utility giant E.ON over the sale of Bouygues' Saur subsidiary failed that year after E.ON decided to focus instead on its electricity and gas operations.

In 2005 Bouygues was more successful when it sought to sell Saur piecemeal. It sold several divisions of the subsidiary (Coved Saur France Saur International and Stereau) to French private equity firm PAI Partners but retained the African and Italian (Sigesa-Crea) divisions of the firm.

Bouygues bought the French government's 21% stake in ALSTOM for $2.5 billion in 2006. The deal was approved on the condition that it not try to control the company for at least three years. Bouygues did build up its holding after the acquisition though eventually holding 29% of the shares.

In 2008 property developer Bouygues Immobilier expanded with the acquisition of Urbis a French rival. That year Colas bought the Gouyer Group of companies (distribution of construction materials) in Martinique and Guadeloupe while Bouygues Telecom acquired a fixed-line network that allowed it to launch the Bbox broadband router and Internet services that include VoIP e-mail Internet access and television; the telecom unit also gained the previously denied right to offer the iPhone 3G.

EXECUTIVES

Deputy CEO, Olivier Bouygues, age 65, $920,000 total compensation

Chairman and CEO, Martin Bouygues, age 63, $920,000 total compensation

Chairman and CEO TF1, Nonce Paolini, age 66

Chairman and CEO Bouygues Construction, Yves Gabriel, age 65, $850,000 total compensation

Chairman and CEO Bouygues Telecom, Olivier Roussat, age 51

CFO, Philippe Marien, age 59

Chairman and CEO Bouygues Immobilier; Director, Francois Bertiere, age 65

Chairman and CEO Colas; Director, Herve Le Bouc, age 64

Auditors: Mazars

LOCATIONS

HQ: Bouygues S.A.
32 avenue Hoche, Paris, Cedex 08 75378

Phone: (33) 1 44 20 10 00

Web: www.bouygues.com

2014 Sales

	% of total
Europe	
France	62
Other countries	16
North America	9
Asia/Pacific	6
Africa & Middle East	5
Central & South America	1
Oceania	1
Total	**100**

PRODUCTS/OPERATIONS

2014 Sales by Segment

	% of total
Construction	80
Telecoms	13
Media	7
Total	**100**

2014 Sales

	% of total
Colas	37
Bouygues Construction	35
Bouygues Telecom	13
TF1	7
Bouygues Immobilier	8
Total	**100**

Selected Subsidiaries and Affiliates

Construction
- Autoroute de liaison Seine-Sarthe SA (33%)
- Bouygues Bâtiment Ile-de-France SA (99.9%)
- Bati-Rénov SA (99.3%)
- Bouygues Bâtiment International SA (99.9%)
- Bouygues Thaï Ltd (49%)
- DTP Singapour Pte Ltd (99.9%)
- Kohler Investment SA (Luxembourg 99.9%)
- Bouygues Construction SA (99.9%)
- ETDE SA (99.9%)
- Exprimm IT (99.9%)
- Icel Maidstone Ltd (UK 99.9%)
- Quille SA (99.9%)
- Westminster Local Education Partnership Ltd (UK 80%)

Media
- Métro France Publications (15%)
- Télévision Française 1 SA (TF1 43%)
- TF1 Vidéo (43%)
- TV Breizh (43%)

Property
- Bouygues Immobilier
- Parque Empresearial Cristalia SL

SNC Bouygues Immobilier Entreprises Íle-de-France
Roads
Cofiroute (16%)
Colas Guadeloupe (97%)
Colas Hungaria (97%)
Colas Polska (97%)
Colas SA (96%)
Spac (97%)
Telecommunications
Bouygues Telecom SA (90%)

COMPETITORS

Alarko
Amec Foster Wheeler
Anglian Water Group
Atlantia
Balfour Beatty
Bechtel
Bilfinger
CANAL+
CSCEC
Dragados
EIFFAGE
Engie
FCC Barcelona
Fluor
Groupe SNEF
HOCHTIEF
Hyundai Engineering and Construction
MWH Global
Orange
Orange Switzerland
SUEZ Environnement
Severn Trent
Skanska
Technip
VINCI

HISTORICAL FINANCIALS

Company Type: Public

Income Statement FYE: December 31

	REVENUE ($ mil.)	NET INCOME ($ mil.)	NET PROFIT MARGIN	EMPLOYEES
12/14	40,409	980	2.4%	127,470
12/13	46,039	(1,042)	—	128,067
12/12	44,357	834	1.9%	133,780
12/11	42,483	1,383	3.3%	130,827
12/10	41,983	1,433	3.4%	133,456
Annual Growth	(1.0%)	(9.0%)	—	(1.1%)

2014 Year-End Financials

Debt ratio: 25.6%
Return on equity: 10.7%
Cash ($ mil.): 5,037
Current ratio: 0.96
Long-term debt ($ mil.): 7,110
No. of shares (mil.): 336
Dividends
Yield: —
Payout: 66.9%
Market value ($ mil.): —

BP p.l.c.

BP is also BO (Big Oil). It is the world's #3 publicly traded integrated oil concern behind Royal Dutch Shell and Exxon Mobil. BP explores for oil and gas in 28 countries and has proved reserves of 17 billion barrels of oil equivalent. The company is the largest oil and gas producer in the US and a top refiner with 15 plants processing more than 3.2 million barrels of crude oil per day; it is also a major producer of petrochemicals. The company supplies fuel and related convenience services to consumers at some 17200 BP-branded retail sites worldwide and markets its products in more than 50 countries.

Geographic Reach

The company operates in 80 countries primarily in North America Europe and Asia but it also manufactures and markets products in Australasia Africa and Central and South America. BP's upstream activities in North America takes place in four main areas: deep-water Gulf of Mexico Lower 48 states Alaska and Canada.

Operations

BP's downstream segment includes fuels lubricants and Petrochemicals. The Upstream segment operates oil and natural gas exploration field development and production and midstream transportation storage and processing. BP also markets and trade natural gas including liquefied natural gas power and natural gas liquids.

Sales and Marketing

The company supplies fuel and related retail services to consumers through company-owned and franchised retail sites as well as other channels including dealer wholesalers and jobbers. BP also supplies commercial customers in the transport and industrial sectors.

Financial Performance

In 2014 BP's net revenues decreased by 7% due to lower liquids realizations partially offset by higher production in higher-margin areas higher gas realizations and higher gas marketing and trading revenues.

The company's net income decreased by 84% in 2014 due to lower net revenues higher impairment charges and losses on sale of businesses and fixed assets stemming from adjustments to prior year disposals in Canada and the North Sea and costs associated with the decision to cease refining operations at Bulwer Island in Australia. Other factors included the write-off of expenses related to unsuccessful drilling activities or lease expiration. In 2014 the company's cash inflow increased by 55% due to changes in working capital as a result of a decline in inventories a drop in other current and non-current assets and a decrease in other current and non-current liabilities.

Strategy

The company took a major hit in 2010 when one of its Gulf of Mexico oil rigs exploded and killed 11 workers. Millions of gallons of crude spilled into the Gulf and BP was forced to set aside $20 billion to pay for related damages in 2011 and 2012.

The spill developed into a major political economic and public relations crisis for the company as it struggled to cap the leaking well clean up the massive spill and mollify Gulf Coast communities which saw their fishing industry decimated and their coastlines inundated by oil. To address the growing crisis in 2010 the company established an escrow account of $20 billion managed by a third party to reimburse claims from people and businesses financially damaged by the oil spill. (It settled with individual and business plaintiffs for $7.8 billion in 2012 but still faced federal state and local government charges). In a plea deal with the US government in 2012 BP pled guilty to criminal misconduct (12 felony counts) and in 2013 agreed to pay $4.5 billion in damages.

A federal court found BP grossly negligent in 2014 for its role in the 2010 spill. In 2015 BP agreed to pay a record $20.8 billion in damages to the US government and five Gulf Coast states that resolved years of litigation over the 2010 Gulf of Mexico oil spill.

The company continues to jettison non-core assets to raise cash. In 2015 BP announced plans to sell its oil storage terminal in Amsterdam. It also agreed to sell its equity in the Central Area Transmission System business in the UK North Sea to Antin Infrastructure Partners for £324 million ($545 million).

After the costly Gulf spill BP embarked on a "shrink to grow" strategy of selling older oilfields around the world to generate cash for settlements and simplify its upstream operations. All told the company has sold about $37 billion in assets. Completed divestitures include one of the largest transactions in the Gulf of Mexico –BP's sale of a number of oil and gas fields in the deepwater Gulf of Mexico region to Plains Exploration & Production for $5.55 billion in 2012. That year it also sold assets in Canada Egypt and the Permian Basin in the US to fellow explorer Apache for about $7 billion. The deal included BP receiving a $5 billion cash advance. (In 2011 BP sold its Colombian assets to Talisman Energy and Ecopetrol for $1.9 billion and properties in Venezuela and Vietnam to its Russian joint venture TNK-BP for $1.8 billion.)

TNK-BP was BP's longtime drilling venture with several Russian partners. After years of feuding with those partners in 2013 BP sold that business to Russian state oil company Rosneft as part of a complex package of deals worth a whopping $55 billion. The transaction gave BP a nearly 20% stake in Rosneft and about $12.3 billion in cash allowing it to pursue offshore drilling opportunities in the Arctic Ocean and settle billions of dollars in US Gulf spill penalties. Several BP competitors Exxon Mobil Italy's Eni and Norway's Statoil already have Russian Arctic drilling deals.In 2014 the company agreed to sell interests in four BP-operated oilfields on the North Slope of Alaska to Hilcorp and its specialist global Aviation Turbine Oils business to Eastman Chemical Company.

On the growth side in 2015 BP signed a deal to sell to China Huadian Corporation up to 1 million tons of liquefied natural gas per year worth up to $10 billion over the next 20 years.

Mergers and Acquisitions

As part of its strategy to be a leading purified terephthalic acid (PTA) regional player in 2014 BP acquired PT Amoco Mitsui PTA Indonesia (AMI). The deal allows the company to assess future opportunities to lower the cost of the production facilities by upgrading to the latest technology as well as opportunities for expansion in the Indonesian market.

HISTORY

The company which was formed in 1998 from the merger of British Petroleum and Amoco grew by buying Atlantic Richfield Company.

BP (formerly BP Amoco) was born on two sides of the Atlantic. In the US Amoco emerged from Standard Oil Trust organized by John D. Rockefeller in 1882. In 1886 he bought Lima (Ohio) oil a high-sulfur crude anticipating the discovery of a sulfur-removing process. Such a process was indeed patented in 1887 and in 1889 Standard organized Standard Oil of Indiana which later established such innovations as company-owned service stations and a research lab at the refinery.

Overseas British Petroleum (BP) was a twinkle in the eye of English adventurer William D'Arcy who began oil exploration of Persia in 1901. In 1908 bankrolled by Burmah Oil D'Arcy's firm was the first to strike oil in the Middle East. D'Arcy and Burmah Oil formed Anglo-Persian Oil in 1909 and the British government took a 51% stake in 1914.

Back in the US Standard was broken up into 34 independent oil companies in 1911. Standard Oil of Indiana kept its oil refining and US marketing operations. In 1925 it added a few Mexican and Venezuelan firms including Pan American Petroleum and Transport which held half of American Oil Co. known for Amoco antiknock gasoline. It began Amoco Chemicals in 1945.

Anglo-Persian took the BP name in 1954 and bought its own Standard Oil: After making a strike in Alaska in 1969 BP swapped Alaskan reserves for a 25% interest (later upped to 55%) in Standard Oil of Ohio (SOHIO). BP also struck North Sea oil in 1970. But falling oil and copper prices in the mid-1980s and a dry hole in the Beaufort Sea hurt earnings. Under Robert Horton SOHIO sold off units. BP also bought livestock feed producer Purina Mills (1986 sold 1998) and the rest of SOHIO (1987).

Standard Oil of Indiana had its own problems including being kicked out of Iran after the Islamic revolution and causing a major oil spill off the French coast in 1978. The firm which became Amoco in 1985 bought Canada's Dome Petroleum in 1988 making it the largest private owner of North American gas reserves but the big purchase proved hard to swallow.

In 1992 Amoco hurled itself into overseas oil exploration. It was the first foreign oil company to explore the Chinese mainland. But by 1995 production was down. That year John Browne often compared to Rockefeller became BP's CEO. In 1996 BP and Mobil merged their European fuel and lubricants operations and the British government sold its remaining stake in BP.

As oil prices tumbled in 1998 BP merged with Amoco in a $52 billion deal that formed BP Amoco. The new oil major agreed the following year to buy US-based Atlantic Richfield (ARCO) in a deal that closed in 2000. BP Amoco sold ARCO's Alaskan properties to Phillips (later ConocoPhillips) for $7 billion to gain regulatory approval for the purchase.

Its stake in Siberian oil fields was nearly taken away in a controversial 1999 bankruptcy sale before BP Amoco and Russia's Tyumen Oil agreed to cooperate. In 2000 BP Amoco and Shell Oil sold their stakes in Altura Energy to Occidental Petroleum for $3.6 billion. Also that year BP Amoco bought motor-oil maker Burmah Castrol for $4.7 billion. It paid $1.5 billion for the 18% of former ARCO exploration and production unit Vastar Resources that it didn't already own.

The company adopted BP as its main worldwide brand in 2000 and it officially shortened its name the next year.

In 2001 BP agreed to swap control of its stake in German natural gas supplier Ruhrgas plus $1.6 billion in cash and $950 million in assumed debt to German utility giant E.ON for a majority interest in Veba Oel owner of Germany's largest gas station chain. Regulators moved to keep E.ON from acquiring the Ruhrgas stake but BP agreed to make up the difference in cash if necessary and the deal proceeded. The agreement allowed BP to take full ownership of Veba Oel in 2002. To recoup some of its investment BP (with E.ON's consent) sold Veba Oel's exploration and production operations to Petro-Canada.

That year BP increased it stake in Russian oil and gas producer Sidanco from 10% to 25%.

In 2003 BP sold its Boqueron field and Desarrollo Zulia Occidental assets both located in Venezuela to Europe's Perenco. In late 2005 BP sold its petrochemical unit Innovene to INEOS for a reported $9 billion.

An explosion and fire in 2005 at BP's Texas City refinery killed 15 workers and injured many more.

In 2006 the company sold its remaining producing properties on the Outer Continental Shelf of the Gulf of Mexico to Apache Corporation for $845 million. That year BP sold its 28% stake in the Shenzi field in the Gulf of Mexico to Repsol for $2.2 billion. It also acquired a $1 billion stake in Rosneft.

In 2006 the discovery of corrosion in a major oil pipeline forced BP to close down part of its Prudhoe Bay oilfield (which represents 8% of daily US crude production) for several weeks.

That year the company also announced plans to invest $3 billion to reconfigure its Whiting Refinery in Indiana to process Canadian heavy crude oil.

In 2007 the company sold its Coryton refinery in the UK to Petroplus Holdings for $1.4 billion. That year BP acquired Chevron's 31% stake in a Netherlands-based refinery and other assets for $900 million.

BP's long-term chief executive John Browne was forced to step down in 2007 over a personal scandal and was replaced by BP veteran Tony Hayward. That year the company announced a major restructuring with a focus on core divisions Exploration & Production and Refining & Marketing and a new Alternative Energy unit dedicated to solar power wind energy and carbon capture technology.

In 2007 BP agreed to pay US authorities $373.5 million in fines relating to the 2005 Texas City refinery explosion the 2006 Alaska oil spill and a propane price-fixing scandal.

In 2008 the company signed a deal with Enbridge to pipe oil sands crude from Canada to the Texas Gulf Coast. Enbridge and BP will spend up to $2 billion to expand existing pipelines and build new connections to deliver up to 250000 barrels a day to Gulf Coast refiners by 2012. In another oil sands move BP and Husky Energy teamed up that same year to create an integrated North American oil sands business through two joint ventures BP-Husky Refinery LLC operated by BP and the Sunrise Oil Sands Partnership (SOSP) operated by Husky. BP committed $2.8 billion to create SOSP.

In 2008 BP acquired 90000 net acres of natural gas assets in the Arkoma Basin Woodford Shale play in the US from Chesapeake Energy for $1.75 billion. It subsequently bought a 25% stake in that company's Fayetteville Shale assets in Arkansas for $1.9 billion.

Boosting its North Sea assets in 2010 the company agreed to buy two oil fields in the Norwegian sector from TOTAL for $991 million. That year BP acquired Devon Energy's international assets for $7 billion in a deal that among other things gave BP a foothold in the emerging major oil play off the coast of Brazil. The company also gained properties in Azerbaijan and the Gulf of Mexico. (In 2010 it agreed to sell four of these mature deepwater oil and gas fields in Gulf of Mexico to Marubeni Oil and Gas for $650 million in order to pay down debt).

The global recession and the slump in demand for oil and gas products saw BP's revenues (along with those of its industry peers) plummet in 2009. Improved market conditions in 2010 lifted revenues. However the company reported a $4.9 billion loss for 2010 as a result of the Gulf oil spill and its aftermath the cost of which was pegged at almost $41 billion.

EXECUTIVES

CEO, Robert W. (Bob) Dudley, $750,000 total compensation
EVP Strategy and Regions, Dev Sanyal
CEO US Business, David C. Lawler, age 47
Chief Executive Upstream, H. Lamar McKay
EVP Corporate Business Activities, Katrina Landis
Group Operating Officer Strategy and Regions Upstream, Andy Hopwood
EVP Safety and Operational Risk, Bob Fryar
COO Production, Bernard Looney
EVP and Group Human Resources Director, Helmut Schuster
CFO, Brian Gilvary
President Russia, David Campbell
President Oman, Yousuf al Ojaili
CEO Downstream, Tufan Erginbilgic
Chairman, Carl-Henric Svanberg, age 63
Auditors: Ernst & Young LLP

LOCATIONS

HQ: BP p.l.c.
1 St. James Square, London SW1Y 4PD
Phone: (44) 20 7496 4000 **Fax:** (44) 20 7496 4570
Web: www.bp.com

PRODUCTS/OPERATIONS

2014 Sales

	% of total
Upstream	8
Downstream	92
Other businesses and corporate	-
Total	**100**

2014 Sales

	% of total
US	35
Other countries	65
Total	**100**

Major Operations

Refining and marketing
- Marketing
- Refining
- Supply and trading
- Transportation and shipping

Exploration and production
- Field development
- Gas processing and marketing
- Oil and gas exploration
- Pipelines and transportation

Gas and power
- Natural gas marketing and trading
- Natural gas liquids

Chemicals
- Chemical intermediates
- Feedstock
- Performance products
- Polymers

Other
- Coal mining
- Solar power

Selected Subsidiaries

Atlantic Richfield Co
BP America Inc. (US)
BP Amoco Chemcal Company (US)
BP Oil Australia
BP Exploration Operating Company
BP Espa?a (Spain)
BP International
BP Norge (Norway)
BP Oil New Zealand
BP Shipping
BP Southern Africa (South Africa)
Burmah Castrol
The Standard Oil Company (US)

COMPETITORS

Apache
Ashland Inc.
BASF SE
BG Group
BHP Billiton
Chevron
ConocoPhillips
Dow Chemical
DuPont
Eni
Exxon Mobil
Hess Corporation
Huntsman International
Imperial Oil
Koch Industries Inc.
Marathon Oil
Norsk Hydro ASA
Occidental Petroleum
PEMEX
PETROBRAS
Petrleos de Venezuela
Repsol
Royal Dutch Shell
Sinclair Oil
Sunoco
TOTAL
Valero Energy

HISTORICAL FINANCIALS

Company Type: Public

Income Statement FYE: December 31

	REVENUE ($ mil.)	NET INCOME ($ mil.)	NET PROFIT MARGIN	EMPLOYEES
12/14	357,783	3,780	1.1%	84,500
12/13	383,102	23,451	6.1%	83,900
12/12	381,589	11,582	3.0%	85,700
12/11	382,333	25,700	6.7%	83,400
12/10	302,545	(3,719)	—	79,700
Annual Growth	4.3%	—	—	1.5%

2014 Year-End Financials

Debt ratio: 18.5%
Return on equity: 3.1%
Cash ($ mil.): 29,763
Current ratio: 1.37
Long-term debt ($ mil.): 45,977
No. of shares (mil.): —
Dividends
Yield: 6.1%
Payout: 1,145.9%
Market value ($ mil.): —

	STOCK PRICE ($) FY Close	P/E High/Low	PER SHARE ($) Earnings	Dividends	Book Value
12/14	38.12	260170	0.20	2.34	5.57
12/13	48.61	39 32	1.23	2.19	6.94
12/12	41.64	79 60	0.60	1.98	6.19
12/11	42.74	36 26	1.34	1.68	5.87
12/10	44.17	— —	(0.20)	2.52	5.05
Annual Growth	(3.6%)	— —	—	(1.8%)	2.5%

Bridgestone Corp (Japan)

Auditors: Deloitte Touche Tohmatsu LLC

LOCATIONS

HQ: Bridgestone Corp (Japan)
3-1-1 Kyobashi, Chuo-ku, Tokyo 104-8340
Phone: (81) 3 6836 3162
Web: www.bridgestone.co.jp

HISTORICAL FINANCIALS

Company Type: Public

Income Statement FYE: December 31

	REVENUE ($ mil.)	NET INCOME ($ mil.)	NET PROFIT MARGIN	EMPLOYEES
12/14	30,792	2,519	8.2%	144,632
12/13	33,991	1,924	5.7%	145,029
12/12	35,292	1,992	5.6%	143,448
12/11	39,081	1,330	3.4%	143,124
12/10	35,181	1,216	3.5%	139,822
Annual Growth	(3.3%)	20.0%	—	0.8%

2014 Year-End Financials

Debt ratio: 0.1%
Return on equity: 15.4%
Cash ($ mil.): 3,272
Current ratio: 1.92
Long-term debt ($ mil.): 3,051
No. of shares (mil.): 783
Dividends
Yield: 1.9%
Payout: 11.8%
Market value ($ mil.): 13,634

	STOCK PRICE ($) FY Close	P/E High/Low	PER SHARE ($) Earnings	Dividends	Book Value
12/14	17.41	— —	3.21	0.34	22.97
12/13	19.10	— —	2.46	0.22	22.67
12/12	51.67	— —	2.54	0.70	21.05
12/11	45.00	— —	1.70	0.00	19.25
12/10	38.73	— —	1.55	0.41	18.48
Annual Growth	(18.1%)	— —	20.0%	(4.7%)	5.6%

British American Tobacco Plc (United Kingdom)

When people pick up smoking British American Tobacco (BAT) picks up steam. BAT is the world's second-largest publicly-traded tobacco company by market share (after Philip Morris International). The company rolls more than 660 billion cigarettes a year sold in 200 markets across 60-plus countries. BAT's five global cigarette brands –Dunhill Kent Rothmans Lucky Strike and Pall Mall – account for more than a third of group sales. BAT also produces loose tobacco and regional cigarette brands giving it a portfolio of more than 200 brands overall. It owns 42% of Reynolds American the #2 US cigarette maker created by the merger of BAT's Brown & Williamson unit with R.J. Reynolds Tobacco. BAT holds about 30% of India's ITC as well.

OperationsThe company sources its product from more than 100000 tobacco farmers worldwide. BAT contributed about £30 billion worth of excise and other taxes to governments worldwide in 2014.BAT's five Global Drive Brands (GDBs) include Dunhill Kent Lucky Strike Pall Mall and Rothmans.Geographic ReachBAT generated 28% of its total revenue from sales in the Asia-Pacific region in 2014 while sales from the Americas; Western Europe; and Eastern Europe Middle East and Africa (EMEA) regions contributed 21% 24% and 27% to total revenue respectively.Sales and MarketingBAT sells its product through retailers wholesalers distributors and logistics providers. About 50% of its global volume is sold by retailers that are supplied by direct distribution or exclusive distributors. Financial PerformanceNote: Growth rates may differ after conversion to US dollars.BAT has struggled to grow its revenues and profits over the past few years as cigarette and tobacco product sales have been dampened worldwide with decreasing use rates.The company's revenue fell by 8% to £13.97 billion ($21.7 billion) in 2014 mostly because of unfavorable foreign exchange rates across its international markets. Not counting this however BAT's revenue rose by nearly 3% as its price mix increased by 4% during the year. The cigarette maker recorded volume growth in Bangladesh Venezuela China Turkey Ukraine Pakistan and Iran; while cigarette sales volumes in Russia Vietnam Brazil and Western Europe shrank by around 1%. The strength of its GDBs drove its share growth higher by 10 basis points in key markets.Declining revenue in 2014 caused BAT's net income to fall by nearly 20% to £3.39 billion ($5 billion) while the company's operating cash fell by 8% to £4.9 billion ($7.6 billion) as cash earnings shrank during the year.

Stategy

BAT in 2015 continued to invest in high-growth markets with a focus on Eastern Europe Africa the Middle East and the Asia-Pacific regions. It also pledged to continue introducing differentiated products and next-generation tobacco products such as its recent Vype brand e-cigarettes and Voke a nicotine inhalation product licensed as medicine in the UK; the company reported that its innovations made up nearly 50% of its Global Drive Brand (GDBs) volume during 2014. The company planned to launch its new tobacco heating product in test markets in 2016.Faced with struggling sales in recent years the firm has had to cut back operations in several markets to keep its profits stable. In 2014 it closed factories in Australia Colombia and in the Democratic Republic of Congo while restructuring factories in Argentina Indonesia Canada Switzerland and Germany. In past years the company has cut costs by closing and downsizing its operations in other countries including Italy Denmark Australia Poland as well as combining businesses in Belgium Luxembourg and the Netherlands. All told the cigarette maker has scaled back the number of factories it operates to 44 from 83 (including acquisitions) in 2000.The cigarette industry continues to consolidate adding possible challenges for BAT in the future. BAT's equity stake in rival Reynolds helps to hedge its bets but it comes with its own set of challenges. In 2014 for example Reynolds American Inc. acquired smaller cigarette maker Lorillard forcing BAT to make a $4.7 billion investment to keep its 42% equity stake in the enlarged Reynolds. Company BackgroundIn fall 2011 it purchased Colombia's second-largest cigarette maker Productora Tabacalera de Colombia (Protabaco) for $452 million. Protabaco's brands include Mustang (the country's #2 selling cigarette) Premier and President. The deal elevates BAT from third place to second place in Colombia's cigarette market.

HISTORY

Company BackgroundAfter a year of vicious price-cutting between Imperial Tobacco (UK) and James Buchanan Duke's American Tobacco in the UK Imperial counterattacked in the US. To end the cigarette price war in the UK the firms created British American Tobacco (BAT) in 1902. The truce granted Imperial the British market American the US market and they jointly owned BAT in the rest of the world.

With Duke in control BAT expanded into new markets. In China it was selling 25 billion cigarettes a year by 1920. When the Communist revolution ended BAT's operations in China the company lost more than 25% of its sales (although China later reemerged as a major export market for the company's cigarettes).

A 1911 US antitrust action forced American to sell its interest in BAT and opened the US market to the company. BAT purchased US cigarette manufacturer Brown & Williamson in 1927 and continued to grow through geographic expansion until the 1960s. In 1973 BAT and Imperial each regained control of its own brands in the UK and Continental Europe. Imperial sold the last of its stake in BAT in 1980.

Fearing that mounting public concern over smoking would limit the cigarette market BAT acquired nontobacco businesses; it changed its name to B.A.T Industries in 1976. The acquisitions of retailers Saks (1973) Argos (UK 1979) Marshall Field (1982) and later insurance firms diversified the company's sales base. After a 1989 hostile takeover bid from Sir James Goldsmith it sold its retail operations and retained its tobacco and financial services.

In 1994 B.A.T acquired the former American Tobacco for $1 billion. In 1997 the company acquired Cigarrera de Moderna (with 50% of Mexico's cigarette sales) and formed a joint venture with the Turkish tobacco state enterprise Tekel.

B.A.T's tobacco operations were spun off in 1998 as British American Tobacco (BAT). The financial services operations were merged with Zurich Insurance in a transaction that created two holding companies: Allied Zurich (UK) and Zurich Allied (Switzerland). With the changes Martin Broughton became chairman of BAT.

The company in 1999 paid $8.2 billion to buy Dutch cigarette company Rothmans International (Rothmans Dunhill) from Switzerland's Compagnie Financiere Richemont and South Africa's Rembrandt Group –both controlled by Anton Rupert. With the purchase BAT received a controlling stake in Canada's Rothmans Benson & Hedges (RBH).

In early 2000 BAT bought the 58% of Canada's Imasco it didn't already own. Imasco sold off its financial services and BAT received Imasco's Imperial Tobacco unit (not related to the UK's Imperial Tobacco Group) in the deal. (Formerly called Imperial Tobacco Company of Canada Imasco was created in 1908 with help from BAT.) BAT also unloaded its share of RBH via a public offering.

In 2001 BAT bought the 40.5% of its BAT Australasia subsidiary (formed in 1999 through the Rothmans merger) it didn't already own. Broughton announced that year that the Chinese government had approved development plans that would allow the company to build a factory in China. The company also announced it would build the first foreign-owned cigarette factory in South Korea at that time the world's #8 tobacco market.

Increasing its Latin American regional presence BAT purchased a controlling stake in Peru's top tobacco company Tabacalera Nacional and several of its suppliers in 2003. However two months later BAT said it would not make the million-dollar investment in the company. The announcement came soon after Peru raised taxes on cigarettes. By the end of the year BAT had purchased tobacco manufacturer Ente Tabacchi Italiani S.p.A. from the Italian government. BAT sold the distribution end of its Italian business to Compañía de Distribución Integral Logista in 2004 the same year that Broughton retired; the company named Jan du Plessis as chairman and Paul Adams as CEO.

In June 2009 the company acquired an 85% stake in Indonesia's fourth largest cigarette maker PT Bentoel Internasional Investama Tbk for £303 million ($494 million) from Rajawali Group. Later that year Richard Burrows became chairman; he replaced du Plessis who had become chairman of Rio Tinto. Replacing Adams Nicandro Durante became CEO in early 2011. BAT in fall 2011 acquired Colombia's second-largest cigarette maker Productora Tabacalera de Colombia (Protabaco) for $452 million.

EXECUTIVES

Chief Executive, Nicandro Durante, age 58, $516,791 total compensation
Finance Director, Ben Stevens, age 55, $528,901 total compensation
Director Special Projects, Jean-Marc L ©y
Regional Director Asia-Pacific, Jack Bowles, age 51
Managing Director Next Generation Products, Des Naughton, age 48
Regional Director Western Europe, Naresh Sethi
Director Operations, Alan Davy
Regional Director Americas, Ricardo Oberlander
Regional Director Eastern Europe Middle East and Africa, Johan Vandermeulen
Chairman, Richard Burrows, age 70
Auditors: PricewaterhouseCoopers LLP

LOCATIONS

HQ: British American Tobacco Plc (United Kingdom)
Globe House, 4 Temple Place, London WC2R 2PG
Phone: (44) 20 7845 1000 **Fax:** (44) 20 7240 0555
Web: www.bat.com

PRODUCTS/OPERATIONS

2014 Cigarettes Sold

	Billion
Pall Mall	92
Kent	64
Dunhill	55
Rothmans	36
Lucky Strike	31
Total	**278**

2014 Sales

	%
Asia-Pacific	28
EEMEA	27
Western Europe	24
Americas	21
Total	**100**

Selected Brands
Benson & Hedges (Asia/Pacific Middle East Africa)
Craven ' A'
Dunhill
John Player Gold Leaf
Kent
Kool
Lucky Strike
Pall Mall
Peter Stuyvesant
Player' s Gold Lead
Rothmans
State Express 555
Viceroy
Vogue

COMPETITORS

Altria
Imperial Tobacco
Japan Tobacco
Philip Morris International
Reemtsma Cigarettenfabriken
Santa Fe Natural Tobacco
Swedish Match
Swisher International
Universal Corporation
Vector Group

HISTORICAL FINANCIALS

Company Type: Public

Income Statement FYE: December 31

	REVENUE ($ mil.)	NET INCOME ($ mil.)	NET PROFIT MARGIN	EMPLOYEES
12/14	21,809	4,862	22.3%	90,118
12/13	25,218	6,451	25.6%	89,820
12/12	24,484	6,191	25.3%	87,485
12/11	23,789	4,781	20.1%	87,813
12/10	23,107	4,470	19.3%	92,285
Annual Growth	(1.4%)	2.1%	—	(0.6%)

2014 Year-End Financials

Debt ratio: 73.1%
Return on equity: 51.3%
Cash ($ mil.): 2,837
Current ratio: 1.04
Long-term debt ($ mil.): 15,265
No. of shares (mil.): 2,026
Dividends
Yield: 4.4%
Payout: 174.2%
Market value ($ mil.): 218,518

	STOCK PRICE ($) FY Close	P/E High/Low	PER SHARE ($) Earnings	Dividends	Book Value
12/14	107.82	70 54	2.60	4.82	4.24
12/13	107.42	61 50	3.38	4.33	5.41
12/12	101.25	57 47	3.18	4.21	5.94
12/11	94.88	61 45	2.41	3.64	6.23
12/10	77.70	54 42	2.24	3.17	7.06
Annual Growth	8.5%	— —	3.8%	11.0%	(11.9%)

BT Group Plc

BT Group isn't the behemoth it used to be but it still wears the crown as the UK's top telecommunications carrier. It offers local and long-distance phone service and provides Internet access and other data and IT services. BT Group operates through several divisions —corporate clients are served through its BT Global Services unit while BT Business provides communications and IT services in the UK and the Republic of Ireland and BT Consumer offers consumer fixed-voice and broadband services in the UK. The BT Wholesale and Openreach divisions are devoted to the broadband and local network needs of other carriers. BT which claims to be the world's oldest communications company is working to adapt to the age of mobile communications.

Operations

BT Global Services the group's enterprise telecommunications division is its largest segment by sales accounting for about 38% of revenue in 2015 (ended March). It provides voice and data communications as well as managed network and IT services to corporate and public sector customers in more than 170 countries; the UK government is the company's largest client. BT Global Services also operates customer contact and data centers and offers customer relationship management and managed network security.

BT Business serves small and medium-sized enterprises (SMEs) in fixed-voice and data; mobility; and IT services. The company has a market share of around 30% in fixed-voice and data but just 1% in mobility and 6% in IT services. The segment accounts for 15% of the BT Group's revenue.

BT Consumer provides broadband TV sports channels and mobile services. The unit also sells services through its Plusnet brand. The segment generates about a quarter of revenue.

BT Wholesale provides network services to more than 1400 communications service providers in the UK. It operates the only network that covers the entire country and many competitors pay to use its network to enable their own services. BT Wholesale manages the network infrastructure for Virgin Media and KCOM while O2 and Vodafone use its fixed-line network for their business customers. It has about 12% of the BT Group's sales.

Openreach is the group's smallest segment with 11% of sales. It was created in 2006 as part of a settlement with regulatory agency Ofcom to ensure that other companies have full access to BT's network. About 500 communications service providers including BT divisions rely on Openreach for network communications.

Geographic Reach

The UK is London-based BT Group's largest market accounting for more than three-quarters of its annual sales. Key European markets for the company include Italy Germany and Spain. In North America BT serves customers from offices in 25 cities. The firm also has a presence in high-growth regions in Asia Pacific Latin America the Middle East and Africa. Overall BT Group has operations in about 170 countries.

Financial Performance

BT Group's revenue declined 2% in 2015 (ended March) versus the prior year to £17.8 billion. BT Global's revenue dropped 7% because of the negative impact from foreign exchange and lower transit revenue. BT Business underlying revenue excluding transit was down with lower call and line volumes as customers moved to broadband and IP services. BT Wholesale underlying revenue fell 7%.

Net income grew 15% in 2015 versus 2014 while cash flow was flat year-to-year.

Strategy

BT Group is looking to spruce up its infrastructure and making improvements to its UK broadband network. The network is more resilient and has the capacity to comfortably accommodate increases in traffic. With its mobile virtual network operator (MVNO) partner EE BT Group is developing new mobile services that enable BT Consumer's jump back into mobile.

Ownership

Asset manager Invesco owns about 10% of BT Group's stock.

HISTORY

Early History

In 1879 the British Post Office (now known as Royal Mail and formerly Consignia) got the exclusive right to operate telegraph systems. When private firms tried to offer phone service the government objected arguing in court that its telegraph monopoly was imperiled. The courts agreed and the Post Office was empowered to license private phone companies collect a 10% royalty and operate its own systems.

The private National Telephone Company emerged as the leading phone outfit competing with the Post Office. When National's license expired in 1911 the Post Office took over and became the monopoly phone company. In 1936 the phone system introduced its familiar red phone booths designed for King George V's jubilee.

Under a 1981 law telecommunications were split from the Post Office and placed under the new British Telecommunications (BT). The government also allowed competitor Mercury Communications –formerly One 2 One and now known as T-Mobile (UK) –to compete. The Thatcher government soon called for BT's privatization.

EXECUTIVES

CEO, Gavin Patterson, age 48
General Counsel and Secretary, Dan Fitz
Group Finance Director and Board Member, Anthony E. A. (Tony) Chanmugam, age 61
CIO, Clive Selley
CEO - BT Global Services, Luis Alvarez
Chairman, Michael D. V. (Mike) Rake, age 67
Auditors: PricewaterhouseCoopers LLP

LOCATIONS

HQ: BT Group Plc
BT Centre, 81 Newgate Street, London EC1A 7AJ
Phone: (44) 20 7356 5000 **Fax:** (44) 20 7356 5520
Web: www.bt.com

2015 Sales

	% of total
Europe Middle East & Africa	
UK	78
Other countries	13
Americas	6
Asia Pacific	3
Total	**100**

PRODUCTS/OPERATIONS

2015 Sales

	% of total
BT Global Services	38
BT consumer	24
BT business	15
BT wholesale	12
Openreach	11
Total	**100**

2015 Sales by Market

	%
ICT & managed networks	36
Calls & lines	33
Broadband & convergence	21
Transit	3
Other	7
Total	**100**

Selected Subsidiaries and Affiliates

Basilica Computing Limited (IT services)
British Telecommunications plc (telecommunication related services and products)
BT Americas Inc. (telecommunication related services and products US)
BT Australasia Pty Limited (telecommunication related services and products Australia)
BT Centre Nominee 2 Limited (property holding company)
BT Communications Ireland Limited (telecommunications services)
BT Conferencing Inc. (Audio video and Web conferencing services US)
BT Convergent Solutions Limited (communications related services and products)
BT ESPAÑA Compa?ía de Servicios Globales de Telecomunicaciones S.A. (telecommunication related services and products Spain)
BT Fleet Limited (fleet management)
BT France SA (telecommunication related services and products)
BT Frontline Pte Ltd (communications related services and products Singapore)
BT (Germany) GmbH & Co. oHG (telecommunication related services and products)
BT Global Services Limited (international telecommunications network systems)
BT Holdings Limited (investment holding company)
BT Hong Kong Limited (telecommunication related services and products)
BT Infrastructures Critiques (IT systems and network services France)
BT INS Inc (Information telecommunication consulting and software US)
BT Italia SpA (telecommunications related services and products Italy 97%)
BT Limited (international telecommunication network systems provider)
BT Nederland NV (telecommunication related services and products The Netherlands)
BT US Investments Limited (investments holding company US)
Communications Global Network Services Limited (telecommunication related services and products Bermuda)
Communication Networking Services (UK) (telecommunication related services and products)
Infonet Services Corporation (global managed network services provider US)
Infonet USA Corporation (global managed network services provider US)
Radianz Americas Inc. (global managed network services provider US)

COMPETITORS

Accenture	Sky plc
COLT Group	THUS Ltd.
Cable & Wireless	TalkTalk
Capgemini	Telecom Italia
Deutsche Telekom	Telecom plus
Easynet	Telefnica
IBM Global Services	Telenor
KCOM Group	TeliaSonera
KPN	Verizon Enterprise Solutions
Orange	Virgin Media
Orange Business Services	Vodafone

HISTORICAL FINANCIALS

Company Type: Public

Income Statement

FYE: March 31

	REVENUE ($ mil.)	NET INCOME ($ mil.)	NET PROFIT MARGIN	EMPLOYEES
03/15	26,571	3,155	11.9%	88,500
03/14	30,444	3,359	11.0%	87,800
03/13	27,379	3,177	11.6%	87,900
03/12	30,280	3,208	10.6%	89,000
03/11	32,301	2,416	7.5%	92,600
Annual Growth	(4.8%)	6.9%	—	(1.1%)

2015 Year-End Financials

Debt ratio: 53.0%	No. of shares (mil.): —
Return on equity: 1,976.8%	Dividends
Cash ($ mil.): 641	Yield: 2.7%
Current ratio: 0.97	Payout: 141.0%
Long-term debt ($ mil.): 11,628	Market value ($ mil.): —

	STOCK PRICE ($) FY Close	P/E High/Low	PER SHARE ($) Earnings	Dividends	Book Value
03/15	65.17	262199	0.39	0.88	0.14
03/14	63.85	271172	0.41	0.76	(0.12)
03/13	42.03	159113	0.39	1.28	(0.05)
03/12	36.16	145100	0.39	1.17	0.25
03/11	30.08	160 92	0.30	0.53	0.38
Annual Growth	21.3% (21.7%)	— —	6.7%	13.8%	

Bunge Ltd.

Bunge's businesses stretch from the farm field to your local supermarket shelf. A leading integrated agribusiness and food company Bunge produces stores and sells agricultural products such as oilseeds and grains which it turns into vegetable oils and protein meals. Customers include animal feed poultry and aquaculture producers. The agribusiness markets vegetable oils used in the biodiesel industry. The company's edible oil products segment sells packaged oils like shortening and margarine under brands Bunge Pro Floriol and Olek. A sugar and bioenergy unit produces sugar and ethanol which are sold primarily in Brazil. Bunge also mixes and distributes crop fertilizers to farmers in South America.

Geographic Reach

Bunge has operations in Africa Asia the Caribbean Europe the Middle East North and South America. Europe is the company's largest market accounting for nearly a third of total sales. The US represents about a quarter of sales while Asia accounts for nearly a fifth.

Operations

The integrated agribusiness and food company divides its operations into four divisions. Agribusiness is the largest accounting for nearly three-quarters of the company's sales. It's primarily involved in the purchase storage transport processing and ultimately the sale of agricultural commodities in North and South America Europe and Asia. Bunge's Food and Ingredients division houses edible oils products and milling products and includes businesses that produce and sell edible oils shortenings margarines mayonnaise and milled products such as wheat flours corn-based products and rice. The Sugar and Bioenergy segment produces and sells sugar and ethanol derived from sugarcane. The firm's shrinking Fertilizer arm makes blends and distributes fertilizer products for the agricultural industry primarily in South America.

Financial Performance

Bunge's sales approached $61 billion in 2012 a 4% increase versus 2011. Agribusiness and Edible Oil Products outperformed the company's other business segments posting sales increases of 15% and 7% respectively. The company's Sugar and Bioenergy operation's sales tumbled 20% in 2012 versus the prior year while sales of milling products declined by nearly 9%. Asia Canada and the US each posted double-digit annual sales comparisons while sales in Europe rose 6%. Brazil posted a 3% gain in 2012 sales while Argentina suffered a 16% decline. Overall 2012 marked the third consecutive year of increasing sales for Bunge although the rate of growth has slowed. Indeed in 2011 sales jumped 29% versus 2010.

Net income plunged 93% in 2012 its second year of steep decline due primarily to an after-tax charge related to the impairment of the Sugar & Bioenergy segment goodwill and a loss of $342 million for results of discontinued operations.

Strategy

Diversified Bunge is building some of its businesses while retrenching in others such as fertilizer. Indeed in 2013 the company sold its Brazilian fertilizer business to Yara International ASA for $750 million in cash. Also in 2012 the firm sold its 28% stake in Soloe LLC its joint venture with DuPont formed in 2003 for $440 million. Bunge will continue to supply fertilizer to farmers as part of its grain organization activities.

Bunge intends to fuel growth by investing in projects that strengthen its leadership in grains oilseeds and food ingredients.

Mergers and Acquisitions

In line with its focus on agriculture and environmental concerns Bunge in 2012 acquired London-based Climate Change Capital Group parent to Climate Change Capital (CCC) a UK-regulated sustainable asset manager and adviser. CCC makes investments in projects companies and technologies focusing on carbon finance private equity and property. Also in 2012 Bunge's subsidiary in India acquired the edible oils and fats business of Amrit Banaspati. The purchase which included the rights to the vanaspati (cooking oil) brand GAGAN furthers Bunge's presence in the Indian consumer foods market. The deal followed Bunge's purchase (through its North American subsidiary) of a pair of margarine production facilities and their assets from The C.F. Sauer Company in mid-2011. Bunge scooped up an assortment of low saturated and trans-fat products for its North American customers which include restaurants and food processors.

In April 2012 Bunge purchased the assets of MCN BioProducts a privately-held Canadian technology company. The purchase creates opportunities for Bunge to provide protein alternatives in existing and new markets.

HISTORY

In 2003 Bunge announced it acquired the India-based edible oils and fats businesses of Hindustan Lever as well as India oilseed-crushing business Prestige Foods Limited. That year it also sold its private-label retail bottled-oil business to ACH Food.

The company also sold the bakery business of its North American subsidiary to Dawn Food Products for about $82 million. The business included Bunge North America's frozen dough mixes syrups and toppings products. These changes allowed Bunge to continue its focus on its edible-oils business. In addition the acquisition of Cereol in 2003 made Bunge the world's largest oilseed producer.

The company is expanding into Eastern Europe and Asia. As part of that effort it purchased Poland's Kama Foods in 2004. Activity in Russia includes the purchase of a grain terminal in Rostov to handle the increase in Russian exports of wheat and barley. Taking its first step into China in 2005 Bunge purchased a controlling interest in a soybean crushing and refining plant in Shandong Province.

Bunge agreed to acquire Corn Products International (renamed Ingredion) in June 2008. In November 2008 Corn Products announced its board withdrew its support for its planned takeover without citing a reason. A week later Bunge issued a statement saying that although the company still believed the takeover was a good fit that it was not in its best interests to do pursue the takeover at that time. Falling corn prices and the weak economy are believed to be the deciding factors in the cancellation of the deal. Bunge is already the #3 agribusiness company in the global marketplace (after #1 Cargill and #2 Archer Daniels Midland). The acquisition of Corn Products would have given Bunge a much stronger presence in corn as well as greater access to markets in Asia and North and South America. Bunge did add to its holdings in 2008 when it acquired the international sugar trading and marketing division of European ingredients giant Tate & Lyle.

Founded in 1818 as a grain trading company in Amsterdam Bunge was held mostly by families descended from founder Johann Bunge until it went public in 2001.

EXECUTIVES

Managing Director Bunge Global Agribusiness; CEO Bunge Product Lines, Raul Padilla, age 59, $731,610 total compensation

Chief Financial Officer; Global Operational Excellence Officer, Andrew J. (Drew) Burke, age 60, $541,667 total compensation

CEO Bunge Asia, Christopher S. White, age 62

Managing Director Food and Ingredients, Gordon Hardie

President and Chief Executive Officer; Bunge Brazil, Pedro Pullen Parente, age 62

Chief Development Officer and Managing Director Sugar and Bioenergy, D. Benedict Pearcy, age 46, $488,333 total compensation

Chief Executive Officer; Director, Soren W. Schroder, age 53

CEO Bunge Argentina, Enrique Humanes

CEO Bunge EMEA, Tommy Jensen

Executive Chairman of the Board, Alberto Weisser, age 59

Deputy Chairman, L. Patrick Lupo, age 64

Auditors: Deloitte & Touche LLP

LOCATIONS

HQ: Bunge Ltd.
50 Main Street, White Plains, NY 10606
Phone: 914 684-2800
Web: www.bunge.com

PRODUCTS/OPERATIONS

Selected Products and Services

Agribusiness
- Purchase storage transport processing and sale of agricultural commodities
- Corn

Rapeseed (
- Soybeans
- Sunflower seed
- Wheat
- Sugar
- Sugar cane-based ethanol

Fertilizer
- Mining and processing of phosphate ore
- Production
- Ammonia
- Ammonium nitrate
- Dicalcium phosphate
- Monoammonium phosphate
- Nitric acid
- Phosphate rock
- Phosphate-based animal feed ingredients
- Phosphoric acid
- Sulfuric acid
- Triple superphosphate
- Urea

Food and food ingredients
- Bulk oils
- Edible oils

Rapeseed (
- Soybean
- Sunflower
- Margarines
- Mayonnaise
- Packaged vegetable oils
- Shortenings

Milling

Brazil
- Bakery mixes
- Wheat flours

North America
- Corn oil
- Corn-based animal feed
- Corn/soy meal
- Dry-milled cornmeal
- Flours
- Grits
- Soy-fortified cornmeal

Selected Joint Ventures

Agribusiness
- AGRI-Bunge LLC (34% AGRI Industries grain origination and Mississippi river terminal operation)
- Biocolza-Oleos E Farinhas de Colza S.A. (40% joint venture with Tagol; rapeseed oil crushing and biodiesel production; Portugal)
- Biodiesel Bilbao S.A. (20% with Acciona Biocombustibles S.A.; biofuel production; Spain)
- Bunge-Ergon Vicksburg LLC (BEV; 50% with Ergon Ethanol Inc.; ethanol production)
- Diester Industries International S.A.S. (DII) (DII; 40% with Diester Industries a subsidiary of Sofiproteol; biodiesel production and marketing; Germany)
- Ecofuel S.A. (50% with AGD; biodiesel production; Argentina)
- Southwest Iowa Renewable Energy LLC (SIRE; 26% with agricultural producers located in Southwest Iowa; ethanol production)

Fertilizer
- Bunge Maroc Phosphore S.A. (50% with Office Cherifien Des Phosphates (OCP); ferlilizer production; Morocco)

Food Products
- Harinera La Espiga S.A. de C.V. (32% with Grupo Neva S.A. de C.V. and Cerrollera S.A. de C.V.; wheat milling and bakery dry mix production; Mexico)

Selected Subsidiaries

Argentina
- Fertimport S.A.
- Guide S.A.

Belgium
- Afrique Initiatives

Bulgaria
- Kaliakra A.D.

Canada
- CF Oils Investments Inc.
- Leblanc & Lafrance Inc.
- Neptune Bulk Terminals (Canada) Ltd.

China
- Bunge Sanwei Oil & Fat Co. Ltd.
- Taixing Zhenhua Oils & Fats Co. Ltd.

Cyprus
- Brea Commodities Limited

France
- Diester Industries International S.A.S.

Italy
- Escercizio Raccordi Ferroviari S.p.A.

Latvia
- Dan Store LSEZ SIA

Mexico
- Harinera La Espiga S.A. de C.V.
- Inmobiliaria A. Gil S.A.
- Inmobiliaria Gilsa S.A.

Poland
- Polska Trade Services S.p.z.o.o.
- Warsaw Mathematical Institute Sp z.o.o.
- Z.T. Kruszwica S.A.

Romania
- SC Interoil S.A.
- SC Muntenia S.A.
- SC Unirea S.A.

Russia
- LLC Bunge CIS
- OJS Kholmsky
- Rostov Grain Terminal LLC

Spain
- Biodiesel Bilbao S.L.
- Estación de Descarga y Carga S.A. (Esdecasa)
- Huelva Belts S.L.
- Moyresa Girasol S.L.

Switzerland
- Ecoinvest Carbon S.A.
- Oleina S.A.

Ukraine
- Black Sea Industries Limited
- Suntrade S.E.

Uruguay

Agritrade S.A.

US

Biofuels Company of America LLC
The Crete Mills Inc.
Delphos Terminal Company Inc.
International Produce Inc.
Renewable Energy Group Inc.
Solae Holdings LLC
Southwest Iowa Renewable Energy LLC

Venezuela

Almacen Terminal Santana C.A.

Vietnam

Baria Joint Stock Company of Services for Import Export of Agro-Forestry Products and Fertilizer

COMPETITORS

ADM
Ag Processing Inc.
Associated British Foods
CHS
Cargill
ConAgra
Cosan
Danisco A/S
Dawn Food Products
General Mills
Ingredion
LifeLine
Louis Dreyfus Group
Mosaic Company
Potash Corp
Repsol
Rich Products
Sadia
Sdzucker
Tereos
Unilever
Ventura Foods
Wilmar

HISTORICAL FINANCIALS

Company Type: Public

Income Statement FYE: December 31

	REVENUE ($ mil.)	NET INCOME ($ mil.)	NET PROFIT MARGIN	EMPLOYEES
12/14	57,161	515	0.9%	35,000
12/13	61,347	306	0.5%	35,000
12/12	60,991	64	0.1%	36,000
12/11	58,743	942	1.6%	34,000
12/10	45,707	2,354	5.2%	33,021
Annual Growth	5.7%	(31.6%)	—	1.5%

2014 Year-End Financials

Debt ratio: 18.0%
Return on equity: 5.6%
Cash ($ mil.): 362
Current ratio: 1.50
Long-term debt ($ mil.): 2,855
No. of shares (mil.): 145
Dividends
Yield: 1.4%
Payout: 29.7%
Market value ($ mil.): —

Canadian Imperial Bank of Commerce

Canadian Imperial Bank of Commerce (CIBC) is both Canadian and imperial when it comes to growing its business. CIBC has more than 1100 domestic branches that offer a range of consumer and business financial services including deposits loans investments and insurance. Its largest segment is Retail and Business Banking which handles consumer and small business banking and credit card services. It also provides a full suite of services through its wholesale banking and wealth management divisions. Founded in 1867 CIBC's assets are worth more than $400 billion making it one of the five largest banks in Canada.

OperationsCIBC operates three main divisions: Retail and Business Banking Wealth Management and Wholesale Banking. The Retail and Business Banking division brings in nearly 65% of total revenue and provides financial advice along with banking investment and authorized insurance products.CIBC's Wealth Management division generates nearly 20% of revenue and offers advisory services and a variety of investment solutions for institutions retail and high net worth clients. The business encompasses asset management retail brokerage and private wealth management activities and is delivered through more than 1500 advisors across Canada and the US.Wholesale Banking accounts for another 15% of revenues and offers credit and capital market products and services investment banking advisory services and research for corporate institutional and government clients from around the world.Sales and MarketingThe bank provides financial products and services to 11 million individual small business commercial corporate and institutional clients from Canada and around the world. CIBC has been increasing its advertising spend over the past few years to go toward strategic initiatives and developing its enhanced travel rewards program. The bank spent C$285 million toward advertising and business development in fiscal 2014 up 21% from its spend in 2013 and up 22% from what it spent in 2012.Financial PerformanceNote: Growth rates may differ after conversion to US dollars.CIBC has enjoyed steady top-line growth over the past few years thanks to higher non-interest fee and commission-based income from its banking insurance and investing-related products and services. Revenue grew by 2% to C$17.4 billion ($15.5 billion) in fiscal 2014 (ended October) thanks to higher fee income from investment management custodial and mutual fund products. The bank was able to generate higher fees as its assets under management grew from its recent acquisition of Atlantic Trust and because asset values rose along with the rising stock market.Despite higher revenue net income fell by 4% to C$3.22 billion ($2.88 billion) in fiscal 2014 after three straight years of profit growth. This is mostly because CIBC incurred significant impairment charges as the CIBC FirstCarribean division's loan assets fell in value in the struggling Carribean economy. The bank also paid employees more in performance-based compensation and spent more on computer software and office equipment.Operations used C$16.57 billion in fiscal 2014 significantly more than in 2013 when operations provided C$5.19 billion mostly as the bank used more cash toward loans and securities purchased under resale agreements. From fiscal 2011 to fiscal 2013 operations had provided more cash than it spent.

Stategy

To grow its Retail and Business Banking division CIBC has shifted its strategy to a client-oriented focus. To do this CIBC aims to make banking easy personalized and flexible which it hopes will deepen client relationships and grow its client base further. Making moves toward this long-term goal in recent years CIBC was the first of Canada's five largest banks to launch eDeposit services for personal and business banking clients. It also took steps to achieve the third-largest branch and ATM network in Canada.Toward CIBC's goal of expanding its wealth management business in North America CIBC in 2013 acquired Atlantic Trust an integrated wealth management solutions provider for high-net worth individuals families foundations and endowments in the US. The purchase helped CIBC broaden its reach into the US private wealth market where high-net-worth personal financial assets were growing 50% faster than those of the average US household. The acquisition also built upon the bank's 2012 purchase of the private-wealth business MFS McLean Budden in Canada which managed more than $1.4 billion in assets.Looking to focus more on its core operations CIBC sold its stake in trust and custody services provider CIBC Mellon to its partner in the joint venture The Bank of New York Mellon for an undisclosed amount in late 2013.

Mergers and AcquisitionsIn 2013 CIBC acquired Atlanta-based Atlantic Trust from Invesco for C$224 million (or $210 million) to expand its Wealth Management business in North America.

HISTORY

In 1858 Bank of Canada was chartered; Toronto financier William McMaster bought the charter in 1866 when investors failed to raise enough money to open it and changed the name to Canadian Bank of Commerce.

The firm opened in 1867 bought the Gore Bank of Hamilton (1870) and expanded within seven years to 24 branches in Ontario as well as Montreal and New York. Led by Edmund Walker the bank spread west of the Great Lakes with the opening of a Winnipeg Manitoba branch in 1893 and joined the Gold Rush with branches in Dawson City Yukon Territory and Skagway Alaska in 1898.

As the new century began the bank's purchases spanned the breadth of Canada from the Bank of British Columbia (1901) to Halifax Banking (1903) and the Merchants Bank of Prince Edward Island (1906). More buys followed in the 1920s; the bank's assets peaked in 1929 and then plunged during the Depression. It recovered during WWII.

In 1961 Canadian Bank of Commerce merged with Imperial Bank of Canada to become Canadian Imperial Bank of Commerce (CIBC). Imperial Bank was founded in 1875 by Henry Howland; it went west to Calgary and Edmonton and became known as "The Mining Bank." It bought Barclays Bank (Canada) in 1956.

As the energy and agriculture sectors declined in the early 1980s two of CIBC's largest borrowers Dome Petroleum and tractor maker Massey-Ferguson defaulted on their loans. Deregulation opened investment banking to CIBC which in 1988 bought a majority share of Wood Gundy one of Canada's largest investment dealers; CIBC also purchased Merrill Lynch Canada's retail brokerage business.

In 1992 CIBC added substantially to its loss reserves (resulting in an earnings drop of 98%) to cover real estate losses from developer Olympia & York and others. This launched more cost-cutting as the company reorganized by operating segments.

Deregulation allowed CIBC to begin selling insurance in 1993; the company built a collection of life credit personal property/casualty and nonmedical health companies.

In 1996 the bank formed Intria a processing and technical support subsidiary. The next year CIBC Wood Gundy became CIBC World Markets and CIBC bought securities firm Oppenheimer & Co. and added its stock underwriting and brokerage abilities to CIBC World Markets.

In 1998 increasing foreign competition prompted CIBC and Toronto-Dominion to plan a merger (as did Royal Bank of Canada and Bank of Montreal); the government halted both plans citing Canada's already highly concentrated banking industry.

Spurned the bank overhauled its operations to spark growth in the late 1990s. To cut costs it eliminated some 4000 jobs and sold its more than $1-billion real estate portfolio. It teamed with the Winn-Dixie (1999) and Safeway (2000) supermarket chains to operate electronic branches in the US. The firm scaled back its disappointing international operations and began selling its insurance units.

In 2000 CIBC created Amicus as a holding company for CIBC World Markets' retail electronic banking business. The following year the bank sold its merchant card services business to US-based Global Payments.

In 2002 the company snagged US-based Merrill Lynch's Canadian retail brokerage asset management and securities operations renaming it CIBC Asset Management Inc. That same year CIBC merged its Caribbean banking business with that of UK-based Barclays to create FirstCaribbean Bank.

The next year CIBC sold the Oppenheimer private client and asset-management divisions to Fahnestock Viner (now Oppenheimer Holdings). It sold Juniper Financial a Delaware-based credit card issuer to Barclays for some $293 million in 2004.

In 2004 and again in 2006 CIBC was sued by creditors of Internet telecommunications company Global Crossing stating that the bank had engaged in insider trading to the tune of $2 billion. Creditors demanded a return of the proceeds. CIBC denied the claims but in 2006 two units of the bank agreed to pay $17.4 million to investors in the ill-fated telecom.

More trouble came in 2005 when CIBC agreed to pay some $2.4 billion in an investor class-action suit to resolve claims that the company helped notorious energy trader Enron to conceal losses.

EXECUTIVES

EVP and General Counsel Legal and Regulatory Compliance, Michael G. Capatides
SEVP and Group Head Wealth Management, Stephen (Steve) Geist
EVP Brand Corporate and Client Relationships, Stephen J. Forbes
President and CEO, Victor Dodig
Managing Director and Head Cash Equities CIBC World Markets, Rik Parkhill
Managing Director and Head Fixed Income Currencies & Distribution CIBC World Markets, Harry Culham
SVP and Chief Auditor, Kevin J. Patterson
EVP Retail Distribution and Channel Strategy, Christina Kramer
SEVP and Group Head Retail and Business Banking, J. David Williamson, age 55, $348,657 total compensation
SEVP and Chief Risk Officer, Laura Dottori-Attanasio
EVP Human Resources, Jacqueline C. Moss
Managing Director and Head Equity Markets, Roman Dubczak
SEVP and CFO, Kevin Glass
Managing Director and Global Head Investment Banking CIBC World Markets, Geoffrey (Geoff) Belsher
Managing Director and Global Head Corporate Banking, Gary W. Brown
Managing Director and Head Capital Markets Trading, Christian Exshaw
EVP Products and Payments, Jenny Fagg
Managing Director and Head CIBC Wood Gundy, Monique Gravel
EVP Human Resources, Sandy Sharman
Chairman and CEO Atlantic Trust, Jack Markwalter
Senior Executive Vice-President Managing Director, Richard E. Venn
Chairman, Charles Sirois, age 61
Auditors: Ernst & Young LLP

LOCATIONS

HQ: Canadian Imperial Bank of Commerce
Commerce Court, Toronto, Ontario M5L 1A2
Phone: 416 980-2211
Web: www.cibc.com

PRODUCTS/OPERATIONS

2014 Sales

	% of total
Interest	
Loans	55
Securities & other	11
Noninterest	
Mutual fund fees	7
Deposits and payments fees	5
Investment management & custodial fees	4
Underwriting & advisory fees	3
Credit fees	3
Card fees	2
insurance fees	2
Commissions on securities transactions	2
Available-for-sale securities gains	1
Other	5
Total	**100**

2014 Revenue by Segment

	% of total
Retail and business banking	63
Wealth management	18
Wholesale banking	15
Corporate and other	4
Total	**100**

COMPETITORS

BMO Financial Group
Barclays
Caisses centrale Desjardins
Citigroup
Goldman Sachs
JPMorgan Chase
National Bank of Canada
RBC Financial Group
Scotiabank
TD Bank

HISTORICAL FINANCIALS

Company Type: Public

Income Statement FYE: October 31

	ASSETS ($ mil.)	NET INCOME ($ mil.)	INCOME AS % OF ASSETS	EMPLOYEES
10/15	352,088	2,717	0.8%	44,201
10/14	370,794	2,875	0.8%	44,424
10/13	380,892	3,253	0.9%	43,039
10/12	394,456	3,340	0.8%	42,595
10/11	385,287	2,878	0.7%	42,239
Annual Growth	(2.2%)	(1.4%)	—	1.1%

2015 Year-End Financials

Return on assets: 0.8%
Return on equity: 17.8%
Long-term debt ($ mil.): —
No. of shares (mil.): 397
Sales ($ mil): 13,241
Dividends
Yield: 0.0%
Payout: 48.4%
Market value ($ mil.): 30,413

	STOCK PRICE ($) FY Close	P/E High/Low		PER SHARE ($) Earnings	Dividends	Book Value
10/15	76.55	9	7	6.74	3.27	40.86
10/14	91.35	12	10	7.02	3.62	41.91
10/13	85.15	10	9	7.87	3.71	43.71
10/12	78.58	10	9	7.87	3.61	41.81
10/11	75.45	13	10	6.74	3.52	39.92
Annual Growth	0.4%	—	—	0.0%	(1.8%)	0.6%

Canon, Inc.

For Canon image is everything. The company makes printers multifunction document equipment and other computer peripherals for home and office use (more than half of sales). It also remains a force in the consumer and professional photography industry making still and video digital cameras LCD projectors lenses and binoculars. Canon also operates an industrial segment featuring such diverse products as semiconductor manufacturing equipment television broadcast lenses and devices used for eye examinations. Customers in its home country of Japan generate just 20% of the company's revenues.

Most of Canon's manufacturing is done in Japan but it also has plants in countries including Brazil France Germany the Netherlands China Malaysia Taiwan Thailand Vietnam and the US. Nearly 60% of Canon's revenues are divided between Europe which has the slightly larger share and the Americas served by subsidiaries including Canon U.S.A. and Canon Canada. The company circulates its products in those regions primarily through large distributors.

Like many companies Canon fell victim to the global recession with 2009 sales falling nearly one-quarter. Although the company recuperated with a 30% gain in 2010 it still hasn't returned to the level of growth it has typically had over the past decade. The deceptive 1% increase in revenues for 2011 when looked at in US currency reaching more than $45 billion was actually a 4% dip to 3.6 trillion albeit by a less-dramatic drop than recession-addled 2009. Net profit of 255 trillion (about $3.2 billion) is much closer to pre-recession levels though it's still essentially flat in domestic currency compared to 2010.

Canon-branded products are the company's primary source of revenue but it also sells equipment that is branded for its partners. Competitor Hewlett-Packard is among those customer-partners accounting for approximately 20% of sales. With the market relatively underpenetrated with color office products Canon and its competitors are pushing to shift customers away from monochrome products for growth in this segment.

While rivals such as Xerox may be digging deep into back office enterprise IT services Canon has stayed more focused on the front office. In 2011 however the company created the Canon Information and Imaging Solutions subsidiary under Canon U.S.A. to focus on the IT services market. The new company will look to cloud computing and other software and services for such areas as business process optimization security services and elements of enterprise resource planning. In 2012 Canon announced it would acquire Belgium-based document management and IT services company I.R.I.S. Group. Canon has partnered with the company for years and bought a 17% stake in it in 2009. Besides bringing in complementary products the purchase will fuel Canon's consultancy aspirations.

Perhaps still best known for its cameras Canon has seen its photographic business steadily decline as traditional camera manufacturers have started to directly compete with electronics manufacturers. However the company remains a leader in the digital camera market where it concentrates on high-end single-lens-reflex (SLR) devices which include professional video cameras used in broadcast and major motion picture production. Canon's third primary product group industry encompasses a diverse portfolio including semiconductor and LCD lithography equipment medical imaging equipment lenses micromotors and large-format printers.

Canon faces stiff competition in all of its segments all over the world. In Japan the digital camera market is particularly heated. Although the company's brand remains strong globally it faces intense rivalries with foes such as Sony Nikon and Panasonic. To increase its competitiveness Canon hopes to find ways to bring products and services to its customers via the cloud and boost its R&D activity in the US and Europe. It will also keep an eye out for acquisitions that could bring in new technologies. The company's sales efforts will focus on strengthening its group companies in developed countries and forging approaches in emerging markets according to the conditions in each region.

HISTORY

Takeshi Mitarai and a friend Saburo Uchida formed Seiki Kogaku Kenkyusho (Precision Optical Research Laboratory) in Tokyo in 1933 to make Japan's first 35mm camera. In 1935 the camera was introduced under the brand name Kwanon (after Quan Yin the Buddhist goddess of mercy) –but later renamed Canon. In response to a pre-WWII military buildup the company made X-ray machines for the Japanese.

In 1947 the company became Canon Camera Company as the brand name gained popularity. Canon opened its first overseas branch in New York in 1955. It diversified into business equipment by introducing the first 10-key electronic calculator (1964) and a plain-paper photocopier (1968) independent of Xerox's patented technology. Canon dropped "Camera Company" from its name in 1969.

The company invented the "liquid dry" copying system which used plain paper and liquid developer in 1972. It failed to produce new cameras and was surpassed by Minolta (now defunct) as Japan's top camera exporter. Sales were sluggish in the early 1970s and in 1975 Canon suspended dividends for the first time since WWII.

At that time Canon's managing director Ryuzaburo Kaku convinced Mitarai that the company's problems stemmed from indecisive leadership and weak marketing. Kaku turned Canon around unleashing the electronic AE-1 in a media blitz that in 1976 included the first-ever TV commercials for a 35mm camera. With automated features the AE-1 appealed to the clumsiest photographers. Its success catapulted Canon past Minolta as the world's #1 camera maker.

In 1979 Canon introduced the first copier to use a dry developer. As the copier market matured in the early 1980s Canon shifted to making other automated office equipment including laser printers and fax machines.

Mitarai died in 1984. Minolta the next year again displaced Canon as the world's #1 camera maker when it introduced a fully automated model. But Canon came back in 1987 with the electronic optical system (EOS) auto-focus camera which returned the company to preeminence in 1990. That year the company initiated an ink cartridge recycling program. Canon teamed up with IBM in 1992 to produce portable PCs. In 1993 Takeshi Mitarai's son Hajime who joined Canon in 1974 was named president and began expanding product development.

In 1995 Canon introduced the world's first color ferroelectric LCD designed to replace cathode ray tubes in computer and TV screens as the industry standard. When Hajime died that year cousin Fujio Mitarai a 34-year Canon employee who served as the head of Canon U.S.A. in the 1980s was named president and CEO. In 1996 the company made Canon Latin America a direct subsidiary of Canon U.S.A. with the "kyosei" idea that regionalized control would make the subsidiary more efficient.

Canon stopped making PCs in 1997. The next year the company unveiled its Hyper Photo System which combines a scanner PC server and printer to produce photo prints and expanded its copier remanufacturing operations. In 1999 after 16 years of production Canon stopped making optical memory cards. The company also opened a research and development facility in the US.

In 2000 Canon and Toshiba began working together to develop technology for flat-panel displays. Canon expanded its line of digital cameras in 2001; the company's sales in that segment almost doubled that year.

The next year the company announced that it would merge two of its office equipment subsidiaries Copyer and Canon Aptex in an effort to improve operating efficiency.

In 2004 Canon formed a joint venture with Toshiba to develop surface-conduction electron-emitter display (SED) products. Canon acquired Toshiba's stake in the company in 2007.

In 2010 Canon acquired Oc ŒEurope's largest manufacturer of printers to solidify its position in that key geographic market. The company maintained the Oc Œbrand following completion of the transaction operating the Dutch supplier of office machines as a division.

Auditors: Ernst & Young ShinNihon LLC

LOCATIONS

HQ: Canon, Inc.
30-2, Shimomaruko 3-chome, Ohta-ku, Tokyo 146-8501
Phone: (81) 3 3758 2111
Web: www.canon.jp

HISTORICAL FINANCIALS

Company Type: Public

Income Statement FYE: December 31

	REVENUE ($ mil.)	NET INCOME ($ mil.)	NET PROFIT MARGIN	EMPLOYEES
12/14	31,239	2,135	6.8%	191,889
12/13	35,546	2,195	6.2%	194,151
12/12	40,401	2,607	6.5%	196,968
12/11	45,969	3,212	7.0%	198,307
12/10	45,573	3,031	6.7%	197,386
Annual Growth	(9.0%)	(8.4%)	—	(0.7%)

2014 Year-End Financials

Debt ratio: 0.0%	No. of shares (mil.): 1,091
Return on equity: 8.6%	Dividends
Cash ($ mil.): 7,078	Yield: 6.2%
Current ratio: 2.60	Payout: 97.7%
Long-term debt ($ mil.): 9	Market value ($ mil.): 34,567

	STOCK PRICE ($) FY Close	P/E High/Low		PER SHARE ($) Earnings	Dividends	Book Value
12/14	31.66	0	0	1.92	1.96	22.86
12/13	32.00	0	0	1.91	1.41	24.38
12/12	39.21	0	0	2.22	1.49	26.17
12/11	44.04	0	0	2.64	1.64	27.44
12/10	51.34	0	0	2.46	1.23	26.48
Annual Growth	(11.4%)	—	—	(6.0%)	12.3%	(3.6%)

Carrefour S.A.

At the junction of groceries merchandise and services you'll find Carrefour (which means "crossroads"). One of the world's largest retailers (behind Wal-Mart and Tesco) Carrefour operates more than 10600 stores under various banners including hypermarkets (Carrefour) supermarkets (Carrefour Market formerly Champion) convenience stores (City Express Proxi) and cash-and-carry outlets (Promocash) in more than 30 countries in Europe Latin America and Asia. France with some 4780 Carrefour stores is the retailer's largest market. Carrefour is struggling to reverse a decade-long sales slump at home while expanding in fast-growing emerging markets in Asia and Latin America.

Operations

Carrefour which pioneered the hypermarket format operates about 1420 of the huge general merchandise and grocery stores on three continents accounting for the majority of its sales. It also operates more than 2900 supermarkets in 19 countries under the Carrefour market and other banners. The French retail giant also operates a growing number of more than 5600 convenience stores 90% of which are operating under franchising agreements. Its cash & carry stores mostly in France combine wholesaling and hypermarkets offering larger quantities to cater to professionals. Carrefour also sells food and nonfood items online in France Brazil Spain and other countries.

Geographic Reach

France is Carrefour's largest market accounting for 47% of sales in 2013. Other countries in Europe including Belgium Italy Poland Romania and Spain contributed about a quarter of its total sales. About 18% of the group's sales are rung up in Latin America (where it has market leading positions in Argentina and Brazil) while Asia (including China) accounts for nearly 9%.

Financial Performance

Carrefour reversed a three-year slide in sales in 2013 posting sales of 74.9 billion ($102 billion) a modest 2% gain at constant exchange rates versus 2012. Notably its sales grew organically by more than 1% in France reversing a prolonged slump at home. Indeed in France Carrefour posted its best year of organic growth since 2007 across all of its store formats with hypermarkets performing particularly well. Beyond France sales grew in by double digits in Latin America driven by strong performance in Brazil and Argentina. While sales declined by 3% overall in Europe they showed signs of improvement particularly in Spain in the second half of 2013. Sales grew more modestly in Asia driven in part by expansion in China where Carrefour opened 20 new hypermarkets over the course of the year.

Net income was essentially flat (up 0.1%) in 2013 versus 2012 while recurring operating income rose 10% over the same period.

Strategy

Under the leadership of CEO Georges Plassat (who took over in May 2012) Carrefour is in the midst of a three-year recovery plan which appears to be meeting with some success. Plassat has reduced the company's exposure to ailing euro zone countries including Greece and Spain. Carrefour in mid-2012 sold its stake in its joint venture Carrefour Marinopoulos –operator of Greece's leading supermarket chain –at a loss to its partner. It also spun off its Dia discount chain though its working to reacquire the French locations. The spinoff enables Carrefour to concentrate on restoring its weaker domestic operations. Other efforts to revive its retail business include the sale of $1.2 billion worth of assets –including its stores in Japan and Mexico –to support lower prices and attract new shoppers.

Emerging markets are the growth driver for Carrefour. Overall the multi-format retailer does business in 34 countries including North Africa and the Middle East (Lebanon Jordan and the UAE). In 2013 Carrefour opened 810 new stores including 20 in China where it is looking to newly developing urban areas. Eastern Europe is also a focus for the company which entered Georgia in fall 2012 and is continuing its expansion in Poland and Romania. While it has been busy trimming the number of hypermarkets and supermarkets it operates Carrefour is growing its convenience store and cash & carry operations which boast smaller stores that can be situated closer to customers.

Mergers and Acquisitions

In late 2014 Carrefour acquired Dia France from Spain's Dia. Carrefour picked up more than 800 Dia stores but it must sell about 55 to satisfy antitrust regulators. (Carrefour previously owned Dia but spun it off in 2011 when the company was listed on the Spanish stock exchange.)

In 2014 Carrefour's convenience store business acquired 128 stores from the Coop Alsace network and bought the RAST supermarket chain of 10 stores in Poland.

HISTORY

Although its predecessor was actually a supermarket opened by Marcel Fournier and Louis Defforey in a Fournier's department store basement in Annecy France the first Carrefour supermarket was founded in 1963 at the intersection of five roads (Carrefour means "crossroads"). That year Carrefour opened a vast store dubbed a "hypermarket" by the media in Sainte-Genevieve-des-Bois outside Paris.

The company opened additional outlets in France and moved into other countries including Belgium (1969) Switzerland (1970 –the year it went public) Italy and the UK (1972) and Spain (1973). Carrefour stepped up international expansion during the mid-1970s after French legislation limited its growth within the country.

Carrefour exported its French-style hypermarkets to the US (Philadelphia) in 1988. Scant advertising limited selection and a union strike led Carrefour to close its US operations in 1993. Carrefour opened its first hypermarket in Taiwan in 1989. The next year it formed Carma a 50-50 joint venture with Groupama to sell insurance. Carrefour paid over $1 billion for two rival chains (the bankrupt Montlaur chain and Euromarche) in 1991.

Daniel Bernard replaced Michel Bon the hard-charging expansion architect in 1992 after a 50% drop in first-half profits. A year later Carrefour partnered with Mexican retailer Gigante to open a chain of hypermarkets in Mexico. (In 1998 Carrefour bought Gigante's share of the joint venture.) In 1996 the company bought a 41% stake in rival GMB (Cora hypermarket chain) and sold its 11% stake in US warehouse retailer Costco (it now owns 20% of Costco UK). The next year Carrefour allowed 16 hypermarkets owned by Guyenne et Gascogne Coop Atlantique and Chareton to operate under the Carrefour name. It expanded into Poland in 1997 and the Czech Republic in 1998.

Its biggest acquisition (at the time) came in 1998 when Carrefour acquired French supermarket operator Comptoirs Modernes (with about 800 stores under the Stoc Comod and March Plus flags). Carrefour also entered the Indonesian market that year.

In August 1999 Carrefour announced a deal even bigger than the one for Comptoirs Modernes –a $16.3 billion merger with fellow French grocer Promodès which operated more than 6000 hypermarkets supermarkets convenience stores and discount stores in Europe. Paul-Auguste Halley and Leonor Duval Lemonnier founded Promodès in Normandy France in 1961. Initially a wholesale food distributor Promodès opened its first supermarket in 1962. This was followed by a cash-and-carry wholesale outlet (1964) a hypermarket (1970) and convenience stores (Shopi and 8 à Huit during the 1970s). To gain regulatory approval for the acquisition Carrefour divested its stake in the Cora chain and sold nearly 40 other stores in France and Spain. The Promodès acquisition was completed in 2000.

The company joined with US retailer Sears and software maker Oracle among others to form Internet-based supply exchange GlobalNetXchange in early 2000. Also that year Carrefour bought Belgian retailer GB (about 500 stores).

In 2001 Carrefour sold its 74%-stake in Picard Surgels (frozen food stores). Carrefour also opened its first Japanese grocery store near Tokyo that year.

The grocer sold its 10% stake in PetSmart Inc. in a public offering in July 2002. That December Carrefour acquired the remaining 20% of the shares of Centro Comerciales Carrefour its Spanish subsidiary it didn't already own in a public tender offer.

In February 2003 Carrefour acquired two hypermarkets in Italy from Hyparlo. In October it entered the Scandinavian market through a franchise partnership and supply agreement with Norwegian grocer NorgesGruppen. Soon after Carrefour Poland acquired two hypermarkets there from troubled Dutch retailer Royal Ahold. In late 2003 Carrefour's discount chain Ed acquired 44 Treff Marche shops in France from German retailer Edeka.

The company sold its seven-hypermarket Chilean division in January 2004 to Distribución Y Servicio. In April Carrefour opened its first Champion supermarket in Beijing. In September it entered Norway with six Meny Champion discount supermarkets in Oslo in partnership with Norway's NorgesGruppen.

In February 2005 Luc Vandevelde the former chairman of troubled British retailer Marks and Spencer succeeded Daniel Bernard as non-executive chairman of Carrefour. Bernard had been with Carrefour for 13 years. No stranger to the company Vandevelde was chief executive of Promodès when it merged with Carrefour in 1999. Concurrently ex-CFO Jos-Luis Durán was named CEO. In March Carrefour sold its 29 hypermarkets in Mexico to Grupo Comercial Chedraui for an undisclosed sum. Also in March Carrefour exited the Japanese market with the sale of its eight hypermarkets there to Japanese retail giant AEON CO. On the plus side Carrefour completed the acquisition of Chris Cash & Carry of Cyprus through its Greek subsidiary Carrefour Marinopoulos. In November the French retailer acquired full ownership of three of its Chinese hypermarket joint ventures from its local partners: Kunming Department Store Co. a unit of China's Kunming Sinobright (Group) Co.; Hunan Yiyou Commercial Trade Co.; and Xinjiang Grandscape Investment Co. Also in 2005 Carrefour swapped 15 of its hypermarkets in Slovakia and the Czech Republic for five outlets in Taiwan operated by rival Tesco exiting both countries.

Carrefour increased its ownership stake in Groupe Hyparlo in late 2005 to 49% (up from 20% in 2004).

In 2006 the company pulled out of South Korea where it held a relatively weak market position. Carrefour sold its 32 stores there to local fashion retailer E.Land for about $1.9 billion. In July Carrefour acquired 98% of the share capital and 99% of the voting rights of Hyparlo which operates stores under the Carrefour banner in France and Romania. The retailer launched its own mobile phone service Carrefour Mobile at all 218 of its hypermarkets in France in late 2006. (Rival Auchan launched a similar product earlier in the year.)

Vandevelde resigned his position in 2007 as non-executive chairman after a falling out with the controlling Halley family. In July Carrefour acquired 250 Spanish discount supermarkets trading under the PLUS banner for about $275 million. About the same time it sold a dozen hypermarkets in Portugal to Sonae the country's largest retailer for about $920 million. In October Carrefour added to its holdings in Romania with the purchase of the Artima supermarket chain there from Polish-based private equity firm Enterprise Investors for about $87 million.

In March 2008 the Halley family split its 13% stake in Carrefour into two separate holding companies –Halley Participations SAS and Comet BV –thereby ceding control of the French retail giant to Blue Capital. In May Robert Halley stepped down as chairman of the company's supervisory board and was replaced by the deputy chairman Amaury de Seze. Blue Capital which recently was granted two seats on the company's supervisory board won a third with the appointment of Bernard Arnault.

Duran stepped down in January 2009 and Lars Olofsson took over as top executive. In June the company opened its first location in Russia: a hypermarket in Moscow. A second Russian store debuted in September.

In November 2010 Carrefour sold its 42 stores in Thailand to Casino Guichard-Perrachon's Big C affiliate there for some 868 million ($1.17 billion).

At Carrefour's annual meeting in June 2011 chairman Amaury de Seze stepped down and Olofsson added the chairman's title. Olofsson retired in May 2012 and was succeeded by Georges Plassat who joined Carrefour as COO in April 2012.

EXECUTIVES

Chairman and CEO, Georges Plassat
Executive Director China and Taiwan, Thierry Garnier, age 48
Executive Director Group Merchandise, ric Legros
Executive Director France, No «l Prioux, age 55
Executive Director Belgium, G ©ard Lavinay
Executive Director Turkey, Guillaume de Colonges
Executive Director Poland, Jean Anthoine
Executive Director Brazil, Luiz Fazzio
Executive Director Europe (excluding France), Thomas M. H bner, age 57
CFO, Pierre-Jean Sivignon
Executive Director Spain, Pascal Clouzard
Executive Director India, Jean-No «l Bironneau
Executive Director Argentina, Daniel Fernandez
Executive Director Taiwan, Patrick Ganaye
Executive Director Romania, Fran §is Melchior de Polignac
Executive Director International Partnerships, St ©phane Thouin
Vice Chairman, Georges Ralli, age 67
Auditors: Deloitte & Associ ©

LOCATIONS

HQ: Carrefour S.A.
33, avenue Emile-Zola, TSA 55 555, Boulogne-Billancourt, Cedex 92649
Phone: (33) 1 41 04 26 00 **Fax:** (22) 1 41 04 26 01
Web: www.carrefour.com

2014 Sales

	% of total
Europe	
France	47
Other countries	26
Latin America	19
Asia	8
Total	**100**

PRODUCTS/OPERATIONS

2014 Stores

	No.
Convenience	3,673
Supermarkets	960
Hypermarkets	237
Cash & Carry	143
Total	**5,013**

Selected Operations and Banners

Hypermarkets
- Carrefour

Supermarkets
- Champion
- GB
- Globi
- GS
- Marinopoulos
- Norte
- Super GB
- Super GS
- Unic

Hard discount stores
- Ed
- Minipreco

Other stores
- Cash-and-carry stores
- Docks Market
- Promocash
- Puntocash

Convenience stores
- 8 à Huit
- Di per Di
- GB Express
- Marché Plus
- Proxi
- Shopi

Other Operations
- Carfuel (petroleum products)
- Comptoirs Modernes (supermarkets)
- Costco UK (20% warehouse club)
- Erteco (hard-discount stores)
- Financiera Pryca (46% consumer credit Spain)
- Fourcar B.V. (investments The Netherlands)
- GlobalNetXchange (Internet-based supply exchange joint venture)
- Ooshop (online shopping)
- Prodirest (catering)
- Providange (auto centers)
- S2P (60% consumer credit)

COMPETITORS

AEON	Ito-Yokado
ALDI	La Rinascente
Auchan	Lianhua Supermarket
Brasileira de Distribui§o	Lidl
	Lotteshopping
Casino Guichard	METRO AG
China Nepstar	Marui Group
Dairy Farm International	Migros
	REWE
Delhaize	Rallye
E.Leclerc	Royal Ahold
Edeka Zentrale	SHV Holdings
Eroski	Super Indo
Falabella	Tengelmann
Galeries Lafayette	Tesco
Globex Utilidades	Wal-Mart
H&M	WuMart
ITM Entreprises	Zara

HISTORICAL FINANCIALS

Company Type: Public

Income Statement FYE: December 31

	REVENUE ($ mil.)	NET INCOME ($ mil.)	NET PROFIT MARGIN	EMPLOYEES
12/14	92,764	1,518	1.6%	381,227
12/13	105,561	1,738	1.6%	364,795
12/12	103,414	1,625	1.6%	364,969
12/11	107,051	479	0.4%	412,443
12/10	122,478	579	0.5%	471,755
Annual Growth	(6.7%)	27.2%	—	(5.2%)

2014 Year-End Financials

Debt ratio: 36.8%
Return on equity: 14.6%
Cash ($ mil.): 3,783
Current ratio: 0.76
Long-term debt ($ mil.): 10,215
No. of shares (mil.): 711
Dividends
Yield: 2.8%
Payout: 6.9%
Market value ($ mil.): 4,283

	STOCK PRICE ($) FY Close	P/E High	P/E Low	PER SHARE ($) Earnings	Dividends	Book Value
12/14	6.02	4	3	2.15	0.17	15.70
12/13	7.88	4	3	2.51	0.28	15.40
12/12	5.15	3	2	2.39	0.90	14.38
12/11	4.48	14	7	0.72	0.99	12.71
Annual Growth	10.4%	—	—	31.3%	(35.7%)	5.4%

Casino Guichard Perrachon S.A.

You won't hit the jackpot at Casino Guichard-Perrachon but odds are you'll go home with the groceries. One of the world's leading food retailers Casino Group owns and operates more than 11700 stores including hypermarkets (mostly G ©ant) supermarkets (Casino and Monoprix to name a few) restaurants (Casino Caf ©©ia) and discount stores (Leader Price). It is the third-largest food retailer (behind Carrefour and Auchan) and the #1 convenience store operator in France (primarily Petit Casino but other banners include Franprix Vival and Spar). Most of its stores are in France but it has outlets in 8 countries in Asia and South America including Brazil Colombia Thailand and Vietnam.

After a blip in 2009 when net sales dipped by just over 1% vs. the previous year Casino's sales (in local currency) rebounded by more than 8% in 2010. Profitability improved as well (up 7.5% for the year). With emerging economies in South America and Asia outperforming France Casino's international operation outperformed its domestic one with net sales overseas increasing by more than 22% while sales at home grew by less than 2%. Indeed international sales are a rapidly-growing part of Casino's revenue stream accounting for 48% of sales in 2011 up from 34% just two years ago. Key international markets for the French firm include Brazil where it operates more than 1500 stores Colombia Thailand and Vietnam.

More than 90% of Casino's growing international business comes from the fast-growing South American and Asian markets where the company is placing its bets. Brazil and Colombia together account for more than two-thirds of the company's overseas sales. Casino owns a 43% stake in Brazil's #1 retailer Companhia Brasileira de Distribuição (CBD) operator of the Pão de Açucar supermarket chain there. The French retailer also operates in the Indian Ocean region where it owns a majority stake in Vindmia an operator of supermarkets and hypermarkets in Asia and Africa. In Thailand Casino's Big C affiliate in late 2010 acquired about 40 stores (including 34 hypermarkets) from rival Carrefour for 868 million (about $1.17 billion). (Casino owns a 36% stake in that country's Big C Supercentre chain which is second in store count in Thailand to UK-owned Tesco Lotus.) The move doubled Big C's presence in Greater Bangkok.

At home price competition from discounters has hurt Casino and its rival Carrefour as French shoppers eschew their traditional hypermarkets and supermarkets for discount stores. In response Casino has strengthened its position in the convenience and discount store markets. Indeed convenience and discount stores are the retailer's most popular formats accounting for 60% of sales in France.

Casino shored up its balance sheet through a plan to dispose of some 1 billion ($1.3 billion) of assets by the end of 2010. The divestments included the sale of 42 superette Casino supermarket and Franprix-Leader price stores in 2008. Future divestments will include the sale of 334 million ($424 million) of soon-to-be-built real estate to Mercialys a property company spun off by Casino in 2006. Mercialys will pay for the properties in stock which will be redistributed to Casino shareholders as a dividend. Casino has been reducing its stake in Mercialys thereby raising 138 million ($182 million). It currently owns about 40% of the property company.

The company's 125-plus Gant hypermarkets (warehouse-style stores that sell groceries and other merchandise) and convenience stores together contribute more than 50% of revenues. Casino Caftria operates about 275 eating places in varying size and cuisines including Poncholito (Tex-Mex) and La Pastaria (Italian). Casino is also active in e-commerce (Cdiscount.com).

Casino is controlled by Euris which is controlled by Jean-Charles Naouri Casino's chairman and CEO.

HISTORY

Frenchman Geoffroy Guichard married Antonia Perrachon a grocer's daughter in 1889 in Saint-tienne France. Three years later Geoffroy took over his father-in-law's general store (a converted "casino" or musical hall). In 1898 the company became Soci ©©des Magasins du Casino. By 1900 when it became a joint stock company Casino had 50 stores; it opened its 100th store in 1904. That year the company introduced its first private-label product: canned sardines. In 1917 Guichard named his two sons Mario and Jean as managers.

By WWI there were about 215 branches more than 50 in Saint- tienne. From 1919 to the early 1920s the company opened several factories to manufacture goods such as food soap and perfumes. In 1925 the elder Guichard retired leaving the day-to-day operations of Casino to his two sons. (Geoffroy died in 1940.) WWII took a heavy toll on the company: About 70 Casino stores were leveled and another 450 were damaged.

The company began opening cafeterias in 1967 and in 1976 it formed Casino USA to run them. Casino USA bought an interest in the California-based Thriftimart volume retailer in 1983 renaming the company after Thriftimart's Smart & Final warehouse stores.

Casino grew by acquiring companies across France including CEDIS (16 hypermarkets 116 supermarkets and 722 smaller stores in eastern France; 1985) and La Ruche Meridionale (18 hypermarkets and 112 supermarkets in southern France 1990). Casino bought nearly 300 hypermarkets and supermarkets from Rallye SA in 1992 giving Rallye about 30% of the company. The company opened its first hypermarket in Warsaw Poland in 1996.

Rival Promod˝s made a roughly $4.5 billion hostile takeover bid for Casino in 1997. Guichard family members voted against the Promod˝s offer instead backing a $3.9 billion friendly offer from Rallye (increasing their stake to nearly 50%). Casino also launched a massive counterattack — buying more than 600 Franprix and Leader Price supermarket stores from food manufacturer TLC Beatrice and acquiring a 21% stake in hypermarket chain Monoprix. Promod˝s withdrew its bid four months later.

Casino expanded internationally in the late 1990s acquiring stakes in food retailers in Argentina (Libertad) Uruguay (Disco) Colombia (Almacenes Exito SA) Brazil (Companhia Brasileira de Distribui § o) and Thailand (Big C the country's largest retailer). It also opened its first hypermarket in Taichung Taiwan.

Expansion in France included a joint venture (called Opera) formed in 1999 with retailer Cora SA to buy food and nonfood goods for the Casino and Cora stores and the acquisition of 100 convenience stores (converted to the Petit Casino banner) in southwest France from retailer Guyenne et Gascogne.

Casino acquired 100 Proxi convenience stores in southeast France in 2000 from Montagne (most became Vival franchises) and more than 400 convenience stores (Eco Service and others) from Auchan. Casino also bought 51% of French online retailer Cdiscount.com (CDs videos CD-ROMs and DVDs) and upped its ownership in several of its international supermarket operations including gaining 100% ownership of Libertad. It also increased its ownership of Monoprix to 49%.

In July 2002 Casino bought a 38% stake in Laurus NV its financially troubled Dutch rival. Laurus operates nearly 2000 supermarkets in the Netherlands Spain and Belgium. (Soon after Casino sold Laurus's unprofitable stores in Spain and Belgium.) Also in 2002 the company sold its wine division Les Chais Beaucairois to wine and spirits company Marie Brizard for $22 million.

Chief executive Pierre Bouchut unexpectedly left Casino in March 2005. Jean-Charles Naouri the company's chairman and controlling shareholder replaced him. In May Casino took joint control of Brazil's leading food retailer Companhia Brasileira de Distribui § o along with the family of Ab lio Diniz. Previously Casino held a minority stake in the supermarket chain. Casino spun off some of its shopping center assets in an October IPO for part of its real estate assets in France including shopping mall properties adjacent to its hypermarket and supermarkets as well as the land under its cafeterias.

In 2006 the French supermarket operator spun off its property company Mercialys. (Following the IPO Casino holds about a 60% stake in Mercialys.) In January 2006 Casino increased its stake in Colombia's biggest retailer Exito to nearly 39%. The company in July sold its 19 hypermarkets in Poland to METRO AG its German rival for about $1.1 billion as part of its asset disposal program. In September Casino sold its 50% stake in its Taiwanese subsidiary Far Eastern G ®nt to its joint venture partner Far Eastern Department Stores.

Real estate sales continued in late 2007 with the announcement that Casino plans to sell nearly $930 million in assets including 255 grocery stores in France. The retailer says it plans to use the proceeds from the sale of these "mature" assets for high-potential projects in France and abroad. In May 2007 Casino sold its 55% stake of the California-based Smart & Final warehouse grocery chain to Apollo Management for $813 million thereby exiting the US market.

Casino acquired in July 2008 about 90% of the French textile maker International Textiles Associes (or INTEXA) from members of the Broyer family. Also Casino exercised its option in 2008 to increase its share in Dutch supermarket operator Super de Boer (formerly Laurus acquired in 2002) to a majority stake. However in December 2009 Casino sold its 57% stake in Super de Boer to Dutch rival Jumbo Groep Holding for €552.5 (nearly $800 million).

In November 2009 Casino acquired the remaining shares of Leader Price and Franprix chains from the Baud family bringing its ownership stake up to 100% in both chains.

EXECUTIVES

Finance Director, Antoine Giscard d'Estaing
Chairman Chief Executive Officer, Jean-Charles Naouri, age 66
Auditors: Deloitte & Associ ©

LOCATIONS

HQ: Casino Guichard Perrachon S.A.
1, Esplanade de France, Saint-Etienne, Cedex 2 42008
Phone: (33) 4 77 45 31 31 **Fax:** (33) 4 77 45 38 38
Web: www.groupe-casino.fr/en/

PRODUCTS/OPERATIONS

2014 Stores

	No.
France	10,416
International	
Argentina	27
Uruguay	54
Brazil	2,143
Colombia	1,258
Thailand	636
Vietnam	40
Total	**14,574**

2014 type of Stores (France)

	No.
Casino hypermarket	127
Supermarkets	444
Monoprix	632
Franprix	860
Leader price	801
Convenience stores	6,825
Indian ocean	129
Other Activities	598
Total	**10,416**

2014 Sales

	% of Total
France Retail	39
Latam Retail	32
Discount	15
Latam Electronics	7
E-Commerce	7
Total	**100**

Selected Operations

Banque du Groupe Casino (60% financial services)
Big C (36% Thailand)
Casino Enterprise (non-food operations)
Cativen (66% Venezuela)
Cdiscount.com (67% e-commerce)
Companhia Brasileira de Distribuição (34% Brazil)
Devoto (97% supermarkets Uruguay)
Exito Colombia SA (55% supermarkets)
Franprix (supermarkets)
Géant (hypermarkets)
Imagica (photo and digital imaging processing)
Leader Price (supermarkets)
Libertad (hypermarkets Argentina)
Vindémia (supermarkets; Madagascar Mauritius Réunion)

COMPETITORS

ALDI
Auchan
Carrefour
E.Leclerc
Groupe Flo
Guyenne et Gascogne
IGA
ITM Entreprises
Kingfisher
METRO AG
Migros
Tesco
Wal-Mart Brazil

HISTORICAL FINANCIALS

Company Type: Public

Income Statement

FYE: December 31

	REVENUE ($ mil.)	NET INCOME ($ mil.)	NET PROFIT MARGIN	EMPLOYEES
12/14	58,943	305	0.5%	335,436
12/13	66,971	1,171	1.7%	329,355
12/12	55,319	1,399	2.5%	318,600
12/11	44,444	734	1.7%	223,050
12/10	38,917	736	1.9%	170,248
Annual Growth	10.9%	(19.8%)	—	18.5%

2014 Year-End Financials

Debt ratio: 36.9%
Return on equity: 3.2%
Cash ($ mil.): 8,944
Current ratio: 0.94
Long-term debt ($ mil.): 11,210
No. of shares (mil.): 113
Dividends
Yield: 4.6%
Payout: —
Market value ($ mil.): 2,092

	STOCK PRICE ($) FY Close	P/E High	P/E Low	PER SHARE ($) Earnings	Dividends	Book Value
12/14	18.49	12	9	2.03	0.86	82.78
12/13	22.95	3	3	10.16	1.55	93.43
12/12	19.37	2	2	12.38	0.79	87.88
Annual Growth	(2.3%)	—	—	(36.4%)	2.0%	(1.5%)

Cathay Financial Holding Co

One of the largest financial services firms in Taiwan Cathay Financial Holding Co. owns companies involved in banking insurance brokerage and more. Its holdings include life accident and health insurer Cathay Life; property/casualty coverage provider Cathay Century; brokerage firm Cathay Securities; and Cathay United Bank which offers consumer banking services such as deposit accounts home mortgages credit cards and car loans as well as international banking and trust services. Cathay Financial Group also has units devoted to venture capital investing. All told the company has more than 700 locations and claims a customer base of more than ten million.

EXECUTIVES

EVP Cathay Life Insurance, Fa-Te Chang
Director; President Cathay Life Insurance, Ming-Ho Hsiung
Chairman Cathay Financial Holdings and Cathay Life Insurance, Hong-Tu Tsai
Vice Chairman; Chairman Cathay United Bank, Gregory K.H. Wang
President and Director, Chang-Ken Lee
CFO and First Deputy Spokesperson, Grace Chen
Director; Managing Director Cathay Life Insurance, Cheng-Ta Tsai
Director; Chairman Cathay Century Insurance, Cheng-Chiu Tsai
Director; Vice Chairman Cathay United Bank, Tsu-Pei Chen
Director; President Cathay Century Insurance, J. H. Hsu
EVP and Director; Chairman Cathay Securities Corporation, David P. Sun
EVP and Spokesperson, Alan Lee
Auditors: Ernst & Young

LOCATIONS

HQ: Cathay Financial Holding Co
No. 296, Sec. 4, Ren Ai Road, Da' an District, Taipei 106
Phone: (886) 2 2708 7698 **Fax:** (886) 2 2325 2488
Web: www.cathayholdings.com.tw

COMPETITORS

Bank of China	Hua Nan Financial
Chang Hwa Bank	Mega Financial
Chinatrust Financial	Shin Kong
E.Sun	SinoPac Holdings
First Financial Holding	Taishin
	Taiwan Business Bank

HISTORICAL FINANCIALS

Company Type: Public

Income Statement FYE: December 31

	ASSETS ($ mil.)	NET INCOME ($ mil.)	INCOME AS % OF ASSETS	EMPLOYEES
12/14	219,329	1,563	0.7%	44,542
12/13	203,777	966	0.5%	44,487
12/12	189,889	555	0.3%	44,678
12/11	165,140	372	0.2%	43,904
12/10	161,137	148	0.1%	42,605
Annual Growth	8.0%	80.3%	—	1.1%

2014 Year-End Financials

Return on assets: 0.7%	Dividends
Return on equity: 13.8%	Yield: —
Long-term debt ($ mil.): —	Payout: —
No. of shares (mil.): —	Market value ($ mil.): —
Sales ($ mil): 13,379	

	STOCK PRICE ($) FY Close	P/E High	P/E Low	PER SHARE ($) Earnings	Dividends	Book Value
12/14	0.00	—	—	0.12	0.34	1.09
12/13	13.41	5	5	0.08	0.15	0.79
12/12	10.00	9	7	0.05	0.10	0.78
12/11	10.60	—	—	0.03	0.00	0.66
Annual Growth	—	—	—	37.7%	—	13.3%

Centrica Plc

Centrica is centered on energy in the UK and North America via five major brands: British Gas Bord Gáis Energy Centrica Energy Centrica Storage and Direct Energy. The UK's largest gas supplier British Gas serves about 11 million homes and 1 million businesses with electricity gas and energy-related services. Direct Energy supplies gas and power to residential customers in Canada and the US. Bord Gáis supplies Irish customers. Centrica is also engaged in gas exploration and production and storage operations. Other activities include gas and electricity production wholesale energy marketing international retail energy marketing drain cleaning services (the Dyno Group) and appliance sales.

Geographic Reach

The company operates in North America Ireland the UK Norway the Netherlands and Trinidad and Tobago.

Operations

The company operates through British Gas Direct Energy Centrica Energy Centrica Storage and Bord Gáis Energy.In addition leading energy supplier and provides energy and/or services to around 11million homes in Britain British Gas provides energy to more than 9000000 UK business supply points. British Gas Services installs repairs and maintains boilers and heating systems. Direct Energy provides of electricity natural gas. and home services across North America via three lines of business: Residential energy supply; Business energy supply; and Residential and business services.Centrica Energy produces natural gas on the UK continental shelf and has a significant international operating portfolio in Norway the Netherlands and North America. It also operate a fleet of gas-fired power stations and offshore wind farms in the UK and holds a 20% stake in eight nuclear power stations in the UK. Centrica Storage store gas on behalf of utilities gas traders and gas producers. Bord Gáis Energy supplies gas and electricity to more than 600000 customers in the Republic of Ireland.

Financial Performance

The company's net revenues have grown over the last few years. Revenues increased by 11% in 2014 due to stronger Direct Energy sales reflecting a full year of revenues from the Hess Energy Marketing acquisition (completed in November 2013).

In 2014 Centrica posted a net loss of 1.01 billion (compared to net income of 950.00 million in 2013) due to higher cost of sales as a result of changes in cost of sales before exceptional items and certain re-measurements and changes in the re-measurement of energy contracts.The company's cash inflow decreased by 59% in 2014 due to a net loss and changes in working capital as a result of changes in receivables and payables.

Strategy

A major aspect of the company's strategy includes growing its core British Gas business and upstream operations (including gas supply storage and renewables) while establishing a leadership position as an integrated North American energy business. Centrica also intends to increase its gas production by 50% –to around 75 million barrels of oil equivalent over the next three to five years – by extending its geographic reach. The company also looks to investing in power generation using offshore wind nuclear and biomass technologies to supply its customers' needs.

In 2015 the company plans to continue to develop its leading position in smart metering innovation and connected homes in the UK. In North America it is looking to expand its offerings to the more valuable customer segments through joint energy and services products solar and innovative partnership agreements. Centrica is also working on reducing capital expenditure through driving efficiencies on in-flight projects and putting a hold on certain new projects.That year Direct Energy agreed to sell its Ontario home services business to EnerCare for C$550 million. In 2014 Centrica sold its 50% non-operated interest in the 90 MW Barrow Offshore Wind Farm located in the East Irish Sea for £50 million. In 2013 the company signed an agreement to sell its Race Bank offshore wind farm project to DONG Energy Power (UK) Limited for £50 million. Centrica will retain equity interests totaling 290 MW in four operational wind farms in the UK.In 2013 Centrica entered into a 4½ year LNG supply agreement with Qatargas for the purchase of up to 3 million tons of liquefied natural gas (LNG) per year. The £4.4 billion deal builds on Centrica's existing agreement with Qatargas signed in February 2011 and could provide gas to meet approximately 13% per cent of UK annual residential gas demand. With increasing global competition from emerging economies for LNG and declining North Sea production this transaction secures important gas supplies for Centrica and the UK to the end of 2018.

Mergers and Acquisitions

In 2015 British Gas acquired AlertMe a UK-based connected homes company that provides innovative energy management products and services. The acquisition gives British Gas ownership of a scalable technology platform software development capability data analytics and a patent portfolio enabling further development of connected homes products and services in other parts of the Centrica Group through Direct Energy in North America and Bord Gáis in Ireland.In 2014 Centrica and Qatar Petroleum International agreed to acquire a package of natural gas assets in the Foothills region of Alberta from Shell Canada Energy for C$50 millionExpanding its geographic presence in 2014 Centrica acquired Bord Gáis Energy's gas and electricity supply business in Ireland and the Whitegate gas-fired power station. In 2013 Direct Energy acquired Texas-based electricity retailer Bounce Energy.

HISTORY

William Murdock invented gas lighting in 1792. In 1812 the Gas Light and Coke Company of London was formed as the world's first gas supplier to the public and by 1829 the UK had 200 gas companies.

In the second half of the 19th century the gas industry began looking for new uses for the fuel. Gas stoves were introduced in 1851 the geyser water heater was invented in 1868 and in 1880 the first gas units to heat individual rooms were developed.

Gas companies countered the emerging electricity industry by renting gas stoves at low prices and installing gas fittings (stove pipe and lights) in poor homes with no installation charges or deposits. By 1914 the UK had 1500 gas suppliers.

The electricity industry soon made major strikes against the gas industry's dominance. In 1926 the government began reorganizing the fragmented electricity supply industry building a national power grid and establishing the Central Electricity Generating Board to oversee it.

The gas industry was nationalized in 1949 and 1050 gas suppliers were brought under the control of the British Gas Council. Still the gas industry was losing. Supplying gas was more expensive than generating electricity: Gas was seen as a power supply of the past. The Gas Council sought to change that image through an aggressive marketing campaign in the 1960s touting gas as a modern clean fuel. Other factors played a part in its re-emergence: The Clean Air Act of 1956 steadily reduced the use of coal for home heating liquefied natural gas was discovered in the North Sea and OPEC raised oil prices in the 1970s. When natural gas was introduced most of the old gasworks were demolished and the British Gas Council (which became the British Gas Corp. in 1973) set about converting free of charge every gas appliance in the UK to natural gas.

As Margaret Thatcher's government began privatizing state industries the British Gas Corp. was taken public in 1986. Freed from government control British Gas expanded its international exploration and production activities. When the US gas industry began deregulating British Gas formed joint venture Accord Energy in 1994 with US gas trader Natural Gas Clearinghouse (now NGC) to sell gas on the wholesale market.

With the opening of the UK gas-supply market (which began regionally in 1996 and went nationwide in 1998) British Gas split into two public companies to avoid a conflict of interest between its supply business and its monopoly transportation business. In 1997 it spun off Centrica the retail operations and BG (now BG Group) which received the transportation business and the international exploration and production operations.

The UK electricity supply market began opening up to competition in 1998 and Centrica won 750000 UK electricity customers most of them also gas customers. In 1999 it bought The Automobile Association which it sold to venture capitalists in 2004. In 2000 Centrica began offering telecom services in the UK.

Centrica moved into North America in 2000 by purchasing two Canadian companies: natural gas retailer Direct Energy Marketing and gas production company Avalanche Energy. It gained a 28% stake in US marketing firm Energy America through the Direct Energy transaction and purchased the remaining 72% from US firm Sempra Energy the next year. Continuing its non-domestic strategy Centrica bought a 50% interest in Belgium energy supplier Luminus.

The firm purchased 60% of the 1260-MW Humber Power station in 2001 its first domestic power plant interest. It also acquired the UK operations of Australia's One.Tel and it bought Enron's European retail supply business Enron Direct for $137 million.

In 2002 Centrica purchased the retail energy services business of Canadian pipeline company Enbridge for $637 million; it also agreed to acquire another Enron-controlled company US retail energy supplier NewPower Holdings for $130 million. But Centrica withdrew its offer to buy NewPower a month after the deal was announced because of concerns about NewPower's potential Enron-related liabilities. Later that year Centrica acquired 200000 retail customer accounts in Ohio and Pennsylvania from NewPower.

In 2004 the company brought all its UK upstream activities together under Centrica Energy.

In 2005 Centrica acquired Oxxio the Netherlands #4 energy supplier.

To pursue green energy options in 2007 British Gas launched British Gas New Energy.

In 2007 Centrica acquired Newfield Exploration's North Sea assets for $486 million and in 2008 it acquired its first gas and oil assets in the Norwegian North Sea for $375 million (from Marathon Oil).

Growing it retail business in 2008 Centrica acquired Electricity Direct a UK commercial retail supplier serving nearly 1 million customers.

In 2008 Centrica's British Gas unit acquired 40000 small and mid-sized business customers from UK retail energy provider BizzEnergy in the wake of the latter's sudden financial collapse.

Centrica began in 2012 a program to save £500 million ($788 million) in costs over the next two years by identifying efficiencies. Although the company plans to continue investing for further growth it has already started cutting 2300 positions company-wide as well as implementing a pay freeze across much of the group. It set out to develop a better relationship with its customers by simplifying the purchase of gas and electricity. It also decided to make the cost of delivery more transparent by giving its customers a breakdown on their bill of the actual costs of providing the energy.

Through its aggressive acquisition strategy in North America the company has gained more than 6 million retail power and gas supply customers in less than a decade as part of its Direct Energy operations. Building on its portfolio of offerings in 2011 it acquired Illinois-based Home Warranty of America (HWA) for £30 million ($48 million). HWA provides whole home warranty plans to more than 70000 customers through a network of 4000 contractors.

Direct Energy also made three acquisitions in 2011 for its residential energy supply business in North America: Gateway Energy Services First Choice Power and Vectren Retail. The deals part of the company's strategy of acquiring smaller suppliers and buying in deregulated markets added more than 750000 customers.

In a major move to grow its upstream business and its Norwegian operations Centrica completed a £936 million ($1.5 billion) deal in 2012 to acquire Norwegian assets from Statoil and ConocoPhillips. Combined the new assets will increase the company's reserves by almost 40% and its production by more than 30%. The acquisition includes proved and probable reserves of 117 million barrels of oil equivalent and production of 34000 barrels of oil evalent per day. The buy also makes Centrica one of Norway's fastest growing companies with a third of its gas and oil production originating from that region. The company's upstream operations also have a presence in Trinidad and the Netherlands.

In spite of the growth of Centrica's gas assets the company decided to raise its gas and electricity prices by 17% in late 2011 to cover the rising wholesale commodity prices in the first half of the year. Mild weather that year led to a decline per household averaging 21% less in gas and 4% less in electricity consumption. With lower residential demand customer bills were 4% lower on average in 2011. Consumer complaints over higher prices for heating homes in the UK led to protests at the offices of utility companies and at town halls early in 2012.

EXECUTIVES

Interim Managing Director British Gas, Ian Peters
CEO, Iain C. Conn
Managing Director International Upstream, Mark Hanafin
CFO, Jeff Bell
Chairman, Richard (Rick) Haythornthwaite
Auditors: PricewaterhouseCoopers LLP

LOCATIONS

HQ: Centrica Plc
Millstream, Maidenhead Road, Windsor, Berkshire SL4 5GD
Phone:
Web: www.centrica.com

2011 Sales

	% of total
UK	69
US	17
Canada	9
Other countries	5
Total	**100**

PRODUCTS/OPERATIONS

2011 Sales

	% of total
UK	
Downstream	
Residential energy supply	36
Business energy supply & services	12
Residential services	7
Upstream	
Gas	13
Power	6
Storage	1
North America	
Business energy supply	12
Residential energy supply	10
Residential & business services	2
Upstream & wholesale energy	1
Total	**100**

COMPETITORS

AGL Resources
Community Energy
Constellation Energy Group
Dominion Resources
E.ON Ruhrgas
E.ON UK
EDF Energy
Electrabel
Gasunie
Green Mountain Energy
IBERDROLA
RWE npower
STASCO
Scottish and Southern Energy
Southern Company
United Utilities
Viridian Group
Western Power Distribution

HISTORICAL FINANCIALS

Company Type: Public

Income Statement FYE: December 31

	REVENUE ($ mil.)	NET INCOME ($ mil.)	NET PROFIT MARGIN	EMPLOYEES
12/14	45,906	(1,579)	—	37,530
12/13	43,910	1,569	3.6%	36,966
12/12	38,591	2,051	5.3%	38,642
12/11	35,259	650	1.8%	39,432
12/10	34,814	3,004	8.6%	34,970
Annual Growth	7.2%	—	—	1.8%

2014 Year-End Financials

Debt ratio: 48.0%
Return on equity: (-25.5%)
Cash ($ mil.): 969
Current ratio: 0.84
Long-term debt ($ mil.): 8,353
No. of shares (mil.): —
Dividends
Yield: 6.4%
Payout: —
Market value ($ mil.): —

	STOCK PRICE ($) FY Close	P/E High/Low	PER SHARE ($) Earnings	Dividends	Book Value
12/14	17.26	— —	(0.32)	1.11	0.86
12/13	23.18	145116	0.30	1.02	1.69
12/12	22.00	90 74	0.39	0.96	1.84
12/11	17.82	262209	0.13	0.87	1.67
12/10	20.64	58 43	0.58	0.76	1.75
Annual Growth	(4.4%)	— —	—	9.9%	(16.3%)

Chiba Bank, Ltd

The Chiba Bank based in Japan's Chiba prefecture — located east of Tokyo — operates 175 branches and sub-branches across Japan. The bank boasts more than 39140 ATMs nationwide and operates international offices in Hong Kong London New York Shanghai and Singapore. Its lending focuses on home mortgages regional businesses and residential construction companies. In addition to providing traditional banking services to individuals and businesses The Chiba Bank offers investment trusts credit cards leasing financial consulting annuities and securities. Subsidiaries include Chibagin Accounting Service (cash and securities analysis) and Chibagin Capital (shareholders consultancy).
Auditors: Ernst & Young ShinNihon LLC

LOCATIONS

HQ: Chiba Bank, Ltd
1-2 Chiba-Minato, Chuo-ku, Chiba 260-8720
Phone: (81) 43 245 1111
Web: www.chibabank.co.jp

HISTORICAL FINANCIALS

Company Type: Public

Income Statement FYE: March 31

	ASSETS ($ mil.)	NET INCOME ($ mil.)	INCOME AS % OF ASSETS	EMPLOYEES
03/15	108,097	475	0.4%	4,420
03/14	116,486	449	0.4%	4,399
03/13	120,878	469	0.4%	4,454
03/12	133,082	497	0.4%	4,491
03/11	127,441	490	0.4%	4,490
Annual Growth	(4.0%)	(0.8%)	—	(0.4%)

2015 Year-End Financials

Return on assets: 0.4%
Return on equity: 7.0%
Long-term debt ($ mil.): —
No. of shares (mil.): 832
Sales ($ mil): 1,911
Dividends
Yield: —
Payout: —
Market value ($ mil.): —

	STOCK PRICE ($) FY Close	P/E High	P/E Low	PER SHARE ($) Earnings	Dividends	Book Value
03/15	0.00	—	—	0.57	0.00	8.59
03/14	30.94	—	—	0.53	0.00	8.77
03/13	28.90	—	—	0.54	0.00	9.01
03/12	29.50	—	—	0.57	0.00	9.21
Annual Growth	—	—	—	0.0%	—	(1.7%)

China Citic Bank Corp Ltd

Commercial enterprises mean money in the bank for China CITIC Bank. One of China's largest commercial banks China CITIC Bank offers corporate small business and retail banking and financial services including business accounts personal savings accounts loans asset management and private banking. The bank operates primarily in China through a network of more than 600 branches many of which are located in China's coastal regions and major economic centers. To a lesser extent China CITIC serves select international markets as well. Founded in 1987 the bank is majority-owned and controlled by state-owned investment firm CITIC Group.

While it is actively expanding its presence throughout China China CITIC Bank has been focused in recent years on building its international banking business. In late 2009 the bank acquired a controlling stake in CITIC International Financial Holdings Limited (CIFH) which has a presence in China and operates offices in Los Angeles and New York. China CITIC Bank intends to leverage CIFH's international presence to expand into markets in Asia the Americas and other regions.

One of China CITIC Bank's shareholders Banco Bilbao Vizcaya Argentaria (BBVA) has itself been actively investing in some of the bank's other growth efforts. The two banks are collaborating to develop auto financing private banking and other retail banking services for markets in Asia. The relationship is also opening up business opportunities for China CITIC Bank in South America a region in which BBVA has a significant presence.

BBVA has ownership stakes in both China CITIC Bank (15%) and CIFH (30%) and has been increasing its investments in and consequently strengthening its relationship with China CITIC Bank since its initial investment in 2006.

Auditors: KPMG Huazhen (Special General Partnership)

LOCATIONS

HQ: China Citic Bank Corp Ltd
No.9 Chaoyangmen Beidajie, Dongcheng District, Beijing 100010
Phone: (86) 10 89938900 **Fax:** (86) 10 85230081
Web: www.bank.ecitic.com

HISTORICAL FINANCIALS

Company Type: Public

Income Statement FYE: December 31

	REVENUE ($ mil.)	NET INCOME ($ mil.)	NET PROFIT MARGIN	EMPLOYEES
12/14	38,250	6,556	17.1%	50,735
12/13	30,388	6,471	21.3%	46,822
12/12	24,705	4,977	20.1%	41,365
12/11	18,945	4,896	25.8%	37,195
12/10	12,332	3,263	26.5%	33,552
Annual Growth	32.7%	19.1%	—	10.9%

2014 Year-End Financials

Debt ratio: —
Return on equity: 16.7%
Cash ($ mil.): 86,763
Current ratio: —
Long-term debt ($ mil.): —
No. of shares (mil.): —
Dividends
Yield: —
Payout: —
Market value ($ mil.): —

	STOCK PRICE ($) FY Close	P/E High	P/E Low	PER SHARE ($) Earnings	Dividends	Book Value
12/14	0.70	0	0	0.14	0.00	0.89
12/13	0.53	0	0	0.14	0.00	0.80
12/12	0.51	0	0	0.11	0.00	0.68
12/11	0.55	0	0	0.11	0.00	0.59
12/10	0.71	0	0	0.08	0.00	0.47
Annual Growth	(0.4%)	—	—	13.8%	—	17.6%

China Communications Constructions Group Ltd

Engineering services nsk

EXECUTIVES

Chairman, Yusheng Chen
Auditors: PricewaterhouseCoopers Zhong Tian LLP

LOCATIONS

HQ: China Communications Constructions Group Ltd
85 De Sheng Men Wai Street, Xicheng District, Beijing 100088
Phone: (86) 10 8201 6562 **Fax:** (86) 10 8201 6524
Web: www.cccltd.cn

HISTORICAL FINANCIALS

Company Type: Public

Income Statement FYE: December 31

	REVENUE ($ mil.)	NET INCOME ($ mil.)	NET PROFIT MARGIN	EMPLOYEES
12/14	58,978	2,253	3.8%	103,357
12/13	54,807	2,076	3.8%	100,874
12/12	47,370	1,964	4.1%	94,629
12/11	46,752	1,869	4.0%	90,674
12/10	41,376	1,496	3.6%	101,030
Annual Growth	9.3%	10.8%	—	0.6%

2014 Year-End Financials

Debt ratio: 5.8%
Return on equity: 13.2%
Cash ($ mil.): 11,572
Current ratio: 1.05
Long-term debt ($ mil.): 22,203
No. of shares (mil.): —
Dividends
Yield: 2.0%
Payout: —
Market value ($ mil.): —

China Construction Bank Corp

Auditors: PricewaterhouseCoopers Zhong Tian LLP

LOCATIONS

HQ: China Construction Bank Corp
No. 25, Financial Street, Xicheng District, Beijing 100033
Phone: (86) 10 6621 5533 **Fax:** (86) 10 6621 8888
Web: www.ccb.com

HISTORICAL FINANCIALS

Company Type: Public

Income Statement FYE: December 31

	ASSETS ($ mil.)	NET INCOME ($ mil.)	INCOME AS % OF ASSETS	EMPLOYEES
12/14	2,697,894	36,709	1.4%	372,321
12/13	2,537,740	35,457	1.4%	368,410
12/12	2,241,301	30,986	1.4%	355,290
12/11	1,951,231	26,890	1.4%	329,438
12/10	1,640,014	20,456	1.2%	313,867
Annual Growth	13.3%	15.7%	—	4.4%

2014 Year-End Financials

Return on assets: 1.4%
Return on equity: 19.7%
Long-term debt ($ mil.): —
No. of shares (mil.): —
Sales ($ mil): 141,641
Dividends
Yield: 5.0%
Payout: 564.2%
Market value ($ mil.): —

	STOCK PRICE ($) FY Close	P/E High	P/E Low	PER SHARE ($) Earnings	Dividends	Book Value
12/14	16.45	18	14	0.15	0.83	0.80
12/13	15.18	21	15	0.14	0.73	0.70
12/12	16.23	22	16	0.12	0.62	0.60
12/11	13.94	30	17	0.11	0.55	0.52
12/10	18.30	98	31	0.08	2.47	0.42
Annual Growth	(2.6%)	—	—	14.6%	(23.9%)	17.3%

China Life Insurance Co Ltd

Controlling about half of its home country's life insurance market China Life Insurance Company is the insurance beast from the East. The firm is by far China's largest life insurance company providing annuity products and life insurance for both individuals and groups. It has more than 90 million individual and group policies in force. China Life sells its individual products primarily through about 640000 of its own agents who are spread across the country at roughly 15000 branch locations; another direct sales force handles marketing of its group policies. In addition to life insurance the company provides asset management services and health and accident insurance.

China Life was formed in 2003 when its state-owned predecessor China Life Insurance (Group) Company (or CLIC) spun off some of its more attractive assets in an IPO on the New York Stock Exchange. CLIC still owns about 68% of China Life with public investors owning the rest of the company.

Though its formidable force of exclusive sales agents is still the firm's core means for selling its products China Life has been diversifying its distribution channels using alliances with banks travel agencies brokerages and others to reach additional customers.

In 2009 the company announced it would buy a stake in China Development Bank as part of China Life's strategy of investing in banks as a way to build a distribution network for its policies. The purchase also matches the company's strategy of buying into unlisted companies.

China Life is also implementing market segmentation initiatives designing products and marketing plans tailored for different income and education levels. China's booming middle and upper classes are among the company's key customer targets.

Through its controlling interest in China Life Insurance Assets Management China Life is the largest insurance asset management company and one of the largest institutional investors in China.

HISTORY

China Life listed on the NYSE in what would become one of the largest IPOs of 2003 valued at more than $3 billion. The company's IPO however was tarnished by subsequent revelations of improper accounting prior to the company's going public; several US lawsuits were filed but in 2006 the SEC's investigation came to an end with no action taken.

EXECUTIVES

President; Executive Director, Feng Wan
COO, Hengping Xu
Chairman of the Board; Executive Director, Mingsheng Yang
Auditors: Ernst & Young Hua Ming LLP

LOCATIONS

HQ: China Life Insurance Co Ltd
16 Financial Street, Xicheng District, Beijing 100033
Phone: (86) 10 63633333 **Fax:** (86) 10 66575722
Web: www.e-chinalife.com

COMPETITORS

AEGON
AXA
Allianz
Aviva
Bank of China
CIGNA
China Minsheng Banking
China Pacific Insurance
Generali
ING
John Hancock Financial Services
Manulife Financial
MetLife
PICC Property
Ping An Insurance
Skandia
Sun Life

HISTORICAL FINANCIALS

Company Type: Public

Income Statement FYE: December 31

	ASSETS ($ mil.)	NET INCOME ($ mil.)	INCOME AS % OF ASSETS	EMPLOYEES
12/14	361,977	5,189	1.4%	101,972
12/13	325,896	4,090	1.3%	100,310
12/12	304,594	1,774	0.6%	100,340
12/11	251,637	2,912	1.2%	100,319
12/10	213,996	5,101	2.4%	103,220
Annual Growth	14.0%	0.4%	—	(0.3%)

2014 Year-End Financials

Return on assets: 1.5%
Return on equity: 12.7%
Long-term debt ($ mil.): —
No. of shares (mil.): —
Sales ($ mil): 71,648
Dividends
Yield: 3.2%
Payout: 116.3%
Market value ($ mil.): —

	STOCK PRICE ($) FY Close	P/E High/Low	PER SHARE ($) Earnings	Dividends	Book Value
12/14	58.71	52 34	0.18	0.64	1.62
12/13	47.25	62 39	0.15	0.29	1.29
12/12	49.69	122 88	0.06	0.47	1.25
12/11	36.97	102 52	0.10	0.28	1.08
12/10	61.17	66 50	0.18	1.37	1.12
Annual Growth	(1.0%)	— —	0.4%	(17.4%)	9.7%

China Merchants Bank Co Ltd

China Merchants Bank (CMB) is out for the business of corporate and small-time merchants. The bank is one of China's top five banks and with 53 million credit cards its largest issuer. CMB offers businesses and individuals a range of financial services including credit cards savings accounts mortgage loans ATMs foreign exchange trading and on-line banking service. Corporate banking accounts for half of its operating income. CMB targets affluent markets through a network of more than 90 branches and 800 sub-branches and 2680 ATMs in more than 100 cities in China. It also maintains branches in New York City and London. CMB has relationships with more than 1600 banks worldwide.

Geographic Reach

CMB is headquartered in Shenzhen and primarily focuses on the Chinese domestic market. CMB operates a branch and a representative office in New York and also representative offices in London and Taipei.

Operations

CMB divides its operations into three main segments: corporate (or wholesale) banking retail banking and treasury. Corporate banking accounted for 63% of the bank's total revenue in 2011; retail banking 37%. The treasury operations lost money for the bank during its fiscal year 2011.

Financial Performance

Since the end of the global Great Recession CMB has seen four straight years of impressive growth. From 2010 to 2011 its net sales increased by 35% and its net income jumped by 40%.

The growth was attributed to a 34% increase in net interest which was mainly due to improvement in yield of interest-earning assets brought about by better risk pricing and positive re-pricing of assets as a result of rising interest rates and a steady expansion of the volume of interest-earning assets. Net fee and commission revenue also surged by 38% due to the increase in commissions from custody and other trustee businesses bank card commissions settlement and clearing fees and financial consultancy fees.

Net income in 2011 increased mainly due to the increase in net sales partially offset by a 25% increase in operating expenses. Staff costs and other general and administrative expenses increased by 27% due to increased headcounts along with business expansion.

Auditors: KPMG Certified Public Accountants

LOCATIONS

HQ: China Merchants Bank Co Ltd
7088 Shennan Boulevard, Futian District, Shenzhen, Guangdong Province 518040
Phone: (86) 755 83198888 **Fax:** (86) 755 83195109
Web: www.cmbchina.com

HISTORICAL FINANCIALS

Company Type: Public

Income Statement FYE: December 31

	ASSETS ($ mil.)	NET INCOME ($ mil.)	INCOME AS % OF ASSETS	EMPLOYEES
12/14	762,415	9,008	1.2%	75,109
12/13	663,440	8,547	1.3%	68,078
12/12	546,693	7,261	1.3%	59,340
12/11	444,040	5,739	1.3%	45,344
12/10	364,480	3,909	1.1%	43,089
Annual Growth	20.3%	23.2%	—	14.9%

2014 Year-End Financials

Return on assets: 1.2%
Return on equity: 19.2%
Long-term debt ($ mil.): —
No. of shares (mil.): —
Sales ($ mil): 45,309
Dividends
Yield: 5.6%
Payout: —
Market value ($ mil.): —

	STOCK PRICE ($) FY Close	P/E High/Low	PER SHARE ($) Earnings	Dividends	Book Value
12/14	2.51	0 0	0.36	0.70	2.01
12/13	2.10	0 0	0.38	0.71	1.74
12/12	2.18	0 0	0.34	0.27	1.49
12/11	2.08	0 0	0.27	0.00	1.21
12/10	2.46	0 0	0.19	0.00	0.94
Annual Growth	0.5%	— —	17.7%	—	20.8%

China Minsheng Banking Corp Ltd

LOCATIONS

HQ: China Minsheng Banking Corp Ltd
No. 2, Fuxingmennei Avenue, Xicheng District, Beijing 100031
Phone: (86) 10 68946790 **Fax:** (86) 10 58560720
Web: www.cmbc.com.cn

HISTORICAL FINANCIALS

Company Type: Public

Income Statement FYE: December 31

	ASSETS ($ mil.)	NET INCOME ($ mil.)	INCOME AS % OF ASSETS	EMPLOYEES
12/14	646,937	7,177	1.1%	59,659
12/13	532,914	6,983	1.3%	54,927
12/12	515,218	6,025	1.2%	49,227
12/11	354,134	4,435	1.3%	40,820
12/10	276,675	2,667	1.0%	31,454
Annual Growth	23.7%	28.1%	—	17.4%

2014 Year-End Financials

Return on assets: 1.2%
Return on equity: 20.3%
Long-term debt ($ mil.): —
No. of shares (mil.): —
Sales ($ mil): 39,633
Dividends
Yield: 1.3%
Payout: 2.2%
Market value ($ mil.): —

	STOCK PRICE ($) FY Close	P/E High/Low		PER SHARE ($) Earnings	Dividends	Book Value
12/14	13.14	0	0	0.20	0.17	1.13
12/13	11.00	0	0	0.20	0.33	0.96
12/12	11.67	0	0	0.18	0.48	0.77
12/11	8.61	0	0	0.14	0.00	0.64
Annual Growth	15.1%	—	—	9.5%	—	15.2%

China Mobile Limited

China Mobile Limited sees unlimited potential. The company is China's (and the world's) leading wireless operator by subscribers which total some 800 million. In terms of sales it trails UK-based global leader Vodafone Group. China Mobile offers domestic and international phone service text messaging and other mobile data services. In addition to its flagship postpaid GoTone brand the company targets the youth and budget-conscious markets with M-Zone and Easy Own prepaid services. State-controlled China Mobile Communications Corporation (CMCC) indirectly holds a majority stake of 75% through intermediary subsidiary China Mobile (Hong Kong) Group Limited.

Revenue rose more than 7% in 2010 over 2009 thanks mainly to upticks in voice usage volume and value-added business besides the more obvious factor of subscriber growth. In the company's main segment of usage and monthly fees (64% of revenue) revenue went up about 4% in 2010 over 2009 a trend that could continue because of tariff decreases that may bring more business. The value-added services segment (31% of revenue) enjoyed an increase of more than 15% in 2010 over 2009 owing mainly to the launch of new products and other business-development efforts.

Like any other major telecom company 3G (Third Generation) and LTE (Long Term Evolution) development have kept China Mobile Limited buzzing recently. After initiating 3G service in 2009 the company has signed up about 27 million customers for it. Efforts to keep 3G service up to speed could result in significant capital expenditures. In addition to that China Mobile has been helping its parent CMCC roll out the LTE network in six Chinese cities as well as installing a demonstration LTE network in Beijing.

Meanwhile China Mobile Limited's organic growth has been fueled in part by the adoption of mobile communications in rural areas that previously had no wired or wireless telephone services. Additionally the company has catered increasingly to corporate clients in a search for higher-margin contracts.

Other efforts to grow its business include the $35.9 million acquisition in 2011 of China Topssion Communication a seller of mobile phones and other electronic devices to build its distribution and retail operations. China Mobile bought state-run fixed-line carrier China Tietong Telecommunications in 2008 as part of a broader restructuring of the telecom industry in China which also involved former rival China Unicom selling its wireless operations to China Telecom. The previous year it grew globally as well with the acquisition of nearly 90% of Pakistani wireless company Paktel Ltd. for about $284 million.

These purchases continued the company's history of using acquisitions to expand operations. From 1998 to 2004 China Mobile purchased 29 regional telecom service providers. The company acquired China Resources Peoples Telephone (later renamed China Mobile Peoples Telephone) a Hong Kong-based telecom service provider for $436 million in 2006.

EXECUTIVES

CEO, Li Yue, age 55
VP and CFO, Xue Taohai, age 58
VP and Executive Director, Sha Yuejia, age 57
VP and Executive Director, Liu Aili, age 52
Chairman, Shang Bing, age 59
Auditors: PricewaterhouseCoopers Zhong Tian LLP

LOCATIONS

HQ: China Mobile Limited
60/F, The Center, 99 Queen' s Road Central,
Phone: (852) 3121 8888 **Fax:** (852) 3121 8809
Web: www.chinamobileltd.com

PRODUCTS/OPERATIONS

2013 Sales

	% of total
Telecommunication Services	
Voice Services	56
Data Services	33
Other	5
Other products & services	6
Total	**100**

COMPETITORS

China Telecom Corporation Limited
China Unicom
City Telecom
Hutchison Telecommunications
PCCW Ltd.
Vodafone

HISTORICAL FINANCIALS

Company Type: Public

Income Statement FYE: December 31

	REVENUE ($ mil.)	NET INCOME ($ mil.)	NET PROFIT MARGIN	EMPLOYEES
12/14	103,353	17,607	17.0%	241,550
12/13	104,094	20,101	19.3%	197,030
12/12	89,892	20,736	23.1%	182,487
12/11	83,883	19,997	23.8%	175,336
12/10	73,613	18,150	24.7%	164,336
Annual Growth	8.9%	(0.8%)	—	10.1%

2014 Year-End Financials

Debt ratio: 0.0%
Return on equity: 13.2%
Cash ($ mil.): 10,754
Current ratio: 1.11
Long-term debt ($ mil.): 804
No. of shares (mil.): —
Dividends
Yield: 3.1%
Payout: 211.7%
Market value ($ mil.): —

	STOCK PRICE ($) FY Close	P/E High/Low		PER SHARE ($) Earnings	Dividends	Book Value
12/14	58.82	12	8	0.86	1.83	6.75
12/13	52.29	10	8	0.99	2.02	6.48
12/12	58.72	9	8	1.02	1.96	5.77
12/11	48.49	8	7	0.99	1.88	5.14
12/10	49.62	9	8	0.89	1.66	4.36
Annual Growth	4.3%	—	—	(0.9%)	2.4%	11.6%

China Pacific Insurance (Group) Co., Ltd.

Auditors: PricewaterhouseCoopers Zhong Tian LLP

LOCATIONS

HQ: China Pacific Insurance (Group) Co., Ltd.
South Tower, Bank of Communications, Financial Building, 190 Central Yincheng Road, Pudong New District, Shanghai 200120
Phone: (86) 21 58767282 **Fax:** (86) 21 68870791
Web: www.cpic.com.cn

HISTORICAL FINANCIALS

Company Type: Public

Income Statement FYE: December 31

	REVENUE ($ mil.)	NET INCOME ($ mil.)	NET PROFIT MARGIN	EMPLOYEES
12/14	34,835	1,780	5.1%	90,829
12/13	31,750	1,529	4.8%	86,893
12/12	26,812	814	3.0%	85,137
12/11	24,707	1,320	5.3%	82,456
12/10	21,440	1,298	6.1%	74,590
Annual Growth	12.9%	8.2%	—	5.0%

2014 Year-End Financials

Debt ratio: —
Return on equity: 10.2%
Cash ($ mil.): 1,807
Current ratio: 2.00
Long-term debt ($ mil.): —
No. of shares (mil.): —
Dividends
Yield: —
Payout: —
Market value ($ mil.): —

	STOCK PRICE ($) FY Close	P/E High/Low		PER SHARE ($) Earnings	Dividends	Book Value
12/14	3.60	0	0	0.20	0.00	2.08
Annual Growth	—	—	—	—	—	—

China Petroleum & Chemical Corp. Inc

China Petroleum and Chemical Corporation (Sinopec Corp.) is China's largest producer and supplier of refined oil products and its second-largest crude oil producer. It is also China's largest petrochemicals producer and distributor and the world's fourth-largest ethylene producer. Operations include oil and gas exploration and production; crude oil processing; oil products trading transportation distribution and marketing; and petrochemicals manufacturing. In 2010 it reported proved reserves of 2.9 billion barrels of oil and 6.5 trillion cu. ft. of natural gas; it also owns more than 29600 gas stations and 34 refineries. China's government controls about 76% of the company through Sinopec Group.

Sinopec Corp. is committed to growing its oil and gas reserves to keep pace with the energy demands from China's booming industrial economy and growing population. The company operates 16 oil and gas production fields in China and also owns vast reserves in Africa. In 2010 the company produced an average of more than 1 billion barrels of oil equivalent per day. For the past few years it has been buying up resources across the globe as it competes with other developing countries for oil and gas reserves.

In late 2011 the company acquired Canada's Daylight Energy for $2.1 billion which gave it access to 69 oil and natural gas assets in the western provinces of British Columbia and Alberta. Daylight is being integrated within an indirect subsidiary of Sinopec Corp. and will operate as Sinopec Daylight Energy. The purchase was made on the heels of the acquisition of OPTI Canada in November by competitor CNOOC another Chinese state-owned company.

In 2013 it purchased a 50% undivided interest in 850000 of Chesapeake's net oil and natural gas leasehold acres in the Mississippi Lime play in northern Oklahoma (425000 acres net to Sinopec) for $1.02 billion.

The acquisitions follow several other purchases Sinopec has made since 2009 including shelling out $7.1 billion for Repsol's assets in Brazil $2.5 billion for Occidental Petroleum's assets in Argentina; $4.7 billion for ConocoPhillips' 9% stake in Syncrude; and $7.5 billion for Addax Petroleum which had reserves in Africa and the Middle East. In late 2010 the company also signed a deal with Chevron to help develop the $6 billion-plus Gendalo-Gehem deepwater natural gas project off the coast of Indonesia.

The shopping spree for oil and gas resources paid off in 2010 when Sinopec Corp. achieved record sales. The company's sales spiked 47% over the previous year and its net income grew by more than 20%. Its exploration and production operations not only grew exponentially but the official launch of the Sichuan-East China Gas project in 2010 also accelerated the company's growth. The pipeline has the capacity to produce about 12 billion cu. meters of gas per year.

Sinopec Corp.'s parent state-owned China Petrochemical (Sinopec Group) reorganized in 2000 and pooled the best of its assets as Sinopec Corp.

EXECUTIVES

Vice Chairman of the Board; President, Wang Tianpu, age 52, $726,000 total compensation
VP and Director General Engineering Department, Zhang Kehua, age 61, $539,000 total compensation
VP and Director General Development and Planning Department, Lei Dianwu, age 52, $362,000 total compensation
Chairman, Wang Yupu
CFO, Dongfen Wen
Vice Chairman, Zhang Yaocang, age 61
Auditors: PricewaterhouseCoopers Zhong Tian LLP

LOCATIONS

HQ: China Petroleum & Chemical Corp. Inc
22 Chaoyangmen North Street, Chaoyang District, Beijing 100728
Phone: (86) 10 5996 0028 **Fax:** (86) 10 5996 0386
Web: www.sinopec.com

PRODUCTS/OPERATIONS

2013 Sales

	% of total
Marketing & distribution	31
Refining	27
Chemicals	9
Exploration & production	5
Corporate & Others	28
Total	**100**

COMPETITORS

BASF SE
BP
Bangchak Petroleum Public
CNOOC
CPC
Chevron
Exxon Mobil
Furmanite
PetroChina
Royal Dutch Shell
TOTAL

HISTORICAL FINANCIALS

Company Type: Public

Income Statement FYE: December 31

	REVENUE ($ mil.)	NET INCOME ($ mil.)	NET PROFIT MARGIN	EMPLOYEES
12/14	455,324	7,486	1.6%	358,571
12/13	475,778	10,923	2.3%	368,953
12/12	446,893	10,246	2.3%	376,201
12/11	398,081	11,633	2.9%	377,235
12/10	290,245	10,892	3.8%	373,375
Annual Growth	11.9%	(8.9%)	—	(1.0%)

2014 Year-End Financials

Debt ratio: 3.6%
Return on equity: 8.0%
Cash ($ mil.): 1,627
Current ratio: 0.60
Long-term debt ($ mil.): 24,318
No. of shares (mil.): —
Dividends
Yield: 4.2%
Payout: 5,371.2%
Market value ($ mil.): —

	STOCK PRICE ($) FY Close	P/E High/Low		PER SHARE ($) Earnings	Dividends	Book Value
12/14	81.01	2601	82	0.06	3.47	0.81
12/13	82.17	2211	20	0.09	3.27	0.81
12/12	114.92	2221	48	0.09	4.25	0.73
12/11	105.05	1791	31	0.10	2.49	0.67
12/10	95.69	1631	20	0.10	2.47	0.56
Annual Growth	(4.1%)	—	—	(9.4%)	8.8%	9.4%

China Railway Construction Corp Ltd

Auditors: Ernst & Young Hua Ming LLP

LOCATIONS

HQ: China Railway Construction Corp Ltd
East, No. 40 Fuxing Road, Haidian District, Beijing 100855
Phone: (86) 10 5268 8600 **Fax:** (86) 10 5268 8302
Web: www.crcc.cn

HISTORICAL FINANCIALS

Company Type: Public

Income Statement FYE: December 31

	REVENUE ($ mil.)	NET INCOME ($ mil.)	NET PROFIT MARGIN	EMPLOYEES
12/14	95,380	1,827	1.9%	249,624
12/13	96,927	1,708	1.8%	246,736
12/12	77,685	1,360	1.8%	244,523
12/11	72,662	1,247	1.7%	241,621
12/10	69,230	644	0.9%	229,070
Annual Growth	8.3%	29.8%	—	2.2%

2014 Year-End Financials

Debt ratio: 3.9%
Return on equity: 13.2%
Cash ($ mil.): 15,804
Current ratio: 1.21
Long-term debt ($ mil.): 13,140
No. of shares (mil.): —
Dividends
Yield: 1.3%
Payout: —
Market value ($ mil.): —

	STOCK PRICE ($) FY Close	P/E High/Low		PER SHARE ($) Earnings	Dividends	Book Value
12/14	12.60	0	0	0.15	0.17	1.19
12/13	10.00	0	0	0.14	0.14	1.08
12/12	11.39	0	0	0.11	0.00	0.94
12/11	5.29	0	0	0.10	0.00	0.83
12/10	11.90	1	1	0.05	0.00	0.71
Annual Growth	1.4%	—	—	29.8%	150.4%	13.9%

China Railway Group Ltd

China Railway Group keeps its infrastructure construction projects on the right track. A subsidiary of state-owned China Railway Engineering Corporation the company designs and constructs railways roads bridges tunnels subways and other structures. It also offers related consulting and engineering services as well as property development and construction services for commercial and residential buildings and other projects. In addition to its core transportation-related projects the company pursues projects from municipal and energy entities in China and abroad. Some of those projects have included hydroelectricity facilities ports and docks.

Operations

China Railway Group operates through five main segments. Its Infrastructure Construction segment generated 82% of its total sales in 2014 and works on railways highways bridges railways irrigation works dams docks airports and municipal works among other projects. Its Property Development segment (5% of revenue) is its next largest and sells or manages residential and commercial properties. The other segments include Survey Design and Consulting Services (2%); Engineering Equipment and Component Manufacturing (2%); and other (9%).Geographic ReachBeyond China the group has worked on construction projects in the Americas Europe Africa and the Asia Pacific. Still the group generated 96% of its total revenue from China in 2014.Sales and MarketingChina Railway Group's largest customer is the China Railway Corporation which accounted for 32% of its total revenue in 2014. Its four next largest customers combined made up another 2.5% of its total revenue.

Financial PerformanceNote: Growth rates may differ after conversion to US dollars. This analysis uses financials from the company's annual report.China Railway Group's annual revenues and profits have grown more than 30% since 2011 thanks mostly to increased demand for infrastructure construction in China with the growing economy.The group's revenue climbed 9% to RMB$590.2 billion ($95.9 billion) during 2014 mostly driven by double-digit growth in its infrastructure construction business with more demand for railways highways building construction and urban rail work. The group's Survey Design and Consulting Services business grew 12% due to a rise in infrastructure project activity while its manufacturing and property development businesses each grew by 6% during the year.Strong revenue growth in 2014 drove China Railway Group's net income higher by 9% to RMB$10.26 billion ($1.67 billion). The group's operating cash levels more than doubled to RMB$19.4 billion ($3.16 billion) in FY2014 mostly as it was able to collect more of its trade receivables with stronger management initiatives.

Stategy

Buoyed by an influx of infrastructure funds from the Chinese government's "One Belt and One Road" policy the group in 2015 planned to build a new China brand for high speed rail and expand its construction projects globally (through its "Go Global" campaign) in new infrastructure markets such as Russia and Israel. The group also planned to invest more in Research Development and Technological Achievements creating some 957 new research projects during 2014 with support from national funds amounting to nearly RMB$29 million.Despite a strategy to expand internationally most of China Railway Group' work still originates in China. Recent projects include new light rail systems and highways in some of China's larger cities. Ultimately a state-owned company China Railway Group receives much of its funding for projects from the Chinese government which has been pushing to expand the country's public transportation infrastructure.

Company Background

China Railway Group traces its roots back to the 1950s. It has completed hundreds of infrastructure projects in more than 50 countries since the 1970s.

EXECUTIVES

President and Director, Zhang Zongyan
Chairman and Executive Director, Shi Dahua
Auditors: Deloitte Touche Tohmatsu Certified Public Accountants LLP

LOCATIONS

HQ: China Railway Group Ltd
918, Block 1, No. 128 South 4th Ring Road West, Fengtai District, Beijing 100070
Phone:
Web: www.crec.cn

COMPETITORS

Bechtel
Beijing Urban Construction
Bouygues
CCCC
CSCEC
Hyundai Engineering and Construction
Shimizu
Zhejiang Expressway

HISTORICAL FINANCIALS

Company Type: Public

Income Statement

FYE: December 31

	REVENUE ($ mil.)	NET INCOME ($ mil.)	NET PROFIT MARGIN	EMPLOYEES
12/14	95,090	1,653	1.7%	293,592
12/13	89,263	1,548	1.7%	289,547
12/12	74,688	1,179	1.6%	289,343
12/11	70,255	1,062	1.5%	294,761
12/10	69,194	1,136	1.6%	285,054
Annual Growth	8.3%	9.8%	—	0.7%

2014 Year-End Financials

Debt ratio: 4.3%
Return on equity: 11.0%
Cash ($ mil.): 11,065
Current ratio: 1.16
Long-term debt ($ mil.): 15,362
No. of shares (mil.): —
Dividends
Yield: 0.0%
Payout: —
Market value ($ mil.): —

	STOCK PRICE ($) FY Close	P/E High	P/E Low	PER SHARE ($) Earnings	Dividends	Book Value
12/14	17.77	1	1	0.08	0.01	0.75
12/13	12.81	1	1	0.07	0.00	0.67
12/12	14.14	1	1	0.06	0.00	0.59
12/11	7.82	1	0	0.05	0.00	0.54
12/10	17.87	1	1	0.05	0.00	0.47
Annual Growth	(0.1%)	—	—	9.8%	7.2%	12.0%

China Resources Beer Holdings Co Ltd

China Resources Beer (CR Beer) has ditched oil for alcohol. Having divested its petroleum distribution business the group is now focused on becoming the largest consumer goods company in mainland China and Hong Kong with a focus on retail stores beer and food and beverage. Its holdings include supermarket and convenience store retail fashion and arts and crafts retail China's best-selling Snow beer brand and food and beverage. Its more than 4400 supermarkets and franchised stores operate under such brands as CR Vanguard Suguo and Fun. Holding company China Resources National Corporation owns a majority stake in CR Beer.

Operations

CR Beer's retail arm operates more than 4400 stores in China of which more than 80% are operated by the company. Types of stores include hypermarkets supermarkets convenience stores and specialty shops under such brands as CR Vanguard Suguo Fun and Ole among others. The company's CR Snow Breweries is a joint venture with SABMiller plc and operates some 85 breweries in China with a combined annual production capacity of more than 18 million kiloliters. Its "Snow" brand beer has a market share of about 22% in China. CR Beer's nonalcoholic Beverage segment makes and sells purified water. The company's Ng Fung division is the the largest supplier of Chinese foodstuffs in Hong Kong and one of the leading integrated food suppliers in China.

Strategy

In 2012 the company divested its marine fishing and aquatic products processing operation and acquired a rice distribution business in keeping with its strategy to focus on high-growth businesses. On the retail front CR Beer is focusing on hypermarkets as its main retail format.

Mergers and Acquisitions

In September 2013 China Resources Snow Breweries acquired the beer business of Kingway Brewery Holdings Ltd. boosting annual production capacity of the beer division to more than 19 million kiloliters. The purchase added another brand to Snow's portfolio and strong market share in Guangdong province.

EXECUTIVES

CEO, Hong Jie, age 47
CFO, Lai (Frank) Ni Hium, age 53
Vice Chairman and CEO Vanguard, Chen Lang, age 50
Vice Chairman, Liu Hongji, age 54
Auditors: PricewaterhouseCoopers

LOCATIONS

HQ: China Resources Beer Holdings Co Ltd
39/F, China Resources Building, 26 Harbour Road, Wanchai,
Phone: (852) 2827 1028 **Fax:** (852) 2598 8453
Web: www.cre.com.hk

PRODUCTS/OPERATIONS

2012 Sales

	% of total
Retail	66
Beer	22
Food	8
Beverage	4
Total	100

Selected Subsidiaries

Callany Limited (transportation services and petroleum trading)
C' estbon Food and Beverage (Shenzhen) Co. Ltd.
China International Fisheries (51% Cayman Islands)
China Resources Chemicals Company Limited (chemical products trading)
China Resources Gas Company Limited (liquefied petroleum gas)
China Resources (Guangzhou) Superstore Co. Ltd.
China Resources Petroleum Company Limited
China Resources Snow (Anhui) Brewery Company Limited (51%)
China Resources Snow Breweries Limited (51%)
China Resources Snow Brewery (Dalian) Company Limited (51%)
China Resources Snowflake Brewery (Jilin) Company Limited (51%)
China Resources Supermarket (Hong Kong) Company Limited (supermarket operations)
China Resources Textiles Company Limited
China Resources Vanguard Co. Ltd.
Chinese Arts & Crafts (H.K.) Limited (retailer)
Chung Kong Luen Livestock Company Limited (36% live pig wholesaling)
CRE Property (Argyle Centre) Limited
CRE Property (Nan Fung Centre) Limited
CRE Property (Silvercord) Limited
Hsin Hung Textiles Limited
Jin Feng S.A. (51% marine fishing Panama)
Ng Fung Frozen Meats & Aquatic Products Co. Limited (94%)
Ng Fung Hong Limited (food distribution)
Suguo Supermarket Co. Ltd.
Victory Return Corporation (51% arine fishing and fishing supplies)
Worldfaith Properties Limited (real estate development)
Tuen Fat Wharf & Godown Company Limited

COMPETITORS

A.S. Watson
Dairy Farm International
Guangdong Investment
Hang Lung Group
Jardine Matheson
Lion
Tsingtao
Weiqiao Textile
Wheelock and Company

HISTORICAL FINANCIALS

Company Type: Public

Income Statement FYE: December 31

	REVENUE ($ mil.)	NET INCOME ($ mil.)	NET PROFIT MARGIN	EMPLOYEES
12/14	21,774	(20)	—	252,000
12/13	18,882	246	1.3%	217,000
12/12	16,284	508	3.1%	211,000
12/11	14,181	364	2.6%	200,000
12/10	11,158	730	6.5%	171,000
Annual Growth	18.2%	—	—	10.2%

2014 Year-End Financials

Debt ratio: 2.0%
Return on equity: (-0.3%)
Cash ($ mil.): 2,662
Current ratio: 0.76
Long-term debt ($ mil.): 2,562

No. of shares (mil.): —
Dividends
Yield: 0.0%
Payout: —
Market value ($ mil.): —

	STOCK PRICE ($) FY Close	P/E High	P/E Low	PER SHARE ($) Earnings	PER SHARE ($) Dividends	PER SHARE ($) Book Value
12/14	4.01	—	—	(0.01)	0.06	2.60
12/13	6.58	9	7	0.10	0.06	2.37
12/12	7.31	5	3	0.21	0.11	2.19
12/11	6.87	8	5	0.15	0.12	1.95
12/10	8.38	4	3	0.30	0.11	1.65
Annual Growth	(16.8%)	—	—	—	(15.3%)	11.9%

China Shenhua Energy Co., Ltd.

China Shenhua Energy Company (CSEC) is an integrated coal mining company in China. CSEC operates four mining groups –two underground and two surface mining projects –in western and northern China. The Shendong Mines account for close to two-thirds of its total coal production which is more than 180 million tons a year. It also markets coal mined by other companies making a total of more than 230 million tons sold annually. CSEC owns and operates four railway lines and port facilities for the transportation of its coal. The company also operates more than a dozen power plants with a total installed capacity of close to 18000 MW. Shenhua Group holds about 75% of the company.

The group announced in early 2006 that it plans to funnel all of its coal-related activities into Shenhua Energy. Shenhua Group's other businesses include power station construction coal chemicals manufacturing and coal-to-oil production.

EXECUTIVES

CFO, Zhang Kehui, age 49
Executive Director and President, Han Jianguo
Chairman, Zhang Yuzhuo, age 53
Vice chairman and Executive director, Ling Wen, age 52
Auditors: Deloitte Touche Tohmatsu Certified Public Accountants LLP

LOCATIONS

HQ: China Shenhua Energy Co., Ltd.
22 Andingmen Xibinhe Road, Dongcheng District, Beijing 100011
Phone: (86) 10 5813 3399 **Fax:** (86) 10 5813 1804
Web: www.csec.com

2008 Sales

	% of total
China	91
Other countries	9
Total	**100**

COMPETITORS

China Yangtze Power
Peabody Energy
Rio Tinto Limited
U.S. China Mining Group
Yankuang
Yanzhou Coal

HISTORICAL FINANCIALS

Company Type: Public

Income Statement FYE: December 31

	REVENUE ($ mil.)	NET INCOME ($ mil.)	NET PROFIT MARGIN	EMPLOYEES
12/14	40,016	6,233	15.6%	92,738
12/13	46,878	7,446	15.9%	91,487
12/12	40,142	7,837	19.5%	89,144
12/11	33,076	7,256	21.9%	82,260
12/10	23,069	5,784	25.1%	65,154
Annual Growth	14.8%	1.9%	—	9.2%

2014 Year-End Financials

Debt ratio: 2.7%
Return on equity: 13.4%
Cash ($ mil.): 5,793
Current ratio: 1.09
Long-term debt ($ mil.): 10,257

No. of shares (mil.): —
Dividends
Yield: 4.0%
Payout: —
Market value ($ mil.): —

	STOCK PRICE ($) FY Close	P/E High	P/E Low	PER SHARE ($) Earnings	PER SHARE ($) Dividends	PER SHARE ($) Book Value
12/14	11.90	6	5	0.31	0.48	2.41
12/13	12.60	8	4	0.37	0.51	2.30
12/12	17.90	19	6	0.39	0.49	2.07
12/11	43.03	23	15	0.36	0.41	1.80
12/10	41.45	29	19	0.29	0.27	1.51
Annual Growth	(26.8%)	—	—	1.9%	15.4%	12.3%

China Taiping Insurance Holding Co., Ltd.

EXECUTIVES

Chairman, Fan Lin
Auditors: PricewaterhouseCoopers

LOCATIONS

HQ: China Taiping Insurance Holding Co., Ltd.
22nd Floor, China Taiping Tower Phase I, 8 Sunning Road, Causeway Bay,
Phone: (852) 2854 6100 **Fax:** (852) 2544 5269
Web: www.ctih.cntaiping.com

HISTORICAL FINANCIALS

Company Type: Public

Income Statement FYE: December 31

	ASSETS ($ mil.)	NET INCOME ($ mil.)	INCOME AS % OF ASSETS	EMPLOYEES
12/14	57,193	521	0.9%	43,933
12/13	40,627	197	0.5%	40,827
12/12	31,339	120	0.4%	37,187
12/11	24,635	63	0.3%	31,661
12/10	19,875	288	1.5%	33,663
Annual Growth	30.2%	15.9%	—	6.9%

2014 Year-End Financials

Return on assets: 1.0%
Return on equity: 13.3%
Long-term debt ($ mil.): —
No. of shares (mil.): —
Sales ($ mil): 10,975

Dividends
Yield: —
Payout: —
Market value ($ mil.): —

	STOCK PRICE ($) FY Close	P/E High	P/E Low	PER SHARE ($) Earnings	PER SHARE ($) Dividends	PER SHARE ($) Book Value
12/14	0.00	—	—	0.19	0.00	1.69
12/13	2.00	0	0	0.10	0.00	1.50
12/12	1.53	0	0	0.07	0.00	1.05
12/11	2.06	0	0	0.04	0.00	0.86
Annual Growth	—	—	—	49.5%	—	18.3%

China Telecom Corp Ltd

China Telecom Corporation Limited is a leading provider of fixed-line (or wireline) phone and Internet broadband services in some 20 provinces and autonomous regions of China. Its principal operations are in four of the most economically developed regions in China including Shanghai and the provinces of Guangdong Jiangsu and Zhejiang. Services include local access domestic and international long-distance Internet access wireless service managed data services leased lines and about 13 million public phones. China Telecom counts 100 million residential landline customers 186 million wireless subscribers 100 million broadband subscribers and about 30 million business wireless subscribers.

Revenues for residential landline customers continue to decrease as fewer households use landlines and instead make their primary phone a cell phone or VoIP service. The number of subscribers dropped 10% in 2009 and the company expects to lose about as many customers in 2010. Enterprise customers however such as corporations and government agencies still require wireline service and that business segment continues to grow by a few million new customers every year. As long as wireline customers switch to a wireless service with China Telecom the company isn't losing anything but the wireless service market is intensely competitive in China. Wireless customers currently make up about 10% of revenue.

Internet service accounts for a quarter of revenue and is the company's second-largest segment. Unlike the US where many customers use their television cable company as an Internet service provider China's television programming is largely state-controlled and thus service is offered through the phone company.

In 2008 the Ministry of Industry and Information the National Development and Reform Commission and the Ministry of Finance reformed the telecommunications industry in China by granting 3G network access to the three main providers – China Telecom China Mobile and China Unicom. As part of the deal China Telecom acquired the CDMA (code division multiple access) mobile communications business from China Unicom and was able to enter the wireless market in order to remain competitive.

China Telecom Corporation Limited is ultimately owned by the Chinese government. It is 71% controlled by the government-owned China Telecommunications Corporation. Chinese law forbids foreign investment and in order to trade on the New York Stock Exchange the company became an operating subsidiary.

Auditors: Deloitte Touche Tohmatsu

LOCATIONS

HQ: China Telecom Corp Ltd
31 Jinrong Street, Xicheng District, Beijing 100033
Phone: (86) 10 6642 8166 **Fax:** (86) 10 6601 0728
Web: www.chinatelecom-h.com

HISTORICAL FINANCIALS

Company Type: Public

Income Statement FYE: December 31

	REVENUE ($ mil.)	NET INCOME ($ mil.)	NET PROFIT MARGIN	EMPLOYEES
12/14	52,267	2,848	5.5%	300,960
12/13	53,120	2,898	5.5%	306,545
12/12	45,406	2,394	5.3%	305,676
12/11	38,930	2,621	6.7%	309,799
12/10	33,355	2,390	7.2%	312,322
Annual Growth	11.9%	4.5%	—	(0.9%)

2014 Year-End Financials

Debt ratio: 3.0%
Return on equity: 6.2%
Cash ($ mil.): 3,292
Current ratio: 0.29
Long-term debt ($ mil.): 10,137
No. of shares (mil.): —
Dividends
Yield: 1.8%
Payout: —
Market value ($ mil.): —

	STOCK PRICE ($) FY Close	P/E High/Low	PER SHARE ($) Earnings	Dividends	Book Value
12/14	58.71	300182	0.04	1.10	0.58
12/13	50.57	271209	0.04	0.99	0.57
12/12	56.85	357238	0.03	0.99	0.53
12/11	57.13	345274	0.03	1.02	0.50
12/10	52.28	300222	0.03	0.98	0.43
Annual Growth	2.9%	— —	5.3%	3.0%	7.3%

China Unicom (Hong Kong) Ltd

China Unicom (Hong Kong) Limited has brought competition to the world's largest telecommunications market. The Chinese government set up China Unicom in 1994 as the first competitor to another government-owned telecommunications monopoly. The state-controlled company provides 437 million subscribers long-distance broadband data and mobile communications services in 31 provinces cities and other regions throughout China. It is the country's #2 mobile phone operator behind former monopoly China Mobile Communications. China Unicom (Hong Kong) Limited operates primarily in the Chinese northern provinces; major cities served include Beijing and Tianjin.

EXECUTIVES

Chairman and CEO, Chang Xiaobing, age 58
Executive Director and President, Lu Yimin, age 51
Executive Director and CFO, Li Fushen, age 52
Auditors: KPMG

LOCATIONS

HQ: China Unicom (Hong Kong) Ltd
75th Floor, The Center, 99 Queen' s Road Central,
Phone: (852) 2126 2018 **Fax:** (852) 2126 2016
Web: www.chinaunicom.com.hk

PRODUCTS/OPERATIONS

2013 Sales

	% of total
Mobile	51
Fixed-line	30
Telecommunication products	19
Total	**100**

COMPETITORS

Beijing Mobile
China Mobile
China Mobile Communications
China Telecom Corporation Limited
China Tietong
Hunan Telecom
Pacnet
Shanghai Mobile

HISTORICAL FINANCIALS

Company Type: Public

Income Statement FYE: December 31

	REVENUE ($ mil.)	NET INCOME ($ mil.)	NET PROFIT MARGIN	EMPLOYEES
12/14	45,869	1,942	4.2%	281,420
12/13	48,735	1,719	3.5%	283,596
12/12	39,928	1,138	2.9%	289,015
12/11	33,230	671	2.0%	297,210
12/10	25,987	584	2.2%	310,030
Annual Growth	15.3%	35.0%	—	(2.4%)

2014 Year-End Financials

Debt ratio: 4.0%
Return on equity: 5.4%
Cash ($ mil.): 4,077
Current ratio: 0.19
Long-term debt ($ mil.): 3,893
No. of shares (mil.): —
Dividends
Yield: 3.0%
Payout: 297.6%
Market value ($ mil.): —

	STOCK PRICE ($) FY Close	P/E High/Low	PER SHARE ($) Earnings	Dividends	Book Value
12/14	13.45	35 23	0.08	0.41	1.53
12/13	15.06	41 28	0.07	0.17	1.52
12/12	16.29	73 42	0.05	0.14	1.43
12/11	21.13	126 83	0.03	0.11	1.39
12/10	14.25	99 68	0.02	0.47	1.33
Annual Growth	(1.4%)	— —	34.3%	(3.7%)	3.7%

China United Network Communications Ltd

Auditors: PricewaterhouseCoopers Zhongtian Certified Public Accountants Co., Ltd.

LOCATIONS

HQ: China United Network Communications Ltd
29th Floor, No. 1033, Changning Road, Changning District, Shanghai 200050
Phone: (86) 21 52732228 **Fax:** (86) 21 52732220
Web: www.chinaunicom-a.com

HISTORICAL FINANCIALS

Company Type: Public

Income Statement FYE: December 31

	REVENUE ($ mil.)	NET INCOME ($ mil.)	NET PROFIT MARGIN	EMPLOYEES
12/14	46,495	641	1.4%	0
12/13	50,170	568	1.1%	0
12/12	41,105	379	0.9%	0
12/11	34,239	224	0.7%	215,954
12/10	26,726	186	0.7%	215,815
Annual Growth	14.8%	36.2%	—	—

2014 Year-End Financials

Debt ratio: 3.7%
Return on equity: 5.2%
Cash ($ mil.): 4,092
Current ratio: 0.19
Long-term debt ($ mil.): 3,847
No. of shares (mil.): —
Dividends
Yield: —
Payout: —
Market value ($ mil.): —

China Vanke Co., Ltd.

China Vanke (known as Vanke) helps the country's emerging middle class become yezhu (homeowners). Vanke is China's largest mainland residential real estate developer. Its high-rise apartment towers single-story suburban developments and luxury gated communities can be seen in 30 cities across the Pearl River Delta the Yangtze River Delta and the Bohai Rim region. Vanke has developed hundreds of properties and has a land bank of 18 million square meters (about 7 sq. mi.). The company was founded in 1984 by chairman Shi Wang and in 1991 it became the second company to list on the Shenzhen Stock Exchange. China Vanke's largest shareholder is China Resources (Holdings) Co. with 15%.

China Vanke said in late 2007 it was considering an IPO on the Hong Kong Stock Exchange which would give it more access to international investors than the Shenzhen Stock Exchange.

While the company does provide property management services that segment only accounts for around 1% of revenues. Vanke announced a joint venture with CBRE in 2008 to provide management services at its high-end properties.

Over the years China Vanke has grown through acquisitions. The company has about 180 subsidiaries of mostly property development companies. In 2007 alone it bought 13 companies either outright or through stock purchases.

EXECUTIVES

Deputy Chairman, Lin Song, age 53
Chairman, Shi Wang, age 64
Auditors: KPMG Huazhen Certified Public Accountants

LOCATIONS

HQ: China Vanke Co., Ltd.
Vanke Center, No. 33, Huanmei Road, Dameisha, Yantian District, Shenzhen, Guangdong Province 518083
Phone: (86) 755 25606666 **Fax:** (86) 755 25531696
Web: www.vanke.com

COMPETITORS

CapitaLand
China Overseas Land & Investment
China Resources Land
Chinese Estates
Evergrande Real Estate Group
New World China Land
New World Development
SRE Group
Shanghai Forte Land
Singapore Land
Xinyuan
Yanlord Land

HISTORICAL FINANCIALS

Company Type: Public

Income Statement FYE: December 31

	REVENUE ($ mil.)	NET INCOME ($ mil.)	NET PROFIT MARGIN	EMPLOYEES
12/14	23,586	2,536	10.8%	0
12/13	22,368	2,497	11.2%	35,330
12/12	16,540	2,013	12.2%	31,019
12/11	10,757	1,529	14.2%	27,951
12/10	7,246	1,104	15.2%	22,850
Annual Growth	34.3%	23.1%	—	—

2014 Year-End Financials

Debt ratio: 2.1%
Return on equity: 19.0%
Cash ($ mil.): 10,104
Current ratio: 1.34
Long-term debt ($ mil.): 7,435
No. of shares (mil.): —
Dividends
Yield: —
Payout: —
Market value ($ mil.): —

Christian Dior SA

This is not your grandmère's Christian Dior. Under now former chief designer John Galliano the fashion house had gone from outfitting ladies who lunch to women who rock. The holding company's operating unit Christian Dior Couture designs and makes some of the world's most coveted haute couture as well as luxury ready-to-wear fashion and accessories for men and women. Christian Dior operates more than 235 boutiques worldwide with plans to open more. Don't let the pious name fool you though; Christian Dior is a wolf in tight-fitting clothing due to its roughly 42% stake in luxury goods giant LVMH. Chairman and LVMH CEO Bernard Arnault and family control Christian Dior.

Geographic Reach

Headquartered in France Christian Dior operates more than 235 boutiques worldwide. It sells its upscale items in Europe the US Asia and internationally. Some 37% of its revenue comes from Asia followed by Europe's 30% and another 22% from the US.

Sales and Marketing

Besides its network of luxury boutiques Christian Dior sells its products online.

Operations

The company which owns a 100% stake in its lucrative Christian Dior Couture operation also runs retail stores under the the banner names DFS Galleria Sephora Le Bon March Ile de Beaut and Ole Henriksen. As part of its business Christian Dior maintains publications that are sold under the Les Echos-Investir and the Royal Van Lent-Feadship titles.

Financial Performance

Christian Dior generated 30.6 billion euros in revenue in fiscal 2013. Its revenue consisted of Fashion and Leather Goods Selective Retailing Wine and Spirits Perfumes and Cosmetics Watches and Jewelry and Christian Dior Couture. Combined Fashion and Leather Goods and Selective Retailing accounted for about 60% of the firm's total revenue. During the same reporting period the luxury retailer posted 1.87 billion euros in profit.

Strategy

Capitalizing on its brand's reputation for timeless elegance the company has been busy growing its network of swank boutiques in markets such as Russia Asia and the Middle East. It plans to continue building its presence in these regions specifically targeting China and Singapore.

In the US Christian Dior plans to open a 10000-sq.-ft. flagship store in San Francisco's Union Square in 2016.

HISTORY

Christian Dior a trained architect opened his own fashion house in 1947 with the backing of flamboyant textile king Marcel Boussac. Dior brightened up a bleak postwar Paris in 1948 when he launched his "New Look" designs. After years of slim cuts (to conserve fabric) and drab colors Dior's looks were feminine glamorous and opulent (skirts often used 40 or more yards of fabric).

Dior opened a store in New York in 1948 and pioneered the concept of licensing with hosiery and ties. Dior died unexpectedly from a stroke in 1957 and was succeeded by 21-year-old assistant Yves Saint-Laurent. By 1960 when Marc Bohan succeeded Saint-Laurent the house of Dior had dressed such famous women as Brigitte Bardot Marlene Dietrich and Eva Perón.

But mismanagement by Boussac took its toll and the company sold its trademark for perfume and cosmetics –potentially its most lucrative licenses –to Moët-Hennessy in 1972. Boussac drained the profits from Dior to finance his company's other struggling divisions and in 1978 the Boussac group was purchased by (also struggling) textile and retailing company Agache-Willot. Agache-Willot wound up in the hands of the French government with the dubious distinction of being France's largest bankruptcy since the war.

In 1984 ambitious but little-known real estate executive Bernard Arnault beat out several more prominent suitors to buy Agache-Willot from the French government; he put up $15 million of his own money and $45 million from investors and renamed the company Financiere Agache. He then laid off 9000 people sold factories and made the company profitable within three years.

Christian Dior SA was born in 1988 when Arnault sold 42% of it to the public to finance his victorious battle for control of newly formed luxury goods conglomerate LVMH Moët Hennessy Louis Vuitton. Meanwhile Arnault had to deal with the fact that Christian Dior's traditional business Dior Couture was losing its luster. Part of the problem was overlicensing –more than 250 licenses existed for everything Dior from sunglasses to sheets. What's more Dior Couture simply looked dowdy compared to other hot young designers.

To turn things around Arnault lured Beatrice Bongibault from Chanel and made her managing director of Dior Couture. She quickly cut nearly a quarter of the company's licenses and centralized control of those that remained improving quality and cutting costs. (Her techniques were quickly copied by other design houses.) She also replaced designer Bohan with Italian Gianfranco Ferr in 1989. Arnault ousted Bongibault in 1990. Dior Couture accused her of embezzlement but the parties settled out of court.

Dior Couture bought back most of its remaining licenses in 1994 and 1995. In 1996 Dior Couture turned to controversial designer John Galliano –already head of LVMH's house of Givenchy –to capitalize on the publicity that followed Galliano's eccentric sometimes bizarre creations.

Aided by its retail expansion Dior Couture bounced back from a 1997 loss with a profit in 1998. The fashion house opened 19 more boutiques in 2000 and introduced the Dior Homme collection of menswear –designed by Hedi Slimane –in January 2001 (now designed by Kris Van Assche).

In 2005 the company launched the perfume brands Miss Dior Chrie and Dior Homme. Christian Dior reclaimed the Baby Dior business in 2006 which had been operated under license. The fashion house celebrated its 60th anniversary in 2007.

In 2008 Christian Dior Couture acquired 87% of the shares of John Galliano SA a company specializing in the creation and concession of fashions and luxury items by the designer. To mark its entrance into the Chinese market the company hosted a major exhibition in Beijing.

Following allegations of anti-Semitic remarks made by its longtime and lucrative designer Christian Dior in March 2011 parted ways with Galliano.

EXECUTIVES

Chairman and CEO, Bernard Arnault, age 66
President Dior Hommes, Serge Brunschwig, age 54
Group Managing Director, Sidney Toledano, age 64
Vice Chairman, Eric Guerlain, age 75
Auditors: ERNST & YOUNG et Autres

LOCATIONS

HQ: Christian Dior SA
30, avenue Montaigne, Paris 75008
Phone: (33) 1 44 13 22 22 **Fax:** (33) 1 44 12 22 23
Web: www.dior-finance.com

2013 Sales

	% of total
Asia	
Japan	8
Rest of Asia	29
Europe	
France	11
Rest of Europe	19
US	22
Other regions	11
Total	**100**

PRODUCTS/OPERATIONS

2013 Product Sales

	% of total
Fashion & leather goods	33
Selective retailing	27
Wine & spirits	14
Perfumes & cosmetics	12
Watches & jewelry	9
Christian Dior Couture	4
Other activities & eliminations	1
Total	**100**

Principal Holdings
Christian Dior Couture SA
- Accessories
- Haute couture
- Luxury ready-to-wear

LVMH Moët Hennessy Louis Vuitton (42%)
- Fragrances and cosmetics
- Leather and fashion
- Retailing
- Watches and jewelry
- Wine and spirits

COMPETITORS

Armani
Bill Blass
Calvin Klein
Chanel
Dolce & Gabbana
Escada
Est©e Lauder
Gianni Versace
Herm□s
Kering
Krizia
L' Or©al
Oscar de la Renta
Prada
Puig
Ralph Lauren
Richemont
Salvatore Ferragamo
Shiseido
Valentino Fashion
Vera Wang

HISTORICAL FINANCIALS

Company Type: Public

Income Statement FYE: June 30

	REVENUE ($ mil.)	NET INCOME ($ mil.)	NET PROFIT MARGIN	EMPLOYEES
06/14	42,306	1,945	4.6%	117,806
06/13*	6,231	282	4.5%	108,837
04/13	39,076	1,871	4.8%	108,546
04/12	11,888	520	4.4%	100,755
12/11	31,855	1,654	5.2%	101,154
Annual Growth	15.2%	8.5%	—	7.9%

*Fiscal year change

2014 Year-End Financials

Debt ratio: 24.1%
Return on equity: 12.4%
Cash ($ mil.): 3,612
Current ratio: 1.25
Long-term debt ($ mil.): 6,007
No. of shares (mil.): 178
Dividends
Yield: 0.0%
Payout: 17.7%
Market value ($ mil.): 8,884

	STOCK PRICE ($) FY Close	P/E High/Low		PER SHARE ($) Earnings	Dividends	Book Value
06/14	49.70	12	10	10.79	1.91	91.44
06/13*	41.59	65	57	1.57	0.73	80.51
04/13	41.50	10	9	10.33	0.73	80.29
04/12	37.75	29	25	2.86	0.59	74.50
Annual Growth	9.6%	—	—	94.4%	79.7%	10.8%

*Fiscal year change

Chubb Ltd

Through subsidiaries Chubb Limited (formerly ACE Limited) sells property/casualty insurance life insurance and reinsurance through subsidiaries around the globe. It primarily provides property/casualty insurance to commercial and personal customers. Policies offered include general liability homeowners auto accident workers' compensation and specialty crop and marine coverage. The company's ACE Tempest Re businesses provide reinsurance to property/casualty insurers in North America and Europe. In early 2016 the former ACE Limited acquired the US's Chubb Corporation for $28 billion and took the Chubb name.

Geographic Reach

The North American insurance segment which includes property/casualty subsidiaries ACE USA ACE Bermuda and ACE Canada is Chubb's largest business segment accounting for about 40% of revenue. The company's ACE International and ACE Global Markets property/casualty insurance units reach into the rest of the world while its smaller ACE Life insurance division primarily operates in emerging markets in Asia Europe and the Americas. ACE Private Risk Services is a property/casualty division catering to high-net-worth individuals

With its operating subsidiaries located in more than 50 countries Chubb serves customers in more than 170 nations.

ACE moved its place of incorporation home from the Caymans to Switzerland in 2008. It kept executive offices in Bermuda and New York.

Strategy

Chubb regularly looks to expand its product offerings and geographical presence through acquisitions and organic measures.

To expand in high-growth geographic markets it established new offices in Turkey and Panama in 2009 and 2008. Then in early 2012 the company opened a representative office in Kiev that will allow it to directly engage in the Ukrainian insurance market.

Mergers and Acquisitions

In recent years Chubb has focused its geographic expansion on smaller acquisitions in emerging global marketplaces. In 2011 it entered two new markets for life insurance in North Asia after acquiring New York Life's life insurance operations in Hong Kong and South Korea for about $425 million.

In 2012 Chubb acquired Indonesian general insurance firm Asuransi Jaya Proteksi for some $130 million. It closed its purchase of Mexican surety insurer Fianzas Monterrey from New York Life for $285 million in 2013 as well as its purchase of another Mexican insurance firm ABA Seguros from Ally Financial for $865 million.

In 2015 the company acquired the Fireman's Fund US personal lines business catering to high-net-worth customers. The deal valued at $365 million and providing access to more than 120000 premier personal lines customers expanded Chubb's position as one of the largest personal lines insurers catering to wealthy individuals.

Later that year the company announced a much larger deal with plans to acquire insurer Chubb which specialized in serving wealthy clients for $28.3 billion. The combined company which operates under the Chubb name became one of the world's largest property/casualty firms. ACE shareholders own 70% of the new company.

EXECUTIVES

EVP Global Underwriting, Jacques Q. Bonneau
EVP and Chief Investment Officer, Timothy A. Boroughs
Chairman and CEO, Evan G. Greenberg, age 61, $1,200,000 total compensation
EVP and CFO, Philip V. Bancroft, age 56, $750,000 total compensation
EVP Global Accident and Health and Life, Edward (Ed) Clancy
Chief Claims Officer, Frank Lattal
Vice Chairman Chubb Limited and Chubb Group and President North America Major Accounts and Specialty Insurance, John Lupica, $775,000 total compensation
EVP Chief Risk Officer and Chief Actuary, Sean Ringsted, $575,000 total compensation
SVP; President ACE Life, Russell G. Bundschuh
SVP; President ACE European Group, Andrew Kendrick
SVP; President ACE Tempest Re Group, James E. Wixtead
Vice Chairman and COO; Chairman Insurance Overseas General, John W. Keogh, age 51, $885,000 total compensation
EVP ACE Group Personal Lines; COO ACE Overseas General, Juan C. Andrade, age 47
SVP; Regional President ACE Latin America, Jorge L. Cazar
SVP; Division President Accident and Health ACE Overseas General, Edward Levin
SVP; President Combined Insurance, Brad Bennett
SVP; Chairman ACE Asia/Pacific, Damien Sullivan
VP and CIO, Kevin Shearan
Regional President ACE UK and Ireland, David Robinson
Regional President ACE Continental Europe, Jeff Moghrabi
Regional President ACE Eurasia and Africa, Giles Ward
SVP; Regional President ACE Asia/Pacific, Juan L. Ortega
Regional President Asia/Pacific Ace Life, Kevin Goulding
Regional President ACE Far East, Jeffery Hager
EVP and General Counsel, Joseph Wayland
SVP; Division President ACE USA, Chris Maleno
VP Global Operations and IT Officer, Charles Brooks
VP and Chief Reinsurance Officer, William O 'Farrell
EVP Professional Risk US, Keith M. Lavigne
EVP Global Reinsurance ACE Overseas General, Neil Bennett
Head of North Africa, Ghassan Wazen
Auditors: PricewaterhouseCoopers LLP

LOCATIONS

HQ: Chubb Ltd
Baerengasse 32, Zurich CH-8001
Phone: (41) 43 456 76 00
Web: www.acegroup.com

PRODUCTS/OPERATIONS

2010 Premiums

	% of total
Insurance - North America	42
Insurance - overseas general	39
Life	11
Global reinsurance	8
Total	**100**

COMPETITORS

AEGON
AIG
AXA
Aetna
Allianz
Allstate
American Financial Group
Berkshire Hathaway
CNA Surety
Fairfax Financial Holdings
General Re
Hannover Re
Humana
ING
Liberty Mutual
Loews
MetLife
Munich Re America
Munich Re Group
Old Republic
Swiss Re
The Hartford
Travelers Companies
W. R. Berkley
White Mountains Insurance Group
XL Group plc

HISTORICAL FINANCIALS

Company Type: Public

Income Statement FYE: December 31

	ASSETS ($ mil.)	NET INCOME ($ mil.)	INCOME AS % OF ASSETS	EMPLOYEES
12/14	98,248	2,853	2.9%	21,000
12/13	94,510	3,758	4.0%	20,000
12/12	92,545	2,706	2.9%	17,000
12/11	87,505	1,585	1.8%	16,500
12/10	83,355	3,108	3.7%	16,000
Annual Growth	4.2%	(2.1%)	—	7.0%

2014 Year-End Financials

Return on assets: 2.9%
Return on equity: 9.7%
Long-term debt ($ mil.): —
No. of shares (mil.): 328
Sales ($ mil): 19,171
Dividends
Yield: 2.7%
Payout: 38.1%
Market value ($ mil.): —

Chubu Electric Power Co., Inc.

Chubu Electric Power is Japan's third-largest electric utility after Tokyo Electric and Kansai Electric. The company supplies power to about 16 million people in central Japan's Chubu region a leading manufacturing region in Japan that includes Nagoya one of the country's largest cities. It has thermal hydroelectric nuclear wind and solar power generating facilities that together have a capacity of more than 32830 GW. It also has power transmission and distribution facilities. In response to deregulation Chubu Electric Power has moved into newer industries including IT natural gas supply real estate management and overseas consulting.

Operations

Chubu Electric Power has about 200 power generation facilities in Japan a transmission line that runs more than 12200 kilometers a distribution line that runs more than 130000 kilometers and nearly 100 transforming substations. The company also maintains major overseas offices in Washington DC London Bangkok and Doha in Qatar.

Financial Performance

Chubu Electric experienced its first operating loss in its history in fiscal 2012 (ends March). While revenues increased just slightly at 5% net income took a steep nose dive from a profit of about $1 billion in fiscal 2011 to a net loss of about $1.1 billion in fiscal 2012 mainly due to swelling thermal power fuel costs attributable to the shutdown of the Hamaoka nuclear power station in mid-2011. Chubu Electric suspended operations at that plant at the request of the national government due to rising concerns over safety after the massive tsunami and Fukushima Daiichi nuclear power plant disaster in March 2011.

Strategy

In order to get its profitability back on track and ensure a stable supply of electricity Chubu Electric is working on a tsunami countermeasure initiative to improve the safety of its power generation facilities including Hamaoka at a cost of about $1.5 billion. Its main efforts to this end are developing flooding prevention measures and enhancing emergency measures.

Although tight conditions at the company are expected to continue until the Hamaoka station resumes operations Chubu Electric's longer-term goals are to continue developing and buying more renewable energy and increase revenues by advancing energy-related infrastructure businesses including power generation in foreign countries.

EXECUTIVES

President, Akihisa Mizuno
EVP, Tomohiko Ohno
EVP, Masatoshi Sakaguchi
EVP, Kazuhiro Matsubara
EVP, Satoru Katsuno
Senior Managing Executive Officer, Ryosuke Mizutani
Senior Managing Executive Officer, Yutaka Watanabe
Senior Managing Executive Officer, Satoshi Onoda
Senior Managing Executive Officer, Masanori Matsuura
Chairman, Toshio Mita
Auditors: KPMG AZSA LLC

LOCATIONS

HQ: Chubu Electric Power Co., Inc.
1 Higashi-Shincho, Higashi-ku, Nagoya, Aichi 461-8680
Phone: (81) 52 951 8211 **Fax:** (81) 52 962 4624
Web: www.chuden.co.jp

PRODUCTS/OPERATIONS

2014 Sales

	% of total
Electric power	90
Energy	3
Other	7
Total	**100**

COMPETITORS

Chugoku Electric Power
Hokkaido Electric Power
Hokuriku Electric Power
KEPCO
Kyushu Electric Power
Osaka Gas
Shikoku Electric
Tohoku Electric Power
Tokyo Electric
Tokyo Gas

HISTORICAL FINANCIALS

Company Type: Public

Income Statement FYE: March 31

	REVENUE ($ mil.)	NET INCOME ($ mil.)	NET PROFIT MARGIN	EMPLOYEES
03/15	25,867	323	1.3%	30,848
03/14	27,535	(632)	—	30,888
03/13	28,153	(341)	—	30,847
03/12	29,858	(1,123)	—	29,859
03/11	28,148	1,021	3.6%	29,583
Annual Growth	(2.1%)	(25.0%)	—	1.1%

2015 Year-End Financials

Debt ratio: 0.4%
Return on equity: 2.7%
Cash ($ mil.): 1,338
Current ratio: 0.83
Long-term debt ($ mil.): 18,749
No. of shares (mil.): 757
Dividends
Yield: —
Payout: —
Market value ($ mil.): —

	STOCK PRICE ($) FY Close	P/E High/Low		PER SHARE ($) Earnings	Dividends	Book Value
03/15	0.00	—	—	0.43	0.00	16.59
Annual Growth	—	—	—	—	—	—

Chugoku Bank, Ltd. (The)

Chugoku Bank hopes to attract individuals and businesses who are looking to bank on the sunny side. The Japanese regional bank serves the Okayama prefecture (known as “the sunny land”) and the neighboring areas of Ehime Hiroshima Hyogo Kagawa and Tottori through some 150 offices and a network of ATMs. The bank also boasts overseas operations with offices in China Hong Kong Singapore and the US. Chugoku Bank subsidiaries and affiliates are involved in such businesses as asset management credit cards credit guarantees financing leasing and pre-paid cards. Japan Trustee Services Bank Ltd. owns a majority stake in the bank.

EXECUTIVES

President, Masato Miyanaga
Auditors: KPMG AZSA LLC

LOCATIONS

HQ: Chugoku Bank, Ltd. (The)
1-15-20 Marunouchi, Kita-ku, Okayama 700-8628
Phone: (81) 86 223 3111
Web: www.chugin.co.jp

PRODUCTS/OPERATIONS

Selected Subsidiaries

CBS Company Limited
Chugin Asset Management Company Limited
Chugin Securities Co. Ltd.
The Chugin Card Company Limited
The Chugin Credit Guarantee Co. Limited
The Chugin Lease Company Limited
The Chugin Operation Center Co. Limited

COMPETITORS

Awa Bank
Hiroshima Bank
Hyakujushi Bank
Mitsubishi UFJ Financial Group
Mizuho Financial
Norinchukin Bank
Resona
Sumitomo Mitsui

HISTORICAL FINANCIALS

Company Type: Public

Income Statement FYE: March 31

	ASSETS ($ mil.)	NET INCOME ($ mil.)	INCOME AS % OF ASSETS	EMPLOYEES
03/15	63,517	205	0.3%	3,537
03/14	67,627	278	0.4%	3,558
03/13	72,051	195	0.3%	3,570
03/12	77,278	232	0.3%	3,574
03/11	75,126	52	0.1%	3,583
Annual Growth	(4.1%)	40.6%	—	(0.3%)

2015 Year-End Financials

Return on assets: 0.3%
Return on equity: 5.0%
Long-term debt ($ mil.): —
No. of shares (mil.): 197
Sales ($ mil): 1,056
Dividends
Yield: —
Payout: —
Market value ($ mil.): —

CIMB Group Holdings Bhd

CIMB Group is the second-largest financial services firm in Malaysia behind Maybank. It is the holding company for CIMB Bank CIMB Investment Bank and CIMB Islamic which provide retail and commercial banking and financial services to 13 million customers throughout Southeast Asia. While it has a presence in more than 15 countries (including a CIMB Securities office in New York City) the bank's main markets are Malaysia Indonesia Singapore Thailand and Cambodia. Altogether the group has more than 1050 branches. CIMB Group's offerings include corporate and consumer banking investment banking Islamic banking stock brokerage asset management and insurance. It was established in 1924 as Bian Chiang Bank.

Mergers and Acquisitions

CIMB Investment Bank became one of the largest investment banking franchises in Asia in 2012 with the acquisition of most of the Asian investment banking business of the Royal Bank of Scotland. The acquisition gave CIMB a presence in Taiwan and Australia and expanded its operations in Hong Kong India and China. RBS kept its business in South Korea.

Auditors: PricewaterhouseCoopers

LOCATIONS

HQ: CIMB Group Holdings Bhd
Level 13, Menara CIMB, Jalan Stesen Sentral 2, Kuala Lumpur Sentral, Kuala Lumpur 50470
Phone: (60) 3 2261 0085 **Fax:** (60) 3 2261 0099
Web: www.cimb.com

PRODUCTS/OPERATIONS

Selected Businesses

Consumer Banking
Wholesale Banking
Islamic Banking

Selected Subsidiaries

CIMB Group
- CIMB Bank Berhard (commercial banking)
- CIMB Futures Sdn Bhd (futures and options)
- CIMB Investment Bank Berhad (investment banking and securities)
- CIMB Islamic Bank Berhard (Islamic banking and finance)
- CIMB-Mapletree Management Sdn Bhd (real estate investment and management 60%)
- CIMP-Principal Asset Management Berhard (50%)

COMPETITORS

AmBank Group
Bank Muamalat
Bank Negara
Bank Pembangunan
DBS Group Holdings
Edaran Otomobil
Guoco
Hong Leong Bank
Malaysian Industrial Development Finance
Maybank
Public Bank
RHB Bank Berhad
RHB Capital

HISTORICAL FINANCIALS

Company Type: Public

Income Statement FYE: December 31

	ASSETS ($ mil.)	NET INCOME ($ mil.)	INCOME AS % OF ASSETS	EMPLOYEES
12/14	118,440	888	0.8%	41,669
12/13	113,225	1,386	1.2%	40,804
12/12	110,085	1,419	1.3%	41,993
12/11	94,731	1,271	1.3%	40,244
12/10	87,399	1,142	1.3%	36,984
Annual Growth	7.9%	(6.1%)	—	3.0%

2014 Year-End Financials

Return on assets: 0.7%
Return on equity: 9.1%
Long-term debt ($ mil.): —
No. of shares (mil.): —
Sales ($ mil): 6,348
Dividends
Yield: —
Payout: —
Market value ($ mil.): —

	STOCK PRICE ($) FY Close	P/E High	P/E Low	PER SHARE ($) Earnings	Dividends	Book Value
12/14	1.91	1	0	0.11	0.00	1.28
12/13	2.31	0	0	0.18	0.00	1.20
12/12	2.44	0	0	0.19	0.00	1.26
Annual Growth	(11.5%)	—	—	(13.4%)	—	0.4%

CITIC Ltd

CITIC Limited (formerly CITIC Pacific) is a chip off the old Communist bloc. The group has investments in steel real estate energy aviation and communications. With stakes in steel plants with an annual capacity of more than 7 million tons CITIC is China's largest producer of specialty steel (heat-resistant anti-corrosion and other enhanced steel). CITIC also owns stakes in facilities that produce raw materials needed in steel production including iron ore mines and coking coal plants. Property developments include office and residential towers and the group owns several land banks in and around Shanghai. State-owned CITIC Group owns more than half of CITIC Limited.

Geographic Reach

The company's headquarters are located in Hong Kong. It performs operations in different parts of China including Beijing Chongqing Guangzhou Hainan Hong Kong Shanghai and Tianjin.

Operations

CITIC's primary businesses are specialty steel manufacturing iron ore mining and property development in mainland China. These three businesses constituted over 70% of total assets at the end of 2012.

Financial Performance

The company's total annual revenue has been strong in recent fiscal years. After claiming a little more than $9 billion in revenue during fiscal 2010 its revenue spiked to $12.8 billion in fiscal 2011 and leveled off at about $12.0 billion in fiscal 2012.

EXECUTIVES

Executive Director and VP, Dou Jianzhong, age 60
Vice Chairman and President, Wang Jiong, age 55
VP, Zhang Jijing, age 59
executive Vice President of CITIC Pacific, Kwok Leung
Chairman, Chang Zhenming, age 58
Auditors: KPMG

LOCATIONS

HQ: CITIC Ltd
32nd Floor, CITIC Tower, 1 Tim Mei Avenue, Central,
Phone: (852) 2820 2111 **Fax:** (852) 2877 2771
Web: www.citic.com

2014 Sales

	% of total
Mainland China	84
Hong Kong and Macau	7
Overseas	9
Total	**100**

PRODUCTS/OPERATIONS

2014 Sales

	% of total
Financial Services	41
Manufacturing	18
Resources and energy	13
Real estate and infrastructure	8
Engineering contracting	4
Others	16
Total	**100**

COMPETITORS

CK Hutchison
Guangdong Investment
Henderson Investment
Jardine Matheson
New World Development
Shanghai Industrial
Sino Land
Sun Hung Kai Properties
Wing Tai

HISTORICAL FINANCIALS

Company Type: Public

Income Statement FYE: December 31

	REVENUE ($ mil.)	NET INCOME ($ mil.)	NET PROFIT MARGIN	EMPLOYEES
12/14	51,852	5,136	9.9%	125,273
12/13	11,354	978	8.6%	36,512
12/12	12,032	897	7.5%	34,781
12/11	12,884	1,188	9.2%	33,295
12/10	9,085	1,146	12.6%	29,886
Annual Growth	54.6%	45.5%	—	43.1%

2014 Year-End Financials

Debt ratio: —
Return on equity: 14.9%
Cash ($ mil.): 115,685
Current ratio: —
Long-term debt ($ mil.): —£
No. of shares (mil.): —
Dividends
Yield: —
Payout: —
Market value ($ mil.): —

	STOCK PRICE ($) FY Close	P/E High	P/E Low	PER SHARE ($) Earnings	Dividends	Book Value
12/14	1.66	0	0	0.21	0.00	2.24
12/13	1.49	0	0	0.27	0.05	3.60
12/12	1.45	0	0	0.25	0.06	2.99
12/11	1.71	0	0	0.33	0.00	2.86
12/10	2.56	0	0	0.31	0.00	2.41
Annual Growth	(10.3%)	—	—	(10.0%)	—	(1.8%)

Clydesdale Bank PLC (United Kingdom)

Clydesdale Bank won't horse around with your money. Founded in 1838 the full-service Scotland-based financial institution is owned by National Australia Bank. Along with standard personal and commercial services such as deposit accounts lending credit cards and financial advice the bank also dabbles in agribusiness and private banking. Clydesdale Bank has some 140 retail branches in Scotland and England. It is one of the only banks in Scotland that issues its own notes. Sister firm Yorkshire Bank also operates as a National Australia Bank brand in the UK.

OperationsClydesdale Bank reports under National Australia Bank's retail and commercial "UK Banking" business. UK Banking consists of banking and wealth management activities operating under the "Clydesdale Bank" and "Yorkshire Bank" brands. Together the two UK brands offer services through a network of retail branches direct banking business and private banking centers and broker channels.The UK Banking business operates under two main segments: Business & Private Banking and Retail Banking. The Retail Banking segment generates nearly 60% of the UK Banking revenues. It provides products and services to personal customers including savings and deposit accounts mortgages overdraft lines of credit personal loans insurance and financial planning.The remaining 40% of revenues come from the Business & Private Banking business which includes business banking centers small business and private banking customers and offers loans wealth management international services treasury solutions and day to day banking services.Geographic Reach-Clydesdale Bank operates 140 retail branches and a network of business and private banking centers in Scotland and across the UK. The bank added two new UK branches in mid-2014 in Princes Square and in Perth.Financial PerformanceThe UK Banking group (which reports the combined results of Clydesdale Bank and Yorkshire Bank) grew its revenue –defined as net interest income plus non-interest income –by 2% to £963 million in fiscal 2014. This is mostly from a 2% increase in net interest income thanks to a combination of higher interest margins increased mortgage business from the Retail segment and low rates of deposit paid to its customers. Non-interest income also grew by 4% in 2014 primarily thanks to gains in the fair value of the bank's investment holdings and hedging ineffectiveness.

Despite revenue growth the UK Banking group's profits continued to be hindered by "legacy conduct" expenses in 2014 as the bank had to set aside millions for customers that were allegedly mislead by the firm's sales payment protection insurance and interest rate hedging products. Because the UK Banking group had £433 million more in such expenses than in 2013 the group suffered a net loss of £178 million –more than four times what it lost in 2013.Cash from operations also suffered with a net outflow of £629 million in 2014 compared to a net inflow of £3.8 billion the year before. While the £162 million drop in before-tax net income played a role the bank also used £1.19 billion toward operating assets in 2014 as it lent out significantly more for mortgage loans. By comparison in 2013 operating assets provided £6.13 billion in cash as the bank sold off many of its assets held for sale.

Stategy

The UK Banking group which includes Clydesdale Bank and Yorkshire Bank is dedicated to being a strong customer focused bank for the communities it serves. With this in mind and for the sake of turning around two years of losses the group will continue to follow a few key strategic objectives.It's first objective is customer and cost oriented and involves the reshaping of the group's Retail Branch network. In March 2014 the group announced that it would close 28 unsustainable branches and relocate three of them to more targeted locations. The group also announced that it would invest in six new flagship branches in heartland locations that would provide access to new in-house facilities services and technology. To that end in mid-2014 Clydesdale Bank opened two new branches (in Perth and Princes Square) that will highlight the bank's new technology and register customers for internet and mobile banking assist with product discussions and collect customer feedback.

In addition the group plans to control its lending risk by creating a better framework for its management teams and intends to grow its credit portfolio with sustainable types of loans such as mortgages. The group has already seen lower risk and higher returns from its Retail Banking segment in 2014 as mortgage lending and interest margins on loans provided £23 million more net interest income compared the prior year. In December 2014 to further this initiative the group announced an aggressive £1000 cash back mortgage offer to new home-buying customers.

EXECUTIVES

COO, Debbie Crosbie
CEO and Director, David Duffy, age 53
CFO, Ian Smith
Chairman, James (Jim) Pettigrew, age 55
Auditors: Ernst & Young LLP

LOCATIONS

HQ: Clydesdale Bank PLC (United Kingdom)
30 St. Vincent Place, Glasgow, Scotland G1 2HL
Phone: (44) 0141 248 7070 **Fax:** (44) 0141 204 0828
Web: www.cbonline.co.uk

COMPETITORS

AIB
Barclays
Co-operative Bank
HSBC
Lloyds Banking Group
Nationwide Building Society
Royal Bank of Scotland
Santander UK

HISTORICAL FINANCIALS

Company Type: Public

Income Statement FYE: September 30

	ASSETS ($ mil.)	NET INCOME ($ mil.)	INCOME AS % OF ASSETS	EMPLOYEES
09/14	60,013	(288)	—	4,521
09/13	58,906	(71)	—	4,570
09/05	39,322	219	0.6%	6,176
09/04	15,873	108	0.7%	6,443
09/03	14,761	184	1.2%	2,881
Annual Growth	13.6%	—	—	4.2%

2014 Year-End Financials

Return on assets: (-0.4%)
Return on equity: (-7.2%)
Long-term debt ($ mil.): —
No. of shares (mil.): —
Sales ($ mil): 2,147
Dividends
Yield: —
Payout: —
Market value ($ mil.): —

CNH Industrial N.V.

Auditors: Ernst & Young LLP

LOCATIONS

HQ: CNH Industrial N.V.
Cranes Farm Road, Basildon, Essex SS14 3AD
Phone: (44) 1 268 292 545 **Fax:** (44) 1 268 292 984
Web: www.cnhindustrial.com

HISTORICAL FINANCIALS

Company Type: Public

Income Statement FYE: December 31

	REVENUE ($ mil.)	NET INCOME ($ mil.)	NET PROFIT MARGIN	EMPLOYEES
12/14	32,957	917	2.8%	69,207
12/13	35,489	1,086	3.1%	71,192
12/12	33,985	1,067	3.1%	68,257
12/11	31,416	807	2.6%	66,998
12/10	28,563	456	1.6%	62,123
Annual Growth	3.6%	19.1%	—	2.7%

2014 Year-End Financials

Debt ratio: 54.5%
Return on equity: 14.0%
Cash ($ mil.): 6,141
Current ratio: 9.08
Long-term debt ($ mil.): 29,701
No. of shares (mil.): 1,355
Dividends
Yield: 2.4%
Payout: 40.6%
Market value ($ mil.): 10,924

	STOCK PRICE ($) FY Close	P/E High/Low	PER SHARE ($) Earnings	Dividends	Book Value
12/14	8.06	18 11	0.68	0.28	5.56
12/13	11.35	21 16	0.87	0.00	5.61
Annual Growth	(29.0%)	— —	(5.9%)	—	(0.2%)

Cnooc Ltd.

CNOOC Limited manages China's offshore oil and gas exploration and production activities in partnership with international oil and gas firms. Under Chinese government-regulated production sharing contracts CNOOC Limited has the sole right to acquire up to 51% of any successful discovery offshore China made by foreign partners. CNOOC Limited has 2.6 billion barrels of oil equivalent in estimated proved reserves primarily in the South China Sea. CNOOC Limited is also engaged in oil refining natural gas processing and refined products marketing. The oil producer has a net production of 469.4 barrels of oil equivalent per day. To grow it global assets in 2012 the company agreed to buy Nexen for $15 billion.

The deal gives CNOOC access to major oil and gas plays including Canadian oil sands and conventional fields in western Canada the North Sea the Gulf of Mexico and Nigeria.

Growin its North American assets in 2010 the company paid about $1.1 billion for a one-third stake in Chesapeake Energy's 600000 oil and natural gas acres in the Eagle Ford shale project in South Texas. It boosted its shale holdings further in 2011 agreeing to spend $570 million to buy a one-third stake in Chesapeake Energy's drilling assets in a shale oil field in northeast Colorado and southeast Wyoming. It also bought oil sands producer OPTI Canada for $2.1 billion.

In another major expansion that year the company acquired a 33% stake in an onshore oilfield in Uganda from Tullow Oil for $1.5 billion.

CNOOC Limited is 64%-owned by China National Offshore Oil Corporation.

EXECUTIVES

EVP, Chen Wei, age 57
EVP development production and Sales, Chen Bi, age 54
EVP, Fang Zhi, age 53
EVP, Yuan Guangyu, age 57
SVP; General Manager CNOOC China Limited Shanghai Branch, Zhang Guohua, age 56
Chief Geologist CNOOC; EVP; General Manager Exploration Department, Zhu Weilin, age 60
CEO, Li Fanrong, age 53
CFO, Zhong Hua
Chairman, Yang Hua, age 54
Auditors: Deloitte Touche Tohmatsu

LOCATIONS

HQ: Cnooc Ltd.
65th Floor, Bank of China Tower, One Garden Road,
Phone: (852) 2213 2500 **Fax:** (852) 2525 9322
Web: www.cnoocltd.com

2007 Sales

	% of total
China	86
Other countries	14
Total	100

PRODUCTS/OPERATIONS

2007 Sales

	% of total
Production sharing contracts	47
Independent operations	35
Trading businesses	18
Total	100

Selected Subsidiaries

CNOOC China Limited (China)
CNOOC Finance (2002) Limited (British Virgin Islands)
CNOOC Finance (2003) Limited (British Virgin Islands)

CNOOC International Limited (British Virgin Islands)
CNOOC Offshore Oil (Singapore) Pte. Ltd.

COMPETITORS

Anadarko Petroleum
Apache
BP
Chevron
Exxon Mobil
PetroChina
Royal Dutch Shell
Sinopec Corp.

HISTORICAL FINANCIALS

Company Type: Public

Income Statement FYE: December 31

	REVENUE ($ mil.)	NET INCOME ($ mil.)	NET PROFIT MARGIN	EMPLOYEES
12/14	44,250	9,699	21.9%	21,046
12/13	47,218	9,326	19.8%	17,553
12/12	39,720	10,216	25.7%	10,063
12/11	38,279	11,161	29.2%	5,377
12/10	27,770	8,254	29.7%	4,650
Annual Growth	12.4%	4.1%	—	45.9%

2014 Year-End Financials

Debt ratio: 3.3%
Return on equity: 16.6%
Cash ($ mil.): 6,082
Current ratio: 1.36
Long-term debt ($ mil.): 16,979
No. of shares (mil.): —
Dividends
Yield: 4.8%
Payout: 3,038.2%
Market value ($ mil.): —

	STOCK PRICE ($) FY Close	P/E High/Low	PER SHARE ($) Earnings	Dividends	Book Value
12/14	135.44	148 94	0.22	6.62	1.37
12/13	187.66	185128	0.21	6.62	1.26
12/12	220.00	164124	0.23	4.99	1.11
12/11	174.68	179 94	0.25	5.92	0.94
12/10	238.37	197119	0.18	4.74	0.73
Annual Growth	(13.2%)	—	—	4.3%	8.7% 16.9%

Co-operative Bank p.l.c. (The) (United Kingdom)

In business for well over a century The Co-operative Bank provides individuals and business with traditional services (checking and savings accounts mortgages loans and credit cards) along with such ethical financial services products as credit cards that benefit charities. The bank also offers insurance (through sister firm Co-operative Insurance Society) and investments such as ISAs unit trusts pensions and trust funds. The institution which has more than 300 branches throughout the UK also operates Internet banking business smile. Founded in 1872 by what is now Co-operative Group the bank was incorporated in 1970.The group's financial service offerings (Co-Operative Bank Co-operative Insurance online bank smile) are operated under the aegis of holding company Co-operative Banking Group (formerly Co-operative Financial Services). They account for about one-fifth of Co-operative Group's revenues.Co-operative Financial Services merged in 2009 with the second-largest building society in the UK Britannia Building Society creating a "super-mutual" financial institution as an alternative to the country's floundering shareholder-owned banks. The combined firm is a wholly owned subsidiary of Co-operative Group.As it complete the integration process Co-operative Bank is also investing in its CFS transformation plan. The group plans to spend some 729 million over the course of three years to update its banking systems and infrastructure. As part of that transformation Co-operative Bank rolled out online banking in 2010.The Financial Times named Co-operative the world's most sustainable bank in 2010.

EXECUTIVES

CEO, Niall S. K. Booker, age 56
CFO, John Baines
COO, R. G. (Bob) Rickert
Managing Director CoAM, Grahame McGirr
Chairman, Dennis Holt, age 67
Auditors: Ernst & Young LLP

LOCATIONS

HQ: Co-operative Bank p.l.c. (The) (United Kingdom)
1 Balloon Street, Manchester M60 4EP
Phone: (44) 161 832 3456 **Fax:** (44) 161 829 4475
Web: www.co-operativebank.co.uk

PRODUCTS/OPERATIONS

2011 Sales

	% of total
Interest & similar	61
Earned premiums	28
Fees & commissions	11
Total	**100**

COMPETITORS

Bank of England
Barclays
HSBC
Lloyds Banking Group
Nationwide Building Society
Royal Bank of Scotland
Santander UK
Standard Life Bank

HISTORICAL FINANCIALS

Company Type: Public

Income Statement FYE: December 31

	ASSETS ($ mil.)	NET INCOME ($ mil.)	INCOME AS % OF ASSETS	EMPLOYEES
12/14	58,667	(353)	—	6,402
12/13	71,715	(1,237)	—	7,526
12/12	79,905	(820)	—	7,754
12/11	75,629	74	0.1%	8,528
12/10	70,771	56	0.1%	8,746
Annual Growth	(4.6%)	—	—	(7.5%)

2014 Year-End Financials

Return on assets: (-0.5%)
Return on equity: (-12.1%)
Long-term debt ($ mil.): —
No. of shares (mil.): 451
Sales ($ mil): 1,950
Dividends
Yield: —
Payout: —
Market value ($ mil.): —

Commerzbank AG (Germany, Fed. Rep.)

Sprechen sie Commerz? The second-largest bank in Germany (behind Deutsche Bank) Commerzbank provides retail and commercial banking services from approximately 1200 branches nationwide and from offices in another 50 countries. The bank serves about 15 million customers primarily individuals and small to midsized businesses in Germany and abroad. Mortgage specialist Eurohypo provides commercial and residential real estate lending and public financing services in Europe and the US. Since Dresdner Bank merged into Commerzbank in 2009 the company has been retooling itself and focusing on its core banking operations.

It took two years for Commerzbank to fully integrate Dresdner Bank and its former Dresdner Kleinwort investment banking operations. It was the largest integration project in German banking history.

As a result of the merger Commerzbank scaled back some of its operations and is focused on becoming a leaner more efficient company. It is in the process of selling several private banking divisions including units acquired in the Dresdner Bank transaction. Units sold include Dresdner Bank of Switzerland Kleinwort Benson Private Bank Dresdner Monaco and Austria's Privatinvest Bank. Additionally Commerzbank has shut down or sold investment banking and securities lending units.

In 2010 the company continued to cut non-core assets selling its Montrada credit card processing unit to Equens and its Commerzbank International Trust Singapore fund management unit to Trident Trust. The company also is seeking buyers for Eurohypo (though finding a buyer for the troubled firm may be difficult).

The financial market and economic crisis dragged down performance of Commerzbank during the recession. However by 2010 Commerzbank returned to profit after posting losses in 2009. The increase in profit was attributed to net trading income and lower loan loss provisions. Charges connected to the integration of Dresdner Bank also were not a factor in 2010. With the integration behind Commerzbank it expects to realize synergies and reduce costs helping increase profits even more. The company also plans to reduce risk as a whole by scaling back its activity in commercial real estate and public finance.

As Commerzbank's performance improves one big goal is to repay the German government for the aid it received during the market turmoil. In 2008 the global economic crisis hit Germany and Commerzbank received a government bailout of 8 billion ($11 billion) to help stimulate lending and promote consumer confidence.

The government stepped in once again in early 2009 with an injection of some 10 billion ($14 billion) to help ensure the merger between Commerzbank and Dresdner Bank. As part of the intervention in which the government assumed one-fourth ownership of the company.

In 2011 Commerzbank started a two-step process to repay the government.

HISTORY

In 1870 a group of merchants and bankers formed Commerz- und Disconto-Bank in Hamburg. Germany boomed after the Franco-Prussian War and the bank expanded quickly into Frankfurt Berlin and London. Its 1905 purchase of Berliner Bank refocused the bank on the German capital.

After WWI hyperinflation led to a rash of mergers among crippled banks; Commerz absorbed regional players including Mitteldeutsche Privat-Bank (1920) and Mitteldeutsche Creditbank (1929). In the late 1920s the bank partnered with Chase National Bank to bring foreign money into Germany. As the Depression swept Europe the government bought a majority stake and merged it with Barmer Bank-Verein. Commerz became one of Germany's six "Berliner Grossbanken".

The bank took its current name after the government sold its stake in 1940. After WWII the Allies overhauled Germany's banking system and Commerzbank was split into three regional banks in 1952. In the late 1950s the rules barring large banks expired and the Commerz trio had regrouped by 1958 minus the company's prewar eastern German offices.

After rebuilding its domestic operations in the early 1960s Commerzbank expanded into Hong Kong the UK and the US among other countries. During the 1970s it acquired stakes in a variety of nonbanking companies spurred by a government fearful that Middle Eastern oil money would take control of the country's struggling industrial giants. It also diversified its services.

Overexpansion bad loans in Latin America and a bloated staff took their toll in the early 1980s. On the verge of failure Commerzbank brought in banker Walter Seipp to lead a recovery. He cut costs and focused on profit; the bank was back in shape by 1984. It then focused on creating an "allfinanz" group lining up with such firms as insurance provider DBV Versicherungen and savings and loan Leonberger Bausparkasse.

After the Berlin Wall fell in 1989 Commerzbank moved back into eastern Germany and made forays into other Eastern European countries. During the 1990s the bank focused on asset and investment management. It bought UK pension fund manager Jupiter Tyndall Group Martingale Asset Management (US) Montgomery Asset Management (US) and other firms and opened investment management offices in Frankfurt Hong Kong London New York and Tokyo. It added money market funds when they were introduced in Germany in 1994.

In 1996 the bank was embroiled in a tax evasion scandal when regulators charged that it had helped clients move assets to Luxembourg. The company was then hit hard by the Asian financial crisis of 1998 especially after the contagion spread to Russia. But as the situation eased in 1999 Commerzbank formed a joint venture with Bangkok Land to build a mall in Bangkok. That year the company announced an alliance with Assicurazioni Generali (which owns about 9% of Commerzbank) to cross-sell their banking and insurance products.

In 2000 Commerzbank and Dresdner Bank (on the rebound from a failed merger with Deutsche Bank) began merger talks. However after German regulators sought to prevent Commerzbank's largest single shareholder Cobra Beteiligungs from exercising its voting rights the bank's share price fell and the companies could not conclude the merger of equals. Amid swirling rumors of other potential alliances Commerzbank sought to strengthen its pan-European alliances and made connections with retail brokers in Japan. (German insurance giant Allianz bought Dresdner in 2001.)

Later in 2000 Commerzbank announced a restructuring plan that included closing about 150 branches and regrouping the bank's business divisions. The next year Commerzbank entered a strategic alliance with China-based China Southern Securities.

Commerzbank's mortgage bank RheinHyp merged with Dresdner Bank's Deutsche Hypothekenbank and Deutsche Bank's Eurohypo in 2002. The combined company was named Eurohypo.

As chief executive Klaus-Peter M ller launched a more performance-driven strategy for Commerzbank and implemented an Anglo-American style of management in an effort to make the bank competitive.

Commerzbank acquired the struggling Schmidt-Bank in 2004 in response to government pressure for consolidation in the banking industry.

In 2006 Commerzbank which owned about 32% of Eurohypo bought Deutsche Bank's 38% stake and Dresdner Bank's 28% interest for $6.9 billion in 2006 bringing Commerzbank's ownership in the venture to some 98%.

Commerzbank acquired rival Dresdner Bank from Allianz in 2009 cementing its position as Germany's second-largest bank. Commerzbank has boosted its Central and Eastern Europe business. It acquired 60% of Ukraine-based Bank Forum in 2009 and the following year increased its stake to 89%.

Auditors: PricewaterhouseCoopers Aktiengesellschaft

LOCATIONS

HQ: Commerzbank AG (Germany, Fed. Rep.)
Kaiserplatz, Frankfurt am Main D-60261
Phone: (49) 69 136 20 **Fax:** (49) 69 28 53 89
Web: www.commerzbank.com

HISTORICAL FINANCIALS

Company Type: Public

Income Statement FYE: December 31

	ASSETS ($ mil.)	NET INCOME ($ mil.)	INCOME AS % OF ASSETS	EMPLOYEES
12/14	677,776	320	0.0%	52,103
12/13	756,737	107	0.0%	52,944
12/12	838,118	7	0.0%	53,601
12/11	855,958	825	0.1%	49,215
12/10	1,009,532	1,913	0.2%	50,489
Annual Growth	(9.5%)	(36.0%)	—	0.8%

2014 Year-End Financials

Return on assets: 0.0%
Return on equity: 1.0%
Long-term debt ($ mil.): —
No. of shares (mil.): 1,138
Sales ($ mil): 19,854

Dividends
Yield: —
Payout: —
Market value ($ mil.): 14,869

	STOCK PRICE ($) FY Close	P/E High/Low	PER SHARE ($) Earnings	Dividends	Book Value
12/14	13.06	76 55	0.28	0.00	27.82
12/13	16.30	— —	(0.12)	3.63	31.42
12/12	1.98	— —	(0.53)	0.00	59.13
12/11	1.69	5 1	2.33	0.00	60.98
12/10	7.36	1 1	16.19	0.00	318.29
Annual Growth	15.4%	— —	(63.8%)	—	(45.6%)

Commonwealth Bank of Australia

Commonwealth Bank of Australia (CBA) one of Australia's Big Four banks offers retail private business and institutional banking services funds management insurance and investment services. CBA's brands include Bankwest wealth manager Colonial First State master trust services provider FirstChoice online brokerage CommSec ASB Bank which provides banking investment and financial services in New Zealand. CBA has more than 1100 branch offices in Australia (plus over 3600 Australia Post locations) as well as operations that reach Asia Europe and the US. CBA is also one of the largest life insurers in Australia and a leading provider of home loans there.

Operations

Broadly speaking CBA generated 75% of its revenue from interest income from its various banking divisions and New Zealand operations in fiscal 2015 (ended June 30) while its insurance premiums and fund management income (from its Wealth Management New Zealand and IFS and other divisions) made up 11% of revenue. The rest came from other banking income and investment revenue.CBA operates seven divisions. Its Retail Banking unit which made up 40% of its revenue in FY2015 provides deposit home loan and consumer loan products to retail customers and small businesses. The Business and Private Banking division (16% of revenue) provides personalized banking services to Agribusiness customers and high-net-worth individuals as well as margin lending through CommSec. Institutional Banking and Markets (12% of revenue) provides debt and equity capital raising financial and commodities price risk management and transactional banking services to corporate institutional and government clients. Its Wealth Management division (10% of revenue) includes its Global Asset Management business (including operations in Asia and Europe) as well as its Platform Administration and Life and General Insurance businesses in Australia. The rest of its revenue comes from its operations in New Zealand (9% of revenue) Bankwest (8% of revenue) and IFS and other divisions (5% of revenue). In addition to banking CBA has life insurance operations in New Zealand (Sovereign) Indonesia (Commonwealth Life) and a joint venture in China called BoCommLife. Its investment products include funds offered by CBA or through its master trust product FirstChoice the largest retail platform in Australia. CBA is one of the country's largest managers of Australian funds.Geographic Reach

CBA generated 83% of its revenue from customers in Australia in FY2015 while its business in New Zealand brought in another 11% of revenue. The bank operates retail banks in New Zealand (ASB) and Indonesia (Commonwealth Bank of Indonesia). It has minority investments in two banks in China and one in Vietnam. It also has banking branch offices in London New York Tokyo Hong Kong Shanghai Singapore Auckland Ho Chi Minh City and Mumbai.Financial PerformanceNote: Growth rates may differ after conversion to US dollars.CBA's revenues and profits have been rising in recent years thanks to growing loan business (especially retail loans for homes) lower interest expense on deposits amidst the low-interest environment and declining loan loss provisions.The bank's revenue rose 2% to A$45.3 billion (around $34 billion) in fiscal 2015 (ended June 30) mostly thanks to higher card and loan commissions from higher transaction volumes and higher trading income stemming from strong market sales and trading volumes. Its interest income inched up by 1% on continued loan business growth.Higher revenue in 2014 drove CBA's net income up 5% to A$9 billion (roughly $7 billion) despite headwinds of higher staff costs and salary increases and regulatory tightening. The bank's operating cash levels jumped 81% to A$7.1 billion ($5.5 billion) on higher cash earnings and favorable changes in working capital.

Strategy

CBA in 2015 continued its focus on four "strategic priorities": people technology productivity and strength. In line with these priorities CBA has been moving toward digital banking channels that are quickly taking the industry by storm allowing the bank to slow expensive branch-expansion plans and cut operating costs significantly while giving customers faster access to banking services. During 2014 it continued improving its CommBank app on mobile phones and introduced the app for smartwatches which allowed customers to find

ATMs and view balances and even pay for items with its "Cardless Cash" feature. That year it also introduced its Innovation Lab in Sydney to provide a place for employees and customers to create new solutions and launched "Albert" its tablet device allowing businesses to create email receipts and invoices split bills up to nine ways record and track payments and collect real-time analytics and business insights. Mergers and AcquisitionsIn 2014 CBA purchased TYME (Take Your Money Everywhere) a South African-based digital banking technology designer and builder. The deal follows the bank's digitization strategy and is expected to unlock opportunities in its emerging markets businesses.

HISTORY

Company BackgroundThe Commonwealth Bank Act of 1911 allowed banks to conduct both savings bank and central bank functions and paved the way for the founding of the Commonwealth Bank of Australia the next year. The bank initially operated through a single main office and in nearly 500 post offices in Victoria; it spread out through the entire country over the next few years.

The young bank was drafted during WWI to help the federal government organize war loans and a merchant shipping fleet. In 1919 the bank took over responsibility for issuing notes from the Federal Treasury. In 1928 it created the Commonwealth Savings Bank from its savings department.

Australia —heavily indebted to British lenders — was devastated by the Great Depression. As banks failed the Commonwealth Bank picked up several other institutions including the state banks in Western Australia and New South Wales. During those years Commonwealth took on more and more of the functions of a central bank.

During WWII the bank again came to the aid of its country acting as an agent for the federal government. After the war when the Australian economy stabilized the bank began offering home loans.

After years of controversy in 1959 two bank acts formally separated the Commonwealth Bank's central bank and savings functions. The Reserve Bank of Australia took over the central bank functions in 1960 and the trading and savings operations were taken over by the new Commonwealth Development Bank later renamed the Commonwealth Banking Corporation (a subsidiary of Commonwealth Bank of Australia).

The bank concentrated on expansion and diversification in the 1970s establishing travel home insurance and financing (CBFC 1978); it set its sights on technology in the 1980s expanding its credit card offerings and introducing electronic banking.

The US's 1987 stock market crash again affected Australia's banks which spent almost a decade recovering. Luckily for Commonwealth Bank it wasn't the hardest hit.

In 1988 Commonwealth Bank moved into life insurance and investment services forming subsidiaries Commonwealth Life and Commonwealth Management Services (now together known as CBA Financial Services). In 1989 the bank bought 75% of New Zealand-based ASB Bank.

Commonwealth faced a bevy of challenges including banking deregulation that began in 1982 foreign competition and 1990's banking-law amendments allowing banks to be publicly traded. All of these factors influenced Commonwealth's decision to reorganize. The government sold approximately 30% of its stake in 1991 in part to help Commonwealth fund its acquisition of the State Bank of Victoria. The government sold the rest of its stake in 1996.

That year the company's push into electronic banking bore fruit —some 60% of all its banking transactions were online; that figure later rose to 80%. The company moved into e-commerce in 1999 putting out a call for an overseas partner; Commonwealth's stated goal was to generate one-quarter of its income outside Australia. Also that year Commonwealth and a division of The Bank of Nova Scotia joined forces to form a commodities trading group specializing in metals. In 2000 the company bought Australian financial services firm Colonial Limited.

In late 2008 the company acquired Australia-based BankWest from British bank HBOS (now part of Lloyds Banking Group). The US$1.5 billion deal included insurer and asset manager St. Andrew's (which was later sold) and bolstered CBA's presence in western Australia. Its 2008 acquisitions of BankWestfrom HBOS bolstered its position in western Australia. In 2010 CBA entered the Chinese insurance market with the launch of a joint venture with Bank of Communications. In 2011 the bank opened branches in China India and Indonesia and bought a 20% sake in Vietnam International Bank. Also that year the bank continued to strengthen its ties to China signing a referral agreement with Agricultural Bank of China to capture potential customers.

EXECUTIVES

CFO, David Craig
Group Executive Group Strategic Development, Grahame A. Petersen
Group Executive Chief Executive and Managing Director ASB, Barbara Chapman
Managing Director and CEO, Ian Narev, age 47
Group Chief Risk Officer, Alden Toevs
Group Executive Wealth Management, Annabel F. Spring
Group Executive International Financial Services, Simon Blair
Group Executive Retail Banking Services, Matt Comyn
Group Executive Enterprise Services and CIO, David Whiteing
Group Executive Institutional Banking and Markets, Kelly Bayer Rosmarin
Chairman, David J. Turner, age 71
Auditors: PricewaterhouseCoopers

LOCATIONS

HQ: Commonwealth Bank of Australia
Ground Floor, Tower 1, 201 Sussex Street, Sydney, New South Wales 2000
Phone: (61) 2 9378 2000 **Fax:** (61) 2 9118 7192
Web: www.commbank.com.au

2015

	%
Australia	83
New Zealand	11
Other locations	5
Total	**100**

PRODUCTS/OPERATIONS

2015

	%
Interest income	75
Other banking income	11
Premiums from insurance contracts	6
Funds management income	5
Investment revenue	2
Investment revenue	1
Total	**100**

2015 Sales by Segment

	% of total
Retail banking services	40
Business & private banking	16
Institutional banking & markets	12
Wealth Management	10
New Zealand	9
Bankwest	8
IFS and Other Divisions	5
Total	**100**

Selected Brands

ASB (New Zealand)
Bankwest
Colonial First State
CommInsure
CommSec
FirstChoice
Sovereign

COMPETITORS

AMP Limited
AXA Asia Pacific
Asteron
Australia and New Zealand Banking
HSBC
Lloyds Banking Group
Macquarie Group
National Australia Bank
QBE
Suncorp-Metway
Westpac Banking

HISTORICAL FINANCIALS

Company Type: Public

Income Statement FYE: June 30

	ASSETS ($ mil.)	NET INCOME ($ mil.)	INCOME AS % OF ASSETS	EMPLOYEES
06/15	671,217	6,964	1.0%	45,948
06/14	743,668	8,109	1.1%	44,329
06/13	695,355	7,081	1.0%	44,969
06/12	731,444	7,220	1.0%	44,844
06/11	715,933	6,853	1.0%	46,060
Annual Growth	(1.6%)	0.4%	—	(0.1%)

2015 Year-End Financials

Return on assets: 1.0%
Return on equity: 17.9%
Long-term debt ($ mil.): —
No. of shares (mil.): 1,622
Sales ($ mil): 34,042
Dividends
Yield: 5.1%
Payout: 72.2%
Market value ($ mil.): 106,489

	STOCK PRICE ($) FY Close	P/E High/Low	PER SHARE ($) Earnings	Dividends	Book Value
06/15	65.62	14 10	4.17	3.36	24.83
06/14	76.50	15 12	4.90	3.53	28.38
06/13	63.35	14 10	4.28	3.26	25.82
06/12	53.69	12 9	4.41	3.08	26.37
06/11	54.70	14 12	4.24	3.36	25.38
Annual Growth	4.7%	— —	(0.4%)	(0.0%)	(0.6%)

Compagnie de Saint-Gobain

One of the world's largest materials groups Compagnie de Saint-Gobain is in a glass by itself. The mega-group develops manufactures and distributes a wide variety of products for construction transportation industrial food storage and solar energy use. Saint-Gobain operates in four primary sectors: Building Distribution Construction Products (insulation roofing and other products) Innovative Materials (Flat Glass and High-Performance Materials such as polymers and glass fabrics) and Packaging (glass bottles). It owns notable brands such as Gyproc Dahl International and CertainTeed. Saint-Gobain dates to the 1660s when it made mirrors for the Palace of Versailles.

The global economy and slowdown in the construction market hurt Saint-Gobain's performance in 2008 and 2009 (when net income dropped by 85%). To weather the financial crisis the group cut costs and worked to improve operating efficiencies. The cost cutting (along with an increase in sales prices) helped. By 2010 the company began to recover. It returned to growth and reported an increase in sales.

Saint-Gobain which operates in about 65 countries around the world is focused on growing organically by constructing new manufacturing plants. It is keen on investing in emerging countries such as Asia Latin America Africa and the Middle East and Eastern Europe. In 2011 it made acquisitions in Turkey to expand it plasterboard business. It also bought a manufacturer of insulation in Russia and a float glass business in India.

Another key strategy is developing more sustainability technologies to take advantage of increasing interest in environmental issues. Some of its products include self-cleaning windows and green insulation systems and water supply systems. Saint-Gobain has a particular focus on solar power. Its solar unit is dedicated to solar-related products including photovoltaic panels and solar heating systems. The company plans to expand that business by more than ten-fold within five years; to that end Saint-Gobain acquired the 70% of solar roof tiles maker Solarwood Technology it didn't already own in 2010. It also bought the rest of photovoltaic panels maker Avancis from Shell. In another deal that year Saint-Gobain bought 50% of SAGE Electrochromics which manufactures tinted glass products. In 2011 Saint-Gobain agreed to acquire Solar Gard which specializes in manufacturing tinted films used to reduce energy consumption.

As part of a renewed focus on the construction sector Saint-Gobain plans to divest its Verallia packaging arm which makes bottles and jars for food and drinks. Verallia planned an initial public offering but that was delayed due to poor market conditions (and fears surrounding the Greek financial crisis). In another deal aimed at sharpening its focus on the construction sector Saint-Gobain sold its advanced ceramics unit to US specialty manufacturer CoorsTek for $245 million.

However construction isn't getting all of the attention. In 2011 Saint-Gobain announced plans to expand its building distribution segment (which represents more than 40% of sales) with the acquisition of the Build Center network from Wolseley. The deal will include 148 builders merchant branches in the UK as well as the French subsidiary Brossette. Saint-Gobain plans to blend the new locations in with its 500-store Jewson retail network

French holding company Wendel Investissement is Saint-Gobain's largest shareholder with a stake of 18%. Wendel also has three seats on the company's board of directors.

HISTORY

Originally called Dunoyer Saint-Gobain (named after the factory location) was founded in 1665 by order of the Sun King Louis XIV who needed mirrors to adorn his palaces. Because Venice had the monopoly on glass Louis lured Venetian artisans to Paris. Some were poisoned by Italian assassins but enough remained to teach Parisians their secrets. Saint-Gobain glass decorates the Palace of Versailles' Hall of Mirrors.

With its decreed glass monopoly in France the company grew steadily until the French Revolution interrupted its prosperity. By the early 1800s however Saint-Gobain was shining again. It set up a sales office in New York in 1830 and its first foreign subsidiary in Germany in 1857. Under chemist Joseph Gay-Lussac's direction Saint-Gobain began dabbling in chemicals in the mid-1800s.

Expanding to Italy (1889) and Spain (1904) the firm was Europe's leading glassmaker by 1913. Saint-Gobain pioneered the production of tempered security glass in the 1920s; it diversified into glass fiber in the 1930s.

Pilkington a UK competitor developed a glassmaking method in 1959 that obviated the need for polishing and therefore slashed production costs. Saint-Gobain refit its factories to use the Pilkington method to keep its 50% EC market share. In 1968 the shareholding Suez Group forced Saint-Gobain to merge with Pont- -Mousson (now Saint-Gobain Canalizaci n) then the world's leading iron pipe maker. The merger led to a much-needed restructuring that included selling Saint-Gobain's chemical interests.

The company acquired a majority interest in US building-material maker CertainTeed in 1976. In 1982 it was forced to divest some of its interests when it was nationalized by France's new socialist government. Despite nationalization the company grew steadily during the 1980s investing in Compagnie G n rale des Eaux the world's largest drinking-water distributor.

In 1986 after a change in France's political climate Saint-Gobain became the first company to be reprivatized. Three years later it purchased G n rale Fran aise de C ramique (clay tile) and a controlling interest in Vetri (glass containers Italy).

Saint-Gobain bought Norton (the world's leader in abrasives) and UK glassmaker Solaglas in 1990. With the 1991 purchases of German glassmakers GIAG and Oberland Saint-Gobain became the world's #1 glass manufacturer within a year.

After the recession of the early 1990s Saint-Gobain sold its paper and packaging interests to Jefferson Smurfit in 1994 raising more than $1 billion for acquisitions. With Ball Corporation it formed a glass container joint venture Ball-Foster Glass in 1995; the next year it bought Ball's stake. Acquisitions in 1997 included industrial ceramics firms in Germany and France and UK abrasives maker Unicorn International. In 1998 Saint-Gobain bought Bird Corp. (roofing materials US) and CALMAR (plastic pump sprayers US). The next year it bought US-based Furon which was absorbed into a new unit Saint-Gobain Performance Plastics.

In 2000 Saint-Gobain acquired Meyer International (a UK building materials supplier) Raab Karcher (a German building materials distributor) and US-based polymer specialist Chemfab. The following year Saint-Gobain bolstered its ceiling systems operations with the acquisition of the Maars Group's metal ceiling grid business. In 2002 Saint-Gobain acquired the 25% of France-based Lapeyre (doors windows cabinetry) stock it didn't own.

The company's most notable deal of 2004 was the E686 million acquisition of Swedish plumbing products distributor Dahl International. Early in 2005 Saint-Gobain raised its stake in Hankuk Glass Industries a Korean glass maker with sales of more than $250 million from 46% to more than 80%.

In August 2005 the company made a hostile $6.5 billion bid for UK drywall/plasterboard maker BPB after friendly overtures were rejected. BPB with operations in some 60 countries rejected Saint-Gobain's initial offer as too low. Saint-Gobain came back with a sweetened $6.68 billion bid which BPB accepted. The transaction closed in 2006.

Also that year the company formed a joint venture with Owens Corning to merge their reinforcements and composites businesses. Owens Corning bought out Saint-Gobain's 40% stake in the venture for $640 million in 2007.

All told Saint-Gobain acquired around 70 companies in 2007. Its purchases that year included US vinyl siding manufacturer Norandex other building products distribution companies in Europe and the UK medical tubing products maker Consolidated Polymer Technologies (folded into its performance plastics group) and construction materials operations primarily in emerging countries. Perhaps its biggest deal was its acquisition of HeidelbergCement's industrial mortars division Maxit. The deal made Saint-Gobain the top producer in Germany and Scandinavia and strengthened its position in the rest of Europe.

Although it had embarked on a notable spending spree Saint-Gobain also sold noncore operations to refocus on its core products. In 2007 it sold 80% of its specialty bottle maker Desjonqueres to two investment funds Sagard and Cognetas. It planned to sell its packaging operations but halted those plans when the global financial markets crashed.

Saint-Gobain bought a 44% stake in Japanese insulation maker MAG in 2008. Later that year Saint-Gobain was fined nearly 900 million ($1.1 billion) by the European Union for alleged price fixing; it was one of the largest fines ever levied against a single firm.

Also in 2008 French holding company Wendel Investissement became Saint-Gobain's largest shareholder with a stake of approximately 20%. Wendel gained two board seats and a third seat in 2009.

Auditors: PricewaterhouseCoopers Audit

LOCATIONS

HQ: Compagnie de Saint-Gobain
Les Miroirs, 18, avenue d' Alsace, Courbevoie 92400
Phone: (33) 1 47 62 30 00
Web: www.saint-gobain.com

HISTORICAL FINANCIALS

Company Type: Public

Income Statement FYE: December 31

	REVENUE ($ mil.)	NET INCOME ($ mil.)	NET PROFIT MARGIN	EMPLOYEES
12/14	49,957	1,158	2.3%	178,799
12/13	57,857	819	1.4%	185,634
12/12	56,937	1,009	1.8%	192,781
12/11	54,475	1,660	3.0%	194,658
12/10	53,694	1,511	2.8%	189,193
Annual Growth	(1.8%)	(6.4%)	—	(1.4%)

2014 Year-End Financials

Debt ratio: 29.0%
Return on equity: 5.3%
Cash ($ mil.): 4,245
Current ratio: 1.35
Long-term debt ($ mil.): 10,590
No. of shares (mil.): 560
Dividends
Yield: 4.0%
Payout: 14.5%
Market value ($ mil.): 4,674

	STOCK PRICE ($) FY Close	P/E High/Low	PER SHARE ($) Earnings	Dividends	Book Value
12/14	8.34	6 4	2.07	0.34	39.07
Annual Growth	—	—	—	—	—

Compagnie Generale des Etablissements Michelin (France)

The Michelin Man may look like a marshmallow but what he's selling is tires. Behind that fluffy white figure is one of the world's top tire manufacturers Compagnie G © ©ale des tablissements Michelin which produces more than 175 million tires annually for all kinds of vehicles. The majority of its sales are made from supplying replacement tires to the passenger car and truck markets. It is also a world leader in aircraft and earthmover tires. Michelin sells to both consumers and vehicle manufacturers. Included in its stable are brands recognized regionally (Kleber in Europe Warrior in China) and worldwide (Michelin BF Goodrich). The company also publishes about 10 million maps and travel guides per year.

The company produces its tires at approximately 70 production sites across the Americas Asia Africa and Europe; its sales network is worldwide. North America is Michelin's second-largest market (with 18 manufacturing facilities) generating about one-third of the company's sales annually. With demand up in Europe and North America as well as in Asia and South America Michelin is building three high capacity plants in Brazil India and China; all of which are scheduled to begin production in 2012.

In fact with such a strong demand from these fast-growing emerging regions Michelin is realigning its business to emphasize the three countries. It is also bumping up its research and development investment from E1 billion (about $1.3 billion) to E1.6 billion (more than $2 billion) per year for the next five years. R&D will weigh the needs of the company's main emerging markets and will cater to the regions accordingly.

With its sights focused on China as a burgeoning region Michelin agreed in spring 2011 to form a joint venture (it will take a 40% stake) with China-based tire maker Double Coin and investment firm Shanghai Huayi to manufacture Warrior-brand car and truck tires for the Chinese market.

With resurging demand and new regional market interest Michelin's 2010 passenger and truck tire sales increased 18% and 26% respectively over 2009. With higher volumes sold and cost cutting measures in place the company realized a respectable overall revenue increase in 2010 of almost 12%; however its net income exceeded expectations at almost $1.4 billion representing an increase in excess of 800% over 2009. As tough as it was the company's Horizon 2010 plan did reduce costs and increased plant productivity by 35%; Michelin's cost-cutting measures and plans to improve efficiency showed up as positive cash flow. Higher prices for its tires and lower materials costs also helped the bottom line.

This positive showing comes not so long after the economic downturn that crushed the automotive industry particularly in North America and Europe. The US was at the forefront of the financial impact in 2009 when Michelin was forced to close its 1000-worker BF Goodrich plant in Opelika Alabama. Michelin chose to close the plant in order to focus on the Michelin brand which the company says is more resilient than other brands. Europe was hit hard as well and it suffered a similar fate with 1000 workers laid off in France; this was also part of a company-wide restructuring to focus on its best-selling brands.

HISTORY

After toying with making rubber balls Edouard Daubr ©and Aristide Barbier formed a partnership in Clermont-Ferrand France in 1863 and entered the rubber business in earnest. Both men soon died but Barbier in-law Andr ©Michelin a successful businessman took over the company in 1886. Andr ©recruited his brother Edouard a Parisian artist to run the company and in 1889 it was renamed Compagnie G © ©ale des tablissements Michelin.

That year Edouard found that air-filled tires made bicycling more comfortable. But pneumatic tires were experimental and because they were glued to the rims required hours to change. In 1891 Edouard made a detachable bicycle tire that took only 15 minutes to change.

The Michelins promoted their tires by persuading cyclists to use them in long-distance races where punctures were likely. They demonstrated the applicability of such tires for cars in an auto race in 1895. In 1898 Andr ©commented that a stack of tires would look like a man if it had arms a notion that led to the creation of Bibendum the Michelin Man. Andr ©launched the "Michelin Guide" for auto tourists in 1900.

Expansion followed as Michelin opened a London office (1905) and began production in Italy (1906) and the US (in New Jersey in 1908). Innovations included detachable rims and spare tires (1906) tubeless tires (1930) treads (1934) and modern low-profile tires (1937). During the Depression Michelin closed its US plant and accepted a stake in Citro «n later converted into a minority stake in Peugeot in lieu of payment for tires.

Michelin patented radial tires in 1946. Expansion was largely confined to Europe in the 1950s but thanks to radials increased worldwide in the 1960s. Sears began selling Michelin radials in 1966. Radials took hold during the 1970s and Michelin returned to manufacturing in the US opening a plant in South Carolina in 1975.

Expanding aggressively (Michelin opened or bought a plant every nine months from 1960 to 1990) the company went into the red when economic conditions dipped in the early 1980s and in 1990 and 1991. The company's $1.5 billion purchase of Uniroyal Goodrich in 1990 contributed to the latter losses but improved Michelin's position in the US the world's largest auto market.

In response to the losses Michelin attacked its bloated infrastructure and reinvented itself along nine product lines (according to tire/vehicle type plus travel suspension and primary product manufacturing). It also consolidated facilities and cut about 30000 jobs. The company continued to focus on R&D bringing out new high-performance tires such as its "green" tire designed to help cars save fuel.

Michelin bought a majority interest in a Polish tire maker in 1995 and the next year it bought 90% of Taurus a Hungarian firm that produces most of that country's rubber. Michelin joined German competitor Continental in 1996 to make private-label tires for independent distributors. The next year Michelin introduced a run-flat tire –capable of traveling 50 miles after a puncture –for the automotive aftermarket. The company acquired Icollantas a Colombian tire group with two factories in Bogot ˜ and Cali in 1998.

After leading the company for more than 40 years patriarch Fran §is Michelin stepped down in 1999 leaving his youngest son Edouard in charge. Almost immediately Edouard announced a restructuring that would cut 7500 jobs in Europe including almost 2000 in France. The company benefited somewhat from Firestone's recall woes in 2000 but Michelin still faced rising material costs and difficult market conditions.

The European Commission fined Michelin nearly $20 million in 2001 claiming the company engaged in anticompetitive behavior by abusing its dominant position in Europe. In 2003 Michelin and TRW Automotive created EnTire Solutions a joint venture to develop a tire pressure monitoring system. Michelin announced a licensing agreement in 2004 for Toyo Tire to make sell and promote PAX system tires (run-flat tires).

Former co-managing partner Edouard Michelin the youngest son of patriarch Fran §is Michelin and the fourth generation of Michelins in the business was killed in a boating accident in May 2006.

The tire market made a huge shift during and after the Great Recession of 2009. While Europe and North American demand faltered emerging countries like China and India as well as countries in South America filled the gap in demand. To take advantage of the burgeoning Asian market Michelin increased its stake in South Korea-based Hankook Tires to about 10% in mid-2008.

Auditors: Deloitte & Associ ©

LOCATIONS

HQ: Compagnie Generale des Etablissements Michelin (France)
23, place des Carmes-Dechaux, Clermont-Ferrand, Cedex 9 63040
Phone: (33) 4 73 32 20 00
Web: www.michelin.com

HISTORICAL FINANCIALS

Company Type: Public

Income Statement FYE: December 31

	REVENUE ($ mil.)	NET INCOME ($ mil.)	NET PROFIT MARGIN	EMPLOYEES
12/14	23,766	1,253	5.3%	112,300
12/13	27,874	1,551	5.6%	112,199
12/12	28,303	2,069	7.3%	107,302
12/11	26,799	1,891	7.1%	115,000
12/10	23,944	1,402	5.9%	111,090
Annual Growth	(0.2%)	(2.8%)	—	0.3%

2014 Year-End Financials

Debt ratio: 12.7%
Return on equity: 10.9%
Cash ($ mil.): 1,418
Current ratio: 1.82
Long-term debt ($ mil.): 1,970
No. of shares (mil.): 185
Dividends
Yield: 3.7%
Payout: 9.1%
Market value ($ mil.): 3,351

	STOCK PRICE ($) FY Close	P/E High/Low		PER SHARE ($) Earnings	Dividends	Book Value
12/14	18.04	4	3	6.62	0.68	62.25
12/13	21.35	4	3	8.23	0.63	68.56
12/12	19.19	2	1	11.08	0.53	61.36
12/11	11.72	2	1	10.31	0.46	58.19
12/10	14.34	3	2	8.89	0.75	61.57
Annual Growth	5.9%	—	—	(7.1%)	(2.4%)	0.3%

Compal Electronics Inc

Computer companies have a friend in Compal Electronics. One of the world's largest notebook computer manufacturers the company makes a variety of notebook computers computer monitors LCD TVs and other devices on a contract basis for leading PC vendors. Its Digital Media Center (DMC) develops portable and handheld consumer electronics. The company counts Acer Dell Nokia Toshiba and Hewlett-Packard among its customers. Founded in 1984 Compal Electronics has manufacturing plants located in Brazil China Taiwan and Vietnam. It has two subsidiaries in the US Bizcom Electronics and Auscom Engineering.

In late 2011 the company announced plans to form a joint venture (JV) with Lenovo valued at $300 million. The JV will produce laptop and all-in-one desktop PC's exclusively for Lenovo. The plant is slated to begin operations in late 2012 to fuel further expansion into the Chinese PC market.

Compal is known for its strong R&D capabilities creating in-house R&D groups for its customers. This allows the company to make design changes quickly essential for clients who need to respond quickly to changes in market demand. Annual sales in 2010 grew by 34% over 2009 becoming one of the top three companies in Taiwan in terms of sales and scale.

The company –along with many of its rivals – is looking to the budding automotive industry in China for growth. Compal is initially developing car audio electronics and portable media products for both the automotive and consumer electronics markets. While the automotive market has been slow to develop in the region that is changing thanks to difficult market conditions in North America and Europe and booming demand for cars in China. As manufacturers continue to set up shop in China looking for lower cost labor and production costs they will tap established contract manufacturers –especially those with extensive design capabilities –to supply products.

Looking to set up manufacturing operations outside of China Compal received government permission to build a $500 million notebook computer manufacturing complex in the Vinh Phuc province of Vietnam approximately 40 kilometers from Hanoi. The plant has the capacity to manufacture 1.5 million notebooks per month.

Compal was one of the few electronics manufacturers to add employees in 2009. Due to higher orders for laptops from Acer Dell and Hewlett-Packard the company hired more than 10000 employees during the first quarter of the year and plans to continue to increase its headcount throughout 2009.

The company spun off its Personal Mobile Communications and Computing (PMCC) division to its handset subsidiary Compal Communications in order to focus on notebooks. The PMCC division made handheld computers GPS-based PDAs Pocket PC Phones and CDMA cellular phone handset products.

EXECUTIVES

SVP and CFO, Gary Lu
Auditors: KPMG

LOCATIONS

HQ: Compal Electronics Inc
No. 581, Ruiguang Road, Neihu District, Taipei 11492
Phone: (886) 2 8797 8588 **Fax:** (886) 2 2658 5001
Web: www.compal.com

COMPETITORS

ASUSTeK
BenQ
Celestica
China Techfaith
First International Computer
Jabil
MiTAC
Pegatron
Quanta Computer
Sanmina
Tatung
Flextronics
Hon Hai
Inventec
TriGem
Wistron

HISTORICAL FINANCIALS

Company Type: Public

Income Statement FYE: December 31

	REVENUE ($ mil.)	NET INCOME ($ mil.)	NET PROFIT MARGIN	EMPLOYEES
12/14	26,708	222	0.8%	0
12/13	23,230	82	0.4%	0
12/12	23,565	220	0.9%	67,156
12/11	22,867	366	1.6%	62,357
12/10	30,482	801	2.6%	63,251
Annual Growth	(3.3%)	(27.4%)	—	—

2014 Year-End Financials

Debt ratio: 0.5%
Return on equity: 7.1%
Cash ($ mil.): 2,359
Current ratio: 1.30
Long-term debt ($ mil.): 647
No. of shares (mil.): —
Dividends
Yield: 0.0%
Payout: 0.3%
Market value ($ mil.): —

	STOCK PRICE ($) FY Close	P/E High	P/E Low	PER SHARE ($) Earnings	Dividends	Book Value
12/14	0.00	0	0	0.05	0.00	0.72
12/13	3.60	0	0	0.02	0.00	0.72
12/12	3.16	0	0	0.05	0.00	0.83
12/11	4.00	—	—	0.08	0.00	0.86
Annual Growth	—	—	—	(11.2%)	—	(4.1%)

Companhia Brasileira de Distribuicao

What began as a São Paulo pastry shop is now Brazil's #1 retailer: Companhia Brasileira de Distribuição (CBD). The company operates more than 1600 stores including: supermarkets under the Pão de Açúcar Sendas and Extra banners; Extra hypermarkets and convenience stores; Ponto Frio electronics and appliance stores; Casas Bahia household appliance and furniture shops; and numerous e-commerce sites. CBD's strategy of operating diversified businesses and acquiring regional chains has enabled it to claim the title of Brazil's leading merchant. The founding Diniz family and French food retailer Casino Guichard-Perrachon own about two-thirds of CBD and share control of the company.

CBD has weathered increased foreign competition from the likes of US giant Wal-Mart (which acquired the Bompreço chain) and France's Carrefour by buying up smaller competitors and sharpening its channeled marketing approach. Indeed CBD is thriving despite the competition with 2010 sales and net income up more than 44% and 24% respectively vs. the previous year. Still it faces increasing competition from both Wal-Mart and Carrefour in the fast-growing and lucrative Brazilian market. Both foreign chains are investing heavily in Brazil.

Plans put forth by Abilio Diniz for a merger between CBD and the Brazilian assets of Carrefour were abandoned in mid-2011 after Casino's board opposed the deal. Indeed Casino's CEO Jean-Charles Naouri says his company plans to exercise its option in 2012 to take full control of CBD.

To defend its turf from foreign chains the firm is busy acquiring local retailers and wholesalers. To that end in late 2009 CBD completed the acquisition of a 70% stake in Globex Utilidades the holding company for the electronics and furniture retailer Ponto Frio for the equivalent of $650 million. The purchase added more than 400 stores and allowed CBD to recapture the title of Brazil's largest retailer which it lost to Carrefour in 2007 and strengthen its presence in retail electronics. CBD later merged Globex's Ponto Frio chain with Casas Bahia another Brazilian retailer that it acquired in 2010 to form the Nova Globex division. Through 2011 CBD is focusing on integrating Ponto Frio's and Casas Bahia's operations and improving corporate governance standards. In 2012 the Brazilian retailer plans to launch initial public offerings for both Nova Globex and its e-commerce unit.

Just months before the Globex Utilidades deal CBD purchased the 40% of wholesaler Assai Atacadista it did not already own. Assai operates more than a dozen stores across São Paulo.

CBD got its start in 1948 as a pastry shop named Pão de Açúcar. Its first supermarket opened in 1959 followed by the first hypermarket in Brazil in 1971.

EXECUTIVES

CEO, Ronaldo Iabrudi dos Santos Pereira, age 56
Auditors: Deloitte Touche Tohmatsu

LOCATIONS

HQ: Companhia Brasileira de Distribuicao
Avenida Brigadeiro Luis Antonio 3142, Sao Paulo, SP 01402-901
Phone: (55) 11 3886 0421 **Fax:** (55) 11 3884 2677
Web: www.gpari.com.br

2014 Sales

	% of total
Brazil	70
Other countries	30
Total	**100**

PRODUCTS/OPERATIONS

2014 Sales

	% of total
Retail	40
Home appliances	35
Cash and Carry	13
E-commerce	12
Total	**100**

COMPETITORS

Carrefour
Lojas Americanas
Makro Atacadista
Rallye
Wal-Mart Brazil

HISTORICAL FINANCIALS

Company Type: Public

Income Statement FYE: December 31

	REVENUE ($ mil.)	NET INCOME ($ mil.)	NET PROFIT MARGIN	EMPLOYEES
12/14	24,658	477	1.9%	0
12/13	24,439	445	1.8%	156,451
12/12	24,907	514	2.1%	151,037
12/11	24,983	385	1.5%	149,070
12/10	19,332	435	2.3%	92,661
Annual Growth	6.3%	2.4%	—	—

2014 Year-End Financials

Debt ratio: 8.1%
Return on equity: 12.6%
Cash ($ mil.): 4,195
Current ratio: 1.01
Long-term debt ($ mil.): 1,179
No. of shares (mil.): 99
Dividends
Yield: 1.0%
Payout: 20.3%
Market value ($ mil.): 3,671

	STOCK PRICE ($) FY Close	P/E High/Low	PER SHARE ($) Earnings	Dividends	Book Value
12/14	36.83	10 8	1.70	0.40	39.94
12/13	44.67	13 10	1.59	0.45	40.27
12/12	44.39	13 9	1.85	0.32	41.68
12/11	36.43	16 11	1.40	0.36	41.02
12/10	41.98	31 14	1.60	0.33	16.59
Annual Growth	(3.2%)	— —	1.5%	4.8%	24.6%

Compass Group PLC (United Kingdom)

Look in almost any direction and you'll likely see a foodservice operation run by this company. Compass Group is the world's largest contract foodservices provider with operations in more than 50 countries. It provides hospitality and foodservice for a variety of businesses and such public-sector clients as cultural institutions hospitals and schools. It also offers vending catering concessions and security services for a number of events and sports venues. Its foodservice brands include Chartwells Crothall and Levy Restaurants. In addition Compass is a franchisee of such well-known chains as Burger King and Starbucks.

Compass became the leader in its industry through aggressive expansion and numerous acquisitions over the years. The company has been especially focused on boosting its presence internationally.

To this end in 2011 Compass acquired the remaining 50% of SOFRA its joint venture in Turkey and entered a deal to buy meal-delivery firm Obasan which serves business in Turkey Bursa and Istanbul. That same year Compass also acquired a pair of companies in India that provide facilities management and foodservice to businesses in Delhi. The twin purchases followed the acquisition of German education and health care foodservices provider Menke Menue for about €5 million (nearly $7 million) in cash and it snapped up a 90% stake in Japanese catering firm Chiyoda Food from Nippon Yusen Kabushiki Kaisha (which retained the remaining shares). In late 2011 Compass acquired UK-based Cygnet Foods a food and support services company for an undisclosed price.

In 2010 the company purchased Australia-based foodservices firm Life's A Party Group for 14 million ($22 million) and Denmark's IDA Service for 17 million ($27 million) from OKF Holding A/S and its management. Also that year Compass bought family-owned Tirumala Hospitality Services a leading caterer for corporate and industrial businesses in western India and France's Caterine Restauration a foodservices firm for the country's education and health care sectors.

The company continues to build on its operations back at home as well. Responding to the requests of its clients Compass extended its reach to the safety business in mid-2010 when it acquired VSG Group a security services firm from Lloyds Development Capital for $81 million. VSG supplies manned guarding electronic surveillance and support services to companies in the UK. VSG's security operations are complementary to Compass' cleaning and catering businesses as customers of these services often ask for security support.

While the global recession and credit crisis have caused hardships in many industries the contract foodservices segment has continued to grow as companies look for new ways to outsource and cut costs. As such Compass Group is focused on winning new services contracts and expanding its business relationships with existing customers. In 2009 and 2010 the company won new business from Visa Google Microsoft Nestl ©and Electrolux.

Compass Group has also been mindful of costs itself pulling out of some unprofitable global markets streamlining operations and strengthening financial controls throughout its expansive network of worldwide subsidiaries. The moves have helped the company to widen its margins.

HISTORY

Compass Group was formed in 1987 when management bought out the catering business of London-based food and spirits giant Grand Metropolitan (now Diageo) for $260 million. The company went public the next year listing on the London Stock Exchange. Gerry Robinson CEO at the time left in 1991 to take a position with British TV programming giant Granada Group (renamed ITV plc in 2004) where he helped that company diversify into food service operations. Finance director Francis Mackay took over as CEO.

Believing that real growth in the catering industry could come from size and economies of scale Mackay orchestrated a $2.5 billion acquisition plan over the next five years. In 1992 Compass bought Traveller's Fare (now Upper Crust) a railway caterer from British Rail. The company expanded into airports the following year with the acquisition of Scandinavian Airlines System's catering operations. Then in 1994 Compass bought Canteen Corporation the US's third-largest vending and food service company.

Compass achieved its goal of becoming the world's largest caterer in 1995 with the acquisition of France's Eurest International putting it ahead of Sodexho Alliance and Granada. Mackay calmed London investors nervous about the pace of Compass' acquisitions by selling off its hospital management operations and paying lip service to focusing on organic growth. Later that year Compass was awarded the world's largest food service contract a $250-million five-year deal with IBM.

By 1996 the company seemed to have forgotten all about organic growth buying Service America and then Daka International and France's SHRM in 1997. French subsidiary Eurest later snatched a $40 million contract from rival Sodexho (later Sodexo) to supply the staff restaurants at Euro Disney one of France's top three catering contracts. The next year Compass solidified its position in the airport markets with a five-year licensing deal for use of the T.G.I. Fridays brand joining Taco Bell Pizza Hut Burger King and Harry Ramsden's fish and chip shops in Compass' quiver of branded airport outlets.

In 1999 CEO Mackay became group chairman leaving the reins to Compass' chief of North American operations Michael Bailey. The company's US acquisitions quickly paid off that year with a contract to serve 90% of the food venues at the 2002 Winter Olympics in Salt Lake City. In 2000 the company merged with UK hospitality giant Granada Group (the combined firm became Granada Compass) which then spun off its media operations as a separate company Granada Media. Late that year it bought Boston-based bakery/caf © chain Au Bon Pain for about $108 million.

The new company got a quick divorce in 2001 when Granada Compass decided to demerge and make Compass Group public again. Compass Group later sold the Le Meridien hotel operations it gained from the Granada merger to Nomura International for nearly $3 billion. (The firm kept the Travelodge chain.) The company then began making purchases including Morrison Management Specialists for $563 million the 66% it didn't already own in Selecta Group UK vending machine company Vendepac and health care services management company Crothall Services. Compass lost seven operating sites during the September 11 terrorist attacks on the World Trade Center. Late in 2001 Compass strengthened its presence in Japan with the $277 million acquisition of Seiyo Food Systems that country's #2 food services group.

In 2002 Compass signed arguably the industry's largest contract ever a $200 million a year deal to feed Chevron employees around the world. In 2003 the company sold its Travelodge motel business and Little Chef diners to private equity firm Permira for $1.14 billion a 5% discount to the asking price. Compass became the first non-Chinese company to provide food in stations and on trains operated by the Shanghai Railway Administration in 2004. In addition the firm bought Creative Host Services in 2004.

In 2005 Compass sold a 75% stake in Au Bon Pain back to a management group retaining a 25% interest in the quick-casual chain. The following year the company sold its travel hospitality businesses including Select Service Partner (now SSP Group) and UK motorway operator Moto to private investors for more than $3 billion. Compass sold its European vending business Selecta to German financial giant Allianz for $1.5 billion in 2007.

In 2009 the firm added the US's Southeast Service Corporation which focuses on education catering for $65 million. Compass also purchased Germany's Plural which provides janitorial and related support services for corporate and health care clients and it took over the remaining 50% of shares it didn't already own in Brazil's GR SA. Touting its expertise in on-the-go food offerings Compass in 2009 purchased about 30 McColls retail locations in UK hospitals from Martin McColl.

EXECUTIVES

Group Chief Executive, Richard J. Cousins, age 56, $313,000 total compensation
Group COO North America, Gary R. Green, age 58
COO Europe, Dominic Blakemore, age 45
Finance Director, Johnny Thompson
Chairman, Paul S. Walsh, age 60
Auditors: KPMG LLP

LOCATIONS

HQ: Compass Group PLC (United Kingdom)
Compass House, Guildford Street, Chertsey, Surrey KT16 9BQ
Phone: (44) 1932 573 000 **Fax:** (44) 1932 569 956
Web: www.compass-group.com

PRODUCTS/OPERATIONS

Selected Operating Units
All Leisure (sports and leisure venues)
Bon Appétit Management Company (on-site dining services)
Canteen (v
Chartwells
Crothall (health care facilities management)
ESS (offshore and remote foodservices)
Eurest (co

FLIK (upsc
Levy Restaurants (fine dining sports and leisure events)
Medirest (health care services)
Morrison Management Specialists (health care foodservice)
Restaurant Associates Managed Services (corporate dining and sporting and leisure events)
Scolarest

COMPETITORS

ARAMARK
Autogrill
Centerplate
Delaware North
Elior
Farsight Security Services
Healthcare Services
Legion Group
Reliance Security
Sodexo

HISTORICAL FINANCIALS

Company Type: Public

Income Statement FYE: September 30

	REVENUE ($ mil.)	NET INCOME ($ mil.)	NET PROFIT MARGIN	EMPLOYEES
09/15	26,698	1,318	4.9%	515,864
09/14	27,605	1,399	5.1%	514,718
09/13	28,340	692	2.4%	506,699
09/12	27,378	979	3.6%	508,714
09/11	24,662	1,133	4.6%	471,108
Annual Growth	2.0%	3.9%	—	2.3%

2015 Year-End Financials

Debt ratio: 50.8%
Return on equity: 46.0%
Cash ($ mil.): 429
Current ratio: 0.74
Long-term debt ($ mil.): 4,073
No. of shares (mil.): 1,656
Dividends
Yield: 2.4%
Payout: 48.5%
Market value ($ mil.): 26,658

	STOCK PRICE ($) FY Close	P/E High/Low		PER SHARE ($) Earnings	Dividends	Book Value
09/15	16.09	36	27	0.79	0.39	1.77
09/14	16.07	35	27	0.79	0.00	1.78
09/13	13.71	63	46	0.38	0.00	2.49
09/12	11.05	37	26	0.52	0.00	2.82
09/11	8.02	25	21	0.60	0.00	2.87
Annual Growth	19.0%	—	—	7.4%	—	(11.3%)

Continental AG (Germany, Fed. Rep.)

Continental AG keeps rolling along as one of Europe's largest manufacturers of tires for cars trucks bicycles and agricultural products. Its Automotive Group is Continental's largest segment manufacturing brake and traction control systems passive safety products sensors and chassis and powertrain products. The Rubber Group comprises its Tires division (sold under the Continental Uniroyal and General brands) as well as its ContiTech division which produces vibration control and power transmission systems as well as conveyor belts. Germany-based bearing and clutch manufacturer Schaeffler controls 46% of Continental AG's shares.

Operations

Continental's Automotive Group generates about 60% of total sales each year while its Rubber Group hauls in the remaining 40%. Automotive comprises the Interior Chassis and Safety and Powertrain segments. Each segment operates through about 80 to 90 locations in about 20 countries.

Financial PerformanceThe company's revenues increased by 4% from 2013 to 2014. The primary reason was a surge in the production of cars station wagons and light commercial vehicles combined with a more favorable vehicle mix. The growth in its automotive division was strongest in NAFTA and in Asia particularly in China. Continental's net income also increased 24% from 2013 to 2014 due to the higher revenue volumes coupled with lower depreciation and amortization costs.

Strategy

For its growth strategy Continental has identified about 25 of the fastest growing automotive groups including navigation systems turbochargers and systems used for reducing emissions. The decision to diversify product lines is also part of the company's strategy to keep its dependence on the automotive industry in check by generating additional sales in industries other than automotive. Continental also intends to tighten its grip in emerging markets in Asia where it already generates about 20% of its total sales. Throughout 2005 it additionally announced initiatives to expand its tire research and development capabilities in both China and Bangalore.

Mergers and Acquisitions

In 2015 Continental bought US-based rubber and plastics maker Veyance Technologies from financial investment firm Carlyle for about EUR 1.4 billion (or US $1.9 billion). The company will integrate Veyance into its ContiTech division.

HISTORY

A group of financiers and industrialists with interests in the rubber industry founded Continental-Caoutchouc und Gutta-Percha Compagnie in Hanover Germany in 1871. The company's products included solid tires for carriages and bicycles rubberized fabrics and various consumer items.

In 1892 Continental was the first German maker of pneumatic bicycle tires. During this period the budding automobile and motorcycle industries created fresh demand for solid tires. Continental began producing pneumatic tires for automobiles in 1898. By 1904 Continental was first to develop a treaded tire. Between 1905 and 1913 Continental expanded into Australia Denmark Italy Norway Romania Sweden and the UK by forming marketing subsidiaries. However the onset of WWI caused a shift to military production and the overseas sales network dissolved.

Poor overall economic conditions atrophied postwar tire industry growth and by the late 1920s the company merged several German rubber firms to create a much larger and stronger Continental. In 1929 the company changed its name to Continental Gummi-Werke AG.

EXECUTIVES

Chairman Executive Board, Elmar Degenhart, age 57
Executive Board Member ContiTech Division, Heinz-Gerhard Wente, age 64
Member Executive Board Chassis and Safety, Ralf Cramer, age 49
Member Executive Board Interior, Helmut Matschi, age 52
Member Executive Board Tire Division, Nikolai Setzer, age 44
Member Executive Board Finance Controlling Compliance Law and IT, Wolfgang Sch □fer, age 56
Member Executive Board Powertrain Division, Jos ©A. Avila, age 60
Chairman Supervisory Board, Wolfgang H. Reitzle, age 66
Deputy Chairman Supervisory Board, Werner Bischoff, age 68
Auditors: KPMG AG Wirtschaftspufungsgesellschaft

LOCATIONS

HQ: Continental AG (Germany, Fed. Rep.)
Vahrenwalder Strasse 9, Hanover 30165
Phone: (49) 511 938 01 **Fax:** (49) 511 938 81 770
Web: www.continental-corporation.com

2014 Sales

	% of total
Europe	
Germany	23
Other countries	30
North America	22
Asia	20
Other regions	5
Total	**100**

PRODUCTS/OPERATIONS

2014 Sales

	% of total
Automotive Group	
Chassis & safety	22
Interior	20
Powertrain	19
Rubber Group	
Tires (passenger & light truck)	28
ContiTech	11
Other/Consolidation	0
Total	**100**

Selected Automotive Group Products

Chassis and Safety
- Chassis components
- Electronic brake systems
- Hydraulic brake systems
- Passive safety and ADAS
- Sensors

Interior
- Body and security
- Commercial vehicles and aftermarket
- Connectivity
- Instrumentation and displays
- Interior modules
- Multimedia

Powertrain
- Engine systems
- Fuel supply
- Hybrid electric vehicle
- Sensors and actuators
- Transmissions

Selected Rubber Group Products

ContiTech
- Air spring systems
- Benecke-Kaliko group
- Conveyor belt group
- Elastomer coatings
- Fluid technology
- Power transmission group
- Vibration control

Tires
- Commercial vehicle
- Passenger and light truck

COMPETITORS

A.G. Simpson
AirBoss of America
Bridgestone
China Enterprises
Cooper Tire & Rubber
DENSO
Dana Holding
Delphi Automotive Systems
Gates Corp.
Goodyear Tire & Rubber
Hankook Tire
Johnson Controls
Kumho Tire
Lear Corp
Magna International
McLaren Performance
Meritor
Michelin
Nokian Tyres
Pirelli
Robert Bosch
Standard Motor Products
Sumitomo Rubber
Toyo Tire & Rubber
Trelleborg
Valeo
Visteon
Yokohama Rubber

HISTORICAL FINANCIALS

Company Type: Public

Income Statement FYE: December 31

	REVENUE ($ mil.)	NET INCOME ($ mil.)	NET PROFIT MARGIN	EMPLOYEES
12/14	41,941	2,887	6.9%	189,168
12/13	45,887	2,647	5.8%	177,762
12/12	43,147	2,482	5.8%	169,639
12/11	39,456	1,606	4.1%	163,788
12/10	34,860	770	2.2%	148,228
Annual Growth	4.7%	39.1%	—	6.3%

2014 Year-End Financials

Debt ratio: 25.7%
Return on equity: 24.1%
Cash ($ mil.): 3,942
Current ratio: 1.32
Long-term debt ($ mil.): 6,171

No. of shares (mil.): 200
Dividends
Yield: 1.1%
Payout: 3.0%
Market value ($ mil.): 8,366

	STOCK PRICE ($) FY Close	P/E High	P/E Low	PER SHARE ($) Earnings	Dividends	Book Value
12/14	41.83	4	3	14.44	0.50	64.86
12/13	44.42	23	5	13.24	0.43	62.03
12/12	117.10	12	7	12.42	0.29	57.78
12/11	62.00	16	8	8.03	0.00	46.21
12/10	78.10	31	15	3.85	0.36	39.21
Annual Growth	(14.5%)	—	—	39.1%	8.3%	13.4%

Coop Switzerland (Switzerland)

Groceries general line nsk

EXECUTIVES

Managing Director, Gerhard Metz
Auditors: PricewaterhouseCoopers AG

LOCATIONS

HQ: Coop Switzerland (Switzerland)
Thiersteinerallee 12, Postfach 2550, Basel CH-4002
Phone: (41) 61 336 66 66 **Fax:** (41) 61 336 60 40
Web: www.coop.ch

HISTORICAL FINANCIALS

Company Type: Public

Income Statement FYE: December 31

	REVENUE ($ mil.)	NET INCOME ($ mil.)	NET PROFIT MARGIN	EMPLOYEES
12/14	27,459	475	1.7%	77,087
12/13	30,264	518	1.7%	74,955
12/12	29,160	493	1.7%	75,309
12/11	28,316	459	1.6%	75,296
12/10	20,266	502	2.5%	53,559
Annual Growth	7.9%	(1.4%)	—	9.5%

CPC Corporation, Taiwan

The Chinese petroleum handled by this company is in the other China –Taiwan. CPC (formerly Chinese Petroleum Corporation) is engaged in the exploration production refining storage transportation and the sale of oil and oil products in Taiwan. To supplement oil supply to hydrocarbon-poor Taiwan the state-owned monopoly has stakes in oil and gas exploration ventures in Australia Chad Ecuador Indonesia Libya the US and Venezuela. Its refineries produce natural gas kerosene fuel oil ethylene propylene and other refined products. CPC owns and operates more than 2030 gas stations as well as boat and aviation refueling stations. The Taiwanese government has CPC on track for privatization.

Geographic Reach

CPC has operations in Taiwan and in 21 active fields in seven countries including Block 16 and 17 in Ecuador; Sanga Sanga Bulungan Amborip VI and Sanga Sanga coal bed methane in Indonesia; Gulf of Paria East and Gulf of Paria West in Venezuela (negotiations are in progress in regard to confiscated prospects); Block AC/P21 and NT/P76 in Australia; Caviar Manahuilla Estrella Garden City Field and Hurricane Creek (Big Horn Shorts Creek Danub Yellowstone) Blocks in the USS; the Murzuq 162 Block in Libya; and the BCO III/BCS 11/BLT I Blocks in Chad. In tandem with CNPC it is also seeking to exploit the Agadem block in Niger.

OperationsIn 2011 CPC sold a total of 15.28 billion cubic meters of natural gas mainly for power generation co-generation industrial and household use in Taiwan.

Financial Performance

In 2011 CPC's revenues increased by 10% and net income decreased by 302%.

Strategy

Because of its dependency of foreign oil and gas sources CPC plans to increase investment in domestic exploration and production in order to protect Taiwan from the rising costs of crude oil imports. In 2012 it signed a joint exploration and production agreement with Husky Energyto develop the deep water oil and gas reserve in the Tainan Basin in the Taiwan Strait southwest of Kaohsiung City.

Growing its marketing presence in 2012 CPC set up CPCI new subsidiary of the company's Overseas Petroleum and Investment Corporation (OPIC) Group as the first ever overseas oil trading unit in Singapore.

The company is also investing in upgrading its refinery infrastructure to increase its processing capacity and efficiency. To streamline refinery configuration and boost value-added profiles in 2012 CPC built a residue fluid catalytic cracking unit with a capacity of 80000 barrels per stream day. To meet the increase in ethylene demand by the local petrochemical industry that year CPC built a naphtha cracker unit with an annual capacity of 600000 metric tons of ethylene.

To comply with environmental regulations and to upgrade gasoline quality in 2011 CPC set up an alkylation unit with a capacity of 14000 barrels per stream day.

Company Background

Boosting its LNG supply base in 2008 CPC signed a deal whereby Woodside Petroleum agreed to supply 2-3 million tons per year for 15 to 20 years.

EXECUTIVES

Director Refining and Manufacturing Research Institute, Sheng-Chung Lin
CEO Natural Gas Business Division, J. Y. Chen
President, Arthur H. Kung
VP; CEO Petrochemical Business Division, J. S. Yang
CEO Marketing Business Division, Cheng-Hsie Liu
CEO Solvent and Chemical Business Division, Jimmy Chang
VP, Ray-Chung Chang
VP, Shane S. I. Lin
VP, Ming-Huei Chen
CEO Exploration and Production Business Division, Jong-Chang Wu
CEO Refining Business Division, Ching-Yang Wu
CEO LPG Business Division, Jung-Lieh Lin
Acting CEO Lubricants Business Division, Ting Pang Chi
Director Refining & Manufacturing Research Institute, Vincent Y.S. Ho
Director Exploration & Development Research Institute, Shin-Tai Hu
Director Project & Construction Division and Acting Director LNG Project Division, Marc W.H. Lin
Director Green Technology Research Institute, Jung-Chung Wu
Director Material Testing & Certification Center, Ta-Tsung Yen
Auditors: Deloitte Taiwan

LOCATIONS

HQ: CPC Corporation, Taiwan
No. 3, Songren Road, Sinyi District, Taipei 11010
Phone: (886) 2 8789 8989 **Fax:** (886) 2 8789 9000
Web: www.cpc.com.tw

PRODUCTS/OPERATIONS

Selected Products

Industrial Oil
LNG Product
LPG Product
Lube Oil
Marine Oil
Motor Oil
RBU Product
SNC Product

COMPETITORS

BP
CNOOC
Cosmo Oil
Exxon Mobil
Formosa Plastics
Royal Dutch Shell
Sinopec Corp.
TOTAL

HISTORICAL FINANCIALS

Company Type: Public

Income Statement FYE: December 31

	REVENUE ($ mil.)	NET INCOME ($ mil.)	NET PROFIT MARGIN	EMPLOYEES
12/14	37,638	(1,066)		14,787
12/13	39,827	110	0.3%	14,819
12/12	39,529	(1,162)		14,977
12/11	33,977	(1,070)	—	15,219
12/10	32,104	549	1.7%	14,871
Annual Growth	4.1%		—	(0.1%)

2014 Year-End Financials

Debt ratio: 1.6%
Return on equity: (-16.0%)
Cash ($ mil.): 73
Current ratio: 0.79
Long-term debt ($ mil.): 6,155

No. of shares (mil.): —
Dividends
Yield: —
Payout: —
Market value ($ mil.): —

CrediCorp Ltd.

Auditors: Paredes, Zaldivar, Burga & Asociados S.C.R.L

LOCATIONS

HQ: CrediCorp Ltd.
Calle Centenario 156, La Molina, Lima 12
Phone: (51) 1 313 2014 **Fax:** (51) 1 313 2121
Web: www.credicorpnet.com

HISTORICAL FINANCIALS

Company Type: Public

Income Statement FYE: December 31

	ASSETS ($ mil.)	NET INCOME ($ mil.)	INCOME AS % OF ASSETS	EMPLOYEES
12/14	45,163	799	1.8%	32,313
12/13	40,820	567	1.4%	27,638
12/12	40,797	788	1.9%	26,541
12/11	30,732	709	2.3%	22,276
12/10	28,413	571	2.0%	19,641
Annual Growth	12.3%	8.8%	—	13.3%

2014 Year-End Financials

Return on assets: 2.7%
Return on equity: 26.2%
Long-term debt ($ mil.): —
No. of shares (mil.): 79
Sales ($ mil): 4,956
Dividends
Yield: 1.1%
Payout: 18.1%
Market value ($ mil.): 12,732

	STOCK PRICE ($) FY Close	P/E High/Low		PER SHARE ($) Earnings	Dividends	Book Value
12/14	160.18	6	4	9.80	1.90	58.91
12/13	132.73	23	16	7.12	2.60	53.25
12/12	146.56	15	11	9.90	2.30	52.50
12/11	109.47	13	9	8.90	1.95	42.76
12/10	118.91	18	10	7.17	1.70	36.17
Annual Growth	7.7%	—	—	8.1%	2.8%	13.0%

Credit Agricole Corporate & Investment Bank

The corporate and investment banking arm of French superbank Cr ©dit Agricole Cr ©dit Agricole Corporate and Investment Bank (or Cr ©dit Agricole CIB formerly Calyon) possesses expertise in capital markets; mergers and acquisitions advice; equity debt and derivatives sales and underwriting; foreign exchange; brokerage; and structured finance. It is active in about 60 countries. The company's Chevreaux affiliate provides equity brokerage and research services primarily in Europe. Calyon changed its name to Cr ©dit Agricole CIB in 2010 in an effort to unite the division with its parent and strengthen the brand.

The company has targeted Asia as a strategic growth market. The region is among the fastest-growing in the world and contains much of the world's wealth. The company hopes to tap into that wealth by developing its distribution network and partnerships with other financial institutions. Structured finance and bonds are among the assets it is promoting in the region. Cr ©dit Agricole CIB traces its roots in Asia to 1874 when it opened its first branch in Vietnam.

Further underscoring its focus on Asia the company announced plans to join forces with China brokerage CITIC Securities in late 2010. If given regulatory and corporate approval the partnership will be a capital markets and equity brokerage leader especially in China.

In 2008 the company merged its US-based Calyon Financial subsidiary which specialized in commodities and futures trading with Soci ©©G ©eral ©s Fimat unit to form Newedge. Cr ©dit Agricole CIB and Soci ©©G ©eral ©each own 50% of the combined firm.

Itself a product of a merger Calyon was formed in 2004 when Cr ©dit Agricole Indosuez combined with the investment banking division of Credit Lyonnais which Cr ©dit Agricole acquired in 2003.

EXECUTIVES

Pr ©sident Directeur G ©n ©ral, Philippe BRASSAC
Board Member, Marc KYRIACOU
Board Member, Jean-frederic Marcel Ivan DREYFUS
Board Member, Anne-Laure NOAT
Board Member, Fabienne HAAS
Board Member, Marie-Claire DAVEU
Auditors: ERNST & YOUNG et Autres

LOCATIONS

HQ: Credit Agricole Corporate & Investment Bank
9, quai du President Paul Doumer, Paris La Defense, Cedex 92920
Phone: (33) 1 41 89 00 00 **Fax:** (33) 1 41 89 12 77
Web: www.ca-cib.fr

COMPETITORS

CIBC World Markets
Citigroup Global Markets Limited
Cowen Group
Goldman Sachs
JPMorgan Chase
Lazard
Merrill Lynch
Morgan Stanley
N M Rothschild & Sons
UBS Investment Bank

HISTORICAL FINANCIALS

Company Type: Public

Income Statement FYE: December 31

	ASSETS ($ mil.)	NET INCOME ($ mil.)	INCOME AS % OF ASSETS	EMPLOYEES
12/14	782,903	1,275	0.2%	9,720
12/13	834,217	770	0.1%	9,993
12/12	1,193,217	(512)		12,154
12/11	1,068,396	882	0.1%	14,863
12/10	958,531	1,345	0.1%	14,703
Annual Growth	(4.9%)	(1.3%)	—	(9.8%)

2014 Year-End Financials

Return on assets: 0.1%
Return on equity: 6.7%
Long-term debt ($ mil.): —
No. of shares (mil.): 268
Sales ($ mil): 9,595
Dividends
Yield: —
Payout: —
Market value ($ mil.): —

Credit Du Nord S.A. (France)

EXECUTIVES

President Directeur G ©n ©ral, Jean-Francois SAMMARCELLI
Auditors: ERNST & YOUNG et Autres

LOCATIONS

HQ: Credit Du Nord S.A. (France)
28, place Rihour, Lille 59000
Phone: (33) 1 40 22 40 22
Web: www.groupe-credit-du-nord.com

HISTORICAL FINANCIALS

Company Type: Public

Income Statement FYE: December 31

	ASSETS ($ mil.)	NET INCOME ($ mil.)	INCOME AS % OF ASSETS	EMPLOYEES
12/14	67,093	413	0.6%	9,033
12/13	78,114	507	0.7%	9,323
12/12	74,813	406	0.5%	9,689
12/11	71,343	407	0.6%	9,850
12/10	62,015	352	0.6%	9,948
Annual Growth	2.0%	4.1%	—	(2.4%)

2014 Year-End Financials

Return on assets: 0.6%
Return on equity: 12.4%
Long-term debt ($ mil.): —
No. of shares (mil.): 111
Sales ($ mil): 3,139
Dividends
Yield: —
Payout: —
Market value ($ mil.): —

Credit Industriel et Commercial France

Auditors: ERNST & YOUNG et Autres

LOCATIONS

HQ: Credit Industriel et Commercial France
6 avenue de Provence, Paris 75009
Phone: (33) 1 45 96 96 96 **Fax:** (33) 1 45 96 96 66
Web: www.cic.fr

HISTORICAL FINANCIALS

Company Type: Public

Income Statement FYE: December 31

	ASSETS ($ mil.)	NET INCOME ($ mil.)	INCOME AS % OF ASSETS	EMPLOYEES
12/14	298,624	1,356	0.5%	19,893
12/13	320,669	1,163	0.4%	20,222
12/12	310,706	920	0.3%	20,654
12/11	301,740	717	0.2%	20,668
12/10	323,934	1,492	0.5%	20,728
Annual Growth	(2.0%)	(2.4%)	—	(1.0%)

2014 Year-End Financials

Return on assets: 0.4%	Dividends
Return on equity: 9.5%	Yield: —
Long-term debt ($ mil.): —	Payout: —
No. of shares (mil.): 37	Market value ($ mil.): —
Sales ($ mil): 16,135	

Credit Suisse Group

Credit Suisse is one of Switzerland's top financial services firms though a distant second to behemoth rival UBS. The group provides investment management private banking and asset management services to clients worldwide. Its investment banking offerings include debt and equity underwriting M&A advisory and other securities services. The group also provides wealth management services and asset management services to individual institutional and government clients. With more than 200 retail branches in Switzerland it operates in more than 50 countries (including the US and UK).

OperationsCredit Suisse operates through two main divisions that each contribute nearly 50% of total revenue: Private Banking & Wealth Management and Investment Banking.The Private Banking & Wealth Management division provides advisory and financial services to private corporate and institutional clients and is made up of three businesses including: Wealth Management Clients Corporate & Institutional Clients and Asset Management businesses. Credit Suisse's Investment Banking division provides a range of financial products and services to client-driven flow-based and capital efficient businesses. Its services include: global securities sales trading and execution prime brokerage and capital raising services corporate advisory and comprehensive investment research. Its investment banking services are delivered through the company's regional and local teams based in major global financial centers. As part of Credit Suisse's integrated business model the Investment Banking division works closely with Private Banking & Wealth Management with the goal of providing customized financial solutions for each of Credit Suisse's clients.Geographic Reach-Switzerland-based Credit Suisse boasts 530 offices and 22 booking centers in more than 50 countries. More than 40% of its revenue comes from the Americas while another 30% is generated in Switzerland. Other major regions include Europe Middle East and Africa (or EMEA which brings in more than 15% of revenue) and the Asia Pacific Region. Sales and MarketingCredit Suisse's Private Banking & Wealth Management business serves more than 2 million clients globally. The firm's Wealth Management Clients business serves ultra-high-net-worth and high-net-worth individuals worldwide as well as wealthy and retail clients in Switzerland. Its Corporate & Institutional Clients business caters to corporations and institutional clients mostly in Switzerland. The Asset Management business offers its investment products globally to governments institutions corporations and individuals.The company's Investment Banking serves corporations governments and institutional investors (including pension and hedge funds) and private individuals.Financial PerformanceNote: Growth rates may differ after conversion to US dollars.While Credit Suisse's financials have stabilized since its low-days in 2008 the bank has struggled to grow significantly in recent years. Revenue in 2014 remained mostly flat at CHF 26.24 billion ($26.52 billion). Fair value gains in the company's credit spreads (compared to credit spread losses in 2013) were the reason Credit Suisse did not lose revenue in 2014 as the Private Banking & Wealth Management division experienced a 6% decline in revenue as it earned lower net interest income and lower transaction- and performance-based revenue. Income from the group's Investment Banking division remained stable thanks to higher fixed income sales as well as higher fee income from trading underwriting and advisory activities. Net income plummeted by 19% to CHF 1.88 billion ($1.89 billion) in 2014 mostly because the bank incurred an 11% hike in general and administrative expenses which were primarily driven by a CHF 1.618 billion ($1.64 billion) litigation charge related to the final settlement of all outstanding US cross-border matters. Cash levels dropped significantly in 2014 with operations using CHF 17.62 billion ($17.81 billion) mostly due to the timing of its trading assets and liabilities which vary significantly in the normal course of business. Management believes that the capital it receives from operations available cash balances and short and long-term borrowings is sufficient to fund the company's operations.

Stategy

With the goal of creating a more client-focused capital-efficient strategy in the midst of a challenging regulatory environment Credit Suisse continues to sell off less profitable businesses to refocus its resources on higher-returning ones. In late 2014 the company sold its Private Banking & Wealth Management's local affluent and upper affluent businesses in Italy along with the associated 1.9 billion ($2.31 billion) in assets under management to Banca Generali S.p.A. It also exited a string of other small businesses in 2014 to free up cash resources including: its private equity fund of funds Customized Fund Investment Group; the group's mid-market leveraged buyout business DLJ Merchant Merchant Banking Partners; and its German-based private banking business in Germany selling the unit to Bethmann Bank AG.That year it also exited its small commodities trading business (part of its global macro products business) planning to refocus instead on its more popular foreign exchange business and simplify it to satisfy client liquidity needs in cash products and derivatives. Additionally in 2014 the company agreed to sell its Prime Fund Services to BNP Paribas. In 2013 Credit Suisse sold its exchange traded funds (ETFs) business to private equity giant BlackRock Inc.

Credit Suisse also continues to make strategic acquisitions to grow the business. In 2014 the company purchased Morgan Stanley's private wealth management businesses in the EMEA region to expand its affluent client base across Europe. In 2012 the company acquired HSBC's private banking operations in Japan.Additionally the company has made moves to grow beyond its main markets in the Americas and Switzerland. In 2015 the company launched its global digital private banking platform in Singapore with plans to provide digital wealth management services to the region while introducing a new 24-hour private banking service delivery model at the same time.Mergers and AcquisitionsIn 2014 Credit Suisse acquired Morgan Stanley's private wealth management businesses in the EMEA region (excluding Switzerland) which expanded its client base among high- and ultra-high-net-worth individual clients across the Europe.

Company Background

The bank has been plagued by litigation charges in recent years. In 2012 Credit Suisse handed over information to the US government as part of an investigation into hidden Swiss bank accounts that are used by wealthy Americans to evade taxes. Credit Suisse was among other Swiss banks that were being investigated. Swiss privacy laws have typically protected wealthy individuals who funnel money through offshore accounts.

HISTORY

In 1856 shortly after the creation of the Swiss federation Alfred Escher opened Credit Suisse (CS) in Zurich. Primarily a venture capital firm CS helped fund Swiss railroads and other industries. It later opened offices in Italy and helped establish the Swiss Bank Corporation.

CS shifted its focus to commercial banking in 1867 and sold most of its stock holdings. By 1871 it was Switzerland's largest bank buoyed by the nation's swift industrialization. In 1895 CS helped create the predecessor of Swiss utility Electrowatt. Foreign activity grew in the 1920s. A run on banks in the Depression forced CS to sell assets at a loss and dip into reserves of unreported retained profits.

Trade declined in WWII but neutrality left Switzerland's institutions intact and made it a major banking center partly due to CS's role as a conduit for the Nazis' plundered gold. Foreign exchange and gold trading became important activities for CS after WWII. Mortgage and consumer credit acquisitions fueled domestic growth in the 1970s.

In 1978 the bank took a stake in US investment bank First Boston and with it formed London-based Credit Suisse-First Boston (CSFB). CS created 44%-owned holding company Credit Suisse First Boston to own First Boston CSFB and Tokyo-based CS First Boston Pacific.

The stock market crash of 1987 led a damaged First Boston to merge with CSFB the next year. In 1990 CS (renamed CS Holding) injected $300 million into CSFB and shifted $470 million in bad loans from its books becoming the first foreign owner of a major Wall Street investment bank.

In the early 1990s CS Holding strengthened its insurance business with a Winterthur Insurance alliance. In 1993 and 1994 acquisitions helped it gain share in its overbanked home market.

In 1996 CS Holding reorganized as Credit Suisse Group and grew internationally including further merging the daredevil US investment banking operations into Credit Suisse's more staid and relationship-oriented corporate banking. It bought Winterthur (Switzerland's #2 insurer) in 1997 as well as Barclays' European investment banking business.

Credit Suisse and other Swiss banks came under fire in 1996 for refusing to relinquish assets from Jewish bank accounts from the Holocaust era and for gold trading with the Nazi regime. In 1997 the banks agreed to establish a humanitarian fund for Holocaust victims. A stream of lawsuits by American heirs and boycott threats from US states and cities led in 1998 to a tentative $1.25 billion settlement (unpopular in Switzerland) with Credit Suisse on the hook for about a third of that.

CS in 1998 expanded its investment banking by buying Brazil's Banco de Investimentos Garantia; it also moved to expand US money management operations by allying with New York-based Warburg Pincus Asset Management. By 1999 that joint venture –which was to give the investment firm access to CS's mutual fund distribution channels in Europe and Asia –had morphed into CS's $650 million purchase of Warburg Pincus Asset Management.

Japan revoked the license of the company's financial products unit for obstructing an investigation (the harshest penalty ever given to a foreign firm at the time); it also accused the company of helping 60 others hide losses and cover up evidence.

In 2000 the company started a mortgage and home-buying Web site and decided to allow searches of Holocaust-era accounts. The next year as a part of its European expansion Credit Suisse acquired Spanish broker and asset manager General de Valores y Cambios.

Under former chairman and CEO Lukas Mühlemann the company expanded Credit Suisse First Boston when it bought US investment firm Donaldson Lufkin & Jenrette in 2000 and renamed it Credit Suisse First Boston (USA).

The collapse of Credit Suisse's share price along with what proved to be an over-ambitious acquisition strategy brought about the downfall of Mühlemann who was pressured out by shareholders in 2002.

In 2005 Credit Suisse merged with its Credit Suisse First Boston subsidiary creating a global Credit Suisse brand and in 2006 reorganized into three distinct operating segments –investment banking private banking and asset management along with insurance.

Credit Suisse sold insurance subsidiary Winterthur to AXA in 2006 for nearly $10 billion. A Winterthur sale had been on Credit Suisse's agenda for a while as a plan to divest noncore operations. Also that year Credit Suisse and General Electric jointly acquired a 50% stake in London City Airport which serves about 2 million travelers a year. The following year as a cost-saving measure Credit Suisse combined four private banks and one securities dealer into Clariden Leu.

The company named Brady Dougan CEO in 2007. Dugan was the first non-German speaker to hold the position.

Globally the investment banking industry was hit hard by the US subprime mortgage crisis and Credit Suisse was no exception. The company reported a net loss of 5.4 billion in 2008 the worst in its history. Credit Suisse turned down a bailout offer from the Swiss government in 2008 but it did receive a capital injection of CHF10 billion ($8.7 billion) from private investors. However the capital infusion couldn't prevent losses as global credit markets froze and consumer and shareholder confidence fell.

The company cut more than 5000 jobs or some 11% of its workforce mostly from its investment banking unit. It also reviewed its results for 2007 and among its findings discovered rogue traders in its ranks à la the beleaguered Socit Gnrale. Credit Suisse reduced its results accordingly.

In 2008 it bought an 80% stake in US firm Asset Management Finance Corporation a division of National Bank of Canada. Also in 2008 it expanded its Middle East franchise when it bought majority ownership in joint venture Saudi Swiss Securities which it renamed Credit Suisse Saudi Arabia. It has added Shariah-compliant banking for Islamic clients and has expanded in other markets including Brazil Kazakhstan and Turkey.

The following year Credit Suisse sold certain fund management assets and businesses to Aberdeen Asset Management in exchange for about 25% of Aberdeen's shares.

EXECUTIVES

Co-President Institutional Securities Credit Suisse First Boston, Brady W. Dougan, age 56
Chief Talent Branding and Communications Officer, Pamela A. Thomas-Graham, age 52
Head Private Banking and Wealth Management, Robert S. (Rob) Shafir, age 58
Head Private Banking and Wealth Management; CEO Region Switzerland, Hans-Ulrich Meister, age 56
CEO, Tidjane C. Thiam, age 53
Head Investment Banking and Fixed Income; CEO Region Europe Middle East & Africa, Ga d de Boissard
Head Investment Banking, James L. Amine
Chief Risk Officer, Joachim Oechslin, age 44
Head Investment Banking Equities, Timothy P O'Hara, age 51
CEO Australia, John Knox
CFO, Rocco DelGuercio
CEO Mexico, Pedro Jorge Villareal
Global Head Investment Strategy, Nannette Hechler-Fayd 'herbe
Chairman, Urs Rohner, age 56
Vice Chair and Lead Independent Director, Noreen Doyle, age 66
Auditors: KPMG AG

LOCATIONS

HQ: Credit Suisse Group
Paradeplatz 8, Zurich CH 8001
Phone: (41) 44 333 6607 **Fax:** (41) 44 333 1790
Web: www.credit-suisse.com

2014 Sales

	% total
Americas	42
Switzerland	31
EMEA	17
Asia Pacific	10
Total	**100**

PRODUCTS/OPERATIONS

2014 Sales

	% of total
Net interest income	35
Non-Interest	
Commissions & fees	50
Trading revenues	8
Other	7
Total	**100**

2014 Sales

	% of total
Private Banking & Wealth Management	48
Investment Banking	48
Non-Controlling interest with SEI	2
Corporte Center	2
Total	**100**

COMPETITORS

AEGON
Barclays
Citigroup
Deutsche Bank
Goldman Sachs
Grupo Santander
HSBC
ING
JPMorgan Chase
Mitsubishi UFJ Financial Group
Mizuho Financial
Morgan Stanley
Nomura Securities
TD Bank
UBS

HISTORICAL FINANCIALS

Company Type: Public

Income Statement FYE: December 31

	ASSETS ($ mil.)	NET INCOME ($ mil.)	INCOME AS % OF ASSETS	EMPLOYEES
12/14	931,534	1,895	0.2%	45,800
12/13	979,520	2,610	0.3%	46,000
12/12	1,008,171	1,617	0.2%	47,400
12/11	1,115,189	2,075	0.2%	49,700
12/10	1,102,816	5,447	0.5%	50,100
Annual Growth	(4.1%)	(23.2%)	—	(2.2%)

2014 Year-End Financials

Return on assets: 0.2%
Return on equity: 4.3%
Long-term debt ($ mil.): —
No. of shares (mil.): 1,599
Sales ($ mil): 26,528
Dividends
Yield: 3.1%
Payout: 65.3%
Market value ($ mil.): 40,116

	STOCK PRICE ($) FY Close	P/E High/Low		PER SHARE ($) Earnings	Dividends	Book Value
12/14	25.08	28	22	1.08	0.79	27.78
12/13	31.04	28	21	1.37	0.14	29.74
12/12	24.56	33	19	0.98	0.82	30.04
12/11	23.48	35	15	1.45	1.36	29.33
12/10	40.41	15	10	4.16	1.78	30.30
Annual Growth	(11.2%)	—	—	(28.6%)	(18.5%)	(2.1%)

CRH Plc

CRH has built its business upon building materials. Through subsidiaries (including Oldcastle) the international company makes and distributes cement concrete aggregate glass and asphalt for commercial residential and infrastructure projects across the globe. CRH has some 4000 operating locations and operates more than 700 wholesale and retail building supply stores under the Professional Builders Merchants GAMMA and Allied Building Products brands. With a presence in some 35 countries CRH has become the top supplier of building materials in North America and the third-largest worldwide.

OperationsCRH's operations are divided into six segments based on its largest service lines in the Americas and Europe. Its Europe Heavyside businesses (which make up 20% of CRH's total revenue) manufacture and supply cement aggregates precast and ready-mixed concrete concrete landscaping and asphalt products while its Americas Materials businesses (nearly 30% of revenue) provide similar products in the Americas. The company's Europe Distribution businesses (20% of revenue) consist of its Do-It-Yourself (DIY) General Merchants and Sanitary Heating and Plumbing (SHAP) businesses that supply bricks cement sanitary heating plumbing and other building products to consumers and small and medium-sized builders. Its Europe Lightside businesses (5% of revenue) make and sell construction accessories shutters and awnings fencing and composite access chambers.CRH's Americas Products businesses (more than 15% of revenue) produce and sell concrete masonry and hardscapes clay brick packaged lawn and garden products cement mixes fencing utility drainage and other construction products. Its Americas Distribution businesses (nearly 10% of revenue) supply exterior products like roofing and siding as well as interior products like gypsum wallboard metal studs and acoustical ceiling systems. Geographic ReachWhile Ireland-based CRH operates in more than 35 countries it generates more than 50% of its sales in the US. More than 10% of sales come from countries in the Benelux region (mainly the Netherlands) while less than 2% of its sales come from its home country. The company also supplies materials in emerging markets in Asia Eastern Europe and South America. Financial PerformanceNote: Growth rates may differ after conversion to US dollars.CRH has struggled to grow its revenues and profits in recent years as the sluggish housing markets and overall economies across Europe have held back demand for its products. CRH's sales rose by 5% to 18.9 billion ($23 billion) in 2014 mostly thanks to higher demand for its products in the US as the housing market and overall economy picked up steam. Business in Europe picked up as well thanks to favorable early season weather while like-for-like sales picked up by 6% in the region.Higher sales and gains from the sale of discontinued operations in 2014 pushed CRH's profits up to 582 million ($707 million) compared to a loss of 296 million in 2013. CRH's operating cash levels jumped by 13% to 1.2 billion ($1.46 billion) thanks to higher cash earnings.

Strategy

Since the company's formation in 1970 acquisitions have been a key part of CRH's growth strategy. The company has historically targeted growth across all business divisions in both developed and emerging regions making strategic bolt-on acquisitions each year. After a brief break from acquisitions after the financial crisis CRH has resumed making acquisitions making its biggest deal yet in 2015 after purchasing cement facilities from rivals Lafarge and Holcim to boost its production capacity and geographic reach.

While the company is growing in some areas it is making cuts in others –particularly in the US. In 2014 the company announced a multi-year divestment program intended to streamline operations to prepare for future growth and make acquisitions that align with that goal. That year it divested 16 units realizing total proceeds of 350 million; most had been bolt-on acquisitions for its existing operations in the Americas. Late in 2014 CRH also announced plans to sell its UK clay and concrete businesses and its US clay business to European funds managed by Bain Capital for £414 million.

Mergers and AcquisitionsIn August 2015 CRH purchased cement assets from Holcim Ltd. and Lafarge SA for a total of 6.5 billion ($7.3 billion) marking its largest acquisition to date. The deal bolstered the company's production capacity and expanded its operations in Canada Brazil the Philippines and several countries in Europe.

EXECUTIVES

Finance Director, Maeve Carton, age 56
CEO, Albert Manifold, age 52
Chairman, Nicky Hartery, age 63
Auditors: Ernst & Young

LOCATIONS

HQ: CRH Plc
Belgard Castle, Clondalkin, Dublin 22
Phone: (353) 1 404 1000 **Fax:** (353) 1 404 1007
Web: www.crh.com

2014 Sales

	% of total
Europe	
Heavysie	21
Distribution	21
Lightside	5
Americas	
Materials	27
Products	17
Distribution	9
Total	**100**

PRODUCTS/OPERATIONS

Selected Activities and Products

Materials
- Aggregates
- Agricultural and chemical lime
- Asphalt
- Cement
- Concrete products
- Ready-mixed concrete

Products
- Architectural concrete
- Building products
- Building envelope products
- Construction accessories
- Clay facing bricks pavers and blocks
- Structural concrete

Distribution
- Builders merchants
- DIY stores

COMPETITORS

BUZZI UNICEM
Boral
CEMEX
CIMPOR
Cementos de Chihuahua
Ciments Fran§ais
Dyckerhoff
Grafton Group
HeidelbergCement
Home Depot
Imerys
Italcementi
Kingspan
LafargeHolcim
Marshalls
Martin Marietta Materials
Saint-Gobain
Tarmac
Titan Cement
Travis Perkins
Vulcan Materials
Wienerberger

HISTORICAL FINANCIALS

Company Type: Public

Income Statement FYE: December 31

	REVENUE ($ mil.)	NET INCOME ($ mil.)	NET PROFIT MARGIN	EMPLOYEES
12/14	22,987	707	3.1%	75,706
12/13	24,823	(407)	—	75,642
12/12	24,593	727	3.0%	76,175
12/11	23,386	763	3.3%	76,433
12/10	22,983	578	2.5%	76,418
Annual Growth	0.0%	5.2%	—	(0.2%)

2014 Year-End Financials

Debt ratio: 32.3%
Return on equity: 5.8%
Cash ($ mil.): 3,964
Current ratio: 2.26
Long-term debt ($ mil.): 6,586
No. of shares (mil.): 744
Dividends
Yield: 3.4%
Payout: 78.4%
Market value ($ mil.): 17,876

	STOCK PRICE ($) FY Close	P/E High/Low		PER SHARE ($) Earnings	Dividends	Book Value
12/14	24.01	33	25	0.96	0.84	16.61
12/13	25.55	—	—	(0.56)	0.82	18.14
12/12	20.34	29	23	1.01	0.80	19.12
12/11	19.82	27	17	1.07	0.81	18.91
12/10	20.80	48	26	0.82	0.81	19.49
Annual Growth	3.7%	—	—	4.0%	0.8%	(3.9%)

CTBC Financial Holdings Ltd

Chinatrust Financial Holding (CFHC) is one of Taiwan's largest financial services groups. It operates Chinatrust Commercial Bank which has more than 140 domestic branches and more than 70 overseas. The group provides general banking services including corporate and consumer loans financial consulting checking and savings accounts letters of credit commercial drafts collections and payments and credit cards. It also offers property/casualty insurance life insurance investments and other related financial services. Overseas the bank operates subsidiaries in the US Canada the Philippines and Indonesia. The predecessor to the family-owned CFHC was founded in 1966.

EXECUTIVES

President Retail Banking Group, Oliver Shang
EVP; Managing Director Commercial Banking, James Chen
EVP; Managing Director Investment Banking Group, Larry Hsu
EVP; Managing Director Retail Banking Group, Su Kuo Huang
Managing Director General Administration, Thomas K. S. Chen
EVP; Managing Director Consumer Finance Group, Eric Wu
EVP; Managing Director Risk Management Group, Jack T. K. Cheng
EVP; Managing Director Audit Management Division, Julie L. Yang
EVP, Jason Wang
EVP, Albert Shiung
Chief Information Officer, Rutian Zhang
Chairman of the Board, Liansong Gu
Auditors: KPMG

LOCATIONS

HQ: CTBC Financial Holdings Ltd
27 & 29F., No. 168, Jingmao 2nd Road, Nangang District, Taipei 115
Phone: (886) 2 3327 7777
Web: www.ctbcholding.com

COMPETITORS

Cathay Financial Holding
Chang Hwa Bank
E.Sun
East West Bancorp
First Financial Holding
Fubon Financial
Hua Nan Financial
Mega Financial
Shin Kong
SinoPac Holdings
Taishin
Taiwan Business Bank

HISTORICAL FINANCIALS

Company Type: Public

Income Statement FYE: December 31

	ASSETS ($ mil.)	NET INCOME ($ mil.)	INCOME AS % OF ASSETS	EMPLOYEES
12/14	115,418	1,245	1.1%	0
12/13	81,308	721	0.9%	0
12/12	72,825	733	1.0%	13,107
12/11	66,632	603	0.9%	12,568
12/10	62,359	485	0.8%	11,562
Annual Growth	16.6%	26.5%	—	—

2014 Year-End Financials

Return on assets: 1.3%
Return on equity: 18.6%
Long-term debt ($ mil.): —
No. of shares (mil.): —
Sales ($ mil): 7,020
Dividends
Yield: —
Payout: —
Market value ($ mil.): —

Dai-ichi Life Insurance Co Ltd

Trying its best to live up to its name (Dai-ichi means "first") Dai-ichi Life Insurance Company is one of Japan's top insurers. The firm sells individual and group life insurance annuities and supplemental medical coverage as well as individual and group pension products. Dai-ichi Life also provides nonlife insurance products through its partnership with Sompo Japan Insurance as well as cancer insurance through a partnership with Aflac. Other services include asset management and risk management. Dai-ichi Life sells its products through its network of thousands of sales representatives.

Sales and Marketing

Dai-ichi Life markets its products through sales representatives at a number of locations –including retail stores call centers and administration centers –as well as through online and direct mail programs.

Strategy

The company has responded to increased competition in the Japanese market by expanding its product offerings including lifetime supplemental medical coverage and annuity products. In expanding its financial services segment the company has become one of the top institutional investors in Japan.

Mergers and Acquisitions

Dai-ichi Life is also investing in overseas subsidiaries in a bid to increase its presence outside of Japan. In mid-2011 it strengthened its international presence by acquiring the balance of Tower Australia Group. (It first purchase a stake in the Australian life insurer in 2008.) Dai-Ichi Life has also made moves into Thailand and Vietnam.

Ownership

Previously named Dai-ichi Mutual Life Insurance the company jumped on the demutualization bandwagon and made its IPO on the Tokyo stock exchange in early 2010. The listing for the renamed Dai-ichi Life Insurance raised some 1 trillion ($11 billion) and the proceeds were used to pad the company's coffers after the drop in value of its securities during the economic recession.

Auditors: Ernst & Young ShinNihon LLC

LOCATIONS

HQ: Dai-ichi Life Insurance Co Ltd
1-13-1 Yuraku-cho, Chiyoda-ku, Tokyo 100-8411
Phone: (81) 3 3216 1211
Web: www.dai-ichi-life.co.jp

HISTORICAL FINANCIALS

Company Type: Public

Income Statement FYE: March 31

	REVENUE ($ mil.)	NET INCOME ($ mil.)	NET PROFIT MARGIN	EMPLOYEES
03/15	57,315	1,187	2.1%	60,647
03/14	54,963	755	1.4%	59,512
03/13	52,947	344	0.7%	60,771
03/12	55,775	248	0.4%	60,305
03/11	51,146	231	0.5%	59,356
Annual Growth	2.9%	50.6%	—	0.5%

2015 Year-End Financials

Debt ratio: 0.0%	No. of shares (mil.): 1,197
Return on equity: 5.1%	Dividends
Cash ($ mil.): 7,824	Yield: —
Current ratio: 0.13	Payout: —
Long-term debt ($ mil.): 4,076	Market value ($ mil.): —

Daimler AG

Daimler's cars may stop on a dime but they cost a little more than that. Daimler's passenger car business Mercedes-Benz includes luxury brands Mercedes and Maybach as well as compact hybrid and electric models including its smart brand. Other major auto brands include Freightliner Western Star BharatBenz Fuso Setra and Thomas Built Buses while financial services brands include Mercedes-Benz Bank Mercedes-Benz Financial moovel and car2go. Its Daimler Trucks North America unit manufactures heavy-trucks in the US. Daimler sells its vehicles in 40 countries but Europe represents around 35% of its net sales.

OperationsThe company operates through five business segments: Mercedes-Benz Cars (55% of net sales) Daimler Trucks (23%) Mercedes-Benz Vans (7%) Daimler Buses (3%) and Daimler Financial Services (12%). Daimler distributes its vehicles in around 200 countries worldwide.

Financial Performance

After posting four straight years of revenue growth Daimler saw its revenues dip 3% from $162 billion in 2013 to $158 billion in 2014. Profits also declined 10% from $9 billion to roughly $8.5 billion over that same time period due to higher interest tax rates and increased expenses.

Strategy

The company's blueprint for growth involves the strengthening of its core business within the emerging markets of Brazil Russia India and China. It is also focused on enhancing its green technologies and vehicular safety operations. It will invest approximately 11 billion in property plant and equipment throughout 2015 and 2016 as well as more than 13 billion in research and development projects.

With its continued focus on the Chinese markets the company in 2013 opened a new production plant for four-cylinder engines in China along with its biggest training center in the world in 2014. Daimler also plans to launch a new research and development center in Beijing.

For the Brazilian markets the company will begin manufacturing its C‑Class and the GLA brands for the local market in Brazil in 2016. The company will also establish its local bus manufacturing operations in India in 2015.

HISTORY

Daimler-Benz was formed by the merger of two German motor companies –Daimler and Benz –in 1926. Daimler-Benz bought Auto Union (Audi) in 1958 (sold to Volkswagen in 1966). The company's Mercedes cars gained international fame and sales expanded worldwide in the 1970s.

Daimler-Benz diversified in the 1980s buying aerospace heavy truck (Freightliner) and consumer and industrial electrical companies. Although diversification continued sales slowed. Losses at its aerospace unit forced Daimler-Benz into the red in 1995. Also that year the company and ABB Asea Brown Boveri (now ABB) formed joint venture Adtranz the #1 train maker in the world and Jürgen Schrempp became chairman of the management board (CEO).

In 1998 Daimler-Benz acquired Chrysler and introduced a subcompact car the smart in Europe. The newly formed DaimlerChrysler rolled both companies' financial services units into Daimler-Chrysler Interservices (DEBIS) in 1999.

EXECUTIVES

Member of the Board of Management; President and CEO Chrysler Group, Dieter Zetsche, age 62, $1,530,000 total compensation

Member Management Board; Head Daimler Trucks and Buses Division, Wolfgang Bernhard, age 55

Member Management Board Finance and Controlling Daimler Financial Services, Bodo Uebber, age 55, $660,000 total compensation

Member Management Board; Head Greater China, Hubertus Troska

Member Management Board; Head Marketing and Sales, Ola K □llenius

CEO Daimler Trucks Korea, Cho Kyu-Sang

President and CEO Daimler Middle East and Levant, Mark De Haes

Chairman Supervisory Board, Manfred Bischoff, age 73

Auditors: KPMG AG Wirtschaftsprufungsgesellschaft

LOCATIONS

HQ: Daimler AG
Mercedesstrasse 137, Stuttgart D-70327
Phone: (49) 711 17 97875 **Fax:** (49) 711 17 94075
Web: www.daimler.com

PRODUCTS/OPERATIONS

Selected Divisions and Brands

Mercedes-Benz Cars
- Maybach
- Mercedes-Benz
- smart

Daimler Trucks
- Freightliner
- Mitsubishi Fuso
- Mercedez-Benz
- Western Star Trucks

Daimler Financial Services
Banking (M
- Fleet management
- Insurance
- Leasing and financing

Mercedes-Benz Vans
Daimler Buses
- Mercedes-Benz (city buses coaches interurban minibuses)
- Mercedes-Benz chassis
- Mitsubishi Fuso (large buses midi-sized buses minibuses)

Orion (cit
- Setra (coaches interurban buses)
- Thomas Built Buses (hybrid school bus school and activity buses)

COMPETITORS

BMW	PACCAR
Fiat Chrysler	PROTON Holdings
Ford Motor	Peugeot
Fuji Heavy Industries	Porsche
General Motors	Renault
Honda	Scania
Isuzu	Toyota
Land Rover	Volkswagen
MAN	Volvo
Navistar International	ZAP
Nissan	

HISTORICAL FINANCIALS

Company Type: Public

Income Statement FYE: December 31

	REVENUE ($ mil.)	NET INCOME ($ mil.)	NET PROFIT MARGIN	EMPLOYEES
12/14	157,860	8,462	5.4%	279,972
12/13	162,430	9,419	5.8%	274,616
12/12	150,649	8,033	5.3%	275,087
12/11	137,804	7,329	5.3%	271,370
12/10	130,840	6,020	4.6%	260,100
Annual Growth	4.8%	8.9%	—	1.9%

2014 Year-End Financials

Debt ratio: 55.5%	No. of shares (mil.): 1,069
Return on equity: 16.1%	Dividends
Cash ($ mil.): 11,750	Yield: 2.7%
Current ratio: 1.15	Payout: 34.5%
Long-term debt ($ mil.): 61,260	Market value ($ mil.): —

Daishi Bank, Ltd.

If everything old is new again then Daishi Bank is hot off the presses. The regional bank which was founded in 1873 and lays claim to being the oldest in Japan serves primarily the Niigata prefecture through some 120 offices there. Daishi Bank also has about 10 additional offices (two in Tokyo and 10 in other prefectures). Daishi Bank and it subsidiaries offer individuals and businesses a range of traditional deposit banking and other products and services including business matching business consulting credit cards credit guarantee credit card settlement and processing financial advice investment banking investment products leasing and venture capital.

Auditors: KPMG AZSA LLC

LOCATIONS

HQ: Daishi Bank, Ltd.
1071-1 Higashiborimae-dori 7-bancho, Chuo-ku, Niigata 951-8066
Phone: (81) 25 222 4111
Web: www.daishi-bank.co.jp

COMPETITORS

Hachijuni Bank
Hokuetsu Bank Ltd.
Mizuho Financial
Resona
Sumitomo Mitsui

HISTORICAL FINANCIALS

Company Type: Public

Income Statement

FYE: March 31

	ASSETS ($ mil.)	NET INCOME ($ mil.)	INCOME AS % OF ASSETS	EMPLOYEES
03/15	43,288	118	0.3%	2,580
03/14	47,735	124	0.3%	2,610
03/13	52,032	114	0.2%	2,635
03/12	57,087	118	0.2%	2,651
03/11	55,720	73	0.1%	2,660
Annual Growth	(6.1%)	12.6%	—	(0.8%)

2015 Year-End Financials

Return on assets: 0.2%
Return on equity: 4.9%
Long-term debt ($ mil.): —
No. of shares (mil.): 350
Sales ($ mil): 817
Dividends
Yield: —
Payout: —
Market value ($ mil.): —

Daiwa House Industry Co Ltd

More than a half-century ago Daiwa House Industry called its first prefabricated homes "Pipe Houses" because they were made from steel pipes. Today the group's eight businesses build lease sell and manage single-family houses condominiums and commercial buildings. Daiwa House's health and leisure segment manages and operates resort hotels golf courses fitness clubs and health care facilities. Other offerings include agency services office relocation and staffing services and vehicle and equipment leasing. Daiwa House Industry has more than 100 branches and factories throughout Japan and in China and Vietnam.OperationsThe company has built leased and/or managed some 1.5 million single-family homes more than 30000 commercial facilities and more than 60000 health care facilities.

Financial Performance

Daiwa House's sales increased 35% to ¥2.7 trillion in fiscal 2013 (ended March). The rise was driven by commercial facilities and rental housing. Net income rose 54% to ¥102 billion over the same period largely due to the increased revenues. Cash flow from operations fell 52% to ¥78.5 billion largely as a result of changes in current assets and liabilities.

Stategy

In 2013 Daiwa House acquired Fujita Corp. a construction business active in Japan and beyond. The purchase strengthens Daiwa House's operations beyond Japan as Fujita is one of the top Japanese contractors in China and supports its Chinese clients operations abroad in countries such as Mexico and Vietnam. Daiwa plans to use Fujita's overseas platform to expand its own presence abroad as well as in the corporate and commercial construction markets.Japan's aging and shrinking population doesn't favor new single-family home construction so Daiwa House has increasingly focused on in its commercial and hotel operations as well as rental housing condominiums and home renovations. The company also operates about a dozen Daiwa Roynet business hotels.In fiscal 2015 Daiwa House entered into a partnership with Malaysian developer Sunway Berhad to develop and sell prefabricated landed houses in Malaysia.

EXECUTIVES

EVP and CFO, Tetsuji Ogawa, age 74
President Nihon Jyutaku Ryutu, Minoru Fujita
President and COO, Naotake Ohno, age 67
Chairman and CEO, Takeo Higuchi, age 77
Senior Managing Executive Officer, Takuya Ishibashi, age 62
Senior Managing Executive Officer, Tatsushi Nishimura, age 66
President Daiwa Royal, Ken Harada
Senior Managing Executive Officer, Shigeru Numata, age 66
President Daiwa Logistics, Isamu Ogata, age 67
Senior Managing Executive Officer, Katsutomo Kawai, age 68
President Daiwa Lease, Shunsaku Morita
President Daiwa Odakyu Construction, Atsushi Kanakubo
President Daiwa Royal Golf, Seishu Umaoka
President Daiwa House Reform, Junichi Sugiura
President Daiwa House Life Support, Toshinori Inaguchi
President Osaka Marubiru, Haruyuki Yoshimoto
President Eneserve, Yoshio Kinoshita
President Higashi-Fuji, Masamichi Yagita
President Daiwa Energy, Hidekazu Matsushima
President Daiwa House Insurance, Shigeru Sasashita
President Fujita, Takuji Ueda
President Daiwa House Asset Management, Yuji Yamada
EVP, Tamio Ishibashi, age 60
President Daiwa Living Management, Masaru Akashi
President Daiwa Rakuda Industry, Masato Shima
President Daiwa Service, Tomoyuki Kido
President Global Community, Takashi Yamada
President Daiwa LifeNext, Yoshinori Watanabe
President Cosmos Initia, Yoshiyuki Takagi
President Daiwa Homes Online, Norio Togashi
President Daiwa Core Factory, Syuji Oda
President Daiwa Lantec, Kazuo Shimoe
President Daiwa Information Service, Katsuyuki Fujita
President Daiwa House REIT Management, Hirotaka Najima
President Media Tech, Mitsuo Adachi
President Daiyoshi Trust, Yoshihiro Oho
President Frameworx, Junichi Akiba
President Daiwa House Financial, Hiroshi Osada
President Royal Home Center, Masaaki Nakayama
President Daiwa Resort, Seiji Kushida
President Sports Club NAS, Yoshinari Shibayama
President Nishiwaki Royal Hotel, Hideaki Tomiyama
President Shinwa Agency, Nobuyuki Otsuji
President Daiwa House California, Takeshi Wakita
Auditors: Deloitte Touche Tohmatsu LLC

LOCATIONS

HQ: Daiwa House Industry Co Ltd
3-3-5 Umeda, Kita-ku, Osaka 530-8241
Phone: (81) 6 6342 1400 **Fax:** (81) 6 6342 1587
Web: www.daiwahouse.co.jp

PRODUCTS/OPERATIONS

2014 Sales

	% of total
Rental housing	24
Business and corporate facilities	21
Commercial facilities	15
Single-family housing	14
Condominiums	9
Existing homes	3
Other businesses	14
Total	100

COMPETITORS

HASEKO
Nishimatsu Construction
Sekisui House
Shimizu
Sumitomo Mitsui Construction
Taisei
Takenaka
Toda
Tokyu Construction

HISTORICAL FINANCIALS

Company Type: Public

Income Statement

FYE: March 31

	REVENUE ($ mil.)	NET INCOME ($ mil.)	NET PROFIT MARGIN	EMPLOYEES
03/15	23,426	976	4.2%	34,903
03/14	26,160	989	3.8%	32,628
03/13	21,340	704	3.3%	30,361
03/12	22,538	404	1.8%	27,130
03/11	20,410	329	1.6%	26,310
Annual Growth	3.5%	31.2%	—	7.3%

2015 Year-End Financials

Debt ratio: 0.1%
Return on equity: 11.2%
Cash ($ mil.): 1,990
Current ratio: 1.39
Long-term debt ($ mil.): 3,443
No. of shares (mil.): 658
Dividends
Yield: 2.5%
Payout: —
Market value ($ mil.): 12,992

	STOCK PRICE ($) FY Close	P/E High/Low	PER SHARE ($) Earnings	Dividends	Book Value
03/15	19.72	— —	1.48	0.51	14.08
03/14	169.35	— —	1.56	5.47	14.59
03/13	196.35	— —	1.22	0.00	13.50
03/12	131.71	— —	0.70	0.00	13.86
03/11	122.46	— —	0.57	1.92	13.25
Annual Growth	(36.7%)	— —	27.0%	(28.3%)	1.5%

Danone

You say Danone I say Dannon; let's call the whole thing one of the largest dairy food and water producers in the world. The company is organized around its core activities: fresh dairy products water and infant and medical nutrition. The company #1 maker of fresh dairy products worldwide offers dozens of worldwide and regional yogurt brands including Dannon and Activia and the organic and Greek yogurt brands Stonyfield Farm and Oikos. The company's Evian Volvic Aqua and other water brands make it #2 worldwide in bottled water. Danone became a player in the baby-food sector with its purchase of Royal Numico and is now the world's #2 baby nutrition company. Its medical nutrition products are #1 in Europe.

HISTORY

In 1965 Antoine Riboud replaced his uncle as chairman of family-run Souchon-Neuvesel a Lyons France-based maker of glass bottles. Antoine quickly made a mark in this field –he merged the firm with Boussois a major French flat-glass manufacturer creating BSN in 1966.

Antoine enlarged BSN's glass business and filled the company's bottles by acquiring well-established beverage and food concerns. In 1970 BSN purchased Brasseries Kronenbourg (France's largest brewer) Socit Europenne de Brasseries (another French brewer) and Evian (mineral water France). The 1972 acquisition of Glaverbel (Belgium) gave BSN 50% of Europe's flat-glass market. The next year BSN merged with France's Gervais Danone (yogurt cheese Panzani pasta; founded in 1919 and named after founder Isaac Carasso's son Daniel). This moved the company into pan-European brand-name foods.

Increasing energy costs depressed flat-glass earnings so BSN began divesting its flat-glass businesses. In the late 1970s it acquired interests in brewers in Belgium Spain and Italy.

BSN bought Dannon the leading US yogurt maker (co-founded by Daniel Carasso who had continued making Danone yogurt in France until WWII) in 1982. It established a strong presence in the Italian pasta market by buying stakes in Ponte (1985) and Agnesi (1986). BSN also purchased Generale Biscuit the world's #3 biscuit maker (1986) and RJR Nabisco's European cookie and snack-food business (1989).

In a series of acquisitions starting in 1986 BSN took over Italy and Spain's largest mineral water companies and several European pasta makers and other food companies. Adopting the name of its leading international brand BSN became Groupe Danone in 1994.

Antoine's son Franck succeeded him as chairman in 1996 and restructured the company to focus on three core businesses: dairy beverages (specifically water and beer) and biscuits. By 1997 Danone had begun shedding non-core grocery products. The company simultaneously stepped up acquisitions of dairy beer biscuit and water companies in developing markets.

The 1998 purchase of AquaPenn Spring Water for $112 million doubled its US water-bottling production capacity. Danone in 1999 completed a merger and subsequent sale of part of its BSN Emballage glass-packaging unit to UK buyout firm CVC Capital Partners for $1.2 billion; Danone retained 44% ownership. Thirsty for the #2 spot in US bottled water sales Danone gulped down McKesson Water (the #3 bottled water firm in the US after Nestl and Suntory) for $1.1 billion in 2000.

Also in 2000 Danone's joint venture Finalrealm (which includes several European equity firms) along with Burlington Biscuits Nabisco and HM Capital Partners (then called Hicks Muse Tate & Furst) acquired 87% of leading UK biscuit maker United Biscuits. Danone then bought Naya (bottled water Canada) and sold its brewing operations (#2 in Europe) to Scottish & Newcastle (later acquired by Heineken and Carlsberg) for more than $2.6 billion.

During 2001 Danone announced restructuring would shutter two LU biscuit plants and eliminate about 1800 jobs; the move met with strikes and legal battles. That same year having been bumped to the #2 spot in the US yogurt market (after General Mills' Yoplait brand) Danone acquired 40% of Stonyfield Farm the #4 yogurt brand in the US and ultimately came to own 84% of the company.

The company launched 2002 with a series of beverage acquisitions including Frucor (New Zealand) and Zywiec Zdroj (the top brand of water in Poland). Danone then struck a deal handing Coca-Cola the distribution and marketing of Evian in North America and formed a joint venture with Coke to distribute its lower-end water brands. Antoine Riboud died that same year at the age of 83.

Danone divested noncore companies during 2002 including the sale of its Italian meat and cheese business Galbani and its Kro Beer Brands (Kronenbourg 1664 brands) to Scottish & Newcastle. Then typical of its consolidation strategy later in 2002 Danone acquired the home and office water delivery companies Chateaud'eau (France) Patrimoine des Eaux du Quebec (Canada) and Canada's Sparkling Spring (now Aquaterra).

In 2004 Danone sold its 10% interest in the Australian dairy firm National Foods. Later that year it announced an alliance with Japanese dairy group Yakult Honsha to focus both companies' efforts with probiotics. Danone is a 20% shareholder of Yakult and has agreed not to increase its share holdings of Yakult for five years and not to pursue majority control for another five. Also in 2004 Danone acquired the Mexican bottled water company Arco Iris.

While its dairy and water businesses bubbled along nicely Danone found its cookies crumbling. Opting for a new recipe in 2004 it joined with Argentine food giant ARCOR Group to merge both companies' biscuits operations in South America. Later that same year Danone sold off its W&R Jacob Ltd. biscuits operations in Ireland to local company Fruitfield Foods. It also sold Italaquae its Italian bottled water business to LGR Holding.

Long after its departure from brewing in 2004 Danone was fined 1.5 million for forming a beer distribution cartel along with Heineken in 1996. In 2005 Danone and Coca-Cola ended their 2002 water-distribution joint venture with Coke buying out Danone's 49% share for about $100 million.

In 2005 Danone got out of the brewing business altogether with the sale of its 33% stake in Spanish brewer Mahou. It sold its HP Foods Group including Amoy Lea & Perrins and HP sauce brands to Heinz and its biscuits businesses in the UK and Ireland. That year it sold its US home and office water-delivery company DS Waters of America to investment firm Kelso & Company. Danone has increased its ownership of Russian dairy and beverage company Wimm-Bill-Dann Foods to almost 20%.

Due to slow sales for its chilled products and competition from lower-priced brands in 2006 Danone introduced Senjà (a soy-based yogurt) in France. It acquired Egyptian fresh dairy products company Olait (which it renamed Danone Dairy Egypt) and Algerian bottled water company Tessala. On the Asian front Danone acquired 23% of fruit-drink company China Huiyuan Juice Group and 51% of Wahaha. (It sold its interest in Huiyuan Juice in 2010.) In the Ukraine it bought fresh dairy company JSC Molochnyi Zavod. In the US it launched the Activia brand yogurt.

Because it wants to introduce more organic products in Europe in 2006 Danone announced the spending of $66 million on the expansion of its subsidiary Stonyfield Farm's New Hampshire production plant. (That year Stonyfield bought a 34% interest in Irish organic dairy Glenisk.)

In 2006 Danone sold its Amoy Asian sauce and chilled foods business to Ajinomoto exiting the sauce business altogether. It then sold virtually all of its grocery activities glass-container business its cheese and cured meat activities (Galbani) and its beer activities in Europe. It also sold New Zealand biscuits maker Griffins Food to investment firm Pacific Equity Partners.

Danone paid 12 billion (about $16 billion) for Numico maker of infant food and medical nutrition (nutritional bars and shakes) in 2007. The Numico products (Cow & Gate Dumex Mellin milupa NUTRICIA) joined Danone's bldina baby-food brand to create a wide array of well-known nutritional products for babies and adults. The purchase made Danone the largest baby-food maker in Europe.

Prior to announcing the Numico purchase Danone announced the sale of its cookie business to Kraft Foods; that deal closed in late 2007. At the time some analysts saw Danone as ripe for a takeover; hence the Numico deal was construed as a way for Danone to remain independent. (The acquisition was viewed as helping ward off predators who might have been attracted to the cash that Danone accrued as a result of the Kraft deal.) As part of its strategy to divest itself of all biscuit/cookie activities in 2009 the company ended its Indian joint venture with the Wadia Group. Danone sold its 50% interest in the operation ABI Holdings to Wadia.

Strengthening its business in Asia in 2007 Danone acquired all of the Japanese joint venture with Ajinomoto and Calpis that it did not already own. Renamed Danone Japan the operation manufactures fresh products for the expanding Japanese dairy market.

Saying it wanted to "regain room for maneuver[ing]" in 2007 it sold off its 20% stake in and terminated its distribution agreement with Shanghai-based Bright Dairy. Danone cited no specifics surrounding the move but the company has had legal disputes with various joint-venture partners in China and India recently relating to how its brands are marketed and produced.

In late 2007 the company exited its joint venture with Chinese company Mengniu Dairy Group citing time frame and other condition difficulties. (Both companies agreed to the termination of the venture which was initiated in 2006.) Turning to South America that same year Danone acquired a 70% holding in Chile's fresh dairy company Vialat.

Among its divestments in 2008 in order to fulfill European Union requirements for its acquisition of Numico the company sold off its French baby milk and baby drinks businesses to Groupe Lactalis. That year it also sold its subsidiary Frucor a maker of non-alcoholic beverages in New Zealand and Australia as well as its international brands V and Mizone (with the exception of in China and Indonesia) to Suntory for some 600 million ($780 million).

Danone took full control of its South African joint venture Danone Clover in 2009. It purchased Clover's 45% stake for R1085 ($145 million). (Clover is one of South Africa's largest dairy companies.) Other partnerships include a joint venture with Weight Watchers formed in 2008. The 51% Weight Watchers-49% Danone operation provides weight-management services to the People's Republic of China.

Following its acquisition of a controlling interest in a venture with Russia's Unimilk in 2010 Danone sold its 18.4% stake in Wimm-Bill-Dann Foods back to the Russian dairy and juice producer for $470 million.

EXECUTIVES

Vice Chairman and Co-COO, Jacques Vincent, age 68, $1,529,800 total compensation
EVP Fresh Dairy Products, Thomas Kunz, age 58
CEO, Emmanuel Faber, age 52, $1,373,620 total compensation
Chairman President and CEO Stonyfield Farm, Gary Hirshberg
Deputy General Manager and Co-COO; Director, Bernard Hours, age 59, $2,863,620 total compensation
General Manager Medical Nutrition, Flemming Morgan, age 59
EVP Research and Development, Jean-Philippe Par ©age 57
Exec. VP Baby Nutrition; Member of the Executive Committee, Felix Garcia
EVP of Research & Development; Member of the Executive Committee, Jean-Philippe Pare
CFO and Member the Executive Committee, Pierre-Andre Terisse
General Manager South-Eastern Europe, Adrian Pascu
Chairman, Franck Riboud, age 59
Auditors: ERNST & YOUNG et Autres

LOCATIONS

HQ: Danone
17, Boulevard Haussmann, Paris 75009
Phone: (33) 1 44 35 20 20 **Fax:** (33) 1 44 35 26 95
Web: www.danone.com

2013 Sales

	% of total
Europe (excluding CIS)	39
Asia-Pacific Latin America Middle East & Africa	39
CIS & North America	22
Total	**100**

PRODUCTS/OPERATIONS

2013 Sales

	% of total
Fresh dairy	56
Early life nutrition	20
Waters	18
Medical nutrition	6
Total	**100**

Selected Products and Brands

Fresh dairy
- Africa (Clover)
- Argentina (La Serenissima Ser)
- China (Bright Dairy)
- France (Danette Danone Senjà)
- International (Actimel Danone)
- Japan (Danone Yakult)
- Latin America (Corpus La Serenisima Mastellone)
- US (Activia Dannon Stonyfield Farm YoCream)

Bottled water
- Argentina (Villa del Sur)
- Asia/Pacific (Aqua)
- Canada (Crystal Springs Evian Labrador Naya)
- France (Badoit Salvetat Arvie)
- International (Evian Volvic)
- Mexico (Bonafont)
- Spain (Font Vella)
- Turkey (Hayat)
- US (Dannon Evian)

Baby nutrition
- Bebelac
- blédina
- Cow & Gate
- Dumex
- Gallia
- Mellin
- milupa
- NUTRICIA

Medical nutrition
- FortiCare
- Fortimel
- Fortisip
- Neocate
- Nutricia
- Nutrini

COMPETITORS

Abbott Nutrition
Ajinomoto
Arla Foods
Associated British Foods
Beech-Nut
Blue Bell
China Mengniu Dairy
Coca-Cola
Dairy Crest
Dairy Farm International
Dairygold
Dean Foods
Dr Pepper Snapple Group
Dreyer' s
Feihe
Fonterra
FrieslandCampina
General Mills
Gerber Products
Glanbia plc
Granarolo
HP Hood
Heinz
Irish Dairy Board
Kellogg
Kerry Group
Lactalis
Leche Pascual
Mead Johnson
Metagenics
Nestl©
Novartis
Parmalat
PepsiCo
Pfizer
Shanghai Bright Dairy & Food
Sodiaal
Unilever NV
Wells' Dairy
Wessanen
WhiteWave
Wimm-Bill-Dann
Yili Group

HISTORICAL FINANCIALS

Company Type: Public

Income Statement

FYE: December 31

	REVENUE ($ mil.)	NET INCOME ($ mil.)	NET PROFIT MARGIN	EMPLOYEES
12/14	25,700	1,360	5.3%	99,927
12/13	29,321	1,957	6.7%	104,642
12/12	27,506	2,203	8.0%	102,401
12/11	24,986	2,161	8.7%	101,885
12/10	22,765	2,502	11.0%	100,995
Annual Growth	3.1%	(14.1%)	—	(0.3%)

2014 Year-End Financials

Debt ratio: 42.6%
Return on equity: 10.0%
Cash ($ mil.): 1,069
Current ratio: 0.70
Long-term debt ($ mil.): 8,019
No. of shares (mil.): 600
Dividends
Yield: 3.0%
Payout: 15.1%
Market value ($ mil.): 7,811

	STOCK PRICE ($) FY Close	P/E High/Low	PER SHARE ($) Earnings	Dividends	Book Value
12/14	13.02	7 6	2.29	0.39	23.69
12/13	14.52	7 6	3.33	0.38	25.11
12/12	13.39	5 4	3.65	0.36	27.08
12/11	12.64	5 4	3.58	0.32	26.06
12/10	12.65	4 4	4.07	0.89	26.11
Annual Growth	0.7%	—	—(13.4%)	(18.3%)	(2.4%)

Danske Bank AS (Denmark)

When you're the largest bank in Denmark there's nowhere to grow but out. Danske Bank serves 3.7 million consumers and businesses through a network of 159 branches in Denmark; 45 branches in Finland (where it operates Sampo Bank); 39 branches in Sweden (Ostgota Enskilda Bank); 32 in Norway (Fokus Bank); and more than 50 branches in Ireland and Northern Ireland where it owns National Irish Bank and Northern Bank respectively. The company also has operations in Germany Poland Russia and the Baltic states. In addition to standard deposit and lending services Danske Bank offers asset management insurance leasing securities trading and research and real estate brokerage services.

Operations Danske Bank operates out of three divisions: Personal Banking Business Banking and Corporates & Institutions.Personal Banking makes up more than 35% of revenue and serves personal and private banking customers with traditional banking services and financial advice to high-net worth clients respectively. Business Banking brings in another nearly 30% of revenue and provides financing investing cash management and risk management services to small and medium-sized businesses through the bank's network of finance centers branches contact centers and online channels. Corporates & Institutions makes up roughly 20% of revenue and provides wholesale banking services to the largest institutional and corporate customers in the Nordic region. The segment's products and services include cash management services; trade finance solutions; custody services; equity bond foreign exchange and derivatives products; corporate finance; and acquisition finance. The bank also offers life insurance and pensions (Danica Pension) services mortgage finance (Realkredit Danmark) asset management (Danske Capital) real estate (home) and leasing (Nordania Leasing) services.

Geographic ReachCopenhagen-based Danske Bank boasts roughly 330 branches in 15 countries with a major presence in Denmark Northern Ireland Finland Sweden Norway Estonia Lithuania and Latvia. It also has branches in London Hamburg Dublin and Warsaw and an office in New York City. Subsidiaries in Luxembourg and St. Petersburg serve private banking and corporate banking customers respectively.Financial PerformanceNote: Growth rates may differ after conversion to US dollars.After years of flat revenue Danske Bank's total income in 2014 jumped by 10% to D$43.9 billion ($7.17 billion) mostly thanks to a combination of: higher net interest income from lower funding costs as the bank paid down its borrowed debt an 11% rise in net fee income thanks to increased business from all banking units and positive developments at Danske Capital and the doubling of its insurance business resulting from the booking of the risk allowance to income (for all four interest rate groups) and booking of part of the shadow account balance. Despite higher revenue and lower operating expenses in 2014 the bank's net income fell by 46% to D$3.8 billion (roughly $620 million) mostly as it paid D$9.1 billion ($1.49 billion) worth of (non-recurring) goodwill impairment charges as a result of weaker long-term economic development expectations in Finland Northern Ireland and Estonia. Before counting these goodwill impairments net profit rose by 82%.Cash levels in 2014 improved significantly with operations using D$7.48 billion ($1.22

billion) mostly as the bank raised more cash from its bonds issued by RealKredit Danmark and borrowed more from other credit institutions and central banks.The bank grew its total loans by 2% to D$1.56 trillion ($255 billion) in 2014 while total deposits declined by 2% to D$763.4 billion ($124.63 billion).

Stategy

While Danske Bank expects slow and fragile economic growth and a continuation of low interest rate levels in its core markets in 2015 it still is optimistic about future profit growth. By the end of 2015 it expects revenue to remain flat but also expects that profit will rise above D$14 billion (roughly $2.15 billion) from lower deposit funding costs higher customer activity and significantly lower impairment charges (as it incurred significant goodwill impairment charges in 2014). The bank plans to continue adding to its market share in its core markets where it controlled more than 25% of the deposit and lending markets in Denmark nearly 10% in Finland and roughly 5% in both the Sweden and Norway markets as of late 2014. In 2014 it built on its Personal Banking market positions in Sweden and Norway by strengthening its management team in both regions signing an agreement with the Akademikerne federation to offer services to more than 100000 of its members in Norway and positioning itself as a full-service bank in Sweden. It also plans to continue reducing its salary consultancy services marketing and other discretionary spending to boost profit. In late 2014 it planned to strengthen its workforce setup with Group Services operations in Lithuania and insourcing of activities in India to support cost reductions in the coming years. It also encouraged its clients to adopt its digital banking services which will help lessen the need for costly brick-and-mortar branch operations.

HISTORY

Company BackgroundLeathersmith-turned-stock trader Gottlieb Gedalia founded Den Danske Landmandsbank Hypothek- og Vexelbank i Kjøbenhavn (The Danish Farmer's Bank Mortgage and Exchange Bank of Copenhagen. It would change its name four times before finally settling on the less-verbose Danske Bank.

Even in its early years Danske Bank never restricted itself to purely agricultural concerns preferring to offer a wide range of banking services that appealed to farmers merchants and businessmen alike. Isak Glückstadt who managed the bank from 1872 until his death in 1910 guided the bank to prominence in Copenhagen's corporate landscape where it became a leading commercial bank. Glückstadt's son Emil succeeded his father as managing director in 1910. Despite his best efforts Danske Bank could not cope with the strains of WWI and the Depression; the Danish government had to rescue the firm from bankruptcy. But the bank survived German occupation during WWII mostly unscathed.

During the 1960s and 1970s Denmark's government encouraged Danish banks to expand internationally. Danske Bank pounced on the opportunity by forming consortium banks with such Nordic neighbors as Skandinaviska Enskilda Banken (aka S-E-Banken). Danske Bank stayed ahead of its competitors through acquisitions including the purchase of two large Danish banks in 1990 making it Denmark's largest bank.

By 1990 the bank also had made its presence felt worldwide but Asian economic crises in the early 1990s caused the bank's international subsidiaries to fall short of expectations. After restructuring its international business the bank focused more energy on its Nordic customers. It bought Sweden's Ostgota Enskilda in 1998 and Norway's Fokus Bank in 1999. In 2000 Danske bought fellow Danish Bank BG Bank. Danske also added a Finnish asset management company and a majority interest in Pol-Can Bank of Poland in the same year. In 2001 Danske and BG trimmed down redundant branches.

Danske Bank bought the banking operations of Finnish insurer Sampo for more than $5 billion in 2007. The acquisition brought in more than 150 branches in Finland Estonia Latvia and Lithuania. It followed Danske Bank's 2005 acquisitions of National Irish Bank and Northern Bank from National Australia Bank for some $1.8 billion.

EXECUTIVES

Group CEO, Thomas F. Borgen, age 51
Member Executive Board and Head Personal Banking, Tonny Thierry Andersen, age 51
Member Executive Board and Head Business Banking, Lars Stensgaard M¸rch, age 43
Member Executive Board and CFO, Henrik Ramlau-Hansen, age 59
Member Executive Board; Head Corporates and Institutions, Glenn Soderholm, age 51
Member Executive Board; Head Group Services and Group IT (COO), Jim Ditmore
Head of Banking Baltic Region, Ivar Pae
Deputy CFO, Jacob Aarup-Andersen, age 37
Vice Chairman of Board, Trond . Westlie, age 50
Chairman, Ole Gjesso Andersen, age 59
Auditors: Deloitte Statsautoriseret Revisionspartnerselskab

LOCATIONS

HQ: Danske Bank AS (Denmark)
Holmens Kanal 2-12, Copenhagen K DK-1092
Phone: (45) 33 44 00 00 **Fax:** 212 370-9564
Web: www.danskebank.com

PRODUCTS/OPERATIONS

2014 Sales

	% of total
Net Interest	53
Net fees	24
Net trading income	15
Net income from insurance business	3
Other	5
Total	**100**

2014 Sales by Segment

	% of total
Personal Banking	36
Business Banking	29
Corporate & Institutions	20
Danica Pension	7
Danske Capital	5
Other Activities	3
Total	**100**

COMPETITORS

ABN AMRO Group
ABN AMRO Group
Citigroup
Citigroup
Credit Suisse
Credit Suisse
Cr©dit Agricole
Cr©dit Agricole
Deutsche Bank
Deutsche Bank
DnB NOR
DnB NOR
ING
ING
Jyske
Jyske
Nordea Bank
Nordea Bank
SEB AB
SEB AB
Svenska Handelsbanken
Svenska Handelsbanken
UniCredit Bank AG
UniCredit Bank AG

HISTORICAL FINANCIALS

Company Type: Public

Income Statement FYE: December 31

	ASSETS ($ mil.)	NET INCOME ($ mil.)	INCOME AS % OF ASSETS	EMPLOYEES
12/15	480,623	1,826	0.4%	19,049
12/14	563,717	585	0.1%	18,478
12/13	595,590	1,313	0.2%	19,122
12/12	615,733	838	0.1%	20,308
12/11	595,800	297	0.1%	21,320
Annual Growth	(5.2%)	57.4%	—	(2.8%)

2015 Year-End Financials

Return on assets: 0.3%
Return on equity: 7.9%
Long-term debt ($ mil.): —
No. of shares (mil.): 976
Sales ($ mil): 15,876

Dividends
Yield: —
Payout: —
Market value ($ mil.): —

DBS Bank (Hong Kong) Limited

Auditors: PricewaterhouseCoopers

LOCATIONS

HQ: DBS Bank (Hong Kong) Limited
11th Floor, The Center, 99 Queen' s Road Central, Central,
Phone:
Web: www.dbs.com.hk

HISTORICAL FINANCIALS

Company Type: Public

Income Statement FYE: December 31

	ASSETS ($ mil.)	NET INCOME ($ mil.)	INCOME AS % OF ASSETS	EMPLOYEES
12/14	40,416	394	1.0%	0
12/13	39,807	454	1.1%	0
12/12	36,787	416	1.1%	0
12/11	35,928	334	0.9%	0
12/10	31,832	314	1.0%	0
Annual Growth	6.2%	5.8%	—	—

2014 Year-End Financials

Return on assets: 0.9%
Return on equity: 9.5%
Long-term debt ($ mil.): —
No. of shares (mil.): —
Sales ($ mil): 1,361

Dividends
Yield: —
Payout: —
Market value ($ mil.): —

DBS Group Holdings Ltd.

DBS Group is the holding company for DBS Bank the largest bank in Singapore and a significant presence throughout Southeast Asia. DBS Bank offers personal and private banking in addition to commercial banking services to small and midsized companies through some 80 branches in its home country. The company also has around 50 locations in Hong Kong plus operations in China India Indonesia Malaysia The Philippines Taiwan and Thailand. DBS Group owns a 20% stake in the Bank of the Philippine Islands (that country's second-largest bank) as well. Other activities include capital markets brokerage fund management private equity and equipment and trade finance.

DBS intends to continue its expansion in Asia. It has opened new branches in India and Indonesia and was the first Singapore bank to establish a local subsidiary in China. In 2011 the company bought the retail and commercial banking operations of Royal Bank of Scotland in China and plans to more than double its presence in that country by 2013.

In 2012 DBS announced plans to acquire PT Bank Danamon Indonesia. The deal would greatly expand DBS' presence in Indonesia and add about 1400 branches.

In addition to expanding geographically DBS is also placing more emphasis on small and midsized businesses large corporations and affluent consumers. Areas of focus include transaction services treasury and markets and wealth management.

The Singapore government (through Temasek) owns more than a quarter of DBS Group.

EXECUTIVES

Group Executive Institutional Banking Group DBS Bank, Jeanette Wong
CFO, Chng Sok Hui
Managing Director & Head Specialised Corporate and Investment Banking DBS Bank, Elbert Pattijn
CEO, Piyush Gupta, age 55
Managing Director and Head Group Technology and Operations, David Gledhill
Managing Director and Group Head Consumer Banking and Wealth Management, Tan Su Shan, age 47
President Director DBS Indonesia, Paulus Sutisna
Group Executive Singapore Country Head DBS Bank, Sim S Lim
CEO DBS Bank (Hong Kong) Limited, Sebastian Paredes
CEO DBS India, Surojit Shome
Chairman, Peter Seah Lim Huat, age 68
Auditors: PricewaterhouseCoopers LLP

LOCATIONS

HQ: DBS Group Holdings Ltd.
12 Marina Boulevard, Marina Bay Financial Centre Tower 3, 018982
Phone: (65) 6878 8888 **Fax:** 213 627-0228
Web: www.dbs.com

2014 Sales

	% of total
Singapore	62
Hong Kong	19
Rest of the greater China	10
South and Southeast Asia	6
Rest of the world	3
Total	**100**

PRODUCTS/OPERATIONS

2014 Sales

	% of total
Institutional Banking	51
Consumer Banking/wealth management	29
Treasury	11
Others	9
Total	**100**

2014 Sales

	% of total
Interest income	73
Net fee and commission income	16
Net Trading income	7
Net income from investment securities	2
Other income	2
Total	**100**

Selected Subsidiaries

DBS Bank
- Bank of the Philippine Islands (20.3%)
- Cholamandalam DBS Finance Limited (37.4%)
- DBS Asia Capital Limited
- DBS Asset Management Ltd
- DBS Diamond Holdings Ltd
- DBS Bank (Hong Kong) Limited
- Hutchison DBS Card Ltd (50%)
- DBSN Services Pte. Ltd.
- DBS Vickers Securities (Singapore) Pte Ltd
- The Islamic Bank of Asia Limited (50%)
- PT Bank DBS Indonesia (99%)

COMPETITORS

AmBank Group
Amara
Bangkok Bank
Bank Central Asia
Bank Mandiri
Bank Rakyat
Bank of China
HSBC
Hong Leong Finance
Maybank
Maybank Kim Eng
Metropolitan Bank and Trust
OCBC Bank
Standard Chartered
United Overseas Bank

HISTORICAL FINANCIALS

Company Type: Public

Income Statement

FYE: December 31

	ASSETS ($ mil.)	NET INCOME ($ mil.)	INCOME AS % OF ASSETS	EMPLOYEES
12/14	333,543	3,062	0.9%	0
12/13	318,213	2,906	0.9%	0
12/12	288,638	3,114	1.1%	0
12/11	262,255	2,335	0.9%	0
12/10	221,253	1,272	0.6%	0
Annual Growth	10.8%	24.5%	—	—

2014 Year-End Financials

Return on assets: 0.9%
Return on equity: 11.2%
Long-term debt ($ mil.): —
No. of shares (mil.): —
Sales ($ mil): 9,477
Dividends
Yield: 2.8%
Payout: 139.5%
Market value ($ mil.): —

	STOCK PRICE ($) FY Close	P/E High/Low		PER SHARE ($) Earnings	Dividends	Book Value
12/14	62.23	38	29	1.22	1.80	11.54
12/13	54.27	38	30	1.17	1.73	11.09
12/12	49.06	31	24	1.28	1.74	10.66
12/11	35.42	37	26	0.97	1.62	9.47
12/10	44.94	70	59	0.53	1.62	9.01
Annual Growth	8.5%	—	—	23.1%	2.6%	6.4%

Dekabank Deutsche Girozentrale

Savings institutions except federal nsk

EXECUTIVES

Chief Executive Officer, Michael R diger
Auditors: KPMG AG Wirtschaftspruefungsgesellschaft

LOCATIONS

HQ: Dekabank Deutsche Girozentrale
Mainzer Landstrasse 16, Frankfurt 60325
Phone: (49) 69 7147 0 **Fax:** (49) 69 7147 1376
Web: www.dekabank.de

HISTORICAL FINANCIALS

Company Type: Public

Income Statement

FYE: December 31

	ASSETS ($ mil.)	NET INCOME ($ mil.)	INCOME AS % OF ASSETS	EMPLOYEES
12/14	137,564	674	0.5%	4,183
12/13	159,801	407	0.3%	4,035
12/12	171,009	375	0.2%	4,040
12/11	172,983	337	0.2%	3,957
12/10	174,395	866	0.5%	3,683
Annual Growth	(5.8%)	(6.1%)		3.2%

2014 Year-End Financials

Return on assets: 0.4%
Return on equity: 13.2%
Long-term debt ($ mil.): —
No. of shares (mil.): 191
Sales ($ mil): 4,716
Dividends
Yield: —
Payout: —
Market value ($ mil.): —

Denso Corp. (Japan)

DENSO knows: When building cars the whole is very little without its parts. Among the world's largest automotive parts manufacturers DENSO supplies OEM and aftermarket components and systems for most of the world's carmakers. Its six product groups make systems for powertrain control information and safety electric electronic small motors and thermal systems. Its lines range from automotive air conditioning systems to radiators and spark plugs. The Information and Safety Systems arm develops car navigation and collision avoidance systems. Non-auto industrial systems and consumer products are also made; subsidiary DENSO WAVE makes bar code readers industrial robots and programmable logic controllers.

DENSO's holistic perspective is demonstrated in all aspects of its automotive business from product development and design to manufacturing and sales. The company touts collaborative efforts with local car manufacturers and suppliers that support each customer's specific regional requirements. Although the company has a global presence with more than 185 subsidiaries and operations in 35 countries more than half of its sales depend on Japanese manufacturers. US operations are overseen by DENSO International America which accounted for 14% of sales in fiscal 2011.

DENSO was spun off from Toyota Motor Corporation in 1949; its former parent remains the largest shareholder owning a 25% stake. Toyota Industries Corporation owns almost 9% while an affiliate of German auto parts giant Robert Bosch owns another 6%. Toyota Motor Corporation is also its largest customer accounting for about 30% of sales in 2011.

Like other auto parts manufacturers DENSO is looking to expand in emerging markets in Brazil China and India. It built a new plant for car air conditioners in Changchun a city in northeast China that is also home to the China FAW Group. The plant will supply AC units to Toyota and Volkswagen models built by China FAW and is expected to open by 2013. It also expanded its car air conditioner and radiator plant in Brazil to increase production capacity and established a joint venture with Indian air conditioning company Subros. It introduced four low-cost heat exchangers for the Indian market. Elsewhere DENSO bought CTR an Italian company that sells air conditioners to aftermarket customers and opened its first sales office in Dubai for customers in the Middle East and North Africa.

With international operations representing about a quarter of overall sales the company is pinning its future growth foremost on product research and development to boost fuel efficiency and reduce carbon dioxide emissions. New products include engines for hybrid and electric vehicles. DENSO is working on cutting costs and improving performance in key products such as inverters DC-DC converters battery monitoring units and electric compressors. It is also developing new products such as battery packs that integrate motor generators batteries battery monitoring units and cooling fans. Its intelligent sensing monitoring and navigation technologies are advancing too with components that promise to help reduce car accidents.

Cost-control measures are playing an equally dominant role in DENSO's operations. The company is shifting its concentration from products for mature markets and premium vehicles to producing low-cost lines that cater to rising demand in developing markets particularly for compact cars which are common in Asia. Business systems at DENSO are evolving as well; more projects are addressed on an interdepartmental basis allowing resources to be pooled and leveraged. The company set a goal to halve the manufacturing costs of 23 key products sold in emerging markets by buying local parts and materials. For fiscal 2011 DENSO managed to cut costs by 40%.

HISTORY

Originally the in-house parts supplier for Toyota Nippondenso Co. (the predecessor to DENSO) was spun off by Toyota in 1949 because Toyota no longer wanted the burden of Nippondenso's troubled financial performance. Nippondenso remained dependent upon Toyota for sales and members of Toyota's controlling family the Toyodas remained involved in management. Nippondenso established a technological partnership with Germany's Robert Bosch in 1953.

As part of its plan to become a major supplier to North American carmakers in 1966 Nippondenso established a sales office in Chicago and branch offices in Los Angeles and Detroit. It then turned to Europe establishing a branch office in Stuttgart Germany in 1970. The following year the company established its first overseas subsidiary Nippondenso of Los Angeles (now DENSO Sales California). In 1972 the company established three more foreign subsidiaries in Australia Canada and Thailand. A European subsidiary (now DENSO Europe) was established in the Netherlands in 1973.

Nippondenso began consignment production for what is now known as Asmo Co. a maker of electric motors in 1978. In 1984 the company joined with Allen Bradley Co. (US) to develop factory automation equipment. That year the predecessor to DENSO Manufacturing Michigan one of the company's largest international subsidiaries was established. Nippondenso expanded into Spain in 1989 by opening a plant in Barcelona.

In 1990 the company formed NDM Manufacturing (now DENSO Manufacturing UK) a joint venture (25%-owned) with Magneti Marelli of Italy for the manufacture of automotive air conditioning and heating systems. The following year Nippondenso and AT&T formed a joint venture for the development of integrated circuit (IC) cards.

Nippondenso established several Chinese manufacturing joint ventures during the mid-1990s. In 1994 the company was recognized by the Guinness Book of Records as the maker of the world's smallest car the DENSO Micro Car.

The company changed its name to DENSO CORPORATION in 1996. In 1999 it acquired the rotating machines business of Magneti Marelli. The next year DENSO agreed to buy out Magneti Marelli's share in the companies' automotive air conditioning and heating joint venture (the deal was completed in 2001).

In 2001 DENSO ceased production of wireless phones in order to focus on making onboard car information systems. Also in 2001 the company merged its industrial equipment subsidiaries (bar code scanners and factory automation robots) and spun them off as majority-owned subsidiary DENSO Wave.

DENSO joined forces with Robert Bosch GmbH in 2003 to form a joint venture for the development of car navigation and multimedia systems.

In 2006 DENSO added four new Chinese production facilities that make navigation systems air conditioner compressors instrument panels and oil filters. It has also established technical centers in China and Thailand.

EXECUTIVES

EVP, Masahiko Miyaki
EVP, Haruya Maruyama
EVP, Yasushi Yamanaka
President and CEO, Koji Arima
CEO North America Thermal Systems Center, Steve Milam
President DENSO Manufacturing Canada, Rich van Oorschot
EVP, Koji Kobayashi
Chairman, Nobuaki Katoh
Auditors: Deloitte Touche Tohmatsu LLC

LOCATIONS

HQ: Denso Corp. (Japan)
1-1 Showa-cho, Kariya, Aichi 448-8661
Phone: (81) 566 25 5850 **Fax:** (81) 566 25 4913
Web: www.denso.co.jp

2011 Sales

	% of total
Japan	56
Rest of Asia	17
North America	14
Europe	11
Other	2
Total	**100**

PRODUCTS/OPERATIONS

2011 Sales

	% of total
Automotive	
Thermal systems	31
Powertrain control systems	25
Information & safety systems	17
Electronic systems	9
Electric systems	9
Small motors	7
Industrial systems & consumer products	1
Total	**100**

Selected Products

Automotive
- Thermal systems
- Air conditioning systems
- Air purifiers
- Cooling fans
- Cooling modules
- Front end modules
- Oil coolers
- Radiators
- Truck refrigeration units
- Powertrain control systems
- Diesel engine management systems
- Gasoline engine management systems
- Transmission control components
- Information and safety systems
- Multi-information display
- Radar system for detecting obstacles in front of vehicle
- Remote touch controller
- Electronic systems
- Car security systems
- Instrument clusters
- Integrated climate control panels
- Rear and corner sonars
- Remote keyless entry controllers
- Smart keys
- Electric systems
- ABS actuators
- Airbag sensors
- Alternators
- Electric power steering motors
- Starters
- Small motors
- Power window motors
- Windshield washer systems
- Windshield wiper systems

Industrial and Consumer
- Bar code readers
- Industrial robots
- Programmable logic controllers

COMPETITORS

APM Automotive
Adept Technology
Aisin Seiki
Delphi Automotive Systems
Garmin
JTEKT
Johnson Controls
KUKA
Key Safety Systems
NGK SPARK PLUG
Prestolite Electric
Remy International
Robert Bosch
Standard Motor Products
Valeo
Visteon
Yazaki
ZF TRW Automotive

HISTORICAL FINANCIALS

Company Type: Public

Income Statement

FYE: March 31

	REVENUE ($ mil.)	NET INCOME ($ mil.)	NET PROFIT MARGIN	EMPLOYEES
03/15	35,921	2,153	6.0%	176,297
03/14	39,672	2,685	6.8%	167,139
03/13	38,057	1,930	5.1%	132,276
03/12	38,456	1,088	2.8%	126,036
03/11	37,816	1,727	4.6%	123,165
Annual Growth	(1.3%)	5.7%	—	9.4%

2015 Year-End Financials

Debt ratio: 0.0%
Return on equity: 8.4%
Cash ($ mil.): 6,604
Current ratio: 2.27
Long-term debt ($ mil.): 2,902
No. of shares (mil.): 797
Dividends
Yield: 2.1%
Payout: 16.2%
Market value ($ mil.): 18,242

	STOCK PRICE ($) FY Close	P/E High/Low		PER SHARE ($) Earnings	Dividends	Book Value
03/15	22.87	0	0	2.70	0.48	34.78
03/14	23.99	0	0	3.37	0.42	34.03
03/13	21.24	—	—	2.41	0.00	32.43
03/12	16.82	—	—	1.35	0.00	32.03
03/11	16.45	—	—	2.14	0.21	31.06
Annual Growth	8.6%	—	—	5.9%	23.3%	2.9%

Deutsche Bahn AG

One of Europe's largest transportation providers Deutsche Bahn gets freight and passengers from Punkt A to Punkt B. The company's DB Mobility Logistics group encompasses logistics and rail operations. About half of the company's sales come from freight transport and logistics led by Schenker AG. Its railway division carries 2.2-plus billion passengers yearly throughout Germany and into neighboring countries over a network of about 34000 km of track. Deutsche Bahn operates bus services in Germany and holds interests in passenger rail franchises dotting Europe. It also manage train stations and infrastructure services. State-owned Deutsche Bahn operates a handful of offices around the world.

Geographic Reach

By far the company's largest geographical segment is Germany representing 58% of total sales. Other European countries account for 31% while other major markets include the Asia/Pacific (6%) and North America (4%).

Mergers and Acquisitions

Deutsche Bahn often grows though the use of acquisitions. In 2013 its DB Schenker subsidiary purchased the assets of its long-standing partner Euro-Line Panamericana in Panama thereby expanding its network in one of the growth markets within Central America.

HISTORY

In 1989 the Federal Cabinet of West Germany adopted a resolution to set up an independent government railway commission. That year the wall between East Germany and West Germany came down and the two nations were united into the Federal Republic of Germany in 1990.

In 1993 the cabinet endorsed a railway reform plan submitted by the federal minister of transport and later that year the plan won approval from the German Parliament and the Federal Council. Deutsche Bahn was then established in 1994 to unify Germany's western (Deutsche Bundesbahn) and eastern (Deutsche Reichsbahn) railway systems as a public company. The Federal Republic of Germany was sole shareholder.

The next year Deutsche Bahn created a subsidiary DBKom to offer telecom services in competition with Deutsche Telekom. In 1996 a consortium led by German conglomerate Mannesmann bought a 50% stake in DBKom. By 1997 Deutsche Bahn had been transformed from a government department into a registered company and split into four operating units: tracks freight local passenger services and intercity passenger services. That year Deutsche Bahn also bought Lufthansa's 33% stake in tour operator Deutsches Reiseb ro (DER) giving it full ownership of the company as well as DER's 20% stake in tour group TUI.

Trouble came in 1998: Deutsche Bahn sent its 59 first-generation high-speed InterCityExpress (ICE) trains for inspections after one of the trains crashed and killed 98 passengers. Investigators believed a broken wheel caused the crash.

Deutsche Bahn and French state-owned railway SNCF announced plans in 1999 to develop a high-speed train capable of traveling up to 320 km (198 miles) per hour. Also that year Hartmut Mehdorn credited with turning around printing equipment manufacturer Heidelberger Druck and Daimler-Chrysler's aerospace unit became Deutsche Bahn's new CEO. Tasked with improving the railway's punctuality Mehdorn pledged to make Deutsche Bahn more efficient by cutting losses and raising productivity. That year the company sold its stake in TUI to conglomerate Preussag and its DER unit to supermarket giant Rewe.

In 2000 the company's DB Cargo unit and Dutch rail freight company N.S. Cargo formed a new group Railion (joined by Danish State Railways' freight unit DSB Gods in 2001). Also in 2000 Germany's transport minister postponed plans to float Deutsche Bahn after it posted losses for the first time since 1994.

Hoping to take advantage of Deutsche Bahn's financial troubles Connex then a subsidiary of French conglomerate Vivendi offered in 2001 to acquire Deutsche Bahn's long-distance express passenger trains. But Mehdorn refused the offer saying the company did not want to give up its long-distance traffic. Deutsche Bahn did agree in 2001 to form a railway telematics (communications system) joint venture with Mannesmann Arcor a company controlled by Vodafone. The agreement called for Deutsche Bahn to keep its 18% stake in Arcor but lose its minority veto rights which Deutsche Bahn had used earlier that year to block an Arcor IPO.

The company in 2002 bought the 65% stake in logistics provider Stinnes held by E.ON. The next year Deutsche Bahn took full ownership of Stinnes.

In 2004 Deutsche Bahn partnered with two UK companies Stagecoach Group and Virgin Group to bid on UK rail franchises. Deutsche Bahn withdrew from the venture before the bidding got very far however.

Deutsche Bahn sold its 83% stake in bus unit Deutsche Touring GmbH to Eurosur SA of Spain for an undisclosed amount in 2005.

Deutsche Bahn enhanced its logistics business in 2006 by acquiring US-based freight forwarder BAX Global. Buying BAX Global expanded Deutsche Bahn's logistics network in the Americas as well as the Asia/Pacific region positioning the company to benefit from Asian and transpacific trade.

Deutsche Bahn began expanding its passenger transportation business into the UK in 2007 by purchasing English Welsh & Scottish Railway (now DB Schenker Rail UK). In 2008 it acquired Laing Rail from construction firm John Laing. The company gained interests in three rail operations including full ownership of Chiltern Railways which operates the main artery between London and Birmingham. It rebranded it DB Schenker Rail UK.

Raising cash through privatization has been a long-held goal for Deutsche Bahn. In preparation for an IPO the company's passenger and freight transportation and logistics businesses were spun off as DB Mobility Logistics in 2008. (The split comprised almost all former operations; DB Mobility Logistics accounts for more than 90% of Deutsche Bahn's revenue.) Plans called for just under 25% of DB Mobility Logistics to be sold to the public while parent Deutsche Bahn –and thus the German government –would maintain a controlling stake. However the IPO was halted due to the international financial crisis. The business climate worsened in 2009; Deutsche Bahn's operating profit plummeted by more than 70% from 2008 levels pressured by declining revenues of about 13%.

In addition Deutsche Bahn in 2008 acquired a majority stake in Spanish logistics company Transportes Ferroviarios Especiales (Transfesa) which specializes in arranging the transportation of freight by rail and by road. The deal bolstered Deutsche Bahn's presence in Western Europe and the Iberian Peninsula. The company has also moved to extend its rail freight operations which are conducted primarily under the DB Schenker Rail brand.

In May 2009 R diger Grube took over as chairman of the company's management board and CEO replacing Hartmut Mehdorn. Grube has served on the boards of Daimler and Airbus. Grube's arrival fell on the heels of accusations that Deutsche Bahn management spied on its employees tarnishing the company's image among employees stakeholders and the general public.

With plans to capitalize on the liberalization of the European transportation industry Deutsche Bahn paid around 2.8 billion (approximately $3.7 billion) in 2010 to buy Arriva one of the UK's largest bus and rail operators. European antitrust laws however are dashing Deutsche Bahn's hopes and forcing it to divest Arriva's German bus and rail business along with other German activities. Late in the year Deutsche Bahn agreed to sell the bus and rail unit to Italy's national railway company Trenitalia (a division of Ferrovie dello Stato) to comply with European Union law.

EXECUTIVES

Member Management Board; Infrastructure and Services, Volker Kefer, age 60
Member Management Board; Finance and Controlling, Richard Lutz, age 51
Chairman and CEO, R diger Grube, age 64
Member Management Board; Human Resources, Ulrich Weber, age 65
Member Management Board; Compliance Privacy Legal Affairs and Corp. Security, Gerd Becht, age 63
Member Management Board; Technology and Environment, Heike Hanagarth, age 56
Chairman Supervisory Board, Utz-Hellmuth Felcht
Auditors: PricewaterhouseCoopers Aktiengesellschaft Wirtschaftspruefungsgesellschaft

LOCATIONS

HQ: Deutsche Bahn AG
Potsdamer Platz 2, Berlin 10785
Phone: (49) 30 297 61030 **Fax:** (49) 30 297 61919
Web: www.deutschebahn.com

2013 Sales

	% of total
Europe	
Germany	58
Other countries	31
Asia/Pacific	6
North America	4
Other regions	1
Total	**100**

PRODUCTS/OPERATIONS

2013 Sales

	% of total
Transport & logistics	49
Passenger transport	43
Infrastructure	6
Other	2
Total	**100**

COMPETITORS

Air Berlin
Air France
British Airways
DHL
Expeditors
FedEx
Geodis
KLM Royal Dutch Airlines
Kuehne + Nagel International
Lufthansa
National Express Group
Panalpina
SNCF
UPS Supply Chain Solutions
Veolia Environnement

HISTORICAL FINANCIALS

Company Type: Public

Income Statement FYE: December 31

	REVENUE ($ mil.)	NET INCOME ($ mil.)	NET PROFIT MARGIN	EMPLOYEES
12/14	51,564	1,174	2.3%	295,763
12/13	57,486	904	1.6%	295,653
12/12	55,239	1,938	3.5%	299,005
12/11	52,302	1,706	3.3%	294,733
12/10	49,007	1,390	2.8%	285,977
Annual Growth	1.3%	(4.1%)	—	0.8%

2014 Year-End Financials

Debt ratio: 44.2%	No. of shares (mil.): 430
Return on equity: 6.6%	Dividends
Cash ($ mil.): 4,899	Yield: —
Current ratio: 0.81	Payout: —
Long-term debt ($ mil.): 23,304	Market value ($ mil.): —

Deutsche Bank AG

Deutsche Bank AG is one of the top financial groups in the world and the largest bank in Germany where it operates about 1845 retail branch locations. It has another 1000 branches in more than 70 countries in Europe the Americas Asia the Pacific Rim and Africa. Deutsche Bank's Corporate Banking & Securities division is its largest business while the Private & Business Clients segment is the next largest. The company's massive Deutsche Asset Management subsidiary which includes US-based companies Deutsche Bank Securities RREEF and DWS Investments serves private and institutional clients and boasts some 711 billion (some $804.8 billion) in assets under management.

OperationsDeutsche Bank operates through five main segments. Corporate Banking & Securities (CB&S) which makes up 40% of the company's total revenue is made up of the company's global Corporate Finance and Markets businesses which offer financial products such as underwriting of stocks and bonds trading services for investors and other company-tailored financial services.The Private & Business Clients (PBC) segment brings in another 30% of revenue and is made up of all private and commercial banking operations under: the Deutsche Bank brand (in Germany); Advisory Banking International (in the rest of Europe); and under its joint-venture with Hua Xia Bank and Postbank which includes Postbank norisbank and BHW (in Asia).Global Transaction Banking (GTB) which makes up roughly 15% of revenue provides commercial banking products and services to corporate clients and financial institutions such as domestic and cross-border payments international trade financing and lending. It also offers provision of trust agency depositary custody and related services.Its Deutsche Asset & Wealth Management (Deutsche AWM) division generates another 15% of overall revenue. Its asset management arm offers traditional active passive and alternative investments spanning all major asset classes to individuals and institutions worldwide. The division also offers wealth management and private banking services to high-net-worth and ultra-high-net-worth (UHNW) individuals and family offices.The Non-Core Operations Unit (NCOU) which makes up roughly 1% of revenue operates alongside Deutsche Bank's core businesses and is designed to highlight the company's non-core positions for management-led risk decisions.Geographic ReachDeutsche Bank operates worldwide through nearly 2815 branches with two-thirds of those in Germany. Roughly 35% of revenue comes from Germany while the Americas generate another 25%. The UK is the next largest market generating 15%. Other large markets include the Asia Pacific region (more than 10% of revenue) the rest of Europe the Middle East and Africa.Sales and MarketingThe bank serves both corporate clients and individuals. It spent 313 million on advertising in 2014 down from 314 million in 2013 and 362 million in 2012.Financial PerformanceNote: Growth rates may differ after conversion to US dollars.Deutsche Bank's revenue has trended downward in recent years. Revenue in 2014 fell to 42.67 billion ($51.88 billion) mostly due to lower interest income from the NCOU division as the bank sold off some of its riskier assets as part of a long-term de-risking initiative. Its CB&S division grew by 9% however thanks to better trading conditions in the bond market compared to a tough 2013 and favorable trading conditions in the equity derivatives market.Despite falling revenue in 2014 profit rose for a second year with net income more than doubling to 1.69 billion ($2.02 billion). The profit boost was mostly driven by the de-risking activities during the year which reduced credit loss provisions by 931 million ($1.13 billion). The bank's general and administrative expenses also fell by 472 million ($573.71 million) mostly thanks to lower litigation costs as well as savings from its Operational Excellence (OpEx) program.

Cash levels fell in 2014 with operations using 630 million ($765.76 million). The drop was mostly because the bank had less inflow from interest-earning time deposits from its bank subsidiaries and other banks.

Stategy

Deutsche Bank has taken a number of cost-cutting and growth initiative measures in recent years to turn around its multi-year revenue decline. In 2014 for example the bank invested 4 billion (roughly $4.8 billion) into its Operational Excellence (OpEx) program which was designed to increase quality and flexibility as well as reinforce controls and establish a cost-efficiency culture in the bank. With plans to achieve 4.5 billion (around $5.1 billion) in annual cost savings by 2015's end the program saved a cumulative 3.3 billion ($4 billion) by the end of 2014 ahead of target.Part of this cost-cutting plan has included investments in technology to streamline operations and transition away from costly brick-and-mortar banking. In early 2015 the company partnered with Hewlett-Packard in a 10-year multi-billion agreement to modernize its global information technology (IT) operations and significantly cut IT infrastructure costs by having HP provide on-demand data center services for the bank including storage platform and hosting. In mid-2014 the company invested 200 million ($272 million) toward its mobile and web-based banking options to allow its retail clients access to more services typically offered through its branches. The bank has also been leveraging its wide variety of services through its different divisions to add new customers and grow business with existing customers. In 2014 for example the bank cross-sold between its CB&S and GTB divisions to better serve multinational corporations in the US helping it obtain 66 new clients over the year.

Company Background

Hoping to take advantage of China's growing economy the bank established an outpost there in 2008. It also built up its stake in the China-based mutual fund manager Harvest Fund and in 2009 became the largest single shareholder in Hua Xia Bank (with a 19.99% stake the maximum allowed for a foreign investor).

HISTORY

Company BackgroundGeorg von Siemens opened Deutsche Bank in Berlin in 1870. Three years later the firm opened an office in London and was soon buying other German banks. In the late 1800s Deutsche Bank helped finance Germany's electrification (carried out by Siemens AG) and railroad construction in the US and the Ottoman Empire. Von Siemens ran the bank until his death in 1901.

The bank survived post-WWI financial chaos by merging with Disconto-Gesellschaft and later helped finance the Nazi war machine. After the war the Allies split the company into 10 banks; it became extinct in Soviet-controlled East Germany.

The bank was reassembled in 1957 and primarily engaged in commercial banking often taking direct interests in its customers. It added retail services in the 1960s. In 1975 to prevent the Shah of Iran from gaining a stake in Daimler-Benz (now Daimler) the bank bought 29% of that company.

The firm opened an investment banking office in the US in 1971 and a branch office in 1978. In the 1980s it expanded geographically buying Bank of America's Italian subsidiary (1986) and UK merchant bank Morgan Grenfell (1989); it also moved into insurance creating life insurer DB Leben (1989).

Terrorists killed chairman Alfred Herrhausen a symbol of German big business in 1989. After German reunification in 1990 successor Hilmar Kopper oversaw the bank's reestablishment in eastern Germany.

In 1994 Deutsche Bank bought most of ITT's commercial finance unit. That year the company suffered scandal when real estate developer Jurgen Schneider borrowed more than DM1 billion and disappeared; he was later found and returned to Germany.

The company grew its global investment banking operations in 1995 under its Morgan Grenfell subsidiary. Corporate culture clashes prompted Deutsche Bank to take greater control of the unit and restructure it in 1998.

Deutsche Bank's global aspirations suffered a setback in 1998 when losses on investments in Russia trimmed its bottom line. Still trying to put WWII behind it the bank accepted responsibility for its wartime dealing in gold seized from Jews but has rejected liability to compensate victims of Nazi forced labor who toiled in industrial companies in which it holds stakes.

In 1999 the bank acquired Bankers Trust. Despite a decision to divest its industrial portfolio that year the company bought Tele Columbus the #2 cable network in Germany and Piaggio the Italian maker of the famed Vespa motor scooter. On the banking front Deutsche Bank bought Chase Manhattan's Dutch auction business and sought a foothold in Japan through alliances with Nippon Life Insurance and Sakura Bank (now part of Sumitomo Mitsui Banking).

In 2000 the company agreed to merge with Dresdner Bank (after which they would spin off their retail banking businesses) but the merger collapsed in part over the fate of investment banking subsidiary Dresdner Kleinwort Benson. German mega-insurer Allianz bought Dresdner in 2001. Deutsche Bank's reorganization plans the same year saw the bank eliminate 2600 jobs worldwide and realign its businesses into two divisions. Deutsche Bank also bought Banque Worms from French insurer AXA.

Looking for a steady supply of cash in 2001 Deutsche Bank's Morgan Grenfall Private Equity bought 3000 English pubs owned by UK-based conglomerate Whitbread plc. In 2002 more shuffling of the executive board members allowed

Deutsche Bank to grow in the international Anglo-American style rather than as a domestic player.

In 2004 Deutsche Bank acquired Berkshire Mortgage (now Deutsche Bank Berkshire Mortgage) one of the top multifamily residential lenders in the US. The next year it bought Russian financial services company United Financial Group and combined its depositary business with its own.

The year 2006 was a bad year for the company from a public relations standpoint. Fallout from former chairman Rolf Breuer's remarks regarding the financial stability of banking client Kirch Holding led to a shake-up in the executive suite and the board that year. Later UK financial regulators charged the bank an $11.1 million fine for market misconduct related to trading activity in 2004. In the US the IRS investigated the bank for alleged abusive tax shelters.

The bank also took a public relations hit when its CEO Josef Ackermann went on trial for illegal bonuses during his tenure at Mannesmann.

To boost its lending operations in the US the company bought MortgageIT a real estate investment trust for some 285 million ($430 million) in 2007. The timing wasn't great: the subsidiary suffered a major loss a victim of the US subprime mortgage crisis. Also that year Deutsche Bank acquired Abbey Life from Lloyds Banking Group for some 1 billion ($2 billion.) This acquisition fared better than MortgageIT finishing out the year in the black.

Deutsche Bank's expansion was slowed in 2008 when its proposed acquisition of some of ABN AMRO's assets –including corporate and commercial units parts of Hollandische Bank Unie and a factoring company –from Fortis was canceled.

On the heels of a global expansion which began in earnest in 2002 Deutsche Bank was hit hard by the worldwide financial crisis. The company reported a fourth-quarter loss of 4.8 billion in 2008 largely due to declines in its trading and asset management businesses. Its Americas business primarily the US operations was hit the hardest by far.

But in 2009 Deutsche Bank's growth seemed to pick back up again as it acquired Dresdner Bank's global agency securities lending business from Commerzbank. The business was merged with Deutsche's trust and securities services unit. The deal expanded Deutsche Bank's custody platform.

EXECUTIVES

Head of Global Banking Division and Global Transaction Banking, J rgen Fitschen, age 67, $600,000 total compensation
CFO, Marcus Schenck, age 50
Co-CEO, John Cryan, age 55
CIO and Head of Operations Corporate and Investment Banking, Pascal Boillat
Chief Risk Officer, Stuart Lewis
COO, Kim Hammonds
Global Head Equities Trading; Head Equities EMEA, Rick Saunders
COO Global Equities Trading, Leonie Ryan
Head Global Markets, Garth Ritchie
Chairman, Paul Achleitner, age 59
Deputy Chairman, Alfred Herling, age 62
Auditors: KPMG AG

LOCATIONS

HQ: Deutsche Bank AG
Taunusanlage 12, Frankfurt am Main D-60325
Phone: (49) 69 910 00 **Fax:** (49) 69 910 34 225
Web: www.deutsche-bank.com

2014 Net Sales

	% of total
Europe Middle East & Africa	
Germany	34
UK	15
Other countries	14
Americas	25
Asia/Pacific	12
Total	**100**

PRODUCTS/OPERATIONS

2014 Sales

	% of total
Interest	
Loans & others	36
Financial assets at fair value through profit or loss	23
Noninterest	
Commission & fee income	29
Other	12
Total	**100**

2014 Sales

	% of total
Corporate Banking & Securities	42
Private & Business Clients	29
Deutsche Asset & Wealthmanagement	15
Global Transaction Banking	13
Non-Core Operations Unit	1
Total	**100**

COMPETITORS

BNP Paribas
Barclays
Citigroup
Citigroup Global Markets
Commerzbank
Cortal Consors
Credit Suisse
Goldman Sachs
Grupo Santander
HSBC
JPMorgan Chase
KfW
Landesbank Berlin
Merrill Lynch
Mizuho Financial
Morgan Stanley
National Australia Bank
Rabobank Group
Soci©t© G©n©rale
TD Bank
UBS
UniCredit Bank AG

HISTORICAL FINANCIALS

Company Type: Public

Income Statement FYE: December 31

	ASSETS ($ mil.)	NET INCOME ($ mil.)	INCOME AS % OF ASSETS	EMPLOYEES
12/14	2,076,936	2,021	0.1%	98,138
12/13	2,218,471	916	0.0%	98,254
12/12	2,652,349	312	0.0%	98,219
12/11	2,799,163	5,344	0.2%	100,996
12/10	2,550,442	3,091	0.1%	102,602
Annual Growth	(5.0%)	(10.1%)	—	(1.1%)

2014 Year-End Financials

Return on assets: 0.1%
Return on equity: 2.6%
Long-term debt ($ mil.): —
No. of shares (mil.): 1,379
Sales ($ mil): 51,875
Dividends
Yield: 2.5%
Payout: 1,071.4%
Market value ($ mil.): —

Deutsche Bundesbank (Germany, Fed. Rep.)

Deutsche Bundesbank is not your local burg's bank. The central bank of Germany Deutsche Bundesbank is a major part of the European System of Central Banks (ESCB). Deutsche Bundesbank supervises the German banking system manages the country's monetary supply collects and publishes economic statistics advises the German government on monetary policy and settles cross-border euro transactions. With the ESCB it participates in monetary decisions for the European Union. Deutsche Bundesbank has nine regional offices that operate 35 branches throughout Germany.

OperationsThe bank generated 75% of its total revenue from interest income (mostly on the euro and foreign currencies) during 2014 while fee and commission income made up just 1%. Income from participating interest in the ECB the BIS and Liquiditats-Konsortia Bank (which was in liquidation) made up another 9% of the bank's total revenue while the rest came from realized gains from financial operations (9%) net result arising from allocation of monetary income (4%) and other income (2%). Geographic ReachFrankfurt-based Deutsche Bundesbank has a regional office in nine German cities including Berlin Düsseldorf Frankfurt am Main Hamburg Hanover Leipzig Mainz Munich and Stuttgart.Financial PerformanceNote: Growth rates may differ after conversion to US dollars. This analysis uses financials from the company's annual report. Deutsche Bundesbank's annual revenues have been declining over the past few years as low interest rates (and interest rate cuts) have eaten into its euro-based revenue.The bank's revenue fell 37% to 5.38 billion ($6.54 billion) during 2014 mostly as lower key interest rates and a decline in Eurosystem-relevent balance sheet items caused its interest income on the euro to be cut nearly in half half. Key interest rates were just over two-thirds lower on an annual average. Falling revenue in 2014 coupled with moderately rising staff costs caused Deutsche's net income to tumble 36% to 2.95 billion ($3.59 billion) for the year. StrategyDeutsche Bundesbank and the European Central Bank (ECB) have been cutting interest rates to spur economic growth in Germany and Europe in recent years. Indeed in December 2015 the ECB said it looked to reduce deposit interest rates at commercial banks from minus 0.2 percent to minus 0.3 percent which was intended to help bank lend more cash instead of leaving it at the central bank.The bank has also becoming more digitized along with the rest of the banking industry to save on operating costs. It's reduced its branch count from a peak of 202 in 1991 to 61 branches in 2006 and has ultimately settled to 35 branches today (as of early 2016).

EXECUTIVES

Member Executive Board Information Technology and Markets, Hans-Helmut Kotz
Chairman Executive Board and President, Jens Weidmann, age 47
Auditors: Ernst & Young GmbH

LOCATIONS

HQ: Deutsche Bundesbank (Germany, Fed. Rep.)
Wilhelm-Epstein-Strasse 14, Frankfurt am Main D-60431
Phone: (49) 69 9566 0 **Fax:** (49) 69 9566 3077
Web: www.bundesbank.de

PRODUCTS/OPERATIONS

2014 Sales

	% of total
Interest Income	75
Realized gain/losses arising from financial operations	9
Income from fees and commissions	1
Income from Participating interest	9
Net result arising from allocation of monetary income	4
Other income	2
Total	**100**

COMPETITORS

Bank of England
Federal Reserve
Reserve Bank of Australia

HISTORICAL FINANCIALS

Company Type: Public

Income Statement FYE: December 31

	ASSETS ($ mil.)	NET INCOME ($ mil.)	INCOME AS % OF ASSETS	EMPLOYEES
12/14	936,962	3,590	0.4%	10,858
12/13	1,102,810	6,320	0.6%	10,822
12/12	1,351,404	875	0.1%	10,825
12/11	1,083,451	831	0.1%	9,743
12/10	898,394	2,952	0.3%	9,560
Annual Growth	1.1%	5.0%	—	3.2%

2014 Year-End Financials

Return on assets: 0.3%
Return on equity: 2.8%
Long-term debt ($ mil.): —
No. of shares (mil.): —
Sales ($ mil): 5,949
Dividends
Yield: —
Payout: —
Market value ($ mil.): —

Deutsche Genossenschafts-Hypothekenbank (Germany, Fed. Rep.)

Commercial banks not chartered

EXECUTIVES

Vorstandsvorsitzender, Frank Westhoff
Auditors: Ernst & Young GmbH

LOCATIONS

HQ: Deutsche Genossenschafts-Hypothekenbank (Germany, Fed. Rep.)
Rosenstrasse 2, P.O. Box 10 14 46, Hamburg D-20095
Phone: (49) 40 33 34 0 **Fax:** (49) 40 33 34 11 11
Web: www.dghyp.de

HISTORICAL FINANCIALS

Company Type: Public

Income Statement FYE: December 31

	ASSETS ($ mil.)	NET INCOME ($ mil.)	INCOME AS % OF ASSETS	EMPLOYEES
12/14	52,159	0	—	449
12/13	68,445	0	—	438
12/12	71,659	0	—	372
12/11	75,041	0	—	433
12/10	84,910	0	—	454
Annual Growth	(11.5%)	—	—	(0.3%)

Deutsche Lufthansa AG (Germany, Fed. Rep.)

Germany's air ambassador Deutsche Lufthansa rivals the world's largest airlines. Operating through some 540 subsidiaries and affiliated companies the global aviation group runs Europe's largest passenger airline. Lufthansa Passenger Airlines operates a global route network of 235 destinations in 78 countries with a fleet of more than 400 aircraft. Its logistics segment is also a market leader in international airfreight transportation through Lufthansa Cargo. The group's other main business segments deal in maintenance repair and overhaul (MRO) services through Lufthansa Technik; airline catering services through LSG Sky Chefs; and IT services through Lufthansa Systems.

Geographic Reach

The company's largest market is still Europe including the former CIS states. This region accounted for 67% of revenue in 2014.

Operations

Lufthansa's passenger airline business segment consists of Lufthansa (which includes Lufthansa Regional and Lufthansa Italia) Austrian Airlines SWISS and Germanwings as well as equity stakes in Brussels Airlines JetBlue and SunExpress. The company is considered to be a leading European premium carrier with hubs in Brussels Frankfurt Munich Vienna and Zurich.

The company is also a member of the Star Alliance a group of 27 member airlines and counting that together cover more than 1100 destinations across the globe and of Atlantic++ the largest transatlantic joint venture which was founded by Lufthansa Air Canada Continental Airlines and United Air Lines. With about 280 daily transatlantic flights Atlantic++ establishes a route network to North America from Europe the Middle East and Africa.

Lufthansa Cargo one of the largest cargo airlines in the world is seeing a dramatic earnings turnaround due to the recovering global economy and a boom in German exports. The Asia/Pacific region is Lufthansa Cargo's most important sales market generating about half of its total traffic revenue.

Lufthansa Technik serves a total of 3290 aircraft on an exclusive basis for almost 800 customers worldwide. It provides maintenance aircraft overhaul technical support for engines components and landing gear and special maintenance services for VIP aircraft. Lufthansa Technik

Financial Performance

In fiscal 2014 Lufthansa's net revenue was m 30 billion which remained stable compared to 2013. While most segments remained flat for 2014 the company's catering segment jumped by 6% and its MRO and IT services segments climbed 3% and 2% respectively.

Lufthansa's net income decreased by m 258 million in 2014 compared to 2013. This decrease was due to additional operating expenses driven by foreign exchanges losses and losses from non-disposable assets.

Strategy

An ongoing positive uptick in passenger air travel is expected to help Lufthansa return to normal economic growth. A fleet modernization program may also prove fruitful over the long-term as Lufthansa ordered 29 new aircraft to be delivered starting in 2014. Overall the Lufthansa Group's order list contains 263 aircraft for delivery by 2025.

HISTORY

The Weimar government created Deutsche Luft Hansa (DLH) in 1926 by merging private German airlines Deutscher Aero Lloyd (founded 1919) and Junkers Luftverkehr (formed in 1921 by aircraft manufacturer Junkers Flugzeugwerke). DLH built what would become Europe's most comprehensive air route network by 1931. It served the USSR through Deruluft (formed 1921; dissolved 1941) an airline jointly owned by DLH and the Soviet government. In 1930 DLH and the Chinese government formed Eurasia Aviation Corporation to develop air transport in China.

DLH established the world's first trans-Atlantic airmail service from Berlin to Buenos Aires in 1934 and went on to develop air transport throughout South America. The outbreak of WWII ended operations in Europe and the Chinese government seized Eurasia Aviation in 1941. Klaus Bonhoeffer head of DLH's legal department led an unsuccessful coup against the Nazi leadership and was executed in 1945. Soon afterward all DLH operations ceased.

In 1954 the Allies allowed the recapitalization of Deutsche Lufthansa. The airline started with domestic routes returned to London and Paris (1955) and then re-entered South America (1956). In 1958 it made its first nonstop flight between Germany and New York and initiated service to Tokyo and Cairo. Meanwhile it started a charter airline with several partners in 1955. Lufthansa bought out its partners in 1959 and renamed the unit Condor two years later.

The carrier resumed service behind the Iron Curtain in 1966 with flights to Prague. The stable West German economy helped Lufthansa maintain profitability through most of the 1970s. The reunification of Germany in 1990 ended Allied control over Berlin airspace allowing Lufthansa which had bought Pan Am's Berlin routes to fly there under its own colors for the first time since the end of WWII.

EXECUTIVES

Chief Officer Hub Management, Harry Hohmeister, age 51
Chairman and CEO, Carsten Spohr, age 49
CEO Eurowings and Aviation Services, Karl U. Garnadt, age 59
CIO, Roland Sch tz, age 47
CFO, Simone Menne, age 56
CEO Austrian Airlines, Kay Kratky, age 57
Auditors: PricewaterhouseCoopers Aktiengesellschaft

LOCATIONS

HQ: Deutsche Lufthansa AG (Germany, Fed. Rep.)
Lufthansa Aviation Center, Airportring, Frankfurt 60546
Phone: (49) 69 696 28008 **Fax:** (49) 69 696 90990
Web: www.lufthansagroup.com

2014 Sales

	% of total
Europe	62
North America	17
Asia/Pacific	13
Middle East	3
Central & South America	3
Africa	2
Total	**100**

PRODUCTS/OPERATIONS

2014 Sales

	% of total
Passenger airline group	75
Maintenance repair & overhaul	9
Logistics	8
Catering	7
IT services	1
Total	**100**

COMPETITORS

AAR Corp.
Aer Lingus
Air Berlin
Air France-KLM
Alitalia
Amadeus IT
American Airlines Group
Aviall
British Airways
Delta Air Lines
Deutsche Bahn
Gate Gourmet
IAG
ITA Software
Japan Airlines
Jeppesen Sanderson
Korean Air
Qantas
Ryanair
SR Technics
TIMCO Aviation
Virgin Atlantic Airways
easyJet

HISTORICAL FINANCIALS

Company Type: Public

Income Statement

FYE: December 31

	REVENUE ($ mil.)	NET INCOME ($ mil.)	NET PROFIT MARGIN	EMPLOYEES
12/14	36,736	66	0.2%	118,781
12/13	41,558	430	1.0%	117,343
12/12	39,868	1,304	3.3%	118,368
12/11	37,345	(16)	—	119,084
12/10	36,790	1,513	4.1%	117,066
Annual Growth	(0.0%)	(54.2%)	—	0.4%

2014 Year-End Financials

Debt ratio: 23.7%
Return on equity: 1.1%
Cash ($ mil.): 1,158
Current ratio: 0.75
Long-term debt ($ mil.): 6,519
No. of shares (mil.): 462
Dividends
Yield: 2.6%
Payout: 264.7%
Market value ($ mil.): 7,707

	STOCK PRICE ($) FY Close	P/E High/Low	PER SHARE ($) Earnings	Dividends	Book Value
12/14	16.66	206110	0.15	0.44	10.42
12/13	21.39	34 26	0.94	0.00	18.08
12/12	19.29	9 5	2.85	0.22	23.61
12/11	11.78	— —	(0.04)	0.55	22.45
12/10	21.76	10 6	3.31	0.00	24.09
Annual Growth	(6.5%)	— —	(54.2%)	—	(18.9%)

Deutsche Post AG

Deutsche Post has outgrown its mailbox origins. Doing business as Deutsche Post DHL the company divides its operations between delivering the mail in Germany (Deutsche Post) and being one of the world's leading providers of express delivery and logistics services (DHL). As Deutsche Post it delivers about 64 million letters a day to more than 40 million customers (about half of the German population). DHL handles the international express delivery freight forwarding global mail and supply chain business. Overall DHL-branded business activities account for the majority of Deutsche Post DHL's sales. The company's largest market is Europe which accounts for about two-thirds of total sales.

Operations

Deutsche Post operates through four divisions: Express Freight Forwarding Global Mail and Supply Chain. Deutsche Post only encompasses the group's German mail service. And as electronic communication grows the company is reevaluating its legacy operations. Demand for mail delivery has trended downward; and while that's good for the earth it's bad for business.

The company expects the most growth to come from its DHL-branded services which handle the international express delivery freight forwarding global mail and supply chain business.

Financial Performance

Deutsche Post's revenue dropped marginally from 2012 to 2013 due to slight decreases in sales from European countries (other than Germany) the Americas and other regions. The company also experienced a revenue drop from its freight segment from 2012 to 2013. (Note: Growth rates may differ after conversion to US dollars.)

Strategy

The company is looking to strengthen its international express services and its freight business. In China DHL-Sinotrans International Air Courier operates as its joint venture with Sinotrans one of the country's top express delivery firms. Deutsche Post will also continue to focus on logistics as its core business with more than 85% of revenue coming from logistics by 2020. In addition it aims to secure its letter business in Germany while also further expanding its services within the e-commerce market.

HISTORY

The German postal system was established in the 1490s when German emperor Maximilian I ordered a reliable and regular messenger service to be set up between Austria (Innsbruck where the emperor had his court) and the farther reaches of his Holy Roman Empire: the Netherlands France and Rome. The von Tassis (later renamed Taxis) family of Italy was responsible for running the network. Family members settled in major cities across Europe to expand the postal business.

Although the family operated what was officially an exclusively royal mail service by the early 1500s the company was also delivering messages for private patrons. In 1600 a family member who served as general postmaster was authorized to collect fees for private mail deliveries. By the early 19th century Thurn und Taxis as the company was then called was the leading postal service in the Holy Roman Empire serving more than 11 million people.

The dissolution of the Holy Roman Empire prompted by Napoleon's military adventures led to the creation of a federation of 39 independent German states. Thurn und Taxis had to make agreements with members of the separate states including Austria and Prussia. After Austria's defeat in 1866 by Prussia the confederation was dissolved and all Thurn und Taxis postal systems were absorbed by Prussia. When Bismarck's Prussian-led German Reich was established in 1870 the new postal administration (Reichspostverwaltung) began issuing postage stamps valid across Germany.

After Germany was defeated in WWII and split into two nations in 1949 two postal systems were established: Deutsche Post (East Germany) and Deutsche Bundespost (West Germany). The fall of the Berlin Wall in 1989 preceded a reunion of the two German states in 1990. That year Deutsche Post led by chairman Klaus Zumwinkel was integrated into Deutsche Bundespost.

EXECUTIVES

CEO, Frank Appel, age 54, $867,167 total compensation
Director Finance and Global Business Services, Lawrence A. Rosen, age 58
CEO DHL Express, Ken Allen, age 60
CEO Post eCommerce Parcel, J rgen Gerdes, age 51, $357,500 total compensation
CEO DHL Supply Chain Williams Lea, John Gilbert
CEO Global Forwarding Freight, Roger A. Crook, age 58
Chair Supervisory Board, Wulf von Schimmelmann
Auditors: PricewaterhouseCoopers Aktiengesellschaft

LOCATIONS

HQ: Deutsche Post AG
Charles-de-Gaulle-Strasse 20, Bonn D-53113
Phone: (49) 228 182 0 **Fax:** (49) 228 14 88 72
Web: www.dpwn.de

2014 Sales

	% of total
Europe	
Germany	31
Other countries	33
Americas	16
Asia/Pacific	16
Other regions	4
Total	**100**

PRODUCTS/OPERATIONS

2014 Sales

	% of total
PeP	27
Supply Chain	26
Global Forwarding Freight	25
Express	21
Total	**100**

Selected Services

Air freight
Contract logistics
Dialog marketing services
European road freight
International express
National and international mail and parcel services
Ocean freight
Outsourcing and system solutions for the mail business

COMPETITORS

CEVA Logistics
DB Schenker Rail Deutschland
Expeditors
FedEx
Geodis
Kuehne + Nagel International
La Poste
Nippon Express
Panalpina
PostNL
Poste Italiane
Royal Mail
TNT Express
UPS
US Postal Service

HISTORICAL FINANCIALS

Company Type: Public

Income Statement

FYE: December 31

	REVENUE ($ mil.)	NET INCOME ($ mil.)	NET PROFIT MARGIN	EMPLOYEES
12/14	68,834	2,517	3.7%	488,824
12/13	75,837	2,878	3.8%	479,212
12/12	73,167	2,185	3.0%	472,321
12/11	68,331	1,504	2.2%	467,188
12/10	68,900	3,400	4.9%	464,471
Annual Growth	(0.0%)	(7.2%)	—	1.3%

2014 Year-End Financials

Debt ratio: —
Return on equity: 21.0%
Cash ($ mil.): 3,619
Current ratio: 1.02
Long-term debt ($ mil.): —
No. of shares (mil.): 1,209
Dividends
Yield: 3.2%
Payout: 47.6%
Market value ($ mil.): 39,254

	STOCK PRICE ($) FY Close	P/E High/Low		PER SHARE ($) Earnings	Dividends	Book Value
12/14	32.45	20	16	1.99	1.07	11.42
12/13	36.70	21	13	2.29	0.89	11.22
12/12	22.12	16	12	1.74	0.87	13.03
12/11	15.42	19	12	1.24	0.83	11.78
12/10	17.09	9	7	2.81	0.76	11.64
Annual Growth	17.4%	—	—	(8.2%)	8.8%	(0.5%)

Deutsche Post RG

Auditors: PricewaterhouseCoopers Aktiengesellschaft Wirtschaftpruefungsgesellschaft

LOCATIONS

HQ: Deutsche Post RG
Charles-de-Gaulle-Str. 20, Bonn 53113
Phone: (49) 228 182 0 **Fax:** (49) 228 182 98 80
Web: www.dp-dhl.com

HISTORICAL FINANCIALS

Company Type: Public

Income Statement FYE: December 31

	REVENUE ($ mil.)	NET INCOME ($ mil.)	NET PROFIT MARGIN	EMPLOYEES
12/14	68,834	2,517	3.7%	488,824
12/13	75,837	2,878	3.8%	480,006
12/12	73,167	2,185	3.0%	473,626
12/11	68,331	1,504	2.2%	471,654
Annual Growth	0.2%	18.7%	—	1.2%

2014 Year-End Financials

Debt ratio: —
Return on equity: 21.5%
Cash ($ mil.): 3,619
Current ratio: 1.04
Long-term debt ($ mil.): —
No. of shares (mil.): 1,209
Dividends
Yield: —
Payout: —
Market value ($ mil.): —

	STOCK PRICE ($) FY Close	P/E High/Low		PER SHARE ($) Earnings	Dividends	Book Value
12/14	0.00	—	—	1.99	0.00	9.42
Annual Growth	—	—	—	—	—	—

Deutsche Postbank AG

Deutsche Postbank is claiming its post as one of Germany's leading retail banks. Spun off from postal service provider Deutsche Post in 2004 the bank offers deposits loans and mortgages asset management insurance and commercial finance including factoring and leasing services through more than 850 branches; it also offers some services through post office locations. The bank performs payment processing services as well with rivals including Deutsche Bank among its biggest customers. Outside Germany Deutsche Postbank offers banking services in Luxembourg and structured finance products to companies in North America. Deutsche Bank controls just over half of the bank.In 2008 there was renewed interest in the acquisition of Deutsche Postbank as its former parent company Deutsche Post sought to sell the bank in order to focus on mail express deliveries and logistics. German banking giant Deutsche Bank acquired 25% of Deutsche Postbank for some $4 billion in 2009; it later upped its stake to more than 50% the next year.Stefan Juette was named CEO of Deutsche Postbank in 2009. He followed Wolfgang Klein who resigned following a clash with members of the board. Juette was a Deutsche Postbank board member responsible for lending and credit management.

EXECUTIVES

Member Management Board; Resources, Ralf Stemmer, age 54, $400,000 total compensation
Member Management Board; Branch Sales, Hans-Peter Schmid, age 57, $433,300 total compensation
CFO, Marc Hess, age 42
Chairman; Group Management and Sales, Frank Strauss, age 45
Member Management Board; Chief Risk Officer, Hanns-Peter Storr, age 56
COO, Ralph M ller, age 44
Member Management Board; Product, Susanne Kl ¶, age 51
Auditors: PricewaterhouseCoopers Aktiengesellschaft Wirtschaftprufungsgesellschaft

LOCATIONS

HQ: Deutsche Postbank AG
Friedrich-Ebert-Allee 114-126, Bonn D-53113
Phone: (49) 228 920 0 **Fax:** (49) 228 920 35151
Web: www.postbank.com

2007 Sales

	% of total
Europe	
Germany	94
Other countries	4
US & Asia	2
Total	100

PRODUCTS/OPERATIONS

2007 Sales by Segment

	% of total
Retail banking	77
Corporate banking	9
Transaction banking	8
Financial markets	6
Total	100

COMPETITORS

ABN AMRO Group
Commerzbank
DZ BANK
Deutsche Bank
Erste Bank
HSBC
UniCredit Bank AG

HISTORICAL FINANCIALS

Company Type: Public

Income Statement FYE: December 31

	ASSETS ($ mil.)	NET INCOME ($ mil.)	INCOME AS % OF ASSETS	EMPLOYEES
12/14	188,946	337	0.2%	14,774
12/13	222,351	454	0.2%	18,223
12/12	255,466	367	0.1%	18,599
12/11	248,319	143	0.1%	19,232
12/10	287,327	184	0.1%	20,361
Annual Growth	(9.9%)	16.3%	—	(7.7%)

2014 Year-End Financials

Return on assets: 0.1%
Return on equity: 4.3%
Long-term debt ($ mil.): —
No. of shares (mil.): 218
Sales ($ mil): 7,922
Dividends
Yield: —
Payout: —
Market value ($ mil.): —

	STOCK PRICE ($) FY Close	P/E High/Low		PER SHARE ($) Earnings	Dividends	Book Value
12/14	0.00	—	—	1.54	0.00	36.64
12/13	41.70	50	50	2.08	0.00	39.06
12/12	42.20	57	52	1.69	0.00	37.98
12/11	30.10	113	99	0.66	0.00	33.73
Annual Growth	—	—	—	23.7%	—	2.1%

Deutsche Telekom AG

Operating the autobahn on the global information superhighway Deutsche Telekom (DT) is a leading telecom company in Europe and one of the largest carriers in the world. The company's core business is its services and products for fixed-network and mobile communications services as well as for enterprise information and communication technology (ICT). Germany's #1 fixed-line telephone operator it provides domestic and international long-distance voice services. It is a leading ISP offering other data and multimedia services such as its Entertain-branded Internet television. DT's T-Systems International delivers ICT services for businesses. About three-quarters of sales come from Europe.

Operations

DT offers goods and services through subsidiaries in 15 European countries including Austria Croatia the Czech Republic Greece (through a 30% stake in OTE) Hungary (Magyar Telekom) the Netherlands and Poland (Polska Telefonia Cyfrowa).

Outside Germany and Eastern Europe the company's key international wireless subsidiaries are T-Mobile USA and T-Mobile (UK). The UK is the group's third-largest market with about 17 million subscribers.

Geographic Reach

Deutsche Telekom (DT) operates through its subsidiary in more than 50 countries worldwide. The company gets about 60% of its revenue from outside Germany. While DT has an impressive global reach customers in Germany still comprise its largest single market accounting for almost 40% of sales; its customers in Europe are essentially in Eastern European countries.

Financial Performance

In 2014 DT's revenue rose 4% on the strength of 21% growth in the US which came from the addition of MetroPCS and new customers. In Germany the company posted a slight decrease in revenue. Revenue from its other European operations was hurt by regulatory decisions and price reductions driven by competition.

DT's net income jumped more than 200% in 2014 from 2013. The increase in product and service revenue was supplemented by a transaction between T-Mobile US and Verizon Communications concerning the acquisition and exchange of spectrum.

Mergers and Acquisitions

DT has built up its operations in Eastern Europe with acquisitions.

It acquired the 40% of T-Mobile Czech Republic it didn't own in order to combine the Czech operations of GTS Group and T-Mobile Czech Republic. In 2015 DT bought out the rest of Slovak Telekom. Those moves followed the previous acquisition of GTS Central Europe to offer telecom services across Europe.

Ownership

The German government and German state-owned development bank KfW together own about 32% of Deutsche Telekom.

HISTORY

Early History

Deutsche Telekom was formed by the 1989 separation of West Germany's telecommunications services from the nation's postal system Deutsche Post. Dating back to the 15th century (when the Thurn und Taxis private postal system was created for German principalities) the service expanded to cover Austria France the Netherlands and most of Germany by the 1850s. After the 1866 Austro-Prussian War it became part of the North German Postal Confederation. When the German Empire was formed in 1871 the postal operation became the Deutsche Reichspost (later the Bundespost). Shortly thereafter the newly invented telephone was introduced in Germany.

Post-WWI inflation shook the Bundespost and the government allowed it to try new organizational structures. A 1924 law allowed the state-run service to operate as a quasi-commercial company. After WWII the American-British zone returned postal authority to Germans and in 1949 the USSR established the state of East Germany.

Only by the 1960s did West Germany's postal and phone services meet modern standards. Privatization of the Bundespost became a political cause when many complained about the monopoly's cost and inefficiency. Efforts to privatize the agency (named Deutsche Telekom in 1989) intensified with the 1990 German reunification. Faced with updating the antiquated phone system of the former East Germany however political opposition to taking Deutsche Telekom public faded.

The company began operating T-D1 its mobile phone network in 1992 and the next year it launched T-Online now Germany's largest online service provider. In 1996 Deutsche Telekom finally went public and raised more than $13 billion in Europe's largest IPO. It also launched Global One with France Telecom (renamed Orange) and Sprint (now Sprint Nextel); as part of the partnership Deutsche Telekom took a 10% stake in Sprint.

In 1998 European Union (EU) member countries opened their phone markets to competition and Deutsche Telekom's long-distance market share quickly eroded. Under EU pressure in 1999 the company said it would sell its cable network which it divided into nine regional units.

EXECUTIVES

Member Management Board Europe and Technology, Claudia Nemat, age 46
CEO, Timotheus Hottges, age 54
Member Board of Management; T-Systems, Reinhard Clemens, age 56
Member Board of Management; Managing Director Telekom Deutschland GmbH, Niek Jan Van Damme, age 55
Member Board of Management; CFO, Thomas Dannenfeldt
Member Board of Management; Data Privacy Legal Affairs and Compliance Acting Chief Human Resources Officer, Thomas Kremer, age 58
Auditors: PricewaterhouseCoopers Aktiengesellschaft

LOCATIONS

HQ: Deutsche Telekom AG
Friedrich-Ebert-Allee 140, Bonn D-53113
Phone: (49) 228 181 4949 **Fax:** (49) 228 181 94004
Web: www.telekom.com

2014 Sales

	% of total
Europe	
Germany	40
Other European countries	23
North America	36
Other countries	1
Total	**100**

PRODUCTS/OPERATIONS

2014 Sales

	% of total
Rendering of services	86
Sale of goods & merchantise	13
The use of entity assets & other	1
Total	**100**

COMPETITORS

BT
COLT Group
Cable & Wireless
Freenet
HP Enterprise Services
Invitel
KPN
Orange
Proximus
QSC
Swisscom
TDC
Tele Columbus
Telecom Italia
Telefnica
Telefnica O2 Germany
Telekom Austria
Telenor
TeliaSonera
United Internet
Versatel
Vodafone
Vodafone GmbH

HISTORICAL FINANCIALS

Company Type: Public

Income Statement FYE: December 31

	REVENUE ($ mil.)	NET INCOME ($ mil.)	NET PROFIT MARGIN	EMPLOYEES
12/14	76,161	3,554	4.7%	227,811
12/13	82,785	1,280	1.5%	228,586
12/12	76,669	(6,926)	—	229,686
12/11	75,864	720	0.9%	235,132
12/10	83,542	2,268	2.7%	246,777
Annual Growth	(2.3%)	11.9%	—	(2.0%)

2014 Year-End Financials

Debt ratio: 51.8%
Return on equity: 11.8%
Cash ($ mil.): 9,144
Current ratio: 1.06
Long-term debt ($ mil.): 54,295
No. of shares (mil.): —
Dividends
Yield: 4.0%
Payout: 102.7%
Market value ($ mil.): —

	STOCK PRICE ($) FY Close	P/E High/Low	PER SHARE ($) Earnings	Dividends	Book Value
12/14	15.89	26 19	0.79	0.65	6.85
12/13	17.26	82 52	0.29	0.90	7.39
12/12	11.36	— —	(1.61)	0.85	7.91
12/11	11.45	113 80	0.17	0.86	10.56
12/10	12.80	36 29	0.52	1.03	11.78
Annual Growth	5.6%	— —	10.9%	(11.0%)	(12.7%)

Dexia Bank Belgium S.A. (Belgium)

Auditors: Deloitte Bedrijfsrevisoren / Reviseurs d'Entreprises

LOCATIONS

HQ: Dexia Bank Belgium S.A. (Belgium)
Boulevard Pacheco 44, Brussels B-1000
Phone: (32) 2 222 11 11 **Fax:** (32) 2 222 11 22
Web: www.belfius.be

HISTORICAL FINANCIALS

Company Type: Public

Income Statement FYE: December 31

	ASSETS ($ mil.)	NET INCOME ($ mil.)	INCOME AS % OF ASSETS	EMPLOYEES
12/14	236,302	561	0.2%	6,817
12/13	251,636	612	0.2%	7,058
12/12	280,674	547	0.2%	7,175
12/11	300,739	(1,767)	—	7,428
12/10	331,785	907	0.3%	7,859
Annual Growth	(8.1%)	(11.3%)	—	(3.5%)

2014 Year-End Financials

Return on assets: 0.2%
Return on equity: 6.3%
Long-term debt ($ mil.): —
No. of shares (mil.): 359
Sales ($ mil): 9,369
Dividends
Yield: —
Payout: —
Market value ($ mil.): —

Dexia S.A.

HISTORY

Dexia which is Greek for both "right" and "treaty" is the product of the Maastricht Treaty of 1991 which called for full economic union within the European Economic Community.

Dexia's earliest antecedent the still-powerful Caisse des D ⓟ 'ts et Consignations (CDC) was formed in 1816 by the restored French monarchy to manage funds for institutions and government entities. It used the funds to finance public infrastructure projects.

In 1860 the Belgian government formed Cr ⓓit Communal de Belgique (known to Flemings as Gemeentekrediet) to provide banking services particularly loans to local governments.

Both banks were state-owned until the 1990s. In 1987 CDC under fire for being too powerful separated its savings and asset management functions from municipal lending packaging the latter into Cr ⓓit Local of which it sold 20% in 1991 (CDC now owns 18%). While France was beginning to deal with its chaotic banking system Belgium was content with its bewildering array of specialty banks until the move toward European economic union forced it to reduce its national debt which stood at 137% of GDP in 1993. Part of the solution was to offload debt through privatization so in 1996 Belgium floated Cr ⓓit Communal.

As European banks began to consolidate both Cr ⓓit Communal and Cr ⓓit Local began looking for ways to grow. Cr dit Local made acquisitions in Germany and the UK and Cr dit Communal linked with Banque Internationale a Luxembourg (BIL formed in 1856 to help finance industrial development throughout Europe).

In 1996 the two companies agreed on a merger modeled on Fortis a cross-border pairing of insurers AG 1824 (Belgian) and AMEV (Dutch). Dexia spent 1997 assimilating its operations but not streamlining them: Both companies retained their full management and directorial rosters. Dexia made acquisitions in Spain and Italy and began adding new services including debt security underwriting; deposit accounting and cash management services; and asset management (using BIL as the nucleus for asset management offerings).

In 1999 Dexia expanded its asset management services into Asia and South America and increased its interest in BIL from about 60% to 99%. It also abandoned its unusual ownership structure merging Dexia France and Dexia Belgium into a single Belgian holding company.

In 2000 the company bought US bond insurer Financial Security Assurance Holdings. It also boosted its private banking operations with the purchase of Dutch bank Labouchere from AEGON N.V..

In 2001 Dexia bought Artesia Banking a private Belgian financial services company. The move bolstered Dexia's already notable size in Belgium. During the merger Dexia closed about 30% of its branches bringing its total down from 1500 to about 1000.

Dexia acquired around 75% of Turkey's DenizBank in 2006. Denizbank offers retail and commercial banking as well as public finance in one of Europe's fastest-growing markets. DenizBank was positioned to be a major growth engine for Dexia. The bank wanted to take advantage of the growing Turkish market by establishing an additional 300 branches there and generating 27% of its income from Turkey.

Dexia was hurt by the global financial crisis which exposed the group to an increase in mortgage defaults (through its former Financial Securities Assurance Holdings arm (FSA)). The company lost billions when a loan to Germany's DEPFA BANK went sour. The governments of Belgium France and Luxembourg first stepped in to bail the bank out in 2008. They injected some 6.5 billion ($9.3 billion) in capital and provided state guarantees for its liabilities. In 2010 Dexia freed itself from the state guarantees and tried to improve liquidity and refocus on financial activities that rely less on capital and reserves.

As part of the rescue Dexia's chairman Pierre Richard and CEO Axel Miller were both fired. Jean-Luc Dehaene and Pierre Mariani were named as their respective replacements.

As Dexia restructured it sold off assets that no longer fit with its mission and cut costs. First off it sold its troubled FSA to Assured Guaranty and cut some 900 jobs. It also halted noncore public-finance operations in Asia North America Europe and Australia.

Next the group sold its Dexia Epargne Pension life insurance subsidiary to a unit of BNP Paribas in early 2010. Also that year Dexia sold its Slovak unit (Slovensko) to Penta Investments in order to meet requirements by the European Commission and sold its majority stake in IT services unit Adinfo. In 2011 Bank of Jerusalem bid $150 million for Dexia's Israeli unit.

Auditors: Deloitte Bedrijfsrevisoren / Reviseurs d' Entreprises

LOCATIONS

HQ: Dexia S.A.
Place du Champ de Mars, 5, Brussels B-1050
Phone: (32) 2 213 50 81
Web: www.dexia.com

HISTORICAL FINANCIALS

Company Type: Public

Income Statement FYE: December 31

	ASSETS ($ mil.)	NET INCOME ($ mil.)	INCOME AS % OF ASSETS	EMPLOYEES
12/14	300,375	(736)	—	1,290
12/13	306,923	(1,491)	—	1,405
12/12	470,820	(3,777)	—	2,429
12/11	533,884	(15,054)	—	14,181
12/10	758,502	967	0.1%	27,148
Annual Growth	(20.7%)	—	—	(53.3%)

2014 Year-End Financials

Return on assets: (-0.2%)
Return on equity: (-19.5%)
Long-term debt ($ mil.): —
No. of shares (mil.): 1,948
Sales ($ mil): 13,642
Dividends
Yield: —
Payout: —
Market value ($ mil.): 312

	STOCK PRICE ($) FY Close	P/E High/Low		PER SHARE ($) Earnings	Dividends	Book Value
12/14	0.16	—	—	(0.38)	0.00	1.69
12/13	0.00	—	—	(0.77)	0.00	2.46
12/12	0.00	—	—	(1.94)	0.00	1.93
12/11	0.50	—	—	(7.72)	0.00	(1.34)
Annual Growth	(31.6%)	—	—	—	—	—

DNB ASA

Financial services 'n real estate are what DnB NOR is for. One of the largest banks in Norway the company serves retail and corporate clients at more than 150 locations in 20 countries operating under the DnB NOR Bank Nordlandsbanken and Postbanken banners. In addition to traditional banking services such as deposits and loans it also provides life and pension insurance (through its Vital subsidiary) credit cards (through Cresco) and mutual funds and institutional asset management in Norway and Sweden (through DnB NOR Asset Management) as well as real estate brokerage and capital markets services. The Norwegian government owns about a third of DnB Nor.

DnB NOR also has banking and insurance operations in Sweden where it operates through Svensk Fastighetsformedling and SalusAnsvar. Elsewhere it provides banking services in Poland Denmark and the Baltic States through DnB NORD and in Russia through DnB NOR Monchebank. The group's strategy for international growth is focused on large corporate clients particularly in the energy shipping and seafood industries. DnB NOR also has limited operations in the US and Asia.

The company acquired the 49% it didn't already own in DnB NORD from German venture partner Norddeutsche Landesbank Girozentrale (NordLB) in late 2010. NordLB had considered buying out DnB NOR in the Baltic venture which had been hit hard by the global economic crisis but ultimately chose not to. DnB NOR instead took over the unit. DnB NORD is still reeling from the downturn but its 2010 losses were about a third of 2009's.

To strengthen the group's identity and streamline operations DnB NOR is uniting itself under one brand. Among its planned changes is the eventual phasing out of the Postbanken name.

Also DnB NOR discontinued its mortgage lending business in Sweden in 2011. It sold its retail customer mortgage loan portfolio to SEB that year.

The Norwegian government owns about a third of DnB NOR.

EXECUTIVES

EVP DNB Markets, Ottar Ertzeid, age 50, $1,600,000 total compensation
EVP Finance, Bj rn Erik N ss, age 61
EVP Wealth Management, Tom Rathke, age 58, $2,604,000 total compensation
EVP IT and Operations, Liv Fiksdahl, age 51, $1,615,000 total compensation
EVP Products, Kari Olrud Moen, age 47
EVP Personal Banking Norway, Trond Bentestuen, age 46
EVP Large Corporates and International, Harald Serck-Hanssen
EVP Corporate Banking Norway, Kjerstin Braathen, age 46
EVP HR, Solveig Hellebust
EVP Risk Management, Terje Turnes
EVP Corporate Communications, Thomas Midteide
Chairman, Anne Carine Tanum, age 62
Vice Chairman, Tore Olaf Rimmereid, age 56
Auditors: Ernst & Young AS

LOCATIONS

HQ: DNB ASA
Dronning Eufemias gate 30, Oslo N-0021
Phone: (47) 915 03000
Web: www.dnb.no

2013 Sales

	% of total
Norway	80
Other international operations	15
Baltics and Poland	5
Total	**100**

PRODUCTS/OPERATIONS

2013 Sales

	% of total
Large corporate and international customers	36
Personal customers	37
Small and medium-sized enterprises	16
Trading	6
Traditional pension products	5
Total	**100**

COMPETITORS

ABN AMRO Group
BNP Paribas
Credit Suisse
Danske Bank
Deutsche Bank
Grupo Santander
HSBC
Nordea Bank
SEB AB
Svenska Handelsbanken
UBS

HISTORICAL FINANCIALS

Company Type: Public

Income Statement FYE: December 31

	ASSETS ($ mil.)	NET INCOME ($ mil.)	INCOME AS % OF ASSETS	EMPLOYEES
12/14	357,047	2,778	0.8%	12,064
12/13	393,236	2,884	0.7%	12,016
12/12	404,904	2,441	0.6%	13,291
12/11	353,609	2,158	0.6%	16,320
12/10	319,028	2,538	0.8%	13,021
Annual Growth	2.9%	2.3%	—	(1.9%)

2014 Year-End Financials

Return on assets: 0.8%
Return on equity: 13.7%
Long-term debt ($ mil.): —
No. of shares (mil.): 1,628
Sales ($ mil): 10,912

Dividends
Yield: 3.0%
Payout: —
Market value ($ mil.): 242,740

	STOCK PRICE ($) FY Close	P/E High/Low		PER SHARE ($) Earnings	Dividends	Book Value
12/14	149.03	0	0	1.71	4.58	13.13
12/13	180.20	0	0	1.77	3.61	14.37
12/12	129.33	1	0	1.49	3.42	14.05
12/11	95.00	1	0	1.33	0.33	12.03
12/10	130.45	0	0	1.48	0.69	11.70
Annual Growth	3.4%	—	—	3.7%	60.8%	2.9%

DZ Bank AG Deutsche Zentral-Genossenschaftsbank

DZ BANK is the central institution for 1000 local cooperative banks which serve 30 million customers from a combined 11000 branch offices across Germany. It provides administrative services for its member banks which are also the company's owners. Additionally DZ BANK provides corporate banking services including commercial lending for small to midsized businesses capital markets services retail and private banking and transaction banking. DZ Bank agreed to acquire WGZ Bank in late 2015 which would effectively make it Germany's third-largest financial institution and lender.

OperationsAs of early 2016 DZ Bank operated nine management units including: DZ BANK; Deutsche Genossenschafts-Hypothekenbank AG Hamburg (DG HYP); TeamBank AG Nürnberg (TeamBank); and the BSH; DVB; DZ PRIVATBANK; R+V; UMH; and VR LEASING subgroups.Subsidiary Union Investment is one of Germany's top fund managers and had some 232 billion ($250 billion) in assets under management as of late 2015. ReiseBank another unit provides foreign cash exchange and transfers from about 100 locations around Germany. Other divisions offer credit processing for financial companies and specialist consumer financing.Broadly speaking the bank made 25% of its total revenue from interest income during 2014 while another 10% came from fee and commission income. About 47% of its revenue came from premiums earned from its insurance businesses. The remainder of its revenue came from non-recurring gains mostly on its insurance business investments.Geographic ReachWhile the vast majority of its branches are in Germany the bank has representative offices and branches in London New York Singapore Hong Kong Dublin (subsidiaries) and other key financial centers around the world.Sales and MarketingThe bank serves retail affluent individuals corporate and institutional clients. It spent 133 million ($161.7 million) on public relations and marketing expenses in 2014 down from 134 million ($184.5 million) in 2013. Financial PerformanceNote: Growth rates may differ after conversion to US dollars. This analysis uses financials from the company's annual report.DZ Bank's annual revenues and profits have been trending higher over the past several years. The bank's revenue jumped 9% to 29.4 million ($35.7 million) during 2014 mostly thanks to a combination of gains on sold investments from its insurance companies which included selling shares in Natixis and selling asset-backed securities; coupled with higher insurance premium earnings as the company integrated its R+V subgroup into its cooperative financial network.Strong revenue growth in 2014 combined with lower interest fee and commission expenses drove DZ Bank's net income higher by 48% to 1.7 billion ($2.1 billion). The company's operating cash levels doubled to 5.1 billion ($6.2 billion) as cash-based earnings rose for the year. StrategyDZ Bank has been moving toward digital banking channels that are quickly taking the industry by storm allowing the bank to slow expensive branch-expansion plans and cut operating costs significantly while giving customers faster access to banking services. As part of its local cooperative banks' omnichannel strategy DZ Bank launched its webErfolg (web success) project aimed at building its online sales channel in 2014. In 2015 it launched its follow-up Kundenfokus 2020 project which was designed to focus on a number of improvements for the bank including "interlinking the depth and breadth of the online and offline sales channels."DZ Bank sometimes acquires other banks to grow its branch reach loan and deposit business keeping the idea of cross-selling its variety of other services later. Its late 2015 announcement to buy WGZ Bank would take DZ Bank from being Germany's fourth-largest financial institution to its third largest.Mergers and AcquisitionsIn November 2015 DZ Bank planned to buy WGZ Bank in a deal that would create Germany's third-largest financial institution. With the acquisition slated for completion in August 2016 the newly merged DZ Bank would control total assets of nearly 500 billion ($535 billion) making it Germany's third-largest lender behind larger lenders Deutsche Bank and Commerzbank and ahead of development bank KfW. Company Background

In 2009 DZ BANK and WGZ BANK the second-largest central institution for Germany's cooperative banking network postponed merger discussions for the fourth time in three years. The deal would have created the third-largest bank in Germany. However the two companies have combined certain operations such as their investment advisory and private banking units.In 2001 GZ-Bank and DG Bank –Germany's primary central institutions for cooperative lenders –merged to create today's DZ BANK.

HISTORY

Company BackgroundCreated as a public entity in 1895 DG Bank began as the Preussische Central Genossenschafts-Kasse (Preussenkasse). The bank controlled liquidity and also managed cashless payment transfers and securities business for central cooperative banks. By 1905 regional co-op banks had taken equity stakes in the Preussenkasse. In the years that followed more central banks began to work with the company and its influence spread to all areas of the cooperative movement as well as outside Prussian borders.

Even the German government took an interest in the Preussenkasse and by 1932 had taken it under its control and renamed it the Deutsche Zentralgenossenschaftskasse. The partition of Germany following WWII affected the bank in two ways: assets of companies in the Soviet zone were seized and the bank's headquarters located in the Soviet-occupied portion of Berlin had to be moved. The bank operated from Marburg and Hamburg until a new headquarters was chosen in 1949. This new bank was based in Frankfurt and called Deutsche Genossenschaftskasse. The entity had a similar structure and public mandate to Preussenkasse and Deutsche Zentralgenossenschaftskasse.

In the following decades the bank started accepting deposits and received trust investment status (1954) began issuing securities (1957) and expanded its investment portfolio. The Deutsche Genossenschaftsbank Act of 1975 formalized the company's development into a commercial bank and gave it the new name Deutsche Genossenschaftsbank to reflect this.

Throughout the late 1980s the bank underwent mergers that expanded its abilities as a cooperative central institution. During this time the bank arose as the central bank of Bavaria northern Germany and parts of Hesse. In 1987 the bank approached the trade union-owned Volksfursorge Group about merging with the R&V Versicherungsgruppe to form an insurance group in an effort to boost bank and insurance cross-marketing. The next year DG solicited a possible merger among West Germany's five cooperative banks. It also took a stake in its Spanish counterpart Cajas Rurales. Both offers fell through in 1989 as some of the other cooperatives dissented and management decided against acquiring a 75% stake in Volksfursorge.

In 1990 several French banks cried outrage over $3.5 billion in bonds that had sunk in value by about $350 million. Inflation and fears over the currency integration with East Germany were the culprits for the devaluation. A vice chairman of the company took responsibility for the dispute and resigned. By 1991 three key DG Bank executive had left or announced their resignations from the company. Bernd Thiemann took the helm to restore credibility to the company which had alienated itself from other cooperative banks and whose plans to be a universal bank made it overextend itself.

With the reunification of Germany in the early 1990s DG assumed the role of the central bank for former East German cooperatives as well as East Germany's Bank für Landwirtschaft und Nahrungsgüterwirtschaft der DDR (Agriculture and Food Industry Bank).

In 1995 the bank started to look outside Germany for expansion and by 1997 it was ready to open an office in Hong Kong. In addition DG purchased a majority stake in Magyar Takarekszovethezeti Bank of Hungary. That year DG Bank along with other state-owned banks in Germany came under fire from the European Commission for receiving illegal public aid.

DG became a publicly traded company in 1998. Early that year the bank began discussions with Rabobank and Crdit Agricole (similarly organized banks in the Netherlands and France) about establishing a European cooperative bank.

In 2000 DG Bank began to securitize mortgages originated by its DG Hypothekenbank unit and scrapped its planned merger with the Netherlands-based Rabobank. DG Bank then found a merger partner in the fellow German cooperative bank GZ Bank. They formed DZ BANK in 2001.

EXECUTIVES

Managing Director, Albrecht Merz
CEO, Wolfgang Kirsch
President DZ Financial Markets, Gerhard Summerer
Managing Director DZ BANK Ireland, Mark Jacob
Managing Director DZ BANK Ireland, Tilmann Gerhards
Chairman of the Supervisory Board, Rolf Hildner
Deputy Chairman of the Supervisory Board, Helmut Gottschalk
Auditors: Ernst & Young GmbH Wirtschaftsprufungsgesellschaft

LOCATIONS

HQ: DZ Bank AG Deutsche Zentral-Genossenschaftsbank
Platz der Republik, Frankfurt am Main 60265
Phone: (49) 69 7447 01 **Fax:** (49) 69 7447 1685
Web: www.dzbank.com

PRODUCTS/OPERATIONS

2014 Sales

	% of total
Premiums earned	47
Interest income and current income and expense	25
Gains and losses on investments held by insurance companies	15
Fee and commission income	10
Others	3
Total	**100**

Selected Subsidiaries

Bausparkasse Schwäbisch Hall
Deutsche Genossenschafts-Hypothekenbank AG (DYG HYP)
DZ PRIVATBANK Group
R+V Versicherung AG
TeamBank
Union Investment Group
VR LEASING

COMPETITORS

BNP Paribas	Deutsche Bank
Barclays	HSBC
BayernLB	KBC
Citibank	UniCredit Bank AG
Commerzbank	WestLB

HISTORICAL FINANCIALS

Company Type: Public

Income Statement FYE: December 31

	REVENUE ($ mil.)	NET INCOME ($ mil.)	NET PROFIT MARGIN	EMPLOYEES
12/14	35,746	2,102	5.9%	29,596
12/13	37,220	1,609	4.3%	28,962
12/12	34,534	910	2.6%	28,227
12/11	31,051	497	1.6%	27,825
12/10	33,971	1,160	3.4%	26,800
Annual Growth	1.3%	16.0%	—	2.5%

2014 Year-End Financials

Debt ratio: —
Return on equity: 15.6%
Cash ($ mil.): 3,686
Current ratio: —
Long-term debt ($ mil.): —
No. of shares (mil.): 1,402
Dividends
Yield: —
Payout: —
Market value ($ mil.): —

E.ON SE

E.ON has transformed itself from a regional conglomerate into a multi-utility and a global player with 26 million customers. Its diversified business consists of power generation natural gas energy trading retail and distribution operations. Subsidiary E.ON Energie is one of Germany's top two power companies (running neck and neck with RWE) with some 17 million electricity gas and water customers; the unit also has about 69000 MW of electric generating capacity across Germany and Central Europe. E.ON operates E.ON Ruhrgas Germany's #1 natural gas supplier. Non-German utility subsidiaries include E.ON UK and E.ON Nordic.

Geographic ReachE.ON operates in Bulgaria the Czech Republic France Germany Hungary Italy the Netherlands Romania Russia Slovakia Spain Sweden and the UK.Financial AnalysisIn 2011 the company reported revenue growth of 22% thanks to a 2% increase in Generation revenue as a result of higher sales volume higher average transfer prices and positive currency-translation effects in Sweden's Nuclear sales. Other factors included high Fossil segment sales a 26% increase in the Renewables segment and an 8% increase in the Gas segment as a result of positive energy price developments. There was also a 50% jump in the Trading segment as a result of an increase in trading activity in power and gas and a 29% increase in Russian sales as a result of a growth in generating capacity coupled with higher power prices.E.ON has a net loss of 130% in 2011 attributable to the 58% decrease in Net book gains compared to 2010 and 3 billion ($4.2 billion) in impairment charges on assets and goodwill mainly at its generation businesses. It also had impairment charges of 1.9 billion ($2.7 billion) in Spain and Italy due to poor regional economic forecasts for the long-term development of power prices regulatory intervention and reduced use of gas-fired and coal-fired power stations.

Stategy

The company is focusing on realigning its businesses to create greater efficiencies putting more emphasis on developing its renewable power operations and reducing its debt.

In response to tightening European regulations regarding carbon emissions E.ON has announced plans to obtain 24% of its generating capacity from renewable energy sources by 2030.In 2012 the company started building the Wysoka (Wysoka 1 und 2) onshore wind farm in Poland growing E.ON's position as one of the leading players on the Polish wind energy market.Creating a foothold in Brazil in 2012 the company formed a power generation joint venture with Brazilian company MPX to develop 20000 MW of capacity in Brazil and Chile.E.ON is seeking to generate about 15 billion ($21 billion) through divestments by the end of 2013. Paying down debt in 2012 E.ON sold Open Grid Europe its gas transmission company in Germany to a consortium led by Macquarie European Infrastructure Fund 4 for about 3.2 billion ($4.5 billion).In 2011 it sold its Italian natural gas distribution network unit (E.ON Rete) to a group of Italian and French investors for EUR290 million (US$392.3 million). It also sold its UK-based Central Networks unit to PPL for $5.7 billion

HISTORY

VEBA (originally Vereinigte Elektrizitats-und Bergwerks AG) was formed in 1929 in Berlin to consolidate Germany's state-owned electricity and mining interests. These operations included PreussenElektra an electric utility formed by the German government in 1927; Hibernia a coal mining firm founded in 1873; and Preussag a mining and smelting company founded in 1923.

In the 1930s VEBA produced synthetic gasoline (essential to the German war machine) from coal at its Hibernia plant. In 1938 the company and chemical cartel I. G. Farben set up Chemische Werke H ls to make synthetic rubber. After WWII VEBA's assets in western Germany were transferred to the government and several executives were arrested. Preussag was spun off in 1959.

In 1965 the government spun off VEBA to the public. That year the company entered trading and transportation by buying Stinnes one of West Germany's largest industrial companies. In 1969 VEBA transferred its coal mining interests to Ruhrkohle and a few years later moved into oil exploration and development. The company shortened its name to VEBA in 1970.

The West German government sold its remaining stake in VEBA in 1987. In a changed regulatory environment large investors were able to accumulate big portions of stock and their dissatisfaction with the company's lackluster results made it a takeover target. In response new chairman Ulrich Hartmann began cutting noncore businesses and reducing staff.

In 1990 VEBA began accumulating mobile communications networking and cable TV companies. It allied with the UK's Cable and Wireless (C&W) in 1995 to develop a European mobile phone business but in 1997 C&W sold its interest to VEBA (as part of the deal VEBA gained a 10% stake in C&W which it sold in 1999). In anticipation of the 1998 deregulation of the German telecom market VEBA and RWE merged their German telecom businesses in 1997.

VEBA acquired a 36% stake in Degussa a specialty chemicals company in 1997; two years later Degussa merged with H ls to form a separately traded chemical company called Degussa-H ls in which VEBA took a 62% stake. VEBA sold a 30% stake in Stinnes to the public in 1999. The company's telecom venture sold its fixed-line telephone business its cable TV unit and its stake in mobile phone operator E-Plus.

These moves however were just the prelude to a bigger deal: a $14 billion merger agreement between VEBA and fellow German conglomerate VIAG. The partners announced plans to dump noncore businesses and beef up their energy and chemicals holdings. VEBA and VIAG completed their merger in 2000 and the combined company adopted the name E.ON. The companies' utilities businesses were combined into E.ON Energie and their chemicals units were brought together as Degussa.

To gain regulatory approval to form E.ON VEBA and VIAG agreed to sell their stakes in German electric utilities Bewag and VEAG and coal producer LAUBAG. E.ON sold its VEAG and LAUBAG interests along with semiconductor and electronics distribution units in 2000 and sold Bewag in 2001.

In 2001 E.ON agreed to acquire UK electricity generator Powergen (now E.ON UK) and it sold off nonutility operations including Degussa and Veba Oel. E.ON swapped a 51% stake in Veba Oel for BP's 26% stake in German natural gas supplier Ruhrgas (now E.ON Ruhrgas). E.ON also sold Kl ¶ckner to UK steel trader Balli and sold its stake in silicon wafer maker MEMC to buyout firm Texas Pacific Group.

In 2002 E.ON sold its VAW Aluminum unit to Norwegian conglomerate Norsk Hydro in a $2.8 billion deal. Regulators moved to prevent E.ON from acquiring BP's stake in Ruhrgas in 2002 but BP agreed to pay for the Veba Oel stake in cash if necessary and the swap was completed later that year. E.ON also acquired Vodafone and ThyssenKrupp's stakes in Ruhrgas in 2002 and it sold its remaining stake in Veba Oel to BP.

Also in 2002 E.ON completed its purchase of Powergen (which included its US subsidiary LG&E Energy) for about $8 billion and it sold its 65% stake in logistics company Stinnes to German railroad operator Deutsche Bahn. In late 2002 E.ON acquired the UK energy supply and generation businesses of TXU Europe in a $2.5 billion deal.

The following year E.ON swapped its majority stake in chemical maker Degussa with coal group RAG for RAG's 18% interest in Ruhrgas. It completed its acquisition of Ruhrgas by purchasing the combined 40% stake held by Royal Dutch Shell Exxon Mobil and TUI (formerly Preussag). It also sold subsidiary Viterra's energy services unit (gas and water meters) to CVC Capital Partners.

In 2005 the company acquired the Enfield power station in the UK for $250.2 million.

In 2007 E.ON acquired Ireland-based wind farm company Airtricity for $1.4 billion.

Pursuing growth in new geographic markets in 2007 E.ON acquired Russia-based power utility OGK-4 for almost $6 billion. Outmaneuvered by its rivals in 2008 it dropped its $56 billion bid to buy Endesa S.A. Spain's largest electric utility settling for the purchase of a number of Endesa's generation assets in Spain and Italy.

In 2009 to counter EDF's acquisition of British Energy E.ON and RWE formed a joint venture to develop 6000 MW of nuclear power capacity in the UK.

That year prompted by the regulatory requirements of the European Commission E.ON and GDF SUEZ agreed to swap generating assets to allow for more competition in their major markets. It sold 860 MW of Germany-based conventional power plants 132 MW of hydroelectric plants and access to 770 MW of nuclear power. In return GDF SUEZ sold to E.ON a similar amount of power generation capacity in France and the Benelux countries. In 2010 also to meet EU anti-monopoly regulations it sold grid operator Transpower to Dutch giant TenneT for $1.1 billion and it swapped 5000 MW of generation capacity with EDF and EnBW.

In 2010 the company sold E.ON U.S. which operates Kentucky's two major utilities for $7.6 billion. Its US assets were no longer considered a core part of its growth strategy and the sale helped to pay down debt. To raise cash that year it also sold its 3.5% stake in Gazprom to Russian investment bank Vnesheconombank for $4.4 billion.

EXECUTIVES

Chairman Uniper, Bernhard Reutersberg, age 62
CFO, Klaus Sch ◻fer, age 48
CEO E.ON Deutschland and CEO E.ON Energie Deutschland, Robert Hienz
Chairman and CEO, Johannes Teyssen
Member Management Board - Human Resources and Generation, Mike Winkel
CEO E.ON E&P, Frank Sivertsen
SVP Technology and Innovation, Susana Quintana-Plaza
Chairman Supervisory Board, Werner Wenning, age 69
Member Management Board - Markets and Services, Ing. Leonhard Birnbaum
Auditors: PricewaterhouseCoopers Aktiengesellschaft Wirtschaftspruefungsgesellschaft

LOCATIONS

HQ: E.ON SE
E.ON-Platz 1, Duesseldorf D-40479
Phone: (49) 211 45 79 0 **Fax:** (49) 211 45 79 5 01
Web: www.eon.com

2014 Sales

	% of total
Europe	
Germany	37
UK	29
Sweden	3
Other countries	28
Other regions	3
Total	**100**

PRODUCTS/OPERATIONS

2014 Sales

	% of total
Electricity	49
Gas	46
Other	5
Total	**100**

Selected Business Areas

Power Generation
Energy Mix
Coal
Natural Gas and Oil
Nuclear
Water
Wind
Solar
Bio Energy
Gas Supply & Production
Exploration & Production
LNG
Sources of Supply
Security of Supply
Gas Storage & Transportation
Underground Storage Facilities
Nord Stream Pipeline
Trading
Power and Emissions Trading
Gas and Oil Trading
Coal Biofuels and Freight Trading
Market Activity
Market Development
Distribution
Power Distribution
Gas Distribution
Technology of the Future

COMPETITORS

BASF SE	EnBW
Bayer AG	Endesa S.A.
Business Group Benelux	Enel
Deutsche Telekom	Engie
Dow Chemical	Eni
DuPont	Orange
EVN	RWE
Electricit© de France	Vattenfall

HISTORICAL FINANCIALS

Company Type: Public

Income Statement FYE: December 31

	REVENUE ($ mil.)	NET INCOME ($ mil.)	NET PROFIT MARGIN	EMPLOYEES
12/14	135,942	(3,841)	—	59,301
12/13	169,067	2,948	1.7%	62,239
12/12	174,687	2,922	1.7%	72,083
12/11	146,751	(2,870)	—	78,889
12/10	125,181	7,833	6.3%	85,105
Annual Growth	2.1%	—	—	(8.6%)

2014 Year-End Financials

Debt ratio: 19.0%
Return on equity: (-10.8%)
Cash ($ mil.): 7,374
Current ratio: 1.20
Long-term debt ($ mil.): 19,185
No. of shares (mil.): 1,932
Dividends
Yield: 3.5%
Payout: —
Market value ($ mil.): 32,847

	STOCK PRICE ($) FY Close	P/E High/Low		PER SHARE ($) Earnings	Dividends	Book Value
12/14	17.00	—	—	(1.99)	0.60	15.46
12/13	18.48	18	15	1.54	1.10	24.15
12/12	18.79	22	16	1.53	0.96	24.16
12/11	21.39	—	—	(1.50)	1.39	24.26
12/10	30.41	13	9	4.11	1.40	29.26
Annual Growth	(13.5%)	—	—	—	(19.0%)	(14.7%)

E.Sun Financial Holdings Co Ltd

Here comes the E.Sun and I say it's providing banking and financial services in Taiwan. Established in 2002 to consolidate the operations of E.Sun Bank and other subsidiaries E.Sun provides commercial banking venture capital securities trading and other financial services to businesses and individuals throughout the country. The group depends on commercial banking services for its bread and butter (90% of annual revenues) and carries out additional financial operations through six subsidiaries. An attempt to acquire Taiwan Business Bank in 2005 broke down amid union protests. A year later the group allied with Singapore's Temasek which would eventually control 6% through Fullerton Financial Holdings.

EXECUTIVES

President, Yung Jen Huang
Auditors: Deloitte Taiwan

LOCATIONS

HQ: E.Sun Financial Holdings Co Ltd
14F., No.117 & 1F, No. 115, Sec.3, Minsheng E. Rd, Songshan District, Taipei
Phone: (886) 2 2175 1313
Web: www.esunfhc.com.tw

PRODUCTS/OPERATIONS

Selected Subsidiaries

E.Sun Bills Finance Corp.
E.Sun Commercial Bank Ltd.
E.Sun Insurance Brokers Co. Ltd.
E.Sun Securities Co. Ltd.
E.Sun Securities Investment Trust Co. Ltd.
E.Sun Venture Capital Co. Ltd.

COMPETITORS

Cathay Financial Holding	Hotung Investment Holdings
Chinatrust Financial	Taiwan Business Bank

HISTORICAL FINANCIALS

Company Type: Public

Income Statement FYE: December 31

	ASSETS ($ mil.)	NET INCOME ($ mil.)	INCOME AS % OF ASSETS	EMPLOYEES
12/14	49,468	332	0.7%	7,678
12/13	46,310	282	0.6%	7,164
12/12	42,931	242	0.6%	6,476
12/11	38,122	114	0.3%	6,009
12/10	37,270	134	0.4%	5,162
Annual Growth	7.3%	25.3%	—	10.4%

2014 Year-End Financials

Return on assets: 0.7%
Return on equity: 11.1%
Long-term debt ($ mil.): —
No. of shares (mil.): —
Sales ($ mil): 1,402
Dividends
Yield: —
Payout: —
Market value ($ mil.): —

East Japan Railway Co.

If you want to ride the rails into Tokyo you could find yourself cruising at 168 mph aboard a bullet train operated by East Japan Railway known as JR East. The company serves 17 million people daily and carries passengers on more than 7510 km (4660 miles) of track in the eastern half of the Japanese mainland including the Tokyo area. JR East's shinkansen (bullet-train) lines connect metropolitan Tokyo with other major cities. Besides its transportation-related operations JR East gets revenue from leasing restaurant and retail space in its stations and from managing shopping centers and office buildings on property that has been developed near its stations.

Geographic Reach

The railway business of JR East spans the eastern half of Hons Shinkansen network which connects Tokyo with regional cities in five directions.

Operations

JR East operates through four segments. Transportation its core business accounted for around 68% of its total revenue for 2014. Station space utilization represented 15% of its sales while shopping centers and office buildings accounted for 9%. Other operations accounted for the remainder of revenue.

The company is one of the six passenger railway companies and serves eastern Honshu (Japan's main island). It operates 70 railway lines 1686 railway stations and 7512.6 operating kilometers.

Financial Performance

In the recent past JR East's balance sheet has been affected by many factors including the Great East Japan Earthquake a sizable strengthening of the yen rising oil prices and the financial debt crisis affecting Europe.

However net sales increased 1% from 2013 to 2014 due to growth from its transportation (1%) and shopping centers and office buildings (5%) segments. Its net income also spiked by 14% in 2014 due to decreased impairment losses on fixed assets and insurance proceeds related to the earthquake.

Strategy

To grow and to maintain consumers' confidence in the safety of its system JR East aims to continue to invest in its rail infrastructure. The company is preparing for higher-speed trains that will travel at 200 mph. It also sees opportunities for additional growth in revenue from its rail-related real estate operations and its electronic ticketing system Suica.

EXECUTIVES

President and CEO, Tetsuro Tomita
Vice Chairman Technology and Overseas Related Affairs, Masaki Ogata
EVP, Yuji Fukasawa
EVP, Naomichi Yagishita
Chairman, Satoshi Seino
Auditors: KPMG AZSA LLC

LOCATIONS

HQ: East Japan Railway Co.
2-2-2 Yoyogi, Shibuya-ku, Tokyo 151-8578
Phone: (81) 3 5334 1111 **Fax:** (81) 3 5334 1110
Web: www.jreast.co.jp

PRODUCTS/OPERATIONS

2014 Sales

	% of total
Transportation	68
Station space utilization	15
Shopping centers & office buildings	9
Other	8
Total	**100**

COMPETITORS

FedEx
Keihin Electric Express Railway
Keio Corporation
Keisei Electric Railway
Kintetsu
Odakyu Electric Railway
UPS

HISTORICAL FINANCIALS

Company Type: Public

Income Statement FYE: March 31

	REVENUE ($ mil.)	NET INCOME ($ mil.)	NET PROFIT MARGIN	EMPLOYEES
03/15	22,972	1,503	6.5%	73,329
03/14	26,186	1,937	7.4%	73,551
03/13	28,395	1,863	6.6%	73,017
03/12	30,868	1,325	4.3%	71,729
03/11	30,641	920	3.0%	71,749
Annual Growth	(6.9%)	13.1%	—	0.5%

2015 Year-End Financials

Debt ratio: 0.3%
Return on equity: 8.0%
Cash ($ mil.): 636
Current ratio: 0.64
Long-term debt ($ mil.): 21,543
No. of shares (mil.): 393
Dividends
Yield: 1.3%
Payout: —
Market value ($ mil.): 5,266

	STOCK PRICE ($) FY Close	P/E High/Low		PER SHARE ($) Earnings	Dividends	Book Value
03/15	13.40	—	—	3.83	0.18	48.86
03/14	12.28	—	—	4.91	0.20	53.99
03/13	13.60	—	—	4.72	0.00	55.02
03/12	10.44	—	—	3.35	0.00	58.25
03/11	9.25	—	—	2.33	0.21	55.99
Annual Growth	9.7%	—	—	13.2%	(3.6%)	(3.3%)

Eaton Corp plc

Auditors: Ernst & Young LLP

LOCATIONS

HQ: Eaton Corp plc
Eaton House, 30 Pembroke Road, Dublin 4 44114-2584
Phone: (1) 353 1637 2900
Web: www.eaton.com

HISTORICAL FINANCIALS

Company Type: Public

Income Statement FYE: December 31

	REVENUE ($ mil.)	NET INCOME ($ mil.)	NET PROFIT MARGIN	EMPLOYEES
12/14	22,552	1,793	8.0%	102,000
12/13	22,046	1,861	8.4%	102,000
12/12	16,311	1,217	7.5%	103,000
12/11	16,049	1,350	8.4%	73,000
12/10	13,715	929	6.8%	70,000
Annual Growth	13.2%	17.9%	—	9.9%

2014 Year-End Financials

Debt ratio: 26.9%
Return on equity: 11.0%
Cash ($ mil.): 781
Current ratio: 1.51
Long-term debt ($ mil.): 8,024
No. of shares (mil.): 467
Dividends
Yield: 2.8%
Payout: 55.3%
Market value ($ mil.): 31,798

	STOCK PRICE ($) FY Close	P/E High/Low		PER SHARE ($) Earnings	Dividends	Book Value
12/14	67.96	21	15	3.76	1.96	33.74
12/13	76.12	20	14	3.90	1.68	35.34
12/12	54.18	15	14	3.46	1.52	32.05
Annual Growth	12.0%	—	—	2.1%	6.6%	1.3%

Eaton Ltd (United Kingdom)

Auditors: Ernst & Young

LOCATIONS

HQ: Eaton Ltd (United Kingdom)
Eaton House, 30 Pembroke Road, Dublin
Phone:
Web: www.eaton.com

HISTORICAL FINANCIALS

Company Type: Public

Income Statement FYE: December 31

	REVENUE ($ mil.)	NET INCOME ($ mil.)	NET PROFIT MARGIN	EMPLOYEES
12/14	22,552	1,793	8.0%	102,227
12/13	22,046	1,861	8.4%	0
12/12	16,311	1,217	7.5%	0
Annual Growth	17.6%	21.4%	—	—

2014 Year-End Financials

Debt ratio: 26.9%
Return on equity: 11.0%
Cash ($ mil.): 1,026
Current ratio: 1.51
Long-term debt ($ mil.): 8,024
No. of shares (mil.): 467
Dividends
Yield: —
Payout: 52.1%
Market value ($ mil.): —

	STOCK PRICE ($) FY Close	P/E High/Low		PER SHARE ($) Earnings	Dividends	Book Value
12/14	0.00	—	—	3.76	1.96	33.74
12/13	0.00	—	—	3.90	1.68	35.34
Annual Growth	—	—	—	(1.8%)	8.0%	(2.3%)

Ecopetrol SA

Ecopetrol performs crude oil and natural gas exploration production refining and transportation. The largest company in Colombia (where it accounts for 60% of national production and is one of the world's 40 largest oil companies) Ecopetrol has two large refineries (Barrancabermeja and Cartagena) strategically located to supply the domestic market and to export oil and oil products to the southern US. Ecopetrol explores for oil and gas across Colombia and is expanding internationally through exploration partnerships in Brazil Peru and the US Gulf of Mexico. In 2013 the company reported proved reserves of more than 1.4 billion barrels of oil equivalent.

Geographic Reach

Headquartered in Bogota Colombia the company has exploration and production activities in Brazil Peru and the US (Gulf of Mexico). In 2013 it derived almost 40% of its revenues from Colombia and nearly 30% from the US.

Sales and Marketing

The company's crude oil export sales are made both in the spot market and through long-term contracts primarily to refiners in the US Gulf Coast Far East Europe and the U. West Coast. It sell natural gas to distribution companies through take-or-pay or swing contracts.

Strategy

The company has ambitious expansion plans including the doubling of refining capacity and the emergence of Ecopetrol as a leader in biofuels production. The company's goal is to produce 1 million barrels of oil equivalent per day by 2015 and 1.3 million of oil equivalent per day in 2020.Ecopetrol's strategy is focused on supplying the local market and exporting crude oil refined products petrochemical products and natural gas to end-users including refineries and wholesalers in order to improve its margins. It also intends to increase its market participation in crude oil and refined products in Asia and Europe.

In an effort to enhance the strategic and logistical framework of Colombia's oil industry in response to the increase in hydrocarbon production and higher sales of crudes and refined products both within Colombia and on the international markets in 2012 the company established Cenit as a wholly-owned subsidiary specializing in logistics and transportation of hydrocarbons within Colombia.

During 2012 the company acquired 23908 kilometers of additional seismic equivalent which includes 13908 kilometers in the US Gulf Coast and 10000 kilometers in Brazil. During the first quarter of 2013 it drilled five stratigraphic wells out of which two exhibited evidence of hydrocarbons (Segua 1 and Circe 1).

EXECUTIVES

VP Development and Production, H ©tor Manosalva Rojas
VP Refining, Federico Maya Molina
Director Colombian Petroleum Institute (ICP), N ©tor Fernando Saavedra
COO, Camilo Marulanda, age 36
VP Exploration, Humberto Fuenzalida
VP Transportation, Jaime Bocanegra
CFO, Magda Manosalva
Manager Procurement, Jaime A. Pineda Dur ˜n
CEO, Juan Carlos Echeverry
Auditors: PricewaterhouseCoopers Ltda.

LOCATIONS

HQ: Ecopetrol SA
Carrera 13 No. 36-24, Bogota
Phone: (57) 1 234 4000 **Fax:** (57) 1 234 5628
Web: www.ecopetrol.com.co

2013 Sales

	% of total
Colombia	38
US	29
Asia	16
Europe	7
Central America and Caribbean	5
South America	3
Others	2
Total	**100**

PRODUCTS/OPERATIONS

2013 Sales

	% of total
Exploration & production	59
Refining activities	34
Transportation & logistics	7
Total	**100**

COMPETITORS

BP
Exxon Mobil
Gran Tierra Energy
HKN
Houston American Energy
Hunt Oil
Nexen
Pacific Exploration
Royal Dutch Shell
Talisman Energy

HISTORICAL FINANCIALS

Company Type: Public

Income Statement FYE: December 31

	REVENUE ($ mil.)	NET INCOME ($ mil.)	NET PROFIT MARGIN	EMPLOYEES
12/14	28,827	3,141	10.9%	11,069
12/13	36,501	6,792	18.6%	10,686
12/12	38,801	8,328	21.5%	9,701
12/11	33,928	7,973	23.5%	8,729
12/10	21,097	4,095	19.4%	7,575
Annual Growth	8.1%	(6.4%)	—	9.9%

2014 Year-End Financials

Debt ratio: 0.0%
Return on equity: 10.7%
Cash ($ mil.): 3,325
Current ratio: 1.21
Long-term debt ($ mil.): 14,161
No. of shares (mil.): —
Dividends
Yield: 13.6%
Payout: —
Market value ($ mil.): —

	STOCK PRICE ($) FY Close	P/E High/Low	PER SHARE ($) Earnings	Dividends	Book Value
12/14	17.12	— —	0.08	2.67	0.70
12/13	38.45	— —	0.17	3.15	0.90
12/12	59.67	— —	0.20	4.38	0.89
12/11	44.52	— —	0.20	0.00	0.69
12/10	43.62	— —	0.10	0.93	0.51
Annual Growth	(20.8%)	— —	(6.8%)	30.0%	8.0%

Electricite de France

State-owned Electricit de France (EDF) has been quick to expand into global deregulated markets. One of the world's top electric utilities (as well as one of the last major state-controlled energy giants in Europe) EDF has a generating capacity of more than 654 TWh (primarily from nuclear sources) and provides power to 28.5 million French customers and 10 million customers in other countries. It's transmission and distribution subsidiaries in France operate 1.3 million km of low and medium voltage power lines and 100000 km of high and very high voltage networks. Its EDF Trading unit trades a range of energy products.

Geographic Reach

The company operates power plants in Europe Africa the Americas Asia and the Middle East.

Operations

EDF operates in three major segments: Generation/Supply –energy generation and energy sales to industry local authorities small businesses and residential consumers. This segment also includes commodity trading activities; Distribution –the management of the low and medium-voltage public distribution network; and Other –energy services (district heating thermal energy services etc.) for industry and local authorities and new businesses mainly aimed at boosting electricity generation through cogeneration and renewable energy sources.

Nuclear plants provide the vast majority of EDF's domestic power supply; other sources include hydroelectric and fossil-fueled plants. Making use of its extensive experience especially in developing nuclear power EDF builds power plants and provides plant management and consulting services worldwide.In the UK EDF's units include EDF Energy Nuclear Generation Ltd and EDF Development Company Ltd. In Italy operations are led by the Edison subgroup TdE and Fenice.

EDF International and the other gas and electricity entities are located in continental Europe the US Latin America and Asia. Other activities include EDF Trading EDF ?nergies Nouvelles Dalkia Tiru ?lectricit de Strasbourg and EDF Investissements Groupe.

Financial Performance

EDF's net revenues increased by 1% in 2014 primarily due to an increase in Other activities driven by organic growth of 22 million as the result of the takeover of former joint venture Dalkia's activities in France in 2014.Net income increased by 5% due to higher revenues changes in net increases in provisions for renewal of property plant and equipment operated under concessions and a share in net income of associates and joint ventures.In 2014 the company's cash inflow decreased by 2% due to changes in working capital as a result of changes in net financial expenses disbursed and income taxes paid.

Strategy

EDF is investing aggressively outside of France. In 2015 the EDF Energies Nouvelles entered into the South American market by setting up a local subsidiary in Brazil EDF EN do Brasil. EDF Energies Nouvelles purchased a portfolio of wind energy development projects from SOWITEC one of the leading international renewable energy developers with a total capacity of about 800 MW.

That year EDF announced additional capacity at the Arada-Montemuro (9.2 MW) and São Pedro (2 MW) wind farms in Portugal. These extensions increased the combined capacity of these two facilities to 133 MW. In 2015 EDF also signed an agreement with China General Nuclear Power Group to share their experience of plant operation and engineering support for existing nuclear fleets with the aim of preserving the highest safety levels and maintaining consistency between French and Chinese procedures and standards. It also signed an agreement with Huadian a leading Chinese electric utility paving the way for future cooperation on joint projects in China and elsewhere.In 2014 the company and the UK government agreed to build a new nuclear power station at Hinkley Point C in Somerset. That year EDF also signed an agreement with Constellation Energy Nuclear Group (CENG) delegating to Exelon operational management of the five nuclear reactors owned by CENG. Exelon also granted to EDF an option to sell its holding in CENG to Exelon between 2016 and 2022. After this deal EDF will continue to hold 49.99% of CENG whilst Exelon will hold 50.01%.In 2013 EDF signed an agreement with Global Energy Holding Company (GEHC) for the creation of a joint venture in nuclear energy Riyadh. The JV will carry out feasibility studies in the context of the Saudi nuclear program based on French technology.

Ownership

The French government owns 85% of the company.

HISTORY

The French government nationalized hundreds of regional private firms to form Electricit de France (EDF) in 1946 as part of an effort to rebuild the nation's badly shaken post-war economy. This was a marked difference from the notoriously complex and inefficient pre-war electrical industry.

By the 1950s EDF had taken advantage of the centralized control and developed massive hydroelectric projects. Hydroelectric power would account for more than 70% of EDF's power.

But in France as elsewhere hydro wasn't enough to keep up with the growing demand for electricity and fossil fuels became an increasingly important power source. Then came the oil shortages of the 1970s and France –with limited domestic supplies of oil and gas –began searching for alternatives to fossil-fueled plants. Nuclear power was determined to be the answer.

The government moved to invest billions of dollars in developing its relatively small nuclear power production facilities. Muddled with Malthusian predictions of power shortages and a preoccupation with having enough energy to be self-reliant France found its nuclear operations left the government with more energy than it could use and more debt than it wanted. The company began to build a cable connecting the Continent to the UK in 1981. With the power grids of the two countries connected in 1986 EDF was finally able to start exporting its power to the Brits.

The 1990s brought with them deregulation. EDF fought to keep the UK-France grid closed to other energy sellers. After the government forbade the utility from diversifying into areas other than electricity in 1995 the company turned its attention to foreign investment especially in Latin America.

The company faced increasing deregulatory pressures from without in the late 1990s. The newly formed European Union required open competition from member states. Begrudgingly and behind schedule EDF opened about 30% of its market to competition in 2000.

Other members of the EU complained that EDF was trying to play it both ways: It was making aggressive acquisitions in the UK liberalized market (it bought London Electricity in 1999) while resisting a competition-enabling breakup or even allowing a foreign competitor to buy a stake in the French market.

EDF in 2001 expanded its stake in Italy's Montedison a conglomerate with substantial energy holdings by forming a consortium (Italenergia) with Italian automaker Fiat and some Italian banks to wrest control of Montedison from Italian bank MEDIOBANCA. Although the consortium owns 94% of Montedison EDF has only 2% of voting rights. (Montedison changed its name to Edison in 2002.)

EDF also purchased a 35% interest in German utility Energie Baden-Württemberg in 2001 and it merged its energy services unit with Dalkia a unit of Vivendi Environnement (now Veolia Environnement) taking a 34% stake in Dalkia (which will eventually be increased to 50%). EDF subsidiary London Electricity agreed to buy $2.4 billion in UK assets from TXU Europe that year including a 2000 MW power plant TXU's Eastern Electricity distribution unit and its interest in TXU/EDF joint venture 24seven; the deals were completed in 2001 and 2002.

In 2002 EDF increased its stake in Brazilian utility Light Serviços de Eletricidade to 88% by swapping Light's interest in São Paulo utility Eletropaulo for AES's 24% interest in Light. Later that year EDF purchased UK electric and gas utility SEEBOARD (1.9 million customers) from US utility AEP in a $2.2 billion deal.

Deregulation of 70% of the French market took effect in July 2004. Between 2000 and 2004 only 30% of the market was deregulated just more than the percentage required by European Union (EU) rulings.

EDF acquired Edison SpA (Italy's second-largest power group) in partnership with Italian utility company AEM SpA in 2005 for an estimated $15.4 billion.

Expanding its presence and its position as a nuclear power provider in the US in 2009 EDF unit EDF Development acquired 49.99% of Constellation Energy's Constellation Energy Nuclear Group LLC for $4.5 billion. (However another joint venture between these two parties aimed at developing new nuclear power plants in the US was terminated in 2010 after strategic disagreements between the principals).

In a move to boost its position as both a major energy and a nuclear power player in Europe in 2009 EDF acquired British Energy with its 1.1 million customer accounts for about $18 billion.

In 2010 EDF signed two new agreements with China National Nuclear Corporation and China Guangdong Nuclear Power Holding Company solidifying its role as a long term partner in China's nuclear development program. (The company has worked in China for 25 years).

To help pay down debt to pay for its expansion in 2010 Hong Kong's Cheung Kong Infrastructure and Hongkong Electric both controlled by Hong Kong-based billionaire Li Ka-shing acquired EDF's three UK distribution UK grids in a deal valued at about $9 billion. In 2011 EDF sold its 45% stake in German power utility Energie Baden-Württemberg for $6.1 billion.

In 2012 EDF acquired the Italy-based energy group Edison by purchasing Delmi's entire investment (50%) in Transalpina Di Energia for a total of 784 million. Following this acquisition the Group held 78.96% of the capital and 80.64% of the voting rights in Edison.

Not to be left out in the competitive renewable energy market EDF is seeking to boost its wind and solar energy output from a few hundred MW in 2008 to 4000 MW (in 2012) and higher in 2013.

The company is working on a 6 billion Flamanville EPR construction project in France. In early 2013 the civil engineering work was 94% complete and 39% of the electro-mechanical equipment was in place. Its other projects included French offshore projects at Saint-Nazaire Courseulles-sur-Mer and Fcamp.

EXECUTIVES

Director Upstream-Downstream Optimisation and Trading Division, Philippe Torrion
SEVP Finance, Thomas Piquemal, age 45
SEVP HR, Marianne Laigneau
Chairman and CEO, Jean-Bernard L ©y, age 59
Chief Executive EDF Energies Nouvelles, Antoine Cahuzac
SEVP Commerce Optimisation and Trading and Island Energy Systems, Henri Lafontaine
SEVP Gas and Southern Europe; Chief Executive Edison, Bruno Lescoeur
Chief Executive EDF Energy, Vincent de Rivaz
Director Hydraulic Production and Engineering Division, Xavier Ursat
Auditors: Deloitte & Associ ©

LOCATIONS

HQ: Electricite de France
22-30 avenue de Wagram, Paris, Cedex 08 75382
Phone: (33) 1 40 42 22 22 **Fax:** (33) 1 40 42 32 17
Web: www.edf.com

2014 Sales

	% of total
France	55
Italy	17
UK	14
Other countries	8
Other activities	6
Total	**100**

COMPETITORS

Business Group Benelux
Centrica
E.ON
ELETROBRS
Endesa S.A.
Enel
Energias de Portugal
Engie
Hydro-Qu©bec
IBERDROLA
International Power
RWE
Scottish and Southern Energy
Vattenfall
Veolia Environnement

HISTORICAL FINANCIALS

Company Type: Public

Income Statement

FYE: December 31

	REVENUE ($ mil.)	NET INCOME ($ mil.)	NET PROFIT MARGIN	EMPLOYEES
12/14	88,578	4,498	5.1%	158,161
12/13	104,072	4,841	4.7%	158,467
12/12	95,860	4,370	4.6%	159,740
12/11	84,471	3,893	4.6%	151,804
12/10	87,215	1,365	1.6%	158,842
Annual Growth	0.4%	34.7%	—	(0.1%)

2014 Year-End Financials

Debt ratio: 25.2%
Return on equity: 10.6%
Cash ($ mil.): 5,714
Current ratio: 1.26
Long-term debt ($ mil.): 56,565
No. of shares (mil.): 1,858
Dividends
Yield: 6.0%
Payout: 13.9%
Market value ($ mil.): 10,091

	STOCK PRICE ($) FY Close	P/E High/Low		PER SHARE ($) Earnings	Dividends	Book Value
12/14	5.43	4	3	2.16	0.33	23.02
12/13	7.01	4	2	2.53	0.33	25.34
12/12	3.71	3	2	2.37	0.29	18.46
12/11	4.81	5	3	2.11	0.30	21.40
12/10	8.30	21	15	0.74	0.29	22.68
Annual Growth	(10.1%)	—	—	30.9%	2.7%	0.4%

Enbridge Inc

Cold spells heated business for Enbridge in North America. Gas Pipelines Processing and Energy Services is Enbridge's largest segment but it also has interests in Gas Distribution Liquids Pipelines and Sponsored Investments. Its gas utilities provide natural gas to about 2 million customers primarily in Ontario and New York. A major crude oil and liquids transporter Enbridge moves about 2.5 million barrels of crude oil a day and operates thousands of miles of natural gas pipeline including a 1500 mile system connecting Alberta and British Columbia to the Chicago area. Its Sponsored Investments business consists of the firm's holdings in Enbridge Energy Partners (25%) and Enbridge Income Fund (72%).

Enbridge operates the world's longest crude oil and liquids pipeline system and transports 65% Western Canada's crude oil exports. It has natural gas gathering transmission and midstream operations and a power transmission business. The company also owns Canada's largest natural gas distribution operations. To meet clean air regulations Enbridge is also investing in geothermal hybrid fuel cell solar and wind power projects and has about 1000 MW of renewable and alternative energy generating capacity.

Enbridge operates in Canada and the US. It has gas distribution customers in Ontario Quebec New Brunswick and New York. Outside of North America the company provides natural gas distribution consulting services in more than 30 countries.

Embridge reported a 26% jump in revenues in 2011 thanks to an improving economy increased product sales and higher commodity oil and natural gas liquids prices. However net income grew by only 1.5% as higher gas commodity costs related to its gas pipelines processing and energy services segment trimmed back its profits.

In North America the company is investing heavily in pipeline construction to expand the reach of its oil and gas assets. In 2012 it teamed up with Spectra Energy and DTE Energy to develop the NEXUS Gas Transmission system a 250-mile pipeline to move natural gas from the Ohio Utica shale to markets in the US Midwest and Ontario. In 2011 Enbridge was eyeing $30 billion in growth opportunities under development extending pipelines from Canadian gas and oil sources for heavily populated markets in the Midwest and Southern US. In 2010 alone Enbridge put into service some $6.5 billion of growth projects including the $3.5 billion Alberta Clipper project the largest liquids pipeline project in the Enbridge's history which provides service between Hardisty Alberta and Superior Wisconsin.

In a major expansion in 2011 Enbridge acquired ConocoPhillips' 50% stake in the Seaway Crude Pipeline System for $1.15 billion and plans to reverse the direction of crude oil flows on the pipeline to enable it to ship oil from Cushing Oklahoma to Gulf Coast refineries.

In 2011 the company acquired Tonbridge Power for $20 million. Tonbridge Power is developing the Montana-Alberta Tie-Line power transmission project a 345-km transmission line from Great Falls Montana to Lethbridge Alberta.

Embridge has also agreed to work with PetroChina International Company to develop the Gateway Pipeline. The proposed pipeline would move 525000 barrels per day of oil sands production from Edmonton Alberta to a port in British Columbia where it would be shipped to California and on to China and other Asian markets.

Enbridge has cut back on its direct investments in international pipeline projects in order to focus on the growing demand and surer financing for pipeline expansion closer to home. (In 2009 Enbridge sold its quarter stake in Colombian pipeline operator Oleoducto Central S.A. to that country's national oil company Ecopetrol for $400 million. Cash from the deal was designated to fund North American crude oil pipeline expansion projects).

In 2016 the company announced the $538 million acquisition of Tupper Main and Tupper West gas plants and associated pipelines in northeastern British Columbiafrom the Canadian subsidiary of Murphy Oil.

EXECUTIVES

EVP Corporate Development, J. Richard Bird, age 66, $540,000 total compensation

President Gas Pipelines and Processing, C. Gregory (Greg) Harper, age 51

EVP and CFO, John K. Whelen

President CEO and Director, Al Monaco, age 56, $437,500 total compensation

EVP People and Partners, Karen L. Radford, age 46

EVP and Chief Legal Officer, David T. Robottom

President Liquids Pipelines, Guy Jarvis

COO, Leon Zupan

President Enbridge Gas Distribution, Glenn Beaumont

Chairman, David A. Arledge, age 71

Auditors: PricewaterhouseCoopers LLP

LOCATIONS

HQ: Enbridge Inc
30th Floor, 425 - 1st Street S.W., Calgary, Alberta T2P 3L8

Phone: 403 231-5935 **Fax:** 403 231-5929

Web: www.enbridge.com

2014 Sales

	% of total
US	60
Canada	40
Total	**100**

PRODUCTS/OPERATIONS

2014 Sales

	% of total
Gas pipelines processing and energy services	61
Sponsored investments	24
Gas distribution	9
Liquids pipelines	6
Total	**100**

Selected Subsidiaries and Affiliates

Gas Pipelines Processing and Energy Services
- Aux Sable Liquids Products Inc. (43%)
- Alliance Pipeline Limited Partnership (50%)
- Tlbury Solar Project
- Vector Pipeline Limited Partnership (60%)

Gas Distribution
- Enbridge Gas Distribution
- Enbridge Gas New Brunswick (63%)
- Gazifère Inc.
- Niagara Gas Transmission Limited

Liquids Pipelines
- Chicap Pipe Line Company (44%)
- Enbridge Energy Partners L.P. (13%)
- Enbridge Pipelines (Athabasca) Inc.
- Enbridge Pipelines (North Dakota) Inc.
- Enbridge Pipelines (NW) Inc.
- Enbridge Pipelines (Toledo) Inc.
- Enbridge Pipelines Inc.
- Frontier Pipeline Company (78%)
- Mustang Pipe Line Partners (30%)
- Olympic Pipe Line (85%)

Sponsored Investments
- Enbridge Income Fund (72%)
- Enbridge Energy Partners L.P. (25.5%)

Corporate
- Noverco Inc. (39%)
- Gaz Métropolitain and Company Limited Partnership (71%)
- Vermont Gas Systems Inc.

COMPETITORS

Con Edison
Dynegy
Hydro One
Koch Industries Inc.
National Fuel Gas
New York Power Authority
ONEOK Partners
TransCanada
Williams Companies

HISTORICAL FINANCIALS

Company Type: Public

Income Statement

FYE: December 31

	REVENUE ($ mil.)	NET INCOME ($ mil.)	NET PROFIT MARGIN	EMPLOYEES
12/14	32,504	1,213	3.7%	11,000
12/13	30,957	591	1.9%	10,000
12/12	25,444	718	2.8%	7,828
12/11	19,019	984	5.2%	0
12/10	15,159	972	6.4%	6,357
Annual Growth	21.0%	5.7%	—	14.7%

2014 Year-End Financials

Debt ratio: 42.6%	No. of shares (mil.): 852
Return on equity: 9.2%	Dividends
Cash ($ mil.): 1,088	Yield: 2.7%
Current ratio: 0.86	Payout: 164.7%
Long-term debt ($ mil.): 28,862	Market value ($ mil.): 43,801

	STOCK PRICE ($) FY Close	P/E High/Low	PER SHARE ($) Earnings	Dividends	Book Value
12/14	51.41	37 28	1.18	1.27	17.01
12/13	43.68	83 72	0.52	1.23	15.27
12/12	43.32	54 46	0.78	1.13	13.11
12/11	37.41	49 21	1.27	0.96	11.10
12/10	56.40	45 35	1.29	0.83	9.85
Annual Growth	(2.3%)	— —	(2.2%)	11.3%	14.7%

ENBW Energie Baden-Wuerttemberg AG

One of Germany's largest utilities Energie Baden-Württemberg (EnBW) is bathing its namesake region with light. EnBW distributes electricity in the state of Baden-Württemberg; the company also provides natural gas and energy and environmental services. The company markets power to retail customers throughout Germany under subsidiary Yello Strom. EnBW also generates distributes and markets energy across Central Europe. The company has 5.5 million energy customers and about 15500 MW of electric generating capacity. EnBW is focusing on energy diversity improving the energy-efficiency of its fossil-fuel powered generation facilities while expanding its renewable power sources.

Geographic Reach

The company's core market is Baden-Württemberg where it is the market leader. It also operates throughout Germany and across Europe.

Operations

As an integrated energy supply company EnBW operates four segments: Sales Grids Renewable Energies and Generation and Trading. The Sales segment encompasses the distribution of electricity and gas and the provision of energy-related services (invoicing energy supply and energy-saving contracting) 45% of EnBW's revenues in 2014.The Grids segment encompasses the transmission and distribution of electricity and gas the provision of grid-related services (such as the operation of grids for third parties) and the supply of water. The Renewable Energies segment is engaged in power generation from renewable energy sources (wind power and hydropower). It is involved in project development construction the efficient operation of green energy plantsThe Generation and Trading segment encompasses the generation and trading of electricity the gas midstream business district heating environmental services and decommissioning of power plants. This business is primarily based on the generation of electricity and heat from thermal power plants (coal gas and pumped storage power plants and nuclear power plants).

Sales and Marketing

The company's core market is Baden-Württemberg. It supplies customers all over Germany through subsidiaries Yello Strom GmbH and Sales & Solutions GmbH. EnBW serves private residential customers commercial enterprises the housing industry and agriculture major commercial enterprises industrial customers and redistributors municipal utilities local authorities and public entities.

Financial Performance

In 2014 EnBW's net revenues increased by 2% due to higher sales from Grids segment and Renewable Energies segment. Revenues in the Grids segment grew significantly as a result of higher EEG revenues while Renewable Energies segment was dueto the sale of two solar parks and higher organic sales.Net income decreased by 417% due to increased amortization and depreciation costs partially offset by increased revenues. In 2014 net cash provided by the operating activities decreased by 7% as the result of a change in net balance of other assets and liabilities and trade receivables and payables.

Strategy

EnBW aims to more than double its share of renewable energies in its generation portfolio raising it from about 19% to more than 40% in 2020. Its capacities derived from onshore wind farms will be increased significantly in the target markets of Germany and Turkey. The company's innovation strategy pursues a goal of developing models for new business segments and rapidly moving them to commercialization.

EnBW invested nearly 2 billion euros in 2014 primarily in the Renewable Energies segment in the expansion of the company's electric grids. Other main areas of investment were the new power plants RDK 8 in Karlsruhe and Lausward in Düsseldorf.

To raise cash to pay down debt and fund growth in 2014 EnBW Group sold 74.9% of the equity in SWS Netzinfrastruktur GmbH Stuttgart to Stadtwerke Stuttgart GmbH Stuttgart on 31 October 2014. The sale is connected with the City of Stuttgart's franchise award process. SWS Netzinfrastruktur GmbH owns the electricity and gas distribution grid in the Stuttgart franchise area. Following the sale of the interest SWS Netzinfrastruktur GmbH is now a joint venture in the EnBW Group and is consolidated using the equity method.That year it also sold 49.98% of the equity in EnBW Onshore Portfolio GmbH Stuttgart in equal shares to Onshore Bündelgesellschaft 1 GmbH Stuttgart Onshore Bündelgesellschaft 2 GmbH Karlsruhe and Onshore Bündelgesellschaft 3 GmbH Stuttgart. As a result of the transaction our interest in EnBW Onshore Portfolio GmbH falls to 50.02%. EnBW continues to fully consolidate EnBW Onshore Portfolio GmbH in its consolidated financial statements.In 2013 EnBW announced plans to shut down a total of four non-core power plant units with a total output of 668 MW at its power plant locations in Marbach and Walheim.

Mergers and Acquisitions

Expanding its Renewable Energies portfolio in 2015 EnBW bought wind power player PROKON Regenerative Energien GmbH. It also acquired the Albatros offshore wind farm project from the consortium partners STRABAG and the Norderland/ETANAX Group. This offshore wind project which has approval for 79 wind turbines of the 5-7 megawatt rating class is located 105 kilometers from the coast in the German sector of the North Sea.

In 2014 EnBW purchased a further 50% of the equity in EnBW Gas VerwaltungsgesellschaftmbH Karlsruhe (previously EnBW Eni Verwaltungsgesellschaft mbH Karlsruhe) and thus indirectly acquired a further 50% of GasVersorgung Süddeutschland GmbH Stuttgart and of terranets bw GmbH Stuttgart from the Italian energy group Eni S.p.A. The 197.9 million deal boosted EnBW's stake in EnBW Gas Verwaltungsgesellschaft mbH to 100%.

Company Background

As part of this green energy push in 2010 EnBW completed its Baltic 1 wind farm (which has 21 turbines and an installed output of 50 MW) just off of Germany's north coast. The company has additional wind farms under construction or in the planning stage.

It is also growing its renewables by acquisition. In 2011 EnBW acquired a 6 MW wind farm from ABO Wind AG through its renewable energy unit EnBW Erneuerbare Energien GmbH. The company had previously acquired a 15 MW wind farm from ABO Wind in 2010.

EnBW has also made selective international energy acquisitions (including renewable sources) to balance the growth of its core German operations. The company moved into Sweden in 2007 via Yello Strom. In 2008 EnBW made a domestic acquisition when it acquired a 26% stake in German gas and electricity distributor EWE for about $3 billion. It also bought stakes in two German coal-fired power plants from E.ON in 2009.

Moving into the Turkish market in 2009 the company announced plans to build up generation capacities of 2000 MW of primarily renewable energy powered plants by 2020 in collaboration with Turkish industrial conglomerate Borusan Holding.

In 2010 with the global economy bouncing back the company benefited from higher commodity prices and greater industrial demand. EnBW saw its revenues and income grow robustly that year led by a 100% jump in its power generating and trading segment revenues.

Electricit de France (EDF) and Oberschwäbische Elektrizitätswerke once each owned 45% of EnBW but in early 2011 EDF sold its stake to the state of Baden-Württemberg for $6.1 billion to raise cash. Baden-Württemberg increased its holdings to 47% in March 2011 through the acquisition of minority stakes.

EXECUTIVES

CTO, Ing. Hans-Josef Zimmer, age 57
CFO and Member the Management Board, Thomas Kusterer
Chairman and CEO, Frank Mastiaux, age 51
Deputy Chairman Supervisory Board, Dietrich Herd
Chairman Supervisory Board, Claus Dieter
Auditors: KPMG AG

LOCATIONS

HQ: ENBW Energie Baden-Wuerttemberg AG
Durlacher Allee 93, Karlsruhe D-76131
Phone: (49) 721 63 00 **Fax:** (49) 721 63 127 25
Web: www.enbw.com

2014 Revenue by Geography

	%
Germany	93
Europe	2
Rest of Europe	5
Total	**100**

PRODUCTS/OPERATIONS

2014 Sales

	% of total
Sales	43
Grids	30
Generation & trading	25
Renewable energies	2
Others	-
Total	**100**

Selected Subsidiaries

EnBW Gas GmbH (natural gas distribution)
EnBW Vertriebs- und Servicegesellschaft mbH (electricity energy and environmental services)
EnBW Kraftwerke AG (electricity generation)
EnBW Regional AG (electricity distribution)
EnBW Trading GmbH (energy marketing)
EnBW Transportnetze AG (electricity transmission)
Yello Strom GmbH (electricity supply)
Gasversorgung Süddeutschland GmbH (GVS district heating and natural gas transmission and supply)

COMPETITORS

Business Group Benelux	Fortum
E.ON	Gasunie
Endesa S.A.	IBERDROLA
Enel	RWE
Energias de Portugal	Vattenfall Europe
Engie	

HISTORICAL FINANCIALS

Company Type: Public

Income Statement

FYE: December 31

	REVENUE ($ mil.)	NET INCOME ($ mil.)	NET PROFIT MARGIN	EMPLOYEES
12/14	25,642	(547)	—	19,966
12/13	28,356	70	0.2%	19,822
12/12	25,410	624	2.5%	20,098
12/11	24,420	(1,121)	—	20,959
12/10	23,531	1,566	6.7%	20,450
Annual Growth	2.2%	—	—	(0.6%)

2014 Year-End Financials

Debt ratio: 26.2%	No. of shares (mil.): 270
Return on equity: (-10.8%)	Dividends
Cash ($ mil.): 3,864	Yield: —
Current ratio: 1.14	Payout: —
Long-term debt ($ mil.): 8,735	Market value ($ mil.): —

Enel Societa Per Azioni

Arrivederci monopolio! Buongiorno diversified energy player. Italy's largest electric utility Enel has given up its monopoly status and raced into the deregulated global power marketplace. Operating in 32 countries Enel distributes electricity and gas to about 61 million customers and has more than 95000 MW of primarily fossil-fueled and hydroelectric generating capacity. The second largest gas distributor in Italy (after Italgas) Enel serves 3.2 million customers in Italy. It also has renewable and international power generation assets. The Italian government owns about a third of Enel.

Geographic Reach

Internationally Enel has built and acquired independent power plants primarily in Europe and the Americas. The company operates in 32 countries across four continents.

In 2014 Italy accounted for 39% of the company's revenues.

Operations

Enel operates through a number of segments. Its Sales Division sells to high-value mass market segments acquiring new electricity and gas customers. Italy-focused Enel Energia serves 55.8 million electricity customers and 4.6 million gas customers. The company's Generation and Energy Management Division generates about 283.1 TWh of power (30% of the Italian market) a year.

The Engineering and Innovation Division carries out numerous research and development initiatives and plant construction projects. The Infrastructure and Networks Division is engaged in energy distribution The Iberia and Latin America Division serve market in Spain and Portugal and South America.

Enel is strongly committed to renewable energy sources and to the research and development of new environmentally friendly technologies. Enel Green Power (the company's publicly listed renewable energy generation business) operating 9500 MW of net installed capacity of hydro wind geothermal solar biomass and co-generation sources in Europe the Americas and Africa.

Financial Performance

In 2014 Enel's revenues decreased by 3.6% due to lower sales of electricity largely due to a fall in amounts sold the adverse impact of changes in the currency exchange rates and the disposal of strategic equity interests.Net income decreased by 84% due to a drop in revenues and increased depreciation amortization and impairment losses. The depreciation amortization and impairment losses reflected the net impact of an increase in impairment of Slovenske elektrarne (held for sale) an increase in impairment of property plant and equipment higher impairment of intangible assets and a decreased impairment of goodwill. In 2014 Enel's net cash provided by the operating activities increased by 39% due to a change in trade payables and receivables.

Strategy

The company is also growing its non-traditional power assets to meet EU regulation on carbon emissions. In 2015 Enel Green Power S.p.A. through its subsidiary Enel Green Power North America Inc. entered into a deal with General Electric Unit GE Energy Financial Services for the sale of a 49% stake in newly created EGPNA Renewable Energy Partners LLC for $440 million.

That year Enel Green Power begun construction of Nojoli wind farm which is located in the Eastern Cape Province in South Africa. The new wind farm will have a total installed capacity of 88 MW.

Enel was the first utility in the world to replace the traditional electromechanical meters with smart meters making it possible to measure consumption in real time and manage contractual relationships remotely. In 2015 some 32 million Italian retail customers are equipped with smart meters developed and installed by Enel. It is deploying an additional 13 million smart meters to its customer base in Spain as well as running pilot tests for the smart cities of Búzios (Brazil) and Santiago (Chile).The company is also expanding in areas where it is already operating such as in Latin America and entering new countries. In 2015 Enel Green Power and Marubeni agreed to cooperate in evaluating potential business opportunities in renewable projects mainly in the Asia-Pacific Region. In 2014 Enel signed a framework agreement with ZTE Corporation a leading Chinese telecommunications equipment and systems company to kick-start cooperation between the two groups in the areas of electric mobility smart grids and renewable generation.To raise cash in 2013 the company disposed of 51% of Buffalo Dunes Wind Project and its remaining stake in Enel Rete Gas.It also disposed its entire 36.2% stake in LaGeo a geothermal generation company in El Salvador and 100% of Enel Green Power France a renewables generator.The Italian government owns about a third of Enel. Italy's Ministry of Economy and Finance directly owns approximately 14% of Enel; it owns another 17% indirectly through the government-controlled bank Cassa Depositi e Prestiti.

HISTORY

Italy's energy consumption doubled in the 1950s as the country experienced a period of rapid industrialization and urbanization. A tight-knit oligopoly controlled the electric power industry and included Edison SADE La Centale SME and Finelettrica. The economic boom pushed into the 1960s and the Italian government created Enel (Ente Nazionale per l'Energia Elettrica) in 1962 to nationalize the power industry. In 1963 Enel began gradually buying some 1250 electric utilities. About 160 municipal utilities and the larger independents such as Edison were left out of the takeover.

The company spent the late 1960s and early 1970s connecting Italy's unwieldy transmission network and building new power plants including the La Spezia thermoelectric plant (600 MW). Construction costs coupled with the high prices Enel was required to pay for its takeover targets caused the utility to become steeped in debt. The Arab oil embargoes of the early 1970s made matters worse and the Italian government helped Enel with an endowment in 1973.

The energy crisis also prompted Enel to build its first nuclear power plant Caorso which came on line in 1980. However nuclear power was short-lived in Italy: After the 1986 Chernobyl accident a national referendum forced Enel to deactivate its nukes in 1987. The firm also stepped up its development of renewable energy sources in the 1980s.

Meanwhile Enel opened its Centro Nazionale de Controllo (CNC) in Rome in 1985 to supervise Italy's power grid. The next year the company turned its first profit.

To begin disassembling Enel's monopoly the Italian government in 1992 opened the power generation market to outside producers and converted Enel into a joint stock company (with the state holding all of the shares). Following the European Union's 1997 directive to deregulate Europe's power industry Enel unbundled its utility activities and began trimming its staff.

Italy's Bersani Decree (passed in 1999) outlined the restructuring process: Enel was ordered to divest 25% of its capacity (15000 MW) and turn over a portion of its municipal distribution networks to local governments to enhance competition in the country's power market. Accordingly it transferred management of the national transmission grid to an independent government-owned operator Gestore della Rete di Trasmissione Nazionale (GRTN) and reduced its customer count by approximately 1 million through municipal distribution asset sales.

Enel had already begun to diversify. It started Wind Telecomunicazioni a joint venture with France Telecom —later renamed Orange —and Deutsche Telekom in 1998. (Deutsche Telekom sold its stake to the other partners in 2000.) Wind first offered fixed-line and mobile telecom services to corporations; it extended the services to residential users in 1999. In addition Enel began building water infrastructure to serve local distributors and purchased three water operations in southern Italy.

Also in 1999 the government floated 32% of Enel in one of the world's largest IPOs at the time. The next year the company bought Colombo Gas (a northern Italian gas distributor with about 75000 customers) and it transferred control of its transmission network to Gestore della Rete di Trasmissione Nazionale (an independent government-owned operator) while retaining ownership of the assets.

Enel bought fixed-line telephone company Infostrada from Vodafone in 2001 acquired two more Italian gas distributors and sold its 5400-MW Elettrogen generation unit to Spain's Endesa for $2.3 billion. That year Enel put its 7000-MW Eurogen generation unit on the auction block. The high bidder with a $2.6 billion offer was a consortium backed by Fiat and ?lectricit de France; the sale was completed in 2002.

Also in 2002 Enel merged Infostrada into Wind Telecomunicazioni to create one of Italy's top telecom companies it purchased Camuzzi Gazometri's gas distribution business (Italy's second-largest) for $870 million from Mill Hill Investments and it bought Endesa's Viesgo unit (2400 MW of generating capacity and 500000 power customers) for about $1.8 billion.

Enel sold its final generation divestment company Interpower (2600 MW) to a consortium of utilities (including Belgian utility Electrabel and Italian utility ACEA) for about $880 million in 2003.

That year Enel purchased France Telecom 's 27% stake in Wind for $1.4 billion making the unit a wholly owned subsidiary. (Enel had flirted with the idea of taking Wind public but instead sold the unit in 2006 to the Egypt-based Weather Investments consortium which had the backing of Orascom Telecom 's chairman and CEO Naguib Sawiris.)

The Italian government began the second round of Enel's privatization process in 2003 by selling a 7% stake to Morgan Stanley for more than $2.3 billion. In 2004 the government further reduced its stake by nearly 20% through a public offering of shares.

In 2005 it acquired power distribution and sales businesses in Romania and in 2006 in Slovakia.

With Italian regulators requiring that Enel divest 80% of its Terna subsidiary (which holds the company's power transmission assets) by 2007 Enel spun off 50% of the unit in an IPO in 2004. The following year it divested another 44% and the company reduced its holding to about 5% by January 2006. Grid management and operational functions were also transferred from GRTN back to Terna.

In 2008 the company set Enel Green Power to develop wind solar geothermal and biomass projects. By 2009 it was operating alternative energy plants worldwide with a generating capacity of 4700 MW. In 2010 Enel Green Power acquired Pagoda Wind Power which is developing 4000 MW of wind projects in California.

In what could have been a large cross-border deal Enel considered making a bid for France's SUEZ (now GDF SUEZ) utility company. Perhaps in reaction to the news of Enel's interest France's Gaz de France made a bid for SUEZ (consummated in 2008) a move that Italy called protectionist.

Unperturbed by its failure to secure SUEZ the company took control of Spain's power giant Endesa in 2007 increasing its market share as a European power player. Hoping to pay down what had become a heavy debt load the company in 2009 sold an 80% stake in gas distributor Enel Rete Gas for $666 million.

In 2012 Enel Green Power consolidated its position in the Greek renewable industry through the launching of two new plants - a wind farm and a photovoltaic plant - both located in the Peloponnese region.

EXECUTIVES

CEO and General Manager, Francesco Starace, age 60
CFO, Alberto De Paoli, age 50
Chairman, Jorge Rosenblut
Auditors: Reconta Ernst & Young spa

LOCATIONS

HQ: Enel Societa Per Azioni
Viale Regina Margherita, 137, Rome I-00198
Phone: (39) 6 8509 3184 **Fax:** (39) 6 8509 5810
Web: www.enel.it

2014 Sales

	% of total
Europe	46
Italy	39
Americas	14
Asia	1
Africa	0
Total	**100**

PRODUCTS/OPERATIONS

2014 Sales

	% of total
Iberia & Latin America	40
Generation & energy management (Italy)	30
Sales (Italy)	20
Infrastructure & networks (Italy)	10
International	7
Renewable energy	4
Other (11)	
Total	**100**

COMPETITORS

A2A	Eni
ABB	HC Energa
ACEA	IBERDROLA
Acque Potabili	International Power
E.ON	Italgas
ERG S.p.A.	RWE
Edison	Risanamento
Electricit© de France	Tractebel Engineering

HISTORICAL FINANCIALS

Company Type: Public

Income Statement

FYE: December 31

	REVENUE ($ mil.)	NET INCOME ($ mil.)	NET PROFIT MARGIN	EMPLOYEES
12/14	92,124	628	0.7%	68,961
12/13	110,875	4,453	4.0%	71,394
12/12	111,966	313	0.3%	73,702
12/11	102,847	5,365	5.2%	75,360
12/10	98,205	5,875	6.0%	78,313
Annual Growth	(1.6%)	(42.8%)	—	(3.1%)

2014 Year-End Financials

Debt ratio: 41.6%
Return on equity: 1.5%
Cash ($ mil.): 15,908
Current ratio: 1.04
Long-term debt ($ mil.): 59,140
No. of shares (mil.): —
Dividends
Yield: 2.5%
Payout: 302.2%
Market value ($ mil.): —

	STOCK PRICE ($) FY Close	P/E High/Low	PER SHARE ($) Earnings	Dividends	Book Value
12/14	4.42	198131	0.06	0.11	4.07
12/13	4.34	25 16	0.47	0.14	5.26
12/12	4.14	254128	0.04	0.22	5.01
12/11	4.00	31 14	0.57	0.44	5.34
12/10	4.96	25 14	0.63	0.18	5.39
Annual Growth	(2.8%)	— —	(44.2%)	(11.9%)	(6.8%)

Engie SA

Engie (formerly GDF SUEZ) channels its energy as Europe's top power gas and infrastructure players. It is engaged in the purchasing production and marketing of natural gas and electricity; the development and maintenance of major natural gas and electricity infrastructures; and the creation and marketing of energy and environmental services. With operations in about 70 countries power producer Engie had 118200 MW of installed capacity in 2011. It is Europe's top importer of liquefied natural gas (LNG) its largest supplier of natural gas the continent's leading supplier of multitechnical energy services and a leading global supplier of water and waste management services.
Geographic Reach

Engie operates around the world. Europe accounted for 80% of the company's revenues in 2011.

OperationsThe company has expertise in four key sectors: liquefied natural gas energy efficiency services independent power production and environmental services. Its environmental services segment offers water management and waste treatment and recovery through its subsidiary SUEZ Environnement.In 2011 Engie operated more than 1200 water production sites producing around 4.5 billion metric meters of drinking water in 2011. In sanitation services it biologically treated around 3.2 billion metric meters of waste water. Internationally in the waste segment it operates 120 composting platforms 48 incineration sites (including 45 that recover energy) 645 sorting and transfer stations and 130 storage centers.In the renewable energy sector Engie had an installed capacity of 16121 MW at the end of 2011. At 11332 MW the company is a hydroelectric operator in France and Brazil where it is continuing to develop large-scale projects. It also has a production capacity of 918 MW in biomass and biogas in Europe the US and Latin America. Wind energy is also a priority with capacity of 3792 MW making the group the leading operator on the French and Belgian markets and the second in Portugal.Financial PerformanceDespite unfavorable weather conditions and flat natural gas prices in France the company's revenues grew by 7% in 2011. In Europe water revenues increased by 3% and waste by 7.1%. Internationally sales from both of these sectors went up by 3.7% that year.
Stategy

Engie is looking to harness its global size and its presence in a mix of energy areas (nuclear natural gas LNG coal and renewables) with its water sanitation and waste management expertise to deliver energy in a way that preserves the environment. The company is constructing 11800 MW of installed power-production capacity. (To raise capital to help fund its expansion between 2011 and 2013 the company sold stakes in power projects in Slovakia Canada the UK and elsewhere).In 2013 Engie announced the construction of the 300 MW Tarfaya wind farm in Morocco which will be the largest wind project in Africa. The project is owned in partnership with Nareva Holding a Moroccan energy company. Engie is also developng Cyberjaya Malaysia's premier cybercity through a joint venture with local partner Cyberview Sdn Bhd of Cyberjaya's district cooling network.In 2012 Engie and its International Power subsidiary expanded its power generation of Tihama power sites in Saudi Arabia by 532 MW following an award from Saudi Aramco.

Dramatically boosting its power generation assets in 2011 the company's GDF SUEZ Energy International merged with UK-based International Power. The $21.5 billion deal created one of the world's largest global independent power generation companies. Engie held 70% of International Power which has generation capacity of 66000 MW in 2011 and bought out the other 30% in 2012 for about $2.2 billion to gain full ownership.

Later that year International Power formed a joint venture with Supreme Energy and Marubeni Corporation to develop the Rantau Dedap geothermal project located in Sumatra.The 220-MW geothermal plant is part of the Indonesian government's long-term plan to meet the country's needs with renewable power.

HISTORY

The first canal in Egypt was dug in the 13th century BC but it was Napoleon who revived the idea of a shorter trade route to India: a canal through Egypt linking the Gulf of Suez with the Mediterranean. Former French diplomat and engineer Ferdinand de Lesseps formed Compagnie Universelle du Canal Maritime de Suez in 1858 to build and eventually operate the canal which opened 11 years later. Egypt's modernization had pushed it into debt and increased its ties to the British government which by 1875 had acquired a 44% stake in the company.

For more than 80 years the Suez Canal was a foreign enclave protected by the British Army since 1936. After Egypt's puppet government fell and as Gamal Abd Al-Nasser assumed power in 1956 British troops exited the Canal Zone which Egypt quickly nationalized. Israel Britain and France attacked but the UN arranged a truce and foreign forces withdrew leaving the Suez in Egypt's control.

With no canal to operate Universelle du Canal Maritime de Suez became Compagnie Financière de Suez in 1958. A year later it created a bank (which became Banque Indosuez in 1974).

In 1967 Financière de Suez became the largest shareholder in Socit Lyonnaise des Eaux et de L'Eclairage a leading French water company. Formed in 1880 Lyonnaise des Eaux had stakes in water (Northumbrian Water) and energy (Elyo). After France's energy firms were nationalized in 1946 Lyonnaise des Eaux dipped deeper into the water industry by acquiring Degrmont (now Ondeo-Degrmont) in 1972. It also purchased stakes in waste management (SITA 1970) and heating systems (Cofreth 1975).

In the 1980s Lyonnaise des Eaux expanded in Spain the UK and the US and diversified into cable TV (1986) and broadcast TV (1987). It merged with construction firm Dumez in 1990.

Meanwhile Financière de Suez became a financial power when it won a controlling stake in Socit Gnrale de Belgique (SGB) in 1988 and bought Groupe Victoire in 1989. But the two buys left the firm (renamed Compagnie de Suez in 1990) deeply in debt.

Losing money Compagnie de Suez disposed of Victoire (1994) and then the valuable Banque Indosuez (1996). In 1996 the company bought a controlling stake in Belgium's top utility Tractebel (now SUEZ-TRACTEBEL). Compagnie de Suez and Lyonnaise des Eaux merged in 1997 to create Suez Lyonnaise des Eaux. The following year Suez Lyonnaise acquired the rest of SGB and bought the European and Asian operations of waste management giant Browning-Ferris Industries; it also began divesting noncore operations.

Suez Lyonnaise in 1999 expanded its core businesses primarily in the US. The company bought Calgon (water treatment US) and Nalco Chemical (water treatment chemicals US) then merged Calgon into Nalco to form Ondeo Nalco. (The company's name was changed back to Nalco when it was divested in 2003.)

In 2000 Suez Lyonnaise bought United Water Resources (now United Water) and acquired the rest of SITA. Through its Elyo subsidiary Suez Lyonnaise bought out minority shareholders in US-based Trigen Energy. The company also merged its construction unit Groupe GTM with French construction rival VINCI; Suez Lyonnaise then sold the VINCI shares that it received from the transaction.

The next year the company shortened its name to Suez (later modified to SUEZ) as part of a global rebranding effort. It also united its water services operations under the ONDEO brand. In 2002 SUEZ made Tractebel a wholly owned subsidiary by purchasing the remaining publicly held shares. Also in 2002 SUEZ sold minority stakes in communications equipment manufacturer Sagem (now SAFRAN) steelmaker Arcelor and motorway operator Autopistas Concesionaria Española (ACESA).

SUEZ divested most of its 11% stake in Belgian insurance firm Fortis for nearly $2 billion in 2003. It also sold its 79% stake in cable company Coditel that year. In 2003 the company merged Tractebel and SGB (Tractebel's former holding company) to form SUEZ-TRACTEBEL.Gaz de France was founded in 1946 by the French government to consolidate the more than 500 (mostly coal-fired) gas works that had existed before WWII. From 1949 on Gaz de France focused on upgrading gas plants and local transmission networks. Its first long-distance pipeline was built in 1953 linking Paris to the Lorraine coal gas fields. With the development of the Lacq gas field in southwestern France annual gas sales increased by 300% between 1957 and 1962.

By 1965 nearly half of the French population was supplied with natural gas. Spurred on by the loss of its Algerian colony which held major oil and gas assets the French government pushed for new gas supplies to supplement its Lacq resources. Gaz de France was able to secure a contract with Algerian natural gas supplier Sonatrach in 1965 and in 1967 it signed an import contract with Dutch supplier Gasunie. The company also diversified in the 1960s helping to build a natural gas liquefaction plant in Algeria and a receiving terminal in Le Havre. It also helped pioneer gas storage engineering.

Following the price shock of the Arab oil embargo of the early 1970s Gaz de France stepped up its search for alternative suppliers including contracts with Russia's largest gas producer Soyouzgazexport (in 1976 1980 and 1984) and four separate Norwegian producers Efofisk (1977) Stafjord (1985) Heimdal (1986) and Gullfaks (1987). The company also renewed contracts with its Dutch and Algerian suppliers.

During the 1990s Gaz de France expanded its international operations as deregulation in the industry accelerated. In 1994 the company gained a foothold in eastern Germany's gas sector by buying gas production and storage company Erdgas Erdol GmbH (EEG). Three years later Gaz de France acquired Italian heating and related services firm Agip Servizi and was awarded a joint venture contract to distribute gas in Berlin in 1997 and in the suburbs of Mexico City in 1998.

Through contracts for North Sea oil and gas with Elf Aquitaine (now owned by TOTAL FINA ELF) British-Borneo and Ruhrgas in 1999 the company increased its natural gas supplies. It also established new gas supply contracts with Nigeria and Qatar.

For the first time in its history Gaz de France became an offshore field operator in 2000 by acquiring exploration and production company TransCanada International Netherlands and a 39% stake in Noordgastransport BV an offshore gas pipeline operator.

In 2001 through the purchase of a 10% interest in Petronet LNG Gaz de France embarked on a project to import liquefied natural gas from Qatar to India.

France's energy and environmental services giants came together when SUEZ merged with Gaz de France in 2008 to form GDF SUEZ. As part of the merger agreement and in order to clear hurdles set up by the EU competition policy SUEZ then spun off its waste and water unit SUEZ Environnement.

Following the 2008 merger of Gaz de France with SUEZ in a move to expand geographically GDF SUEZ acquired a 90% stake in Izmit Gaz Dagitim San Ve Tic AS (Turkey's third-largest natural gas distributor) for $232 million.

In 2009 the company made further geographic realignments prompted by the regulatory requirements of the European Commission for GDF SUEZ and Germany's E.ON to allow for more competition in their major markets by swapping some generation capacity. It acquired from E.ON 860 MW of Germany-based conventional power plants 132 MW of hydroelectric plants and through subsidiary Electrabel access to 770 MW of nuclear power. In return GDF SUEZ sold to E.ON a similar amount of power generation capacity in France and the Benelux countries.

Ramping up its nuclear assets in 2011 GDF SUEZ formed a joint venture with IBERDROLA and Scottish and Southern Energy. NuGeneration planned to develop up to 3600 MW of nuclear power in the UK. Late in 2011 SSE announced plans to sell its 25 percent in NuGen to GDF SUEZ and IBERDROLA and return to its renewable energy strategy.

EXECUTIVES

Executive Vice-President Energy Service, J ©´me Tolot, age 64
EVP International Relations Global Gas & LNG, Jean-Marie Dauger, age 63
EVP Communications and Sustainable Development, Val ©e Bernis, age 57
Chairman and CEO; Chairman SUEZ-TRACTEBEL GDF SUEZ Energy Services and SUEZ Environnement, G ©ard Mestrallet, age 66
EVP Electricity and Gas International; CEO Tractebel Electricity and Gas International, Dirk Beeuwsaert, age 68
Chairman and CEO ONDEO-Degr ©mont, Jean-Louis Chaussade, age 64
Vice Chairman and President, Jean-Fran §ois Cirelli, age 57
EVP and COO, Isabelle Kocher, age 48
CEO of GDF SUEZ Energy International, Willem van Twembeke, age 50
Head Energy France, Henri Ducr ©age 59
Group CIO, Yves Le G ©ard
Executive Vice-President Infrastructures, Jean-Claude Depail, age 67
Director of Group Purchasing, Claire Brabec-Lagrange
Director of the Group Sales and Marketing, Jean-Louis Blanc
CEO Elengy, Martin Lestang
EVP and CFO, Judith Hartmann
Auditors: Deloitte & Associ ©

LOCATIONS

HQ: Engie SA
1, Place Samuel de Champlain, Courbevoie 92400
Phone: (33) 1 44 22 00 00
Web: www.gdfsuez.com

2011 Sales

	% of total
Europe	80
Asia Pacific & Middle East	8
North America	6
Latin America	5
Africa	1
Total	1

PRODUCTS/OPERATIONS

2011 Sales

	% of total
Electricity	33
Environmental Services	33
Natural gas & other	34
Total	100

COMPETITORS

BG Group
Bouygues
CANAL+
Centrica
Covanta
Dragados
E.ON
Electricit© de France
Electricit© de Strasbourg
Enel
Eni
Gas Natural SDG
Gasunie
Gazprom
Italgas
National Grid
RWE
SABESP
United Utilities
Vattenfall
Veolia Environnement

HISTORICAL FINANCIALS

Company Type: Public

Income Statement FYE: December 31

	REVENUE ($ mil.)	NET INCOME ($ mil.)	NET PROFIT MARGIN	EMPLOYEES
12/14	91,317	2,965	3.2%	152,882
12/13	122,942	(12,788)	—	147,199
12/12	127,900	2,042	1.6%	139,781
12/11	117,281	5,177	4.4%	240,303
12/10	113,063	6,177	5.5%	236,116
Annual Growth	(5.2%)	(16.8%)	—	(10.3%)

2014 Year-End Financials

Debt ratio: 28.1%
Return on equity: 5.0%
Cash ($ mil.): 10,387
Current ratio: 1.07
Long-term debt ($ mil.): 34,063
No. of shares (mil.): —
Dividends
Yield: 11.4%
Payout: 115.2%
Market value ($ mil.): —

	STOCK PRICE ($) FY Close	P/E High/Low	PER SHARE ($) Earnings	Dividends	Book Value
12/14	23.30	26 20	1.22	2.67	25.18
12/13	23.67	— —	(5.38)	1.99	27.97
12/12	21.04	42 29	0.88	3.00	33.41
12/11	27.17	22 13	2.33	1.87	36.77
12/10	36.04	19 15	2.81	3.07	37.43
Annual Growth	(10.3%)	— —	(18.9%)	(3.4%)	(9.4%)

ENI S.p.A.

It's not teeny it's Eni —and it's huge. One of Italy's largest companies Eni operates in the oil and natural gas petrochemicals and oil field services industries and has expanded into power generation. Its main subsidiaries and affiliates include EniPower (power generation) Italgas (natural gas transmission) Saipem (oil field services) pipeline operator Snam Rete Gas and Snamprogetti (contracting engineering). As one of the world's leading oil enterprises in 2010 Eni had proved reserves of 6.8 billion barrels of oil equivalent most of it in Italy and in Africa. The Italian government owns 27% of Eni.

The company's oil and gas holdings and exploration and production efforts extend into more than 30 countries on five continents. Eni has expanded outside its traditional bases of Africa and Italy with ventures in the Americas the Asia/Pacific region Europe and the Middle East.

In response to the opening up of Italy's energy markets Eni is increasing its natural gas holdings and adding electricity generating power units. In 2007 the company bought Dominion Resources' US oil and gas assets in the Gulf of Mexico for $4.75 billion. To expand its Asian and Algerian holdings in 2008 Eni acquired Burren Energy and First Calgary Petroleums. It was able to benefit from SUEZ's acquisition of Gaz de France by buying up GDF SUEZ's majority stake in Belgian gas company Distrigas. Eni now owns 100% of Distrigas.

In 2009 to raise cash to pay down debt the company sold its 20% stake in Gazprom Neft to strategic partner Gazprom for $4.2 billion. To save operating costs that year Eni consolidated its gas divisions and sold Italgas and Stogit (gas storage) to subsidiary Snam Rete Gas.

Expanding its Central European market share in 2010 it acquired Exxon Mobil's 135 gas stations and other downstream assets in Austria.

In the wake of the global recession the company saw its revenues and income bounce back in 2010 thanks to higher commodity prices and stronger demand. The unrest in Libya in 2011 had a material impact of Eni which gets 15% of it production from the North African country. To compensate the company is investing heavily in growing production in other areas. Looking to expand in China in 2011 Eni signed a strategic alliance with Chinese oil major PetroChina.

In order to comply with an EU anti-trust ruling in 2011 the company sold its 89% stake in the TAG Pipeline (which transports gas from Russia to Italy) to Cassa Depositi e Prestiti for $986 million.

HISTORY

Although the Italian parliament formed Ente Nazionale Idrocarburi (National Hydrocarbon Agency) in 1953 Enrico Mattei is the true father of Eni. In 1945 Mattei a partisan leader during WWII was appointed northern commissioner of Agip a state-owned petroleum company founded in 1926 by Mussolini and ordered to liquidate the company. Mattei instead ordered the exploration of the Po Valley where workers found methane gas deposits in 1946.

When Eni was created in 1953 Mattei was named president. His job was to find energy resources for an oil-poor country. He initiated a series of joint ventures with several Middle Eastern and African nations offering better deals than his large oil company rivals which he dubbed the Seven Sisters.

Mattei didn't stick to energy: By the time he died in a mysterious plane crash in 1962 Eni had acquired machinery manufacturer Pignone finance company Sofid Milan newspaper Il Giorno and textile company Lane Rossi. Eni grew during the 1960s partly because of a deal made for Soviet crude in 1958 and a joint venture with Esso in 1963. It also expanded its chemical activities.

By the early 1970s losses in Eni's chemical and textile operations the oil crisis and the Italian government's dumping of unprofitable companies on Eni hurt its bottom line. Former finance minister Franco Reviglio took over in 1983 and began cutting inefficient operations.

EniChem merged with Montedison Italy's largest private chemical company in 1988 but clashes between the public agency and the private company made Montedison sell back its stake in 1990. Eni became a joint stock company in 1992 but the government retained a majority stake.

Franco Bernabe took over Eni following a 1993 bribery scandal and began cutting noncore businesses. The Italian government began selling Eni stock in 1995. In 1996 Eni signed on to develop Libyan gas resources and build a pipeline to Italy. A year later the company merged its Agipa exploration and production subsidiary into its main operations. Eni also took a 35% stake in Italian telecom company Albacom (which has since been sold to British Telecom Group).

The government cut its stake in Eni from 51% to 38% in 1998. That year Vittorio Mincato a company veteran succeeded Bernabe as CEO. In 1999 Eni and Russia's RAO Gazprom the world's largest natural gas production firm agreed to build a controversial $3 billion natural gas pipeline stretching from Russia to Turkey. Eni agreed to invest $5.5 billion to develop oil and gas reserves in Libya; it also sold interests in Saipem and Nuovo Pignone as well as some of its Italian service stations.

In 2000 Eni paid about $910 million for a 33% stake in Galp a Portuguese oil and gas company that also has natural gas utility operations. Also that year Eni bought British-Borneo Oil & Gas in a $1.2 billion deal and in 2001 it paid $4 billion for UK independent exploration and production company LASMO topping a bid by US-based Amerada Hess.

The Italian government sold off another 5% of Eni in 2001 reducing its stake to about 30% and announced that it was considering selling its entire investment. In an effort to reduce noncore holdings the company sold property management subsidiary Immobiliare Metanopoli to Goldman Sachs. Also that year Eni sold a minority stake in its gas pipeline unit Snam Rete Gas to the public.

In 2002 Eni entered discussions to acquire Enterprise Oil but lost out to a rival bid from Royal Dutch Shell. Later that year Eni's oil field services unit Saipem gained control of Bouygues Offshore.

In 2006 Eni and Gazprom formed an international alliance to launch joint mid and downstream gas projects and collaborate in upstream and in technological activities.

EXECUTIVES

CEO, Claudio Descalzi, age 61
SEVP Corporate Affairs and Governance, Roberto Ulissi
SEVP Internal Audit, Marco Petracchini
SEVP Retail Market g&p, Angelo Zaccari
EVP Procurement Department, Rita Marino
EVP Government Affairs Department, Pasquale Salzano
EVP External Communication Department, Marco Bardazzi, age 49
Chairman, Emma Marcegaglia, age 51
Auditors: Reconta Ernst & Young S.p.A.

LOCATIONS

HQ: ENI S.p.A.
1, piazzale Enrico Mattei, Rome 00144
Phone: (39) 2 52041730 **Fax:** (39) 2 52041765
Web: www.eni.com

2014 Sales

	% of total
Europe	
Italy	27
Other EU countries	27
Other countries	11
Africa	11
Americas	8
Asia	15
Other Areas	1
Total	**100**

PRODUCTS/OPERATIONS

2014 Sales

	% of total
Refining & marketing	42
Gas & power	21
Exploration & production	22
Engineering & construction	10
Petrochemicals	4
Corporate & financial	1
Total	**100**

Selected Subsidiaries and Affiliates

Distrigas NV (gas Belgium)
EniPower SpA (power generation)
Italgas SpA (natural gas supply)
Saipem SpA (42.9% oil field services)
Snam Rete Gas SpA (52.5% gas pipeline)
Snamprogetti SpA (contracting and engineering)

COMPETITORS

A2A
Ashland Inc.
BASF SE
BG Group
BP
Chevron
ConocoPhillips
ERG S.p.A.
Edison
Exxon Mobil
Hellenic Petroleum
Marathon Oil
Occidental Petroleum
PEMEX
PETROBRAS
Petrleos de Venezuela
Royal Dutch Shell
Sunoco
TOTAL

HISTORICAL FINANCIALS

Company Type: Public

Income Statement

FYE: December 31

	REVENUE ($ mil.)	NET INCOME ($ mil.)	NET PROFIT MARGIN	EMPLOYEES
12/14	134,857	1,569	1.2%	84,405
12/13	159,816	7,103	4.4%	83,887
12/12	169,719	10,264	6.0%	77,838
12/11	142,954	8,873	6.2%	78,686
12/10	133,139	8,455	6.4%	79,941
Annual Growth	0.3%	(34.4%)	—	1.4%

2014 Year-End Financials

Debt ratio: 21.5%
Return on equity: 2.1%
Cash ($ mil.): 8,039
Current ratio: 1.46
Long-term debt ($ mil.): 23,478
No. of shares (mil.): —
Dividends
Yield: 6.4%
Payout: 468.1%
Market value ($ mil.): —

	STOCK PRICE ($) FY Close	P/E High/Low	PER SHARE ($) Earnings	Dividends	Book Value
12/14	34.91	137 89	0.44	2.24	20.17
12/13	48.49	38 30	1.95	2.31	22.12
12/12	49.14	23 19	2.83	2.14	21.54
12/11	41.27	25 16	2.44	1.91	19.81
12/10	43.74	29 22	2.33	1.87	18.92
Annual Growth	(5.5%)	— —	(34.2%)	4.7%	1.6%

Ergo Versicherungsgruppe AG

ERGO Insurance Group thinks logically: people need insurance ergo they sell it! The company comprises a number of firms specializing in life health property casualty and legal expenses insurance as well as pensions. Property/casualty and life policies are offered under the ERGO brand while health legal and travel insurance are provided through the DKV D.A.S. and ERV divisions. The company targets individuals and small to midsized businesses. ERGO is controlled by reinsurance giant Munich Re; the two companies have formed joint venture MEAG MUNICH ERGO AssetManagement to provide financial services.

ERGO sells its products through a vast network of self-employed agents direct sales employees and brokers. ERGO's marketing efforts target private individuals who account for the lion's share of premiums.

In 2009 the company consolidated its property/casualty and life operations under the ERGO brand withdrawing the Victoria and Hamburg-Mannheimer brands from the German market. ERGO also renamed its majority-owned KarstadtQuelle Insurance subsidiary which provides insurance and financial advice to department stores and mail-order customers through a partnership with Arcandor (formerly Karstadt Quelle) as ERGO Direct. ERGO also has cooperative agreements with banker HVB.

ERGO's health insurance and legal expenses products are its biggest sellers in Germany and Europe. In 2009 the company introduced a new product in those markets the "Home and Walkies" insurance package which covers liabilities related to dogs (such as fights with others' dogs while out for a walk or doggie messes left on apartment rugs or hotel floors).

ERGO has been strengthening its foreign operations through acquisitions and joint ventures. The company operates in approximately 30 countries; focus areas for growth include Eastern Europe including Poland and Turkey as well as Asian countries such as India and China. To that end ERGO acquired a majority stake in Turkish insurer ISVICRE and formed an Indian joint venture HDFC Ergo General Insurance with Housing Development Finance Corporation.

It expanded its Baltic States operations in 2008 by forming a European Public Company to offer health insurance and then merging its existing life insurance operations into the new company becoming the first non-government health insurer in the Baltics. The company operates in Estonia and Lithuania.

HISTORY

In 1843 Otto Crelinger applied for a royal license to create a railway insurance company in Prussia; King Friedrich Wilhelm IV of Prussia granted it 10 years later. By 1861 the company was selling life insurance as well and in 1875 it took the name VICTORIA.

VICTORIA was the first German company to offer life insurance to the public without the need to see a doctor (a plan modeled after Prudential's operations in the UK) and it gradually extended its reach to several other European countries and expanded into other areas of insurance including property casualty and automobile. By 1900 it was Germany's largest insurance company and on the eve of WWI it was the largest in Europe.

The war took a severe toll on VICTORIA but careful planning kept it on its feet. By 1927 it was back to prewar asset levels. In 1932 the company accounted for 80% of foreign premiums collected by German insurance companies.

WWII would prove to be an even more trying period for VICTORIA. Among the company's many misfortunes was the destruction of its main offices in Berlin. However cautious planning again kept the company afloat. By 1953 it was back on top of its game now mainly operating from Düsseldorf.

West Germany's economy flourished in the 1960s. During this decade VICTORIA bought D.A.S. then a relatively small legal expenses insurer that would grow to be the leader in its market. The 1970s saw a downturn in the world economy but VICTORIA weathered the decade well even expanding into the health insurance market.

In 1997 German reinsurer Munich Re decided to bring together three insurance companies in which it held stakes: VICTORIA Hamburg-Mannheimer (primarily a life and accident insurer) and DKV (a health insurer). The group instantly became Germany's second-largest insurer behind Allianz. All of these companies served mostly individual customers in Germany and abroad with secondary focuses on small to midsized businesses and some government institutions. Munich Re owned about 54% of the new holding company which was called ERGO Insurance Group (Versicherungsgruppe). ERGO shares went public in February 1998. Later that year Munich Re increased its stake to about 63%.

The new insurance conglomerate continued strengthening its international presence acquiring Spain's fifth-largest insurer Previasa. In 1999 ERGO acquired the Netherlands' health insurer Levob and Spain's Nordica. In 2000 the company acquired Italy's Bayerische Vita (life insurance) and Bayerische Assicurazioni (property and casualty insurance) an additional Netherlands insurer and majority stakes in Poland's Compensa Zycie (a life insurer) and a new life and accident insurer in Slovakia.

Also in 2000 the company's joint venture with Munich Re MEAG MUNICH ERGO AssetManagement began providing financial services and ERGO forged a strategic partnership with Deutsche Telekom to develop an online marketplace for insurance and financial services. The company together with affiliate Österreichische Volksbanken also made a bid for the Austrian Post Office Savings Bank.

In 2001 ERGO took a majority stake in PREVENTA Lithuania's third biggest insurer.

Since then the company has been focused on continuing to grow its foreign operations primarily through acquisitions. To that end the company has made about five major buys over the past few years.

EXECUTIVES

Chairman of the Management Board, Markus Riess, age 50
Chief Investment Officer, Daniel von Borries, age 50
Management Board Member Composite Segment; Chairman Victoria Versicherung and Hamburg-Mannheimer Sachversicherungs, Christian Diedrich, age 59
CFO, Christoph Jurecka, age 41
Chairman Supervisory Board, Nikolaus von Bomhard
Deputy Chairwoman, Anne Horstmann
Auditors: KPMG Bayerische Treuhandgesellschaft Aktiengesellschaft

LOCATIONS

HQ: Ergo Versicherungsgruppe AG
Victoriaplatz 2, Duesseldorf D-40198
Phone: (49) 211 477 0 **Fax:** (49) 211 477 1500
Web: www.ergo.com

COMPETITORS

AEGON
AOK
AWD
AXA
Ageas Insurance International
Allianz
Generali
Generali Deutschland
Helvetia Group
Prudential plc
Vienna Insurance Group
Zurich Insurance Group

HISTORICAL FINANCIALS

Company Type: Public

Income Statement FYE: December 31

	ASSETS ($ mil.)	NET INCOME ($ mil.)	INCOME AS % OF ASSETS	EMPLOYEES
12/14	190,245	738	0.4%	28,019
12/13	203,027	571	0.3%	29,595
12/12	194,027	363	0.2%	29,768
12/11	180,237	432	0.2%	31,311
12/10	186,373	460	0.2%	32,997
Annual Growth	0.5%	12.5%	—	(4.0%)

2014 Year-End Financials

Return on assets: 0.4%
Return on equity: 12.1%
Long-term debt ($ mil.): —
No. of shares (mil.): 75
Sales ($ mil): 32,735
Dividends
Yield: —
Payout: —
Market value ($ mil.): —

Ericsson

Ericsson opens all lines of communication. The world's leading maker of mobile broadband infrastructure gear provides the equipment that telecom carriers use to build and expand their networks. The company also provides wireline broadband metro area Ethernet LTE modems and optical transport equipment. Its services unit handles operations ranging from systems integration to network deployment and management. Ericsson's multimedia arm provides content-related products including Internet television systems. The company traces its roots back to 1876 when Lars Magnus Ericsson opened up a telegraph repair shop in Stockholm.

Operations

Ericsson's core business comprises three segments: networks professional services and support solutions. The networks segment which accounts for more than half of the company's sales develops and deploys the latest generation of mobile broadband networks (LTE) and maintains and refines older networks (GSM WCDMA etc.) for its network operator customers. The segment also provides equipment for Internet protocol (IP) microwave transport and core networks including IP routers core routers and switches cables and interconnect products microwave radio links optical transport components radio base stations and wireline network access equipment.

Serving network operators Ericsson's professional services segment supports its customers network operations through its consulting customer support network design and integration and training services. The segment also offers managed services like application hosting and network operations. The growing professional services unit is supported by four global service centers in India China Mexico and Romania. The services segment accounts for about 40% of the company's net sales.

The company's multimedia support solutions segment offers software for consumer-facing applications including mobile and Internet television messaging and music as well as billing support systems for telecommunications network operators.

Financial Performance

For 2012 Ericsson reported modest revenue growth and a 50% drop in its net income from 2011 levels. While its networks segment struggled its growing professional services segment finished strong in 2012. The company attributed the group-wide drop in profitability to operating losses in its ST-Ericsson joint venture (which it dissolved in late 2013) as well as to high research and development and other costs tied to the ongoing modernization of its networks product line. Geographically North America and northeast Asia were Ericsson's strongest markets where demand for mobile products continues to climb.

Strategy

Capitalizing on the booming mobile communications industry Ericsson's is focusing on growing its broadband network equipment and services businesses while divesting non-core businesses. In 2012 Ericsson sold its 50% stake in Sony Ericsson to Sony for more than 1 billion (about $1.5 billion) in cash. Ericsson which is now focused on global wireless connectivity surrendered the handset portion of the Sony Ericsson business to Sony. Sony and Ericsson plan to work together on a wireless connectivity initiative Ericsson's primary expertise and a pivotal component of Sony's device convergence strategy.

In 2013 semiconductor manufacturer STMicroelectronics (ST) sold its stake in ST-Ericsson a now-dissolved joint venture with Ericsson. The two companies split the joint venture's assets with Ericsson taking over the development and sales of the newer LTE multimedia thin modems (which complement its mobile broadband business) and ST taking a portion of the existing ST-Ericsson modem product line. Other assets including a global navigation satellite system were sold to third parties.

Mergers and Acquisitions

Ericsson is using acquisitions to bolster its product portfolio and expand further into international markets to capitalize on demand for the mobile broadband services that its equipment supports and fuel the growth of its global services organization. The company bought New Jersey-based Telcordia in 2012 for more than $1 billion in cash to expand its mobile broadband and business communications software holdings particularly in the areas of operations support systems and business support systems applications and to further expand its North American business. Telcordia brought in about $740 million in revenue for its 2011 fiscal year.

Ericsson kept pouring money into boosting its wireless portfolio with the 2012 purchase of BelAir Networks which provides carrier-grade Wi-Fi equipment in North America. Ericsson also established a stronger presence as a provider of managed services for broadcasters that year when it bought a related division from Technicolor for nearly 20 million (about $25 million). The acquisition extended its reach beyond Sweden into France the Netherlands and the UK and became a leading provider in Europe.

HISTORY

Lars Magnus Ericsson opened a telegraph repair shop in Stockholm in 1876 the same year Alexander Graham Bell applied for a US patent on the telephone. Within two years Ericsson was making telephones. His company grew rapidly supplying equipment first to Swedish phone companies and later to other European companies. In 1885 Ericsson crafted a combination receiver-speaker in one handset.

In 1911 Ericsson and SAT the Stockholm telephone company merged under the Ericsson banner. The company adopted its present name in 1926. In 1930 international financier Ivar 'The Match King" Kreuger owner of the Swedish Match Co. won control of Ericsson. His triumph was short-lived. Krueger committed suicide in 1932 and one of his creditors Sosthenes Behn's ITT took over.

ITT in 1960 sold its interest in Ericsson to the top Swedish industrialist family the Wallenbergs. In 1975 Ericsson introduced its computer-controlled exchange called AXE. Buoyed by AXE's success the company unveiled the "office of the future" in the early 1980s diversifying into computers and office furniture.

However Ericsson's timing was off: The demand for office automation never materialized and profits plunged. Electrolux chairman Hans Werthen was recruited to split his time between the two companies and rescue Ericsson. The company sold its computer business to Nokia in 1988 and refocused on telephone equipment. It dusted off its aging AXE system for the burgeoning cellular market and quickly won key contracts.

The company and aircraft maker Saab merged their military aviation electronics operations as Ericsson Saab Avionics in 1996. (It was dissolved in 1998.) In 1998 manager Sven-Christer Nilsson was appointed CEO. He reorganized the company and laid off 14000 workers.

After Ericsson fought bitterly with rival QUALCOMM over wireless standards and patents the companies settled in 1999 agreeing to push for the standardization of third-generation technology based on QUALCOMM's code-division multiple access (CDMA) technology. As a part of the deal Ericsson purchased QUALCOMM's infrastructure business. To expand its Internet offerings Ericsson bought Internet router maker Torrent and Internet telephony company Touchwave.

By 1999 Nilsson was pushed out for moving too slowly on restructuring plans and was replaced as CEO by chairman Lars Ramqvist who put many of the duties on president Kurt Hellstr ¶n. Hellstr ¶n immediately set out to simplify the company's managerial and accounting structure trim its workforce and slow-growth businesses and push new phone models to market.

The next year Ericsson sold noncore businesses including its private radio systems power supply and equipment shelter operations. The company also agreed to develop a standard for secure wireless transactions with Nokia and Motorola and formed a joint venture with Web router maker Juniper Networks to sell routers for mobile Internet applications.

Fierce competition an industrywide slowdown in handset sales and manufacturing glitches led Ericsson to outsource the manufacture of its phones to Flextronics and form a joint venture (Sony Ericsson Mobile Communications) with Sony to link the development and marketing of their handsets in 2001. Ericsson also sold its direct enterprise sales and service unit outsourced IT operations in Europe to Electronic Data Systems (which later became HP Enterprise Services) and cut more than 20000 jobs that year. Hellstr ¶n became CEO in 2001.

Chairman Ramqvist became honorary chairman in 2002; Electrolux CEO Michael Treschow was named as the acting chairman. Ericsson announced 20000 more layoffs in 2002. That year the company sold its semiconductor unit to Infineon for about $380 million.

Ericsson sold its optoelectronic components business in 2003. Hellstr ¶n retired later that year and Carl-Henric Svanberg former CEO of Assa Abloy was appointed as company president and CEO. In 2005 Ericsson acquired certain telecom hardware assets from troubled Marconi (later renamed telent) for about $2.1 billion.

The company acquired seven companies in 2007 the largest of which were Redback Networks ($1.9 billion) and TANDBERG Television ($1.4 billion). The Redback buy gained Ericsson broadband IP routers while the TANDBERG Television purchase brought software and services for the cable television market. It also picked up fiber-access technology company Entrisphere in an effort to expand its broadband access offerings in North America.

Looking to broaden its multimedia offerings the company purchased Mobeon a Swedish provider of IP-based voice and video mail. Other 2007 acquisitions included German customer care software provider LHS Swedish mobile service deliver platform developer Drutt and Spanish IPTV specialist HyC. In an effort to refocus its multimedia operations on key areas such as service delivery and provisioning Ericsson sold its enterprise PBX products business to Aastra Technologies for about $100 million in 2008.

To expand its North American business Ericsson bought bankrupt Nortel Network's CDMA and LTE-based wireless business there in 2009 for $1.1 billion. The deal significantly boosted its profile as a provider of mobile networking gear to wireless carriers on the continent. The company's other acquisitions that year complemented its manufacturing and services activities. These purchases included the manufacturing operations of Estonian electronics maker Elcoteq as well as Turkish systems integrator Bizitek.

In 2010 EVP/CFO Hans Vestberg took over as president and CEO of Ericsson succeeding Carl-Henric Svanberg who resigned to become chairman of BP.

Auditors: PricewaterhouseCoopers AB

LOCATIONS

HQ: Ericsson
Torshamnsgatan 21, Kista, Stockholm SE-164 83
Phone: (46) 10 719 0000
Web: www.ericsson.com

HISTORICAL FINANCIALS

Company Type: Public

Income Statement FYE: December 31

	REVENUE ($ mil.)	NET INCOME ($ mil.)	NET PROFIT MARGIN	EMPLOYEES
12/14	29,492	1,496	5.1%	118,055
12/13	35,465	1,872	5.3%	114,340
12/12	34,964	886	2.5%	110,255
12/11	32,901	1,768	5.4%	104,525
12/10	30,325	1,662	5.5%	90,261
Annual Growth	(0.7%)	(2.6%)	—	6.9%

2014 Year-End Financials

Debt ratio: 1.0%
Return on equity: 8.1%
Cash ($ mil.): 5,302
Current ratio: 2.00
Long-term debt ($ mil.): 2,828

No. of shares (mil.): —
Dividends
Yield: 2.5%
Payout: —
Market value ($ mil.): —

	STOCK PRICE ($) FY Close	P/E High/Low		PER SHARE ($) Earnings	Dividends	Book Value
12/14	12.10	3	3	0.46	0.30	5.65
12/13	12.24	4	3	0.58	0.77	6.77
12/12	10.10	6	5	0.27	0.35	6.52
12/11	10.13	4	2	0.55	0.00	6.46
12/10	11.53	4	3	0.52	0.28	6.76
Annual Growth	1.2%	—	—	(2.9%)	2.1%	(4.4%)

Erste Group Bank AG

First there was Erste. Erste Group Bank is the holding company of Erste Bank Austria's first savings bank founded in 1819. However the company has grown beyond its home country to number some 2800 branches throughout Central and Eastern European that serve some 16.5 million customers. The company has operating subsidiaries in Austria Croatia the Czech Republic Montenegro Moldova Romania Serbia Slovakia and Hungary. Erste Group banks provide financial services such as savings and lending to individuals and small to medium-size businesses. It also has a private banking arm. Erste Bank is Austria's largest lender.

As Austrian banks consolidated the group increased its presence in surrounding nations. Since the early 2000s the holding company has expanded its market by purchasing stakes in or acquiring outright banks in Austria Bosnia Russia and the Ukraine. Each of its subsidiaries is focused on local operations.

Erste Group slowed its acquisitions during the economic downturn and focused instead on cutting costs and making good lending decisions. The choices helped the company weather the financial crisis rather well. Over the long term Central and Eastern European countries are expected to record economic growth. Erste Group expects loan growth and an increased demand for asset management services in those emerging countries.

The company has sharpened its focus on its core banking activities by selling non-core insurance subsidiaries. It sold most its insurance brokerage operations to Austrian firm GrECo International in 2010.

In 2011 Erste Group made its first acquisitions in several years when it took control of Intermarket Bank –the largest factoring bank in Austria. Erste Group already owned more than 20% of Intermarket Bank and it acquired an additional 56%. The transaction was part of Erste Group's strategy to offer broad services to corporate customers. Also in 2011 Erste offered to buy the rest of majority-held Romanian unit Banca Comerciala Romana it doesn't already own.

HISTORY

In 1819 a bank was born and its name was Erste oesterreichische Spar-Cassa. Called Die Erste for short the bank was Austria's first commercial and savings bank. Unlike Austria's community savings banks Die Erste was independent –not backed by government guarantees.

For more than 150 years Die Erste operated as a local savings bank serving Vienna. Then in 1979 the Austrian government passed a law that would alter the face of the banking industry in that country. The Banking Act of 1979 placed banks and savings institutions in direct competition with each other by allowing them both to take part in all aspects of the banking business. As a result of the enhanced competition Die Erste began expanding its domestic branch network.

Meanwhile the Austrian savings banks had established their own central institution in 1937 and called it Girovereinigung der osterreichischen Sparkassen or Girozentrale for short. Girozentrale focused on managing the liquidity reserves of the savings banks and helping them with their syndication and securities businesses. The bank also endeavored to improve the non-cash payment system and to promote mortgage savings. Concentrating on international and investment banking rather than retail banking Girozentrale eventually became the country's third-largest bank.

Throughout the late 1980s and into the 1990s rumors began to spread about a possible merger between Girozentrale and Die Erste (both were associated with the nation's conservative People's Party). In 1992 Girozentrale merged with Österreichisches Credit-Institut (ÖCI) to create GiroCredit giving the central savings bank a branch network for the first time. But it also made GiroCredit a direct competitor with its two largest shareholders –Bank Austria (now part of HypoVereinsbank) and Die Erste who were also fierce competitors with each other.

Between 1992 and 1994 Die Erste and Bank Austria struggled to find a solution to the problem of GiroCredit's ownership. In 1994 Bank Austria emerged the victor by winning the majority stake in GiroCredit in a move that was characterized by Die Erste as "unfriendly."

Throughout the next two years Die Erste attempted to secure a stake in Creditanstalt Austria's second-biggest bank as the Austrian government began moves to privatize it. Die Erste acted as a part of a consortium of Austrian German and Italian entities interested in obtaining stakes in the bank. But in 1997 Bank Austria won that battle too managing to take over Creditanstalt. In turn Die Erste bought Bank Austria's majority stake in GiroCredit. The resulting company was given the name Erste Bank which went public that year in the largest stock issue in Austrian history. In 1998 it became the first major Austrian company to allow for the election of small shareholder representatives to its supervisory board.

In 2000 Erste Bank bought a majority stake in Ceská Sporitelna the largest retail bank in the Czech Republic from the Czech government. Later in the year the Slovak government allowed Erste Bank to become a major shareholder in the previously state-owned Slovenská sporitel'na. Erste Bank was also one of several Austrian banks to be accused by the European Commission of fixing foreign exchange fees.

In 2001 Erste Bank took control of Slovenská Sporitel'na and acquired majority ownership of Tiroler Sparkasse Bank AG. The following year Erste Bank took full control of Czech Republic-based Czeska Sporitelna. Ever acquisitive in 2005 the company completed its acquisition of Serbia's Novosadska banka.

Erste in 2006 acquiered Romanian bank Banca Comerciala Romana the largest bank in that country and previously state-owned.

Erste switched to a holding company structure in 2008. That year the company also sold most of its insurance business to Vienna Insurance Group.

EXECUTIVES

Chairman, Andreas Treichl, $1,245,000 total compensation

Management Board Member Controlling and Information Management, Gernot Mittendorfer, age 51

Management Board Member Enterprise wide Risk Management, Andreas Gottschling, age 48

Management Board Member Investment Banking and Steering and Operating Office Corporates, Jozef Sikela

First Vice Chairman, Georg Winckler, age 72

Chairman, Friedrich R – DLER, age 65

Second Vice Chairman, Jan Homan, age 68

Auditors: Ernst & Young Wirtschaftsprufungsgesellschaft

LOCATIONS

HQ: Erste Group Bank AG
Milchgasse 1, Vienna A-1010
Phone: (43) 50100 17 693 **Fax:** (43) 50100 9 13112
Web: www.erstegroup.com

PRODUCTS/OPERATIONS

2013 Sales

	% of total
Interest income	77
Fee & commission income	23
Total	**100**

Selected Subsidiaries

Banca Comerciala Romana S.A. (BCR)
Ceská Sporitelna (Czech Republic)
Erste Bank a.d. Novi Sad (Serbia)
Erste Bank Croatia (Erste & Steiermärkische Bank d.d.)
Erste Bank der oesterreichen Sparkassen AG
  Autoleasing EBV
  Sparkasse Salzburg
  Wohnbaubank
Erst Bank Hungary Nyrt.
Erste Bank Ukraine (formerly Bank Prestige)
Slovenská sporitelna a.s. (Slovakia)

COMPETITORS

BAWAG
Banca Comerciala Romana
Bank Austria
Credit Suisse
Deutsche Bank
Deutsche Post
Deutsche Postbank
Erste & Steierm□rkische Bank
Investkredit
OTP Bank
Oberbank AG
RZB Group
UBS
UniCredit Bank AG

HISTORICAL FINANCIALS

Company Type: Public

Income Statement FYE: December 31

	ASSETS ($ mil.)	NET INCOME ($ mil.)	INCOME AS % OF ASSETS	EMPLOYEES
12/14	238,588	(1,752)	—	46,067
12/13	275,176	83	0.0%	45,670
12/12	281,830	637	0.2%	49,381
12/11	271,633	(929)	—	50,452
12/10	275,621	1,359	0.5%	50,272
Annual Growth	(3.5%)	—	—	(2.2%)

2014 Year-End Financials

Return on assets: (-0.7%)
Return on equity: (-13.6%)
Long-term debt ($ mil.): —
No. of shares (mil.): 409
Sales ($ mil): 5,757

Dividends
Yield: 1.1%
Payout: —
Market value ($ mil.): 4,694

	STOCK PRICE ($) FY Close	P/E High/Low		PER SHARE ($) Earnings	Dividends	Book Value
12/14	11.45	—	—	(4.10)	0.13	29.17
12/13	17.60	—	—	(0.08)	0.21	37.56
12/12	16.05	19	9	1.15	0.00	45.10
12/11	8.65	—	—	(2.95)	0.00	41.92
12/10	23.77	10	7	3.11	0.28	50.23
Annual Growth	(16.7%)	—	—	—	(17.9%)	(12.7%)

Etablissements Delhaize Freres et Cie Le Lion S.A. (Belgium)

This Belgian's roar can be heard from Brussels to Bali to Baltimore. Food retailer Delhaize Group runs about 3500 stores –including flagship banner Delhaize Le Lion –in the US Southeastern Europe and Asia. Food retailing accounts for a lion's share of the company's profits but it also engages in food wholesaling and the sale of pet food and pet products in Belgium. Delhaize Group's sales network consists of company-operated affiliated and franchised stores 85% of which conform to the supermarket format. Other store formats include neighborhood convenience and specialty stores. US subsidiary Delhaize America is one of the largest supermarket operators on the East Coast from Maine to Florida.

The operation of retail supermarkets accounts for nearly 90% of Delhaize Group's sales. Its US subsidiary Delhaize America is the third-largest operator of grocery stores along the East Coast of the US where it operates some 1500 stores in 17 states from Maine to Florida. Stores banners include Food Lion and Hannaford. It also operates two of fast-growing off-price formats: Bloom and the Bottom Dollar chain of limited-assortment discount supermarkets. In its home market of Belgium (including the Grand Duchy of Luxembourg) Delhaize operates a multi-format network of about 820 stores under about a half a dozen banners. It does business in Greece through some 250 Alfa-Beta stores and in five Balkan countries through the recently-acquired Delta Maxi chain of supermarkets. In Indonesia its 51%-owned PT Lion Super Indo chain operates stores on the island of Java where it has about an 11% share of the retail food market. Beyond retailing Delhaize supplies food to affiliated stores and independent customers. The company also sells pet food and pet products at about 135 Tom & Co. stores in Belgium.

Brussels-based Delhaize rings up nearly two-thirds of its sales and earns more than 60% of its operating profit in the US where it operates about 1650 supermarkets. Belgium and Luxembourg account for more than 20% of sales with Southern Europe (Albania Bosnia and Herzegovina Bulgaria Greece Montenegro Romania and Serbia) and Indonesia making up the rest.

Despite continued shaky economic conditions in Europe (including an economic catastrophe in Greece) and parts of the US Delhaize Group rang up more than 21 billion ($29.4 billion) in sales in 2011 a 1.3% increase vs. 2010. The company's operating profit fell 21% over the same period. The US operation outperformed Belgium with sales up more than 2% vs. 1% respectively. While growth in the US was modest it was an improvement over the past few years when Delhaize America posted declining annual sales comparisons. Delhaize's Southeastern Europe and Asia segment saw sales climb by nearly a third driven by the acquisition half way through the year of Delta Maxi's 485 retail stores in the Baltic states and expansion in Indonesia. Looking ahead Delhaize expects Delta Maxi to generate approximately 1.3 billion in revenues in 2012.

To grow Delhaize Group is setting its sights on newer and faster growing opportunities. The purchase of the Delta Maxi stores in Southeastern Europe fits the bill. Delhaize in July 2011 it acquired Serbia's leading food retail chain for about 630 million (nearly $875 million) from businessman Miroslav Miskovic. Delta Maxi operates about 485 retail stores in Albania Bosnia Bulgaria Montenegro and Serbia. Combined with its existing operations in Greece where it owns the #2 food retailer Alfa-Beta and Romania (Mega Image) the Belgian retailer is now a leading player with about 850 grocery stores in the seven countries. Fast-growing Indonesia is another focus of growth for the Belgian retailer. In 2011 the company added 16 new stores bringing the total to about 90 supermarkets there. Other growth formats include limited-assortment low-cost supermarkets: Bottom Dollar in the US and Red Market (launched in 2009) in Europe.

HISTORY

Two brothers and a brother-in-law –all teachers –founded Delhaize in 1867 in Charleroi Belgium. A professor of commercial sciences Jules Delhaize wanted to try out his ideas about food retailing such as creating a network of stores and a centralized warehouse and charging set prices for items. He enlisted the aid of his brother Edouard and his brother-in-law Jules Vieujant. The trio picked the symbol that has become synonymous with the company –the lion because it represented strength and it was the emblem of their native country. A third brother Adolphe later started his own food-retailing operation also with multiple branches. (His operations were merged into Delhaize in 1950.)

The company moved to Brussels in 1871. In the early 1880s the company moved closer to a rail line for better transportation services opened a large warehouse and other operations and began setting up factories to produce its own brand-name foods and beverages.

Although it still had stores only in Belgium (more than 500 by 1914) the company had an international presence because of its appearance at exhibitions such as the St. Louis World's Fair in 1904. After WWI the company began investigating possibilities for international trade by sending a delegation to the US and Canada.

At the beginning of WWII Delhaize had 744 branches and 1500 affiliated shops including several in the Belgian Congo. At war's end Delhaize started closing some of its factories although it kept a few.

Taking a page from the American supermarkets it had been studying Delhaize in 1957 opened Europe's first full self-serve supermarket complete with pre-packaged meat frozen foods and fresh produce and the look of American stores –bright colors checkout stands and fluorescent lighting. Delhaize went public in 1962 as S.A. Delhaize Fr¨res et Cie "Le Lion."

In 1972 Jacques LeClercq the great-grandson of Jules Delhaize persuaded the Delhaize board that future opportunities for growth lay in the US. Two years later with the enactment of "padlock laws" to halt the spread of hypermarkets in Belgium and similar restrictions occurring elsewhere in Europe the company bought 32% of Food Town an American chain with 19 stores. (Delhaize bought a controlling interest in Food Town in 1976.) A few years later Delhaize bought Food Giant in Atlanta and began expanding beyond the supermarket in Belgium setting up the Di body care shops and in 1981 the AD (Delhaize Affiliates) chain to offer wholesale and management advice services.

Food Town became Food Lion in 1983. Two years later Delhaize opened a new chain Cub Food in Atlanta. In 1989 it set up Caddy-Home a home-delivery service and Tom & Co stores selling pet foods and supplies.

International expansion was the byword for the 1990s. Delhaize set up Delvita in 1991 in the Czech Republic. Further acquisitions included controlling interests in Alfa-Beta Vassilopoulos (Greece 1992) the Kash n' Karry chain (US 1996) and interests in supermarket chains in Thailand and Indonesia (1997). Acquisitions in 1999 included 49% of Shop n Save (Singapore) and 28 Farmer Jack stores (US).

Expansion continued in 2000 with further acquisitions in Thailand and Romania and the mid-year US acquisition of Hannaford Bros. In April 2001 Delhaize acquired all of Delhaize America merging its US operations and listing on the New York Stock Exchange (the only Belgian company on that august body). In late 2001 the company shut down its Atlanta-based joint venture 19 Super Discount Markets in which it held a 60% ownership stake.

In October 2003 Delhaize Group completed the acquisition of 43 Harveys supermarkets in Florida and central and southern Georgia filling in an area where Food Lion has a limited presence. Following the acquisition Harveys became the Delhaize Group's fourth US banner. In November Delhaize agreed to sell its 49% stake in Singapore food retailer Shop N Save to Cold Storage Singapore for 21.9.

Delhaize Group shut down its Food Lion Thailand operation in August 2004 with the sale of 20 stores there to Central Food Retail Co. and the closure of its remaining locations. In November the company –through its US subsidiary Hannaford Bros. –acquired the 19-store Victory Super Markets chain Massachusetts and New Hampshire for $175 million. At year end Baron Gui de Vaucleroy retired down as chairman of the board and was succeeded by Georges Jacobs.

In May 2005 Delhaize Group completed the acquisition of Cash Fresh a chain of 43 supermarkets mainly in northeastern Belgium for about 169 million (including real estate). In June the company sold all 11 Delvita stores in Slovakia to Germany's Rewe exiting that market.

Stiff competition in its home market from discounters including ALDI Lidl and French hypermarket operator Carrefour led Delhaize Group to cut prices on some 1000 items in early 2006.

The following year the Belgian grocer sold its Delvita stores in the Czech Republic also to Rewe. Also the last of the company's Kash n' Karry stores in Florida were converted to the Sweetbay banner.

In April 2008 Delhaize through its Alfa-Beta subsidiary in Greece acquired 34 Plus Hellas supermarkets there from Germany's Tengelmann for about $108 million. Mega Image in 2008 nearly doubled its store network through acquisitions including the purchase of the 14-store La Fourmi chain for 19 million (about $26 million).

To streamline its European operations the company in July 2009 sold its four stores in Germany to rival REWE. (Delhaize entered the German market in 2003.)

In 2010 the company added 110 new stores: 40 in the US 28 in Belgium 14 in Greece 21 in Romania and seven in Indonesia. Delhaize acquired all of the minority shares in Alfa-Beta and delisted the company from the Athens Stock Market in 2010.

In July 2011 Delhaize acquired Serbia's Delta Maxi chain of stores from businessman Miroslav Miskovic for about 630 million (nearly $875 million). Delta Maxi is Serbia's #1 food retailer with 365 stores there. The grocery chain operates about 100 other stores in Bulgaria Bosnia and Herzegovina Montenegro and Albania.

In June 2014 Delhaize sold its Sweetbay Reid's and Harveys chains in the southeastern US to rival BI-LO Holding for $246 million. In a separate transaction the company sold its distribution center in Plant city Florida to C&S Wholesale Grocers for $28 million.

Auditors: Deloitte Bedrijfsrevisoren/Reviseurs d'Entreprises

LOCATIONS

HQ: Etablissements Delhaize Freres et Cie Le Lion S.A. (Belgium)
Square Marie Curie 40, Brussels 1070
Phone: (32) 2 412 22 11 **Fax:** (32) 2 412 22 22
Web: www.delhaizegroup.com

HISTORICAL FINANCIALS

Company Type: Public

Income Statement FYE: December 31

	REVENUE ($ mil.)	NET INCOME ($ mil.)	NET PROFIT MARGIN	EMPLOYEES
12/14	25,964	108	0.4%	152,000
12/13	29,060	246	0.8%	160,000
12/12	29,968	138	0.5%	158,000
12/11	27,316	614	2.2%	160,000
12/10	27,905	768	2.8%	138,622
Annual Growth	(1.8%)	(38.7%)	—	2.3%

2014 Year-End Financials

Debt ratio: 27.5%
Return on equity: 1.6%
Cash ($ mil.): 1,944
Current ratio: 1.24
Long-term debt ($ mil.): 3,252
No. of shares (mil.): 101
Dividends
Yield: 2.0%
Payout: 31.8%
Market value ($ mil.): 1,843

	STOCK PRICE ($) FY Close	P/E High/Low	PER SHARE ($) Earnings	Dividends	Book Value
12/14	18.12	73 17	1.06	0.38	65.10
12/13	59.42	41 24	2.42	0.33	68.94
12/12	40.55	59 32	1.37	0.41	67.82
12/11	56.35	17 11	6.05	0.42	69.56
12/10	73.71	16 11	7.60	0.36	67.45
Annual Growth	(29.6%)	— —	(38.9%)	0.9%	(0.9%)

Eurobank Ergasias SA

Eurobank Ergasias has a lot of branches for shaking the money tree. The bank operates some 500 branches business centers and ATMs in its home country Greece and about 1250 more in about half-a-dozen other central and southeastern European countries. In addition to traditional retail banking and consumer lending Eurobank offers business banking factoring insurance leasing investment banking and wealth management services. The bank was founded in 1990 as Euromerchant Bank. Swiss-based EFG Bank European Financial Group owns about 44% of Eurobank.

Plans to merge with rival Alpha Bank fell through in 2012. The merger was aimed at strengthening both banks which hold much of Greece's troubled debt that caused fear of another worldwide recession. By joining forces the companies would have created the nation's largest lender. However Alpha scrapped merger plans after the Greek government restructured its sovereign debt.

Unlike many banks in Europe Eurobank increased its lending activity in 2008. It saw the biggest increases in mortgage small business and corporate loans to customers in its Eastern European and Greek markets.

In addition Eurobank saw a rise in deposit activity in 2008. The bank attributed this increase to its expansion of low-cost deposit products which brought in more consumer and professional customers. It also made heavy investments in products and services outside its home country and aims to become a banking leader in Romania Serbia Bulgaria Turkey Cyprus the Ukraine and other European countries.

In 2012 EFG Eurobank Ergasias sold a majority stake in its Polbank subsidiary in Poland. Raiffeisen Bank International acquired 70% of Polbank for €490 million ($640 million).

EXECUTIVES

Chief Executive Officer, Fokion Christos Karavias
Chairman, Nikolaos Basil Karamouzis
Vice Chairman, Spyridon Loudovikos Lorentziadis
Auditors: PricewaterhouseCoopers SA

LOCATIONS

HQ: Eurobank Ergasias SA
8 Othonos Street, Athens 105 57
Phone: (30) 210 333 7000 **Fax:** (30) 210 323 3866
Web: www.eurobank.gr

COMPETITORS

Alpha Bank
Emporiki Bank
National Bank of Greece
Piraeus Bank S.A.

HISTORICAL FINANCIALS

Company Type: Public

Income Statement FYE: December 31

	ASSETS ($ mil.)	NET INCOME ($ mil.)	INCOME AS % OF ASSETS	EMPLOYEES
12/14	91,792	(1,481)	—	18,428
12/13	106,815	(1,588)	—	20,053
12/12	89,170	(1,915)	—	17,662
12/11	99,365	(7,124)	—	19,156
12/10	116,690	91	0.1%	22,717
Annual Growth	(5.8%)	—	—	(5.1%)

2014 Year-End Financials

Return on assets: (-1.5%)
Return on equity: (-24.6%)
Long-term debt ($ mil.): —
No. of shares (mil.): —
Sales ($ mil): 4,177
Dividends
Yield: —
Payout: —
Market value ($ mil.): —

	STOCK PRICE ($) FY Close	P/E High/Low	PER SHARE ($) Earnings	Dividends	Book Value
12/14	0.12	— —	(0.13)	0.00	0.47
12/13	0.11	— —	(0.56)	0.00	1.07
12/12	0.30	— —	(3.03)	0.00	(2.23)
12/11	0.18	— —	(13.10)	0.00	1.40
12/10	2.60	— —	(0.20)	0.00	14.37
Annual Growth	(53.7%)	— —	—	—	(57.6%)

Faurecia S.A. (France)

Faurecia is one of Europe's largest automotive seat makers. In addition to car seats it also manufactures exhaust systems vehicle interiors and doors and front-end systems. Although Europe accounts for 75% of sales it supplies most major carmakers including GM Ford Mercedes BMW and Volkswagen. Faurecia also owns Faurecia Exhaust Systems and took over EMCON Technologies in 2010 –both are US-based makers of emission control technologies. Bertrand Faure and ECIA a Peugeot S.A. subsidiary merged in 1999 to create Faurecia. Peugeot is Faurecia's largest customer followed by Renault-Nissan. Faurecia's CEO seat has been hard to keep filled turning over the title three times in less than five years.

CEO Yann Delabrière in office since 2007 is navigating the company's rebound. Faurecia took a drastic hit during the global economic downturn that all but decimated the automotive industry. Its earnings have a sketchy history; since 2005 the company's net losses have widened on sales that peaked in 2007 and plummeted during the following two years by more than 25%.

Even as troubled as the automotive industry has been the company is focusing on opportunities for acquisitions triggered by the recession. Included among those efforts was a deal to acquire the automotive interior components business of Ford's Automotive Components Holding (ACH) subsidiary in 2012. The business which annually brings in about $1.1 billion provides cockpit modules instrument panels door panels and center consoles for operations at eight Ford plants. The acquisition made Faurecia the largest interior systems supplier in North America.

Faurecia's investments have also looked to bump up its market share particularly in the promising small-car segment. The company completed its purchase of US-based exhaust systems manufacturer EMCON Technologies (formerly known as Arvin Industries) from One Equity Partners in early 2010. The 300 million ($400 million) acquisition which served as the catalyst for creating Faurecia Emissions Control Technologies business doubles the size of Faurecia's exhaust systems operations giving it an entre into the commercial vehicle market dominated by US-based Tenneco. Faurecia's roster of commercial vehicle customers promises to include such blue chip OEMs as Volvo Trucks John Deere Fiat Cummins DAF and Iveco as well as passenger car makers Honda and Toyota. Following the acquisition of EMCON Technologies Peugeot's stake in Faurecia dwindled to 57% from more than 70%.

Closer to home in the spring of 2010 Faurecia acquired the German operations of Plastal Holding AB a Swedish company whose European assets were under administration due to its bankruptcy filing. The approximate 23 million ($32 million) deal significantly enhances Faurecia's portfolio beyond its core bumper offerings paving the way the company to become Europe's largest supplier of exterior plastic parts for major auto OEMs Ford and Porsche as well as Volkswagen/Audi and BMW. Plastal Spain was subsequently incorporated into Faurecia. In late 2010 Faurecia also agreed to acquire Angell-Demmel Europe a German manufacturer of real-metal automotive interior parts. Faurecia Interior Systems is set to inherit Angell-Demmel's operations.

In the meantime the company is working to move many of its European manufacturing sites to lower-cost countries. Faurecia has opened new facilities in Slovakia (seats instrument panels and bumpers) and Poland (seating foam and components). Faurecia has one plant in Russia which makes parts for Logan sedans made by a Renault facility outside of Moscow. Plans to build more factories in Russia stalled in the face of declining regional sales in 2009.

Faurecia is simultaneously implementing a restructuring program that includes closing down a number of manufacturing operations in France and reducing its workforce in Spain and elsewhere. Reductions spread west in 2008 when the company announced it would close one of its nearly 30 Canadian plants. In 2008 the company sold its France-based Sieto subsidiary to Toyota Boshoku; the subsidiary manufactured seats solely for Toyota's Yaris.

In the field of seating systems the company maintains a competitive edge in making lighter components which help to improve vehicle fuel efficiency. It has designed seats that are thinner and lighter than those used in most US vehicles. Faurecia in 2010 acquired the pneumatic seat comfort technology from German-based HOERBIGER Automotive. The addition strengthens Faurecia's seating know-how in the premium brand market. In other areas Faurecia has developed a cockpit without a crossbar that is lighter in weight as well as an exhaust system that warms up small-engine hybrids on cold days.

HISTORY

Bertrand Faure opened his workshop in Levallois-Perret France in 1914 to manufacture cushions and spring backs for automotive seats; spring pads were developed in 1929. The company diversified into bedding in 1954. The following year it opened a factory near Etampes.

Throughout the 1960s and 1970s Bertrand Faure continued to grow through geographic and product-line expansion. The company boosted its metal and foam seat-making operations in France and in 1971 it expanded into Germany with the purchase of automotive seating component manufacturer Schmitz. Faure bought French bedding maker Mrinos in 1973 and then changed its company name to Epda-Bertrand Faure. Between 1977 and 1978 Epda-Bertrand Faure expanded its automotive seating business through acquisitions in Spain and Portugal.

Epda-Bertrand Faure diversified into the luggage business with the 1982 purchase of Delsey. That year the company was floated on the French stock exchange. In 1983 Epda-Bertrand Faure further strengthened its car-seat business in France with the purchase of Autocoussin (structures and foam) and Cousin Frères (mechanisms). Another plant in Germany was opened in 1986 to supply BMW. That year Epda-Bertrand Faure invested in Canadian CASE a leading North American maker of car-seat mechanisms. The company also reorganized its automotive activities under the name Bertrand Faure Automobile.

Epda-Bertrand Faure acquired Luchaire a defense materials and aerospace and automotive equipment manufacturer in 1987. The following year the company bought automotive seating structures maker Sicam (Italy) and seating foam and structures firm Molaflex (Portugal). In 1989 the company forged joint ventures in the UK Japan and Canada for the manufacture of car seating.

By 1990 the company had reorganized into four product segments: automotive seats bedding luggage and aerospace equipment. The automotive seating business was conducted under the name Bertrand Faure while the rest of the group changed its name to EBF. Bertrand Faure purchased RHW a leading German maker of car seats in 1991.

The following year EBF's board of directors decided to focus the company on automotive seating and initiated a vast restructuring plan. EBF sold its bedding concerns in 1994. As part of its restructuring EBF changed its name back to Bertrand Faure. Two years later Bertrand Faure opened offices in Beijing and São Paulo.

Peugeot S.A. subsidiary ECIA and Bertrand Faure merged in 1999 to form Faurecia. In 2000 Faurecia bolstered its North American presence by purchasing US-based automotive exhaust system maker AP Automotive Systems; it renamed the subsidiary Faurecia Exhaust Systems. The company acquired Sommer Allibert's car interiors business early in 2001.

Expanding in Asia Faurecia purchased Chang Heung Precision Co. Ltd. a Korean maker of exhaust systems in 2003.

Since 2004 the headcount at high-cost Western European locations has been reduced while headcount in low-cost regions has increased.

In 2006 the company opened a new plant in China for the manufacture of automotive seats and interior modules for Ford.

In 2006 CEO Pierre Levi stepped down amid a corruption scandal involving Faurecia employees who allegedly offered kickbacks to managers at customers including Volkswagen and BMW. CFO Frank Imbert was named interim CEO then director Gregoire Olivier followed as CEO. Yann Delabrière succeeded him in early 2007.

In 2007 sales in North America grew by 42%. The company opened seven new plants in the US in 2006 and 2007 —in Michigan (seats interior modules front end modules) Ohio (interior modules and exhaust systems) and South Carolina (seats).

In Asia Faurecia's sales grew by 21% in 2007 over the previous year. To keep up momentum Faurecia continues to invest in the region.

EXECUTIVES

EVP Faurecia North America, Jacques Mauge
EVP Faurecia Emissions Control Technologies, Christophe Schmitt
EVP Faurecia Group Human Resources, Jean-Pierre Sounillac
EVP Faurecia Automotive Seating, Patrick Koller
Chairman and CEO, Yann Delabriere
EVP Faurecia and Group CFO, Michel Favre
EVP Faurecia Interior Systems, Jean-Michel Renaudie
Auditors: PricewaterhouseCoopers Audit

LOCATIONS

HQ: Faurecia S.A. (France)
2, rue Hennape, Nanterre 92000
Phone: (33) 1 72 36 70 00 **Fax:** (33) 1 72 36 70 07
Web: www.faurecia.com

2014 Sales

	% of total
Europe	55
North America	24
Asia	16
South America	4
Other countries	1
Total	**100**

PRODUCTS/OPERATIONS

2014 Sales

	% of total
Interior modules	
Automotive seating	28
Interior systems	25
Other modules	
Emissions control technologies	36
Automotive exteriors	11
Total	**100**

2014 Sales by Customer

	% of total
VW Group	19
Ford group	13
PSA Peugeot Citroën	12
Renault & Nissan	9
Daimer	8
GM	7
BMW	5
Others	27
Total	**100**

COMPETITORS

Benteler Group
DURA Automotive
IAC Group
Johnson Controls
Kongsberg Automotive
Lear Corp
Magna International
Magneti Marelli
Meritor
Tenneco
Visteon

HISTORICAL FINANCIALS

Company Type: Public

Income Statement FYE: December 31

	REVENUE ($ mil.)	NET INCOME ($ mil.)	NET PROFIT MARGIN	EMPLOYEES
12/14	22,886	201	0.9%	99,281
12/13	24,820	120	0.5%	97,419
12/12	22,887	187	0.8%	93,918
12/11	20,941	480	2.3%	84,179
12/10	18,464	269	1.5%	75,676
Annual Growth	5.5%	(7.1%)	—	7.0%

2014 Year-End Financials

Debt ratio: 32.2%
Return on equity: 10.3%
Cash ($ mil.): 1,236
Current ratio: 0.74
Long-term debt ($ mil.): 1,250
No. of shares (mil.): 123
Dividends
Yield: —
Payout: 22.3%
Market value ($ mil.): —

Fiat Chrysler Automobiles NV

Auditors: Reconta Ernst & Young S.p.A.

LOCATIONS

HQ: Fiat Chrysler Automobiles NV
25 St. James' Street, London SW1A 1HA
Phone: (44) 20 776 0311
Web: www.fcagroup.com

HISTORICAL FINANCIALS

Company Type: Public

Income Statement FYE: December 31

	REVENUE ($ mil.)	NET INCOME ($ mil.)	NET PROFIT MARGIN	EMPLOYEES
12/14	116,797	690	0.6%	228,690
12/13	119,258	1,244	1.0%	229,053
12/12	110,406	57	0.1%	218,311
12/11	77,036	1,550	2.0%	197,021
Annual Growth	14.9%	(23.6%)	—	5.1%

2014 Year-End Financials

Debt ratio: 40.7%	No. of shares (mil.): 1,284
Return on equity: 5.2%	Dividends
Cash ($ mil.): 27,762	Yield: —
Current ratio: 1.44	Payout: —
Long-term debt ($ mil.): 40,991	Market value ($ mil.): —

	STOCK PRICE ($) FY Close	P/E High/Low		PER SHARE ($) Earnings	Dividends	Book Value
12/14	0.00	—	—	0.56	0.00	12.70
Annual Growth	—	—	—	—	—	—

Finatis SA

Finatis finesses its way through a variety of activities. The French holding company has interests in commercial real estate including the leasing of shopping malls in France and Poland through a majority stake in Fonciere Euris. It is also involved in the distribution of food and sporting goods in France through retail giant Rallye owner of Groupe Casinoand Groupe Go Sport and food in South America through Companhia Brasileira de Distribui § o. Through Euristates Finatis has interests in US property investment funds. Groupe Euris founded by president Jean-Charles Naouri controls Finatis.

EXECUTIVES

Managing Director, Jean-Marie Grisard, age 72
Finance Director, Pierre Feraud
Chairman and CEO, Jean-Charles Naouri, age 66
Auditors: ERNST & YOUNG et Autres

LOCATIONS

HQ: Finatis SA
83, rue du Faubourg Saint-Honore, Paris 75008
Phone: (33) 1 44 71 14 00
Web: www.finatis.fr

COMPETITORS

Auchan	Kl©pierre
Carrefour	SFL
GECINA	Unibail-Rodamco
ITM Entreprises	

HISTORICAL FINANCIALS

Company Type: Public

Income Statement FYE: December 31

	REVENUE ($ mil.)	NET INCOME ($ mil.)	NET PROFIT MARGIN	EMPLOYEES
12/14	60,481	(9)	—	340,060
12/13	68,383	108	0.2%	333,723
12/12	56,709	224	0.4%	321,386
12/11	45,885	(23)	—	227,997
12/10	40,465	18	0.0%	175,383
Annual Growth	10.6%	—	—	18.0%

2014 Year-End Financials

Debt ratio: 44.9%	No. of shares (mil.): 5
Return on equity: (-0.0%)	Dividends
Cash ($ mil.): 9,341	Yield: —
Current ratio: 0.92	Payout: —
Long-term debt ($ mil.): 14,723	Market value ($ mil.): —

First Commercial Bank

EXECUTIVES

President, Ching Nien Tsai
Auditors: PricewaterhouseCoopers

LOCATIONS

HQ: First Commercial Bank
30, Chung-King S. Road, Sec. 1, Taipei 100-05
Phone: (886) 2 2348 1111 **Fax:** (886) 2 2361 0036
Web: www.firstbank.com.tw

HISTORICAL FINANCIALS

Company Type: Public

Income Statement FYE: December 31

	ASSETS ($ mil.)	NET INCOME ($ mil.)	INCOME AS % OF ASSETS	EMPLOYEES
12/14	72,533	422	0.6%	7,286
12/13	73,997	356	0.5%	7,207
12/12	71,424	357	0.5%	7,133
12/11	67,153	284	0.4%	7,279
12/10	68,812	217	0.3%	7,178
Annual Growth	1.3%	18.0%	—	0.4%

2014 Year-End Financials

Return on assets: 0.5%	Dividends
Return on equity: 9.4%	Yield: —
Long-term debt ($ mil.): —	Payout: —
No. of shares (mil.): —	Market value ($ mil.): —
Sales ($ mil): 1,661	

First Gulf Bank

EXECUTIVES

Director & Chairman, Sheikh Tahnoon Bin Zayed Al Nahyan
Auditors: Ernst & Young

LOCATIONS

HQ: First Gulf Bank
P.O. Box 6316, Abu Dhabi
Phone: (971) 2 681 6666 **Fax:** (971) 2 681 3169
Web: www.firstgulfbank.ae

HISTORICAL FINANCIALS

Company Type: Public

Income Statement FYE: December 31

	ASSETS ($ mil.)	NET INCOME ($ mil.)	INCOME AS % OF ASSETS	EMPLOYEES
12/14	57,767	1,539	2.7%	0
12/13	53,098	1,299	2.4%	1,452
12/12	47,650	1,130	2.4%	1,112
12/11	42,874	1,009	2.4%	930
12/10	38,321	931	2.4%	956
Annual Growth	10.8%	13.4%	—	—

2014 Year-End Financials

Return on assets: 2.7%	Dividends
Return on equity: 17.3%	Yield: —
Long-term debt ($ mil.): —	Payout: —
No. of shares (mil.): —	Market value ($ mil.): —
Sales ($ mil): 3,000	

Flextronics International Ltd.

Having factories on four continents would make you flexible too. Flextronics International offers turnkey manufacturing services to the world's leading electronics companies including Apple Cisco Ericsson HP Huawei Lenovo Microsoft BlackBerry and Xerox. The company's services range from design engineering through manufacturing and assembly to distribution and warehousing. It manufactures and assembles printed circuit boards electromechanical components subsystems and complete systems for a wide range of makers of networking and telecommunications equipment computers consumer electronics and medical instrumentation.

Flextronics has reorganized its market segments into four areas: high-reliability solutions (automotive aerospace and defense medical) high-velocity solutions (game consoles mobile handsets and smartphones printers enterprise PC manufacturing) industrial and emerging industries (clean technology including solar industrial semiconductor capital equipment) and integrated network solutions (connected home data networking servers and storage and telecommunications infrastructure equipment). The company has exited the original design manufacturing (ODM) personal computers business which generated $1.6 billion in sales and $113 million in losses. It continues to provide ODM products —where customers buy products designed and manufactured by Flextronics —in the automotive industrial infrastructure medical and power supply sectors among others.

Flextronics maintains facilities in more than 30 countries. Much of its manufacturing capacity is located in regions with lower labor costs including Brazil China Hungary India Malaysia Mexico Poland and Ukraine. China (38% of sales) and Mexico (14%) lead the way among Flextronics's manufacturing operations. Sales outside the US account for 90% of sales.

Overall sales were $29.4 billion in fiscal 2012 an increase of around 3% over 2011. Flextronics recorded growth across nearly all of its product groups as the company benefited from an improved global economy and more balanced portfolio of products. Net income was down 18% for the year due in part to an out-of-period adjustment to cost of sales (the errors were related to one of its foreign locations for fiscal periods 2009-2011) and a writedown of inventory related to one of its solar customers. While sales to customers in its high velocity solutions (HVS) market segment make up 40% of sales Flextronics is looking to further shift its product balance to non-HVS businesses with a target of 70% of sales coming from non-HVS businesses.

The majority of Flextronics' growth in fiscal 2012 was organic.The company mirrors its customers to align with changes in their marketing strategy and to take advantage of changes in outsourcing trends. Flextronics has also diversified its business across and within many different end markets in order to protect against shifts in demand and to expand the range of opportunities available in each market. Like many contract electronics manufacturers the company is increasingly offering more aftermarket supply chain services including product order fulfillment refurbishment repair recycling and warranty management.

Flextronics' continuous expansion has elevated it into the top ranks of the consolidating contract electronics manufacturing business. The company has to be able to expand capacity during periods of high demand while keeping costs low enough to maintain profitability in a low-margin industry. New facilities were opened during 2011 for the company's medical and logistics business operations. Flextronics Medical is a contract manufacturer for medical devices (customers include Insulet and Waters Corporation) and Flextronics Global Services offers post-manufacturing supply chain logistics. A medical equipment plant in Romania was expanded to better serve the emerging market of Eastern Europe. Flextronics Global Services added facilities in India and Turkey. The Indian facility provides repair services to a smartphone manufacturer and the Turkish facility is the new inbound distribution hub for a computer manufacturer. Also that year Flextronics and solar company SunPower joined together to open a small solar panel assembly plant in California.

In 2012 Flextronics acquired Stellar Microelectronics an EMS provider based in California that specializes in custom packaging services for the aerospace defense and medical manufacturing markets. The move is part of the company's plan to expand services in those markets which often have to meet specific regulations for product manufacturing. It also acquired Michigan-based EMS provider Saturn Electronics & Engineering that year. The following year in a move that underscores its commitment to expand its services to the healthcare market Flextronics acquired RIWISA a European provider of injection molding and other services for medical consumer and industrial applications.

Part of expanding is a willingness to part with assets that are not core to future growth. In 2012 Flextronics sold its Vista Point camera module business to DigitalOptics a subsidiary of Tessera Technologies. The sale included the brand intellectual property and China-based manufacturing assets. Flextronics retained part of Vista Point's assets but plans to use them to expand other manufacturing services.

HISTORY

Flextronics International formed in 1990 followed two earlier contract manufacturers named Flextronics formed in 1969 and 1980. The latter iteration used acquisitions to expand throughout Asia and the US. In 1988 it opened the first US-managed contract electronics plant in China and that year sales topped $200 million.

But acquisitions burdened Flextronics with debt and left it with disparate operations. It divested its US-based manufacturing operations and laid off 75% of its workforce. The company brought in a management team to sell its healthy Asian operations to pay off debt. These operations formed the current incarnation of Flextronics International.

A revitalized Flextronics based in Singapore went public in 1994. It quickly joined the industry rush toward consolidation and globalization. Acquisitions included nCHIP (California 1996) FICO Plastics (Hong Kong 1997) Neutronics Electronic Industries (Austria 1997) and Kyrel EMS Oyj (Finland and France 1999).

In 2000 Flextronics acquired rival The DII Group which propelled the company to the #4 spot in contract manufacturing (behind Solectron SCI Systems and Celestica). The company was also selected by Microsoft to build the software juggernaut's Xbox video game console. Later that year Motorola and Flextronics signed one of the largest outsourcing deals ever worth an estimated $30 billion over five years. The company expanded further in Asia when it acquired JIT Holdings a Singapore-based electronics manufacturer.

In 2001 Flextronics announced a deal with telecommunications giant Ericsson; under the pact Flextronics assumed management of Ericsson's mobile phone manufacturing operations worldwide. Later that year the company announced that it would cut its workforce by about 10% and that the multibillion-dollar deal with Motorola unraveled due to a continuing market slowdown. Flextronics also repurchased Motorola's 5% stake in the company.

Also that year Flextronics bought Telcom Global Solutions a supplier of planning and design services for telecommunications providers. Flextronics later announced a deal with Xerox to acquire Xerox facilities in Brazil Canada Malaysia and Mexico for about $220 million and to provide manufacturing services to Xerox for five years. Later that year the company laid off 10000 workers – about 15% of its staff –in a cost-cutting move. Flextronics also acquired a 91% stake in Orbiant a telephone network services spinoff of Swedish telecom giant Telia for $100 million in cash (along with future payments pegged to the unit's performance).

In 2002 the company made a deal with CASIO COMPUTER under which Flextronics bought two CASIO plants in Asia then supplied the Japanese electronics maker with finished products in a three-year pact. Also that year the company significantly expanded its presence in southern China with the purchase of Hong Kong-based NatSteel Broadway (printed circuit boards plastic and metal components) for about $367 million.

In 2004 Flextronics took over optical wireless and enterprise manufacturing as well as optical design operations from Nortel Networks in a four-year supply deal generating about $2.5 billion in annual revenues. Flextronics later closed several former Nortel facilities in Canada France and Northern Ireland.

Flextronics also acquired a majority ownership stake in India-based software services provider Hughes Software Systems (HSS) in 2004. The following year Flextronics purchased Agilent's mobile communications camera module business. The company sold its semiconductor division to AMIS Holdings (now part of ON Semiconductor) and its Flextronics Network Services division was merged with a company called Telavie and renamed Relacom; Flextronics retained a 30% stake.

Flextronics set plans in 2005 to build an industrial park in Chennai India to supplement its existing operations on the subcontinent where it previously employed more than 5000 people. The development added to the two manufacturing facilities and three design centers Flextronics had in India.

To focus on its core electronics manufacturing services business in 2006 Flextronics sold its Flextronics Software Systems business (renamed Aricent) to an affiliate of KKR for about $900 million in cash and notes. Flextronics retained a 15% equity interest in the software development business which was primarily based in India (it sold the remaining stake in 2009). Divestitures of its software and semiconductor businesses took a small chunk out of the company's revenues –$278 million in fiscal 2006.

Flextronics then acquired International DisplayWorks a contract manufacturer of small LCDs and LCD modules for cell phones and other consumer electronics for stock valued at approximately $243 million. International DisplayWorks became a wholly owned subsidiary of Flextronics operating within the company's Components Group. Also in 2006 nLight Corp. acquired the assets of Flextronics Photonics including a line of fiber-coupled and hybrid microelectronic devices.

In 2007 Flextronics purchased rival contract manufacturer Solectron in a deal valued at $3.6 billion. The combination vaulted the company into the position of the second-largest contract electronics manufacturer in the world trailing only Hon Hai Precision Industry the maker of products for Apple Dell and many other companies.

The next year it bought contract disposable device maker Avail Medical Products a private company with around $250 million in sales to further the expansion of its Flextronics Medical segment. Also in 2008 Flextronics inked a deal to acquire Elcoteq's ZAO Elcoteq subsidiary and plant in St. Petersburg Russia. Flextronics however later terminated the transaction and was forced to pay a fee for noncompletion.

In 2009 it sold its stake in Aricent a privately held communications software company to investment firms KKR and CPP Investment Board for about $250 million. The sale was part of a plan to sell noncore assets as Flextronics tried to bolster its balance sheet during the economic downturn. At the end of the year it bought SloMedical S.R.O. a leading maker of disposable medical devices for the European market. In addition to adding disposable devices for the medical and surgical market in Eastern Europe SloMedical (based in Slovenia) gave Flextronics an FDA-compliant clean room-enabled production site with low production costs.

In 2012 Flextronics acquired Stellar Microelectronics an EMS provider based in California that specializes in custom packaging services for the aerospace defense and medical manufacturing markets as part of a plan to expand services for the highly regulated markets. Also that year Flextronics sold its Vista Point camera module business to Tessera Technologies' subsidiary DigitalOptics; the sale included the brand intellectual property and China-based manufacturing assets.

EXECUTIVES

EVP and General Counsel, Jonathan S. (Jon) Hoak, age 65, $500,000 total compensation
President Americas Operations, Michael M. (Mike) McNamara, age 58, $1,250,000 total compensation
President Automotive, Christopher J. Obey
President Innovation and New Ventures, Jeannine P. Sargent, age 50
CFO, Christopher (Chris) Collier, age 47, $538,750 total compensation
President Industrial and Emerging Industries, Douglas (Doug) Britt, age 50
President Power Solutions, Christopher Cook
President Global Operations and Components, Fran $is Barbier, age 56, $625,000 total compensation
President High Reliability Solutions, Paul Humphries, $625,000 total compensation
President Consumer Technologies Group, Mike Dennison
President Integrated Network Solutions, Caroline Dowling
President Strategic Partnerships, Ruvi Shaibel
President Multek, Franck Lize
President Manufacturing Operations, Tzahi Rodrig
CTO, Erik H. Volkerink
SVP and CIO, Gus Shahin
Chairman, H. Raymond Bingham
Auditors: Deloitte & Touche LLP

LOCATIONS

HQ: Flextronics International Ltd.
2 Changi South Lane, 486123
Phone: (65) 6876 9899
Web: www.flextronics.com

2012 Sales

	$ mil.	% of total
China	11,148	38
Mexico	4,005	14
US	3,006	10
Malaysia	2,869	10
Hungary	2,123	7
Other countries	6,234	21
Total	**29,387**	**100**

PRODUCTS/OPERATIONS

2012 Sales by Market

	$ mil.	% of total
High velocity solutions	11,645	40
Integrated network solutions	11,358	39
Industrial & emerging industries	3,989	13
High reliability solutions	2,394	8
Total	**29,387**	**100**

Selected Services

Assembly and manufacturing
- Box build (complete systems)
- Complex electromechanical components
- Printed circuit boards (PCBs)
- Subsystems (including those that incorporate PCBs)

Engineering
- Design
- Prototyping
- Test development

Materials procurement and management
- Planning
- Purchasing
- Warehousing

Network support
- Installation and maintenance of telecommunications systems and corporate networks

Packaging
Plastic and metal components
Product distribution
Recycling and refurbishment
Testing of PCBs subsystems and systems
Warranty repair

COMPETITORS

ASUSTeK
Benchmark Electronics
Cal-Comp Electronics
Celestica
Compal Electronics
Hon Hai
Jabil
Kimball International
MiTAC
Nam Tai
Plexus
Quanta Computer
SYNNEX
Sanmina
TTM Technologies
Universal Scientific
Venture Corp.
Wistron

HISTORICAL FINANCIALS

Company Type: Public

Income Statement FYE: March 31

	REVENUE ($ mil.)	NET INCOME ($ mil.)	NET PROFIT MARGIN	EMPLOYEES
03/15	26,147	600	2.3%	150,000
03/14	26,108	365	1.4%	150,000
03/13	23,569	277	1.2%	149,000
03/12	29,387	488	1.7%	159,000
03/11	28,679	596	2.1%	176,000
Annual Growth	(2.3%)	0.2%	—	(3.9%)

2015 Year-End Financials

Debt ratio: 17.8%
Return on equity: 26.5%
Cash ($ mil.): 1,628
Current ratio: 1.29
Long-term debt ($ mil.): 2,037
No. of shares (mil.): 563
Dividends
Yield: —
Payout: —
Market value ($ mil.): —

Fonciere Euris SA

Foncire Euris is a holding company that engages in specialty distribution and real estate. Through main majority held subsidiary Rallye Foncire Euris is involved in food distribution to supermarkets hypermarkets convenience stores and discount stores in France and abroad via Casino Guichard-Perrachon and sporting goods distribution in France and Poland via Groupe Go Sport. Foncire Euris also holds directly or indirectly a handful of shopping centers in operation and shopping centers under construction in France Germany and Poland. Most of the company's sales are made in France but it also generates significant sales in South America and to a lesser extent Asia among other regions.

Operations

Among Foncire Euris' property holdings are three shopping centers in operation in Tours France Lotz Poland and Frankfurt Germany. It has two shopping centers under construction in Paris and Gdynia Poland.

Ownership

Parent company Finatis controls about 80% of Foncire Euris.

EXECUTIVES

Chairman & Managing Director, Michel SAVART
Board Member, Christian PEENE
Board Member, Jean-louis BRUNET
Auditors: ERNST & YOUNG et Autres

LOCATIONS

HQ: Fonciere Euris SA
83, rue du Faubourg Saint-Honore, Paris 75008
Phone: (33) 1 44 71 14 00
Web: www.fonciere-euris.fr

COMPETITORS

Bayerische Immobilien
Fonci□re des R©gions
Kl©pierre
SFL
Unibail-Rodamco

HISTORICAL FINANCIALS

Company Type: Public

Income Statement FYE: December 31

	REVENUE ($ mil.)	NET INCOME ($ mil.)	NET PROFIT MARGIN	EMPLOYEES
12/14	60,481	2	0.0%	340,060
12/13	68,383	123	0.2%	333,723
12/12	56,709	242	0.4%	321,386
12/11	45,883	(12)	—	227,996
12/10	40,459	20	0.0%	175,382
Annual Growth	10.6%	(41.0%)	—	18.0%

2014 Year-End Financials

Debt ratio: 44.6%
Return on equity: 0.0%
Cash ($ mil.): 9,341
Current ratio: 0.91
Long-term debt ($ mil.): 14,542
No. of shares (mil.): 9
Dividends
Yield: —
Payout: —
Market value ($ mil.): —

Formosa Petrochemical Corp

Formosa Petrochemical Corporation (FPCC) is second only to Chinese Petroleum Corporation for oil refining in Taiwan. The company produces refined petroleum products (jet fuel liquid petroleum gas and gasoline) and petrochemicals (ethylene propylene and butadiene) from its naphtha cracking operations. It owns gas stations through subsidiary Formosa Oil. FPCC also sells electricity and steam from its co-generation plants. Its engineering and maintenance divisions carry out planning construction and daily maintenance services on behalf of group companies.

Geographic Segment

FPCC sells its products worldwide. In 2011 Taiwan accounted for 58% of the company's revenues.

Sales and Marketing

In 2011 Formosa Chemicals & Fibers accounted for 19% of sales; Formosa Plastics 13%.

Financial Performance

FPCC's revenues increased by 7% in 2011 and its net income decreased by 45%.

StrategyIn 2011 the company restarted its 700000 tons-per-year No. 1 naphtha cracker after a four-month shutdown due to a fire.

Ownership

Formosa Plastics owns 29% of FPCC; affiliates Formosa Chemicals & Fibers and Nan Ya Plastics also own 25% and 24% respectively.

Company Background

The three group companies formed FPCC in 1992 to build and run a giant integrated petrochemicals facility called the No. 6 Naphtha Cracking Project.

EXECUTIVES

President and Director, Wilfred Wang
Chief Financial Officer, Ming-Hsiung Shih
Chairman, Chen Bao-Lang
Auditors: Ernst & Young

LOCATIONS

HQ: Formosa Petrochemical Corp
No. 1-1, Taisu Industrial Park, Mailiao Township, Yunlin County 638
Phone: (886) 5 6812345
Web: www.fpcc.com.tw

COMPETITORS

BASF-YPC
CPC
ExxonMobil Chemical
OCI Company
Total Petrochemicals

HISTORICAL FINANCIALS

Company Type: Public

Income Statement FYE: December 31

	REVENUE ($ mil.)	NET INCOME ($ mil.)	NET PROFIT MARGIN	EMPLOYEES
12/14	28,836	286	1.0%	4,864
12/13	31,230	900	2.9%	3,978
12/12	30,817	93	0.3%	6,507
12/11	0	0	—	6,426
12/10	25,736	1,406	5.5%	5,604
Annual Growth	2.9%	(32.8%)	—	(3.5%)

2014 Year-End Financials

Debt ratio: 1.2%
Return on equity: 3.7%
Cash ($ mil.): 1,283
Current ratio: 2.49
Long-term debt ($ mil.): 3,841
No. of shares (mil.): —
Dividends
Yield: —
Payout: —
Market value ($ mil.): —

Fresenius SE & Co KGaA

Fresenius takes a free hand with dialysis and infusion products and services. The company offers a wide range of health products and services through its four core business segments: Fresenius Medical Care Fresenius Kabi Fresenius Helios and

Fresenius Vamed. The company's Medical Care division specializes in treating chronic kidney failure at some 3350 dialysis clinics worldwide. Fresenius Kabi provides nutrition infusion and IV therapies and related equipment. Fresenius Helios operates private hospitals in Germany while Fresenius Vamed offers facility management project development and other services to hospitals and health facilities. Fresenius has operations in more than 100 countries.

Operations

Fresenius Helios operates 110 hospitals (including 86 acute-care facilities and seven maximum-care hospitals) with more than 34000 beds in Germany. Fresenius Vamed provides project development planning technical and operation management and turnkey construction services to hospitals and other health care facilities around the world.

In addition to its four core segments the Corporate and Other segment comprises the holding activities of Fresenius as well as its internal IT service provider Fresenius Netcare.

Geographic Reach

North America and Europe are the German health care company's largest markets contributing 40% and 44% of annual revenue respectively. The Asia/Pacific region (China Japan) accounts for about 10% of revenue followed by Latin America (5%) and South Africa (2%).

The company also has production facilities in other European countries and in Latin America the Asia/Pacific region and South Africa.

Sales and Marketing

Fresenius offers its products and services to hospitals and other health care organizations.

Financial Performance

Fresenius has seen revenue growth over the past few years. In 2014 revenue rose 14% to 23.2 billion primarily due to 54% growth in the Helios segment which saw growth due to the addition of acquired hospitals from Rhon-Klinikum (which contributed 1.8 billion) as well as an increase of admissions and hospital services price increases. The Medical Care segment grew 8% that year while Kabi and Vamed rose 3% and 2% respectively.

The higher revenues led to a 6% increase in net income which reached 1.1 billion. Cash flow from operations also increased rising 11% to 2.5 billion; this was led by a decline in cash used in inventories and an increase in trade accounts payable accrued expenses and other liabilities.

Strategy

The company has been aggressively expanding its core operating segments through both organic growth and acquisitions. Its majority-owned Fresenius Medical Care subsidiary which accounts for more than half of the firm's revenues has expanded its dialysis service and its equipment manufacturing operations through acquisitions. Though Fresenius Medical Care primarily grows through purchases of single clinics or small dialysis groups it occasionally makes larger acquisitions. The division is also widening its operations in the fields of home dialysis and renal pharmaceuticals.

Fresenius Kabi is a market leader in infusion therapy and clinical nutrition in Europe and in key markets in the Asia/Pacific region and Latin America. Fresenius has expanded Kabi's operations through a number of acquisitions in recent years. In 2014 for instance Kabi acquired the privately held Brazilian pharmaceutical company Novafarma Industria Farmacêutica to further its strategy to expand its market presence in emerging markets. In addition Fresenius Kabi is working to expand in the generic injectables market by developing and releasing new IV pharmaceutical products and expanding distribution of existing drugs both in the US and international markets. Kabi is also working to increase its offerings of infusion and nutrition equipment such as feeding tubes and drug delivery pumps. In 2014 the unit was granted US approval for products in the fields of clinical nutrition and medical devices.

In 2015 Kabi sold subsidiary CFL a specialist in IV oncology drug compounding in order to focus on parenteral nutrition products.

Fresenius Vamed provides hospitals with engineering equipment planning and other upkeep-related services. Helios is seeking to increase brand recognition and add more facilities as Germany's hospitals become increasingly privatized while Vamed is focused on growth of engineering and other specialty services. A hard-won acquisition in 2014 of a rival German hospital operator has made Fresenius Helios the leading private hospital operator in Europe with 117 hospitals across Germany.

Mergers and Acquisitions

In a move that created the largest private hospital operator in Europe in February 2014 Fresenius Helios acquired 38 hospitals and 11 outpatient facilities from Rhon-Klinikum for $4.1 billion. The purchase gave Fresenius Helios 117 hospitals across Germany. The deal came a year after Fresenius attempted to acquire all of Rhon-Klinikum but failed. The purchase will add about 2 billion in annual sales.

Later that year Fresenius Medical Care acquired US-based Cogent Healthcare to become the nation's largest private provider of hospitalist and intensivist services. Its majority-owned Sound Inpatient Physicians division now serves more than 180 hospitals.

Also in 2014 Fresenius bought National Cardiovascular Partners which provides endovascular vascular and cardiovascular services in outpatient settings.

HISTORY

Fresenius was founded as the Hirsch Pharmacy in 1462. The Fresenius family took over its ownership in the 18th century and converted it into a pharmaceutical manufacturing entity in 1912.

Fresenius entered the dialysis equipment market in 1966. The company formed its Fresenius Medical Care unit in 1996 when it merged its dialysis systems division with National Medical Care (NMC).

In 1999 Fresenius formed its Fresenius Kabi division by combining its infusion pharmaceutical operations with the former infusion solution business of drugmaker Pharmacia & Upjohn which it acquired the previous year.

The company conducted a number of expansion efforts within the Kabi division in the following decade including the 2007 purchase of IV drug manufacturing firms Labesfal (Portugal) and Filaxis (Argentina) as well as German medical device maker Clinico. Also that year the company bought the artificial colloid product business of Kyorin to build up a presence in the Tokyo market.

It then purchased Indian oncology drug manufacturer Dabur Pharma in 2008. Also that year the unit expanded its reach in the US market for injectable drugs by acquiring US generics maker APP Pharmaceuticals for $3.7 billion plus debt.

Following the acquisition of German private clinic operator Helios Kliniken Fresenius refreshed its acute care operations by separating its hospital division (Fresenius ProServe) into two business segments Fresenius Helios and Fresenius Vamed in 2008.

EXECUTIVES

Chairman Managing Board, Ulf M. (Mark) Schneider, age 49
CEO Fresenius Medical Care, Rice Powell, age 59
CFO, Stephan Sturm, age 52
CEO Fresenius Kabi AG, Mats Henriksson, age 48
CEO Fresenius Helios, Francesco De Meo, age 51
CEO Fresenius Vamed, Ernst Wastler, age 56
Deputy Chairman, Gerhard Rupprecht, age 67
Chairman, Gerd Krick, age 77
Auditors: KPMG AG

LOCATIONS

HQ: Fresenius SE & Co KGaA
Else-Kroener-Strasse 1, Bad Homburg D-61352
Phone: (49) 6172 608 0 **Fax:** (49) 6172 608 2488
Web: www.fresenius.com

2014 Sales

	% of total
North America	40
Europe	44
Asia Pacific	9
Latin America & other regions	7
Total	**100**

PRODUCTS/OPERATIONS

2014 Sales

	% of total
Fresenius Medical Care	51
Fresenius Kabi	22
Fresenius Helios	23
Fresenius Vamed	4
Total	**100**

Selected Services

Fresenius Medical Care
- Dialysis facility operation
- Disease management
- Disposable dialysis supplies
- Hemodialysis equipment
- Peritoneal dialysis equipment

Fresenius Kabi
- Blood volume replacement
- Enteral nutrition
- Infusion and IV devices
- Infusion therapies
- IV generic drugs
- Parenteral nutrition
- Tranfusion products

Fresenius Helios
- HELIOS Kliniken Group (61 private hospitals Germany)

Fresenius Vamed
- Construction management
- Facility planning
- Maintenance services
- Operational management
- Project development
- Staff recruitment and training

COMPETITORS

Asahi Kasei
B. Braun Melsungen
Baxter International
Becton Dickinson
Bio-Reference Labs
DaVita
Dialysis Clinic Inc
Hospira
Johnson & Johnson
NxStage
Ranbaxy Laboratories
Renal Advantage
Terumo
Teva

HISTORICAL FINANCIALS

Company Type: Public

Income Statement FYE: December 31

	REVENUE ($ mil.)	NET INCOME ($ mil.)	NET PROFIT MARGIN	EMPLOYEES
12/14	28,237	1,296	4.6%	216,275
12/13	27,990	1,391	5.0%	178,337
12/12	25,425	1,220	4.8%	169,324
12/11	21,370	892	4.2%	149,351
12/10	21,376	832	3.9%	137,552
Annual Growth	7.2%	11.7%	—	12.0%

2014 Year-End Financials

Debt ratio: 47.0%
Return on equity: 13.0%
Cash ($ mil.): 1,428
Current ratio: 1.41
Long-term debt ($ mil.): 16,756
No. of shares (mil.): 541
Dividends
Yield: 1.1%
Payout: 5.4%
Market value ($ mil.): 7,024

	STOCK PRICE ($) FY Close	P/E High/Low		PER SHARE ($) Earnings	Dividends	Book Value
12/14	12.97	9	6	2.38	0.14	20.95
12/13	19.35	10	7	2.58	0.12	20.93
12/12	14.40	9	7	2.32	0.10	18.82
12/11	11.70	8	8	1.80	0.00	15.77
Annual Growth	3.5%	—	—	7.2%	—	7.4%

Fuji Heavy Industries, Ltd.

Fuji Heavy Industries (FHI) is the parent of Subaru of America the automotive company known for its all-wheel-drive (AWD) technology found in cross-over vehicles (a sedan drive with SUV looks) such as the Forester and Outback and in the Impreza Legacy and Tribeca models. Through some 80 subsidiaries FHI has manufacturing operations in China Japan Taiwan and the US where it operates through Subaru of America. Other FHI businesses include Aerospace (aircraft and structural components) and Industrial Products (general-purpose engines agricultural machinery and machine tools). However its core business is Subaru automobiles representing more than 90% of sales.

Financial Performance

Strong momentum at Subaru of America the company's core business is driving sales and profit growth for Fuji Heavy Industries (FHI). Indeed in fiscal 2014 (ended March) FHI reported sales of $23.4 billion up 15% versus the prior year. Net income rose 59% to $2 billion over the same period. Subaru sold 424683 vehicles in the US in 2013 and the company expects to sell at least 500000 in 2014 marking its fifth straight year of record sales here. Subaru represented 93% of FHI's total fiscal 2014 revenue while the Aerospace business accounted for 5%.

FHI's Aerospace arm posted a 40% increase in sales in fiscal 2014 versus the prior year while the Industrial Products division saw its sales dip 1%. The company credited increased sales to Japan's Ministry of Defense and Boeing to support the Boeing 777 and 787 jetliners for the rise in its Aerospace business.

Strategy

The company is focused on advancing transportation technology with innovations that include the horizontally-opposed Boxer Engine Symmetrical All-Wheel drive the advanced driving support system "EyeSight" in the automotive business and the unmanned aircraft system in its aerospace business.

Fuji Industrial Products holds a large share in the global general-purpose engine market with more than 2000 models one of which is the Robin engine which is sold in more than 70 countries. Fuji's Eco Technologies supplies vehicles (Fuji Mighty sanitation truck) used to collect and transport waste products as well as wind-power systems. Its Clean Robot division was the first to commercialize floor-cleaning robots for high-rise buildings.

Fuji Aerospace manufactures main wings and other structural aircraft components. It is the primary contractor of the AH-64D combat helicopter to the Japan Defense Agency (JDA). Fuji Aerospace also supplies JDA with fixed-wing aircraft and primary trainers and manufactures components for Boeing aircraft (767/777); its center wing box is part of the Boeing 787 Dreamliner. Other technology includes unmanned aircraft and development of a Fuji Aerial Robot (FABOT) system that uses GPS navigation and handles takeoffs and landings by small fixed-wing aircraft.

HISTORY

Chikuhei Nakajima started the Aircraft Research Laboratory north of Tokyo in 1917 renaming it the Nakajima Aircraft Company in 1931. Amid the ashes of WWII Nakajima formed Fuji Sangyo to make products with aircraft technology in 1945. His motor scooters used bomber tail wheels and he later added buses with unibody frames. Nakajima died in 1949.

Fuji Sangyo joined four other firms in 1953 and Fuji Heavy Industries was born. The Subaru car division debuted in 1958 and FHI went public two years later. The firm expanded product lines throughout the 1960s and in 1968 Nissan Motor invested in FHI. The relationship lasted more than 30 years.

Subaru expanded to the US in 1968 with the help of furniture retailer Harvey Lamm. Lamm visiting Japan saw Subaru's utilitarian front-wheel-drive station wagon and recognized its potential. He convinced FHI to make him its US importer and he set up Subaru of America. Lamm ultimately became chairman and CEO of the US subsidiary.

In 1975 FHI exported the four-wheel-drive Subaru GF to the US; it was the country's first four-wheel-drive car for the mass market. High energy prices and the appeal of a four-wheel-drive car drove sales in the 1970s and early 1980s. By 1986 Subaru achieved 12 straight years of record sales and profits.

The next year however a rising yen boosted Japanese car prices and sales dips fueled round after round of incentives. Profits tanked and Subaru responded by expanding trim levels and power train choices. The misstep confused shoppers and sales nose-dived.

Also in 1987 FHI and Isuzu teamed up to build an assembly plant (Subaru-Isuzu Automotive) in Indiana while other makers introduced minivans and sport utility vehicles. Focusing on cars Subaru missed the start of the SUV boom. Even the arrival of the Legacy in 1989 failed to jumpstart sales. Lamm left Subaru in 1990 and two years later Subaru's US arm posted a record loss of $250 million.

Veteran CFO George Muller took over as president and COO of Subaru of America in 1993. Saddled with inventory plummeting sales and a poor brand image he promptly launched one of the greatest turnarounds in US automotive history.

Muller refined the niche Lamm carved out in the 1970s. He cut every product from the lineup that lacked all-wheel-drive. Enlisting the Legacy a car-SUV hybrid (Outback) was created in 1995 by lifting the body a few inches and adding beefy-looking body attachments.

Muller took aggressive steps at the corporate level to cut costs and build a culture of risk-taking initiative and speed. By 1999 profits were back to record levels. In Japan though trouble at parent FHI overshadowed Subaru's rejuvenation.

In 1998 revelations surfaced that FHI bribed legislator Yojiro Nakajima (a former official in Japan's defense agency and grandson of Chikuhei) to secure government contracts for a sea rescue aircraft. FHI had also illegally funneled cash to Nakajima to help his 1996 election bid. Nakajima along with FHI's chairman and several former executives was arrested. He later committed suicide and FHI was barred from bidding on defense contracts for one year.

GM bought 20% of FHI for $1.5 billion in 1999. The deal included the 4% held by FHI's largest investor Nissan. GM won access to FHI's all-wheel-drive technology and provided FHI resources to develop more-efficient fuel systems. Midway through 2000 Muller resigned from Subaru.

FHI struck a deal with Airbus in 2001 develop the company's new Airbus A380 airliner. Subaru and GM also unveiled plans to jointly produce an all-wheel-drive sport wagon to be built at the Subaru-Isuzu plant in the US.

FHI announced in 2002 that it would cease production of bus bodies and railway cars by March 2003. Later that year FHI bought Isuzu Motors' 49% stake in the companies' carmaking joint venture Subaru-Isuzu Automotive. FHI renamed the company Subaru of Indiana Automotive.

That same year FHI implemented sweeping changes in an effort to focus on its core business —building cars. The Fuji Dynamic Revolution-1 plan (FDR-1) aimed to increase sales by 35% by 2007 and to remake Subaru as a luxury brand. Part of the original plan was for the company to leverage its relationship with GM to reduce procurement and purchasing costs. GM however decided largely to terminate its relationship with FHI and has sold its 20% stake in the Japanese manufacturer about 9% of it going to Toyota Motor. It sold the remaining 11% through Fuji's open-market share-buyback program and through regular market sales.

In the first product tie-up since Toyota became FHI's largest shareholder the two companies announced in early 2006 that Toyota Camrys would be built at FHI's Subaru of Indiana plant. That production began the following year.

In 2006 FHI made a few adjustments to its FDR-1 plan. The company restructured its sales networks and layed off about 700 workers to meet its cost reduction goals. The notion of transforming into a luxury brand however was deemed to be infeasible from a cost standpoint. FDR-1's successes were mixed. FHI managed to increase sales but profits were hurt by poor sales at home in Japan and meager sales of higher-end Subaru models in the US which were likely slowed by high fuel prices.

In 2007 FHI established its Overseas Sales and Marketing Divisions I & II. The first overseas division is dedicated to centralizing control of manufacturing and sales activities in the US. The move aimed to bring refinement and sophistication to the Subaru brand in the US while capitalizing on its reputation of offering affordable compelling AWD vehicles.

EXECUTIVES

Deputy President, Jun Kondo
EVP, Naoto Muto
President and CEO, Yasuyuki Yoshinaga, age 39
EVP, Akira Mabuchi
EVP, Takeshi Tachimori
EVP, Hisashi Nagano
VP, Mitsuru Takahashi
EVP, Masahiro Kasai
EVP, Shuzo Haimoto
Auditors: KPMG AZSA LLC

LOCATIONS

HQ: Fuji Heavy Industries, Ltd.
1-20-8 Ebisu, Shibuya-ku, Tokyo 150-8554
Phone: (81) 3 6447 8825 **Fax:** (81) 3 6447 8184
Web: www.fhi.co.jp

2014 Sales by Unit

	% of total
US	441,799
Japan	181,601
China	44,807
Europe	31,756
Australia	39,515
Canada	36,013
Russia	15,314
Other	34,293
Total	**825,098**

PRODUCTS/OPERATIONS

2014 Sales

	% of total
Automobiles	94
Aerospace	5
Industrial products	1
Other	-
Total	**100**

2014 Sales by Unit

	% of total
Legacy	201,673
Forester	267,745
Impreza	271,899
Minicars (discontinued)	55,454
OEM	2,113
Tribeca	6,414
Subaru BRZ	19,202
Other	598
Total	**825,098**

Selected Products and Divisions

Aerospace
- AH-64D combat helicopter
- Center-wing section (Boeing B-777)
- Design and training simulators
- Fixed-wing aircraft
- T-1 Trainer
- Unmanned aircraft

Automobiles
- Dex
- Dias Wagon
- Exiga
- Forester
- Impreza (wagon sedan)
- Legacy (touring B4 Outback)
- Outback (sport wagon sedan)
- Sambar (van truck wagon)
- Stella (R1 R2 Pleo)
- Tribeca

Eco Technologies
- Clean Robot floor-cleaning system
- Intermediate refuse collection systems
- Maintenance and sanitation vehicles
- Refuse management systems
- Special purpose vehicles
- Sweepers and scrubbers
- Wind-power systems

Industrial Products
- Agricultural machinery
- Construction machinery
- Forestry machinery
- General-purpose engines (Robin)
- Other machine tools and their components

Selected Subsidiaries:

Fuji Heavy Industries U.S.A. Inc.
Fuji Machinery Co. Ltd. (Japan)
Subaru Canada Inc.
Subaru of China Ltd.
Subaru Europe N.V./S.A. (Belgium)
Subaru of America Inc. (US)
Subaru of Indiana Automotive Inc.

COMPETITORS

Daimler
FCA US
Ford Motor
General Motors
Honda
Kawasaki Heavy Industries
MPM Technologies
Mazda
Mitsubishi Heavy Industries
Mitsubishi Motors
Nissan
Sumitomo Heavy Industries
Suzuki Motor
Toyota
Volvo Trucks

HISTORICAL FINANCIALS

Company Type: Public

Income Statement

FYE: March 31

	REVENUE ($ mil.)	NET INCOME ($ mil.)	NET PROFIT MARGIN	EMPLOYEES
03/15	23,986	2,182	9.1%	29,774
03/14	23,330	2,001	8.6%	28,545
03/13	20,330	1,270	6.3%	27,509
03/12	18,494	468	2.5%	27,123
03/11	19,087	607	3.2%	27,296
Annual Growth	5.9%	37.7%	—	2.2%

2015 Year-End Financials

Debt ratio: 0.0%
Return on equity: 29.2%
Cash ($ mil.): 1,907
Current ratio: 1.69
Long-term debt ($ mil.): 1,045
No. of shares (mil.): 780
Dividends
Yield: 1.7%
Payout: —
Market value ($ mil.): 52,036

	STOCK PRICE ($) FY Close	P/E High/Low	PER SHARE ($) Earnings	Dividends	Book Value
03/15	66.68	— —	2.80	1.16	11.01
03/14	54.40	— —	2.57	0.59	9.56
03/13	31.66	— —	1.63	0.00	8.13
03/12	16.18	— —	0.60	0.00	7.05
03/11	64.74	— —	0.78	0.54	6.41
Annual Growth	0.7%	— —	37.6%	21.3%	14.5%

FUJIFILM Holdings Corp

FUJIFILM still has film in its name but FUJIDOCS or FUJI INFO might be more apt. The company's imaging unit is its smallest by far making photographic films and papers digital cameras photofinishing equipment and chemicals. FUJIFILM's main businesses about 85% of revenue together are document operations and information-related products and services. Its document business includes joint venture Fuji Xerox offering copy machines printers and production services. The information unit provides medical imaging large-scale printing recording media optical and flat panel display devices and components. Customers overseas account for about 60% sales.

Operations

The company's document solutions business generates 47% of revenue with information solutions accounting for 38%. The imaging unit provides 15% of revenue.

Document solutions includes the company's production services and global services office products and office printers.

Product groups in the information unit are medical and life sciences systems products and services for graphic arts applications flat panel displays industrial products and electronic materials and recording media and optical devices.

Imaging is a much smaller slice of FUJIFILM's pie now about 15% of sales though the company is still a major global force there. Photo imaging sells film paper chemicals photo finishing and lab services and electronic imaging consists of digital cameras.

Financial Performance

Revenue rose 2% in 2015 (ended March) from 2014. Sales increased for photo imaging medical systems electronic materials and the document business. That was almost balanced by decreases in sales in the optical devices electronic imaging and flat panel display materials.

Net income jumped 46% higher with help from reduced research and developed costs in 2015. Cash from continuing operations dropped from 2014 to 2015.

Strategy

FUJIFILM is making investments in three core markets: healthcare highly functional materials and document business. Particularly in health care the company is looking to build its pharmaceuticals business and regenerative medicine businesses and maintain stable profits from medical systems.

Mergers and Acquisitions

FUJIFILM acquired Cellular Dynamics International a developer and manufacturer of fully functioning human cells in industrial quantities to precise specifications in 2015. The purchase provide FUJIFILM's with more advanced capabilities in its bid to build its life sciences business. It continues a series of health and life science related acquisitions FUJIFILM has made in recent years.

HISTORY

Mokichi Morita president of Japan's leading celluloid maker (Dainippon Celluloid Company founded 1919) decided to start making motion picture film in the early 1930s. Movies were becoming popular in Japan but there was no domestic film supplier. Working with a grant from the government Dainippon Celluloid established Fuji Photo Film Co. an independent company in 1934 in Minami Ashigara Village near Mount Fuji.

At first the company had trouble gaining acceptance in Japan as a quality film producer. However German emulsion specialist Dr. Emill Mauerhoff helped Fuji overcome its product deficiencies producing black-and-white photographic film (1936) and the first Japanese-made color film (1948). In the meantime Fuji added 35mm photographic film 16mm motion picture film and X-ray film to its product line. By the early 1940s the company was operating four factories and a research laboratory in Japan. Its first overseas office opened in Brazil in 1955 was followed by offices in the US (1958) and Europe (1964).

Fuji continued to expand its product line adding magnetic tape in 1960. Two years later it formed Fuji Xerox a Japanese joint venture with Xerox to sell copiers in Japan and the Pacific Rim. It operated as a private-label film supplier in the US and did not market its products under its own brand name until 1972.

International marketing VP Minoru Ohnishi became Fuji's youngest president in 1980 at age 55. To decrease dependence on Japanese film sales he built sales in the US (agreeing to sponsor the 1984 Los Angeles Olympics after Eastman Kodak refused to was key) and pumped money into the production of videotapes floppy disks and medical diagnostic equipment. Fuji introduced Fujicolor Quicksnap the world's first 35mm disposable camera in 1986. It began establishing manufacturing operations in the US two years later.

The company created the FUJIFILM Microdevices subsidiary to produce image-processing semiconductors in 1990. In 1992 Fuji scientists completed a crude artificial "eye" (a possible forerunner of more efficient eyes for robots). The following year it launched the Pictrostat instant print system which produces color prints in one minute from photos slides and objects.

Fuji was forced to temporarily raise US prices in 1994 after Kodak accused it of illegally dumping its photographic paper exported to the US. But Fuji skirted the problem in 1995 by making the paper at its US plant. That year Kodak asked for economic sanctions against Fuji and the Japanese government saying that the government encouraged Fuji to use exclusive contracts to control film distribution thus keeping Kodak from selling film in many stores. (The case was rejected by the World Trade Organization in 1997.)

The firm unveiled the Advanced Photo System (co-developed with Kodak and three other companies) in 1996 combining conventional photography with digital-image processing and printing technology. Also that year Fuji bought six off-site wholesale photofinishing plants from Wal-Mart (the largest US provider of photofinishing services) and won contracts to provide supplies to all of Wal-Mart's in-store one-hour photo labs.

In 1997 it chopped film prices in the US and began making film at its US plant. In 1999 Fuji introduced a high-quality image sensor for digital cameras (Super CCD) and Instax an instant picture camera. Fuji and Sony launched HiFD a floppy disk with 140 times the storage capacity of traditional disks in early 2000. Fuji later announced plans to develop more efficient low-cost ink jet printers through an alliance with Xerox and Sharp Corp.

In March 2001 Fuji acquired half of Xerox's 50% stake in the companies' Fuji Xerox joint venture. In 2002 the company acquired Japanese film processing company Jusphoto Co. and in 2003 purchased additional shares of Process Shizai Co. renaming it Fujifilm Graphic Systems Co. Ltd.

It bought Sericol from Saratoga Partners in 2005 for $230 million and Avecia Inkjet in 2006 for $260 million. Also that year the company adopted a new holding company structure and changed its name to FUJIFILM Holdings. Also that year the firm acquired US-based Problem Solving Concepts a manufacturer of medical imaging information systems for cardiology; TSR Holding S.A. a medical equipment service and maintenance supplier; and the remaining shares of Fuji Medical Systemes France S.A. a medical imaging products distributor.

In January 2008 FUJIFILM Holdings acquired Germany's IP Labs GmbH a developer of online photo service systems. The consolidation of Toyama Chemical into a consolidated subsidiary in March marked the holding company's entry into the pharmceutical business. In November it purchased Empiric Systems LLC a US-based maker of radiology information systems.

EXECUTIVES

Chairman and CEO, Shigetaka Komori
President and COO, Shigehiro Nakajima
President FUJIFILM Holdings America Corporation and President and CEO FUJIFILM North America Corporation, Ryutaro (Ray) Hosoda
President and CEO FUJIFILM Sonosite, Naohiro Fujitani
Auditors: Ernst & Young ShinNihon LLC

LOCATIONS

HQ: FUJIFILM Holdings Corp
9-7-3 Akasaka, Minato-ku, Tokyo 107-0052
Phone: (81) 3 6271 1111
Web: www.fujifilmholdings.com

2015 Sales

	% of total
Domestic	41
Overseas	59
Total	**100**

PRODUCTS/OPERATIONS

2015 Sales

	% of total
Document	47
Information	38
Imaging	15
Total	**100**

2015 Sales

	% of total
Sales	86
Rentals	14
Total	**100**

Selected Products

Document
- Business process outsourcing
- Digital color printers
- Digital multifunction printer/copiers
- Digital photo printers
- On-demand publishing systems

Imaging
- Color photo printing paper and chemicals
- Digital cameras and accessories
- Electronic imaging systems
- Film processing services
- Motion picture films
- Photo lab equipment
- Photographic films

Information
- Data storage media
- LCD materials
- Medical imaging systems and films
- Nutraceuticals
- Pharmaceuticals
- Plate-making supplies films and chemicals
- Printer inks
- X-ray films

COMPETITORS

Agfa
Bayer AG
Brother Industries
Canon
Datapulse Technology
Eastman Kodak
Electronics for Imaging
GlaxoSmithKline
HP
Hitachi
IBM
Imation
Konica Minolta
Kyocera
Kyocera Document Solutions
Lexmark
Mitsubishi Paper Mills
NEC
Nikon
Novartis
Olympus
Panasonic Corp
Pfizer
Philips Electronics
Ricoh Company
Samsung Electronics
Sharp Corp.
Sony
Toshiba
Xerox

HISTORICAL FINANCIALS

Company Type: Public

Income Statement FYE: March 31

	REVENUE ($ mil.)	NET INCOME ($ mil.)	NET PROFIT MARGIN	EMPLOYEES
03/15	20,775	988	4.8%	88,662
03/14	23,638	784	3.3%	87,726
03/13	23,537	576	2.5%	89,324
03/12	26,762	533	2.0%	90,373
03/11	26,774	771	2.9%	86,700
Annual Growth	(6.1%)	6.4%	—	0.6%

2015 Year-End Financials

Debt ratio: 0.0%
Return on equity: 5.5%
Cash ($ mil.): 6,217
Current ratio: 3.12
Long-term debt ($ mil.): 2,609
No. of shares (mil.): 482
Dividends
Yield: 1.4%
Payout: 22.2%
Market value ($ mil.): 17,172

	STOCK PRICE ($) FY Close	P/E High	P/E Low	PER SHARE ($) Earnings	Dividends	Book Value
03/15	35.61	0	0	2.04	0.51	38.59
03/14	26.86	0	0	1.62	0.40	40.62
03/13	19.64	0	0	1.15	0.40	41.22
03/12	23.51	0	0	1.06	0.39	43.57
03/11	31.01	0	0	1.46	0.32	43.19
Annual Growth	3.5%	—	—	8.8%	12.2%	(2.8%)

Fujitsu Ltd.

Fujitsu Limited's supply of high-tech offerings seems almost limitless. The company provides customers worldwide with products ranging from computers and electronic components to air conditioners and bar code scanners. Fujitsu's computer products include PCs servers storage systems and peripherals. One of the top IT services firms in the world it provides consulting infrastructure management and systems integration. Other lines include a wide range of software telecommunications transmission equipment consumer electronics and semiconductors. Fujitsu also owns Nifty one of Japan's leading ISPs. The company gets the vast majority of its sales in Japan.

Already struggling amid the global economic slump –with a year-over-year decline in net sales of 3% in 2010 –Fujitsu booked an extraordinary loss of 11.6 billion ($150.8 million) and operating income fell 13 billion ($169 million) primarily as a result of the Great East Japan Earthquake in March 2011. Year-over-year net sales were again down 3% in 2011 but rose 1.4% to $55.4 billion the following year.

The company's Technology Solutions unit generates the largest portion of its revenue. In addition to consulting and outsourcing this division provides systems integration application development hardware installation and other services. Fujitsu Services is among the company's key IT services subsidiaries. Fujitsu's software offerings include customer relationship management (CRM) supply chain management (SCM) and enterprise resource planning (ERP) applications. Revenue for technology solutions declined about 4% in 2011.

Fujitsu's ubiquitous solutions division includes PCs tablets mobile phones and audio and navigation equipment. Ubiquitous solutions (22% of sales) rose 0.5% in 2011. The device solutions segment which includes LSI devices and electronic components and represents 12% of revenue rose 7% in 2011.

In 2012 Fujitsu spun off its access network business as a new company called Access Network Technology Ltd. The venture is 52.8% owned by Fujitsu with the remainder held by NTT DoCoMo (19.9%) NEC (17.8%) and Fujitsu Semiconductor (9.5%). The joint venture will develop chips that control wireless communications and signals but will outsource production of those chips. The move is intended to take take on industry leader QUALCOMM in the fast-growing market for mobile communications chips used smartphones and tablets.

The Access Network Technology venture was the result of a failed attempt by the company to establish a partnership with NTT Docomo Fujitsu Semiconductor NEC Panasonic Mobile Communications and Samsung Electronics earlier in 2012. Intended to give the companies a way to develop and market their own cellphone chips the venture was abandoned after the partners were unable to come to an agreement over details.

In 2010 the company combined its cell phone business with that of key rival Toshiba in hopes that the new business (anticipated to be the largest cell phone maker in Japan) would be better able to compete with global industry leaders. Fujitsu carried an 80% stake in the new company Fujitsu Toshiba Mobile Communications Limited until it bought Toshiba's remaining 20% in 2012 making the company a subsidiary Fujitsu Mobile Communications Limited.

Fujitsu generates most of its revenues in Japan but its growth strategy includes strengthening its international operations with a goal of increasing the percentage of sales outside Japan to 40%. To increase its international operations the company acquired KAZ Group the IT arm of Australian telecom Telstra in 2009. It also bought out Siemens' stake in their European computer joint venture Fujitsu Siemens for E450 million ($570 million) in 2009. The unit is now called Fujitsu Technology Solutions.

Fujitsu's efforts to strengthen its North American operations have included consolidating a number of its subsidiaries in the region. In 2009 the company combined three of its US-based subsidiaries –Fujitsu Consulting Fujitsu Computer Systems and Fujitsu Transaction Solutions –to form Fujitsu America.

HISTORY

Furukawa Electric and Siemens created Fuji Electric in 1923 to produce electrical equipment. Fuji Electric spun off Fujitsu its communications division in 1935. Originally a maker of telephone equipment Fujitsu produced anti-aircraft weapons during WWII. After the war it became one of four major suppliers to state-owned monopoly Nippon Telegraph and Telephone (NTT) and continued to benefit from Japan's rapid economic recovery in the 1950s and 1960s.

With encouragement from Japan's Ministry of International Trade and Industry (MITI) Fujitsu developed the country's first commercial computer in 1954. MITI erected trade barriers to protect Japan's computer industry and in the early 1960s sponsored the production of mainframe computers directing Fujitsu to develop the central processing unit. The company expanded into semiconductor production and factory automation in the late 1960s. Its factory automation business was spun off as Fujitsu Fanuc in 1972.

Fujitsu gained badly needed technology when it bought 30% of IBM-plug-compatible manufacturer Amdahl in 1972. By 1979 Fujitsu had passed IBM to become Japan's #1 computer manufacturer. In Europe Fujitsu entered into computer marketing ventures with Siemens (1978) and UK mainframe maker ICL (1981). In the US it teamed with TRW to sell point-of-sale systems (1980) assuming full control of the operation in 1983. Fujitsu released its first supercomputer in 1982.

Fujitsu bought 80% of ICL (from the UK's Standard Telephones & Cables) in 1990 for $1.3 billion. In 1993 it formed a joint venture with Advanced Micro Devices to make flash memory products.

The company doubled its share of Japan's PC market in 1995 to more than 18% and the next year expanded its PC business globally. In 1997 Fujitsu paid about $878 million for the 58% of Amdahl it didn't already own. The next year it bought the 10% of ICL it didn't own. Fujitsu's 1998 earnings suffered from a slump in the semiconductor market Amdahl-related expenses and a weak Asian economy.

Also in 1998 Naoyuki Akikusa son of a former NTT president became head of Fujitsu. He began trimming some operations while ramping up the company's Internet activities. Fujitsu in 1999 became full owner of online services provider Nifty Serve making it Japan's largest Internet service provider. It merged Nifty with the operations of another ISP called InfoWeb. Also that year Siemens and Fujitsu combined their European computer operations in a 50-50 joint venture (Fujitsu Siemens Computers) as one part of a larger global alliance. A restructuring of Fujitsu's semiconductor operations caused losses for 1999.

Akikusa's reorganization continued in 2000. Fujitsu overhauled its server business (subsidiary Amdahl ceased production of IBM-compatible mainframes) and accelerated production of flash memory. Responding to a global slump in its markets in 2001 Fujitsu announced that it would cut more than 16000 jobs –about 10% of its workforce –to control costs. Soon after it announced the cutting of an additional 4500 jobs.

In 2002 Fujitsu moved to outsource its semiconductor test and assembly operations when it agreed to sell its Kyushu Fujitsu Electronics subsidiary to Amkor Technology; the deal was terminated however when Amkor and Fujitsu were unable to agree to terms.

In 2003 the company formed a joint venture with AMD called Fujitsu AMD Semiconductor Ltd. or FASL to manufacture flash memory. (Renamed Spansion in 2004 the company went public in 2005 filed for Chapter 11 in 2009 and emerged from bankruptcy reorganization in 2010.)

In 2005 Fujitsu sold Hitachi its stake in Fujitsu Hitachi Plasma Display a company it formed with Hitachi to develop plasma display panels for televisions. Fujitsu sold its LCD business Fujitsu Display Technologies to Sharp in 2005.

Fujitsu spun off its advanced semiconductor business as a separate subsidiary Fujitsu Microelectronics (now Fujitsu Semiconductor) in 2008. The following year it sold its hard-disk drive business to Toshiba but retained about a 20% stake in the business which was renamed Toshiba Storage Device. Late in 2010 Toshiba bought Fujitsu's remaining shares.

Auditors: Ernst & Young ShinNihon LLC

LOCATIONS

HQ: Fujitsu Ltd.
Shiodome City Center, 1-5-2 Higashi-Shimbashi, Minato-ku, Tokyo 105-7123
Phone: (81) 3 6252 2220
Web: www.fujitsu.com

HISTORICAL FINANCIALS

Company Type: Public

Income Statement FYE: March 31

	REVENUE ($ mil.)	NET INCOME ($ mil.)	NET PROFIT MARGIN	EMPLOYEES
03/15	39,616	1,167	2.9%	176,150
03/14	46,139	1,096	2.4%	179,859
03/13	46,568	(774)	—	168,733
03/12	54,462	520	1.0%	173,155
03/11	54,686	665	1.2%	172,336
Annual Growth	(7.7%)	15.1%	—	0.5%

2015 Year-End Financials

Debt ratio: 0.1%
Return on equity: 20.6%
Cash ($ mil.): 3,017
Current ratio: 1.24
Long-term debt ($ mil.): 3,384
No. of shares (mil.): 2,068
Dividends
Yield: 1.0%
Payout: 59.1%
Market value ($ mil.): 70,482

	STOCK PRICE ($) FY Close	P/E High/Low		PER SHARE ($) Earnings	Dividends	Book Value
03/15	34.07	1	0	0.56	0.36	3.18
03/14	30.32	1	0	0.53	0.00	2.65
03/13	21.05	—	—	(0.37)	0.00	4.67
03/12	26.44	—	—	0.25	0.00	5.69
03/11	28.00	—	—	0.31	0.57	5.57
Annual Growth	5.0%	—	—	16.0%	(10.7%)	(13.0%)

Fukoku Mutual Life Insurance Co (Japan)

Fukoku Mutual Life Insurance Company is one of Japan's major life insurers. As part of its business it sells products through a network of nearly 10000 agents as well as through more than 60 branch locations and about 470 field offices. It operates primarily through half a dozen subsidiaries that extends its reach to London New York and Singapore. Fukoku Mutal sells both face-to-face in the field and through call centers offering life and non-life insurance products (such as medical and nursing care insurance) as well as a variety of financial products and services. Fukoku Mutal's typical clients include private individuals and business owners. Fukoku Mutual was founded in 1923.OperationsIn addition to selling life insurance Fukoku Mutual provides investment management services information systems development and maintenance services staffing services and research on its industry in Asia (through subsidiary Fukoku Life Research Singapore). Sales and MarketingThe company sells its policies through its own sales representatives and through financial institutions.Financial PerformanceIn fiscal 2015 (ended March) net revenue grew 12% to ¥1 trillion (versus ¥936 billion in fiscal 2014). Net income also increased growing 34% to ¥70 billion. That gain was primarily due to a decrease in losses on disposal of fixed assets and higher surplus before income taxes.Cash flow from operations increased 52% to ¥260 billion that year.

Stategy

Fukoku Mutual's traditional strategies –investing conservatively and targeting government agencies as customers –have earned it a reputation as one of the more stable insurers in an industry that has experienced heavy losses primarily stemming from the weak economy and slumping stock markets. The firm is looking to continue diversifying its practices in such areas as borrower and loan periods.

EXECUTIVES

Deputy President and Executive Officer, Katsumasa Furuya
President and CEO, Yoshiteru Yoneyama
Director and Managing Executive Officer, Hitoshi Sakai
Director and Managing Executive Officer, Toshihiro Hayashi
Board Member, Kenji Hirai
Director and Managing Executive Officer, Tadashi Akikawa
Chairman, Tomofumi Akiyama
Auditors: Kisaragi Audit Corp.

LOCATIONS

HQ: Fukoku Mutual Life Insurance Co (Japan)
2-2-2 Uchisaiwaisho, Chiyoda-ku, Tokyo, injike- 100-0011
Phone: (81) 3 3508 1101 **Fax:** (81) 3 3591 6446
Web: www.fukoku-life.co.jp

PRODUCTS/OPERATIONS

Selected Subsidiaries and Affiliates
Fukoku Capital Management Inc.
Fukoku Information Systems Co. Ltd.
Fukoku Lif
Fukoku Lif
Fukoku Shinyo Hosho Company Limited
Fukokushinrai Life Insurance Company

COMPETITORS

Asahi Mutual Life
Dai-ichi Life
Daido Life
Gibraltar Life Insurance
Meiji Yasuda Life
Mitsui Life
Nippon Life Insurance
Sony Financial
Sumitomo Life
T&D Holdings
Taiyo Life

HISTORICAL FINANCIALS

Company Type: Public

Income Statement FYE: March 31

	ASSETS ($ mil.)	NET INCOME ($ mil.)	INCOME AS % OF ASSETS	EMPLOYEES
03/15	69,400	0	—	12,677
03/14	75,738	0	—	12,999
03/13	80,122	0	—	13,488
03/12	85,745	0	—	13,502
03/11	80,553	0	—	13,702
Annual Growth	(3.7%)	—	—	(1.9%)

2015 Year-End Financials

Return on assets: —
Return on equity: —
Long-term debt ($ mil.): —
No. of shares (mil.): —
Sales ($ mil): 8,728
Dividends
Yield: —
Payout: —
Market value ($ mil.): —

Galp Energia, SGPS, SA

Portugal's primary oil and gas group Galp Energia (formerly Petróleos de Portugal) produces transports refines distributes and sells crude oil natural gas and oil products. It operates mainly in Portugal and Spain but also has operations in a half-dozen former Portuguese colonies. Although Galp Energia is primarily a refining and marketing company with more than 1450 gas stations it is seeking to expand its exploration and production efforts. The company has significant exploration and production activities in Angola Brazil and Portugal and holds gas and power infrastructure assets in Portugal. Italian energy giant Eni and Portuguese investment firm Amorim Energia each own 33% of the company.

EXECUTIVES

CCO Corporate Services and Biofuel Business Unit, Carlos Pina
CFO, Filipe Cris stomo Silva
COO, Carlos Nuno Gomes da Silva
COO, Thore E. Kristiansen
CCO and Head Procurement and Asset Management Division, Jos ©Carlos da Silva Costa
Vice Chairman and CEO, Manuel Ferreira De Oliveira
Chairman Supervisory Board, Daniel Bessa Fernandes Coelho
Chairman Executive Board, Am ©co Ferreira de Amorim
Vice Chairman, Lu s Palha da Silva
Auditors: PricewaterhouseCoopers & Associados

LOCATIONS

HQ: Galp Energia, SGPS, SA
Rua Tomas de Fonseca, Torre C, Lisbon 1600-209
Phone: (351) 21 240 866 **Fax:** (351) 21 242 965
Web: www.galpenergia.com

PRODUCTS/OPERATIONS

2013 Sales

	% of total
Refining & marketing	83
Gas & power	17
Total	**100**

Selected Subsidiaries
Galp Power (electricity generation and sales)
Galpgeste (management and operation of service stations)
GDP Gás de Portugal
Petróleos de Portugal (Petrogal; exploration and production refining transport distribution and sales of oil products)
Sacor Maritima (marine transport)
Sopor (51% distribution and sale of oil products)
Transgás Armazenagem (natural gas underground storage)

COMPETITORS

BP
Endesa S.A.
Exxon Mobil
Repsol
Royal Dutch Shell
TOTAL

HISTORICAL FINANCIALS

Company Type: Public

Income Statement FYE: December 31

	REVENUE ($ mil.)	NET INCOME ($ mil.)	NET PROFIT MARGIN	EMPLOYEES
12/14	22,032	(210)	—	6,855
12/13	27,210	259	1.0%	6,968
12/12	24,573	452	1.8%	7,241
12/11	21,972	559	2.5%	7,381
12/10	19,040	590	3.1%	7,311
Annual Growth	3.7%	—	—	(1.6%)

2014 Year-End Financials

Debt ratio: 33.7%
Return on equity: (-3.4%)
Cash ($ mil.): 1,390
Current ratio: 2.29
Long-term debt ($ mil.): 4,085
No. of shares (mil.): 829
Dividends
Yield: 2.3%
Payout: —
Market value ($ mil.): 4,163

	STOCK PRICE ($) FY Close	P/E High/Low		PER SHARE ($) Earnings	Dividends	Book Value
12/14	5.02	—	—	(0.26)	0.12	7.34
12/13	8.14	68	57	0.32	0.17	8.57
12/12	7.82	39	23	0.54	0.21	8.58
12/11	8.53	43	25	0.67	0.11	4.50
12/10	9.50	36	23	0.71	0.56	4.32
Annual Growth	(14.7%)	—	—	—	(32.3%)	14.1%

Gas Natural SDG, S.A.

A latter-day Spanish "conquistador" Gas Natural is venturing into markets in both the Old World and the New. Gas Natural operates a group of energy companies that supply natural gas and electricity serving 20 million customers primarily in Spain but also in France Italy and Latin America. The largest natural gas supplier in Spain Gas Natural is also a leading liquefied natural gas (LNG) supplier. The company has a generating capacity of 15400 MW (including 4400 MW in Latin America). In 2009 Gas Natural greatly expanded its power business acquiring Spanish utility Uni n Fenosa in a $26 billion deal and in 2010 adopted Gas Natural Fenosa as its new corporate brand name.
Auditors: PricewaterhouseCoopers Auditores, S.L.

LOCATIONS

HQ: Gas Natural SDG, S.A.
Placa del Gas, 1, Barcelona 08003
Phone: (34) 93 219 9199 **Fax:** (34) 93 402 5870
Web: www.gasnatural.com

HISTORICAL FINANCIALS

Company Type: Public

Income Statement FYE: December 31

	REVENUE ($ mil.)	NET INCOME ($ mil.)	NET PROFIT MARGIN	EMPLOYEES
12/14	30,074	1,777	5.9%	21,961
12/13	34,375	1,989	5.8%	14,982
12/12	32,824	1,899	5.8%	15,959
12/11	27,260	1,713	6.3%	16,202
12/10	26,272	1,607	6.1%	17,347
Annual Growth	3.4%	2.5%	—	6.1%

2014 Year-End Financials

Debt ratio: 48.9%
Return on equity: 10.6%
Cash ($ mil.): 4,341
Current ratio: 1.28
Long-term debt ($ mil.): 21,465
No. of shares (mil.): 1,000
Dividends
Yield: 0.0%
Payout: 8.5%
Market value ($ mil.): 5,114

	STOCK PRICE ($) FY Close	P/E High/Low		PER SHARE ($) Earnings	Dividends	Book Value
12/14	5.11	4	3	1.77	0.15	17.18
12/13	5.05	4	3	1.98	0.17	18.50
12/12	3.50	2	1	1.91	0.15	17.47
12/11	3.51	3	2	1.80	0.06	16.68
12/10	3.00	3	2	1.74	0.15	16.53
Annual Growth	14.2%	—	—	0.5%	0.7%	1.0%

Gazprom Neft PJSC

One of Russia's largest integrated oil companies and its third largest refiner Gazprom Neft explores for produces refines and markets petroleum products. Its retail operations include about 1750 gas stations. The company with proved reserves of 9.7 billion barrels of oil equivalent controls refineries in Moscow Mozyr Noyabrsk and Omsk that produce more than 45.7 million tonnes of petroleum products per year. It refines about 80% of the oil it produces a high ratio for Russia. Gazprom Neft also shares ownership of major natural gas project SeverEnergia with NOVATEK the country's largest independent gas producer. State-owned gas giant Gazprom controls Gazprom Neft.

HISTORY

In the aftermath of the fall of the Soviet Union in the early 1990s Sibneft was formed in 1995 as part of Russia's privatization of state industries. Sibneft included western Siberian oil producer Noyabrskneftegas and the Omsk oil refinery. The Russian government was to retain a 51% stake for three years while limiting foreign ownership to 15%. Finance Oil Company (FNK) controlled by business oligarch Boris Berezovsky the man reportedly behind Sibneft's formation gained a controlling stake in Sibneft. The new integrated oil company's prize asset was the Omsk refinery. Built in the mid-1980s it was Russia's largest and most modern refinery.

In 1997 Sibneft became the first Russian company to issue a Eurobond. Despite an economic crisis in 1998 Sibneft continued to service all of its financial obligations. That year Sibneft made plans to merge with rival oil company Yukos (controlled by oligarch Mikhail Khodorkovsky) but falling oil prices led the two firms to scuttle the proposed union.

Also in 1998 Sibneft published a corporate governance charter compiled by leading European experts to bring the company in line with international practices. This move was followed up with the appointment of three non-executives to the company's board of nine directors. A year later Sibneft became the first major Russian oil company to publish its financial accounts (audited by Arthur Andersen) according to US generally accepted accounting principles. In 1999 Sibneft also formed alliances with two Western oil services firms US-based Schlumberger and Canadian-based BJ Services to enhance its extraction of oil and gas.

During the 1999 Russian Duma elections reclusive oligarch Roman Abramovich (who had acquired a 12% stake in Sibneft in 1996) claimed to control Sibneft whereas Berezovsky (also elected to the Duma) was said to have only a background role in Sibneft.

The company announced plans in 2000 to invest $52 million to modernize the Omsk refinery upgrading its capacity to produce lead-free gasoline. That year Sibneft also agreed to acquire majority stakes in two refined products retailers in the Urals region which together controlled 132 service stations and 20 storage sites.

Sibneft lost out in its bid to gain control of Onako another former state-owned oil company that was privatized in 2000. Sibneft had teamed up with two other oil companies Yukos and Stroitransgaz (a unit of Russian gas giant Gazprom) to bid for Onako but lost out to rival Tyumen Oil Co. (TNK). However Sibneft which had gained control of a 40% stake in Onako's main oil producing subsidiary Orenburgneft reportedly made an arrangement with TNK to swap its Orenburgneft shares for a minority stake in Onako. Also in 2000 Sibneft and other Russian oil companies were investigated by Russian authorities after allegations of tax evasion.

In 2001 the company announced plans to search for oil in the Chukotka autonomous district. (Abramovich is the governor of Chukotka). This unexplored area has a similar geological structure to Alaska's oil-rich North Slope. Later that year Sibneft acquired a 36% stake in a Moscow refinery from oil giant LUKOIL allowing the company to supply markets in European Russia.

In 2002 Sibneft opened its first gas station in Moscow.

Gazprom Neft (as Sibneft) was once controlled by UK-residing Chelsea soccer club-owning Russian oligarch Roman Abramovich through investment company Millhouse Capital. In 2005 Gazprom bought its majority stake in Sibneft from Millhouse Capital for $11 billion. The company changed its name to Gazprom Neft the next year and ENI acquired 20% of Gazprom Neft in 2007 following the bankruptcy of Yukos. Gazprom had the option to buy ENI's stake within two years and exercised that right in 2009 paying just more than $4 billion to ENI. Gazprom now directly owns or indirectly controls through subsidiaries about 95% of Gazprom Neft.

EXECUTIVES

Chairman and CEO, Alexander V. Dyukov, age 48
Deputy chairman and Deputy CEO for Logistics Processing and Sales, Anatoly Cherner, age 62
Deputy CEO Foreign Asset Management, Kirill Kravchenko, age 39
Deputy Chairman and First Deputy CEO, Vadim Yakovlev, age 45
Deputy Chairman and Deputy CEO Administration, Vitaliy Baranov
Deputy CEO International Business Development, Vladislav Baryshnikov
Deputy CEO Economics and Finance, Alexei Yankevich
Chairman, Alexei B. Miller, age 54
Auditors: ZAO PricewaterhouseCoopers Audit

LOCATIONS

HQ: Gazprom Neft PJSC
G3-5 Pochtamtskaya St., St. Petersburg 190000
Phone: (7) 812 363 31 52 **Fax:** (7) 812 363 31 51
Web: www.gazprom-neft.ru

PRODUCTS/OPERATIONS

2013 Sales

	% of total
Petroleum Products	81
Crude Oil	14
Gas	2
Other	3
Total	**100**

COMPETITORS

BP
Bashneft JOSC
Devon Energy
Exxon Mobil
JX Nippon Oil & Energy
LUKOIL
Mitsui
Occidental Petroleum
Rosneft
Royal Dutch Shell
Surgutneftegas
TOTAL
Tatneft
Transneft

HISTORICAL FINANCIALS

Company Type: Public

Income Statement FYE: December 31

	REVENUE ($ mil.)	NET INCOME ($ mil.)	NET PROFIT MARGIN	EMPLOYEES
12/14	23,925	2,074	8.7%	0
12/13	38,569	5,413	14.0%	0
12/12	40,415	5,791	14.3%	0
12/11	44,172	5,352	12.1%	0
12/10	32,772	3,148	9.6%	0
Annual Growth	(7.6%)	(9.9%)	—	—

2014 Year-End Financials

Debt ratio: 0.4%
Return on equity: 12.1%
Cash ($ mil.): 903
Current ratio: 1.88
Long-term debt ($ mil.): 8,533
No. of shares (mil.): —
Dividends
Yield: 10.7%
Payout: 38.2%
Market value ($ mil.): —

	STOCK PRICE ($) FY Close	P/E High/Low		PER SHARE ($) Earnings	Dividends	Book Value
12/14	11.77	1	0	0.44	1.27	3.84
12/13	22.60	1	0	1.15	1.70	6.14
12/12	23.76	1	1	1.23	0.95	5.81
12/11	23.33	24	15	1.13	0.16	4.98
12/10	20.95	44	24	0.67	0.47	3.96
Annual Growth	(13.4%)	—	—	(10.0%)	28.1%	(0.8%)

GlaxoSmithKline Plc

GlaxoSmithKline (GSK) gives anxiety asthma and other ailments the ax. One of the top five pharmaceutical firms in the world GSK's bestsellers include respiratory neurological cardiovascular and dermatology drugs as well as vaccines and antivirals. Its top product is asthma medication Advair (aka Seretide) which combines two of its other asthma products Flovent and Serevent. Other bestsellers include epilepsy treatment Lamictal cholesterol medicine Lovaza prostate enlargement drug Avodart and antibiotic Augmentin as well as Cervarix and Pediarix vaccines. GSK's consumer products include Tums dental care products Aquafresh and Sensodyne and smoking-cessation products NicoDerm and Nicorette.

Operations

GSK operates through two primary segments — Pharmaceuticals and Vaccines (which accounts for more than 80% of revenue) and Consumer Healthcare (which accounts for the remainder).

Within the Pharmaceuticals and Vaccines segment the pharmaceuticals business develops and makes medicines that treat a wide variety of acute and chronic diseases. Respiratory drugs is its largest sales category primarily due to blockbuster Advair which brings in more than £4 billion annually. Other respiratory products include Ventolin Relvar and Anoro Ellipta. GSK also has a strong presence in the HIV market (through majority-owned ViiV Healthcare) as well as the central nervous system cardiovascular urogenital dermatology (through its Stiefel division) virology infectious disease and metabolism treatment markets.

Meanwhile the vaccines business is a global leader with more than 30 pediatric adolescent adult and travel vaccines on the market. Its Infanrix childhood vaccine for diptheria and tetanus leads the pack followed by products for the prevention of hepatitis pneumonia rotavirus and influenza. More than 80% of the group's vaccines are distributed in the developing world.

Consumer Healthcare products fall into the oral health wellness nutrition and skin health categories with top sellers including Sensodyne Panadol and Horlicks. The segment also makes key brands Theraflu Polident and Abreva. GSK sells these products in more than 100 countries around the world. In 2015 GSK combined its consumer health care operations with those of Novartis to create a global leader in that market.

Sales and Marketing

The company markets its products directly to hospitals pharmacies doctors and other health care consumers; it also uses wholesale distributors in some markets and serves customers in more than 150 countries overall.

Geographic Reach

GSK has more than 80 manufacturing facilities in 36 countries. The group's major R&D centers are located in the UK the US Belgium and China.

The US is the company's largest market representing about a third of total earnings. Europe and emerging markets (including the Asia/Pacific and Latin America) each account for about a quarter of revenue and Japan accounts for nearly 10%.

Financial Performance

Note: Growth rates may differ after conversion to US dollars.

After remaining relatively stable GSK's revenue took a dip in 2014. That year revenue fell 13% to £23 billion when compared to 2013 revenue. (The company has restated its 2013 revenue to reflect £903 million in divestments; this comparison is to the original 2013 figure of £26.5 billion.) The decline was attributed to lower sales in all categories –pharmaceuticals vaccines and consumer healthcare. Pharmaceuticals sales fell an overall 5% due largely to declines in the US and despite growth in emerging markets and Japan as well as in the ViiV Healthcare unit. Vaccines sales dropped 1% as did consumer healthcare.

Profit after taxation fell 50% to £2.8 billion in 2014 primarily as a result of the decreased revenue. Net cash flow from operating activities dropped 28% to £5.2 billion due to the negative impact of foreign exchange rates.

Strategy

In 2014 GSK announced a major transaction with Novartis that reshaped its operations. It paid Novartis $7.1 billion for that company's vaccine business while collecting up to $16 billion for handing over its oncology line. The two companies are also combining their consumer products lines to create the world's top provider of over-the-counter (OTC) medicines. Altogether the three-part deal is expected to add £1.3 billion to GSK's bottom line and strengthen its core OTC and vaccine businesses.

As sales in GSK's largest market the US account for about a third of pharmaceutical sales maintaining a rich portfolio of US patent-protected products can make or break the company's future. For example cardiovascular drug Lovaza began facing generic competition in 2014 and fell 54% that year. Other established products that have experienced sales slumps due to patent losses include best-selling herpes drug Valtrex and anti-depressant Paroxetine (marketed as Seroxat and Paxil).

The development of new potential blockbusters is the best way to alleviate these losses. GSK has some 25 pharmaceutical candidates in trials for conditions such as HIV respiratory immuno-inflammation and cardiovascular disease as well as some 15 vaccine candidates for the prevention of diseases including shingles hepatitis C tuberculosis malaria and Ebola.

GSK is also working to pump potential new blockbusters into its pipeline by acquiring promising research firms and forming development agreements with other drug companies. The company is working with pharmaceutical firms Pfizer and Shionogi on HIV medications through ViiV Healthcare; many of the company's HIV and vaccine development programs aim to provide affordable disease preventions and treatments to developing countries. ViiV Healthcare sale rose 15% in 2014 largely due to the successful launches of antiretroviral drugs Tivicay and Triumeq.

A major trend among pharmaceutical companies is to focus on growing in emerging markets which represent an opportunity for big sales because of a relatively untapped consumer base. Towards that end GSK has established a presence in select Asian African Latin American and Middle Eastern nations.

CEO Andrew Witty is intent on keeping the company focused on small strategic acquisitions and expansion in fast-growing markets including vaccines biopharmaceuticals and consumer health products. He is also carrying forth ongoing cost-cutting measures which aim to reduce operational expenses through measures such as simplifying its administrative infrastructure narrowing its R&D programs and consolidating its drug development and manufacturing sites. To focus on its top selling drugs and R&D investments the company is also divesting assets where it sees fit.

HISTORY

Englishman Joseph Nathan started an import-export business in New Zealand in 1873. He obtained the rights to a process for drying milk and began making powdered milk in New Zealand selling it as baby food Glaxo.

Nathan's son Alec dispatched to London to oversee baby food sales in Britain increased Glaxo's name recognition by publishing the Glaxo Baby Book a guide to child care. After WWI the company began distribution in India and South America.

In the 1920s Glaxo launched vitamin D-fortified formulations. It entered the pharmaceutical business with its 1927 introduction of Ostelin a liquid vitamin D concentrate and continued to grow globally in the 1930s introducing Ostermilk (vitamin-fortified milk).

Glaxo began making penicillin and anesthetics during WWII; it went public in 1947. A steep drop in antibiotic prices in the mid-1950s led Glaxo to diversify; it bought veterinary medical instrument and drug distribution firms.

In the 1970s the British Monopolies Commission quashed both a hostile takeover attempt by Beecham and a proposed merger with retailer and drugmaker Boots. Glaxo launched US operations in 1978.

Glaxo shed nondrug operations in the 1980s to concentrate on pharmaceuticals. A 1981 marketing blitz launched antiulcer drug Zantac (to vie with SmithKline's Tagamet) in the US where Glaxo's sales had been small. The company boosted outreach by contracting to use Hoffmann-La Roche's sales staff. The Zantac sales assault gave Glaxo leadership in US antiulcer drug sales.

Under CEO Sir Richard Sykes Glaxo in 1995 made a surprise bid for UK rival Wellcome. Founded in 1880 by Americans Silas Burroughs and Henry Wellcome to sell McKesson-Robbins' products outside the US Burroughs Wellcome and Co. began making its own products two years later. By the 1990s the company which fostered Nobel Prize-winning researchers led the world in antiviral medicines. Its primary drug products were Zovirax (launched 1981) and Retrovir (1987).

Though an earlier bid by Glaxo had been rejected Sykes won the takeover with backing from Wellcome Trust Wellcome's largest shareholder.

In 1997 the company formed a new genetics division buying Spectra Biomedical and its gene variation technology. That year the company pulled diabetes drug Romozin (Rezulin in the US) from the UK market over concerns that it caused liver damage.

Glaxo in 1998 ended its joint venture with Warner-Lambert (begun 1993) selling its former partner the Canadian and US marketing rights to acid blocker Zantac 75.

In 1999 Glaxo trimmed its product line pulling hepatitis treatment Wellferon because of slow sales and selling the US rights to several anesthesia products. It also cut some 3400 jobs (half from the UK). Also that year Glaxo threatened to leave the UK after the National Health Service opted not to cover antiflu inhalant Relenza claiming the drug is not cost-effective.

The FDA in 2000 approved Glaxo's Lotronex for irritable bowel syndrome but several hospitalizations linked to the drug prompted the FDA to ask the company to withdraw it from the US market. Later that year Glaxo completed its merger with former UK rival SmithKline Beecham to create GlaxoSmithKline (GSK).

EXECUTIVES

CEO, Andrew Witty, age 51, $1,059,000 total compensation
President Consumer Healthcare Worldwide, Emma Walmsley
President North America Pharmaceuticals, Deirdre P. Connelly, age 54
Chairman Global Vaccines, Moncef Slaoui, age 55, $1,180,000 total compensation
President Pharmaceuticals R&D, Patrick Vallance
President Global Pharmaceuticals, Abbas Hussain
SVP Core Business Services and Chief Information Officer, Bill Louv
CFO, Simon Dingemans, $699,000 total compensation
President Global Manufacturing & Supply, Roger Connor
CEO GlaxoSmithKline (GSK) Korea, Kim Suekyung, age 61
Chairman, Philip Hampton, age 62
Auditors: PricewaterhouseCoopers LLP

LOCATIONS

HQ: GlaxoSmithKline Plc
980 Great West Road, Brentford, Middlesex TW8 9GS
Phone: (44) 20 8047 5000 **Fax:** (44) 20 8047 7807
Web: www.gsk.com

2014 Sales

	% of total
US	32
Europe	28
Emerging markets	27
Japan	7
Other	6
Total	**100**

PRODUCTS/OPERATIONS

2014 Sales

	% of total
Pharmaceuticals	67
Consumer healthcare	19
Vaccines	14
Total	**100**

Selected Products

Pharmaceuticals
- Respiratory
  - Beconase (allergies)
  - Becotide/Beclovent (asthma and chronic obstructive pulmonary disease)
  - Flixonase/Flonase (allergies)
  - Flixotide/Flovent (asthma and chronic obstructive pulmonary disease)
  - Seretide/Advair (asthma and chronic obstructive pulmonary disease)
  - Serevent (asthma and chronic obstructive pulmonary disease)
  - Ventolin (asthma and chronic obstructive pulmonary disease)
  - Veramyst/Avamys (rhinitis)
- Cardiovascular and urogenital
  - Arixtra (deep vein thrombosis and pulmonary embolism)
  - Avodart (prostatic hyperplasia)
  - Benlysta (systemic lupus erychematosus with HGS)
  - Coreg CR (heart failure and hypertension)
  - Fraxiparine (deep vein thrombosis and pulmonary embolism)
  - Levitra (erectile dysfunction with Bayer)
  - Lovaza (coronary heart disease)
  - Vesicare (overactive bladder)
  - Volibris (pulmonary hypertension)
- Central nervous system disorders
  - Horizant (post-herpetic neuralgia or restless leg syndrome)
  - Imigran/Imitrex (migraines)
  - Lamictal (epilepsy and bipolar disorder)

Potiga/Trobalt (epilepsy and partial seizures)
Requip (Parkinson' s disease)
Seroxat/Paxil (depression)
Treximet (migraine)
Wellbutrin SR (depression)
ViiV Healthcare (HIV with Pfizer)
Combivir/Biovir (reverse transcriptase inhibitor for HIV/AIDS)
Epivir/3TC (reverse transcriptase inhibitor for HIV/AIDS)
Epizicom/Kivexa (combination of Epivir and Ziagen for HIV/AIDS)
Lexiva/Telzir (protease inhibitor for HIV/AIDS)
Selzentry (HIV)
Trizivir (three reverse transcriptase inhibitors for HIV/AIDS)
Antibacterials
Amoxil and Augmentin (antibiotics non-US only)
Dermatology
Bactroban (skin infections)
Duac (acne vulgaris)
Zovirax (herpes infections shingles chicken pox and cold sores)
Antivirals
Relenza (influenza)
Hepsera (hepatitis B)
Valtrex/Zelitrex (shingles and genital herpes)
Zeffix/Septavir/Heptodin/Epivir HBV (hepatitis B)
Vaccines
Cervarix (human papilloma virus)
Fluarix (influenza)
FluLaval (influenza)
Infanrix/Pediarix (diphtheria tetanus pertussis polio and hepatitis B)
Rotarix (rotavirus)
Synflorix (pneumonia)
Twinrix (hepatitis A and hepatitis B)
Metabolic
Avandia Avandamet (type 2 diabetes)
Boniva/Bonviva (osteoporosis with Roche)
Consumer products
Over-the-counter medicines
Abreva (cold sores)
alli (weight loss)
Breathe Right (nasal strips)
Citrucel (laxative)
Commit (smoking-cessation)
Contac (respiratory product)
Nicabate/NicoDerm/NiQuitin CQ (smoking-cessation)
Nicorette (smoking-cessation)
Panadol (analgesic)
Tums (antacid)
Oral care
Aquafresh (toothpaste and toothbrushes)
Corega (denture care)
Dr Best (toothbrushes)
Macleans (toothpaste)
Odol (toothpaste)
Polident (denture cleaner)
Poli-Grip (denture adhesive)
Sensodyne (toothpaste)
Nutritional health care
Horlicks (milk-based malted food and chocolate drinks)
Lucozade (glucose energy drink)
Ribena (line of juice drinks rich in vitamin C)

COMPETITORS

Abbott Labs	Mylan
Amgen	Novartis
AstraZeneca	Novo Nordisk
Bayer AG	Pfizer
Biogen	Procter & Gamble
Bristol-Myers Squibb	Ranbaxy Laboratories
Colgate-Palmolive	Reckitt Benckiser
Dr. Reddy' s	Roche Holding
Eli Lilly	Sanofi
Gilead Sciences	Takeda Pharmaceutical
Johnson & Johnson	Teva
Merck	UCB

HISTORICAL FINANCIALS

Company Type: Public

Income Statement FYE: December 31

	REVENUE ($ mil.)	NET INCOME ($ mil.)	NET PROFIT MARGIN	EMPLOYEES
12/14	35,912	4,302	12.0%	97,921
12/13	43,801	8,983	20.5%	99,817
12/12	42,603	7,358	17.3%	98,681
12/11	42,308	8,127	19.2%	97,401
12/10	44,082	2,537	5.8%	98,485
Annual Growth	(5.0%)	14.1%	—	(0.1%)

2014 Year-End Financials

Debt ratio: 72.1%	No. of shares (mil.): —
Return on equity: 48.9%	Dividends
Cash ($ mil.): 6,771	Yield: 6.2%
Current ratio: 1.10	Payout: 282.5%
Long-term debt ($ mil.): 24,728	Market value ($ mil.): —

	STOCK PRICE ($) FY Close	P/E High/Low	PER SHARE ($) Earnings	Dividends	Book Value
12/14	42.74	93 72	0.89	2.65	1.37
12/13	53.39	52 40	1.83	2.41	2.38
12/12	43.47	53 46	1.47	2.48	1.91
12/11	45.63	44 34	1.59	2.10	2.46
12/10	39.22	128108	0.50	2.00	2.66
Annual Growth	2.2%	— —	15.6%	7.3%	(15.3%)

Glencore PLC

Auditors: Deloitte LLP

LOCATIONS

HQ: Glencore PLC
Baarermattstrasse 3, P.O. Box 777, Baar CH-6341
Phone: (41) 41 709 2000 **Fax:** (41) 41 709 3000
Web: www.glencorexstrata.com

HISTORICAL FINANCIALS

Company Type: Public

Income Statement FYE: December 31

	REVENUE ($ mil.)	NET INCOME ($ mil.)	NET PROFIT MARGIN	EMPLOYEES
12/14	221,073	2,308	1.0%	0
12/13	232,694	(7,402)		0
12/12	214,436	1,004	0.5%	0
12/11	186,152	4,048	2.2%	0
12/10	144,978	1,291	0.9%	0
Annual Growth	11.1%	15.6%	—	—

2014 Year-End Financials

Debt ratio: 34.6%	No. of shares (mil.): —
Return on equity: 4.6%	Dividends
Cash ($ mil.): 2,824	Yield: 3.3%
Current ratio: 1.21	Payout: 95.0%
Long-term debt ($ mil.): 40,688	Market value ($ mil.): —

	STOCK PRICE ($) FY Close	P/E High/Low	PER SHARE ($) Earnings	Dividends	Book Value
12/14	9.23	71 48	0.18	0.31	3.74
12/13	10.42		(0.67)	0.29	3.81
12/12	11.67	112 66	0.14	0.28	4.40
12/11	12.14	20 16	0.69	0.05	4.23
Annual Growth	(8.7%)	— —	(28.5%)	57.5%	(3.0%)

Great Eastern Holdings Ltd. (Singapore)

Great Eastern Holdings Limited holds quite a few insurance companies in the far east and they all want to be great. The company through its subsidiaries has operations in Singapore and Malaysia where it is the largest and oldest insurer as well as in Brunei Indonesia China (via joint venture) and Vietnam. It offers asset management investment holding management services life insurance (through Great Eastern Life Assurance) and other financial services. Great Eastern Holdings' 20000 dedicated agents sell its products; representatives at major banks also offer its wares. The company which was incorporated in 1908 is owned by Oversea-Chinese Banking Corp.

Great Eastern Holdings which plans to eventually have branches across all of Asia operates in China through a joint venture with Chongqing Land Properties Group. The JV Great Eastern Life Assurance (China) has opened six offices and continues petitioning the Chinese government for permission to set up more.

The company opened its Vietnam office in Ho Chi Minh City in 2008. Shortly thereafter a second branch in Hanoi opened its doors.

Also in 2008 12-year CEO Tan Beng Lee retired and was replaced by insurance industry veteran Ng Keng Hooi. Ng was formerly the regional managing director of Asia for Prudential.

EXECUTIVES

Chief Executive Officer, Christopher Wei
Chief Finance Officer, Tony Cheong
Director & Chairman, Norman Ka Cheung Ip
Auditors: Ernst & Young LLP

LOCATIONS

HQ: Great Eastern Holdings Ltd. (Singapore)
1 Pickering Street #16-01, Great Eastern Centre, 048659
Phone: (65) 6248 2000 **Fax:** (65) 6438 3889
Web: www.greateasternlife.com

COMPETITORS

China Life Insurance	Guoco
China Pacific Insurance	Ping An Insurance
Edaran Otomobil	Prudential plc

HISTORICAL FINANCIALS

Company Type: Public

Income Statement FYE: December 31

	ASSETS ($ mil.)	NET INCOME ($ mil.)	INCOME AS % OF ASSETS	EMPLOYEES
12/14	49,711	665	1.3%	0
12/13	48,214	534	1.1%	0
12/12	48,811	972	2.0%	0
12/11	42,781	296	0.7%	0
12/10	41,623	395	1.0%	0
Annual Growth	4.5%	13.9%	—	—

2014 Year-End Financials

Return on assets: 1.3%	Dividends
Return on equity: 16.0%	Yield: 0.0%
Long-term debt ($ mil.): —	Payout: 57.9%
No. of shares (mil.): 473	Market value ($ mil.): —
Sales ($ mil): 818	

STOCK PRICE ($) FY Close	P/E High/Low		PER SHARE ($) Earnings	Dividends	Book Value
12/14 0.00	16	15	1.41	0.82	9.39
Annual Growth —	—	—	—	—	—

Great-West Life Assurance Co

Great-West Life Assurance has a great big array of insurance benefits and investment products for individuals and businesses large and small in Canada and Europe. Through its operating subsidiaries Canada Life and London Life the company provides group and individual life insurance supplemental health insurance disability and critical illness insurance and investment and retirement plans. Its European business is focused on the UK Ireland and Germany where it provides asset management individual insurance and reinsurance. Great-West Life Assurance is a subsidiary of Great-West Lifeco and part of the Power Financial group of companies.

While it has experienced organic growth the company has been acquisitive picking up businesses in both Canada and the UK. In 2009 the company acquired the Canadian group retirement and savings business of Fidelity Investments Canada. The acquisition gave Great-West Life Assurance about 100 plan sponsors nearly 500 retirement plans and about 100000 new members in Canada.

(For those wondering why the company's Canada Life operates in the UK but its London Life operates in Canada –the "London" in London Life refers to its hometown of London Ontario.)

Great-West Life Assurance's sister company Great-West Life & Annuity Insurance Company offers a more limited portfolio of products in the US including life insurance annuity and retirement products.

Founded in 1891 in Winnipeg Great-West Life Assurance is a leading provider of employee benefits programs in Canada and serves clients with large and small employee groups. The company is led by CEO D. Allen Loney who took over for Raymond McFeetors when he was named chairman of the board in 2008

EXECUTIVES

Chairman, Raymond L. McFeetors, age 70
Auditors: Deloitte LLP

LOCATIONS

HQ: Great-West Life Assurance Co
100 Osborne Street North, Winnipeg, Manitoba R3C 1V3
Phone: 204 946-1190 **Fax:** 204 946-4139
Web: www.greatwestlife.com

COMPETITORS

AGF Management
Aviva
CPP Investment Board
Desjardins Financial Security
ING
Mackenzie Financial
Manulife Financial
RBC Insurance
Sun Life
Western Financial Group

HISTORICAL FINANCIALS

Company Type: Public

Income Statement FYE: December 31

	ASSETS ($ mil.)	NET INCOME ($ mil.)	INCOME AS % OF ASSETS	EMPLOYEES
12/14	249,304	2,246	0.9%	0
12/13	250,015	2,110	0.8%	0
12/12	202,090	1,754	0.9%	0
12/11	185,218	1,910	1.0%	0
12/10	182,644	1,355	0.7%	12,600
Annual Growth	8.1%	13.5%	—	—

2014 Year-End Financials

Return on assets: 0.9%
Return on equity: 13.7%
Long-term debt ($ mil.): —
No. of shares (mil.): 2
Sales ($ mil): 27,821
Dividends
Yield: —
Payout: —
Market value ($ mil.): —

Great-West Lifeco Inc.

Great-West writes policies for the Great White North and beyond. Holding company Great-West Lifeco majority-owned by Power Financial is one of Canada's largest insurance organizations but its reach extends to the US and to Europe. Through subsidiaries (including Great-West Life Assurance in Canada and Great-West Life & Annuity in the US) the company offers a range of individual and group life and health insurance retirement savings and investment products reinsurance and services to financial institutions. Great-West Life Assurance's two major subsidiaries Canada Life and London Life Insurance provide individual insurance and wealth-management products in Canada Germany Ireland and the UK.

Operations

In the US Great-West Life & Annuity (GWL&A) provides retirement savings plans to employers. Great-West Lifeco's companies also provide reinsurance to niche markets in the US and Europe. Great-West Lifeco has more than $705 billion in assets under administration.

The company divides its business geographically: it offers financial services and asset management in the US its largest market individual and group insurance and wealth management services in Canada and insurance and annuities along with reinsurance in Europe. Its US asset management line of business brings in the largest part of revenue at 40%.

Financial Performance

A decline in European results balanced with increases in Canada and the US sales to result in flat revenue for 2012. Net income dropped due to higher commissions and general expenses.

Strategy

Going forward Great-West Lifeco intends to keep expanding geographically and across product lines. It believes multiple brands and distribution channels positions it well for growth. It continues to seek unique opportunities to support larger and more complex accounts especially in its wealth management business which is developing retirement income products as that segment of the population grows.

Mergers and Acquisitions

In 2013 Great-West Lifeco acquired Irish Life Group Limited for some 1.3 billion ($1.75 million) from the Irish government. The purchase gives Great-West a leading position in life insurance pension and investment management markets in Ireland. Following the transaction Great-West Lifeco moved its existing Irish subsidiary Canada Life (Ireland) into the Irish Life division.

EXECUTIVES

President and CEO U.S., Robert L. Reynolds, age 63
EVP and CFO, William W. Lovatt
EVP General Counsel and Compliance, Andrew D. Brands
President and CEO, Paul A. Mahon
EVP Actuarial and Risk, Garry MacNicholas
President and COO Canada, J. Dave Johnston
President and Chief Operating Officer Europe, Arshil Jamal
EVP and Chief Investment Officer, S. Mark Corbett
EVP Chief Human Resources Officer, Grace Palombo
Auditors: Deloitte LLP

LOCATIONS

HQ: Great-West Lifeco Inc.
100 Osborne Street North, Winnipeg, Manitoba R3C 1V3
Phone: 204 946-1190 **Fax:** 204 946-4139
Web: www.greatwestlifeco.com

2012 Sales

	$ mil.	% of total
US		
Asset management	23	40
Financial services	6	10
Canada		
Wealth management	9	16
Group insurance	7	12
Individual insurance	3	7
Europe		
Insurance & annuities	5	8
Reinsurance	4	7
Total	**59**	**100**

PRODUCTS/OPERATIONS

Selected Subsidiaries & Affiliates

The Great-West Life Assurance Company
Canada Life Financial Corporation
The Canada Life Assurance Company
Canada Life Capital Corporation Inc.
The Canada
Canada Life International Re Limited
Canada Life Irish Holding Company Limited
Crown Life Insurance Company
Laketon Investment Management Ltd.
London Insurance Group
London Life Insurance Company
London Reinsurance Group Inc.
GWL&A Fina
Great-West Life & Annuity Insurance Company
Advised Assets Group LLC
FASCore LLC

COMPETITORS

AXA Financial
CIBC
Industrial Alliance Insurance and Financial Servic
John Hancock Financial Services
Liberty Mutual
Manulife Financial
Nationwide Financial
Prudential
RBC Financial Group
RBC Insurance
Sun Life

HISTORICAL FINANCIALS

Company Type: Public

Income Statement FYE: December 31

	ASSETS ($ mil.)	NET INCOME ($ mil.)	INCOME AS % OF ASSETS	EMPLOYEES
12/14	308,036	2,303	0.7%	0
12/13	306,494	2,264	0.7%	20,970
12/12	255,102	1,940	0.8%	17,870
12/11	234,062	2,076	0.9%	17,350
12/10	229,909	1,704	0.7%	17,450
Annual Growth	7.6%	7.8%	—	—

2014 Year-End Financials

Return on assets: 0.7%
Return on equity: 14.4%
Long-term debt ($ mil.): —
No. of shares (mil.): 996
Sales ($ mil): 33,834
Dividends
Yield: 0.0%
Payout: 48.3%
Market value ($ mil.): 28,925

	STOCK PRICE ($) FY Close	P/E High/Low	PER SHARE ($) Earnings	Dividends	Book Value
12/14	29.02	11 10	2.20	1.06	16.68
12/13	30.70	13 10	2.16	1.16	16.60
12/12	24.42	13 11	1.91	1.24	15.95
12/11	20.04	13 9	2.07	1.21	14.32
12/10	26.50	17 14	1.70	1.23	13.49
Annual Growth	2.3%	— —	6.7%	(3.7%)	5.4%

Groupama S.A. (France)

Group and individual insurance policies are the name of the game at Groupama. Multi-line insurer Groupama is the operating company responsible for a group of regional mutual insurance companies that provide life health and property/casualty insurance throughout France. The group also offers retirement savings products as well as banking and asset management services. Through brand names including Groupama Gan Franck Cammas and Amaguiz.com the company caters to private individuals and small and midsized businesses. The company operates in about a dozen countries in Europe and Asia. Groupama is owned indirectly (through a holding company) by the mutual companies it operates.

Groupama has been in expansion mode snapping up companies in foreign markets particularly in central and eastern Europe. In 2008 it picked up a Hungarian bank a Romanian insurer and a Turkish insurer. In 2009 the firm slowed its acquisition pace and focused on consolidating some of its European subsidiaries to strengthen its competitive position. Groupama is also working to open new branch locations and enter new partnerships to expand its European distribution network.

In 2010 the company made bold Asian expansion moves when it formed a joint venture with Aviation Industry Corporation of China to begin offering property/casualty insurance in the Chinese market. It also gained regulatory approval to form its own independent insurance subsidiary in China.

In addition to international expansion the company is looking to strengthen its core French business through distribution partnerships new products and mobile and Internet sales. Through a deal with Dexia for instance Groupama provides insurance and risk management products to local municipalities.

Though it became known as Groupama in 1986 the company traces its roots back more than a hundred years when it was formed by farmers as a leading agricultural insurer. The F © ©ation Nationale Groupama the association of mutual companies that form the core of the company still acts as an agricultural trade organization.

In 2011 Groupama completed a consolidation plan that reduced the number of regional mutual members from about 20 to 10 to increase efficiencies and improve communication in its organization. The firm is also working to streamline its information systems to reduce costs.

EXECUTIVES

CFO, Christian Collin, age 62
Managing Director Insurance France, Thierry Martel, age 50
Managing Director IT Systems Logistics Management and Purchasing, Francis Thomine, age 53
Director Groupama National Federation, Maurice Faure, age 60
General Secretary Strategy and Human Resources, Philippe Carraud, age 61
Auditors: Mazars

LOCATIONS

HQ: Groupama S.A. (France)
8-10 rue d' Astorg, Paris, Cedex 08 75383
Phone: (33) 1 44 56 77 77
Web: www.groupama.com

2009 Sales

	% of total
France	76
Southeastern Europe	12
Southwestern Europe	6
Central & eastern Europe	3
UK	3
Total	**100**

PRODUCTS/OPERATIONS

2009 Sales

	% of total
Life and health insurance	49
Property and casualty insurance	49
Asset management and other financial activities	2
Total	**100**

COMPETITORS

AXA
April Group
Assurances G©n©rales de France
Aviva
BNP Paribas
CNP Assurances
Generali
Mutualit© Fran$aise

HISTORICAL FINANCIALS

Company Type: Public

Income Statement FYE: December 31

	ASSETS ($ mil.)	NET INCOME ($ mil.)	INCOME AS % OF ASSETS	EMPLOYEES
12/14	120,063	18	0.0%	15,675
12/13	125,829	185	0.1%	16,009
12/12	115,917	(819)	—	17,142
12/11	115,619	(2,343)	—	0
12/10	124,555	517	0.4%	21,857
Annual Growth	(0.9%)	(56.7%)	—	(8.0%)

2014 Year-End Financials

Return on assets: 0.0%
Return on equity: 0.3%
Long-term debt ($ mil.): —
No. of shares (mil.): 329
Sales ($ mil): 14,849
Dividends
Yield: —
Payout: —
Market value ($ mil.): —

Grupo Financiero Banorte S.A. BDE C V

EXECUTIVES

Director General, Alejandro Valenzuela
Auditors: Galaz, Yamazaki, Ruiz Urquiza, S.C. (member of Deloitte & Touche Tohmatsu)

LOCATIONS

HQ: Grupo Financiero Banorte S.A. BDE C V
Prolongacion Reforma 1230, Col. Cruz Manca Santa Fe, Mexico, Distrito Federal 05300
Phone: (52) 55 1103 4000
Web: www.banorte.com

HISTORICAL FINANCIALS

Company Type: Public

Income Statement FYE: December 31

	ASSETS ($ mil.)	NET INCOME ($ mil.)	INCOME AS % OF ASSETS	EMPLOYEES
12/14	74,703	1,036	1.4%	27,943
12/13	76,883	1,031	1.3%	27,549
12/12	70,538	837	1.2%	26,212
12/11	59,365	609	1.0%	24,027
12/10	47,636	540	1.1%	19,759
Annual Growth	11.9%	17.6%	—	9.1%

2014 Year-End Financials

Return on assets: 1.4%
Return on equity: 13.2%
Long-term debt ($ mil.): —
No. of shares (mil.): —
Sales ($ mil): 7,604
Dividends
Yield: 1.0%
Payout: —
Market value ($ mil.): —

	STOCK PRICE ($) FY Close	P/E High/Low	PER SHARE ($) Earnings	Dividends	Book Value
12/14	27.62	— —	0.37	0.28	3.02
12/13	35.04	— —	0.41	0.39	2.94
12/12	32.51	— —	0.36	0.18	2.71
12/11	15.17	— —	0.27	0.00	2.19
12/10	23.49	— —	0.27	0.00	1.84
Annual Growth	4.1%	— —	8.7%	—	13.1%

Gunma Bank, Ltd. (The) (Japan)

Gunma Bank hopes that you have more than just a yen for its services. Through more than 140 branches The Gunma Bank provides banking services in the Gunma prefecture and surrounding areas of Japan through some 150 branches. The Gunma Bank also operates a subsidiary in Hong Kong and a branch in New York City. As the company's name might imply the Gunma prefecture (known for its industry and agriculture-based economy) accounts for more than 80% of deposits. Besides deposits Gunma Bank's services include loans to companies individuals and the government securities insurance and exchange. The Gunma Bank was founded in 1932.
Auditors: Ernst & Young ShinNihon LLC

LOCATIONS

HQ: Gunma Bank, Ltd. (The) (Japan)
194 Motosoja-machi, Maebashi, Gunma 371-8611
Phone: (81) 27 252 1111
Web: www.gunmabank.co.jp

COMPETITORS

77 Bank	Ito-Yokado
Hachijuni Bank	Japan Post

HISTORICAL FINANCIALS

Company Type: Public

Income Statement FYE: March 31

	ASSETS ($ mil.)	NET INCOME ($ mil.)	INCOME AS % OF ASSETS	EMPLOYEES
03/15	62,935	215	0.3%	3,339
03/14	69,189	192	0.3%	3,405
03/13	72,746	218	0.3%	3,405
03/12	78,760	228	0.3%	3,399
03/11	75,207	209	0.3%	3,347
Annual Growth	(4.4%)	0.8%	—	(0.1%)

2015 Year-End Financials

Return on assets: 0.3%
Return on equity: 5.3%
Long-term debt ($ mil.): —
No. of shares (mil.): 455
Sales ($ mil): 1,105
Dividends
Yield: —
Payout: —
Market value ($ mil.): —

Hachijuni Bank, Ltd. (Japan)

The Hachijuni Bank operates more than 150 branches in Japan primarily in the central prefecture of Nagano. It serves individuals and businesses with traditional products as deposit services and loans. The bank also owns subsidiaries active in financial services including leasing consumer loan guarantee investment advisory venture capital for high-tech firms and credit cards. Overseas Hachijuni has a branch in Hong Kong and representative offices in China Singapore and Thailand. The company was founded in Nagano City in 1931.

The Hachijuni Bank is looking to expand both through opening additional offices and through beefing up its offerings in such areas as investment production sales and consultation services.

Auditors: Deloitte Touche Tohmatsu LLC

LOCATIONS

HQ: Hachijuni Bank, Ltd. (Japan)
178-8 Aza Okada, Oaza Nakagosho, Nagano 380-8682
Phone: (81) 26 227 1182
Web: www.82bank.co.jp

HISTORICAL FINANCIALS

Company Type: Public

Income Statement FYE: March 31

	ASSETS ($ mil.)	NET INCOME ($ mil.)	INCOME AS % OF ASSETS	EMPLOYEES
03/15	66,797	226	0.3%	3,679
03/14	73,510	256	0.3%	3,713
03/13	77,105	235	0.3%	3,756
03/12	80,473	211	0.3%	3,800
03/11	76,006	244	0.3%	3,862
Annual Growth	(3.2%)	(1.8%)	—	(1.2%)

2015 Year-End Financials

Return on assets: 0.3%
Return on equity: 4.4%
Long-term debt ($ mil.): —
No. of shares (mil.): 501
Sales ($ mil): 1,448
Dividends
Yield: 1.4%
Payout: —
Market value ($ mil.): 34,618

	STOCK PRICE ($) FY Close	P/E High/Low	PER SHARE ($) Earnings	Dividends	Book Value
03/15	69.05	— —	0.45	1.00	11.51
03/14	57.89	— —	0.51	1.14	11.37
03/13	59.46	— —	0.46	0.00	11.83
03/12	58.85	— —	0.41	0.00	11.75
03/11	57.56	— —	0.47	0.75	10.99
Annual Growth	4.7%	— —	(1.0%)	7.5%	1.2%

Haci Omer Sabanci Holding A.S.

Haci Ömer Sabanci is one of Turkey's largest industrial and financial conglomerates with interests in the energy banking retail cement textile and other industries. Its primary holding is a stake in Turkish banking firm Akbank which provides commercial retail and private banking as well as investment and foreign trade services. Other holdings include stakes in domestic energy company Enerjisa and supermarket operator Carrefoursa a joint venture with Carrefour. Sabanci's portfolio spans some 20 countries in Europe Africa Asia and the Americas. It also has several partnerships with multinationals such as Bridgestoneand Philip Morris. The wealthy Sabanci family owns 60% of the company.

HISTORY

Haci Ömer Sabanci's eponymous empire traces back to the 1930s. Sabanci left his native village Akcakaya at the age of 14 to become a laborer in a cotton plantation in the Adana region of Turkey in 1921. By 1932 he had become a shareholder in a cotton ginning plant. During the next decade he grabbed stakes in two vegetable oil plants: Türk Nebati Yaglar Fabrikasi (1943) and Marsa (1946; renamed in 1993 as Marsa KJS a joint venture with Kraft).

Quickly broadening his portfolio Sabanci along with more than 80 citizens of Adana and surrounding regions became a founding shareholder in Akbank (named for Sabanci's native village) in 1948. He further diversified with investments in Bossa a flour and cotton ginning mill in 1951. Sabanci's second financial holding the Aksigorta insurance business was formed in 1960 as a subsidiary of Akbank.

By the time Sabanci died in 1966 Akbank had opened its 100th branch office. Sabanci's five sons took the helm of their father's companies and moved the group's headquarters to the more cosmopolitan Istanbul in 1974 in accordance with Sabanci's growing stance as a global entity. Domestic operations continued to grow however; fabric producer Yünsa was founded in 1973 and the Çimsa unit began producing cement two years later.

The 1980s marked the Haci Ömer Sabanci group's emergence as a multinational and the beginnings of its signature business style: growth through partnerships with major players. In 1985 Akbank joined with Banque Nationale de Paris (now BNP Paribas) to create BNP-Ak Bank; leading German bank Dresdner joined the companies three years later to form BNP-Ak-Dresdner Bank. A joint venture with DuPont in 1987 created nylon yarn producer Dusa. The following year the company renamed its Lassa tire manufacturing concern Brisa after sealing a deal with Bridgestone of Japan. By the end of the decade the Sabanci family were billionaires.

The group continued developing powerful partnerships in the next decade. Two joint ventures with Philip Morris (1991 and 1994) involved Haci Ömer Sabanci in the manufacturing marketing and selling of the maker's cigarettes in Turkey. A trinational deal in 1997 with US conglomerate Koch Industries and Mexican billionaire Isaac Saba's Imasab created Sakosa a polyester tire cord and industrial yarn manufacturer. Another joint venture with DuPont in 1999 (DuPontsa BV) linked the companies' operations to create Europe's largest polyester producer.

An attempt to break into telecommunications stalled that year when the almost $3 billion price tag in Turkey's mobile phone license auction proved too steep for the Sabanci group. However the company was able to purchase Turk.Net Turkey's largest ISP for $25 million. By 2000 Haci Ömer Sabanci had ceased seeking out partnerships and ventures in disparate sectors planning instead to narrow its focus to select industries including energy the Internet and telecommunications.

In 2001 the company teamed up with DuPont to form global nylon industrial yarn and tire cord joint venture DUSA International. It also sold its stake in automotive joint venture Toyotasa to partner Toyota.

Chairman Sakip Sabanci's lifelong dream of creating a world-class museum in Turkey was realized in 2002 with the opening of the Sakip Sabanci Museum. Sabanci died two years later.

Also in 2004 Sabanci bought BNP Paribas and Dresdner Bank out of their BNP-Ak-Dresdner Bank venture.

Belgian partner Bekaert bought out Sabanci's share of their Beksa steel cord and metal fiber joint venture in 2008. Sabanci sold stakes in other holdings including its edible oils operations financial services companies and another joint venture with Toyota.

The group teamed up with Austria-based Verbund to own and operate a regional electricity distributor in Turkey in 2008. The landmark $1 billion deal was part of the Turkish government's plan to privatize and transform the country's power industry.

EXECUTIVES

CFO, Faruk Bilen, age 46
CEO; Board Member, Zafer Kurtul
President Energy, Selahattin Hakman, age 63
President Industry SBU, Mehmet N. Pekarun

President Cement, Mehmet Gocmen, age 58
President of Retailing and Insurance Unit, Haluk Dincer, age 53
Chief Information Officer, Gungor Kaymak
Vice Chairman, Erol Sabanci, age 77
Chairman and Managing Director, Guler Sabanci
Auditors: DRT BAGIMSIZ DENETIM VE SERBEST MUHASEBECI MALI M SAVIRLIK A.S.

LOCATIONS

HQ: Haci Omer Sabanci Holding A.S.
Sabanci Center 4, Levent, Istanbul 34330
Phone: (90) 212 385 80 80 **Fax:** (90) 212 385 88 88
Web: www.sabanci.com

PRODUCTS/OPERATIONS

Selected Investments

Cement
- Akçansa
- Çimsa

Energy
- Enerjisa

Financial services
- Akbank
- Aksigorta

Retail
- Carrefoursa
- Teknosa

Industrial
- Brisa
- Kordsa Global
- Temsa
- Sasa
- Yunsa

Other
- Bimsa
- Philip Morrissa
- Philsa
- Tursa

COMPETITORS

Alarko
Alfa Group
Berkshire Hathaway
Dogan Holding
Global Yatirim
Koş
Yazicilar

HISTORICAL FINANCIALS

Company Type: Public

Income Statement FYE: December 31

	ASSETS ($ mil.)	NET INCOME ($ mil.)	INCOME AS % OF ASSETS	EMPLOYEES
12/14	99,034	893	0.9%	60,170
12/13	96,571	809	0.8%	58,907
12/12	97,929	1,036	1.1%	57,556
12/11	80,059	994	1.2%	57,374
12/10	84,258	1,077	1.3%	57,209
Annual Growth	4.1%	(4.6%)	—	1.3%

2014 Year-End Financials

Return on assets: 0.9%
Return on equity: 11.4%
Long-term debt ($ mil.): —
No. of shares (mil.): —
Sales ($ mil): 12,273
Dividends
Yield: 0.0%
Payout: 0.1%
Market value ($ mil.): —

	STOCK PRICE ($) FY Close	P/E High/Low		PER SHARE ($) Earnings	Dividends	Book Value
12/14	0.75	0	0	4.38	0.01	0.04
12/13	4.00	—	—	3.97	0.01	0.04
12/12	4.00	0	0	5.08	0.01	0.04
12/11	1.50	—	—	4.87	0.01	0.04
12/10	1.50	—	—	5.28	0.01	(0.00)
Annual Growth	(15.9%)	—	—	(4.6%)	(9.8%)	—

Hang Seng Bank Ltd.

Hang Seng Bank whose name means "ever-growing" in Chinese is one of Hong Kong's largest banks. It has more than 220 branches and automated banking centers –including one in every subway station –throughout the city. It also boasts more than 45 outlets in mainland China and has locations in Macao Singapore and Taiwan. The bank provides corporate and retail banking services such as deposit accounts credit cards mortgages business and personal loans and insurance as well as investment products and services the likes of securities trading and mutual funds. With total assets of HK$1.1 billion at the end of 2013 it also offers personal wealth management and private banking services.
Auditors: PricewaterhouseCoopers

LOCATIONS

HQ: Hang Seng Bank Ltd.
83 Des Voeux Road Central,
Phone: (852) 2198 1111 **Fax:** (852) 2868 4047
Web: www.hangseng.com

HISTORICAL FINANCIALS

Company Type: Public

Income Statement FYE: December 31

	ASSETS ($ mil.)	NET INCOME ($ mil.)	INCOME AS % OF ASSETS	EMPLOYEES
12/14	162,986	1,951	1.2%	10,192
12/13	147,504	3,440	2.3%	9,856
12/12	138,949	2,506	1.8%	9,680
12/11	125,572	2,147	1.7%	9,834
12/10	117,967	1,919	1.6%	9,642
Annual Growth	8.4%	0.4%	—	1.4%

2014 Year-End Financials

Return on assets: 1.2%
Return on equity: 12.2%
Long-term debt ($ mil.): —
No. of shares (mil.): 1,911
Sales ($ mil): 6,371
Dividends
Yield: 3.8%
Payout: —
Market value ($ mil.): 31,660

	STOCK PRICE ($) FY Close	P/E High/Low		PER SHARE ($) Earnings	Dividends	Book Value
12/14	16.56	2	2	1.02	0.64	9.39
12/13	16.28	1	1	1.80	0.61	7.27
12/12	15.49	2	1	1.31	0.72	6.23
12/11	11.80	2	1	1.12	0.60	5.30
12/10	16.49	2	2	1.00	0.60	4.71
Annual Growth	0.1%	—	—	0.4%	1.6%	18.8%

Hannover Rueckversicherung SE

Who insures insurance companies over and over? Hannover! Hannover Rück (Hannover Re) is the second-largest German reinsurance company (Munich Re is #1) and the fourth-largest such company in the world. Through more than 100 subsidiaries the company provides property and casualty (Hannover Re's largest segment) financial life and health reinsurance products in about 150 countries worldwide. Financial reinsurance is provided through Hannover Re Advanced Solutions a Dublin-based consortium managed jointly with HDI Reinsurance (Ireland); both Hannover Re and HDI Reinsurance (Ireland) are subsidiaries of HDI Haftpflichtverband der Deutschen Industrie.

Hannover Re is 50%-owned by German mutual insurance group Talanx AG part of HDI Haftpflichtverband der Deutschen Industrie.

Like nearly all other insurers Hannover Re saw its investment income for 2008 shrink significantly. But an uptick in demand for reinsurance in 2009 along with a decrease in catastrophe losses and a more than 300% increase in investment returns put group results back in line with pre-financial crisis levels. In the second quarter of 2010 however the company experienced higher-than-expected major losses with the sinking of the Deepwater Horizon oil rig operated by BP.

The property/casualty unit of the ever-diversifying Hannover Re accounts for more than 55% of all premiums and is geared toward markets in the US Germany and Japan. Its life/health business is marketed through subsidiary Hannover Life Re and focuses on treaty (groups of risks) rather than facultative (individual risk) policies.

To boost its presence in the US the company purchased a portfolio of life reinsurance from Scottish Re in 2009. The deal gave Hannover a business it attempted to buy from ING Groep in 2004 but lost out to Scottish Re. In 2011 Scottish Re offloaded another chunk of life reinsurance which Hannover Re readily purchased.

While Hannover Re's traditional brot und butter has been property and casualty reinsurance the firm has expanded its life and health lines which are contributing closer and closer to half of all premiums. Hannover Re has also adopted American accounting practices and become more transparent in order to remain a compelling stock in investors' eyes.

HISTORY

Hannover Re was founded in 1966 as the Aktiengesellschaft für Transport und Rückversicherung (ATR) by the Feuerschadenverband Rheinisch-Westfaelischer Zechen (FSV) a mutual insurer specializing in fire damage in the town of Bochum. Within five years ATR had expanded into international reinsurance markets. In 1970 FSV merged with another mutual HDI Haftpflichtverband der Deutschen Industrie which owned reinsurer Eisen und Stahl Rückversicherungs-AG. ATR's headquarters relocated to Hannover and six years later it was renamed Hannover Rückversicherungs-Gesellschaft.

Jointly managed by HDI Hannover Re and Eisen und Stahl operated separately until 1996: Hannover Re targeted international markets while Eisen und Stahl operated mostly within Germany.

Hannover Re maintained its foreign focus throughout the 1970s and 80s expanding in Europe and South Africa and making its first forays into the US. In 1990 the firm acquired US life insurer Reassurance Company of Hannover.

Hannover Re went public in 1994 selling 25% of its stock. Also that year the firm formed an Australian subsidiary. The next year Hannover Re acquired Eisen und Stahl (renamed E+S Ruck 1996) which then assumed total control of the company's domestic business.

In 1998 Hannover Re became the first reinsurer to securitize life insurance business (reinsurers often securitize non-life policies to protect against natural catastrophe risks) through an agreement with Interpolis an Irish reinsurance subsidiary of the Netherlands' Rabobank. Also that year the firm expanded its financial reinsurance business reorganizing the Irish consortium it formed with another subsidiary of HDI into Hannover Re Advanced Solutions.

As various natural disasters offset earnings in Hannover Re's property & casualty division in 1998 and 1999 its life and health segment boomed. To facilitate further growth the firm restructured these operations into a new subsidiary Hannover Life Re. Also in 1999 the firm acquired the Clarendon Insurance Group of New York. In 2001 Hannover Re joined Inreon an online reinsurance trading exchange set up by rivals Munich Re and Swiss Re. Also in 2001 the company established a Bermuda-based subsidiary focused on catastrophe business. The following year Hannover Re split its stock in order to stimulate demand and become a more widely held company.

Like many other insurers the company was hit hard by the attacks of September 11 2001 falling stock markets and in 2005 damages in the Gulf of Mexico caused by hurricanes Katrina and Rita.

Late in 2006 China loosened its regulation of a number of industries and insurance was one of them –Hannover Re was one of the first to gain permission to enter the Chinese market for life and health reinsurance.

At about the same time the company announced plans to cut down on its noncore business operations. The first move in this direction was the sale of its US-based Praetorian Group subsidiary to QBE's US-based subsidiary for a sum in excess of $800 million. Hannover Re used the proceeds to shore up its property/casualty and life/health reinsurance businesses.

EXECUTIVES

Executive Board Member Property and Casualty Treaty Reinsurance Germany Austria Switzerland and Italy; Credit Surety & Political Risk worldwide; Group Legal Services; Run Off Solutions, Michael Pickel, age 55
CFO, Roland Vogel
Executive Board Member Life and Health, Klaus Miller, age 55
Executive Board Member Property and Casualty Specialty Lines Worldwide, Sven Althoff
Executive Board Member Life and Health, Claude Ch¨vre
Executive Board Member Property and Casualty Coordination and Global Reinsurance, J rgen Gr□ber
Deputy Chairman, Klaus Sturany, age 69
Chairman, Ulrich Wallin, age 54
Chairman, Herbert K. Haas
Auditors: KPMG AG Wirtschaftsprufungsgesellschaft

LOCATIONS

HQ: Hannover Rueckversicherung SE
Karl-Wiechert-Allee 50, Hannover D-30625
Phone: (49) 511 5604 0 **Fax:** (49) 511 5604 1188
Web: www.hannover-re.com

2013 Premiums Written

	% of total
Europe	
Germany	9
UK	19
France	4
Other countries	12
North America	
US	24
Other countries	5
Asia	12
Australia	6
Africa	3
Other regions	6
Total	**100**

COMPETITORS

Everest Re
General Re
Lloyd' s
Munich Re Group
PartnerRe
Reinsurance Group of America
SCOR
Swiss Re
XL Group plc

HISTORICAL FINANCIALS

Company Type: Public

Income Statement FYE: December 31

	ASSETS ($ mil.)	NET INCOME ($ mil.)	INCOME AS % OF ASSETS	EMPLOYEES
12/14	73,486	1,198	1.6%	2,534
12/13	74,227	1,232	1.7%	2,376
12/12	72,244	1,131	1.6%	2,263
12/11	64,500	783	1.2%	2,210
12/10	62,535	1,002	1.6%	2,130
Annual Growth	4.1%	4.6%	—	4.4%

2014 Year-End Financials

Return on assets: 1.7%
Return on equity: 14.6%
Long-term debt ($ mil.): —
No. of shares (mil.): 120
Sales ($ mil): 16,891
Dividends
Yield: 0.0%
Payout: 13.3%
Market value ($ mil.): 5,493

	STOCK PRICE ($) FY Close	P/E High	P/E Low	PER SHARE ($) Earnings	Dividends	Book Value
12/14	45.55	6	4	9.93	1.32	76.10
12/13	43.22	6	5	10.23	1.43	67.22
12/12	38.93	6	3	9.38	0.98	66.19
12/11	24.82	6	4	6.49	1.06	53.31
12/10	26.70	4	3	8.31	0.96	50.04
Annual Growth	14.3%	—	—	4.6%	8.4%	11.1%

HDFC Bank Ltd

HDFC Bank serves nearly 30 million customers worldwide and provides a variety of wholesale retail and depository financial services through more than 3400 branches and some 11500 ATMs throughout India. Established by financial institution Housing Development Finance Corporation in 1994 the bank offers deposit accounts loans credit cards insurance investments and related services. Subsidiary HDFC Securities provides online brokerage services. HDFC Bank targets individual customers in the middle and upper-class as well as trusts small businesses and not-for-profit organizations in the country.
Auditors: KPMG

LOCATIONS

HQ: HDFC Bank Ltd
HDFC Bank House, Senapati Bapat Marg, Lower Parel, Mumbai 400 013
Phone: (91) 22 66521000 **Fax:** (91) 22 24960737
Web: www.hdfcbank.com

HISTORICAL FINANCIALS

Company Type: Public

Income Statement FYE: March 31

	ASSETS ($ mil.)	NET INCOME ($ mil.)	INCOME AS % OF ASSETS	EMPLOYEES
03/15	100,073	1,586	1.6%	76,286
03/14	85,359	1,321	1.5%	68,165
03/13	80,517	1,138	1.4%	69,065
03/12	70,194	978	1.4%	66,076
03/11	0	924	****************%	55,752
Annual Growth	—	14.5%	—	8.2%

2015 Year-End Financials

Return on assets: 1.7%
Return on equity: 15.4%
Long-term debt ($ mil.): —
No. of shares (mil.): —
Sales ($ mil): 9,283
Dividends
Yield: 0.5%
Payout: 47.6%
Market value ($ mil.): —

	STOCK PRICE ($) FY Close	P/E High	P/E Low	PER SHARE ($) Earnings	Dividends	Book Value
03/15	58.89	2	0	0.65	0.32	4.79
03/14	41.03	1	1	0.55	0.26	3.69
03/13	37.42	2	1	0.48	0.22	3.63
03/12	34.10	7	1	0.42	0.19	3.31
03/11	169.94	11	8	0.39	0.15	(0.00)
Annual Growth	(23.3%)	—	—	13.2%	21.1%	—

Heineken Holding NV (Netherlands)

Trusts nec
Auditors: KPMG Accountants N.V.

LOCATIONS

HQ: Heineken Holding NV (Netherlands)
Tweede Weteringplantsoen 5, Amsterdam 1017 ZD
Phone: (31) 20 622 11 52 **Fax:** (31) 20 625 22 13
Web: www.heinekenholding.com

HISTORICAL FINANCIALS

Company Type: Public

Income Statement FYE: December 31

	REVENUE ($ mil.)	NET INCOME ($ mil.)	NET PROFIT MARGIN	EMPLOYEES
12/14	23,406	923	3.9%	76,136
12/13	26,437	940	3.6%	80,933
12/12	24,229	1,946	8.0%	76,191
12/11	22,147	927	4.2%	64,252
12/10	21,591	963	4.5%	65,730
Annual Growth	2.0%	(1.1%)	—	3.7%

2014 Year-End Financials

Debt ratio: 41.0%
Return on equity: 12.9%
Cash ($ mil.): 811
Current ratio: 0.71
Long-term debt ($ mil.): 11,546
No. of shares (mil.): 288
Dividends
Yield: 1.4%
Payout: 33.7%
Market value ($ mil.): —

Heineken N.V. (Netherlands)

HISTORY

Every Sunday morning Gerard Heineken's mother was appalled by crowds of drunken Dutchmen who had consumed too much gin the night before. Heineken who wanted his mother's financial backing insisted that drunkenness would decrease if people drank beer instead of gin and pointed out that there were no good beers in Holland. His strategy worked. In 1863 Heineken's mother put up the money to buy De Hooiberg (The Haystack) a 271-year-old brewery in Amsterdam.

Gerard proved his aptitude for brewing and within 10 years had established a brewery in Rotterdam. He named the business Heineken in 1873 and launched the company's lucrative foreign trade by exporting beer in 1876 to France. (By the 1950s half the beer brewed by the company was for export.) The company perfected a yeast strain (Heineken A-yeast) in 1886 that is still in use today.

In 1917 Gerard's son Dr. Henri Pierre Heineken inherited the firm and expanded operations to the US. Making a voyage to that country Henri Pierre met Leo van Munching a ship's bartender who displayed a remarkable knowledge of beer. Recognizing van Munching's talent Henri Pierre hired him as Heineken's US importer. Prohibition killed the US operations although the company entered new markets elsewhere; after repeal Heineken was the first foreign beer to re-enter the US market.

After WWII Henri Pierre sent his son Alfred to learn the business under van Munching who had created a national distribution system in the US. Alfred succeeded his father in 1953 and stepped down in 1989.

Heineken bought the Amstel Brewery in Holland (founded 1870) in 1968. Two years later it became a producer of stout through the acquisition of James J. Murphy in Cork Ireland. Facing a consolidation of the European market Heineken launched a campaign in the 1980s to expand its European beer operations purchasing breweries in France Greece Ireland Italy and Spain.

In 1991 Heineken bought the van Munching US import business and a majority interest in Hungarian brewer Komaromi Sorgyar its first Eastern European investment. Two years later Karel Vuursteen was appointed chairman.

The firm cut more than 1300 jobs in 1993 and sold its spirits and wine operations the next year. In 1995 Heineken began a major spending spree acquiring Interbrew Italia and 66% of Zlaty Bazant the largest Slovakian brewery and maltworks (it acquired the rest in 1999). The company bought Birra Moretti Italy's third-largest brewery in 1996. It also purchased interests in two African breweries. All the acquisitions led to high integration costs and lower profits.

To boost its sales in Poland in 1998 Heineken raised its stake in brewer Zaklady Piwowarskie W. Zywcu (Zywiec) to 75% bought a minority stake in Brewpole and merged the companies to create the largest Polish brewer. That year Heineken bought about 25% of Pivara Skopje the largest brewery in the former Yugoslav republic of Macedonia through its Brewinvest joint venture. In 1999 the company bought about 18% of Israel's leading brewer Tempo (Goldstar and Maccabee beers).

In 2000 Heineken bought 99% of Spanish brewer Cruzcampo most of it from Diageo. Cruzcampo later merged with Heineken's Spanish brewer El guila to create Heineken Espa ±a. In February 2001 Heineken created a joint venture BrauHolding International with Bayerische BrauHolding to sell Paulaner Weiss beer and to give Heineken access to two German beer makers.

VP Anthony Ruys replaced Vuursteen as CEO in 2002. Heineken also announced it would launch its premium Heineken beer in the UK in 2003 and eventually withdraw its Heineken Cold Filtered and Heineken Export beers from that market. It also signed a deal allowing Belgium's Interbrew (now Anheuser-Busch InBev) to brew and sell Murphy's Irish Stout in Britain. Heineken also gained EU approval that year to buy a stake in German brewer Karlsberg.

Also in 2002 Heineken agreed to buy stakes in two Central American breweries: Costa Rica's Florida Ice and Farm Company (FIFCO) and Nicaragua's Consorcio Cervecero Centroamericano (COCECA). With FIFCO and Coca-Cola bottler Panamerican Beverages Heineken purchased Cervecer as Brau-Panam ˘ the country's second-largest brewer for $138 million. The company later purchased Russian brewer Bravo International (which changed its name to Heineken Brewery in 2003). Heineken also bought a controlling stake in Egyptian brewer Al Ahram Beverages in 2002. Ak Agram produces Fayrouz a nonalcoholic beer favored by Muslims. The brewer also agreed to increase its stake in Lebanese brewer Almaza from 10% to 79%.

In 2003 Heineken purchased Austrian brewer BBAG –sterreichische Brau-Beteiligungs-AG for $1.7 billion. It combined its regional operations with BBAG creating Brau Union AG. That year Heineken sold all of its shares (15% of outstanding shares) in Quilmes to Beverage Associates Corp. (BAC); AmBev (now InBev) acquired 8.6% of the Quilmes shares from BAC.

Making a strong play for the growing US Hispanic market Heineken inked a three-year deal with FEMSA Cerveza in 2004 making it the sole importer of FEMSA's Mexican beers Tecate Sol Dos Equis Carta Blanca and Bohemia. Heineken recognized the growing number of people using online music stores. That year it entered a joint venture with Lion Nathan Limited to sell its flagship brand in Australia. Heineken also began an aggressive push into Russia that year when it purchased Sobol Beer in West Siberia and the Volga and Shikhan breweries. Heineken also grew steadily in new markets such as Asia and South America. In 2004 it joined its Chinese operations with those of Asia Pacific Breweries to form Heineken Asia Pacific Breweries China (HAPBC) and that year HAPBC bought an approximate 21% stake in China's Kingway Brewery.

In order to compete with competitors' low-calorie low-carb beers in 2005 the company introduced Heineken Premium Light in select markets in the US market. Also in 2005 the company formed a partnership with Diageo to produce and distribute Guinness in Russia. It also acquired approximately 91% of German brewer W rzburger Hofbr ¤u.

In 2006 the company focused on growth in Indo-China. Its Asian joint venture with Fraser and Neave Asia Pacific Breweries made a number of strategic acquisitions including the Fosters brewing assets in Vietnam and the Quang Nam Brewery in Vietnam. In addition it announced an acquisition in Laos and acquired shares in Tunisian distribution company Soci ©@de Production et de Distribution des Boissons.

Heineken was one of three Dutch brewers (along with Grolsch and Bavaria Brewery) that in 2007 were fined by the European Commission for price fixing surrounding sales to Dutch bars and restaurants in the late 1990s. Heineken's fine amounted to 219 million (about $297 million).

In 2008 Heineken and Denmark's Carlsberg acquired Scottish & Newcastle (S&N) which it renamed Heineken UK. The $15.3 billion takeover resulted in Heineken owning the US Indian (37% of United Breweries maker of Kingfisher beer) UK and other European operations of the noted Irish brewer. Carlsberg took over 100% ownership of Baltic Beverage Holdings (BBH) the 50-50 joint venture it had with S&N as well as its Chinese French Greek and Vietnamese operations. As if that weren't enough for the its bean counters the company added more operations in 2008 as well. Upping its presence in the Czech market Heineken acquired Drinks Union and its national brand Zlatopramen among others. Other notable wheeling and dealing included an agreement to buy the beverage operations of Swiss company Eichhof Holding and the purchase of Romanian brewer Bere Mures.

EXECUTIVES

Director, Marcus Goumans
Auditors: KPMG Accountants N.V.

LOCATIONS

HQ: Heineken N.V. (Netherlands)
Tweede Weteringplantsoen 21, Amsterdam 1017 ZD
Phone: (31) 20 5239 239 **Fax:** (31) 20 627 9684
Web: www.theheinekencompany.com

HISTORICAL FINANCIALS

Company Type: Public

Income Statement FYE: December 31

	REVENUE ($ mil.)	NET INCOME ($ mil.)	NET PROFIT MARGIN	EMPLOYEES
12/14	23,406	1,842	7.9%	76,136
12/13	26,437	1,877	7.1%	80,933
12/12	24,229	3,886	16.0%	76,191
12/11	22,147	927	4.2%	64,252
12/10	21,591	963	4.5%	65,730
Annual Growth	2.0%	17.6%	—	3.7%

2014 Year-End Financials

Debt ratio: 41.0%
Return on equity: 12.7%
Cash ($ mil.): 811
Current ratio: 0.71
Long-term debt ($ mil.): 11,546
No. of shares (mil.): 574
Dividends
Yield: 1.3%
Payout: 13.2%
Market value ($ mil.): 20,301

	STOCK PRICE ($) FY Close	P/E High/Low	PER SHARE ($) Earnings	Dividends	Book Value
12/14	35.33	15 10	3.20	0.47	26.25
12/13	33.76	17 14	3.26	0.48	27.30
12/12	33.57	7 6	6.75	0.00	53.50
Annual Growth (16.3%)	2.6%	— —	(17.0%)	—	

Hennes & Mauritz AB

H&M Hennes & Mauritz targets the Hip & Modish. The firm designs cheap yet chic clothing mainly for men and women ages 18 to 45 children's apparel and its own brands of cosmetics. Fast-growing H&M operates some 2470 stores in some 35 countries and offers online shopping in eight countries. Germany is its #1 market accounting for more than 20% of sales. The firm doesn't own factories but buys its goods from suppliers primarily in Asia and Europe. H&M opened its first women's clothing store in 1947 as Hennes (Swedish for "hers"); it later bought the hunting and men's clothing store Mauritz Widforss. H&M is controlled by the family of chairman Stefan Persson (the billionaire son of founder Erling Persson).

H&M's cheap-chic strategy and global retail presence has largely insulated the company from the global economic downturn. Indeed fiscal 2010 (ends November) sales were up 7% vs. the prior year after climbing 15% in the previous annual comparison. (The retailer also enjoyed double-digit sales growth in 2008 vs. 2007.) International expansion has been the hallmark of H&M's business plan in recent years. Indeed the fast-growing chain added about 220 stores in 2010 including its first locations in South Korea Israel and Turkey. Also in 2010 H&M launched an e-commerce site in the UK H&M's second-largest market. Going forward H&M plans to stick to its ambitious target to increase the number of stores by 10% to 15% per year. Despite its rapid growth H&M has been overtaken by Spain's Inditex owner of the Zara chain as Europe's largest apparel retailer.

Taking a page from Inditex which also operates Zara Home the Swedish retailer in early 2009 quietly launched a catalog and Internet H&M Home business in Austria Germany the Netherlands and the Nordic region. Longer-term the H&M Home brand of pillows towels curtains and other home textiles may support retail stores. Moving up market H&M has launched a chain called COS —for Collection of Style. Aimed at the premium market the first COS store debuted in London in 2007. The chain has since grown to about 35 locations in Belgium Denmark France Ireland Germany the Netherlands Spain and the UK.

In late 2010 H&M acquired the remaining 40% of the shares in FaBric Scandinavien AB which runs the store chains Weekday and Monki as well as the Cheap Monday brand. The brands will continue to operate as separate retail concepts.

H&M generates "buzz" and drives shoppers to its stores through tie ups with big name designers and celebrities. The company's latest collaboration is with the Italian brand Marni and its founder and creative director Consuelo Castiglioni. Marni will design a spring collection for H&M in 2012. Previous design partners have included Karl Lagerfeld Stella McCartney Comme des Gar $ons Jimmy Choo Lanvin and Versace.

Women's clothing accounts for 60% of sales; private-label brands include Hennes L.O.G.G. (Label of Graded Goods) and the plus-size BiB (Big is Beautiful) line.

HISTORY

Swedish salesman Erling Persson visited the US in 1947 and returned intrigued by the low-price high-turnover clothing store he saw on his trip. That year Persson opened his first Hennes store (Swedish for "hers" because it only sold women's apparel) in V □ster s Sweden. The company expanded opening its first foreign stores in Norway in 1964 and Denmark in 1967. As it grew and increased volume the retailer was able to offer lower prices. The company bought hunting and men's clothing shop Mauritz Widforss in 1968 and began offering men's clothing in Mauritz stores.

The firm took its fashions to a different market in 1974 when its stock was listed on the Swedish stock exchange. H&M Hennes & Mauritz introduced cosmetics in 1975 and began opening stores in London the following year. Also in 1976 the company introduced its teenage clothing stores under the Impulse banner.

By the end of the 1970s the company had moved into Switzerland (1978) and Germany (1980) and introduced baby clothes. In 1980 H&M also purchased mail-order company Rowell.

Stefan Persson took over as CEO from his father Erling in 1982. He expanded throughout northern Europe and H&M boasted 200 stores in 1985. By 1988 the company was sustaining annual sales growth rates of 25%-30% to the delight of investors. H&M saw fashion globalization coming and knew that more and more people would be dressing similarly even if they lived in different countries. At the same time however the company maintained local flavor in its stores so shoppers would feel as if they were shopping with a hometown merchant rather than a foreign company.

The firm's European expansion continued and by 1998 H&M had entered six more countries including France Austria Finland and the Benelux countries. By this time the company had also consolidated its men's women's children's and teens' stores under the H&M banner. Stefan gave up his CEO position and became executive chairman of the board in 1998. The company's purchasing director Fabian M nsson succeeded him as CEO. In 1998 and 1999 H&M began selling online first in Sweden then in Denmark and Finland.

The company moved into the US and Spain in 2000. The openings considered a success by H&M put a strain on earnings which sent the stock into a dive. Before the drop the company had the second-largest market cap on the Swedish exchange. In a move the company said was unrelated M nsson resigned and was replaced by Danish subsidiary CEO Rolf Eriksen.

In 2001 the company said it was planning to have 85 stores in the US by 2003 but it scaled back its US expansion plans somewhat in early 2002. In October founder Erling Persson died at the age of 85.

In 2004 Gap Inc. sold H&M the entirety of its German operations including ten stores which were later converted to H&M stores. That fall H&M hired fashion industry giant Karl Lagerfeld best known for his bringing back the Chanel brand for a collection of 30 pieces. The following year the Swedish retailer enlisted Stella McCartney to design a one-time women's collection of some 40 items under the label "Stella McCartney for H&M."

In November 2005 H&M opened a pair of stores in San Francisco the company's first on the West Coast. Overall in 2005 the company opened 145 stores and closed 20; new markets included Ireland and Hungary with a major expansion in Spain.

In September 2006 the company opened its first two stores in Dubai in the Mall of the Emirates as well as its first store in Southern California (in Pasadena). In 2007 the retailer expanded in Asia with stores in Hong Kong and Shanghai. In 2008 H&M added more than 230 shops worldwide. H&M also acquired a 60% share in FaBric Scandinavien AB in 2008. (The company exercised its option to buy the remaining 40% of FaBric in late 2010.)

Karl-Johan Persson —son of chairman Stefan Persson —took the helm at H&M in July 2009 when CEO Rolf Eriksen retired. Persson is a member of the board and served in the executive post responsible for expansion and business development. Also in 2009 the chain opened its first store in Russia.

Auditors: Ernst & Young AB

LOCATIONS

HQ: Hennes & Mauritz AB
Master Samuelsgatan 46A, Stockholm SE-106 38
Phone: (46) 8 796 55 00 **Fax:** (46) 8 796 55 44
Web: www.hm.com

HISTORICAL FINANCIALS

Company Type: Public

Income Statement FYE: November 30

	REVENUE ($ mil.)	NET INCOME ($ mil.)	NET PROFIT MARGIN	EMPLOYEES
11/14	20,419	2,693	13.2%	93,351
11/13	19,646	2,621	13.3%	81,099
11/12	18,170	2,537	14.0%	72,276
11/11	15,988	2,299	14.4%	64,874
11/10	15,402	2,652	17.2%	59,440
Annual Growth	7.3%	0.4%	—	11.9%

2014 Year-End Financials

Debt ratio: —
Return on equity: 41.2%
Cash ($ mil.): 1,900
Current ratio: 2.11
Long-term debt ($ mil.): —
No. of shares (mil.): 1,655
Dividends
Yield: 0.0%
Payout: 15.5%
Market value ($ mil.): 14,118

	STOCK PRICE ($) FY Close	P/E High/Low		PER SHARE ($) Earnings	Dividends	Book Value
11/14	8.53	1	1	1.63	0.25	4.20
11/13	8.45	1	1	1.58	0.29	4.18
11/12	6.42	1	1	1.53	0.27	3.98
11/11	6.25	1	1	1.39	0.31	3.87
11/10	6.74	1	1	1.60	0.41	3.79
Annual Growth	6.1%	—	—	0.4%	(11.5%)	2.6%

Hiroshima Bank, Ltd. (The) (Japan)

Few banks have deeper roots in the Hiroshima Prefecture than the Hiroshima Bank. Established in 1878 the bank serves Japan's Chugoku and Shikoku regions through more than 175 offices and 830 ATMs. Hiroshima organizes its business approach into three distinct areas: financial intermediation risk management assistance and information provision. It offers the traditional array of financial services including investment and private banking products real estate appraisal banking software venture capital support and assistance with corporate restructuring.

EXECUTIVES

President, Koji Ikeda
Auditors: KPMG AZSA LLC

LOCATIONS

HQ: Hiroshima Bank, Ltd. (The) (Japan)
1-3-8 Kamiya-cho, Naka-ku, Hiroshima 730-0031
Phone: (81) 82 247 5151 **Fax:** (81) 82 247 5234
Web: www.hirogin.co.jp

COMPETITORS

Aozora Bank
Chugoku Bank
Higo Bank
Mitsubishi UFJ Financial Group
Miyazaki Bank
Shizuoka Bank

HISTORICAL FINANCIALS

Company Type: Public

Income Statement FYE: March 31

	ASSETS ($ mil.)	NET INCOME ($ mil.)	INCOME AS % OF ASSETS	EMPLOYEES
03/15	65,986	221	0.3%	3,231
03/14	69,808	221	0.3%	3,187
03/13	75,050	184	0.2%	3,207
03/12	81,075	168	0.2%	3,274
03/11	77,165	166	0.2%	3,371
Annual Growth	(3.8%)	7.4%	—	(1.1%)

2015 Year-End Financials

Return on assets: 0.3%
Return on equity: 6.6%
Long-term debt ($ mil.): —
No. of shares (mil.): 623
Sales ($ mil): 1,094

Dividends
Yield: —
Payout: —
Market value ($ mil.): —

Hitachi, Ltd.

Hitachi which means "risen sun" is looking for a new dawn of profits from its galaxy of businesses. The company's Information & Telecommunications Systems (semiconductors servers mainframes ATMs) brings in the most revenue followed by Social Infrastructure (elevators escalators industrial machinery) and High Functional Materials (wire cables specialty steel circuit boards). Its Electronic Systems & Equipment segment includes specialized manufacturing equipment and power tools. The company is a world leader in consumer goods ranging from TVs to washing machines and in power generation equipment. Hitachi also has operations in financial services automotive systems and construction machinery.

Operations

Responding to such IT changes as cloud computing and business globalization the company announced it would merge Information & Telecommunication Systems' units Hitachi Electronics Services (HES) and Hitachi Information Systems (Hitachi Joho) to create Hitachi Systems. Effective in 2011 the combination is designed to strengthen the company's data center services business in Japan. The move follows Hitachi's efforts to focus on its most profitable segments and streamline sector management.

Financial Analysis

When the company announced fiscal 2011 results it showed improved revenue on the strength of an increase in global demand amid economic recovery and the company's restructuring and cost-cutting measures. Revenue had declined 10% the prior year due to falling demand though belt tightening in 2009 had begun to have a positive effect on net income.

Strategy

Hitachi plans to put many of its eggs in the Social Innovation basket where its Social Infrastructure unit works with its other four leading business units –Information & Telecom Power Construction Machinery and High Functional Materials –to create IT power and transportation systems for urban and industrial segments. The eggs in the basket are about 2.6 trillion in capital expenditures strategic investments and R&D spending on Social Innovation through fiscal 2014. Other targets include improving Hitachi's overall business structure and expanding globally especially in China Germany and the US.

In a move aimed at improving its ability to compete in an increasingly global marketplace in early 2011 Hitachi formed an alliance with Mitsubishi Heavy Industries (MHI) and Mitsubishi Electric Corp to spin off and integrate their hydroelectric power businesses. The joint venture 98% owned by Hitachi with 1% for each of the other partners is tentatively named HM Hydro. The companies' variable-speed technology could give them an advantage over other power players if smart grids continue to expand in global markets. The joint venture is a way for Hitachi and its partners to better compete for international projects against market leaders such as Toshiba and Voith Hydro (a joint venture between Voith and Siemens). The domestic market for hydroelectric power systems in Japan has stopped growing which has forced companies there to rely on maintenance services to stay afloat.

An increasingly competitive climate along with expected growth in the small and midsized display market prompted another alliance in this case with Sony and Toshiba. Each of the three companies will integrate their businesses in this niche under a new company to be set up and run by Innovation Network Corporation of Japan (INCJ). INCJ will hold 70% of the voting stock in the company while the remaining shares will be evenly divided among the other three companies.

As part of its strategy to refocus on its infrastructure businesses in 2012 Hitachi sold its Hitachi Global Storage Technologies (HGST) disk drive subsidiary to Western Digital in a $4.3 billion cash and stock transaction. The deal gave Hitachi a 10% stake in Western Digital and board representation along with an estimated $3.5 billion in cash. Hitachi originally planned on an IPO for HGST which became profitable in 2011 after five years of losses. HGST was not considered core to ongoing operations. Also in 2012 Hitachi's display business was folded into a new joint venture with Sony and Toshiba called Japan Display Inc. The company was launched on the same day as South Korea-based rival Samsung Display Co. Ltd. and focuses on small and midsized displays for mobile devices automotive and industrial applications.

Mergers and Acquisitions

In 2012 Hitachi announced it would buy the UK Horizon nuclear project from Germany's E.ON and RWE for $1.12 billion to build four to six new nuclear power stations. It hopes to have the first of the 1300 megawatt (MW) nuclear power plants operations by the mid-2020s. Together the plants could provide electricity to 14 million homes for more than 60 years. Hitachi along with British companies Babcock International and Rolls-Royce will use Horizon to create a strong and permanent base of nuclear skills in the UK.

HISTORY

Namihei Odaira an employee of Kuhara Mining in the Japanese coastal city of Hitachi wanted to prove that Japan did not have to depend on foreigners for technology. In 1910 he began building electric motors in Kuhara's engineering and repair shop. Japanese power companies were forced to buy Odaira's generators when WWI made imports scarce. Impressed they reordered and in 1920 Hitachi (meaning "risen sun") became an independent company.

During the 1920s acquisitions and growth turned Hitachi into a major manufacturer of electrical equipment and machinery. In the 1930s and 1940s Hitachi developed vacuum tubes and light bulbs and produced radar and sonar for the Japanese war effort. Postwar occupation forces removed Odaira and closed 19 Hitachi plants. Reeling from the plant closures war damage and labor strife Hitachi was saved from bankruptcy by US military contracts during the Korean War.

In the 1950s Hitachi became a supplier to Nippon Telegraph and Telephone (NTT) the state-owned telecommunications monopoly. Japan's economic recovery led to strong demand for the company's communications and electrical equipment. Hitachi began mass-producing home appliances radios TVs and transistors. The group spun off Hitachi Metals and Hitachi Cable in 1956 and Hitachi Chemical in 1963.

With the help of NTT the Ministry of International Trade and Industry and technology licensed from RCA (bought by General Electric in 1986) Hitachi produced its first computer in 1965. Hitachi built factories in Southeast Asia and started manufacturing integrated circuits.

Hitachi launched an IBM-compatible computer in 1974. The company sold its computers in the US through Itel until 1979 when Itel was bought by National Semiconductor and afterward through National Semi's National Advanced Systems (NAS) unit. In 1982 FBI agents caught Hitachi staff buying documents allegedly containing IBM software secrets. Settlement of a civil lawsuit required Hitachi to make payments to IBM for eight years as compensation for the use of IBM's software.

When the rising Japanese yen hurt exports Hitachi focused on its domestic market and invested heavily in factory automation in the late 1980s. But a recession at home caused earnings to fall. In 1988 the company and Texas Instruments joined in the costly development and production of 16-megabyte DRAMs. In 1989 Hitachi bought 80% of NAS giving it direct control of its US distribution.

Despite its rivalry with IBM in 1991 Hitachi began to resell IBM notebook PCs under its own name in Japan. In a major move to combat sluggish consumer electronics sales in 1994 Hitachi merged with its marketing subsidiary Hitachi Sales Corp. Hitachi used joint ventures to beef up its international presence including a 1995 agreement with India's Tata Group.

Tokyo police in 1997 began investigating Hitachi charging that the company and others had paid off a corporate racketeer. A slump in semiconductor prices coupled with the Asian economic turmoil hurt Hitachi in 1998. Etsuhiko Shoyama became president the next year replacing Tsutomu Kanai who became chairman. Hitachi posted its then-worst loss in history in 1999; the firm combined some subsidiaries and announced layoffs. It also formed a joint venture with Fujitsu to make plasma display panels. The JV was called Fujitsu Hitachi Plasma Display (FHP).

Hitachi spun off its DRAM business into Elpida Memory a joint venture with NEC that began operations in 2000. That year Hitachi launched the Internet & Network Services Group to focus on Internet business development; in 2001 it joined with NEC to develop semiconductors for LCD panels and cell phone displays.

Hitachi teamed with Sun Microsystems in 2002 in a multibillion-dollar storage software distribution and cross-licensing agreement. The company also formed a joint venture with IBM for Hitachi to acquire IBM's disk drive operations which was launched the following year as Hitachi Global Storage Technologies.

In 2002 Hitachi merged its system chip unit with that of Mitsubishi Electric to form a new company Renesas Technology.

In early 2003 the company unveiled a three-year program to reorganize its businesses known as Hitachi Plan II. The plan called for the company to exit certain businesses and to focus on targeted businesses using a process it called "future inspiration value."

In 2003 the company unveiled a finger vein authentication system for use in confirming user identities. Hitachi also increased its investment in Elpida Memory by $80 million along with NEC and added Intel as an investor in the memory semiconductor business. Intel put in $100 million. Later that year Hitachi merged Hitachi netBusiness (established 2000) with Hitachi Information Systems.

It sold its Hitachi Printing Solutions subsidiary to Ricoh in 2004. To strengthen its automotive business Hitachi merged its TOKICO affiliate with its Hitachi Unisia Automotive subsidiary consolidating the operations within the company. Hitachi also announced plans for an LCD television joint venture with Toshiba and Matsushita Electric in 2004 and a plasma television JV with Matsushita Electric in 2005. It collaborated with NEC again on forming another ALAXALA Networks to make backbone routers and switches for communications networks. Hitachi took a 60% interest in ALAXALA.

In early 2005 Hitachi assumed control of Fujitsu Hitachi Plasma Display by buying 30% of FHP from Fujitsu leaving Hitachi with 80% of the JV. That year the company sold shares in Elpida Memory reducing its ownership to nearly 20%. Hitachi launched a computer server systems business in North America as part of Hitachi America. Hitachi Plant Engineering & Construction Hitachi Kiden Kogyo and Hitachi Industries merged in 2006 along with part of Hitachi's Industrial Systems Group to become Hitachi Plant Technologies. Hitachi Mobile in which Hitachi held an equity stake of about 65% became a wholly owned subsidiary of Hitachi. Hitachi Mobile was established in 1950 to repair automobiles and to sell car parts; it later offered auto and mobile communication equipment.

Hitachi Renesas and Toshiba set up a joint-venture planning company in early 2006 to study whether the three chip makers should go into the silicon foundry business (contract manufacturing of semiconductors) together. By midyear however Hitachi concluded that such a move was not feasible under industry conditions at the time. The three chip makers along with NEC Electronics agreed on standardizing technology among them for fabricating semiconductors with features as small as 45 nanometers.

Etsuhiko Shoyama president and CEO of Hitachi since mid-2003 became chairman of the company in early 2006. EVP Kazuo Furukawa was promoted to president and CEO at the same time.

In late 2006 Hitachi took control of Clarion a manufacturer of audio and navigation systems for motor vehicles. In 2000 the company had established a joint venture with Clarion HCX and in 2004 Hitachi became Clarion's largest shareholder buying nearly 15% of the company. Through a tender offer Hitachi increased its ownership to nearly 64% spending almost 32 billion (about $260 million). The acquisition was expected to strengthen its position in the car information systems market.

Hitachi decided to exit the consumer PC market in late 2007. The company scaled back production of PCs at its factory in Toyokawa Japan to focus on manufacturing computer servers for business applications. Hitachi had previously contracted out some PC production to Hewlett-Packard. According to MM Research Institute Hitachi was eighth in the Japanese PC market with a share of only 4.5% well behind competitors Dell Fujitsu NEC and Toshiba.

The economic downturn and slow recovery forced change across Hitachi's businesses. In 2009 Renesas Technology Corp. a joint venture between Hitachi and Mitsubishi Electric merged with NEC Electronics. Yasushi Akao Renesas president took the reins as president of the merged company. It also created a joint venture with NEC Corp. and CASIO COMPUTER to compete in the growing global cell phone market.

Continuing the streamlining in 2009 Hitachi established new units designed to take advantage of synergies. It created a Battery Systems Division bringing together its work in lithium-ion batteries and a Renewable Energy & Smart Grid Division both in the Power Systems Group. The company launched a Material Resource Recycling Office in the Business Incubation Division for recycling home appliances and other products. It also merged communication subsidiaries in the US to create Hitachi Communication Technologies America.

In 2012 Hitachi sold its Hitachi Global Storage Technologies disk drive subsidiary to Western Digital in a cash and stock deal valued at around $4.3 billion. The move was part of Hitachi's plan to focus on its social infrastructure businesses.

Auditors: Ernst & Young ShinNihon LLC

LOCATIONS

HQ: Hitachi, Ltd.
1-6-6 Marunouchi, Chiyoda-ku, Tokyo 100-8280
Phone: (81) 3 3258 1111
Web: www.hitachi.co.jp

HISTORICAL FINANCIALS

Company Type: Public

Income Statement — FYE: March 31

	REVENUE ($ mil.)	NET INCOME ($ mil.)	NET PROFIT MARGIN	EMPLOYEES
03/15	81,471	1,812	2.2%	385,262
03/14	93,162	2,567	2.8%	369,116
03/13	96,087	1,863	1.9%	374,775
03/12	117,833	4,232	3.6%	369,722
03/11	112,500	2,884	2.6%	406,149
Annual Growth	(7.8%)	(11.0%)	—	(1.3%)

2015 Year-End Financials

Debt ratio: 0.2%
Return on equity: 7.7%
Cash ($ mil.): 5,848
Current ratio: 1.23
Long-term debt ($ mil.): 17,470
No. of shares (mil.): —
Dividends
Yield: 1.5%
Payout: 114.7%
Market value ($ mil.): —

	STOCK PRICE ($) FY Close	P/E High	P/E Low	PER SHARE ($) Earnings	Dividends	Book Value
03/15	68.57	1	1	0.84	1.05	5.08
03/14	74.30	2	1	0.53	0.98	5.32
03/13	57.90	2	1	0.39	1.05	4.58
03/12	64.69	1	1	0.88	0.72	4.66
03/11	51.63	1	1	0.60	0.59	3.85
Annual Growth	7.4%	—	—	9.0%	15.2%	7.2%

Hochtief AG

HOCHTIEF is a giant in Germany and beyond. In addition to doing business throughout Europe the construction-related services provider operates in the Americas and the Asia/Pacific region and is among the world's largest general builders. US subsidiaries Turner and Flatiron provide building and infrastructure construction. CIMIC (formerly Leighton Holdings) based in Australia provides engineering and construction services for the infrastructure and mining industries. The group also operates in such European countries as the Czech Republic Poland Russia and the UK. All of HOCHTIEF's businesses focus on the Americas Asia Pacific Europe and concessions.

Spanish construction group Actividades de Construcciones y Servicios (ACS) is HOCHTIEF's largest shareholder controlling more than 65% of its capital (and more than 50% voting rights). (A Qatar sovereign wealth fund sold its 10% stake in 2015; about half of that went to ACS). ACS has been building up its ownership for several years.

HOCHTIEF aims to provide services that span the lifecycle of a construction project. The company is known for building private projects such as warehouses and retail complexes. But its growing concessions and public-private partnership (PPP) division works on major federal state and municipal projects such as power plants toll roads tunnels and water treatment facilities. HOCHTIEF is continually growing and has its sights set on areas of growth especially in places where the PPP market is expanding as it is in North America. Other growth areas include the wind power market. Geographically HOCTIEF plans to expand into India.

Through its concessions division the group also is active in airport projects and it runs public buildings such as schools hospitals and prisons. HOCHTIEF AirPort has grown to become one of the world's largest independent airport managers. The division also takes ownership stakes in projects; its portfolio encompasses principal airports in Athens; Budapest Hungary; Düsseldorf and Hamburg Germany; Sydney; and Tirana Albania. HOCHTIEF in 2013 agreed however to sell its airport portfolio to Public Sector Pension Investment Board of Canada. The deal values the business at 1.5 billion Euros ($2 billion) giving HOCHTIEF about 1.1 billion Euros after its other business partners are paid. Also in 2011 HOCHTIEF sold several of its Leighton mining assets in Australia as a way to boost profit.

The company's former real estate and services divisions merged into the Europe division in 2011. The restructuring helped streamline business and save the company money. The Europe division includes HOCHTIEF Solutions which plans develops and markets large real estate properties such as hotels office buildings and retail and residential projects in Europe.

In addition to building and developing properties HOCHTIEF also makes sure those properties stay running. Its services division includes facility management and energy management providers. The division specializes in servicing the automotive industry chemical and pharmaceutical plants financial services facilities airports and health care and event facilities.

HISTORY

Brothers Philipp and Balthasar Helfmann mill and farm workers from Kelsterbach Germany started construction company Fa. Gebr. Helfmann Bauunternehmer in Frankfurt am Main in 1875. The firm primarily built houses until 1878 when it was contracted to build the university at Giessen.

In 1884 the company was made a general partnership. Projects of this era included Frankfurt's Hotel Continental and Wiesbaden's Hotel Kaiserhof. When Balthasar died in 1896 Philipp converted the business to a joint stock company and renamed it Actien-Gesellschaft für Hoch- und Tiefbauten. Three years later with new capital for expansion the company won its first contract abroad —construction of a pneumatic conveyer-equipped granary in the harbor at Genoa (its first reinforced-concrete project).

Philipp Helfmann died in 1899 but the company continued operating. The battlefields of WWI took away most of the workforce and construction slowed to a near halt. But in the years following the war the company grew. In 1921 German industrialist Hugo Stinnes began buying stakes in the company and was its major shareholder by 1923.

The company decided in 1922 to relocate to Essen closer to the Stinnes Group's operations and in 1923 it was renamed HOCHTIEF Aktiengesellschaft für Hoch- und Tiefbauten vorm. Gebr. Helfmann.

Stinnes died in 1924 and two years later his empire collapsed. But German banks helped keep HOCHTIEF alive and operating as an independent company. That year Rheinisch-Westfälische-Elektrizitätswerke AG (RWE) the electric utility that Stinnes helped create became the main shareholder in HOCHTIEF with a 31% stake.

Many of RWE's facilities were damaged during WWII including its Essen headquarters and the RWE staff used the HOCHTIEF building until 1961. Postwar reconstruction kept the company active including Germany's first nuclear reactor built by HOCHTIEF and commissioned in 1966. After the war RWE began increasing its stake in HOCHTIEF until it became the majority shareholder (56%) in 1989.

As a division of the RWE Group HOCHTIEF began acquiring former state-owned companies throughout Germany. By 1996 it had added financing and operation of major projects to its services. That year it led a consortium to build and operate an international airport in Athens. In 1997 it teamed with Ireland's Aer Rianta to build new terminals and manage the airport in Düsseldorf Germany. The next year HOCHTIEF won a bid to build and operate Berlin's new airport but a rival's allegations of bidding irregularities led to a raid by prosecutors on HOCHTIEF's headquarters. Charges were dismissed but the company was disqualified from the project.

The company sought to expand internationally with an agreement to take a 49% stake in the US holdings of its main rival Philipp Holzmann (1997). But when these plans failed and HOCHTIEF was blocked by regulators from increasing its 20% stake in the competitor (held since 1981) it lost interest and relinquished its shares.

HOCHTIEF like many of its competitors expanded abroad in 1999 by helping engineer Canadian firm Armbro's takeover of rival BFC (and then grabbing a 49% share in the merged firm now Aecon Group) and by acquiring US construction giant Turner. The company suffered a $75 million operating loss in 2000 because of a slowdown in the German construction industry and expenses related to acquisitions.

It secured a contract to build a rail tunnel under the River Thames in London in 2001. Also that year it merged its building and civil units into HOCHTIEF Construction and made plans to join former rival IVG Immobilien to bid on building Berlin's new airport Berlin-Brandenburg. HOCHTIEF reorganized in 2001 to reflect its increasingly international operations.

By 2002 Philipp Holzmann was in insolvency and HOCHTIEF initially made plans to bid on its former rival's technical services group HSG. However after reviewing the unit's prospectus HOCHTIEF withdrew from the bidding.

Longtime shareholder and German energy giant RWE sold its 56% stake in HOCHTIEF in 2004 to European and US institutional investors. It was the largest such transaction involving a German stock.

HOCHTIEF subsidiary Leighton and joint venture partner Downer EDI won a 100 million contract to build a four-lane highway in New Zealand in 2006. The project is expected to be finished in 2010.

In 2007 the company acquired the energy contracting business of Vattenfall Europe adding to its existing service portfolio of energy contracting and management operations. Also that year HOCHTIEF acquired Flatiron Construction from Royal BAM Group. That deal provided the group with entry into infrastructure PPP markets in the US and Canada.

EXECUTIVES

President and CEO Turner Construction, Peter J. Davoren, age 60
CEO Flatiron Construction, John A. DiCiurcio, age 60
CFO and Member Executive Board, Peter Sassenfeld, age 50
Chief Executive Officer CEO, Rainer Eichholz, age 60
CEO Leighton Holdings Limited, Hamish G. Tyrwhitt, age 52
CEO HOCHTIEF Solutions, Nikolaus Graf von Matuschka, age 52
COO HOCHTIEF AG and HOCHTIEF Solutions., Jos Ggnacio Legorburo, age 50
Auditors: Deloitte & Touche GmbH Wirtschaftspraefungsgesellschaft

LOCATIONS

HQ: Hochtief AG
Opernplatz 2, Essen D-45128
Phone: (49) 201 824 0 **Fax:** (49) 201 824 2777
Web: www.hochtief.com

2013 Sales

	% of total
Australia	47
Americas	32
Asia	10
Germany	8
Rest of Europe	3
Total	**100**

PRODUCTS/OPERATIONS

2013 Sales

	% of totoal
HOCHTIEF Asia Pacific	57
HOCHTIEF Americas	32
HOCHTIEF Europe	11
Total	**100**

Selected Subsidiaries and Associates

Airport
- HOCHTIEF AirPort Capital Verwaltungs GmbH & Co. KG
- HOCHTIEF AirPort GmbH

Construction Services Americas
- Flatiron Construction Corp. (US)
- HOCHTIEF Americas GmbH
- HOCHTIEF do Brasil S.A. (92%)
- The Turner Corporation (US)

Construction Services Asia Pacific
- HOCTHIEF Asia Pacific GmbH

Construction Services Europe
- DURST-BAU GmbH (Austria)
- HOCHTIEF Construction AG

Development
- Deutsche Bau-und Siedlungs-Gesellschaft mbH
- HOCTHIEF Aurestis Beteiligungsgesellschaft mbH

COMPETITORS

Acciona
Avionic Services International
Bechtel
Bilfinger
Bouygues
Cheung Kong Infrastructure
Dragados
Fluor
Heathrow Airport Holdings
KBR Building Group
PCL Employees Holdings
Parsons Corporation
Peter Kiewit Sons'
STRABAG SE
Skanska
Tutor Perini
VINCI

HISTORICAL FINANCIALS

Company Type: Public

Income Statement FYE: December 31

	REVENUE ($ mil.)	NET INCOME ($ mil.)	NET PROFIT MARGIN	EMPLOYEES
12/14	26,824	305	1.1%	68,426
12/13	35,265	235	0.7%	80,912
12/12	33,767	208	0.6%	79,987
12/11	29,928	(207)	—	75,449
12/10	27,187	385	1.4%	70,657
Annual Growth	(0.3%)	(5.6%)	—	(0.8%)

2014 Year-End Financials

Debt ratio: 32.0%
Return on equity: 11.3%
Cash ($ mil.): 3,142
Current ratio: 1.35
Long-term debt ($ mil.): 3,721
No. of shares (mil.): 68
Dividends
Yield: —
Payout: —
Market value ($ mil.): 4,974

	STOCK PRICE ($) FY Close	P/E High/Low		PER SHARE ($) Earnings	Dividends	Book Value
12/14	72.65	42	29	4.42	0.00	38.67
12/13	85.25	68	47	3.26	0.00	40.51
12/12	51.91	58	33	2.83	0.00	45.20
12/11	57.60	—	—	(2.82)	0.00	43.65
12/10	84.00	37	24	5.77	0.00	51.58
Annual Growth	(3.6%)	—	—	(6.4%)	—	(6.9%)

Hokuhoku Financial Group Inc

Short on cash and passing through the Hokuriku or Hokkaido districts of Japan? You might want to check in with this group. The Hokuhoku Financial Group's core business is banking primarily through its chief subsidiaries: The Hokuriku Bank and The Hokkaido Bank. Through both banks' approximately 325 branches the financial services group targets the Toyama Ishikawa and Fukui Prefectures. In addition to banking Hokuhoku Financial Group provides credit cards leasing services venture capital and financing products. Hokuriku Bank (founded in 1877) merged with Hokkaido Bank in 2004 to form Hokuhoku Financial Group which today operates in the Hokuriku and Hokkaido district and Tokyo Osaka and Nagoya.
Auditors: Deloitte Touche Tohmatsu LLC

LOCATIONS

HQ: Hokuhoku Financial Group Inc
1-2-26 Tsutsumicho-dori, Toyama 930-8637
Phone: (81) 76 423 7331
Web: www.hokuhoku-fg.co.jp

PRODUCTS/OPERATIONS

Selected Subsidiaries and Affiliated Companies

Hokugin Lease Co. Ltd.
Hokugin Software Co. Ltd.
Hokuriku Capital Co. Ltd.
Hokuriku Card Co. Ltd.
Hokuriku Hosho Services Co. Ltd.
Nihonkai Services Co. Ltd.
The Hokkaido Bank Ltd.
- Dogin Business Service Ltd.
- Dogin Card Co. Ltd.

The Hokuriku Bank Ltd.

Hokugin Business Services Co. Ltd.
Hokugin Corporate Co. Ltd.
Hokugin Office Services Co. Ltd.
Hokugin Real Estate Services Co. Ltd.
Hokugin Shisankanri Co. Ltd.
Hokuriku International Cayman Limited

COMPETITORS

Bank of Nagoya
Hachijuni Bank
Hokkoku Bank
Hyakujushi Bank
Mitsubishi UFJ Financial Group
Sapporo Hokuyo

HISTORICAL FINANCIALS

Company Type: Public

Income Statement

FYE: March 31

	ASSETS ($ mil.)	NET INCOME ($ mil.)	INCOME AS % OF ASSETS	EMPLOYEES
03/15	97,375	235	0.2%	5,412
03/14	107,681	264	0.2%	5,510
03/13	116,686	192	0.2%	5,569
03/12	129,578	172	0.1%	5,573
03/11	127,828	222	0.2%	5,447
Annual Growth	(6.6%)	1.4%	—	(0.2%)

2015 Year-End Financials

Return on assets: 0.2%
Return on equity: 5.2%
Long-term debt ($ mil.): —
No. of shares (mil.): 1,339
Sales ($ mil): 1,617
Dividends
Yield: —
Payout: —
Market value ($ mil.): —

Hon Hai Precision Industry Co Ltd

Hon Hai Precision Industry may be the biggest electronics company you never heard of. The company more commonly known by its trade name Foxconn is the world's largest contract electronics manufacturer. It manufactures computers consumer electronics communications and other products including connectors cable assemblies enclosures flat-panel displays game consoles motherboards servers and televisions. Hon Hai also provides design engineering and mechanical tooling services. The global company's customers include Apple Cisco Dell Nokia and Sony. Chairman Terry Gou founded Hon Hai in 1974 to make plastic switches for TVs.

Hon Hai's operations are closely tied to consumer demand for computers and consumer electronics. Because of its size the company is able to take on significant new orders in a relatively short time. The company was tapped by Microsoft in 2009 to supply Xbox consoles for the holiday shopping season shortly after Hon Hai landed the contract to provide Sony with PS3 consoles. The company's sales also increased after Microsoft released its Windows 7 operating system. It also makes several products for Apple –the iPod Nano music player the iPhone the iPad and the iMac – all products that are in greater demand during the holiday season.

After having a 30% growth rate for years in 2010 the company lowered its growth forecasts. Computer sales are predicted to slow throughout 2011 and demand for iPhones and iPads has not offset shrinking PC sales. In 2011 the company's sales were up just 11% to $113 billion and its net income rose a mere 2%.

Hon Hai has tried to expand its focus beyond consumer electronics with biotechnology nanotechnology and media content mentioned as industries the company is interested in as it tries to sustain growth. The company is also targeting the budding automotive market in China (the company makes automotive connectors) smartbooks (mini-laptops that use smartphone technology) and e-book readers for the Taiwan market. (Hon Hai already makes about 80% of e-book readers made globally including the Amazon Kindle reader.)

In another move aimed at expanding its reach Hon Hai has tried to reach a deal with Sharp which is spiraling downward along with prices for flat-panel TVs. Sharp which has had too narrow a focus on TVs in the last few years also makes displays for Hon Hai's Apple products something Hon Hai is eager to get its hands on. In 2012 Hon Hai offered to buy nearly 10% of Sharp for around $1.7 billion. But Sharp's market value plummeted as it later widened expectations for a record loss and its credit was downgraded to junk status. Hon Hai wants to renegotiate the initial deal including lowering the price and having a hand in Sharp's operations. Chairman Gou left negotiations in Japan a day early and without a deal when Sharp's management balked at the idea. Hon Hai is also looking at buying plants in Mexico and China from Sharp; the two companies are joint owners in the Sakai LCD panel factory which has been running below capacity and contributed to the losses at Sharp.

Hon Hai focuses more on internal development than growth through acquisitions stating that it had paid too much for some acquisitions. The company has expanded its product lines and design capabilities through a number of select acquisitions including Finland-based Eimo renamed Foxconn Oy which makes plastic moldings for cell phone components. It also bought Taiwan-based Ambit Microsystems for $1.1 billion; Ambit makes routers modems and networking equipment. Hon Hai has also boosted its manufacturing capacity through acquisitions such as its purchase of the PC manufacturing assets in Hungary Mexico and the US with associated logistics services from rival Sanmina-SCI which is getting out of the PC-making business.

Hon Hai subsidiary INNOLUX Display acquired flat-panel display manufacturer Chi Mei Optoelectronics through a share swap in 2010 creating a company called Chimei Innolux. Through Chimei Innolux Hon Hai will compete with big display makers in South Korea and Taiwan which dominate the market.

Outside of acquisitions Hon Hai grows organically by investing in new manufacturing facilities as it prepares to enter new markets. The company is investing about $1 billion to build a new manufacturing facility in China as part of its environmental protection technology initiative. The plant will develop and make products for the alternative energy market including LED (light-emitting diode) backlights and LCD display modules. Hon Hai subsidiary Foxsemicon is working with semiconductor manufacturing equipment maker Applied Materials to develop products for solar energy manufacturing equipment.

A spate of suicides by workers at its Shenzhen production facilities sent Hon Hai reeling in 2010. The company responded by increasing wages at its largest facilities and relocating some production facilities inland closer to the hometowns of much of the workforce. It has also hired a significant number of employees (in 2011 the number of employees rose by 85%) and restricted the number of hours that can be worked. The moves increased production costs for Hon Hai not all of which could be recouped by raising the prices charged to manufacturers. After reports of poor working conditions at some facilities Apple took heat for continuing to source products from Hon Hai.

A Hon Hai affiliate Foxconn International Holdings (FIH) has struggled after handset orders from major clients declined. The company makes handsets for companies including Nokia which are losing market share to smartphones like the iPhone and devices based on Google's Android operating system. FIH which began relocating some of its Chinese facilities in 2007 also moved some production to northern China and to India to lower costs.

In 2013 Hon Hai embarked on an extensive restructuring effort to create more nimble business units and streamline decision-making. The company may spin off one or more of its business units as part of the initiative.

EXECUTIVES

Chairman and CEO, Terry T.M. Gou
Director and President; Chairman Xin-Xi Technology Co. Inc., Tai Jeng-wu
Director and President, Lu Fang-ming
Director and President, Chien Yi-bin
Auditors: PricewaterhouseCoopers Taiwan

LOCATIONS

HQ: Hon Hai Precision Industry Co Ltd
No. 66, Zhongshan Road, Tucheng Industrial Zone, Tucheng District, New Taipei 236
Phone: (886) 2 2268 3466
Web: www.foxconn.com

PRODUCTS/OPERATIONS

Selected Products

Cable assemblies
CD-ROMs
Connectors
E-book readers
Enclosures
Flat-panel displays
Game consoles
Handsets
Keyboards
LCD (liquid-crystal display) TVs
Mobile phones
Motherboards
Personal computers
Servers
Smartphones
Switches
Tablets
Thermal products

COMPETITORS

ASUSTeK
Amphenol
BenQ
Cal-Comp Electronics
Celestica
First International Computer
Flextronics
Hosiden
Inventec
Jabil
MiTAC
Nam Tai
Quanta Computer
Sanmina
TPV Technology
Universal Scientific
Venture Corp.
Wistron

HISTORICAL FINANCIALS

Company Type: Public

Income Statement FYE: December 31

	REVENUE ($ mil.)	NET INCOME ($ mil.)	NET PROFIT MARGIN	EMPLOYEES
12/14	133,055	4,122	3.1%	0
12/13	132,534	3,577	2.7%	0
12/12	134,567	3,261	2.4%	1,290,000
12/11	113,912	2,703	2.4%	961,000
12/10	103,000	2,593	2.5%	836,000
Annual Growth	6.6%	12.3%	—	—

2014 Year-End Financials

Debt ratio: 0.5%
Return on equity: 15.4%
Cash ($ mil.): 21,444
Current ratio: 1.48
Long-term debt ($ mil.): 5,016
No. of shares (mil.): —
Dividends
Yield: 0.0%
Payout: 24.2%
Market value ($ mil.): —

	STOCK PRICE ($) FY Close	P/E High/Low		PER SHARE ($) Earnings	Dividends	Book Value
12/14	5.45	1	1	0.26	0.06	1.89
12/13	5.10	1	1	0.23	0.06	1.66
12/12	5.82	1	1	0.21	0.05	1.45
12/11	5.27	—	—	0.17	0.00	1.33
12/10	8.00	—	—	0.17	0.06	1.17
Annual Growth	(9.1%)	—	—	11.5%	1.3%	12.8%

Honda Motor Co., Ltd.(Honda Giken Kogyo Kabushiki Kaisha) (Japan)

According to Honda you might want to do your Civic duty and get Fit. Honda Motor is Japan's #2 automaker (after Toyota) and the world's largest motorcycle producer. The company's car models include the Accord CR-V Civic Element and Fit; gasoline-electric hybrid versions of the Civic and Accord; and seven models of the luxury Acura line. Honda's line of motorcycles includes everything from scooters to superbikes. The company also makes a line of ATVs and personal watercraft. Honda's power products division makes commercial and residential machinery (lawn mowers snow blowers and tillers); portable generators; and outboard motors. Almost 75% of Honda Motor sales come from outside Japan.

Geographic Reach

The company's major geographic areas are concentrated in North America (the US Canada and Mexico); Europe (the UK Germany France Belgium and Russia); and Asia (Thailand Indonesia China India and Vietnam). It also has a major presence in Brazil and Australia. Japan accounts for 24% of net sales while North America generates 45%. Asia brings in 21% and Europe 4%.

Operations

Honda's operations are divided across the segments of automobile (73% of net sales) motorcycle (14%) financial services (12%) and power product and other (2%).

Financial PerformanceHonda's revenue increased 7% from 2014 to 2015 due to increased sales across all its segments. Its net income however decreased 16% in 2015 due to additional selling general and administrative expenses resulting from increased product warranty expenses related to airbag inflators. (Note: growth rates may differ after conversion to the US dollar.)

Motorcycle segment sales grew 9% in 2015 largely due to a spike in sales in India and Vietnam. Financial services revenue grew 17% as a result of a rise in operating lease revenues and the positive effects of foreign currency translations. Automobile sales surged by 5% primarily due to the launch of new automobile models in Indonesia and India. In addition power product and other segment sales increased by 3% in 2015 resulting from positive foreign currency translation effects.

StrategyHonda is enjoying brisk motorcycle sales particularly in Asia where motorcycles are a popular mode of transportation. Motorcycle sales account for almost 15% of revenues. The company is beefing up production capacity in India to keep up with demand. Indonesia is the world's third-largest market for motorcycles (after China and India). To meet demand in 2014 Honda opened a second factory in Indonesia.Throughout 2015 the company expanded its sales of the HondaJet for the first time to South America. With the expansion into Brazil the HondaJet dealer network spans three continents and includes 11 territories spanning North America Europe and South America.

HISTORY

Soichiro Honda spent six years as an apprentice at Tokyo service station Art Shokai before opening his own branch of the repair shop in Hamamatsu in 1928. He also raced cars and in 1931 received a patent for metal spokes that replaced wood in wheels.

Honda started a piston ring company in 1937. During WWII the company produced metal propellers for Japanese bombers. When bombs and an earthquake destroyed most of his factory Honda sold it to Toyota in 1945.

In 1946 Honda began motorizing bicycles with war-surplus engines. When this proved popular Honda began making engines. The company was renamed Honda Motor Co. in 1948 and began producing motorcycles. Soichiro Honda hired Takeo Fujisawa in 1949 to manage the company so Honda could focus on engineering. Honda's innovative overhead valve design made its early 1950s Dream model a runaway success. In 1952 the smaller Cub sold through bicycle dealers accounted for 70% of Japan's motorcycle production.

Funded by a 1954 public offering and Mitsubishi Bank Honda expanded capacity and began exporting. American Honda Motor Company was formed in Los Angeles in 1959 accompanied by the slogan "You meet the nicest people on a Honda" in a campaign crafted to counter the stereotypical biker image. Honda added overseas factories in the 1960s and began producing lightweight trucks sports cars and minicars.

The company began selling its tiny 600 model in the US in 1970 but it was the Civic introduced in 1973 that first scored with the US car market. Three years later Honda introduced the Accord which featured an innovative frame adaptable for many models. In 1982 Accord production started at the company's Ohio plant.

EXECUTIVES

EVP; President Honda North America, Tetsuo Iwamura, age 64
Operating Officer; President and Director Honda Manufacturing of Alabama LLC, Takashi Yamamoto
Managing Officer; President Honda Motor Europe, Manabu Nishimae
Managing Officer; President Asian Honda Motor, Hiroshi Kobayashi, age 61
Senior Managing Officer, Sho Minekawa, age 61
Senior Managing Officer; President and CEO Honda North America Services, Hidenobu Iwata
Operating Officer; President and CEO Honda Engineering, Hiroshi Sasamoto
Operating Officer; President and Director Honda Siel Cars India, Masahiro Takedagawa
Managing Officer; President Honda Motor India, Yoshiyuki Matsumoto
Operating Officer; President Honda Motor (China) Investment, Seiji Kuraishi, age 57
Managing Operating Officer European Operations, Toshiaki Mikoshiba
Operating Officer; President Honda Aircraft, Michimasa Fujino
Operating Officer; President Honda R&D Europe (U.K.), Soichiro Takizawa
Operating Officer; COO Motorcycle Operations, Shinji Aoyama
President and CEO, Takahiro Hachigo, age 56
Chairman, Fumihiko Ike, age 63
Auditors: KPMG AZSA LLC

LOCATIONS

HQ: Honda Motor Co., Ltd.(Honda Giken Kogyo Kabushiki Kaisha) (Japan)
1-1, Minami-Aoyama 2-chome, Minato-ku, Tokyo 107-8556
Phone: (81) 3 3423 1111 **Fax:** (81) 3 5412 1515
Web: www.honda.co.jp

2014 Sales

	% of total
North America	40
Japan	28
Asia	19
Europe	5
Other region	8
Total	100

PRODUCTS/OPERATIONS

2014 Sales

	% of total
Automobiles	78
Motorcycles	14
Financial services	5
Power products & other	3
Total	100

Selected Acura Models

CSX (Canada)
MDX
RDX
RL
TL
TSX
ZDX

Selected Honda Car and Truck ModelsPassenger cars

CBR600RR
CBR1000RR
Elite (scooter)
Fury
Gold Wing
Interstate
NT700V
Nighthawk
PCX (scooter)
Ruckus (scooter)
Sabre
SH150i (scooter)
Shadow RS
Silver Wing (scooter)
Stateline
ST1300
VFR1200F

Selected ATVs

Utility ATVs

FourTrax Foreman 4x4
FourTrax Rancher
FourTrax Rancher AT
FourTrax Recon
FourTrax Rincon
Multipurpose Utility Vehicles
Big Red

Selected Personal Watercraft

AquaTrax F-15
AquaTrax F-15X

Selected Power Products

Cogeneration Units
Commercial mowers
Engines
Lawn mowers
Marine motors
Portable generators
Pumps
Snowblowers
Tillers

COMPETITORS

BMW	Kia Motors
Briggs & Stratton	Land Rover
Brunswick Corp.	Mahindra Renault
Caterpillar	Mazda
Daihatsu	Mitsubishi Motors
Daimler	Nissan
Deere	Peugeot
Exmark Manufacturing	Renault
FCA US	Suzuki Motor
Fiat Chrysler	Tata Motors
Ford Motor	Textron
Fuji Heavy Industries	Toro Company
General Motors	Toyota
Harley-Davidson	Triumph Motorcycles
Hyundai Motor	Viper Motorcycle
Indian Motorcycle	Volkswagen
Isuzu	Volvo
Kawasaki Heavy Industries	Yamaha Motor

HISTORICAL FINANCIALS

Company Type: Public

Income Statement FYE: March 31

	REVENUE ($ mil.)	NET INCOME ($ mil.)	NET PROFIT MARGIN	EMPLOYEES
03/15	111,086	4,246	3.8%	204,730
03/14	114,730	5,562	4.8%	198,561
03/13	104,981	3,902	3.7%	190,338
03/12	96,892	2,578	2.7%	187,094
03/11	107,924	6,449	6.0%	179,060
Annual Growth	0.7%	(9.9%)	—	3.4%

2015 Year-End Financials

Debt ratio: —
Return on equity: 7.8%
Cash ($ mil.): 12,266
Current ratio: 1.19
Long-term debt ($ mil.): —
No. of shares (mil.): 1,802
Dividends
Yield: 2.4%
Payout: 31.3%
Market value ($ mil.): 59,043

	STOCK PRICE ($) FY Close	P/E High	P/E Low	PER SHARE ($) Earnings	Dividends	Book Value
03/15	32.76	0	0	2.36	0.80	32.87
03/14	35.34	0	0	3.09	0.99	31.82
03/13	38.26	0	0	2.17	0.76	29.71
03/12	38.43	0	0	1.43	0.73	29.78
03/11	37.51	0	0	3.57	0.60	29.82
Annual Growth	(3.3%)	—	—	(9.9%)	7.3%	2.5%

Hong Leong Bank Berhad

One of Malaysia's largest banks Hong Leong Bank operates about 200 branches in its home country. It offers loans deposits credit cards investments and insurance to retail customers. The bank's offerings for corporate and commercial clients include loans trade financing economic research and debt capital markets services. Hong Leong Bank also provides Syariah-compliant banking services and Takaful (insurance) to Islamic customers. Its Singapore branch focuses on private banking investment banking Islamic banking treasury and asset management. The bank also has an office in Hong Kong. Started in 1905 as Kwong Lee Mortgage and Remittance Hong Leong Bank is a subsidiary of Hong Leong Group.

Hong Leong Bank has been expanding throughout Southeast Asia. In late 2008 the company established commercial banking operations in Vietnam and it created a consumer lending joint venture in China the following year; it's the first Malaysian bank to have operations in each country. Hong Leong offered nearly $1.5 billion to acquire smaller Malaysian banking company EON Capital in 2010. After initially rejecting the bid EON's board eventually accepted the buyout deal. The merger also was held up by a lawsuit filed by one of Eon Capital's largest shareholders who argued that the deal was illegal. However the lawsuit was dismissed and the deal was completed in 2011.

Auditors: PricewaterhouseCoopers

LOCATIONS

HQ: Hong Leong Bank Berhad
Level 8, Wisma Hong Leong, 18 Jalan Perak, Kuala Lumpur 50450
Phone: (60) 3 2164 8228 **Fax:** (60) 3 2164 2503
Web: www.hlb.com.my

COMPETITORS

AmBank Group	Edaran Otomobil
Bank Muamalat	Hang Seng Bank
Bank of China	Maybank
Berjaya Group	Norinchukin Bank
CIMB Group	Sime Darby

HISTORICAL FINANCIALS

Company Type: Public

Income Statement FYE: June 30

	ASSETS ($ mil.)	NET INCOME ($ mil.)	INCOME AS % OF ASSETS	EMPLOYEES
06/15	48,796	592	1.2%	0
06/14	53,048	654	1.2%	0
06/13	51,775	587	1.1%	0
06/12	49,668	518	1.0%	0
06/11	48,145	375	0.8%	0
Annual Growth	0.3%	12.0%	—	—

2015 Year-End Financials

Return on assets: 1.2%
Return on equity: 14.2%
Long-term debt ($ mil.): —
No. of shares (mil.): 1,798
Sales ($ mil): 2,081
Dividends
Yield: —
Payout: —
Market value ($ mil.): —

HSBC Bank Canada

HSBC Bank Canada is one of the largest foreign-owned banks in Canada. Through approximately 250 locations including some 140 bank branches it provides a range of commercial and retail financial services including deposit accounts loans and mortgages import and export financing equipment leasing and investment capital financing. Through subsidiaries the bank also offers brokerage services insurance mutual funds merchant banking trust services and portfolio management and investment counseling. HSBC Bank Canada is controlled by one of the largest banks on the planet UK-based financial services heavyweight HSBC Holdings.The bank's loan portfolio is dominated by residential mortgages and real estate loans to businesses and government entities. Nearly half of all the bank's loans are originated in British Columbia.HSBC Bank Canada's operations fall into four segments: retail banking and wealth management commercial banking global banking and markets and consumer finance (which is being wound down). The retail banking and wealth management segment has seen growth by providing specialized services for high-net-worth individuals and families. In commercial banking the company's growth centers around clients including small businesses and midsized Canadian companies doing business overseas. HSBC Banks Canada's global banking and markets segment is also focused on international growth offering trading and investment banking services.The final segment consumer finance provided products including mortgages loans specialty insurance and credit cards through subsidiary HSBC Financial. In 2012 as part of parent HSBC's restructuring efforts to create a leaner group HSBC Bank Canada announced plans to wind down the consumer finance segment. The decision was made after no buyer could be found for the business.The closure follows the 2011 sale of the full-service investment advisory business of HSBC Securities (Canada) to National Bank of Canada. Both divestitures reflect the group's strategy to focus on commercial banking retail banking and wealth management.HSBC Bank Canada's profits rose 14% from 2010 to 2011 as the company reported lower loan impairment charges and fee income grew. The growth was slightly offset by decreased interest income (primarily due to lower interest rates) and net trading income. The company also recorded a one-time charge for a write down in the value of investment property which lowered its other operating income by about half.

EXECUTIVES

EVP Commercial Banking; Regional President Central and Eastern Canada, Linda Seymour
EVP Personal Financial Services and Wealth Management, Margaret Willis
Co-Head Global Markets, Jason Henderson
CFO, Jacques Fleurant
President and CEO, Sandra Stuart
Chairman, Samuel (Sam) Minzberg, age 65
Auditors: KPMG LLP

LOCATIONS

HQ: HSBC Bank Canada
885 West Georgia Street, Vancouver, British Columbia V6C 3E8
Phone: 604 685-1000 **Fax:** 604 641-3098
Web: www.hsbc.ca

PRODUCTS/OPERATIONS

Selected Subsidiaries

Household Trust Company
HSBC Capit
HSBC Financial Corporation Limited
HSBC Globa
HSBC Inves
HSBC Loan
HSBC Mortg
HSBC Secur
HSBC South
HSBC Trust

COMPETITORS

BMO Financial Group
CIBC
Canadian Western Bank
IGM Financial
Laurentian Bank
National Bank of Canada
RBC Financial Group
Scotiabank
TD Bank

HISTORICAL FINANCIALS

Company Type: Public

Income Statement FYE: December 31

	ASSETS ($ mil.)	NET INCOME ($ mil.)	INCOME AS % OF ASSETS	EMPLOYEES
12/14	76,168	529	0.7%	6,150
12/13	79,241	579	0.7%	6,050
12/12	81,154	693	0.9%	0
12/11	78,418	620	0.8%	7,900
12/10	78,183	532	0.7%	8,200
Annual Growth	(0.7%)	(0.1%)	—	(6.9%)

2014 Year-End Financials

Return on assets: 0.7%
Return on equity: 12.6%
Long-term debt ($ mil.): —
No. of shares (mil.): 498
Sales ($ mil): 2,480
Dividends
Yield: 5.0%
Payout: —
Market value ($ mil.): 10,860

	STOCK PRICE ($) FY Close	P/E High/Low	PER SHARE ($) Earnings	Dividends	Book Value
12/14	21.78	18 18	1.06	1.15	8.31
12/13	23.52	20 19	1.17	1.23	9.21
12/12	25.84	19 18	1.39	1.28	10.35
12/11	25.19	20 18	1.24	1.25	9.78
12/10	23.45	23 19	1.06	1.28	8.89
Annual Growth	(1.8%)	—	(0.0%)	(2.7%)	(1.7%)

HSBC Bank Plc (United Kingdom)

EXECUTIVES

Director, Jonathan Symonds
Auditors: KPMG Audit Plc

LOCATIONS

HQ: HSBC Bank Plc (United Kingdom)
8 Canada Square, London E14 5HQ
Phone: (44) 20 7991 8888
Web: www.hsbc.co.uk

HISTORICAL FINANCIALS

Company Type: Public

Income Statement FYE: December 31

	ASSETS ($ mil.)	NET INCOME ($ mil.)	INCOME AS % OF ASSETS	EMPLOYEES
12/14	1,244,586	2,113	0.2%	68,035
12/13	1,341,390	4,123	0.3%	69,824
12/12	1,314,446	3,842	0.3%	74,190
12/11	1,279,092	3,597	0.3%	80,013
12/10	1,239,773	4,594	0.4%	77,932
Annual Growth	0.1%	(17.6%)	—	(3.3%)

2014 Year-End Financials

Return on assets: 0.1%
Return on equity: 3.9%
Long-term debt ($ mil.): —
No. of shares (mil.): 796
Sales ($ mil): 28,591
Dividends
Yield: —
Payout: —
Market value ($ mil.): —

HSBC Holdings Plc

HSBC would be a real alphabet soup if the company's name reflected its geographic diversity. One of the world's largest banking groups by assets (and the leader in customer deposits with more than $1 trillion) HSBC Holdings owns subsidiaries throughout Europe Hong Kong and the rest of the Asia/Pacific region the Middle East and Africa and the Americas. All told the company has some 6100 locations in more than 70 countries. Its activities include consumer and commercial banking credit cards private banking investment banking and leasing. Its North American operations include HSBC USA HSBC Bank Canada HSBC Bank Bermuda and Grupo Financiero HSBC in Mexico.

Operations

HSBC operates four core business segments that serve roughly 51 million customers. Its Retail Banking and Wealth Management (RBWM) division which accounted for 45% of the firm's total revenue in 2014 provides traditional banking products and services to retail customers as well as insurance investment products global asset management and financial planning services to mass affluent individuals. Commercial Banking (CMB) which brought in another 22% of total revenue provides credit and lending international trade and receivables finance commercial insurance and investments and treasury and cash management-related services to small and medium-sized enterprises (SMEs) as well as mid-market enterprises and corporations.HSBC's Global Banking and Markets (GB&M) division generated another 22% of revenues and offers financing advisory and transaction services for major government corporate and institutional clients and private investors around the globe. Its Global Private Banking (GPB) division made up the bank's remaining revenue in 2014 and provides investment services to high-net-worth individuals and families.The bank has always had a bent toward international expansion even from its inception. Founded in Hong Kong in 1865 HSBC owns all or parts of HSBC Bank plc in the UK The Hongkong and Shanghai Banking Corporation HSBC France The Saudi British Bank and Hong Kong's Hang Seng Bank. The company was also one of the first foreign banks to receive regulatory approval to incorporate in China. It owns about 20% of Bank of Communications one of the largest commercial banks in the country.Geographic ReachHSBC operates in more than 70 countries. It generates nearly 40% of its revenue from its business in Asia while operations in Europe bring in another 35%. The bank's other largest markets are in North America (10% of revenues) Latin America (10%) and the Middle East and North Africa (MENA) which brings in another 5% of its business.Financial PerformanceHSBC's revenues and profits have been trending lower in recent years mostly due to fee income declines and shrinking interest margins on loans amidst the low-interest environment.The bank's revenue fell by 3% to $94.4 billion in 2014 mostly as its net trading income from its Foreign Exchange business declined by 22% during the year on lower volatility reduced client inflows and lower net gains on security sales. The bank's interest income declined slightly with lower interest margins while its fee income also shrank by 2% on unfavorable exchange rates and lost revenue on the sale of its Panama operations in 2013. Lower revenues coupled with slightly higher employee and general and administrative expenses in 2014 caused HSBC's net income to fall by 16% to $13.7 billion despite a nearly $2 billion decline in loan impairment and credit risk provisions as its loan portfolio's creditworthiness improved. HSBC's operating cash levels also fell sharply with operations using $21 billion mostly due to lower cash earnings and cash outflows from changes in operating liabilities.

Strategy

HSBC maintained in 2015 that it would continue making moves toward emerging markets in Asia Latin America and the MENA region for long-term growth. The company believes the global economy will shift toward those markets over the next few decades –expecting those markets in particular to grow by "four-fold" by 2050 –and plans to be in place to provide them with cross-border trade and capital flow services.

Struggling to grow in the meantime HSBC has been making big cuts in under-performing global markets in recent years to free up resources for stronger investments elsewhere. HSBC in 2015 stated that it planned to reduce its risk-weighted assets by $290 billion (or 25%) while cutting up to 25000 jobs worldwide aiming to save between $4.5 billion to $5 billion by the end of 2017. In initiating its second sweeping restructuring in four years the bank in 2015 agreed to sell its Brazilian operations to Banco Bradesco for $15.2 billion not long after setting up the sale of its operations in Turkey; both sales were designed to shed some $110 billion worth of risk-weighted assets. In 2014 the bank sold its UK pensions business to ReAssure Limited part of Admin Re Group and Swiss Re Group. The company also sold off its 15.6% stake in Chinese insurer Ping An to Thailand's CP Group for $9.4 billion.In Asia HSBC sold its private banking operations in Japan to Credit Suisse in 2012. It also shut down its retail banking operations in Japan though it continues to offer corporate banking there. HSBC sold its US credit card portfolio worth some $30 billion to Capital One in 2012 and sold 195 US bank branches mainly in upstate New York to First Niagara Financial Group for £613 million ($1 billion).

HISTORY

Company BackgroundScotsman Thomas Sutherland and other businessmen in 1865 opened the doors to Hongkong & Shanghai Bank financing and promoting British imperial trade in opium silk and tea in East Asia. It soon established a London office and created an international branch network emphasizing China and East Asia. It claims to have been the first bank in Thailand (1888).

War repeatedly disrupted but never demolished the bank's operations. During WWII the headquarters were temporarily moved to London. (They moved back on a permanent basis in 1991.) The bank's chief prewar manager Sir Vandeleur Grayborn died in a Japanese POW camp. After the Communists took power in China in 1949 the bank gradually withdrew; by 1955 only its Shanghai office remained and it was later closed. The bank played a key role in Hong Kong's postwar growth by financing industrialists who fled there from China.

In the late 1950s Hongkong & Shanghai Bank's acquisitions included the British Bank of the Middle East (founded 1889; now The Saudi British Bank) and Mercantile Bank (with offices in India and Southeast Asia). In 1965 the company bought 62% of Hang Seng Hong Kong's #2 bank. It also added new subsidiaries including Wayfoong (mortgage and small-business finance 1960) and Wardley (investment banking Hong Kong 1972).

In the late 1970s and into the 1980s China began opening to foreign business. The bank added operations in North America to capitalize on business between China and the US and Canada. Acquisitions included Marine Midland Bank (US 1980) Hongkong Bank of Canada (1981) 51% of treasury securities dealer Carroll McEntee & McGinley (US 1983) most of the assets and liabilities of the Bank of British Columbia (1986) and Lloyds Bank Canada (1990).

Following the 1984 agreement to return Hong Kong to China Hongkong & Shanghai Bank began beefing up in the UK buying London securities dealer James Capel & Co. (1986) and the UK's #3 bank Midland plc (1992). In 1993 the company formed London-based HSBC Holdings and divested assets most notably its interest in Hong Kong-based Cathay Pacific Airways.

HSBC then began expanding in Asia again particularly in Malaysia where its Hongkong Bank Malaysia became the country's first locally incorporated foreign bank. The company returned to China with offices in Beijing and Guangzhou. It also added new European branches.

Latin American banks acquired in 1997 were among the non-Asian operations that cushioned HSBC from the worst of 1998's economic crises. Nonetheless The Hong Kong Monetary Authority took a stake in the bank to shore up the stock exchange and foil short-sellers.

In 1999 China's government made HSBC a loan for mainland expansion. That year the company was foiled in its attempt to buy South Korea's government-owned Seoulbank but did buy the late Edmond Safra's Republic New York Corporation and his international bank holding company Safra Republic Holdings (it negotiated a $450 million discount on the $10 billion deal after a Japanese probe of Republic's securities division caused delays).

The company unveiled several online initiatives in 2000 including Internet ventures with CK Hutchison Holdings and Merrill Lynch and bought CCF (then called Crdit Commercial de France now HSBC France). However HSBC's plans to buy a controlling stake in Bangkok Metropolitan Bank fell through before the year's end.

In 2001 HSBC agreed to pick up Barclays Bank's fund management operations in Greece. Later in response to the slowing economy it froze the salaries of 14000 employees. Argentina's 2001 peso devaluation cost the company half a billion dollars in currency conversion losses alone. Total charges pertaining to Argentina equaled more than $1 billion that year.

HSBC expanded its consumer finance operations with the purchase of US-based Household International (now HSBC Finance) in 2003.

The next year HSBC acquired The Bank of Bermuda as well as Marks and Spencer Financial Services (aka M&S Money) one of the UK's leading credit card issuers. It bought US credit card company Metris the following year.

HSBC's Latin American operations at this point were primarily in Argentina Brazil and Mexico. The company expanded its presence in Central America and the Caribbean with the 2006 purchase of Panama-based Banistmo a banking group with offices in the Bahamas Colombia Costa Rica El Salvador Honduras and Nicaragua.

HSBC asold its regional banking operations in France to Banque Populaire in 2008. The deal included eight banks with around 400 branches. Also that year the company canceled its proposed $6 billion acquisition of Lone Star's 51% stake in Korea Exchange Bank a deal that had been held up for months by an investigation by the South Korean government. HSBC cited weakened asset values in the global financial markets for the cancellation.

Beset by mortgage defaults the group closed its Decision One US-based wholesale subprime lending unit in 2007. In 2009 it shuttered its North American consumer lending business placing related portfolios (excluding credit cards) in run-off. To further reduce its exposure to consumer credit it sold a $4 billion car loan portfolio and servicing platform to an affiliate of Santander USA.

The company acquired a majority stake in Indonesian lender Bank Ekonomi in 2009 doubling its presence in the nation.

In 2010 HSBC sold HSBC Insurance Brokers to Marsh & McLennan in a £135 million ($218 million) cash-and-stock deal. As part of the transaction the companies entered into a strategic partnership under which Marsh markets insurance and risk management services to HSBC's corporate and private clients ahead of other providers.

In late 2011 the Financial Services Authority (the UK regulator of financial services providers) fined HSBC £10.3 million after it was found that salespeople at its NHFA Limited subsidiary had sold inappropriate and unsuitable five-year bonds to nearly 3000 elderly customers. HSBC which had alerted the FSA once it was made aware of the issue closed NHFA to new business that year.

EXECUTIVES

Group Chief Executive, Stuart T. Gulliver, age 55, $800,000 total compensation
Chief Executive Global Banking and Markets, Samir Assaf, age 55
Group Chief Operating Officer, Sean P. O'Sullivan
Chief ExecutiveThe Hong Kong and Shanghai Banking Corporation, Peter T. S. Wong, age 64
Group Chief Information Officer, Darryl West
Chief Executive Global Private Banking, Peter W. Boyles, age 59
Executive Director and Chief Risk Officer, Marc Moses
Group Director Finance, Iain J. Mackay, age 53
Group Head Human Resources and Corporate Sustainability, Ann Almeida, age 58
President and Chief Executive HSBC USA, Irene M. Dorner, age 60
Chief Executive Retail Banking and Wealth Management, John Flint
Chief Legal Officer, Stuart Levey
CEO Ireland, Alan Duffy
CEO Hong Kong and Regional Head Asia-Pacific HSBC Global Asset Management, Pedro Bastos
CEO HSBC Bangladesh, Francois de Maricourt
Chief Executive Global Commercial Banking, Simon Cooper
Chief Executive Latin America and the Caribbean, Antonio Losada
CEO HSBC Vietnam, Pham Hong Hai, age 41
CEO Saudi Arabia, Majed Najm
President and CEO HSBC Bank Canada, Sandra Stuart
CEO HSBC Latin America, Paulo Maia
CEO HSBC Thailand, Kelvin Tan
CEO HSBC Bank plc and CEO Europe, Antonio Simoes
EVP and General Counsel, Julie Davenport
EVP and Corporate Secretary, Karen Pisarczyk
SEVP and COO, Vittorio Severino
Chief Executive Global Commercial Banking (CMB), Noel Quinn
CEO Asset Management India, Ravi Menon
Head Asset Management Southeast Asia, Puneet Chaddha
Chairman, Douglas J. Flint, age 60
Auditors: KPMG Audit Plc

LOCATIONS

HQ: HSBC Holdings Plc
8 Canada Square, London E14 5HQ
Phone: (44) 20 7991 8888 **Fax:** (44) 20 7992 4880
Web: www.hsbc.com

2014 Income

	% of total
Asia	38
Europe	35
North America	13
Latin America	10
MENA	4
Total	**100**

PRODUCTS/OPERATIONS

2014 Sales

	% of total
Interest	54
Fees	21
Net earned insurance premiums	13
Net trading income	7
Other	5
Total	**100**

2014 Sales by Segment

	% of total
Retail banking & wealth management	45
Global banking & markets	22
Commercial banking	22
Global private banking	3
Other	8
Total	**100**

Selected Subsidiaries

Hang Seng Bank Limited (62% Hong Kong)
The Hong Kong and Shanghai Banking Corporation Limited
HSBC Asset Finance (UK) Ltd.
HSBC Bank Argentina S.A. (99.9%)
HSBC Bank A.S. (Turkey)
HSBC Bank Australia Limited
HSBC Bank Bermuda Limited
HSBC Bank Brasil S.A. - Banco Múltiplo
HSBC Bank Canada
HSBC Bank (China) Company Limited
HSBC Bank Egypt S.A.E. (95%)
HSBC Bank International Limited (Jersey)
HSBC Bank Malaysia Berhad
HSBC Bank Malta p.l.c. (70%)
HSBC Bank Middle East Limited
HSBC Bank (Panama) S.A.
HSBC Bank plc
HSBC Bank USA N.A.
HSBC Finance Corporation (US)
HSBC France
HSBC Mexico S.A. Institución de Banca Múltiplo Grupo Financiero HSBC (99.9%)
HSBC Private Banking Holdings (Suisse) S.A. (Switzerland)
HSBC Securities (USA) Inc.
HSBC Trinkaus & Burkhardt AG (80% Germany)
Marks and Spencer Retail Financial Services Holdings Limited

COMPETITORS

BBVA
Bank of America
Lloyds Banking Group
Mitsubishi UFJ

Bank of China	Financial Group
Barclays	Mizuho Financial
CIBC	Prudential plc
Citigroup	RBC Financial Group
Credit Suisse	Royal Bank of Scotland
Deutsche Bank	Standard Chartered
Intesa Sanpaolo	UBS
JPMorgan Chase	

HISTORICAL FINANCIALS

Company Type: Public

Income Statement FYE: December 31

	ASSETS ($ mil.)	NET INCOME ($ mil.)	INCOME AS % OF ASSETS	EMPLOYEES
12/14	2,634,139	13,688	0.5%	266,000
12/13	2,671,318	16,204	0.6%	263,000
12/12	2,692,538	14,027	0.5%	284,186
12/11	2,555,579	16,797	0.7%	305,984
12/10	2,454,689	13,159	0.5%	302,327
Annual Growth	1.8%	1.0%	—	(3.1%)

2014 Year-End Financials

Return on assets: 0.5%	Dividends
Return on equity: 7.3%	Yield: 5.1%
Long-term debt ($ mil.): —	Payout: 355.0%
No. of shares (mil.): —	Market value ($ mil.): —
Sales ($ mil): 96,963	

	STOCK PRICE ($) FY Close	P/E High/Low	PER SHARE ($) Earnings	Dividends	Book Value
12/14	47.23	81 67	0.69	2.45	9.91
12/13	55.13	70 60	0.84	2.40	9.66
12/12	53.07	72 52	0.74	2.50	9.48
12/11	38.10	64 39	0.91	1.95	8.88
12/10	51.04	81 61	0.72	1.70	8.35
Annual Growth	(1.9%)	— —	(1.1%)	9.6%	4.4%

Hua Nan Commercial Bank, Ltd.

EXECUTIVES

President, Teng Chen Liu
Auditors: Deloitte & Touche

LOCATIONS

HQ: Hua Nan Commercial Bank, Ltd.
No. 123, Songren Road, Xinyi District, Taipei
Phone: (886) 2 23713111 **Fax:** (886) 2 23316741
Web: www.hncb.com.tw

HISTORICAL FINANCIALS

Company Type: Public

Income Statement FYE: December 31

	ASSETS ($ mil.)	NET INCOME ($ mil.)	INCOME AS % OF ASSETS	EMPLOYEES
12/14	69,827	392	0.6%	7,034
12/13	71,012	320	0.5%	7,196
12/12	69,718	300	0.4%	7,109
12/11	63,883	276	0.4%	7,163
12/10	63,136	204	0.3%	7,161
Annual Growth	2.6%	17.7%	—	(0.4%)

2014 Year-End Financials

Return on assets: 0.5%	Dividends
Return on equity: 9.1%	Yield: —
Long-term debt ($ mil.): —	Payout: —
No. of shares (mil.): —	Market value ($ mil.): —
Sales ($ mil): 1,500	

Huaneng Power International, Inc.

Huaneng Power International is one of China's largest independent power producers. Its nearly 50 power plants in about 20 provinces have a capacity of more than 66700 MW; nearly all of the company's power is produced from coal. Huaneng Power International which is always expanding also owns Singapore's electricity retailer Tuas Power. Huaneng Power International sells power to local utilities primarily in China's coastal provinces. Huaneng International Power Development Corporation a subsidiary of the China Huaneng Group owns 36% of Huaneng Power International; China Huaneng Group 16%. Huaneng Power International was formed in 1994.

Huaneng Power International has been steadily increasing power generation through the acquisition on new power plants and in response to rapid increases in power consumption in the regions where the company operates.

In 2008 the company acquired SinoSing Power from parent China Huaneng Group. It also acquired 40% of Huating Coal Mining Group the largest coal producer in northwestern China's Gansu province.

Expanding its renewable sources in 2009 it agreed to acquire a 65% stake in Qidong Windpower.

EXECUTIVES

Chairman, Peixi Cao, age 60
President, Guoyue Liu, age 52
Chief Engineer, Yong He
VP and Chief Accountant, Hui Zhou, age 52
Vice Chairman, Guo Junming, age 50
Chaiman, Xiangdong Ye, age 48
Auditors: KPMG Huazhen (Special General Partnership)

LOCATIONS

HQ: Huaneng Power International, Inc.
Huaneng Building, 6 Fuxingmennei Street, Xicheng District, Beijing 100031
Phone: (86) 10 6322 6999 **Fax:** (86) 10 6322 6888
Web: www.hpi.com.cn

2013 Sales

	% of total
PRC power	89
Singapore	11
Total	**100**

COMPETITORS

AES	Hong Kong and China Gas
CLP Holdings	Huadian Power
China Power	Korea Electric Power
China Resources Power	Power Assets
Datang Power	

HISTORICAL FINANCIALS

Company Type: Public

Income Statement FYE: December 31

	REVENUE ($ mil.)	NET INCOME ($ mil.)	NET PROFIT MARGIN	EMPLOYEES
12/14	20,206	1,733	8.6%	37,737
12/13	22,106	1,722	7.8%	37,729
12/12	21,488	884	4.1%	36,326
12/11	21,196	187	0.9%	35,903
12/10	15,825	507	3.2%	33,811
Annual Growth	6.3%	35.9%	—	2.8%

2014 Year-End Financials

Debt ratio: 9.1%	No. of shares (mil.): —
Return on equity: 16.2%	Dividends
Cash ($ mil.): 2,031	Yield: 4.0%
Current ratio: 0.36	Payout: 1,804.6%
Long-term debt ($ mil.): 13,150	Market value ($ mil.): —

	STOCK PRICE ($) FY Close	P/E High/Low	PER SHARE ($) Earnings	Dividends	Book Value
12/14	54.17	74 41	0.12	2.21	0.78
12/13	36.25	68 46	0.12	1.19	0.73
12/12	37.15	95 55	0.06	0.26	0.64
12/11	21.02	310199	0.01	1.12	0.58
12/10	21.38	94 76	0.04	1.09	0.58
Annual Growth	26.2%	— —	30.3%	19.4%	7.8%

Husky Energy Inc.

This husky has a voracious appetite for oil. Husky Energy has emerged as one of Canada's largest oil and gas enterprises. The company's main energy assets are in Alberta and Saskatchewan although it has oil and gas operations worldwide (including in China Greenland and Libya). In 2010 it reported net proved reserves of 1.9 billion barrels of oil and bitumen and 3 trillion cu. ft. of natural gas. The firm has a 82000-barrel-per-day heavy oil upgrader (Lloydminster) and also operates 555 gas stations in Canada. Hong Kong billionaire Li Ka-shing and his flagship company CK Hutchison Holdings control Husky Energy. Li's son Victor is a co-chair of Husky Energy.

Supporting Husky Energy's strategy to expand its downstream business and become a fully integrated oil business in 2008 the company swapped a half-share in the Sunrise (oil sands) field in Alberta in return for 50% of BP's Toledo oil refinery as part of a deal that formed a major BP/Husky heavy oil production partnership. With an eye to further exploiting Canada's abundant oil sands Husky also acquired 110000 acres of oil sands leases at McMullen in the Athabasca oil sands deposit in northern Alberta for $105 million. It further added to its heavy oil assets in 2009 when it acquired properties in Alberta and Saskatchewan (producing more than 6000 barrels per day and containing reserves of 20.5 million barrels of oil equivalent) from Penn West Energy Trust.

Looking to beef up its near-term natural gas production in 2010 the company acquired assets in the Alberta Foothills adding more than 65 million cu. ft. per day of natural gas production. The deal also helped to optimize the use of its Ram River Gas Plant by providing abundant supply. In 2011 it bought conventional oil and gas assets in Alberta and British Columbia from Exxon Mobil for $860 million. The deal added about 113 million barrels of proved and probable oil equivalent reserves to Husky's portfolio.

Husky saw its revenues drop sharply in 2009 as the result of the global recession causing weak demand and lowering commodity prices. However cost-cutting measures helped the company still post a healthy net income of more that 9%. A stronger economy and higher oil prices helped to lift the company's revenues in 2010 although higher expenses trimmed net income.

To help give the company a boost as a global player in 2010 the company appointed Asia Ghosh who led Vodafone Essar from a startup to a global cellular phone player as president and CEO. Retiring CEO John Lau was reassigned to help develop the company's holdings in the Asia/Pacific region which in late 2010 was named as a major growth area (to be exploited in collaboration with CNOOC).

EXECUTIVES

CFO, Jonathan McKenzie
President and CEO, Asim Ghosh
COO, Robert J. Peabody, $700,000 total compensation
SVP Exploration, Brad Allison
Co-Chairman, Victor T. K. Li, age 51
Co-Chairman, Canning K. N. Fok, age 64
Deputy Chairman, William Shurniak, age 83
Auditors: KPMG LLP

LOCATIONS

HQ: Husky Energy Inc.
707, 8th Avenue S.W., Calgary, Alberta T2P 1H5
Phone: 403 298-7333 **Fax:** 403 298-7323
Web: www.huskyenergy.ca

2014 Sales

	% of total
United States	49
Canada	48
Other countries	3
Total	**100**

PRODUCTS/OPERATIONS

2014 Sales

	% of total
Downstream	
US refining & marketing	40
Canadian refined products	15
Upgrading	8
Midstream	
Infrastructure & marketing	28
Upgrading	9
Upstream	-
Total	**100**

COMPETITORS

BP
Canadian Natural
Devon Energy
Encana
Imperial Oil
Nexen
Shell Canada
Suncor
Talisman Energy

HISTORICAL FINANCIALS

Company Type: Public

Income Statement

FYE: December 31

	REVENUE ($ mil.)	NET INCOME ($ mil.)	NET PROFIT MARGIN	EMPLOYEES
12/14	20,804	1,086	5.2%	5,774
12/13	21,928	1,720	7.8%	5,479
12/12	22,557	2,033	9.0%	5,178
12/11	22,903	2,180	9.5%	4,726
12/10	17,143	949	5.5%	4,380
Annual Growth	5.0%	3.4%	—	7.2%

2014 Year-End Financials

Debt ratio: 12.3%
Return on equity: 6.1%
Cash ($ mil.): 1,094
Current ratio: 0.77
Long-term debt ($ mil.): 3,765
No. of shares (mil.): 983
Dividends
Yield: 0.0%
Payout: 100.0%
Market value ($ mil.): 23,305

	STOCK PRICE ($) FY Close	P/E High/Low		PER SHARE ($) Earnings	Dividends	Book Value
12/14	23.69	25	15	1.04	1.04	18.06
12/13	31.76	17	14	1.74	1.13	19.20
12/12	29.65	14	11	2.07	1.21	19.61
12/11	24.00	12	9	2.29	1.18	18.20
12/10	26.63	28	22	1.05	1.20	16.40
Annual Growth	(2.9%)	—	—	(0.4%)	(3.7%)	2.4%

Hyakugo Bank Ltd. (Japan)

Serving its primary business base in the Mie Prefecture Hyakugo Bank is a Japanese regional bank offering traditional banking services such as electronic corporate and consumer banking as well as international and securities offerings. Hyakugo Bank serves its products through more than 100 branches and 26 sub-branches and also owns foreign offices in Singapore and Shanghai. Listed subsidiaries include Hyakugo Business Service Company Hyakugo Staff Service Company and Hyakugo Property Research Company. The bank goes all the way back to 1878 when it was established as The 105th National Chartered Bank.
Auditors: KPMG AZSA LLC

LOCATIONS

HQ: Hyakugo Bank Ltd. (Japan)
21-27 Iwata, Tsu, Mie 514-8666
Phone: (81) 59 227 2151 **Fax:** (81) 59 228 2010
Web: www.hyakugo.co.jp

COMPETITORS

Aozora Bank
Iyo Bank
Mie Bank
Mitsubishi UFJ Financial Group
Shizuoka Bank

HISTORICAL FINANCIALS

Company Type: Public

Income Statement

FYE: March 31

	ASSETS ($ mil.)	NET INCOME ($ mil.)	INCOME AS % OF ASSETS	EMPLOYEES
03/15	44,462	88	0.2%	2,947
03/14	49,139	111	0.2%	2,917
03/13	50,855	100	0.2%	2,925
03/12	55,017	94	0.2%	2,923
03/11	52,349	89	0.2%	2,879
Annual Growth	(4.0%)	(0.3%)	—	0.6%

2015 Year-End Financials

Return on assets: 0.2%
Return on equity: 3.3%
Long-term debt ($ mil.): —
No. of shares (mil.): 253
Sales ($ mil): 673
Dividends
Yield: —
Payout: —
Market value ($ mil.): —

Hyundai Heavy Industries Co., Ltd.

Not afraid to play the heavy Hyundai Heavy Industries (HHI) is the world's largest shipbuilder and among the top five manufacturers in heavy industries. Started in 1972 HHI's shipbuilding division builds containerships tankers bulk/petrochemical carriers drill ships and specialty vessels. HHI also offers offshore construction and exploration services and it has expanded into robotic systems and large industrial pumps and presses. Additionally HHI makes diesel engines and engine parts for industrial and marine applications. Other HHI offerings include electric systems (circuit breakers switchgear transformers) and construction equipment (excavators forklifts and loaders).

Operations

HHI operates through several business divisions: Construction Equipment Electro Electric System Engine and Machinery Green Energy Industrial Plant and Engineering Offshore and Engineering Financial Services Oil Refining and its bread and butter Shipbuilding.

The Construction Equipment segment is capitalizing on China's infrastructure market flooded with government stimulus funding. HHI's excavators claim more than a 10% share of China's excavator market. The company operates manufacturing plants in China as well as India that position HHI to capture an increasing share of the countries' construction equipment growth.

The Offshore and Engineering business operates a 292-acre offshore yard and fabrication shop for engineering and construction of offshore oil and gas facility projects. The Industrial Plant and Engineering business works on industrial plant projects for power generation desalination and oil and gas processing and capitalizes on burgeoning work in the Middle East and South America. Despite a drop in marine engine and power engine demand pressured by the slow economy the Engine and Machinery business continues to benefit from HHI's move into China India and other developing markets.

Another small business of HHI is its Electro Electric Systems segment which manufactures and installs electrical systems in power plants locomotives subways and marine vessels. The business' performance is buoyed by the increase in replacement electrical equipment for renovating and upgrading power transformers and other facilities in North America as well as building new facilities in the Middle East and other rapidly modernizing regions.

Financial Performance

Research and development is also bolstering HHI's reach into profitable niche markets related to its established presence. Shipbuilding HHI's largest business represents roughly 35% of sales and revenues. In fiscal 2013 its net sales decreased 1% compared to 2012. The primary cause of the marginal dip in sales was a decrease in sales from its Oil Refining and Offshore and Engineering segments.

EXECUTIVES

President and COO HHI Group Planning Team, Kwon Oh-gab
President and COO, Kim Jung Rae
CEO, O.G. Kwon
Auditors: Samjong Accounting Corporation (A Member Firm of KPMG)

LOCATIONS

HQ: Hyundai Heavy Industries Co., Ltd.
1000, Bangeojinsunhwando-ro Dong-gu, Ulsan 682-792
Phone: (82) 52 202 2114 **Fax:** (82) 52 202 3432
Web: www.hhi.co.kr

2014 Sales

	% of total
Korea	86
Asia	12
North America	1
Europe	1
Total	**100**

PRODUCTS/OPERATIONS

2014 Sales

	% of total
Shipbuilding	34
Oil Refining	15
Financial Services	10
Construction Equipment	5
Offshore and Engineering	4
Engine and Machinery	3
Electro Electric Systems	3
Industrial Plant and Engineering	2
Green Energy	1
Others	23
Total	**100**

Selected Divisions Products and Services

Construction Equipment
- Excavators
- Forklifts
- Skid loaders
- Wheel loaders

Electro Electric Systems
- Low- and Medium-voltage circuit breakers
- Power electronics and control systems
- Rotating machinery
- Transformers gas insulated switchgear switchgear

Engine and Machinery
- Diesel and gas power plant engines
- Industrial and marine pumps industrial robots side thrusters
- Propellers and crankshafts
- Presses conveyor systems steel strip process lines
- Steam turbines and turbochargers
- Two-stroke diesel engines four-stroke (HiMSEN) engines

Green Energy

Industrial Plant and Engineering
- Plant equipment
- Power plants
- Process plants

Offshore and Engineering
- Floating units
- Fix platforms
- Land-based modules
- Offshore installations
- Pipelines and subsea facilities

Shipbuilding
- Containerships bulk carriers OBO carriers
- Drillships
- LNG carriers LPG carriers
- Ro-pax ships ro-ro ships pure car carriers tankers/VLCCs
- Submarines destroyers frigates
- VLCCs tankers product carriers chemical tankers

COMPETITORS

ALSTOM
Aker Solutions
BWX Technologies
Baltija Shipbuilding
Bechtel
Bharat Heavy Electricals
Caterpillar
China State Shipbuilding
China Yuchai
Crown Equipment
DSME
Doosan Infracore
Ebara
Evergreen Marine
General Dynamics
Gulf Island Fabrication
Hanjin Heavy Industries & Construction
Harbison-Fischer
Hitachi Zosen
Huntington Ingalls
KBR
Kawasaki Heavy Industries
Komatsu
McDermott
Mitsubishi Heavy Industries
Mitsui Engineering & Shipbuilding
NASSCO
Oceaneering International
Samsung Heavy Industries
Siemens Industry Automation
Stolt-Nielsen
Sumitomo Heavy Industries
Technip USA

HISTORICAL FINANCIALS

Company Type: Public

Income Statement

FYE: December 31

	REVENUE ($ mil.)	NET INCOME ($ mil.)	NET PROFIT MARGIN	EMPLOYEES
12/14	48,059	(1,617)	—	28,291
12/13	51,526	265	0.5%	27,246
12/12	51,487	921	1.8%	26,255
12/11	46,355	2,208	4.8%	24,948
12/10	33,303	3,704	11.1%	24,222
Annual Growth	9.6%	—	—	4.0%

2014 Year-End Financials

Debt ratio: 0.0%
Return on equity: (-10.9%)
Cash ($ mil.): 2,951
Current ratio: 1.08
Long-term debt ($ mil.): 6,800
No. of shares (mil.): 61
Dividends
Yield: —
Payout: —
Market value ($ mil.): —

Hyundai Mobis Co Ltd (South Korea)

South Korean auto parts giant Hyundai Mobis keeps drivers mobile with automotive modules and systems including chassis brakes air bags telematics and electronic devices. Established as a container manufacturer in 1977 the Hyundai (HMC) affiliate has since reinvented itself as a leading auto parts manufacturer supplying components in all Hyundai and Kia vehicles; other customers include BMW GM and Chrysler. The company has taken aggressive steps toward expanding beyond its Korean borders with forays into Japan China and Eastern Europe. Mobis markets its products in North America Australia Southeast Asia the Middle East and Europe.

Geographic Reach

Hyundai Mobis' main markets are Korea and China which collectively account for 70% of its total annual revenue. The US generates around 15% while the continent of Europe accounts for roughly 10%.

Operations

Hyundai Mobis has two reportable segments: auto parts (80% of total sales) and after sales services (20%).

Financial Performance

The company's net revenues increased 19% from 2010 to 2011 while its profits jumped by 11% over that same period. It was helped by a 16% surge in demand for its auto parts in Korea and a 19% increase in China.

Ownership

Kia Motors owns nearly 17% of Hyundai Mobis.

EXECUTIVES

Vice Chairman and CEO, Suk Soo Chung, age 63
Auditors: Samjong Accounting Corporation (A Member Firm of KPMG)

LOCATIONS

HQ: Hyundai Mobis Co Ltd (South Korea)
140-2 Gangnam-gu, Seoul 135-916
Phone: (82) 2 2018 5114 **Fax:** (82) 2 2018 6000
Web: www.mobis.co.kr

PRODUCTS/OPERATIONS

Selected Products

Airbags
Brake systems
Chassis modules
Cockpit modules
Wheel and deck assemblies

COMPETITORS

Autoliv
Dana Holding
Delphi Automotive Systems
Johnson Controls
Robert Bosch
Visteon
ZF TRW Automotive

HISTORICAL FINANCIALS

Company Type: Public

Income Statement

FYE: December 31

	REVENUE ($ mil.)	NET INCOME ($ mil.)	NET PROFIT MARGIN	EMPLOYEES
12/14	33,072	3,128	9.5%	8,068
12/13	32,519	3,253	10.0%	7,615
12/12	28,836	3,332	11.6%	7,085
12/11	22,693	2,608	11.5%	6,663
12/10	19,748	2,419	12.3%	6,244
Annual Growth	13.8%	6.6%	—	6.6%

2014 Year-End Financials

Debt ratio: 0.0%
Return on equity: 15.8%
Cash ($ mil.): 2,661
Current ratio: 2.20
Long-term debt ($ mil.): 1,028
No. of shares (mil.): 95
Dividends
Yield: —
Payout: —
Market value ($ mil.): —

Hyundai Motor Co., Ltd.

Hyundai vehicles run the gamut from budget cars to luxury sedans to commercial trucks. South Korea's leading carmaker Hyundai Motor produces compact and luxury cars SUVs minivans trucks buses and other commercial vehicles. Its cars are sold in 180 countries through some 6000 dealerships. Hyundai generates about half of its sales in South Korea but its vehicles are also popular in emerging markets such as China and India. The company operates a dozen manufacturing plants in China the Czech Republic India Russia South Korea Turkey and the US. It sold 3.6 million passenger cars in 2010 but only 500000 in the US where it does business as Hyundai Motor America. Hyundai also owns a 34% stake in Kia Motors.

Although South Korea accounts for half of Hyundai's sales and vehicle production capabilities the company is focused on growth in other markets. China's two plants now account for about 20% of production and construction on a third plant began in 2011. The plant a 50/50 joint venture with Beijing Automotive Industry Holding Co. Ltd. will be the company's largest in China capable of producing 400000 small and mid-size vehicles specifically designed for the Chinese market. (Hyundai's other two plants can make 300000 cars per year each). When the plant opens in 2012 Hyundai will be manufacturing 1 million cars a year in China.

Hyundai also established a second 50/50 joint venture in spring 2011 to begin making commercial trucks and buses in China. Both Hyundai and Sichuan Nanjun Automobile are investing about $275 million each to build Sichuan Hyundai a plant with an annual production capacity of 160000 units (150000 trucks and 10000 buses) starting in 2013. Sichuan Hyundai will make two types of trucks –value models sold under the Nanjun brand and higher-priced models sold under the Hyundai brand. Still the market for commercial vehicles in China is very tight and Hyundai only expects to sell 160000 trucks and buses per year by 2015 for a market share of 3%. A previous joint venture with Baotou Bei Ben Heavy-Duty Truck signed in late 2009 fell through.

To keep pace with markets in Europe Hyundai has manufacturing plants in the Czech Republic Russia and Turkey. The Russian plant opened in early 2011 and can manufacture 150000 Solaris sedans a model specifically designed to withstand Russia's cold climate. Hyundai exports another 10 models to Russia including the Elantra sedan the Sonata sedan and the Santa Fe SUV. Together the company's plants in the Czech Republic and Turkey produce about 7% of Hyundai's vehicles while all of Europe accounts for about 15% of sales.

The company is also setting up shop in Brazil to target the fast-growing Latin American market. Construction on a $600 million manufacturing plant began in early 2011 with the government providing Hyundai with free land and tax breaks. The plant will first produce a small hatchback specifically designed for the market with a goal of manufacturing 150000 ethanol flex-fuel cars per year. Currently top models for the Brazilian market include the compact i30 the Azera and Sonata sedans and the Veracruz and ix35 SUVs.

Hyundai is a leading brand in India as well trailing domestic players Maruti Suzuki India and Tata Motors. India accounts for more than 15% of the company's total production and is the company's international base for economy vehicles. Its newest compact vehicle for India the Eon launched in October 2011.

HISTORY

Hyundai Motor Company was established in 1967 and it initially began manufacturing cars and light trucks through a technology collaboration with Ford's UK operations. By the early 1970s Hyundai was ready to build cars under its own nameplate. The company debuted the subcompact Hyundai Pony in 1974 at Italy's annual Turin Motor Show.

The Pony was an instant domestic success and soon propelled Hyundai to the top spot among South Korea's carmakers. During the mid-1970s the company began exporting the Pony to El Salvador and Guatemala.

By the 1980s Hyundai was ready to shift into high gear and begin high-volume production in anticipation of penetrating more overseas markets. The company began exporting to Canada in 1983.

Hyundai introduced the Hyundai Excel in 1985. That year the company established its US subsidiary Hyundai Motor America. By 1986 Hyundai was exporting Excels for sale in the US. Sales of the Excel soared the next year so Hyundai decided to build a factory in Bromont Quebec.

But by the time the factory was finished in 1989 consumers were tiring of the aging compact car and the quality problems that came with it. Hyundai closed the plant after just four years of operation.

The company introduced its first sports car the Scoupe in 1990. The following year it developed the first Hyundai-designed engine called the Alpha. Two years later the carmaker unveiled its second-generation proprietary engine the Beta.

By 1998 Hyundai was beginning to feel the pinch of the Asian economic crisis as domestic demand dropped drastically. However the decrease in Korean demand was largely offset by exports. That year Hyundai took a controlling stake in Korean competitor Kia Motors.

In hopes of increasing its share of the Asian automotive market Daimler AG took a 10% stake in Hyundai in 2000 (sold 2004). The deal included the establishment of a joint venture to manufacture commercial vehicles as well as an agreement among Hyundai Daimler and Mitsubishi Motors to develop small cars for the global market.

In 2001 Hyundai decreased its stake in Kia Motors to about 46%.

The following year Daimler announced it would exercise its option to take a 50% stake in Hyundai's heavy truck business.

In 2004 Hyundai CEO Kim Dong-Jin was indicted in South Korea on charges that he violated campaign finance laws and engaged in managerial negligence. The charges stemmed from a general crackdown on campaign finance violations during which more than a dozen members of South Korea's parliament were either indicted or detained. Later in 2004 Kim was convicted of the charges against him and sentenced to a suspended two-year prison term.

To increase its presence in the US Hyundai completed construction of a new manufacturing plant Hyundai Motor Manufacturing Alabama in 2005. The plant's annual production was about 300000 cars.

In 2006 Hyundai's legal woes persisted when two executives were arrested as part of a Korean bribery investigation. The pair were accused of creating a slush fund that was allegedly used to fund a lobbyist who sought favors for Hyundai from the South Korean government. Officials were also investigating whether the slush fund was created at the behest of Hyundai chairman Chung Mong-Koo.

Chung then was indicted and arrested on charges that he embezzled Hyundai company cash to finance bribes for Korean government officials in exchange for corporate favors. After two months of incarceration Chung was released from jail on $1 million bail.

He was convicted early in 2007. Under Korean law Chung faced a potential life sentence but received only a three-year prison term as the judge in the case said Chung contributed hugely to the development of the Korean economy. During his trial Chung admitted some wrongdoing when he said "I admit to my guilt to some extent." However Chung appealed the conviction. Three other Hyundai officials were also convicted but they received suspended sentences. Chung's son Kia Motors boss Chung Eui-Sun also was under investigation but prosecutors did not indict him.

Later in 2007 Chung's three-year prison sentence was suspended by an appeals court with a three-judge panel citing his importance to Korea's economy. The appellate judges however required the Hyundai executive to maintain a clean record for five years to avoid prison and to fulfill a promise he made to donate $1.1 billion of his personal assets to society.

EXECUTIVES

CEO Hyundai Steel, Kang Hak-Seo
President China Operations, Choi Sung-kee, age 65
President, Kim Choong Ho
President Ulsan Plant, Yoon Gap Han
Chairman, Chung Mong-Koo, age 67
Vice Chairman, Chung Eui-Sun, age 44
Auditors: Anjin & Co. (A Member Firm of Deloitte Touche Tohmatsu)

LOCATIONS

HQ: Hyundai Motor Co., Ltd.
12, Heolleung-ro Seocho-gu, Seoul 137-938
Phone: (82) 2 3464 1114 **Fax:** (82) 2 3463 3484
Web: www.hyundai-motor.com

2010 Sales

	% of total
South Korea	49
North America	22
Rest of Asia	15
Europe	14
Total	**100**

PRODUCTS/OPERATIONS

2010 Sales

	% of total
Automotive	95
Financial services	5
Total	**100**

Selected Models

Commercial vehicles
- Aero (large city bus)
- Aero Town (medium bus)
- County (small bus)
- e-Mighty (light commercial truck)
- Super Aero City (bus)
- Universe (large coach bus)

Passenger cars
- Accent (compact coupe)
- Atos Prime (subcompact)
- Avante XD
- Azera (sedan)
- Elantra (sedan)
- Entourage (minivan)
- Equus/Centennial (premium sedan)
- Genesis (premium coupe)
- Getz (compact sedan)
- Santa Fe (SUV)
- Sonata (sedan)
- Tiburon (coupe)
- Tucson (SUV)
- Trajet (SUV)
- Veracruz (SUV)

COMPETITORS

BYD
Chery Automobile
Daihatsu
Daimler
Dongfeng Motor
FCA US
Fiat Chrysler
Ford Motor
GM Korea
General Motors
Hindustan Motors
Honda
Isuzu
Maruti Suzuki
Mazda
Nissan
Peugeot
Renault
Ssangyong Motor
Tata Motors
Toyota
Volkswagen

HISTORICAL FINANCIALS

Company Type: Public

Income Statement FYE: December 31

	REVENUE ($ mil.)	NET INCOME ($ mil.)	NET PROFIT MARGIN	EMPLOYEES
12/14	81,579	6,714	8.2%	64,956
12/13	83,019	8,122	9.8%	63,099
12/12	79,113	8,018	10.1%	59,831
12/11	67,142	6,607	9.8%	57,105
12/10	59,740	4,964	8.3%	56,137
Annual Growth	8.1%	7.8%	—	3.7%

2014 Year-End Financials

Debt ratio: 0.0%
Return on equity: 13.4%
Cash ($ mil.): 6,486
Current ratio: 1.85
Long-term debt ($ mil.): 34,487
No. of shares (mil.): 208
Dividends
Yield: 1.6%
Payout: —
Market value ($ mil.): 11,841

	STOCK PRICE ($) FY Close	P/E High/Low	PER SHARE ($) Earnings	Dividends	Book Value
12/14	56.75	— —	24.71	0.96	252.56
12/13	58.00	— —	29.90	0.86	235.97
12/12	30.15	— —	29.52	0.00	197.10
12/11	25.25	— —	24.34	0.00	153.06
12/10	27.69	— —	18.30	0.00	(0.00)
Annual Growth	19.6%		7.8%	—	—

Iberdrola SA

Holding companies nec nsk

HISTORY

The 1992 merger of two private utilities – Hidroel ©trica Espa ±ola (Hidrola) and Hidroel ©trica Iberia Iberduero –created IBERDROLA. Iberduero's forebear Hidroel ©trica Ib ©ica was born in 1901 in Spain's industrialized north; its first power plant began operations in 1904.

In 1918 Saltos del Duero began producing hydroelectric power along the Duero River. The two companies merged to become Iberduero in 1944 five years after the reign of Gen. Francisco Franco began. Neither Iberduero nor Hidrola (founded in 1907 to electrify Madrid and Valencia) grew much during Spain's isolationist years.

Hoping to make friends the US pumped money into Spain in the 1950s. As industrial production picked up both Hidrola and Iberduero completed construction on several large power plants between 1957 and 1969.

Dependent on imported oil Spain was shaken by the 1970s oil crisis. In 1975 a few months before Franco died the government began to promote nuclear energy. Both firms invested heavily in nukes but by 1984 overcapacity high building costs and inflation led the government to freeze nuclear construction. Hidrola Iberduero and other private utilities were left deeply in debt.

In the late 1980s the government arranged nuclear and hydro asset swaps to spread the debt around. Ultimately more power was shifted to the state utility Endesa. In 1992 with Endesa gobbling up smaller utilities and European deregulation in the wings Iberduero and Hidrola merged in self-defense. The result was IBERDROLA Spain's largest privately owned utility and Endesa's only real competition. IBERDROLA and Endesa stayed at odds particularly over stranded costs from the stalled nuclear program and the government's mandate that the private utilities buy Endesa's energy to repay Endesa for taking over their power plants. Finally in 1996 the government agreed to issue bonds to cover most of the debt.

IBERDROLA began piling up Latin American interests in 1992 by buying stakes in Argentina's Gas Litoral and the G emes power plant. It soon grabbed holdings in Bolivian electricity distributors Electropaz and Elfeo (1995) two Chilean utilities (1996) gas and electric companies in Brazil and a gas company in Colombia (1997).

To create a more horizontal business structure in 1995 IBERDROLA created Iberinco an engineering firm and Iberener to manage Latin American energy holdings. It formed telecom joint venture Utilitel with Telef nica in 1997 and founded data management firm Iberdrola Sistemas in 1998.

IBERDROLA agreed to cooperate with oil company Repsol on developing energy projects in 1997 a year before Spain's deregulation began. With Electricidade de Portugal and the US's TECO Energy it acquired Guatemala's Empresa El ©trica in 1998 and with Telef nica bought interests in Brazilian wireless phone companies.

In 1999 IBERDROLA took over US company Energy Works (which managed electricity buys for industrial customers) allied with German giant RWE to compete throughout Europe and made plans to exit the Utilitel venture.

IBERDROLA bought Brazilian electric distributor CELPE for $1 billion in 2000. Later that year the company itself agreed to be acquired by rival Endesa for $12.9 billion but the deal was abandoned in 2001. Also in 2001 IBERDROLA sold its Latin American telecommunications interests to Telef nica.

In 2002 the company sold controlling stakes in its Spanish water utilities (Pridesa and Ondagua) to RWE's Thames Water unit for $96 million. IBERDROLA also sold its power transmission assets to Infraestructuras de Alta Tension (INALTA) which is owned by CVC Capital Partners (75%) and Red El ©trica de Espa ±a (25%).

IBERDROLA expanded in Latin America to include electric generation and distribution companies in Brazil Bolivia Chile Guatemala and Mexico.

The company sold off noncore assets including some domestic water utility and real estate assets its Latin American gas businesses and two Chilean hydroelectric plants. Spanish construction giant ACS acquired 10% of IBERDROLA in 2006 for $2.7 billion. That year the company acquired two UK-based wind power projects with a combined power capacity of more than 20MW its first such acquisition in the UK.

IBERDROLA became a major global force in 2007 with the friendly takeover of Scottish Power for $22.5 billion. Scottish Power was the third-largest electricity distributor and largest wind power producer in the UK. In 2008in a major move into the US power market IBERDROLA acquired Energy East (now Iberdrola USA) for $4.5 billion. Iberdrola USA distributes and markets power and natural gas to Connecticut Maine Massachusetts New Hampshire and New York.

EXECUTIVES

Authorised Signing Officer, Fernando Julio Arias Coterillo
Auditors: Ernst & Young, S.L.

LOCATIONS

HQ: Iberdrola SA
Tomas Redondo, 1, Madrid 28033
Phone: (34) 91 784 2742 **Fax:** (34) 91 784 2977
Web: www.iberdrola.es

HISTORICAL FINANCIALS

Company Type: Public

Income Statement FYE: December 31

	REVENUE ($ mil.)	NET INCOME ($ mil.)	NET PROFIT MARGIN	EMPLOYEES
12/14	36,504	2,827	7.7%	28,021
12/13	45,167	3,540	7.8%	30,678
12/12	45,078	3,744	8.3%	31,338
12/11	40,935	3,627	8.9%	31,885
12/10	40,728	3,842	9.4%	31,344
Annual Growth	(2.7%)	(7.4%)	—	(2.8%)

2014 Year-End Financials

Debt ratio: 36.7%
Return on equity: 6.5%
Cash ($ mil.): 2,194
Current ratio: 0.84
Long-term debt ($ mil.): 28,339
No. of shares (mil.): —
Dividends
Yield: 5.8%
Payout: —
Market value ($ mil.): —

	STOCK PRICE ($) FY Close	P/E High/Low	PER SHARE ($) Earnings	Dividends	Book Value
12/14	26.91	78 60	0.44	1.58	6.84
12/13	25.55	64 48	0.56	1.22	7.80
12/12	21.32	55 30	0.60	0.99	7.25
12/11	24.10	70 48	0.62	0.00	7.23
12/10	30.65	69 46	0.71	2.26	7.10
Annual Growth	(3.2%)	— —	(10.9%)	(8.5%)	(0.9%)

ICICI Bank Ltd (India)

You see ICICI Bank is India's #2 bank (after State Bank of India) and its largest private bank boasting over $130 billion in assets. The bank has some 4000 branches nationwide as well as locations in about 20 other countries. The Retail banking group offers lending and deposit services to small businesses and individuals while Wholesale Banking does the same for corporate clients in India and abroad. The rural and government banking unit offers micro-loans and agricultural banking. Its International Banking unit deals with the bank's foreign operations and international trade finance-related service. The bank also offers life and property/casualty insurance through subsidiaries.

OperationsServing some 52 million customers the bank operates three core business segments: Retail Banking (30% of revenue); Wholesale Banking (30% of revenue) which serves corporate customers in India and overseas in providing working capital finance export finance trade transaction and commercial banking and foreign currency term loans; and Treasury (40% of revenue) which manages the bank's investment portfolio and includes the Proprietary Trading Group Markets Group and Asset Liability Management Group.Key subsidiaries include ICICI Prudential Life Insurance (the largest private sector life insurer in the country) ICICI Lombard General Insurance (property/casualty coverage) ICICI Prudential Asset Management (mutual funds) ICICI Securities (investment banking and brokerage) and ICICI Venture Funds Management (venture capital).

Geographic ReachWhile it operates in 17 countries ICICI generates more than 90% of its total revenue in its home country. The bank has an international presence through its ICICI Bank UK and ICICI Bank Canada subsidiaries in the UK and Canada respectively. It also has branches in the US

China Singapore Hong Kong Dubai Sri Lanka Bahrain South Africa Bangladesh Malaysia and Indonesia.Financial PerformanceNote: Growth rates may differ after conversion to US dollars. This analysis uses the company-provided financials from its 2015 Annual Report.ICICI Bank's revenues and profits have been steadily rising over the past few years mostly as its overall loan business (particularly loans to its Retail customers) has continued to grow with aggressive domestic branch expansion.The bank's revenue rose by 12% to R$613 billion ($10 billion) in fiscal 2015 (ended March) mostly thanks to double-digit interest income growth as its Retail and Wholesale loan assets grew by 10% and as interest margins ticked up slightly during the year. ICICI's fee income rose by 7% on higher transaction banking fees third-party referral fees and commercial banking fees. The bank's Treasury segment grew by 12% thanks to higher gains on government securities and other fixed income securities exchange gains on overseas operations dividend income from subsidiaries and gains on its equity and mutual fund investment portfolio.Higher revenue in FY2015 drove ICICI's net income higher by 13% to R$111 billion (nearly $2 billion) for the year. The bank's operating cash levels fell sharply during the year with operations using R$48.2 billion ($769 million) after unfavorable changes in working capital related to its investments advances deposits and other assets liabilities and provisions.

Stategy

ICICI Bank has continued to move toward digital banking channels that are quickly taking the industry by storm allowing the bank to slow expensive branch-expansion plans and cut operating costs significantly while giving customers faster access to banking services. As India's first bank to offer mobile banking (its iMobile app) and its first bank to offer money transfer via Twitter (and the second Globally) pioneering ICICI Bank had more than 100 electronic Touch Banking branches across 33 Indian cities in 2015 which allowed customers to have full 24/7 bank access without the need for a physical branch. During FY2015 it also launched its "Pockets" digital mobile wallet app which offered customers a full suite of bank and e-commerce services; as well as its "Tap n Pay" solution that enabled customers to tap their cards for fast payment transactions.But that doesn't mean it's done growing its physical branch network. Already boasting a vast network of more than 4050 domestic branches ICICI in 2015 continued to expand what is the largest branch network among private sector banks in India. It's also been expanding abroad opening its first branch in China in 2015.

Ownership

Deutsche Bank Trust owned 29% of ICICI Bank at the FY2015.

EXECUTIVES

Managing Director and CEO, Chanda D. Kochhar, age 54
Executive Director, N. S. Kannan, age 50
Executive Director, Krishnaswamy Ramkumar, age 54
President, Zarin Daruwala
Executive Director, Rajiv Sabharwal
President, Vijay Chandok
CFO, Rakesh Jha
Chairman, Mahendra Kumar Sharma, age 68
Auditors: KPMG

LOCATIONS

HQ: ICICI Bank Ltd (India)
ICICI Towers, Bandra-Kurla Complex, Mumbai 400 051
Phone: (91) 22 2653 1414 **Fax:** (91) 22 2653 1122
Web: www.icicibank.com

PRODUCTS/OPERATIONS

2015 Sales by Segment

	% of total
Treasury	39
Wholesale Banking	30
Retail Banking	30
Other Banking	1
Total	**100**

COMPETITORS

BNP Paribas
Bank of Baroda
Bank of India
Canara Bank
Citigroup
GE Money India
HDFC Bank
HSBC
ING
Industrial Development Bank of India
Punjab National Bank
Standard Chartered
State Bank of India
UCO Bank

HISTORICAL FINANCIALS

Company Type: Public

Income Statement FYE: March 31

	ASSETS ($ mil.)	NET INCOME ($ mil.)	INCOME AS % OF ASSETS	EMPLOYEES
03/15	132,079	1,958	1.5%	90,486
03/14	124,533	1,838	1.5%	94,204
03/13	0	1,769****************% 85,217		
03/12	118,759	1,502	1.3%	81,254
03/11	119,719	1,366	1.1%	79,978
Annual Growth	2.5%	9.4%	—	3.1%

2015 Year-End Financials

Return on assets: 1.5%
Return on equity: 15.2%
Long-term debt ($ mil.): —
No. of shares (mil.): —
Sales ($ mil): 14,424
Dividends
Yield: 1.4%
Payout: 43.7%
Market value ($ mil.): —

	STOCK PRICE ($) FY Close	P/E High/Low		PER SHARE ($) Earnings	Dividends	Book Value
03/15	10.36	3	0	0.33	0.15	2.34
03/14	43.80	2	1	0.32	0.13	2.20
03/13	42.90	3	2	0.31	0.12	(0.00)
03/12	34.87	—	—	0.26	0.00	2.09
03/11	49.83	—	—	0.24	0.10	2.15
Annual Growth	(32.5%)	—		8.8%	10.3%	2.1%

Idemitsu Kosan Co Ltd

As long as Japanese drive Toyotas there will be a role for Idemitsu Kosan. The company is the #2 oil refiner in Japan (behind Nippon Oil). At its four refineries in Japan (processing 640000 barrels per day) Idemitsu Kosan produces petroleum products such as gasoline and other fuels kerosene and lubricants. It markets its fuel products through a network of 4600 service stations. Idemitsu Kosan sells heavy oil and jet fuels to industries and kerosene and liquefied petroleum gas (LPG) to the residential sector. The company also has interests in oil exploration and production as well as coal and uranium. OperationsIdemitsu Kosan has three reportable segments: Its petroleum products business includes fuel oil and petrochemical products. Its petrochemical products operations consist of the basic chemicals business which jointly operates an ethylene complex with Mitsui Chemicals and the functional materials business which develops functional flexible polypropylene. The company's resources businesses is engaged in exploration activities to expand its oil reserves.In addition to its oil and gas businesses the company has a number of New Growth activities including agro-business (pesticides) and green energy (wind solar and geothermal). Idemitsu Kosan is also developing electronic materials (organic light-emitting diode luminous materials with Sony Corporation) and lithium battery development.Geographic ReachIdemitsu Kosan has offices in Africa Asia (East South East and South West) Australia Europe (including Russia) the Middle East and North and South America.Financial PerformanceIn 2012 the company's revenues increased by 18% due to increases in the prices of crude oil and naphtha significant rises in coal prices and an increase in the volume of products sold. Japan accounted for 84% of the company's revenues that year.Net income increased by 6% in 2012 thanks to higher revenues and the result of progress in streamlining activities in production sales and distribution as well as improved product margins for petrochemical products despite a contraction of margins for petroleum products.

Business StrategyTo meet increased demand Idemitsu Kosan is enhancing its petroleum products business in the growing overseas markets centered on the Pacific Rim. As part of this process in 2012 it acquired Freedom an independent Australian petroleum products distributor that sells petroleum products wholesale and operates about 40 gas stations on Australia's east coast.That year it also opened an office in China formed a joint venture in Taiwan and set up a lubricant manufacturing and sales company in Vietnam.

Idemitsu Kosan unified its ethylene production with Mitsui Chemicals in 2010 to promote efficiency.

Company Background

Pooling their LPG resources and expertise in 2006 Idemitsu Kosan merged its LPG operations with those of Mitsubishi to form Astomos Energy.

EXECUTIVES

EVP, Kenichi Matsui
EVP and Director, Kazuhisa Nakano, age 68
Managing Director, Junjiro Kuramochi
EVP, Takashi Tsukioka
Managing Director, Yasunori Maeda
Managing Director, Osamu Kamimae
EVP, Yoshihisa Matsumoto
Auditors: Deloitte Touche Tohmatsu LLC

LOCATIONS

HQ: Idemitsu Kosan Co Ltd
3-1-1 Marunouchi, Chiyoda-ku, Tokyo 100-8321
Phone: (81) 3 3213 3150
Web: www.idemitsu.co.jp

2014 Sales

	% of total
Japan	81
Asia & Oceania	10
North America	6
Europe	2
Other regions	1
Total	**100**

PRODUCTS/OPERATIONS

2014 Sales

	% of total
Petroleum products	82
Petrochemical products	13
Resources	4
Other	1
Adjustments	-
Total	**100**

Selected Subsidiaries

Apollo Service Co. Ltd.
Idemitsu Apollo Corp. (US)
Idemitsu Engineering Co. Ltd.
Idemitsu International (Asia) Pte. Ltd. (Singapore)
Idemitsu International (Europe) PLC (UK)
Idemitsu Oil & Gas Co. Ltd.
Idemitsu Oil Development Co Ltd.
Idemitsu Oita Chinetsu Co. Ltd.
Idemitsu Petrochemical Co. Ltd.
IS Electrode Materials Co. Ltd.
Munakata Shipping Co. Ltd.

COMPETITORS

Cosmo Oil
JX Holdings
JX Nippon Mining & Metals
JX Nippon Oil & Energy
SK Innovation
Showa Shell Sekiyu

HISTORICAL FINANCIALS

Company Type: Public

Income Statement FYE: March 31

	REVENUE ($ mil.)	NET INCOME ($ mil.)	NET PROFIT MARGIN	EMPLOYEES
03/15	38,587	(1,149)	—	8,829
03/14	48,779	351	0.7%	8,749
03/13	46,493	533	1.1%	8,684
03/12	52,545	784	1.5%	8,243
03/11	44,190	732	1.7%	8,201
Annual Growth	(3.3%)	—	—	1.9%

2015 Year-End Financials

Debt ratio: 0.3%	No. of shares (mil.): 159
Return on equity: (-21.3%)	Dividends
Cash ($ mil.): 941	Yield: —
Current ratio: 0.96	Payout: —
Long-term debt ($ mil.): 5,023	Market value ($ mil.): 1,435

	STOCK PRICE ($) FY Close	P/E High/Low	PER SHARE ($) Earnings	Dividends	Book Value
03/15	8.97	— —	(7.19)	0.00	32.85
03/14	10.54	— —	2.20	0.00	45.05
03/13	21.97	— —	3.33	0.00	45.71
03/12	26.72	— —	4.91	0.00	46.83
03/11	29.45	— —	4.58	0.00	40.83
Annual Growth	(25.7%)	— —	—	—	(5.3%)

Imperial Brands PLC

Auditors: PricewaterhouseCoopers LLP

LOCATIONS

HQ: Imperial Brands PLC
121 Winterstoke Road, Bristol BS3 2LL
Phone: (44) 117 963 6636 **Fax:** (44) 117 933 7430
Web: www.imperial-tobacco.com

HISTORICAL FINANCIALS

Company Type: Public

Income Statement FYE: September 30

	REVENUE ($ mil.)	NET INCOME ($ mil.)	NET PROFIT MARGIN	EMPLOYEES
09/15	38,383	2,566	6.7%	36,400
09/14	43,088	2,301	5.3%	33,900
09/13	45,631	1,512	3.3%	35,300
09/12	46,277	1,098	2.4%	37,200
09/11	45,520	2,797	6.1%	38,200
Annual Growth	(4.2%)	(2.1%)	—	(1.2%)

2015 Year-End Financials

Debt ratio: 71.5%	No. of shares (mil.): 957
Return on equity: 32.5%	Dividends
Cash ($ mil.): 3,099	Yield: 3.9%
Current ratio: 0.82	Payout: 149.6%
Long-term debt ($ mil.): 18,593	Market value ($ mil.): 99,059

	STOCK PRICE ($) FY Close	P/E High/Low	PER SHARE ($) Earnings	Dividends	Book Value
09/15	103.50	60 43	2.69	4.04	8.45
09/14	86.77	61 48	2.40	4.00	8.56
09/13	74.15	85 71	1.55	3.38	9.31
09/12	74.04	124101	1.10	3.26	9.87
09/11	67.10	39 31	2.75	2.86	11.80
Annual Growth	11.4%	— —	(0.6%)	9.0%	(8.0%)

Imperial Oil Ltd.

Imperial Oil Canada's second-largest oil integrated company behind Suncor Energy holds sway over a vast empire of oil and gas resources. Imperial is one of Canada's top natural gas producers a leading refiner and marketer of petroleum products and a major supplier of petrochemicals. It sells petroleum products including gasoline heating oil and diesel fuel under the Esso name and other brand names. The company reported proved reserves in 2013 of 3.6 billion barrels of oil-equivalent including 62 million barrels of liquids 678 billion cu. ft. of natural gas 579 million barrels of synthetic oil and 2.9 billion barrels of bitumen. Exxon Mobil owns about 70% of Imperial.

Geographic Reach

Most of the company's production comes from fields in Alberta and the Northwest Territories.

Operations

Imperial has three main segments: Upstream Downstream and Chemical. Upstream operations include the exploration for and production of crude oil natural gas synthetic oil and bitumen; Downstream operations consist of the transportation and refining of crude oil blending of refined products and the distribution and marketing of those products; and its Chemical operations consist of the manufacturing and marketing of various petrochemicals such as ethylene benzene aromatic and aliphatic solvents plasticizer intermediates and polyethylene resin.

In addition to its conventional upstream operations Imperial owns 25% of Syncrude Canada which operates the world's largest oil sands development with synthetic oil and bitumen/heavy oil end products.

The Downstream segment owns and operates three refineries. The Strathcona and Sarnia refineries process Canadian crude oil and the Nanticoke refinery processes a combination of Canadian and foreign crude oil. The Strathcona refinery operates lubricating oil production facilities. The company maintains a nationwide distribution system including 22 primary terminals to handle bulk and packaged petroleum products moving from refineries to market by pipeline tanker rail and road transport. It also owns and operates natural gas liquids and products pipelines in Alberta Manitoba and Ontario and has interests in the capital stock of one crude oil and two products pipeline companies.

Sales and Marketing

The company sells gasoline to motorists at more than 1700 primarily Esso-branded gas stations across Canada.

It markets more than 550 petroleum products throughout Canada to all types of customers. It also serves the Canadian agriculture residential heating and small commercial markets through 28 branded resellers and sells petroleum products to large industrial and commercial accounts as well as to other refiners and marketers.

Financial Performance

Imperial's revenues grew by 6% in 2013 primarily due to increased Upstream sales partially offset by lower Downstream and Chemical sales.Upstream segment revenue growth was fueled by higher production of both conventional crude oil and natural gas (as the result of the Celtic acquisition and the Horn River pilot which more than offset normal field decline) as well as priced. The improvement was partially offset by lower production of Cold Lake bitumen.Downstream segment revenues declined due to reduced refinery throughput of 426000 barrels per day in 2013 (compared to 435000 barrels per day in 2012) as well as the closing of its Dartmouth refinery. This was partially offset by increased production higher product sales and reduced maintenance activities.The chemical segment revenue decline was due to a lower volume of petrochemical sales in 2013.Imperial's net income declined by 25% in 2013 due to significantly lower industry refining margins higher Kearl bitumen project costs (as production contribution was more than offset by start-up and operating costs) lower volumes at Syncrude and a lower contribution from Cold Lake as well as an after-tax charge associated with the conversion of the Dartmouth refinery to a terminal.

Cash flow generated from operating activities decreased by $1.4 billion in 2013 primarily due to lower net income and working capital effects.

Strategy

Reorganizing its portfolio in 2014 Imperial sold its interests in assets located in Boundary Lake Cynthia/West Pembina and Rocky Mountain House in Western Canada to Whitecap Resources Inc. for C$855 million (US$785 million).

In 2013 the company converted its underperforming Dartmouth refinery to a fuels terminal. That year Imperial invested about $8 billion in capital and exploration expenditures primarily in the Upstream segment related to Celtic and Clyden acquisitions and post-acquisition investments and the advancement of the Kearl expansion and Nabiye projects. In 2012 the company entered into a $2 billion expansion of the company's Cold Lake operation in northeastern Alberta. The expansion called Nabiye will bring on additional commercial bitumen production of more than 40000 barrels per day at Cold Lake. The project (which has access to 280 million barrels of recoverable reserves) is expected to start up by the end of 2014.In 2013 the company's research expenditures were $199 million and were mainly targeted on developing technologies to reduce the environmental impact and improve bitumen recovery in the upstream segment and for supporting environmental and process improvements in the refineries as well as accessing Exxon Mobil's data worldwide.

Mergers and Acquisitions

In 2013 following the acquisition of Celtic Exploration by ExxonMobil Canada Imperial acquired 50% of Celtic from ExxonMobil Canada for $1.6 billion. A general partnership was formed to hold and operate the assets of Celtic under the name of XTO Energy Canada.That year Imperial and ExxonMobil Canada also acquired ConocoPhillips' interest in the Clyden oil sands lease.

HISTORY

London Ontario boomed from the discovery of oil in the 1860s and 1870s but when the market for Canadian kerosene became saturated in 1880 16 refiners banded together to form the Imperial Oil Company.

The company refined sulfurous Canadian oil nicknamed "skunk oil" for its powerful smell. Imperial faced tough competition from America's Standard Oil which marketed kerosene made from lighter less-odorous Pennsylvania crude. Guided by American expatriate Jacob Englehart Imperial built a better refinery and hired a chemist to develop a process to clean sulfur from the crude.

By the mid-1890s Imperial had expanded from coast to Canadian coast. Cash-starved from its expansion the company turned to old nemesis Standard Oil which bought a controlling interest in Imperial in 1898. That interest is today held by Exxon Mobil.

After the turn of the century Imperial began producing gasoline to serve the new automobiles. The horseless carriages were spooking the workhorses at the warehouse where fuel was sold so an Imperial manager in Vancouver opened the first Canadian service station in 1907. The company marketed its gas under the Esso banner borrowed from Standard Oil.

An Imperial crew discovered oil in 1920 at Norman Wells in the remote Northwest Territories. In 1924 a subsidiary sparked a new boom with a gas well discovery in the Turner Valley area northeast of Edmonton. But soon Imperial's luck ran as dry as the holes it was drilling; it came away empty from the next 133 consecutive wells. That string ended in 1947 when it struck oil in Alberta at the Leduc No. 1. To get the oil to market Imperial invested in the Interprovincial Pipe Line from Alberta to Superior Wisconsin.

The company began research in 1964 to extract bitumen from the oil sands in Cold Lake Alberta. During the 1970s oil crisis Imperial continued to search for oil in northern Canada. It found crude on land near the Beaufort Sea (1970) and in its icy waters (1972). The company formed its Esso Resources Canadian Ltd. subsidiary in 1978 to oversee natural resources production.

In 1989 Texaco (acquired by Chevron in 2001) still reeling from a court battle with Pennzoil sold Texaco Canada to Imperial. To diminish debt and comply with regulators Imperial agreed to sell some of Texaco Canada's refining and marketing assets in Atlantic Canada its interests in Interhome Energy and oil and gas properties in western Canada.

Imperial reorganized in 1992 centralizing several units and in 1993 closed its refinery at Port Moody British Columbia. It sold most of its fertilizer business in 1994 disposed of 339 unprofitable gas stations in 1995 and the next year closed down Canada's northernmost oil refinery at Norman Wells.

In 1997 Imperial announced an ambitious program to expand Syncrude's oil sands bitumen upgrading plant. In 1998 Exxon agreed to buy Mobil which had substantial Canadian oil assets. In 1999 Canada preapproved the potential merger of Imperial Oil and Mobil Canada. Later that year Exxon completed its purchase of Mobil to form Exxon Mobil.

Expanding its exploration and production assets in 2007 Imperial and ExxonMobil Canada acquired exploration rights for a development parcel in the Beaufort Sea and in 2008 in the Horn River area of northeastern British Columbia.

EXECUTIVES

Chairman President and CEO, R. M. (Rich) Kruger, $4,837,802 total compensation

SVP Finance and Administration and Treasurer, Paul J. Masschelin, age 61, $499,694 total compensation

SVP Upstream, B.P. (Bart) Cahir

VP and General Counsel, W.J. (Bill) Hartnett, $434,333 total compensation

Treasurer, David Bailey

VP Fuels Lubricants and Specialties Marketing, B.G. Merkel, $424,333 total compensation

Auditors: PricewaterhouseCoopers LLP

LOCATIONS

HQ: Imperial Oil Ltd.
237 Fourth Avenue S.W., Calgary, Alberta T2P 3M9
Phone: 416 968-8145 **Fax:** 416 968-5345
Web: www.imperialoil.ca

PRODUCTS/OPERATIONS

2013 Sales

	% of total
Downstream	70
Upstream	26
Chemical	4
Total	**100**

COMPETITORS

Abraxas Petroleum
Ashland Inc.
BHP Billiton
BP
Barnwell Industries
Canadian Natural
ConocoPhillips
Devon Energy
Dominion Resources
DuPont
Encana
Eni
Hunting
Husky Energy
Koch Industries Inc.
Marathon Oil
Murphy Oil
Occidental Petroleum
PEMEX
PETROBRAS
Petrleos de Venezuela
Pioneer Natural Resources
Royal Dutch Shell
Suncor
Sunoco
TOTAL
Talisman Energy

HISTORICAL FINANCIALS

Company Type: Public

Income Statement FYE: December 31

	REVENUE ($ mil.)	NET INCOME ($ mil.)	NET PROFIT MARGIN	EMPLOYEES
12/14	31,922	3,268	10.2%	5,500
12/13	30,967	2,659	8.6%	5,300
12/12	31,358	3,786	12.1%	5,100
12/11	30,108	3,304	11.0%	5,085
12/10	25,145	2,214	8.8%	4,970
Annual Growth	6.1%	10.2%	—	2.6%

2014 Year-End Financials

Debt ratio: 10.3%
Return on equity: 18.0%
Cash ($ mil.): 185
Current ratio: 0.60
Long-term debt ($ mil.): 4,242
No. of shares (mil.): 847
Dividends
Yield: 1.2%
Payout: 11.8%
Market value ($ mil.): 36,472

	STOCK PRICE ($) FY Close	P/E High	P/E Low	PER SHARE ($) Earnings	Dividends	Book Value
12/14	43.03	11	9	3.84	0.47	22.95
12/13	44.23	13	11	3.12	0.47	21.66
12/12	43.00	11	9	4.44	0.48	19.43
12/11	44.48	13	9	3.87	0.43	15.41
12/10	40.52	17	14	2.60	0.41	13.21
Annual Growth	1.5%	—	—	10.3%	3.4%	14.8%

Industria De Diseno Textil (Inditex) SA

Industria de Dise ±o Textil (Inditex) makes disposable chic fashions that are here today and gone tomorrow. The Spanish designer-cum-retailer uses technology and an armada of designers to master cheap chic. Inditex sells on a global scale with some 4900 shops in about 75 countries under eight different banners: Zara Oysho Massimo Dutti Pull and Bear Bershka Stradivarius Zara Home and Uterq e. Located mostly in Europe the firm's stores answer to popular trends by telling designers in Spain what customers are asking for locally. Inditex responds in about two weeks with new designs. Amancio Ortega Gaona Spain's wealthiest businessman founded Zara in 1975 and later created Inditex as a holding company.

Inditex's worldwide presence and low-price selling strategy have served it well during the global recession and the nascent recovery. Sales were up 9% (at constant exchange rates) in fiscal 2010 (ends January) after rising 12% in fiscal 2009 while those of many other retailers fell. Indeed while competitors were closing stores Inditex added about 340 new shops (an 8% increase in selling space) across its varied banners in fiscal 2010. Recent stops on the retailer's world tour included New Delhi and Mumbai India where the company has begun opening Zara stores in partnership with Trent Ltd. (part of India's Tata Group). In 2011 the partnership was extended to set up Massimo Dutti stores there.

Inditex is focusing its expansion efforts on China and in Europe in such countries as Italy Turkey France Germany Poland and Russia. The Spanish firm is growing quickly in China with some 110 shops there since entering the market in 2006. It also has more than 55 stores in Japan and about 90 others in Indonesia Malaysia Singapore South Korea Thailand and the Philippines.

More than two-thirds of the company's sales are made outside of Spain where Inditex operates more than 1900 stores. Beyond Europe Inditex operates stores in Asia the Americas the Middle East and North Africa. Inditex's US presence is slight (only about 50 Zara stores) compared to its massive European footprint. After a seemingly splashy US debut the company has decided to grow slowly there while it focused on expanding in Europe. However a deal Inditex inked in early 2011 indicates that the holding company has big plans for its Zara banner. Inditex is investing in retail space on swanky Fifth Avenue in Manhattan to be "one of Zara's most emblematic flagships worldwide." The company has agreed to pay $400 million to occupy a 32000-sq.-ft. retail space at 666 Fifth Avenue that once was an NBA store. The deal includes the purchase price plus fewer than three years left on NBA's lease.

The company's fashion-forward flagship Zara chain navigates the prevailing winds of the fickle fashion world with an army of about 1485 stores in more than 70 countries. Zara's team of more than 200 designers produces 20000 items each year. In order to respond to popular demand and draw repeat business new merchandise is sent to Zara stores twice each week. Zara controls prices through vertical integration. Indeed Zara's low prices and rapid response to fashion trends has positioned it to challenge Gap Inc. for top ranking among global clothing vendors.

Capitalizing on Zara's success Inditex has launched two brand extensions: Zara Home and Zara Kids as well as an e-commerce site for Zara Home in Europe. Zara Home which has grown to about 270 stores in some 25 countries sells home furnishings tableware and linens for the table bedroom and bathroom. Overall Zara sales account for nearly two-thirds of its parent company's total revenue.

Inditex designs manufactures and distributes garments to clothe all kinds of customers: Zara (fashion forward apparel for men women and kids) Oysho (lingerie) Pull and Bear (urban youth ages 14 to 28) Massimo Dutti (upscale fashion boutiques) and two brands targeted at young women Stradivarius and Bershka. The company's newest banner is Uterq e (launched in 2008) which sells leather goods numbers about 70 shops in 15 countries worldwide.

HISTORY

Holding company Industria de Dise ±o Textil (Inditex) got its start as Confecciones Goa in 1963 making women's lingerie and housecoats in La Coru ±a Spain.

Founder Amancio Ortega learned the rag trade as a boy when at age 13 he made deliveries for a shirtmaker. Managing a tailor shop when he was a young man Ortega spied an expensive negligee for sale and he thought he could make copies and sell them for half the price. From there he made nightshirts and pajamas before he opened the first Zara store in La Coru ±a in 1975 where Ortega began expanding his offerings for women.

Ortega formed Inditex as a holding company for his growing operations in 1985. Inditex ran nearly 100 Zara stores before venturing out of the country to Portugal in 1988. New York City and Paris stores opened in 1989.

The company created the Pull & Bear clothing chain in 1991. About that time Inditex purchased a 65% stake in the Massimo Dutti group. (Inditex owns it all now.) The group continued to open stores around the globe: Mexico in 1992 Greece in 1993 Belgium and Sweden in 1994 Malta and Cyprus in 1996 and Israel and Norway in 1997.

In 1998 Inditex opened the Berksha chain to lure young females. The company further expanded that year into Argentina Japan Lebanon the UK and Venezuela.

Inditex then acquired 90% of Stradivarius a young women's chain with about 80 stores mostly in Spain. Meanwhile that year Inditex moved into nine more countries: Bahrain Brazil Canada Chile Germany the Netherlands Poland Saudi Arabia and Uruguay.

In 2000 the company announced it would open 150 new stores in the next two years including perhaps 40 in the US. Later in the year however the company said it would hold off on US expansion to concentrate on European growth. To fuel the growth of its Zara chain Inditex floated 26% of the company in a public offering in May 2001.

Over the course of 2001 Inditex entered six new markets: the Czech Republic Iceland Ireland Jordan Luxembourg and Puerto Rico.

In 2003 the first Zara Home stores opened and Inditex entered new markets in Malaysia Russia Slovakia and Slovenia. The following year the group surpassed the 2000 store count and entered Estonia Hungary Latvia Lithuania Morocco Panama and Romania.

Early in 2005 Inditex stopped selling fur items in all of its stores worldwide. In June Pablo Isla lvarez de Tejera succeeded Jos ©Mar a Castellano R os as chief executive of the Spanish fashion giant. Castellano remained a non-executive vice chairman of the company until September when he resigned unexpectedly following a disagreement with Inditex's chairman Amancio Ortega over his failed bid for Fenosa a Spanish utility company. Castellano's departure ended a 31-year partnership between the two men.

Overall Inditex opened about 450 stores in 2005 and in the process became Europe's largest apparel retailer ahead of Sweden's H&M Hennes & Mauritz.

In February 2006 the first Zara store opened its doors in Shanghai the first Inditex shop in China.

In 2007 80% of new stores opened were located outside of Spain. Overall the group added 560 stores in some 50 countries. Also in 2007 the group's Kiddy's Class business segment combined operations with Zara Childrenswear. In October Zara Home launched an online shopping site. The online portal is a first for Inditex which has focused on the international expansion of its fashion chains.

In 2009 Inditex signed a joint venture with the Tata Group to open stores in India beginning in 2010. Also in 2009 the firm opened its first stores in Syria.

EXECUTIVES

Chairman and CEO, Pablo Isla
Auditors: DELOITTE, S.L.

LOCATIONS

HQ: Industria De Diseno Textil (Inditex) SA
Avda. de la Diputacion s/n, Edificio INDITEX, La Coruna, Arteixo 15142
Phone: (34) 98 118 5400
Web: www.inditex.es

2010 Sales

	% of total
Europe	
Spain	32
Other countries	46
America	10
Asia & other regions	12
Total	**100**

2010 Stores

	No.
Europe	
Spain	1,916
Other countries	2,006
Americas	390
Asia & other regions	595
Total	**4,907**

PRODUCTS/OPERATIONS

2010 Stores

	No.
Zara	1,483
Bershka	698
Pull & Bear	663
Stradivarius	573
Massimo Dutti	519
Oysho	422
Zara Home	272
Zara Kids	205
Uterqüe	72
Total	**4,907**

2010 Sales

	% of total
Zara	64
Bershka	11
Massimo Dutti	7
Pull & Bear	7
Stradivarius	6
Oysho	3
Zara Home	2
Uterqüe	-
Total	**100**

COMPETITORS

Adolfo Domnguez
Arcadia
Benetton
Carrefour
Cortefiel
Diesel SpA
El Corte Ingl©s
Fast Retailing
French Connection
H&M
IKEA
Kering
L Brands
LVMH
NEXT plc
Prada
Selfridges
The Gap

HISTORICAL FINANCIALS

Company Type: Public

Income Statement FYE: January 31

	REVENUE ($ mil.)	NET INCOME ($ mil.)	NET PROFIT MARGIN	EMPLOYEES
01/15	20,563	2,838	13.8%	137,054
01/14	22,657	3,220	14.2%	128,313
01/13	21,613	3,199	14.8%	120,314
01/12	18,180	2,546	14.0%	109,512
01/11	17,128	2,368	13.8%	100,138
Annual Growth	4.7%	4.6%	—	8.2%

2015 Year-End Financials

Debt ratio: 0.0%
Return on equity: 25.4%
Cash ($ mil.): 4,310
Current ratio: 1.90
Long-term debt ($ mil.): 2
No. of shares (mil.): —
Dividends
Yield: 0.0%
Payout: —
Market value ($ mil.): —

	STOCK PRICE ($) FY Close	P/E High/Low	PER SHARE ($) Earnings	Dividends	Book Value
01/15	14.70	32 14	0.91	0.21	3.80
01/14	29.79	43 33	1.03	0.44	4.02
01/13	27.90	39 23	1.03	0.35	3.67
01/12	17.45	30 22	0.82	0.35	3.14
01/11	15.05	32 20	0.76	0.24	2.80
Annual Growth	(0.6%)	— —	4.6%	(3.9%)	7.9%

Industrial Alliance Insurance & Financial Services Inc

Industrial Alliance Insurance and Financial Services covers all of Canada with its individual and group insurance savings and retirement products. The company sells life health and disability insurance as well as retirement savings plans and annuities to individuals and employers across the country. To a much lesser extent it offers life insurance products in parts of the US. The company manages mutual funds through its IA Clarington unit and it brokers securities and funds through Investia FundEX Investments and Industrial Alliance

Securities. Industrial Alliance also sells auto and homeowners insurance. Its products are distributed by some 17500 agents across Canada.

Financial Performance

Because it straddles both general insurance and financial services Industrial Alliance measures growth both in its premium revenues and the assets it has under administration. Both measurements have generally reflected positive growth.

Strategy

Industrial Alliance worked to diversify its product offerings and geographical presence and it's been largely successful on both fronts through acquisitions and organic growth. Historically limited to the Quebec market the firm has expanded its services into every Canadian province and is now making more than half its sales outside of Quebec. It has augmented its financial services and wealth management offerings through acquisitions.

Industrial Alliance has moved into new insurance coverage niches. Through acquisitions it entered the individual disability and health insurance markets. Used car insurance is a non-glamorous niche that IA has snuggled into through the acquisition of National Warranties MRVW and three Quebec-based specialty insurers that offer creditor insurance and replacement warranty products to car dealers

While the US contributes only a small fraction to Industrial Alliance's revenues the company is intent on establishing a solid base to the south. Through careful acquisitions it has built up life insurance holdings in the US with increased distribution through its IA American Life Insurance Company.

Mergers and Acquisitions

To further grow its financial services offerings the company acquired CTL Corporation a subprime auto lender operating across Canada in 2015. That deal broadens the products Industrial Alliance offers through car dealerships.

Company Background

Founded in 1892 the insurer converted from a mutual to a public company in 2000.

EXECUTIVES

SVP Group Insurance, Jacques Parent
President and CEO, Yvon Charest
President Investia, Louis H. DeConinck
EVP and Chief Actuary, Ren @Chabot
EVP and Chief Investments Officer, Michel Tremblay
Auditors: Deloitte LLP

LOCATIONS

HQ: Industrial Alliance Insurance & Financial Services Inc
1080 Grande Allee West, P.O. Box 1907, Station Terminus, Quebec City, Quebec G1K 7M3
Phone: 418 780-5945 **Fax:** 418 684-5192
Web: www.inalco.com

PRODUCTS/OPERATIONS

Selected Acquisitions

COMPETITORS

AEGON
CPP Investment Board
Canada Life
Desjardins Financial Security
E-L Financial
Great-West Lifeco
ING
Manulife Financial
Power Financial
RBC Insurance
Standard Life
Sun Life
Wawanesa Mutual

HISTORICAL FINANCIALS

Company Type: Public

Income Statement FYE: December 31

	ASSETS ($ mil.)	NET INCOME ($ mil.)	INCOME AS % OF ASSETS	EMPLOYEES
12/14	43,470	373	0.9%	0
12/13	41,407	362	0.9%	6,317
12/12	41,974	343	0.8%	6,152
12/11	36,703	124	0.3%	4,109
12/10	34,180	276	0.8%	3,756
Annual Growth	6.2%	7.8%	—	—

2014 Year-End Financials

Return on assets: 0.9%
Return on equity: 11.3%
Long-term debt ($ mil.): —
No. of shares (mil.): 100
Sales ($ mil): 8,359
Dividends
Yield: 0.0%
Payout: 26.7%
Market value ($ mil.): 4,383

	STOCK PRICE ($) FY Close	P/E High/Low		PER SHARE ($) Earnings	Dividends	Book Value
12/14	43.49	10	9	3.43	0.92	33.72
12/13	44.56	13	8	3.36	0.92	34.72
12/12	30.43	9	7	3.33	0.99	36.41
12/11	26.39	34	22	1.16	0.96	30.10
12/10	35.41	12	11	2.94	0.98	30.21
Annual Growth	5.3%	—	—	3.9%	(1.7%)	2.8%

Industrial and Commercial Bank of China (Asia) Limited

National commercial banks nsk

EXECUTIVES

Chief Executive Officer, Aiping Chen
Auditors: KPMG

LOCATIONS

HQ: Industrial and Commercial Bank of China (Asia) Limited
33/F., ICBC Tower, 3 Garden Road, Central,
Phone: (852) 2588 1188 **Fax:** (852) 2805 1166
Web: www.icbcasia.com

HISTORICAL FINANCIALS

Company Type: Public

Income Statement FYE: December 31

	ASSETS ($ mil.)	NET INCOME ($ mil.)	INCOME AS % OF ASSETS	EMPLOYEES
12/14	87,762	821	0.9%	2,395
12/13	73,480	677	0.9%	2,317
12/12	54,914	517	0.9%	1,845
12/11	52,131	405	0.8%	0
12/10	34,343	386	1.1%	1,543
Annual Growth	26.4%	20.7%	—	11.6%

2014 Year-End Financials

Return on assets: 1.0%
Return on equity: 13.2%
Long-term debt ($ mil.): —
No. of shares (mil.): 2,064
Sales ($ mil): 2,517
Dividends
Yield: —
Payout: —
Market value ($ mil.): —

Industrial and Commercial Bank of China Ltd

Boasting assets of roughly $3.35 trillion Industrial and Commercial Bank of China (ICBC) is one of China's biggest banks –and one of the largest in the world. The bank provides corporate retail and investment banking as well as asset management trust financial leasing insurance and other financial services to more than 5 million corporate clients and some 465 million individuals through 17000-plus branches across China and nearly 400 overseas branches and offices in more than 40 countries in six continents. The Chinese government controls about 70% of ICBC.

OperationsICBC operates three business segments. Corporate Banking which brings in nearly 50% of the bank's total operating income provides traditional banking products institutional and international banking settlement and cash management services trade finance investment banking underwriting asset trading and various other financial services to corporations. Its Personal Banking division makes up around 40% of the bank's total revenue and provides deposit and loan products as well as private banking services to individuals. Its Treasury operations (nearly 10% of total revenues) manage the bank's money market and investment securities.

In addition to these divisions the bank also provides wealth management asset custody and pension services and has a Metal business Franchise Treasury business and Asset Securitization business. ICBC owns most of Bank Halim Indonesia a majority stake in South Africa-based Standard Bank Group and an approximately 80% stake in ICBC (Macau). The company also has an 80% stake in Bank of East Asia's Canadian unit –now ICBC (Canada).Altogether the bank made 84% of its total revenue from interest income in 2014 (mostly from loans and advances followed by investment interest) while 14% came from fee and commission income.Geographic ReachThe bank generates roughly 95% of its revenues from China while the remainder comes from 40 other countries.Sales and MarketingThe bank reaches its large customer base through its massive branch network and more than 2000 correspondent banks worldwide. It also offers its services through its E-Banking network via internet and telephone banking and self-service banking centers.Financial PerformanceNote: Growth rates may differ after conversion to US dollars.ICBC's revenues and profits have risen at a healthy clip over the past few years mostly thanks to its fast-growing client base double-digit loan business growth and the doubling of its net fee and commission income from other services since 2010. The bank's revenue jumped by 11% to C¥1015.4 billion (around $165 billion) in 2014 thanks mostly to higher interest income on double-digit growth of its loan and advances asset balances. The banks interest income on investments also increased thanks to a high-yield bond investment opportunity while fee and commission income grew thanks to the bank's growing card private banking and wealth management businesses. The boost in revenue coupled with strong cost controls also pushed the bank's net income higher by 5% to C¥276 billion ($44.8 billion). The bank's operating cash rose sharply to C¥201 billion ($32.7 billion) thanks to higher cash earnings mostly after adjusting for a $18 billion increase in non-cash impairment losses on loans and advances to customers.

Stategy

ICBC reiterated in 2015 its core plans for growth which included: focusing on product innovation and bolstering its service lines; diversifying its operations; continuing its aggressive global expansion plans; and continuing to invest in IT-based banking developments. Although it doesn't have the international presence of fellow Chinese group Bank of China ICBC has had its eyes on growth abroad over the past few years. In 2015 the bank's acquisitions expanded its business into Turkey as well as in several new locations in the UK US Japan and the UAE. And during 2014 the bank expanded its global reach in opening its businesses in New Zealand opening new branches in Kuwait and London and obtaining regulatory approval for its Yangon branch and Mexico subsidiary.Mergers and AcquisitionsIn May 2015 expanding its operations into Turkey for the first time ICBC bought a 75.5% stake in Tekstilbank from GSD Holding AS making it the first business institution operating in Turkey by a Chinese Bank.In February 2015 with its eye on global expansion ICBC purchased a controlling 60% stake in Standard Bank PLC from Standard Bank Group Limited for $690 million. The joint-venture deal boasted operations in London New York Singapore Dubai Tokyo Hong Kong and Shanghai and would provide trading services in commodities foreign exchange interest rates credit and equities to clients worldwide.In 2012 ICBC purchased a majority of the Bank of East Asia's US operations including more than a dozen bank branches in New York and California. The deal marked the first time that a US retail bank was acquired by a Chinese company.

Company Background

ICBC ventured into the US broker-dealer business in 2010 when it acquired the Prime Dealer Services unit of Fortis Securities from BNP Paribas.

EXECUTIVES

Vice Chairman Executive Director and President, Yi Huiman, age 51
Chief Risk Officer, Wei Guoxiong, age 60
SEVP, Zhang Hongli
SEVP, Wang Xiquan
SEVP, Zheng Wanchun
SEVP, Gu Shu
SEVP, Wang Jingdong
CIO, Lin Xiaoxuan
Chairman and Executive Director, Jiang Jianqing, age 62
Chairman, Zhao Lin
Auditors: KPMG Huazhen (Special General Partnership)

LOCATIONS

HQ: Industrial and Commercial Bank of China Ltd
No. 55 Fuxingmennei Avenue, Xicheng District, Beijing 100140
Phone: (86) 10 66106114 **Fax:** (86) 10 66107571
Web: www.icbc.com.cn

2014 Sales

	% of total
Mainland China	94
Overseas and other	6
Total	**100**

PRODUCTS/OPERATIONS

2014 Sales

	% of total
Interest	84
Noninterest	
Fees & commissions	14
Other	2
Total	**100**

2014 Sales by Segment

	% of total
Corporate banking	49
Personal banking	37
Treasury operations	13
Other	1
Total	**100**

COMPETITORS

Agricultural Bank of China
Bank of China
Bank of Communications
CITIC International Financial
China Construction Bank
China Merchants Bank
HSBC
Hua Xia Bank

HISTORICAL FINANCIALS

Company Type: Public

Income Statement FYE: December 31

	ASSETS ($ mil.)	NET INCOME ($ mil.)	INCOME AS % OF ASSETS	EMPLOYEES
12/14	3,320,774	44,439	1.3%	462,282
12/13	3,124,889	43,385	1.4%	441,902
12/12	2,813,847	38,261	1.4%	427,356
12/11	2,458,831	33,087	1.3%	408,859
12/10	2,041,783	25,055	1.2%	397,339
Annual Growth	12.9%	15.4%	—	3.9%

2014 Year-End Financials

Return on assets: 1.4%
Return on equity: 19.6%
Long-term debt ($ mil.): —
No. of shares (mil.): —
Sales ($ mil): 162,341

Dividends
Yield: —
Payout: —
Market value ($ mil.): —

Industrial Bank Co., Ltd.

There's nothing average about Industrial Bank. Founded in 1988 Industrial Bank is one of China's first joint stock commercial banks. Through some 95 branches and more than 815 sub-branches across China Industrial Bank offers standard deposit loan wealth management credit card and e-banking products and services to personal and commercial banking customers. Fujian Finance Department a government institution controls nearly a fifth of Industrial Bank while Hong Kong's Hang Seng Bank owns more than 10%.

EXECUTIVES

Director and President, Li Renjie, age 60
Chairman, Gao Jianping
Chairman Supervisory Board, Kang Kang
Auditors: Fujian Huaxing Certified Public Accountants Ltd.

LOCATIONS

HQ: Industrial Bank Co., Ltd.
154 Hudong Road, Fuzhou, Fujian Province 350003
Phone: (86) 591 87824863 **Fax:** (86) 591 87842633
Web: www.cib.com.cn

PRODUCTS/OPERATIONS

Selected Products and Services

Credit cards
Corporate banking
Electronic banking
Financial markets
Personal banking
Private banking

COMPETITORS

Bank of China
Bank of East Asia
Bank of Shanghai
China Construction Bank
China Merchants Bank
China Minsheng Banking
Shanghai Pudong Development Bank

HISTORICAL FINANCIALS

Company Type: Public

Income Statement FYE: December 31

	ASSETS ($ mil.)	NET INCOME ($ mil.)	INCOME AS % OF ASSETS	EMPLOYEES
12/14	709,980	7,595	1.1%	0
12/13	607,449	6,807	1.1%	0
12/12	521,470	5,568	1.1%	0
12/11	382,689	4,052	1.1%	0
12/10	280,610	2,809	1.0%	0
Annual Growth	26.1%	28.2%	—	—

2014 Year-End Financials

Return on assets: 1.1%
Return on equity: 20.6%
Long-term debt ($ mil.): —
No. of shares (mil.): —
Sales ($ mil): 20,176

Dividends
Yield: —
Payout: —
Market value ($ mil.): —

ING Bank N.V. (Netherlands)

ING Groep is a Dutch hybrid of banking insuring and asset-managing services. One of the world's largest banking and financial services companies its operations are focused on its home Benelux market as well as the rest of Europe; it also has operations in the Americas and Asia. Its banking operations include commercial and retail banking mortgage lending and online retail banking (ING Direct). Key insurance products include life insurance pensions and retirement services. ING provides asset management for individuals and institutions through both its insurance and banking units. The firm sold off insurance operations as well as some banking and investment businesses to repay government bailout loans.

Operations

Amid the global financial crisis of 2008 ING accepted a 10 billion (about $13 billion) bailout loan from the Dutch government to shore up its capital position and reassure wary investors. Since then ING has been focused on enacting strategic measures to further offset losses including layoffs and asset sales. Under requirements for the bailout funds ING has also been working to separate its banking and insurance operations through the sale of the insurance assets (as well as some banking assets). In late 2014 it completed paying off the debt.

The company is focused on its European banking operations –including divisions in the Netherlands Belgium and Germany –which provide a full range of services including savings and investment products. Due to the restructuring efforts banking operations now account for 60% of revenues (insurance was previously the core business).

ING's retail banking operations are primarily delivered online which reduces overhead and offers potential savings to customers.

Geographic Reach

ING operates in more than 40 countries in Europe North America Latin America Asia and the Asia/Pacific region. The Netherlands is its largest single market accounting for about 30% of its total interest income followed by Belgium (some 20%). The rest of Europe represents nearly 40% of total interest. (North America was previously the largest segment but the company sold its US retail bank in 2014 as well as insurance operations on both sides of the Atlantic as it continues to streamline operations.)

Sales and Marketing

ING uses a multi-channel distribution model to reach customers including individuals families small business entities large corporations government agencies and institutions. Marketing and sales methods include Internet banking mobile banking call centers mailings and branch and outbound sales representative efforts. ING has more than 33 million private corporate and institutional customers.

In 2014 the company spent 405 million on advertising and public relations (slightly up from 404 million spent in 2013).

Financial Performance

ING's revenues have seen a steady decline over the past five years largely due to asset disposal efforts. In 2014 revenue fell 9% to 51.7 billion due to declines in its commercial banking operations and investment income. Net income which has fluctuated in recent years fell 78% to 1.1 billion as values on non-trading derivatives declined.

After ING reported an 8 billion cash outflow in 2013 cash flow from operations rose to 12 billion in 2014 as the group generated funds due from banks and trading liabilities.

Strategy

ING has been divesting many of its holdings to create a stronger more streamlined operation with a renewed focus on banking in the Netherlands Belgium and Germany. Its restructuring plan which is nearly complete encompasses the sale or spin-off of all of its insurance operations which have included life insurance and non-life insurance businesses in Europe the Americas and the Asia/Pacific. In early 2014 the company raised $1.18 billion by selling off a majority stake in its US insurance unit. The plan also includes the divestiture of the company's insurance-related investment management operations as well as select non-core banking operations. The company is now focused on building strong domestic retail and commercial banking units as well as strong banking positions in other Central and Eastern European markets.

The company has made more than 50 divestitures over the past five years. Some of its largest sales have included banking firms ING Direct USA ING Direct Canada and ING Direct UK; it sold its investment management business in South Korea as well as insurance assets in China Hong Kong Macau and Thailand. In 2014 it agreed to sell its Taiwanese asset management business to Nomura Asset Management. Also that year it exited its equity investment business in the Middle East and North Africa as well as its insurance business in Brazil. In India the company exited the Vysya insurance business; in 2015 its ING Vysya bank merged with Kotak Mahindra Bank with ING retaining a small stake in the combined entity.

Some of ING's divestitures are being conducted through public offerings. ING U.S. (since renamed Voya Financial) went public in 2013 raising some $1.3 billion. ING retained a 75% stake in ING U.S. which holds ING's remaining US-based life insurance retirement and investment management operations. The company divested its holding in Voya Financial in early 2015.

ING conducted an IPO to sell part of its stake in NN Group its European life insurance and investment management operations in 2014. The group's insurance segment was eliminated after the IPO as those businesses were classified as discontinued operations. ING further reduced its holdings in NN Group in 2015 and plans to exit the business completely by 2016.

Company Background

Prior to the economic meltdown ING took aim at becoming a financial services player in all four corners of the world and made acquisitions accordingly. Along with much of the insurance industry it shifted its base from traditional life insurance products to investment-backed products which favor companies that can sell through banks. ING utilized its owns banks to distribute such products. The company also targeted expansion in growing economies such as South Korea Turkey and Thailand to meet anticipated consumer demand for new banking and retirement options. In more mature markets like North America and Europe the company had the aging population in its sights and placed retirement planning and pensions as sources of future growth.

HISTORY

HCING Groep's roots go back to 1845 when its earliest predecessor the Netherlands Insurance Co. was founded. The firm began expanding geographically; in 1903 it added life insurance. In 1963 it merged with the century-old Nationale Life Insurance Bank to form Nationale-Nederland (NN). Over the next three decades the company grew primarily through acquisitions in Europe North America and Australia. In 1986 NN became the first European life insurance company to be licensed in Japan.

Another predecessor the Rijkspostspaarbank was founded in 1881 to provide Dutch citizens with simple post office savings accounts. In 1918 the Postcheque-en Girondienst (giro) system was established to allow people to use vouchers drawn on their savings accounts to pay bills. This system became the main method of settling accounts (instead of bank checking accounts).

Rijkspostspaarbank and Postcheque merged in 1986 to become Postbank. Postbank merged in 1989 with the Nederlandse Middenstandsbank (founded 1927) to become NMB Postbank. The vast amounts of cash tied up in the post office savings and giro systems fueled NMB's business.

In 1991 as the European economic union became a reality and barriers between banking and insurance began to fall NN merged with NMB Postbank to form Internationale Nederland Groep (ING). ING began cutting costs shedding redundant offices and unprofitable operations in both its segments. In the US where insurance and banking were legally divided the company "debanked" itself in order to keep its more lucrative insurance operations (but retained the right to provide banking services to those operations).

ING sought to increase its investment banking and finance operations in the 1990s. In 1995 it took over UK-based Barings Bank (personal banker to the Queen of England) after Nicholas Leeson a trader in Barings' Singapore office lost huge sums of money in derivatives trading. The acquisition gave the firm a higher profile but cost more than anticipated and left it embroiled in lingering legal actions.

In 1996 ING bought Poland's Bank Slaski (the company had first entered Poland in 1994). The next year it expanded its securities business by acquiring investment bank Furman Selz doubled its US life insurance operations by purchasing Equitable of Iowa and listed on the NYSE. In 1998 ING's acquisition strategy again involved Europe and North America: It bought Belgium's Banque Bruxelles Lambert and Canadian life insurer Guardian Insurance Co. (from Guardian Royal Exchange now part of AXA UK).

ING turned eastward in 1999 kicking off asset management operations in India and buying a minority stake in South Korea's HC&B (formerly Housing & Commercial Bank). In 2000 the company bulked up its North American operations with the purchase of 40% of Savia SA a Mexican insurance concern. It also bought US firm ReliaStar Financial in a $6 billion deal and Charterhouse Securities from CCF (then called Crdit Commercial de France).

In 2004 ING realigned its management structure dividing the company's operations into six business lines: Insurance Americas Insurance Europe Insurance Asia-Pacific Wholesale Banking Retail Banking and ING Direct. ING boosted its North American insurance operations with the acquisition of Allianz's Canadian property and casualty operations.The company struggled with investment banking arm ING Barings. The unit was reorganized and streamlined for cost-savings purposes but ultimately was put on the block. Its Asian equities operations were sold to Macquarie Bank in 2004. Barings Private Equity Partners unit was sold to its management. The Barings investment management operations were sold to MassMutual in 2005 while Northern Trust bought up its fund administration trust and custody operations.

ING sold most of ING BHF-Bank to Sal. Oppenheim during 2004. The next year ING turned over its US life reinsurance operations to Scottish Re and sold subsidiary Life Insurance Company of Georgia to Jackson National Life.

During 2005 ING acquired a 20% stake in the Bank of Beijing as part of a strategic alliance. In 2006 the company sold off its UK brokerage business Williams de Broë to The Evolution Group.

In 2008 the company acquired CitiStreet a leading US administrator of defined-contribution retirement savings pension health and other plans; it paid about $900 million for the firm.

After the global financial crisis hit in 2008 ING accepted a 10 billion (more than $13 billion) bailout loan from the Dutch government. The bailout was intended to shore up the company's capital position and reassure wary investors. Strategic measures to further offset losses and repay debt were enacted in 2009 including layoffs and asset sales. CEO Michael Tilmant stepped down and was replaced by former chairman Jan Hommen. By the end of 2009 job cuts totaled about 10% of its workforce. The company also outlined plans to split the company in half by separating its insurance and banking operations.

Prior to the bailout ING has already been working to simplify and streamline its operations through a "Back to Basics" strategy. Restructuring measures under the strategy include the refocusing of ING's banking operations on (mostly Central) Europe and the reduction of the company's US financial product offerings.

In early 2009 the company sold its ING Canada property/casualty business which was then renamed Intact Financial. ING sold its life insurance joint venture stake in Australia and New Zealand to partner ANZ and offloaded its noncore annuity and mortgage businesses in Chile to life insurer Corp Group Vida Chile in late 2009. The company also sold its Taiwanese life insurance business to Fubon Financial Holding in a deal worth 447 million ($600 million) in mid-2009. ING gained a 5% stake in Fubon through the deal which it sold the following year for another 395 million ($522 million).

In early 2010 ING completed sales of the company's Swiss Private Banking unit to Julius Baer for $506 million and its Asian Private Banking unit (operating in Hong Kong the Philippines and Singapore) to OCBC Bank for nearly $1.5 billion. In addition the company sold its North American reinsurance operations to RGA and most of its US insurance brokerage operations to Lightyear Capital in early 2010. ING has also agreed to sell its stake in one of its Chinese life insurance ventures (Pacific Antai with China Pacific Insurance) to China Construction Bank.

In 2011 ING sold its Asian and European real estate investment management (REIM) operations as well as select US REIM assets for about $940 million to broker CBRE Group (formerly CB Richard Ellis Group). The firm sold its remaining US REIM assets to Lightyear Capital for some $100 million. Also that year the firm agreed to sell its Australian investment management business to UBS for an undisclosed sum.

Farther south in 2011 the company sold its Latin American insurance operations to Columbian insurer GrupoSura for $3.7 billion. The sale included insurance savings and investment management operations in Chile Colombia Mexico Uruguay and Peru. It also sold ING Car Least to BMW.

EXECUTIVES

Chairman Executive Board and CEO, R.A.J.G. (Ralph) Hamers
CFO, P.G. (Patrick) Flynn
Chief Risk Officer, W.F. (Wilfred) Nagel
Chairman Supervisory Board, Jeroen van der Veer
Auditors: Ernst & Young Accountants LLP

LOCATIONS

HQ: ING Bank N.V. (Netherlands)
Bijlmerplein 888, Amsterdam 1102 MG
Phone: (31) 20 5639111 **Fax:** (31) 20 5760950
Web: www.ing.com

2014 Total Income

	% of total
Europe	
The Netherlands	29
Belgium	21
Other countries	37
North America	3
Asia	4
Australia	3
Other	3
Total	**100**

PRODUCTS/OPERATIONS

2014 Interest Income

	% of total
Commercial banking	60
Retail Netherlands	15
Retail Belgium	5
Retail Germany	7
Retail rest of world	9
Corporate line banking	4
Total	**100**

2014 Sales

	% of total
Interest income banking operations	93
Commission income	4
Investment income	1
Result on disposals of group companies	1
Net trading income	1
Share of result from associates & joint ventures	-
Other income	-
Total	**100**

COMPETITORS

ABN AMRO Group
ABN AMRO Group
AEGON
AEGON
Achmea
Achmea
Ageas Insurance International
Ageas Insurance International
Barclays
Barclays
Citigroup
Citigroup
Credit Suisse
Credit Suisse
Delta Lloyd
Delta Lloyd
Deutsche Bank
Deutsche Bank
Deutsche Bundesbank
Deutsche Bundesbank
HSBC
HSBC
KBC
KBC
Rabobank Group
Rabobank Group
UBS
UBS

HISTORICAL FINANCIALS

Company Type: Public

Income Statement

FYE: December 31

	REVENUE ($ mil.)	NET INCOME ($ mil.)	NET PROFIT MARGIN	EMPLOYEES
12/14	63,766	3,335	5.2%	55,945
12/13	77,155	4,216	5.5%	64,373
12/12	86,064	4,105	4.8%	66,879
12/11	90,271	5,180	5.7%	71,175
12/10	99,292	6,015	6.1%	71,287
Annual Growth	(10.5%)	(13.7%)	—	(5.9%)

2014 Year-End Financials

Debt ratio: —	No. of shares (mil.): 465
Return on equity: 7.7%	Dividends
Cash ($ mil.): 14,855	Yield: —
Current ratio: —	Payout: —
Long-term debt ($ mil.): —	Market value ($ mil.): —

ING Groep N.V.

ING Groep is a Dutch hybrid of banking insuring and asset-managing services. One of the world's largest banking and financial services companies its operations are focused on its home Benelux market as well as the rest of Europe; it also has operations in the Americas and Asia. Its banking operations include commercial and retail banking mortgage lending and online retail banking (ING Direct). Key insurance products include life insurance pensions and retirement services. ING provides asset management for individuals and institutions through both its insurance and banking units. The firm sold off insurance operations as well as some banking and investment businesses to repay government bailout loans.

Operations

Amid the global financial crisis of 2008 ING accepted a 10 billion (about $13 billion) bailout loan from the Dutch government to shore up its capital position and reassure wary investors. Since then ING has been focused on enacting strategic measures to further offset losses including layoffs and asset sales. Under requirements for the bailout funds ING has also been working to separate its banking and insurance operations through the sale of the insurance assets (as well as some banking assets). In late 2014 it completed paying off the debt.

The company is focused on its European banking operations –including divisions in the Netherlands Belgium and Germany –which provide a full range of services including savings and investment products. Due to the restructuring efforts banking operations now account for 60% of revenues (insurance was previously the core business).

ING's retail banking operations are primarily delivered online which reduces overhead and offers potential savings to customers.

Geographic Reach

ING operates in more than 40 countries in Europe North America Latin America Asia and the Asia/Pacific region. The Netherlands is its largest single market accounting for about 30% of its total interest income followed by Belgium (some 20%). The rest of Europe represents nearly 40% of total interest. (North America was previously the largest segment but the company sold its US retail bank in 2014 as well as insurance operations on both sides of the Atlantic as it continues to streamline operations.)

Sales and Marketing

ING uses a multi-channel distribution model to reach customers including individuals families small business entities large corporations government agencies and institutions. Marketing and sales methods include Internet banking mobile banking call centers mailings and branch and outbound sales representative efforts. ING has more than 33 million private corporate and institutional customers.

In 2014 the company spent 405 million on advertising and public relations (slightly up from 404 million spent in 2013).

Financial Performance

ING's revenues have seen a steady decline over the past five years largely due to asset disposal efforts. In 2014 revenue fell 9% to 51.7 billion due to declines in its commercial banking operations and investment income. Net income which has fluctuated in recent years fell 78% to 1.1 billion as values on non-trading derivatives declined.

After ING reported an 8 billion cash outflow in 2013 cash flow from operations rose to 12 billion in 2014 as the group generated funds due from banks and trading liabilities.

Strategy

ING has been divesting many of its holdings to create a stronger more streamlined operation with a renewed focus on banking in the Netherlands Belgium and Germany. Its restructuring plan which is nearly complete encompasses the sale or spin-off of all of its insurance operations which have included life insurance and non-life insurance businesses in Europe the Americas and the Asia/Pacific. In early 2014 the company raised $1.18 billion by selling off a majority stake in its US insurance unit. The plan also includes the divestiture of the company's insurance-related investment management operations as well as select non-core banking operations. The company is now focused on building strong domestic retail and commercial banking units as well as strong banking positions in other Central and Eastern European markets.

The company has made more than 50 divestitures over the past five years. Some of its largest sales have included banking firms ING Direct USA ING Direct Canada and ING Direct UK; it sold its investment management business in South Korea as well as insurance assets in China Hong Kong Macau and Thailand. In 2014 it agreed to sell its Taiwanese asset management business to Nomura Asset Management. Also that year it exited its equity investment business in the Middle East and North Africa as well as its insurance business in Brazil. In India the company exited the Vysya insurance business; in 2015 its ING Vysya bank merged with Kotak Mahindra Bank with ING retaining a small stake in the combined entity.

Some of ING's divestitures are being conducted through public offerings. ING U.S. (since renamed Voya Financial) went public in 2013 raising some $1.3 billion. ING retained a 75% stake in ING U.S. which holds ING's remaining US-based life insurance retirement and investment management operations. The company divested its holding in Voya Financial in early 2015.

ING conducted an IPO to sell part of its stake in NN Group its European life insurance and investment management operations in 2014. The group's insurance segment was eliminated after the IPO as those businesses were classified as discontinued operations. ING further reduced its holdings in NN Group in 2015 and plans to exit the business completely by 2016.

Company Background

Prior to the economic meltdown ING took aim at becoming a financial services player in all four corners of the world and made acquisitions accordingly. Along with much of the insurance industry it shifted its base from traditional life insurance products to investment-backed products which favor companies that can sell through banks. ING utilized its owns banks to distribute such products. The company also targeted expansion in growing economies such as South Korea Turkey and Thailand to meet anticipated consumer demand for new banking and retirement options. In more mature markets like North America and Europe the company had the aging population in its sights and placed retirement planning and pensions as sources of future growth.

HISTORY

HCING Groep's roots go back to 1845 when its earliest predecessor the Netherlands Insurance Co. was founded. The firm began expanding geographically; in 1903 it added life insurance. In 1963 it merged with the century-old Nationale Life Insurance Bank to form Nationale-Nederland (NN). Over the next three decades the company grew primarily through acquisitions in Europe North America and Australia. In 1986 NN became the first European life insurance company to be licensed in Japan.

Another predecessor the Rijkspostspaarbank was founded in 1881 to provide Dutch citizens with simple post office savings accounts. In 1918 the Postcheque-en Girondienst (giro) system was established to allow people to use vouchers drawn on their savings accounts to pay bills. This system became the main method of settling accounts (instead of bank checking accounts).

Rijkspostspaarbank and Postcheque merged in 1986 to become Postbank. Postbank merged in 1989 with the Nederlandse Middenstandsbank (founded 1927) to become NMB Postbank. The vast amounts of cash tied up in the post office savings and giro systems fueled NMB's business.

In 1991 as the European economic union became a reality and barriers between banking and insurance began to fall NN merged with NMB Postbank to form Internationale Nederland Groep (ING). ING began cutting costs shedding redundant offices and unprofitable operations in both its segments. In the US where insurance and banking were legally divided the company "debanked" itself in order to keep its more lucrative insurance operations (but retained the right to provide banking services to those operations).

ING sought to increase its investment banking and finance operations in the 1990s. In 1995 it took over UK-based Barings Bank (personal banker to the Queen of England) after Nicholas Leeson a trader in Barings' Singapore office lost huge sums of money in derivatives trading. The acquisition gave the firm a higher profile but cost more than anticipated and left it embroiled in lingering legal actions.

In 1996 ING bought Poland's Bank Slaski (the company had first entered Poland in 1994). The next year it expanded its securities business by acquiring investment bank Furman Selz doubled its US life insurance operations by purchasing Equitable of Iowa and listed on the NYSE. In 1998 ING's acquisition strategy again involved Europe and North America: It bought Belgium's Banque Bruxelles Lambert and Canadian life insurer Guardian Insurance Co. (from Guardian Royal Exchange now part of AXA UK).

ING turned eastward in 1999 kicking off asset management operations in India and buying a minority stake in South Korea's HC&B (formerly Housing & Commercial Bank). In 2000 the company bulked up its North American operations with the purchase of 40% of Savia SA a Mexican insurance concern. It also bought US firm ReliaStar Financial in a $6 billion deal and Charterhouse Securities from CCF (then called Crdit Commercial de France).

In 2004 ING realigned its management structure dividing the company's operations into six business lines: Insurance Americas Insurance Europe Insurance Asia-Pacific Wholesale Banking Retail Banking and ING Direct. ING boosted its North American insurance operations with the acquisition of Allianz's Canadian property and casualty operations.The company struggled with investment banking arm ING Barings. The unit was reorganized and streamlined for cost-savings purposes but ultimately was put on the block. Its Asian equities operations were sold to Macquarie Bank in 2004. Barings Private Equity Partners unit was sold to its management. The Barings investment management operations were sold to MassMutual in 2005 while Northern Trust bought up its fund administration trust and custody operations.

ING sold most of ING BHF-Bank to Sal. Oppenheim during 2004. The next year ING turned over its US life reinsurance operations to Scottish Re and sold subsidiary Life Insurance Company of Georgia to Jackson National Life.

During 2005 ING acquired a 20% stake in the Bank of Beijing as part of a strategic alliance. In 2006 the company sold off its UK brokerage business Williams de Broë to The Evolution Group.

In 2008 the company acquired CitiStreet a leading US administrator of defined-contribution retirement savings pension health and other plans; it paid about $900 million for the firm.

After the global financial crisis hit in 2008 ING accepted a 10 billion (more than $13 billion) bailout loan from the Dutch government. The bailout was intended to shore up the company's capital position and reassure wary investors. Strategic measures to further offset losses and repay debt were enacted in 2009 including layoffs and asset sales. CEO Michael Tilmant stepped down and was replaced by former chairman Jan Hommen. By the end of 2009 job cuts totaled about 10% of its workforce. The company also outlined plans to split the company in half by separating its insurance and banking operations.

Prior to the bailout ING has already been working to simplify and streamline its operations through a "Back to Basics" strategy. Restructuring measures under the strategy include the refocusing of ING's banking operations on (mostly Central) Europe and the reduction of the company's US financial product offerings.

In early 2009 the company sold its ING Canada property/casualty business which was then renamed Intact Financial. ING sold its life insurance joint venture stake in Australia and New Zealand to partner ANZ and offloaded its noncore annuity and mortgage businesses in Chile to life insurer Corp Group Vida Chile in late 2009. The company also sold its Taiwanese life insurance business to Fubon Financial Holding in a deal worth 447 million ($600 million) in mid-2009. ING gained a 5% stake in Fubon through the deal which it sold the following year for another 395 million ($522 million).

In early 2010 ING completed sales of the company's Swiss Private Banking unit to Julius Baer for $506 million and its Asian Private Banking unit (operating in Hong Kong the Philippines and Singapore) to OCBC Bank for nearly $1.5 billion. In addition the company sold its North American reinsurance operations to RGA and most of its US insurance brokerage operations to Lightyear Capital in early 2010. ING has also agreed to sell its stake in one of its Chinese life insurance ventures (Pacific Antai with China Pacific Insurance) to China Construction Bank.

In 2011 ING sold its Asian and European real estate investment management (REIM) operations as well as select US REIM assets for about $940 million to broker CBRE Group (formerly CB Richard Ellis Group). The firm sold its remaining US REIM assets to Lightyear Capital for some $100 million. Also that year the firm agreed to sell its Australian investment management business to UBS for an undisclosed sum.

Farther south in 2011 the company sold its Latin American insurance operations to Columbian insurer GrupoSura for $3.7 billion. The sale included insurance savings and investment management operations in Chile Colombia Mexico Uruguay and Peru. It also sold ING Car Least to BMW.

EXECUTIVES

Chairman Executive Board and CEO, R.A.J.G. (Ralph) Hamers
CFO, P.G. (Patrick) Flynn
Chief Risk Officer, W.F. (Wilfred) Nagel
Chairman Supervisory Board, Jeroen van der Veer
Auditors: Ernst & Young Accountants LLP

LOCATIONS

HQ: ING Groep N.V.
Bijlmerplein 888, Amsterdam 1102 MG
Phone: (31) 20 563 6710
Web: www.ing.com

2014 Total Income

	% of total
Europe	
The Netherlands	29
Belgium	21
Other countries	37
North America	3
Asia	4
Australia	3
Other	3
Total	**100**

PRODUCTS/OPERATIONS

2014 Interest Income

	% of total
Commercial banking	60
Retail Netherlands	15
Retail Belgium	5
Retail Germany	7
Retail rest of world	9
Corporate line banking	4
Total	**100**

2014 Sales

	% of total
Interest income banking operations	93
Commission income	4
Investment income	1
Result on disposals of group companies	1
Net trading income	1
Share of result from associates & joint ventures	-
Other income	-
Total	**100**

COMPETITORS

ABN AMRO Group	Credit Suisse
ABN AMRO Group	Delta Lloyd
AEGON	Delta Lloyd
AEGON	Deutsche Bank
Achmea	Deutsche Bank
Achmea	Deutsche Bundesbank
Ageas Insurance International	Deutsche Bundesbank
Ageas Insurance International	HSBC
Barclays	HSBC
Barclays	KBC
Citigroup	KBC
Citigroup	Rabobank Group
Credit Suisse	Rabobank Group
	UBS
	UBS

HISTORICAL FINANCIALS

Company Type: Public

Income Statement

FYE: December 31

	ASSETS ($ mil.)	NET INCOME ($ mil.)	INCOME AS % OF ASSETS	EMPLOYEES
12/14	1,200,561	1,170	0.1%	68,431
12/13	1,482,196	6,301	0.4%	83,690
12/12	1,531,742	4,295	0.3%	92,572
12/11	1,647,314	6,130	0.4%	104,419
12/10	1,663,388	3,716	0.2%	106,139
Annual Growth	(7.8%)	(25.1%)	—	(10.4%)

2014 Year-End Financials

Return on assets: 0.0%
Return on equity: 2.1%
Long-term debt ($ mil.): —
No. of shares (mil.): —
Sales ($ mil): 62,304
Dividends
Yield: 0.0%
Payout: 200.0%
Market value ($ mil.): —

	STOCK PRICE ($) FY Close	P/E High/Low	PER SHARE ($) Earnings	Dividends	Book Value
12/14	12.97	237 193	0.07	0.15	14.69
12/13	14.01	13 7	1.46	0.00	15.77
12/12	9.49	14 9	0.91	0.00	17.95
12/11	7.17	14 7	1.10	0.00	15.18
12/10	9.79	18 12	0.83	0.00	15.35
Annual Growth	7.3%	— —	(45.6%)	—	(1.1%)

International Consolidated Airlines Group SA

A member of the royal family of European airlines British Airways (BA) carries passengers and cargo to more than 160 destinations in some 75 countries from hubs at London's Heathrow Gatwick and London City airports. The carrier operates a fleet of more than 250 aircraft (with another 20 on order) consisting mainly of Airbus and Boeing jets. BA extends its network to more than 400 total destinations via joint business agreements and code-sharing relationships with AMR's American Airlines and members of the Oneworld alliance such as Qantas. In 2011 BA merged with Spain's #1 airline Iberia forming International Airlines Group (IAG).

Operations

Upon its formation IAG joined the wave of multinational air carriers namely Air France-KLM and Lufthansa (which owns Austrian Brussels and SWISS). Although BA and Iberia continue to fly under their own names the merger created Europe's third largest scheduled airline by revenue and one of the world's top five airline groups. The deal also marked the end of more than two decades of trading under the British Airways name. Under the merger's terms BA owns 56% and Iberia holds the remaining 44% of IAG. In addition to its brand name each carrier maintains its own hub.

The Passenger segment which includes both scheduled and unscheduled services accounts for nearly 90 percent of revenue. The Cargo segment operated with scheduled passenger services represents 7% of revenue. The Passenger and Cargo segments are operated as one business unit. The Other segment accounts for 5% of revenue.

Financial Performance

BA's revenue increased slightly (8%) due to increased ticket prices and a boost from the purchase of British Midland Airways (bmi). However continued high fuel costs contributed to a 110% increased in net loss. The company also disposed of two of bmi's subsidiaries adding to the loss. Consequently cash flow was down more than 170%.

Strategy

To compensate for the rise of fuel cost which accounts for one-third of expenses BA has been focusing on working with suppliers to drive down controllable costs. The company also cushions itself against the high price of fuel by buying oil derivatives in forward markets.

To further hedge its bets on fuel and go a little green BA has partnered with Solena Group to build a sustainable jet fuel plant where fuel will be created from waste biomass. The facility which is the first of its kind in Europe is expected to be in operation by 2015.

To stand out from its competition in a soft market the company is investing more than 5 billion to purchase new Airbus A380 and Boeing 787 aircraft upgrade its cabins and lounges and new technology all in an effort to persuade air travelers to choose BA.

Mergers and Acquisitions

IAG acquired British Midland Airways from Lufthansa in 2012 and began integrating it with BA's operations. Also BA Iberia and American Airlines rolled out a transatlantic joint venture a step up from their code-sharing alliance that defends their routes between the US and UK. Other transatlantic joint ventures include SkyTeam (including Delta and Korean Air Lines) and Star Alliance (United Continental and Lufthansa among its members).

HISTORY

British Airways has a jet trail winding back to 1916 and its biplane-flying ancestor Aircraft Transport and Travel which in 1919 launched the world's first daily international air service (between London and Paris). Concerned about subsidized foreign competition British authorities in 1924 merged Aircraft Transport and Travel successor Daimler Airways with other fledgling British carriers –British Air Marine Navigation Handley Page and Instone Air Line –to form Imperial Airways.

Imperial pioneered routes from London to India (1929) Singapore (1933) and –in partnership with Qantas Empire Airways –Australia (1934). Competition on European routes emerged in the 1930s from upstart British Airways; in 1939 the government troubled by the threat to Imperial nationalized and merged the two airlines to form British Overseas Airways Corporation (BOAC).

After WWII BOAC continued as the UK's international airline but state-owned British European Airways (BEA) took over domestic and European routes. In 1972 the government combined the duo to form British Airways (BA).

BA and Air France jointly introduced supersonic passenger service in 1976 with the Concorde –a PR victory that contributed to years of losses. Colin Marshall became CEO in 1983 and reduced manpower and routes.

In 1987 the government sold BA to the public and the airline bought chief UK rival British Caledonian. Hoping to become a globe-spanning carrier in 1992 BA tried to gain a 44% stake in USAir (which became US Airways). American Airlines United and Delta strongly objected demanding equal access to UK markets. BA settled for a 25% stake the maximum foreign ownership allowed by US law in 1993. It also bought 25% of Qantas.

That year BA settled a libel suit brought by UK competitor Virgin Atlantic Airways which accused BA of waging a smear campaign against it. The settlement cost BA about $5 million and Virgin Atlantic followed with a $1 billion antitrust suit in the US (dismissed in 1999). In 1994 BA paid out $4 million to settle yet another Virgin Atlantic suit this one claiming BA had done sloppy maintenance on Virgin aircraft. BA also sold British Caledonian.

In 1996 Marshall turned over the CEO job to Bob Ayling who had joined BA in 1985. BA and American Airlines agreed to coordinate prices and schedules and to share market data for their transatlantic routes. Though the deal met regulatory obstacles from the start in 1997 BA sold its stake in US Airways. BA and American also took the lead in forming the Oneworld global alliance (which took effect in 1999).

The next year BA launched low-fare European carrier Go. In 1999 BA and American all but abandoned plans for their comprehensive transatlantic linkup after US regulators denied antitrust immunity. Meanwhile as fuel prices rose and passenger numbers fell BA announced it would cut unprofitable routes and use smaller planes.

Ayling resigned in 2000 and Marshall stepped in as temporary CEO before Rod Eddington a veteran of Cathay Pacific and Ansett was appointed. Also that year BA took a 9% stake in Iberia and sold its interest in France's Air Libert ©

BA grounded its Concordes in 2000 (flights resumed in 2001) three weeks after the crash of an Air France Concorde outside Paris in which 113 people were killed. The airline put its no-frills carrier Go up for sale that year and in 2001 sold the airline to venture capital firm 3i Group. Also in 2001 BA and American announced plans to once again seek regulatory approval for a code-sharing partnership.

That year BA laid off 5200 employees as a result of decreased demand for air travel after the terrorist attacks in New York and Washington DC. The layoffs were on top of 1800 job cuts the airline made earlier in the year reducing BA's workforce by 10%.

BA's long-negotiated trans-Atlantic alliance with American Airlines received tentative approval from the US Department of Transportation in 2002. But the airlines chose to abandon the deal rather than accept regulators' terms which called for BA and American to give up more landing slots at London's Heathrow airport than they were willing to relinquish. The next year the carriers won approval for an extensive code-sharing agreement that did not include routes between London and US cities.

The year 2003 also saw the retirement of the BA's Concorde fleet a longtime symbol of the airline's trans-Atlantic dominance. That year the carrier acquired four additional slots at London's Heathrow Airport from rival United Airlines which was reorganizing under bankruptcy protection.

BA sold its 19% stake in Qantas in 2004 to help cut down on its debt. Eddington stepped down as CEO in 2005 and former Aer Lingus chief Willie Walsh was named to replace him.

In 2006 BA was a target of an investigation by US and UK government agencies into alleged price-fixing on fuel surcharges by airlines. Two company officials commercial director Martin George and communications head Iain Burns were placed on leave and then resigned in connection with the inquiry. The next year BA settled the charges by agreeing to pay fines of about $300 million to the US and about $247 million to the UK.

As early as 2007 BA has started working steadily to cut costs throughout its business and eliminate unprofitable operations in order to focus on core long-haul offerings. Toward that end the company sold most of the operations of its money-losing BA Connect regional business to rival Flybe.

BA moved to augment its transatlantic service in June 2008 by launching a new carrier OpenSkies. The startup which began operations by flying between Paris and New York was inspired by the Open Skies treaty between the US and the EU which allows European airlines to serve city pairs that don't include their home countries and enables US airlines to directly serve more European destinations. OpenSkies which uses a custom-configured Boeing 757 from the BA fleet hopes to simultaneously differentiate itself from its parent and benefit from BA's strong brand and deep pockets. To strengthen OpenSkies BA in July 2008 paid about $107 million for French startup carrier L'Avion which also uses 757s to provide business-class service between Paris and Newark New Jersey. L'Avion's operations were integrated into those of OpenSkies.

In the meantime BA attempted to merge with leading Australian airline Qantas. In December 2008 BA announced it was in talks with Qantas but the talks quickly fizzled out. Among other hurdles BA disagreed with Qantas owning more than 50% of the combined firm. (Australian law states that Qantas has to remain majority-owned by Australian investors with its head office residing in Australia.) Qantas also was apprehensive about BA's merger talks with Iberia occurring at the same time it was trying to reach an agreement with Qantas.

In 2008 BA reach a long-awaited milestone when it moved its Heathrow operations to a new facility Terminal 5. The new terminal was seen as a major step up both for passengers and for employees; functions such as security and baggage handling for example were designed to be easier to manage. However Terminal 5's opening was marred as not all of the bugs had been worked out of the new baggage-handling system. Hundreds of flights were canceled during the first week of operations because of problems with the baggage system —causing BA's reputation for customer service to suffer. In late 2009 BA announced it would merge with Iberia.

British Airways faced ongoing difficulties in 2010 with the eruption of the Iceland volcano Eyjafjallajokull in April. The airline sustained millions of pounds in losses a day due to the airspace closure.

Auditors: Ernst & Young, S.L.

LOCATIONS

HQ: International Consolidated Airlines Group SA
2 World Business Centre, Newall Road, London
Heathrow Airport, Hounslow TW6 2SF
Phone: (44) 20 8564 2800
Web: www.iairgroup.com

HISTORICAL FINANCIALS

Company Type: Public

Income Statement FYE: December 31

	REVENUE ($ mil.)	NET INCOME ($ mil.)	NET PROFIT MARGIN	EMPLOYEES
12/14	24,516	1,193	4.9%	59,484
12/13	25,564	167	0.7%	60,089
12/12	23,879	(1,242)	—	59,574
12/11	20,828	726	3.5%	56,791
12/10	8,944	210	2.3%	39,828
Annual Growth	28.7%	54.4%	—	10.5%

2014 Year-End Financials

Debt ratio: 34.0%
Return on equity: 26.5%
Cash ($ mil.): 6,009
Current ratio: 0.76
Long-term debt ($ mil.): 7,176
No. of shares (mil.): 2,040
Dividends
Yield: —
Payout: —
Market value ($ mil.): 75,524

	STOCK PRICE ($) FY Close	P/E High/Low	PER SHARE ($) Earnings	Dividends	Book Value
12/14	37.02	78 50	0.56	0.00	2.08
12/13	33.55	524252	0.09	0.00	2.65
12/12	15.45	— —	(0.67)	0.00	3.38
12/11	11.38	76 32	0.38	0.00	3.75
12/10	21.15	279131	0.18	0.00	2.55
Annual Growth	15.0%	— —	32.7%	—	(5.0%)

Intesa Sanpaolo S.P.A.

Intesa Sanpaolo provides retail and commercial banking services in Italy through its Banca dei Territori division. The company serves 11.1 million customers from 4500 branches throughout Italy and an additional 1400 locations in Central and Eastern Europe as well as North African areas. Intesa Sanpaolo also provides investment banking corporate finance public and infrastructure finance factoring and trade financing services. The company offers life property and casualty insurance through Fideuram Vita and other insurance subsidiaries. Asset management is handled by Eurizon Capital while Banca Fideuram arm provides financial planning services.

OperationsBanca dei Territori is the company's flagship brand generating more than 60% of total revenue. It boasts more than 4000 branches that provide traditional banking and loan products. More than 80% of the group's loan portfolio is made up of commercial banking loans half of which are mortgages with the other half being current accounts and advances and other loans. Nonperforming loans make up roughly 10% of the overall loan portfolio. The division's affiliates include the company's small to medium enterprises (SME) finance hub Mediocredito Italiana non-profit organization lender Banca Prossima and payment systems provider Setefi. Corporate and Investment Banking makes up nearly 20% of total revenue and offers investment banking and capital market services through Banca IMI via a network of more than 40 branches in Italy. The International Subsidiary Banks division bring in another roughly 10% of revenue. This division serves more than 8 million customers in 11 countries through more than 1100 branches in select countries in Central-Eastern Europe and the Middle East and North Africa region. The other divisions include Private Banking (under the Banca Fideuram brand) which offers wealth management services to high net worth individuals; the Asset Management division (under the Eurizon Capital brand) which manages more than 200 billion in assets under management for the individuals as well as institutional clientele; and the Insurance division (under Intesa Sanpaolo Vita Fideuram Vita and Intesa Sanpaolo Assicura brands) which boasts more than 25 billion in premiums and more than 110 billion in technical reserves. Capital Light Bank a non-core segment manages non-performing loans and repossessed assets (including those of Pravex-Bank in Ukraine). Geographic ReachIntesa Sanpaolo and its subsidiary banks boasts nearly 4500 branches across Italy more than 1200 branches in select countries in Central and Eastern Europe. It also has more than 150 branches in Africa and the Middle East and a handful of branches and representative offices in America and Asia. Nearly 80% of revenue comes from business in Italy while Europe makes up more than 15%.Sales and MarketingThe banking group serves individuals (including households in financial difficulty) small to mid-size enterprises (SMEs) startup and large businesses consumer associations public entities and industrial associations. In all the group serves more than 19 million customers with the average customer holding an account for more than 12 years.The company spent 160 million on advertising and promotional expenses in 2014 up from 154 million spent in 2013.Financial PerformanceNote: Growth rates may differ after conversion to US dollars.Intesa Sanpaolo's financial performance has been volatile in recent years as the bank has been grappling with recession in Italy and as it has been working to derisk its portfolio in the years following the financial crisis. Revenue in 2014 rose by double digits to 16.9 billion ($20.5 billion) mostly thanks to a combination of higher net fee and commission income and increased income from the insurance business. Net fee and commission income grew thanks to higher collections and payment services fees higher guarantee fees and higher credit and debit card fees. The insurance business grew by 16% thanks to strong investment performance. Higher revenue and lower operating costs in 2014 pushed Intesa Sanpaolo back into profitability as net income jumped to 1.31 billion (roughly $1.6 billion) compared to a net loss of 4.55 billion ($6.3 billion) in 2013. Cash from operations rose thanks to higher cash earnings.

Stategy

Intesa Sanpaolo is working to strengthen its retail banking operations and maintain a diversified presence in international markets. For now its focus is on its flagship Banca dei Territori division which handles domestic commercial banking and is responsible for retail customers individual customers and small businesses. Leaning on its Banca dei Territori business in 2014 the company introduced its growth-oriented Banca 5 project designed to cross sell its banking customers on the group's insurance and investing products and services from its other divisions.Intesa Sanpaolo has also formed strategic partnerships with other financial companies to extend into new financial markets. In 2015 for example the company partnered with GSO Capital Partners (the credit investment arm of Blackstone) to provide alternative funding to Italian middle market businesses which have faced a tight private credit market for the past several years.

Company Background

Intesa Sanpaolo is the result of the 2007 mega-merger between Banca Intesa and Sanpaolo IMI. After the merger the company reshuffled its assets and sold off some branches in order to comply with antitrust orders and raise capital.

HISTORY

Company BackgroundIn Italy charity begins at home and often heads to the financial institutions. In 1563 Turin citizens founded Compagnia di San Paolo a foundation that provided education and dowries to orphaned girls and aid to impoverished nobility. In 1579 the organization began a pawn shop the Monte di Pieta or Mountain of Mercy (founded in 1519 and reopened by the Compagnia). The foundation grew over the next 200 years fattened by bequests and inheritances from wealthy Piedmontese families.The French Republican government in Piedmonte gradually took control of the foundation's operations and closed it in 1802. The Monte di Pieta was reopened in 1804 and under the French influence became more bank-like. In 1848 the charitable and financial operations were formally divided.Industrialization came slowly to Italy after its unification in the 1860s (the country remained largely agricultural until after WWII) and the organization survived a banking crisis from 1887 to 1894 by operating conservatively. It contributed to the WWI effort by purchasing government bonds. In 1928 the foundation separated Monte di Pieta's credit and pawn operations and adopted the name Istituto di San Paolo di Torino - Beneficenza e Credito (San Paolo).Specialized institutions were founded in the 1920s to finance utilities and transportation; one of them La Centrale Societa per il Finanziamento di Imprese Elettriche e Telefoniche was formed in 1925 to help finance Italy's energy and telecommunications industries. In 1965 this entity enlarged its focus and changed its name to La Centrale Finanziaria Generale a forerunner of Banca Intesa.La Centrale's interests in energy were transferred to ENEL the state holding company in 1985 leaving it with banking finance and insurance holdings. That year the bank merged with Nuovo Banco Ambrosiano formerly Banco Ambrosiano.Banco Ambrosiano was founded in 1896 by Guiseppi Tovino whose good works and sturdy faith made him a saint (he was beatified in 1998). Betraying his legacy in 1981 chairman Roberto Calvi was found hanging under the Blackfriars Bridge in London. Calvi called "God's Banker" for his connections to the Vatican left behind a tangle of debt phony holding companies and fraud that implicated the Catholic Church brought down an archbishop and involved a secretive Masonic lodge. Banco Ambrosiano was taken over by a group of creditor banks and its name was changed to Nuovo Banco Ambrosiano.In 1989 Nuovo Banco Ambrosiano merged with its subsidiary Banco Cattolica del Veneto and became known as Banco Ambroveneto. It bought La Cassa di Risparmio delle Provincie Lombarde (Cariplo) Italy's biggest savings bank in 1997; they merged to form Banca Intesa the following year. Cariplo was founded by the Austro-Hungarian government in 1823 when the region was still recovering from Napoleon's depredations. Count Giovanni Pietro Porro wanted to allow artisans and day laborers to set aside money and the company remained true to that mission throughout Italy's unification and two world wars.Italy began its race toward privatization in 1990 to counter the growing interest of foreign banks in the Italian market and help the nation meet the criteria for joining the European Union. In 1992 San Paolo was one of the first banks to sell a 20% stake in itself (it sold another 20% in 1997). The bank bought several regional and national banks over the next few years and in 1998 merged with investment bank Istituto Mobiliare Italiano or IMI (founded 1931) to form Sanpaolo IMI.Banca Intesa was the product of a combination of the staid Cassa di Risparmio delle Provincie Lombarde (Cariplo) and the somewhat more colorful Banco Ambroveneto whose history helped inspire the plot of The Godfather Part III . It took over Banca Commerciale Italiana (BCI or Comit) in 2000 creating one of Italy's largest banks. Banca Intesa integrated BCI to form IntesaBci the following year and then in late 2002 rebranded as Banca Intesa.Banca Intesa and Sanpaolo IMI merged in 2007. After the deal antitrust authorities ordred the company to sell some 200 branches to France-based Crdit Agricole. In late 2008 the Italian banking group sold 36 branches to Veneto Banca for 274 million ($401 million).A good portion of its branches were acquired in 2007 when Intesa Sanpaolo increased its stake in Banca CR Firenze to some 60% in preparation for taking over the bank outright. Banca CR Firenze added about 550 locations in Tuscany and surrounding regions to Intesa Sanpaolo's network.The next year the bank upped its stake in Cassa dei Risparmi di Forli e della Romagna to about 70% increasing its influence in northern Italy. During more reshuffling of assets Intesa Sanpaolo sold a 30% stake in Cassa di Risparmio di Fano to Credito Valtellinese in 2009.

EXECUTIVES

Chief Risk Officer, Bruno Picca, age 66
Head of Planning and Control, Carlo Messina, age 54
Head of Italian and International Subsidiary Banks Divisions, Giovanni Boccolini, age 62
Chief Economist, Gregorio de Felice
Chief Lending Officer, Eugenio Rossetti, age 60
CFO, Stefano Del Punta
Head Corporate and Investment Banking Division, Gaetano Micciche
COO, Eliano Omar Lodesani
Chairman Supervisory Board, Giovanni Bazoli, age 83
Deputy Chairman Supervisory Board, Mario Bertolissi, age 67
Chairman Management Board, Gian Maria Gros-Pietro
Senior Deputy Chairman Management Board, Marcello Sala
Auditors: KPMG S.p.A.

LOCATIONS

HQ: Intesa Sanpaolo S.P.A.
Piazza San Carlo, 156, Torino 10121
Phone: (39) 11 5551
Web: www.intesasanpaolo.com

2014 Sales

	% of total
Italy	79
Europe	17
Rest of the world	4
Total	**100**

PRODUCTS/OPERATIONS

2014 Sales

	% of total
Net interest income	50
Net fee and commission income	40
Profits on tradings	5
Income from insurance business	5
Total	**100**

Selected Subsidiaries

Banca CR Firenze
Banca dell' Adriatico
Banca di Credito Sardo
Banca di Trento e Bolzano
Banca Fideuram
Banca IMI
Banca Intesa
Banca Intesa Beograd
Banca Monte Parma
Banca Prossima
Banco di Napoli
Bank of Alexandria
Banka Koper
Cassa dei Risparmi di Forlì e della Romagna
Cassa di Risparmio del Friuli Venezia Giulia
Cassa di Risparmio del Veneto
Cassa di Risparmio della Provincia di Viterbo (CARIVIT)
Cassa di Risparmio di Civitavecchia
Cassa di Risparmio di Pistoia e della Lucchesia
Cassa di Risparmio di Rieti (CARIRI)
Cassa di Risparmio di Venezia
Cassa di Risparmio in Bologna
Casse di Risparmio dell' Umbria
CIB Bank
Epsilon Associati SGR
Equiter
Eurizon A.I. SGR
Eurizon Capital
IMI Fondi Chiusi SGR
IMI Investimenti
Infogroup

COMPETITORS

BBVA
BNL bc
Banca Popolare di Milano
Banco Popolare
Dexia
Mediobanca
Monte dei Paschi di Siena
UniCredit

HISTORICAL FINANCIALS

Company Type: Public

Income Statement

FYE: December 31

	ASSETS ($ mil.)	NET INCOME ($ mil.)	INCOME AS % OF ASSETS	EMPLOYEES
12/14	785,735	1,520	0.2%	89,486
12/13	862,226	(6,264)	—	93,945
12/12	887,669	2,115	0.2%	96,170
12/11	826,801	(10,593)	—	100,118
12/10	881,662	3,620	0.4%	102,501
Annual Growth	(2.8%)	(19.5%)	—	(3.3%)

2014 Year-End Financials

Return on assets: 0.2%
Return on equity: 2.8%
Long-term debt ($ mil.): —
No. of shares (mil.): —
Sales ($ mil): 52,845
Dividends
Yield: 1.7%
Payout: 279.3%
Market value ($ mil.): —

	STOCK PRICE ($) FY Close	P/E High/Low	PER SHARE ($) Earnings	Dividends	Book Value
12/14	17.32	238163	0.10	0.31	3.43
12/13	14.95	— —	(0.39)	0.57	3.96
12/12	10.64	126 68	0.13	0.28	4.22
12/11	9.94	— —	(0.72)	1.10	3.93
12/10	16.22	123 74	0.28	0.41	6.05
Annual Growth	1.7%	— —	(23.3%)	(6.8%)	(13.2%)

Israel Discount Bank Ltd.

Who doesn't love a discount? Israel Discount Bank the third-largest bank in Israel has about 150 locations across the country. The bank offers standard consumer services like deposits loans and credit cards in addition to private banking international trade and commercial banking activities. Israel Discount Bank oversees four subsidiaries – Discount Mortgage Bank Mercantile Discount Bank (which has about 75 branches) Israel Discount Bank of New York and IDB (Swiss) Bank Ltd. It also owns a 26% stake in First International Bank of Israel the country's fifth-largest bank. In 2015 IDB sold Uruguay-based subsidiary Discount Bank Latin America to Bank of Nova Scotia in a deal worth $65 million.

Company BackgroundIn 2010 Israel Discount Bank announced it was selling off Tachlit Investment House its portfolio management subsidiary that has about $3 billion in assets under management.

Auditors: Ziv Haft

LOCATIONS

HQ: Israel Discount Bank Ltd.
23 Yehuda Halevi Street, Tel-Aviv 65136
Phone: (972) 3 514 5555 **Fax:** (972) 3 514 5346
Web: www.discountbank.net

COMPETITORS

Bank Hapoalim
Bank Leumi le-Israel
First International Bank of Israel
Mizrahi Tefahot

HISTORICAL FINANCIALS

Company Type: Public

Income Statement FYE: December 31

	ASSETS ($ mil.)	NET INCOME ($ mil.)	INCOME AS % OF ASSETS	EMPLOYEES
12/14	53,256	153	0.3%	9,215
12/13	57,783	251	0.4%	9,877
12/12	53,893	215	0.4%	9,942
12/11	52,966	244	0.5%	10,211
12/10	52,437	204	0.4%	10,221
Annual Growth	0.4%	(6.9%)	—	(2.6%)

2014 Year-End Financials

Return on assets: 0.2%
Return on equity: 4.6%
Long-term debt ($ mil.): —
No. of shares (mil.): 105
Sales ($ mil): 2,313

Dividends
Yield: —
Payout: —
Market value ($ mil.): —

	STOCK PRICE ($) FY Close	P/E High/Low		PER SHARE ($) Earnings	Dividends	Book Value
12/14	0.00	—	—	0.15	0.00	32.34
12/13	1.50	2	2	0.24	0.00	33.45
12/12	0.96	2	1	0.20	0.00	30.14
12/11	1.42	2	2	0.21	0.00	26.67
Annual Growth	—	—	—	(8.8%)	—	4.9%

Itau Unibanco Holding S.A.

Itaú Unibanco is one way of saying "really big bank." The Brazilian bank offers a variety of standard retail and commercial banking services as well as consumer credit financial management leasing foreign exchange and trade financing. It is one of Brazil's largest credit card issuers. It also provides investment banking securities brokerage and insurance services. Besides its network of more than 3900 Brazilian branches the firm boasts operations in other South America countries and in North America the Caribbean Asia and Europe. It leverages acquisitions such as its 2013 Credicard purchase to boost its presence. Banco Itaú merged with Unibanco in 2009 to become Itaú Unibanco.

The deal to combine the two Brazilian megabanks established the largest private financial conglomerate in South America. Itaú Unibanco is now better equipped to compete on an international level as it expands its global presence. The merger also allowed the bank to expand credit and increase its range of products and services. Since joining forces the group has more than doubled its earnings.

In 2012 the bank agreed to buy the 49.99% it doesn't already own in card payment processing firm Redecard for some R11.8 billion (approximately $6.8 billion). The deal will help boost earnings from credit and debit card usage; it should also help Redecard compete in the growing payment-processing sector.

Itaú Unibanco is controlled by holding company IUPAR itself controlled by the Egydio de Souza Aranha family. The Moreira Salles family which previously controlled Unibanco holds a stake of about 25% of the bank. Together the families have board representation with five company directors (including president and CEO Egydio Setubal).

EXECUTIVES

Vice Chairman and CEO, Roberto Egydio Setubal, age 60
EVP and Investor Relations, Alfredo Egydio Setubal, age 60
EVP, Candido Botelho Bracher, age 56
CFO and EVP, Caio Ibrahim David, age 46
Chairman, Pedro Moreira Salles, age 56
Vice Chairman, Alfredo Egydio Arruda Villela Filho, age 45
Auditors: PricewaterhouseCoopers Auditores Independentes

LOCATIONS

HQ: Itau Unibanco Holding S.A.
Praca Alfredo Egydio de Souza Aranha, 100, Sao Paulo 04344-902
Phone: (55) 11 5019 1267
Web: www.itau-unibanco.com

PRODUCTS/OPERATIONS

2013 Sales

	% of total
Interest & similar income	72
Banking service fees	17
Foreign exchange results & exchange variation on transaction	5
Income from insurance private pension & capitalization	5
Other	1
Total	**100**

COMPETITORS

Banco Bradesco
Banco Franc©s
Banco Santander
Banco do Brasil
Caixa Econ´mica Federal

HISTORICAL FINANCIALS

Company Type: Public

Income Statement FYE: December 31

	ASSETS ($ mil.)	NET INCOME ($ mil.)	INCOME AS % OF ASSETS	EMPLOYEES
12/15	322,276	6,498	2.0%	90,320
12/14	424,191	8,111	1.9%	93,175
12/13	434,889	6,952	1.6%	95,696
12/12	468,153	6,179	1.3%	96,977
12/11	438,678	7,419	1.7%	104,542
Annual Growth	(7.4%)	(3.3%)	—	(3.6%)

2015 Year-End Financials

Return on assets: 2.1%
Return on equity: 24.3%
Long-term debt ($ mil.): —
No. of shares (mil.): —
Sales ($ mil): 47,703

Dividends
Yield: 6.1%
Payout: 29.0%
Market value ($ mil.): —

	STOCK PRICE ($) FY Close	P/E High/Low		PER SHARE ($) Earnings	Dividends	Book Value
12/15	6.51	2	1	1.08	0.40	4.79
12/14	13.01	4	3	1.48	0.37	6.83
12/13	13.57	5	3	1.40	0.31	13.99
12/12	16.46	7	5	1.36	0.38	16.22
12/11	18.56	7	4	1.64	0.45	17.32
Annual Growth	(23.0%)	—	—	(9.8%)	(2.8%)	(27.5%)

ITOCHU Corp. (Japan)

Itochu Enex is totally immersed in Japan's oil and gas markets. The company operates more than 20 subsidiaries. The home life segment supplies liquefied petroleum gas (LPG) to more than 1 million homes and businesses throughout Japan. The company's car life and industrial materials divisions operate full service gas stations and sells gasoline kerosene and oil to service stations. Additionally they cater to the manufacturing trucking and shipping industries selling them oil LPG and coal as well as secondary energy like electricity and heat and industrial materials such as asphalt and cement. The energy trade division engages in global oil product trading and logistics.

HISTORY

Chubei Itoh was only 18 when he organized his own wholesale linen business C. Itoh & Co. in 1858. As Japan opened to foreign trade in the 1860s the company prospered and was one of Osaka's largest textile wholesalers by the 1870s. C. Itoh established a trade office in San Francisco in 1889.

By 1919 C. Itoh had trading offices in New York Calcutta Manila and four cities in China. Although it was not one of the "zaibatsu" (industrial groups) that flourished in Japan during the period between the world wars C. Itoh benefited from the general increase in trade.

C. Itoh merged in 1941 with two other trading operations Marubeni and Kishimoto into a new company Sanko Kabushiki Kaisha. C. Itoh and Marubeni were separated in 1949. C. Itoh supplied UN troops with provisions during the Korean War; profits were used to diversify into petroleum machinery aircraft and automobiles.

After the oil crisis of 1973 demonstrated Japan's vulnerability to oil import disruptions C. Itoh actively participated in the development of petroleum production technology. To prevent the failure of Japan's 10th-largest trading company Ataka the Japanese government arranged a merger in 1977 making C. Itoh the third-largest "sogo shosha."

The company established Japan Communications Satellite (JCSAT) with Mitsui and Hughes Communications in 1985. JCSAT launched its first two satellites in 1989 and 1990. The following year C. Itoh and Toshiba joined Time Warner in a limited partnership Time Warner Entertainment Company to produce and distribute movies and television programs and to operate cable TV systems in the US. C. Itoh Time Warner and Toshiba formed another joint venture to distribute Warner Bros. films and develop amusements parks in Japan.

C. Itoh changed its name to ITOCHU a transliteration of its Japanese name in 1992. After sales dropped the next year ITOCHU began selling poorly performing subsidiaries reducing its investment portfolio by more than one-third.

In 1996 the company formed an alliance with US oil company Atlantic Richfield to buy Coastal Corp.'s western US coal operations and it took a stake in a massive project led by Amoco and British Petroleum to develop oil and gas deposits in the Caspian Sea. That year PerfecTV! (a joint venture with Sumitomo and other Japanese companies) began satellite broadcasting. Also in 1996 ITOCHU bought stakes in the Asia Broadcasting and Communications Network a satellite communications company.

To help cover its losses from the Asian currency crisis the company sold 40% of its stake in Time Warner in 1998; in 1999 ITOCHU sold its remaining stake. ITOCHU also sold low-performing real estate investments and laid plans to divest about one-third of its subsidiaries.

Two of ITOCHU's agricultural subsidiaries were liquidated in 2000. The company also sought out partnerships in order to offset costs incurred in new ventures: it joined with Japan's other top trading companies and Brazil's Petrobras to develop oil fields in South America. And in response to the rapid consolidation of Japan's steel industry ITOCHU and Marubeni agreed to integrate their steel operations in 2001 to better compete.

In 2002 ITOCHU formed a partnership with Bally International to expand the European fashion brand's presence in Japan. In 2004 the company sold its interest in Utah-based Canyon Fuel Co. to Arch Coal Inc. for $112 million and dissolved its subsidiary ITOCHU Coal International Inc. Also that year the company formed a joint venture with Ishimori Shotaro Pro Inc. to establish Ishimori Entertainment which produces movies television programs and publications based on Shotaro Ishimori titles including the popular MASKED RIDER.

ITOCHU established a fund with Turner Broadcasting to finance Japanese animation in 2005. It also acquired two US medical-device-distribution companies Products for Surgery and Flanagan Instruments marking ITOCHU's first step into that market.

In 2008 the company partnered with BayCorp Holdings and Energy Management to form American Renewables to develop build and operate biomass-fueled power-generation facilities in the US. Also that year it acquired 41% of Medical Collective a Japanese company that provides marketing assistance to pharmaceutical companies.

In 2010 ITOCHU bought China-based daily goods wholesaler Hangzhou New Huahai Business & Trading boosting its presence in that market. That same year ITOCHU agreed to acquire a 15% stake in Kalahari Minerals PLC which holds uranium gold copper and other base metal interests in Namibia.

Also that year ITOCHU made deals to move into the US energy market joining Chubu Electric Power in a joint venture to buy five natural-gas fired power plants from Tenaska and acquire a 25% interest in the Niobrara shale oil mining project in southeastern Wyoming. With the latter transaction ITOCHU became the first Japanese company to participate in a US shale oil project. The company had acquired 85% of US-based solar power systems maker Solar Net LLC in 2009.

Masahiro Okafuji was named president of ITOCHU in 2010. He replaced Eizo Kobayashi who was named the company's chairman. Okafuji was previously ITOCHU's EVP.

EXECUTIVES

President, Kenji Okada
Auditors: Deloitte Touche Tohmatsu LLC

LOCATIONS

HQ: ITOCHU Corp. (Japan)
3-1-3 Umeda, Kita-ku, Osaka 530-8448
Phone: (81) 6 7638 2121
Web: www.itochu.co.jp

PRODUCTS/OPERATIONS

2014 Sales

	% of total
Energy Trade	25
Car-Life	59
Total	13
Power and Utility	3
Other	-
Total	100

COMPETITORS

Marubeni
Showa Shell Sekiyu
TonenGeneral

HISTORICAL FINANCIALS

Company Type: Public

Income Statement FYE: March 31

	REVENUE ($ mil.)	NET INCOME ($ mil.)	NET PROFIT MARGIN	EMPLOYEES
03/15	46,603	2,505	5.4%	142,178
03/14	54,132	2,376	4.4%	134,010
03/13	48,673	2,978	6.1%	98,272
03/12	52,066	3,663	7.0%	94,366
03/11	44,074	1,943	4.4%	84,589
Annual Growth	1.4%	6.5%	—	13.9%

2015 Year-End Financials

Debt ratio: 0.3%
Return on equity: 13.4%
Cash ($ mil.): 5,836
Current ratio: 1.45
Long-term debt ($ mil.): 21,241
No. of shares (mil.): 1,577
Dividends
Yield: 4.0%
Payout: 50.7%
Market value ($ mil.): 34,297

	STOCK PRICE ($) FY Close	P/E High/Low		PER SHARE ($) Earnings	Dividends	Book Value
03/15	21.74	0	0	1.56	0.88	12.86
03/14	23.38	0	0	1.50	0.81	12.56
03/13	24.49	0	0	1.88	1.01	11.89
03/12	21.85	0	0	2.32	0.62	10.54
03/11	20.90	1	0	1.23	1.24	8.84
Annual Growth	1.0%	—	—	6.2%	(8.2%)	9.8%

Iyo Bank, Ltd. (Japan)

With 15-plus branches and about a dozen subsidiaries The Iyo Bank targets customers across the four prefectures of Shikoku and the seven prefectures surrounding the Seto Inland Sea. The institution which has grown to become Japan's #1 regional bank offers retail products including deposits leasing services trusts and pension products and mergers and acquisitions support services. The Iyo Bank also operates a securities brokerage business arm. Its Corporate Consulting Division helps companies galvanize their operations and capital. Established in 1941 the bank owns and operates branch offices in Hong Kong Shanghai and New York. It boasts alliances with banks in China Thailand Indonesia and India.

EXECUTIVES

President, Iwao Otsuka
Senior Managing Director, Ippei Nagai
Managing Director, Shuichi Miyazaki
Managing Director, Hiroyuki Takaoka
Managing Director, Kenji Takata
Managing Director, Muneaki Todo
Executive Officer, Kenji Morioka
Executive Officer, Kenji Miyoshi
Executive Officer, Hideyo Nishimoto
Executive Officer, Yuichi Matsuura
Chairman, Koji Morita
Auditors: KPMG AZSA LLC

LOCATIONS

HQ: Iyo Bank, Ltd. (Japan)
1 Minami-Horibata-cho, Matsuyama, Ehime 790-8514
Phone: (81) 89 941 1141 **Fax:** 212 688-6420
Web: www.iyobank.co.jp

Selected Branch Locations

Head Offic
Aichi
Fukuoka
Hiroshima
Hyogo
Kagawa
Kochi
Oita
Okayama
Osaka
Tokushima
Tokyo
Yamaguchi

PRODUCTS/OPERATIONS

Selected Subsidiaries

Computer Services Inc. Iyogin
Iyogin Business Service Co. Ltd.
Iyogin Capital Co. Ltd.
Iyogin guarantee Ltd.
Iyogin Leasing Co. Ltd.
Iyogin Securities Co. Ltd.
Ltd. Iyo silver Regional Center for Economic Research
Ltd. Iyogin Dee Sea card

COMPETITORS

Aozora Bank
Joyo Bank
Miyazaki Bank
Shizuoka Bank
Toho Bank

HISTORICAL FINANCIALS

Company Type: Public

Income Statement FYE: March 31

	ASSETS ($ mil.)	NET INCOME ($ mil.)	INCOME AS % OF ASSETS	EMPLOYEES
03/15	54,804	225	0.4%	2,977
03/14	59,337	253	0.4%	2,937
03/13	63,817	195	0.3%	2,872
03/12	69,151	224	0.3%	2,857
03/11	64,794	182	0.3%	2,888
Annual Growth	(4.1%)	5.4%	—	0.8%

2015 Year-End Financials

Return on assets: 0.4%
Return on equity: 5.0%
Long-term debt ($ mil.): —
No. of shares (mil.): 316
Sales ($ mil): 1,033

Dividends
Yield: —
Payout: —
Market value ($ mil.): —

J Sainsbury PLC

J Sainsbury's trolley is filled with more than groceries. The UK's third-largest food retailer (after Tesco and ASDA) operates the Sainsbury's Supermarkets chain of some 570 stores throughout the UK. Its Sainsbury's online home delivery shopping service covers more than 90% of the UK population. In addition to supermarkets it operates a fast-growing convenience store business with 440 shops under the Sainsbury's Local banner. The firm also owns half of Sainsbury's Bank (in a 50-50 joint venture with Lloyds Banking Group) and a pair of property joint ventures. Sainsbury also sells apparel and home goods including cookware and bedding in its supermarkets and online. The company agreed to buy Home Retail Group for $1.9 billion in February 2016.

Mergers and Acquisitions In February 2016 Sainsbury's agreed to buy Home Retail Group for £1.3 billion (around $1.9 billion).

Company Background

Sainsbury bought the online entertainment company from MBL Group plcfor £1 billion ($1.57 billion) in October. The grocery chain which launched its own entertainment Web site in late 2010 said the acquisition will support its drive into the growing online and digital entertainment market. Global Media Vault's digital database includes more than three million music film and game assets for the UK market.

After losing the #2 slot in the UK grocery market years ago to Wal-Mart-owned ASDA Sainsbury has made a strong comeback battling back and forth with ASDA for second place. The two rivals are enmeshed in an ongoing price war with market leader Tesco and other domestic and foreign food retailers including deep-discounters such as ALDI and Lidl. (Sainsbury enjoys an even stronger position in populous London with about 25% of the market.)

HISTORY

Newlyweds John James and Mary Ann Sainsbury established a small dairy shop in their London home in 1869. Customers flocked to the clean and efficient store a far cry from most cluttered and dirty London shops. They opened a second store in 1876. By 1914 115 stores had been opened and the couple's sons had entered the business.

During WWI the company's stores established grocery departments to meet demand for preserved products such as meat and jams which were sold under the Sainsbury's label.

Mary Ann died in 1927 and John James the next year. Son John Benjamin wholly devoted to the family business took charge. (He is reported to have said on his deathbed "Keep the stores well lit.") In the 1930s he engineered the company's first acquisition the Thoroughgood stores.

Sales dropped by 50% during WWII and some shops were destroyed by German bombing. Under third-generation leader Alan John Sainsbury the company opened its first self-service store in 1950 in Croydon. The 75000-sq.-ft. store opened in 1955 in Lewisham was considered to be the largest supermarket in Europe.

J Sainsbury went public in 1973. It established a joint venture with British Home Stores in 1975 forming the Savacentre hypermarkets (the company bought out its partner in 1989).

Sainsbury partnered with Grand Bazaar Innovation Bon Marche of Belgium in 1979 to establish Homebase a do-it-yourself chain. (It bought the remaining 25% in 1996 and then sold the company in 2001 retaining only 18%.)

By 1983 most of Sainsbury's 229 stores were clustered in the south of England. A mature market and stiff competition forced the company to look elsewhere –both overseas and close to home. It began buying out US-based Shaw's Supermarkets in New England and in 1984 opened its first Scottish hypermarket. By 1987 the grocer owned 100% of Shaw's which had 60 stores in Massachusetts Maine and New Hampshire.

In 1991 Sainsbury came under competitive pressure from Tesco and the Argyll Group (later renamed Safeway plc) which also began building superstores. It responded with an expansion drive of its own including opening its first Scottish supermarket (in Glasgow) the next year.

In 1994 the company purchased a $325 million stake in Maryland-based Giant Food. Sainsbury bought home improvement retailer Texas Homecare from UK leisure concern Ladbroke in 1995 and integrated it into its Homebase unit. The following year it bought 12 supermarkets in Connecticut from Dutch retailer Royal Ahold (the purchase lowered its profits for the year) and entered Northern Ireland.

A year later the company opened Sainsbury's Bank. Royal Ahold bought Giant Food including Sainsbury's 20% stake in 1998. David Sainsbury –a great-grandson of the founders –retired as chairman in 1998 to pursue politics marking the first time a Sainsbury had not headed up the company in its more-than-a-century history.

As a cost-cutting effort in 1999 Sainsbury cut 2200 jobs more than half in management. It also launched its convenience store concept called Sainsbury's Local. Also that year Sainsbury bought the 53-store Star Markets chain of Massachusetts merging it into its Shaw's operations. In March 2000 Sir Peter Davis took over as CEO of Sainsbury's Supermarkets replacing David Bremner.

In 2001 Sainsbury acquired 19 Grand Union stores in the US (17 of which were converted to the Shaw's banner) and opened 25 new stores in the UK. The company also exited the Egyptian market and sold its home-and-garden chain Homebase to private equity firm Permira.

In 2002 Shaw's Supermarkets bought control of 18 stores in New England from bankrupt discounter Ames.

In November 2003 Sainsbury reached a £2 million out-of-court settlement with designer Jeff Banks over termination of his contract to revamp its clothing line in a bid to emulate rival ASDA's success with its George line of apparel.

In January 2004 the grocery chain acquired Swan Infrastructure (an Accenture affiliate) the company that ran its information technology systems for about $1 billion. The move brought the grocers information technology operations which were outsourced in 2000 back in-house.

In February 2004 Sainsbury acquired 54 Bells convenience stores. (Bells Stores was founded in 1968 by Les Bell and was owned by the Bell family until its acquisition.) Justin King (formerly of Marks & Spencer) joined Sainsbury as its CEO in March 2004 succeeding Sir Peter Davis who became chairman of the board. In April Sainsbury sold JS USA Holdings which operated 203 Shaw's and Star Markets stores in New England to US grocery chain Albertson's in a deal worth about $2.4 billion. The retailer also disposed of JS Developments its property development operation in fiscal 2004. Davis stepped down as chairman of Sainsbury on July 1 2004 one year ahead of schedule and following a prolonged dispute with investors that culminated in a fight over his compensation.

Philip Hampton (former finance director of Lloyds TSB (now Lloyds Banking Group) BT Group and BG Group) joined Sainsbury as its new chairman on July 19 2004. Hampton's appointment and experience with mergers and acquisitions fueled speculation that the struggling grocery chain may become a takeover target. In August Sainsbury acquired Jacksons Stores Ltd. and its wholly owned subsidiary Jacksons Stores 2002 Ltd. for about £100 million. In September Sainsbury agreed to pay ex-chairman Davis £2.6 million despite shareholder protests in July that forced the grocery retailer to withdraw a similar offer. At that time Lord Levene of Portsoken and Keith Butler-Wheelhouse both non-executive directors of the company and members of the remuneration committee resigned from the board.

In October 2004 Sainsbury said it was writing off £140 million against information technology systems and an another £120 million linked to ineffective supply chain equipment as a result of a huge infrastructure investment program instituted by ex-chairman Davis that failed. In November the company acquired JB Beaumont a convenience store chain with six stores in the East Midlands. In 2005 the grocery chain acquired the five-store SL Shaw chain in southeastern England. Sainsbury renamed the shops Sainsbury's Local. The acquisitions pushed Sainsbury's convenience store count to nearly 300 outlets throughout the UK giving the company a 2% share of the convenience market.

The company sold 5% of its majority stake in Sainsbury's Bank in February 2007 to its joint venture partner HBOS for about £21 million ($40 million). As a result the bank became a 50-50 joint venture between the two firms. Also in 2007 the company shutdown its online entertainment division Sainsbury's Entertain You which offered books CDs DVDs videos computer games and a DVD rental service citing stiff competition in the online arena. The company removed hydrogenated fats from its branded products in 2007.

In mid-2008 Qatar Holding-backed real estate investment group Delta Two increased its stake in Sainsbury to about 25% fueling speculation that it may attempt to take over the British grocer. (In 2007 Delta Two made a bid to buy the remainder of the company but withdrew the offering in November amid turmoil in the credit markets.) Delta Two was the second suitor to leave the grocery chain at the altar. The company and key shareholders from the founding Sainsbury family rebuffed a group of private equity investors led by CVC Capital earlier in the year.

In mid-2009 the grocery chain launched online sales of some 8000 non-food items such as kitchenware and furniture. It also extended its online home grocery delivery service to an additional 200 stores. The company welcomed David Tyler formerly chairman of Logica as its new chairman in November 2009. Tyler succeeded Sir Philip Hampton.

In November 2010 the company launched Sainsbury's Entertainment a digital download service that provides customers with access to more than 150000 books DVDs Blu-rays CDs and games to purchase online.

EXECUTIVES

MD of General Merchandise Clothing & Logistics, Roger Burnley
Property Director, John Rogers
IT Director, Rob Fraser
CEO, Mike Coupe
Chairman, David A. Tyler, age 62
Auditors: PricewaterhouseCoopers LLP

LOCATIONS

HQ: J Sainsbury PLC
33 Holborn, London EC1N 2HT
Phone: (44) 20 7921 6000
Web: www.j-sainsbury.co.uk

PRODUCTS/OPERATIONS

2015 segment

	%
Retailing	99
Financial services	1
Property investments	0
Total	**100**

2015 Stores

	No.
Sainsbury's Supermarkets	597
Convenience stores	707
Total	**1,304**

PRODUCTS
Summer
Fruit & ve
Meat & fis
Dairy eggs
Bakery
Frozen
Food cupboard
Drinks
Health & b
Baby
Household
Pet
Home
Cook event

COMPETITORS

ALDI
ASDA
Co-operative Group
Costcutter Supermarkets
Iceland Foods
Lidl
METRO AG
Marks & Spencer
Musgrave Retail Partners
SNAX 24
SPAR (UK)
Tesco
Waitrose
Wm Morrison Supermarkets

HISTORICAL FINANCIALS

Company Type: Public

Income Statement

FYE: March 14

	REVENUE ($ mil.)	NET INCOME ($ mil.)	NET PROFIT MARGIN	EMPLOYEES
03/15	35,195	(245)	—	161,100
03/14	39,747	1,188	3.0%	160,500
03/13	35,322	930	2.6%	157,000
03/12	35,079	940	2.7%	152,000
03/11	34,073	1,033	3.0%	148,400
Annual Growth	0.8%	—	—	2.1%

2015 Year-End Financials

Debt ratio: 24.7%
Return on equity: (-2.8%)
Cash ($ mil.): 1,902
Current ratio: 0.65
Long-term debt ($ mil.): 3,709
No. of shares (mil.): 1,919
Dividends
Yield: 0.0%
Payout: —
Market value ($ mil.): 29,540

	STOCK PRICE ($) FY Close	P/E High/Low		PER SHARE ($) Earnings	Dividends	Book Value
03/15	15.39	—	—	(0.13)	1.02	4.27
03/14	21.14	74	54	0.61	1.12	5.22
03/13	21.84	67	52	0.49	0.98	4.59
03/12	19.10	71	51	0.50	0.95	4.70
03/11	22.60	74	59	0.55	0.98	4.68
Annual Growth	(9.2%)	—	—	—	0.9%	(2.3%)

Jardine Matheson Holdings Ltd.

EXECUTIVES

Presidente, Benjamin William Keswick
Presidente Junta Directiva, Henry Keswick
Auditors: PricewaterhouseCoopers LLP

LOCATIONS

HQ: Jardine Matheson Holdings Ltd.
4th Floor, Jardine House, 33-35 Reid Street, Hamilton HM 12
Phone: (441) 292 0515 **Fax:** (441) 292 4072
Web: www.jardines.com

HISTORICAL FINANCIALS

Company Type: Public

Income Statement

FYE: December 31

	REVENUE ($ mil.)	NET INCOME ($ mil.)	NET PROFIT MARGIN	EMPLOYEES
12/14	39,921	1,710	4.3%	430,000
12/13	39,465	1,566	4.0%	390,000
12/12	39,593	1,688	4.3%	0
12/11	37,967	3,449	9.1%	0
12/10	30,053	3,084	10.3%	0
Annual Growth	7.4%	(13.7%)	—	—

2014 Year-End Financials

Debt ratio: 17.2%
Return on equity: 9.0%
Cash ($ mil.): 5,315
Current ratio: 1.40
Long-term debt ($ mil.): 7,416
No. of shares (mil.): 305
Dividends
Yield: 2.1%
Payout: 28.6%
Market value ($ mil.): 18,514

	STOCK PRICE ($) FY Close	P/E High/Low		PER SHARE ($) Earnings	Dividends	Book Value
12/14	60.70	14	11	4.61	1.32	63.17
12/13	52.81	16	12	4.25	1.29	60.68
12/12	62.23	14	10	4.62	1.19	59.34
12/11	47.51	6	5	9.46	1.10	54.89
12/10	44.26	6	3	8.34	0.91	46.32
Annual Growth	8.2%	—	—	(13.8%)	9.8%	8.1%

Jardine Strategic Holdings Ltd (Bermuda)

Jardine Strategic Holdings (JSH) has a garden of multinationals. Primary interests include Dairy Farm International with 5800 locations hotel group Mandarin Oriental with 45 hotels holding company Jardine Cycle & Carriage (the largest engine manufacturer in Indonesia) financial services firm Rothchilds Continuation and real estate developer Hongkong Land. JSH and its Hong Kong-based affiliate Jardine Matheson Holdings share these interests and are operated together in a complex ownership structure. Jardine Matheson provides services to JSH owns about 80% of its stock. Formed after the breakup of the East India Company's tea monopoly in 1832 JSH was instrumental in the formation of Hong Kong.

The company was originally formed in the wake of the breakup of the East India Company's tea trade monopoly in 1832. Following Jardines' founding it was a key company that promoted the founding of Hong Kong.

EXECUTIVES

Group Finance Director, James Riley
Director, David Hsu
Chairman, Henry Keswick
Chairman and Managing Director, Ben Keswick
Deputy Chairman and Deputy Managing Director, Adam Keswick
Auditors: PricewaterhouseCoopers LLP

LOCATIONS

HQ: Jardine Strategic Holdings Ltd (Bermuda)
Jardine House, 33-35 Reid Street, Hamilton
Phone:
Web: www.jardines.com

PRODUCTS/OPERATIONS

2013 Sales

	% of total
Astra	56
Dairy Farm	32
Hong-Kong Land	6
Jardine Cycle & Carriage	4
Mandarin Oriental	2
Intersegment transaction	0
Total	**100**

2013 Sales

	% of total
Motor Vehicles	35
Retail	32
Mining	10
Property and hotels	8
Engineering and Construction	5
Agribusiness	4
Financial Services	4
Logistics and IT Services	2
Resturants	0
Total	**100**

2013 Sales

	% of total
Southeast Asia	78
Greater China	21
United Kingdom	0
Rest of World	1
Total	**100**

Subsidiaries

Astra International
Dairy Farm
Hongkong Land
Jardine Cy
Jardine Lloyd Thompson
Jardine Matheson
Jardine Motors
Jardine Pacific
Mandarin Oriental

COMPETITORS

Accor	Hyatt
China Resources Beer	ITOCHU
Continental Automotive Group	Marriott
	Marubeni
Daiei	McDonald' s
HSBC	Royal Ahold
Hopewell Holdings	Swire Pacific

HISTORICAL FINANCIALS

Company Type: Public

Income Statement FYE: December 31

	REVENUE ($ mil.)	NET INCOME ($ mil.)	NET PROFIT MARGIN	EMPLOYEES
12/14	32,236	1,832	5.7%	0
12/13	32,666	1,700	5.2%	0
12/12	33,098	1,839	5.6%	0
12/11	31,049	3,943	12.7%	0
12/10	25,498	3,535	13.9%	0
Annual Growth	6.0%	(15.2%)	—	—

2014 Year-End Financials

Debt ratio: 16.8%
Return on equity: 8.1%
Cash ($ mil.): 5,074
Current ratio: 1.46
Long-term debt ($ mil.): 7,260
No. of shares (mil.): 196
Dividends
Yield: 0.0%
Payout: 3.8%
Market value ($ mil.): 3,348

	STOCK PRICE ($) FY Close	P/E High	P/E Low	PER SHARE ($) Earnings	Dividends	Book Value
12/14	17.08	6	5	3.02	0.12	118.33
12/13	16.01	7	6	2.79	0.11	112.39
12/12	17.76	23	5	2.99	0.42	106.72
12/11	54.92	11	8	6.34	0.10	98.26
12/10	55.20	10	6	5.54	0.37	78.99
Annual Growth	(25.4%)	—	—	(14.1%)	(25.2%)	10.6%

JBS SA

Carnivores have a friend in JBS. With a daily slaughter capacity of 86000 head of cattle JBS is the world's biggest beef (and pork poultry and lamb) processor and exporter. In addition to fresh and processed beef and pork (it is the #3 pork producer in the US) JBS offers cooked and canned meats ready-to-eat meals as well as hides and dairy products. JBS sells beef domestically under the Friboi brand. It also owns about 75% of US poultry giant Pilgrim's Pride. JBS exports products worldwide; top markets include Japan the Middle East and Africa and Mexico. Positioned as an integrated food company JBS is expanding in the US and Australia. The Batista family through FB Parti $pac µes owns 47% of JBS.

Managing its growth strategy is challenging the company's already full plate of activities. JBS posted almost a 60% increase in year-over-year revenues in 2010 fueled in part by its business acquisitions and marking it as Brazil's third largest company by revenue. Earnings before interest and taxes soared too. Nonetheless net earnings plummeted to roughly a $180 million loss eroded by debt which swelled by more than 20% and other costs. Among them the cost to restructure its US operations (including consolidation of Pilgrim's Pride) simultaneous with incorporating Bertin (a Brazilian meatpacker taken over in late 2009) with the JBS Mercosul food division has taken a toll on working capital resulting in higher financial expenses.

Adding to its frustration after two unsuccessful runs at Sara Lee in 2011 and late 2010 JBS ended its attempt to buy the iconic cheesecake maker. A takeover of Sara Lee's packaged meat business (Ball Park Jimmy Dean) would have consolidated JBS's power as a global integrated meat producer rivaling US-based Tyson Foods and Smithfield Foods. Following JBS's second failed bid Wesley Batista succeeded his brother Joesley as company CEO. Wesley formerly head of JBS USA Holdings has more than two decades of experience in the company.

Under Joesley Batista JBS undertook an aggressive international expansion strategy culminating in alliances and acquisitions in Argentina Australia Europe and the US. Late 2010 JBS entered a 50/50 joint venture with Jack Link's Beef Jerky a maker of the top US meat snack brand. Concurrently Jack Link's purchased a beef jerky manufacturing plant from JBS and JBS agreed to supply raw meat to Jack Link's for processing packaging and distribution.

Significant acquisitions have included taking over the ailing Pilgrim's Pride (2009). The deal marked JBS's entry into the US poultry industry and rank as the #2 poultry producer in the world with a daily slaughtering capacity of 7.9 million birds. After acquiring its initial stake in Pilgrim's Pride JBS upped its holding to more than 67% in late 2010 and later to 75% in 2012.

JBS also bought out US beef producer Swift Foods (2007) now JBS USA. To diversify its funding resources and raise money for acquisitions the company in 2009 filed to take JBS USA public. It delayed the IPO and paid an approximately $315 million penalty for its inaction (which added to the company's loss in 2010). In early 2011 JBS withdrew the IPO.

HISTORY

After nearly two decades in operation JBS began to expand its business significantly and steadily during the 1970s by purchasing independent slaughterhouses and cattle processing facilities throughout Brazil. These acquisitions continued through the end of the century at which point JBS also began to turn an acquisitive eye toward Argentina.

In 2005 the Brazilian meat giant took its first step abroad buying 85% of Swift Armour Argentina's largest beef processor for $200 million. In 2007 the company acquired US-based Swift Foods for $225 million and assumed its heavy debt load estimated at more than $1 billion a few months after going public on the Sao Paulo Stock Exchange.

In 2008 JBS acquired Australian-based beef producer Tasman Group for $107 million in cash. Also that year it bought US processor Smithfield Beef from Smithfield Foods for $565 million. In Europe it formed a 50:50 joint venture with Italy's Cremonini and subsidiary Inalca with plants in Italy Russia and Africa for $328 million.

In 2009 JBS filed with US regulators to hold a $2 billion initial public offering for JBS USA Holdings (It withdrew the proposed IPO in 2011.) Also in 2009 JBS acquired a 64% stake in restructured US poultry producer Pilgrim's Pride for $800 million. Prior to declaring bankruptcy in 2008 Pilgrim was the #1 US chicken producer and despite selling off some of its operations was still a huge poultry operation. Other than saying it hoped to increase Pilgrim's competitiveness both domestically and internationally JBS made no other statement as to Pilgrim's future. In late 2009 JBS acquired Australia's Tatiara Meat Company from the Dutch company VION Food Group for $28 million. Tatiara is Australia's largest exporter of fresh lamb meat; it also offers value-added lamb products. It was integrated into JBS's Swift Australia operations. At home JBS bought #2 Brazilian beef producer Bertin with 38 plants at home and abroad in an all-stock deal in 2009.

Eyeing acquisitions on the other side of the globe JBS in September 2010 bought Australia's Rockdale Beef from joint owners Itoham Foods and Mitsubishi Corporation. The deal valued at about $38 million boosted the firm's processing capacity by some 550 cattle per day and secured its foothold in the country. In February 2011 Wesley Batista succeeded his brother Joesley Batista as CEO of the company. Wesley formerly head of the company's US subsidiary is a 22-year veteran of JBS. Joesley Batista continued as chairman. In March JBS terminated its joint venture with Italy's Cremonini after a protracted dispute by selling its 50% stake in Inalca back to Cremonini for $304 million.

In March 2012 JBS through its subsidiary JBS USA Holdings increased its stake in Pilgrim's Pride to more than 75% through the purchase of nearly 19 million shares owned by Lonnie Bo Pilgrim for about $107 million.

Auditors: BDO RCS Auditores Independentes SS

LOCATIONS

HQ: JBS SA
Avenida Marginal Direita do Tiete, 500, Sao Paulo, SP 05118-100
Phone: (55) 11 3144 4000 **Fax:** (55) 11 3144 4279
Web: www.jbs.com.br

HISTORICAL FINANCIALS

Company Type: Public

Income Statement FYE: December 31

	REVENUE ($ mil.)	NET INCOME ($ mil.)	NET PROFIT MARGIN	EMPLOYEES
12/14	45,335	766	1.7%	216,000
12/13	39,328	392	1.0%	185,000
12/12	37,024	351	0.9%	0
12/11	33,134	(40)	—	0
12/10	33,166	(182)	—	0
Annual Growth	8.1%	—	—	—

2014 Year-End Financials

Debt ratio: 18.3%
Return on equity: 8.8%
Cash ($ mil.): 5,611
Current ratio: 1.51
Long-term debt ($ mil.): 9,931
No. of shares (mil.): —
Dividends
Yield: 0.0%
Payout: 0.0%
Market value ($ mil.): —

	STOCK PRICE ($) FY Close	P/E High/Low		PER SHARE ($) Earnings	Dividends	Book Value
12/14	8.48	0	0	265.87	0.05	3.11
12/13	7.34	0	0	136.87	0.05	3.24
12/12	6.00	0	0	121.22	0.00	3.54
12/11	6.31			(14.89)	0.00	3.74
12/10	8.67			(73.16)	0.02	4.25
Annual Growth	(0.6%)	—	—	—	20.7%	(7.5%)

JFE Holdings Inc

JFE Holdings has an iron will unmatched in Japan and much of the rest of the world. The "J" in JFE stands for Japan; "F" is for Fe the chemical symbol for iron; and "E" stands for engineering. JFE Holdings' steel business unit JFE Steel accounts for about 85% of total sales and manufactures steel products such as bars pipes steel frames tubes and stainless steel for the automotive construction and petroleum industries. JFE is among the world's largest steel companies ranking behind ArcelorMittal Japan's Nippon Steel & Sumitomo Metal and China's Hebei Iron and Steel and Baosteel.

Geographic Reach

While most of its steel production facilities are in Japan JFE's reach is global and it has offices in 12 other countries.

Operations

JFE's engineering unit makes designs and builds facilities such as gasifying and melting furnaces water purification plants steelworks plants and equipment and steel structures used in the energy environmental and steel structural sectors. Its shipbuilding unit constructs both merchant and military vessels in several Japanese ports including Kyoto and Yokahama. JFE's urban development unit develops large-scale condominium complexes using large plots of undeveloped land while its microelectronics (LSI) division includes Kawasaki Microelectronics which produces integrated circuits for digital cameras.

Financial Performance

The company's revenues decreased by a marginal 1% (in local currency) in fiscal year 2012 to a decrease in sales in the steel urban development and LSI segments due to a decline in demand which was partially offset by an increase in sales in the engineering and shipbuilding segments.

However its net income decreased by 163% in local currency in fiscal year 2012 due to a drop in operating income and ordinary income and a loss on the valuation of overseas investments.

Strategy

The company buys and sell steel companies and other assets as it seeks to deliver the best returns for its shareholders.

In 2012 JFE Steel agreed to acquire threading business and related assets of US-based Benoit Machine LLC through holding company Benoit Holding jointly owned by JFE Steel and Kanematsu USA a subsidiary of Kanematsu. The deal will enable JFE Steel and Kanematsu to establish a total supply chain for the manufacture threading and distribution of oilfield tubing and downhole accessories and thereby meet diversified needs in the oil and gas industry and capture growing demand for oilfield tubing going

On the other side of the ledger in 2012 JFE Steel sold part of its stake in South Korean steelmaker Hyundai Hysco to the Hyundai Group for an undisclosed amont. The stake was cut to below 8%. JFE Steel supplies hot-rolled steel sheet to Hyundai Hysco for the construction and automobile industries but Hyundai has stepped up its steel production and reduced the need for imports.

In 2010 JFE Steel acquired all shares of Toyohira Steel it did not already own taking full control of the company. Toyohira a Sapporo-based electronic furnace steelmaker is a wholly owned subsidiary of JFE Steel.

That same year JFE Steel acquired a 24% stake in Pancheng Yihong Pipe Co. a China-based maker of seamless pipes for oilfields in a stock-purchase deal. Following the investment JFE jointly owns the company along with China's Chengdu Steel & Vanadium Co. (51%) and another Japanese company Marubeni-Itochu Steel (25%).

EXECUTIVES

President JFE Engineering, Sumiyuki Kishimoto
Director and SVP Corporate Planning and Controller, Eiji Hayashida
President and CEO JFE Shoji Trade Corporation, Tsutomu Yajima
SVP Finance and Investor Relations, Shinichi Okada
Auditors: Ernst & Young ShinNihon LLC

LOCATIONS

HQ: JFE Holdings Inc
2-2-3 Uchisaiwai-cho, Chiyoda-ku, Tokyo 100-0011
Phone: (81) 3 3597 4321
Web: www.jfe-holdings.co.jp

PRODUCTS/OPERATIONS

2014 Sales

	% of total
Steel	48
Trading	42
Engineering	10
Adjustment	0
Total	**100**

COMPETITORS

ArcelorMittal
Baosteel
BlueScope Steel
Kobe Steel
Nippon Steel & Sumitomo Metal Corporation
Nippon Yakin
Nisshin Steel
Severstal
Shougang Corp.
United States Steel

HISTORICAL FINANCIALS

Company Type: Public

Income Statement FYE: March 31

	REVENUE ($ mil.)	NET INCOME ($ mil.)	NET PROFIT MARGIN	EMPLOYEES
03/15	32,091	1,161	3.6%	58,856
03/14	35,524	991	2.8%	57,210
03/13	33,894	420	1.2%	57,044
03/12	38,601	(446)	—	54,133
03/11	38,590	707	1.8%	54,400
Annual Growth	(4.5%)	13.2%	—	2.0%

2015 Year-End Financials

Debt ratio: 0.2%
Return on equity: 7.6%
Cash ($ mil.): 715
Current ratio: 1.54
Long-term debt ($ mil.): 9,449
No. of shares (mil.): 576
Dividends
Yield: —
Payout: —
Market value ($ mil.): —

Jiangxi Copper Co., Ltd.

EXECUTIVES

Chairman, Baomin Li
Auditors: Deloitte Touche Tohmatsu Certified Public Accountants LLP

LOCATIONS

HQ: Jiangxi Copper Co., Ltd.
7666 Changdong Avenue, High and New Technology Development Zone, Nanchang, Jiangxi Province 330096
Phone: (86) 791 82710016 **Fax:** (86) 791 82710114
Web: www.jxcc.com

HISTORICAL FINANCIALS

Company Type: Public

Income Statement FYE: December 31

	REVENUE ($ mil.)	NET INCOME ($ mil.)	NET PROFIT MARGIN	EMPLOYEES
12/14	31,945	467	1.5%	21,366
12/13	28,955	587	2.0%	22,425
12/12	25,344	829	3.3%	22,596
12/11	18,606	1,046	5.6%	22,500
12/10	11,550	756	6.6%	27,879
Annual Growth	29.0%	(11.4%)	—	(6.4%)

2014 Year-End Financials

Debt ratio: 4.7%
Return on equity: 6.4%
Cash ($ mil.): 3,124
Current ratio: 1.65
Long-term debt ($ mil.): 1,116
No. of shares (mil.): —
Dividends
Yield: 4.2%
Payout: 59.6%
Market value ($ mil.): —

Joyo Bank, Ltd.

Tracing its roots back to 1938 The Joyo Bank offers regional banking services for Japan's Ibaraki Prefecture and its surrounding regions. Backed by more than 170 branches Joyo offers deposits loans investment portfolios international business and other traditional retail banking products. Subsidiaries and affiliated companies include Joyo Computer Service Co. (calculation software) Joyo Lease Co. (machinery and equipment leasing) Joyo Credit Guarantee Co. (housing loans credit) and Joyo Cash Service Co. (ATM and CD management and maintenance).

EXECUTIVES

President, Kazuyoshi Terakado
Auditors: Ernst & Young ShinNihon LLC

LOCATIONS

HQ: Joyo Bank, Ltd.
2-5-5 Minami-machi, Mito, Ibaraki 310-0021
Phone: (81) 29 231 2151
Web: www.joyobank.co.jp

COMPETITORS

Aozora Bank
Iyo Bank
Mitsubishi UFJ Financial Group
Miyazaki Bank
Norinchukin Bank
Shizuoka Bank
Towa Bank

HISTORICAL FINANCIALS

Company Type: Public

Income Statement FYE: March 31

	ASSETS ($ mil.)	NET INCOME ($ mil.)	INCOME AS % OF ASSETS	EMPLOYEES
03/15	75,558	239	0.3%	3,687
03/14	82,703	242	0.3%	3,713
03/13	87,871	241	0.3%	3,766
03/12	97,589	221	0.2%	3,783
03/11	89,827	168	0.2%	3,793
Annual Growth	(4.2%)	9.1%	—	(0.7%)

2015 Year-End Financials

Return on assets: 0.3%
Return on equity: 5.1%
Long-term debt ($ mil.): —
No. of shares (mil.): 722
Sales ($ mil): 1,316
Dividends
Yield: —
Payout: —
Market value ($ mil.): —

Juroku Bank, Ltd.

The Juroku Bank is industriously working to serve its customers in the prefectures of Gifu and Aichi both part of the industrial region of Chubu. The regional bank has about 150 offices in its primary service areas as well as offices in Osaka and Tokyo and overseas offices in Hong Kong and Shanghai. In addition to traditional deposit banking products and services The Juroku Bank and its subsidiaries do business in such areas as credit cards credit guarantees investments and leasing. The bank joined with five other regional banks to form the Tokai-Kinki PFI Financial Network which is intended to help its member strengthen their abilities related to private finance initiatives.In 2005 the bank fell prey to an ATM scam in 2005 the same year Juroku Bank signed on to use Hitachi's finger-vein authentication system to verify identification at its cash machines.

EXECUTIVES

President, Hakumi
Auditors: Deloitte Touche Tohmatsu LLC

LOCATIONS

HQ: Juroku Bank, Ltd.
8-26 Kanda-machi, Gifu 500-8516
Phone: (81) 58 265 2111
Web: www.juroku.co.jp

PRODUCTS/OPERATIONS

690571450

COMPETITORS

Mie Bank
Mitsubishi UFJ Financial Group
Mizuho Financial
Resona
Sumitomo Mitsui

HISTORICAL FINANCIALS

Company Type: Public

Income Statement FYE: March 31

	ASSETS ($ mil.)	NET INCOME ($ mil.)	INCOME AS % OF ASSETS	EMPLOYEES
03/15	50,746	190	0.4%	3,445
03/14	55,667	163	0.3%	3,497
03/13	60,236	246	0.4%	3,565
03/12	66,902	145	0.2%	3,689
03/11	64,124	112	0.2%	3,704
Annual Growth	(5.7%)	14.1%	—	(1.8%)

2015 Year-End Financials

Return on assets: 0.3%
Return on equity: 7.0%
Long-term debt ($ mil.): —
No. of shares (mil.): 373
Sales ($ mil): 1,066
Dividends
Yield: —
Payout: —
Market value ($ mil.): —

JX Holdings, Inc.

Japan's JX Holdings is an integrated energy holding company that combines the businesses of two of the country's top oil refiners Nippon Oil and Nippon Mining Holdings which merged to become a powerhouse with diverse operations in petroleum refining and marketing oil and natural gas exploration and production and metals (mainly copper). JX Holdings produces 128000 barrels of oil equivalent from its exploration and production asserts. Its refineries have the capacity to process roughly 1.7 million barrels of crude oil per day representing more than a quarter of the total amount of crude oil processed per day in Japan. In 2015 JX Holdings agreed to merge with TonenGeneral Sekiyu.

Geographic Reach

The company markets refined products across Japan; is engaged in exploration development and production of oil and gas in 14 countries around the world; and has stake in a copper mine in Chile.

Operations

JX Holding operates through three major subsidiaries: JX Nippon Oil & Energy; JX Nippon Oil & Gas Exploration; and JX Nippon Mining & Metals.

The company's petroleum refining and marketing business accounted for 87% of total revenues in fiscal 2014. Among its refined petroleum products are gasoline and gas oil for automobiles and trains; jet fuel for aircraft; kerosene for heating homes; lubricant oil for machinery and engines; naphtha for production of petrochemicals; petrochemicals for manufacturing synthetic fibers paints and plastics; and fuel oils and other heavy oils for heating buildings and operating heavy machinery.

Its energy business consists of petroleum refining and marketing basic chemical products lubricants specialty and performance chemicals coal electricity gas and new energy and oil and natural gas exploration development and production.

Its Metals segment includes non-ferrous metal resources development and mining copper gold silver sulfuric acid copper foils materials for rolling and processing thin film materials non-ferrous metal recycling and industrial waste treatment transportation by ships of products including metal business products and titanium.Other businesses include asphalt paving civil engineering work construction work electric wires land transportation real estate leasing business and common JX Group activities including fund procurement.JX Holdings has a nearly 40% market share in Japan of both fuel oil marketing and lubricating oil marketing.

Financial Performance

The company has reported an increase in net revenues over the last four years.In fiscal 2014 net sales increased by 10.6%.In the Oil and Natural Gas E&P business sales volume declined due primarily to the spontaneous reduction of production volume. Nonetheless as a result of the depreciation of the yen cash flow increased and ordinary income was up year on year.In the Metals business the copper price was low but the depreciation of the yen had a positive effect on ordinary income and results were about the same level as in the previous year.

The company has seen it net income decline trend over the last four years.In fiscal 2014 JX Holdings' net income declined by 33% due to an increase in impairment losses expenses on suspended mines a growth in deferred taxes and an increase in cost of sales.

Cash from operating activities grew by 15% thanks to income before income taxes and minority interests of ¥220.3 billion and depreciation and amortization of ¥183.6 billion outpace the decline in cash from operating activities from a decrease in notes and accounts payable-trade of ¥84.2 billion.

Strategy

JX Holdings allocates profits and cash reserves from its Japan-based petroleum refining and marketing operations and from other existing businesses to the development of petroleum natural gas and mineral resources as well as new energy businesses. In the near future it plans to formulate a new long-term vision for 2030.

In the meantime JX Holdings is working to strengthen its sales network by opening new service stations and converting others to self service. It is also reevaluating its card strategy and expanding the number of service stations that offer the Dr. Drive car care service. The group is aiming to increase its production volume of 200000 barrels per day.

Company Background

The merger of Nippon Oil and Nippon Mining in 2010 was spurred on by changes in the Japanese oil industry including excess refining capacity due to the continued decline in domestic demand for refined petroleum products a growing consumer awareness of environmental issues and alternative energy options and a sluggish Japanese economy. Such trends prompted the two to consider restructuring and integrating their businesses to strengthen competitiveness. Following the merger JX Nippon set up upstream oil business JX Nippon Oil & Gas Exploration and metals unit JX Nippon Mining and Metals as operating subsidiaries.

Petroleum refining and marketing will continue to be a core segment that JX Holdings plans to expand further throughout Asia and arpund the world. However it may also look for future opportunities to engage in new energy markets such as fuel cells and photovoltaic power generation to keep up with the growing green trend.

In 2012 the company's wholly owned subsidiary JX Nippon Exploration and Production (U.K.) Limited signed sale and purchase agreements to acquire an extensive portfolio of non-operated oil and gas assets in the UK Continental Shelf from ENI. The assets give JX a substantial long-term oil and gas production base in the UK.

EXECUTIVES

President, Isao Matsushita, age 68
Executive Officer, Yuji Nakajima
Executive Officer, Satoru Uchida

Executive Officer, Susumu Hara
Executive Officer, Ichiro Yamamoto
Chairman, Yasushi Kimura, age 68
Auditors: Ernst & Young ShinNihon LLC

LOCATIONS

HQ: JX Holdings, Inc.
2-6-3 Otemachi, Chiyoda-ku, Tokyo 100-8161
Phone: (81) 3 6275 5009
Web: www.hd.jx-group.co.jp

2014 Sales

	% of total
Japan	74
China	19
Other countries	7
Total	**100**

PRODUCTS/OPERATIONS

2014 Sales

	% of total
Energy	87
Metals	8
Oil & natural gas exploration & production	2
Other	3
Total	**100**

COMPETITORS

Cosmo Oil
Exxon Mobil
Honeywell International
Idemitsu Kosan
Mitsubishi Electric
Mitsui Mining and Smelting
SK Innovation
Showa Shell Sekiyu
Singapore Petroleum
Sumitomo Metal Mining

HISTORICAL FINANCIALS

Company Type: Public

Income Statement FYE: March 31

	REVENUE ($ mil.)	NET INCOME ($ mil.)	NET PROFIT MARGIN	EMPLOYEES
03/15	90,702	(2,310)	—	26,415
03/14	120,248	1,037	0.9%	26,616
03/13	119,239	1,694	1.4%	25,569
03/12	130,730	2,079	1.6%	24,236
03/11	116,348	3,764	3.2%	24,691
Annual Growth	(6.0%)	—	—	1.7%

2015 Year-End Financials

Debt ratio: 0.2%
Return on equity: (-13.6%)
Cash ($ mil.): 2,744
Current ratio: 0.98
Long-term debt ($ mil.): 11,620
No. of shares (mil.): —
Dividends
Yield: —
Payout: —
Market value ($ mil.): —

	STOCK PRICE ($) FY Close	P/E High/Low		PER SHARE ($) Earnings	Dividends	Book Value
03/15	7.99	—	—	(0.93)	0.00	8.16
03/14	9.50	—	—	0.42	0.00	10.26
03/13	11.39	—	—	0.68	0.00	9.93
03/12	11.80	—	—	0.84	0.00	10.02
03/11	13.75	—	—	1.51	0.00	9.16
Annual Growth	(12.7%)	—	—	—	—	(2.8%)

Jyske Bank A/S

Jyske Bank is a leading independent Danish bank offering a variety of financial services to private customers and small and medium-sized businesses. The shareholder-owned bank operates a decentralized network of around 110 domestic branches that operate separately under a guiding set of policies and goals. Securities and currency transactions asset management investment services and leasing are among Jyske Bank's primary offerings. The bank was established in 1967 as the result of a merger of four Danish banks. It has international branch operations in Switzerland Gibraltar Germany France and the Netherlands.

EXECUTIVES

Chief Executive Officer, Anders Christian Dam
Auditors: Deloitte Statsautoriseret Revisionsaktieseiskab

LOCATIONS

HQ: Jyske Bank A/S
Vestergade 8-16, Silkeborg DK-8600
Phone: (45) 89 89 89 89 **Fax:** (45) 89 89 19 99
Web: www.jyskebank.dk

COMPETITORS

Danske Bank
Nordea Bank
Sydbank

HISTORICAL FINANCIALS

Company Type: Public

Income Statement FYE: December 31

	ASSETS ($ mil.)	NET INCOME ($ mil.)	INCOME AS % OF ASSETS	EMPLOYEES
12/14	88,431	504	0.6%	4,191
12/13	48,355	333	0.7%	3,774
12/12	45,625	104	0.2%	3,728
12/11	47,014	85	0.2%	3,802
12/10	43,831	135	0.3%	3,886
Annual Growth	19.2%	38.8%	—	1.9%

2014 Year-End Financials

Return on assets: 0.7%
Return on equity: 13.7%
Long-term debt ($ mil.): —
No. of shares (mil.): 95
Sales ($ mil): 2,639
Dividends
Yield: —
Payout: —
Market value ($ mil.): —

	STOCK PRICE ($) FY Close	P/E High/Low		PER SHARE ($) Earnings	Dividends	Book Value
12/14	0.00	—	—	5.73	0.00	47.34
12/13	0.00	0	0	4.68	0.00	45.17
12/12	7.20	1	1	1.50	0.00	38.68
Annual Growth	—	—	—	39.8%	—	5.2%

Kansai Electric Power Co., Inc. (Kansai Denryoku K. K.) (Japan)

Japan's #2 electric utility (behind Tokyo Electric) the Kansai Electric Power Company (KEPCO) provides electricity to 13.3 million customers in Japan's Kansai region. The utility has a generating capacity of 348580 MW which is produced at hydroelectric fossil-fueled and nuclear power plants. As deregulation takes effect KEPCO is moving into new business arenas including retail natural gas sales in Japan. Additionally KEPCO is engaged in information technology telecommunications construction and engineering services environmental services home security real estate transportation leasing and other energy-related operations. It has about 50 main affiliated companies primarily in Japan.

Operations

The company's power plant portfolio includes some 150 hydroelectric plants about a dozen fossil-fired plants and three nuclear plants. It has123804 km of overhead distribution lines and 6245 km of underground lines. It also has 14101 km of overheads transmission lines and 4413 km of underground transmission lines.

Geographic Reach

KEPCO's supply area includes all of Osaka Kyoto Nara Shiga and Wakayama prefectures and portions of Fukui Gifu and Mie prefectures.

Financial Performance

The company's revenues increased by 2% in fiscal year 2012 due to a 0.5% increase in the sale of electrical power to other power companies and an 8% increase in IT/communications revenues as the group worked to acquire customers through aggressive sales activities in a fiercely competitive climate. Contracts for Internet phone and television services services reached 1.3 million as of the end of the fiscal year resulting in an increase in IT/Communications segment revenues and a 5% increase in other revenues due to higher sales volumes and the growth in the price of gas. An increase in the number of condominiums in lifecycle-related businesses also led to an increase in overall revenues.

However KEPCO's net loss increased by 297% in fiscal year 2012 due to an increase in other expenses because of higher impairment losses on securities holdings and other factors.

Company Background

The company was established in 1951.

KEPCO has a longstanding relationship with Australia's North West Shelf liquefied natural gas (LNG) joint venture. One of the venture's first customers in 1989 the company in 2009 signed a new deal guaranteeing the Japanese utility some 3.3 million metric tons a year in LNG supply.

EXECUTIVES

Managing Director, Masafumi Ikari
Managing Director, Makoto Yagi
Managing Director, Masao Ikoma
Managing Director, Yuzuru Hiroe
EVP and Director, Hideki Toyomatsu
EVP and Director, Jiroh Kagawa
Managing Director, Noriaki Hashimoto
Managing Director, Youichi Mukae
Managing Director, Yoshihiro Doi
Managing Director, Ryohei Shirai
EVP and Director, Shigeki Iwane
Managing Director, Masahiro Iwatani
Managing Director, Yasuhiro Yashima
Chairman, Shosuke Mori, age 75
Auditors: Deloitte Touche Tohmatsu LLC

LOCATIONS

HQ: Kansai Electric Power Co., Inc. (Kansai Denryoku K. K.) (Japan)
3-6-16 Nakanoshima, Kita-ku, Osaka 530-8270
Phone: (81) 6 6441 8821
Web: www.kepco.co.jp

PRODUCTS/OPERATIONS

2014 Sales

	% of total
Electri power	86
IT/Communications	5
Other	9
Total	**100**

Selected Subsidiaries

Kanden E House Corporation (housing design and electric appliances)
Kanden Gas and Co-generation Co. Inc. (90% gas sales and energy services)
The Kanden Industries Inc. (real estate management)
Kanden Joy Life Co. Ltd. (retirement homes)
Kanden Kakoh Co. Inc. (environmental protection facilities and waste management)
Kanden Real Estate Co. Ltd. (real estate sales leasing and management)
Kanden Security of Society (71% home security services)
Kansai Tech Corporation (electrical construction and petroleum transportation)
Sakai LNG Co. Inc. (70% LNG terminal construction and operation)

COMPETITORS

Chubu Electric Power
Chugoku Electric Power
Hokkaido Electric Power
Hokuriku Electric Power
Internet Initiative Japan
KDDI
Kobe Steel
Kyushu Electric Power
NTT
Nippon Steel & Sumitomo Metal Corporation
Osaka Gas
SOFTBANK MOBILE
Shikoku Electric
Tohoku Electric Power
Tokyo Electric
Tokyo Gas

HISTORICAL FINANCIALS

Company Type: Public

Income Statement FYE: March 31

	REVENUE ($ mil.)	NET INCOME ($ mil.)	NET PROFIT MARGIN	EMPLOYEES
03/15	28,388	(1,236)	—	33,539
03/14	32,237	(943)	—	33,657
03/13	30,385	(2,587)	—	33,537
03/12	34,273	(2,953)	—	32,961
03/11	33,448	1,487	4.4%	32,418
Annual Growth	(4.0%)	—	—	0.9%

2015 Year-End Financials

Debt ratio: 0.4%
Return on equity: (-13.3%)
Cash ($ mil.): 1,319
Current ratio: 0.63
Long-term debt ($ mil.): 29,394
No. of shares (mil.): 937
Dividends
Yield: —
Payout: —
Market value ($ mil.): 4,287

	STOCK PRICE ($) FY Close	P/E High/Low		PER SHARE ($) Earnings	Dividends	Book Value
03/15	4.57	—	—	(1.38)	0.00	9.42
03/14	5.37	—	—	(1.06)	0.00	13.16
03/13	4.55	—	—	(2.90)	0.00	15.21
03/12	7.65	—	—	(3.31)	0.00	20.88
03/11	12.66	—	—	1.66	0.00	24.78
Annual Growth	(22.5%)	—	—	—	—	(21.5%)

Kasikornbank Public Co Ltd

Thais take their money –and their investing needs –straight to the KASIKORNBANK (known as KBank). One of Thailand's largest commercial banks KBank operates some 1050 domestic branches. It offers banking and financial services through offices in the Cayman Islands greater China Hong Kong Japan and the US. Its services include retail and commercial banking asset management consumer lending trade finance factoring and securities handling as well as hire purchase and leasing businesses. The bank which was established in 1945 and listed on the Thai stock exchange in 1976 boasted total assets of Baht 2.3 million total deposits of Baht 1.6 million and total loans of Baht 1.5 million in 2013.

EXECUTIVES

Chairman and CEO, Banthoon Lamsam
President, Teeranun Srihong
Division Head Capital Markets Business Division, Thiti Tantikulanan
SEVP Retail Business Division, Pakorn Partanapat
President and Director, Kattiya Indaravijaya, age 50
Division Head Investment Banking Business Division, Panop Ansusinha
EVP SME Business Division, Patchara Samalapa
EVP Corporate Secretariat Division, Adit Laixuthai
EVP Corporate Strategy Management Division, Ampol Polohakul
EVP Corporate Strategy Management Division, Prasopsuk Damrongchietanon
EVP Corporate Strategy Management Division, Chongrak Rattanapian
EVP Compliance and Audit Division, Surasak Dudsdeemaytha
EVP Corporate Business Division, Vasin Vanichvoranun
EVP Corporate and SME Products Division, Vallop Vongjitvuttikrai
EVP Retail Business Division, Thawee Teerasoontornwong
EVP Retail Business Division, Chatchai Payuhanaveechai
Head Private Banking Business, Jirawat Supornpaibul
EVP WorldBusiness Division, Pipit Aneaknithi
EVP Customer Service Fulfillment Division, Pipatpong Poshyanonda
EVP Enterprise Risk Management Division, Wirawat Panthawangkun
EVP Systems Division, Somkid Jiranuntarat
EVP Human Resource Division, Krit Jitjang
Vice Chairman, Krisada Lamsam
Vice Chairman, Somchai Bulsook
Auditors: KPMG Phoomchai Audit Ltd.

LOCATIONS

HQ: Kasikornbank Public Co Ltd
1 Soi Rat Burana 27/1, Rat Burana Road, Rat Burana Sub-District, Rat Burana District, Bangkok 10140
Phone: (66) 2 222 0000 **Fax:** (66) 2 470 1144
Web: www.kasikornbank.com

PRODUCTS/OPERATIONS

2013 Sales

	% of total
Interest income	53
Fees & service income	14
Other income	33
Total	**100**

Selected Companies

Kasikorn asset management co. ltd
Kasikorn factory & equipment co. ltd.
Kasikorn leasing co. ltd.
Kasikorn research center co. ltd.
Kasikorn securities pcl

COMPETITORS

Bangkok Bank
Bank of Ayudhya
Thanachart Capital
United Overseas Bank

HISTORICAL FINANCIALS

Company Type: Public

Income Statement FYE: December 31

	ASSETS ($ mil.)	NET INCOME ($ mil.)	INCOME AS % OF ASSETS	EMPLOYEES
12/14	72,661	1,403	1.9%	21,614
12/13	69,950	1,262	1.8%	19,303
12/12	67,890	1,152	1.7%	17,389
12/11	54,748	769	1.4%	16,580
12/10	51,495	667	1.3%	15,677
Annual Growth	9.0%	20.4%	—	8.4%

2014 Year-End Financials

Return on assets: 1.9%
Return on equity: 19.3%
Long-term debt ($ mil.): —
No. of shares (mil.): —
Sales ($ mil): 7,273
Dividends
Yield: 1.2%
Payout: —
Market value ($ mil.): —

	STOCK PRICE ($) FY Close	P/E High/Low		PER SHARE ($) Earnings	Dividends	Book Value
12/14	28.12	2	1	0.59	0.35	3.27
12/13	19.53	2	1	0.53	0.32	2.80
12/12	25.65	2	1	0.48	0.26	2.53
12/11	15.80	2	1	0.32	0.00	2.06
Annual Growth	21.2%	—	—	16.2%	—	12.3%

KB Financial Group, Inc.

KB Financial Group holding company for Kookmin Bank provides commercial and consumer banking services in South Korea. It offers asset management and life insurance through alliances with Netherlands-based ING Groep. The bank's lending activities mainly entail residential mortgages home equity loans consumer loans and corporate loans. Kookmin Bank has more than 1200 branches in its home country where it claims some 26 million customers or about half of the population of South Korea. The bank provides corporate services such as foreign exchange and securities trading from offices at home and abroad in New York London Hong Kong Tokyo and Auckland New Zealand.

KB Financial became a bank holding company in 2008 and made no bones about its ambitions to stretch its wings with acquisitions. It has been eyeing brokerage firms as well as other financial services companies.

It is reportedly interested in acquiring troubled Korea Exchange Bank. This is the second time KB Financial has wanted to buy KEB; in 2006 its $7 billion offer was stymied by KEB's parent US-based private equity firm Lone Star Funds. In 2008 the South Korean government blocked HSBC's acquisition of KEB putting the bank in play once more.

A proposed KEB acquisition is just one part of KB Financial's strategy. Seeking strategic opportunities in emerging markets the bank has opened representative offices in Kazakhstan the Ukraine and Vietnam and is mulling moves into other Central and Southeast Asian nations. In 2008 it bought a 30% stake in Kazakhstan bank JSC Bank CenterCredit; it eventually intends to build up to a controlling stake of that bank.

In the meantime the company sold its nearly 14% stake in PT Bank International Indonesia to Malayan Banking Berhad for some $309 million.

Kookmin Bank spun off its credit card business in 2011 and KB Financial took it over. The new company KB Kookmin Card Co. will focus on credit card/telecommunications services and include a mobile credit card. Other services include consumer financing and insurance.

In 2006 erstwhile Kookmin Bank CEO Kim Jung-tae resigned in the face of disciplinary sanctions imposed by financial regulators after he was accused of accounting irregularities. Some South Korean newspapers speculated that a disciplinary warning issued by the Financial Supervisory Commission was retaliation for Kim's opposition to government-led bailouts of financially troubled companies.

Citigroup owns around 17% of KB Financial.

EXECUTIVES

Chairman and CEO, Young-Rok Lim
Deputy President and CFO, Woong-Won Yoon
Senior Managing Director and Chief Risk Officer, Ki-Bum Lee
Senior Managing Director and CIO, Jae-Youl Kim
Auditors: Samil Accounting Corporation (A Member Firm of PircewaterhouseCoopers)

LOCATIONS

HQ: KB Financial Group, Inc.
84 Namdaemun-ro Jung-gu, Seoul 100-703
Phone: (82) 2 2073 2844 **Fax:** (82) 2 2073 2848
Web: www.kbfng.com

PRODUCTS/OPERATIONS

Selected Subsidiaries

KB Asset M
KB Credit
KB Data Sy
KB Futures
KB Investm
KB Real Es
Kookmin Bank
Kookmin Bank Hong Kong Ltd.
Kookmin Bank International Ltd.

COMPETITORS

Busan Bank
Citigroup
Daegu Bank
Hana Bank
Industrial Bank of Korea
Korea Exchange Bank
Samsung Life Insurance
Shinhan Financial
Woori

HISTORICAL FINANCIALS

Company Type: Public

Income Statement

FYE: December 31

	ASSETS ($ mil.)	NET INCOME ($ mil.)	INCOME AS % OF ASSETS	EMPLOYEES
12/14	281,834	1,280	0.5%	168
12/13	277,505	1,198	0.4%	151
12/12	264,124	1,594	0.6%	157
12/11	239,580	2,048	0.9%	148
12/10	230,781	130	0.1%	155
Annual Growth	5.1%	76.9%	—	2.0%

2014 Year-End Financials

Return on assets: 0.4%
Return on equity: 5.2%
Long-term debt ($ mil.): —
No. of shares (mil.): 386
Sales ($ mil): 13,485
Dividends
Yield: 1.4%
Payout: 13.8%
Market value ($ mil.): 12,603

	STOCK PRICE ($) FY Close	P/E High/Low		PER SHARE ($) Earnings	Dividends	Book Value
12/14	32.62	0	0	3.30	0.48	64.62
12/13	40.51	0	0	3.09	0.53	63.14
12/12	35.90	0	0	4.12	0.64	59.42
12/11	31.34	0	0	5.56	0.10	51.19
12/10	52.89	0	0	0.38	0.21	42.70
Annual Growth	(11.4%)	—	—	71.6%	23.7%	10.9%

KBC Group NV

HISTORY

KBC Group traces its roots back to 1931 when a commercial bank named Algemeene Bankvereeniging responded to the global financial crisis by restructuring. The bank decided to regroup its assets in Belgium and Hungary and create a new holding company Algemene Maatschappij voor Nijverheidskrediet –or Almanij for short.

In 1935 Almanij helped organize a new bank Kredietbank in exchange for a majority stake in the company. Within the next few years Almanij managed to accrue a large debt to Kredietbank; in order to pay it back the company was forced to sell its shares in other firms. The debt was finally cleared by 1945.

Kredietbank quickly grew to be one of Belgium's leading banks. In 1949 it set up private bank KB Luxembourg which would later operate as an independent company majority-controlled by Almanij. In the ensuing years Almanij benefited from Belgium's ability to bounce back after WWII relative to the rest of Europe.

Fears that the Belgian government would like the French nationalize the country's banks led Almanij to make some changes in 1978. The company sliced Kredietbank and KB Luxembourg into two firms and refocused its investments into three major branches: Kredietbank KB Luxembourg and insurance and leasing entities such as the insurer Fidelitas. Though the 1980s were a shaky time for Belgian banks Almanij endured and industry conditions improved toward the end of the decade.

In 1991 the Banking and Finance Commission in Brussels announced changes in the regulations for Belgian banks; these changes included the stipulation that the main shareholders of banks make up the majority on their boards. The new regulations allowed holding companies like Almanij to have more influence over banks' strategies while also forcing them to drum up more capital for the banks.

Almanij acquired a majority stake in investment firm Gevaert in 1997. The following year it hit the big time with the creation of KBC Bank and Insurance Holding Company which went on to become one of the top financial services firms in Belgium. In 1999 Almanij formed Almafin a wholly owned consulting services subsidiary.

Almanij ran into some trouble in 2000 when the government began investigating Kredietbank and KBC Bank and Insurance for possible tax fraud. That year Cera Holding spun off most of its stake in Almanij in the form of a new holding company called Almancora.

Late in 2004 KBC Bank and Almanij announced that KBC would acquire Almanij to streamline operations; the deal which created KBC Group was completed early in 2005.

The company then expanded through a variety of deals. It acquired the Czech-based Ceskoslovenska Obchodni Banka (CSOB Bank) which it later split into two entities separately serving the Czech Republic and Slovakia. KBC also acquired complete ownership of Hungary-based K&H Bank. Other deals included acquisitions in Romania and Bulgaria. In 2008 the group bought Slovakia's eighth largest bank Istrobanka which it merged into CSOB Bank.

Auditors: Ernst & Young Bedrijfsrevisoren BCVBA

LOCATIONS

HQ: KBC Group NV
Havenlaan 2, Brussels 1080
Phone: (32) 2 429 49 16 **Fax:** (32) 2 429 44 16
Web: www.kbc.com

HISTORICAL FINANCIALS

Company Type: Public

Income Statement

FYE: December 31

	ASSETS ($ mil.)	NET INCOME ($ mil.)	INCOME AS % OF ASSETS	EMPLOYEES
12/14	298,010	2,141	0.7%	36,187
12/13	332,214	1,397	0.4%	38,167
12/12	338,588	806	0.2%	48,026
12/11	369,127	16	0.0%	51,127
12/10	429,380	2,489	0.6%	52,110
Annual Growth	(8.7%)	(3.7%)	—	(8.7%)

2014 Year-End Financials

Return on assets: 0.7%
Return on equity: 11.4%
Long-term debt ($ mil.): —
No. of shares (mil.): 417
Sales ($ mil): 13,353
Dividends
Yield: —
Payout: —
Market value ($ mil.): 11,669

	STOCK PRICE ($) FY Close	P/E High/Low		PER SHARE ($) Earnings	Dividends	Book Value
12/14	27.93	16	11	4.04	0.00	48.08
12/13	28.37	53	29	1.42	0.43	46.71
12/12	17.83	—	—	(1.44)	0.00	49.31
12/11	6.10	—	—	(2.50)	0.69	61.01
12/10	17.39	11	8	4.98	0.00	70.49
Annual Growth	12.6%	—	—	(5.1%)	—	(9.1%)

KDDI Corp

Auditors: Kyoto Audit Corp.

LOCATIONS

HQ: KDDI Corp
3-10-10 Iidabashi, Chiyoda-ku, Tokyo 102-8460
Phone: (81) 3 6678 0712
Web: www.kddi.com

HISTORICAL FINANCIALS

Company Type: Public

Income Statement FYE: March 31

	REVENUE ($ mil.)	NET INCOME ($ mil.)	NET PROFIT MARGIN	EMPLOYEES
03/15	38,116	3,566	9.4%	28,172
03/14	41,984	3,119	7.4%	27,073
03/13	38,922	2,566	6.6%	20,238
03/12	43,546	2,908	6.7%	19,680
03/11	41,476	3,080	7.4%	18,418
Annual Growth	(2.1%)	3.7%	—	11.2%

2015 Year-End Financials

Debt ratio: 0.1%
Return on equity: 14.9%
Cash ($ mil.): 2,202
Current ratio: 1.78
Long-term debt ($ mil.): 6,870

No. of shares (mil.): —
Dividends
Yield: 3.0%
Payout: —
Market value ($ mil.): —

	STOCK PRICE ($) FY Close	P/E High/Low	PER SHARE ($) Earnings	Dividends	Book Value
03/15	16.98	— —	1.42	0.34	10.78
03/14	14.52	— —	1.29	0.39	11.28
03/13	20.80	— —	1.02	0.00	10.77
03/12	16.24	— —	1.15	0.00	11.32
03/11	62.18	— —	1.17	0.19	10.30
Annual Growth	(27.7%)	— —	5.0%	16.1%	1.1%

Kia Motors Corp. (South Korea)

South Korea's #2 carmaker (behind Hyundai Motor) Kia Motors produces about 3 million vehicles a year at 10 manufacturing and assembly plants in five countries which are then sold through a network of distributors and dealers covering 150 countries. Its compact Kia picanto is the second-best selling car in South Korea. Other popular models include the Forte the Sorento and the Soul. Kia also makes a number of commercial vehicles. Its high-capacity plants outside Korea are in the US Slovakia and China. After Korea Kia's second-largest market is the US. Part of the Hyundai Kia Automotive Group Kia operates as an affiliate of Hyundai Motor.

Geographic Reach

Kia has established manufacturing plants in key regions two in China (set up as joint partnerships with Yueda and Dongfeng Motor) a Slovakia assembly plant in Eastern Europe (that also produces Hyundai vehicles) and one in the US (in Georgia). In 2014 it invested $1 billion to launch a new manufacturing plant in Monterrey Mexico.

Strategy

Kia is focused on edging out the competition with its stylish design that doesn't come with a European price tag. By strengthening its platform to smaller lighter cars Kia aims to rapidly respond to changes in consumer demand. The company markets its value in design esthetics and fuel efficiency. None of its vehicles are gas guzzlers and its Optima sedan came with a hybrid engine option. Most of its vehicles have a gasoline direct injection (GDI) engine that results in better fuel economy.

HISTORY

Kia's conglomerate ownership is also fundamental to its operation. Favoring its founding family former president of Kia Hyundai Motors vice chairman Chung Eui-sun is the son of Hyundai Kia Automotive Group chairman Chung Mong-koo. The elder Chung is the son of Hyundai's founder and controls the car company through a series of cross-holdings involving auto-parts maker Hyundai Mobis and steelmaker Hyundai Steel. In 2010 he stepped down from Kia Motors' board. To fill his vacancy the role of CEO was jointly held by Kia vice chairman Chung Sung-eun and Kia president Seo Young-jong until late 2010 when Chung Sung-eun resigned amidst the recall of some 100000 automobiles. President and COO Lee Hyoung-keun was named as Chung's replacement.

Leadership has had other rough patches as well. A court found then-chairman Chung guilty of embezzlement and fraud in a slush fund scandal that passed corporate control and wealth from father to son hurting shareholders' value. An appeals court suspended the chairman's prison sentence to community service citing the executive's irreplaceable role in the company and country's economic well-being. He was subsequently pardoned by the South Korean president.

EXECUTIVES

Vice Chairman and Co-CEO, Hyoung-Keun (Hank) Lee
Co-CEO, Han-Woo Park
Chairman, Chung Mong-Koo, age 67
Auditors: Samjong Accounting Corporation (A Member Firm of KPMG)

LOCATIONS

HQ: Kia Motors Corp. (South Korea)
12 Heolleung-ro Seocho-gu, Seoul 137-130
Phone: (82) 2 3464 1114 **Fax:** (82) 2 3464 6813
Web: www.kia.co.kr

2013 Sales

	% of total
South Korea	17
China	20
US	19
Europe	12
Rest of world	32
Total	**100**

PRODUCTS/OPERATIONS

Selected Models

Commercial vehicles
- K2700/Strong/3000s/2500TCI
- K4000G

Passenger cars
- Cadenza
- cee' d
- cee' d_sw
- Cerato/Forte
- Cerato/Forte Koup
- Optima
- Picanto
- pro_cee' d
- Rio
- Soul

SUV & MP
- Borrego/Mohave
- Carens/Rondo
- Carnival/Sedona
- Sorento
- Sportage
- Venga

COMPETITORS

BYD	Isuzu
Chery Automobile	Mazda
China FAW	Nissan
Daimler	Peugeot
FCA US	Renault
Fiat Chrysler	Shanghai Automotive
Ford Motor	Ssangyong Motor
Fuji Heavy Industries	Suzuki Motor
GM Korea	Toyota
General Motors	Volkswagen
Honda	

HISTORICAL FINANCIALS

Company Type: Public

Income Statement FYE: December 31

	REVENUE ($ mil.)	NET INCOME ($ mil.)	NET PROFIT MARGIN	EMPLOYEES
12/14	43,046	2,736	6.4%	34,112
12/13	45,260	3,629	8.0%	33,576
12/12	44,247	3,619	8.2%	32,756
12/11	37,275	2,947	7.9%	32,411
12/10	31,951	2,392	7.5%	32,599
Annual Growth	7.7%	3.4%	—	1.1%

2014 Year-End Financials

Debt ratio: 0.0%
Return on equity: 14.0%
Cash ($ mil.): 2,265
Current ratio: 1.39
Long-term debt ($ mil.): 2,634

No. of shares (mil.): 404
Dividends
Yield: —
Payout: —
Market value ($ mil.): —

Koc Holdings AS

In Turkey Ko § (pronounced "coach") class equals first class. Led by its energy businesses Ko § Holding is Turkey's dominant industrial conglomerate. The company's Tofas unit an alliance with Fiat is Turkey's champion carmaker; Ko §s joint venture with Ford Motor sells imported Ford models. Other businesses include consumer goods such as large household appliances (Ar §lik teaming up with LG Electronics) and energy (distribution of liquefied petroleum gas). Subsidiaries engage in food production construction international trading and hospitality and tourism. Ko §also operates banking securities brokerage and insurance businesses. The Ko §family one of the wealthiest in Turkey controls the company.

OperationsKo §s business activities include the acquisition disposal and exchanging of shares of domestic and foreign corporations and limited liability companies for all types of commercial industrial agricultural and financial activities.

Ko §and Royal Dutch Shell together continue to drive a 51% stake in oil refiner T PRAS. T PRAS the 8th largest refining company in Europe controls 40% ownership in the fuel distribution company Opet Petrol I k.The company's finance segment includes three main groups; banking insurance and consumer finance. Leasing factoring portfolio management custody and brokerage services are included in the banking sector.Financial PerformanceKo §s revenues increased by 41% in 2011 thanks to a growth in revenues from all of its segments. Higher revenues fueled the company's net income growth of 23% that year.

Stategy

Ko § is reaching far across the Bosporus while simultaneously refocusing its efforts in consumer goods automotive finance and energy markets. The company's strategy is to buy and sell assets to achieve portfolio diversification to minimize sector and regional risks. It is also focusing on expanding its operations in developing markets through acquisitions and joint ventures.

In 2011 its Arcelik subsidiary acquired the South Africa-based Defy which is engaged in the production of refrigerators freezers dryers ovens cooking appliances and the selling and marketing of all kinds of durable home appliances across Southern Africa.

That year Ko §established a shipping subsidiary Sariyer Tankercilik. To raise cash it also agreed to sell Ko §Net Haberlesme Teknolojileri ve Iletisim Hizmetleri A.S. (Ko §net) to Vodafone.

Expanding its role in power production and responding to the Turkish government's plan to privatize power generation in Turkey in 2010 Ko § formed a joint venture with energy powerhouse AES to develop new power plants. AES-Entek aims to become one of the top five independent power producers in Turkey by 2015.

Ownership

With a combined stake of more than 69% members of the Ko §family direct the operations of Ko § Holding.

HISTORY

In 1917 16-year-old Vehbi Ko §and his father opened a small grocery store in Ankara Turkey. With the fall of the Ottoman Empire after WWI Turkey's capital was moved to Ankara which was then only a village. The Ko § recognized an opportunity and expanded into construction and building supplies winning a contract to repair the roof of the Turkish parliament building. By age 26 Ko § was a millionaire.

Ford Motor made Ko §its Turkish agent in 1928. In 1931 Mobil Oil and Ko §entered an exclusive agreement to search for oil in Turkey. The company incorporated in 1938 as Ko §Ticaret Corporation the first Turkish joint stock company with an employee stock-ownership program.

Despite Turkey's neutrality in WWII the fighting disrupted Ko §s business. The nation became isolationist after the war and restricted foreign concerns to selling through local agents; Ko §benefited by importing foreign products.

General Electric and Ko §entered a joint venture in 1946 to build Turkey's first lightbulb factory. In 1955 Ko §set up Ar §lik the first Turkish producer of refrigerators washing machines and water heaters; T rk Demir D §k m the first Turkish producer of radiators and later auto castings; and Turkay the country's first private producer of matches. In 1959 Ko §constructed Turkey's first truck assembly plant (Otosan).

Other firsts followed in the 1960s as the company leveraged its size and government influence to attract more ventures. These included a tire factory (with Uniroyal) a cable factory (with Siemens) production of electric motors and compressors (with GE) and the production of Anadol the first car to be made entirely in Turkey (by Otosan under license from Ford). In 1974 Ko §expanded into retailing with the purchase of Migros Turkey's largest chain of supermarkets.

The Turkish military imposed martial law in 1980 and restricted foreign exchange payments forcing Ko §to limit its operations. In 1986 a year after foreign companies were allowed to export products directly to Turkey Ko §and American Express started Ko §Amerikan Bank (which Ko § bought out and renamed Ko §bank in 1992). In the late 1980s Vehbi's only son Rahmi took over the company's leadership. Vehbi Ko §died in 1996.

Auto sales fell sharply in 1996 as buyers awaited the country's entry into the European Union's customs union. In an effort to offset market risks Ko § forged a number of alliances in 1997. It participated in a British-Canadian-Turkish consortium that was building a large power plant in central Turkey.

Reflecting a greater willingness to open the company to foreign investors Ko §announced plans to offer $250 million in shares in a public offering in 1998 but it soon canceled the offering because of market volatility. A year later the company completed an auto plant in Samarkand Uzbekistan to build Otoyol-Iveco buses and trucks.

Ko §entered into a joint venture –Ko §Finansal Hizmetler –with Unicredito Italiano in 2002 in an effort to further consolidate its financial holdings.

Significant company moves in 2008 included selling its Otomotiv Lastikleri Tevzi (Oltas) to Germany's Continental AG. Oltas had distributed Continental tires and related products since 2003. The company's interest in supermarkets dwindled to less than 50% with the sale of its stake in Migros. Its sway however in the IT data processing business of Ko §Net Haberlesme Teknolojileri ve Iletisim Hizmetleri A.S. increased to almost 100%. The company picked up military aero and marine tech simulator Kaletron an arm of Kale Group too.

In 2009 the global recession curtailed industrial output and demand and hurt the company's revenues. However its diversified portfolio and cost saving measures enabled it to post a modest improvement in net income.

EXECUTIVES

President Tourism Food and Retailing Group, Tamer Hasimoglu
President Energy Group, Erol Memio ľu, age 61
CFO, Ahmet Ashabolu
President Defense Industry Other Automotive and IT Group, Kudret Onen
President Automotive Group, Cenk Cimen
President Banking and Insurance Group, Faik Acikalin
CEO, Levent akiroglu
Chairman, Mustafa V. Ko § age 55
Auditors: Guney Bagimsiz Denetim ve Serbest Muhasebeci Mali Musavirlik Anonim Sirketi

LOCATIONS

HQ: Koc Holdings AS
Nakkastepe, Azizbey Sok No. 1, Istanbul, Kuzguncuk 34674
Phone: (90) 216 531 0000 **Fax:** (90) 216 531 0099
Web: www.koc.com.tr

PRODUCTS/OPERATIONS

2011 Sales

	% of total
Energy	63
Automotive	13
Consumer durables	11
Finance	8
Other	5
Total	**100**

Core Businesses
Automotive
Construction and mining
Durable goods
Food/Beverage/Tobacco
Energy
Financial services
Information technology
International trade
Marinas
New business development
Tourism and services

COMPETITORS

Adam Opel
Caterpillar
Electrolux
Hellenic Petroleum
Honda
International Power
Renault
Robert Bosch
Sabanci
Siemens AG
Yazicilar

HISTORICAL FINANCIALS

Company Type: Public

Income Statement FYE: December 31

	REVENUE ($ mil.)	NET INCOME ($ mil.)	NET PROFIT MARGIN	EMPLOYEES
12/14	29,480	1,164	3.9%	85,517
12/13	30,940	1,252	4.0%	80,996
12/12	47,364	1,292	2.7%	82,158
12/11	40,127	1,125	2.8%	80,987
12/10	34,861	1,123	3.2%	73,063
Annual Growth	(4.1%)	0.9%	—	4.0%

2014 Year-End Financials

Debt ratio: 13.3%
Return on equity: 14.1%
Cash ($ mil.): 4,256
Current ratio: 1.31
Long-term debt ($ mil.): 6,186
No. of shares (mil.): —
Dividends
Yield: 1.1%
Payout: 57.4%
Market value ($ mil.): —

	STOCK PRICE ($) FY Close	P/E High/Low	PER SHARE ($) Earnings	Dividends	Book Value
12/14	26.39	25 15	0.46	0.29	0.03
12/13	20.61	26 18	0.49	0.41	0.03
12/12	26.16	29 17	0.51	0.27	0.04
12/11	14.88	25 16	0.47	0.50	0.03
12/10	24.45	35 20	0.47	0.38	(0.00)
Annual Growth	1.9%	— —	(0.3%)	(6.1%)	—

Komercni Banka A.S. (Czech Republic)

EXECUTIVES

predseda predstavenstva, Henri Bonnet
Auditors: Ernst & Young Audit, s.r.o.

LOCATIONS

HQ: Komercni Banka A.S. (Czech Republic)
Na Prikope 33, Praha 1 114 07
Phone: (420) 485 262 800 **Fax:** (420) 224 243 020
Web: www.kb.cz

HISTORICAL FINANCIALS

Company Type: Public

Income Statement FYE: December 31

	ASSETS ($ mil.)	NET INCOME ($ mil.)	INCOME AS % OF ASSETS	EMPLOYEES
12/14	41,812	569	1.4%	8,520
12/13	43,407	629	1.5%	8,604
12/12	41,267	731	1.8%	8,758
12/11	37,824	474	1.3%	8,918
12/10	37,218	710	1.9%	8,689
Annual Growth	3.0%	(5.4%)	—	(0.5%)

2014 Year-End Financials

Return on assets: 1.4%
Return on equity: 12.9%
Long-term debt ($ mil.): —
No. of shares (mil.): 38
Sales ($ mil): 1,761

Dividends
Yield: 115.0%
Payout: 66.9%
Market value ($ mil.): 7,602

	STOCK PRICE ($) FY Close	P/E High	P/E Low	PER SHARE ($) Earnings	Dividends	Book Value
12/14	200.00	1	1	15.08	11.39	122.74
12/13	218.00	1	1	16.66	11.47	123.80
12/12	220.00	1	0	19.37	7.91	134.96
12/11	166.00	1	1	12.53	13.53	104.44
12/10	230.15	1	1	18.84	9.06	104.90
Annual Growth	(3.4%)	—	—	(5.4%)	5.9%	4.0%

Kommunalbanken A/S (Norway)

Auditors: Ernst & Young AS

LOCATIONS

HQ: Kommunalbanken A/S (Norway)
Haakon VIIs gate 5B, Oslo N-0110
Phone: (47) 21 50 20 00 **Fax:** (47) 21 50 20 01
Web: www.kbn.org

HISTORICAL FINANCIALS

Company Type: Public

Income Statement FYE: December 31

	ASSETS ($ mil.)	NET INCOME ($ mil.)	INCOME AS % OF ASSETS	EMPLOYEES
12/14	61,382	66	0.1%	56
12/13	59,561	178	0.3%	56
12/12	62,385	335	0.5%	54
12/11	61,022	120	0.2%	50
12/10	52,725	126	0.2%	48
Annual Growth	3.9%	(15.0%)	—	3.9%

2014 Year-End Financials

Return on assets: 0.1%
Return on equity: 5.9%
Long-term debt ($ mil.): —
No. of shares (mil.): 2
Sales ($ mil): 713

Dividends
Yield: —
Payout: —
Market value ($ mil.): —

Koninklijke Ahold NV

A tattered prince of global food retailing Royal Ahold owns or has an interest in more than 3200 supermarkets and specialty stores in five countries in Europe and North America. While its status as one of the world's largest grocery retailers has been greatly diminished it still ranks as a leading supermarket operator along the East Coast of the US under names including Giant Food and Stop & Shop which account for about 60% of its total sales. Royal Ahold also operates Albert Heijn (the #1 food retailer in The Netherlands) as well as stores in Germany Belgium and the Czech Republic. Other interests include the US online grocery ordering and delivery service Peapod and Gall & Gall liquor stores.

HISTORY

Albert Heijn and his wife took over his father's grocery store in Ootzaan Netherlands in 1887. By the end of WWI the company had 50 Albert Heijn grocery stores in Holland and at WWII's end it had almost 250 stores. In 1948 the company went public.

It opened its first self-service store in 1952 and its first supermarket in 1955. Growing into the #1 grocer in the Netherlands Albert Heijn opened liquor and cosmetic stores in 1973. (It changed its name to Ahold that year to better reflect its range of businesses.) Ahold expanded outside the Netherlands in 1976 when it founded supermarket chain Cadadia in Spain (sold 1985).

Ahold entered the US in 1977 by purchasing BI-LO and furthered its expansion in 1981 by adding Pennsylvania-based Giant Food Stores. In 1987 in honor of its 100th anniversary Ahold was granted the title Koninklijke (Dutch for "royal"). In 1988 it bought a majority stake in Dutch food wholesaler Schuitema.

The company added New York-based TOPS Markets in 1991. That year Royal Ahold founded food retailer and distributor Euronova (now called Ahold Czech Republic) and in 1992 it acquired 49% of Portuguese food retailer Jerónimo Martins Retail. In 1993 Cees van der Hoeven was promoted to chief executive and Royal Ahold was listed on the NYSE.

Other acquisitions included New England grocery giant The Stop & Shop Companies in 1996. That year saw the beginning of several Asian joint ventures that gave Royal Ahold stores in Singapore Malaysia and Thailand. It also formed a joint venture in 1998 with Argentina's Velox Retail Holdings (owner of about 90% of supermarket operators DISCO and Santa Isabel) and Royal Ahold added Maryland-based grocer Giant Food Inc. (unrelated to Royal Ahold's Giant Food Stores).

Royal Ahold's moves in 1999 included the acquisition of several Spanish supermarket chains (with a total of about 200 stores) the purchase of Dutch institutional food wholesaler Gastronoom and the acquisition of 50% of Sweden's top food seller ICA AB. In Central America it acquired half of La Fragua an operator of supermarkets and discount stores. However North American expansion plans hit a snag when Royal Ahold backed out of a deal to buy Pathmark Stores.

In 2000 Royal Ahold acquired Spanish food retailer Kampio+ #2 and #4 foodservice distributors U.S. Foodservice and PYA/Monarch US convenience store chains Sugar Creek and Golden Gallon and all of the voting stock of Brazilian retailer Bompreço. In June the firm bought a 51% stake in online grocer Peapod. Royal Ahold took over food retailer Superdiplo which runs more than 300 stores in Spain (including the Canary Islands) in late 2000.

In March 2001 Royal Ahold began buying the remaining outstanding shares of Bompreço with the intention of delisting the company from the Brazilian Luxembourg and New York stock exchanges (which it did in late December). Chicago-based Peapod became a wholly owned Royal Ahold subsidiary in 2001. The retailer also expanded its bricks-and-mortar US presence in 2001 by purchasing Alliant Exchange parent of Alliant Foodservice which distributes food to more than 100000 customers and Bruno's Supermarkets which operates more than 180 stores in the Southeast. In December Ahold also agreed to buy the 32-store G. Barbosa supermarket chain which would add to its holdings in Brazil.

Royal Ahold reported its first net loss in nearly 30 years in the second quarter of 2002. In August 2002 Royal Ahold assumed full control of Disco Ahold International Holdings its former joint venture company with Velox Retail Holdings. Soon after the company increased its ownership stake in Chilean grocery chain Santa Isabel from 70% to 97% in a tender offer. In October the company integrated its Polish Czech and Slovak operations under the umbrella of Ahold Central Europe (ACE). ACE will manage more than 400 Albert supermarkets and Hypernova hypermarkets in Central Europe. In late 2002 subsidiary U.S. Foodservice agreed to buy Allen Foods a major independent foodservice distributor in the Central Plains region.

In February 2003 CEO Cees van der Hoeven and CFO Michiel Meurs resigned following an announcement that the grocery giant would restate its financial results by at least $500 million because of accounting irregularities at U.S. Foodservice. (van der Hoeven is facing charges by Dutch prosecutors in connection with the scandal at U.S. Foodservice.) Chairman Henny de Ruiter became acting CEO of the company and Dudley Eustace a British national who serves as a director of several Dutch companies was named interim CFO in March. In May 2003 IKEA veteran Anders Moberg became acting CEO; de Ruiter remained chairman. Soon after Ahold said it would restate earnings downward by $880 million (much more than the original $500 million projection) because of the accounting scandal at U.S. Foodservice. Further accounting investigations uncovered about $29 million in irregularities at the company's TOPS Markets US subsidiary.

In May Ahold completed the sale of its De Tuinen natural product stores to NBTY's British subsidiary Holland & Barrett Europe. In June it sold its Jamin chain of candy stores to Jamin management. The Santa Isabel chain in Chile was sold in July to Cencosud for about $95 million far less than the $150 million originally discussed. Adding to its woes in July the public prosecutor in Amsterdam launched a criminal investigation into possible falsification of accounts by the company. Soon after Ahold completed the sale of 22 stores in Indonesia to PT Hero Supermarket as well as its Malaysian retail business. In September the board of directors of Royal Ahold approved the appointment of Moberg and Ryopponen as CEO and CFO respectively. Later in the month the global grocer sold its operations in Paraguay (Supermercados Stock S.A.) to A.J. Vierci for about $4 million.

In October 2003 Royal Ahold published its long-awaited 2002 results revealing a $1.27 billion loss which the retailer attributed to special charges related to overstated profits at U.S. Foodservice. That month the company completed the sale of its 138-store Golden Gallon convenience chain to The Pantry for about $187 million and de Ruiter resigned and was succeeded by Karel Vuursteen previously a board member. In November Royal Ahold sold two hypermarkets in Poland to Carrefour Poland as part of its overall strategy to restructure its retail portfolio. In December the Peruvian operations of its Santa Isabel chain were sold to Grupo Interbank and other investors led by Nexus Group.

In March 2004 Royal Ahold sold its 118-store Bompreço chain in Brazil to Wal-Mart Stores and its credit card business (Hipercard) there to Unibanco S.A. for a combined price of about $500 million. Also in March the Dutch chain sold its stake in CRC Ahold operating in Thailand to its partner the Central Food Retail Co. completing the company's withdrawal from Asia. At a shareholders meeting in March Ahold placed the blame for the accounting scandal which nearly bankrupted the company in 2003 squarely on the shoulders of Jim Miller the former CEO of U.S. Foodservice. (Later Miller and Ahold agreed in late 2007 to settle litigation related to the matter with Miller paying Ahold $8 million.) In August Karel Vuursteen resigned as chairman of the supervisory board for personal reasons as was succeeded by Ren Dahan. In September Ahold reached a settlement with the Dutch public prosecutor in which the company agreed to pay 8 million. In return the Dutch prosecutor agreed not to undertake proceedings against Royal Ahold. In October the company reached a settlement with the US Securities and Exchange Commission that imposed no fines on Royal Ahold due in part to its "extensive co-operation" with the investigation. The company also finalized a deal to increase its stake in its Scandinavian retail joint venture ICA AB. It paid its 811 million for a 20% stake in the partnership sold by Canica. In December Ahold completed the sale of its retail activities in Spain and the Canary Islands (nearly 600 stores) to the Permira Funds.

In January 2005 the grocery giant sold its BI-LO and Bruno's chains in the southeastern US to an affiliate of Lone Star Funds for some $660 million. In February the Dutch retailer completed the sale of a dozen Hypernova hypermarkets in Poland to rival Carrefour followed by the sale of a single large hypermarket to a local Polish firm two months later. Also in April Royal Ahold completed its exit from Brazil with the sale of 32 G. Barbosa hypermarkets there to ACON Investments a US-based investment firm. In May the company announced completion of the sale of its 50% stake in Spanish winery Bodegas Williams & Humbert (formerly known as Luis Paez) to its joint venture partner Jose Medina y Cia SA for an undisclosed sum. In June Ahold completed the sale of its chain of 198 Wilson Farms and Sugarcreek convenience stores part of its TOPS Markets subsidiary in the US to WFI Acquisition for an undisclosed sum. In September Ahold sold its Deli XL foodservice operation in Belgium and the Netherlands to a subsidiary of South Africa-based The Bidvest Group for about 140 million.

CFO Hannu Ryopponen resigned at the end of August 2005 to join Stora Enso an integrated paper packaging and forest products company. In October Royal Ahold completed the acquisition of 56 stores in the Czech Republic from Julius Meinl a.s. In November the company settled a US class action lawsuit by paying $1.1 billion to shareholders who purchased stock between July 3 1999 and February 23 2003; just before the 2003 accounting scandal broke. Concurrently the company reached an agreement to settle litigation with the Dutch Shareholders' Association.

The grocery chain also sold 13 large Hypernova hypermarkets in Poland to Carrefour and a local operator in early 2005. The company also moved its corporate headquarters from Zaandam to Amsterdam later in the year.

In 2006 the company sold three shopping centers in Poland and the Czech Republic for about 108 million. In April Jose Alvarez was named president and CEO of the combined Stop & Shop/Giant-Landover organization succeeding Marc Smith who retired. In September Royal Ahold was reported to be in talks with its Belgian counterpart Delhaize regarding a possible merger. However negotiations were later suspended. In November the Dutch grocer completed the acquisition of 27 Konmar stores in the Netherlands from Laurus B.V. for about $130 million.

More than three years after teetering on the brink of bankruptcy as a result of one of Europe's largest financial scandals a Dutch court found former CEO Cees van der Hoeven and former CFO Michael Meurs guilty of fraud. Van der Hoeven and Meurs were accused of improperly booking sales from four subsidiaries in Scandinavia Argentina and Brazil. Both men were fined and given suspended sentences. Former executive board member Jan Andreae who headed Ahold's European operations was sentenced to four months in jail suspended for two years and fined.

CEO Anders Moberg left the company in July 2007. Also in July U.S. Foodservice was finally sold to a consortium of Clayton Dubilier & Rice and Kohlberg Kravis Roberts & Co. for about $7.1 billion. In November John Rishton Ahold's CFO who had been serving as interim chief executive since Moberg's departure was named to the post permanently. In December Royal Ahold sold its underperforming TOPS Markets chain to Morgan Stanley Private Equity for about $310 million.

In June 2008 the company completed sold its 73% stake in Schuitema N.V. to private equity firm CVC Capital Partners in return for cash and the transfer of 50-plus Schuitema stores to Ahold.

In 2009 Royal Ahold's Albert/Hypernova business in the Czech Republic and Slovakia closed 23 underperforming stores and downsized a dozen hypermarkets. It also finished converting its Hypernova stores to the Albert brand in the Czech Republic.

In February 2010 Ahold acquired 25 Ukrop's Super Market stores inventory equipment and leases in a $140 million transaction. The Ukrop's chain became part of Ahold USA's Giant-Carlisle division.

In March 2013 the company sold its 60% stake in the Sweden's largest food retailer ICA AB to Sweden's Hakon Invest for SEK 21.2 billion ($3.3 billion) in cash to better stick to its strategy of focusing on businesses it controls.

EXECUTIVES

CEO, A. Dick Boer, age 58, $625,000 total compensation
COO Europe, Sander van der Laan, age 46
CFO, Jeff Carr, age 55
COO Ahold USA, James McCann, age 46
Vice Chairman, Tom de Swaan, age 70
Chairman, Ren ©Dahan, age 74
Auditors: PricewaterhouseCoopers Accountants N.V.

LOCATIONS

HQ: Koninklijke Ahold NV
Provincialeweg 11, Zaandam 1506 MA
Phone: (31) 88 659 5100
Web: www.ahold.com

2014 Stores

	No.
The Netherlands	2,105
US	768
Czech Republic	333
Total	**3,206**

2014 Sales

	% of total
US	60
Europe	
The Netherlands	36
Other	4
Total	**100**

PRODUCTS/OPERATIONS

Selected Operations

Retail
Europe
Albert (supermarkets Czech Republic and Slovakia)
Albert Heijn (supermarkets convenience stores)
Etos (drugstores online shopping)
Gall & Gal
US
Giant-Carl
Giant-Land
Stop & Sho

COMPETITORS

A&P
ALDI
BJ' s Wholesale Club
Big Y Foods
Carrefour
Costco Wholesale
Delhaize
Golub
Kooperativa F¶bundet
Kroger
Lidl
METRO AG
NorgesGruppen
Safeway
Shaw' s
Target Corporation
Tesco
Wal-Mart
Wegmans
Whole Foods

HISTORICAL FINANCIALS

Company Type: Public

Income Statement FYE: December 28

	REVENUE ($ mil.)	NET INCOME ($ mil.)	NET PROFIT MARGIN	EMPLOYEES
12/14	39,945	723	1.8%	227,000
12/13	45,217	3,517	7.8%	222,000
12/12*	43,286	1,090	2.5%	225,000
01/12	39,154	1,315	3.4%	218,000
01/11	39,475	1,140	2.9%	213,000
Annual Growth	0.3%	(10.7%)	—	1.6%

*Fiscal year change

2014 Year-End Financials

Debt ratio: 27.5%
Return on equity: 10.4%
Cash ($ mil.): 1,979
Current ratio: 1.00
Long-term debt ($ mil.): 3,695
No. of shares (mil.): 822
Dividends
Yield: 0.1%
Payout: 213.3%
Market value ($ mil.): 14,700

	STOCK PRICE ($) FY Close	P/E High/Low		PER SHARE ($) Earnings	Dividends	Book Value
12/14	17.87	26	21	0.82	1.74	7.18
12/13	18.21	8	6	3.31	0.65	9.20
12/12*	13.33	18	15	1.03	0.00	7.61
01/12	13.45	15	11	1.15	0.00	7.17
01/11	13.19	20	16	0.96	0.00	6.90
Annual Growth	7.9%	—	—	(4.0%)	—	1.0%

*Fiscal year change

Koninklijke Philips NV

Auditors: KPMG Accountants N.V.

LOCATIONS

HQ: Koninklijke Philips NV
Philips Center, Amstelplein 2, Amsterdam 1096 BC
Phone: (31) 20 59 77 777
Web: www.philips.com

HISTORICAL FINANCIALS
Company Type: Public

Income Statement FYE: December 31

	REVENUE ($ mil.)	NET INCOME ($ mil.)	NET PROFIT MARGIN	EMPLOYEES
12/14	26,000	504	1.9%	113,678
12/13	32,117	1,609	5.0%	116,681
12/12	32,671	297	0.9%	118,087
12/11	29,204	(1,675)	—	125,241
12/10	34,020	1,935	5.7%	119,001
Annual Growth	(6.5%)	(28.5%)	—	(1.1%)

2014 Year-End Financials

Debt ratio: 17.5%
Return on equity: 3.7%
Cash ($ mil.): 2,276
Current ratio: 1.34
Long-term debt ($ mil.): 4,511
No. of shares (mil.): 914
Dividends
Yield: 3.1%
Payout: 177.7%
Market value ($ mil.): 26,517

	STOCK PRICE ($) FY Close	P/E High/Low	PER SHARE ($) Earnings	Dividends	Book Value
12/14	29.00	76 56	0.55	0.93	14.45
12/13	36.97	29 22	1.75	0.83	16.90
12/12	26.54	107 72	0.32	0.80	16.05
12/11	20.95	— —	(1.76)	0.00	17.26
12/10	30.70	23 17	2.05	0.79	21.28
Annual Growth	(1.4%)	— —	(28.1%)	4.0%	(9.2%)

Korea Electric Power Corp

Korea Electric Power (KEPCO) is slowly relinquishing its status as South Korea's electric utility monopoly. The company is still the country's primary power distributor serving 12 million households. It generates 87% of Korea's power supply with an installed capacity of more than 65380 MW (primarily from thermal and nuclear plants). KEPCO also buys capacity from independent power producers. Industrial demand accounts for more than 50% of the company's annual output. In response to deregulation the company plans to divest more than half of its Korean-based generation assets while it builds an extensive power plant portfolio in other countries. The Korean government controls 51% of KEPCO.

In a government effort to restructure the power industry KEPCO is required to spin off all of its fossil-fueled power generation operations which have been split up into five new subsidiaries; the utility will retain its nuclear and hydroelectric plants. However due to market conditions the privatization plans have been delayed. The government looked at options to allow competition in the country's power distribution market but these plans have also been suspended.

KEPCO is looking to become both a leader in the use of green technology (pushing "smart" grid deployment and cleaner burning power plants and wind farms). With power use beginning to plateau in Korea KEPCO is looking to become a global power player (a "Global Top Five Energy and Engineering Company by 2020"). In 2010 the company was engaged in power plant and related projects in a wide range of countries including Australia China Egypt Nigeria the Philippines Russia and the US and had more than 5420 MW of installed capacity outside of Korea. All told it was involved in 84 international projects in nuclear hydro and thermal power plants transmission and distribution projects and energy resources development initiatives.

To improve its coal self-sufficiency in 2010 KEPCO acquired the Bylong coal mine in Australia from Anglo American PLC for $340 million.

The reviving economy higher commodity prices and increased energy demand helped to lift sales and net income in 2010.

In 2011 the company agreed to set up a 66%-owned joint venture with Germany's Uhde GmbH. Kepco-Uhde Inc. will work on joint projects in Korea relating to integrated gasification combined cycle and synthetic natural gas.

Auditors: Samjong Accounting Corporation (A Member Firm of KPMG)

LOCATIONS

HQ: Korea Electric Power Corp
512 Yeongdong-daero Gangnam-gu, Seoul 135-882
Phone: (82) 2 3456 3114 **Fax:** (82) 2 3456 4298
Web: www.kepco.co.kr

HISTORICAL FINANCIALS
Company Type: Public

Income Statement FYE: December 31

	REVENUE ($ mil.)	NET INCOME ($ mil.)	NET PROFIT MARGIN	EMPLOYEES
12/14	52,531	2,455	4.7%	20,223
12/13	51,384	57	0.1%	20,000
12/12	46,287	(2,965)	—	19,568
12/11	37,570	(2,908)	—	19,579
12/10	35,233	(106)	—	19,927
Annual Growth	10.5%	—	—	0.4%

2014 Year-End Financials

Debt ratio: 0.0%
Return on equity: 5.1%
Cash ($ mil.): 1,641
Current ratio: 0.78
Long-term debt ($ mil.): 51,183
No. of shares (mil.): 641
Dividends
Yield: 0.2%
Payout: 10.3%
Market value ($ mil.): 12,428

	STOCK PRICE ($) FY Close	P/E High/Low	PER SHARE ($) Earnings	Dividends	Book Value
12/14	19.36	0 0	0.39	0.04	76.31
12/13	16.61	0 0	0.09	0.00	76.71
12/12	13.97	— —	(4.76)	0.00	75.00
12/11	10.98	— —	(4.67)	0.00	73.79
12/10	13.51	— —	(0.17)	0.00	81.38
Annual Growth	9.4%	— —	—	—	(1.6%)

Korea Gas Corp. (South Korea)

As the world's largest importer of liquefied natural gas (LNG) KOGAS single-handedly helps South Koreans stay warm and chill out. The company is the sole provider of LNG to the country (about 25 million tons imported annually) operating three terminals and a nationwide pipeline network. KOGAS supplies LNG to power plants and utility companies throughout South Korea and produces and supplies LNG products to domestic and overseas markets. It imports come around the world including from Indonesia Malaysia Myanmar Oman Qatar and Russia. KOGAS development initiatives include natural gas vehicles LNG chiller/heater systems for homes and fuel cells.

Geographic Reach

The company is headquartered in Taegu South Korea. The company has presence in Korea Mexico Australia Canada Iraq Russia Mozambique Timor and Cyprus.

Operations

KOGAS operates four LNG terminals (Pyeongtaek Incheon Tongyeong and Samcheok) and a nationwide pipeline network spanning over 4240 km. The company imports LNG and distributes it to consumers across South Korea. It has storage capacity of 9.46 million in 63 facilities. Ten power generation companies (17 power generation plants) supply the gas to end users within their respective regions.

It major business lines include: Construction and Operation of LNG Terminals and Natural Gas Distribution Network; Exploration and Import/Export of Natural Gas and LNG; Production and Distribution of Natural Gas (including Purification and Sales of By-products); and Research and Technical Development.

Sales and Marketing KOGAS safely delivers natural gas supplied from LNG regasification terminals to pipelines of city gas companies. As a public enterprise KOGAS is in charge of wholesale of natural gas in the domestic market while 30 private city gas companies are granted with exclusive retail sales rights within their respective regions.

Financial Performance

In 2014 the company's net revenues (in local currency) decreased by 2%.Net income saw a strong improvement from previous year's loss mainly due to the benefit from income tax.KOGAS' cash from operating activities increased by 34% due to the changes in trade accounts receivable and other receivables.

Strategy

It has expanded its research and development's core competencies in upstream businesses new energy and future growth engines and is expanding its network by adding domestic and overseas energy research and development institutes.

KOGAS plans to increase its LNG storage ratio to 21% by 2027 to stabilize supply and demand. It continues to conduct overseas resource development projects to secure a stable gas supply in Korea and enhance national energy security. In this regard in 2015 it teamed up with Exxon Mobil and the Korea Institute of Energy Technology Evaluation and Planning to hold discussions concerning natural gas technologies and new energy technologies. KOGAS aims to secure the oil and gas resources of 400 million tons (10% of the energy demand forecast of Korea in 2020) and the annual production volume is expected to reach 10 million tons (25% of Korea'sl energy consumption). It also plans further stabilize the supply and demand by increasing storage facilities securing storage capacity and exporting its gas technologies.

Company Background

KOGAS was incorporated by the Korean government in 1983.

In 2006 KOGAS acquired an 8% interest in China Gas Holdings as a strategic partner. The deal paved the way for further expansion in China's gas distribution market. KOGAS additionally acquired four LNG tankers in a joint venture with three other South Korean companies. The move pointed to a broadening of its overall LNG business.

In 2011 KOGAS signed on to an LNG joint development project in Indonesia and in 2010 it secured development and production rights in the oil and gas fields in Zubair and Badra in Iraq and an equity partnership in Australia's Gladstone LNG project.

The Korean government owns about 26% of the company KEPCO 20.5%.

EXECUTIVES

CEO, Kangsoo Choo
Auditors: Samil Accounting Corporation (A Member Firm of PircewaterhouseCoopers)

LOCATIONS

HQ: Korea Gas Corp. (South Korea)
171, Dolma-ro Bundang-gu, Seongnam-si, Gyeonggi-do 463-754
Phone: (82) 31 710 0114 **Fax:** (82) 31 710 0399
Web: www.kogas.or.kr

COMPETITORS

BP
Exxon Mobil
GS Caltex
JX Nippon Oil & Energy
SK Innovation

HISTORICAL FINANCIALS

Company Type: Public

Income Statement FYE: December 31

	REVENUE ($ mil.)	NET INCOME ($ mil.)	NET PROFIT MARGIN	EMPLOYEES
12/14	34,078	408	1.2%	3,349
12/13	36,193	(190)	—	3,202
12/12	32,809	343	1.0%	2,999
12/11	24,591	156	0.6%	2,815
12/10	20,280	246	1.2%	2,797
Annual Growth	13.9%	13.4%	—	4.6%

2014 Year-End Financials

Debt ratio: 0.0%
Return on equity: 4.7%
Cash ($ mil.): 191
Current ratio: 1.40
Long-term debt ($ mil.): 20,409
No. of shares (mil.): 87
Dividends
Yield: —
Payout: —
Market value ($ mil.): —

Krung Thai Bank Public Co. Ltd.

One of Thailand's largest financial institutions Krung Thai Bank provides banking and financial services to consumers and corporate clients throughout the country. It offers deposit accounts credit and debit cards loans mortgages and leasing as well as life insurance commercial insurance wealth management and access to investments such as securities and mutual funds. In addition to approximately 1160 domestic locations Krung Thai Bank also operates a fleet of some 90 mobile vans that provide on-the-go banking services in remote areas and at tourist destinations and festival sites. Founded in 1966 Krung Thai Bank listed on the Stock Exchange of Thailand in 1989.
Auditors: Office of the Auditor General of Thailand

LOCATIONS

HQ: Krung Thai Bank Public Co. Ltd.
35 Sukhumvit Road, Klong Toey Nua Subdistrict, Bangkok, Wattana 10110
Phone: (66) 2 255 2222 **Fax:** (66) 2 255 9391
Web: www.ktb.co.th

PRODUCTS/OPERATIONS

Selected Group Companies
Credit-Related Business Krung Thai IBJ
Krungthai Card Pcl.
KTB Leasing Co. Ltd.
Leasing Co. Ltd.
Capital Market Business
Krung Thai Asset Management Pcl.
KT ZMICO Securities Co. Ltd.
KTB Advisory Co. Ltd.
Holding Business
KTB Capital Holding Co. Ltd.
Insurance Business
Krungthai Panich Insurance Pcl.
Krungthai-AXA Life Insurance Pcl.
Support Business
KTB Computer Services Co. Ltd.
KTB General Services Co. Ltd.
KTB Law Co. Ltd.

COMPETITORS

Bangkok Bank
Bank of Ayudhya
KASIKORNBANK
Thanachart Capital

HISTORICAL FINANCIALS

Company Type: Public

Income Statement FYE: December 31

	ASSETS ($ mil.)	NET INCOME ($ mil.)	INCOME AS % OF ASSETS	EMPLOYEES
12/14	83,313	1,009	1.2%	23,014
12/13	76,815	1,036	1.3%	20,770
12/12	73,652	768	1.0%	20,121
12/11	62,440	541	0.9%	18,428
12/10	58,680	496	0.8%	18,032
Annual Growth	9.2%	19.4%	—	6.3%

2014 Year-End Financials

Return on assets: 1.2%
Return on equity: 15.1%
Long-term debt ($ mil.): —
No. of shares (mil.): —
Sales ($ mil): 4,510
Dividends
Yield: 0.0%
Payout: 593.4%
Market value ($ mil.): —

	STOCK PRICE ($) FY Close	P/E High/Low		PER SHARE ($) Earnings	Dividends	Book Value
12/14	13.55	7	4	0.07	0.43	0.51
12/13	11.00	7	4	0.07	0.22	0.45
12/12	13.04	7	6	0.07	0.00	0.42
Annual Growth	1.9%	—	—	2.5%	—	4.6%

KT Corp (Korea)

KT keeps South Korea wired (and wireless). The former state-run monopoly is the country's #1 phone company. With 20 million phone lines it controls most of the fixed-line telephone and pay phone service market and is the largest provider of broadband Internet service with 7 million subscribers and more than 40% of the market. (South Korea's population is about 50 million). KT's wireless unit ranks behind only SK Telecom in the mobile telecom segment. The company also provides business customers with IT services such as consulting and systems integration and other subsidiaries are involved in real estate development and rental car services.
Auditors: Samil Accounting Corporation (A Member Firm of PircewaterhouseCoopers)

LOCATIONS

HQ: KT Corp (Korea)
90 Buljeong-ro Bundang-gu, Sungnam-si, Gyeonggi-do 463-711
Phone: (82) 31 727 0850 **Fax:** (82) 31 727 0949
Web: www.kt.co.kr

HISTORICAL FINANCIALS

Company Type: Public

Income Statement FYE: December 31

	REVENUE ($ mil.)	NET INCOME ($ mil.)	NET PROFIT MARGIN	EMPLOYEES
12/14	21,407	(964)	—	23,371
12/13	22,641	(154)	—	32,451
12/12	22,281	990	4.4%	32,186
12/11	18,978	1,248	6.6%	31,981
12/10	18,127	1,155	6.4%	31,155
Annual Growth	4.2%	—	—	(6.9%)

2014 Year-End Financials

Debt ratio: 0.0%
Return on equity: (-9.5%)
Cash ($ mil.): 1,726
Current ratio: 0.88
Long-term debt ($ mil.): 9,043
No. of shares (mil.): 244
Dividends
Yield: 2.7%
Payout: —
Market value ($ mil.): 3,457

	STOCK PRICE ($) FY Close	P/E High/Low		PER SHARE ($) Earnings	Dividends	Book Value
12/14	14.12	—	—	(3.94)	0.38	38.60
12/13	14.87	—	—	(0.63)	0.88	45.83
12/12	16.74	0	0	4.06	0.88	47.30
12/11	15.64	0	0	5.13	1.04	41.52
12/10	20.80	0	0	4.75	0.89	40.82
Annual Growth	(9.2%)	—	—	—	(18.9%)	(1.4%)

L'Oreal S.A. (France)

Business services nec nsk

EXECUTIVES

Pr ©sident, Lo c ARMAND
Auditors: Deloitte & Associ ©

LOCATIONS

HQ: L' Oreal S.A. (France)
14, rue Royale, Paris 75008
Phone: ( ) **Fax:** (33) 1 47 56 86 42
Web: www.loreal.com

HISTORICAL FINANCIALS

Company Type: Public

Income Statement FYE: December 31

	REVENUE ($ mil.)	NET INCOME ($ mil.)	NET PROFIT MARGIN	EMPLOYEES
12/14	27,387	5,968	21.8%	78,611
12/13	31,632	4,072	12.9%	77,452
12/12	29,606	3,779	12.8%	72,637
12/11	26,312	3,153	12.0%	68,886
12/10	26,092	2,997	11.5%	66,619
Annual Growth	1.2%	18.8%	—	4.2%

2014 Year-End Financials

Debt ratio: 9.8%
Return on equity: 22.9%
Cash ($ mil.): 2,330
Current ratio: 0.95
Long-term debt ($ mil.): 81

No. of shares (mil.): 554
Dividends
Yield: 2.0%
Payout: 5.9%
Market value ($ mil.): 18,473

	STOCK PRICE ($) FY Close	P/E High	P/E Low	PER SHARE ($) Earnings	Dividends	Book Value
12/14	33.33	4	3	10.20	0.69	44.27
12/13	35.15	8	6	6.70	0.60	51.96
12/12	27.98	6	4	6.25	0.52	46.11
12/11	20.83	6	4	5.28	0.47	38.37
12/10	22.46	6	5	5.07	0.40	33.74
Annual Growth	10.4%	—	—	19.1%	14.9%	7.0%

Landesbank Baden-Wurttemberg

Landesbank Baden-W rttemberg (LBBW) acts as the central bank to savings banks in the German states of Baden-W rttemberg Rhineland Palatinate and Saxony. The bank handles large transactions (wholesale banking financial securities foreign exchange) too costly for the smaller state savings banks. Through its regional banks Baden W rttembergische Bank and Sachsen Bank and Rheinland-Pfalz Bank LBBW also provides traditional retail banking services such as real estate and commercial loans and portfolio management at more than 200 branches. Other subsidiaries provide leasing factoring venture capital and equity financing services.

LBBW operates offices worldwide that assist export-oriented companies and other German-based customers. LBBW has offices in New York London Singapore Seoul and Mexico City. Those operations are supplemented by four German Centres of Industry in Beijing Mexico City Singapore and India.

Banks all over the world felt the impacts of the global financial crisis and LBBW was not immune. Solid income from its corporate financial markets and private customer segments was not enough to protect the bank from overall losses due to a slowdown in the banking sector and exposure to toxic assets in 2008 and 2009.

In order to strengthen its capital base and provide LBBW with enough liquidity for it to continue functioning as a financing partner the company's government owners pumped in about €5 billion ($6.5 billion) to the bank in 2009. The state of Baden-W rttemberg also provided a €13 billion ($16.5 billion) protection guarantee against risks. As a condition of the bailout the European Commission ordered LBBW to undergo restructuring.

Under the plan the bank was forced to scale back its credit substitute business and cut costs by selling equity investments and eliminating 2500 jobs. At the end of the restructuring LBBW will be smaller and more focused on its core business with corporations private customers and savings banks. It also plans to grow its financial markets and real estate financing business.

As part of the restructuring LBBW agreed to sell its LBBW Securities to Guggenheim Partners in 2010. LBBW Securities is the US broker/dealer for LBBW and handles repurchase agreements securities lending and other financing transactions.

The Savings Banks Association of Baden-W rttemberg owns about 40% of LBBW. The state of Baden-W rttemberg its capital of Stuttgart and Landesbeteilgungen Baden-W rttemberg each controls about 20%.

HISTORY

Landesbank Baden-W rttemberg traces its roots to three German institutions. The oldest Landesgirokasse - – ffentliche Bank und Landessparkasse was founded in 1818 in Stuttgart Germany and eventually grew to be a medium-sized regional savings bank.

Landeskreditbank Baden-W rttemberg was formed in 1924 and throughout the rest of the 20th century Landeskreditbank operated as a public-sector bank serving the western German state of Baden-W rttemberg.

S dwestdeutsche Landesbank Girozentraler (S dwestLB) was formed in 1988 by the merger of Badische Kommunale Landesbank Girozentrale (Bakola) and Landesbank Stuttgart Girozentrale (formerly W rttembergische Kommunale Landesbank Girozentrale).

S dwestLB established itself as the first Landesbank to be wholly owned by the state's savings banks. In 1990 S dwestLB became the first regional bank to take a stake in WestDeutsche Landesbank at the time Germany's largest public-sector financial institution; the move was intended to increase S dwestLB's presence abroad. S dwestLB then joined with WestDeutsche Landesbank Girozentrale in 1992 to purchase Chartered WestLB a pan-European corporate finance company.

In 1998 S dwestLB agreed to merge with Landesgirokasse and the commercial banking unit of Landeskreditbank. The merger which took effect on January 1 1999 resulted in the formation of Landesbank Baden-W rttemberg (LBBW). LBBW immediately became one of the top public-sector banks in Germany.

In 2005 LBBW focused on growing its retail banking business. It acquired Baden W rttembergische Bank (BW Bank) in Landesbank Rheinland-Pfalz (renamed Rheinland-Pfalz Bank). Three years later LBBW looked to broaden its retail banking reach in Central Germany. It acquired Sachsen LB in 2008 which was integrated under the name Sachsen Bank.

EXECUTIVES

Financial Markets, Siegfried Jaschinski
Deputy Chairman Board of Managing Directors, Michael Horn
Head of Capital Markets Trading and Sales, Ralf Winkelmann
Auditors: KPMG AG Wirtschaftsprufungsgesellschaft

LOCATIONS

HQ: Landesbank Baden-Wurttemberg
Am Hauptbahnhof 2, Stuttgart D-70173
Phone: (49) 7 11 127 0 **Fax:** (49) 7 11 127 43544
Web: www.LBBW.de

PRODUCTS/OPERATIONS

Select Subsidiaries and Affiliates

Baden-Württembergische Equity Gesellschaft mit beschränketer Haftung
Baden-Württembergische L-Finance
BW Capital Markets Inc.
BWK GmbH
Cellent AG
Cellent Finance Solutions AG
Deutsche Mittelstandsinformatik GmbH
Landesbank Baden-Württembergische Capital Markets plc
LBBW Asset Management Investmentgesellschaft mbH
LBBW Bank CZ a.s.
LBBW Dublin Management GmbH
LBBW Equity Partners GmbH & Co. KG
LBBW Immobilien GmbH
LBBW Leasing GmbH
LBBW Pensionsmanagement GmbH
LBBW Structured Investment LLC
LBBW (Schw
LBBW Venture Capitala GmbH
LHI Leasing GmbH
MKB Mittelrheinische Bank GmbH
SüdFactoring GmbH
Süd Beteiligungen GmbH
SüdWERT Wohnungsprivatisierungsgesellschaft mbH
Vorarlberger Landes- und Hypothekendbank AG

COMPETITORS

BayernLB
Commerzbank
DZ BANK
Deutsche Bank
UniCredit Bank AG

HISTORICAL FINANCIALS

Company Type: Public

Income Statement FYE: December 31

	ASSETS ($ mil.)	NET INCOME ($ mil.)	INCOME AS % OF ASSETS	EMPLOYEES
12/14	323,603	527	0.2%	11,117
12/13	376,568	472	0.1%	11,308
12/12	443,294	525	0.1%	11,642
12/11	482,533	113	0.0%	12,231
12/10	501,103	(464)	—	13,906
Annual Growth	(10.4%)	—	—	(5.4%)

2014 Year-End Financials

Return on assets: 0.1%
Return on equity: 3.2%
Long-term debt ($ mil.): —
No. of shares (mil.): —
Sales ($ mil): 22,118

Dividends
Yield: —
Payout: —
Market value ($ mil.): —

Landesbank Hessen-Thueringen Girozentrale (Helaba) (Germany, Fed. Rep.)

Savings institutions except federal nsk

EXECUTIVES

Chief Executive Officer, Hans-Dieter Brenner
Auditors: PricewaterhouseCoopers Aktiengesellschaft Wirtschaftprufungsgesellschaft

LOCATIONS

HQ: Landesbank Hessen-Thueringen Girozentrale (Helaba) (Germany, Fed. Rep.)
Neue Mainzer Strasse 52-58, Frankfurt am Main D-60311
Phone: (49) 69 91 32 01 **Fax:** (49) 69 29 15 17
Web: www.helaba.de

HISTORICAL FINANCIALS

Company Type: Public

Income Statement FYE: December 31

	ASSETS ($ mil.)	NET INCOME ($ mil.)	INCOME AS % OF ASSETS	EMPLOYEES
12/14	218,169	487	0.2%	6,274
12/13	245,173	484	0.2%	6,293
12/12	262,688	417	0.2%	6,284
12/11	212,106	513	0.2%	5,748
12/10	222,496	400	0.2%	6,180
Annual Growth	(0.5%)	5.1%	—	0.4%

2014 Year-End Financials

Return on assets: 0.2%
Return on equity: 5.5%
Long-term debt ($ mil.): —
No. of shares (mil.): —
Sales ($ mil): 7,269

Dividends
Yield: —
Payout: —
Market value ($ mil.): —

Landwirtschaftliche Rentenbank (Germany, Fed. Rep.)

EXECUTIVES

Vorstandsmitglied, Hans Bernhardt
Auditors: KPMG AG Wirtschaftspr fungsgesellschaft

LOCATIONS

HQ: Landwirtschaftliche Rentenbank (Germany, Fed. Rep.)
Hochstrasse 2, Frankfurt am Main D-60313
Phone: (49) 69 2107 0 **Fax:** (49) 69 2107 6444
Web: www.rentenbank.de

HISTORICAL FINANCIALS

Company Type: Public

Income Statement FYE: December 31

	ASSETS ($ mil.)	NET INCOME ($ mil.)	INCOME AS % OF ASSETS	EMPLOYEES
12/14	107,992	73	0.1%	269
12/13	112,799	633	0.6%	257
12/12	116,512	321	0.3%	250
12/11	114,958	(89)	—	239
12/10	112,132	203	0.2%	227
Annual Growth	(0.9%)	(22.5%)	—	4.3%

2014 Year-End Financials

Return on assets: 0.0%
Return on equity: 1.8%
Long-term debt ($ mil.): —
No. of shares (mil.): —
Sales ($ mil): 4,067

Dividends
Yield: —
Payout: —
Market value ($ mil.): —

Legal & General Group PLC (United Kingdom)

Legal & General Group is one of the UK's biggest life insurers. The holding company operates four main divisions: investment management risk savings and international. Its investment management arm generates more than 50% of revenues as the UK's largest pension fund manager serving institutional and retail investors. Its risk businesses provide groups and individuals with life insurance annuities and homeowners insurance. Personal savings products include unit trusts investment bonds and savings accounts. International offers life insurance group benefits and wealth management products. The firm operates in the US as Banner Life Insurance Company and William Penn Life Insurance Company of New York.

As part of its distribution network Legal & General's Mortgage Club serves as a marketplace for mortgage advisors to shop for lenders and other services.

The company serves more than 7 million individual corporate and institutional customers. It mainly distributes its insurance products in the UK through retail independent financial advisers (IFAs) and employee benefit consultants which make up more than 70% of it distribution mix. Banks and building societies including Sainsbury's Bank and Barclays also distribute its products.

Strategically Legal & General is focused on broadening its core product offerings finding new markets building its brand recognition and widening its distribution network to provide a variety of ways to access its products. Additionally the company is pursuing growth opportunities both domestically and overseas to expand its global reach in response to customer demand particularly in North America the Gulf and Asia. Other key strategic goals include improving customer engagement by 2014 increasing cash generation and delivering strong return on equity results through capital management and improving organizational production responsiveness and diversity. Achieving positive results toward its objectives has put the company in a postion of strength in the midst of economic uncertainties and regulatory changes.

Legal & General managed to serve up positive results in 2011 with across-the-board increases in its sales operational cash generation and operating profits in each of its divisions even though its revenues of 18.3 million ($28.5 million) for the year represented a decrease of more than 50% from 2010 and its net income fell nearly 12% to 0.7 million ($1.1 million) mainly due to a 63% drop in investment returns.

HISTORY

The Legal in Legal & General's name comes from its founding mission –to provide life insurance to members of the legal profession. The company was started in 1836 by six lawyers as the Legal & General Life Assurance Society; its first customer solicitor Thomas Smith ill-manneredly died four years later after paying less than 200 pounds on a 1000-pound policy.

Throughout that century and into the next the company made loans to individuals and corporations; it also moved into real estate. After struggling under claims during WWI and the 1918 flu pandemic it moved into fire and accident coverage in 1920. It opened membership to nonlawyers in 1929. The company took over the UK operations of the US firm Metropolitan Life (MetLife) in 1933.

In 1934 Legal & General bought Gresham Life Assurance and Gresham Fire and Accident to gain a presence in Australia. During WWII the company was hit hard by German air attacks both physically (it had to relocate away from London for a time) and at the bottom line.

The postwar years were a time of expansion as the company moved into South Africa and also broadened its operations at home. In 1949 it moved into marine insurance and in 1956 inaugurated life insurance in Australia.

The company began expanding its product offerings in the 1970s with managed pension funds and retail unit trusts. It established a direct sales force for life and pensions in 1977. The company also formed alliances with several European insurance companies and sold its Gresham life subsidiary. In 1979 it formed Legal & General Group Limited as a holding company for its now-separate insurance international and investment management operations.

In 1981 Legal & General bought US auto insurer GEICO's two-thirds interest in Government Employees Life Insurance Company changing the subsidiary's name to Banner Life. Three years later it bought the Dutch operations of Unilife Assurance and created a subsidiary in the Netherlands. Despite all this activity however the company's performance during the 1980s was poor and it brought in David Prosser (who became CEO in 1991) to goose its asset management operations.

In 1989 the company bought William Penn Life Insurance from Continental Corp. and opened its first real estate agency –just in time for the real estate market crash. Legal & General and other mortgage guarantee insurers were also squeezed by the resulting increase in mortgage default rates as homebuyers were caught between high interest rates and high unemployment.

The company formed a joint venture with Woolwich Building Society to provide Woolwich customers with insurance products in 1995. The next year it followed the insurance industry trend by establishing a bank of its own.

With each succeeding merger of its rivals Legal & General became the target of rumors about its own fate. The company has remained adamantly independent with Prosser claiming that Legal & General could instead benefit by picking up business left behind by the new entities.

In 1998 the British insurance industry was stung by scandalous revelations regarding improper pension sales in the late 1980s and early 1990s. Legal & General set aside about $1 billion to compensate victims; it also sold its Australian operations. In 1999 banking company National Westminster and Legal & General talked takeover but the deal fell through. (NatWest was eventually bought by Royal Bank of Scotland.)

In 2001 Legal & General announced a deal with UK-based Barclays to provide the bank's customers with life insurance and pension products. In 2002 Legal & General extended its marketing agreement with UK financial services company Alliance & Leicester.

The company then discontinued its health insurance offerings and reduced its venture capital investment operations. In 2005 the company sold its Gresham Insurance subsidiary to Barclays Bank.

EXECUTIVES

CEO Legal & General Assurance Society, John Pollock, age 56, $370,000 total compensation
CEO Legal & General Investment Management, Mark Zinkula

CEO Legal & General Investment Management America Inc, Robert Moore
Interim President and CEO Legal & General America, Gene Gilbertson
CEO Legal & General Gulf, Peter Drummond
Group CEO, Nigel Wilson
CFO, Mark Gregory
Managing Director Legal & General Retirement, Kerrigan Procter
Managing Director Legal & General Capital, Paul Stanworth
Vice Chairman, Rudy H. P. Markham, age 69
Chairman, John M. Stewart, age 66
Auditors: PricewaterhouseCoopers LLP

LOCATIONS

HQ: Legal & General Group PLC (United Kingdom)
One Coleman Street, London EC2R 5AA
Phone: (44) 20 3124 2000 **Fax:** (44) 20 3124 2500
Web: www.legalandgeneralgroup.com

PRODUCTS/OPERATIONS

2011 Revenues by Segment

	% of total
Investment management	52
Risk (life & property insurance)	33
Savings	9
International	6
Group capital & financing	-
Total	**100**

2011 Distribution Channels

	% of total
Retail independent financial advisers (IFA)	37
Employee benefit consultants	35
Bancassurance	23
Direct	3
Tied agents	2
Total	**100**

Selected Acquisitions

COMPETITORS

AEGON
AXA
Allianz
Aviva
ING
Lloyds Banking Group
MetLife
Prudential
Prudential plc
Royal London Mutual
Standard Life
Zurich Insurance Group

HISTORICAL FINANCIALS

Company Type: Public

Income Statement FYE: December 31

	ASSETS ($ mil.)	NET INCOME ($ mil.)	INCOME AS % OF ASSETS	EMPLOYEES
12/14	623,711	1,537	0.2%	11,038
12/13	600,157	1,475	0.2%	11,163
12/12	558,191	1,310	0.2%	9,864
12/11	504,733	1,121	0.2%	9,138
12/10	502,858	1,273	0.3%	8,662
Annual Growth	5.5%	4.8%	—	6.2%

2014 Year-End Financials

Return on assets: 0.2%
Return on equity: 16.8%
Long-term debt ($ mil.): —
No. of shares (mil.): —
Sales ($ mil): 80,419
Dividends
Yield: 4.0%
Payout: 279.0%
Market value ($ mil.): —

	STOCK PRICE ($) FY Close	P/E High/Low		PER SHARE ($) Earnings	Dividends	Book Value
12/14	19.27	117	97	0.26	0.77	1.59
12/13	18.45	123	81	0.25	0.59	1.58
12/12	12.42	87	60	0.22	0.49	1.49
12/11	7.95	77	54	0.19	0.35	1.37
12/10	7.67	59	40	0.22	0.27	1.28
Annual Growth	25.9%	—	—	4.6%	30.0%	5.6%

Lenovo Group Ltd

Workhorse Lenovo Group has risen to the top of the worldwide PC market ahead of #2 HP and #3 Dell. The China-based group is a global supplier of Think-branded commercial PCs and Idea-branded consumer PCs holding a dominant position in China. The company makes tablets smartphones laptops desktops workstations servers software and accessories and it is developing and launching mini ultrabooks and ideapads. Lenovo offers services for enterprise small business and home office markets. Certain products and services are geared specifically at the growing education government and health care verticals. Lenovo formed out of the acquisition of IBM's Personal Computing division in 2005.

Geographic Reach

Hong Kong-based Lenovo serves customers in more than 160 countries. The company generates more than 40% of its sales in China where it holds more than 30% market share in PCs. Elsewhere it generates about 20% of its sales in both Europe the Middle East and Africa and in the Asia-Pacific and Latin America regions. Lenovo is also increasing sales in other emerging markets.

Operations

Lenovo has operations in more than 60 countries across the globe. It has operations hubs in Beijing Paris and North Carolina and a marketing hub in Bangalore India. It also has major research centers in Yokohama Japan and in China in Beijing Shanghai and Shenzhen. Aiming to boost sales growth Lenovo in 2013 began producing PCs in Raleigh North Carolina at a new assembly plant. As part of this effort the company is devoting more investment dollars to domestic manufacturing.

Financial Performance

Lenovo's sales jumped 15% in fiscal 2013 (ended March) versus the prior year to an all-time high of $33.9 billion. Indeed the company's sales have more than doubled over the past four years while profits have risen steadily. Driving the strong performance in fiscal 2013 was a 7% year-over-year increase in notebook computer sales and a 6% jump in sales of desktop computers. Sales of mobile Internet and digital home products more than doubled to $3.1 billion driven largely by brisk smartphone sales in China. The company saw growth in all of its geographic markets with China and Europe the Middle East and Africa posting the strongest results. Buoyed by rising sales net income rose 33% to $631.3 million.

Strategy

Lenovo has invested heavily in acquisitions and infrastructure over the past several years to bolster its PC business with stellar results. Between 2011 and 2013 Lenovo jumped from being the world's fourth-largest PC vendor to the largest surpassing HP in worldwide PC shipments and market share in the second quarter of 2013. More impressively while the global PC industry is in a slump (down 5.6% in 2013) Lenovo is the only PC vendor that is growing. Indeed Lenovo shipped almost 54 million PCs in 2013 up slightly from just over 52 million in 2012. Dell and HP both posted declines in shipments in 2013. With demand for PCs declining worldwide Lenovo has diversified into smartphones tablets and other mobile devices as well as into the enterprise sector such as servers.

In addition to being the #1 PC company in the world Lenovo is also the top PC company for large enterprises and the public sector. Lenovo used a different growth strategy than most of its big competitors to reach this market spot expanding East to West. New products are introduced in China then spread across the globe.

Although it has long been the leader in China Lenovo does not rest on its laurels when it comes to increasing additional share in the Asia/Pacific region. To maintain supremacy in this market Lenovo's Hefei China-based joint venture with Compal Electronics began mass producing notebooks in 2013. Lenovo which holds a 51% stake and Compal which owns the remaining 49% will invest a total of $300 million in the JV's expansion.

In Japan Lenovo leverages the strength of that country's #1 PC company NEC through a joint venture called NEC Lenovo Japan Group. That JV of which Lenovo holds a majority stake is the dominant PC maker in Japan with about a 25% share of the market. Prior to the JV's formation in 2011 NEC had been the market leader in Japan but was not turning a profit when it made the deal. The JV helps give NEC access to cheaper Chinese supplies and manufacturing.

Mergers and Acquisitions

In the last two years Lenovo has made acquisitions to beef up its hardware offerings and support expansion in select markets. In January 2014 it agreed to pay more than $5 billion to acquire two new major product lines. First it announced plans to buy IBM's low-end x86 server business for $2.3 billion. The business includes System x BladeCenter and Flex System blade servers and switches x86-based Flex integrated systems NeXtScale and iDataPlex servers and associated software blade networking and customer service operations. The 7500 employees who work for IBM are expected to be transferred to Lenovo. The acquisition frees up IBM to focus on its cloud computing business.

A few weeks later it agreed to pay $2.9 billion for Motorola Mobility. Google bought Motorola's smartphone business in 2012 with big plans for its Android phones. However the division continued to suffer losses in the highly competitive smartphone market and Motorola Mobility was forced to cut staff and close locations. As part of the deal Lenovo will own the brands Moto X Moto G and the DROID Ultra series while Google will own the patent portfolio.

In 2012 the company acquired US-based Stoneware to expand its secure cloud computing portfolio. The deal add new technologies and added capabilities for both commercial and consumer cloud offerings particularly the ability to provide secure content across multiple devices in education and government. Also in September of that year Lenovo made strides in Latin America by acquiring Brazil's CCE a regional leader in PCs and consumer electronics. It added manufacturing facilities; an extensive selection of consumer products such as PCs tablets smartphones and televisions; and a robust supply chain.

Across the Atlantic Lenovo's growth in Europe was supported by a majority stake acquisition in mid-2011 of Germany-based computer and electronics reseller MEDION. The MEDION buy doubled Lenovo's market share in Germany and made it the third-largest PC company in Europe's largest PC market.

HISTORY

Liu Chuanzhi an engineer at the Chinese Academy of Sciences who wrote industry research reports established Legend Group Holdings Co. in 1984 in Beijing. Backed by a modest investment from the academy Liu who went on to become something of an entrepreneurial hero in China and 10 other engineers were given a green light to form a retail business. They first bought and sold items ranging from TVs to roller skates but later focused on distributing computer products and eventually moved into manufacturing PCs for AST Research. Legend introduced its first proprietary product a Chinese character system for PCs in 1985.

In 1988 the company formed Legend Holdings Limited which was originally a Hong Kong-based PC distributor. The following year the parent company began designing and manufacturing motherboards and added systems integration services to its offerings. In 1990 China reduced import tariffs a move that opened the trade door for companies such as IBM and Compaq. That year Legend Group Holdings began making its own brand of PCs.

Legend Holdings went public in 1994 and the following year began absorbing operations from its parent company which retained approximately 60% ownership in the subsidiary. By 1996 it was tied with IBM for PC market share in China; it became the country's top brand the following year.

In 1998 parent company Legend Group Holdings transferred Beijing Legend Group to its Hong Kong-based subsidiary. The following year Microsoft looking to extend its operating system dominance into China teamed up with Legend Holdings to create set-top boxes. In 2000 the company partnered with Pacific Century CyberWorks to provide broadband Internet services. The following year Legend spun off its distribution business Digital China as a separate public company. In 2001 Yang Yuanqing was named CEO of the company.

In 2002 Legend Holdings changed its English company name to Legend Group Limited. The company launched a corporate brand Lenovo the following year and in 2004 it officially adopted Lenovo as its English name. It also sold its non-telecom IT services business to AsiaInfo Holdings renamed AsiaInfo-Linkage in 2004.

Lenovo acquired IBM's worldwide PC operations for approximately $1.75 billion in 2005. IBM executive Stephen Ward was named CEO of Lenovo at the time of the merger but he was replaced by William Amelio before year's end. Amelio headed Dell's Asia/Pacific operations before joining Lenovo. In 2006 Lenovo launched a unit called Lenovo Services.

In 2007 Lenovo stopped using the IBM PC brand to which it still held the rights and began offering only Lenovo-branded machines. The following year it sponsored and supported the Olympic Summer Games in Beijing providing more than 30000 pieces of equipment and 600 engineers.

Looking to focus on its core PC operations Lenovo sold its mobile phone business Lenovo Mobile Communications to Hony Capital in 2008. Hony the private equity arm of Legend Holdings paid $100 million for the unit.

A year later Lenovo bought back the mobile communications business for about $200 million in cash and stock. The company cited the growth of the mobile Internet market and the increasing convergence between the PC and wireless handset sectors for the about-face in product strategy. Lenovo's move came as Dell introduced a mobile phone for the Chinese market.

Citing a flagging economy Lenovo announced a restructuring plan in 2009 that included a workforce reduction of 11% executive pay cuts and the consolidation of its China and the Asia/Pacific units. The company also initiated a management shakeup including its chairman taking over as CEO. The change may in part have reflected a strategy shift for Lenovo. With corporate spending flagging particularly in the US the company planned to focus on China and other emerging markets with an emphasis on consumers.

EXECUTIVES

SVP and Chief Marketing Officer, David A. Roman
Chairman and CEO, Yang Yuanqing, age 52, $894,000 total compensation
SVP Centralized Services, Wang Xiaoyan, age 54
SVP and President EMEA, Eric Cador
Assistant President; Head of Sales Commercial Department, Chen Xudong
President, Gianfranco Lanci, age 60
SVP and CTO, Peter D. Hortensius, age 55
COO Asia Pacific and Chairman Lenovo India, Amar Babu
SVP and CFO, Wong Wai Ming, age 57
EVP and COO PC and EBG Business Groups, Gerry P. Smith, age 52
SVP and President North America, Aymar de Lencquesaing
SVP and CIO, Zhou Qingtong
President Motorola Mobility, Rick Osterloh
Managing Director Lenovo India, Rahul Agarwal
SVP and President Ecosystem and Cloud Business Group, He Zhiqiang
Auditors: PricewaterhouseCoopers

LOCATIONS

HQ: Lenovo Group Ltd
23rd Floor, Lincoln House, Taikoo Place, 979 King' s Road, Quarry Bay,
Phone: (852) 2590 0228 **Fax:** (852) 2516 5384
Web: www.lenovo.com

2013 Sales

	$ mil.	% of total
China	14,538	43
Europe Middle East &Africa	7,535	22
Asia Pacific &Latin America	6,860	20
North America	4,939	15
Total	**33,873**	**100**

PRODUCTS/OPERATIONS

2013 Sales

	$ mil.	% of total
Personal computer		
Desktop	17,935	53
Notebook	10,524	31
Mobile Internet &digital home	3,039	9
Others	2,373	7
Total	**33,873**	**100**

COMPETITORS

ASUSTeK
Acer
Apple Inc.
BlackBerry
Dell
Digital China
Founder Holdings
Fujitsu
Great Wall Technology
HP
HTC Corporation
Hedy Holding
Hitachi
IBM
LG Electronics
Microsoft
NEC
Nokia
Panasonic Corp
Positivo Informtica
Samsung Electronics
Siemens AG
Sony
Toshiba
Wipro

HISTORICAL FINANCIALS

Company Type: Public

Income Statement FYE: March 31

	REVENUE ($ mil.)	NET INCOME ($ mil.)	NET PROFIT MARGIN	EMPLOYEES
03/15	46,295	828	1.8%	60,000
03/14	38,707	817	2.1%	54,000
03/13	33,873	635	1.9%	35,026
03/12	29,574	472	1.6%	27,000
03/11	21,594	273	1.3%	27,039
Annual Growth	21.0%	32.0%	—	22.1%

2015 Year-End Financials

Debt ratio: 11.2%
Return on equity: 24.8%
Cash ($ mil.): 2,855
Current ratio: 0.90
Long-term debt ($ mil.): 1,885
No. of shares (mil.): —
Dividends
Yield: 1.9%
Payout: 753.2%
Market value ($ mil.): —

	STOCK PRICE ($) FY Close	P/E High/Low		PER SHARE ($) Earnings	Dividends	Book Value
03/15	29.15	423280		0.08	0.58	0.35
03/14	22.09	354211		0.08	0.48	0.27
03/13	20.10	377225		0.06	0.33	0.24
03/12	17.98	398229		0.05	0.19	0.23
03/11	11.30	557355		0.03	0.15	0.18
Annual Growth	26.7%	—	—	29.6%	40.3%	17.3%

LG Chem Ltd (New)

LG Chem got there first. Founded in 1947 it was Korea's first chemical company. The company produces a variety of products including cosmetics personal care products petrochemicals pharmaceuticals and specialty chemicals. It's divided into two segments. The Petrochemicals unit makes basic chemicals like ethylene propylene and their derivatives as well as PVC acrylates and engineering plastics. The company's Information and Electronic Materials segment produces rechargeable batteries and display materials. It boasts 12 manufacturing subsidiaries and 20-plus marketing subsidiaries. Formerly the chemical division of the LG Group the company went public in 2001 while LG still owns a third of LG Chem.

After the global recession of 2008 LG Chem saw a significant rise in profitability in 2009 with growth in its petrochemical business due to a booming Chinese economy and improvements in its information and electronic materials business due to a general rise in worldwide demand. Overall LG Chem's sale grew about 8% in 2009 while its net income jumped more than 55%.

In 2009 the company spun off its Industrial Materials unit saying that the business was sufficiently different from LG Chem's core operations that it made more sense to operate it separately. The new company called LG Hausys manufactures window frames flooring materials and other construction-industry products.

The company gets about half of its sales domestically but China accounts for a rapidly growing percentage of its foreign sales around 25%. (Domestic sales accounted for less than half of 2008's total sales marking the first time that has happened for the company.) LG Chem is looking to grow its already strong position in the Chinese PVC market.

Further expanding it geographic assets in 2011 the company announced that a joint venture would invest $4 billion to build a petrochemical complex in Kazakhstan.

EXECUTIVES

Vice Chairman and CEO, Jin Soo Park
President and CFO, Suk-Jeh Cho
President, Young-Su Kwon
President, Young-Ki Park
Research Chairman, Lee Jin-kyu
Chairman, Peter Bahnsuk Kim
Auditors: Samil Accounting Corporation (A Member Firm of PircewaterhouseCoopers)

LOCATIONS

HQ: LG Chem Ltd (New)
LG Twin Towers, 128 Yeouido-dong, Youngdeungpo-gu, Seoul 150-721
Phone: (82) 2 3777 1114 **Fax:** (82) 2 3773 7813
Web: www.lgchem.com

2013 Sales

	% of total
China	38
Korea	36
America	6
Southeast Asia	5
Western Europe	4
Other	11
Total	**100**

PRODUCTS/OPERATIONS

2013 Sales

	% of total
Petrochemicals	76
Information & Electronic Materials	13
Batteries	11
Total	**100**

COMPETITORS

Mitsubishi Chemical
OCI Company
Sumitomo Chemical

HISTORICAL FINANCIALS

Company Type: Public

Income Statement FYE: December 31

	REVENUE ($ mil.)	NET INCOME ($ mil.)	NET PROFIT MARGIN	EMPLOYEES
12/14	20,635	793	3.8%	13,623
12/13	22,007	1,203	5.5%	12,617
12/12	21,787	1,399	6.4%	11,683
12/11	19,569	1,845	9.4%	10,722
12/10	17,365	1,924	11.1%	9,304
Annual Growth	4.4%	(19.9%)	—	10.0%

2014 Year-End Financials

Debt ratio: 0.0%
Return on equity: 7.3%
Cash ($ mil.): 903
Current ratio: 1.69
Long-term debt ($ mil.): 665
No. of shares (mil.): 65
Dividends
Yield: —
Payout: 0.0%
Market value ($ mil.): —

	STOCK PRICE ($) FY Close	P/E High/Low		PER SHARE ($) Earnings	Dividends	Book Value
12/14	0.00	—	—	10.78	0.00	168.34
12/13	99.00	—	—	16.37	0.00	167.31
12/12	99.00	—	—	19.03	0.00	151.04
12/11	99.00	—	—	25.09	0.00	125.09
Annual Growth	—	—	—	(19.0%)	—	7.7%

LG Display Co Ltd

The world is truly flat for LG Display –as in flat-panel displays. The company is one of the world's top producers of TFT-LCDs (thin-film transistor liquid-crystal displays) the svelte screens that go into laptop and notebook computers desktop PC monitors TV sets wireless handsets and a variety of applications in automotive navigation avionics consumer electronics instrumentation and medical equipment. LG Electronics and Philips merged their LCD businesses in 1999. Philips no longer holds any equity in LG Display. The company gets about 70% of its sales from customers in the Asia/Pacific region.

The global economic downturn had little effect on LG Display's sales which rose by 23% in 2009 and by 13% in 2008. Driven by demand for larger and wider screens the increase in unit sales for large-size panels –particularly those for televisions and desktop monitors –more than offset the decrease in average selling prices for the years. The company's profitability remained relatively strong as well; its net income for 2009 was $954 million about a 20% increase over 2008 but around 17% lower than reported in 2007. The lower profits for 2008 and 2009 were due in part to higher raw material costs and higher salary and bonus expenses related to growth in sales and employees. In addition 2008 and 2009 included payments related an antitrust-related settlement. In 2008 LG Display pleaded guilty to fixing prices on LCD panels under charges brought by the US Department of Justice and paid a fine of $424 million.

The company has a limited number of end-brand customers with its top three customers –LG Electronics Philips and Hewlett-Packard –accounting for more than 40% of sales. HP became a significant customer after LG Display agreed to supply panels to HP in 2005 in a three-year deal worth $5 billion. The contract was renewed for another three years in 2008. The flat panels are installed in HP notebook computers and PC monitors.

The flat-panel display industry has grown rapidly but is also highly cyclical and subject to rapid price declines. LG Display counters these declines by carefully allocating its production and development capacity. It also shifts its product mix towards large panels which fetch premium prices. In 2009 the company focused on large-size wide-format panels for desktop monitors notebook computers and televisions. Panels for LCD TVs account for close to half of the company's sales.

LG Display also makes small to midsized panels which are primarily used in handheld applications such as mobile phones GPS units digital photo frames and e-book readers. The average selling price for the panels is significantly lower that other panels and the market is extremely competitive though global demand for products that use the panels continues to grow.

The company must also contend with shifts in display technologies as advanced techniques for making displays challenge the mainstream LCD trade. In 2008 LG Display acquired the active-matrix organic light-emitting diode (AMOLED) business of LG Electronics for nearly $5 million in cash. AMOLEDs are an advanced type of display; OLED displays which are starting to show up in TV sets and other consumer electronics products don't require a backlight like LCDs do and they can offer superior images. The company had worked on AMOLED technology with Eastman Kodak (where the OLED was originally invented) and produced a flexible AMOLED monotone display in 2008 that can function as an "e-newspaper" after introducing a flexible color e-book display in 2007. In 2009 LG Display and its affiliates formed a joint venture company –Global OLED Technology LLC –that acquired Kodak's OLED business. LG Display holds 49% of the JV.

A bright spot for South Korean LCD flat-panel makers came in December 2009 when the South Korean government gave approval for LG Display and Samsung Electronics to export their TFT-LCD technology to China allowing the companies to move forward with plans to build plants there. LG Display has announced it will set up a joint venture to build a $4 billion 8th generation LCD plant in China giving the company expanded access to the rapidly growing Chinese LCD TV market.

Most of LG Display's production and assembly facilities are located in South Korea and China. In order to better serve its customers in the European market LG Display invested $533 million in building and expanding an LCD component factory in Poland which began mass production in 2007.

Philips gradually sold off its equity stake in LG Display. In 2007 Philips reduced its stake in LG Display from 33% to around 20% selling 46.4 million shares for about $2.2 billion. The following year Philips sold another 24 million shares cutting its stake by nearly 7%. The company got slightly more than $1 billion for those shares. In 2009 the Dutch giant sold its last remaining shares in LG Display for about $803 million.

In light of Philips selling its interests in the company shareholders voted in 2008 to change the name of the company from LG.Philips LCD to LG Display. LG Electronics continues to own about 38% of LG Display.

EXECUTIVES

CTO and EVP, Sang-Deog (Eddie) Yeo, age 60
CEO and President, Sang-Beom Han
Chief Production Officer and EVP, Cheol-Dong Jeong
CFO and SVP, Don Kim
Head TV Business Unit and EVP, Yong-Kee Hwang
Head IT/Mobile Business Unit and SVP, Kyong-Deuk Jeong
Chairman, Yu Sig Kang
Auditors: Samjong Accounting Corporation (A Member Firm of KPMG)

LOCATIONS

HQ: LG Display Co Ltd
12th Floor, 128 LG Twin Tower, Youngdengpo-gu, 128 Yeoi-daero, Seoul 150-875
Phone: (82) 2 3777 5114 **Fax:** (82) 2 3777 0797
Web: www.lgdisplay.com

2014 Sales

	% of total
Asia/Pacific	
China	60
Other countries	11
Europe	6
Americas	8
Poland	5
Total	**100**

PRODUCTS/OPERATIONS

2014 Sales

	% of total
TFT-LCD televisions	39
Desktop monitors	18
Tablet products	13
Notebook computers	10
Mobile and others	20
Total	**100**

Products Selected
TV Display
Commercial Display
Monitor Display
Notebook Display

Mobile Display
Auto Display
IPS
AIT
Transparent flexible display
3D

COMPETITORS

AU Optronics
Amax
BOE Technology
Chimei Innolux
Chunghwa Picture Tubes
Delta Electronics Thailand
HannStar Display
JDI
Mitsubishi Electric
NEC Display Solutions
SVA Group
Samsung Electronics
Sharp Electronics
Sony
Truly International
Varitronix
ViewSonic
Wintek

HISTORICAL FINANCIALS

Company Type: Public

Income Statement FYE: December 31

	REVENUE ($ mil.)	NET INCOME ($ mil.)	NET PROFIT MARGIN	EMPLOYEES
12/14	24,180	826	3.4%	32,434
12/13	25,705	405	1.6%	33,643
12/12	27,563	218	0.8%	34,657
12/11	20,964	(665)	—	34,803
12/10	22,752	1,031	4.5%	30,117
Annual Growth	1.5%	(5.4%)	—	1.9%

2014 Year-End Financials

Debt ratio: 0.0%
Return on equity: 8.2%
Cash ($ mil.): 2,208
Current ratio: 1.22
Long-term debt ($ mil.): 2,997
No. of shares (mil.): 357
Dividends
Yield: —
Payout: —
Market value ($ mil.): 5,421

	STOCK PRICE ($) FY Close	P/E High/Low		PER SHARE ($) Earnings	Dividends	Book Value
12/14	15.15	0	0	2.31	0.00	29.20
12/13	12.14	0	0	1.13	0.00	28.20
12/12	14.48	0	0	0.61	0.00	26.72
12/11	10.53	—	—	(1.86)	0.22	24.40
12/10	17.75	0	0	2.81	0.22	27.51
Annual Growth	(3.9%)	—	—	(4.8%)	—	1.5%

LG Electronics Inc

LG Electronics (LGE) makes the products that have tech-savvy consumers chomping at the bit in the kitchen in the media room and on the go. A leader in consumer electronics mobile communications and home appliances LGE operates through more than 100 subsidiaries worldwide that design and make flat panel TVs audio and video products mobile handsets air conditioners washing machines refrigerators and more. Asia and North America are its two largest markets each contributing about a quarter of LGE's sales. LGE owns Zenith Electronics (acquired in 1995) and LG Display. Founded in 1958 as Goldstar LGE established a North American headquarters in 2004. South Korea's LG Corp. owns about one-third of LGE.

Geographic Reach

Seoul-based LG Electronics (LGE) rings up nearly 15% of its sales at home in South Korea. North America accounts for nearly a quarter of its total sales. Other important markets for geographically-diversified LGE include Central and South America (15%) and Europe. About 15% of the company's sales come from emerging markets including India China and Russia. The Middle East and Africa accounts for about 10%. The company controls 114 local subsidiaries across the globe.

Operations

Home entertainment including OLED and Ultra HD TVs and other video and audio products is LGE's largest business accounting for a 45% of sales. Home appliances and mobile communications products each represent about 20% of sales.

Financial Performance

The consumer electronics giant rang up $53.1 billion in sales and a net profit of $203.7 million in 2013 marking an improvement over 2012 results. LGE's operating profit increased modestly in 2013 to nearly $1.2 billion up from $1.1 billion in 2012. The company's mobile communications business posted a 29% jump in annual sales with help from stronger smartphone sales including its G2 and Nexus 5 models. Smartphone shipments rose 54% year over year. LGE's air conditioning and home appliance businesses also posted annual sales gains of 8% and 5% respectively. The laggard was home entertainment which suffered a 5% decline in annual sales despite higher demand for LCD TVs in North America Asia and the CIS countries.

Strategy

LGE is focusing on boosting its mobile communication handset business and enhancing its share of the LCD TV market. Indeed the company is looking to sell about 20% more cell phones. To that end LGE will enter the world's largest 4G mobile market —China —with the introduction of its LG-E985T smartphone through China Mobile (the world's largest mobile operator with nearly 750 million subscribers). The company is also going after the premium kitchen appliance market with the establishment in 2013 of a new division focused exclusively on high-end kitchen packages. The new division will initially focus on the US and Korean markets. The Korean company has formed a strategic relationship with GE to share patents on kitchenware and refrigerators. LGE also has alliances with other companies including Prada (phones) Siemens (air conditioners) and Hitachi (optical storage).

LGE is continuing to invest heavily in marketing to boost its position as one of the world's top consumer electronics brands up there with rivals Sony Samsung and Panasonic. The company is also focused on boosting sales of its commercial air conditioners drum washing machines and side-by-side (aka French door) refrigerators. LGE and US rival Whirlpool have been trading patent infringement claims over refrigerator technology.

Mergers and Acquisitions

In February 2013 LGE acquired the webOS operating system technology from Hewlett-Packard to support its next-generation Smart TV technology. LGE acquired the source code and other assets associated with webOS. The purchase will allow LGE to offer an intuitive user experience and Internet services across a range of consumer electronics devices.

To bolster production of large-scale air conditioning systems both in South Korea and abroad LGE acquired the A/C business of industrial machinery manufacturer LS Mtron for $134 million in early 2011. The deal included a factory in Jeonju South Korea as well as a research and development team. LS Mtron operated as part of LG Group until 2003 when its operations were spun off.

EXECUTIVES

President and CEO Mobile Communications; Director, Cho Jun-Ho
President CFO and Director, Do-Hyun (David) Jung
President and CEO Home Entertainment Company, Bong-Suk Kwon
President and CEO Home Appliances and Air Solutions; Director, Jo Seong-jin
President Business to Business Sector, Lee Sang-bong
President and CEO Vehicle Components, Lee Woo-Jong
Chairman, Bon-Joon Koo, age 63
Auditors: Samil Accounting Corporation (A Member Firm of PircewaterhouseCoopers)

LOCATIONS

HQ: LG Electronics Inc
LG Twin Towers, 128 Yeouido-dong, Yeongdeungpo-gu, Seoul 150-721
Phone: (82) 2 3777 1114 **Fax:** (82) 2 3777 3428
Web: www.lge.com

2012 Sales

	% of total
North America	23
Central & South America	15
Korea	14
Europe	12
Middle East & Africa	11
Commonwealth of Independent States	8
Southeast Asia	7
India	5
China	3
Japan	2
Total	**100**

PRODUCTS/OPERATIONS

2012 Sales

	% of total
Home entertainment	45
Home appliance	22
Mobile communications	20
Air conditioning & energy products	9
Other	4
Total	**100**

Selected Major Products & Services

Home Entertainment (LCD TVs plasma TVs audio video & optical storage)
Mobile Communication (mobile handsets mobile accessory)
Home Appliance (washing machines refrigerators cooking appliances vacuum cleaners built-in appliances)
Air Conditioning (residential air conditioners commercial air conditioners home solution compressors)
Business Solutions (monitors commercial displays car infotainment security business)

COMPETITORS

Apple Inc.
BSH Home Appliances
Electrolux
GE Appliances & Lighting
Haier Group
Panasonic Corp
Philips Electronics
SANYO
Samsung Electronics
Sony
Technicolor
Toshiba
Whirlpool

HISTORICAL FINANCIALS

Company Type: Public

Income Statement FYE: December 31

	REVENUE ($ mil.)	NET INCOME ($ mil.)	NET PROFIT MARGIN	EMPLOYEES
12/14	53,962	365	0.7%	37,835
12/13	55,285	168	0.3%	38,363
12/12	47,728	62	0.1%	36,376
12/11	46,825	(405)	—	35,286
12/10	49,723	1,094	2.2%	32,972
Annual Growth	2.1%	(24.0%)	—	3.5%

2014 Year-End Financials

Debt ratio: 0.0%	No. of shares (mil.): 162
Return on equity: 3.4%	Dividends
Cash ($ mil.): 2,113	Yield: —
Current ratio: 1.11	Payout: —
Long-term debt ($ mil.): 5,874	Market value ($ mil.): —

Linde AG (Germany, Fed. Rep.)

Linde's business is lighter than air and bigger than everyone else's. Operating in more than 100 countries it is the world's largest producer of industrial and medical gases. Linde also has an engineering unit that builds process plants for companies in the petrochemical pharmaceutical and gas manufacturing industries; the gases unit accounts for more than three-quarters of its sales. A third division provides logistics and supply chain services to a broad range of commercial and industrial sectors including electronics grocery retail and gas. The company still does about half of its business in Europe but its presence is growing in emerging markets in Asia and Africa.

Linde operates through a number of subsidiaries including Eibl Homecare GmbH Linde BOC Process Plants African Oxygen Spectra Gases Hoek Loos Linde Medical Devices GmbH and Linde Finance. Linde's business is organized in three divisions: Industrial Gases and Healthcare Engineering and Gist. Industrial Gases and Healthcare is Linde's largest division and has operating segments in Europe the Americas Asia and Africa. Its Engineering division specializes in constructing plants for the production of hydrogen oxygen and olefins. It also builds plants for natural gas treatment. Linde's Gist division provides supply chain services for businesses that include Marks & Spencer British Airways Carlsberg and Dairy Crest.

Acquisitions and joint ventures play a key role in Linde's efforts to grow. On the health care side 2012 was a big year for acquisitions by the company. Linde acquired US-based homecare health company Lincare Holdings for $4.6 billion and it acquired Air Products' homecare business in continental Europe for $751 million. The latter's oxygen- sleep- and infusion-therapy operations serve more than 250000 patients in Belgium France Germany Portugal and Spain. Linde expects to double its sales from this area which would make it one of Europe's top suppliers of homecare respiratory products.

Additionally joint ventures are allowing it to gain entry into emerging markets such as China. In 2011 the company formed a joint venture to build and operate a large gas plant with Chongqing Chemical & Pharmaceutical Holding Company in China. Based in Chongqing the plant will produce carbon monoxide hydrogen and synthesis gas to the production facilities of BASF SE. It will be operational by 2014.

The following year in mid-2012 Linde made a major stride in Southeast Asia by winning a long-term contract to supply Vietnamese steel company POSCO SS-Vina (PSSV) with industrial gases. As part of the deal Linde will invest in and build the country's largest air separation unit in the Vung Tau province. The unit is slated to commence production also in 2014.

Linde's sales increased 7% in fiscal 2011 reaching 13.7 billion ($16.7 billion). Its Gases and Healthcare Division's sales rose 8% that year following an increase in global demand for gases. Its net income also rose nearly 16% in fiscal 2011 to 1.2 billion ($1.5 billion). Sales in the Gases division grew most significantly in the emerging economies of Asia as well as in South America. The division achieved strong growth in its on-site business which supplies gases on site to major customers. Its Engineering Division experienced a 3% increase over the previous year and saw a higher number of orders from the Gases Division than the previous year.

HISTORY

German engineer Karl von Linde perfected the ammonia-compression refrigeration machine in 1876. For the first time ice could be produced commercially instead of being cut in blocks from lakes. In 1879 Gesellschaft fur Linde's Eismaschinen was founded to sell the machines. Its first customers were brewers who wanted to make beer in the summer; the company later designed a refrigerator for the home.

Von Linde granted technology licenses to foreign firms but many licensees couldn't create working systems. Von Linde bought his patents back and in 1885 he set up his first affiliate outside of Germany the Linde British Refrigeration Company which built a London ice factory.

A decade later Von Linde a pioneer in cryogenics patented a process for the liquefaction of air — he had discovered the means to mass produce liquid oxygen. At the same time a similar process was developed by a Frenchman George Claude. To beat his rival Von Linde built an oxygen factory near Munich in 1902 and set up Linde Air Products (now Praxair) in the US in 1907.

After Germany's defeat in WWI the overseas businesses were seized. In the 1920s Linde's Eismaschinen bought German engine manufacturers including Guldner-Motoren-Gesellschaftin (1929). Von Linde died in 1934 at the age of 92. Then came WWII and in the aftermath the company again lost its industrial rights and investments overseas. (In the US Air Products had supplied oxygen to Allied fighter pilots.)

The recovering company launched Hydrocar the first platform truck with a hydrostatic drive in 1955. In 1958 Guldner began making forklift trucks and hydraulic equipment.

Renamed Linde AG in 1965 the firm won its first industrial construction contract to build a petrochemical plant. Switching gears Linde sold its home appliances business to AEG in 1967 and in 1969 Guldner stopped building tractors and diesel engines in favor of materials handling equipment and hydraulics. The forklift operations expanded further with the acquisition of SE Fahrzeugwerke (now STILL) in 1973.

Linde established branches to make industrial gases in Brazil and Australia (1974) and bought forklift manufacturers: Fenwick in France (1984); UK firm Lansing (1989); and a 51% stake in Italy's FIAT OM Carrelli Elevatori (1992). In 1992 it also increased its holding in Hoek's Machine-en Zurstoffabriek (aka Hoek Loos) the Netherland's largest industrial gases supplier to 60%. Other major acquisitions followed including Italian supplier Caracciolossigeno (1994) Czech gases firm Technoplyn (1995) and US engineering firm Pro-Quip (1996).

The company also built up its lines of refrigerated cases. It had taken a stake in CRIOSBANC an Italian manufacturer in 1992 (buying the rest in 1998). Linde acquired UK supplier Radford Retail Systems in 1997 and the next year gained controlling stakes in Brazilian supplier Seral do Brasil and in European distributor Chief Group.

In 1998 Linde also bought Thyssen Krupp Stahl's air separation plants in Duisburg-Ruhrort. A year later Linde reorganized its gases division as a separate operating company (Linde Technische Gase) and in 2000 it acquired Swedish industrial gases giant AGA in a deal that made Linde the world's #4 gas supplier. That year after abandoning plans to take over rival Messer Griesheim's gas operations Linde inked a deal with Japan's Komatsu Forklift for global collaboration. The demise of the Messer Griesheim merger led Linde to restructure its gas and engineering business segment and its refrigeration operations in 2001.

In 2004 Linde sold its refrigeration equipment and cooling systems business to Carrier (a subsidiary of United Technologies Corporation) for $400 million.

Linde became the world's largest gas manufacturer ahead of France's L'Air Liquide in the mid-2000s after it acquired UK gas producer BOC Group. Following the BOC acquisition Linde separated its material handling division and sold it to Kohlberg Kravis Roberts and Goldman Sachs Capital Partners for about $5 billion.

EXECUTIVES

Member Executive Board, Aldo Belloni, age 65, $720,000 total compensation

Member Executive Board, Sanjiv Lamba, age 52

Member Executive Board; CFO, Georg Denoke, age 50, $564,000 total compensation

CEO, Wolfgang Buchele

Member Executive Board, Thomas Blades

Second Deputy Chairman, Michael Diekmann, age 61

Chairman, Manfred Schneider, age 77

Deputy Chairman, Hans-Dieter Katte

Auditors: KPMG AG

LOCATIONS

HQ: Linde AG (Germany, Fed. Rep.)
Klosterhofstrasse 1, Munich, Bavaria 80797

Phone: (49) 89 357 57 1332 **Fax:** (49) 89 35757 1398

Web: www.linde.com

2014 Sales

	% of total
Europe	
Germany	7
Other countries	31
Asia/Australia	30
North America	25
Africa	3
South America	4
Total	**100**

PRODUCTS/OPERATIONS

2014 Sales

	% of total
Linde Gas	82
Linde Engineering	18
Other	0
Total	**100**

COMPETITORS

Air Products
Fluor
GEA Group
L' Air Liquide
Praxair

HISTORICAL FINANCIALS

Company Type: Public

Income Statement FYE: December 31

	REVENUE ($ mil.)	NET INCOME ($ mil.)	NET PROFIT MARGIN	EMPLOYEES
12/14	20,720	1,339	6.5%	65,591
12/13	22,929	1,813	7.9%	63,487
12/12	20,139	1,647	8.2%	61,965
12/11	17,832	1,518	8.5%	50,417
12/10	17,222	1,345	7.8%	48,430
Annual Growth	4.7%	(0.1%)	—	7.9%

2014 Year-End Financials

Debt ratio: 34.8%
Return on equity: 8.4%
Cash ($ mil.): 1,382
Current ratio: 0.93
Long-term debt ($ mil.): 10,407
No. of shares (mil.): 185
Dividends
Yield: 1.5%
Payout: 6.5%
Market value ($ mil.): 3,426

	STOCK PRICE ($) FY Close	P/E High/Low		PER SHARE ($) Earnings	Dividends	Book Value
12/14	18.46	6	5	7.18	0.28	87.78
12/13	21.00	6	4	9.75	0.24	94.70
12/12	17.69	5	3	9.19	0.22	93.19
12/11	14.91	5	3	8.82	0.39	87.74
12/10	15.15	5	3	7.84	0.16	85.25
Annual Growth	5.1%	—	—	(2.2%)	16.1%	0.7%

Lloyds Banking Group Plc

Don't confuse Lloyds Banking Group with that "other" Lloyds. Unrelated to Lloyd's of London Lloyds Banking Group was formed by the 2009 merger of UK banks Lloyds TSB and HBOS. Its retail banking services include deposit accounts credit cards loans and wealth management. Lloyds Banking Group is also one of the nation's top home mortgage lenders. Other products include insurance and investment services through Scottish Widows and wholesale and international banking for UK corporate clients and multinationals. Lloyds Banking Group which operates under the brands Lloyds TSB Halifax and Bank of Scotland has some 2900 branches with representative offices in the Middle East Asia and the Americas.

The UK government owns slightly less than 40% of Lloyds after bailing it out in 2008. After the bailout the company embarked on one of the largest-ever capital raisings in Europe. Although the merger with HBOS nearly destroyed Lloyds — HBOS had a much higher risk tolerance than Lloyds and the company has faced billions in losses since the deal —the combined company controls some 30% of the UK's mortgage market and half of the savings market.

The company has been compelled by European authorities to sell the 600 retail banking branches associated with the Lloyds TSB brand along with a large part of its Cheltenham & Gloucester network. It has received some interest from Virgin Money; another option would be spinning them off to the public. Lloyds Banking Group has divested some noncore businesses such as its fund management arm Insight which was sold to Bank of New York Mellon for 235 million ($386 million); its Irish retail unit which lost billions in toxic loans and its Australian and New Zealand property and corporate loans for $684 million. The company also may spin off its private equity unit Lloyds TSB Development Capital. In late 2013 the company sold its remaining stake in St. James's Place Plc for about 680 pounds ($1.1 billion) to focus on its primary retail and commercial businesses.

As part of its strategic review and after some layoffs related to the ill-fated HBOS acquisition the company announced another round of job cuts in 2011 (mostly back-office and middle management positions). Lloyds has already shed 27500 jobs and will cut another 15000 in the process. The group's strategy for growth include simplifying operations (it completed the integration of HBOS in 2011) while investing in core areas and strengthening its balance sheet and liquidity position.

The restructuring efforts have helped to cut the company's losses. In 2011 Lloyds lost 342 million before taxes a large improvement over the 2010 losses of 2.9 billion. Net interest grew 1% to 12.7 million a modest increase as retail lending markets remained pressured. However revenues declined that year 32% to 17.2 billion largely due to the ongoing economic challenges in the UK and Ireland. Fees and commissions as well as net trading income declined in 2011. The wholesale business' profits decreased by 67% that year as a result of lower asset balances and losses on asset disposals. Earnings were also affected by some 3.6 billion in provisions including a 375 million provision for the mis-selling of payment protection insurance to customers from 2007 to 2011.

HISTORY

In 1765 John Taylor and Sampson Lloyd II founded Taylors and Lloyds bank in Birmingham England; five years later their sons opened a London agency. In 1852 the last Taylor involved with the bank died. In 1865 the bank converted to joint stock form and became Lloyds Banking Company Ltd. Over the next half century it grew by merging with some 50 banks becoming one of England's largest banks by the turn of the century.

Despite the post-WWI roller-coaster economy the bank acquired Capital and Counties Bank (1918 bringing foreign connections); Fox Fowler & Company (1921); and Cox & Company (1923). During both wars deposits grew while lending dropped. After WWII growth was hampered by high inflation.

Lloyds added branches and products in the 1960s. By 1971 it had branches in 43 countries. It moved into insurance (1972) home mortgages (1979) real estate agency services (1982) and merchant banking (1986).

In 1987 Latin American bank defaults pummeled Lloyds. Refocusing on domestic operations the bank sold overseas subsidiaries (including Lloyds Bank Canada in 1990) and acquired 58% of life insurer Abbey Life (1988) and Cheltenham & Gloucester Building Society (1994). HSBC outbid Lloyds for Midland Bank in 1992; Lloyds bought TSB Group in 1995.

TSB Group evolved from the trustee savings banks (TSBs) formed in the 1800s. By 1860 there were 600 such banks mainly in northern England and Scotland. During WWI many TSBs consolidated or closed. By WWII about 100 remained and the mergers continued.

In the 1960s TSBs began offering checking accounts and trust services. Loans credit cards and other services came in 1973. In 1986 the four remaining TSBs (TSB Channel Islands TSB England and Wales TSB Northern Ireland and TSB Scotland) agreed to merge and go public in order to gain equal footing with stock banks. TSB Group was born.

Flush with cash from its offering TSB group defied the late 1980s recession to buy Target Group (life insurance sold 1993) Hill Samuel (merchant banking) and other units; the purchases sent TSB sprawling.

As debt rose in the 1990s TSB Group refocused on banking and insurance. TSB and Lloyds merged in 1995 linking their geographically complementary branch networks to fend off competition.

After the merger Lloyds TSB focused on loans and insurance and dabbled in consumer finance including the sale and delivery of big-ticket items (cars large appliances). Returning overseas it bought the consumer finance unit of Brazil's Banco Multiplic.

In late 1997 and 1998 the bank overhauled its operations to eliminate redundancies and began rebranding under one green and blue banner. In 1999 Lloyds TSB bailed out Abbey Life which had nearly been bankrupted by the cost of settling pension mis-selling claims.

The bank in 2000 bought Scottish Widows to boost its fund management services. It sold the Abbey Life name and its new business to Zurich Financial Services' Allied Dunbar; Abbey Life continued to service existing business for Lloyds. Also that year Lloyds TSB bought consumer and auto finance unit Chartered Trust from Standard Chartered. After a yearlong battle to buy London-based mortgage lender Abbey National the UK government in 2001 blocked the merger attempt because of concerns for the consumer.

Earlier in 2001 Lloyds TSB closed Bahamas-based subsidiary British Bank of Latin America because of alleged money-laundering links revealed in a US Senate report.

Lloyds TSB's asset finance operations bought First National Vehicle Holdings and Abbey National Vehicle Finance from Abbey National plc in 2002. The division also acquired Chartered Trust and Dutton-Forshaw Group a car dealership. Lloyds TSB sold National Bank of New Zealand to Australia and New Zealand Bank Group in 2003.

Commerzbank unit Comdirect Bank sold its UK subsidiary Comdirect Ltd to Lloyds TSB unit Executive Services Group in 2004.

The company sold its Abbey Life unit to Deutsche Bank for nearly $2 billion in 2007. (The life insurer had been closed to new business since 2000.) The group also sold Lloyds TSB Registrars and car dealership The Dutton-Forshaw Group which were noncore units of its wholesale and international business.

The global economic crisis was a difficult time for Lloyds. The UK government took a 40% stake in the company after bailing it out along with seven other top banks in 2008. Lloyds accepted some 17 billion ($25 billion) in taxpayer money. The government hoped the infusion of cash would loosen up credit markets and restore confidence in the financial system. As part of a restructuring plan (and to repay the UK government) Lloyds Banking Group launched one of the largest-ever capital raisings in Europe which included a 9 billion ($13 billion) debt exchange and a nearly 14 billion ($20 billion) rights issue.

Around the same time of the government bailout Lloyds TSB agreed to take over struggling HBOS the UK's top mortgage lender. The controversial 12 billion ($22 billion) deal was announced after HBOS shares fell dramatically amid rising concerns surrounding the vitality of financial services companies worldwide. The combined bank served about one of every three UK consumers and controlled more than a quarter of the UK residential mortgage market. The UK government further capitalized the deal to ensure its viability.

Within weeks though Lloyds Banking Group revealed that HBOS had incurred some 11 billion ($18 billion) in losses and shareholder unrest grew concerning the billions of pounds in toxic assets gained with the acquisition. The merger meant drastic cost cuts and job losses as the company announced more than 42000 job cuts.

Needless to say not everyone was happy with the HBOS merger. At Lloyds Banking Group's annual meeting in 2009 a large group of shareholders loudly criticized the company's board for the HBOS deal demanding resignations and threatening lawsuits over the merger. In 2010 one group of disgruntled shareholders launched legal action in order to recoup up to 14 billion ($20 billion) that they claim they lost as a result of the merger.

Lloyds Banking Group defended the merger though saying it helped improve the company's strategic position by improving its market position (it controlled about half of the savings market) brand recognition and expanding its customer base. Although the deal brought short-term costs company leaders were convinced that it was better positioned for future growth.

Auditors: PricewaterhouseCoopers LLP

LOCATIONS

HQ: Lloyds Banking Group Plc
25 Gresham Street, 5th Floor, London EC2V 7HN
Phone: (44) 20 7356 1274 **Fax:** (44) 20 7356 1038
Web: www.lloydsbankinggroup.com

HISTORICAL FINANCIALS

Company Type: Public

Income Statement FYE: December 31

	ASSETS ($ mil.)	NET INCOME ($ mil.)	INCOME AS % OF ASSETS	EMPLOYEES
12/14	1,334,512	2,204	0.2%	84,490
12/13	1,399,784	(1,384)	—	97,869
12/12	1,490,254	(2,300)	—	113,617
12/11	1,499,351	(696)	—	120,449
12/10	1,539,557	(496)	—	122,979
Annual Growth	(3.5%)	—	—	(9.0%)

2014 Year-End Financials

Return on assets: 0.1%
Return on equity: 3.2%
Long-term debt ($ mil.): —
No. of shares (mil.): —
Sales ($ mil): 62,198
Dividends
Yield: 0.0%
Payout: 241.1%
Market value ($ mil.): —

	STOCK PRICE ($) FY Close	P/E High/Low	PER SHARE ($) Earnings	Dividends	Book Value
12/14	4.64	322264	0.02	0.06	1.06
12/13	5.32	— —	(0.02)	0.07	0.90
12/12	3.20	— —	(0.03)	0.06	1.01
12/11	1.57	— —	(0.01)	0.00	1.03
12/10	4.11	— —	(0.01)	0.00	1.05
Annual Growth	3.1%	— —	—	—	0.3%

Loblaw Cos. Ltd.

Auditors: KPMG LLP

LOCATIONS

HQ: Loblaw Cos. Ltd.
22 St. Clair Avenue East, Suite1901, Toronto, Ontario M4T 2S7
Phone: 416 490-2699 **Fax:** 416 490-2771
Web: www.loblaw.ca

HISTORICAL FINANCIALS

Company Type: Public

Income Statement FYE: January 3

	REVENUE ($ mil.)	NET INCOME ($ mil.)	NET PROFIT MARGIN	EMPLOYEES
01/15*	36,528	45	0.1%	195,000
12/13	30,394	591	1.9%	138,000
12/12	31,776	653	2.1%	134,000
12/11	30,634	753	2.5%	135,000
01/11	30,916	676	2.2%	136,000
Annual Growth	4.3%	(49.1%)	—	9.4%

*Fiscal year change

2015 Year-End Financials

Debt ratio: 31.1%
Return on equity: 0.5%
Cash ($ mil.): 856
Current ratio: 1.47
Long-term debt ($ mil.): 9,465
No. of shares (mil.): 412
Dividends
Yield: 0.0%
Payout: 696.4%
Market value ($ mil.): 22,220

	STOCK PRICE ($) FY Close	P/E High/Low	PER SHARE ($) Earnings	Dividends	Book Value
01/15*	53.87	384254	0.12	0.84	26.56
12/13	39.43	21 16	2.08	0.88	23.34
12/12	41.20	18 14	2.29	0.85	22.91
12/11	37.82	15 13	2.66	0.82	20.93
01/11	40.50	18 14	2.39	0.84	20.02
Annual Growth	7.4%	— —	(52.6%)	(0.2%)	7.3%

*Fiscal year change

Lotte Shopping Co Ltd

Lotte Shopping's department stores offer more than the usual shopping experience. The company is a leading retailer in South Korea with some 30 department and discount stores across the nation. It owns one of the largest retail chains in the country with facilities that are part of vast retail complexes that often include cinemas shopping malls hotels theme parks and wedding halls. It also has a store in Moscow (opened in 2007). In China where Lotte Shopping is looking to grow its 2009 purchase of Times Ltd. an operator of 65 hypermarkets and supermarkets in east China boosted its retail presence there to about 75 stores. Lotte Shopping which was established in 1979 is looking to grow overseas.

To bolster its position in South Korea's retail arena Lotteshopping in February 2010 agreed to acquire three department stores more than a dozen large discout stores from its smaller rival GS Retail (owned by GS Holdings) for about $1.15 billion. Also the company plans to open another department store in South Korea in 2010 and a second department store in China in 2011. Lotteshopping in fall 2009 agreed to buy grocer Times Ltd. in a deal worth about $629 million thereby substantially expanding its retail footprint in China. Previous foreign acquisitions for the South Korea company include Makro Indonesia which operates about 20 outlets there.

EXECUTIVES

CEO, Lee Won Joon
Auditors: Samjong Accounting Corporation (A Member Firm of KPMG)

LOCATIONS

HQ: Lotte Shopping Co Ltd
81 Namdaemun-ro Jung-gu, Seoul 100-721
Phone: (82) 2 771 2500 **Fax:** (82) 2 2118 2028
Web: www.lotteshopping.com

COMPETITORS

Bailian Group
Costco Wholesale
GS Holdings
Tesco
WuMart

HISTORICAL FINANCIALS

Company Type: Public

Income Statement FYE: December 31

	REVENUE ($ mil.)	NET INCOME ($ mil.)	NET PROFIT MARGIN	EMPLOYEES
12/14	25,682	481	1.9%	27,880
12/13	26,826	749	2.8%	26,943
12/12	23,455	1,011	4.3%	24,976
12/11	19,205	804	4.2%	24,801
12/10	16,960	922	5.4%	9,877
Annual Growth	10.9%	(15.0%)	—	29.6%

2014 Year-End Financials

Debt ratio: 0.0%
Return on equity: 3.2%
Cash ($ mil.): 1,762
Current ratio: 1.19
Long-term debt ($ mil.): 7,455
No. of shares (mil.): 29
Dividends
Yield: —
Payout: —
Market value ($ mil.): —

LVMH Moet Hennessy Louis Vuitton

LVMH Moët Hennessy Louis Vuitton is the world's largest luxury goods company with brands that are bywords for the good life and everything showy. LVMH makes wines and spirits (Dom Prignon Moët & Chandon Veuve Clicquot and Hennessy) perfumes (Christian Dior Guerlain and Givenchy) cosmetics (Bliss Fresh and BeneFit) fashion and leather goods (Donna Karan Givenchy Kenzo and Louis Vuitton) and watches and jewelry (TAG Heuer Bulgari). LVMH's selective retail division includes Sephora cosmetics stores Le Bon March Paris department stores and 61% of DFS Group (duty-free shops). Chairman Bernard Arnault and his family through Groupe Arnault own about 46% of LVMH.

Geographic Reach

The Paris-based luxury powerhouse operates some 3385 stores across Asia (including China and Japan) Europe and North America. While more than a third of its stores are in Europe Asia is the company's single largest market accounting for more than 35% of sales. LVMH rings up about 30% of its sales in Europe (including France with 11%). The US represents more than 20%.

Financial Performance

After a period of relatively flat sales during the global financial crisis LVMH has experience four consecutive years of accelerating revenue growth. Indeed sales topped 29.1 billion ($40 billion) in 2013 an 8% increase in organic revenue versus 2012 and an all-time record for the luxury goods company. Profits have risen as well with net income topping $4.7 billion in 2013 up 5% over 2012. Like its customers the company is cash rich reporting more than $4 billion in cash flow from operations in 2013.

Driving revenue growth in 2013 were the company's Selective Retailing business which reported a double-digit increase in sales and to a lesser extent Wines & Spirits and Perfumes & Cosmetics. Fashion & Leather Goods and Watches & Jewelry posted year-over-year declines in sales. On a regional basis Asia (excluding Japan) contributed a growing share (30%) of the group's revenue in 2013 while Japan and Europe (excluding France) accounted for less. Challenging economic conditions kept a lid on growth in Europe and France.

Strategy

With the market for luxury goods on a tear –especially in fast-growing markets in Asia –LVMH is flush with cash for acquisitions and organic growth. Indeed the company is growing its stores base in all of its markets except for Japan where it held steady at 370 shops in 2013. LVMH added 180 stores in 2013 after adding about 165 in 2012. China is a huge emerging market for luxury goods including wines & spirits and a pillar of growth for the French company.

The company has been focusing on controlling as much of its distribution across its 60 brands as possible. LVMH has more than 3380 retail outlets (87% are outside France). Nearly half belong to its Selective Retailing business which consists primarily of Sephora cosmetics stores. About 40% are fashion and leather goods shops led by Louis Vuitton and also include Fendi boutiques and hundreds of other shops under the Celine Givenchy Donna Karan Thomas Pink Pucci and Marc Jacobs brands among others. LVMH's namesake Louis Vuitton brand as well as Fendi and Marc Jacobs are proving resilient in Europe despite the economic slowdown there and posting strong revenue gains in Asia.

Striking out in a new direction the luxury goods firm has entered the hotel business via a partnership with Egypt's Orascom Development Holding. Together the two are developing upmarket resorts in Egypt and Oman with LVMH overseeing the design and running of the hotels.

Mergers and Acquisitions

LVMH expanded its products portfolio in mid-2013 when it purchased an 80% stake in Italian cashmere company Loro Piana for $2.57 billion more than three times the $900 million in sales the company had expected to post in 2013. LVMH values Loro Piana for its products' unique quality and craftsmanship and its six generations of leadership. As part of the transaction the cashmere company's owners will retain a stake in the business.

Putting its ample cash to good use in late 2011 the French luxury goods firm completed a 3.7 billion ($5 billion) tender offer for the shares of Rome-based jeweler Bulgari. Bulgari is the smallest of the major luxury jewelry and watch makers and the deal doubles LVMH's watch and jewelry business. The Bulgari deal was announced soon after LVMH acquired a pair of niche brands: Ole Henriksen and Nude skin care. In late 2010 LVMH bought more than 20% of the shares of its rival Hermes International. While LVMH described the move as friendly and said it would not launch a takeover bid for Hermes it nevertheless led to speculation regarding further consolidation in the luxury goods industry as LVMH is known for its predatory nature.

HISTORY

Woodworker Louis Vuitton started his Paris career packing dresses for French Empress Eugenie. He later designed new types of luggage and in 1854 he opened a store to sell his designs. In 1896 Vuitton introduced the LV monogram fabric that the company still uses. By 1900 Louis Vuitton had stores in the US and England and by WWI Louis' son Georges had the world's largest retail store for travel goods.

Henry Racamier a former steel executive who had married into the Vuitton family took charge in 1977 repositioning the company's goods from esoteric status symbols to designer must-haves. Sales soared from $20 million to nearly $2.5 billion within a decade. Concerned about being a takeover target Racamier merged Louis Vuitton in 1987 with Moët Hennessy (which made wines spirits and fragrances) and adopted the name LVMH Moët Hennessy Louis Vuitton.

Moët Hennessy had been formed through the 1971 merger of Moët et Chandon (the world's #1 champagne maker) and the Hennessy Cognac company (founded by Irish mercenary Richard Hennessy in 1765). Moët Hennessy acquired rights to Christian Dior fragrances in 1971.

Racamier tried to reverse the merger when disagreements with chairman Alain Chevalier arose. Racamier invited outside investor Bernard Arnault to increase his interest in the company. Arnault gained control of 43% of LVMH and became chairman in 1989. Chevalier stepped down but Racamier fought for control for another 18 months and then set up Orcofi a partner of cosmetics rival L'Oral.

LVMH increased its fashion holdings with the purchases of the Givenchy Couture Group (1988) Christian Lacroix (1993) and Kenzo (1993). The company also acquired 55% of French media firm Desfosses International (1993) Celine fashions (1996) the Château d'Yquem winery (1996) and duty-free retailer DFS Group (1996). Next LVMH bought perfume chains Sephora (1997) and Marie-Jeanne Godard (1998). In 1998 LVMH integrated the Paris department store Le Bon March which was controlled by Arnault.

LVMH accumulated a 34% stake in Italian luxury goods maker Gucci in early 1999 and planned to buy all of it. Fellow French conglomerate Pinault-Printemps-Redoute (PPR) later thwarted LVMH by purchasing 42% of Gucci.

Through its LV Capital unit in 1999 LVMH began acquiring stakes in a host of luxury companies including a joint venture with fashion company Prada to buy 51% of design house Fendi (LVMH bought Prada's 25.5% stake for $265 million in November 2001). It has since upped its Fendi stake to about 70%. LVMH later added the Ebel Chaumet and TAG Heuer brands to its new watch division.

In early 2000 LVMH bought Miami Cruiseline Services which operates duty-free shops on cruise ships auction house L'Etude Tajan and 67% of Italian fashion house Emilio Pucci. The company later purchased 35% of French video game retailer Micromania and 51% of department store Samaritaine. In late 2000 LVMH acquired Gabrielle Studio which owns all Donna Karan licenses. In 2001 the company bought Donna Karan International.

LVMH bought in 2001 the Newton and MountAdam vineyards for about $45 million. It then began marketing De Beers diamond jewelry in a 50-50 joint venture with the diamond powerhouse. In March LVMH prompted the investigation of a Dutch court into the PPR-Gucci alliance. The company sold its stake in Gucci to PPR for $806.5 million in October.

In October 2002 LVMH ceased trading on the Brussels and Nasdaq exchanges to concentrate on its Euronext investors. In October 2003 the company sold Canard-Duchene to the Alain Thienot Group. LVMH shed several of the less productive of its 50 brands in 2003 including auction house Phillips de Pury & Luxemborg and fashion brand Michael Kors.

LVMH opened its biggest store –a four-story emporium on New York's Fifth Avenue –in February 2004. A few months later the company added whisky-maker Glenmorangie PLC to its subsidiary roster. LVMH also made its debut in the South African market in October 2004 opening its first sub-Saharan boutique in Johannesburg. Also during the year Bliss spas was sold off.

In early 2004 LVMH won a landmark lawsuit against Morgan Stanley alleging that the firm had used biased research in misstatements about the financial health of LVMH that caused damage to the company's image. The presiding Parisian court ordered Morgan Stanley to pay 100 million euros (about $38 million) in damages. Morgan Stanley appealed the ruling later that year.

In late 2005 LVMH opened its largest store to date on the Champs-Elyses in Paris and the De Beers brand was introduced in the US with stores in New York and Los Angeles. Also that year LVMH was the winning bidder for whisky maker Glenmorangie PLC for which it paid £300 million. On the sell side LVMH divested fashion design house Christian Lacroix SNC.

In May 2007 LVMH acquired a 55% stake in Chinese distillery Wenjun for an undisclosed amount. (Jiannanchun the distillery's previous owner retained a 45% stake in Wenjun.) In December 2007 the luxury goods firm acquired the French newspaper Les Echos from publisher Pearson. LVMH controls Les Echos' rival the financial daily La Tribune but has agreed to sell it. Group Les Echos deal includes the newspaper Web site business magazine Enjeux and other financial information services.

In late 2008 Sephora SA acquired a 45% stake in the Russian perfume and cosmetics chain Ile de Beaut. (The agreement which gave Sephora the option to become a majority shareholder allowed LVMH to up its share to 65% in mid-2011.) The firm acquired the luxury yacht-maker Royal Van Lent.

In August 2009 LVMH acquired 50% stakes in two French wine makers: privately-held Cheval Blanc; and La Tour du Pin owner of the Chateau Quinault l'Enclose estate.

In early 2010 LVMH acquired a 40% stake in Dondup an Italian apparel and denim brand for more than $43 million (or 30 million euros). Its plans are to expand Dondup's business internationally. Later in 2010 the company purchased a 70% stake in the Brazilian fragrance and cosmetics retailer Sack's. The acquisition estimated to be worth R$250 million is a move on LVMH's part to expand its Sephora beauty chain in Brazil one of the fastest-growing beauty markets in the world.

Adding to its vast portfolio of luxury brands in February 2011 LVMH acquired Ole Henriksen a leading luxury botanical skincare company founded and owned by its namesake. Later that same week LVMH bought a 70% stake in Nude Brands skin care as the company continues to acquire niche brands. The four-year-old line - described as "biocompatible luxury skin care" - was founded by Bryan Meehan and Ali Hewson wife of U2 front man Bono. In March LVMH fired Dior star designer John Galliano amid charges of anti-Semitism. In September LVMH completed its tender offer from Rome-based Bulgari acquiring about 98% of the shares.

EXECUTIVES

Chairman and CEO, Bernard Arnault, age 66
COO, Antonio (Toni) Belloni, age 61
Director Strategy, Jean-Baptiste Voisin, age 48
Managing Director Groupe Arnault, Nicolas Bazire, age 58
Chairman and CEO Louis Vuitton, Michael Burke, age 58

Group EVP Human Resources and Synergies, Chantal Gaemperle
CFO, Jean-Jacques Guiony, age 54
CEO Sephora, Chris de Lapuente, age 50
CEO Moet Hennessy, Christophe Navarre
Chairman LVMH Investment Funds, Daniel Piette, age 70
Chairman and CEO LVMH Fashion Group, Pierre-Yves Roussel
Chairman and CEO DFS Group, Philippe Schaus, age 52
Vice Chairman, Pierre Gode, age 71
Auditors: ERNST & YOUNG et Autres

LOCATIONS

HQ: LVMH Moet Hennessy Louis Vuitton
22, avenue Montaigne, Paris 75008
Phone: (33) 1 44 13 22 22 **Fax:** (33) 1 44 13 21 19
Web: www.lvmh.com

2013 Stores

	No.
Europe	
France	443
Other countries	926
Asia	
Japan	370
Other countries	749
US	669
Other regions	227
Total	**3,384**

2013 Sales

	% of total
Europe	
France	11
Other countries	19
Asia	
Japan	7
Other countries	30
US	23
Other regions	10
Total	**100**

PRODUCTS/OPERATIONS

2013 Sales

	% of total
Fashion & leather goods	34
Selective retailing	29
Wines & spirits	14
Perfumes & cosmetics	13
Watches & jewelry	10
Total	**100**

Selected Brands and Operations

Fashion and leather goods
- Berluti
- Celine
- Donna Karan
- Emilio Pucci
- Fendi
- Gabrielle Studio (Donna Karan label)
- Givenchy
- Kenzo
- Loewe
- Loro Piana
- Louis Vuitton
- Marc Jacobs
- Thomas Pink

Retailing
- DFS Group
- La Samaritaine
- Le Bon Marché
- Miami Cruiseline Services (duty-free shops)
- Sephora

Fragrances and cosmetics
- Aqua di Parma
- BeneFit
- Bliss
- Fresh
- Guerlain
- Kenzo Parfums
- Make Up For Ever
- Marc Jacobs Fragrances
- Nude skin care
- Ole Henriksen
- Parfums Christian Dior
- Parfums Givenchy

Spirits and wines
- 10 Cane
- Belvedere
- Canard-Duchene
- Chandon Estates
- Château d' Yquem
- Dom Perignon
- Hennessy
- Krug
- Mercier
- Moet & Chandon
- MountAdam
- Newton
- Ruinart
- Veuve Clicquot

Watches and jewelry
- Bulgari
- Chaumet
- De Beers
- Ebel
- Fred
- Omas
- TAG Heuer
- Zenith

Media (Desfosses International Group)
- Investir
- La Tribune
- Les Echos
- Radio Classique

Other
- Royal van Lent (luxury yachts)

COMPETITORS

Armani	Kirin Holdings Company
Asprey	L' Or©al
Avon	MacAndrews & Forbes
Bacardi	Oscar de la Renta
Brown-Forman	Patek Philippe
Calvin Klein	Prada
Chanel	Puig
Douglas Holding	Ralph Lauren
E. & J. Gallo	Richemont
Escada	Rolex
Est©e Lauder	R©my Cointreau
Galeries Lafayette	Shiseido
Gianni Versace	Swatch
Harry Winston	Taittinger
Herm□s	Tiffany & Co.
Hugo Boss	Unilever
Inditex	Vera Wang
Kering	

HISTORICAL FINANCIALS

Company Type: Public

Income Statement FYE: December 31

	REVENUE ($ mil.)	NET INCOME ($ mil.)	NET PROFIT MARGIN	EMPLOYEES
12/14	37,234	6,865	18.4%	121,289
12/13	40,130	4,730	11.8%	114,635
12/12	37,041	4,513	12.2%	106,348
12/11	30,601	3,964	13.0%	97,559
12/10	27,195	4,057	14.9%	83,542
Annual Growth	8.2%	14.0%	—	9.8%

2014 Year-End Financials

Debt ratio: 21.0%
Return on equity: 23.3%
Cash ($ mil.): 4,972
Current ratio: 1.49
Long-term debt ($ mil.): 6,143
No. of shares (mil.): 501
Dividends
Yield: 2.4%
Payout: 5.6%
Market value ($ mil.): 17,282

	STOCK PRICE ($) FY Close	P/E High/Low		PER SHARE ($) Earnings	Dividends	Book Value
12/14	34.44	3	3	13.63	0.83	52.71
12/13	36.60	6	5	9.40	0.79	73.44
12/12	37.69	5	4	8.99	0.76	64.75
12/11	28.10	5	4	8.06	0.58	58.29
12/10	33.15	5	3	8.46	0.50	48.08
Annual Growth	1.0%	—	—	12.7%	13.6%	2.3%

LyondellBasell Industries NV

Auditors: PricewaterhouseCoopers LLP

LOCATIONS

HQ: LyondellBasell Industries NV
Delftseplein 27E, Rotterdam 3013 AA
Phone: (31) 10 275 5500
Web: www.lyondellbasell.com

HISTORICAL FINANCIALS

Company Type: Public

Income Statement FYE: December 31

	REVENUE ($ mil.)	NET INCOME ($ mil.)	NET PROFIT MARGIN	EMPLOYEES
12/15	32,735	4,476	13.7%	13,000
12/14	45,608	4,174	9.2%	13,100
12/13	44,062	3,857	8.8%	13,300
12/12	45,352	2,848	6.3%	13,500
12/11	51,035	2,147	4.2%	14,000
Annual Growth	(10.5%)	20.2%	—	(1.8%)

2015 Year-End Financials

Debt ratio: 35.2%
Return on equity: 60.2%
Cash ($ mil.): 924
Current ratio: 2.25
Long-term debt ($ mil.): 7,671
No. of shares (mil.): 440
Dividends
Yield: —
Payout: 31.7%
Market value ($ mil.): —

Macquarie Group Ltd

One of the few domestically owned investment banks in the Land Down Under Macquarie Group does business at home in Australia and beyond. Boasting assets of nearly A$190 billion ($145 billion) the holding company for Macquarie Bank and other subsidiaries operates an investment banking practice that performs financing trading strategic advisory equities research and other services for corporate and government clients. Other operations include asset management retail banking and lending and wealth management. Through its Macquarie Energy arm the company participates in the international private-equity market focusing on the energy sector. Founded in 1969 Macquarie Group has offices in nearly 30 countries.

OperationsMacquarie Group operates six divisions. This includes three "annuity style" businesses (that generated nearly 70% of overall profit in fiscal 2015 ended March): Macquarie Asset Management (35% of profit) or MAM which offers infrastructure and real asset management securities investment management and other fund and equity investment services; Corporate and Asset Finance (27% of profit) or CAF which provides specialty asset finance for corporations and and real estate credit lending; and Banking and Financial Services (7% of profit) or BFS which provides personal and business banking and wealth management services. The other three "capital markets facing" business divisions include: the Macquarie Securities Group (1% of profit) which covers sales research equity capital markets execution and derivatives trading; Macquarie Capital (10% of profit) which provides corporate finance services such as M&A equity and debt capital markets and principal investments across six key industry groups and Commodities and Financial Markets (20% of profit) or CFM which provides risk and capital solutions across physical and financial markets.The bank enjoys a diversified revenue base. It generated 41% of its revenue from interest and similar income during 2015 (ended March 31) while fees and commission income made up another 39%. The rest was made from non-recurring income sources such as net trading income (14% of revenue) and other operating income and charges (6%). It had a staff of more than 14000 at the end of FY2015.Geographic ReachThe Sydney-based group generates over 35% of its operating income from customers in the Americas while Australia contributes another 30%. Macquarie generates the rest of its operating income from the Europe Middle East and Africa region (22%) and the Asia Pacific region (12%).Financial PerformanceNote: Growth rates may differ after conversion to US dollars. This analysis uses financials from the company's annual report.Macquarie Group's revenues and profits have been rising each year since 2013. The company's revenue rose 22% to $A12.2 billion ($9.4 billion) in fiscal 2015 (ended March 31) mostly driven by 33% growth in its annuity-style businesses as MAM enjoyed an increase in base and performance fee income CAF's loan and lease volumes grew and as BFS' grew its Australian mortgage business lending and deposits volumes. The groups capital markets facing businesses grew 19% with Macquarie Capital generating higher fee income across all product classes (mostly M&A and debt capital markets) and increased investment sale gains and with CFM generating higher performance from its commodities business increased income across interest rates and foreign exchange platforms and increased fee income and debt capital markets activity in the US.Higher revenue during FY2015 drove Macquarie Group's net income higher by 27% to A$1.6 billion ($1.2 billion). Its operating cash levels declined during the year with operations using A$2.4 billion ($1.9 billion) mostly due to unfavorable working capital changes mostly related to its net payments on trading portfolio assets and other financial assets/liabilities. StrategyMacquarie Group outlined its medium-term strategy in 2015 which listed several goals including: building its annuity-style businesses (such as asset and wealth management specialty financing and investment and retail banking services) and capital markets-facing businesses in a diversified way that produces steady returns in a range of market conditions; diversifying its businesses across different locations and with different service offerings to limit risk and create steady returns; continuing to leverage the group's deep expertise in its target sectors; acquire or grow into business lines that complement existing ones; promoting ideas and innovation for growth; and maintaining a strong balance sheet with capital levels above ordinary requirements. As part of its goals toward growing into complementary business lines Macquarie in August 2015 entered the US ETF market-making business adding to its market-making service lines already offered for ETFs domiciled in Asia and Europe.The company in 2015 continued to boast its "deep knowledge of Asia-Pacific financial markets" and "deep expertise" that has led to market-leading positions in the resources and commodities energy financial institutions infrastructure and real estate sectors. Mergers and Acquisitions

In 2015 a subsidiary of Macquarie Bank Limited agreed to purchase an aircraft operating lease portfolio of 90 modern current-generation commercial passenger aircraft leased to 40 airlines from AWAS Aviation Capital Limited. The deal helped to grow its Corporate and Asset Finance (CAF) division specifically its Macquarie Aviation leasing business.

HISTORY

Company BackgroundMacquarie has made a slew of acquisitions in its past. It acquired several North America-based financial services companies including investment bank Fox-Pitt Kelton Cochran Caronia Waller. In 2010 Macquarie expanded upon its individual and institutional asset management business when it acquired US-based Delaware Investments. It also bought the Canadian investment dealing business of Blackmont Capital and rebranded it as Macquarie Private Wealth.

Two more US acquisitions were designed to enhance Macquarie Capital's advisory business. In 2010 Macquarie bought US-based specialist Presidio Partners which performs real estate advisory and capital raising advisory services. Macquarie also bought Los Angeles-based investment bank Regal Capital Advisors a specialist in strategic and financial advice for the gaming lodging and leisure industries. Overseas Macquarie acquired the cash equities sales and research business of German private bank Sal. Oppenheim Jr. & Cie. in 2010. The acquisition broadened Macquarie's European business bolstering its presence in several key markets. Macquarie is looking to buy trading and investment banking businesses in Europe.The company has also used acquisitions to bolster its position in the energy and other non-traditional banking markets.

In 2009 it acquired Canadian boutique investment bank Tristone Capital which served the oil and gas industry. Macquarie also acquired the downstream natural gas trading operations of Constellation Energy. The company then combined that business with its Macquarie Cook Energy business to form Macquarie Energy a larger North American wholesale gas company. In 2010 Macquarie Energy acquired the wholesale electric marketing and trading portfolio of Integrys Energy Services in a deal that more than doubled Macquarie Energy's customer base and strengthened its position in key North American power markets. Also that year subsidiary Macquarie Aerospace agreed to purchase a portfolio of 53 aircraft from AIG unit International Lease Finance Corporation.

EXECUTIVES

Head Risk Management Group and Chief Risk Officer, Stephen Allen
Managing Director and CEO, Nicholas W. Moore, age 56, $517,573 total compensation
Head Commodities and Financial Markets, Andrew J. Downe, $479,234 total compensation
Deputy Managing Director and Head Banking and Financial Services Group, Greg C. Ward
Head Macquarie Asset Management, Shemara Wikramanayake
Head Macquarie Capital (USA), Tim Bishop
Co-Head Corporate and Asset Finance Group, Garry Farrell
Head Macquarie Securities Group, Stevan Vrcelj
Country Head USA, Michael McLaughlin
COO, Nicole Sorbara
Head Financial Management Group and CFO, Patrick Upfold
Co-Head Corporate and Asset Finance Group, Ben Brazil
Managing Director and CEO Macquarie Bank, Mary Reemst
CIO Asia-Pacific, Justin Raoul Moffitt
Chairman, H. Kevin McCann, age 74
Chairman, Peter H. Warne, age 59
Auditors: PricewaterhouseCoopers

LOCATIONS

HQ: Macquarie Group Ltd
50 Martin Place, Sydney, New South Wales 2000
Phone: (61) 2 8232 3333 **Fax:** (61) 2 8237 1899
Web: www.macquarie.com.au

2015 Sales

	% of total
Americas	39
Australia	35
Europe Middle East Africa	16
Asia/Pacific	10
Total	**100**

PRODUCTS/OPERATIONS

2015 Sales

	% of total
Lending	36
Financial markets	27
Asset & wealth management	22
Capital Markets	15
Total	**100**

2015 Sales

	% of total
Interest and similar income	41
Fee and commission income	39
Net trading income	14
Other operating income and charges	6
Others	-
Total	**100**

COMPETITORS

Citigroup
Deutsche Bank
Goldman Sachs
HSBC
Merrill Lynch
Morgan Stanley
UBS Investment Bank

HISTORICAL FINANCIALS

Company Type: Public

Income Statement FYE: March 31

	ASSETS ($ mil.)	NET INCOME ($ mil.)	INCOME AS % OF ASSETS	EMPLOYEES
03/15	142,854	1,218	0.9%	14,085
03/14	142,035	1,167	0.8%	13,913
03/13	157,029	886	0.6%	13,663
03/12	159,857	759	0.5%	14,202
03/11	163,063	989	0.6%	15,556
Annual Growth	(3.3%)	5.4%	—	(2.5%)

	STOCK PRICE ($) FY Close	P/E High	P/E Low	PER SHARE ($) Earnings	Dividends	Book Value
03/15	58.79	12	8	3.68	2.54	34.07
03/14	53.40	14	9	3.41	0.00	32.82
03/13	38.72	16	10	2.56	0.00	34.96
03/12	30.22	18	10	2.11	0.00	33.44
03/11	38.04	19	12	2.86	0.00	34.03
Annual Growth	11.5%	—	—	6.5%	—	0.0%

Magna International Inc.

Through its various subsidiaries and divisions Magna International makes just about everything needed to put together a motor vehicle. Magna Steyr its largest division offers vehicle engineering and assembly. Magna's interior and exterior systems division makes trim lighting sealing systems instrument and door panels and sound insulation. Cosma International makes body and chassis systems. Magna Powertrain offers transaxles transmission systems and engine parts while Magna Mirrors makes mirrors and driver assistance products. Other Magna operations include Seating E-Car Systems Electronics Roof and Closures. Its geographic markets include North America Europe Africa and Asia.

OperationsThe company based in Ontario Canada operates segments along geographic lines to be more responsive to customers' needs. Its segments include North America (which generated 53% of Magna's total revenue in 2014) Europe (40% of revenue) Asia (5% of revenue) and Rest of World (2% of revenue). The "Rest of World" markets include developing regions such as Africa Asia Eastern Europe and South America. Magna boasts almost 320 manufacturing facilities and roughly 85 product development engineering and sales centers in nearly 30 countries. Magna follows a decentralized mode of operation meaning its businesses operate independently.By product exterior and interior system sales generated 35% of Magna International's total revenue in 2014 while body systems and chassis system sales contributed another 22% to sales. The rest of its total revenue came from powertrain system sales (14% of total sales); complete vehicle assembly sales (8%); tooling engineering and other services (8%); vision and electronic system sales (7%) and closure system sales (6%).

Sales and Marketing

BMW Daimler Fiat/Chrysler Ford GM and VW accounted for approximately 83% of Magna's total sales in 2014.

Financial Performance

Magna has enjoyed sizable revenue and profit growth since 2009 as demand for new cars continues to strengthen around the world. The company's sales rose 5% to a record $36.6 billion during 2014 mostly thanks to business growth in North America with the launch of new programs and as light vehicle production in North America grew by 5% to 17 million units. Total sales were also helped by 18% sales growth in Asia driven by new program launches with Magna content (particularly in China) and higher light vehicle production in Asia. Revenue growth in 2014 drove Magna International's net income higher by 21% to a record $1.88 billion for the year. The company's operating cash levels climbed 9% to $2.79 billion during the year thanks to higher cash earnings.

Strategy

Magna International ranked as the world's second-largest parts supplier behind Robert Bosch GmbH and ahead of ZF as of mid-2015. To satisfy automakers' demand for more of a one-stop-shop in auto part manufacturing the company regularly expands its product lines and expertise through acquisitions of auto parts manufacturers.That said it's also been selective on what auto part manufacturing businesses it wants to be in favoring more profitable business lines and "key areas" of the vehicle. In August 2015 for example Magna sold its interiors operations business including some 36 manufacturing facilities and 12000 employees to Grupo Antolin for $525 million. Magna International often uses strategic partnerships to grow or complement its product lines and extend its reach into new geographic markets. In 2015 subsidiary body and chassis maker Cosma International effectively expanded Magna's reach and product offerings to customers in fast-growing China after it formed a joint venture with Chongqing Xingqiaorui. Also in 2015 Magna International partnered with Argus Cyber Security to offer automotive electronic systems that featured Argus' intrusion prevention system service and cloud-based monitoring service designed to prevent cyber-attacks. In 2014 Magna formed a 50/50 joint venture with Tata AutoComp Systems to provide seating systems to the Indian commercial vehicle industry. Mergers and AcquisitionsIn July 2015 Magna International purchased German transmission manufacturer Getrag for $1.9 billion as part of its continued plan to expand its service and product lines for auto makers.

Company BackgroundMagna International has historically expanded its product lines through acquisitions of other auto parts manufacturers. In early 2011 Magna Seating acquired Germany-based Vogelsitze GmbH which made seats for buses and passenger trains. In 2012 Magna obtained Verwaltungs GmbH a maker of automotive vacuum engine and transmission pumps with two facilities in Germany and one in each of China and Bulgaria. Also in 2012 to strengthen its automotive pump operations Magna purchased the remaining 50% interest it didn't already own of STT Technologies which made transmission and engine related pumps for the North American market.

HISTORY

Company BackgroundMagna International is rooted in a tool and die shop founded by Frank Stronach and friend Tony Czapka in Ontario Canada in 1957. Austrian-born Stronach immigrated to Canada in 1954. By the end of 1957 the business called Multimatic had 10 employees. Multimatic delved into car parts when it landed a contract in 1960 to make sun visor brackets for a General Motors division in Canada.

To go public Multimatic underwent a reverse merger in 1969 with Magna Electronics a publicly traded maker of components for aerospace defense and industrial markets. (Stronach retained control of the company.) Annual sales reached $10 million that year. The company expanded its automotive operations during the early 1970s by adding more stamped and electronic components. Magna was renamed Magna International in 1973.

With sales increasing steadily among its auto parts businesses Magna sold its aerospace and defense business (now part of Heroux-Devtek) in 1981. The new Magna consisted of five distinct automotive divisions that made seat tracks door latches electronic components and other auto parts. During the 1980s the company expanded by adding factories and product lines. It also capitalized on car makers' penchant for outsourcing labor and bypassing unions. By 1987 when sales reached $1 billion the company was producing systems for every area of the automobile. Stronach didn't spend all his time on cars however; he owned race horses and restaurants. He had opened restaurants tried various publishing ventures (which failed) and even made an unsuccessful run for a Canadian parliament seat in 1988.

Aggressive expansion during the 1980s eventually caught up with the company and in 1989 Magna began to restructure selling assets to pay off its debt. The company also was bailed out in part by two of its principal customers –General Motors and Chrysler. Having recovered somewhat Magna began acquiring small auto parts companies in Europe in 1992.

Magna expanded its European presence with the purchase of Austria-based Steyr-Daimler-Puch in 1998 adding about $1 billion in annual sales. The deal steered Magna into the auto assembly business. Stronach also added Santa Anita Park to his holdings that year. In late 1999 the company's racetrack interests were spun off as Magna Entertainment with Magna retaining a 78% stake. Stronach's horse Red Bullet won the 2000 Preakness. Later that year Magna sold its 50% stake in Webasto Sunroofs to privately-owned German auto parts maker Webasto.

Early in 2001 Stronach's daughter Belinda was named vice chairman and CEO. The company then prepared to spin off Magna Steyr and Intier (now Magna's interiors and seating divisions) as public companies; Intier was spun off later in 2001.

Magna acquired rival automotive mirror maker Donnelly in 2002 in a stock-and-debt deal worth $320 million. The company divested its stake in Magna Entertainment in 2003.

Belinda Stronach stepped down as president CEO and director in order to make a bid for the leadership of Canada's new Conservative Party. Her father assumed the role of interim president in early 2004. Ms. Stronach's bid for the leadership of the Conservative Party was not successful. Mr. Stronach ran the company until 2005 when Magna adopted a co-CEO management structure with Donald Walker and Siegfried Wolf at the helm.

Magna and Daimler announced in 2004 that Magna would buy Daimler's drivetrain manufacturing subsidiary New Venture Gear for about $435 million. After approval by the European Commission New Venture Gear was acquired by a newly created joint venture called New Process Gear with Magna holding an 80% interest; Daimler held 20% until 2007 when Magna bought out its stake.

Russian conglomerate Basic Element led by Russian aluminum magnate Oleg Deripaska spent about $1.5 billion to purchase 20% of Magna in 2007. The transaction gave Magna entry to the Russian market but late in 2008 Deripaska's bank BNP Paribas made a margin call that forced the businessman to give up his shares. In 2008 Magna International acquired Technoplast a Russia-based manufacturer of plastic automotive interior and exterior parts which bolstered its capacity in Eastern Europe and Russia.

On the heels of the General Motors bankruptcy filing in 2009 the German government selected Magna International as a partner for Adam Opel and agreed to provide about 1.5 billion (around $2 billion) in bridge loans while GM and Magna finalized the contract. A trusteeship for Opel was arranged to keep European operations separate from the Chapter 11 proceedings of GM.

Magna teamed up with Russian banking firm Sberbank to purchase a 55% interest in Opel and its UK-based Vauxhall unit. While GM initially agreed to the sale in September 2009 it backed out in November. The GM board decided to restructure Opel and its European operations instead because business conditions were improving and the Opel brand was important to its global strategy. In Europe the decision was met with demands by the German government that its 1.5 billion in bridge loans be returned as well as protests and planned work stoppages by the German labor union.

The GM bankruptcy was brought on by the economic crisis of 2008 and 2009. Magna responded by implementing cost cutting measures which included reducing its headcount by approximately 11500 representing a 14% cutback between 2007 and 2009. It also sold off some of its non-core assets.

Founder and chairman Frank Stronach stepped down in 2010 citing the trend toward more regulatory limitations on company management as one of the reasons. He gave up his controlling share in the company and with it his voting control. The company purchased and cancelled all of its Class B shares held by the Stronach Group and issued Class A Common shares. This capital transaction ended the company's dual class stock structure. The former premier of Ontario Mike Harris took Stronach's place. Co-CEO Siegfried ("Sigi") Wolf also resigned which made co-CEO Donald Walker the sole CEO of Magna International as of mid-2011.In early 2011 Magna Seating acquired Germany-based Vogelsitze GmbH which made seats for buses and passenger trains. In 2012 Magna obtained Verwaltungs GmbH a maker of automotive vacuum engine and transmission pumps with two facilities in Germany and one in each of China and Bulgaria.

EXECUTIVES

President, Guenther Apfalter
Vice President, Paul Brock
Vice President, Gary Cohn
Vice President, Joanne Horibe
Vice President, Robert Merkley
Vice President, Atul Mehta
Vice President, Thomas Schultheiss
Vice President, Bassem Shakeel
Chairman Of The Board, William Young
Auditors: Deloitte LLP

LOCATIONS

HQ: Magna International Inc.
337 Magna Drive, Aurora, Ontario L4G 7K1
Phone: 905 726-2462 **Fax:** 905 726-2603
Web: www.magna.com

PRODUCTS/OPERATIONS

2014 Sales

	$ mil.	% of total
Exterior & interior systems	12,840	35
Body systems & chassis systems	8,079	22
Powertrain systems	4,954	14
Complete vehicle assembly	3,067	8
Tooling engineering & other	2,971	8
Vision & electronic systems	2,644	7
Closure systems	2,086	6
Total	**36,641**	**100**

2014 Sales

	$ mil.	% of total
North America	19,603	53
Europe	14,494	40
Asia	1,837	5
Rest of world	694	2
Corporate & Other	13	-
Total	**36,641**	**100**

Selected Operations Products and Services

Cosma International Inc. - body and chassis systems
- Body systems
- Chassis systems
- Design and engineering
- Finishing
- Metal forming technologies
- Stampings

Decoma International - exterior and interior systems
- Body side systems
- Bumper systems (front and rear)
- Cargo management
- Carpet and loadspace
- Cockpit systems
- Engineered glass
- Exterior trim
- Greenhouse systems
- Lighting systems
- Plastic body panels
- Polymeric glazing systems
- Sealing systems
- Vehicle enhancement packages

Magna Car Top Systems - roof systems
- Soft tops
- Removable roof systems
- Retractable hard tops
- Sliding roof systems

Magna Closures - closure systems
- Door modules
- Driver controls
- Handle assemblies
- Power closures and latching systems
- Window systems

Magna E-Car Systems
- Battery cells and packs
- Hybrid and electric vehicle development and production

Magna Electronics - electronic systems
- Body electronics
- Driver assistance and safety systems
- Engine electronics
- Intelligent power systems
- Lighting systems
- Liquid sensors

Magna Mirrors - vision systems
- Actuators
- Electronic vision systems
- Exterior and interior mirrors

Magna Powertrain - powertrain systems
- Automatic overdrives
- Die castings
- Differentials
- Engine systems
- Fluid pressure and controls
- Power take-offs
- Stampings
- Transaxles
- Transfer cases
- Transmission systems

Magna Seating - seating systems
- Seat mechanism systems
- Seating systems

Magna Steyr - complete vehicle manufacturing and OEM engineering
- Energy storing systems
- Fuel systems

COMPETITORS

A.G. Simpson
Aisin Seiki
American Axle & Manufacturing
Benteler Automotive
BorgWarner
Calsonic Kansei
Commercial Vehicle
DENSO
DURA Automotive
Dana Holding
Delphi Automotive Systems
Faurecia
Ficosa
GKN
Gentex
Haldex
Hella
Johnson Controls
KUO
Lacks Enterprises
Lear Corp
Linamar Corp.
Meritor
Plastic Omnium
Prodrive
Robert Bosch
Tenneco
Textron
Torotrak
Tower International
Toyota Auto Body
Valeo
Visteon
ZF Friedrichshafen

HISTORICAL FINANCIALS

Company Type: Public

Income Statement FYE: December 31

	REVENUE ($ mil.)	NET INCOME ($ mil.)	NET PROFIT MARGIN	EMPLOYEES
12/14	36,641	1,882	5.1%	131,000
12/13	34,835	1,561	4.5%	125,000
12/12	30,837	1,433	4.6%	119,000
12/11	28,748	1,018	3.5%	108,275
12/10	24,102	973	4.0%	96,600
Annual Growth	11.0%	17.9%	—	7.9%

2014 Year-End Financials

Debt ratio: 5.6%
Return on equity: 20.5%
Cash ($ mil.): 1,253
Current ratio: 1.31
Long-term debt ($ mil.): 811
No. of shares (mil.): 410
Dividends
Yield: 2.8%
Payout: 34.9%
Market value ($ mil.): 44,598

	STOCK PRICE ($) FY Close	P/E High/Low		PER SHARE ($) Earnings	Dividends	Book Value
12/14	108.69	26	18	4.35	1.52	21.10
12/13	82.06	25	15	3.38	1.28	21.76
12/12	50.02	16	11	3.05	1.10	20.22
12/11	33.31	29	15	2.10	0.50	17.52
12/10	52.00	47	23	2.09	0.42	16.62
Annual Growth	20.2%	—	—	20.1%	37.9%	6.1%

Malayan Banking Berhad

Malayan Banking Berhad (better known as Maybank) is Malaysia's largest financial services group. Boasting assets of RM640 billion ($145 billion) the firm and its subsidiaries provide deposit services mortgages credit cards and other loan products to businesses and individuals through some 400 branches in Malaysia nearly 430 branches in Indonesia over 20 branches in Singapore and 30-plus branches across Southeast Asia. The firm also offers investment banking asset management online banking brokerage insurance unit trusts and other investments and corporate finance services through 2400 offices in 20 countries. Amanah Raya a trust company controlled by the Malaysian government owns over 45% of Maybank.

OperationsMaybank also in 2014 ranked as South East Asia's fourth-largest bank the largest Islamic financing bank in Malaysia and the third-largest Islamic financing bank globally by assets. As Malaysia's largest bank it controlled an 18.4% market share of the loans advances and financing market in Malaysia as well as a 27.6% share of the savings deposit market and 21.1% share of the checking account market.The bank categorizes its financial services under three key business pillars. Its Community Financial Services (which generated 35% of the company's net operating income or NOI in 2014) includes consumer banking SME and business banking services. The Global Banking pillar includes corporate banking (12% of NOI) investment banking (7%) global markets (8%) transaction banking and asset management. The Insurance & Takaful (8% of NOI) pillar offers insurance and Islamic services and also consists of Maybank's international business operations (28% NOI). Islamic financial services are also offered across all of its business units.Broadly speaking Maybank generates about half of its operating income from net interest income (mostly from loans and advances including from Islamic Banking Scheme operations). Around 20% of its operating income comes from net earned insurance premiums. The company had 46000 employees at the end of 2014.Geographic ReachMaybank's home markets are in Malaysia Singapore and Indonesia; which contributed nearly 89% of the group's profit before tax (PBT) in fiscal 2014. About 60% of its loans and 71% of its PBT were originated in Malaysia alone during the fiscal year. Singapore made up about 14% of its PBT. Outside of these markets Maybank operates in 20 countries (including 10 ASEAN countries) in major financial centers such as Hong Kong Shanghai London New York and Bahrain. It also has associates in Pakistan (MCB Bank's 1242 branches) and Vietnam (An Binh Bank's 145 branches). Sales and MarketingThe firm serves more than 22 million individuals organizations and businesses (including those of Muslim faith).Financial PerformanceNote: Growth rates may differ after conversion to US dollars. This analysis uses financials from the company's annual report. Maybank's revenues and profits have risen more than 30% since 2011 thanks largely to strong loan business growth.The company's revenue rose by 7% to RM35.7 billion ($10.2 billion) in 2014 mostly thanks to higher interest income as its loan advances and financing assets grew by 13% driven by a 47.5% jump in international loan growth and buoyed by better-than-industry loan growth in Malaysia and Singapore. Its financial investment portfolio assets also grew 8% during the year which boosted interest income further. Higher revenue in 2014 drove Maybank's net income up 3% to a record RM6.7 billion ($1.91 billion) for the year. The company's operating cash levels fell by 39% to RM5.27 billion ($1.5 billion) despite higher earnings due to unfavorable working capital changes mostly related to financial assets purchased under resale agreements and because it used more cash toward loans advances and financing. Strategy

Maybank's strategic objectives over the past five years (2010 through 2015) have included: being Malaysia's no. 1 retail financial services provider in 2015; be the leading ASEAN Wholesale bank expanding into the Middle East China and India; be Malaysia's leading Insurance and Takaful provider and an emerging regional player in the field as well; become a "truly regional organization" with around 40% of pre-tax profit coming from international operations by 2015; and becoming a global leader in Islamic Finance.Some of Maybank's fastest growing businesses include Islamic financing and Takaful (insurance) services that adhere to Islamic law which prohibits the collection of interest but allows profit-sharing and the sale and buy-back of homes (instead of the origination of mortgages). Serving Muslim individuals organizations and businesses the company is opening branches at home and abroad that offer such services. Indeed Islamic Financing grew by 25% during 2014 which increased its proportion of total Malaysia loans to 43.8% at the end of 2014 (from 38.9% at the end of 2013). The growth also solidified Maybank as the largest Islamic bank in Malaysia and the third-largest globally by assets.

Maybank also continues to expand its global reach beyond its home markets. During 2014 it opened its first branch in Myanmar and its third branch in Kunming China. That year it also launched its Etiqa Insurance and Private Wealth businesses in Singapore.

Company Background

Maybank has made several acquisitions in the past to boost its international presence. In 2011 the company acquired 100% of Singapore brokerage Kim Eng Holdings. The addition boosted Maybank's international profile and expanded its distribution capabilities. In 2008 the bank completed its acquisition of the 250-branch Bank Internasional Indonesia (BII). The deal had stalled when banking regulator Bank Negara Malaysia prohibited the transaction but that decision was reversed and the acquisition was ultimately allowed. Also in 2008 the bank acquired minority stakes in Pakistan's MCB Bank and Vietnam's An Binh Bank (ABBank) as well as Kookmin Bank's minority stake in PT Bank International Indonesia.

Auditors: Ernst & Young

LOCATIONS

HQ: Malayan Banking Berhad
14th Floor, Menara Maybank, 100, Jalan Tun Perak, Kuala Lumpur 50050
Phone: (60) 3 2070 8833 **Fax:** (60) 3 2032 4775
Web: www.maybank.com

PRODUCTS/OPERATIONS

2013 Sales

	% of total
Interest income	65
Income from islamic banking scheme operations	11
Non-interest income	24
Total	**100**

Selected Subsidiaries

BinaFikir Sdn. Bhd.
Etiqa Insurance Berhad
Etiqa Life International (L) Ltd.
Etiqa Takaful Berhad
Maybank (PNG) Limited2
Maybank Ageas Holding Berhad (formerly known as Maybank Fortis Holdings Berhad)
Maybank Allied Credit & Leasing Sdn. Bhd.
Maybank International (L) Ltd.
Maybank Investment Bank Berhad
Maybank Islamic Berhad
Maybank Philippines Incorporated1
Maysec Sdn. Bhd.
PT Bank Internasional Indonesia TBK1
PT Bank Maybank Syariah Indonesial
PT BII Finance Centre1
PT Wahana Ottomitra Multiartha TBK1

COMPETITORS

AmBank Group
Bank Muamalat
Bank of China
Bank of East Asia
CIMB Group
Hang Seng Bank
Hong Leong Bank
Malaysian Industrial Development Finance
OCBC Bank
Public Bank
RHB Capital
Standard Chartered

HISTORICAL FINANCIALS

Company Type: Public

Income Statement FYE: December 31

	ASSETS ($ mil.)	NET INCOME ($ mil.)	INCOME AS % OF ASSETS	EMPLOYEES
12/14	183,112	1,920	1.0%	47,000
12/13	171,082	2,000	1.2%	47,771
12/12	161,627	1,876	1.2%	47,233
12/11*	142,407	815	0.6%	45,000
06/11	136,387	1,473	1.1%	42,000
Annual Growth	7.6%	6.9%	—	2.9%

*Fiscal year change

2014 Year-End Financials

Return on assets: 1.1%
Return on equity: 13.5%
Long-term debt ($ mil.): —
No. of shares (mil.): —
Sales ($ mil): 8,800

Dividends
Yield: 5.7%
Payout: 74.2%
Market value ($ mil.): —

Manulife Financial Corp.

Manulife the holding company for The Manufacturers Life Insurance Company and John Hancock Financial Services has gone mano a mano with its competitors. Manulife provides individual life insurance group life and health group pension products variable annuities wealth management and financial products in nearly two dozen countries and territories worldwide. North America and Asia make up its largest operations. Manulife's reinsurance division provides life health and accident reinsurance and was one of North America's top life retrocessionaires (firms that reinsure reinsurers) until it sold that division in 2011. The company also provides investment management real estate and lending services.

Operations

Along with its John Hancock subsidiary Manulife is one of the top five life insurers in North America and is a top 10 global life insurer based on market capitalization. North American financial products are offered primarily under the John Hancock brand while life insurance is offered through Manufacturers Life. Other brands and subsidiaries include Portland Investment Counsel (mutual funds retail investment funds) and Pottruff & Smith (travel insurance).

Geographic Reach

Sales in the US still make up about a third of Manulife's annual revenue (though the market there has shrunk in response to the flagging economy); Canada and Asia each account for about 30% of Manulife's premium income. Its efforts to grow in China through partnerships have paid off with the company's sales there challenging those in Canada (formerly its second-largest market after the US).

Strategy

Besides building up its more successful offerings and divesting those with higher risks Manulife's strategy for growth includes maintaining a diversified mix and hedging its in-force public equity and interest rate risks over time. The company's objective is to increase its earnings to $4 billion by 2015.

Manulife also grows through collaborations such as its partnership with Edward Jones which helped the company expand its sales network in the US and add agents to increase its distribution presence in Asia. Its Manulife-Sinochem (MSL) partnership with Sinochem has also allowed the company to deepen its reach in China. With operations in 50 Chinese cities MSL has the broadest geographic footprint of any foreign invested joint venture firm in that country. Manulife also has a 49% interest in ABN AMRO TEDA Fund Management in China. The Manulife-TEDA partnership allows the company to expand in China's wealth management market.

Further expansion in China is in the company's plans as is increasing sales of wealth management products. In 2012 for example Manulife Asset Management procured licensure to provide institutional asset management services in Korea's fast-growing market.

Mergers and Acquisitions

The firm's future growth strategy is focused on individual and group life health and group pensions. Towards those ends it has agreed to buy the Hong Kong pension business of Standard Chartered. The deal also includes a 15-year exclusive distribution deal with the UK bank's Hong Kong customers.

Manulife's mutual fund business is an area the company is making great effort to grow. It purchased Wellington West Financial Services from National Bank Financial Group in 2012 for an undisclosed price adding about 40 advisors and some $900 in assets under management to its Canadian investment unit (Manulife Securities) in the deal.

In 2013 Manulife expanded in Canada's mortgage creditor insurance market through the purchase of Benesure Canada. Benesure provides distribution and third-party administration of life and disability creditor policies to mortgage brokerage entities.

Company Background

Manulife acquired US financial services giant John Hancock in a $10 billion deal in 2004 bringing Manulife into the top ranks of US and global life insurers. Manulife subsequently rebranded its US financial products with the more-recognizable John Hancock name and logo. Manulife also consolidated John Hancock's Canadian subsidiary Maritime Life Assurance Company into its flagship subsidiary The Manufacturers Life Insurance Company.

EXECUTIVES

President and CEO, Donald A. Guloien, $774,835 total compensation
SEVP and COO, Paul L. Rooney
SEVP and Chief Investment Officer; Chairman Manulife Asset Management, Warren A. Thomson
EVP Global Head of Wealth and Asset Management; President and CEO Manulife Asset Management, Kai R. Sotorp
President and CEO Manulife Canada; SEVP and General Manager Canadian Division, Marianne Harrison
President John Hancock Financial Services; SEVP and General Manager US Division, Craig R. Bromley
EVP General Account Investments, Scott S. Hartz
EVP Human Resources, Stephani E. Kingsmill
EVP and Chief Actuary, Cindy L. Forbes
EVP and Chief Risk Officer, Rahim Hirji
SEVP and CFO, Stephen B. (Steve) Roder
EVP and General Counsel, Stephen P. Sigurdson
EVP and CIO, Greg Framke
SEVP and General Manager Asia; President and CEO Manulife Asia, Roy Gori
EVP and Chief Innovation Officer, Timothy W. Ramza
Chairman, Richard B. DeWolfe
Auditors: Ernst & Young LLP

LOCATIONS

HQ: Manulife Financial Corp.
200 Bloor Street East, North Tower 10, Toronto, Ontario M4W 1E5
Phone: 416 926-3427 **Fax:** 416 926-5657
Web: www.manulife.com

2010 Revenues

	% of total
US	32
Canada	30
Asia	30
Other	8
Total	**100**

PRODUCTS/OPERATIONS

2010 Revenues

	% of total
Premiums	
Life & health insurance	37
Annuities & pensions	12
Investment income	34
Other	17
Total	**100**

Selected Subsidiaries & Affiliates

Elliott & Page Limited
FNA Financial Inc.
John Hancock Financial Network Inc. (US)
John Hancock Financial Services Inc. (US)
John Hancock Investment Management Services LLC (US)
John Hancock Life Insurance Company (U.S.A.)
John Hancock Life Insurance Company of New York
Manulife International Holdings Limited (Bermuda)
Manulife (Singapore) Pte. Ltd.
Manulife (Vietnam) Limited
Manulife Bank of Canada
Manulife Life Insurance Company (Japan)
Manulife Sinochem Life Insurance Co. Ltd. (China)
NAL Resources Management Limited
P.T. Asuransi Jiwa Manulife Indonesia
The Manufacturers Investment Corporation (US)
The Manufacturers Life Insurance Co. (Philippines) Inc.
The Manufacturers Life Insurance Company

COMPETITORS

AEGON
AIG
Allianz
Canada Life
China Life Insurance
Dai-ichi Life
Fairfax Financial Holdings
Generali
Great-West Lifeco
ING
Industrial Alliance Insurance and Financial Servic
Liberty Mutual
Meiji Yasuda Life
MetLife
Nationwide
New York Life
Nippon Life Insurance
Power Financial
Principal Financial
Prudential
Sun Life
Swiss Re
T&D Holdings
The Hartford
Tokio Marine

HISTORICAL FINANCIALS

Company Type: Public

Income Statement FYE: December 31

	ASSETS ($ mil.)	NET INCOME ($ mil.)	INCOME AS % OF ASSETS	EMPLOYEES
12/14	500,346	3,023	0.6%	0
12/13	483,036	2,943	0.6%	0
12/12	488,707	1,745	0.4%	28,000
12/11	452,995	126	0.0%	26,000
12/10	425,672	(1,666)	—	25,000
Annual Growth	4.1%	—	—	—

2014 Year-End Financials

Return on assets: 0.6%
Return on equity: 11.2%
Long-term debt ($ mil.): —
No. of shares (mil.): 1,864
Sales ($ mil): 47,082

Dividends
Yield: 2.9%
Payout: 29.5%
Market value ($ mil.): 35,584

	STOCK PRICE ($) FY Close	P/E High/Low	PER SHARE ($) Earnings	Dividends	Book Value
12/14	19.09	11 9	1.55	0.52	15.50
12/13	19.73	12 8	1.52	0.51	14.58
12/12	13.59	16 11	0.88	0.52	14.08
12/11	10.62	938500	0.02	0.51	13.32
12/10	17.18	— —	(0.99)	0.51	13.68
Annual Growth	2.7%	— —	—	0.6%	3.2%

Mapfre SA

To whom do you turn when your vehicle intersects with the "Running of the Bulls?" Through its subsidiaries MAPFRE provides customers with property/casualty (especially auto) coverage life insurance and reinsurance. The firm does business primarily in its home country of Spain where it is a top insurer and in about 45 other nations including many in North and South America. Individual and group offerings include funeral home medical and agricultural insurance. It additionally provides financial services such as investment and pension funds. MAPFRE also maintains a very successful alliance with Spanish banking company Caja Madrid through which the companies cross-market each other's products.

Geographic Reach

MAPFRE operates a network of 15000 branches half of which are located in Spain. Of the international locations about 2000 offices are located in Latin American countries. International operations account for about 60% of MAPFRE's annual revenues.

Operations

MAPFRE conducts its operations through about 240 subsidiaries. The group's activities are divided into four segments: life direct motor direct other non-life direct and reinsurance and other activities.

Sales and Marketing

MAPFRE's products are primarily marketed through distribution agreements with third parties especially banks; it also has direct sales operations in Spain. The company has relationships with some 9700 bank branches and other retail outlets. MAPFRE and Caja Madrid run CCM Vida Y Pensiones a 50/50 joint venture to develop and sell life and pension insurance at the bank and banking products through insurance agents. The company also markets products through a network of 70000 agents and brokers in the Americas.

Financial Performance

MAPFRE achieved 15% revenue growth and doubled net income in 2011. Progress was attributed to its diversification activities and strong returns from the international direct insurance and reinsurance operations. Efforts to strengthen the distribution network in Spain also led to stabilization of sales in the domestic auto life and homeowner's insurance markets. The company has also attributed growth to its prudent financing and investment strategies. MAPFRE has reported increased revenues each year since 2007.

Strategy

MAPFRE is focused on expanding its operations through geographic diversification and continued acquisitions in high-growth markets are key to MAPFRE's expansion plans as domestic markets contract. In South America it has moved to become one of the largest non-life insurers in countries including Brazil and Argentina. The company has a partnership with Banco do Brazil to collaborate on the marketing of property insurance in the Brazilian market. Other areas of expansion have included the emerging markets of India Panama and Ecuador.

North America has been another area of focus for MAPFRE's international expansion strategy. Its MAPFRE U.S.A. unit sells car insurance in Massachusetts and more than a dozen other states.

To increase efficiencies and streamline operations in 2011 the company reorganized its domestic distribution network to focus on retail and corporate customers. It is also revamping its international sales networks to maximize returns.

To increase direct sales in Spain the company launched its VERTI internet and phone sales organization in 2011 for home and auto insurance products. MAPFRE also formed a joint venture with Euler Hermes to market credit and surety products in Spain Portugal and Latin America in 2011.

Auditors: Ernst & Young, S.L.

LOCATIONS

HQ: Mapfre SA
Paseo de Recoletos, 25, Madrid 28004
Phone: (34) 91 581 1100 **Fax:** (34) 91 581 1143
Web: www.mapfre.es

HISTORICAL FINANCIALS

Company Type: Public

Income Statement FYE: December 31

	ASSETS ($ mil.)	NET INCOME ($ mil.)	INCOME AS % OF ASSETS	EMPLOYEES
12/14	81,720	1,027	1.3%	35,871
12/13	78,234	1,088	1.4%	36,280
12/12	75,106	877	1.2%	34,962
12/11	70,953	1,245	1.8%	32,798
12/10	65,141	1,249	1.9%	35,704
Annual Growth	5.8%	(4.8%)	—	0.1%

Marubeni Corp.

Marubeni's name combines the Japanese words for "circle" and "red" and Marubeni hopes the comprehensive range of products manufactured and traded by its circle of operating units will keep the company out of the red. One of Japan's largest sogo shosha (general trading companies) Marubeni has a broad range of operating segments: Chemicals; Energy; Finance Logistics & IT Business; Food; Forest Products; Lifestyle; Metals & Mineral Resources; Real Estate Development; Plant & Industrial Machinery; Power Projects & Infrastructure; and Transportation Machinery.

In 2011 the trading company simplified its reporting structure into four broad segments: Machinery (Plant & Industrial Machinery Power Projects & Infrastructure and Transportation Machinery); Resources (Energy and Metals & Mineral Resources); Materials (Chemicals Forest Products and General Merchandise); and Consumer Products (Finance Logistics & IT Business Food Lifestyle and Real Estate Development.)

Marubeni has hundreds of operating companies in 70 countries.

A recovering economy and a robust growth in commodity prices lifted Marubeni's revenues and income in 2012. In fiscal 2012 the company reported a 19% increase in revenues driven by a 17% jump in the volume of Marubeni's trading transactions especially from higher oil prices. Energy accounted for 29% of total trading volume in 2012 and was 22% greater in actual volume than in 2011. Marubeni's higher overall revenues in 2012 outpaced increased expenses enabling the trading house to post a 26% jump in net income.

The group has been particularly active in Asia where its diversity has enabled it to develop local industries and to help build utility and industrial infrastructures such as telephone systems power plants and water systems. The company has championed international expansion since the mid-1990s but Japan's credit crunch and the Asian economic crisis have hurt the company's production and processing operations across Southeast Asia. Marubeni has been reducing debt controlling operating costs and investing in commodity trading natural resources projects and international power generation schemes.

Growing its commodity business in 2012 the company agreed to acquire US-based grain fertilizer and energy commodities distribution and natural gas network Gavilon for $3.6 billion.

Taking advantage of BP's need to raise cash in the wake of its Gulf of Mexico oil disaster in 2011 Marubeni bought four mature producing deepwater oil and gas fields in Gulf from BP for $650 million. In 2013 it also agreed to acquire a 49% stake in Williams Partners' floating production platform project for Tubular Bells Field in the Gulf of Mexico.

In 2011 Marubeni formed a joint venture with Supreme Energy and International Power to develop the Rantau Dedap geothermal project located in Sumatra. The 220 MW geothermal plant is part of the Indonesian government's long-term plan meet its country's needs with renewable power.

It also entered a new market that year airplane leasing with a deal with Deucalion Limited to set up a company in Singapore to invest into aircraft assets.

In 2011 the company announced a medium-term growth plan focusing on natural resources (primarily copper) infrastructure environmental products (especially water businesses) and essential living commodities (building up its grain position in China).

HISTORY

Marubeni's origins are closely linked to those of another leading Japanese trading company. ITOCHU founder Chubei Itoh set up Marubeni Shoten K. K. in 1858 as an outlet in Osaka for his textile trading business (originally C. Itoh & Co.). The symbol for the store was a circle (maru) drawn around the Japanese word for red (beni). As C. Itoh's global operations expanded the Marubeni store served as headquarters.

Marubeni was split off from C. Itoh in 1921 to trade textiles although it soon expanded its operations to include industrial and consumer goods. To mobilize for WWII the Japanese government reunited Marubeni and C. Itoh in 1941 merging them with another trading company Kishimoto into a new entity Sanko Kabushiki Kaisha. In 1944 Sanko Daido Boeki and Kureha Spinning were ordered to consolidate into a larger entity to be called the Daiken Co. but the war ended before all operations were fully integrated.

Spun off from Daiken in 1949 Marubeni began trading internationally. It opened a New York office in 1951 and diversified into food metals and machinery. During the Korean War Marubeni benefited from the UN's use of Japan as a supply base.

In 1955 Marubeni merged with Iida & Company and changed its name to Marubeni-Iida. It received a government concession to supply silicon steel and iron sheets critical to the growing Japanese auto and appliance industries. The company expanded into engineering –building factories aircraft and a nuclear reactor for the Japan Atomic Energy Research Institute –and into petrochemicals fertilizers and rubber products.

Marubeni-Iida was behind the Fuyo keiretsu formed in the early 1960s. Fuyo (another word for Mt. Fuji) is a powerful assemblage of some 150 companies including Canon Hitachi and Nissan that form joint ventures and develop think tanks.

The firm became Marubeni Corp. in 1972 and a year later it bought Nanyo Bussan another trading company. In 1973 Marubeni's image was tarnished by allegations that it had hoarded rice for sale on the Japanese black market.

In the 1990s Marubeni won several major construction contracts. Among them Marubeni formed a venture in 1998 with John Laing and Turkey's Alarko Alsim to rebuild three airports in Uzbekistan.

Marubeni had begun offering Internet access in 1995 and two years later it launched an Internet-based long-distance telephone service. In 1999 the trading house formed two ventures with US firm Global Crossing one to start operating Pacific Crossing One (the Japan-US cable) and another to lay a cable network in Japan.

That year Marubeni tied up with fellow trading company ITOCHU to integrate their steel processing subsidiaries in China to try to keep their Chinese businesses afloat. In 2000 ITOCHU and Marubeni formed an online steel trading joint venture with US-based e-commerce company MetalSite. The two companies also integrated their entire steel divisions in 2001 forming the Marubeni-Itochu Steel joint venture among the largest steel companies in Japan.

Taking responsibility for the sharp downturn in Marubeni's financial performance chairman Iwao Toriumi announced in 2001 that he would step down. The company launched a major restructuring effort the next year that was designed to give more autonomy to the managers of individual business units.

In 2005 Marubeni launched a large power and water project in Abu Dhabi.

In 2007 Marubeni entered into the finance leasing industry in the US launching subsidiary CoActiv Capital Partners.

In 2008 Marubeni acquired US-based The PIC Group Inc. an independent global provider of services and programs focused on power generation and other industrial facilities and services. In 2009 it acquired 49% of Invenergy Thermal Financing LLC which owns three natural-gas fired power plants (with 1014 MW of generating capcity) in the US.

In 2009 the company completed the Laffan Refinery in Qatar which began commercial operations that year. It also signed a $2 billion deal to build the Shuweihat S2 Independent Water and Power Producer project in the United Arab Emirates.

EXECUTIVES

President and CEO, Fumiya Kokubu
Senior Managing Executive Officer, Shigeru Yamazoe
Senior Managing Executive Officer, Mitsuru Akiyoshi
Senior Managing Executive Officer, Yutaka Nomura
Managing Executive Officer, Shoji Kuwayama
Managing Executive Officer, Daisuke Okada
Managing Executive Officer, Kazuaki Tanaka
Managing Executive Officer, Yukihiko Matsumura
Managing Executive Officer, Masumi Kakinoki
Executive Corporate Officer General Affairs Department Corporate Accounting Department Finance Department; Vice Chairman of Investment and Credit Committee; Executive Corporate Officer Investor Relations, Teruo Asada
Auditors: Ernst & Young ShinNihon LLC

LOCATIONS

HQ: Marubeni Corp.
1-4-2 Ohtemachi, Chiyoda-ku, Tokyo 100-8088
Phone: (81) 3 3282 2111 **Fax:** (81) 3 3282 4241
Web: www.marubeni.co.jp

2014 Sales

	% of total
Japan	60
US	29
Singapore	4
Other countries	7
Total	**100**

PRODUCTS/OPERATIONS

2014 Sales

	% of total
Consumer Products	55
Materials	21
Resources	15
Machinery	9
Total	**100**

COMPETITORS

ITOCHU
Jardine Matheson
Kanematsu
LG Group
Largo Vista
Mitsubishi Corp.
Mitsubishi International
Mitsui
Nissan Chemical
Rio Tinto plc
Samsung Group
Seika
Showa Denko
Sime Darby
Sojitz
Sojitz Corporation of America
Sumikin Bussan
Sumitomo
Sumitomo Heavy Industries

HISTORICAL FINANCIALS

Company Type: Public

Income Statement FYE: March 31

	REVENUE ($ mil.)	NET INCOME ($ mil.)	NET PROFIT MARGIN	EMPLOYEES
03/15	65,297	880	1.3%	47,925
03/14	68,356	2,043	3.0%	49,996
03/13	51,665	2,186	4.2%	42,937
03/12	53,521	2,098	3.9%	41,503
03/11	44,487	1,648	3.7%	38,700
Annual Growth	10.1%	(14.5%)	—	5.5%

2015 Year-End Financials

Debt ratio: 0.3%
Return on equity: 7.2%
Cash ($ mil.): 3,909
Current ratio: 1.19
Long-term debt ($ mil.): 23,721
No. of shares (mil.): 1,735
Dividends
Yield: 3.9%
Payout: 413.6%
Market value ($ mil.): 100,947

	STOCK PRICE ($) FY Close	P/E High	P/E Low	PER SHARE ($) Earnings	Dividends	Book Value
03/15	58.17	1	1	0.51	2.31	7.29
03/14	67.80	1	1	1.18	2.40	7.73
03/13	76.48	1	0	1.26	2.36	6.93
03/12	72.50	1	0	1.21	1.99	5.98
03/11	72.43	1	1	0.95	1.26	5.38
Annual Growth	(5.3%)	—	—	(14.5%)	16.4%	7.9%

Mazda Motor Corp. (Japan)

Mazda and its Zoom-Zoom spirit races alongside the top automakers in Japan. Selling more than 1.2 million vehicles annually Mazda makes passenger cars commercial vehicles and crossover SUVs. It comprises more than 50 subsidiaries including sales companies: Mazda Motor of America Europe and Australia. The company manufactures in Japan China and Thailand. Models include the Mazda 2 3 6 and 8 passenger vehicles; MX-5 (Miata) RX-8 sports cars; E-series commercial vehicles; and B-Series pickup trucks. Mazda added crossover SUVs to its lineup with the Tribute Mazda5 (Premacy) Verisa Biante CX-7 and CX-9. Ford Motor holds a 3.5% stake in Mazda.

Just as the automotive industry was getting back on course natural catastrophe in the form of the Great Tohoku Kanto Earthquake and subsequent tsunamis struck Japan in March 2011. Many industries ground to a halt temporarily including Mazda's manufacturing facilities in Hiroshima and Hofu –limited production continued through the end of the month picking up to full production in April. Compounding factors to this event include political unrest in various regions of the world and rising oil prices. Still the company experienced sales increases in certain regions particularly in North America (10% increase) as well as emerging markets such as Russia China and other Asian countries. Mazda realized a 7% increase in overall sales for 2011 but this total was offset by sluggish sales in Japan and European countries as well as a strong yen. Before the fiscal year ended the earthquake struck and Mazda felt the aftershock to its 2011 bottom line posting an almost 60% loss over 2010.

Mazda had started on the road to recovery after the economic crisis in 2009. It weathered the worst of the downturn by implementing cost-saving measures –its workforce was reduced temporary workers' contracts were not renewed and inventory adjustments were made to match demand. Additionally Mazda executives agreed to take a 20% salary cut.

As a result of the recession Mazda's business plan revised target numbers and put an emphasis on brand and technology. Both areas are being served through new models and features. With an added emphasis on innovative technologies Mazda introduced its SKYACTIV technologies in 2011 with the claim that it will improve the fuel efficiency of its vehicles 30% by 2015. The SKYACTIV vision includes the redesign of Mazda's transmissions bodies and chassis for inclusion in its upcoming models. The SKYACTIV-G is a direct-injection gas engine that can achieve 30% fuel economy without the use of an electric motor; it is scheduled for release in Australia in 2011. The Demio (Mazda2) sporting the new engine was released in Japan early in 2011. Prior technology releases included Mazda's Smart Idle Stop System (iStop) which automatically shuts down the engine when the vehicle is stationary. The Mazda Premacy Hydrogen RE (Rotary Engine) Hybrid vehicle is the first of its kind to be made available through leasing; the RX-8 Hydrogen RE was introduced to Norway in 2009.

Ford once held a majority stake in Mazda but it cut its 33% interest to 13% in 2008 because it needed cash. As of 2011 Ford held only 3.5% of Mazda. Following the independence from Ford Takashi Yamanouchi took over as president and CEO of Mazda in 2008 assuming the responsibility of shoring up tumbling profits caused by an unstable yen and a decrease in demand. Former president Hisakazu Imaki continues serving as chairman but plans to retire in the near future; insiders report that Yamanouchi will assume the chairmanship. The management shakeup means Yamanouchi who is a proponent of expanding into the Chinese automobile market may speed up the process of the company's independent development strategy in China.

HISTORY

Ingiro Matsuda founded cork producer Toyo Cork Kogyo in Hiroshima in 1920. The company changed its name to Toyo Kogyo in 1927 and began making machine tools. Impressed by Ford trucks used in 1923 earthquake-relief efforts Matsuda had the company make a three-wheel motorcycle/truck hybrid in 1931.

During the 1930s the company supplied products to the Sumitomo industrial conglomerate. The Sumitomo Bank became a major shareholder of Toyo Kogyo.

The second Sino-Japanese War forced Toyo Kogyo to make rifles and cut back on its truck production. Although the company built a prototype passenger car in 1940 the outbreak of WWII refocused it on weapons. The August 1945 bombing of Hiroshima killed more than 400 Toyo Kogyo workers but the company persevered producing 10 trucks that December. By 1949 it was turning out 800 per month.

The company launched the first Mazda a two-seat minicar in 1960. The next year Toyo Kogyo licensed AUDI's new rotary engine technology. After releasing a string of models the company became Japan's #3 automaker in 1964. Toyo Kogyo introduced the first Mazda powered by a rotary engine Cosmo/110S in 1967 followed by the Familia in 1968.

The company grew rapidly and began exporting to the US in 1970. However recession high gas prices and concern over the inefficiency of rotary engines halted growth in the mid-1970s. Sumitomo Bank bailed out Toyo Kogyo. The company shifted emphasis back to piston engines but managed to launch the rotary engine RX-7 in 1978.

Ford's need for small-car expertise and Sumitomo's desire for a large partner for its client led to Ford's purchase of 25% of Toyo Kogyo in 1979. The company's early 1980s GLC/323 and 626 models were sold as Fords in Asia Latin America and the Middle East.

Toyo Kogyo changed its name to Mazda Motor Corporation in 1984. ("Mazda" is loosely derived from Matsuda's name but the carmaker has never discouraged an association with the Zoroastrian god of light Ahura Mazda.) The company opened a US plant in 1985 but a strong yen expensive increases in production capacity and a growing number of models led to increased overhead soaring debt and shrinking margins. By 1988 Mazda had begun to focus on sporty niche cars launching the hot-selling Miata in 1989.

The company faced more problems with the early 1990s recession. In 1992 Mazda introduced a new 626 model. That year Mazda also sold half its interest in its Flat Rock Michigan plant to Ford. As the yen development costs and prices for its cars in the US all rose sales in the US fell. In 1993 Mazda reorganized subsidiary Mazda of America by cutting staff.

Ford sank $481 million into Mazda in 1996 increasing its stake to 33%. That year the Ford-appointed former EVP of Mazda Henry Wallace became Mazda's president making history as the first non-Japanese to head a major Japanese corporation. In 1997 Wallace resigned to become CFO of Ford's European operations and former Ford executive James Miller replaced him. That year Mazda consolidated four US operations into Mazda North American Operations.

Restructuring continued in 1998 as Mazda consolidated some European operations and closed a plant in Thailand. In 1999 Mazda sold its credit division to Ford and its Naldec auto parts unit to Ford's Visteon unit. It announced plans to sell its stake in South Korean carmaker Kia Motors. Later in the year another American Ford's Mark Fields took over as president.

In 2000 Mazda recalled 30000 of that year's MPV minivans to fix a powertrain control module and asked owners of all 2000 MPVs to bring in their vehicles for front-bumper reinforcement. Mazda also announced plans to close about 40% of its North American dealership outlets over the next three years. The following year Mazda completed a program to assume direct control over distribution in some European markets including France Italy Spain and the UK.

In 2007 Mazda opened a new vehicle assembly plant in Nanjing China and also began building its passenger vehicle plant in Thailand. To strengthen its sales in Japan the company introduced the Mazda Advantage Loan in 2007 in cooperation with PRIMUS Financial Services. Mazda acquired a 40% stake in PRIMUS in March 2008 to strengthen its auto financing business.

Ford's 33% stake in the company was reduced to about 13% in 2008 after the cash-starved company sold off approximately 20% of its holdings. A consortium of Hiroshima Bank Panasonic (both Mazda business partners) and Mazda itself paid a combined sum of about $540 million to bring control of the company back to Japan.

EXECUTIVES

EVP, Akira Marumoto
Managing Executive Officer; President and CEO Mazda Motor Manufacturing de M ©xico, Keishi (Keith) Egawa
Senior Managing Executive Officer, Nobuhide Inamoto
Managing Executive Officer; President and CEO Mazda Motor of America, James J. (Jim) O'Sullivan
Executive Officer Strategic Review Project, Jeffrey H. Guyton
Executive Officer; General Manager Hofu Plant, Masamichi Kogai
Senior Managing Executive Officer; COO Europe Asia & Oceania Middle East Africa and New and Emerging Markets, Yuji Nakamine
Senior Managing Executive Officer, Koji Kurosawa
Senior Managing Executive Officer, Yuji Harada
Managing Executive Officer, Masahiro Moro
Managing Executive Officer, Takashi Furutama
Managing Executive Officer; President Mazda Engineering & Technology, Takahisa Sori
Executive Officer Domestic Sales General Manager Domestic Sales Division and President Mazda Chuhan Co. Ltd., Kazuyuki Fukuhara
Executive Officer New Emergin Market Operation (excepting Latin America); President Mazda South East Asia Ltd., Hiroshi Inoue
Managing Executive Officer Research and Development, Seita Kanai
Auditors: KPMG AZSA LLC

LOCATIONS

HQ: Mazda Motor Corp. (Japan)
3-1 Shinchi, Fuchu-cho, Aki-gun, Hiroshima 730-8670
Phone: (81) 82 282 1111
Web: www.mazda.co.jp

2014 Sales

	% of total
North America	31
Japan	24
Europe	20
Other regions	25
Total	**100**

PRODUCTS/OPERATIONS

Selected Models
B-Series (
E-Series (vans and commercial vehicles)
CX-7 (cros
CX-9 (cros
Mazda 2 (Demio)
Mazda 3 (Axela hatchback sedan)
Mazda 5 (P
Mazda 6 (s
Mazda 8 (MPV)
Mazda Bian
Mazda Tribute
MX-5 Miata
RX-8 (spor
Tribute (S

Selected Subsidiaries and Affiliates
Mazda Australia Pty. Ltd.
Mazda Motor Logistics Europe NV (Belgium)
Mazda Motor of America Inc.

COMPETITORS

BMW	Isuzu
Daimler	Kia Motors
FCA US	Nissan
Fiat Chrysler	Peugeot
Ford Motor	Renault
Fuji Heavy Industries	Suzuki Motor
General Motors	Toyota
Honda	Volkswagen

HISTORICAL FINANCIALS

Company Type: Public

Income Statement FYE: March 31

	REVENUE ($ mil.)	NET INCOME ($ mil.)	NET PROFIT MARGIN	EMPLOYEES
03/15	25,286	1,323	5.2%	44,035
03/14	26,082	1,314	5.0%	40,892
03/13	23,437	364	1.6%	37,745
03/12	24,784	(1,313)	—	37,617
03/11	28,085	(725)	—	38,117
Annual Growth	(2.6%)	—	—	3.7%

2015 Year-End Financials

Debt ratio: 0.2%
Return on equity: 20.7%
Cash ($ mil.): 3,149
Current ratio: 1.45
Long-term debt ($ mil.): 4,069
No. of shares (mil.): 597
Dividends
Yield: 0.2%
Payout: —
Market value ($ mil.): 6,068

	STOCK PRICE ($) FY Close	P/E High/Low	PER SHARE ($) Earnings	Dividends	Book Value
03/15	10.15	— —	2.21	0.02	12.43
03/14	44.50	— —	2.20	0.00	10.97
03/13	29.99	— —	0.61	0.00	9.12
03/12	17.50	— —	(3.52)	0.00	9.67
03/11	21.06	— —	(2.05)	0.00	14.69
Annual Growth	(16.7%)	— —	—	—	(4.1%)

Mediobanca Banca Di Credito Finanziario SpA

There's not much room for mediocrity at Mediobanca. A leading Italian investment bank the firm offers underwriting M&A support wholesale banking and financial advisory to corporate clients worldwide. It also offers retail banking private banking factoring credit management and leasing services. Despite being known as a top investment bank nearly 50% of Mediobanca's revenue comes from its Retail and Consumer Banking businesses which include Compass Futuro Compass RE Creditech and CheBanca! About 40% of its revenue comes from its Corporate and Investment Banking division. Mediobanca's international offices are in Frankfurt Istanbul London Madrid Mexico City New York and Paris.

Operations

Mediobanca operates four divisions. The bank's Retail and Consumer Banking (RCB) business (which made up 48% of its total revenue during fiscal 2015 ended June 30 2015) counts its consumer credit and retail banking business which includes Compass Futuro Compass RE Creditech and CheBanca! Mediobanca's Corporate and Investment Banking (CIB) division (37% of revenue) consists of the Wholesale Banking (WSB) unit which includes lending structured finance and investment banking; as well as the Private Banking (PB) unit which counts Compagnie Monegasque de Banque Spafid and Prudentia and 50% of Banca Esperia pro rata. The Principal Investing (PI) division (12% of revenue) mostly counts the bank's 13% equity stake in Assicurazioni Generali. The Corporate division (3% of revenue) houses other businesses including the leasing business.Broadly speaking about 75% of Mediobanca's revenue came from interest and similar income (about three-fourths of which came from retail loans) in FY2015 while about 15% came from fee and commission income. Around 47% of its 30 billion loan book was tied to RCB loans while about 44% was tied to CIB loans.Geographic ReachMediobanca generates most of its business in Italy though it operates international branches and subsidiary offices in Frankfurt Istanbul London Madrid Mexico City New York and Paris. About 80% of its banking revenue came from Italy during FY2015 while 20% came from other parts of Europe. Around 55% of its wholesale banking revenue came from Italy that year while 24% came from the UK and another 16% was split between Germany France and Spain.Sales and MarketingAbout 48% of Mediobanca's revenue came from consumer finance and retail clients in FY2015 while 31% came from wholesale banking clients and 12% came from principal investing clients.Financial PerformanceNote: Growth rates may differ after conversion to US dollars. This analysis uses financials from the company's annual report.Mediobanca's annual revenues and profits have been growing over the past few years with revenue growing more than 25% since fiscal 2013 (ended June). The bank's revenue jumped 12% to 2.05 billion ($2.27 billion) during FY2015 while net profit rose 27% to 590 million ($654.57 million).

Stategy

Mediobanca plans to continue building its capital-light fee-generating businesses to boost its overall profitability. Indeed during FY2015 the bank generated 47% of its before-tax profit from its Corporate and Investment Banking (CIB) division despite it making up 37% of its revenue. By comparison Mediobanca's interest-focused Retail and Consumer Banking (RCB) division generated nearly half of the group's revenue but only 17% of its profit. Mergers and AcquisitionsIn August 2015 Mediobanca agreed to buy a 51% majority interest in London-based credit asset manager and advisory firm Cairn Capital Group. The move would continue to build on Mediobanca's international Alternative Asset Management business which involves strategic partnerships with asset managers with strong track records "high quality" management teams and scalable platforms.

HISTORY

Company BackgroundIn 1946 the three Italian "banks of national interest" Banca Commerciale Italiana (Comit) Credito Italiano (now Unicredito Italiano) and Banco di Roma (now part of Banca di Roma) founded Mediobanca to offer medium-term credit a market they were barred from.

Enrico Cuccia was with Comit at the time Mediobanca was formed and moved over to head the new institution. In 1955 he created the shareholder structure that later caused a twin uproar in Italian banking and politics: Although the state owned well more than half of the bank's shares a group of wealthy shareholders who together owned less than 10% of the bank wielded the power.

Over the next several decades Cuccia and Mediobanca operated on the behalf of these powerful shareholders and their family businesses devising deals on terms that other companies could not get. Mediobanca also created a web of cross-holdings in other banks which made money for the bank by selling its funds and other services.

In the 1960s and 1970s the bank was at the center of a number of deals not all of which were stellar successes. The bank engineered a merger between Pirelli and Dunlop which fizzled and also pushed the merger of chemical companies Montecatini and Edison into Montedison which took a beating in the marketplace.

In 1982 Cuccia ostensibly retired taking the title of honorary chairman. However his influence never waned and the 1980s brought a war for the soul of Italian business. In 1985 Romano Prodi head of IRI the state-run organization (liquidated in 2000) that owned nearly 60% of the bank planned to privatize the bank. Instead the noble wing came up with its own privatization plan: The private shareholders requested that the state bring its stake in Mediobanca to below 50% by selling some of its shares to the Mediobanca cabal. In 1988 the privatization went through but as part of the pact it was stipulated that the new shareholders would share decision-making powers with the Ala Nobile.

If the 1980s were wild the 1990s were out of control. Italy's banking industry hampered by red tape and old alliances was left behind the rest of Europe. Many of Italy's banks became stock companies when banking laws changed and many merged to compete in the European Union. Many of those deals threatened Mediobanca's hegemony so it tried to block them. The bank nixed Unicredito's 1998 bid for Comit (which instead merged with Banca Intesa) as well as Sanpaolo IMI's 1999 offer for Banca di Roma.

In 2000 the bank still keeping a grip on the wheels of finance orchestrated investment firm Compart's buyout of Montedison (the merged entity took the Montedison name). That year the company launched an online private banking joint venture with Banca Mediolanum.

Also in 2000 its 46-year relationship with Lazard ended when the international investment banker announced plans to sell back to Mediobanca its 4% stake in the company along with its nearly 5% stake in Assicurazioni Generali.

After Cuccia's death in 2000 successor Vincenzo Maranghi battled such controlling shareholders as the Agnelli and Pirelli families and Deutsche Bank over the bank's future. These shareholders wanted to bring Mediobanca into the modern world by possibly merging it with another top Italian bank or even separating its investment management operations from its investment banking which generates a large majority of Mediobanca's profits.

However in a bid to stick to the old ways Maranghi arranged for backing (in exchange for a small stake in Mediobanca) from Swiss Life. Maranghi was blamed in part for the bank's decline: He forced out some of the investment banking division's top talent in the late 1990s and eventually resigned in 2003

Despite efforts to become more open some of the mystery surrounding Mediobanca remains. The shareholder dispute erupted after the death of Cuccia (whose body was subsequently robbed from its grave and later found).

Maranghi's replacement Gabriele Galateri di Genola had his work cut out for him repairing cracks in Mediobanca's image but he saw profits rise considerably. Under his watch the group has made its first foray into operations abroad opening an office in Paris. By 2004 the company posted improved financial results for a second consecutive year including a 20% increase in investment banking fees.

Galateri di Genola resigned from Mediobanca in 2007 after he lost the support of the supervisory board. He was succeeded by Alberto Nagel the company's general manager.

EXECUTIVES

President Titolare, RENATO PAGLIARO
Amministratore Delegato, ALBERTO NAGEL
Vice Presidente, MARCO TRONCHETTI PROVERA
Vice Presidente, MAURIZIA ANGELO COMNENO
Consigliere, MARIE BOLLORE'
Consigliere, GILBERTO BENETTON
Consigliere, ALEXANDRA YOUNG
Consigliere, MAURIZIO COSTA
Consigliere, VANESSA FRANCOISE MARIE LABERENNE
Consigliere, FRANCESCO SAVERIO VINCI
Auditors: PricewaterhouseCoopers S.p.A.

LOCATIONS

HQ: Mediobanca Banca Di Credito Finanziario SpA
Piazzetta Enrico Cuccia 1, Milan 20121
Phone: (39) 02 8829 1 **Fax:** (39) 02 882 9367
Web: www.mediobanca.it

PRODUCTS/OPERATIONS

2015 Sales

	% of total
Retail and consumer banking	50
Corporate and private banking	32
Principal investing	15
Corporate center	3
Total	**100**

COMPETITORS

Banca Carige
Banca Popolare di Milano
Banco di Desio
CREDEM
Credit Suisse
Deutsche Bank
Gemina
Goldman Sachs
Interbanca
Intesa Sanpaolo
Lazard
Morgan Stanley
UBS Investment Bank
UniCredit
Vontobel

HISTORICAL FINANCIALS

Company Type: Public

Income Statement

FYE: June 30

	ASSETS ($ mil.)	NET INCOME ($ mil.)	INCOME AS % OF ASSETS	EMPLOYEES
06/15	79,005	658	0.8%	3,790
06/14	96,213	634	0.7%	3,688
06/13	95,201	(235)	—	3,673
06/12	99,026	101	0.1%	3,652
06/11	109,031	533	0.5%	3,571
Annual Growth	(7.7%)	5.4%	—	1.5%

2015 Year-End Financials

Return on assets: 0.8%
Return on equity: 7.0%
Long-term debt ($ mil.): —
No. of shares (mil.): 867
Sales ($ mil): 3,409
Dividends
Yield: 0.0%
Payout: 14.5%
Market value ($ mil.): 6,686

	STOCK PRICE ($) FY Close	P/E High/Low	PER SHARE ($) Earnings	Dividends	Book Value
06/15	7.71	11 11	0.75	0.11	11.42
06/14	5.31	— —	0.72	0.00	12.83
06/13	5.31	— —	(0.26)	0.04	10.76
06/12	3.50	58 36	0.11	0.00	9.85
Annual Growth	30.1%	— —	60.3%	—	3.8%

Medipal Holdings Corp.

In Japan Medipal Holdings keeps drug and household products retailers well-stocked. Its primary business is the wholesale distribution of prescription and OTC pharmaceuticals medical supplies cosmetics and personal sundries. In addition to supplying some 300000 Japanese pharmacies and retail stores Medipal distributes to hospitals and provides information technology support to its customers through its numerous subsidiaries and affiliates including Mediceo Everlth Atol and Paltac. Its MP Agro subsidiary distributes animal health products.

Operations

Medipal's Animal Health Products Wholesale business sells animal health products raw materials for processing food and food additives.

Geographic Reach

The company operates from more than 300 bases in Japan.

Sales and Marketing

Medipal has more than 4000 sales representatives working nationwide.

Financial Performance

Medipal has experienced rising revenues over the past few years but saw a 3% decline in revenue to ¥2.9 trillion in fiscal 2015 (ended March) as all segments —Prescription Pharmaceutical Wholesale; Cosmetics Daily Necessities and OTC Pharmaceutical Wholesale; and Animal Health Products Wholesale —slipped. Net income decreased 7% to ¥23 billion due to the lower revenue and lower non-operating income such as research fee earnings.

However the company reported an operating cash inflow of ¥80 billion in fiscal 2015 (versus an outflow in 2014) due to changes in notes and accounts receivable.

Strategy

Medipal is focused on marketing of new prescription products as well as niche prescription offerings including subsidized vaccines and lifestyle disease drugs. In addition it is investing in R&D firms to contribute to the development of new pharmaceuticals with the condition that it receives an option to exclusively market the drugs if they gain regulatory approval. The company is also adding new services for retail cosmetic and OTC outlets such as point-of-sale marketing tools.

The company is also investing in its distribution infrastructure including in the area of disaster readiness so that stock-outs are prevented.

Company Background

Medipal was formed when Mediceo Holdings took over household products distributor Paltac in 2005. Paltac brought with it a distribution network and logistical prowess which allowed the new firm to move further into the OTC and non-drugs business. Previously Mediceo Holdings become Japan's largest drug wholesaler in 2004 when it was formed through the merger of three smaller drug wholesalers (Kuraya Pharmaceuticals Sanseido and Tokyo Iyakuhin).

EXECUTIVES

Director and General Manager Sales Division; President and Chief Executive Director KURAYA SANSEIDO, Shuichi Watanabe
Managing Executive Officer, Toshio Hirasawa
Director, Takuro Hasegawa
Director, Kazushi Takao
Executive Officer; Deputy Chief Director of System, Kazuki Kakutani
President of Subsidiary; Director, Koji Orime

Executive Officer; Deputy Chief Director of Business Development, Kuniaki Imagawa
Executive Officer, Masanori Kawara
President of Subsidiary; Director, Yasuhiro Chofuku
Auditors: KPMG AZSA LLC

LOCATIONS

HQ: Medipal Holdings Corp.
2-7-15 Yaesu, Chuo-ku, Tokyo 104-8461
Phone: (81) 3 3517 5800 **Fax:** (81) 3 3517 5811
Web: www.medipal.co.jp

PRODUCTS/OPERATIONS

2015 Sales

	% of toal
Prescription Pharmaceutical Wholesale	71
Cosmetics Daily Necessities and OTC Pharmaceutical Wholesale	28
Animal Health Products Wholesale	1
Total	0 100

Selected Divisions and Brands

Atol Co.
Butsuryu 24
Everlth Co.
Kuraya (USA)
Mediceo
M.I.C. (Medical Information College)
MM Corporation
MP Agro
Paltac
Tokimo Co.
Trim Co.

COMPETITORS

Alfresa
Suzuken
Toho Pharmaceutical

HISTORICAL FINANCIALS

Company Type: Public

Income Statement FYE: March 31

	REVENUE ($ mil.)	NET INCOME ($ mil.)	NET PROFIT MARGIN	EMPLOYEES
03/15	23,945	197	0.8%	10,930
03/14	28,558	246	0.9%	10,930
03/13	29,874	198	0.7%	11,115
03/12	33,527	142	0.4%	11,194
03/11	32,157	20	0.1%	11,661
Annual Growth	(7.1%)	76.0%	—	(1.6%)

2015 Year-End Financials

Debt ratio: 0.0%
Return on equity: 6.4%
Cash ($ mil.): 1,513
Current ratio: 1.16
Long-term debt ($ mil.): 41
No. of shares (mil.): 226
Dividends
Yield: —
Payout: —
Market value ($ mil.): 2,541

	STOCK PRICE ($) FY Close	P/E High/Low		PER SHARE ($) Earnings	Dividends	Book Value
03/15	11.23	—	—	0.87	0.00	16.85
03/14	14.94	—	—	1.09	0.00	17.47
03/13	12.21	—	—	0.87	0.00	18.01
03/12	12.43	—	—	0.60	0.00	18.51
03/11	8.60	—	—	0.09	0.00	17.56
Annual Growth	6.9%	—	—	77.6%	—	(1.0%)

Medtronic PLC

LOCATIONS

HQ: Medtronic PLC
20 On Hatch, Lower Hatch Street, Dublin 55432
Phone: (353) 1 438 1700
Web: www.medtronic.com

HISTORICAL FINANCIALS

Company Type: Public

Income Statement FYE: April 24

	REVENUE ($ mil.)	NET INCOME ($ mil.)	NET PROFIT MARGIN	EMPLOYEES
04/15	20,261	2,675	13.2%	92,000
04/14	17,005	3,065	18.0%	49,247
04/13	16,590	3,467	20.9%	46,659
04/12	16,184	3,617	22.3%	44,944
04/11	15,933	3,096	19.4%	45,000
Annual Growth	6.2%	(3.6%)	—	19.6%

2015 Year-End Financials

Debt ratio: 33.9%
Return on equity: 7.3%
Cash ($ mil.): 4,843
Current ratio: 3.36
Long-term debt ($ mil.): 33,752
No. of shares (mil.): 1,421
Dividends
Yield: 0.3%
Payout: 10.5%
Market value ($ mil.): —

Mega International Commercial Bank Co Ltd

EXECUTIVES

President, Yu Tsai Tsai
Auditors: PricewaterhouseCoopers, Taiwan

LOCATIONS

HQ: Mega International Commercial Bank Co Ltd
No. 100, Chi-lin Road, Taipei 10424
Phone: (886) 2 2563 3156 **Fax:** (886) 2 2356 8936
Web: www.megabank.com.tw

HISTORICAL FINANCIALS

Company Type: Public

Income Statement FYE: December 31

	ASSETS ($ mil.)	NET INCOME ($ mil.)	INCOME AS % OF ASSETS	EMPLOYEES
12/14	93,953	820	0.9%	5,600
12/13	94,550	630	0.7%	5,542
12/12	84,186	654	0.8%	5,471
12/11	76,711	495	0.6%	5,803
12/10	76,068	383	0.5%	5,608
Annual Growth	5.4%	20.9%	—	(0.0%)

2014 Year-End Financials

Return on assets: 0.9%
Return on equity: 12.3%
Long-term debt ($ mil.): —
No. of shares (mil.): —
Sales ($ mil): 2,189
Dividends
Yield: —
Payout: —
Market value ($ mil.): —

Meiji Yasuda Life Insurance Co.

Meiji Yasuda Life Insurance knows the value of life. The company one of Japan's largest life insurers offers individual life and annuities group life and pensions and investment products. It also has some general insurance health care and investment and financial services operations. Meiji Yasuda provides its products to a range of customers including individuals small businesses and corporations. The company has about ¥204 billion of life insurance policies in force and some 6.6 million policy holders. While most of its operations are in Japan Meiji Yasuda operates in Asia Europe and North America.

Operations

The company's operating segments include Individual Insurance Marketing Group Insurance Marketing General Agent Marketing and Asset Management.

Geographic Reach

Meiji Yasuda is headquartered in Tokyo. It also has about 75 regional offices 20 marketing centers and some 1000 agency locations. It has international affiliate locations in 10 global cities: Beijing Frankfurt Hong Kong Honolulu London Los Angeles New York Seoul Shanghai and Warsaw.

Sales and Marketing

The company sells its products through an internal sales force of about 30000 personnel. It makes some sales to banks and other financial institutions through general agents.

Financial Performance

Meiji Yasuda reported a 1% revenue increase to ¥4781 billion (about $46 billion) in 2013 due to higher interest and dividends on investment securities as well as gains on securities sold and redeemed. Net income increase 2% to ¥240 billion that year as a result of the higher earnings and lower claims paid.

Cash flow from operations slipped 11% to ¥1138 billion in 2013 due to changes in noninvestment assets and an increase in reinsurance accounts payable.

Strategy

Meiji Yasuda is especially focused on growth in international markets. Through a partnership with Talanx for instance the company is investing in the German insurance market. It has also expanded its operations in countries including Poland Indonesia and China through partnerships and by investing in minority ownership of global insurance entities. In the US the company is buying StanCorp Financial Group for $5 billion. That company will be Meiji Yasuda's primary US unit.

In addition Meiji Yasuda works to expand its domestic life insurance business as well as on entering other health related markets in Japan such as the nursing home business. In 2013 the company introduced an educational endowment insurance product to help customers prepare for educational expenses; it also launched bicycle insurance and medical insurance for child dependents (including hospitalization coverage).

Also in 2013 Meiji Yasuda introduced its Meister Mobile tablet terminals designed to make the application process easier and faster.

Other strategies include increasing risk management efforts across the company's operations to strengthen its finances and its capital base.

Mergers and Acquisitions

To take advantage of the growing Indonesian life insurance market Meiji Yasuda bumped up its stake in Indonesian partner PT Avrist Assurance from 23% to nearly 30% in 2013.

Company Background

Tracing its roots back to 1881 Meiji Yasuda in its current incarnation was formed through the merger of Meiji Life Insurance and Yasuda Mutual Life in 2004. Prior to their merger Meiji Life and Yasuda Mutual Life were part of the Mitsubishi Group and Mizuho Financial Group respectively.

EXECUTIVES

President, Akio Negishi
Senior Managing Executive Officers, Yasushi Wada
Chief General Manager Tokyo Marketing Headquarters, Katsunari Maeda
Senior Managing Executive Officers, Hiroshi Tokuoka
Chief Executive Investment, Toshihiko Yamashita
Chief Executive Individual Insurance Marketing, Takashi Ito
Chief Executive General Agent Marketing, Tatsuo Ogoshi
Managing Executive Officers, Hiromasa Suzuki
Managing Executive Officers, Masahiro Ifuku
Managing Executive Officers, Kikuo Asano
Chief Executive Group Marketing, Akio Sakai
Managing Executive Officers, Masahiko Sagara
Managing Executive Officers, Shigeru Kawamoto
Chief General Manager Nagoya Marketing Headquarters, Kazuhito Nakakuma
Managing Executive Officers, Tadashi Onishi
General Manager Product Development Department, Shinya Makino
General Manager Agency Department, Takashi Tsunematsu
General Manager Corporate Market Development Department, Tetsuo Maejima
Chief General Manager Osaka Marketing Headquarters, Takashi Kikugawa
General Manager General Agent Channel Department, Yasuyuki Ayai
General Manager International Business Department, Kazunori Yamauchi
Chairman of the Board, Nobuya Suzuki

LOCATIONS

HQ: Meiji Yasuda Life Insurance Co.
2-1-1 Marunouchi, Chiyoda-ku, Tokyo 100-0005
Phone: (81) 3 3283 8293 **Fax:** (81) 3 3215 8123
Web: www.meijiyasuda.co.jp

PRODUCTS/OPERATIONS

Selected Subsidiaries

Meiji Yasuda America Incorporated
Meiji Yasuda Asia Limited
Meiji Yasuda Europe Limited
Meiji Yasuda Realty USA Incorporated
Pacific Guardian Life Insurance Company Limited
Pacific Guardian Life Insurance Company Limited

COMPETITORS

AXA Life Insurance
American Life Insurance
Asahi Mutual Life
Dai-ichi Life
Daido Life
Fukoku Mutual
Gibraltar Life Insurance
Mitsui Life
Nippon Life Insurance
Prudential
Samsung Life Insurance
Sumitomo Life
T&D Holdings
Taiyo Life
Tokio Marine

HISTORICAL FINANCIALS

Company Type: Public

Income Statement FYE: March 31

	REVENUE ($ mil.)	NET INCOME ($ mil.)	NET PROFIT MARGIN	EMPLOYEES
03/15	37,189	2,212	5.9%	40,793
03/14	44,758	2,331	5.2%	37,129
03/13	48,296	2,515	5.2%	0
03/12	71,958	2,105	2.9%	0
03/11	55,968	1,586	2.8%	0
Annual Growth	(9.7%)	8.7%	—	—

2015 Year-End Financials

Debt ratio: —
Return on equity: 7.5%
Cash ($ mil.): 2,000
Current ratio: 1,033.07
Long-term debt ($ mil.): —
No. of shares (mil.): —
Dividends
Yield: —
Payout: —
Market value ($ mil.): —

Metallurgical Corp China Ltd

EXECUTIVES

Chairman, Heting Shen
Auditors: PricewaterhouseCoopers Zhong Tian CPAs Limited Company

LOCATIONS

HQ: Metallurgical Corp China Ltd
MCC Tower, 28 Shuguang Xili, Chaoyang District, Beijing 100028
Phone: (86) 10 59868666 **Fax:** (86) 10 59868999
Web: www.mccchina.com

HISTORICAL FINANCIALS

Company Type: Public

Income Statement FYE: December 31

	REVENUE ($ mil.)	NET INCOME ($ mil.)	NET PROFIT MARGIN	EMPLOYEES
12/14	34,768	638	1.8%	0
12/13	33,480	492	1.5%	0
12/12	35,468	(1,115)	—	0
12/11	36,496	674	1.8%	127,746
12/10	31,312	807	2.6%	126,987
Annual Growth	2.7%	(5.7%)	—	—

2014 Year-End Financials

Debt ratio: 4.5%
Return on equity: 8.6%
Cash ($ mil.): 5,383
Current ratio: 1.14
Long-term debt ($ mil.): 6,972
No. of shares (mil.): —
Dividends
Yield: —
Payout: —
Market value ($ mil.): —

	STOCK PRICE ($) FY Close	P/E High	P/E Low	PER SHARE ($) Earnings	Dividends	Book Value
12/14	0.00	—	—	0.03	0.00	(0.00)
12/13	3.36	—	—	0.03	0.00	(0.00)
12/12	3.36	—	—	(0.06)	0.00	(0.00)
12/11	4.79	1	1	0.03	0.00	0.40
Annual Growth	—	—	—	(0.8%)	—	—

Metro AG

A ride on this METRO could be a shopper's delight. Germany's über retailer the company ranks fourth in the world (behind Wal-Mart Carrefour and Tesco). METRO owns and operates more than 2200 wholesale stores supermarkets hypermarkets department stores and the fast-growing Media Markt and Saturn consumer electronics chains. More than 930 of its shops are in Germany but METRO also has stores in about 30 other countries including China Egypt France India Russia and Vietnam. Store banners include METRO and Makro Cash & Carry wholesale outlets Real hypermarkets and Galeria Kaufhof department stores. METRO is also launching e-commerce platforms for each of its retail businesses.

Operations

The German retail group comprises five units: Metro Cash & Carry self-service wholesale stores (about half of revenue); Media Markt Saturn and Redcoon consumer electronics stores; Real hypermarkets; Galeria Kaufhof department stores in Germany and Belgium; and METRO Properties the group's international real estate arm with properties in about 30 countries. METRO Cash & Carry and Makro wholesale outlets which sell food and other grocery and non-grocery items to businesses and institutional customers account for nearly 50% of group sales while Media-Saturn is Europe's #1 seller of consumer electronics with about 985 locations in 15 countries. With about 140 department stores Galeria Kaufhof is a leading Germany department store chain. Real operates about 425 hypermarkets mostly in Germany but also in Eastern Europe including Poland and Romania.

Geographic Reach

Germany is METRO AG's largest market accounting for about a quarter of sales. About 25 other countries in Western and Eastern Europe account for another quarter while Asia and Africa (4%) and a blanket International category (37%) make up the rest.

Financial Performance

Euro zone currency and debt woes have negatively impacted METRO AG's operations over the years causing fluctuations in revenue and net income. In fiscal 2014 revenue was 63 billion or about 4% lower than the previous year. A "very negative" currency environment the disposal of some assets and generally lower sales all contributed to the result. A decrease in selling and in interest expenses lead to a 162 gain in net income from a net loss the previous year.

Strategy

METRO AG is focused on growth - of products number of stores and the bottom line. To that end it has been working to streamline its organization and use technology to introduce new products and services. The company is also interested in expanding outside its home market particularly by opening new stores in locations where it already has a foothold namely Brazil Russia India and

China. In 2014 it invested more than 1200 million in modernizing and refurbishing stores as well as purchasing real estate for its Galeria Kaufhof unit.

HISTORY

Otto Beisheim founded METRO SB-Grossmarkte in the German town of Mulheim in 1964. A wholesale business serving commercial customers it operated under the name METRO Cash & Carry. Three years later Beisheim received backing from the owners of Franz Haniel & Cie (an industrial company founded in 1756) and members of the Schmidt-Ruthenbeck family (also in wholesaling). This allowed METRO to expand rapidly in Germany and in 1968 into the Netherlands under the name Makro Cash & Carry via a partnership with Steenkolen Handelsvereeniging (SHV). During the 1970s the company expanded its wholesaling operations within Europe and moved into retailing.

METRO's foray into retailing was aided during the next decade by the acquisition of department store chain Kaufhof AG. By the 1980s the rise of specialty stores had many department stores on the defensive and Kaufhof's owners sold it to METRO and its investment partner Union Bank of Switzerland.

As METRO's ownership interest in Kaufhof rose above 50% the chain began converting some of its stores from department stores into fashion and sporting goods sellers. Kaufhof began acquiring a stake in computer manufacturer and retailer Vobis in 1989. In 1993 METRO now operating as METRO Holding AG acquired a majority interest in supermarket company Asko Deutsche Kaufhaus which owned the Praktiker building materials chain. The reclusive Beisheim retired from active management the following year.

To cut costs and prepare for expansion into Asia in 1996 METRO Holding merged its German retail holdings –Kaufhof; Asko; another grocery operation Deutsche SB Kauf; and its German cash-and-carry operations –into one holding company METRO AG.

EXECUTIVES

Chairman, Olaf Koch, age 45
CFO, Mark Frese, age 51
Vice Chairman, Werner Klockhaus, age 55
Chairman, Franz M. Haniel, age 60
Auditors: KPMG AG

LOCATIONS

HQ: Metro AG
Metro-Strafe 1, Duesseldorf 40235
Phone: (49) 211 6886 0 **Fax:** (49) 211 68 86 20 00
Web: www.metrogroup.de

2014 Sales

	% of total
International	37
Germany	25
Western Europe(excl. Germany	19
Europe	15
Asia & Africa	4
Consolidation	-
Total	**100**

2014 Stores

	No.
Western Europe	
Germany	951
Other countries	620
Eastern Europe	498
Asia & Africa	131
Total	**2,200**

PRODUCTS/OPERATIONS

2014 Sales

	% of total
Cash & carry	48
Media-Saturn	33
Real	14
Galeria Kaufhof	5
Other	-
Total	**100**

2014 Stores

	No.
Media Markt & Saturn	986
METRO Cash & Carry	766
Real	311
Galeria Kaufhof	137
Total	**2,200**

Selected Operations

Wholesale Stores
- Makro
- Metro Cash & Carry (wholesale stores)

Food
- Extra (supermarkets)
- Real (hypermarkets)

Nonfood Specialty Stores
- Media Markt (consumer electronics)
- Saturn (consumer electronics)

Department Store
- Galeria Kaufhof

Other Operations
Dinea Gastronomie (restaurants/catering)
METRO MGE Einkauf (purchasing)
METRO MGI Informatik (IT services)
METRO Real Estate Management (construction services)
METRO Werbegesellschaft (advertising)
METRO Online AG (Internet retailer)
MGB METRO Buying Group Hong Kong Ltd.
(purchasing Asia and Non-European Union countries)

COMPETITORS

ALDI
Best Buy
Carrefour
Casino Guichard
Darty
Delhaize
Edeka Zentrale
Lidl
Marktkauf
Maxeda
REWE
Royal Ahold
Tengelmann
Tesco
Wal-Mart

HISTORICAL FINANCIALS

Company Type: Public

Income Statement

FYE: September 30

	REVENUE ($ mil.)	NET INCOME ($ mil.)	NET PROFIT MARGIN	EMPLOYEES
09/15	66,393	753	1.1%	233,962
09/14	79,352	159	0.2%	264,142
09/13*	62,520	(95)	—	278,594
12/12	87,965	3	0.0%	288,107
12/11	86,275	816	0.9%	280,856
Annual Growth	(6.3%)	(2.0%)	—	(4.5%)

*Fiscal year change

2015 Year-End Financials

Debt ratio: 29.8%
Return on equity: 13.2%
Cash ($ mil.): 4,949
Current ratio: 0.92
Long-term debt ($ mil.): 5,304
No. of shares (mil.): 324
Dividends
Yield: 2.4%
Payout: 5.6%
Market value ($ mil.): 1,766

	STOCK PRICE ($) FY Close	P/E High/Low	PER SHARE ($) Earnings	Dividends	Book Value
09/15	5.45	4 2	2.31	0.13	17.92
09/14	6.48	24 16	0.49	0.00	19.37
09/13*	7.98	— —	(0.30)	0.17	21.57
12/12	5.60	832547	0.01	0.23	24.50
12/11	7.81	8 4	2.50	0.22	25.40
Annual Growth	(8.6%)	— —	(1.9%)	(12.3%)	(8.4%)

*Fiscal year change

Minmetals Development Co Ltd

Minmetals Development does the maximum to help China develop. The company works in raw materials and steel trading as well as distribution and logistics. It imports steel iron ore and hulks and exports coal coke billet ferrosilicon ferrosilicomanganese fluorite magnesium ferromolybdenum and carborundum. Through its logistics subsidiaries it is also engaged in international shipping and forwarding storage and warehousing international tendering and bidding. Minmetals also has its hands in luxury hotels high and new technology financing and industrial manufacturing. Minmetals Development is owned by minerals company China Minmetals.

EXECUTIVES

CFO and Finance Manager, Ren Jianhua
Vice Chairman, Feng Guiquan
General Manager, He Jianzeng
Auditors: Ascenda Certified Public Accountants

LOCATIONS

HQ: Minmetals Development Co Ltd
Block B, No. 5, Sanlihe Road, Haidian District, Beijing 100044
Phone: (86) 10 68494205 **Fax:** (86) 10 68494207
Web: www.minlist.com.cn

PRODUCTS/OPERATIONS

Selected Business

Bidding business
Industrial Investment
Logistics business
Metallurgical raw materials supply business
Ferroalloy business
Raw materials business
Steel distribution and products business
Steel & Products Business
Steel distribution business

HISTORICAL FINANCIALS

Company Type: Public

Income Statement FYE: December 31

	REVENUE ($ mil.)	NET INCOME ($ mil.)	NET PROFIT MARGIN	EMPLOYEES
12/14	21,680	33	0.2%	0
12/13	33,574	46	0.1%	0
12/12	23,962	(61)	—	0
12/11	25,745	85	0.3%	8,492
12/10	19,944	58	0.3%	7,861
Annual Growth	2.1%	(12.7%)	—	—

2014 Year-End Financials

Debt ratio: 6.3%
Return on equity: 2.4%
Cash ($ mil.): 311
Current ratio: 1.02
Long-term debt ($ mil.): 714

No. of shares (mil.): —
Dividends
Yield: —
Payout: —
Market value ($ mil.): —

Mitsubishi Chemical Holdings Corp

Mitsubishi Chemical Holdings is the largest chemical manufacturer in Japan. Subsidiary Mitsubishi Chemical Corporation produces a wide variety of petrochemicals specialty chemicals and the like. Another unit Mitsubishi Plastics manufactures plastics and films data storage devices such as CDs and DVDs as well as chemicals for semiconductor manufacturing. Mitsubishi Tanabe Pharma makes pharmaceutical products for central nervous system cardiovascular and gastrointestinal disorders in addition to OTC and anti-inflammatory drugs. Mitsubishi Rayon as its fourth business unit.Mitsubishi Chemical Holdings serves customers in the performance products health care and industrial material markets. Its major products include optical recording media polymer films plastics pharmaceuticals purified terephthalic acid synthetic fibers and a range of polymers. It has more than 340 consolidated subsidiaries and more than 60 affiliated companies.The company has major operations in Australia India North Asia Southeast Asia Europe and the US.In Fiscal 2012 Mitsubishi Chemical Holdings reported a 1% drop in revenues (in local currency) as the company's growth in production was offset by weak economic conditions in Japan (still recovering from the major earthquake in 2011) the appreciation of the yen Europe's economic slowdown and the industrial disruption caused by floods in Thailand. However it posted a 36% drop in net income (in local currency) largely due to higher current and deferred taxes.

In 2010 Mitsubishi Chemical Holdings spent $2.4 billion to purchase Mitsubishi Rayon a manufacturer of monomers and polymers which became the holding company's fourth line of business. It is also the world's #1 maker of methyl methacrylate (a common and versatile plastic also known as MMA) through its 2008 acquisition of Lucite.

Earlier the company merged the former Mitsubishi Pharma with the former Tanabe Seiyaku to form Mitsubishi Tanabe of which it owns about half. In 2008 the company split off its Performance Products segment into a separate operating subsidiary.

Mitsubishi Chemical Holdings was formed in 2005 as the parent of Mitsubishi Chemical Corporation. The company is a subsidiary of Mitsubishi Corporation.

EXECUTIVES

Member of the Board and Managing Executive Officer and Director, Shotaro Yoshimura
Senior Managing Executive Officer, Noboru Tsuda
Executive Officer; General Manager Human Resources Department, Noriyoshi Ohira
Managing Executive Officer, Masanori Karatsu
President and CEO, Hitoshi Ochi
CFO, Kenkichi Kosakai
Chairman, Yoshimitsu Kobayashi
Auditors: Ernst & Young ShinNihon LLC

LOCATIONS

HQ: Mitsubishi Chemical Holdings Corp
1-1-1 Marunouchi, Chiyoda-ku, Tokyo 100-8251
Phone: (81) 3 6748 7115
Web: www.mitsubishichem-hd.co.jp

2014 Sales

	% of total
Japan	69
Other countries	31
Total	**100**

PRODUCTS/OPERATIONS

2014 Sales

	% of total
Chemicals	26
Polymers	25
Designed Materials	23
Health Care	15
Electronics	4
Other	7
Total	**100**

COMPETITORS

Asahi Kasei
Astellas
BASF SE
Bayer AG
Chugai
Daicel Chemical
Daiichi Sankyo
DuPont
Evonik Degussa
Hitachi Chemical
Kyowa Hakko Kirin
Mitsui Chemicals
Nissan Chemical
SABIC Innovative Plastics
Sinopec Group
Sumitomo Chemical
Sumitomo Dainippon Pharma
Takeda Pharmaceutical
Tokai Carbon
Tokuyama

HISTORICAL FINANCIALS

Company Type: Public

Income Statement FYE: March 31

	REVENUE ($ mil.)	NET INCOME ($ mil.)	NET PROFIT MARGIN	EMPLOYEES
03/15	30,474	507	1.7%	68,263
03/14	33,897	312	0.9%	56,031
03/13	32,825	197	0.6%	55,131
03/12	39,109	432	1.1%	53,979
03/11	38,243	1,009	2.6%	53,882
Annual Growth	(5.5%)	(15.8%)	—	6.1%

2015 Year-End Financials

Debt ratio: 0.3%
Return on equity: 6.4%
Cash ($ mil.): 1,968
Current ratio: 1.19
Long-term debt ($ mil.): 7,167

No. of shares (mil.): 1,464
Dividends
Yield: —
Payout: —
Market value ($ mil.): 44,541

	STOCK PRICE ($) FY Close	P/E High	P/E Low	PER SHARE ($) Earnings	PER SHARE ($) Dividends	PER SHARE ($) Book Value
03/15	30.42	—	—	0.34	0.00	9.04
03/14	20.81	—	—	0.21	0.00	8.70
03/13	23.85	—	—	0.13	0.00	8.67
03/12	26.99	—	—	0.28	0.00	9.46
03/11	31.81	—	—	0.65	0.52	9.12
Annual Growth	(1.1%)	—	—	(14.8%)	—	(0.2%)

Mitsubishi Corp

In Japanese mitsubishi means "three diamonds" and Mitsubishi Corporation is one of Japan's crown jewels. The sogo shosha or trading company operates through six main business groups: living essentials (agricultural products food and beverages textiles and construction materials); metals; machinery (power generation equipment electrical systems automobiles); energy (liquefied natural gas crude oil); and chemicals (petrochemicals fertilizers plastics). Its other main business group is industrial finance which handles banking asset management construction and logistics. The company generated most of its fiscal 2012 gross profit from living essentials (42%) metals (24%) and machinery (16%).

Mitsubishi Corporation is part of the Mitsubishi keiretsu a network of affiliated companies that has no official status as a group but within which there is some cross-ownership and considerable business activity. Other affiliates include Mitsubishi Heavy Industries The Bank of Tokyo-Mitsubishi Mitsubishi Electric Mitsubishi Motors and Nikon.

Mitsubishi operates a network of more than 500 group companies in about 90 countries.

Buoyed by higher energy commodity prices and earlier investments in its chemicals segment the company posted an 8% rise in revenues in fiscal 2012. However lower metals income (due in part to a strike which disrupted coal operations in Australia) and lower automobile manufacturing production (due to flooding in Thailand) dragged down Mitsubishi's net income by 2%.

The Sendai earthquake and tsunami in 2011 severely disrupted the Japanese economy and affected Mitsubishi's operations and domestic revenues and net income that year (limited as it occurred late in the fiscal year). Nevertheless Mitsubishi was able to post an overall growth in revenues and net income thanks to a stronger global economy and an increase in demand for steel products and higher oil prices among other factors.

Mitsubishi has set about strengthening its financial position and devised a strategic growth plan that involves focusing on new operational initiatives including new energy sources and on environment and financial services.

Energy plans include the development of biofuels solar and wind energy technologies as industrial emissions-reducing technologies. It is also looking to ramp up its holdings in the global water business to meet growing water infrastructure demand from emerging economies.

On the financial front Mitsubishi is leveraging the group's financial assets and sheer size to facilitate the financing of its own as well as other companies' growth efforts. With its financial services operations the group is targeting real estate development aircraft and other industrial leasing services and it is considering strategic acquisitions of additional financial services assets.

Growing its metals assets in 2011 Mitsubishi acquired nearly 25% of Anglo American Sur a Chile-based copper mining and smelting company owned by Anglo American plc. Anglo American Sur's copper assets include the Los Bronces mine El Soldado mine and Chagres smelter. The purchase is expected to boost Mitsubishi's attributable copper production to 250000 metric tons per year.

To further expand its metals operations Mitsubishi agreed in 2012 to invest about $95 million to acquire a 25% stake in Stillwater Mining's Marathon PGM (platinum group metals) project in Ontario Canada. The project is expected to produce about 200000 ounces of PGMs and 17000 metric tons of copper per year for about 11 1/2 years. Mitsubishi also has the option to purchase up to 100% of the PGM production. PGMs are used in applications such as automobile catalysts electronic devices and fuel cells.

In 2012 Mitsubishi along with Indian fertilizer company Zuari Industries acquired a 30% stake in Fasfatos del Pacifico (FOSPAC) from a Peruvian cement manufacturer Cementos Pacasmayo. Pacasmayo explores for and produces rock phosphate in Peru and the investment will allow the companies to acquire FOSPAC's rock phosphate production (after fulfillment of local demand) for 20 years. The initial production capacity is expected to be about 2.5 million metric tons per year.

That year the company entered the Indonesian geothermal power market through the acquisition of 20% of Star Energy Geothermal Pte Ltd. Mitsubishi is looking to become further involved in geothermal power generation in countries that possess promising geothermal resources including Japan.

Growing another segment in 2013 the company agreed to buy Kirin's Food Science Business.

To raise cash in 2011 Mitsubishi sold its subsidiary Jicoux Datasystems Inc. to NEC Corp. Jicoux offers a fleet management service for commercial vehicles that includes automatic creation of daily reports based on speed route and distance data collected from in-vehicle devices over the internet. NEC plans to absorb the Jicoux's employees and operations and liquidate the company.

Along with the rest of the Mitsubishi companies Mitsubishi Corporation has been hurt by Japan's persistent economic stagnation. The company has restructured and reduced its workforce in the past decade and it has divided the operations of its former information technology and electronics business among its other groups.

HISTORY

Yataro Iwasaki's close ties to the Japanese government (along with subsidies and monopoly rights) ensured the success of his shipping and trading company Mitsubishi. Founded in 1870 Mitsubishi diversified into mining (1873) banking (1885) and shipbuilding (1887); it began to withdraw from shipping in the 1880s. During the next decade it invested in Japanese railroads and property.

In 1918 the Mitsubishi zaibatsu (conglomerate) spun off its central management arm Mitsubishi Trading (the forerunner of Mitsubishi Corporation). By WWII the group was a huge amalgam of divisions and public companies. During the war it made warplanes ships explosives and beer.

The zaibatsu were dissolved by US occupation forces and Mitsubishi was split into 139 entities. After the occupation the Japanese government encouraged many of the former business groups to reunite around the old zaibatsu banks. In 1954 Mitsubishi Trading became the leader of the Mitsubishi Group and established Mitsubishi International (US) which became a leading exporter of US goods.

The 1964 merger of three Mitsubishi companies created Mitsubishi Heavy Industries a top Japanese maker of ships aircraft plants and heavy machinery. Mitsubishi Kasei separated from Asahi Glass and Mitsubishi Rayon by a US fiat became Japan's #1 chemical concern. Mitsubishi Electric emerged as one of the country's leading electrical equipment and electronics manufacturers. In 1971 Chrysler invested in Mitsubishi Motors which began making cars for the US automaker. That year Mitsubishi Trading was renamed Mitsubishi Corporation.

Through the 1980s Japan seemed economically invincible. Then its "bubble economy" burst. The group fell behind in electronics and autos in the US consumer demand dried up at home and Mitsubishi Bank was left with a heavy burden of bad loans. Group members which traditionally provided materials supplies and sales outlets for each other began loosening old keiretsu ties during Japan's recession of the 1990s.

In 1993 Chrysler sold its stock in Mitsubishi Motors and two years later the companies severed production ties. This loss and declining demand in the US for Mitsubishi cars hurt auto sales.

Mitsubishi Bank merged with Bank of Tokyo in 1996 to form the biggest bank in the world The Bank of Tokyo-Mitsubishi (BTM). In 1997 several Mitsubishi companies admitted paying off a corporate racketeer setting off a wave of executive resignations.

By 1999 BTM had tumbled from the top spot and was unable to keep the money freely flowing to fellow Mitsubishi members.

Hit hard by the Asian economic crisis all the struggling Mitsubishi companies had to look outside of the keiretsu for help. In 1999 Mitsubishi Motors found a foreign partner Volvo for its truck making operations. Mitsubishi Oil merged with an outsider Nippon Oil to form Nippon Mitsubishi Oil (later renamed Nippon Oil). In 2000 Daimler-Chrysler (now Chrysler and Daimler) acquired a controlling stake in Mitsubishi Motors for $2.1 billion.

Executives at Mitsubishi Motors were charged in 2001 after they allegedly kept the lid on thousands of reported defects in Mitsubishi cars instead of issuing recalls. Stung by this and the after-effects of scandals from the previous decade Mitsubishi unveiled a new corporate philosophy as part of a strategy to revive the group's reputation.

In 2003 Mitsubishi disbanded its information technology and electronics business unit. The unit's operations were divided between the new business and machinery groups. In 2004 the company formed an alliance with GE Yokogawa Medical Systems (GEYMS) to provide GEYMS with help in developing its presence in the Japanese diagnostic imaging market.

In 2004 the company formed a food distribution joint venture with five Japanese food wholesalers comprising national wholesaler Meidi-ya and four regional companies. The joint venture called Alliance Network became one of Japan's largest food wholesalers. Mitsubishi had a 51% stake in Alliance Network. Later in 2004 Mitsubishi acquired the food beverage additive and pharmaceutical active and excipient businesses of Ashland Distribution.

In 2006 Mitsubishi bolstered its automotive operations when it acquired shares in Isuzu from General Motors; Mitsubishi ended up with a 10% stake in Isuzu. Mitsubishi and Isuzu soon after formed a European joint venture to market light-duty trucks throughout the continent. Later that year Mitsubishi bought the Avon Automotive subsidiary of Avon Rubber in a deal worth $120 million.

The following year Mitsubishi bought majority control of Nosan Corporation a manufacturer of livestock feed. In late 2007 the company acquired the majority interest in Kentucky Fried Chicken Japan.

On the medical health care front Mitsubishi shifted the focus of certain of its subsidiaries to providing services to hospitals and nursing care facilities. It established the Trinity Healthcare Fund in 2007 to provide management support for the restructuring of hospitals and other medical institutions. Other Mitsubishi subsidiaries focused on medical services include ProCure which is a medical equipment wholesale distributor and Apprecia which provides hospital construction consulting services.

During 2007 the group began investing in energy-related assets as part of this strategy. It acquired nearly 40% of Encore Energy Pte. which in turn owns 51% of Medco Energy an Indonesian oil and gas concern. The deal was valued at about $350 million and gave Mitsubishi a 20% stake in Medco. Mitsubishi was already working with Medco on an Indonesian gas plant and the two companies plan to pursue further international energy partnerships.

In 2009 it entered the solar energy business buying 34% of a subsidiary of Spanish renewable energy firm Acciona SA

Mitsubishi in 2010 it merged subsidiaries Mitsubishi Corporation Unimetals and Mitsubishi Shoji Light Metal Sales Corporation. The resulting company was named Mitsubishi Corporation Unimetals and remained a subsidiary of Mitsubishi. The merger was made to concentrate the company's management expertise in the non-ferrous metals industry.

EXECUTIVES

EVP; Group CEO Industrial Finance Logistics and Development Group, Eiichi Tanabe
EVP; General Manager Nagoya Branch, Ichiro Ando
SEVP, Hideto Nakahara
EVP; Regional CEO Asia and Oceania, Toru Moriyama
EVP; Regional CEO Latin America, Seiji Shiraki
President and CEO, Ken Kobayashi
SEVP and CIO, Hideyuki Nabeshima
SEVP, Jun Yanai
EVP; Group COO Metals Group and Division COO Ferrous Raw Materials Division, Jun Kinukawa
EVP; Group CEO Global Environment and Infrastructure Business Group, Nobuaki Kojima
SEVP, Takahisa Miyauchi
EVP; Regional CEO Middle East and Central Asia, Shigeaki Yoshikawa
EVP; Group CEO Machinery Group, Kozo Shiraji
EVP; President Americas, Yasuyuki Sugiura
EVP and CFO, Shuma Uchino
EVP; Group CEO Business Service Group, Toshimitsu Urabe
EVP; Regional CEO East Asia, Shunichi Matsui
EVP; Group CEO Living Essentials Group, Takehiko Kakiuchi
Chairman, Yorihiko Kojima
Auditors: Deloitte Touche Tohmatsu LLC

LOCATIONS

HQ: Mitsubishi Corp
2-3-1 Marunouchi, Chiyoda-ku, Tokyo 100-8086
Phone: (81) 3 3210 2121
Web: www.mitsubishicorp.com

2014 Sales

	% of total
Japan	71
U.S.A	8
Other countries	21
Total	**100**

2014 Sales

	% of total
Living Essential	31
Energy Business	25
Chemicals	19
Metal	12
Machinery	11
Industrial Finance Logistics & Development	2
Global Environmental & Infrastructure Business	0
Others	0
Total	**100**

PRODUCTS/OPERATIONS

Selected Products and Services

Metals
- Bullion and metals futures
- Fabricated steel structures
- Metallurgical and thermal coal
- Nonferrous metal products
- Nonferrous metals
- Nuclear fuel and components
- Precious metals
- Raw materials for steel
- Semifinished products
- Steel materials
- Specialty steel

Living Essentials
- Apparel
- Canned foods
- Ceramic materials
- Cigarettes
- Coffee beans coffee and beverages
- Confections and snacks
- Contract food services
- Dairy foods and processed foods
- Fabrics
- Feedstuffs
- Fresh and frozen foods
- Grains and agricultural products
- Marine products
- Meat and livestock
- Mineral water
- Oils and fats
- Photosensitized materials
- Pulp paper and packaging materials
- Soft drinks
- Sweeteners
- Textile raw materials
- Textiles for industrial use
- Tires
- Wood wood products and construction materials

Machinery
- Automobiles
- Commercial aviation
- Defense systems and equipment
- Electronics products
- Industrial agricultural construction and other general machinery
- Plant and machinery for power generation electricity oil/gas/chemicals steel/cement and environmental protection
- Project development and construction
- Satellite communications
- Ships
- Space systems
- Transportation systems

Energy
- Carbon materials and products
- Crude oil
- LNG
- LPG
- Orimulsion
- Petroleum products

Industrial Finance Logistics and Development
- Commerce services
- Consumer services
- Financial services
- Logistics

Chemicals
- Fertilizers
- Fine and specialty chemicals
- Inorganic chemicals
- Petrochemicals
- Plastics

COMPETITORS

ITOCHU
Marubeni
Mitsui
Samsung Group
Sime Darby
Sumitomo

HISTORICAL FINANCIALS

Company Type: Public

Income Statement

FYE: March 31

	REVENUE ($ mil.)	NET INCOME ($ mil.)	NET PROFIT MARGIN	EMPLOYEES
03/15	63,923	3,338	5.2%	90,048
03/14	73,970	3,500	4.7%	86,190
03/13	63,435	3,826	6.0%	83,891
03/12	67,851	5,532	8.2%	82,792
03/11	62,879	5,593	8.9%	77,494
Annual Growth	0.4%	(12.1%)	—	3.8%

2015 Year-End Financials

Debt ratio: 0.3%
Return on equity: 7.5%
Cash ($ mil.): 14,379
Current ratio: 1.53
Long-term debt ($ mil.): 40,299
No. of shares (mil.): 1,620
Dividends
Yield: 3.5%
Payout: 63.2%
Market value ($ mil.): 65,535

	STOCK PRICE ($) FY Close	P/E High/Low		PER SHARE ($) Earnings	Dividends	Book Value
03/15	40.45	0	0	2.05	1.42	28.65
03/14	37.12	0	0	2.12	1.19	29.78
03/13	37.53	0	0	2.32	1.24	26.97
03/12	46.76	0	0	3.36	1.74	25.99
03/11	55.33	0	0	3.39	1.08	24.12
Annual Growth	(7.5%)	—	—	(11.9%)	6.9%	4.4%

Mitsubishi Electric Corp.

If it has an "on" switch chances are Mitsubishi Electric makes it or makes a part for it. The company part of the Mitsubishi Corporation operates across five primary sectors: Energy and Electric Systems (power generation plants supervisory systems and escalators); Industrial Automation Systems (programmable controllers measurement and control systems); Home Appliances (air-conditioning systems TVs and Blu-ray disc recorders); Information and Communication Systems (satellites wireless systems and network systems); and Electronic Devices (power devices LCD displays). Mitsubishi Electric has operations in about 40 countries but it earns the majority of its sales from Japan.

Energy and Electric Systems representing 25% of sales which the company terms its social infrastructure business includes building systems with elevators and escalators. The AXIEZ elevator features LED lighting and speed-adjustment technology that reduces waiting time. The segment also installs power plants for operations that range from utility companies to the individual sites of companies seeking in-house power generation.

Industrial Automation Systems making up 23% of sales provides such products as programmable logic controllers under the MELSEC brand; the MELSERVO-J4 used for the manufacturing of semiconductors flat panel display equipment and industrial machinery; no-fuse circuit breakers and earth leakage circuit breakers for wiring protection and short-circuit protection; and electrical discharge machines for the manufacturing of automobiles home electronics and IT-related devices. Home Appliances accounting for 20% of sales includes KIRIGAMINE air conditioners photovoltaic generation heat pumps LED lighting RakuRaku-UD technology that enhances the performance of appliances as well as products that go beyond the domestic market such as digital signage and other visual equipment.

Information and Communication Systems 12% of sales offers services that include information systems monitoring server integration and such products as satellite platforms vehicle-mounted satellite communication equipment broadband optical access systems and digital closed-circuit TV systems. Electronic Devices 5% include products for cutting power losses and power consumption integrated circuits for electric vehicles high-electron mobility transistor amplifiers and LCD modules for high brightness and contrast. The company's Other segment 15% of sales mainly comprises materials procurement and engineering.

Mitsubishi Electric has more than 20 manufacturing plants in Japan as well as factories in other countreis that include China Malaysia Thailand the US and the UK.

Consolidated net sales were flat year-over-year from 2011 to fiscal 2012 falling a fraction of a percentage point. By segment Energy and Electric Systems' net sales were also flat falling likewise a fraction of a percentage point. The segment struggled with falling orders in the Japanese public utility and rolling-stock equipment markets.

Supported by demand in the Asian smartphone and tablet markets as well as the automotive equipment markets in the developing world and North America Industrial Automation Systems' sales headed up about 6% in fiscal 2012 compared with 2011. Home Appliances was down 8% in fiscal 2012 versus 2011 as a result in part of lower demand for photovoltaic systems in Europe and weak demand for hot water supply and induction heating cooking systems.

Thanks in part to large orders for submarine line terminal equipment and demand for communications infrastructure systems integration network and system operations and electronics Information and Communication Systems increased 6% over the period between 2011 and fiscal 2012. Electronic Devices rose 14% in fiscal 2012 versus 2011 to meet a strong demand for power modules in the industrial commercial automotive and railcar markets. The Other segment headed up just a fraction of a percentage point in 2012 versus 2011. During that period the company's net income declined about 10% mainly due to a tax adjustment.

Looking ahead each segment has specific goals for product development. The Energy and Electric Systems segment is focused on research and development to improve rotating machines for generators electric motors switches and transformers transportation systems and elevators and escalators. The segment is also concentrating its R&D efforts on IT for supervision and control power information systems and building management systems.

Industrial Automation Systems is focused on improving motors mechatronics equipment automotive components electric power steering and auto multimedia systems. Information and Communication Systems is emphasizing network systems for telecommunication operators and space systems.

Electronic Devices is tasked with product development in semiconductors while Home Appliances is focused on energy saving recycling universal design and digital imaging systems. The Other segment is focused on work that helps the entire group. This segment's accomplishments include a robot system for bulk components and a multi-band power amplifier.

Each segment has also enjoyed some significant capital expenditures. Energy and Electric Systems received investments for more production capacity. Factory automation systems and automotive equipment operations were the focus for Industrial Automation. Home Appliance spending favored increasing production capacity for air-conditioning equipment. Improving research and development received the most capital expenditure focus in Information and Communication Systems and the Other segment. Electronic Devices concentrated on improvements for its power device operations.

In 2012 Mitsubishi Electric acquired the Messung Group which makes programmable logic controllers and human machine interfaces and had served as a sales and distribution partner in India.

HISTORY

Mitsubishi Electric was among 10 companies fined in 2007 by the European Commission (EC) for allegedly conspiring to fix prices for gas-insulated switchgear industrial equipment used by electric utilities. Along with Fuji Electric Hitachi Toshiba and other Japanese manufacturers the company was accused of colluding with ALSTOM AREVA Schneider Electric and Siemens to reserve European markets for Europe-based manufacturers while European companies generally stayed out of the Japanese market. Mitsubishi Electric was fined a mere E118.5 million ($1 million) for its part in the price-fixing cartel.

Auditors: KPMG AZSA LLC

LOCATIONS

HQ: Mitsubishi Electric Corp.
2-7-3 Marunouchi, Chiyoda-ku, Tokyo 100-8310
Phone: (81) 3 3218 2272
Web: www.mitsubishielectric.co.jp

HISTORICAL FINANCIALS

Company Type: Public

Income Statement FYE: March 31

	REVENUE ($ mil.)	NET INCOME ($ mil.)	NET PROFIT MARGIN	EMPLOYEES
03/15	36,031	1,956	5.4%	129,249
03/14	39,279	1,486	3.8%	124,305
03/13	37,911	738	1.9%	120,958
03/12	44,367	1,366	3.1%	117,314
03/11	44,022	1,503	3.4%	114,443
Annual Growth	(4.9%)	6.8%	—	3.1%

2015 Year-End Financials

Debt ratio: 0.0%
Return on equity: 13.9%
Cash ($ mil.): 4,738
Current ratio: 1.63
Long-term debt ($ mil.): 1,813
No. of shares (mil.): 2,143
Dividends
Yield: 1.5%
Payout: 36.1%
Market value ($ mil.): 51,139

	STOCK PRICE ($) FY Close	P/E High/Low		PER SHARE ($) Earnings	Dividends	Book Value
03/15	23.86	0	0	0.91	0.37	7.16
03/14	22.62	0	0	0.69	0.24	6.89
03/13	16.40	1	0	0.34	0.24	6.45
03/12	17.78	0	0	0.64	0.32	6.44
03/11	23.85	2	0	0.70	0.22	5.92
Annual Growth	0.0%	—	—	6.8%	14.0%	4.9%

Mitsubishi Heavy Industries Ltd.

Japanese industrial behemoth Mitsubishi Heavy Industries (MHI) is heavy into machinery manufacturing for a myriad of markets. A member of the Mitsubishi keiretsu the group builds and supplies everything from nuclear power plants bridges and aircraft to engines ships and air conditioners to various industries and customers around the world. MHI operates through six business segments: Power Systems Machinery & Steel Structures Aerospace General Machinery & Special Vehicles Shipbuilding & Ocean Development and Others. The company's core market is Japan but it also does business in other parts of Asia North America Europe Central and South America Africa and the Middle East.

As the world continues to transition to a low-carbon society MHI is focused on four key areas for growth. It is trying to meet growing demand for gas turbines especially as industrialized nations work to replace aging facilities in line with tougher environmental regulations. To this end it is trying to commercialize its J-series gas turbines which offer the highest level of heat efficiency in the world. Second it reached an agreement with UK-based utility Scottish and Southern Energy to develop low-carbon energy. Third it took a capital stake in Italy's ATLA to strengthen its gas turbine service network in Europe. Overall service business sales are projected to account for 35% of sales by fiscal 2014. And fourth the company seeks to expand into fast-growing emerging markets such as India and China.

MHI is specifically pushing for greater localization in these emerging markets. Through two joint ventures with Mumbai-based Larsen & Toubro MHI completed two plants in India to manufacture supercritical-pressure boilers as well as steam turbines and generators in response to India's strong electricity demand. In 2010 it launched a Shanghai subsidiary to oversee its air conditioning and refrigeration business. The subsidiary will manufacture commercial air conditioners and truck refrigeration systems with the goal of doubling sales within the first two years.

In more developed countries like the US MHI is building gas and wind turbine assembly plants to expand its network of overseas production sites. In Japan the group's largest market by sales MHI continues to receive orders for gas turbine combined-cycle thermal power plants to replace aging facilities. In the wake of the catastrophic earthquake that struck eastern Japan in early 2011 the company's efforts are focused on trying to improve the safety of its pressurized water reactor plants and collaborating with Hitachi Ltd. to support recovery and stabilize operations at the Fukushima Daiichi Nuclear Power Plant.

In fiscal 2011 MHI's consolidated net sales remained around the same level as in 2010. Sales in 2010 fell nearly 13% from their record high in 2009 as a result of the global economic crisis. Net sales for 2011 rose in the Shipbuilding & Ocean Development segment on increased deliveries of new vessels and in General Machinery & Special Vehicles on increased orders for engines in China turbochargers in Europe and forklifts in Asia and the Middle East. The Others segment consisting of air conditioning and refrigeration systems also reported both in an increase in orders and higher sales of automotive thermal systems and residential and commercial air conditioners. However net sales decreased in the Power Systems Aerospace and Machinery & Steel Structures segments. Lackluster sales of wind turbines commercial aircraft and defense- and space-related products as well as customer postponement of steel and transportation projects contributed to the decrease in sales in these segments.

EXECUTIVES

President and CEO, Shunichi Miyanaga, age 67
SEVP and President and CEO Energy and Environment, Atsushi Maekawa, age 65
EVP and Assistant to President and CEO Energy and Environment, Koji Hiramoto
EVP and Chairman Mitsubishi Heavy Industries America Inc., Masahiko Arihara, age 63
SEVP and President and CEO Commercial Aviation and Transportation Systems, Yoichi Kujirai, age 64
EVP and President and CEO Integrated Defense & Space Systems, Hisakazu Mizutani, age 64
EVP and Senior General Manager Nuclear Energy Systems Division Energy & Environment, Ei Kadokami
EVP and President Mitsubishi Heavy Industries America Inc. andChairman PW Power Systems Inc., Kenji Ando
EVP Human Resources Labor Relations and Global Personnel, Mutsuo Hiroe
EVP Chief Administrative Officer and Chief Risk Officer, Takashi Funato, age 63
EVP and Head of Monozukuri Innovation Planning Dept of Technology & Innovation Headquarters, Yukio Kodama, age 61
SVP, Yoshihiro Shiraiwa
EVP and President and CEO Machinery Equipment and Infrastructure, Kazuaki Kimura
EVP CFO and Head of Business Strategy Office, Masanori Koguchi
EVP CTO Head of Technology and Innovation Headquarters and Head of Global Business Planning & Operations Headquarters, Michisuke Nayama
EVP VP Commercial Aviation and Transportation Systems and President Mitsubishi Aircraft Corporation, Hiromichi Morimoto
Chairman, Hideaki Omiya, age 69
Auditors: Ernst & Young ShinNihon LLC

LOCATIONS

HQ: Mitsubishi Heavy Industries Ltd.
2-16-5 Konan, Minato-ku, Tokyo 108-8215
Phone: (81) 3 6716 3111 **Fax:** (81) 3 6716 5800
Web: www.mhi.co.jp

2015 Sales

	% of total
Asia/Pacific	
Japan	47
Other countries	17
North America	17
Europe	9
Africa	3
Middle East	3
Latin America	3
Other regions	1
Total	**100**

PRODUCTS/OPERATIONS

2015 Sales

	% of total
Energy & environment	39
Machinery equipment and infrastructure	32
Commercial aviation & transportation systems	13
Integrated defence & space systems.	12
Others	4
Total	**100**

Selected Products

Aerospace

- Aeroengines
- Civil aircraft
- Defense aircraft
- Guided weapon systems
- Laser radar surveillance system
- Launch vehicles
- Rocket engines
- Space stations

General Machinery & Special Vehicles
- Agricultural machinery
- Construction machinery
- Forklift trucks
- Medium- and small-sized engines
- Tractors
- Turbochargers

Machinery & Steel Structures
- Air brakes
- Automated people movers
- Chemical plants
- CO2 recovery plants
- Crane and material handling systems
- Flue gas desulphurization plants
- Injection molding machines
- Monorails
- Production robots
- Rail transit systems
- Sludge treatment systems
- Testing equipment

Power Systems
- Boilers
- Desalination plants
- Fans and blowers
- Diesel engines
- Gas turbines
- Hydraulic equipment (actuators generators motors pumps and water pressure systems)
- Instrumentation and control systems
- Lithium-ion secondary batteries
- Solid oxide fuel cells
- Steam turbines
- Thin-film photovoltaic module
- Wind turbines

Shipbuilding & Ocean Development
- Cargo ships
- Floating facilities
- Marine engines
- Marine machinery
- Passenger ships
- Pure car carriers
- Special-purpose ships
- Tankers

Others
- Air conditioning and refrigeration systems
- Automotive thermal systems
- Centrifugal chillers
- Machine tools

COMPETITORS

ALSTOM
Aker Solutions
BWX Technologies
Baltija Shipbuilding
Bharat Heavy Electricals
Caterpillar
Chiyoda Corp.
DSME
Doosan Heavy Industries
GE
Hanjin Heavy Industries & Construction
Hitachi
Hyundai Heavy Industries
IHI Corp.
Kajima
Kawasaki Heavy Industries
Komatsu
Kubota
MAN
Marubeni
Mitsui Engineering & Shipbuilding
Nippon Sharyo
Nishimatsu Construction
Obayashi
Samsung Heavy Industries
Siemens AG
Sumitomo Heavy Industries
Suzlon Energy Limited
Taisei

HISTORICAL FINANCIALS

Company Type: Public

Income Statement FYE: March 31

	REVENUE ($ mil.)	NET INCOME ($ mil.)	NET PROFIT MARGIN	EMPLOYEES
03/15	33,273	920	2.8%	81,845
03/14	32,451	1,554	4.8%	80,583
03/13	29,948	1,034	3.5%	68,213
03/12	34,388	299	0.9%	68,887
03/11	35,066	363	1.0%	68,816
Annual Growth	(1.3%)	26.1%	—	4.4%

2015 Year-End Financials

Debt ratio: 0.1%
Return on equity: 6.6%
Cash ($ mil.): 3,062
Current ratio: 1.46
Long-term debt ($ mil.): 5,399

No. of shares (mil.): —
Dividends
Yield: —
Payout: —
Market value ($ mil.): —

Mitsubishi UFJ Financial Group Inc

Mitsubishi UFJ Financial Group (MUFG) is the largest banking group in Japan (ahead of Mizuho Financial and Sumitomo Mitsui Financial) and one of the largest in the world. The group provides retail banking corporate banking asset management securities brokerage leasing and trust services. Subsidiary The Bank of Tokyo-Mitsubishi UFJ (BTMU) boasts over 1100 branches across Japan and another 1150 across more than 40 countries. Mitsubishi UFJ Trust and Banking (MUTB) oversees some ¥30 trillion ($250 billion) in assets under management. Other holdings include investment bank Mitsubishi UFJ Securities California-based MUFG Union Bank and private bank Mitsubishi UFJ Morgan Stanley PB Securities (MUMSS).

OperationsMUFG operates an integrated business group system that concentrates on five main business areas: Retail Banking which includes its domestic retail banking trust banking and securities business; Corporate Banking which includes its domestic corporate-focused commercial banking investment banking trust banking and securities businesses; Trust Assets Business Group which covers asset management and administrative services for pension trusts and security trusts through MUTB and globally through BTMU; Global covers its overseas commercial investment retail and trust banking and securities; and Global Markets which provides asset and liability management and strategic investments of BTMU and MUTB and sales and trading of financial products for BTMU MUTB and MUSHD.The firm's variety of service offerings give it a diversified revenue stream. About 40% of its total revenue comes from loan interest (including fees) while about 20% comes from interest income on investments trading account assets and deposits in other banks. Fees and Commissions income makes up 30% of total revenue while investment security gains and equity earnings (if applicable) make up the remainder.MUFG is a member of the Mitsubishi group a mlange of about 30 different companies —active in manufacturing transportation insurance and other industries —that shared common ownership before WWII but have been operated autonomously since. The group also includes credit card company Mitsubishi UFJ NICOS and Mitsubishi UFJ Lease & Finance.Geographic ReachThe company operates in the US Japan and more than 40 countries in Europe Asia/Oceania. About 52% of its revenue came from Japan in fiscal 2015 (ended March 31) down from 70% in FY2014. Another 12% came from the US.Sales and MarketingMUFG mainly markets its products through sales agents.Financial PerformanceNote: Growth rates may differ after conversion to US dollars.MUFG's revenues and profits have trended higher over the past few years thanks to a combination of growing loan and deposit business growing non-interest revenues from its investment businesses lower interest expenses in the low-interest environment a declining loan loss provisions as as its loan portfolio's credit quality has improved with higher property valuations in the strengthened economy.The group's revenue rose more than double digits to nearly ¥5740 billion ($48 billion) fiscal 2015 (ended March 31) mostly thanks to net trading account profits of ¥1.15 billion (compared to net trading account losses of ¥34 billion in FY2014) which were buoyed by higher foreign bond valuations and lower interest rates in the US. MUFG's interest income and fee and commission revenue also grew in the high-single digits.Higher revenue and declines in loan loss provisions helped MUFG's net income jump more than 50% to ¥1531 billion ($12.8 billion) in FY2015. The group's operating cash levels more than doubled to ¥2384 billion ($20 billion) thanks to higher cash earnings.

Strategy

With the stagnant Japanese economy MUFG has increasingly looked to emerging markets in Asia Latin America and Central and Eastern Europe for growth. In 2015 it continued its plans to expand its businesses in the fast-growing Southeast Asia region (including through select acquisitions of large banks like it did with its $5 billion-acquisition of Krungsri bank) and grow its consumer banking business in Asia targeting India Indonesia and the Philippines. Toward that end in 2015 MUFG showed interest in acquiring United Coconut Planters Bank from the Philippine government who wanted to sell its 74% stake in the bank for $350 million.MUFG has also begun pivoting toward growing its asset management business in recent years. In 2015 it purchased an investment management unit from UBS Group AG Global Asset Management. In 2014 MUFG and MUTB and MUFJ Securities Holdings effectively created a new organization structure to strengthen the group's asset management business after merging Mitsubishi UFJ Asset Management (MUAM) with KOKUSAI Asset Management Co (KAM).In the US subsidiary MUFG Union Bank has been expanding through the acquisition of other community banks. MUFG is also looking to strengthen its alliance with Morgan Stanley to grow its global investment banking operations.

Mergers and AcquisitionsIn mid-2015 as part of its asset management expansion strategy MUFG agreed to purchase UBS Group AG Global Asset Management's Alternative Fund Services unit which offers investment services for ¥30 billion ($250 million).In December 2013 the company expanded its banking business further into Southeast Asia after subsidiary The Bank of Tokyo-Mitsubishi UFJ (BTMU) acquired a 72% stake in Thailand-based The Bank of Ayudhya Public Company (Krungsri) for ¥545.8 billion (around $5 billion) cash. Krungsri became a subsidiary of BTMU after the deal.In November 2013 US subsidiary MUFG Union Bank acquired First Bank Association Bank Services a unit of first bank that offered a full suite of banking services to homeowners associations and community management companies which added $570 million in deposits as part of the deal.In September 2013 bolstered its asset management lines after its subsidiary MUTB purchased Butterfield Fulcrum Group for ¥30.2 billion ($250 million) cash and changed its name to Mitsubishi UFJ Fund Services Holdings Limited.

Company Background

In 2010 MUFG became the first Japanese bank to acquire an interest in a Chinese asset manager when it bought out BNP Paribas Asset Management's 33% stake in a joint venture with Shenyin & Wanguo Securities. The following year it acquired some 15% of AMP Limited in Australia. The moves should allow it to expand its investment services to pension funds and other institutional investors as part of a plan to expand its trust operations.

MUFG was formed in the 2005 merger of Mitsubishi Tokyo Financial Group and UFJ Holdings.

HISTORY

Company BackgroundMitsubishi Bank emerged from the exchange office of the original Mitsubishi zaibatsu (industrial group) in 1885. It evolved into a full-service bank by 1895 and became independent in 1919 though its primary customers were Mitsubishi group companies. The bank survived WWII but a US fiat dismantled the zaibatsu after the war. Mitsubishi Bank reopened as Chiyoda Bank in 1948. After reopening offices in London and New York the bank readopted the Mitsubishi name.

In the 1950s Mitsubishi Bank became the lead lender for the reconstituted Mitsubishi group (keiretsu). In the 1960s it followed its Mitsubishi partners overseas helping finance Japan's growing international trade. In 1972 it acquired the Bank of California and began doing more business outside the group.

Japan's overinflated real estate market of the 1980s devastated many of the country's banks including Nippon Trust Bank of which Mitsubishi owned 5%. Japan's Ministry of Finance (MoF) urged Mitsubishi to bail Nippon out; as a reward for raising its stake in Nippon to 69% and assuming a mountain of unrecoverable loans the MoF allowed Mitsubishi to begin issuing debt before other Japanese banks. In 1995 Mitsubishi Bank and Bank of Tokyo agreed to merge.

Bank of Tokyo (BOT) was established in 1880 as the Yokohama Specie Bank; the Iwasaki family founders of the Mitsubishi group served on its board. With links to the Imperial family the bank was heavily influenced by government policy. With Japan isolated after the Sino-Japanese War its international operations suffered greatly even before WWII. Completely dismantled after WWII the bank was re-established in 1946 as the Bank of Tokyo a commercial city bank bereft of its foreign exchange business. During the 1950s the government restored it as a foreign exchange specialist but regulations limited its domestic business.

BOT evolved into an investment bank in the 1970s; its reputation as the leading foreign exchange bank brought in international clients and successful derivatives trading and overseas banking. By the time BOT and Mitsubishi Bank agreed to merge BOT had 363 foreign offices (only 37 in Japan) with more foreign than Japanese employees.

The two banks merged in 1996 to form The Bank of Tokyo-Mitsubishi (BTM); Mitsubishi was the surviving entity. Their California banks merged to create Union Bank of California (UnionBanCal). The next year BTM reorganized its operations but had problems assimilating its disparate corporate cultures.

In 1998 Japanese banking regulators doled out nearly $240 billion to the industry to prop up failing banks and to strengthen healthier ones. Also that year BTM was fined for bribing MoF officials with entertainment gifts and posted a huge loss after writing off $8.4 billion in bad debt. Losses continued in 1999 and the bank responded by reorganizing operationally cutting jobs and offices and selling stock in UnionBanCal.

In 2000 BTM announced plans to form a financial group with Mitsubishi Trust Bank and Nippon Trust Bank. The following year the three banks unified and formed Mitsubishi Tokyo Financial Group. Before rolling into Mitsubishi Trust Financial Group BTM paid back the money showered upon it by the Japanese government in 1998.

In 2004 MTFG introduced a new organizational structure that focused on its three core markets – retail corporate and trust asset businesses. The company planned to unify business within each division and to improve decision-making companywide. The group also introduced a new executive officer system with the idea of separating company oversight and business execution. A mechanism for credit risk control was also added.

It was all to change in 2005 however. During this time Mitsubishi Tokyo Financial Group merged with UFJ Holdings emerging (at that time) as the world's largest bank by assets. As a result of the merger the group was renamed Mitsubishi UFJ Financial Group (MUFG).As with most of its peers MUFG was not immune to the global credit crisis that began in 2007. Its NICOS consumer lending subsidiary had a disappointing year due to the credit crunch. The unit sold its installment credit car loan and car leasing businesses to JACCS in 2008. In 2009 MUFG announced plans to close 50 branches and cut nearly 1000 jobs as a part of a long-term restructuring plan. In addition the bank shut down some 200 ATMs and relocated another 1000 employees.

In 2008 the group bought the rest of UnionBanCal and Mitsubishi UFJ NICOS it didn't already own and acquired a stake in bulge-bracket firm Morgan Stanley. MUFG also bought a 10% stake in UK-based Aberdeen Asset Management that year. (It later upped its interest to around 17%.)

EXECUTIVES

President, Ichiro Hamakawa, age 60
Senior Managing Director Chief Financial Officer, Taihei Yuki, age 63
Deputy President, Masaaki (Masa) Tanaka, age 62
Managing Director, Akihiko Kagawa
Chairman, Takao Kawanishi, age 67
Deputy Chairman, Tatsuo Wakabayashi
Auditors: Deloitte Touche Tohmatsu LLC

LOCATIONS

HQ: Mitsubishi UFJ Financial Group Inc
7-1, Marunouchi 2-chome, Chiyoda-ku, Tokyo 100-8330
Phone: (81) 3 3240 8111 **Fax:** (81) 3 3240 7073
Web: www.mufg.jp

2014 Sales

	% of total
Asia/Oceania	
Japan	72
Other countries	13
US	5
Europe	3
Other regions	7
Total	**100**

PRODUCTS/OPERATIONS

2014 Sales

	% of total
Interest	
Loans including fees	38
Investment securities	8
Trading account assets	9
Other	2
Noninterest	
Fees & commissions	29
Investment securities gains	6
Other	8
Total	**100**

COMPETITORS

Aozora Bank	ORIX
BNP Paribas Bangkok	Resona
Citigroup	Shinsei Bank
HSBC	Sony
Japan Post	Sumitomo Mitsui
Mizuho Financial	Sumitomo Mitsui Trust Holdings
Mizuho Trust & Banking Ltd	

HISTORICAL FINANCIALS

Company Type: Public

Income Statement FYE: March 31

	ASSETS ($ mil.)	NET INCOME ($ mil.)	INCOME AS % OF ASSETS	EMPLOYEES
03/15	2,341,122	12,761	0.5%	137,200
03/14	2,457,493	9,837	0.4%	135,300
03/13	2,450,358	11,362	0.5%	112,100
03/12	2,623,454	5,074	0.2%	110,500
03/11	2,449,821	5,576	0.2%	113,000
Annual Growth	(1.1%)	23.0%	—	5.0%

2015 Year-End Financials

Return on assets: 0.5%
Return on equity: 11.3%
Long-term debt ($ mil.): —
No. of shares (mil.): —
Sales ($ mil): 36,351
Dividends
Yield: 2.6%
Payout: 16.5%
Market value ($ mil.): —

	STOCK PRICE ($) FY Close	P/E High	P/E Low	PER SHARE ($) Earnings	Dividends	Book Value
03/15	6.22	0	0	0.90	0.16	8.73
03/14	5.54	0	0	0.68	0.14	8.35
03/13	6.00	0	0	0.79	0.13	7.97
03/12	4.98	0	0	0.34	0.15	7.40
03/11	4.60	0	0	0.38	0.14	7.13
Annual Growth	7.8%	—	—	24.3%	4.1%	5.2%

Mitsui & Co., Ltd.

Part of a network of companies that was founded by a samurai centuries ago Mitsui & Co. now does battle in the marketplace. Mitsui & Co. spearheads the Mitsui Group one of Japan's largest "keiretsu" (companies loosely connected through cross-ownership). A leading Japanese general trading firm (sogo shosha) Mitsui & Co. has about 320 subsidiaries in a wide range of industries. Its major business units are engaged in the production and sale of chemicals electronics and information energy foods iron and steel nonferrous metals textiles and machinery. The company's largest revenue generators are its trading activities in the energy and chemical sectors.

Geographic Reach

The company maintains a global network of 151 offices in 67 countries as well as about 320 subsidiaries in a wide range of industries and associated companies worldwide.

Operations

Mitsui & Co.'s operating units include Americas; Asia Pacific; Basic Chemicals; Consumer Service; Energy; Europe the Middle East and Africa; Financial & New; Food Products & Services; Food Resources; Infrastructure Projects; Iron & Steel Products; IT; Marine & Aerospace; Mineral & Metal Resources; Motor Vehicles & Construction Machinery; Performance Chemicals; and Transportation Logistics.

Financial Performance

After a decline in its revenues in fiscal years 2010 over 2009 due to the impact of the recession and the major tsunami Mitsui & Co. experienced significant growths in revenues in both fiscal years 2011 and 2012. In fiscal year 2012 the company's revenues increased by 12% and profits grew by 42%. The increase in the revenues was due to the positive impact of the recovering global economy. The growth in profits was due to the increases in commodity prices including crude oil gas iron ore and coal as well as the reversal effect of the previous year's settlement payment related to the Deepwater Horizon oil spill incident in the Gulf of Mexico. (Mitsui & Co. had a minority interest in the doomed rig. Mitsui's energy sector through its MOEX Offshore 2007 subsidiary saw impairment losses on property equipment and mineral rights from its involvement with the massive oil rig fire and subsequent oil spill in the Gulf of Mexico during the summer of 2010).

Strategy

Mitsui & Co.'s strategic role as a sogo shosha brings together marketing financing logistics risk management and IT and process development functions on behalf of its many subsidiaries. It grows through acquisitions and by forming joint ventures and strategic partnerships.

In 2013 Mitsui & Co. agreed to acquire Total E&P Energia Italia S.r.l which owns a 25% stake in the Tempa Rossa onshore oil field in the Gorgoglione concession in Italy. That year the company also formed a joint venture with JGC Corporation and Chongqing Liangjiang New Area Development & Investment Group Co. Ltd. The joint venture company will produce an urban development master plan for the Yulin Business Park to be developed in the Chongqing Liangjiang New Area and will also be involved in promotional activities for inward investment for the Business Park. Liangjiang New Area Development & Investment will hold a 50% stake in the joint venture company and Mitsui and JGC will own 25% respectively.

Mitsui & Co. entered a 50-50 joint venture with Dow Chemical in 2010 to build and operate a membrane chlor-alkali facility located at Dow's Freeport Texas complex. The new facility is expected to begin operations in mid-2013. Mitsui formed yet another joint venture with Dow in 2011 to develop biofuels and biopolymers or organic plastics in Brazil. The 50-50 operation will use Dow's sugar cane production to develop ethanol and packaging materials offering a "green alternative" and replacement product for the flexible packaging hygiene and medical markets.

In 2011 Mitsui & Co. raised its stake in Brazilian grain broker Multigrain SA to almost 90% by buying a 44% stake from US grain company CHS Inc. for $480 million. Mitsui which hopes to improve its competitiveness on the global grain market previously owned about half of the company.

Also that year Mitsui & Co. entered a joint venture with Russian automaker Sollers to construct Toyota vehicles in a production facility in Vladivostok. The venture would be the first Japanese auto assembly operation in Russia's Far East region. The deal calls for the the Mitsui/Sollers JV to manufacture about 30000 vehicles a year and distribute them throughout the Russian Federation via the Trans-Siberian Railway.

Mitsui & Co. also acquired Mercian Corporation's pharmaceutical and chemical businesses in 2011. Mercian's drug and chemical businesses known as MBS Company utilize fermentation technology. Mitsui aims to boost its business in substances such as anti-cancer bioagents and will position MBS as part of its core group.

HISTORY

In the 17th century unemployed samurai (warrior nobleman) Sokubei Mitsui opened a sake and soy sauce brewery at the urging of his wife Shuho. After parental encouragement their youngest son Hachirobei went to Edo (now Tokyo) and opened a dry goods store in 1673. Breaking with Japanese retailing tradition the store offered merchandise at fixed prices on a cash-and-carry basis.

Hachirobei in 1683 opened a currency exchange that evolved into Mitsui Bank. The bank became the Osaka government's official money changer in 1691 and was the first bank to offer money orders in Japan. Before his death in 1694 Hachirobei drafted a unique succession plan to hand down control of the company to every related family not just the eldest son's side.

The shogun's government called upon Mitsui in the mid-1800s to help finance its war against rebels. The family hired Rizaemon Minomura an outsider with influence in the government to protect the company from increasing demands for money. Mitsui became the bank of the Meiji government after Minomura astutely switched support to the winning rebels. Government industrialization pushed Mitsui into textiles paper goods and machinery. Minomura emphasized foreign trade and banking creating Mitsui Bussan (now Mitsui & Co.) and Mitsui Bank in 1876. In the late 1800s Mitsui Bussan profited from a Japanese military buildup formed a shipping line to take on Mitsubishi's monopoly and bought coal mines. The Mitsui family withdrew from Mitsui Bussan management in 1936 following attacks by right-wing terrorists who opposed its democratic leanings.

Mitsui prospered during the 1930s as Japan's military prepared for war. After the defeat occupation forces disbanded Japan's "zaibatsu" industrial groups slicing Mitsui into more than 200 separate entities. By 1950 more than two dozen leaders of the former Mitsui companies began gathering the Mitsui Group back together. Trading firm Mitsui & Co. was established in 1959. The oil crises of the 1970s stalled the oil-dependent Japanese economy prompting Mitsui companies to expand operations overseas and move into industries such as technology and aluminum.

The mammoth Sakura Bank was formed in 1990 with the merger of Mitsui Bank and Taiyo Kobe Bank. Other major ventures were to follow: In 1992 Mitsui & Co. joined with Marathon and Royal Dutch Shell and others to search for oil and gas off Russia's Sakhalin Island; and Mitsui & Co. and other Japanese traders were enlisted by Oman in 1993 for a $9 billion liquefied natural gas transport venture. As cable TV emerged in Japan Mitsui & Co. teamed up the next year with National Media Corp. to launch a home-shopping network.

In anticipation of deregulation in Japan's financial markets four Mitsui Group firms' pension funds –Sakura Bank Mitsui Marine & Fire Insurance Mitsui Mutual Life Insurance and Mitsui Trust and Banking –were linked in 1998. The next year Sakura Bank set aside old loyalties and agreed to merge with Sumitomo Bank the Sumitomo "keiretsu's" main bank; the deal closed in 2001. The group's Mitsui Trust and Banking merged with Chuo Trust and Banking to form Chuo Mitsui Trust and Banking part of Mitsui Trust Holdings.

Mitsui & Co. was implicated in bid-rigging and bribery scandals in 2002 and the company's chairman and CEO resigned. In 2003 the company moved into the German pesticide market by acquiring an 80% stake in Spiess-Urania Chemical a subsidiary of Norddeutsche Affinerie. Later that year it entered the biotechnology market by creating TM Cell Research a 35%-owned joint venture created with Toyobo. The company also entered the telecommunications market by acquiring a 30% stake in Shineedotcom from Shin Corp.

In 2003 Mitsui turned its focus back to the expansion of its current operations. The company acquired a 15% stake in Valepar a holding company of Brazilian-based iron ore producer Companhia Vale do Rio Doce. Mitsui and International Power completed the acquisition of the 1200 MW gas-fired Saltend Power plant in the UK from Calpine Corporation. In 2005 Mitsui acquired a stake in G˜s Participa §ões (Gaspart) a Brazil-based gas distribution company.

To help pay down debt related to its purchase of Uni n Fenosa in 2009 Gas Natural sold power assets in Mexico to Mitsui and Tokyo Gas for $1.2 billion.

Mitsui sold its share of the TAMCO steel mini-mill joint venture to Gerdau Ameristeel in 2010 for about $40 million. Its other partners Ameron and Tokyo Steel also sold their shares in the project to Gerdau.

Eyeing opportunities in the North American gas market Mitsui in 2010 announced plans to invest $1.4 billion to develop a shale gas project in Pennsylvania with Anadarko Petroleum. It also teamed up with Penn West Energy Trust to form an $850-million natural-gas joint venture to develop an oil shale play in British Columbia.

Also in 2010 Mitsui teamed up with US fertilizer company Mosaic for a joint venture in a phosphorus ore development project in Peru. Mitsui will spend $275 million to acquire a 25% stake and voting rights in a subsidiary of Vale while Mosaic will hold a 24% stake. Mitsui is seeking to obtain a steady supply of phosphate which is used in its fertilizer production operations.

Mitsui entered the water infrastructure business in China in 2010 through a 50-50 joint venture with Singapore's Hyflux Ltd. a major provider of integrated water management services. Mitsui plans to do business with local governments and in areas with many industrial complexes by leveraging Hyflux's technological expertise and its own business network.

Auditors: Deloitte Touche Tohmatsu LLC

LOCATIONS

HQ: Mitsui & Co., Ltd.
1-3 Marunouchi 1-chome, Chiyoda-ku, Tokyo 100-8631
Phone: (81) 3 3285 1111 **Fax:** (81) 3 3285 9821
Web: www.mitsui.com

HISTORICAL FINANCIALS

Company Type: Public

Income Statement FYE: March 31

	REVENUE ($ mil.)	NET INCOME ($ mil.)	NET PROFIT MARGIN	EMPLOYEES
03/15	45,048	2,554	5.7%	58,257
03/14	55,531	3,391	6.1%	60,660
03/13	52,200	3,272	6.3%	61,898
03/12	64,020	5,296	8.3%	64,218
03/11	56,510	3,703	6.6%	59,404
Annual Growth	(5.5%)	(8.9%)	—	(0.5%)

2015 Year-End Financials

Debt ratio: 0.3%	No. of shares (mil.): 1,792
Return on equity: 7.7%	Dividends
Cash ($ mil.): 11,675	Yield: 0.0%
Current ratio: 1.67	Payout: 775.7%
Long-term debt ($ mil.): 33,594	Market value ($ mil.): 482,255

	STOCK PRICE ($) FY Close	P/E High/Low		PER SHARE ($) Earnings	Dividends	Book Value
03/15	269.00	2	1	1.42	11.05	19.06
03/14	282.07	2	1	1.86	0.48	20.62
03/13	279.00	2	1	1.79	10.54	18.53
03/12	330.63	2	1	2.90	13.14	17.64
03/11	359.10	2	1	2.03	7.42	15.66
Annual Growth	(7.0%)	—	—	(8.5%)	10.5%	5.0%

Mitsui Life Insurance Co., Ltd.

Auditors: Deloitte Touche Tohmatsu LLC

LOCATIONS

HQ: Mitsui Life Insurance Co., Ltd.
1-1-20 Aomi, Koto-ku, Tokyo 135-8222
Phone: (81) 3 6831 8000
Web: www.mitsui-seimei.co.jp

HISTORICAL FINANCIALS

Company Type: Public

Income Statement FYE: March 31

	ASSETS ($ mil.)	NET INCOME ($ mil.)	INCOME AS % OF ASSETS	EMPLOYEES
03/14	69,986	125	0.2%	10,259
03/13	76,823	81	0.1%	11,552
03/12	87,382	167	0.2%	12,118
03/11	87,242	171	0.2%	12,610
03/10	80,300	49	0.1%	13,868
Annual Growth	(3.4%)	26.3%	—	(7.3%)

2014 Year-End Financials

Return on assets: 0.1%	Dividends
Return on equity: 3.9%	Yield: —
Long-term debt ($ mil.): —	Payout: —
No. of shares (mil.): 278	Market value ($ mil.): —
Sales ($ mil): 8,558	

Mizrahi Tefahot Bank Ltd

Mizrahi Tefahot Bank one of Israel's largest banks offers a variety of international commercial domestic and personal banking services. It also commands more than 40% of the country's mortgage market. Subsidiaries provide financial services including portfolio and fund management and capital market advice. The bank has more than 125 domestic branches and representative offices in the US Switzerland Germany the UK Mexico and the Cayman Islands. The bank was created in 2004 after the merger of United Mizrahi Bank and subsidiary Tefahot Israel Mortgage Bank. The Ofer and Wertheim families control approximately 46% of Mizrahi Tefahot's shares.

Mizrahi Tefahot has been working to grow its customer base. It improved its position in the retail market and expanded its branch network when it bought a 50% stake in Bank Yahav from Bank Hapoalim in 2008. The remaining shares of the Bank Yahav which caters to government employees is held by the government and the Culture & Economic Projects for State Workers. Also in 2008 Mizrahi Tefahot received an option to buy 10% of Israel Credit Cards-Cal. As part of the deal ICC-Cal will begin issuing Mizrahi-Tefahot brand credit cards.

Auditors: Brightman Almagor Zohar & Co.

LOCATIONS

HQ: Mizrahi Tefahot Bank Ltd
7 Jabotinsky Street, P.O. Box 3450, Ramat Gan 5252007
Phone: (972) 3 7559000 **Fax:** (972) 3 7559210
Web: www.mizrahi-tefahot.co.il

HISTORICAL FINANCIALS

Company Type: Public

Income Statement FYE: December 31

	ASSETS ($ mil.)	NET INCOME ($ mil.)	INCOME AS % OF ASSETS	EMPLOYEES
12/14	51,099	278	0.5%	5,864
12/13	51,761	310	0.6%	5,827
12/12	43,527	288	0.7%	5,670
12/11	39,300	273	0.7%	5,518
12/10	37,608	226	0.6%	5,252
Annual Growth	8.0%	5.3%	—	2.8%

2014 Year-End Financials

Return on assets: 0.5%	Dividends
Return on equity: 10.3%	Yield: —
Long-term debt ($ mil.): —	Payout: —
No. of shares (mil.): 233	Market value ($ mil.): —
Sales ($ mil): 1,790	

Monte dei Paschi di Siena (Italy)

The city of Siena knows its way around a horse race –and also the world of banking. It's the home to one of Italy's largest banks Banca Monte dei Paschi di Siena (BMPS) which provides consumer business and other banking services to 6 million clients through nearly 2200 branches throughout the country. BMPS also has limited operations in several other nations. It is split into a public institution (chiefly active in benevolent works grants and public assistance) and the incorporated banking arm (focused on profits). The bank which claims to be the oldest in the world was founded in 1472 to help the poor. It is owned and controlled by Fondazione Monte dei Paschi.

OperationsBoasting total assets of roughly 180 billion (roughly $220 billion) BMPS operates three main business segments and a corporate segment. Retail and Commercial Banking which generates roughly 75% of the bank's overall revenue consists of traditional retail banking products and services for individuals and businesses. Its Private Banking business (5% of overall revenue) provides mutual funds wealth management services pension funds and life insurance products.Corporate and Investment Banking makes up more than 10% of revenue and provides project finance merchant banking and financial advisory services. It also includes the sales activities for key clients foreign branches and subsidiaries MPS Capital Services Banca per le Impresse and MPS Leasing & Factoring.Additionally the bank has a Financial Advisory and Digital Banking segment which counts its Financial Advisory Network and its digital banking subsidiary WIDIBA (established in 2014).BMPS' Corporate Center counts the results of several business centers including: banks under foreign law (MP Banque and MPS Belgio); Group support operations including IT system management and development (MPS Consorzio Operativo di Gruppo); companies consolidated at equity and held for sale; and other minor operating units such as proprietary finance ALM Treasury and Capital Management.Geographic ReachBMPS boasts more than 2180 bank branches in Italy alone. BMPS also has around 40 international branches and representative offices located in New York City Europe (London France Belgium and Central-Eastern regions) Asia (Hong Kong Shanghai India and China) and North Africa.Sales and MarketingBMPS serves some 6 million total customers. More than 5 million are retail customers about 70% of which are families 20% are affluent more than 5% are small businesses. About 35% of these retail customers are located in Central Italy with another 35% from South Italy. The rest come from the North East and North West regions.Financial PerformanceBMPS has seen slow revenue declines but has steadily climbed back in recent years from deep losses in 2011 mostly as it has worked to de-risk its credit portfolio selling off less credit-worthy loan assets and pocketing gains from most transactions.BMPS's revenue in 2014 fell by 7% to 7.56 billion ($9.19 billion) mostly as interest income fell by 12% as interest margins shrank from a runoff of higher-yielding loans and a replacement of lower-yielding loans in the low interest rate environment.Following years of improvement the bank's losses deepened to 5.34 billion ($6.49 billion) in 2014 (compared to its 1.43 billion loss in 2013) mostly as the bank incurred higher (non-recurring) loan impairment charges after its Asset Quality Review parameters changed for the year.Cash levels improved with operations providing 419.4 million ($509.77 million) mostly because 2014 earnings grew after adjusting for the bank's 8.5 billion ($10.33 million) in (non-cash) impairment losses.

Stategy

As of mid 2015 with Italy having been in recession even years after the financial crisis BMPS has struggled with declining revenue and heavy losses as its loan portfolio has been plagued with non-performing loan assets (a problem that several Italian banks have shared). To deal with the problem the bank has been closing hundreds of branches cutting thousands of jobs (more than 8000) and selling off less credit-worthy loan assets to strengthen its balance sheet. These moves helped the bank return to profitability in mid-2015 after nearly four years of losses but the European Central Bank (ECB) maintained that BMPS needed to be bought by a more stable institution as the bank was still not strong enough to stand on its own. Profitability increased the likelihood that BMPS would be bought sooner but financial troubles may haunt the bank in the meantime.

Company Background

BMPS in 2008 announced restructuring plans under which banking subsidiaries Banca Agricola Mantovana Banca Antonveneta and Banca

Toscana would be integrated into the group. Banca Agricola Mantovana which operated some 300 branches in northeastern Italy was absorbed in September 2008. The integration of Banca Antonveneta acquired from Banco Santander in 2008 followed shortly after. Finally the group absorbed Banca Toscana which operated more than 400 branches (mostly in Tuscany and Umbria) in early 2009.

HISTORY

Company BackgroundAnd the Rockefellers think they come from old money!

In 1472 Monte di Pietà was founded by the courts of the State of Siena with the mission of offering banking services to people hard hit by local economic conditions. Soon after the bank increased its array of services. In 1624 the bank's nature was transformed through legal and political developments. The State of Siena was absorbed into the Grand Duchy of Tuscany and Grand Duke Ferdinando II of Tuscany stepped forward to guarantee the bank's deposits. The bank took the name Banca Monte dei Paschi di Siena (BMPS) the same year.

Following the unification of Italy in 1861 the bank continued its geographical and financial expansion offering more services along the way. After WWI BMPS helped merge Credito Toscano with Banca di Firenze to create Banca Toscana.

In 1936 BMPS through a new law was declared a public credit institute. Such an arrangement endured until 1995 when the Treasury Ministry split BMPS into two entities: BMPS a public lending institution and BMPS S.p.A. The former retained the original mission of providing public assistance as well as funding for scientific research and artistic educational and health projects with an emphasis on Siena and its surrounding region. The latter inherited the for-profit operations which by 1995 included finance and insurance divisions. The move also positioned BMPS to survive the free trade zone created among EU member nations allowing the sizable BMPS to take advantage of the provincial and fragmented state of Italian banking.

Given the license to increase its for-profit activities BMPS wasted no time in restructuring its brittle operations and snapping up shares of other Italian banks. Between 1995 and 1999 BMPS sold off its control of MPS Australia and Spain-based Sindibank integrated its information systems and incorporated its once-separate leasing and factoring operations. At the same time BMPS took minority shares in Banca Popolare di Spoleto Banca Monte Parma and Cassa di Risparmio di San Miniato. Its 1999 acquisition of Banca Agricola Mantovana helped reinforce its presence in northern Italy.

In 2000 BMPS bought the majority of Banca del Salento changed its name to Banca 121 and expanded its telephone-based banking services. The buying spree continued the following year with the acquisition of Florence-based Banca Steinhauslin and a stake in Finsoe the holding company for insurer Unipol.

EXECUTIVES

CEO and General Manager, Fabrizio Viola, age 58
Deputy General Manager Vicar Head of Credit, Angelo Barbarulo
COO, Alfredo Montalbano
Head of Risk, Andrea Rovellini
Head of Retail and Network, Marco Bragadin
Head of Corporate and Investment Banking, Sergio Vicinanza
Deputy Chairman, Roberto Isolani
Chairman, Massimo Tononi
Auditors: Reconta Ernst & Young S.p.A.

LOCATIONS

HQ: Monte dei Paschi di Siena (Italy)
Piazza Salimbeni 3, Siena I-53100
Phone: (39) 0577 294111 **Fax:** (39) 0577 294313

PRODUCTS/OPERATIONS

2014 Sales

	% of total
Retail and commercial banking	77
Investment banking and proprietary finance	11
Consumer lending	4
Foreign banking	2
Corporate finance	1
Leasing and factoring	1
Others	4
Total	**100**

2014 Sales

	% of total
Interest income and similar revenue	69
Fee and commission income	28
Net profit from trading	1
Others	2
Total	**100**

COMPETITORS

BNL bc
Banca Fideuram
Banca Popolare dell' Etruria
Banca Popolare di Milano
Banco Popolare
Intesa Sanpaolo
UniCredit

HISTORICAL FINANCIALS

Company Type: Public

Income Statement FYE: December 31

	ASSETS ($ mil.)	NET INCOME ($ mil.)	INCOME AS % OF ASSETS	EMPLOYEES
12/14	222,976	(6,494)	—	25,961
12/13	274,116	(1,981)	—	28,417
12/12	288,497	(4,178)	—	30,265
12/11	311,336	(6,060)	—	31,170
12/10	326,936	1,318	0.4%	31,495
Annual Growth	(9.1%)	—	—	(4.7%)

2014 Year-End Financials

Return on assets: (-2.7%)
Return on equity: (-88.1%)
Long-term debt ($ mil.): —
No. of shares (mil.): —
Sales ($ mil): 9,532
Dividends
Yield: —
Payout: —
Market value ($ mil.): —

Morrison (Wm.) Supermarkets Plc

Wm Morrison Supermarkets moved up the UK food chain with the acquisition of its larger rival Safeway plc. As the UK's fourth-largest grocery chain Morrison runs about 515 stores and nearly 155 convenience stores throughout England and Scotland. Morrison's supermarkets offer a variety of food and nonfood items most notably through its Market Street specialty departments. About 330 of the locations sell gas. Founded by its namesake in 1899 its purchase of the UK's Safeway chain transformed Wm Morrison into a national brand with about an 11% share of the UK grocery market.

OperationsThe chain is known as the master of small to medium-sized supermarkets as most of the company's stores fall into the 25000-to-40000 sq. ft. range. The shops are noted for their Market Street departments a collection of in-store specialty shops that ring the perimeter of the store. They include a bakery butcher shop and deli. Market Street departments also offer pizza pies and curry. Outlets also have in-store cafes. As the UK's second-largest fresh food manufacturer Morrison is vertically integrated including operating facilities for processing packing and distributing meat and produce. Its Farmers Boy unit supplies its stores with fresh food including pizzas cooked meats and other prepared foods. The company operates seven distribution centers and one national center that serviced its supermarkets and three convenience distribution centers.The company generated more than 75% of its revenue from its online and in-store sales in fiscal 2015 (ended February 1) while another 21% of revenue came from fuel sales from its gas stations.Geographic ReachMorrison boasts more than 500 stores scattered across the UK in East England East Midlands Greater London North East North West Scotland South East South West Wales West Midlands Yorkshire and Gibraltar.Sales and MarketingThe retailer spent £291 million ($438 million) on advertising and marketing in FY2015 (ended February 1) up from £280 million ($460 million) in FY2014.Financial PerformanceNote: Growth rates may differ after conversion to US dollars.Wm Morrison's sales and profits have been in decline over the past few years due to declining same-store sales amidst intense competition in the grocers market and stagnating consumer finances with sluggish economic growth in the UK. The retailer's revenue fell by 5% to £16.8 billion ($25.3 million) in fiscal 2015 (ended February 1) mostly as comparable physical store sales declined by 6% (online sales grew by 0.6%) and new store sales fell by nearly 3%. Fuel sales also shrank by 10% as the retailer passed lower oil prices on to the customer.Wm Morrison went even deeper into the red in FY2015 with a loss of £761 million ($1.14 billion) mostly due to a combination of lower revenue and £372 million ($560 million) in additional impairment and onerous lease provision costs during the year as its property and brand value deteriorated compared to its book asset values. The retailer's operating cash levels rose by 21% to £874 ($1.32 billion) as the company received £10 million ($15 million) in tax benefits compared to tax payments of £220 million ($331.2 million) in FY2014.

Stategy

Wm Morrison outlined its strategic objectives in 2015 which involved a £1 billion investment over three years through: permanently lowering prices to attract new customers; making fewer more selective promotions; boosting the value of its Morrison brand products and Market Street credentials; continually improve its product quality and range; improving its store layout to boost sales; and offering customer-loyalty-focused reward programs.Toward its low-cost growth strategy the retailer continues to lower its prices to drive customers from competitors. During fiscal 2015 the retailer cut prices on 130 high-volume everyday product lines by an average of 22%. In 2014 it cut its prices by an average of 17% on some 1200 store products starting with Produce and Meat products through its "I'm Cheaper" campaign. It also launched its Match & More price-match and points card program to gain customer loyalty (with special incentives for its Morrison-brand products) and take customer market share from top competitors Aldi and Lidl. For FY2016 the company targeted another £800 million more in cost savings for customers.Wm Morrison has also been making a number of moves to cut operational costs and boost profits with plans to unlock £1 billion worth of savings from 2014 through 2017. During FY2015 the retailer developed a sales-based ordering program with plans to roll it out to its Frozen food category and others to optimize its stocking inventories for significant cost savings. Also that year the company restructured its in-store teams to make lines of responsibility clearer and boost in-store efficiencies and focused on reducing its shrinkage waste and markdown costs.It's also been expanding its store base particularly its convenience stores. During FY2015 the retailer opened 68 new stores of which 57 were convenience stores.

HISTORY

Company BackgroundA former grocer's apprentice William Morrison founded his company in Bradford UK in 1899 as a wholesale seller of eggs and butter. Named William Morrison (Provisions) the business eventually expanded into retail by opening grocery stalls and by the 1920s was operating counter service shops as well.

Self-service stores became popular in the UK during the late 1940s and 1950s and the company began opening self-service outlets during that time. William's son Ken (born when William was 57 years of age) joined the company in 1950 and became chairman in 1956. The chain opened its first supermarket in Bradford in 1962 by converting an abandoned cinema. Wm Morrison Supermarkets went public five years later.

In 1979 Wm Morrison moved into Lancashire by purchasing the 10-store grocery chain Whelans Discount founded by Dave Whelan an ex-football star who also founded JJB Sports. Two years later it bought the Mainstop chain. The company's sales grew by a factor of 10 during the 1980s and 1990; it added about 50 stores in the 1990s. In 1993 Wm Morrison began opening stores on Sundays and in 1997 it teamed up with Midland Bank to offer in-store banking.

The company had operated mostly in northeastern England but a new distribution center that opened in 1996 in Cheshire allowed it to handle more distribution duties and gave it the base to expand west. Wm Morrison also turned south opening superstores in three southern regions (Oxford Essex and Kent) in 1998. The retailer also acquired two stores from Food Giant and three superstores (one near London) from Co-operative Retail Services that year. Wm Morrison expanded its Farmers Boy food processing operations by opening a new 180000-sq.-ft. facility in 1999. It opened four new stores in 2000 and bought three others.

The company's highly regarded Managing Director John Dowd resigned in March 2002 because of ill health. Soon after Marie Melnyk and Robert Stott were promoted to the positions of joint managing director. Morrison added six stores in fiscal year 2003 (ended January 2003).

On January 9 2003 Morrison made an offer of 1.32 Morrison shares for each share of Safeway plc. In March the company's bid for its rival lapsed after the Office of Fair Trading referred the bid to the Competition Commission.

Following clearance from Britain's High Court the company's acquisition of Safeway closed on March 8 2004. (Morrison shareholders own 60% of the enlarged company with Safeway shareholders left with 40%.)

In June 2006 the company named Marc Bolland formerly COO of brewer Heineken as CEO succeeding Bob Stott who retired. Stott became CEO in 2005.

Sir Kenneth Morrison retired as chairman in March 2008 after 55 years with the company. Morrison who was named honorary president was succeeded by former deputy chairman Sir Ian Gibson. The grocery chain opened eight new supermarkets in fiscal 2008.

In 2009 Morrisons acquired about 40 Co-operative Group and former Somerfield stores for about £220 million (about $330 million). In November Bolland resigned to join Marks and Spencer. He was succeeded by Dalton Philips who joined the business in March 2010.

In 2011 Morrisons acquired about 18 Netto UK stores from ASDA. In June it bought Flower World an importer and wholesaler of flowers in the UK in a bid to improve the flower offering at its supermarkets.

EXECUTIVES

CEO, Dalton T. Philips, age 47
CFO, Trevor Strain
CIO, Daniel Beecham
Chairman, Andrew T. Higginson, age 57
Auditors: PricewaterhouseCoopers LLP

LOCATIONS

HQ: Morrison (Wm.) Supermarkets Plc
Hilmore House, Gain Lane, Bradford BD3 7DL
Phone: (44) 845 611 5000
Web: www.morrisons.co.uk

PRODUCTS/OPERATIONS

2012 Sales

	% of total
Food & general merchandise	76
Fuel	23
Total	**100**

COMPETITORS

ALDI	Lidl
ASDA	Marks & Spencer
BP	Musgrave Retail Partners
Co-operative Group	Royal Dutch Shell
Exxon Mobil	SPAR (UK)
J Sainsbury	Tesco
John Lewis	

HISTORICAL FINANCIALS

Company Type: Public

Income Statement FYE: February 1

	REVENUE ($ mil.)	NET INCOME ($ mil.)	NET PROFIT MARGIN	EMPLOYEES
02/15	25,366	(1,147)	—	119,778
02/14	29,105	(391)	—	127,403
02/13*	28,681	1,024	3.6%	128,705
01/12	27,743	1,083	3.9%	131,207
01/11	26,247	1,006	3.8%	132,074
Annual Growth	(0.9%)	—	—	(2.4%)

*Fiscal year change

2015 Year-End Financials

Debt ratio: 41.4%	No. of shares (mil.): —
Return on equity: (-18.4%)	Dividends
Cash ($ mil.): 363	Yield: 0.0%
Current ratio: 0.54	Payout: —
Long-term debt ($ mil.): 3,783	Market value ($ mil.): —

	STOCK PRICE ($) FY Close	P/E High	P/E Low	PER SHARE ($) Earnings	Dividends	Book Value
02/15	13.46	—	—	(0.49)	0.91	2.32
02/14	19.81	—	—	(0.17)	0.93	3.31
02/13*	19.74	91	74	0.42	0.79	3.53
01/12	22.89	97	79	0.41	0.83	3.35
01/11	20.97	103	85	0.37	0.61	3.25
Annual Growth	(10.5%)	—	—	—	10.4%	(8.1%)

*Fiscal year change

MS&AD Insurance Group Holdings

MS&AD Insurance Group has insurance in Japan covered. MS&AD Insurance Group is the holding company for several large Japanese insurance companies including Mitsui Sumitomo Insurance (MSI) Aioi Nissay Dowa Insurance (ADI) Mitsui Direct General MSI Aioi Life and MSI Primary Life. Together the insurance companies offer property/casualty (e.g. auto personal fire marine) and life insurance as well as asset management (mutual funds financial consulting) and risk management services. MS&AD Insurance's 50 subsidiaries which serve individuals and businesses in Japan also offer products and services to customers in more than 40 countries in Europe Asia and the Americas.

Operations

The group has five primary operating divisions: domestic non-life (property/casualty) insurance domestic life insurance overseas business financial services and risk-related services. Each of its non-life firms underwrites policies in the fire and allied marine personal accident automobile and other arenas. The life insurers underwrite individual policies individual annuity insurance group insurance and other products.

Subsidiary MSI provides insurance and financial services around the world. In Japan it has a network of some 500 sales offices nearly 40000 agencies and about 230 service centers. MSI Primary Life is one of Japan's top individual annuity providers.

Sales and Marketing

MSI has 500 sales offices and more than 200 service centers in Japan. It also has about 900 locations in 40 countries around the globe. ADI has an almost identical range of domestic and international locations.

Mitsui Direct General sells automobile policies directly to individuals online and via telephone. MSI Aioi Life markets its products through financial institutions life insurance agencies and a direct sales force.

Financial Performance

Revenue increased 7% to ¥4689.6 billion in fiscal 2015 (ended March) primarily due to an increase in net premiums written and deposit premiums. Investment income also grew that year. With the increase in revenue net income rose 45% to ¥136 billion.

Cash flow from operations rose 28% to ¥628 billion in fiscal 2015.

Strategy

MS&AD is focused on expanding its domestic property/casualty operations its domestic life insurance business and its overseas operations. Its Next Challenge 2017 strategic plan was designed to promote the group's development.

Part of that plan included restructuring operations by function with MS&AD Holdings MSI ADI and MSI Aioi Life as its core businesses. Among the initiatives already completed was the 2014 establishment of ADI and MSI Aioi Life and the integration of certain business systems. Another key initiative is to promote enterprise risk management.

To expand abroad subsidiaries Mitsui Sumitomo Marine Management (U.S.A.) and Aioi Nissay Dowa Insurance Company of America opened new offices in the Dallas area during 2014. The group is also seeking acquisitions in Southeast Asia.

Mergers and Acquisitions

In 2014 subsidiary ADI and its European subsidiary acquired a 75% stake in UK-based telematics automobile insurer Box Innovation Group.

Company Background

Formed in 2008 as a holding company for the Mitsui Sumitomo operations MS&AD Insurance became the parent of a larger group of insurance companies through a three-way merger between Mitsui Sumitomo Aioi Insurance and Nissay Dowa General Insurance in 2010.

EXECUTIVES

Chairman MSI, Toshiaki Egashira, age 67
President CEO and Representative Director, Yasuyoshi Karasawa, age 65
Executive Officer Marketing and Sales, Masaaki Nishikata
Executive Officer Administration and Information Systems, Tetsuya Yoshikawa
Chairman, Hisahito Suzuki, age 65
Auditors: KPMG AZSA LLC

LOCATIONS

HQ: MS&AD Insurance Group Holdings
27-2, Shinkawa 2-chome, Chuo-ku, Tokyo 104-0033
Phone: (81) 3 5117 0270
Web: www.ms-ad-hd.com

PRODUCTS/OPERATIONS

2015 Sales

	% of total
Underwriting income	83
Investment income	17
Other ordinary income	-
Total	**100**

Selected Products

Compulsory Automobile Liability
Fire and Allied Insurance
Life
Marine
Personal Accident
Voluntary Automobile

COMPETITORS

Allianz
Allstate
Citigroup
Dai-ichi Life
Fuji Fire and Marine
Hyundai Marine & Fire
ING
Prudential
Prudential plc
Samsung Fire & Marine
Sompo Holdings
Sumitomo Life
Tokio Marine
Zurich Insurance Group

HISTORICAL FINANCIALS

Company Type: Public

Income Statement FYE: March 31

	REVENUE ($ mil.)	NET INCOME ($ mil.)	NET PROFIT MARGIN	EMPLOYEES
03/15	38,961	1,135	2.9%	38,358
03/14	42,171	905	2.1%	37,055
03/13	45,785	888	1.9%	36,643
03/12	45,775	(2,065)	—	36,929
03/11	40,878	65	0.2%	36,538
Annual Growth	(1.2%)	104.1%	—	1.2%

2015 Year-End Financials

Debt ratio: 0.0%
Return on equity: 5.1%
Cash ($ mil.): 12,498
Current ratio: 0.19
Long-term debt ($ mil.): 1,885
No. of shares (mil.): 612
Dividends
Yield: 1.8%
Payout: —
Market value ($ mil.): 8,574

	STOCK PRICE ($) FY Close	P/E High/Low	PER SHARE ($) Earnings	Dividends	Book Value
03/15	14.01	— —	1.84	0.26	41.34
03/14	11.38	— —	1.46	0.27	35.72
03/13	11.02	— —	1.43	0.00	34.55
03/12	10.26	— —	(3.32)	0.00	29.64
03/11	11.27	— —	0.10	0.31	31.72
Annual Growth	5.6%	— —	104.8%	(4.9%)	6.8%

Muenchener Hypothekenbank EG (Germany, Fed. Rep.)

Commercial banks not chartered

EXECUTIVES

Vorstandsvorsitzender, Konrad Irtel
Auditors: DGRV - Deutscher Genossenschafts- und Raiffeisenverband e.V.

LOCATIONS

HQ: Muenchener Hypothekenbank EG (Germany, Fed. Rep.)
Karl-Scharnagl-Ring 10, Munich D-80539
Phone: (49) 89 5387 800 **Fax:** (49) 89 5387 900
Web: www.muenchenerhyp.de

HISTORICAL FINANCIALS

Company Type: Public

Income Statement FYE: December 31

	ASSETS ($ mil.)	NET INCOME ($ mil.)	INCOME AS % OF ASSETS	EMPLOYEES
12/14	44,171	19	0.0%	462
12/13	48,046	9	0.0%	351
12/12	48,297	7	0.0%	410
12/11	48,308	6	0.0%	375
12/10	47,144	14	0.0%	366
Annual Growth	(1.6%)	7.4%	—	6.0%

2014 Year-End Financials

Return on assets: 0.0%
Return on equity: 1.5%
Long-term debt ($ mil.): —
No. of shares (mil.): —
Sales ($ mil): 1,435
Dividends
Yield: —
Payout: —
Market value ($ mil.): —

Muenchener Rueckversicherungs-Gesellschaft AG (Germany)

Some companies live with risk... Münchener Rückversicherungs-Gesellschaft (Munich Re) on the other hand thrives on risk. Reinsurance coverage (insurance for insurers) includes fire life motor and liability policies on both a facultative (individual risk) and treaty (categorized risk) basis. The company also provides direct insurance including life health and property coverage through Germany-based ERGO and other subsidiaries and it provides asset management services through MEAG MUNICH ERGO. Through Munich Re America Munich Re enjoys greater access to the US market. As one of the world's largest reinsurance and risk management firms the company operates in some 160 countries.

Operations

The company operates in six segments: life reinsurance property/casualty reinsurance ERGO life and health Germany ERGO property/casualty Germany ERGO international and Munich health (global health reinsurance and non-German health coverage). Reinsurance operations accounted for more than half of Munich Re's earnings in 2014 while ERGO accounted for 35%; Munich Health represented another 11%.

Munich Re's reinsurance and primary insurance segments respectively account for about 50% and 40% of annual premiums. After focused growth efforts in the primary insurance segment the ERGO division has grown to insure clients in 30 countries in Europe and Asia.

The company's health insurance operations are handled through the company's Deutsche Krankenversicherung unit (DKV a subsidiary of ERGO) in Germany and through the Munich Health division (which also holds Munich Re's health reinsurance operations) in international countries. The MEAG asset management unit holds some 200 billion ($260 billion) in investments.

Geographic Reach

North America is Munich Re's largest market accounting for about 45% of gross premiums written in 2014 (up from 25% in 2010 due to acquisitions and organic growth in the US). Europe is its second-biggest market (accounting for about 30% of premiums in 2014) and the company has expanded its European presence over the years through acquisitions and internal growth programs.

Financial Performance

Revenues declined 4% to 47.3 billion in 2014 primarily due to a decline in the reinsurance segments including both life and property/casualty reinsurance earnings. Canada life reinsurance sales went down primarily as the result of the restructuring of a large-volume treaty. Europe and Latin America property/casualty reinsurance also slowed down as did the special and financial risks division. Munich Health slipped 16% that year while primary insurance dropped mainly due to the sale of the Windsor Health Group.

Due to the revenue decline net income fell 5% to 3.1 billion in 2014. However cash flow from operations more than tripled to 7.5 billion due to a change in deposits retained and accounts receivable and payable.

Strategy

Though reinsurance is its largest operating segment the company hopes to continue the growth of its traditional insurance segment in the core German market and other European markets focusing on personal lines. As part of this strategy the company is widening the presence of the ERGO brand across its insurance operations in its European markets (especially in Germany).

Additionally Munich Re is working to extend the ERGO brand into new markets especially in emerging markets in Eastern Europe and parts of Asia.

In the North American market Munich Re is expanding in the specialty property/casualty and health insurance markets primarily through acquisitions. It is also working to expand its presence in the growing health care insurance arena in emerging markets like India.

Ownership

Billionaire investment mogul Warren Buffett who controls a number of insurance and reinsurance players through Berkshire Hathaway has taken notice of Munich Re. Buffett increased his stake in the company to 10% in 2010.

HISTORY

Investors Carl Thieme and Theodor Cramer-Klett founded Munich Re in 1880. Within a month Munich Re opened offices in Hamburg Berlin Vienna and St. Petersburg establishing treaties with German and Danish insurers. In 1888 Munich Re went public; two years later it opened an office in London and helped finance the creation of Allianz which would soon come to dominate the German insurance industry. In 1892 the firm opened a branch in the US (it incurred severe losses from the 1906 San Francisco earthquake).

WWI interrupted Munich Re's UK and US operations. The company recovered after 1918 only to be hobbled again by the Great Depression. In 1933 Munich Re executive Kurt Schmitt became minister of economic affairs for the Nazis. Objecting to the evolving policies of National Socialism he left after a year returning to Munich Re where he became chief executive in 1938.

Hitler's ignition of WWII wasn't quite the boom Munich Re needed; its international business was again disrupted. After the war the Allies further limited overseas operations. Because of his involvement with the Nazi government Schmitt was replaced by Eberhard von Reininghaus in 1945. The division of Germany further hampered the company's recovery.

Jump-started by the Marshall Plan in 1950 the West German Wirtschaftswunder (economic miracle) kicked into high gear as the devastated country rebuilt. Relaxation of occupation-era trading limits also helped as the company rebuilt its foreign business. By 1969 Munich Re's sales topped DM 2 billion. Amid the global oil crisis and a rash of terrorist acts in Germany the firm reported its first-ever reinsurance loss in 1977.

German reunification in 1990 provided new markets for Munich Re but advantages from new business in the East were wiped out by claims arising from that year's harsh winter.

In 1992 an investigation by the German Federal Cartel Office prompted a realignment in the insurance business –Allianz ceded its controlling interests in three life insurers (Hamburg-Mannheimer Versicherungs Karlsruher Lebensversicherung and Berlinische Lebensversicherung) to Munich Re bringing it into direct insurance. Munich Re took over Deutsche Krankenversicherung (DKV) in 1996. Also that year Munich Re acquired American Re.

During the 1990s reinsurance sales dwindled as competition increased forcing lower premiums and alternatives to insurance and reinsurance became more common. Munich Re looked to direct insurance particularly individual property/casualty and life insurance to compensate. In 1997 it merged Hamburg-Mannheimer and DKV with another insurer Victoria AG to form ERGO Versicherungsgruppe. Within a year ERGO's insurance income accounted for half of all revenues.

Munich Re and ERGO launched asset management firm MEAG Munich ERGO AssetManagement in 1999. That year Munich Re experienced its worst year ever after natural disasters hit its reinsurance business hard. To recoup its losses the next year the firm expanded both its reinsurance and primary insurance operations into key markets in Europe North and South America and Asia. Also in 2000 Munich Re bought CNA Financial's life reinsurance operations. Together with Swiss Re the company launched Inreon an online reinsurance exchange in 2001.

As one of the companies hit hardest financially by the World Trade Center tragedy Munich Re paid out some $2 billion in claims. In 2003 Allianz and Munich Re terminated their cooperation agreement as their shareholdings in each other fell to under 15%. (The two companies gradually sold off nearly all of their ownership interests in following years.)

In 2004 Munich Re entered its first Asian market by forming a joint venture in China.

EXECUTIVES

Member Board of Management Special and Financial Risks and Information Technology, Torsten Jeworrek, age 55, $600,000 total compensation

Management Board Member Germany Asia Pacific and Africa Division, Ludger Arnoldussen, age 54, $400,000 total compensation

Management Board Member Special and Financial Risks Division, Thomas Blunck, age 50, $432,500 total compensation

Management Board Member Life Division, Joachim Oechslin, age 50

Management Board Member Europe and Latin America Division, Giuseppina Albo, age 53

CFO, J ¶g Schneider, age 57

Management Board Member Health Division, Doris H ¶pke, age 49

Chairman Management Board, jur. Nikolaus von Bomhard, age 59

Chairman Supervisory Board, Ing. Bernd Pischetsrieder

Deputy Chairman Supervisory Board, Marco N ¶renberg

Auditors: KPMG Bayerische Treuhandgesellschaft AG

LOCATIONS

HQ: Muenchener Rueckversicherungs-Gesellschaft AG (Germany)
Koeniginstrasse 107, Munich D-80802
Phone: (49) 89 38 91 0 **Fax:** (49) 89 39 90 56
Web: www.munichre.com

2014 Premiums

	% of total
Europe	30
North America	45
Asia & Australasia	17
Latin America	5
Africa Near & Middle East	3
Total	100

PRODUCTS/OPERATIONS

2014 Sales

	% of total
Reinsurance	
Property/casualty	34
Life	20
ERGO	
Life and health Germany	21
Property/casualty Germany	7
International	7
Munich Health	11
Total	100

Selected Brands

ERGO (primary insurance)
- Deutscher Automobil Schutz (D.A.S. auto insurance)
- Deutsche Krankenversicherung (DKV)
- ERV

ERGO Direkt (commercial customer consulting)
DKV (domestic health insurance)
Munich Health (international health insurance domestic and international health reinsurance)
Munich Re
Munich Re America
- American Modern Insurance (specialty property/casualty insurance life insurance reinsurance)
- Hartford Steam Boiler (HSB specialty property/casualty insurance and reinsurance)

COMPETITORS

AEGON
AIG
AXA
Allianz
Allstate
Berkshire Hathaway
Bloise-Holding
Chubb Limited
Everest Re
General Re
Hannover Re
Helvetia Group
ING
Manulife Financial
MetLife
Nippon Life Insurance
OdysseyRe
PartnerRe
Prudential plc
Reinsurance Group of America
RenaissanceRe
Swiss Re
Transatlantic Holdings
XL Group plc

HISTORICAL FINANCIALS

Company Type: Public

Income Statement

FYE: December 31

	ASSETS ($ mil.)	NET INCOME ($ mil.)	INCOME AS % OF ASSETS	EMPLOYEES
12/14	331,807	3,832	1.2%	43,316
12/13	350,087	4,561	1.3%	44,665
12/12	340,531	4,211	1.2%	45,437
12/11	320,232	908	0.3%	47,206
12/10	316,335	3,241	1.0%	46,915
Annual Growth	1.2%	4.3%	—	(2.0%)

2014 Year-End Financials

Return on assets: 1.2%
Return on equity: 11.2%
Long-term debt ($ mil.): —
No. of shares (mil.): 168
Sales ($ mil): 76,441

Dividends
Yield: 3.4%
Payout: —
Market value ($ mil.): 3,343

	STOCK PRICE ($) FY Close	P/E High/Low		PER SHARE ($) Earnings	Dividends	Book Value
12/14	19.84	1	1	22.26	0.69	216.63
12/13	22.24	1	1	25.47	0.62	199.46
12/12	18.03	1	1	23.70	0.55	199.76
12/11	12.28	4	3	5.10	0.56	166.33
12/10	15.11	1	1	17.48	0.54	161.79
Annual Growth	7.0%	—	—	6.2%	6.3%	7.6%

Nanto Bank, Ltd.

The Nanto Bank primarily serves the Nara region of Japan. The bank operates from about 135 offices branches and other facilities located in the Hyogo Kyoto Mie Nara Osaka Tokyo and Wakayama areas of the country. Nanto Bank provides a selection of financial services including consumer banking credit card services securities leasing and lending. The bank traces its historical roots back to 1934. Major subsidiaries include Nanto Credit Guarantee Co. Nanto Lease co. Nanto Estate Co. Nanto Staff Service Co. and Nanto Investment Management Co.

Strategy

The Nanto Bank aims to increase its balance of loans deposits and assets by expanding its branch net work mainly through the establishment of new branches. In Osaka Prefecture identified as an important strategic area two new branches –the Eiwa branch and the Wakaeiwata branch —were built and opened in Higashiosaka City in September 2012. The company also opened in 2013 its Joto corporate business office and the Hokusetsu corporate business office with a plan to eventually developing these into branches.

EXECUTIVES

President, Takashi Hashimoto
Auditors: KPMG AZSA LLC

LOCATIONS

HQ: Nanto Bank, Ltd.
16 Hashimoto-cho, Nara 630-8677
Phone: (81) 742 22 1131
Web: www.nantobank.co.jp

COMPETITORS

Aozora Bank
Kiyo Bank
Mitsubishi UFJ Financial Group
Shizuoka Bank
Towa Bank

HISTORICAL FINANCIALS

Company Type: Public

Income Statement FYE: March 31

	ASSETS ($ mil.)	NET INCOME ($ mil.)	INCOME AS % OF ASSETS	EMPLOYEES
03/15	44,413	82	0.2%	2,813
03/14	50,254	87	0.2%	2,866
03/13	53,405	81	0.2%	2,889
03/12	58,631	42	0.1%	2,928
03/11	55,654	79	0.1%	2,882
Annual Growth	(5.5%)	0.9%	—	(0.6%)

2015 Year-End Financials

Return on assets: 0.1%
Return on equity: 4.3%
Long-term debt ($ mil.): —
No. of shares (mil.): 268
Sales ($ mil): 682
Dividends
Yield: —
Payout: —
Market value ($ mil.): —

National Australia Bank Ltd.

National Australia Bank (NAB) is one of Australia's Big Four banks (along with ANZ Westpac and Commonwealth Bank of Australia). It provides banking wealth management and investment banking services in Australia as well as in New Zealand through its Bank of New Zealand (BNZ) subsidiary. NAB also offers debt risk management and investment products for institutional clients. The company and its subsidiaries have more than 1500 branches and service centers in the two regions. During 2015 the bank announced it would sell its Clydesdale Bank and Yorkshire Bank subsidiaries in the UK and its Great Western Bancorp subsidiary in the US to focus on its top markets in Australia and New Zealand.

OperationsNAB operates three business segments: Australian Banking which generated 69% of the company's operating income in fiscal 2015 (ended September 30 2015) and counts its business in Australia; NAB Wealth (10% of operating income) which counts NAB's insurance and investment solutions for retail corporate and institutional clients; and NZ Banking (10% of operating income) which counts NAB's business in New Zealand through BNZ. NAB's fourth segment UK Banking (10% of operating income) was discontinued in 2015 after it sold its Clydesdale Bank and Yorkshire Bank subsidiaries.Broadly speaking NAB generated 70% of its total revenue from interest income (mostly on loans) during FY2015 while investment revenue made up another 12%. The rest came from premium and related revenue (4% of total revenue) fee income (1%) financial instrument gains (4%) and other operating income (9%).Sales and MarketingNAB served more than 12 million customers during FY2015. Its Australian Banking segment serves retail and business customers ranging from small and medium-sized enterprises to Australia's largest institutions. Its NAB segment serves retail corporate and institutional clients. BNZ serves retail business corporate agribusiness and insurance clients in New Zealand.NAB spent A$248 million ($173 million) on advertising and marketing expenses in FY2015 compared to A$242 million ($211 million) in FY2014. Financial PerformanceNote: Growth rates may differ after conversion to US dollars. This analysis uses financials from the company's annual report.NAB's annual operating income (including net interest income) and profits have been trending higher since 2011 mostly thanks to 20% growth in loan assets over the period.The bank's revenue dipped 3% to A$43.65 billion ($30.5 billion) in fiscal 2015 (ended September 30 2015) mostly due to a decrease in investment revenue during the year. Its net interest income however grew by 4% on higher housing and business lending volumes lower borrowing costs and favorable interest rate risk outcomes. The company's NAB Wealth segment grew the fastest (27% growth in cash earnings) thanks to strong insurance results and rising investment markets.Despite revenue declines in FY2015 NAB's net income climbed 20% to A$6.34 billion ($4.4 billion) for the year mostly thanks to favorable foreign exchange rate movements and non-recurring items though low borrowing costs helped as well. The bank's operations used A$13 billion ($9.1 billion) for the year nearly twice as much cash as in FY2014 mostly because it used more cash to extend loans and advances to customers but also because of deposit repayments and various unfavorable working capital changes.

Strategy

Australia remains the core market for NAB making up nearly 70% of its total revenue in FY2015. As such the company continues to invest in building its business banking personal banking and wealth businesses; improving its loan asset quality; and drive mortgage and deposit growth at home.Abroad NAB has been exiting certain geographic markets and business lines in recent years. In October 2015 NAB reached a broad agreement to sell 80% of its life insurance business to Japan's Nippon Life for a little more than ¥2 billion. If the deal goes through the bank will retain 20% ownership of the business and will continue to market insurance products at its branches. Also in 2015 the bank sold its US-based subsidiary Great Western Bancorp in July and also announced it would exit the UK market by selling its Clydesdale Bank and Yorkshire Bank subsidiaries (slated for completion in February 2016).

HISTORY

Company BackgroundFormed in 1858 in Melbourne National Bank of Australasia (NBA) just missed the peak of the Victoria gold rush. The bank expanded across the territory and was one of the first to lend to farmers and ranchers using land deeds as security. In the late 1870s drought imperiled Victoria. Seeking greener pastures NBA entered New South Wales in 1885 then headed into Western Australia. Economic instability continued; in 1893 the bank experienced its first panic and was shuttered for eight weeks. NBA reopened only to close a quarter of its branches between 1893 and 1896.

During the Australian commonwealth's early years Western Australia was the bank's salvation as the economies in Victoria and South Australia stagnated. NBA helped fund Australia's WWI efforts through public loans. A postwar consolidation wave in banking swept up NBA which made acquisitions in 1918 and 1922.

Overdue farm and ranch loans weakened the bank during the Depression. As WWII raged the Commonwealth Bank (established in 1912) took greater control of Australia's banks. With competition among banks primarily limited to branch growth NBA acquired Queensland National Bank in 1948 and Ballarat Banking Co. in 1955. The bank diversified into consumer finance through acquisition. In the 1960s Australia experienced an economic boom as immigration and industrialization grew. The boom went bust in the 1970s as the world sunk into recession. Still under the Commonwealth Bank's tight control the banks watched business that had once been theirs lost to building societies merchant banks and credit unions.

The 1980s brought banking deregulation. To vie with foreign banks entering Australia NBA in 1981 merged with Commercial Banking Co. of Sydney and became the National Commercial Banking Corp. of Australia in 1982. (It took its present name in 1984.) Throughout the 1980s the bank diversified and moved into the US and Japan. It invested in property and made loans to foreign countries. All too quickly though property values sank and countries defaulted on loans.

To fight recession NAB looked abroad for opportunities. In 1987 it bought Clydesdale Bank Northern Bank and National Irish Bank from Midland Bank Group (now part of HSBC Holdings). Three years later NAB bought Yorkshire Bank then turned the four banks around by linking them and tightening loan operations. In 1992 it bought the troubled Bank of New Zealand again tightening loan operations. Three years later NAB claimed Michigan National in the US.

After the mid-1990s economic recovery NAB bought HomeSide to try to adapt the US mortgage firm's efficient operations for all its banks.

NAB in 2000 bought Lend Lease's MLC fund management group. It also announced plans to launch a separate stock for its European businesses fueling speculation it might be on the prowl to buy or merge with a large UK bank. The Australian Competition and Consumer Commission (ACCC) that year accused NAB of credit card transaction price-fixing; the bank faced a possible fine of nearly $6 million but the ACCC dropped litigation against the group the following year.

Also in 2001 NAB sold US-based Michigan National Bank to ABN AMRO and sold mortgage lender HomeSide International to Washington Mutual the following year. In fiscal year 2002 the bank cut some 2000 jobs mostly in back-office operations.

During fiscal year 2003 the company booked pre-tax losses of some $360 million due to unauthorized trading in the company's foreign currency options department. By the end of March 2004 chairman Charles Allen chief executive Frank Cicutto and the heads of global markets and foreign exchange had resigned. Three more executives and at least five traders were fired. The fallout continued the next year as the company struggled to regroup.

NAB sold its Irish banks –National Irish Bank and Northern Bank –to Danske Bank in 2005. It retained its UK banks Yorkshire Bank (England) and Clydesdale Bank (Scotland).

In 2006 NAB sold its Custom Fleet vehicle leasing division to GE Capital as well as its Asian life insurance and wealth management operations. The downsizing was part of the company's move to streamline operations.

To establish a foothold in the US NAB acquired Great Western Bancorporation for $A836 million (nearly US$800 million) in 2008.

Also that year NAB took a 20% stake in Chinese property trust Union Trust and Investment. The deal made NAB the first foreign bank to buy into a Chinese trust firm.

EXECUTIVES

Group Executive Governance and Reputation, Michaela J. Healey, age 48
Managing Director and Group CEO, Andrew Thorburn
Group Executive Personal Banking, Gavin R. Slater
Group Chief Risk Officer, David Gall
Managing Director and CEO Bank of New Zealand, Anthony J. Healy
Group Executive NAB Wealth, Andrew Hagger
Group Executive Finance and Strategy, Craig Drummond
Group Executive Product and Markets, Antony Cahill
Group Executive Business Banking, Angela Mentis
Group Executive Enterprise Services and Transformation, Renee Roberts
Chairman, Michael A. Chaney, age 65
Chairman, Kenneth R. (Ken) Henry
Auditors: Ernst & Young

LOCATIONS

HQ: National Australia Bank Ltd.
Level 1, 800 Bourke Street, Docklands, Melbourne, Victoria 3008
Phone: (61) 3 8872 2461
Web: www.nabgroup.com

PRODUCTS/OPERATIONS

2015 Cash Earnings

	% of total
Australian banking	69
NZ banking	10
UK banking	10
NAB Wealth	8
Corporate function and others	3
Total	**100**

Selected Subsidiaries

Calibre Asset Management
Great Western Bancorporation
nabCapital (formerly Institutional Markets & Services)
National Australia Group Europe Limited
 Clydesdale Bank PLC
 Yorkshire Bank Home Loans Limited
 Yorkshire Bank Investments Limited
 National Australia Group Europe Services Limited
National Australia Group (NZ) Limited
 Bank of New Zealand
 BNZ International Funding Limited
National Australia Trustees Limited
National Wealth Management Holdings Limited
MLC Limited
 National Wealth Management International Holdings Limited

COMPETITORS

Australia and New Zealand Banking
Commonwealth Bank of Australia
Westpac Banking

HISTORICAL FINANCIALS

Company Type: Public

Income Statement FYE: September 30

	ASSETS ($ mil.)	NET INCOME ($ mil.)	INCOME AS % OF ASSETS	EMPLOYEES
09/14	769,692	4,613	0.6%	42,602
09/13	753,097	5,078	0.7%	42,000
09/12	796,373	4,260	0.5%	0
09/11	732,251	5,070	0.7%	0
09/10	664,069	4,089	0.6%	0
Annual Growth	3.8%	3.1%	—	

2014 Year-End Financials

Return on assets: 0.6%
Return on equity: 11.2%
Long-term debt ($ mil.): —
No. of shares (mil.): —
Sales ($ mil): 39,006
Dividends
Yield: 9.1%
Payout: 42.7%
Market value ($ mil.): —

	STOCK PRICE ($) FY Close	P/E High	P/E Low	PER SHARE ($) Earnings	Dividends	Book Value
09/14	14.18	14	6	1.90	1.30	18.06
09/13	32.19	14	9	2.12	1.78	18.90
09/12	26.43	16	13	1.82	0.94	20.35
09/11	21.15	12	8	2.25	1.65	19.03
09/10	24.54	16	11	1.85	1.27	18.07
Annual Growth	(12.8%)	—	—	0.8%	0.6%	(0.0%)

National Bank of Abu Dhabi

Auditors: KPMG

LOCATIONS

HQ: National Bank of Abu Dhabi
P.O. Box 4, Abu Dhabi
Phone:
Web: www.nbad.com

HISTORICAL FINANCIALS

Company Type: Public

Income Statement FYE: December 31

	ASSETS ($ mil.)	NET INCOME ($ mil.)	INCOME AS % OF ASSETS	EMPLOYEES
12/14	102,401	1,518	1.5%	0
12/13	88,500	1,288	1.5%	0
12/12	81,833	1,179	1.4%	0
12/11	69,606	1,009	1.5%	0
12/10	57,560	1,002	1.7%	4,216
Annual Growth	15.5%	10.9%	—	—

2014 Year-End Financials

Return on assets: 1.5%
Return on equity: 15.3%
Long-term debt ($ mil.): —
No. of shares (mil.): —
Sales ($ mil): 3,555
Dividends
Yield: —
Payout: —
Market value ($ mil.): —

National Bank of Canada

What's the bank for the Quebecois? The National Bank of Canada says "C'est moi!" Also known as National Bank Financial Group the company offers personal and commercial banking services through about 450 branches in Canada primarily in Quebec. The bank's offerings include deposits mortgages loans and credit cards. Through subsidiaries it also provides insurance trust services wealth management online brokerage and private banking. The company with $185 billion in assets manages more than 50 proprietary mutual funds under the National Bank Omega and Altamira banners. Its Natbank unit has two branches in Florida for snowbirds.

Through some 85 locations the company's National Bank Financial subsidiary offers investments portfolio management and group insurance plans. The unit manages more than $50 billion of client assets. It also performs investment banking and brokerage services such as mergers and acquisitions advice institutional trading securities clearing and corporate finance.

To boost its institutional services business National Bank of Canada agreed in late 2013 to acquire The Toronto-Dominion Bank's TD Waterhouse Institutional Services business for $250 million.

In 2012 National Bank of Canada sold its Natcan Investment Management arm to Fiera Sceptre (since renamed Fiera Capital) for more than $309 million. As part of the deal the bank received voting shares representing about 35% of Fiera. National Bank of Canada's strategy is to develop partnerships to grow in the wealth management business. In years prior the bank had been growing its wealth management segment hoping to capitalize on an aging Canadian populace investing toward retirement.

National Bank of Canada has benefited from a relatively strong Canadian economy and a rebound in employment in Quebec in particular. It reported more than $1 billion in net income in 2010 and enjoys one of the lowest loan loss ratios among financial institutions in the country. The company is focusing on referrals between its banking and financial markets segments to foment growth.

EXECUTIVES

President and CEO, Louis Vachon, age 53, $800,000 total compensation
EVP Human Resources and Corporate Affairs, Lynn Jeanniot
SVP Internal Audit, Ghislain Parent
EVP Wealth Management; Co-President and Co-CEO National Bank Financial, Luc Paiement, $300,000 total compensation
SVP; Co-President and Co-CEO National Bank Financial, Ricardo Pascoe, $300,000 total compensation
EVP Risk Management, William Bonnell
EVP Operations, Brigitte H ©ert
EVP Personal and Commercial Banking, Diane Giard
EVP Marketing, Karen Leggett
EVP Information Technology and Organizational Performance, Dominique Fagnoule
EVP Operations, St ©hane Bilodeau
Chairman, Jean Houde
Auditors: Deloitte LLP

LOCATIONS

HQ: National Bank of Canada
600 De La Gauchetiere Street West, 4th Floor, Montreal, Quebec H3B 4L2
Phone: 514 394-5000 **Fax:** 514 394-8434
Web: www.nbc.ca

PRODUCTS/OPERATIONS

2010 Sales

	% of total
Interest	
Loans	37
Securities & other	18
Noninterest	
Trust services & mutual funds	7
Securities brokerage commissions	6
Securitization revenue	5
Underwriting & advisory fees	5
Deposit & payment service charges	4
Lending fees	3
Other	15
Total	**100**

Selected Subsidiaries

Natbank (banking US)
NATCAN (75% portfolio management and investments)
National Bank Direct Brokerage (online brokerage)
National Bank Financial (investment banking)
National Bank General Insurance (home and auto coverage)
National Bank Insurance Firm (insurance brokerage)
National Bank Life Insurance Company
National Bank Securities (mutual funds)
National Bank Trust (trust services)

COMPETITORS

BMO Financial Group
CIBC
Caisses centrale
Desjardins
Laurentian Bank
RBC Financial Group
Scotiabank
TD Bank

HISTORICAL FINANCIALS

Company Type: Public

Income Statement FYE: October 31

	ASSETS ($ mil.)	NET INCOME ($ mil.)	INCOME AS % OF ASSETS	EMPLOYEES
10/15	164,216	1,142	0.7%	19,764
10/14	183,589	1,277	0.7%	19,955
10/13	179,938	1,375	0.8%	19,691
10/12	178,387	1,522	0.9%	19,920
10/11	167,519	1,141	0.7%	19,431
Annual Growth	(0.5%)	0.0%	—	0.4%

2015 Year-End Financials

Return on assets: 0.7%
Return on equity: 14.8%
Long-term debt ($ mil.): —
No. of shares (mil.): 337
Sales ($ mil): 5,809
Dividends
Yield: 0.0%
Payout: 45.2%
Market value ($ mil.): 11,133

	STOCK PRICE ($) FY Close	P/E High/Low		PER SHARE ($) Earnings	Dividends	Book Value
10/15	33.01	9	7	3.43	1.55	23.78
10/14	46.87	19	9	3.86	1.73	26.34
10/13	86.95	19	16	4.21	3.35	23.88
10/12	77.36	17	14	4.67	3.06	22.44
10/11	72.47	23	18	3.47	2.77	20.27
Annual Growth	(17.8%)	—	—	(0.3%)	(13.5%)	4.1%

National Bank Of Greece S A

Like the ancient ruins that dominate the landscape of Greece National Bank of Greece (NBG) dominates the banking landscape of the Mediterranean. In addition to holding the top position at home NBG has taken a leading position in the Balkans by acquiring controlling stakes in banks throughout the region. The bank offers such services as commercial and consumer banking asset management investment banking brokerage services financing and insurance. It has more than 500 domestic branches and another 1200 in nearly a dozen outside countries. NBG once served as the Greek central bank but the government sold its stake in the company in 2004.

OperationsBroadly speaking NBG generates 75% of its revenue in the form of interest income (mostly from loans) while the remainder comes from a mix of insurance income deposit account charges and other fees and commissions credit card fees and gains available-for-sale securities.NBG's Turkish Operations is the bank's largest segment generating more than 40% of the bank's total revenue. The unit offers a variety of commercial banking services through Finansbank and its subsidiaries in Turkey.

The Retail Banking division makes up another 20% of revenue and serves individual customers professionals small-medium and small sized companies (identified as businesses with revenues up to 2.5 million or roughly $2.8 million) in Greece. Corporate & Investment Banking (20% of revenue) lends to large and medium-sized companies and also offers shipping finance and investment banking services.

The bank's International business (roughly 10% of revenue) offers commercial banking services including commercial and retail credit trade financing foreign exchange and traditional deposit banking to countries outside of Greece and Turkey. In addition to Finansbank in Turkey NBG's seven other non-Greek subsidiaries include: United Bulgarian Bank (UBB) Vojvodjanska Banka Banca Romaneasca Stopanska Banka the National Bank of Greece (Cyprus) Ltd. (NBG Cyprus) Banka NBG (NBG Albania) South African Bank of Athens (SABA) and NBG Bank (Malta) Ltd. (NBG Malta).NBG also has an Insurance business (5% of revenue) as well as a Global Markets & Asset Management business. Other services include proprietary real estate management and hotel and warehousing services which make up less than 5% of revenue.Geographic Reach

In addition to Greece NBG operates banks in Albania Bulgaria Cyprus Egypt Romania Serbia and FYROM South Africa and Turkey. While most of the bank's revenue comes from its home country about 40% of revenue comes from its operations in Turkey while another roughly 10% comes from countries outside of Greece and Turkey.Sales and MarketingNBG markets its products and services through agents and independent insurance brokers. It spent 53 million ($64.4 million) on promotion and advertising in 2014 up from 68 million ($82.65 million) in 2013.Financial PerformanceNote: Growth rates may differ after conversion to US dollars.The bank has come a long way from its low point in 2011 caused by heavy trading losses and political turmoil in its home country. Still after two years of growth revenue in 2014 plunged by 27% to 5.09 billion ($6.19 billion) mostly due to losses on its derivative investments but also because the bank collected less interest income from a rise in non-performing loans. NBG returned to the red in 2014 reporting a net loss of 2.5 billion ($3 billion) mostly due to a combination of lower revenue and higher loan loss provisions as the quality of its domestic loan portfolio worsened in the midst of intense political uncertainty and bad economic conditions in Greece. The bank's operations provided more cash in 2014 as most of its losses were related to non-cash loan loss provisions. StrategyGiven the poor economic climate in Greece and heated political battles ensuing related to the country's debt levels NBG has been operating in a challenging business climate. To turn around its struggling loan portfolio which has been suffering from domestic property devaluations in troubled Greece and resulting loan asset impairments the bank has been focusing on strengthening its capital position in raising cash from share offerings and selling off riskier loan assets in favor of safer ones. The bank has also been relying heavily on its Turkish Operations to generate loan business in Turkey where roughly 40% of its revenue came from in 2014. Mergers and AcquisitionsIn 2013 NGB made several acquisitions to expand its branch reach and loan business. In mid-2013 for example it purchased selected assets from the troubled banks Probank S.A. and First Business Bank S.A. (FBB) for a total of around 1 billion ($1.3 billion) adding 19 FBB branches and 112 Probank branches to the NBG branch network.

HISTORY

Company BackgroundThe National Bank of Greece (NBG) can trace its banking heritage back to Pasion a metic (non-Greek) former slave living in Athens in the fourth century BC. To help his former master rebuild after one of Greece's many wars he obtained a small private bank that had been formed a few decades earlier and became one of Athens' greatest bankers.

The bank as it exists today though was established in 1841 and for most of its existence served as Greece's central bank. It listed on the Athens Stock Exchange in 1880. NBG survived WWI and Germany's occupation of Greece during WWII. It weathered the civil war in the late 1940s the military coup that overthrew the constitutional monarchy in the 1960s and democratic reformation in the 1970s.

As the 1980s dawned and Andreas Papandreou's socialist government came to power in Greece the bank launched a joint venture in Paris with Crdit Lyonnais and other investors. NBG caused plenty of problems for its privately owned competitors during the early part of the decade — as deposits declined profits shrank and labor costs rose the bank was able to undercut competitors thanks to its government backing.

A banking scandal involving NBG and Papandreou helped topple the socialist government in the late 1980s. The bank's US subsidiary Atlantic Bank of New York was one of two Greek banks charged with money laundering to the tune of $700 million. Rival political parties called for Papandreou already ailing to resign. (In 1992 the former leader was acquitted of corruption charges stemming from the scandal.)

Under the leadership of a different government in the early 1990s the bank looked to shake up its holdings to improve profits. It sold off a number of subsidiaries including a chain of luxury hotels an insurance unit and Traders Credit Bank a small commercial bank. These divestitures were just the beginning as the Greek government looked to privatize a number of its holdings. Turmoil in the Greek economy in the mid-1990s forced the bank to limit withdrawals hike interest rates and take other conservative measures as the government tried to prevent a devaluation of the native currency.

In the late 1990s Greece looked to join the Euro zone and its institutions began shaping up. Doing its part NBG took measures to clean up its balance sheet writing off a number of bad loans it had been pressured to make by the government. The bank focused on retail operations absorbed the National Mortgage Bank and transformed its ETEVA development banking subsidiary into a full-fledged investment bank. It began shoring up flagging overseas operations listed on the NYSE (1999) and looked to expand in the Balkans.

In 1997 the bank opened offices in Albania and three years later bought controlling interests in Macedonia's Skopanska Banka and United Bulgarian Bank. As the 20th century drew to a close NGB won more freedom from the Greek government when the finance ministry announced it would no longer appoint the bank's executive officers instead allowing NGB's board of directors and shareholders to make the decisions.

In 2000 the company launched subsidiary NBG Venture Capital which concentrates on Greece southeast Europe and the eastern Mediterranean. The government sold 10% of its stake in the bank in 2003 as part of its privatization program. Although the move dropped its holdings to 30% the government retained management control. The state divested its interest in the company in 2004.

EXECUTIVES

Deputy CEO, Petros Christodoulou, age 55, $299,693 total compensation

General Manager Risk Management, Michael Oratis, age 58, $323,450 total compensation

Manager Strategic Planning & Research Division, Paul Mylonas, age 57, $292,390 total compensation

General Manager of Corporate Banking Chairman of the Board of Directors at Ethniki Insurance Co, Dimitrios G. Dimopoulos, age 69, $213,254 total compensation

General Manager of Retail Banking, Nelly Tzakou-Lambropoulou, age 54, $205,284 total compensation

General Manager Real Estate, Aristotelis Karytinos, age 60, $344,833 total compensation

CEO, Leonidas Fragkiadakis, age 50, $241,674 total compensation

Chief Financial Officer, Paula N. Hadjisotiriou, age 58

General Manager Group Retail Collections, Marianna Politopoulou

Chief Credit Officer, Dimitris Frangetis

Group CIO, Nikos Christodoulou

Chair, Louka T. Katseli

Auditors: Deloitte Hadjipavlou Sofianos & Cambanis S.A.

LOCATIONS

HQ: National Bank Of Greece S A
86 Eolou St., Athens 10232
Phone: (30) 210 334 1000 **Fax:** (30) 210 334 2235
Web: www.nbg.gr

PRODUCTS/OPERATIONS

2014 Sales

	% of total
Turkish operation	41
Retail banking	19
International	12
Insurance	5
Corporate and investment banking	21
Others	2
Total	**100**

COMPETITORS

Alpha Bank
Bank of Cyprus
Citibank
EFG Eurobank Ergasias
Emporiki Bank
HSBC
Piraeus Bank S.A.
Royal Bank of Scotland

HISTORICAL FINANCIALS

Company Type: Public

Income Statement FYE: December 31

	ASSETS ($ mil.)	NET INCOME ($ mil.)	INCOME AS % OF ASSETS	EMPLOYEES
12/14	131,776	(3,010)	—	34,628
12/13	147,091	50	0.0%	37,591
12/12	133,328	(3,344)	—	35,573
12/11	133,829	(18,806)	—	34,530
12/10	158,907	(474)	—	36,866
Annual Growth	(4.6%)	—	—	(1.6%)

2014 Year-End Financials

Return on assets: (-2.3%)
Return on equity: (-104.8%)
Long-term debt ($ mil.): —
No. of shares (mil.): 235
Sales ($ mil): 6,302
Dividends
Yield: —
Payout: —
Market value ($ mil.): —

National Grid plc

It's not gridlock but a lock on the Grid that is a good thing for National Grid. It is the sole owner and operator of the electricity transmission system in England and Wales. It transmits electricity through about 4500 miles of overhead and underground lines to distribution utilities serving more than 52 million people. National Grid also operates the UK natural gas transmission and distribution system (serving 10.9 million homes and businesses) through its National Grid Gas subsidiary. However it is the company's Northeastern US gas distribution and power generation transmission and distribution operations led by National Grid USA that bring in the bulk of the company's revenues.

Geographic Reach

In fiscal 2015 (March year end) the US accounted for 53% of revenues; the UK 47%.

Operations

In the US the company distributes power to about 3.5 million customers in Massachusetts New Hampshire New York and Rhode Island and natural gas to 3.6 million clients in those states. It also manages the electricity distribution network in Long Island.

National Grid owns the high-voltage electricity transmission network in England and Wales and operates the high pressure gas transmission system in Britain.The electricity industry connects generation sources to homes and businesses through transmission and distribution networks. National Grid produces electricity from fossil fuel and nuclear power stations as well as renewable sources such as wind and solar. In the US National Grid owns and operates 50 fossil fuel-powered stations on Long Island and 4.6 MW of solar generation in Massachusetts.It operates the transmission network in England and Wales and also operates Scottish networks. The company is working in a joint venture with Scottish Power Transmission to construct an interconnector to reinforce the transmission system between Scotland and England and Wales. In the US it jointly operates transmission facilities spanning upstate New York Massachusetts New Hampshire Rhode Island and Vermont.The company's gas industry connects producers processors storage transmission and distribution network operators as well as suppliers to industrial commercial and domestic users. Gas used in the UK is mainly sourced from gas fields in the North and Irish seas piped from Europe and imported as LNG. Gas used in the US is produced mainly in North America. National Grid owns and operate Grain LNG an importation terminal and storage facility at the Isle of Grain in Kent.

Sales and Marketing

The company sells electricity under a long-term contract power supply agreement. It delivers gas to 10.9 million consumers in the UK and 3.6 million customers in the US. The customers buy gas in U.S. via independent providers.

Financial Performance

In fiscal 2015 National Grid's net revenues increased by 3% (in local currency) driven by higher revenues in the UK Electricity Transmission business reflecting increases in allowed Transmission Owner revenues and higher core allowances and pass-through costs in UK Gas Transmission.Revenues in the UK Gas Distribution business were slightly lower as a result of changes in allowed revenues for replacement expenditure. US Regulated businesses revenues were also lower as a result of the end of the LIPA Management Services Agreement in the previous year partially offset by revenue increases from existing rate plans together with additional income from gas customer growth and the impact of the strengthening US dollar.Net income decreased by 18% (in local currency) due to an increase in operating costs as the result of higher controllable costs (including the impact of inflation and additional costs to improve data quality and bring regulatory filings up to date); higher US bad debt costs following an exceptionally cold winter; and higher depreciation and amortization as a result of continued investment programs. These cost increases were partly offset by a reduction in spend on US financial systems implementation and stabilization upgrades.National Grid's cash from operating activities increased by 25% (in local currency) due to changes in exceptional items re-measurements and stranded cost recoveries working capital (principally in the US due to the collection of high winter charges and other settlements including Superstorm Sandy reinsurance claims and LIPA receipts).

Strategy

The company's long-term strategy is to focus on large-scale power and gas systems in the UK and the US and to better integrate its various operations.

National Grid continues to work on developing additional interconnector projects (including opportunities for interconnection with Iceland Denmark and a further link with France). In the UK it is expanding gas system enhancement investment programs and developing electric grid modernization plans.The company also continues investments in US programs investing in electricity and gas infrastructure to improve resilience and help reduce the impact of service interruptions. It is also investing in mobile technology.

HISTORY

The National Grid Company was formed in 1990 as part of the privatization of the electricity industry in England and Wales. Until then the Central Electricity Generating Board (CEGB) a state monopoly responsible for power generation in England and Wales owned the national power grid (transmission system) and sold power to 12 area boards the regional authorities that distributed electricity to customers.

The Electricity Act of 1989 paved the way for competition; in 1990 the CEGB was split into The National Grid Company and three power-generating firms: National Power PowerGen and Nuclear Electric. The 12 area boards transferred their assets to 12 regional companies which jointly owned National Grid. The company keeping its monopoly status was charged to develop and operate an efficient coordinated and economical transmission system and to facilitate competition among power producers.

The company moved outside the UK when it invested in Citelec in 1993. An international consortium Citelec controlled Transener the surviving transmission system after Argentina privatized its electric utilities.

Also in 1993 National Grid set up Energis as a telecommunications firm to provide service to businesses. Piggybacking its fiber-optic lines on National Grid's transmission network Energis introduced national services in 1994 and by 1996 it had won several major customers including the BBC and Microsoft.

In 1995 National Grid went public as The National Grid Group. It also secured concessions to build transmission lines in Pakistan but in 1997 a new Pakistani government put the project on hold. That year it also upped its stake in Citelec from 15% to 41% which increased its control over the development of Argentina's transmission system. With partner CINergy Global it also acquired 80% of the Power Division of Zambia Consolidated Copper Mines in 1997 and it was chosen as a joint venture partner by India's Karnataka Electricity Board to build a transmission line in that state.

The company sold 26% of Energis in 1997; in 1998 it announced plans to sell the rest of Energis and launch a new company under the National Grid banner to set up telecom firms overseas. That year it laid plans to enter the US by agreeing to acquire New England Electric System (NEES). (The $3.2 billion purchase closed in 2000.)

In 1999 the company cut its stake in Energis to 46% and announced plans to shop for more US energy holdings. A deal was struck to purchase New York Utility Niagara Mohawk Holdings the following year. (The deal was completed in 2002.) Also in 2000 and 2001 the company continued to slim its stake in Energis (33%).

National Grid sold some noncore businesses in 2001 including UK metering company Datum Services and US energy marketer Allenergy and pulled out of the transmission project in India. It also agreed to manage the Alliance Regional Transmission Organization (RTO) in the US. In 2002 National Grid sold Niagara Mohawk's 50% interest in Canadian Niagara Power to Canadian utility Fortis.

The firm changed its name to National Grid Transco in 2002 upon completion of its acquisition of Lattice Group in a $21.5 billion deal.

In 2005 National Grid Transco sold four of its regional gas distribution networks; the North England network was acquired by a consortium that includes United Utilities and Cheung Kong Infrastructure; the South of England and Scotland networks were sold to Scottish and Southern Energy Borealis Infrastructure and Ontario Teachers' Pension Plan; and the Wales & West distribution network was purchased by a consortium managed by Macquarie Bank Limited. The company dropped Transco from its name in 2005.

National Grid dramatically boosted its North American assets in 2007 by acquiring gas distributor KeySpan for more than $7 billion. To comply with federal regulations connected to the KeySpan deal in 2008 National Grid sold its 2480-MW Ravenswood Generating Station in New York City to TransCanada for $2.9 billion.

In the second half of the decade to raise cash and narrow its operational focus the company jettisoned a number of noncore operations. National Grid sold its stakes in the alternative telecommunications network industry. The company also sold its telecom interests in Chile Argentina and Poland and wrote off its 33% stake in bankrupt UK telecommunications firm Energis which uses fiber-optic cable strung along National Grid's power lines. National Grid also sold former Lattice Group subsidiary 186k (fiber-optic networking) to Hutchison Whampoa and exited its telecom venture in Brazil. It also sold its electricity interconnector linking Australia to the island state of Tasmania.

In 2010 a National Grid and TenneT joint venture began laying the first section of a high-voltage cable that will link the power grids in the UK and the Netherlands bolstering power supply in both countries. The project will help the companies meet environmental goals by facilitating power flows from low-carbon generation plants.

With an eye on meeting ambitious European Union goals for carbon emission reductions in 2009 National Grid released a report that by 2020 half of the UK's heating needs could be provided by biogas (converted from sewage and injected into the national gas distribution system) compensating for a decline in North Sea gas supply. In 2010 the company had one renewable gas plant under development in the US and two in the UK.

The company reported a major jump in revenues and income in 2010 primarily driven by a rebounding economy (prompting increased demand for power and gas) and by improved rates in the US market. Revenues grew by 40% in 2011 and net income by 30% thanks to strong demand and higher prices in the UK and increased rates in the US.

In 2011 National Grid announced plans to save $200 million in a restructuring of its US operations including cutting 1200 jobs. Late in 2011 the company sold the Seneca-Upshur Petroleum subsidiary for approximately $152 million. The deal is a further move to return to core business operations in gas and electricity distribution. That year it also agreed to sell its non-regulated metering business in the UK (Onstream) to Macquarie Bank for about $440 million.

EXECUTIVES

Finance Director, Andrew R. J. Bonfield, age 52, $712,000 total compensation
CEO and Director, Steven J. (Steve) Holliday, age 59, $1,000,000 total compensation
Global CIO, David W. Lister
President US Operations, Dean S. Seavers, age 55
CEO, John Pettigrew
Chairman, Peter Gershon, age 68
Auditors: PricewaterhouseCoopers LLP

LOCATIONS

HQ: National Grid plc
1-3 Strand, London WC2N 5EH
Phone: (44) 20 7004 3000 **Fax:** (44) 20 7004 3004
Web: www.nationalgrid.com

2014 Sales

	% of total
US	53
UK	47
Total	**100**

PRODUCTS/OPERATIONS

2014 Sales

	% of total
US Regulated	52
UK Electricity Transmission	25
UK Gas distribution	12
UK Gas Transmission	6
Other activities	5
Total	**100**

COMPETITORS

Con Edison
Enterprise Group
Eversource Energy
HomeServe
IBERDROLA
Northern Electric
Northern Ireland Electricity
Northern Powergrid
Scottish and Southern Energy

HISTORICAL FINANCIALS

Company Type: Public

Income Statement FYE: March 31

	REVENUE ($ mil.)	NET INCOME ($ mil.)	NET PROFIT MARGIN	EMPLOYEES
03/15	22,466	2,983	13.3%	24,274
03/14	24,654	4,122	16.7%	23,909
03/13	21,820	3,487	16.0%	25,224
03/12	22,164	3,262	14.7%	25,645
03/11	23,077	3,473	15.1%	27,089
Annual Growth	(0.7%)	(3.7%)	—	(2.7%)

2015 Year-End Financials

Debt ratio: 69.5%
Return on equity: 16.9%
Cash ($ mil.): 175
Current ratio: 0.82
Long-term debt ($ mil.): 33,818
No. of shares (mil.): —
Dividends
Yield: 5.3%
Payout: —
Market value ($ mil.): —

	STOCK PRICE ($) FY Close	P/E High/Low	PER SHARE ($) Earnings	Dividends	Book Value
03/15	64.61	132112	0.79	3.45	4.73
03/14	68.74	106 90	1.10	3.15	5.14
03/13	58.01	93 77	0.95	0.00	4.24
03/12	50.48	93 79	0.91	0.00	4.15
03/11	48.04	83 62	1.02	7.03	4.00
Annual Growth	7.7%	— —	(6.3%)	(16.3%)	4.3%

National Westminster Bank Plc

One of the retail banking arms of The Royal Bank of Scotland (RBS) National Westminster Bank (NatWest) provides banking and financial services to individual and small business clients in the UK. The bank offers deposits mortgages credit cards and personal loans through a network of 1500 bank branches. It also offers phone and Internet banking as well as a network of cash machines and mobile banking units. Subsidiary Ulster Bank has some 240 branches across the island of Ireland. Other offerings include life insurance pensions private banking services carbon offsets and other more prosaic business services as well as investment and retirement management.

NatWest was formed by the 1968 merger of National Provincial Bank (established in 1833) and Westminster Bank (1836). RBS acquired the company in 2000 in the UK's largest bank takeover to date.

The bank has struggled through the global financial crisis which deeply crippled parent RBS. RBS became 84% owned by the UK government after it received a series of bailouts in 2008 and 2009. NatWest reported a loss in 2010 as the result of lower gains on redemption of own debt higher costs and higher impairment losses.

As part of RBS' agreement with the European Commission the company is selling more than 300 of its branches and locations including seven NatWest branches in Scotland to Spanish bank Santander. The transaction (aimed at cutting costs) is expected to close in 2012.

EXECUTIVES

Chief Executive, Stephen A. M. Hester, age 50
Chairman, Philip Hampton, age 62
Auditors: Deloitte LLP

LOCATIONS

HQ: National Westminster Bank Plc
135 Bishopsgate, London EC2M 3UR
Phone: (44) 131 626 4099 **Fax:** (44) 131 626 3081
Web: www.natwest.com

PRODUCTS/OPERATIONS

2010 Sales

	% of total
Net interest income	39
Non interest income	61
Total	**100**

COMPETITORS

AIB
Barclays
Clydesdale Bank
Grupo Santander
HSBC
Lloyds Banking Group
Yorkshire Bank

HISTORICAL FINANCIALS

Company Type: Public

Income Statement FYE: December 31

	ASSETS ($ mil.)	NET INCOME ($ mil.)	INCOME AS % OF ASSETS	EMPLOYEES
12/14	482,268	2,705	0.6%	24,600
12/13	584,120	(9,854)	—	25,600
12/12	612,451	(5,280)	—	24,100
12/11	567,814	(5,950)	—	26,900
12/10	569,092	(3,502)	—	27,300
Annual Growth	(4.1%)	—	—	(2.6%)

2014 Year-End Financials

Return on assets: 0.5%
Return on equity: 11.6%
Long-term debt ($ mil.): —
No. of shares (mil.): 1,678
Sales ($ mil): 15,137
Dividends
Yield: 7.4%
Payout: —
Market value ($ mil.): 43,834

	STOCK PRICE ($) FY Close	P/E High/Low		PER SHARE ($) Earnings	Dividends	Book Value
12/14	26.12	—	—	(0.00)	1.94	15.68
12/13	25.18	—	—	(0.00)	1.94	12.68
12/12	24.78	—	—	(0.00)	1.94	19.88
12/11	16.78	—	—	(0.00)	1.87	14.85
12/10	21.73	—	—	(0.00)	1.94	13.93
Annual Growth	4.7%	—	—	—	(0.0%)	3.0%

NATIXIS SA

Natixis operates in the nexus of the money movers and the money shakers. The company is the corporate banking asset management and specialized financial services arm of French banking giant Groupe BPCE. Natixis serves commercial and financial institutions and wealthy individuals in some 70 countries worldwide. It has some E540 billion (some $790 billion) of assets under management. Other activities include real estate finance brokerage employee benefits planning and payment processing services. Subsidiary Coface provides credit insurance and credit management services. BPCE which was formed in 2009 through the merger of Banques Populaires and Caisses d'Epargne controls some 70% of Natixis.

Natixis has been working to recover from steep revenue declines in 2008 and 2009 some of the toughest years on the global financial sector in several decades. It has restructured itself to streamline operations consolidating units and selling others. The company is also increasingly taking advantage of its connection to BPCE and the cross-selling opportunities that offers as well as investing in new business lines such as exchange-traded funds. Although revenues continued to sink in 2010 the company returned to profitability that year.

The company is looking abroad for future growth. It recently established new offices in Asia where it hopes to build its asset management business. Natixis is beefing up its operations in the US as well.

In 2011 Natixis Global Asset Management (NGAM) acquired Darius Capital Partners an investment advisory and consulting firm with offices in Paris and New York. The addition will help the firm address a growing demand from institutional investors for for transparency liquidity and risk management. NGAM has been gaining momentum in Europe. It also acquired French-based OSSIAM and London-based H2O Asset Management.

HISTORY

Natexis Banques Populaires traces its roots back to end of both world wars. Cr dit National was formed in 1919 at the end of WWI to oversee reconstruction grants. The bank specialized in long-term loans for industry and energy companies.

Banque Fran aise du Commerce Ext rieur (BFCE) was formed in 1946 to provide loans for France's postwar foreign trade. BFCE made commercial loans and offered credits for importers and exporters. Both Cr dit National and BFCE were "quasi state-controlled" and fulfilled institutional roles set up by the French government.

In the 1980s stagnation in international trade the end of subsidized interest rates and deregulation in the French banking industry meant French banks would have to become more competitive. Unfortunately for Cr dit National and BFCE the limited structure of their state-mandated business left them woefully unprepared to do other sorts of business. Rather than redirect their business aim Cr dit National and BFCE looked for partners who would complement them.

In 1996 Cr dit National and BFCE merged to become Natexis Group. The new entity linked Cr dit National's domestic client base with BFCE's international operations. The name "Natexis" was chosen because it was easy to pronounce and inoffensive to clients in any of dozens of countries where the company was active.

In 1997 Groupe Banques Populaires (GBP) in an effort to develop more international business and widen its range of services acquired a 23% interest in Natexis Group. Natexis benefited from the financial stability and depth of its new shareholder. The next year GBP upped its stake in Natexis to 71%. The acquisition rounded out GBP's mostly retail products with large and midsized corporate banking lines.

In 1999 GBP merged its main subsidiary Caisse Centrale des Banques Populaires (France's fifth-largest retail banker) with Natexis to form Natexis Banques Populaires. This regrouping paired Natexis with Banques Populaires' regional business to create a single full-service European bank.

In 2000 Natexis bought an 80% share of London Metals Exchange trader Sogemin Metals.

Natixis was formed in 2006 when Natexis Banques Populaires merged with CNCE's investment divisions including Ixis Corporate and Investment Bank and Ixis Asset Management.

In 2007 Natixis sold its bond insurance business CIFG Holding to parents CNCE and GPB for E1.1 billion ($1.5 billion). The move was intended to preserve CIFG's AAA debt rating which is integral to its business.

The following year the company restructured its corporate and investment banking businesses. It announced plans to stop offering credit and structured credit proprietary investments as well as complex capital investments such as complex fixed-income derivates. It also dropped plans to develop in India and Korea and closed an office in South America. The firm opened an office in Taiwan in 2009.

Also in 2009 the firm named Laurent Mignon as its CEO replacing Dominique Ferrero who was not renewed to the post by the board of directors.
Auditors: Deloitte & Associ ©

LOCATIONS

HQ: NATIXIS SA
30, avenue Pierre Mendes France, Paris 75013
Phone: (33) 1 58 32 30 00
Web: www.natixis.com

HISTORICAL FINANCIALS

Company Type: Public

Income Statement FYE: December 31

	ASSETS ($ mil.)	NET INCOME ($ mil.)	INCOME AS % OF ASSETS	EMPLOYEES
12/14	717,663	1,383	0.2%	20,287
12/13	702,315	1,217	0.2%	19,632
12/12	696,417	1,187	0.2%	20,198
12/11	656,701	2,020	0.3%	20,451
12/10	612,986	2,318	0.4%	19,576
Annual Growth	4.0%	(12.1%)	—	0.9%

2014 Year-End Financials

Return on assets: 0.2%
Return on equity: 6.1%
Long-term debt ($ mil.): —
No. of shares (mil.): —
Sales ($ mil): 21,830
Dividends
Yield: 0.0%
Payout: 453.6%
Market value ($ mil.): —

STOCK PRICE ($) FY Close	P/E High/Low	PER SHARE ($) Earnings	Dividends	Book Value
12/14 68.46	201162	0.43	1.93	7.37
12/13 53.50	202153	0.37	8.35	7.96
12/12 32.50	133122	0.36	0.86	8.34
12/11 31.20	129 69	0.56	3.02	8.69
12/10 58.50	131131	0.62	0.00	9.65
Annual Growth 4.0%	— —	(8.8%)	—	(6.5%)

NEC Corp

Radio and t.v. communications equipment

HISTORY

A group of Japanese investors led by Kunihiko Iwadare formed Nippon Electric Company (NEC) in a joint venture with Western Electric (US) in 1899. Starting as an importer of telephone equipment NEC soon became a maker and a major supplier to Japan's Communications Ministry. Western Electric sold its stake in NEC in 1925. The company became affiliated with the Sumitomo "keiretsu" (industrial group) in the 1930s and went public in 1949.

After Nippon Telegraph and Telephone (NTT) was formed in 1952 NEC became one of its four leading suppliers. The post-WWII need to repair Japan's telephone systems and the country's continuing economic recovery resulted in strong demand from NTT for NEC's products. In the 1950s and 1960s NTT business represented more than half of sales even though NEC expanded overseas diversified into home appliances and formed a computer alliance with Honeywell. NTT which began acquiring shares in the company decades earlier and owned as much as 59% of NEC sold its stake in the 1960s.

In the 1970s Honeywell's lagging position in computers hurt NEC; the company recovered through in-house development efforts and a mainframe venture with Toshiba. In 1977 CEO Koji Kobayashi articulated his revolutionary vision of NEC's future as an integrator of computers and communications through semiconductor technology.

NEC invested heavily in R&D and expansion becoming the world's largest semiconductor maker in 1985. Despite its proprietary operating system NEC garnered more than 50% of the Japanese computer market in the 1980s. NEC entered into a mainframe computer partnership with Honeywell and France's Groupe Bull in 1987.

By the early 1990s NEC lost its status as the world's largest semiconductor maker to Intel. NEC bought 20% of US computer maker Packard Bell in 1995 and merged most of its PC business outside Japan with that company creating Packard Bell NEC in 1996. Also in 1996 NEC created US subsidiary Holon Net Corp. to make hardware and software for Internet and intranet markets.

NEC took control of Packard Bell NEC in 1998 upping its stake to 53%. A sluggish Japanese economy and slumping memory prices contributed to NEC's drop in income for fiscal 1998. A defense contract scandal involving overbilling and improper hiring by an NEC unit forced the resignation of chairman Tadahiro Sekimoto and later president Hisashi Kaneko.

President Koji Nishigaki the first at NEC without an engineering background led a sweeping reorganization to cut 10% of the company's workforce –15000 employees –over three years. He revamped NEC operations around Internet application hardware software and services. In 1998 NEC formed a rare pact with a Japanese rival allying with Hitachi to consolidate memory chip operations. The restructuring of Packard Bell NEC (NEC by then owned 88%) helped cause a $1.3 billion loss for fiscal 1999 NEC's worst-ever drop. NEC folded up its Packard Bell NEC division later that year imposing layoffs of about 80% of its staff divesting it from the US retail market and excising the historic Packard Bell brand name in that region.

NEC restructured again in 2000 splitting into more autonomous units and streamlining its PC operations. That year the company launched an aggressive spending program in a move to lead the broadband mobile networking market. In 2001 NEC ended a long-running dispute with Cray investing $25 million in the company and granting distribution rights to its vector supercomputers in North America –a deal contingent upon Cray's dropping an antidumping suit that led to heavy import taxes being placed on NEC supercomputers sold in the US.

Nishigaki became vice chairman in 2004 and Akinobu Kanasugi was named president. Kanasugi held the post just two years until poor health forced him to turn the reins over to SVP Kaoru Yano. Yano stepped down as president in April 2010 but retained his position as chairman. SVP Nobuhiro Endo who has been with the company since 1981 was promoted to president.

In 2004 NEC took public its DRAM joint venture Elpida Memory thereby reducing its stake in the company and the volatile memory sector. NEC also sold its plasma display business to Pioneer that same year. In 2005 the company dissolved its monitor joint venture with Mitsubishi and took full ownership of the unit (NEC Display Solutions). The next year it sold its European PC operations Packard Bell to Lap Shun "John" Hui a co-founder of eMachines.

The company joined with Sumitomo Electric Industries in 2008 to acquire fiber-optic submarine cable manufacturer OCC Holdings; NEC and Sumitomo acquired 75% and 25% stakes respectively.

Kaoru Yano stepped down as president of NEC in 2010 but retained his position as chairman. SVP Nobuhiro Endo who has been with the company since 1981 was promoted to president.

Auditors: KPMG AZSA LLC

LOCATIONS

HQ: NEC Corp
5-7-1 SHiba, Minato-ku, Tokyo 108-8001
Phone: (81) 3 3454 1111
Web: www.nec.co.jp

HISTORICAL FINANCIALS

Company Type: Public

Income Statement FYE: March 31

	REVENUE ($ mil.)	NET INCOME ($ mil.)	NET PROFIT MARGIN	EMPLOYEES
03/15	24,466	477	2.0%	98,882
03/14	29,481	326	1.1%	100,914
03/13	32,644	323	1.0%	102,375
03/12	37,020	(1,344)	—	109,102
03/11	37,622	(151)	—	115,840
Annual Growth	(10.2%)	—	—	(3.9%)

2015 Year-End Financials

Debt ratio: 0.1%
Return on equity: 7.5%
Cash ($ mil.): 1,331
Current ratio: 1.47
Long-term debt ($ mil.): 3,187
No. of shares (mil.): —
Dividends
Yield: —
Payout: —
Market value ($ mil.): —

	STOCK PRICE ($) FY Close	P/E High/Low	PER SHARE ($) Earnings	Dividends	Book Value
03/15	2.82	— —	0.18	0.00	2.84
03/14	2.75	— —	0.13	0.00	2.86
03/13	2.55	— —	0.12	0.00	3.42
03/12	1.95	— —	(0.52)	0.00	3.65
03/11	2.12	— —	(0.06)	0.04	4.07
Annual Growth	7.4%	— —	—	—	(8.6%)

Nedbank Group Ltd

Nedbank Group provides commercial and personal financial services in South Africa and other parts of the continent. The company offers a range of wholesale and retail banking services through principal business clusters Nedbank Corporate Nedbank Retail Nedbank Wealth Nedbank Business Banking and Nedbank Capital (investment banking and capital markets). Other services include property finance private banking credit card processing insurance and foreign exchange and securities trading. UK-based insurer Old Mutual owns a controlling stake in Nedbank Group.

In addition to about 500 retail and commercial banking branches located primarily in South Africa's urban and suburban areas Nedbank Group has some 400 banking outlets inside Pick 'n Pay grocery stores and more than 40 other locations elsewhere in southern Africa. To grow its retail business Nedbank is looking to underserved markets such as youth senior citizens and small and medium-sized enterprises. It is also building its wealth management operations. As part of an effort to increase its motor vehicle and asset finance business the company in 2010 acquired the nearly 49% of Imperial Bank that it did not already own.

Nedbank strengthened its presence in Africa in 2008 when it announced a strategic alliance with Ecobank an institution that operates mainly in west and central Africa. The deal which gives clients access to both banking networks covering more than 30 countries is part of Nedbank's overall strategy to expand internationally and within Africa.

UK-based global banking firm HSBC was in exclusive talks to acquire a majority stake in Nedbank from Old Mutual. However negotiations broke down in 2010 and the deal fell through. Neither side gave a reason why the talks came to an end. Also that year Mike Brown was named CEO of Nedbank. He succeeded Tom Boardman who retired but remained on the company's board of directors.

EXECUTIVES

CEO, Michael W. T. (Mike) Brown, age 48
Managing Executive Nedbank Capital, Brian Kennedy, age 54
Group Risk Officer, Philip Wessels, age 56
Managing Executive Nedbank Corporate, Mfundo Nkuhlu, age 48
Managing Executive Business Banking, Sandile Shabalala, age 47

CIO, Fred Swanepoel, age 51
CFO, Raisibe K. Morathi, age 46
Chief Risk Officer, Trevor Adams
COO, Graham Wayne Dempster
Chairman, Vassi Naidoo
Auditors: KPMG Inc.

LOCATIONS

HQ: Nedbank Group Ltd
Nedbank 135 Rivonia Campus, 135 Rivonia Road, Sandown, Johannesburg 2196
Phone: (27) 11 294 4444 **Fax:** (27) 11 294 6540
Web: www.nedbankgroup.co.za

COMPETITORS

Absa
Citigroup
FirstRand
Investec
Standard Chartered

HISTORICAL FINANCIALS

Company Type: Public

Income Statement FYE: December 31

	ASSETS ($ mil.)	NET INCOME ($ mil.)	INCOME AS % OF ASSETS	EMPLOYEES
12/14	70,057	847	1.2%	30,499
12/13	71,165	819	1.2%	29,513
12/12	80,221	878	1.1%	28,748
12/11	80,032	764	1.0%	28,494
12/10	91,622	724	0.8%	27,525
Annual Growth	(6.5%)	4.0%	—	2.6%

2014 Year-End Financials

Return on assets: 1.2%
Return on equity: 15.3%
Long-term debt ($ mil.): —
No. of shares (mil.): 465
Sales ($ mil): 6,318
Dividends
Yield: 3.2%
Payout: 36.6%
Market value ($ mil.): 9,986

	STOCK PRICE ($) FY Close	P/E High/Low		PER SHARE ($) Earnings	Dividends	Book Value
12/14	21.45	1	1	1.77	0.70	12.46
12/13	20.07	1	1	1.73	0.68	12.48
12/12	22.54	1	1	1.87	0.73	13.86
12/11	17.66	3	1	1.66	0.61	13.28
12/10	40.34	4	3	1.58	1.18	14.80
Annual Growth	(14.6%)	—	—	2.9%	(12.4%)	(4.2%)

Nestle S.A.

With instant coffee baby food and bottled water in the mix Nestl crunches more than just chocolate. The world's #1 food and drinks company in terms of sales Nestl is also the world leader in coffee (Nescaf). It also makes coffee for the home-brewing system Nespresso. Nestl is one of the world's top bottled water makers (Nestl Waters) one of the biggest frozen pizza makers (DiGiorno) and a big player in the pet food business (Friskies Purina). Its most well-known global food brands include Buitoni Dreyer's Maggi Milkmaid Carnation and Kit Kat. The company also owns Gerber Products. North America is Nestl's most important market.

HISTORY

Henri Nestl purchased a factory in Vevey Switzerland in 1843 that made products ranging from nut oils to rum. In 1867 he developed a powder made from cow's milk and wheat flour as a substitute for mother's milk. A year earlier Americans Charles and George Page had founded the Anglo-Swiss Condensed Milk Company in Cham Switzerland using Gail Borden's milk-canning technology. In 1875 Nestl sold his eponymous company then doing business in 16 countries. When Anglo-Swiss launched a milk-based infant food in 1878 Nestl's new owners responded by introducing a condensed-milk product. In 1905 a year after Nestl began selling chocolate the companies ended their rivalry by merging under the Nestl name. Hampered by limited milk supplies during WWI the company expanded into regions less affected by the war such as the US. In 1929 it acquired Cailler the first company to mass-produce chocolate bars and Swiss General inventor of milk chocolate. An investment in a Brazilian condensed-milk factory during the 1920s paid an unexpected dividend when Brazilian coffee growers suggested the company develop a water-soluble "coffee cube." Released in 1938 Nescaf instant coffee quickly became popular. Other new products included Nestl's Crunch bar (1938) Quik drink mix (1948) and Taster's Choice instant coffee (1966). Nestl expanded during the 1970s with acquisitions such as Beringer Brothers wines (sold in 1995) Stouffer's and Libby's. Moving beyond foods in 1974 Nestl acquired a 49% stake in Gesparal a holding company that controls the French cosmetics company L'Oral. It acquired pharmaceutical firm Alcon Laboratories three years later. Helmut Maucher was named chairman and CEO in 1981. He began beefing up Nestl's global presence. Boycotters had long accused Nestl of harming children in developing countries through the unethical promotion of infant formula and Maucher acknowledged the ongoing boycott by meeting with the critics and setting up a commission to police adherence to World Health Organization guidelines. Nestl bought Carnation in 1985. Maucher doubled the company's chocolate business in 1988 with the purchase of UK chocolate maker Rowntree (Kit Kat). Also in the 1980s Nestl acquired Buitoni pastas. The company expanded in the 1990s with the purchases of Butterfinger and Baby Ruth candies Source Perrier water Alpo pet food and Ortega Mexican foods. Company veteran Peter Brabeck-Letmathe succeeded Maucher as CEO in 1997. He cleaned out Nestl's pantry by selling non-core businesses (Contadina tomato products Libby's canned meat products) but restocked with San Pellegrino (mineral water) and Dalgety's Spillers (pet food) in 1998. By 1999 the company started rolling out its Nestl Pure Life bottled water. It also sold its Findus brand (fish vegetables) and its non-instant US coffee brands. That year Nestl merged its US novelty ice-cream unit with operations of Pillsbury's Häagen-Dazs to form Ice Cream Partners USA. In 2000 Nestl purchased snack maker PowerBar. In 2001 it bought Ralston Purina for $10.3 billion making it the world's largest pet food maker. To win FTC approval the companies agreed to sell Meow Mix and Alley Cat dry cat food brands to Hartz Mountain. In a deal that gives Nestl a 99-year license to use the Häagen-Dazs brand in the US the company agreed to pay $641 million to General Mills (which has bought Pillsbury from Britain's Diageo) for the other half of Ice Cream Partners. In 2002 Nestl acquired German ice-cream maker Schoeller Holding Group as well as US food company Chef America maker of Hot Pockets and Lean Pockets. That same year Nestl also spun off eyecare subsidiary Alcon Laboratories but retained about 75% ownership of it. The company renamed its water unit from Perrier Vittel SA to Nestl Waters and bought Russian bottled water company Saint Springs. The company sold its savory flavor business Food Ingredients Specialties (FIS) to Swiss flavoring company Givaudan and its UK and Ireland ambient foods business to HM Capital Partners (then named Hicks Muse Tate & Furst). It also formed a joint venture with New Zealand dairy co-op Fonterra to produce and distribute dairy products in the Americas. Nestl and Cadbury Schweppes (now Cadbury) made a joint $10.5 billion bid for The Hershey Company in 2002 but Hershey called the sale off later that year. While Nestl already owned 30% of US ice cream powerhouse Dreyer's in 2002 it proposed a merger of its US ice cream businesses. After months of antitrust scrutiny the final deal gave Nestl 67% of Dreyer's. Seeking to further strengthen its position in the worldwide ice cream market Nestl acquired the ice cream and related products of Movenpick a Swiss food company 2003. The acquisition brought Nestl licensing agreements with companies in Egypt Finland Germany Norway Sweden and Saudi Arabia. Other transactions in 2003 included the Nestl USA unit selling its Ortega brand Mexican food products to B&G Foods and the parent company selling Mont Blanc France's leading dessert brand to French investment firm Activa Capital. Also that year the company added to its bottled-water business by acquiring Hutchison Whampoa's Powwow which operates in Denmark France Germany Italy the Netherlands Portugal and the UK. In addition it acquired Clear Water a bottled-water home-and-office delivery company located in Russia. In line with its strategy to concentrate on value-added products in 2004 Nestl sold its cocoa-processing facilities in Germany and the UK to Cargill. Also in 2004 the company acquired Finnish dairy company Valid's Valiojäätelo ice cream business and increased its stake in Israeli bakery company Osem to 53%. In addition Nestl sold its German frozen food distributor Eastman that year and Nestl España bought Nestl Portugal for about $682 million. Nestl was ordered by the Brazilian government to sell its Chocolates Garoto in 2004 on the grounds that ownership of Garoto presented unfair market competition. Later that same year CEO Peter Brabeck-Letmathe announced he was considering reducing the number of outside directorships that he held because of increased demands as the leader of Nestl. At the time Brabeck-Letmathe sat on the boards of Alcon Credit Suisse Dreyer's Grand Ice Cream L'Oral Roche Holding and "Winterthur" Swiss Insurance Company. (He has since left the "Winterthur" board.) And that year in a tangle with a French union over retirement benefits Nestl threatened to sell Perrier or produce its popular water from another source. However the company reached a settlement with the union and the production of Perrier continued. Long-time chairman Rainer Gut retired in 2005 and Brabeck-Letmathe replaced him. In 2005 it became a 90% owner of Dreyer's Grand Ice Cream. The next year Nestl became the owner of more than 90% of Dreyer's as the result of an exercise of a Put Right whereby Nestl was required to purchase certain shareholders' Class A Callable Puttable Common Stock (or Class A shares). As a result of this "short form merger" Dreyer's ceased trading on the Nasdaq stock exchange. In keeping with its strategy to concentrate on value-added products during 2006 Nestl sold its cocoa processing facilities in Germany and the UK to Cargill. Adding to its dominance in the European ice cream sector the company acquired Finnish dairy company Valid's Valiojäätelo's ice cream business and Greece's Delta Ice cream which has operations in Bulgaria Greece Macedonia Montenegro Romania and Serbia. Later that year Nestl bought the Australian breakfast cereal snack and soup operations of Uncle Tobys from Burns Philp for $670 million. The cereal portion was integrated into Cereal Partners Worldwide. In another streamlining move the company agreed to sell its canned liquid milk businesses in Southeast Asia to Singapore-based Fraser and Neave. Hedging its bets considering its food products (candy bars ice cream) are on the opposite end of the waistline wars Nestl acquired Jenny Craig for $600 million in 2006. In 2007 the company purchased the medical-nutrition business of Novartis for 1.88 billion ($2.5 billion). The business which has operations in 40 countries worldwide makes food for hospital patients. The purchase was seen as a move by Nestl to concentrate on higher-margin products. Brands in the acquisition included Boost and Resource nutritional supplements and Optifast dieting products. Nestle divested some operations in France and Spain in order to settle competitive concerns surrounding the deal voiced by the European Commission. On the food front Nestl subsidiary Dreyer's purchased the Eskimo Pie and Chipwich brands from Canadian ice cream maker CoolBrands in 2007 for almost $19 million. Nestl spooned out $5.5 billion in cash to purchase Gerber Products from Novartis in 2007. The deal made Nestl the world's largest baby food company.

Due to the increased workload as chairman Peter Brabeck-Letmathe stepped down as CEO in 2008; he remained in an active role as board chairman. Paul Bulcke former head of Zone Americas for Nestl replaced Brabeck-Letmathe as CEO.

The company it added to its "out of home food and beverage" operations (i.e. foodservice) in 2009 with the purchase of Tampa-based Vitality Foodservice. Vitality provides commercial and non-commercial beverage services worldwide.

In August 2010 Nestl acquired Liverpool-based Vitaflo a maker of clinical nutrition products for people with metabolic disorders. Also in August it completed the sale of Alcon to Novartis. The pharmaceutical maker acquired Nestl's stake in Alcon in two steps beginning with the sale of a 25% stake for $11 billion in July 2008. Novartis exercised its option to buy Nestl's remaining percentage of Alcon for $28 billion in 2010.

In November 2011 Nestl acquired the Oscar stocks and sauces business from Paulig Group building Nestl Professional's presence in the culinary flavors sector.

In July 2014 Nestl acquired L'Oreal's 50% stake in Galderma a joint venture formed by the two companies in 1981. Going forward Galderma will operate as the pharmaceutical arm of Nestl Skin Health S.A. established in June 2014 as a fully-owned Nestl subsidiary.

EXECUTIVES

Deputy EVP GLOBE Programme Information Systems Strategic Supply Chain eNestl © and Group Information Security, Chris Johnson, age 54
President and CEO Nestl © Health Science, Luis Cantarell, age 63
EVP Operations and GLOBE (Global Business Excellence), Jose Lopez
CEO, Paul Bulcke, age 61, $2,000,000 total compensation
EVP Strategic Business Units; Marketing Sales and Nespresso, Patrice Bula, age 60
EVP; Head Asia Oceania and Africa (AOA), Wan Ling Martello
EVP Head of Nestl © Waters, Marco Settembri, age 57
EVP Zone Director for Europe, Laurent Freixe, age 53
Deputy EVP; CEO Nestl © Professional, Martial C. Rolland
EVP Zone Director for Asia Oceania Africa and Middle East, Nandu Nandkishore
EVP and CFO, Fran $is-Xavier Roger
Chairman and Managing Director South Africa, Ian Donald
EVP; CTO Head of Innovation Technology Research & Development, Stefan Catsicas
Deputy EVP Head of Human Resources and Centre Administration, Peter R. Vogt
Chair and CEO Nestl © Indochina, Audrey Liow
Chairman, Peter Brabeck-Letmathe, age 71
First Vice Chairman, Andreas N. Koopmann, age 64
Second Vice Chairman, Rolf H □nggi
Auditors: KPMG SA

LOCATIONS

HQ: Nestle S.A.
Avenue Nestle 55, Vevey CH-1800
Phone: (41) 21 924 2111 **Fax:** (41) 21 924 4800
Web: www.nestle.com

2014 Factories

	No.
Americas	163
Asia Oceania & Africa	143
Europe	136
Total	**442**

2014 Sales

	% of total
Zone Americas	30
Zone Asia Oceania and Africa	20
Zone Europe	17
Nestlé Nutrition	10
Nestlé Waters	8
Other businesses	15
Total	**100**

PRODUCTS/OPERATIONS

2014 Product Sales

	% of total
Powdered & liquid beverages	22
Milk products & ice cream	18
Prepared dishes & cooking aids	15
Nutrition & health care	14
Pet care	12
Confectionery	11
Water	8
Total	**100**

Selected Products and Brands

Bouillons soups seasonings pasta and sauces
- Buitoni
- Maggi
- Thomy
- Winiary

Chilled Nestlé
- Chiquitin
- La Laitière
- La Lechera
- LC1
- Molico
- Ski
- Sveltesse
- Svelty
- Yoco

Chocolate confectionery and biscuits
- Aero
- Baci
- Butterfinger
- Cailler
- Crunch
- Galak/Milkybar
- Kit Kat
- Nestlé
- Polo
- Smarties

Coffee
- Bonka
- Loumidis
- Nescafé
- Nespresso
- Ricoré Ricoffy
- Taster' s Choice
- Zoégas

Foodservice and professional products
- Chef
- Davigel
- Minor' s
- Santa Rica

Frozen foods (prepared dishes pizzas)
- Buitoni
- California Pizza Kitchen (licensed)
- Delissio (Canada only)
- Hot Pockets
- Jack' s Pizza
- Lean Cuisine
- Maggi
- Stouffer' s
- Tombstone

Healthcare and nutrition
- Clinutren
- Modulen
- Nutren
- Peptamen

Ice cream
- Antica Gelateria del Corso
- Chipwich
- Dreyer' s
- Drumstick/Extrême
- Edy' s
- Eskimo Pie
- Häagen-Dazs
- Maxibon/Tandem
- Mega
- Mövenpick
- Parar
- Sin Parar/Sem

Infant food and nutrition
- Beba
- Cérélac
- Gerber
- Good Start
- Guigoz
- Lactogen
- Nan
- Neslac
- Nestlé
- Nestogen
- Nestum

Other beverages
- Carnation
- Caro
- Libby' s
- Milo
- Nescau
- Nesquik
- Nestea

Performance nutrition
- PowerBar
- Pria

Pet care
- Alpo
- Beneful
- Cat Chow
- Dog Chow
- Fancy Feast
- Felix
- Gourmet
- Pro Plan
- Purina Friskies
- Purina ONE
- Tidy Cats

Refrigerated products (cold meat products dough pasta pizzas sauces)
- Buitoni
- Herta
- Nestlé
- Toll House

Shelf-stable products
- Bear Brand
- Carnation
- Coffee-Mate
- Gloria
- Klim
- La Lechera
- Milkmaid
- Moça
- Molico
- Nestlé Omega
- Nido
- Ninho
- Svelty

Water
- Acqua Panna
- Al Manhal
- Arrowhead
- Contrex
- Deer Park

Hépar
Ice Mountain
Levissima
Nestlé Aquarel
Nestlé Pure Life
Nestlé Vera
Ozarka
Perrier
Poland Spring
Quézac
S.Pellegrino
San Bernardo
Vittel
Zephyrhills

Selected Subsidiaries Joint Ventures and Affiliates

Beverage Partners Worldwide (50% with The Coca-Cola Company US)
Cereal Partners Worldwide (50% with General Mills US)
Galderma and Laboratoires innéov (29% with L' Oreal cosmetic and nutritional supplement products)
Gerber Products Company (infant nutrition US)
Jenny Craig Inc. (weight-loss centers and foods US)
Uncle Tobys (soups breakfast cereal snacks Australia)

COMPETITORS

Abbott Labs
Associated British Foods
Atkins Nutritionals
Bally Total Fitness
Barilla
Beech-Nut
Campbell Soup
Coca-Cola
ConAgra
Danone
Danone Water
Dean Foods
Dreyer' s
Fit America
GNC
General Mills
Goya
HMG
Heinz
Hershey
Indofood
Kellogg
Kent Gida
Kerry Group
Lindt & Sprngli
Mars Incorporated
Medifast
Mondelez International
Nutrisystem
PepsiCo
Procter & Gamble
Revlon
Russell Stover
Slim-Fast
Smucker
Starbucks
Suntory Holdings
Tata Global Beverages
United Biscuits
Weight Watchers International
Wimm-Bill-Dann
World' s Finest Chocolate
eDiets.com
maxingvest

HISTORICAL FINANCIALS

Company Type: Public

Income Statement

FYE: December 31

	REVENUE ($ mil.)	NET INCOME ($ mil.)	NET PROFIT MARGIN	EMPLOYEES
12/14	92,869	14,614	15.7%	339,000
12/13	103,667	11,239	10.8%	333,000
12/12	100,713	11,575	11.5%	339,000
12/11	89,041	10,084	11.3%	328,000
12/10	117,250	36,581	31.2%	281,005
Annual Growth	(5.7%)	(20.5%)	—	4.8%

2014 Year-End Financials

Debt ratio: 16.0%
Return on equity: 21.7%
Cash ($ mil.): 8,978
Current ratio: 1.03
Long-term debt ($ mil.): 12,531

No. of shares (mil.): —
Dividends
Yield: 3.3%
Payout: 47.0%
Market value ($ mil.): —

	STOCK PRICE ($) FY Close	P/E High	P/E Low	PER SHARE ($) Earnings	Dividends	Book Value
12/14	72.95	16	14	4.57	2.42	22.38
12/13	73.59	25	21	3.51	2.16	22.02
12/12	65.17	20	17	3.62	2.11	20.85
12/11	57.71	20	16	3.15	1.99	19.03
12/10	58.82	6	5	10.81	1.38	20.30
Annual Growth	5.5%	—	—	(19.4%)	15.1%	2.5%

Nippon Steel & Sumitomo Metal Corp

When it comes to steel Nippon Steel & Sumitomo Metal rates as Japan's heavy lifter. The company the world's second-largest steelmaker after ArcelorMittal manufactures pig iron and ingots steel bars plates sheets pipes and tubes as well as specialty processed and fabricated steel products. Nippon Steel & Sumitomo Metal's annual crude steel output is 48 million tons. The company's operations include engineering construction chemicals nonferrous metals ceramics electricity supply information and communications and urban development (theme parks and condominiums). In 2012 Nippon Steel acquired fellow Japanese steel maker Sumitomo Metal Industries to form a global metals giant.

The $24 billion acquisition of Sumitomo Metal Industries mating Japan's #1 and #3 steelmakers boosted the expended company's market share against ArcelorMittal and other Asian rivals in an increasingly competitive marketplace. Similar consolidation has been happening in other countries —particularly China and Russia —aimed at elevating their steel industries to compete in the international market.

Nippon Steel & Sumitomo Metal makes a range of products including pig iron and ingots steel bars plates sheets pipes and tubes and specialty processed and fabricated steel items. Other operations include engineering construction chemicals nonferrous metals ceramics electricity supply information and communications and urban development. It also provides energy finance and insurance services.

Nippon Steel & Sumitomo Metal's primary operations are in Japan but it also has major subsidiaries in Australia Brazil China Indonesia Thailand and the US.

Prior to the acquisition in fiscal 2012 (FYE March 31 2012) Nippon Steel reported flat revenues (in local currency). Increased demand from industrial machinery and carmakers in Japan was offset by a slump in demand from flood-ravaged Thailand and the slowing of other Asian economies. Nippon Steel reported a 37% drop in net income (in local currency) that year as higher selling general and administrative expenses and steeper losses on securities significantly outpaced revenues.

The company has experienced steady growth in its overall business over the past several years due to an increase in exports primarily to East Asia and more specifically China. The rising demand for steel has brought its own challenges such as bottlenecked production.

Part of its strategy to meet demand calls for alliances with other major steelmakers including one with POSCO where Nippon Steel & Sumitomo Metal has transferred its direct-melting gasification technology. Nippon Steel & Sumitomo Metal has also formed an alliance with Kobe Steel to acquire equity stakes in East Asia United Steel which will share semi-finished products. The then Nippon Steel and Sumitomo Metal Industries integrated their building products units (structural steel sheet) and civil engineering materials operations creating two new joint ventures.

In 2013 ArcelorMittal formed a joint venture with Nippon Steel & Sumitomo Metal to buy ThyssenKrupp Steel USA from ThyssenKrupp for $1.5 billion. The deal is expected to deliver $60 million in annual savings.

The company set up a joint venture in 2011 with China's Wuhan Iron & Steel Co. to make and sell tin plate in China. Nippon and Wuhan China's third-largest steelmaker will each take a 50% stake in the $293 million venture. When operational in 2013 the Hubei province-based plant will have a 400000-ton-per-year annealing and processing line and a 200000-ton-per-year electrolytic tinning line. It also increased its holding in a joint venture with Baosteel to make steel sheets for China's booming automotive market. ArcelorMittal agreed to sell its 12% stake in Baosteel-NSC/Arcelor Automotive Steel Sheets Co. (known as BNA) to Nippon Steel in 2011 making the then Nippon Steel a 50% owner.

Nippon Steel and Ternium agreed to form a joint venture in Monterrey Mexico in 2010 to manufacture and sell hot-dip galvanized and galvannealed steel sheets to serve the Mexican automobile market. Production at the $350 million Tenigal SRL de CV facility is set to begin in 2013.

HISTORY

As Japan prepared for war the government in 1934 merged Yawata Works its largest steel producer and other Japanese steelmakers into one giant company —Japan Iron & Steel. During postwar occupation Japan Iron & Steel was ordered to dissolve. Yawata Iron & Steel and Fuji Iron & Steel emerged from the dissolution and with Western assistance the Japanese steel industry recovered from the war years. In the late 1960s Fuji Steel bought Tokai Iron & Steel (1967) and Yawata Steel took over Yawata Steel Tube Company (1968).

Yawata and Fuji merged in 1970 and became Nippon Steel the world's largest steelmaker. In the 1970s the Japanese steel industry was criticized in the US; American competitors complained that Japan was "dumping" low-cost exports. Meanwhile Nippon Steel aggressively courted China.

The company diversified in the mid-1980s to wean itself from dependence on steel. It created a New Materials unit in 1984 retraining "redundant" steelworkers to make silicon wafers and forming an Electronics Division in 1986. Nippon Steel began joint ventures with IBM Japan (small computers and software) Hitachi (office workstations) and C. Itoh (information systems for small and midsized companies) in 1988 as increased steel demand for construction and cars in Japan's "bubble economy" took the company to new heights.

In an atmosphere of economic optimism the company spent more than four times the expected expense to build an amusement park capable of competing with Tokyo Disneyland. The company plowed ahead spending some $230 million on the park. Space World amusement park opened on the island of Kyushu in 1990. The company's bubble burst that year. (The theme park declared bankruptcy in May 2005 and was sold to Kamori Kanko later that year.)

In response Nippon Steel cut costs and intensified its diversification efforts by targeting electronics information and telecommunications new materials and chemicals markets. Seeking to remake its steel operations the company began a drastic phased restructuring in 1993 that included a step most Japanese companies try to avoid —cutting personnel. A semiconductor division was organized that year as part of the company's diversification strategy.

Upgrading its steel operations Nippon Steel and partner Mitsubishi in 1996 introduced the world's first mass-production method for making hot-rolled steel sheet directly from smelted stainless steel. Profits were hurt that year by a loss-making project in the information and communications segment and by a steep decline in computer memory-chip prices.

The company began operation of a Chinese steelmaking joint venture Guangzhou Pacific Tinplate in 1997. The next year its Singapore-based joint venture with Hitachi Ltd. began mass-producing computer memory chips in hopes of stemming semiconductor losses. But falling prices convinced Nippon Steel to get out of the memory chip business and in 1999 it sold its semiconductor subsidiary to South Korea's United Microelectronics.

That year the US imposed antidumping duties on the company's steel products. The next year Nippon Steel agreed to form a strategic alliance with South Korea-based Pohang Iron and Steel (POSCO) at that time the world's #1 steel maker. The deal called for the exploration of joint ventures shared research and joint procurement as well as increased equity stakes in each other (at 2%-3%). Also in 2000 Nippon Steel agreed to provide Sumitomo Metal Industries and Nisshin Steel Co. with stainless steel products.

Early in 2001 Nippon Steel formed a cooperative alliance –focused on automotive sheet products –with French steel giant Usinor (now a part of ArcelorMittal). At the end of the year Nippon Steel decided to form an alliance with Kobe Steel to pare down costs and share in distribution and production facilities. In 2002 the company continued its series of comprehensive alliances by forming alliances with Japanese steelmaker Nippon Metal Industry to exchange its semi-finished stainless steel technologies and with POSCO to build environment-related businesses.

The company reported a loss of ¥51.69 billion ($430 million) for fiscal 2003 due to securities valuation losses and group restructuring charges. In 2004 Nippon Steel formed a joint venture with Baoshan Iron & Steel and Arcelor to manufacture high-grade automotive steel sheets.

Nippon Steel moved into the South American market in 2006 forming alliances with steelmaker Usiminas and iron miner CVRD. And the next year it created a JV with Baosteel and ArcelorMittal that produces automotive steel sheets.

The company joined up with Sumitomo Metal Industries in 2009 when the two companies agreed to form a joint venture that will combine their arc-welded stainless steel pipe and tube operations. Sumitomo will own 60% of the JV. The operations that make up the new company which will be called Sumikin & Nippon Steel Stainless Steel Pipe Co. achieved sales of more than $250 million in 2008.

EXECUTIVES

President and COO, Hiroshi Tomono, age 70
Chairman and CEO, Shoji Muneoka, age 69
EVP, Syuichiro Kozuka, age 67
EVP, Masakazu Iwaki, age 66
EVP, Kosei Shindo
EVP, Shinya Higuchi
EVP, Katsuhiko Ota
EVP, Akihiro Miyasaka
Auditors: KPMG AZSA LLC

LOCATIONS

HQ: Nippon Steel & Sumitomo Metal Corp
2-6-1 Marunouchi, Chiyoda-ku, Tokyo 100-8071
Phone: (81) 3 6867 4111 **Fax:** (81) 3 6867 5607
Web: www.nssmc.com

2012 Sales

	% of total
Asia	
Japan	67
Other countries	24
Other regions	9
Total	**100**

PRODUCTS/OPERATIONS

2015 Sales

	% of total
Steelmaking & Steel Fabrication	86
Engineering	6
Chemicals	4
Systems Solutions	3
New Materials	1
Total	**100**

Selected Products and Services

Steelmaking and Steel Fabrication
- Fabricated and processed steels
- Pig iron and ingots
- Pipes and tubes
- Plates and sheets
- Sections
- Specialty sheets

Engineering and Construction
- Building construction
- Civil engineering
- Marine construction
- Plant and machinery
- Technical cooperation

Chemicals
- Aluminum products
- Ammonium sulfate
- Cement
- Ceramic products
- Coal tar
- Coke
- Ferrite
- Metallic foils
- Slag products

System Solutions
- Communications services
- Computers and equipment
- Data processing
- Systems development and integration

Urban Development
- Condominiums
- Theme parks

New Materials
- Semiconductor bonding wire
- Silicon wafers
- Titanium products
- Transformers

Other operations
- Services
- Energy services
- Financial services
- Insurance services
- Transportation
- Loading and unloading
- Marine and land transportation
- Warehousing

Selected Subsidiaries and Affiliates

Subsidiaries
- Nippon Steel & Sumikin Coated Sheet Corporation
- Nippon Steel & Sumikin Metal Products Co. Ltd.
- Nippon Steel & Sumikin Stainless Steel Corporation
- Nippon Steel & Sumikin Welding Co. Ltd.
- Nippon Steel Australia Pty. Limited
- Nippon Steel Blast Furnace Slag Cement Co. Ltd.
- Nippon Steel Drum Co. Ltd. 1654
- Nippon Steel Logistics Co. Ltd.
- Nippon Steel Shipping Co. Ltd.
- Nippon Steel Transportation Co. Ltd.
- Nippon Steel U.S.A. Inc.
- Nittetsu Cement Co. Ltd.
- Nittetsu Elex Co. Ltd.
- Nittetsu Finance Co. Ltd.
- Nittetsu Steel Pipe Co. Ltd. 4832
- Nittetsu Tokai Steel Wire Co. Ltd.
- NS Preferred Capital Limited
- Osaka Steel Co. Ltd.
- Siam Nippon Steel Pipe Co. Ltd.
- The Siam United Steel (1995) Co. Ltd.

Affiliates
- Daiwa Can Company
- Geostr Corporation
- Godo Steel Ltd.
- Japan Casting & Forging Corporation
- Krosaki Harima Corporation
- Mitsui Mining Co. Ltd.
- Nichia Steel Works Ltd.
- Nippon Steel Trading Co. Ltd.
- Sanko Metal Industrial Co. Ltd.
- Sanyo Special Steel Co. Ltd.
- Sanyu Co. Ltd.
- Suzuki Metal Industry Co. Ltd.
- Taihei Kogyo Co. Ltd.
- Topy Industries Ltd.

COMPETITORS

ArcelorMittal
BlueScope Steel
JFE Holdings
Kobe Steel
Marubeni
Mitsubishi Corp.
POSCO
Tata Europe
ThyssenKrupp Steel
United States Steel
Vale
Yamato Kogyo

HISTORICAL FINANCIALS

Company Type: Public

Income Statement

FYE: March 31

	REVENUE ($ mil.)	NET INCOME ($ mil.)	NET PROFIT MARGIN	EMPLOYEES
03/15	46,758	1,786	3.8%	84,447
03/14	53,441	2,351	4.4%	84,361
03/13	46,655	(1,323)	—	83,187
03/12	49,871	712	1.4%	60,508
03/11	49,631	1,125	2.3%	59,183
Annual Growth	(1.5%)	12.2%	—	9.3%

2015 Year-End Financials

Debt ratio: 0.2%
Return on equity: 7.5%
Cash ($ mil.): 948
Current ratio: 1.38
Long-term debt ($ mil.): 13,050
No. of shares (mil.): 913
Dividends
Yield: —
Payout: —
Market value ($ mil.): —

Nippon Telegraph & Telephone Corp. (Japan)

Nippon Telegraph and Telephone (NTT) executed an AT&T-style breakup but unlike Ma Bell's gang the family stuck together. One of the world's largest telecom companies NTT owns a controlling stake in Japan's dominant cellular carrier NTT DoCoMo (60 million subscribers) and it is a holding company for regional phone companies NTT East and NTT West which enjoy de facto monopolies in their respective markets. NTT provides long-distance international and data networking services through subsidiary NTT Communications. The company also operates an ISP and provides IT services through majority-owned NTT DATA. NTT has foreign holdings in Europe the Pacific Rim and the US. The Japanese state owns 34% of the company.

Geographic Reach

NTT does business principally in Japan although the company has investments and operations throughout the Pacific Rim –including holdings in Australia Hong Kong Malaysia the Philippines Singapore –as well as in Europe Latin America and the US. The company is investing in its international operations particularly in the areas of data networking and IT services through strategic partnerships and acquisitions primarily to address the needs of its globalized corporate clientele.

Operations

NTT's key Asian holdings include minority stakes in Philippine Long Distance Telephone and

Mumbai-based Tata Teleservices. The company operates in the US through enterprise communications services subsidiary NTT America and it owns Colorado-based Web-hosting and data services provider Verio. NTT also operates a submarine communications system known as Pacific Crossing which directly links NTT's network in Japan with carriers in the US. The company does business in Europe through UK-based NTT Europe and Germany-based itelligence Cirquent and Integralis.

Financial Performance

The company brings in billions every year but its revenue has been declining year-over-year. NTT's net income has remained relatively stable in recent fiscal years despite the decreased revenue during the past two fiscal periods. The company's cash flow increased slightly in fiscal 2014 compared to fiscal 2013 levels.

Strategy

Like most large carriers NTT is investing in upgrades to its landline and mobile networks to improve and expand existing services and enable new functionality. The company has extended the reach of its domestic broadband Internet network and fiber optic video services as landline voice subscriptions continue to decline. While sales from NTT's wireless business have slipped due to decreased voice revenue the company has added mobile subscribers and improved profits by offering more robust data services and improving customer retention.

HISTORY

In 1889 the Japanese Ministry of Communications began telephone service operated as a monopoly after 1900. In 1952 the ministry formed Nippon Telegraph and Telephone Public Corporation (NTT). Regulated by the Ministry of Posts and Telecommunications NTT was charged with rebuilding Japan's war-ravaged phone system. Another company Kokusai Denshin Denwa (now KDD) was created in 1953 to handle international phone service.

Japanese authorities cast NTT in the image of AT&T but prohibited it from manufacturing to encourage competition among equipment suppliers. Nonetheless NTT bought most equipment from favored Japanese vendors. By the late 1970s NTT was a large bureaucracy perceived as inefficient and corrupt. NTT's president quipped that the only equipment the firm would buy overseas was telephone poles and mops but in 1981 NTT was forced to allow US companies to bid. The phone firm spent heavily in the 1980s installing a nationwide fiber-optic network and high-speed ISDN lines.

In 1985 Japan privatized NTT as a precursor to deregulation. At its IPO NTT became the world's most valuable public company. NTT International was established to provide overseas telecom engineering and NTT Data Communications Systems Japan's largest systems integrator was formed in 1988.

As Japan's stock market bubble burst in 1990 NTT chose AT&T Motorola and Ericsson to develop a digital mobile phone system and the next year formed NTT Mobile Communications Network (NTT DoCoMo) as its mobile carrier. Following the deregulation of Japan's cellular market NTT launched its Personal Handyphone Service (PHS) in 1995.

The Japanese government unveiled a plan to break up NTT in 1996 a year before the World Trade Organization spearheaded a historic agreement to open international telecom markets. Meanwhile the government forced NTT to allow rivals to connect to its new all-digital systems. Overseas NTT made its first significant investment in the US by buying a 12.5% stake in local carrier Teligent (later reduced).

In 1998 tiny Tokyo Telecommunications Net (a Tokyo Electric Power affiliate) offered discount phone rates spurring NTT to do the same. NTT spun off DoCoMo in the world's largest IPO at the time.

NTT lost its 1999 bidding war with the UK's Cable and Wireless for International Digital Communications. That year NTT split into three carriers two near-monopoly regional local phone providers –NTT East and NTT West –and a long-distance and international carrier called NTT Communications. Unlike AT&T's breakup in 1984 this split featured a holding company –the new NTT – that owns the three carriers. Criticized for continuing to promote last-generation ISDN as the key to high-speed Internet access NTT in 1999 began to test higher-speed digital subscriber line (DSL) service and planned to cut 21000 jobs at NTT West and NTT East over three years.

The company pressed forward with international investments taking a 49% stake in HKNet of Hong Kong and a 49% stake in Davnet Telecommunications a subsidiary of Australia's Davnet Limited (both were later increased to 100%). In 2000 the Japanese government said it would sell another 6% of NTT. That year NTT paid $5.5 billion for the 90% of US Web-hosting firm Verio that it didn't already own.

NTT purchased mobile phone application developer Panasonic Mobile Communications from parent Panasonic Corporation (formerly Matsushita Electric) in 2008.

In 2010 the company acquired a 70% stake in Singapore-based Emerio GlobeSoft in a further effort to boost its international technology services business. Active primarily in the Asia/Pacific region Emerio specialized in custom software development and support IT network support and business process outsourcing services such as account processing. Additionally NTT established a wireless subsidiary in China through NTT DoCoMo to tap into the booming market there.

Auditors: KPMG AZSA LLC

LOCATIONS

HQ: Nippon Telegraph & Telephone Corp. (Japan)
Otemachi First Square, East Tower, 5-1 Otemachi, 1-Chome, Chiyoda-Ku, Tokyo 100-8116
Phone: (81) 3 6838 5481 **Fax:** (81) 3 6838 5499
Web: www.ntt.co.jp

HISTORICAL FINANCIALS

Company Type: Public

Income Statement FYE: March 31

	REVENUE ($ mil.)	NET INCOME ($ mil.)	NET PROFIT MARGIN	EMPLOYEES
03/15	92,476	4,317	4.7%	241,600
03/14	105,844	5,672	5.4%	340,211
03/13	113,726	5,569	4.9%	324,713
03/12	128,091	5,701	4.5%	313,586
03/11	124,446	6,154	4.9%	302,226
Annual Growth	(7.2%)	(8.5%)	—	(5.4%)

2015 Year-End Financials

Debt ratio: 0.1%
Return on equity: 6.0%
Cash ($ mil.): 7,077
Current ratio: 1.33
Long-term debt ($ mil.): 31,032
No. of shares (mil.): 2,117
Dividends
Yield: 2.6%
Payout: 37.7%
Market value ($ mil.): 65,252

	STOCK PRICE ($) FY Close	P/E High	P/E Low	PER SHARE ($) Earnings	Dividends	Book Value
03/15	30.82	0	0	1.97	0.82	34.29
03/14	27.24	0	0	2.47	0.80	37.26
03/13	21.74	0	0	2.30	0.80	37.29
03/12	22.62	0	0	2.23	0.79	39.26
03/11	22.49	0	0	2.33	0.69	36.60
Annual Growth	8.2%	—	—	(4.0%)	4.2%	(1.6%)

Nippon Yusen Kabushiki Kaisha

Nippon Yusen Kabushiki Kaisha known as NYK Line is at home in ports around the globe. With a fleet of about 875 vessels the company is one of the world's largest marine transportation providers. The NYK Line fleet includes bulk carriers containerships tankers and a variety of specialized vessels including car carriers and liquefied natural gas (LNG) carriers; overall the fleet has a capacity of more than 50 million deadweight tons (DWT). In conjunction with its marine transportation business NYK Line offers such logistics services as customs clearance supply chain management and warehousing and operates more than 40 marine terminals.

Geographic Reach

NYK Line has some 450 logistics locations around the world. About 150 are located in South Asia and Oceania 88 in East Asia 76 in Europe 72 in Japan and 67 in the Americas.

Japan represented 75% of the company's total sales in 2015. Other markets include Asia (9%) North America (8%) Europe (7%).

Operations

NYK Line divides its operations into several segments. Global Logistics is its largest (and includes liner trade terminal and harbor transport air cargo and logistics) contributing 52% of the company's total sales in 2015. Bulk shipping generated 42% of the company's revenue. Its real estate operations accounted for the remainder of sales.

Financial Performance

NYK Line's revenues jumped 7% from 2014 to 2015 due to large gains from its Global Logistics segment particularly within North America Japan and Asia. Its net income also increased by 44% in 2015 compared to 2014. This was sparked by the increased revenue a gain on sales of shares of subsidiaries and affiliates and additional foreign exchange earnings.

Strategy

NYK Line is banking on increased demand for oil. About 80% of the company's new vessels are intended for use in the natural resources and energy transportation. Many of which are under long term contracts to customers in growing economies such as Brazil China and India.

Mergers and Acquisitions

The company often improves its geographical footprint through the use of acquisitions. In 2014 it purchased Tranco Terminal the largest car-terminal operating company in Kazakhstan. NYK Line projects that auto sales will rapidly increase in Kazakhstan. In addition the deal caters to the demand for transnational inland transport from the China and Russia areas bordering Kazakhstan and will provide a service to fulfill the various transport needs of its customers.

EXECUTIVES

Senior Managing Corporate Officer; Chief Executive Technical, Naoya Tazawa
President, Tadaaki Naito
Managing Corporate Officer; President and CEO Nippon Cargo Airlines, Fukashi Sakamoto
Senior Managing Corporate Officer and CFO, Kenji Mizushima
Senior Managing Corporate Officer; Chief Executive Energy Division, Hitoshi Nagasawa
Corporate Officer; President and CEO NYK Group Europe, Takuji Nakai
Managing Corporate Officer and CIO, Hidetoshi Maruyama
Senior Managing Corporate Officer; Chief Executive Automotive Transportation, Koichi Chikaraishi
Senior Managing Corporate Officer; Chief Executive Dry Bulk Division, Masahiro Samitsu
Managing Corporate Officer; Chief Executive General Affairs, Yoshiyuki Yoshida
Corporate Officer; Chairman and CEO NYK Ship Management, Tomoyuki Koyama
Chairman, Yasumi Kudo
Auditors: Deloitte Touche Tohmatsu LLC

LOCATIONS

HQ: Nippon Yusen Kabushiki Kaisha
2-3-2 Marunouchi, Chiyoda-ku, Tokyo 100-0005
Phone: (81) 3 3284 6220
Web: www.nyk.com

2015 Sales

	% of total
Japan	75
Asia	9
North America	8
Europe	7
Other area	1
Total	**100**

PRODUCTS/OPERATIONS

2015 Sales

	% of total
Bulk shipping	42
Liner trade	28
Logistics	20
Air cargo transport	4
Cruise	2
Real estate	0
Other	4
Total	**100**

List of Items
Bulk Shipping Business
- Car Transport
- Dry Bulk Transport
- Offshore Business

Tanker Tra
- Tanker Transport (Petroleum Chemical and LPG Transport)

Global Logistics
- Air Cargo Transportation Business
- Liner Trade Business
- Logistics Business
- Terminal and Harbor Transport Business

Real Estate Business
Others
Worldwide Service Network

COMPETITORS

A.P. M̧ller - M̧rsk
CMA CGM
COSCO Group
DHL
DP World
Dynagas LNG Partners LP
Evergreen Marine
Expeditors
Hanjin Shipping
Hutchison Port Holdings
Kawasaki Kisen
Lufthansa Cargo
Mediterranean Shipping Company
Mitsui O.S.K. Lines
Mitsui-Soko
Neptune Orient
PSA International
Polar Air Cargo

HISTORICAL FINANCIALS

Company Type: Public

Income Statement

FYE: March 31

	REVENUE ($ mil.)	NET INCOME ($ mil.)	NET PROFIT MARGIN	EMPLOYEES
03/15	20,018	396	2.0%	33,520
03/14	21,674	320	1.5%	32,342
03/13	20,162	200	1.0%	28,865
03/12	22,038	(887)	—	28,498
03/11	23,297	948	4.1%	28,361
Annual Growth	(3.7%)	(19.6%)	—	4.3%

2015 Year-End Financials

Debt ratio: 0.3%
Return on equity: 6.2%
Cash ($ mil.): 2,174
Current ratio: 1.57
Long-term debt ($ mil.): 8,203
No. of shares (mil.): 1,695
Dividends
Yield: 1.6%
Payout: —
Market value ($ mil.): 9,752

	STOCK PRICE ($) FY Close	P/E High/Low	PER SHARE ($) Earnings	Dividends	Book Value
03/15	5.75	— —	0.23	0.09	4.33
03/14	5.84	— —	0.19	0.08	4.42
03/13	5.07	— —	0.12	0.00	4.38
03/12	6.26	— —	(0.52)	0.00	4.47
03/11	7.86	— —	0.56	0.19	5.18
Annual Growth	(7.5%)	— —	(19.6%)	(16.2%)	(4.4%)

Nishi-Nippon City Bank Ltd.

The Nishi-Nippon City Bank is more of a community bank. It operates about 200 branches in the Kyushu region of southern Japan (poplation 14.5 million) for a customer base of mainly individuals and small and midsized businesses. Nishi-Nippon City Bank offers traditional banking services such as checking and savings accounts as well as securities credit guarantees credit cards and credit management and business consulting services. In addition to the parent bank it operates through eight subsidiaries. It also maintains representative offices in Hong Kong Seoul and Shanghai. Tracing its roots back to 1944 the bank took its current form in 2004 when Nishi-Nippon Bank acquired Fukuoka City Bank.

EXECUTIVES

President, Isao Kubota
Auditors: Ernst & Young ShinNihon LLC

LOCATIONS

HQ: Nishi-Nippon City Bank Ltd.
3-1-1 Hakata-ekimae, Hakata-ku, Fukuoka 812-0011
Phone: (81) 92 476 1111
Web: www.ncbank.co.jp

COMPETITORS

Aozora Bank
Awa Bank
Bank of Kyoto
Bank of Yokohama
Chiba Bank
Chugoku Bank
Eighteenth Bank Ltd.
Fukuoka Financial Group
Hokkoku Bank
Hokuhoku Financial Group
Mitsubishi UFJ Financial Group
Nanto Bank
Norinchukin Bank
Shiga Bank
Shinsei Bank
Shizuoka Bank
Sumitomo Mitsui
Sumitomo Mitsui Trust Holdings
Suruga Bank
Tokyo Tomin Bank
Towa Bank

HISTORICAL FINANCIALS

Company Type: Public

Income Statement

FYE: March 31

	ASSETS ($ mil.)	NET INCOME ($ mil.)	INCOME AS % OF ASSETS	EMPLOYEES
03/15	71,627	207	0.3%	4,211
03/14	77,767	232	0.3%	4,259
03/13	82,627	195	0.2%	4,392
03/12	93,513	219	0.2%	4,534
03/11	89,386	644	0.7%	4,677
Annual Growth	(5.4%)	(24.7%)	—	(2.6%)

2015 Year-End Financials

Return on assets: 0.3%
Return on equity: 5.8%
Long-term debt ($ mil.): —
No. of shares (mil.): 790
Sales ($ mil): 1,268
Dividends
Yield: —
Payout: —
Market value ($ mil.): —

Nissan Motor Co., Ltd.

Nissan Motor one of Japan's leading automakers wants to get big by going small. Through its small-car initiative the company primarily produces low-cost and fuel-efficient small cars with standard comfort safety style and performance. Nissan's models include Maxima and Sentra cars and Altima and Infiniti upscale sedans as well as pickups SUVs and sports cars. It is also one of the world's largest manufacturers of forklifts. Renault holds a 43% stake in Nissan Motor and Nissan has a 15% stake in Renault constituting the Renault-Nissan Alliance.

Geographic Reach

Nissan manufactures in about 20 countries and sells and services products in more than 160 countries. The company operates 14 production facilities in Japan along with seven R&D facilities. Its facilities are also spread across North America (five production facilities); Europe (four); Asia (13); Oceania (one); Mexico Latin America and Caribbean (five); and the Middle East Gulf States and Africa (two).

Financial Performance

Nissan's net sales increased 20% in 2014 compared to 2013 and its net income spiked by 14%. In Japan total industry volumes rose by 9% to 5.7 million units as Nissan out-performed the market with unit sales up 11% to 719000 representing a market share of 12%. This improvement was driven by strong sales of its DAYZ series as well as strong demand for its first CMF model and the new X-Trail.In China Nissan out-performed overall market growth. The total industry within China was up 14% to 20.75 million units while Nissan sales increased 17% to 1.27 million units. Its Qashqai and the all-new Sylphy along with new models from Venucia and Infiniti contributed to the improvement. In North America Nissan achieved significant sales growth. The total US industry was up 6% at 15.65 million units while Nissan sales volume increased by 13% to 1.29 million units amid strong demand for the new Rogue and the Altima.

Strategy

The Nissan Power 88 plan calls for attaining 8% global market share and an 8% operating profit margin by 2017. A major element of Power 88 is the development of about 90 new technologies including a next-generation XTRONIC continuously variable transmission technology. The plan additionally includes investing 70% of research and development expenses into green technology.

Nissan also has set a goal of increasing the percentage of fully built units that are locally made in the Americas to 85% by 2015. New plants in Brazil and Mexico are tasked with increasing production in the Americas from 1.2 million units a year in 2011 to 2 million units annually by 2014. The Great East Japan of Earthquake of 2011 and other contingencies also lead the company to create more efficient business continuity procedures for parts purchasing.

HISTORY

In 1911 US-trained Masujiro Hashimoto established Tokyo-based Kwaishinsha Motor Car Works to repair import and manufacture cars. Kwaishinsha made its first car sporting its DAT ("fast rabbit" in Japanese) logo in 1913. Renamed DAT Motors in 1925 and suffering from a strong domestic preference for American cars the company consolidated with ailing Jitsuyo Motors in 1926. DAT introduced the son of DAT in 1931 —the Datsun minicar ("son" means "damage or loss" in Japanese hence the spelling change).

Tobata Casting (cast iron and auto parts) bought Datsun's production facilities in 1933. Tobata's Yoshisuke Aikawa believed there was a niche for small cars and the car operations were spun off as Nissan Motors that year.

During WWII the Japanese government limited Nissan's production to trucks and airplane engines; Nissan survived postwar occupation in part due to business with the US Army. The company went public in 1951 and signed a licensing agreement the next year with Austin Motor (UK) which put it back in the car business. A 40% import tax allowed Nissan to compete in Japan even though it had higher costs than those of foreign carmakers.

Nissan entered the US market in 1958 with the model 211 using the Datsun name; it established Nissan Motor Corporation in Los Angeles in 1960. Exports rose as factory automation led to higher quality and lower costs. In the 1970s Nissan expanded exports of fuel-efficient cars such as the Datsun B210. The company became the leading US car importer in 1975.

The company's name change in the US from Datsun to Nissan during the 1980s confused customers and took six years to complete. In 1986 Nissan became the first major Japanese carmaker to build its products in Europe. It launched its high-end Infiniti line in the US in 1989.

EXECUTIVES

Chairman President and CEO, Carlos Ghosn, age 61
EVP Manufacturing and SCM, Hidetoshi Imazu
EVP and CFO, Joseph G. (Joe) Peter, age 52
Vice Chairman EVP and Chief Competitive Officer, Hiroto Saikawa, age 62
EVP, Kimiyasu Nakamura
EVP, Takao Katagiri
Corporate VP and CIO, Celso Guiotoko
EVP Alliance RNPO Global Purchasing, Yasuhiro Yamauchi
EVP, Jose Munoz
EVP and Chief Performance Officer, Trevor Mann
SVP; President Dongfend Motor, Jun Seki
SVP; President Infiniti, Roland Kr ger
Corporate VP Global Sales, Allan Rushforth
Vice Chairman, Toshiyuki Shiga
Auditors: Ernst & Young ShinNihon LLC

LOCATIONS

HQ: Nissan Motor Co., Ltd.
1-1-1 Takashima, Nishi-ku, Yokohama 220-8686
Phone: (81) 45 523 5523
Web: www.nissan-global.com

PRODUCTS/OPERATIONS

2014

	%
Automobile	94
Sales Financing	6
Total	**100**

Selected Products

Forklifts
- Engine-powerd forklifts
- Electric-powered forklifts
- Warehouse products
- Order pickers
- Pallet stackers
- Pallet transporters
- Reach trucks

Infiniti
- Infiniti G
- Infiniti G convertible
- Infiniti G coupe
- Infiniti M
- Infiniti EX
- Infiniti FX
- Infiniti JX
- Infiniti QX

Nissan
- Altima
- Altima coupe
- Altima hybrid
- Armada
- Cube
- Frontier
- GT-R
- Maxima
- Murano
- Pathfinder
- Rogue
- Sentra
- Titan
- Versa
- Xterra

Nissan Marine outboard motors

COMPETITORS

BMW
CLARK Material Handling
Crown Equipment
Daihatsu
Daimler
Deere
FCA US
Fiat Chrysler
Ford Motor
Fuji Heavy Industries
General Motors
Honda
Hyundai Motor
Isuzu
Kia Motors
Mazda
Mitsubishi Motors
NACCO Industries
Peugeot
Suzuki Motor
Tata Motors
Toyota
Volkswagen
Volvo

HISTORICAL FINANCIALS

Company Type: Public

Income Statement FYE: March 31

	REVENUE ($ mil.)	NET INCOME ($ mil.)	NET PROFIT MARGIN	EMPLOYEES
03/15	94,809	3,813	4.0%	151,710
03/14	101,555	3,769	3.7%	147,939
03/13	102,342	3,639	3.6%	160,530
03/12	114,701	4,162	3.6%	157,365
03/11	105,946	3,855	3.6%	155,098
Annual Growth	(2.7%)	(0.3%)	—	(0.6%)

2015 Year-End Financials

Debt ratio: 0.3%
Return on equity: 9.9%
Cash ($ mil.): 6,343
Current ratio: 1.61
Long-term debt ($ mil.): 31,931
No. of shares (mil.): —
Dividends
Yield: 2.8%
Payout: —
Market value ($ mil.): —

	STOCK PRICE ($) FY Close	P/E High/Low	PER SHARE ($) Earnings	Dividends	Book Value
03/15	20.33	— —	0.91	0.57	9.74
03/14	17.87	— —	0.90	0.84	10.08
03/13	19.20	— —	0.87	0.00	9.64
03/12	21.47	— —	1.00	0.00	9.37
03/11	17.65	— —	0.92	0.12	8.82
Annual Growth	3.6%	— —	(0.4%)	48.4%	2.5%

Noble Group Ltd

Noble Group Limited obliges its customers by maintaining an unlimited appetite for raw materials. The investment holding company is principally engaged in the international supply of raw materials to customers in the agriculture energy metals minerals and ores and logistics markets. Noble Group conducts business through a network of more than 120 offices in almost 40 countries providing supply chain services for the sourcing marketing processing and transportation of industrial and agricultural products (grains coal metal ores alternative fuels and much more). The group is also involved in technical ship management services trade finance and coal mining.

The company relies on its diversified portfolio and integrated supply chains to offset downturns in particular sectors and create more operational efficiencies. Noble Group's "pipeline" supply chain strategy allows it to indentify and secure profits at every step of a product's journey from raw material to finished good (such as in the case of an agricultural product through seeking profits from fertilizer sales storage fees refining fees etc).

The company gets the bulk of its profit from agricultural and energy commodities and is investing heavily in both sectors and in 2009 and 2010 has invested in $214 million oil tank terminal in Netherlands warehouses and sugar refineries in Brazil and coal mining assets in Indonesia and Australia. Further diversifying its portfolio in 2010 the company acquired 51% of PT Henrison Inti Persada of Indonesia marking the company's first move into palm oil production. It also picked up the Sempra Energy Solutions unit of RBS Sempra Commodities' joint venture for $318 million.

In 2010 as part of its expansion in South America Noble Group acquired two mills from Brazilian ethanol producer Grupo Cerradinho for a $941 million.

With commodity prices rebounding from the 2009 global recession in 2010 the company reported a jump in revenues and net income led by the strong performance of its energy segment which doubled its revenues that year.

Korea Investment Corporation (KIC) acquired a 21% stake in Noble Group Limited in 2011. KIC and Noble established a co-operative business and strategic partnership to jointly invest in infrastructure assets and supply chain management activities. Investment firm China Investment Corp. is also a strategic partner in agricultural projects across Asia.

Also in 2011 to raise cash Noble Group sold its Donaldson Coal holdings to its 65%-owned Australian coal miner group Gloucester Coal in a transaction valued at $381 million. The deal bolsters Gloucester's production capacity and provides access to additional port capacity.

In 2012 Chinese-controlled coal miner Yancoal Australia (a subsidiary of Yanzhou Coal Mining Company) acquired Noble's Gloucester Coal in a cash-and-stock deal for about $637.4 million. As part of the deal Noble will ultimately get about 22% of the merged company.

EXECUTIVES

Vice Chairman and CFO, Stephen J. Marzo
Executive Director and President, William Randall
CEO and Executive Director, Yusuf A. Alireza
CEO and Director, Richard Samuel Elman
Auditors: Ernst & Young

LOCATIONS

HQ: Noble Group Ltd
18th Floor, MassMutual Tower, 38 Gloucester Road,
Phone: (852) 2861 3511 **Fax:** (852) 2527 0282
Web: www.thisisnoble.com

2010 Sales

	% of total
North America	53
Asia	
China	10
Other countries	12
Europe	13
South America	6
Africa	3
India	2
Australia	1
Total	**100**

2014 Sales

	% of total
North America	65
Asia-Pacific	17
Europe	9
South America	6
Africa	3
Total	**100**

PRODUCTS/OPERATIONS

2010 Sales

	% of total
Energy	65
Agriculture	21
Metals Minerals & Ores	12
Logistics	2
Total	**100**

2015 Sales

	% of total
Energy	85
Metals Minerals & Ores	15
Total	**100**

COMPETITORS

ADM
Cargill
Glencore
ITOCHU
Marubeni
Mitsui
Sime Darby

HISTORICAL FINANCIALS

Company Type: Public

Income Statement FYE: December 31

	REVENUE ($ mil.)	NET INCOME ($ mil.)	NET PROFIT MARGIN	EMPLOYEES
12/14	85,816	132	0.2%	1,900
12/13	97,878	243	0.2%	15,649
12/12	94,045	471	0.5%	15,000
12/11	80,732	431	0.5%	14,000
12/10	56,696	605	1.1%	8,000
Annual Growth	10.9%	(31.7%)	—	(30.2%)

2014 Year-End Financials

Debt ratio: 19.8%	No. of shares (mil.): —
Return on equity: 2.5%	Dividends
Cash ($ mil.): 903	Yield: —
Current ratio: 1.33	Payout: 241.3%
Long-term debt ($ mil.): 2,933	Market value ($ mil.): —

Nomura Holdings Inc

Nomura Holdings is the parent company of Nomura Securities Japan's leading investment bank and brokerage house. The company performs trading equity and bond underwriting research and mergers and acquisitions (M&A) advisory services. It also makes private equity and venture capital investments and oversees some ¥110 trillion in retail client assets. Subsidiary Nomura Asset Management is Japan's largest asset management firm in terms of assets under management in investment trusts which it offers to retail investors and through institutional funds. Nomura Holdings has operations in more than 30 countries; Nomura Securities International is the company's US trading and investment banking unit.

OperationsNomura operates through three business divisions. Wholesale which generated 50% of revenue in fiscal 2015 (ended March 31) includes the firm's global markets and investment banking operations and provides corporate and institutional products and services. Its Retail division (30% of revenue) provides investment products and offers investment consultation services to individuals and businesses from nearly 160 Nomura Securities locations across Japan. Its Asset Management division (6% of revenue) which operates through Nomura Asset Management develops and manages investment trusts and provides investment advisory services. Additional units include Nomura Trust & Banking big-ticket financing firm Nomura Babcock & Brown and the Nomura Institute of Capital Markets Research.The firm's revenue streams are fairly diversified. About 23% of its total revenue came from commissions in FY2015 with another 5% coming from its investment banking fees. The firm's interest and dividend income and asset management/portfolio service fees made up 23% and 11% of total revenue respectively. The remainder of its revenue came from non-recurring sources such as net gains on trading (28% of revenue) and gains on equity investments (1%).Geographic ReachNearly 70% of the firm's revenue came from Japan in fiscal 2015 (ended March) while business in the Americas and Europe each made up 13% of revenue. The remaining 5% of revenue came from the Asia and Oceania region. Its operations are mostly in Japan but subsidiaries are also in the US the UK Singapore and Hong Kong Special Administrative Region.Sales and MarketingThe firm offers its variety of financial services to individuals corporations financial institutions governments and governmental agencies.Financial PerformanceNote: Growth rates may differ after conversion to US dollars.Nomura Holdings has struggled to grow its revenues in recent years though its profits have been steadily climbing as its managed to cut non-interest expenses and pay lower income tax rates with more deductible expenses related to foreign subsidiaries.The firm's revenue climbed 6% to ¥1.9 trillion in fiscal 2015 (ended March 31) mostly thanks to a double-digit jump in net gains on trading. The firm's Wholesale business drove most of the recurring revenue growth with its income rising by 3% on weaker Yen an increase in overseas equity revenue and higher overseas M&A and fundraising activity. Its Asset Management business grew by 15% as its assets under management grew with inflows from its investment trust and investment advisory businesses and from new revenue from its recently acquired subsidiary in Taiwan. Nomura's retail business shrank by 7% on decreasing commissions from the distribution of investment trusts and brokerage services.Higher revenue during FY2015 drove Nomura's net income higher by 5% to ¥224.8 million for the year. The firm's cash levels fell sharply with operations using ¥77 million during the year mostly as it purchased more securities under agreements to resell. Strategy

Nomura is well-positioned to take advantage of expected growth in other Asian nations. The company expressed in 2015 that it expected Asia to account for half of global GDP by 2050 providing Nomura with Wholesale business opportunity as corporations continue to develop with higher demand for funding. It also expected that the region's growing middle class would increase demand for personal financial services over the next several decades creating another growth opportunity for its retail business.Additionally the firm's wide variety of financial services gives its tremendous cross-selling opportunities that integrate both its Retail and Wholesale operations.

HISTORY

Company BackgroundTokushichi Nomura started a currency exchange Nomura Shoten in Osaka in 1872 and began trading stock. His son Tokushichi II took over and in 1910 formed Nomura's first syndicate to underwrite part of a government bond issue. It established the Osaka Nomura Bank in 1918. The bond department became independent in 1925 and became Nomura Securities. The company opened a New York office in 1927 entering stock brokerage in 1938.

The firm rebuilt and expanded retail operations after WWII. It encouraged stock market investing by promoting "million ryo savings chests" —small boxes in which people saved cash (ryo was an old form of currency). When savings reached 5000 yen savers could buy into investment trusts. Nomura distributed more than a million chests in 10 years.

Nomura followed clients overseas in the 1960s helped underwrite a US issue of Sony stock and opened a London office. It became Japan's leading securities firm after a 1965 stock market crash decimated rival Yamaichi Securities. The firm grew rapidly in the 1970s ushering investment capital in and out of Japan and competing with banks by issuing corporate debt securities.

As the Japanese economy soared in the 1980s the company opened Nomura Bank International in London (1986) and bought 20% of US mergers and acquisitions advisor Wasserstein Perella (1988 sold 2001).

Then the Japanese economic bubble burst. Nomura's stock toppled 70% from its 1987 peak and underwriting plummeted. In 1991 and 1992 amid revelations that Nomura and other brokerages had reimbursed favored clients' trading losses the firm was accused of manipulating stock in companies owned by Japanese racketeers. Nomura's chairman and president —both named Tabuchi —resigned admitting no wrongdoing.

The firm trimmed staff and offices and focused on its most efficient operations. From 1993 to 2000 it seesawed from red to black and back again.

Junichi Ujiie became president after the payoff scandal; he restructured operations to prepare for Japan's financial deregulation. Nomura invested in pub chain Inntrepreneur and William Hill a UK betting chain. It also created an entertainment lending unit to lend against future royalties or syndication fees and spun off a minority stake in its high-risk US real estate business which ceased lending altogether the next year.

In 1998 Nomura was dealt a double blow when Asian economies collapsed and Russia defaulted on its debts. Incurring substantial losses the firm refocused on its domestic market and reduced overseas operations. That year it teamed with Industrial Bank of Japan for derivatives sales in the UK and pension plan consulting in Japan.

In 1999 Nomura bailed out ailing property subsidiary Nomura Finance which had been crippled by the sinking Japanese real estate market. It also invested heavily in UK real estate and bought 40% of the Czech beer market with South African Breweries.

The next year the firm agreed to buy the business services arm of Welsh utilities firm Hyder; it also bought 114000 flats in Germany with local government authorities its first European deal outside the UK. Also in 2000 Nomura sold its assets in pachinko parlors and "love" hotels Japanese cultural traditions with less-than-sparkling reputations. British authorities that year fined Nomura traders in relation to charges of trying to rig Australia's stock market in 1996.

The company converted to a holding company structure in 2001 and months later made its debut on the NYSE. It made two big deals in the UK that year buying hotel chain Le Mridien and becoming the nation's largest pub owner via the purchase of some 1000 locations from Bass. The company also bought a stake in Thomas Weisel Partners to increase its participation in M&A action between US and Japanese firms. In 2002 the company decided to sell the network of more than 4100 pubs to a consortium of private investors for some $3 billion.

In 2007 Nomura acquired global agency brokerage Instinet. The deal allowed the company to begin offering electronic trading services.

In 2008 Japanese regulators chose a consortium led by Nomura to take control of troubled Ashikaga Bank from the government; Nomura's private equity arm took a stake of about 45% in Ashikaga. The deal marked Nomura's first foray into retail banking.

The global financial crisis heavily impacted Nomura which reported steep declines in 2008 and 2009. The company lost some ¥208 billion ($2 billion) in 2009 alone on trading and equity investments. The US subprime mortgage bust further hurt the group which lost money on mortgage-backed securities.

In response Nomura cut operating costs and fine-tuned its offerings. The following year the company boosted its global investment banking capabilities by acquiring parts of the fallen bulge-bracket firm Lehman Brothers including operations in Asia Europe and the Middle East as well as the India-based back office operations. (In its post-acquisition transition the company laid off some 11% of its UK workforce or about 1000 employees in its London office.) In an effort to boost its domestic asset management business Nomura bought NikkoCiti Trust and Banking from Citigroup in 2009. The company also exited the US residential mortgage-backed securities business entirely.

The Lehman Brothers acquisition helped boost Nomura's profile in European equities and fixed-income trading. Adding on to that purchase Nomura bought London-based Tricorn Partners –a move that further complements its UK corporate finance advisory business.

Nomura Asset Management also bought a 35% stake in LIC Mutual Fund Asset Management Company of India. The deal gave Nomura a larger foothold in the Indian market and strengthened its credentials as an international asset manager.

EXECUTIVES

President and COO, Atsushi Yoshikawa, age 61
Senior Managing Director, Paul Spanswick
Executive Managing Director; CEO Wholesale, Tetsu Ozaki, age 58
Senior Managing Director; Regional Co-CEO Europe Middle East and Africa, Yasuo Kashiwagi
Senior Managing Director and Regional CEO Americas; Chairman and CEO Nomura Securities International, Shigesuke Kashiwagi, age 56
Senior Managing Director, Hiromasa Yamazaki
Senior Managing Director, Naoki Matsuba
Chairman and CEO China, Zhizhong Yang
Senior Managing Director and CIO, Masahide Nakamura
Executive Managing Director, Shoichi Nagamatsu, age 64
Senior Managing Director and Legal, Noriaki Nagai, age 58
Senior Managing Director, Yuji Nakata
Senior Managing Director, Noriaki Miyano
Senior Management Director, Toshihiro Iwasaki
CEO; President Nomura Securities, Koji Nagai
Senior Managing Director, Kenji Kimura
President and CEO Nomura International (Hong Kong), Minoru Shinohara
Executive Managing Director; CEO Asset Management, Kunio Watanabe
Senior Managing Director, Kentaro Okuda
Senior Managing Director, Junko Nakagawa
Senior Managing Director; Regional CEO Americas, David Findlay
Senior Managing Director, Steven Ashley
Senior Managing Director; Regional Co-CEO Americas, Toshiya Hasegawa
Senior Managing Director, Eiji Miura
Senior Managing Director, Hisato Miyashita
Executive Managing Director; CEO Retail, Toshio Morita
Senior Managing Director, Lewis O'Donald
Senior Managing Director and Co-CIO, Naohiro Sako
Senior Managing Director; President and CEO Nomura Trust and Banking, Chie Shimpo
Senior Managing Director, Yo Akatsuka
Senior Managing Director, Juntaro Kimura
President and CEO India, Vikas Sharma
CEO Europe Middle East and Africa, Jonathan Lewis
Auditors: Ernst & Young ShinNihon LLC

LOCATIONS

HQ: Nomura Holdings Inc
9-1 Nihonbashi 1-chome, Chuo-Ku, Tokyo 103-8645
Phone: (81) 3 5255 1000
Web: www.nomuraholdings.com

2014 Sales

	% of total
Japan	69
Americas	13
Europe	13
Asia and Oceania	5
Total	**100**

PRODUCTS/OPERATIONS

2014 Sales

	% of total
Net gain on trading	28
Commissions	23
Interest and dividends	23
Asset management & portfolio service fees	11
Fees from investment banking	5
Gain on investments in equity securities	1
Other	9
Total	**100**

2014 Sales

	% of total
Wholesale	50
Retail	30
Asset Management	6
Others	14
Total	**100**

COMPETITORS

Bank of America
Barclays
Boom Securities
Daiwa Securities Group
Deutsche Bank
Goldman Sachs
HSBC
SMBC Nikko Securities
UBS Investment Bank

HISTORICAL FINANCIALS

Company Type: Public

Income Statement FYE: March 31

	ASSETS ($ mil.)	NET INCOME ($ mil.)	INCOME AS % OF ASSETS	EMPLOYEES
03/15	348,253	1,873	0.5%	28,672
03/14	421,629	2,069	0.5%	27,670
03/13	403,248	1,139	0.3%	27,956
03/12	435,172	141	0.0%	34,395
03/11	443,117	346	0.1%	26,871
Annual Growth	(5.8%)	52.5%	—	1.6%

2015 Year-End Financials

Return on assets: 0.5%
Return on equity: 8.6%
Long-term debt ($ mil.): —
No. of shares (mil.): —
Sales ($ mil): 8,359
Dividends
Yield: 2.3%
Payout: 24.8%
Market value ($ mil.): —

	STOCK PRICE ($) FY Close	P/E High/Low		PER SHARE ($) Earnings	Dividends	Book Value
03/15	5.87	0	0	0.50	0.14	6.27
03/14	6.43	0	0	0.54	0.14	6.55
03/13	6.17	0	0	0.30	0.04	6.57
03/12	4.41	2	1	0.04	0.10	7.01
03/11	5.20	1	1	0.09	0.09	6.98
Annual Growth	3.1%	—	—	51.5%	11.0%	(2.7%)

Nordea Bank AB

Nordea Bank is one of the largest financial services groups in the Nordic and Baltic Sea regions. Sweden is its home but Nordea also has a major presence in Denmark Finland Norway and Russia. The bank splits its operations into three main divisions: retail banking wholesale banking and wealth management. The bank also provides life and pension products. Originally founded in the 1820s Nordea Bank now boasts a network of about 700 branches and serves some 11 million customers including about 1 million corporate clients –a key customer segment for Nordea. About 55% of its lending activity is to corporations.

OperationsThe bank operates through three main segments. Retail Banking generates roughly 55% of the bank's overall income and offers a wide range of traditional deposit and loan products for both household customers and corporate clients mostly in the Nordic markets and the Baltic countries. Wholesale Banking brings in another 25% of total revenue and provides banking and other financial services to large Nordic and global corporate institutional and public companies. This division also serves financial sector clients with funds and equity products as well as consulting services within asset allocation and fund sales. Nordea Bank Russia offers a full range of bank services to corporate and private customers in Russia. Capital Markets unallocated includes the result in Capital Markets which is not allocated to the main business areas. Roughly 15% of revenue comes from the Wealth Management division which provides investment savings and risk management products. It also manages customers' assets and gives financial advice to affluent and high net worth individuals and institutional investors. Additionally Nordea offers financing and other services to clients in the Shipping Offshore & Oil Services industries. The bank also has a Life & Pensions business and an Asset Management division that is responsible for all actively-managed investment products.Geographic ReachNordea Bank has an international network of branches subsidiaries and representative offices in almost 20 countries around the world with most of its operations in Denmark Finland Norway and Sweden. More than 30% of revenue comes from Denmark while Sweden generates another nearly 25%. Finland and Norway markets contribute more than 15% each. Other large markets include the Baltic countries and Russia.Sales and MarketingThe bank serves private customers (from general retail to the highly-affluent) corporations financial institutions and other global institutional customers.Nordea's mobile banking activity has been growing. In 2014 transaction volume from its mobile bank channels grew by 90% with the number of active mobile banking users growing by 1000 per day.Financial PerformanceNote: Growth rates may differ after conversion to US dollars.Nordea's annual revenues have remained mostly stable for the past few years while profits have steadily been rising. Revenue in 2014 grew by 3% to 10.22 billion ($12.42 billion) mostly thanks to higher commission income from investment and lending services from the bank's growing Wealth Management and Retail Banking divisions.Higher revenue in 2014 pushed profit higher for a third straight year with net income rising by 7% to 3.33 billion ($4.05 billion). Also helping the bank's bottom line net loan loss provisions declined by 26% as its loan portfolio gained credit strength.Cash levels fell despite higher earnings in 2014 with operations using 10.82 billion ($13.15 billion) primarily as deposit funding from credit institutions and the broader public declined over the year.

Stategy

Nordea Bank has continued to focus more on its four key markets in the Nordic and Baltic regions (including Denmark Finland Norway and Sweden). In mid-2014 to better concentrate resources on these key markets Nordea exited its banking life and financing businesses in Poland through the sale of its Nordea Bank Polska S.A. to PKO Bank Polski SA for 694 million ($927 million). As the industry moves from brick-and-mortar branch banking to digital banking Nordea has also been expanding its electronic offerings via its mobile tablet Netbank and Facebook platforms. Indeed during 2014 the bank reported that the number of mobile transactions grew by 90% reflecting the change in consumer tastes in the banking industry. In late 2014 the company announced that it would increase its IT investments by 30-35% over the coming years building new core banking and payment platforms to keep up with the digital banking trend. Company Background

Sampo owns more than 20% of Nordea. The Swedish government held a nearly 20% stake in the bank but reduced that to 13% in 2011 as part of its plan to raise capital. It plans to sell more and possibly all of its Nordea stake over time.

Growth in European markets has been a focus for Nordea. In 2009 the company purchased a 75% stake in Russian bank JSB Orgresbank rebranding it as OJSC Nordea Bank. Nordea also bought the Polish life insurance operations of Finnish banking group Sampo doubling Nordea's customer base in Poland. However Nordea put the breaks on aggressive growth and completely halted branch expansion in Russia and the Baltic countries in light of the global financial crisis.

HISTORY

Company BackgroundNordea traces its roots to 1974 when two Swedish government-owned banks Postbanken and Sveriges Kreditbank merged to form the country's largest bank Post-och Kreditbanken (PKbanken) in order to compete with S-E-Banken and Svenska Handelsbanken.

PKbanken didn't hold on to the top spot long. By the early 1980s a recession and languid profits sank the company to third. However the firm did expand teaming with Norway's Christiana Bank og Kreditkasse to open joint offices in Hong Kong Houston London São Paolo and Singapore.

As regulatory restrictions in Sweden eased the government spun off 15% of its interest in the company on the Stockholm Stock Exchange in 1984.

PKbanken pulled out of its deal in London with Christiana Bank in 1986 but it bought a stake in London-based English Trust Group to expand its merchant banking services. In 1988 PKbanken acquired government-owned Carnegie Fondkommission Sweden's largest brokerage and in 1989 purchased the state-controlled Swedish Investment Bank a provider of funding to small and midsized businesses.

A year later PKbanken acquired regional Swedish bank Nordbanken and assumed the smaller firm's name. Soon after the government axed the combined firm's top officers and installed new management. The purging didn't help as another recession and a real estate market crash hammered the company's bottom line. In 1992 the Swedish government intervened again acquiring all of the outstanding shares of Nordbanken that it did not already own. The company rebounded quickly after selling bad loans to the state and cutting staff by a fifth.

In 1994 the Swedish government transferred its ownership of Gota Bank to Nordbanken. The company resumed trading on the Stockholm Stock Exchange the following year.

Across the border in Finland rivals Union Bank of Finland and Kansallis-Osake-Pankki merged in 1995 to create Merita Bank the country's largest.

In 1997 Nordbanken and Merita Bank combined to form MeritaNordbanken but their parents Nordbanken Holdings and Merita Ab remained separate. In 2000 the company bought Danish bank Unidanmark. MeritaNordbanken's holding companies united and assumed the name Nordic Baltic Holding. Later the company changed its name to Nordea an amalgamation of "Nordic" and "idea."

In 2001 Nordea bought Christiania Bank og Kreditkasse and later that year attached the Nordea Bank name to its banking subsidiaries in Denmark Finland Norway and Sweden.

By 2003 the company composed primarily of the four national banking groups –Nordea Bank Denmark Nordea Bank Finland Nordea Bank Norway and Nordea Bank Sweden –decided to change its complex legal structure and create one European company under the Nordea Bank banner.

Nordea acquired Denmark's Fionia Bank in 2009 including the bank's staff and its 29 branches but excluding some 2000 troubled corporate customers. The Denmark government had taken control of the failing bank earlier in the year.

EXECUTIVES

EVP Chief Risk Officer Head Group Risk Management Country Senior Executive Finland, Ari Kaperi, age 55

CEO Nordea Estonia, Petri Nikkil ¤, age 44

President and Group CEO, Casper von Koskull

Executive Vice President Head of Wealth Management Country Senior Executive in Norway, Gunn W ¦rsted, age 60

Executive Vice President Head of Retail Banking Country Senior Executive in Sweden, Lennart Jacobsen, age 49

Deputy CEO and COO, Torsten Hagen J ̣rgensen

Executive Vice President Chief Operating Officer of Wholesale Banking Country Senior Executive in Denmark, Peter Nyegaard, age 52

Group CFO, Heikki Ilkka, age 45

Chairman, Bj ¶n Wahlroos, age 63

Deputy Chairman, Marie Ehrling, age 60

Auditors: KPMG AG

LOCATIONS

HQ: Nordea Bank AB
Smalandsgatan 17, Stockholm SE-105 71

Phone: (46) 8 614 78 00 **Fax:** (46) 8 10 50 69

Web: www.nordea.com

2014 Sales

	% of total
Denmark	31
Sweden	24
Finland	18
Norway	17
New European markets	4
Other	6
Total	**100**

PRODUCTS/OPERATIONS

2014 Sales

	% of total
Banking products	61
Capital markets products	19
Savings products and asset management	10
Life and pensions	5
Other	5
Total	**100**

2014 Sales

	% of total
Retail Banking	56
Wholesale Banking	24
Wealth Management	16
Group Corporate Centre	4
Total	**100**

2014 Sales

	% of total
Net Interest income	54
Net Fee abd commission income	28
Net results on items at fair value	14
Other Operating income	4
Total	**100**

COMPETITORS

BNP Paribas
Citigroup
Danske Bank
Deutsche Bank
HSBC
JPMorgan Asset Management
KBC
SEB AB
Schroders
Skandia
Svenska Handelsbanken

HISTORICAL FINANCIALS

Company Type: Public

Income Statement FYE: December 31

	ASSETS ($ mil.)	NET INCOME ($ mil.)	INCOME AS % OF ASSETS	EMPLOYEES
12/14	813,588	4,050	0.5%	29,397
12/13	867,940	4,289	0.5%	29,429
12/12	892,873	4,111	0.5%	31,466
12/11	926,375	3,397	0.4%	33,068
12/10	777,378	3,556	0.5%	33,809
Annual Growth	1.1%	3.3%	—	(3.4%)

2014 Year-End Financials

Return on assets: 0.5%
Return on equity: 11.2%
Long-term debt ($ mil.): —
No. of shares (mil.): —
Sales ($ mil): 19,076

Dividends
Yield: 5.1%
Payout: 51.8%
Market value ($ mil.): —

	STOCK PRICE ($) FY Close	P/E High/Low	PER SHARE ($) Earnings	Dividends	Book Value
12/14	11.55	16 13	1.01	0.59	8.99
12/13	13.51	18 13	1.06	0.44	9.97
12/12	9.61	13 10	1.03	0.35	9.23
12/11	7.82	18 10	0.84	0.38	8.32
Annual Growth	13.9%	— —	4.7%	12.1%	2.0%

Nordea Bank Denmark A/S

EXECUTIVES

Bankdirekt ̧r, J ̧rgen H ̧holt
Auditors: Ernst & Young Godkendt Revisionspartnerselskab

LOCATIONS

HQ: Nordea Bank Denmark A/S
Strandgade 3, P.O. Box 850, Copenhagen C DK-0900
Phone: (45) 33 33 33 33 **Fax:** (45) 33 33 63 63
Web: www.nordea.com

HISTORICAL FINANCIALS

Company Type: Public

Income Statement FYE: December 31

	ASSETS ($ mil.)	NET INCOME ($ mil.)	INCOME AS % OF ASSETS	EMPLOYEES
12/14	133,427	930	0.7%	6,325
12/13	152,484	676	0.4%	6,440
12/12	149,322	267	0.2%	6,584
12/11	156,922	380	0.2%	7,885
12/10	178,967	624	0.3%	7,968
Annual Growth	(7.1%)	10.5%	—	(5.6%)

2014 Year-End Financials

Return on assets: 0.6%
Return on equity: 13.3%
Long-term debt ($ mil.): —
No. of shares (mil.): 50
Sales ($ mil): 4,811

Dividends
Yield: —
Payout: —
Market value ($ mil.): —

North Pacific Bank Ltd

Sapporo Hokuyo Holdings supposes it has what customers need in the way of banking and financial services. The company was formed in 2001 to serve as the holding company for North Pacific Bank and The Sapporo Bank; together the regional banks have some 230 offices in Hokkaido as well as an office in Tokyo and two offices in China. North Pacific Bank which is the largest bank in Hokkaido accounts for most of the holding company's sales; the bank traces its roots to 1917. The company also has subsidiaries active in credit cards and leasing; bank subsidiaries engage in such activities as financing.

EXECUTIVES

President, Ryuzo Yokouchi
Auditors: KPMG AZSA LLC

LOCATIONS

HQ: North Pacific Bank Ltd
3-7 Odori Nishi, Chuo-ku, Sapporo, Hokkaido 060-8661
Phone: (81) 11 261 1311
Web: www.hokuyobank.co.jp

COMPETITORS

Hokkoku Bank
Hokuhoku Financial Group
Hyakujushi Bank
Mitsubishi UFJ Financial Group
Mizuho Financial
Resona
Sumitomo Mitsui

HISTORICAL FINANCIALS

Company Type: Public

Income Statement FYE: March 31

	ASSETS ($ mil.)	NET INCOME ($ mil.)	INCOME AS % OF ASSETS	EMPLOYEES
03/15	68,031	131	0.2%	3,640
03/14	76,415	842	1.1%	3,744
03/13	83,029	206	0.2%	3,808
03/12	93,947	294	0.3%	3,730
03/11	89,384	148	0.2%	3,797
Annual Growth	(6.6%)	(2.9%)	—	(1.1%)

2015 Year-End Financials

Return on assets: 0.2%
Return on equity: 4.6%
Long-term debt ($ mil.): —
No. of shares (mil.): 398
Sales ($ mil): 1,200

Dividends
Yield: —
Payout: —
Market value ($ mil.): —

Novartis AG Basel

Although it's based in neutral Switzerland Novartis has been aggressive in attacking illnesses on multiple fronts including pharmaceuticals vaccines and consumer health. Its largest division Pharmaceuticals develops and manufactures prescription drugs for blood pressure cancer and other ailments. Novartis' Sandoz subsidiary produces generic drugs and active pharmaceutical ingredients while the Vaccine and Diagnostics segment makes immune health and blood-screening tools. Its Alcon division makes ophthalmic drugs surgery systems and contact lenses. The Consumer Health unit includes OTC medications such as Excedrin and Theraflu as well as agricultural animal and pet care products.

Geographic Reach

Novartis has operations in 140 countries around the world including sales administrative research and manufacturing locations. The US is the company's largest geographic market accounting for about one-third of revenues followed by Japan Germany and France (each accounting for less than 10% of sales).

Operations

Prescription drugs account for more than half of Novartis' annual revenues. Its blockbusters include high blood pressure treatment Diovan leukemia drug Gleevec/Glivec age-related macular degeneration drug Lucentis and Zometa an intravenous treatment for bone tumors caused by prostate lung and breast cancers. Other strong products include hormone balancing drug Sandostatin Exelon for Alzheimer's disease and Femara which is used to treat postmenopausal women with early and advanced breast cancer.

The company's Sandoz and Alcon units each account for nearly 20% of sales. Sandoz is currently among the largest manufacturers of generic drugs in the world while Alcon is a leader in cataract and vision correction surgical equipment.

Financial Analysis

Novartis' steady growth pace has produced rising revenues over the past decade including a 15% increase to some $59 billion in 2011. The annual sales increase was largely attributed to the acquisition of Alcon as well as to positive currency impacts and sales of newly launched products. However net income dropped 7% to $9.1 billion in 2011 due to acquisition and restructuring costs as well as increased sales marketing manufacturing and other operational expenses.

Like most large drugmakers Novartis is facing increasing pressure to keep its operations lean and develop new blockbusters in the face of patent expiration and rising levels of generic competition. Several of the company's former best sellers including Famvir (antiviral) Lotrel (high blood pressure) and Trileptal (epilepsy treatment) are experiencing dwindling sales due to launches of generic versions in recent years. The company is especially hurting as top seller Diovan which previously accounted for more than $6 billion in sales (or 20% of the firm's annual pharmaceutical revenues) lost patent protection in the US market in 2012 and in Europe in 2011.

To balance out the reduced sales from off-patent products Novartis is conducting cost-cutting programs including a number of workforce reduction plant closure divestiture and outsourcing measures announced in 2011 and 2012.

Strategy

To ward off competitive pressures and support its prescription drug business Novartis maintains a healthy drug pipeline with about 140 candidates in clinical development stages. Novartis relies upon a steady regimen of internal development partnerships and acquisitions to keep its pipeline up and running. R&D programs are focused on core therapeutic areas including cardiology metabolism oncology neurology respiratory ophthalmic and infectious disease. The company is especially focused on increasing its development of biologic (protein and gene-based) drugs. Recently launched products in the US market include chronic obstructive pulmonary disease (COPD) treatment Arcapta in 2011. In addition oncology drug Afinitor gained FDA approval to treat pancreatic tumors and breast cancer in 2012.

In addition Novartis is counting on its new drug for multiple sclerosis Gilenya (licensed from Mitsubishi Tanabe) to be a big revenue earner in the coming years. Gilenya was launched in the US market in 2010 and is the first oral treatment for MS. It is also among the most expensive drugs for the disease. The drug was approved in the European Union market in 2011.

Though the Alcon Sandoz consumer health and vaccines and diagnostics units are smaller than the core pharmaceuticals business Novartis maintains strong acquisition and internal research programs in those divisions as well. For instance to further its goals in personalized medicine Novartis is working to develop more sensitive molecular diagnostics that can be used to monitor patients and determine which medicines will most effectively treat their ailments.

Mergers Acquisitions & Divestitures

Along with new drugs the company's other pharma growth efforts are conducted through numerous acquisitions. Making a bold move in the eye-care market Novartis made ocular drug and vision care company Alcon a wholly owned subsidiary in 2011 after a drawn-out series of share purchases: Novartis first acquired about 77% of Alcon from Nestl ©for some $39 billion (through two transactions in 2008 and 2010). Then in early 2011 Novartis acquired the remaining shares in Alcon through a public tender offer worth nearly $13 billion. Novartis then combined its existing CIBA Vision eye care unit into Alcon which became Novartis' fifth operating segment.

To expand its Sandoz division Novartis completed a $1.5 billion deal to acquire generic drugmaker Fougera Pharmaceuticals in 2012. The purchase strengthened Sandoz's position in the global dermatology medication market.

Additionally the company periodically divests underperforming or noncore assets to focus on its key areas of growth. For instance in 2011 the company sold global rights to eczema treatment Elidel to Meda for some $420 million.

In 2014 the company announced it would spend up to $16 billion depending on milestones to purchase GlaxoSmithKline's oncology unit. At the same time it will sell its vaccine business to GSK for about $7 billion and the two will combine their consumer products. The deal brings Tafinlar and Mekinist two recently approved skin cancer drugs into the Novartis camp. Annual revenue will drop slightly but profits will rise as it picks up higher margin products.

HISTORY

Johann Geigy began selling spices and natural dyes in Basel Switzerland in 1758. A century later the Geigy family began producing synthetic dyes. About that time Alexander Clavel also entered the synthetic dye trade in Basel forming the Gesellschaft fur Chemische Industrie Basel (Ciba). Ciba was Switzerland's #1 chemical firm at century's end.

After WWI Ciba Geigy and Sandoz (a Basel synthetic dye maker founded in 1886) formed the Basel AG cartel to compete with German rival I.G. Farben. Basel used its profits to diversify into pharmaceuticals and other chemicals and to gain a foothold in the US. In 1929 Basel merged with its German and later French and British counterparts but WWII shattered the so-called Quadrapartite Cartel in 1939 leaving only Basel AG intact.

Basel scientist Paul Muller won a Nobel Prize in 1948 for inventing DDT. Basel AG voluntarily dissolved itself back into its component parts in 1951.

Ciba Geigy and Sandoz continued to diversify. Finding new markets in agricultural chemicals Geigy had passed Ciba in sales by 1967. That year Sandoz bought the Wander group of companies (dietetic products). Ciba and Geigy merged in 1970 and began a series of US acquisitions including Funk Seeds in 1974. Sandoz bought Minneapolis-based Northrup King & Co. (1976) and Dutch seed company Zaadunie (1980).

Ciba-Geigy and US biotech company Chiron started a joint venture in 1986 to produce and market genetically engineered vaccines (Ciba-Geigy acquired 50% of Chiron in 1994). Sandoz also bought shares in US biotechnology companies including Genetic Therapy and SyStemix in 1991. It bought Gerber (founded 1927) in 1994.

Ciba-Geigy and Sandoz rejoined to form Novartis in 1996. To win approval for the merger Sandoz (whose Daniel Vasella became CEO of the new company) sold its corn herbicide and US animal health businesses. Novartis spun off its specialty chemicals unit in 1997 and bought Merck's insecticide and fungicide operations.

In 1998 the company merged its OTC health and nutrition businesses into a new consumer health division and in the following year sold several units including cracker maker Wasa to focus the new division's operations. Chairman Alex Krauer who had overseen the formation of Novartis stepped down that year leaving the post to Vasella.

To boost its market share CIBA Vision bought colored contact lens maker Wesley Jessen VisionCare in 2000. Novartis spun off its crop protection and seed units merging them with AstraZeneca's Agrochemicals unit to create Syngenta.

Novartis Ophthalmics split off from the CIBA Vision division to become a separate eye health care unit under the Pharmaceutical Division of Novartis in 2001. The firm's joint venture with BioTransplant successfully cloned genetically altered pigs whose organs would be more suitable for human transplants. Attempting to refine the company's focus on pharmaceuticals Novartis made several acquisitions in 2002 including two animal vaccine companies Grand Laboratories and Immtech Biologies and generic manufacturer Lek Pharmaceuticals while divesting its food and beverage division to Associated British Foods. The remaining assets including sports nutrition health and weight loss products were grouped under the Nutrition & Sant ©banner and were sold to management in 2004.

Novartis engineered one of the largest deals in European pharma in 2004 when it acquired the rights to a prospective inhaled chronic obstructive pulmonary disease (COPD) treatment from UK drug concerns Arakis and Vectura Group.

Novartis' consumer health business got a Boost literally when it purchased Mead Johnson's adult nutrition business in 2004. The buy included brands such as Boost nutritional drinks and feeding tube products Isocal and Ultracal. In a move to further bolster its consumer offerings that same year the company purchased the US and Canadian consumer products division of Bristol-Myers Squibb which brought headache remedy Excedrin cold and flu treatment Comtrex and Keri moisturizers into the company's consumer products stable.

To bulk up Sandoz (which had refocused strictly on generic pharmaceuticals over the years) in 2004 Novartis bought a Canadian maker of generic injectable drugs and a Danish generics maker to increase market share in key regional markets. In 2005 the firm acquired Hexal AG one of Germany's top generics makers and a controlling stake in Hexal's sister firm Eon Labs a US generics manufacturer.

The constant appetite of its drug pipeline was briefly sated in mid-2006 when Novartis acquired NeuTec Pharma a UK-based biopharmaceutical company with two drug candidates that target otherwise drug-resistant "superbugs." That year Novartis spent $5.1 billion to acquire struggling vaccine and biopharmaceuticals products maker Chiron despite Chiron's board rebuffing an earlier offer. Novartis then created a Vaccine and Diagnostics division composed of its existing vaccine operations and Chiron's diagnostics.

Putting its focus entirely on health care Novartis sold off the last of its non-health care businesses in 2007 when Nestl ©purchased Novartis' medical nutrition business for $2.5 billion and its Gerber baby products business for $5.5 billion. Also in 2007 Novartis formed a new unit to focus on biologic drug development which already made up 25% of its preclinical research pipeline.

In 2008 Novartis purchased Speedel the Swiss biotech drugmaker with which it developed blood pressure medication Rasilez (known as Tekturna in the US) for $888 million. It also completed a $400 million acquisition of US biopharmaceutical development company Protez Pharmaceuticals which added a late-stage candidate for drug-resistant Staphylococcus infections. Later that year the company also acquired the pulmonary drug delivery R&D business of Nektar Therapeutics for $115 million. The two companies had already collaborated on the development of an inhaled powder therapy for lung infections and the deal brought that treatment fully under Novartis' roof.

Also in 2008 Novartis struck a deal with Nestl © to acquire its majority stake (about 77%) in eye care firm Alcon. The deal took place over the course of two years and included a $10.4 billion purchase in mid-2008 and a $28.3 billion transaction in mid-2010.

In 2009 it completed a $1.3 billion acquisition of the specialty generic injectables arm of Austrian-based Ebewe Pharma. The buy gave Sandoz a line of oncology drugs that are widely considered to be essential to adhering to standard-of-care guidelines for treating a range of cancers.

To increase the capacity of its Vaccine and Diagnostics division Novartis opened a new vaccine plant in North Carolina in 2009 and in 2010 the company launched Menveo a new meningitis vaccine.

Novartis conducted an executive management shift in early 2010 when Daniel Vasella stepped down as CEO after holding the job for 14 years but remained chairman. Joe Jimenez moved from his position as head of the company's pharmaceutical division to become CEO.

Schizophrenia treatment Fanapt was approved by the FDA in early 2010. Novartis added some late-stage heart failure drugs to its pipeline that year by acquiring privately held drug developer Corthera for $120 million plus up to $500 million in potential milestones. The firm also sold the US rights to overactive bladder treatment Enablex to Warner Chilcott for $400 million in 2010.

Auditors: PricewaterhouseCoopers AG

LOCATIONS

HQ: Novartis AG Basel
Lichtstrasse 35, Basel CH-4056
Phone: (41) 61 324 1111 **Fax:** (41) 61 324 7826
Web: www.novartis.com

HISTORICAL FINANCIALS

Company Type: Public

Income Statement FYE: December 31

	REVENUE ($ mil.)	NET INCOME ($ mil.)	NET PROFIT MARGIN	EMPLOYEES
12/14	53,634	10,210	19.0%	133,413
12/13	58,831	9,175	15.6%	135,696
12/12	57,561	9,505	16.5%	127,724
12/11	59,375	9,113	15.3%	123,686
12/10	51,561	9,794	19.0%	119,418
Annual Growth	1.0%	1.0%	—	2.8%

2014 Year-End Financials

Debt ratio: 16.2%
Return on equity: 14.0%
Cash ($ mil.): 13,023
Current ratio: 1.39
Long-term debt ($ mil.): 13,799
No. of shares (mil.): —
Dividends
Yield: 2.9%
Payout: 66.8%
Market value ($ mil.): —

	STOCK PRICE ($) FY Close	P/E High/Low		PER SHARE ($) Earnings	Dividends	Book Value
12/14	92.66	23	19	4.13	2.76	29.50
12/13	80.38	21	17	3.70	2.43	30.64
12/12	63.30	16	13	3.89	2.48	28.54
12/11	57.17	17	13	3.78	2.36	27.36
12/10	58.95	14	10	4.26	1.95	27.60
Annual Growth	12.0%	—	—	(0.8%)	9.1%	1.7%

NTT DoCoMo Inc

Mobile phone carrier NTT DoCoMo is one of the world's largest wireless network operators in terms of subscribers behind global leader Vodafone. NTT DoCoMo (which means "anywhere") boasts about 65 million subscribers to its FOMA-branded wireless voice network in Japan (giving it about half of market share) while about 49 million customers subscribe to its i-mode mobile Internet services. The company also sells wireless telephone handsets under the DoCoMo brand and it provides emergency satellite services primarily for maritime use. NTT DoCoMo is the wireless spinoff of Japan's leading telecommunications carrier Nippon Telegraph and Telephone (NTT); NTT owns two-thirds of NTT DoCoMo.

The company saw sales slip in 2010 mainly due to the decline of its core voice segment. Meanwhile NTT DoCoMo improved its profits for the year due to decreased costs of equipment and reduced network costs. The company has said that it expects profits to increase in 2011 due to ongoing efforts to further bring down costs as well as initiatives to drive customer usage of data services by offering reduced pricing options and expanded mobile services such as original content delivery and wireless Internet tethering between wireless devices and portable computers.

DoCoMo means "anywhere" and NTT DoCoMo is everywhere in the Japanese market for mobile communication services. However faced with a mature market and stiff competition at home NTT DoCoMo has renewed its efforts to tap into growth markets abroad particularly in the Asia/Pacific region.

In 2011 the company agreed to a deal with JG Summit that gives it the option to buy additional shares in Philippine Long Distance Telephone (PLDT) for around $263 million. NTTDoCoMo already owns about 10% of PLDT.

Its largest purchase in this overseas push was the 2009 acquisition of about one-quarter of India-based Tata Teleservices for about $2.7 billion. The company hopes to tap into the burgeoning Indian market through this alliance with the telecommunications arm of the Tata Group. Also that year NTT DoCoMo bought a 35% stake in US multimedia software maker PacketVideo to bolster its internal efforts to develop applications for mobile video services. It acquired the rest of the company from parent NextWave Wireless for about $115 million in 2010.

NTT DoCoMo's efforts to garner higher subscription fees from its existing customer base in Japan and improve retention have included an increase in the variety of mobile services it offers the introduction of cell phones offering a broader set of features (email music playback and gaming) and ongoing investments in its network infrastructure to enable bandwidth-hungry streaming content such as video programming. The company is counting on increased data usage to fuel profits as sales of voice services decline.

HISTORY

Formed in 1952 by the Japanese Ministry of Communications to rebuild Japan's war-ravaged phone system Nippon Telegraph and Telephone (NTT) enjoyed a monopoly on phone services for more than four decades.

NTT first went into mobile communications with a maritime phone service in 1959 and in 1968 the company began offering paging services. Other telecommunications services followed: car phone service (1979) in-flight phone service (1986) and mobile phone service (1987).

In 1991 NTT established a subsidiary to adopt these wireless segments; it launched operations in 1992 as NTT Mobile Communications Network under the leadership of NTT executive Kouji Ohboshi. The firm quickly took on the DoCoMo nickname. The year closed with slightly more than a million analog mobile phone users in Japan —a market DoCoMo shared with upstart telecom companies DDI and IDO (later bought by DDI). Paging service was more popular and DoCoMo won more than 3 million customers.

DoCoMo in 1993 launched digital mobile phone service based on a scheme called PDC (personal digital cellular) —a system incompatible with the digital standards that would take root in Europe and the US. Liberalization of the cellular phone market in 1994 triggered unexpected growth: Customers who previously had to lease mobile phones from the network operators could now buy them at retail stores. Further competition emerged in 1995 with the launch of personal handyphone services or PHS (parent company NTT was among the companies providing PHS) but DoCoMo's subscriber count passed 3.5 million mobile phone users —about half the market.

DoCoMo's pager business peaked in 1996 before commencing a long-term decline; the mobile phone market where DoCoMo had more than 8 million subscribers overtook it. The company launched a satellite-based mobile phone system that year to serve customers beyond the range of cell sites reaching ships and mountainous regions.

Financial crises rocked the Pacific Rim in 1997 and Japan's Fair Trade Commission rocked NTT by ordering it to cut its 95% ownership of DoCoMo. Customers continued to flock to mobile phones despite economic turmoil and DoCoMo passed the 15-million-subscriber mark. In 1998 DoCoMo gave hope to Japan's low-flying market when it left the nest: Its mammoth IPO raised more than $18 billion.

Meanwhile DDI (now KDDI) had become the first Japanese carrier to launch a digital mobile phone network based on CDMA (code division multiple access) technology. Though DoCoMo still used PDC it redoubled its efforts to help develop and standardize a next-generation wideband version of CDMA.

In 1999 DoCoMo took over NTT's unprofitable PHS unit and rolled out a high-speed data service over the PHS network. That year it acquired a 19% stake in the telecom unit of Hong Kong's Hutchison Whampoa but failed expectations led the company to sell its stake in Hutchison 3G UK to Hutchison Whampoa in 2005 for 120 million.

In 2000 the company adopted NTT DoCoMo as its corporate name. To promote its new data services NTT DoCoMo launched a joint venture in Japan with Microsoft (Mobimagic). It took the i-mode service international in 2001 when the company teamed up with Telecom Italia Mobile to introduce the 3G service in Europe. The next year NTT DoCoMo became the largest shareholder in America Online Japan but it sold the more than 40% stake to America Online in 2003.

The company staked its claim in the US too by paying $9.8 billion for a 16% stake in AT&T Wireless in 2001. NTT DoCoMo sold its stake following the 2004 takeover of AT&T Wireless by rival Cingular Wireless (now AT&T Mobility) in a deal valued at $41 billion.

The company in 2002 took full ownership of its eight majority-owned regional operating subsidiaries and began consolidating operations. The company also has liquidated several other subsidiaries including an operating unit in Brazil and it has reorganized its European holdings under a single subsidiary DoCoMo Europe Ltd.

It also continued to advance digital wireless technologies through partnerships that include an alliance (formed in 2000) with Hutchison Whampoa and Dutch mobile phone company KPN Mobile to bid on European operating licenses. It also paid $4.5 billion for a 15% stake in KPN Mobile. (The stake was reduced to 2% then sold back to parent firm KPN. An i-mode affiliation continues however.)

After the number of paging service subscribers fell to less than 300000 from a high of 6.5 million (in 1996) NTT DoCoMo ended the service in early 2007. It additionally dissolved allucher a marketing and consulting services provider to mobile phone users and its animation-related Web portal management and marketing business known as Hive. NTT DoCoMo also discontinued its Personal Handyphone Service (PHS) and its CITYPHONE digital mobile service in 2008.

NTT DoCoMo in 2008 bought stakes in operators in Bangladesh (TM International 30%) and the Philippines (PLDT 20%). Additionally the company has i-mode network technology licensing agreements with about a dozen GSM network operators in Europe including Russia and Greece as well as in the Asia/Pacific region.

EXECUTIVES

President and CEO PacketVideo, Mark Tapling
EVP Consumer Sales, Takashi Tanaka, age 60
SEVP Chief Privacy Officer and Chief Information Security Officer, Fumio Iwasaki, age 63
SEVP and CFO, Kazuto Tsubouchi, age 63
EVP and Managing Director Network, Kiyoshi Tokuhiro
EVP and CIO, Seiji Nishikawa
EVP Marketing, Tsutomu Shindou
EVP and Managing Director of Corporate Strategy & Planning Department, Kazuhiro Yoshizawa
EVP Managing Director Corporate Strategy and Planning and Board Member, Kaoru Kato, age 64
EVP and CTO, Seizo Onoe
EVP Multimedia Services, Hiroyasu Asami
President CEO Director Oricon Inc, Koh Koike
EVP, Masaaki Shintaku
President DoCoMo Pacific, Jonathan Kriegel
Auditors: KPMG AZSA LLC

LOCATIONS

HQ: NTT DoCoMo Inc
Sanno Park Tower, 11-1, Nagata-cho 2-chome, Chiyoda-ku, Tokyo 100-6150
Phone: (81) 3 5156 1111 **Fax:** (81) 3 5156 0271
Web: www.nttdocomo.co.jp

PRODUCTS/OPERATIONS

2013 Sales

	% of total
Mobile communication services	71
Equipment sales	17
Other operating revenues	12
Total	**100**

Selected Services

Cellular
i-mode (wireless Internet access)
In-flight telephone
Mobile multimedia
Satellite mobile communications
Third-generation (3G) wireless (W-CDMA)
World Call (direct international calling)

Selected Regional Operating Subsidiaries

DOCOMO Business Net Inc.
DOCOMO Engineering Chugoku Inc.
DOCOMO Engineering Hokkaido Inc.
DOCOMO Engineering Hokuriku Inc.
DOCOMO Engineering Inc.
DOCOMO Engineering Kansai Inc.
DOCOMO Engineering Kyushu Inc.
DOCOMO Engineering Shikoku Inc.
DOCOMO Engineering Tohoku Inc.
DOCOMO Engineering Tokai Inc.
DOCOMO I Kyushu Inc.
DOCOMO Mobile Inc.
DOCOMO Mobile Tokai Inc.
DOCOMO Mobile Media Kansai Inc.
DOCOMO Service Chugoku Inc.
DOCOMO Service Hokkaido Inc.
DOCOMO Service Hokuriku Inc.
DOCOMO Service Inc.
DOCOMO Service Kansai Inc.
DOCOMO Service Kyushu Inc.
DOCOMO Service Shikoku Inc.
DOCOMO Service Tohoku Inc.
DOCOMO Service Tokai Inc.
DOCOMO Support Inc.
DOCOMO Systems Inc.
DOCOMO Technology Inc.

COMPETITORS

BT
China Mobile
EMOBILE
Hutchison Telecommunications
KDDI
Optus
SK Telecom
SOFTBANK MOBILE
Telstra
Vodafone

HISTORICAL FINANCIALS

Company Type: Public

Income Statement FYE: March 31

	REVENUE ($ mil.)	NET INCOME ($ mil.)	NET PROFIT MARGIN	EMPLOYEES
03/15	36,534	3,418	9.4%	37,412
03/14	43,220	4,502	10.4%	36,253
03/13	47,507	5,267	11.1%	35,426
03/12	51,688	5,655	10.9%	32,244
03/11	51,013	5,923	11.6%	31,157
Annual Growth	(8.0%)	(12.8%)	—	4.7%

2015 Year-End Financials

Debt ratio: 0.0%
Return on equity: 7.4%
Cash ($ mil.): 879
Current ratio: 2.17
Long-term debt ($ mil.): 1,836
No. of shares (mil.): —
Dividends
Yield: 3.1%
Payout: 59.0%
Market value ($ mil.): —

	STOCK PRICE ($) FY Close	P/E High	P/E Low	PER SHARE ($) Earnings	Dividends	Book Value
03/15	17.43	0	0	0.85	0.55	11.59
03/14	15.77	0	0	1.09	0.61	13.22
03/13	14.87	0	0	1.27	0.62	13.91
03/12	16.67	0	0	1.36	0.66	14.88
03/11	17.59	0	0	1.42	0.59	14.13
Annual Growth	(0.2%)	—	—	(12.2%)	(2.1%)	(4.8%)

Oesterreichische Nationalbank

Central reserve depository nec

EXECUTIVES

Chairman, Ewald Nowotny
Auditors: KPMG Austria GmbH Wirtschaftspruefungs- und Steuerberatungsgesellschaft

LOCATIONS

HQ: Oesterreichische Nationalbank
Otto-Wagner-Platz-3, Vienna 1090
Phone: (43) 1 40420 6666 **Fax:** (43) 1 40420 042299
Web: www.oenb.at

HISTORICAL FINANCIALS

Company Type: Public

Income Statement FYE: December 31

	ASSETS ($ mil.)	NET INCOME ($ mil.)	INCOME AS % OF ASSETS	EMPLOYEES
12/14	112,832	31	0.0%	1,084
12/13	134,211	27	0.0%	1,233
12/12	144,154	37	0.0%	1,222
12/11	128,502	24	0.0%	1,146
12/10	106,757	29	0.0%	1,145
Annual Growth	1.4%	1.5%		(1.4%)

Ogaki Kyoritsu Bank, Ltd.

The Ogaki Kyoritsu Bank provides banking and other financial services in the Gifu prefecture in central Japan. The bank serves consumers and businesses from more than 140 domestic branch locations and from 3 international offices in Hong Kong Shanghai and New York. Services include banking credit cards credit guaranty and leasing. Ogaki Kyoritsu Bank was established in 1896.

EXECUTIVES

President, Takashi Tsuchiya
Auditors: KPMG AZSA LLC

LOCATIONS

HQ: Ogaki Kyoritsu Bank, Ltd.
3-98 Kuruwa-machi, Ogaki, Gifu 503-0887
Phone: (81) 584 74 2111
Web: www.okb.co.jp

COMPETITORS

Aozora Bank
Mitsubishi UFJ Financial Group
Shizuoka Bank

HISTORICAL FINANCIALS

Company Type: Public

Income Statement FYE: March 31

	ASSETS ($ mil.)	NET INCOME ($ mil.)	INCOME AS % OF ASSETS	EMPLOYEES
03/15	42,988	94	0.2%	3,452
03/14	47,234	92	0.2%	3,417
03/13	48,836	106	0.2%	3,346
03/12	52,878	97	0.2%	3,285
03/11	50,637	100	0.2%	3,205
Annual Growth	(4.0%)	(1.4%)	—	1.9%

2015 Year-End Financials

Return on assets: 0.2%
Return on equity: 4.6%
Long-term debt ($ mil.): —
No. of shares (mil.): 347
Sales ($ mil): 959
Dividends
Yield: —
Payout: —
Market value ($ mil.): —

Oil and Natural Gas Corp. Ltd.

The crown jewel of India's oil and gas assets state-owned Oil & Natural Gas Corporation (ONGC) is India's largest exploration and production company. It is also the country's largest multinational corporation. In a country reliant on imported fuels ONGC which has estimated proved and probable reserves of 6.4 billion metric tonnes of oil equivalent accounts for the 78% of India's oil and gas production. ONGC operates a more than 15000-km. pipeline network and owns nearly 72% of Mangalore Refinery & Petrochemicals Ltd. (MRPL). International exploration and production subsidiary ONGC Videsh has established exploration activities in 17 countries. India's government owns 74% of ONGC.

ONGC has been searching for ways to expand its stakes in oil patches around the world.

Through its ONGC Videsh subsidiary the company joined rival China National Petroleum Corporation (CNPC) to acquire a 38% stake in Syria's largest oil company from Petro-Canada. The Syrian company Al Furat Petroleum is 62%-owned by Royal Dutch Shell. ONGC had lost out to CNPC in an earlier bid in 2005 for PetroKazakhstan.

In 2006 ONGC acquired Exxon Mobil's 30% stake in a field in the Campos Basin of Brazil for $1.4 billion. Other partners in the field are the state-owned Petrobras and Royal Dutch Shell which each own 35%. ONGC had lost out to Chinese rivals in previous bids for assets in South America.

In 2008 ONCG Videsh announced plans to acquire Imperial Energy for $2.6 billion giving it a foothold in the Siberian oil market.

EXECUTIVES

Director Finance, Dinesh Kumar Sarraf
Director Finance, Aloke Kumar Banerjee
Director Exploration, Narendra Kumar Verma
Director Technology and Field Services, Shashi Shanker
Director Offshore, Tapas Kumar Sengupta
Auditors: Khandelwal Jain and Co.

LOCATIONS

HQ: Oil and Natural Gas Corp. Ltd.
Tel Bhavan, Dehradun, Uttaranchal 248 003
Phone: (91) 135 275 9561 **Fax:** (91) 11 2331 6413
Web: www.ongcindia.com

COMPETITORS

BP
Cairn Energy
Exxon Mobil
Occidental Petroleum
Royal Dutch Shell
TOTAL
Talisman Energy

HISTORICAL FINANCIALS

Company Type: Public

Income Statement FYE: March 31

	REVENUE ($ mil.)	NET INCOME ($ mil.)	NET PROFIT MARGIN	EMPLOYEES
03/15	266,779	29,313	11.0%	33,185
03/14	302,058	44,144	14.6%	33,988
03/13	309,278	44,615	14.4%	32,923
03/12	298,969	55,319	18.5%	32,909
03/11	277,788	50,366	18.1%	33,273
Annual Growth	(1.0%)	(12.7%)	—	(0.1%)

2015 Year-End Financials

Debt ratio: 0.2%
Return on equity: 10.4%
Cash ($ mil.): 25,736
Current ratio: 1.06
Long-term debt ($ mil.): 76,078
No. of shares (mil.): —
Dividends
Yield: —
Payout: —
Market value ($ mil.): —

Old Mutual Plc

The name belies its demutualized status: Financial services group Old Mutual provides banking insurance and asset management services in about 30 nations in southern Africa Europe Asia and the Americas. Founded in 1845 Old Mutual owns a majority stake of South Africa's Nedbank Group which provides commercial banking finance investment banking and other services. It also owns Old Mutual (US) Holdings also known as Old Mutual Asset Management (US) or OMAM (US). Skandia Insurance offers insurance products and mutual funds primarily in the UK and Sweden. Old Mutual has some £262 billion (some $357 billion) in funds under management.

Geographic Reach

London-based Old Mutual generated more than 40% of its fiscal 2012 revenue from emerging markets. This includes business in Africa operations in Colombia and Mexico and joint ventures in India and China.

Operations

Old Mutual operates through several business lines: long-term savings and investments US asset management banking and short-term insurance. Long-term savings and investments accounted for 70% of the company's fiscal 2012 revenue.

Old Mutual's Asset Management arm offers clients access to more than 115 investment strategies through its affiliated investment firms.

Sales and Marketing

The financial firm boasts more than 14 million customers worldwide. Clients buy products directly from Old Mutual or indirectly through an intermediary such as an independent financial advisor. Old Mutual reaches out to customers through a combined strategy of tied agents and independent financial advisors as well as via the Internet and call center functionality.

Strategy

Old Mutual aims to expand in South Africa Africa and other selected emerging markets. In 2013 the firm purchased a majority stake in Ghana-based Provident Life Assurance Company Limited and entered a strategic partnership with Faulu Kenya DTM LTD by buying a controlling stake in its emerging marketing business. To boot Old Mutual acquired Oceanic Life the life assurance operations of the former Oceanic Bank of Nigeria to extend its reach into the Nigerian market. Focused on strengthening its distribution capabilities in Latin America Old Mutual in 2012 acquired AIVA Business Platforms (AVIA) one of the largest financial groups globally.

It's also working to develop and grow its Old Mutual Wealth and US Asset Management businesses even including a partial IPO of its US Asset Management unit when economic conditions are favorable. For its Nedbank business Old Mutual is focused on boosting non-interest revenue growing the retail business via client-centered strategies and effective risk management and shifting the focus of its portfolio on profit-enhancing products and services.

Stung in the US Old Mutual has been restructuring its operations to recover from the financial crisis. To this end it exited several underperforming markets and sold noncore businesses. The group sold its US life insurance operations to Harbinger Group for $350 million in 2011. Old Mutual also sold its Skandia's business in the Nordic region and rebranded its remaining Skandia units Old Mutual Wealth to unify its brand. By divesting certain businesses Old Mutual can concentrate on its core long-term savings and investments operations. Proceeds from the sales are being used to reduce debt.

Not content with just making divestitures Old Mutual remains as aggressive as practical in target areas such as developing new investment products for distribution in emerging markets. The company has also seen marked improvements in returns due to an upswing in the economy. By streamlining its expansive structure while investing in growth Old Mutual is positioning itself to take advantage of the expected economic recovery.

HISTORY

Old Mutual was founded in 1845 as the Mutual Life Assurance Society of the Cape of Good Hope to sell life insurance in the Cape Colony. When South Africa gained self-governance from the UK in 1910 Old Mutual chairman John Merriman became the colony's first premier. In 1927 the company made its first international expansion into Zimbabwe (then called Rhodesia).

Life insurance remained the firm's sole line of business until 1948 when it acquired a controlling stake in what would become Mutual & Federal a general insurer. To better administer its mutual fund and trust businesses the firm formed the South African Mutual Unit Trust Company in 1966.

Old Mutual diversified in 1986 buying a controlling stake in the Nedcor banking group. Also that year the firm made its first major acquisition outside Africa buying UK life insurer Providence Capitol. In 1995 the firm expanded into Hong Kong and the US where it opened Old Mutual Investment Advisers in Boston. Seeking a way into the UK financial services market the company acquired asset managers Capel-Cure Myers and Albert E Sharp in 1997 and 1998 respectively merging them into Capel-Cure Sharp.

The firm further globalized its asset management operations in 1999 establishing an alliance with Japanese insurer Sumitomo Life to cross-market trust and investment services. Also that year its Nedcor banking subsidiary launched a hostile takeover bid for Standard Bank Investment Corporation (of which Old Mutual already owned 20%); the merger would have created South Africa's largest bank but government regulators nixed the deal.

Old Mutual demutualized in 1999 listing on both the London and Johannesburg stock exchanges. In 2000 the company sold its UK insurance operations to XL Mid Ocean Reinsurance and Century Group then acquired UK brokerage Gerrard Group and started an infrastructure investment joint venture with Australia's Macquarie Bank. Old Mutual also bought US-based United Asset Management (selling its Murray Johnstone Holdings subsidiary to Aberdeen Asset Management). Meanwhile Nedcor (now Nedbank) bought 50.1% of Imperial Bank a South African bank with a large vehicle finance business.While the firm's Old Mutual (US) operations proved successful other areas of growth were less salutary. Three years after forming Gerrard Limited in 2000 as part of a bid to boost the UK business the asset manager was sold to Barclays.Old Mutual gained control of insurer and mutual fund manager Skandia Insurance in 2006 through a nearly £4 billion ($7 billion) hostile takeover bid. The acquisition brought more life insurance asset management and banking to Old Mutual and gave it deeper access into Asia Europe Latin America and the UK.Satisfied with the results of its asset management operations in the US the company began expanding its asset management services in South Africa and the UK. In a shift from operating its businesses regionally the company took to grouping them by their primary operations.

EXECUTIVES

Group Chief Executive and Director, Julian V. F. Roberts, age 58, $830,000 total compensation
Group Finance Director, Ingrid Johnson, age 48
CEO Nedbank Group, Michael W. T. (Mike) Brown, age 48
CEO Old Mutual Wealth, Paul Feeney
Group Strategy Director, Ian Gladman
President and CEO OM Asset Management, Peter L. Bain
Group Risk Officer, Sue Kean
CEO Singapore and Southeast Asia, Steve Hickman
CEO Old Mutual Emerging Markets, Ralph Mupita
Chairman, Patrick H. O'Sullivan, age 66
Auditors: KPMG Audit Plc

LOCATIONS

HQ: Old Mutual Plc
5th Floor, Millennium Bridge House, 2 Lambeth Hill, London EC4V 4GG
Phone:
Web: www.oldmutual.com

Selected Subsidiaries

Old Mutual (South Africa) Ltd
Old Mutual
Old Mutual Life Assurance Company (South Africa) Ltd
Old Mutual
Nedbank Group Ltd
Nedbank Ltd
Mutual & Federal Insurance Company Ltd

Old Mutual
Old Mutual (US) Holdings Inc
Old Mutual
Acadian Asset Management LLC
Barrow Hanley Mewhinney & Strauss LLC
Rogge Global Partners plc
OM Group (
Old Mutual Wealth Management Limited

PRODUCTS/OPERATIONS

2012 Revenue

	% of total
Long-term savings	
Emerging markets	43
Old mutual wealth	27
NedBank	25
M&F	3
US Asset Management	2
Total	**100**

COMPETITORS

Absa	FirstRand
Alliance Trust	Investec
Allianz	PineBridge Investments
Aviva	Russell
Fidelity Worldwide Investment	Sanlam
	Standard Bank Group

HISTORICAL FINANCIALS

Company Type: Public

Income Statement FYE: December 31

	ASSETS ($ mil.)	NET INCOME ($ mil.)	INCOME AS % OF ASSETS	EMPLOYEES
12/14	222,470	908	0.4%	61,583
12/13	231,908	1,165	0.5%	56,812
12/12	231,298	1,890	0.8%	54,368
12/11	250,861	1,030	0.4%	57,430
12/10	300,516	(437)	—	55,730
Annual Growth	(7.2%)	—	—	2.5%

2014 Year-End Financials

Return on assets: 0.4%
Return on equity: 7.9%
Long-term debt ($ mil.): —
No. of shares (mil.): —
Sales ($ mil): 24,202

Dividends
Yield: 4.4%
Payout: 540.3%
Market value ($ mil.): —

	STOCK PRICE ($) FY Close	P/E High/Low	PER SHARE ($) Earnings	Dividends	Book Value
12/14	23.50	208169	0.18	1.04	2.36
12/13	25.40	199152	0.23	1.02	2.45
12/12	23.00	92 58	0.37	0.19	2.58
12/11	16.88	139 93	0.18	0.00	2.26
12/10	15.25	— —	(0.09)	0.00	2.44
Annual Growth	11.4%	— —	—	—	(0.9%)

OMV AG (Austria)

Oil and chemicals group OMV is Austria's largest industrial company. A leading oil and gas company in Central and Eastern Europe it explores for natural gas and crude oil; refines crude oil; and imports transports and stores gas. In 2014 OMV reported proved reserves of 1.1 billion barrels of oil equivalent; it produced about 309000 barrels of oil equivalent per day and sold 13 billion cu. ft. of gas. The bulk of OMV's sales come from refining and marketing with the company operating three refineries and more than 4100 gas stations in 11 countries. OMV is focusing on growing its exploration and production assets.

Geographic Reach

OMV gets the bulk of its oil and gas from Austria and Romania but it also has assets in Africa Norway and the UK. The company operates refineries in Schwechat (Austria) Burghausen (Germany) and Petrobrazi (Romania).

Operations

The company operates in three major segments. OMV Exploration and Production's core countries in Romania and Austria OMV is focusing on reducing the natural decline and on enhancing the recovery rates from mature fields. It is looking to find new growth areas within the Caspian Middle East and Africa regions.

OMV Gas and Power ensures the supply of natural gas to its customers via a 2000 km gas pipeline in Austria. Its natural gas network serving about 90% of Austria's natural gas demand draws gas supplies from Russia Norway and Germany as well as from domestic reserves. Austria's gas market now dominated by OMV is slated for full competition and OMV is among state-controlled companies set for full privatization.

The company operates a gas pipeline network in Austria and owns gas storage facilities with a capacity of 2.7 bcm (30 TWh).

OMV Refining and Marketing serves about 1.5 million people a day through retail gas stations in 11 countries and is the market leader in Central and South Eastern Europe.

A fourth segment OMV Solutions is the integrated shared service center for all of the OMV Group companies. Its portfolio spans IT financial services and human resources administration.

Sales and Operations

The company sells its product through industrial customers local distribution companies and wholesalers which focus on multi-country customers.

Financial Performance

OMV's revenues decreased by 15% in 2014 primarily due to decrease in gas and power sales due to the impairments of the Brazi power plant in Romania and the goodwill related to the Petrol Ofisi acquisition.The company's net income declined by 69% in 2014 due to lower revenues and changes in interest expenses.OMV's cash inflow decreased by 11% that year primarily due to lower net income and changes in working capital as a result of changes in short-term provisions.

Stategy

Reorganizing tp be more operationally efficient in 2015 OMV integrated the Gas and Power and Refining and Marketing business segments. In 2014 the company sold its 45% stake in the German Bayernoil refinery network. The remaining OMV refineries are integrated into crude and/or petrochemicals with the associated competitive advantages in its core markets. Exploration and production is the growth driver of OMV. As part of OMV's strategy to build up a new exploration business in the region of Sub-Saharan Africa in 2014 the company signed an agreement with Tullow Oil an exploration-led company successful in finding and developing new resources in Africa. The first steps were taken with entries into offshore Madagascar Gabon and Namibia.In 2013 the company announced plans to direct more than two-thirds of future investments towards exploration and production of oil and gas. It also plans to grow its integrated natural gas assets and restructure its downstream business by selling non-core refining and marketing assets.

Mergers and Acquisitions

As part of OMV's strategy of focusing on exploration and production in politically stable markets in 2013 the company acquired assets in Norway and the UK (West of Shetland area) from Statoil. It bought 19% in the producing Gullfaks field and 24% in the Gudrun field; both offshore oil and gas fields on the Norwegian Continental Shelf. In addition OMV took over 30% in Rosebank and 5.88% in Schiehallion both located west of the Shetland Islands and assets where OMV already holds a stake in.

Ownership

OMV's largest shareholders are Austrian state holding company ÖIAG (32%) and the International Petroleum Investment Company (IPIC) of Abu Dhabi (20%).

HISTORY

Oil exploration began in Austria in the 1920s largely as joint ventures with foreign firms such as Shell and Socony-Vacuum. Full-scale production did not get underway until 1938 when the Anschluss (the absorption of Austria by Germany) paved the way for Germany to exploit Austria's natural resources to fuel its growing war machine. In the division of spoils following WWII Russia gained control of Austria's oil reserves.

The Russian-administered oil assets were transferred to the new Austrian government in 1955 which authorized the company Österreichische Mineralolverwaltung (ÖMG) in 1956 to control state oil assets. ÖMG state-controlled by the Austrian Mineral Oil Administration set about building a major refinery in 1960 and acquiring marketing companies Martha and ÖROP in 1965.

In 1968 ÖMG became the first Western company to sign a natural gas supply contract with Russia. In 1974 the company commissioned the Trans-Austria Gas Pipeline which enabled the supply of natural gas to Italy. That year ÖMG changed its name to ÖMV Aktiengesellschaft (ÖMV became OMV in 1995 for international markets).

During the 1970s OMV expanded its crude supply arrangements tapping supplies from Iran Iraq Libya and other Middle Eastern countries. It moved into oil and gas exploration in the mid-1980s forming OMV Libya (acquiring 25% of Occidental's Libyan production) and OMV UK.

With Austria moving toward increasing privatization in 1987 about 15% of OMV's shares were sold to the public. The government sold another 10% two years later. In 1989 OMV acquired PCD Polymere. With the aim of merging state-owned oil and chemical activities OMV acquired Chemie Linz in 1990. The company also opened its first OMV-branded service station that year. In 1994 OMV reorganized itself as an integrated oil and gas group based in Central Europe with international exploration and production activities and with other operations in the chemical and petrochemical sectors.

In 1995 OMV acquired TOTAL-AUSTRIA expanding its service stations by 59. The company introduced OMV lubricants to the Greek market in 1996. It also expanded its OMV service station network in Hungary to 66 stations after acquiring 31 Q8 (Kuwait) sites. In 1997 the Stroh Company's retail network in Austria was merged into OMV.

Expanding its retail network even farther OMV acquired BP's retail network in the Czech Republic Slovakia and Hungary in 1998. It also sold its stake in Chemie Linz and acquired a 25% stake in major European polyolefin producer Borealis which in turn acquired PCD Polymere. In 1999 the company pushed its retail network into Bulgaria and Romania. That year OMV also acquired Australian company Cultus Petroleum.

OMV and Shell agreed to develop North Sea fields together in 2000. That year OMV also formed a joint venture with Italy's Edison International to explore in Vietnam and acquired more than 9% of Hungarian rival MOL. It upped that stake to 10% in 2001.

In 2002 OMV opened its first gas station in Serbia and Montenegro. It also increased its German gas station count from 79 to 151 with the purchase of 32 units from Royal Dutch Shell and 40 stations from Martin GmbH & Co.

In 2003 the company acquired Preussag Energie's exploration and production assets for $320 million. That year the company moved into Bosnia-Herzegovina opening nine gas stations.

During 2004 the company bought up 51% of Romania's Petrom making it the top oil and gas producer in Central Europe. As part of the deal OMV chose to divest itself of its quarter-chunk of Rompetrol.

In 2006 Russian energy giant Gazprom signed long-term contracts for gas deliveries with OMV.

In a major consolidation move in 2006 OMV agreed to buy Austrian power firm Verbund for $17 billion but the move was rebuffed by government regulators. The next year the company announced plans to merge with Hungary's energy powerhouse MOL but those plans were called off as well due to European Commission regulatory concerns in 2008.

After plans to merge with Hungary's MOL went south OMV the next year sold its 21% stake in it to Russian oil company Surgutneftegas for 1.4 billion ($1.85 billion). Also in 2009 in keeping with its focus on retail markets in the Danube region southeastern Europe and the Black Sea region OMV sold subsidiary OMV Italia; San Marco Petroli acquired the network of about 100 gas stations in the northern Italian region of Triveneto.

OMV has been disposing of some of its heating oil operations. In 2008 it unloaded Bayern GmbH and it plans to sell its OMV Wärme VertriebsgmbH by the end of 2010. At that point the sale of heating oil to private clients will be handled by partners but OMV will continue to service corporate customers.

Eyeing new areas of exploration that year OMV also acquired a 10% stake in Pearl Petroleum giving it access to gas-condensate fields in Iraq.

In 2010 the company boosted its share of Turkey-based oil products company Petrol Ofisi (renamed OMV Petrol Ofisi) from 42% to 96% by acquiring a 54% stake from Doğan Holding for about $1.4 billion. The deal gave OMV access to not only Turkey but the Caspian region and the Middle East.

The acquisition of full control (in 2010) of Petrol Ofisi Turkey's leading filling station and retail business with the only nationwide filling station network in the country (approximately 2300 stations) built a strategic bridge in the growth market of Turkey.

In a further push to grow in the Middle East in 2011 the company acquired two Tunisia-based exploration and production units from Pioneer Natural Resources for $866 million. It also boosted its footprint in Pakistan acquiring Petronas Carigali (Pakistan) Ltd. in 2011.In 2012 the company sold its gas station subsidiary in Croatia. That year it boosted it E&P assets entering Abu Dhabi and acquiring natural gas assets in Norway.

EXECUTIVES

Deputy Chairman Executive Board and CFO, David C. Davies, age 61, $831,000 total compensation
CEO, Rainer Seele, age 55
Executive Board Member Downstream (Refining Gas and Power and Marketing), Manfred Leitner
CFO, Reinhard Florey, age 51
Executive Board Member Upstream, Johann Pleininger, age 53
Deputy Chairman, Wolfgang C. Berndt, age 73
Chairman, Peter Oswald, age 53
Auditors: Ernst & Young Wirtschaftspruefungsgesellschaft m.b.H.

LOCATIONS

HQ: OMV AG (Austria)
Trabrennstrasse 6-8, Vienna 1020
Phone: (43) 1 40440 0 **Fax:** (43) 1 40440 27900
Web: www.omv.com

COMPETITORS

BP	MOL
Eni	PKN ORLEN
Exxon Mobil	Royal Dutch Shell
Hellenic Petroleum	Unipetrol

HISTORICAL FINANCIALS

Company Type: Public

Income Statement FYE: December 31

	REVENUE ($ mil.)	NET INCOME ($ mil.)	NET PROFIT MARGIN	EMPLOYEES
12/14	43,652	433	1.0%	25,505
12/13	58,393	1,600	2.7%	26,863
12/12	56,213	1,796	3.2%	28,658
12/11	44,046	1,375	3.1%	29,800
12/10	31,215	1,232	3.9%	31,398
Annual Growth	8.7%	(23.0%)	—	(5.1%)

2014 Year-End Financials

Debt ratio: 18.7%	No. of shares (mil.): 326
Return on equity: 3.0%	Dividends
Cash ($ mil.): 788	Yield: 4.8%
Current ratio: 0.94	Payout: 85.8%
Long-term debt ($ mil.): 5,641	Market value ($ mil.): 8,662

	STOCK PRICE ($) FY Close	P/E High/Low		PER SHARE ($) Earnings	Dividends	Book Value
12/14	26.55	39	22	1.32	1.28	43.47
12/13	47.79	15	11	4.89	1.16	49.01
12/12	36.70	9	7	5.50	1.05	48.09
12/11	30.38	13	8	4.36	0.96	43.52
12/10	41.80	14	11	4.11	1.00	40.67
Annual Growth	(10.7%)	—	—	(24.6%)	6.4%	1.7%

Orange

For many in Europe and elsewhere the telecom landscape has an Orange glow. Formerly France Telecom Orange provides fixed-line and mobile voice and data services to consumers and commercial clients around the world. The company serves some 250 million customers in about 30 countries. It is a leading European wireless operator and broadband service provider with more than 190 million mobile customers and some 16 million broadband subscribers. Orange's services for corporate clients are provided by its Orange Business Services unit which offers a wide range of managed business networking and data services. The company had been coalescing around its Orange brand since 2006 culminating in the mid-2013 name change.

Geographic Reach

Orange divides up its primary business –mobile and fixed-line telephony along with Internet access services –by region with France comprising nearly half of total operations. Spain and Portugal are its other two major regions with these services. The rest of the world makes up nearly a fifth of total revenues. The remaining business about 15% of sales is largely the company's enterprise services operations.

Sales and Marketing

Most of Orange's sales come through its own retail locations as well as other retail outlets In France the company operates nearly 550 stores.

Financial Performance

Orange reported its seventh straight year of declining revenue in 2014 with sales off 15% for the year. The company has been hit by pricing competition diminishing demand for legacy landline services and regulation of data transfer prices for customers traveling abroad. Net income drop 56% in 2014 on lower revenue and higher taxes. Cash flow from operations rose slightly for 2014 from 2013.

Strategy

In 2015 Orange unveiled Essentials 2020 a strategic plan to provide customers will a full spectrum of digital communications services. A top goal is to triple average data speeds on fixed and mobile networks in four years ending 2018. The company is investing in fiber networks in France Spain and Poland. In France for example the company intends to increase the number of homes it serves with high-speed service from 3.6 million in 2014 to 12 million in 2018 and to 20 million in 2022.

The company's near-term strategy includes looking beyond France for new business including doubling revenues in Africa and the Middle East by 2015 and expanding in Europe. That expansion will not only benefit Orange's core business but also its enterprise services success.

Mergers and Acquisitions

Orange acquired Jazztel in Spain making Orange the second biggest fixed-line broadband operator and a significant element Spain's mobile market.

HISTORY

Early History

Shortly before he abdicated King Louis Philippe laid the groundwork for France's state-owned telegraphic service. Established in 1851 the operation became part of the French Post Office in the 1870s about the time Alexander Graham Bell invented the telephone. The French government licensed three private companies to provide telegraph service and during the 1880s they merged into the Socit Gnrale de Tlphones (SGT). In 1883 the country's first exchange was initiated in Rheims. Four years later an international circuit was installed connecting Paris and Brussels. The government nationalized SGT in 1889.

By the turn of the century France had more than 60000 phone lines and in 1924 a standardized telephone was introduced. Long-distance service improved with underground cabling and phone exchanges in Paris and other leading cities became automated during the 1930s.

WWII proved a major setback to the French government's telephone operations Direction Gnrale des Tlcommunications (DGT) because a large part of its equipment was destroyed or damaged. For the next two decades France lagged behind other nations in telephony infrastructure development. An exception to this technological stagnation was Centre National d'Etudes des Tlcommunications (CNET) the research laboratory formed in 1944 that eventually became France Telecom's research arm.

In 1962 DGT was a key player in the first intercontinental television broadcast between the US and France via a Telstar satellite. The company began to catch up with its peers when it developed a digital phone system in the mid-1970s. In 1974

CNET was instrumental in the launch of France's first experimental communications satellite. In another technological advance DGT began replacing its paper directories with the innovative Minitel online terminals in 1980.

The French government created France Telecom in 1988. In 1993 France Telecom and Deutsche Telekom (DT) teamed up to form the Global One international telecommunications venture and Sprint joined the next year. Global One was formally launched in 1996. Also that year France Telecom began providing Internet access though Minitel still reigned as the country's top online service.

In 1997 the government sold about 20% of France Telecom to the public. With Europe's state telephone monopolies ending in 1998 France Telecom reorganized and brought prices in line with those of its competitors.

EXECUTIVES

Deputy CEO European Operations, Gervais Pellissier, age 56
Deputy CEO Africa and the Middle East (AMEA), Bruno Mettling, age 57
Chairman and CEO, St ©phane Richard, age 54
Deputy CEO General Secretary Operators (France) and Purchasing, Pierre Louette, age 53
Deputy CEO Customer Experience and Mobile Financial Services, Marc Rennard, age 58
Deputy CEO Finance and Strategy and CFO, Ramon Fernandez, age 48
Deputy CEO Orange Business Services (OBS), Thierry Bonhomme, age 58
CEO Orange Spain, Laurent Paillassot
SEVP Human Resources, J ©´me Barr ©
Senior Executive Orange France, Fabienne Dulac
Auditors: Deloitte & Associes

LOCATIONS

HQ: Orange
78 rue Olivier de Serres, Paris 75015
Phone: (33) 1 44 44 21 05
Web: www.orange.com

2014 Sales

	% of total
France	47
Enterprise	18
Spain	15
Poland	9
Rest of the world	7
International carriers & shared services	4
Total	**100**

PRODUCTS/OPERATIONS

Selected Operations

Audience and advertising (Internet advertising business)
Content (partnerships with content providers and development of related technology platforms)
Enterprise communication services (communication services to companies)
Health (services to the health care industry)
Home communication services (residential communication services especially fixed-line broadband)
Personal communication services (communication services for individuals using mobile devices)

COMPETITORS

AT&T
BT
Bouygues
COLT Group
Cable & Wireless
Deutsche Telekom
Equinix Group
HP Enterprise Services
IBM Global Services
KPN
Maroc T©l©com
Proximus
Sky plc
TalkTalk
Telecom Italia
Telefnica
Telefnica Europe
Tiscali
Unisys
Virgin Mobile
Vivendi
Vodafone

HISTORICAL FINANCIALS

Company Type: Public

Income Statement

FYE: December 31

	REVENUE ($ mil.)	NET INCOME ($ mil.)	NET PROFIT MARGIN	EMPLOYEES
12/14	47,684	1,124	2.4%	156,233
12/13	56,063	2,578	4.6%	165,488
12/12	57,009	1,080	1.9%	170,531
12/11	58,438	5,038	8.6%	171,949
12/10	60,881	6,531	10.7%	168,694
Annual Growth	(5.9%)	(35.6%)	—	(1.9%)

2014 Year-End Financials

Debt ratio: —
Return on equity: 3.4%
Cash ($ mil.): 8,214
Current ratio: 0.72
Long-term debt ($ mil.): —
No. of shares (mil.): —
Dividends
Yield: 5.4%
Payout: 224.3%
Market value ($ mil.): —

	STOCK PRICE ($) FY Close	P/E High/Low		PER SHARE ($) Earnings	Dividends	Book Value
12/14	16.92	57	34	0.38	0.92	13.56
12/13	12.35	21	14	0.98	0.68	12.77
12/12	11.05	52	34	0.41	1.84	12.19
12/11	15.66	15	10	1.89	1.72	13.54
12/10	21.08	13	10	2.44	1.91	14.70
Annual Growth	(5.3%)	—	—	(37.3%)	(16.6%)	(2.0%)

Orix Corp. (Japan)

An international financing leviathan ORIX is one of Japan's largest public financial services firms. The company finances leases of everything from computers and measuring equipment to aircraft and ships; it rents out some 30000 different items and is adding more. ORIX also engages in consumer and corporate finance investment banking brokerage car rental and property development and management services in Japan and more than 35 other countries. Its retail offerings include banking life insurance credit cards and trust services. ORIX even has its own professional baseball team the Kobe-based ORIX Buffaloes.

OperationsORIX operates six main business segments: Corporate Financial Services which is the lending leasing and fee business; Maintenance Leasing which provides automobile leasing and rentals car sharing and test and measurement instruments as well as IT-related equipment rentals and leasing; Real Estate which focuses on development rental and financing facility operation REIT asset management and real estate investment advisory services; Investment and Operation which invests in environment and energy-related business principal investment and loan servicing (asset recovery); Retail which offers life insurance banking and card loans; and Overseas Business which provides leasing lending investment in bonds investment banking asset management and ship- and aircraft-related financing.Overall ORIX generated 35% of its total revenue from services income in fiscal 2015 (ended March 31) while sales of goods and real estate contributed another 20%. Life insurance premiums (and related investment income) and operating lease income each made up more than 15% of revenues. The remainder of revenues came from finance revenues (9%) and investment gains and dividends (3%).ORIX USA acts as the holding company for the firm's operations in the US. Among its holdings are Los Angeles-based investment bank Houlihan Lokey which specializes in middle-market mergers and acquisitions. The firm also owns Japanese condominium builder DAIKYO.

Geographic Reach

The company operates nearly 1300 offices in Japan (where it earns more than 70% of its revenues) and 540 more overseas. The Americas is ORIX's second-largest market comprising another 10% of total revenues.Sales and MarketingORIX has ramped up its advertising spend in recent years. It spent ¥20329 million ($215.7 million) on advertising in fiscal 2015 (ended March 31) compared to ¥15270 million ($162 million) and ¥11579 million ($122.9 million) in FY2014 and FY2013 respectively.Financial PerformanceNote: Growth rates may differ after conversion to US dollars.ORIX's revenues and profits have been rising in recent years thanks to its growing life insurance real estate and services businesses coupled with declining interest expenses as its debt interest has been shrinking.The firm's revenue jumped by 58% to ¥2174.3 billion ($21 billion) in fiscal 2015 (ended March 31) mostly thanks to exceptional growth across its Retail Investment and Operation and Overseas divisions. The firm's Investment and Operation division (its largest) revenues swelled by 181% thanks to continued growth in environment and energy business with government support newly acquired subsidiaries and the consolidation of its DAIKYO real estate builder subsidiary. Its Retail division (its 2nd largest) nearly doubled its revenues thanks to a gain on the sale of shares of Monex Group acquired revenue from its acquisition of Hartford Life Insurance KK an increase in finance revenue from the banking business and policy number growth in the life insurance business. Its Overseas Business revenues rose by 36% thanks to higher fee revenues from operations in the US and by the acquired asset management business of Robeco.Higher revenue in FY2015 drove ORIX's net income higher by 25% to a record ¥234.95 billion (around $2 billion). The firm's operating cash fell by 46% to ¥257.6 billion (more than $2 billion) despite higher earnings mostly due to a net decrease in policy liabilities and policy account balances after its consolidation of Hartford Life Insurance KK.

Strategy

ORIX reiterated in 2015 that it plans to strengthen its non-finance business in the US expand its leasing business and make new investments in Asia build its quality asset base in the ship- and aircraft-related business and grow its asset management business through it recently acquired Robeco subsidiary. It also plans to continue expanding its already diverse array of offerings by moving into energy and environmental products. To this end in 2014 ORIX partnered with its asset manager subsidiary Robeco and the Asian Development Bank to launch a private equity fund to invest in environment and energy-related projects including low-carbon projects in Asia with plans to expand the business in the years ahead. Mergers and AcquisitionsIn July 2014 subsidiary ORIX Life Insurance Corporation bought Tokyo-based Hartford Life Insurance KK for ¥98355 million (roughly $970 million) with the goal of enhancing its capital strength and improving its management to accelerate its growth.In July 2013 ORIX purchased a 90% equity stake in mid-size global asset manager Robeco Groep from Cooperative Centrale Raiffeisen-Boerenleenbank (Rabobank) for a total price of ¥255163 million (around $2.5 billion).

EXECUTIVES

President ORIX Baseball Club, Hiroaki Nishina, age 71
Deputy President and CIO, Tamio Umaki, age 67
Corporate EVP, Shintaro Agata, age 65
CEO ORIX USA, Brian F. Prince
Corporate EVP, Yuki Oshima, age 68
Deputy President and CFO, Haruyuki Urata, age 61
EVP; President ORIX Real Estate, Yoshiyuki Yamaya, age 59
SVP; President ORIX Auto, Katsunobu Kamei
EVP; President NS Lease, Katsutoshi Kadowaki
President and COO, Mikoto Inoue, age 63
Corporate EVP, Kazuo Kojima
SVP; President ORIX Credit, Masatoshi Kemmochi
Auditors: KPMG AZSA LLC

LOCATIONS

HQ: Orix Corp. (Japan)
World Trade Center Building, 2-4-1 Hamamatsu-cho, Minato-ku, Tokyo 105-6135
Phone: (81) 3 3435 3000 **Fax:** (81) 3 3435 3154
Web: www.orix.co.jp

2015 Sales

	% of total
Japan	73
Americas	10
Others	17
Total	**100**

PRODUCTS/OPERATIONS

2015 Sales

	% of total
Service income	35
Goods and real estate	20
Operating leases	17
Life insurance premiums and related investments income	16
Finance revenue	9
Gains on investment securities and dividends	3
Total	**100**

Selected Subsidiaries and Segments

ORIX Aircraft (aircraft leasing)
ORIX Asset Management & Loan Services Corporation (commercial mortgage servicing)
ORIX Auto (car rental and leasing)
ORIX Baseball Club (professional baseball team)
ORIX Life Insurance
ORIX Real Estate (real estate development and investment)
ORIX Real Estate Investment Advisors (asset management)
ORIX Rentec (rental operations)
ORIX Trust and Banking
ORIX USA
SUN Leasing Corporation (medical equipment leasing)

COMPETITORS

CIT Group
GE Capital
ILFC
Mitsubishi UFJ Financial Group
Mizuho Financial
Rentokil Initial
Sumitomo

HISTORICAL FINANCIALS

Company Type: Public

Income Statement

FYE: March 31

	ASSETS ($ mil.)	NET INCOME ($ mil.)	INCOME AS % OF ASSETS	EMPLOYEES
03/15	95,380	1,958	2.1%	31,035
03/14	87,865	1,809	2.1%	25,977
03/13	89,696	1,189	1.3%	19,043
03/12	101,851	1,050	1.0%	17,488
03/11	103,634	812	0.8%	17,578
Annual Growth	(2.1%)	24.6%	—	15.3%

2015 Year-End Financials

Return on assets: 2.2%
Return on equity: 11.5%
Long-term debt ($ mil.): —
No. of shares (mil.): 1,308
Sales ($ mil): 17,924
Dividends
Yield: 1.5%
Payout: 63.8%
Market value ($ mil.): 92,050

	STOCK PRICE ($) FY Close	P/E High	P/E Low	PER SHARE ($) Earnings	Dividends	Book Value
03/15	70.34	0	0	1.49	1.12	13.71
03/14	70.47	1	0	1.38	0.65	14.20
03/13	63.58	1	0	0.93	0.48	14.30
03/12	48.25	1	0	0.82	0.48	15.83
03/11	46.57	1	1	0.64	0.40	14.82
Annual Growth	10.9%	—	—	23.7%	29.1%	(1.9%)

Oversea-Chinese Banking Corp. Ltd. (Singapore)

Singapore bank Oversea-Chinese Banking Corporation (OCBC Bank) operates more than 470 branches and offices in 15 countries including some 350 offices in Indonesia through its Bank OCBC NISP subsidiary. The company offers traditional banking services for individuals and businesses as well as financial services such as brokerage and asset management. Private banking for high-net-worth families is offered through the Bank of Singapore while Great Eastern Holdings which provides life and property/casualty insurance is the largest insurance company in Singapore and Malaysia. OCBC Bank was founded in 1912 to serve the Chinese business community of Singapore and other parts of Asia but now serves the general public.

Geographic Reach

The bank's main operations are in its home country of Singapore which accounts for 60% of business. Malaysia where it operates as OCBC Bank Malaysia and offers Islamic banking services through OCBC Al-Amin Bank accounts for about 20% of business. Indonesia and China each account for less than 10% of business.

In addition to its core markets OCBC also has a presence in Australia Brunei Dubai Hong Kong Japan The Philippines South Korea Taiwan Thailand the UK the US (in New York and Los Angeles) and Vietnam through branches and representative offices.

Strategy

With Singapore's population only 5 million people the bank has targeted China Indonesia and Malaysia as international growth markets. It plans to increase its Islamic banking and insurance operations in Malaysia home to almost 30 million people. In Indonesia (population 247 million) the bank consolidated its banking subsidiaries in order to grow the OCBC NISP brand there. And in China with 1.3 billion people the bank plans to cater to wealthy citizens by offering private banking services through the Bank of Singapore.

EXECUTIVES

COO, Ching Wei Hong, age 55
Group CEO, Samuel N. (Sam) Tsien, age 60
SEVP and Head of Global Treasury and Investment Banking, Lam Kun Kin, age 52
Executive Vice President, Gilbert Kohnke, age 56
Head Group Operations and Technology, Lim Khiang Tong, age 55
CFO, Darren S. P. Tan, age 44
Head of Global Commercial Banking, Linus T. L. Goh, age 52
EVP and Head of Global Corporate Banking, George L. W. Lee
CEO Bank of Singapore, Renato de Guzman
CEO OCBC Bank China, Kng Hwee Tin
CEO OCBC Bank Malaysia, Ong Eng Bin
Chairman, Ooi Sang Kuang, age 67
Auditors: KPMG LLP

LOCATIONS

HQ: Oversea-Chinese Banking Corp. Ltd. (Singapore)
65 Chulia Street, #06-00 OCBC Centre, 049513
Phone: (65) 6318 7222 **Fax:** (65) 6533 7955
Web: www.ocbc.com

2012 Sales

	% of total
Singapore	63
Malaysia	20
Indonesia	7
China	7
Rest of Asia	2
Rest of world	1
Total	**100**

PRODUCTS/OPERATIONS

2012 Sales

	% of total
Interest	59
Noninterest	
Fees & commissions	12
Life insurance	7
General insurance	1
Rental income	1
Dividends	1
Other	19
Total	**100**

Selected Subsidiaries

Banking
- Bank of Singapore Limited
- OCBC Al-Amin Bank Berhad
- OCBC Bank (Malaysia) Berhad
- Singapore Island Bank Limited

Insurance
- Great Eastern Life Assurance (Malaysia) Berhad
- Overseas Assurance Corporation (Malaysia) Berhad
- The Great Eastern Life Assurance Company Limited
- The Overseas Assurance Corporation

Asset management
- Lion Global Investors Limited
- Great Eastern Holdings Limited

Stockbroker
- OCBC Securities Private Limited

COMPETITORS

ABN AMRO Group
AmBank Group
BNP Paribas
Bank Central Asia
Bank Danamon Indonesia
Bank Mandiri
Bank Rakyat
Citigroup
DBS Group Holdings
HSBC
Hong Leong Finance
Maybank
Standard Chartered
United Overseas Bank

HISTORICAL FINANCIALS

Company Type: Public

Income Statement FYE: December 31

	ASSETS ($ mil.)	NET INCOME ($ mil.)	INCOME AS % OF ASSETS	EMPLOYEES
12/14	303,690	2,908	1.0%	29,512
12/13	267,902	2,190	0.8%	25,350
12/12	241,962	3,264	1.3%	24,628
12/11	213,713	1,779	0.8%	22,892
12/10	178,808	1,757	1.0%	21,585
Annual Growth	14.2%	13.4%	—	8.1%

2014 Year-End Financials

Return on assets: 1.0%
Return on equity: 13.6%
Long-term debt ($ mil.): —
No. of shares (mil.): —
Sales ($ mil): 15,723
Dividends
Yield: —
Payout: —
Market value ($ mil.): —

	STOCK PRICE ($) FY Close	P/E High	P/E Low	PER SHARE ($) Earnings	Dividends	Book Value
12/14	7.88	5	4	0.78	0.00	5.91
12/13	7.92	8	6	0.60	0.00	5.79
12/12	7.92	5	3	0.92	0.00	6.15
12/11	6.18	8	5	0.50	0.00	5.05
12/10	7.72	7	5	0.51	0.00	4.86
Annual Growth	0.5%	—	—	10.8%	—	5.0%

P.T. Argo Pantes (Indonesia)

Auditors: Anwar, Sugiharto & Rekan

LOCATIONS

HQ: P.T. Argo Pantes (Indonesia)
Wisma Agro Manunggal, 2nd Floor, Jln. Jend. Gatot Subroto No 95. Kav. 22, Jakarta 12930
Phone: (62) 21 2520065 **Fax:** (62) 21 2520108

HISTORICAL FINANCIALS

Company Type: Public

Income Statement FYE: December 31

	REVENUE ($ mil.)	NET INCOME ($ mil.)	NET PROFIT MARGIN	EMPLOYEES
12/14	104,819	(30,333)	—	2,295
12/13	109	6	6.2%	5,344
12/12	103	(12)	—	4,650
12/11	93	(11)	—	4,617
12/10	73	(13)	—	3,817
Annual Growth	513.7%	—	—	(11.9%)

2014 Year-End Financials

Debt ratio: 76.2%
Return on equity: (-19.8%)
Cash ($ mil.): 717
Current ratio: 0.41
Long-term debt ($ mil.): 78,742
No. of shares (mil.): 335
Dividends
Yield: —
Payout: —
Market value ($ mil.): —

Panasonic Corp

Panasonic has been one of the world's most prolific electronics manufacturers since 1919. The company spans multiple fields: Its consumer business consists of AVC (audio video and communications) equipment along with hardware and software for linking it together and home appliances (washing machines vacuum cleaners personal grooming aids and commercial HVAC). In the field of devices Panasonic covers multimedia and eco-car equipment industrial electronic components and batteries. The company's solutions equipment targets environmentally conscience businesses manufacturers and health care firms.

Geographic Reach

The company sells its products and services in Asia Europe and North and South America. Japan accounts for just over 50% of net sales while other major markets include North and South America (16%) and Europe (10%).

Operations

Within the company's businesses are five segments: automotive and industrial systems (34% of net sales) appliances (23%) eco solutions (20%) AVC networks (14%) and other (9%).

Panasonic is financially diversified across its segments with the digital AVC networks segment consisting of imaging equipment AVC network equipment such as flat-panel TVs blu-ray disc recorders digital cameras notebook PCs projectors and in-flight entertainment systems. Its appliances segment manufactures products like air conditioners refrigerators washing machines and other home appliances.

Eco solutions supplies lighting fixtures electric lamps wiring devices solar photovoltaic systems interior furnishing materials water-related products ventilation and air-conditioning equipment and air purifiers among other products. The automotive and industrial segment maintains a broad spectrum of expertise across car-use-multimedia-related equipment automotive electronics electronics components automation controls electronic materials semiconductors batteries systems optical devices and manufacturing facility systems.

Sales and Marketing

Panasonic's consumer products are mainly sold to mass-merchandisers through sales subsidiaries. Housing products are sold through agencies and sales subsidiaries. AVC networks products are sold through retail distributors logistics service providers and public institutions. The company also markets its products through print ads and TV commercials.

Financial Performance

Panasonic's overall sales for fiscal 2015 (ends March 31) declined marginally by under 1% due to declines from its appliances and eco solutions segments. These segments were negatively affected by weakening demand after a consumption tax hike and a negative impact from sharp price declines of TVs in Japan.

Strategy

In Japan Panasonic is expanding into the housing improvement market where future growth is expected. In addition to renovating its showrooms in Japan to make them more compatible with the housing improvement market and targeting new customers the company is strengthening its direct marketing to clients through PanaHome Reform Corporation which was established in 2014.

Mergers and AcquisitionsThe company is using acquisitions as a means for growth within its satellite-based communications portfolio. In 2015 it acquired ITC Global a provider of satellite communication services for the energy mining and maritime markets. With regional headquarters in Houston; Sion Switzerland; and Perth Australia ITC Global serves customers at more than 1200 remote sites across 70 countries and all the world's oceans.

HISTORY

Grade school dropout Konosuke Matsushita took $50 in 1918 and went into business making electric plugs (with his brother-in-law Toshio Iue founder of SANYO). His mission to help people by making high-quality low-priced conveniences while providing his employees with good working conditions earned him the sobriquet "god of business management." Matsushita Electric Industrial grew by developing inexpensive lamps batteries radios and motors in the 1920s and 1930s.

During WWII the Japanese government ordered the firm to build wood-laminate products for the military. Postwar occupation forces prevented Matsushita from working at his firm for four years. Thanks to unions' efforts he rejoined his namesake company shortly before it entered a joint venture with Dutch manufacturer Philips in 1952. The following year it moved into consumer goods making televisions refrigerators and washing machines and later expanding into high-performance audio products. Matsushita bought a majority stake in Victor Company of Japan (JVC originally established by RCA Victor) in 1954. Its 1959 New York subsidiary opening began Matsushita's drive overseas.

Sold under the National Panasonic and Technics names the firm's products were usually not cutting-edge but were attractively priced. Under Masaharu Matsushita the founder's son-in-law who became president in 1961 the company became Japan's largest home appliance maker introducing air conditioners microwave ovens stereo components and VCRs in the 1960s and 1970s. JVC developed the VHS format for VCRs which beat out Sony's Betamax format.

Matsushita built much of its sales growth on new industrial and commercial customers in the 1980s. The company expanded its semiconductor office and factory automation auto electronics audio-visual housing and air-conditioning product offerings that decade. Konosuke died in 1989.

EXECUTIVES

EVP, Yasuo Katsura, age 68
Managing Director Industrial Sales and Board Member, Yoshihiko (Yoshi) Yamada, age 64
Managing Executive Officer; President Automotive Systems Company, Kazuhiro Tsuga
Managing Executive Officer; President Panasonic Electronic Devices, Toshiaki Kobayashi
Executive Officer; Director Corporate Management Division Asia and Oceania and President Panasonic Asia Pacific, Ikuo Miyamoto
Managing Executive Officer and Head China and Northeast Asia, Hidetoshi Osawa
Executive Officer; Director Corporate Management Division for North America; Chairman and CEO North America, Joseph M. (Joe) Taylor
Managing Director; President AVC Networks Company, Yoshiyuki Miyabe
Senior Managing Director and President Appliances Company, Kazunori Takami, age 61
Managing Director Accounting and Finance, Hideaki Kawai
Executive Officer; President Panasonic France, Laurent Abadie
EVP and President Eco Solutions Company, Shusaku Nagae
Managing Executive Officer and Head Asia the Middle East and Africa, Yorihisa Shiokawa

Managing Director Technology Intellectual Property and Information Systems, Mamoru Yoshida
President Panasonic Healthcare Co. Ltd., Kenji Yamane
President CEO*, Patrick D. O'Brien
Chairman, Kunio Nakamura, age 76
Vice Chairman, Masayuki Matsushita, age 70
Chairman, Fumio Ohtsubo, age 70
Auditors: KPMG AZSA LLC

LOCATIONS

HQ: Panasonic Corp
1006 Oaza Kadoma, Kadoma, Osaka 571-8501
Phone: (81) 6 6908 1121
Web: www.panasonic.co.jp

2015 Sales

	% of total
Japan	49
North & South America	16
Europe	9
Asia & others	26
Total	**100**

PRODUCTS/OPERATIONS

2015 Sales

	% of total
Automotive and industrial systems	34
Appliance	23
Eco Solutions	20
AVC network	14
Other	9
Total	**100**

Selected Segments and Products

AVC Networks
- Camcorders
- Computer drives (CD-ROM DVD-ROM/RAM)
- Computers (PCs)
- Digital cameras
- DVD players and recorders
- Fax machines
- Printers
- Telephones
- TVs (color LCD plasma display)

PEW and PanaHome
- Automation controls
- Beauty and personal care products
- Electronic and plastic materials
- Home security systems
- Interior furnishings

Home appliances
- Air conditioners and purifiers
- Dishwashers
- Dryers
- Fans
- Refrigerators
- Vacuum cleaners
- Water heaters
- Washing machines

Components and devices
- Batteries (dry rechargeable)
- Displays (CRTs LCDs PDPs)
- Electric motors
- General components (capacitors resistors printed circuit boards)
- Magnetic recording heads
- Semiconductors

Selected Brands

National
Panasonic
Quasar
Technics
Victor

COMPETITORS

A123 Systems
Apple Inc.
BSH Bosch und Siemens Hausgerāte
BYD
Canon
Dell
Eastman Kodak
Electrolux
Fujitsu Technology Solutions
GE Appliances & Lighting
HP
Haier Group
IBM
Intel
Konica Minolta
LG Electronics
Motorola Solutions
NEC
Nokia
Olympus
Philips Electronics
Procter & Gamble
Samsung Electronics
Sharp Corp.
Sony
TE Connectivity
Technicolor
Toshiba
Truly International
Whirlpool
Yuasa Battery Thailand

HISTORICAL FINANCIALS

Company Type: Public

Income Statement

FYE: March 31

	REVENUE ($ mil.)	NET INCOME ($ mil.)	NET PROFIT MARGIN	EMPLOYEES
03/15	64,303	1,495	2.3%	254,084
03/14	74,952	1,166	1.6%	271,789
03/13	77,615	(8,016)	—	293,742
03/12	95,650	(9,413)	—	330,767
03/11	104,975	893	0.9%	366,937
Annual Growth	(11.5%)	13.7%	—	(8.8%)

2015 Year-End Financials

Debt ratio: 0.1%
Return on equity: 10.6%
Cash ($ mil.): 10,825
Current ratio: 1.25
Long-term debt ($ mil.): 5,937
No. of shares (mil.): —
Dividends
Yield: 1.1%
Payout: 20.4%
Market value ($ mil.): —

	STOCK PRICE ($) FY Close	P/E High/Low		PER SHARE ($) Earnings	Dividends	Book Value
03/15	13.13	0	0	0.65	0.14	6.62
03/14	11.44	0	0	0.50	0.05	6.53
03/13	7.33	—	—	(3.47)	0.05	5.85
03/12	9.25	—	—	(4.07)	0.12	10.18
03/11	12.59	1	0	0.43	0.11	14.93
Annual Growth (18.4%)	1.1%	—	—	10.6%	6.0%	

Pegatron Corp

Pegatron sounds like the mythical robot that gave humans the gift of electronics but it is one of many contract manufacturers of computers communication devices and consumer electronics. The company formed in 2008 when computer maker ASUSTeK spun off its contract manufacturing business. Pegatron's design and manufacturing capabilities include desktop PCs notebooks netbooks digital photo frames e-readers game consoles handheld devices LCD TVs mobile Internet devices and cable set-top boxes. In addition the company makes the iPod Shuffle for Apple and the iPhone used by China Telecom. Pegatron generates more than two-thirds of sales in Asia. Its former parent ASUSTeK owns 25% of its stock.

The company divides its products into three segments –computers consumer electronics and communication devices. As an original design manufacturer (ODM) and original equipment manufacturer (OEM) the company performs all the aspects of product design and development product testing component sourcing manufacturing and distribution.

Pegatron got its start making motherboards and graphics cards for ASUSTeK and computing products remain its largest segment accounting for more than 65% of overall sales in 2009. Portable computers such as notebooks and netbooks are in the most demand and account for about two-thirds of that segment's revenues while motherboards and desktop PCs make up the other third of sales. Pegatron plans to manufacture about 20 million portable computers in 2011. It manufactures notebooks and netbooks primarily to ASUSTeK its top customer. In fact Pegatron sells more than 35% of its computer products back to ASUSTek. (The company was initially spun off to allow ASUSTek to focus on its own branded ASUS products).

Pegatron's second-largest segment is consumer electronics which accounted for about 20% of revenues in 2009 down from about 30% in 2008 its first operating year. The consumer electronics segment is more prone to fluctuation without a steady customer such as ASUSTeK. It primarily makes game consoles handheld devices and LCD TVs and depending on consumer demand can make digital photo frames and e-readers.

The market for consumer electronics is fiercely competitive and pits companies against each other in terms of innovation. Pegatron is incorporating durable e-ink technology into its e-readers to enhance shock absorption and developing solar-powered e-reader covers to charge the device's batteries. For its digital frames the company is developing GPS functions for customized services and embedded software to modify photo size. Recent contracts for Apple's iPhone in China and rumors of its contract to make the iPhone for Verizon in the US could boost the segment's revenues in 2011.

Communication devices such as routers IP set-top boxes handsets cable modems and wireless adapters make up the company's smallest segment (about 10% of sales). In this area Pegatron is working on a new product that would incorporate broadband connectivity to LCD TVs. Other minor business segments include motherboard manufacturer Advansus a joint venture with embedded computer maker Advantech and Unihan a manufacturer of metal parts and molds (such as plastic casings for electronics) acquired in the ASUSTeK spinoff.

Outside Taiwan Pegatron has three manufacturing plants in China one in the Czech Republic and one in Mexico. In February 2011 the company announced it would lay off most of its 1500 employees in the Czech Republic. At the same time it plans to increase production in China. Pegatron is building a fourth production plant in Chongqing its first in the central part of the country where labor and other costs are less expensive than the urban coastal areas. At a cost of about $49 million the plant to be named Shi Shao Technology will focus on initial-stage notebook PC production.

Pegatron is also upping its investments in manufacturers of parts and components. Under the vertical integration model the company claims owning its own suppliers is cost effective efficient and allows for more product control as consumer electronics have short lifecycles and components need to be upgraded often. In 2010 Pegatron bought two Shanghai-area companies Ri-Teng Computer and Ri-Min Computer that produce mechanical parts and modules.

Pegatron listed on the Taiwan's stock exchange in June 2010. While ASUSTeK is its largest shareholder the former parent does not have a presence on Pegatron's board of directors. The company did that in order to avoid a conflict of interest concerning customers' new product designs and technologies and ensure that ASUSTek has no knowledge of what its competitors are up to.

EXECUTIVES

President, Tzu Hsien Tung
Auditors: KPMG

LOCATIONS

HQ: Pegatron Corp
5/F., No. 76, Ligong Street, Beitou District, Taipei 112
Phone: (886) 2 8143 9001 **Fax:** (886) 2 8143 7984
Web: www.pegatroncorp.com

2014 Sales

	% of total
Taiwan	22
USA	30
Ireland	25
Japan	6
China	5
Others	12
Total	**100**

PRODUCTS/OPERATIONS

2014 Sales

	% of total
DMS	89
Investment Group	11
Total	**100**

COMPETITORS

BenQ
Compal Electronics
Elitegroup Computer Systems
First International Computer
Flextronics
Foxconn International
Foxconn Technology
Giga-Byte Technology
Hedy Holding
Hon Hai
Inventec
Jabil
Lite-On Technology
MiTAC
Micro-Star International
Nam Tai
Quanta Computer
TPV Technology
TriGem
Universal Scientific
Venture Corp.
Wistron

HISTORICAL FINANCIALS

Company Type: Public

Income Statement FYE: December 31

	REVENUE ($ mil.)	NET INCOME ($ mil.)	NET PROFIT MARGIN	EMPLOYEES
12/14	32,204	462	1.4%	6,783
12/13	31,848	320	1.0%	0
12/12	30,363	219	0.7%	177,948
12/11	19,793	109	0.6%	112,318
12/10	18,231	364	2.0%	104,608
Annual Growth	15.3%	6.2%	—	(49.5%)

2014 Year-End Financials

Debt ratio: 0.3%	No. of shares (mil.): —
Return on equity: 12.1%	Dividends
Cash ($ mil.): 3,400	Yield: —
Current ratio: 1.39	Payout: —
Long-term debt ($ mil.): 440	Market value ($ mil.): —

Peoples Insurance Company (Group) of China Ltd (The)

Auditors: Deloitte Touche Tohmastu

LOCATIONS

HQ: Peoples Insurance Company (Group) of China Ltd (The)
28 Qinghua West Road, Haidian District, Beijing 100084
Phone: (86) 10 6261 6611 **Fax:** (86) 10 6262 4880
Web: www.picc.com

HISTORICAL FINANCIALS

Company Type: Public

Income Statement FYE: December 31

	REVENUE ($ mil.)	NET INCOME ($ mil.)	NET PROFIT MARGIN	EMPLOYEES
12/14	56,634	2,112	3.7%	184,644
12/13	50,337	1,341	2.7%	0
Annual Growth	12.5%	57.5%	—	—

2014 Year-End Financials

Debt ratio: —	No. of shares (mil.): —
Return on equity: 15.9%	Dividends
Cash ($ mil.): 6,333	Yield: —
Current ratio: —	Payout: —
Long-term debt ($ mil.): —	Market value ($ mil.): —

	STOCK PRICE ($) FY Close	P/E High/Low	PER SHARE ($) Earnings	Dividends	Book Value
12/14	0.00	— —	0.05	0.00	0.35
12/13	0.00	— —	0.03	0.00	0.28
/0.00	—	—(0.00)	0.00	(0.00)	
Annual Growth	—	— —	—	—	—

Permanent TSB Group Holdings Plc

Taking the "Ireland first" motto to heart permanent tsb Group Holdings (formerly Irish Life & Permanent) provides financial services across the grassy hills of Ireland. The company provides banking mortgage loans and asset management services to its home country. The permanent tsb banking unit operates more than 70 retail branches while its Capital Home Loans subsidiary provides residential mortgage loans. Slow to recover from economic troubles the firm has been restructuring in recent years; its efforts culminated with the sale of its life insurance operations to Ireland's Minister for Finance office in 2012. The Irish government also holds a majority stake in permanent tsb Group Holdings.The company's Irish Life unit provides life insurance and investment products to individuals through its own sales force independent agents and the branches of permanent tsb. In addition Irish Life owns 30% of Allianz-Irish Life; German insurance giant Allianz is the majority owner of the nonlife insurance firm. Overall IL&P serves 1.6 million customers.In addition to its banking and insurance divisions other divisions provide asset management and group pension and insurance products. Like many Irish banks and lenders the company has been hurt by the global credit crunch and subprime mortgage market collapse. It stopped writing home loans in the UK market late in 2008. Early the following year Irish Life & Permanent came under fire for financial transactions conducted with Anglo Irish Bank (renamed Irish Bank Resolution Corporation Limited in 2011) during 2008 and during the ensuing regulatory investigation CEO Denis Casey resigned. Kevin Murphy took over the CEO role the following year.By mid-2009 the company had turned to its "worst-case scenario" for dealing with bad loan losses. It then announced plans to split apart its insurance banking and asset management operations into separate companies.Irish Life is the result of a 1999 merger between Irish Life and Irish Permanent.

HISTORY

One of the two strands that make up Irish Life & Permanent began in 1884 with the founding of The Irish Temperance Permanent Benefit Building Society. In 1940 however the company was refitted with the more manageable moniker: The Irish Permanent Building Society. This was also the event that kicked off the company's efforts to advertise and build a major national brand name.

During the 1940s and 1950s the Irish Permanent Building Society continued to put its energy into developing its reputation and brand through advertising. This strategy paid off in spades and by the end of the 1960s the company had nearly 200 locations in Ireland.

With the passing of the Building Societies Act at the end of the 1980s Irish Permanent Building Society began to set up subsidiaries to handle other business ventures. Its Irish Permanent Finance provided unsecured lending and leasing and its Irish Permanent Life & Pensions sold pension policies and life insurance.

In 1994 Irish Permanent bought Prudential Life of Ireland a company whose life assurance and pensions business in Ireland helped Irish Permanent in its campaign to expand its product range. That year the company also picked up private bank Guinness & Mahon. The buying spree continued in 1996 as Irish Permanent acquired Capital Home Loans a mortgage lender operating in the UK.

On the other side of the family Irish Life Assurance was founded in 1939 from several Irish and British life assurance companies. This (and subsequent) dealings left Ireland's Minister of Finance with a 90% share of the company.

Irish Life Assurance was restructured as Irish Life and listed on the Irish and London stock exchanges in the summer of 1991. This event began the Minister of Finance's dissolution of most of his stake in the company (a purging that was complete by 1995). In 1992 the company came to Belfast and London moving beyond Ireland for the first time.

Then in 1999 Irish Life and Irish Permanent came together effectively pairing the Emerald Isle's biggest life insurer and biggest mortgage firm. Both companies boasted a market share above 20 percent in their respective industries and while life insurance is still its bread and butter the company is angling to become an ever-more central player in Ireland's burgeoning personal financial services market. In 2001 the company completed its acquisition of Irish retail banker TSB.In line with Irish Life & Permanent's strategy to focus on its domestic market the company sold the last of several US insurance subsidiaries in 2003.

LOCATIONS

HQ: Permanent TSB Group Holdings Plc
56 - 59, St. Stephen' s Green, Dublin 2
Phone:
Web: www.permanenttsbgroup.ie

COMPETITORS

AIB
Azimut
Bank of Ireland
Jupiter Fund Management
National Irish Bank
Royal Bank of Scotland
St. Andrew' s Group
Shannon

HISTORICAL FINANCIALS

Company Type: Public

Income Statement FYE: December 31

	ASSETS ($ mil.)	NET INCOME ($ mil.)	INCOME AS % OF ASSETS	EMPLOYEES
12/14	44,117	(123)	—	2,321
12/13	51,766	(359)	—	2,041
12/12	53,933	(1,316)	—	2,305
12/11	93,176	(553)	—	4,407
12/10	101,313	(171)	—	4,338
Annual Growth	(18.8%)	—	—	(14.5%)

2014 Year-End Financials

Return on assets: (-0.2%)
Return on equity: (-4.3%)
Long-term debt ($ mil.): —
No. of shares (mil.): 276
Sales ($ mil): 1,151
Dividends
Yield: —
Payout: —
Market value ($ mil.): 14

	STOCK PRICE ($) FY Close	P/E High/Low		PER SHARE ($) Earnings	Dividends	Book Value
12/14	0.05	—	—	(0.00)	0.00	10.03
Annual Growth	—	—	—	—	—	—

PetroChina Co Ltd

If you want petroleum in China or elsewhere then PetroChina is your company. A subsidiary of state-owned China National Petroleum Corporation (CNPC) PetroChina produces two-thirds of China's oil and gas. The company has proved reserves of 10.8 billion barrels of oil and 69.3 trillion cu. ft. of natural gas. In China it owns more than 53400 kilometers of natural gas and refined products pipeline and operates 29 refineries and 13 chemical plants. PetroChina was created in 2000 as a separate company to initially manage the domestic operations –and in recent years some key international assets –of CNPC.

Strategy

PetroChina is taking advantage of the growing consumption of natural gas in China by expanding its transmission infrastructure. It is also expanding its oil reserves and refining operations through the purchase of international oil fields and refineries including several assets from its parent.

In 2015 the company agreed to sell 50% of Central Asia Natural Gas Pipeline Co. to Mansong Holdings Ltd a subsidiary of China Reform Holdings Corp. Ltd. for 15 billion to 15.5 billion yuan.

EXECUTIVES

Vice Chairman and President, Wang Dongjin
VP and General Manager Exploration and Production, Zhao Zhengzhang, age 58
VP and General Manager PetroChina Natural Gas and Pipelines, Huang Weihe, age 57
Chief Engineer, Lin Aiguo, age 56
VP and General Manager PetroChina Refining and Chemical, Xu Fugui
VP and General Manager PetroChina International Company Limited (China National United Oil Corporation), Wang Lihua
VP and General Manager PetroChina International Exploration and Development and China National Exploration and Development, Lu Gongxun
CFO, Zhao Dong, age 45
Chairman, Wang Yilin, age 62
Auditors: KPMG Huazhen (Special General Partnership)

LOCATIONS

HQ: PetroChina Co Ltd
No. 9 Dongzhimen North Street, Dongcheng District, Beijing 100007
Phone: (86) 10 5998 5667 **Fax:** (86) 10 6209 5667
Web: www.petrochina.com.cn

2013 Sales

	% of total
Mainland China	67
Other countries	33
Total	**100**

PRODUCTS/OPERATIONS

2013 Sales

	% of total
Marketing	51
Refining & chemicals	23
Exploration & production	20
Natural gas & pipeline	6
Total	**100**

COMPETITORS

Bangchak Petroleum Public
CNOOC
Chevron
Exxon Mobil
Sinopec Shanghai Petrochemical

HISTORICAL FINANCIALS

Company Type: Public

Income Statement FYE: December 31

	REVENUE ($ mil.)	NET INCOME ($ mil.)	NET PROFIT MARGIN	EMPLOYEES
12/14	367,841	17,268	4.7%	534,652
12/13	373,003	21,407	5.7%	544,083
12/12	352,134	18,498	5.3%	548,355
12/11	318,353	21,123	6.6%	552,810
12/10	222,315	21,237	9.6%	552,698
Annual Growth	13.4%	(5.0%)	—	(0.8%)

2014 Year-End Financials

Debt ratio: 3.6%
Return on equity: 9.2%
Cash ($ mil.): 11,887
Current ratio: 0.67
Long-term debt ($ mil.): 59,664
No. of shares (mil.): —
Dividends
Yield: 4.2%
Payout: 4,927.4%
Market value ($ mil.): —

	STOCK PRICE ($) FY Close	P/E High/Low	PER SHARE ($) Earnings	Dividends	Book Value
12/14	110.96	251157	0.10	4.70	1.04
12/13	109.74	211145	0.12	4.21	1.02
12/12	143.78	246189	0.10	4.47	0.93
12/11	124.31	223156	0.12	4.90	0.87
12/10	131.49	180139	0.12	3.80	0.78
Annual Growth	(4.2%)	—	(4.7%)	5.4%	7.4%

Petroleo Brasileiro S.A.

PETRÓLEO BRASILEIRO (PETROBRAS) isn't brash but it is Brazil's top company. The integrated energy company (controlled by the Brazilian government) explores for oil and gas and produces refines and transports oil and gas products. With extensive offshore assets in 2014 PETROBRAS reported proved reserves of 16.6 billion barrels of oil equivalent. In Brazil it also operates 15 refineries an extensive oil and gas pipeline network and more than 7710 gas stations. Petrobras Distribuidora is Brazil's #1 retailer of oil products and fuel alcohol. Petrobras Argentina is a top Argentine oil firm. Other units operate electricity (10 power plants) petrochemicals and natural gas assets.

Geographic Reach

Petrobras Internacional also known as Braspetro conducts exploration worldwide including in Angola Nigeria Tanzania Portugal the US and across Latin America. PETROBRAS has a presence in 17 countries.

Operations

The company operates through six business segments: Exploration and Production (crude oil NGL and natural gas exploration development and production in Brazil). In 2014 the company reported proved developed oil and gas reserves of 8.1 billion barrels of oil equivalent and proved undeveloped reserves of 4.6 billion barrels of oil equivalent in Brazil. The bulk of PETROBRAS' production comes from its operations in Brazilian waters; the company is recognized as a leader in offshore drilling technology and deepwater wells. Refining Transportation and Marketing (refining logistics transportation trading operations oil products and crude oil exports and imports and petrochemical investments in Brazil).Distribution (oil products ethanol biodiesel and natural gas to wholesalers and through PETROBRAS' Petrobras Distribuidora S.A. retail network in Brazil).Gas and Power (transportation and trading of natural gas and LNG produced in or imported into Brazil as well as generation and trading of electric power and the fertilizer business.Biofuel (production of biodiesel and its co-products and ethanol-related activities such as equity investments production and trading of ethanol sugar and the excess electricity generated from sugarcane bagasse). PETROBRAS is a major ethanol producer and plans (through Petrobras Transporte S.A. which oversees oil and derivatives ethanol biofuels and natural gas transportation and storage activities) to invest billions of dollars in biofuel development to ensure Brazil's fuel independence as its economy and population grows.International (exploration and production of oil and gas refining transportation and marketing distribution and gas and power operations).PETROBRAS main subsidiaries include Petrobras Distribuidora S.A. Petrobras Biocombustível Petrobras Transporte S.A. Petrobras Gás S.A. and Liquigás Distribuidora S.A.

Sales and Marketing The company serves industries such as Automotive Industrial Agriculture Rail Maritime and Aviation. It distributes its oil products through a company-owned retail network wholesale channels and by supplying other fuel wholesalers and retailers.

Financial Performance

PETROBRAS' net revenues increased by 2% in 2014 due to an increase in Gas & Power and Distribution sales.The increase was primarily driven by higher oil product prices in the Brazil due to diesel and gasoline price increases applied in 2013 and 2014 and the impact of the appreciation of the US dollar against the real (9%) on the price of oil products adjusted to reflect international prices (such as jet fuel and naphtha) as well as higher electricity and natural gas prices.Revenues were also affected by a 3% increase in the demand for oil products in Brazil mainly diesel (2%) gasoline (5%) and fuel oil (21%) and higher crude oil export volumes (12%) partially offset by a decrease in oil product export volumes (15%).Foreign currency translation effects reduced the increase of sales revenues in US dollars. Excluding those effects sales revenues increased by 11% when expressed in reals.PETROBRAS posted a net loss of 166% in 2014 primarily due to an increase in impairment of assets resulting from individualized impairment testing of a second refining unit of Refinaria Abreu e Limaand Complexo Petroquímico do Rio de Janeiro and lower international crude oil prices and lower valuataion of petrochemical assets.In 2014 the company's cash inflow increased by 1% due to changes in working capital as a result of a decrease in inventories and increase in other liabilities.

Strategy

The company's 2014-2018 Business and Management Plan foresees investments in the order of $220.6 billion. Exploration & Production will get $153.9 billion mainly to develop the pre-salt and the post-salt production. Downstream will see investments of $38.7 billion to enhance refining capacity and achieve operational improvements.As per the 2030 Strategic Plan PETROBRAS is aiming to produce an average of 4 million barrels of oil equivalent per day between 2020 and 2030 and keep growing in biofuels ethanol and biodiesel to support the Brazilian diesel and gasoline markets.

To raise cash in 2015 PETROBRAS sold a 49% stake in its natural gas distribution subsidiary Gaspetro to Mitsui for $490.2 million.

HISTORY

"O petróleo nosso!"

"The oil is ours!" proclaimed the Brazilian nationalists' slogan in 1953 and President Getúlio Vargas approved a bill creating a state-run monopoly on petroleum discovery development refining and transport. The same year that PETRÓLEO BRASILEIRO (PETROBRAS) was created a team led by American geologist Walter Link reported that the prospects of finding petroleum in Brazil were slim. The report outraged Brazilian nationalists who saw it as a ploy for foreign exploitation. PETROBRAS proved it could find oil but Brazil continued to import crude oil and petroleum products. By 1973 the company produced about 10% of the nation's needs.

When oil prices soared during the Arab embargo the government instead of encouraging exploration for domestic oil pushed PETROBRAS into a program to promote alcohol fuels. The company was forced to raise gasoline prices to make the more costly gasohol attractive to consumers. During the 1979 oil crunch the price of gasohol was fixed at 65% of gasoline. But during the oil glut of the mid-1980s PETROBRAS' cost of making gasohol was twice what it cost to buy gasoline —in other words PETROBRAS lost money.

PETROBRAS soon began overseas exploration. In 1980 it found an oil field in Iraq an important trading partner during the 1980s. The company also drilled in Angola and through a 1987 agreement with Texaco in the Gulf of Mexico.

In the mid-1980s PETROBRAS began production in the deepwater Campos basin off the coast of Rio de Janeiro state. Discoveries there in 1988 in the Marlim and Albacora fields more than tripled its oil reserves. It plunged deep into the thick Amazon jungle in 1986 to explore for oil and by 1990 Amazon wells were making a significant contribution to total production. That year to ease dependence on imports PETROBRAS launched a five-year $16.9 billion plan to boost crude oil production. It also began selling its mining and trading assets.

Before the invasion of Kuwait Brazil relied heavily on Iraq trading weapons for oil. After the invasion spawned increases in crude prices PETROBRAS raised pump prices but yielding to the government's anti-inflation program still did not raise them enough to cover costs. It lost $13 million a day.

The company sold 26% of Petrobras Distribuidora to the public in 1993 and privatized several of its petrochemical and fertilizer subsidiaries. A 1994 presidential order bent on stabilizing Brazil's 40%-per-month inflation cut the prices of oil products. In 1995 the government loosened its grip on the oil and gas industry and allowed foreign companies to enter the Brazilian market. In the wake of this reform PETROBRAS teamed up with a Japanese consortium to build Brazil's largest oil refinery.

In 1997 PETROBRAS appealed a $4 billion judgment from a 1992 shareholder lawsuit; the suit alleged PETROBRAS had undervalued shares during the privatization of the loss-making Petroquisa affiliate. (The appeal was granted in 1999.)

As part of an effort to boost oil production PETROBRAS also began to raise money abroad in 1999. The next year PETROBRAS and Spanish oil giant Repsol YPF agreed to swap oil and gas assets in Argentina and Brazil in a deal worth more than $1 billion.

In 2000 the company announced plans to change its corporate name to PETROBRAX but fierce political and popular reaction forced the company to abort this plan in 2001. In an even greater public relations disaster that year one of PETROBRAS' giant rigs sank off of Brazil and 10 workers were killed. In 2001 PETROBRAS announced that it was going to spend as much as $3 billion to buy an oil company in order to increase its production in the Gulf of Mexico.

In 2002 the company expressed an interest in buying Argentina's major oil company (YPF) from Spanish/Argentine energy giant Repsol YPF. That year PETROBRAS bought control (59%) of Argentine energy company Perez Companc in a deal valued at $1 billion. PETROBRAS also reported its first oil find in Argentina in 2002.

In 2006 the company acquired a 50% stake in a deepwater block in Equatorial Guinea from a private group of companies for an undisclosed sum.

The company also restructured the Brazilian petrochemical industry to make it more efficient. Its actions included the purchase of the petrochemical assets of the Ipiranga Group in 2007 and Suzano Petroquímica a leader in Latin American polypropylene resin production in 2008.

In 2007 PETROBRAS announced a major offshore oil discovery in the Tupi. In 2008 it reported it had discovered a major natural gas field near the Tupi find.

In 2011 it was operating more than 130 production platforms. PETROBRAS has made a number of major offshore oil discoveries in offshore Brazil since 2000 including the Tupi field (found in 2007) and which has the potential to boost Brazil's oil reserves by 40%. In 2010 PETROBRAS announced another major discovery a 3.7 to 15 billion-barrels-of-oil-reserves find (offshore of Rio de Janeiro) that could double Brazil's known reserves.

Streamlining its Petrobras Argentina operations in 2011 the company acquired that unit's Brazilian petrochemicals business (Innova SA) for $332 million.

In 2012 it teamed up with GE Oil & Gas in a $1.1 billion deal through which the GE unit will supply 380 subsea wellhead systems to a number of PETROBRAS' oil and gas fields in offshore Brazil.

Brazil's government owns more than 55% of PETROBRAS.

EXECUTIVES

CFO and Investor Relations Director, Ivan de Souza Monteiro, age 55
Exploration and Production Officer; Member of the Executive Board, Guilherme Estrella
President, Aldemir Bendine
CEO Transpetro, Ant´nio Rubens Silva Silvino
Chairman, Luiz Nelson Guedes de Carvalho
Auditors: PricewaterhouseCoopers Auditores Independentesâ‑PwC

LOCATIONS

HQ: Petroleo Brasileiro S.A.
Avenida Republica do Chile, 65, Rio de Janeiro 20031-912
Phone: (55) 21 3224 4477
Web: www.petrobras.com.br

2010 Sales

	% of total
Brazil	74
Other countries	28
Total	**100**

PRODUCTS/OPERATIONS

2010 Sales

	% of total
Refining transportation & marketing	46
Exploration & production	26
Distribution	18
International	6
Gas & power	4
Total	**100**

Selected Subsidiaries

Downstream Participações S.A. (asset exchanges between Petrobras and Repsol-YPF)
Petrobras Argentina (59%; oil and gas Argentina)
Petrobras Comercializadora de Energia Ltda
Petrobras Distribuidora SA (BR; distribution and marketing of petroleum products fuel alcohol and natural gas)
Petrobras Gás SA (Gaspetro management of the Brazil-Bolivia pipeline and other natural gas assets)
Petrobras Internacional SA (Braspetro; overseas exploration and production marketing and services)
Petrobras International Finance Company - PIFCO (oil imports)
Petrobras Negócios Eletrônicos S.A.
Petrobras Química SA (Petroquisa petrochemicals)
Petrobras Transporte SA (Transpetro oil and gas transportation and storage)

COMPETITORS

Ashland Inc.
BHP Billiton
BP
Chevron
Devon Energy
Eni
Exxon Mobil
Imperial Oil
Koch Industries Inc.
Marathon Oil
Norsk Hydro ASA
Occidental Petroleum
PEMEX
Petrleos de Venezuela
Royal Dutch Shell
Sunoco
TOTAL

HISTORICAL FINANCIALS

Company Type: Public

Income Statement FYE: December 31

	REVENUE ($ mil.)	NET INCOME ($ mil.)	NET PROFIT MARGIN	EMPLOYEES
12/14	143,657	(7,367)	—	80,908
12/13	141,462	11,094	7.8%	86,111
12/12	144,103	11,034	7.7%	85,065
12/11	145,915	20,121	13.8%	81,918
12/10	120,052	19,184	16.0%	80,492
Annual Growth	4.6%	—	—	0.1%

2014 Year-End Financials

Debt ratio: 44.2%
Return on equity: (-5.5%)
Cash ($ mil.): 16,655
Current ratio: 1.63
Long-term debt ($ mil.): 120,274
No. of shares (mil.): —
Dividends
Yield: 8.4%
Payout: —
Market value ($ mil.): —

	STOCK PRICE ($) FY Close	P/E High/Low	PER SHARE ($) Earnings	Dividends	Book Value
12/14	7.30	— —	(0.56)	0.61	8.91
12/13	13.78	24 14	0.85	0.21	11.39
12/12	19.47	38 21	0.85	0.86	12.87
12/11	24.85	27 14	1.54	0.93	13.48
12/10	37.84	25 16	1.94	0.99	24.39
Annual Growth	(33.7%)	— —	—(11.3%)		
(22.2%)					

Peugeot S.A.

Peugeot S.A. enjoys its space under L'Arc de Triomphe besting rival Renault to claim the top spot in the battle for auto sales in France. Peugeot makes cars and light commercial vehicles under the Peugeot and Citro «n brands. Peugeot is among the top manufacturers in European passenger car and commercial vehicle sales. Also part of Peugeot's automotive operations are Faurecia (auto parts) GEFCO (transportation and logistics) and Banque PSA Finance (financial services for dealers and customers). Other group products include motorcycles and scooters. Peugeot makes most of its sales in Europe. The Peugeot family controls about 38% of the voting stock.

The Peugeot brand rolled out more than 2.1 million vehicles in 2011. Sales outside Europe accounted for 48% of the total. Peugeot models include the Peugeot 508 RXH the Peugeot 3008 crossover and the RCZ coupe. Citro «n sold more than 1.4 million cars in 2011. Citro «n models include the DS4 DS5 C3 Picasso C4 and C-Crosser. Both brands boast electric cars the Peugeot iOn and the Citro «n C-ZERO as well as electric commercial vehicles the Peugeot Partner Origin and Citro «n Berlingo First. The company has sold about 4000 electric vehicles and has orders for more than 6000.

Financing vehicle sales as well as vehicle and replacement part inventories at dealers Banque PSA Finance operates in more than 20 countries. It annually provides financing for more than 840000 vehicles. Deriving about 38% of its sales from non-Peugeot clients Gefco provides upstream and downstream logistics services in about 150 countries. Peugeot plans to sell all or part of Gefco in 2012. Faurecia 57% owned by Peugeot focuses its automotive equipment operations on automotive seating emissions control technologies interior systems and automotive exteriors. Faurecia operates at about 240 locations and about 40 research and development centers in more than 30 countries.

Peugeot's consolidated sales and revenue rose about 7% in 2011 compared with 2010. By segment the automotive division's consolidated revenue increased 3% over the same period. New vehicle sales similarly went up about 3%. By region the division responded to strong demand in Latin America China and Russia. Also the percentage of premium cars sold rose from 13% in 2010 to 18% in 2011.

Faurecia soared 17% in 2011 versus 2010. Sales of the division's catalytic converter monoliths rose about 24% while sales of R&D tooling and prototypes headed up 19%. The division also enjoyed strong sales in all regions. European sales were up 11 while North America jumped about 33% Asia headed up 15% South America surged about 15% and the rest of the world increased about 31%.

Gefco jumped about 13% in 2011 versus 2010 supported by the acquisition of 70% of the Italy-based Mercurio group which transports vehicles worldwide in May 2011. The Mercurio acquisition boosted the segment's business in downstream logistics. Services for external customers rose 19%.

Banque PSA Finance inched up about 3%. The segment financed about 28% of all new Peugeot and Citro «n cars in 2011. It enjoyed especially strong demand in Argentina Brazil and Russia.

While Peugeot is anticipating a contraction of auto sales in the European auto market it expects to see strong growth in China Latin America and Russia. In China where the company has a market share of more than 3% the Peugeot brand boasts more than 500 sales outlets while Citro «n has about 860. To boost Latin American sales the company has launched two locally produced models the Peugeot 408 and Citro «n C3 Picasso. In Russia the two brands operate more than 140 sales outlets that cover 90% of the country.

In 2012 Peugeot and General Motors announced that they would form an alliance to share vehicle platforms components and modules and to establish a global purchasing joint venture. The companies hope the partnership will create annual savings of $2 billion within five years. As part of the deal GM will pay $400 million to $470 million (depending on market conditions) for a 7% stake in Peugeot. The company's engine partnership with BMW gave birth to a 50/50 joint venture in 2011 to produce powertrain components such as battery packs power electronics and software for hybrid vehicles. The main components used in BMW's and Peugeot's hybrid vehicles will be standardized thus saving manufacturing and development costs for both car companies.

HISTORY

In 1810 brothers Fr © ©c and Jean-Pierre Peugeot made a foundry out of the family textile mill in the Alsace region of France and invented the cold-roll process for producing spring steel. Bicycle production began in 1885 at the behest of avid cyclist Armand Peugeot Jean-Pierre's grandson.

Armand turned to automobiles and built Peugeot's first car a steam-powered three-wheeler in 1889. A gas-fueled Peugeot tied for first place in the 1894 Paris-Rouen Trials the earliest auto race on record. That year the budding carmaker built the first station wagon followed in 1905 by the first compact the 600-pound 'Le B © ©

Peugeot built factories in France including one in Sochaux (1912) that remains the company's main plant. It made the first diesel passenger car in 1922. The 1929 introduction of the reliable 201 model was followed by innovations such as synchromesh gears in 1936. The company suffered heavy damage in WWII but quickly bounced back and began expanding overseas after the war.

In 1954 CEO Roland Peugeot rebuffed a board proposal calling for global expansion that would place the company in competition with US automakers. By 1976 the French government persuaded Peugeot to merge with Citro «n.

Andr ©Citro «n founded his company in 1915 and in 1919 it became the first in Europe to mass-produce cars. Citro «n hit the skids during the Depression and in 1934 handed Michelin a large block of stock in lieu of payment for tires. Citro «n never fully recovered though by 1976 the company's line ranged from the 2CV minicar (discontinued in 1990) to limousines.

In 1978 Peugeot bought Chrysler's aging European plants and withering nameplates including Simca (France) and Rootes (UK). Peugeot changed the nameplates to Talbot but sales continued to slide. It lost nearly $1.2 billion from 1980 to 1984.

Jacques Calvet took over as CEO in 1984. He cut 30000 jobs and spent heavily on modernization. Aided by the strong launch of the 205 superminicar Peugeot returned to profitability in 1985 and by 1989 had halved its production break-even point. In the 1980s Peugeot inked production deals with Renault (industrial vehicles motors gearboxes) and Fiat (light trucks) and introduced a reasonably priced electric van in 1990.

Peugeot withdrew from the US in 1991 after five years of declining sales. A year later Renault and Peugeot developed electric cars and set up servicing centers throughout France. Citing an economic slump in 1993 Peugeot suffered its first loss ($239 million) since 1985. A French government incentive to replace cars more than 10 years old boosted 1994 sales.

Peugeot and rival Renault together introduced a V6 engine in 1996. Jean Martin Folz replaced Calvet as managing board chairman in 1997; Folz headed up Peugeot for 10 years and was replaced by Christian Streiff in 2007. In 1998 the company began building Peugeots and Citro «ns in the same plants and created its Faurecia unit when its ECIA subsidiary merged with car parts maker Bertrand Faure. In an effort to capitalize on the growing South American car market the company purchased more than 80% of Argentina's Sevel and built a plant in Brazil. In 1999 the company sold its flight systems supplier SAMM to TRW's Lucas Aerospace unit.

With demand for its cars falling steeply in South America due to the region's continuing economic crisis Peugeot restructured its Brazil operations in 2000 and formed a new subsidiary Citro «n do Brasil.

In 2001 Peugeot announced that it was building an engine plant in Brazil and agreed to produce a subcompact car for the European market with Toyota.The following year Peugeot formed an alliance with BMW to develop and build a line of small diesel engines for use in vehicles made by both companies.

In 2005 Peugeot achieved a major milestone when for the first time it sold more than 1 million units outside its traditional market of Western Europe or 30% of total sales. Large gains were made in South America and even more so in China. In 2006 the company repeated the feat. With Western Europe a mature market Peugeot was looking to three key emerging markets to drive future growth: China the Mercosur region (Argentina Brazil Paraguay and Uruguay) and Central and Eastern Europe.

EXECUTIVES

EVP Operational Director Asia and South-East Asia, Gr ©oire Olivier

EVP Director Supply Chain and Manufacturing, Yann Vincent, age 58
Chairman Managing Board, Carlos Tavares, age 56
EVP Operational Director India-Pacific, Emmanuel Delay
EVP Operational Director Middle-East & Africa, Jean-Christophe Qu @ard
EVP Operational Director Europe, Denis Martin
EVP Operational Director Eurasia, Christophe Bergerand, age 51
EVP Finance, Jean-Baptiste de Chatillon
CEO DS Brand, Yves Bonnefont
CEO Peugeot Brand, Maxime Picat
CEO Citro «n Brand, Linda Jackson
EVP Research and Development, Gilles Le Borgne
EVP Purchasing, Yannick Bezard
EVP Human Resources, Philippe Dorge
EVP Operational Director Latin America, Carlos Gomes
EVP Programs and Strategy, Patrice Lucas
Chairman of Board, Louis Gallois, age 67
Auditors: ERNST & YOUNG et Autres

LOCATIONS

HQ: Peugeot S.A.
75, avenue de la Grande-Armee, Paris 75116
Phone: (33) 1 40 66 55 11 **Fax:** (33) 1 40 66 54 14
Web: www.psa-peugeot-citroen.com

2011 Sales

	% of total
Europe	73
Latin America	9
Asia	5
Russia	3
Rest of the world	10
Total	**100**

PRODUCTS/OPERATIONS

2011 Sales

	% of sales
Automotive division	66
Faurecia	25
Gefco	6
Banque PSA Finance	3
Total	**100**

2011 Sales

	Units
% of total	
Peugeot brand	60
Citroën brand	40
Total	**100**

Selected Subsidiaries

Citroën
Peugeot
Banque PSA Finance
Faurecia (57% automotive components)
GEFCO (transportation and logistics services)

COMPETITORS

BMW	Kia Motors
CRCAM IDF CCI	Mazda
Daimler	Nissan
FCA US	Piaggio & Co.
Fiat Chrysler	Renault
Ford Motor	Suzuki Motor
General Motors	Toyota
Honda	Volkswagen
Isuzu	Yamaha Motor

HISTORICAL FINANCIALS

Company Type: Public

Income Statement FYE: December 31

	REVENUE ($ mil.)	NET INCOME ($ mil.)	NET PROFIT MARGIN	EMPLOYEES
12/14	65,159	(858)	—	189,786
12/13	74,467	(3,189)	—	196,885
12/12	73,080	(6,603)	—	204,287
12/11	77,493	760	1.0%	0
12/10	75,030	1,517	2.0%	198,200
Annual Growth	(3.5%)	—	—	(1.1%)

2014 Year-End Financials

Debt ratio: 26.3%
Return on equity: (-8.7%)
Cash ($ mil.): 12,105
Current ratio: 0.71
Long-term debt ($ mil.): 7,855
No. of shares (mil.): 770
Dividends
Yield: 0.2%
Payout: —
Market value ($ mil.): 9,382

	STOCK PRICE ($) FY Close	P/E High/Low	PER SHARE ($) Earnings	Dividends	Book Value
12/14	12.18	— —	(1.40)	3.29	14.63
Annual Growth	—	— —	—	—	—

PFA Pension Forsikringsaktieselskab (Denmark)

Pension health and welfare funds nsk

EXECUTIVES

Chairman, Jens Peter Due Olsen
Auditors: Deloitte Statsautoriseret Revisionspartnerselskab

LOCATIONS

HQ: PFA Pension Forsikringsaktieselskab (Denmark)
Sundkrogsgade 4, Copenhagen DK-2100
Phone: (45) 39 17 50 00 **Fax:** (45) 39 17 59 50
Web: www.pfa.dk

HISTORICAL FINANCIALS

Company Type: Public

Income Statement FYE: December 31

	ASSETS ($ mil.)	NET INCOME ($ mil.)	INCOME AS % OF ASSETS	EMPLOYEES
12/14	90,177	95	0.1%	1,277
12/13	77,051	39	0.1%	1,235
12/12	65,365	67	0.1%	0
12/02	23,678	148	0.6%	1,007
12/01	18,279	(437)	—	847
Annual Growth	13.1%	—	—	3.2%

PICC Property and Casualty Co Ltd

PICC Property and Casualty (PICC P&C) is the leading property/casualty (P&C) insurer in bustling China. Founded in 1949 as the state-owned People's Insurance Company of China (now known as PICC Group) PICC P&C was spun off in 2003. It operates throughout most of China with more than 10000 branch offices providing primarily auto insurance (more than 70% of sales). Additional types of coverage include commercial property liability accident and homeowners insurance. PICC Group holds 70% of the company while US firm AIG holds 10% of its shares.

Founded just 20 days after ceremonies marking the founding of China PICC P&C survived a 20-year suspension of insurance activities within China. It eventually came to control 70% of the P&C market in spite of increasing competition both from China-based insurers and from foreign companies entering the burgeoning marketplace.

The company has sisters: PICC Life Insurance Company and PICC Health Insurance Company which offer complementary coverage.

EXECUTIVES

Chairman, Wu Yan
Vice Chairman, Guo Shengchen
EVP, Wang He
Auditors: Deloitte Touche Tohmatsu Certified Public Accountant LLP

LOCATIONS

HQ: PICC Property and Casualty Co Ltd
Tower 2, No. 2 Jianguomenwai Avenue, Chaoyang District, Beijing 100022
Phone: (86) 10 85176084 **Fax:** (86) 10 85176084
Web: www.piccnet.com.cn

COMPETITORS

Allianz Guangzhou	China Pacific Property Insurance
CNinsure	Ping An Insurance
China Life Insurance	

HISTORICAL FINANCIALS

Company Type: Public

Income Statement FYE: December 31

	ASSETS ($ mil.)	NET INCOME ($ mil.)	INCOME AS % OF ASSETS	EMPLOYEES
12/14	58,992	2,435	4.1%	161,310
12/13	52,763	1,744	3.3%	160,190
12/12	46,585	1,669	3.6%	156,364
12/11	42,203	1,275	3.0%	140,942
12/10	30,612	790	2.6%	60,629
Annual Growth	17.8%	32.5%	—	27.7%

2014 Year-End Financials

Return on assets: 4.4%
Return on equity: 21.1%
Long-term debt ($ mil.): —
No. of shares (mil.): —
Sales ($ mil): 36,272
Dividends
Yield: 0.0%
Payout: —
Market value ($ mil.): —

	STOCK PRICE ($) FY Close	P/E High	P/E Low	PER SHARE ($) Earnings	Dividends	Book Value
12/14	51.00	1	1	0.17	0.06	0.93
12/13	36.80	1	1	0.13	0.05	0.70
12/12	32.21	1	1	0.14	0.02	0.59
12/11	25.30	2	1	0.11	0.04	0.46
Annual Growth	26.3%	—	—	12.0%	13.7%	19.6%

Ping An Bank Co Ltd

Auditors: Ernst & Young Hua Ming

LOCATIONS

HQ: Ping An Bank Co Ltd
Shenzhen Devolopment Bank Building, No. 5047, Shennan East Road, Shenzhen, Guangdong Province 518001
Phone: (86) 755 82080387 **Fax:** (86) 755 82080386
Web: www.bank.pingan.com

HISTORICAL FINANCIALS

Company Type: Public

Income Statement FYE: December 31

	ASSETS ($ mil.)	NET INCOME ($ mil.)	INCOME AS % OF ASSETS	EMPLOYEES
12/14	352,292	3,190	0.9%	0
12/13	312,483	2,515	0.8%	0
12/12	257,695	2,149	0.8%	0
12/11	199,888	1,632	0.8%	0
12/10	110,384	953	0.9%	0
Annual Growth	33.7%	35.3%	—	—

2014 Year-End Financials

Return on assets: 0.9%
Return on equity: 16.3%
Long-term debt ($ mil.): —
No. of shares (mil.): —
Sales ($ mil): 11,834
Dividends
Yield: —
Payout: —
Market value ($ mil.): —

Ping An Insurance (Group) Co of China Ltd.

Ping An Insurance is China's second-largest life insurance company (after China Life Insurance Company) and offers a variety of products including fire marine cargo and accident insurance as well as a home protection plan. The company also provides stock trading equity investment funds and bonds property leasing and asset management services through Ping An Trust; and its Shenzhen Ping An Bank subsidiary offers retail banking and other consumer services such as credit card and mortgage lending. In addition Ping An Insurance founded in 1988 has launched Ping An Health Insurance Company of China.

While insurance is still the company's main staple it is hoping to secure a prime spot in China's developing asset management industry.

London-based HSBC Holdings which has had operations in China for more than 140 years doubled its stake in Ping An to about 20% in 2006 through a $1 billion deal with shareholders Goldman Sachs Group and a unit of the private equity business of Morgan Stanley.

In 2008 Ping An agreed to acquire half of the asset management business of Fortis in an attempt to diversify its operations and make them more global in scope. However the deal valued at nearly $3.4 billion was terminated when Fortis foundered in late 2008.

Meanwhile the company's insurance arm set to investigating and paying claims from the 2008 earthquake and aftershocks in the Sichuan province. By 2009 the company had already paid out its largest claim ever: $105 million to Lafarge Shui Cement the worlds' largest cement manufacturer for damages to several cement plants it operated in that area.

EXECUTIVES

Chairman and CEO, Ma Mingzhe
EVP, Sun A
Chief Investment Officer, Chen Dexian
Chief Actuary, Yao Bo
Auditors: PricewaterhouseCoopers Zhong Tian LLP

LOCATIONS

HQ: Ping An Insurance (Group) Co of China Ltd.
Offices at 15, 16, 17, 18 Floors, Galaxy Development Center, Fu Hua No. 3 Road, Futian District, Shenzhen, Guangdong Province 518048
Phone: (86) 400 8866 338 **Fax:** (86) 755 8243 1029
Web: www.pingan.com

PRODUCTS/OPERATIONS

2007 Revenues

	% of total
Life insurance	56
Property/casualty insurance	11
Banking	8
Securities	8
Other businesses	17
Total	**100**

Selected Subsidiaries & Affiliates

China Ping An Insurance Overseas (Holdings) Limited
China Ping An Insurance (Hong Kong) Company Limited (75%)
Ping An of China Asset Management (Hong Kong) Company Limited
China Ping An Trust & Investment Co. Ltd.
Ping An Securities Co. Ltd.
Ping An Annuity Insurance Company of China Ltd.
Ping An Health Insurance Company of China Ltd.
Ping An Life Insurance Company of China Ltd.
Ping An Property & Casualty Insurance Company of China Ltd.
Shenzhen Ping An Bank Co. Ltd.

COMPETITORS

CNinsure
China Insurance
China Life Insurance
China Pacific Insurance
China Pacific Property Insurance
PICC Property

HISTORICAL FINANCIALS

Company Type: Public

Income Statement FYE: December 31

	ASSETS ($ mil.)	NET INCOME ($ mil.)	INCOME AS % OF ASSETS	EMPLOYEES
12/14	645,451	6,328	1.0%	235,999
12/13	555,066	4,650	0.8%	203,366
12/12	456,232	3,216	0.7%	190,284
12/11	363,088	3,094	0.9%	175,136
12/10	177,745	2,626	1.5%	128,808
Annual Growth	38.0%	24.6%	—	16.3%

2014 Year-End Financials

Return on assets: 1.0%
Return on equity: 16.6%
Long-term debt ($ mil.): —
No. of shares (mil.): —
Sales ($ mil): 81,267
Dividends
Yield: 0.8%
Payout: 23.8%
Market value ($ mil.): —

	STOCK PRICE ($) FY Close	P/E High	P/E Low	PER SHARE ($) Earnings	Dividends	Book Value
12/14	20.39	8	6	0.38	0.09	2.62
12/13	18.03	11	7	0.29	0.06	1.91
12/12	17.19	14	10	0.20	0.05	1.62
12/11	13.11	19	8	0.20	0.07	1.31
12/10	22.45	21	14	0.17	0.05	1.11
Annual Growth	(2.4%)	—	—	21.2%	14.1%	23.9%

Piraeus Bank SA

Greece is the word and Piraeus has most certainly heard. Piraeus Bank provides retail banking investment banking leasing and insurance services in the Mediterranean and in Central and Eastern Europe. Its network of branches across Greece numbers more than 1000 plus it has about 400 more in Albania (Tirana Bank) Romania Bulgaria Serbia the Ukraine and the US (New York's Marathon Bank). Piraeus Bank also provides its services through its electronic Winbank business which includes about 1900 ATMs Internet and phone banking. The company maintains a diverse loan portfolio with energy and transportation loans making up 30% of its portfolio. Piraeus Bank was founded in 1916 and under state control until 1991.Since Piraeus Bank was privatized it has grown rapidly through acquisitions of other banks in Greece. The company also has expanded internationally into Central and Eastern Europe and elsewhere in the Mediterranean. It acquired Bulgarian Eurobank (now Piraeus Bank Bulgaria) Atlas Bank (renamed Piraeus Bank Beograd) Egyptian Commercia Bank (Piraeus Bank Egypt) Share Capital of International Commerce Bank in the Ukraine and the Cyprus branch network of Arab Bank (Piraeus Bank Cyprus).In 2009 Piraeus Bank teamed with BNP Wealth Management to begin offering wealth management services. In another partnership that year the company signed an agreement with Victoria General Insurance Group in order to offer insurance. Piraeus Bank continues to seek investments for further growth.

EXECUTIVES

Chief Executive Officer, Anthimos Konstantinos Thomopoulos
Chairman, Michail George Sallas
Vice Chairman, Apostolos Stavros Tamvakakis
Vice Chairman, Nikolaos Michail Christodoulakis

Vice Chairman, Stavros Michail Lekkakos
Auditors: PricewaterhouseCoopers S.A.

LOCATIONS

HQ: Piraeus Bank SA
4 Amerikis str., Athens 105 64
Phone: (30) 210 333 5000 **Fax:** (30) 210 333 5080
Web: www.piraeusbankgroup.com

Branch Locations

	No.
Greece	1,037
Romanis	140
Bulgaria	83
Albania	53
Serbia	42
Egypt	41
Ukraine	37
Cyprus	14
London	1
Frankfurt	1
Total	**1,449**

PRODUCTS/OPERATIONS

Selected Subsidiaries

ATEbank
ETBA Industrial Areas S.A.
Marathon B
OJSC Pirae
Picar S.A.
Piraeus Asset Management Mutual Funds S.A.
Piraeus Ba
Piraeus Bank Bulgaria AD
Piraeus Ba
Piraeus Bank Egypt SAE
Piraeus Capital Management
Piraeus Card Services
Piraeus Direct Services S.A.
Piraeus Insurance and Reinsurance Brokerage S.A.
Piraeus Insurance Agency S.A.
Piraeus Factoring S.A.
Piraeus Leaases SA
Piraeus Leasing Bulgaria
Piraeus Bank Romania S.A.
Piraeus Leasing Romania
Piraeus Private Equity
Piraeus Real Estate S.A.
Piraeus Securities S.A.
Piraeus Wealth Management
Tirana Ban
Tirana Lea

COMPETITORS

Alpha Bank
Bank of Cyprus
EFG Eurobank Ergasias
Emporiki Bank
National Bank of Greece

HISTORICAL FINANCIALS

Company Type: Public

Income Statement

FYE: December 31

	ASSETS ($ mil.)	NET INCOME ($ mil.)	INCOME AS % OF ASSETS	EMPLOYEES
12/14	108,532	(2,396)	—	22,372
12/13	126,672	3,505	2.8%	22,718
12/12	92,798	(671)	—	18,872
12/11	63,834	(8,554)	—	12,806
12/10	77,038	(27)	—	13,320
Annual Growth	8.9%	—	—	13.8%

2014 Year-End Financials

Return on assets: (-2.1%)
Return on equity: (-25.2%)
Long-term debt ($ mil.): —
No. of shares (mil.): —
Sales ($ mil): 4,918
Dividends
Yield: —
Payout: —
Market value ($ mil.): —

	STOCK PRICE ($) FY Close	P/E High/Low		PER SHARE ($) Earnings	Dividends	Book Value
12/14	2.18	—	—	(0.41)	0.00	1.44
12/13	4.11	5	1	1.28	0.00	1.81
12/12	6.45	—	—	(0.58)	0.00	(1.30)
12/11	6.45	—	—	(7.91)	0.00	(1.08)
12/10	6.45	—	—	(0.04)	0.00	10.20
Annual Growth	(23.8%)	—	—	—	—	(38.7%)

PJSC Gazprom

With prominent gas assets Gazprom Russia's largest company has proved and probable oil and gas reserves of 29.2 billion tons of coal equivalent and produces about 513 billion cu. meters of natural gas a year. With 18% of the world's gas reserves it is also the world's #1 gas producer. Majority-owned by the Russiangovernment Gazprom is engaged in oil and gas exploration processing transport and marketing. It operates Russia's domestic gas pipeline network and delivers gas across Central Asia and Europe. It also holds stakes in Russian financial institutions a polypropylene plant and a telecom network and produces 17% of Russia's electricity. Gazprom accounts for about 25% of Russia's tax revenues.

Geographic Reach

Gazprom exports gas to more than 30 countries within and beyond the borders of the former Soviet Union. The company has offices in Algiers Astana Ashkhabad Bishkek Dokha Ekaterinburg Kiev Kishinev Krasnodar Minsk Moscow Novy Urengoy Peking Riga Rio de Janeiro Samara St. Petersburg Tehran Tomsk Khabarovsk and Yuzhno-Sakhalinsk.

Operations

Gazprom operates one of the largest gas pipeline systems in the world and is responsible for the major part of gas production and high pressure gas transportation in the Russian Federation and is a major supplier of gas to European countries. It is engaged in oil production refining activities electric and heat energy generation. Its reportable segments are: Production of gas; Transport; Distribution; Gas storage; Production of crude oil and gas condensate; Refining; and Electric and heat energy generation and sales.

The company owns the world's largest gas transmission network – the Unified Gas Supply System of Russia with the total length of over 168 thousand kilometers.

In addition to natural gas Gazprom holds a 5% global share of the production of liquefied natural gas (LNG). It also holds 79% of oil producer Gazprom Neft. It also holds stakes in Russian financial institutions a polypropylene plant and its own telecom network and produces 17% of Russia's electric power.

Financial Performance

In 2014 Gazprom's net sales increased by 6% (in local currency) due to higher sales from production of gas segment refining and gas storage.Its net income dropped by 1 trillion rubles (87%) compared to 2013. In fiscal 2014 net cash provided by the operating activities increased by 12% (in local currency) primarily due to a change in other current assets settlements on tax payable and accounts payable and accrued charges excluding interest dividends and capital construction.

Strategy

Gazprom's strategic goal is to establish itself as a leader among global energy companies by diversifying sales markets ensuring reliable supplies increasing operating efficiency and exploring its scientific and technical potential.To grow its gas and condensate transmission in Western Siberia the company is expanding and retrofitting the Urengoy Condensate Treatment Plant in order to increase its annual throughput to 12 million tons of de-ethanized condensate; completing treatment and transmission facilities for oil and Achimov condensate; building sections of the Urengoy Surgut condensate pipeline; as well as expanding and retrofitting its Surgut Condensate Stabilization Plant.Gazprom's export strategy is based on the long-term contract system under the take-or-pay principle with the contractual gas price pegged to the petroleum product price as the industry benchmark.

Gas exports to Europe are critical to Gazprom which is burdened by debt because of the insolvency of Russian consumers and hordes of non-paying customers. Gazprom holds strategic partnerships with Western energy companies including Germany's E.ON Ruhrgas. Other partners include Royal Dutch Shell Eni of Italy and Finland's Fortum. In addition Gazprom has a deal with German chemical conglomerate BASF that grants BASF minority shares in both the proposed North Europe Gas Pipeline and the West Siberia field that will feed it. The company is also working on the South Stream Pipeline a massive project aimed at linking Russia's southern gas fields to Western markets via Bulgaria.

Establishing a major new market (China) in 2014 the company tied up a 30-year $400 billion-plus gas supply deal with China National Petroleum.

While natural gas is its core asset the company is also ramping up its other segments as part of a diversification drive to broaden its revenue base and enhance its profile as an integrated energy producer

In the power industry the company is engaged in the diversification of tariff regulation risks optimization of the fuel balance and achieving synergies by combining natural gas and electric power businesses. The major focus is to be placed on construction of cutting-edge combined cycle power plants which will use of natural gas. By 2020 the aggregate capacity of Gazprom's generating facilities will reach 44.8 GW.

Mergers and Acquisitions

In 2014 Gazprom acquired 100% of the South Stream Transport B.V. (the company responsible for the offshore part of the South Stream project) by acquiring EDF International S.A.S. Wintershall Holding GmbH and ENI International B.V. shares in the project for Euro 883 million.In 2013 it bought a 89.98% interest in OAO Moscow Integrated Power Company (OAO MIPC) and heat assets from the Moscow Government. The primary business activity of OAO MIPC is thegeneration purchase and supply heating and hot water to commercial and residential customers in the City of Moscow.

HISTORY

Following the breakup of the Soviet Union in the early 1990s one of the first priorities of the Russian government was to move some state monopolies toward a free-market economic system. A presidential decree in 1992 moved the company toward privatization by calling for the formation of a Russian joint-stock company to explore for and produce gas gas condensates and oil; provide for gas processing; operate gas wells; and build gas pipelines and storage facilities.

By 1993 the government had converted its natural gas monopoly Gazprom into a joint-stock company; the company had dated back to the 1940s and the USSR Ministry of the Gas Industry had kept all of its assets when it became a corporation in 1989.

The new Gazprom was 15%-owned by Gazprom workers and 28% by people living in Russia's gas-producing regions. The state retained about a 40% share (boosted to 51% in 2003). The company inherited all of the former Soviet republics' export contracts to Western and Central Europe.

Thanks to the power of Viktor Chernomyrdin (Gazprom's former Soviet boss and gas industry minister who became Russia's prime minister in 1992) the company was able to enjoy large tax breaks and maintain its role as a monopoly –even as other industries were being more deeply privatized. However the privatization of Gazprom was later attacked as being manipulated to profit the company's top management including Chernomyrdin. Top managers were rumored to have each received 1%-5% of shares –holdings potentially worth $1.2 billion-$10 billion each.

Needing to raise cash in 1996 Gazprom offered 1% of its stock to foreigners the first sale of stock to foreign investors. In 1997 Gazprom and Royal Dutch/Shell formally became partners. That year Gazprom began building its Blue Stream pipeline across the Black Sea to Turkey. Italian group Eni helped back the project and became a partner by 1999.

In 1998 Gazprom acquired a stake in Promostroibank Russia's fourth-largest financial institution. German energy powerhouse Ruhrgas acquired a 3% stake in Gazprom in 1998 which it increased to nearly 4% the next year. Also in 1999 Gazprom started building its Yamal-Europe pipeline which was to stretch to Germany for exports to Europe.

The next year an attempt by Gazprom to muscle into Hungary's chemicals sector by offering cheaper raw materials was blocked by Hungary's TVK and Borsodchem and their allies. Also in 2000 Gazprom became embroiled in a politically controversial issue when it called for the country's leading private media holding group Media-MOST to sell shares to the gas giant in order to settle millions of dollars of debt. Because Media-MOST held NTV television a major critic of Russian President Vladimir Putin the deal was alleged to have been directed by the Kremlin. A government probe into the deal was later ordered. (By 2002 Gazprom owned a significant stake in NTV which it sold that year so it could focus on its core energy businesses.)

The alignment of Gazprom's board changed in 2000 after the annual shareholder's meeting. For the first time in Gazprom's history company managers did not have a majority of seats. A new chairman Dmitri Medvedev second in command to Putin was elected to replace Chernomyrdin. In 2001 the board fired CEO Rem Vyakhirev and replaced him with Deputy Energy Minister Alexei Miller a Putin ally.

Gazprom had announced plans in 2004 to acquire Rosneft (effectively giving the Russian government control of Gazprom) though the deal was complicated by Rosneft's acquisition of the Yugansk assets acquired from YUKOS. In 2005 Gazprom abandoned plans to merge with Rosneft and acquired Sibneft in an effort to add significant oil operations to its business. Millhouse Capital a holding company controlled by Russian oligarch Roman Abramovich sold its majority stake in what was then a major exploration and production company called Sibneft (now Gazprom Neft) to Gazprom for a reported $13 billion. At the time Sibneft was Russia's fifth-largest oil company.

In 2006 Gazprom signed long-term contracts for gas deliveries with Austrian energy giant OMV. That year Royal Dutch/Shell agreed to give control of the $22 billion Sakhalin-2 project (run by Sakhalin Energy Investment) in Russia's Far East to Gazprom.

Former Gazprom chairman Dmitri Medvedev was elected president of Russia in 2008.

The company became embroiled in a pricing dispute with neighbor Ukraine in 2009 resulting in the disruption of gas supplies to Ukraine and because of its transnational pipelines to dozens of other countries in Europe.

Wanting to expand its Russian and international assets and diversify its profile in 2009 Gazprom acquired Italian energy titan ENI's 20% share in oil producer Gazprom Neft raising the Russian giant's direct ownership to 79%. ENI had acquired its stake in 2007 following the bankruptcy of YUKOS. Gazprom had the option to buy ENI's stake within two years and exercised that right in 2009 paying just more than $4 billion to ENI. Gazprom directly owns or indirectly controls through subsidiaries about 95% of Gazprom Neft.

In 2010 the company made its first entry into the US gas market when it began trading and marketing natural gas though Gazprom Marketing & Trading USA. It also signed a strategic partnership with Royal Dutch Shell to develop oil and gas assets in Russian Siberia and the Far East and process and market products in Russia and Europe.

To raise cash to pay down debt in 2010 the company sold its controlling stake in SeverEnergia (a natural gas project partly owned by ENI) to a joint venture owned by Gazprom Neft and OAO Novatek for $1.5 billion. To raise cash it sold 9% of its 19% stake in Novatek to Gazprombank for $2.8 billion.

In 2011 it installed 1.9 GW of combined heat and power generation units and deployed an offshore production platform at the Prirazlomnoye oil field in the Pechora Sea in the Arctic.

Expanding its energy footprint in 2011 Gazprom agreed to acquire power generation KES Holding (which owns four power companies) to create Russia's largest power company. KES Holding will hold 25% of the new joint venture.

To expand its gas supply in 2012 the company announced that it planned to spend 43 billion rubles (US $1.4 billion) that year to develop gas infrastructure projects (gas fields and pipelines) in the Sakhalin region of Eastern Russia. In 2011 Gazprom acquired TNK-BP's east Siberian Kovykta gas field for about $770 million. The purchase opens up the possibility of a major supply agreement with China.

EXECUTIVES

Deputy Chairman and CEO, Alexei B. Miller, age 54
Deputy Chairman Management Committee; Director General OOO Gazprom export, Alexander I. Medvedev, age 60
Member Management Committee; Head Marketing and Processing of Gas and Liquid Hydrocarbons Department; Director General OOO Mezhregiongaz, Kirill Gennadievich Seleznev, age 41
Member Management Committee; Head Legal Department, Nikolay N. Dubik, age 44
Member Management Committee; Director General OOO Gazprom komplektatsiya, Igor Y. Fyodorov, age 50
Head Information Policy Department, Alexander D. Bespalov, age 65
Member Management Committee and Head Department Gas Transportation Underground Storage and Utilization Department, Oleg E. Aksyutin
Member Management Committee; Head Gas Gas Condensate and Oil Production, Vsevolod Cherepanov, age 49
Deputy CFO, Alexander Ivannikov
Member of the Management Committee Department Head Gazprom, Sergey Prozorov, age 57
Head of Department 840, Natalia Borisenko, age 38
Chairman, Victor A. Zubkov, age 74
Auditors: ZAO PricewaterhouseCoopers Audit

LOCATIONS

HQ: PJSC Gazprom
Nametkina St., 16, V-420, GSP-7, Moscow 117997
Phone: (7) 495 719 3001 **Fax:** (7) 495 719 8333
Web: www.gazprom.com

PRODUCTS/OPERATIONS

2014 Sales

	% of total
Distribution	53
Refining	29
Electric and heat energy generation and sales	7
Production of crude oil and gas condensate	4
Transport	3
Gas storage	0
Production of gas	0
All other segments	4
Total	**100**

COMPETITORS

BP
Centrica
E.ON Ruhrgas
Gasunie
LUKOIL
Qatar Petroleum
Rosneft
Sakhalin Energy
Surgutneftegas
Tatneft

HISTORICAL FINANCIALS

Company Type: Public

Income Statement FYE: December 31

	REVENUE ($ mil.)	NET INCOME ($ mil.)	NET PROFIT MARGIN	EMPLOYEES
12/14	94,585	2,701	2.9%	0
12/13	159,918	34,664	21.7%	459,500
12/12	156,607	38,850	24.8%	417,000
12/11	143,741	40,490	28.2%	401,000
12/10	118,085	31,741	26.9%	393,000
Annual Growth	(5.4%)	(46.0%)	—	—

2014 Year-End Financials

Debt ratio: 0.3%
Return on equity: 1.6%
Cash ($ mil.): 17,638
Current ratio: 1.86
Long-term debt ($ mil.): 37,785
No. of shares (mil.): —
Dividends
Yield: 15.1%
Payout: 196.9%
Market value ($ mil.): —

	STOCK PRICE ($) FY Close	P/E High/Low		PER SHARE ($) Earnings	Dividends	Book Value
12/14	4.53	1	1	0.12	0.68	7.26
12/13	8.65	0	0	1.51	0.29	12.34
12/12	9.73	0	0	1.69	0.46	12.00
12/11	10.68	1	0	1.76	0.19	10.06
12/10	25.44	1	0	1.38	0.12	8.91
Annual Growth	(35.0%)	—	—	(46.0%)	53.7%	(5.0%)

PJSC Lukoil

Russians look to LUKOIL for their energy needs. Russia's #1 integrated oil company produces refines and sells oil and oil products; it accounts for 16% of Russia's crude oil production. In 2012 LUKOIL reported proved reserves of 17.3 billion barrels of oil equivalent the majority of which is located in Russia. The company explores for oil and gas in Russia and in about a dozen other countries in Eastern Europe the Middle East Asia and South America. It owns refineries in five countries and marketing and distribution assets in nearly 30 including about 6000 gas stations. In addition LUKOIL has power generation assets in Russia Bulgaria Romania and Ukraine.

Operations

It operates five refineries in Russia one each in Ukraine Bulgaria Romania the Netherlands and Italy; LUKOIL's gas stations are located in Russia the Baltic states Central and Eastern Europe and the US.

LUKOIL Russia's second-largest company behind natural gas monopoly Gazprom is steadily transforming itself from a top-heavy bureaucratic enterprise into a decentralized entrepreneurial company competing in free markets through joint ventures and strategic relationships.

Financial Performance

The company has seen a few years of robust growth in revenues and net income due in part to the expansion of its activities (including increased hydrocarbon production and the growth of its gas station network) but largely because of the recovering global economy's effect on increasing demand and lifting commodity prices.

Ownership

LUKOIL president Vagit Alekperov controls about 20% of the company. ING Bank Eurasia holds about 70% of LUKOIL's shares on behalf of other investors.

HISTORY

LUKOIL was formed from the combination of three major state-owned oil and gas exploration companies –Langepasneftegaz Uraineftegaz and Kogalymneftegaz –that traced their origins to the discovery of oil in western Siberia in 1964. More than 25 years later after the Soviet Union broke up the oil and gas sector was one of the first industries marked for privatization.

In 1992 the government called for Langepasneftegaz Uraineftegaz and Kogalymneftegaz to merge and LUKOIL was created the next year. (The LUK of LUKOIL comes from the initials of the three companies.) Russian president Boris Yeltsin appointed Siberian oil veteran Vagit Alekperov as the company's first president. The Russian government also formed several other large integrated oil companies including Yukos Surgutneftegaz Sidanco and Sibneft.

LUKOIL went public on the fledgling Russian Trading System in 1994. The next year the company absorbed nine other enterprises including oil exploration companies Astrakhanneft Kaliningradmorneftegaz and Permneft. That year LUKOIL became the first Russian oil company to set up an exploration and production trading arm. In 1996 LUKOIL acquired a 41% stake in Izvestia Russia's major independent newspaper.

Chevron and LUKOIL with seven other oil and gas companies and three governments agreed in 1996 to build a 1500-kilometer pipeline to link the Kazakhstan oil fields to world markets.

In 1997 LUKOIL became the first Russian corporation to sell bonds to international investors and the government sold 15% of its stake in the company. That year LUKOIL's 50%-owned Nexus Fuels unit opened its first gas stations located in the parking lots of US grocery stores (the partnership dissolved and Nexus went bankrupt in 2000).

LUKOIL began a partnership with Conoco (later ConocoPhillips) in 1998 to develop oil and natural gas reserves in Russia's northern territories. LUKOIL also acquired 51% of Romania's Petrorel refinery. In 1999 it acquired control of refineries in Bulgaria and Ukraine and in a petrochemical firm in Saratov. It also acquired oil company KomiTEK in one of Russia's largest mergers.

The government sold a 9% stake in LUKOIL to a Cyprus-based unit Reforma Investments held in part by LUKOIL's "boss of bosses" Vagit Alekperov (gained at the bargain price of $200 million). Critics cited the sale as Yeltsin's bid to gain Alekperov's political support.

The company announced the first major oil find in the Russian part of the Caspian Sea in 2000 and formed a joint venture (Caspian Oil Company) with fellow Russian energy giants Gazprom and Yukos to exploit resources in the Caspian. The next year LUKOIL acquired more than 1300 gas stations on the East Coast of the US when it bought Getty Petroleum Marketing.

That year LUKOIL also acquired Bitech a Canadian oil exploration and production firm with operations in the Republic of Komi in the Russian Federation. In 2002 the company sold its oil service business a move that cut its overall workforce by some 20000 and resulted in savings of $500 million annually.

With an appetite for expansion the company upped its production with refinery acquisitions and invested heavily in new oil patches such as the Caspian Sea. In 2005 LUKOIL acquired Finland-based Oy Teboil AB and Suomen Petrooli Oy affiliated refined oil products companies for an undisclosed amount. LUKOIL also acquired Nelson Resources which had oil and gas interests in Western Kazakhstan for about $2 billion.

The next year the company acquired Marathon Oil's assets in Khanty-Mansiysk Autonomous Region –Yugra of Western Siberia –for $787 million. LUKOIL also acquired 376 European gas stations from ConocoPhillips in 2006.

In 2007 LUKOIL signed a strategic exploration and production agreement with Qatar Petroleum.

In 2008 the company diversified its operations further creating a power generation segment which encompasses its own generators at well sites and a number of generating units in Bulgaria Romania and Ukraine.

In 2008 it began to re-engage in Iraq where it had held oil concessions prior to the US-led invasion in 2003. It also acquired a retail network in Turkey in 2008 for $500 million.

EXECUTIVES

First VP Economics and Finance, Sergei P. Kukura, age 62

First EVP Exploration and Production, Ravil U. Maganov, age 61

President and Director, Vagit Y. Alekperov, age 65

SVP Finance, Alexander K. Matytsyn, age 54

VP; CEO of LUKOIL-West Siberia, Vladimir I. Nekrasov, age 58

SVP Oil and Gas Production, Azat Shamsuarov, age 52

Chairman, Valery I. Grayfer, age 86

Auditors: ZAO KPMG

LOCATIONS

HQ: PJSC Lukoil
11 Sretensky Boulevard, Moscow 101000
Phone: (7) 495 627 4444 **Fax:** (7) 495 625 7016
Web: www.lukoil.com

2012 Sales

	$ mil.	% of total
Russia	64,725	36
Other countries	114,001	64
Adjustments	(39555)	-
Total	**139,171**	**100**

PRODUCTS/OPERATIONS

2012 Sales

	$ mil.	% of total
Refined products	103,407	95
Crude oil	27 670	3
Gas & gas products	3,477	2
Petrochemicals	1,410	-
Sales of energy & related services	1,394	-
Other	1,813	-
Total	**139,171**	**100**

COMPETITORS

Ashland Inc.
BP
Exxon Mobil
Gazprom Neft
Imperial Oil
Norsk Hydro ASA
Occidental Petroleum
PEMEX
PETROBRAS
Petrleos de Venezuela
Rosneft
Royal Dutch Shell
Surgutneftegas
TOTAL
Tatneft

HISTORICAL FINANCIALS

Company Type: Public

Income Statement

FYE: December 31

	REVENUE ($ mil.)	NET INCOME ($ mil.)	NET PROFIT MARGIN	EMPLOYEES
12/14	144,167	4,746	3.3%	0
12/13	141,452	7,832	5.5%	0
12/12	139,171	11,004	7.9%	0
12/11	133,650	10,357	7.7%	0
12/10	104,956	9,006	8.6%	0
Annual Growth	8.3%	(14.8%)	—	—

2014 Year-End Financials

Debt ratio: 12.1%
Return on equity: 5.9%
Cash ($ mil.): 3,004
Current ratio: 1.60
Long-term debt ($ mil.): 11,361
No. of shares (mil.): 754
Dividends
Yield: 6.8%
Payout: 42.2%
Market value ($ mil.): 28,949

	STOCK PRICE ($) FY Close	P/E High/Low		PER SHARE ($) Earnings	Dividends	Book Value
12/14	38.35	10	5	6.20	2.62	107.48
12/13	63.12	7	5	10.18	3.66	104.10
12/12	67.50	5	4	14.17	3.05	96.98
12/11	53.20	6	4	13.04	1.71	87.34
12/10	57.22	6	4	10.94	1.39	75.76
Annual Growth	(9.5%)	—	—	(13.2%)	17.2%	9.1%

Polski Koncern Naftowy Orlen S.A.

Crudely moving into the private market PKN ORLEN is the largest refiner and distributor of oil in Poland. The company owns a total of seven refineries (including three in the Czech Republic and one in Lithuania) and has some 2700 retail sites in the Czech Republic Germany Lithuania and Poland. PKN ORLEN owns chemical maker Anwil has holdings in several other Polish companies and controls Czech refiner and retailer UNIPETROL. Two former state monopolies Petrochemia Plock (Poland's largest refinery) and Centrala Produktow Naftowych (Poland's #1 petroleum distributor) merged in 1999 to create PKN ORLEN. The Polish government still owns 27% of the company.

The company also manufactures liquefied propane-butane gas (LPG) for use at industrial plants and for heating public buildings. Other PKN ORLEN products include polyvinyl chloride plastics used in foils containers bottles cable insulation and auto parts; nitric fertilizers; asphalts for construction of roads airports and sports facilities; and basic industrial and engine oils.

Its Eko subsidiary burns hazardous waste while its ORLEN Transport division handles the distribution of fuel to its gas stations. Its Solino holdings (70%) produce salt and brine and use salt caverns for underground storage of petroleum and fuels.

HISTORY

The merger between Petrochemia Plock Poland's largest refiner and petrochemicals maker and CPN (Centrala Produktow Naftowych) the nation's largest motor fuel distributor created Polski Koncern Naftowy (PKN) in 1999.

Poland's oil industry stretches back to the late 1800s when five refineries were built in the nation's southern region. The Polish Oil Monopoly was formed in 1944 to oversee the country's oil distribution operations; it assumed the CPN name a year later.

While the rest of the world increasingly turned to oil as an energy source after WWII Poland continued to rely on coal and its oil industry grew slowly. CPN was split into 17 regional branches in 1955. The branches controlled local operations and the head office in Warsaw handled pricing and purchasing.

In the late 1950s the Soviet Union began building the Friendship pipeline to deliver crude oil to East Germany and Poland. The Polish government responded by forming Petrochemia to develop a refinery next to the pipeline in the city of Plock.

The Petrochemia refinery began producing refined products in 1964; four years later it started processing crude oil to make fuels lubricants and bitumen. The refinery also began making products such as detergents and plastics from processed refinery gases and other hydrocarbons. It added petrochemicals in 1970.

Because of the oil industry's slow growth in Poland the country managed to avoid some of the impact of the 1970s energy crisis. (Even as late as 1995 oil accounted for only 17% of Poland's energy consumption.) But it was forced to pay higher prices for Russian crude. In 1975 the government decided to expand its refining operations and created a second major refiner Rafineria Gdanska to focus on motor oils.

Locked behind the Iron Curtain Poland was not able to build its oil operations until the early 1990s. In 1992 Petrochemia began expanding its refinery facilities to reach a production capacity of 820000 barrels per day within 10 years.

After Communism's demise the Polish government started planning the privatization of its oil operations. After several plans were adopted and discarded in the early 1990s the government finally decided in 1996 to split CPN up among the nation's refineries. Holding company Nafta Polska was formed that year to own 75% stakes in Poland's refineries and in CPN and carry out the privatization process.

In 1997 CPN was stripped of its fuel depots and rail transport operations which were placed under the Nafta Polska umbrella. Displeased with the plan to carve up CPN the distributor's management rallied against the government's plan. The Polish government gave in and went back to the drawing board.

A successful plan was formed in 1998 namely to merge Petrochemia and CPN. The companies were combined in 1999 and 30% of the new PKN was floated on the Warsaw and London stock exchanges. The next year the government spun off an additional 42% stake and the company added ORLEN to its name (combining the Polish words for eagle and energy). Also in 2000 the government began preparing to float Refineria Gdanska. PKN hoped to get a piece of its regional rival but the state left PKN out of the bidding to encourage competition.

PKN acquired some 494 gas stations in Germany from BP who sold them to meet German antitrust regulations for its merger with Veba Oel in late 2002.

In 2004 PKN purchased 63% of UNIPETROL; the European Commission's Competition Directorate granted approval of the purchase in mid-2005.

EXECUTIVES

VP and CFO, Slawomir R. Jedrzejczyk, age 47
Member Management Board Refinery Operations, Krystian Pater, age 52
President and CEO, Dariusz J. Krawiec
Member of Management Board Petrochemical Operations, Piotr Chelminski
Auditors: KPMG Audyt Sp. z o.o.

LOCATIONS

HQ: Polski Koncern Naftowy Orlen S.A.
Chemikow 7, Plock 09-411
Phone: (48) 24 256 81 80 **Fax:** (48) 24 367 77 11
Web: www.orlen.pl

COMPETITORS

BP	OMV
Exxon Mobil	Royal Dutch Shell
LUKOIL	Statoil
MOL	TOTAL

HISTORICAL FINANCIALS

Company Type: Public

Income Statement FYE: December 31

	REVENUE ($ mil.)	NET INCOME ($ mil.)	NET PROFIT MARGIN	EMPLOYEES
12/14	30,339	(1,650)	—	20,305
12/13	37,762	58	0.2%	21,565
12/12	38,822	758	2.0%	21,956
12/11	31,044	685	2.2%	22,380
12/10	28,238	801	2.8%	22,040
Annual Growth	1.8%	—	—	(2.0%)

2014 Year-End Financials

Debt ratio: 6.4%	No. of shares (mil.): 427
Return on equity: (-25.9%)	Dividends
Cash ($ mil.): 1,118	Yield: —
Current ratio: 1.55	Payout: —
Long-term debt ($ mil.): 2,746	Market value ($ mil.): —

POSCO (South Korea)

POSCO has steeled itself for any set of business conditions. The company makes hot- and cold-rolled steel products (plate steel stainless steel electrical steel and wire rods) which it sells to the auto shipbuilding home appliance engineering and machinery industries. It produces more than 39 million tons of steel a year making it the world's #3 steelmaker behind ArcelorMittal and Nippon Steel. Majority-owned POSCO Engineering & Construction builds industrial facilities such as steel plants and energy plants. POSCO Energy is Korea's largest private power generator and subsidiary Daewoo International is a global steel and raw materials trading company. Most of POSCO's sales are to Korean markets.

POSCO's hot- and cold-rolled products segments account for about two-thirds of sales. Hot-rolled products are used in the construction of automobile chassis buildings and bridges industrial pipes and tanks and railway rolling stocks. The company's cold-rolled products such as cold-rolled coils and galvanized cold-rolled products are used in the automotive industry to manufacture car body panels and for other uses like household goods electrical appliances and engineering and metal parts. It produces most of its steel at its integrated steel facilities Pohang Works and Gwangyang Works. POSCO also engages in steel and raw materials trading and invests in energy and mineral development projects around the world though its Daewoo International unit.

South Korea has little native iron ore and POSCO has had to look elsewhere for its raw materials. It purchases iron ore or coal from Australia Brazil Canada South Africa and the US from companies such as Vale Rio Tinto and BHP Billiton. To expand its production operations POSCO has developed joint ventures with companies in China Southeast Asia and Latin America.

In 2011 the company reported an 11% rise in revenues (a more than 40% increase in local revenues) thanks in part to higher selling prices for its steel and wire rod products but primarily because of a 200%-plus growth in trading revenues as the result of the Daewoo acquisition in 2010. However POSCO reported a drop of 13% in net income for the year as major cost increases related to the Daewoo purchase outpaced revenue growth.

To geographically expand its operations POSCO has an alliance with long-time rival Nippon Steel whereby each has taken a small stake in the other; it has also formed a joint venture with Steel Authority of India and plans to establish agreements with other steelmakers in China and Europe.

POSCO is looking to expand into the energy industry market for steel plate (used in the construction oil platforms). In 2012 it secured a steel supply contract from rig maker Samkang M&T for North Sea rigs and has set its sights on getting a 10% global share of the oil and gas industry's steel plate market by 2020.

In 2011 POSCO entered a $6 billion joint venture with Vale's Mozambique operations to mine coal in the southern part of that country. The mine expected to produce 11 million tons of metallurgical coal a year will help POSCO maintain a steady supply of raw materials for its steel mills. At the same time POSCO agreed to set up a similar joint mining venture in neighboring Zimbabwe with Anchor Holdings to develop chrome coal iron ore and other minerals.

That same year POSCO acquired a 20% stake in US-based graphene company XG Sciences in a move to diversify its business. Graphene is a raw material used to manufacture high-tension nanocarbon. POSCO also moved to acquire all of Thailand-based stainless steel producer Thainox Stainless pcl in 2011. POSCCO already owned a 16% stake but had waited for political stability to return to Thailand before acquiring the balance.

HISTORY

After the Korean War South Korea the US and its allies wanted to rebuild South Korea's infrastructure as quickly as possible. Steel was given a high priority and before long about 15 companies were making various steel products. Quality was a problem though as the companies used dated production processes.

With the backing of South Korean president Chung Hee Park momentum for a large steel plant grew in the late 1960s. In 1967 the South Korean government and Korean International Steel Associates (KISA) —a consortium of seven Western steelmakers - signed an agreement that called for the completion of an integrated mill by 1972. Pohang Iron & Steel Co. (POSCO) the operating company was incorporated in 1968. Efforts to raise the necessary capital failed however and KISA was dissolved in 1969.

Undaunted the South Koreans turned to the Japanese who arranged loans covering most of the mill's costs and the early phases of planning and construction. The Japanese also transferred the technology needed to run such a plant. Slow and deliberate planning resulted in a plant far away from Seoul (part of a plan to locate industries throughout the country) and a design that lent itself to future expansion. The first stage including a blast furnace and two steel converters was completed in 1973. By the time the fourth stage of construction began in 1979 the Koreans had gained enough confidence to take over many of the tasks. When the last stage was completed in 1981 the plant had an annual capacity of 8.5 million tons.

To ensure steel of acceptable quality POSCO focused first on plain high-carbon steel for general construction rather than on specialized (and difficult to produce) varieties. The company gradually broadened its specialized offerings.

In 1985 POSCO began construction on a second integrated steel plant located in Kwangyang. That plant was also built in four stages; its annual production capacity when it was completed in 1992 was 11.4 million tons. By 1987 POSCO was exporting almost 3 million tons of steel a year and using its knowledge to assist in plant construction projects in other countries.

By the mid-1990s POSCO was exporting 6 million tons of steel annually. The South Korean government sold a 5% stake in POSCO to the public in 1998 and vowed to open up the primary steelmaking industry to competition. However facing a severe downturn in steel demand that year because of sluggishness in Asian and domestic markets the company canceled two projects in China and suspended two in Indonesia. In 1999 POSCO merged its two subsidiaries Pohang Coated Steel and Pohang Steel Industries to create Pohang Steel Co. That same year POSCO Machinery & Engineering POSEC-HAWAII and P.T. Posnesia Stainless Steel Industry were joined to form POSCO Machinery Co. The South Korean government continued selling off its 13% stake in 1999.

In 2000 POSCO sold its 51% stake in telecommunications company Shinsegi Telecom to SK Telecom in exchange for cash and a 6.5% stake in SK Telecom. It also formed a strategic alliance –exploration of joint ventures shared research and joint procurement –with Nippon Steel the world's #1 steelmaker. The deal also calls for each to take increased equity stakes (2% or 3%) in the other. After about 30 years of government control the South Korean government sold its remaining shares of POSCO in 2001.

In June 2002 Chairman Yoo was indicted for influencing POSCO subsidiaries and contractors to buy inflated shares of Tiger Pools International (South Korea's sole sports lottery business) for Kim Hong-Gul the third son of South Korean President Kim Dae-Jung. That same year Pohang Iron & Steel Co. officially changed its company name to POSCO to try and strengthen brand recognition.

In 2003 Yoo resigned ahead of the company's shareholder meeting amid his possible involvement in illegal stock transactions.

The company invested in its Mexican operations in 2006 announcing a joint venture coil processing facility with Daewoo International to serve local carmakers. In 2010 POSCO acquired a majority stake in Daewoo International. Daewoo shareholders voted to put the company's depressed shares up for sale after the South Korean government gave its approval for the deal early in 2010.

EXECUTIVES

President, Hwang Eun-Yeon, age 57
CEO, Oh-Joon Kwon, age 64
President and Head Steel Production Division, Jin-Il Kim, age 62
SEVP and Head Corporate Infrastructure Division, Dong-Jun Yoon, age 56
SEVP and Head Finance and Investment Division, Young-Hoon Lee, age 55
SEVP and Head Steel Business Division, In-Hwan Oh, age 56
SEVP and Department Manager Legal Affairs, Se-Bin Song, age 52
SEVP and Head Technical Research Laboratories, Sung-Ho Park, age 58
SEVP and General Superintendent Gwangyang Works, Tong-Il An, age 55
SEVP and General Superintendent Pohang Works, Hag-Dong Kim, age 55
SEVP and Department Manager Value Management, Chung-Myong Cho, age 54
EVP and Department Manager Corporate Audit, Woo-Kyu Lee, age 57
EVP and General Manager Europe, Chang-Hee Yim
EVP and Department Manager Labor and Outside Services, Suk-Bum Ko, age 57
EVP and Project Manager Regional Head Office Establishment Team Indonesia, Jhi-Yong Kim, age 53
EVP and Department Manager New Business Development Department, Seong Yu, age 58
EVP and Department Manager Steel Solution Marketing, In-Hwa Chang, age 59
EVP and Department Manager External Relation, Dong-chang Jung, age 56
EVP and Project Manager Regional Head Office Establishment Team Vietnam, Sik Nam, age 58
EVP and President PT Krakatau POSCO Co. Ltd., Kyung-Zoon Min, age 56
EVP and Department Manager Energy and Shipbuilding Materials Marketing, Tak Jeong, age 55
EVP and Department Manager safety and Production Strategy, Tae-Ju Lee, age 56
EVP and Department Manager Steel Planning, Hong-Soo Kim, age 57
EVP and Department Manager Steel Business Strategy, Chang Hwan Son, age 54
Auditors: Samjong Accounting Corporation (A Member Firm of KPMG)

LOCATIONS

HQ: POSCO (South Korea)
6261 Donghaean-ro Nam-gu, Pohang-si, Gyeongsangbuk-do 790-300
Phone: (82) 54 220 0114 **Fax:** (82) 54 220 6000
Web: www.posco.co.kr

COMPETITORS

ArcelorMittal
Baosteel
Bechtel
Fluor
Hitachi
Hyundai Steel
JFE Holdings
Kobe Steel
Mitsubishi Steel Mfg.
Nippon Steel & Sumitomo Metal Corporation
Samsung Group
Severstal
Tata Steel
ThyssenKrupp Steel
United States Steel

HISTORICAL FINANCIALS

Company Type: Public

Income Statement

FYE: December 31

	REVENUE ($ mil.)	NET INCOME ($ mil.)	NET PROFIT MARGIN	EMPLOYEES
12/14	59,499	572	1.0%	17,877
12/13	58,826	1,308	2.2%	17,832
12/12	59,571	2,305	3.9%	17,623
12/11	59,496	3,148	5.3%	17,553
12/10	42,707	3,661	8.6%	16,390
Annual Growth	8.6%	(37.1%)	—	2.2%

2014 Year-End Financials

Debt ratio: 0.0%
Return on equity: 1.5%
Cash ($ mil.): 3,483
Current ratio: 1.49
Long-term debt ($ mil.): 13,922
No. of shares (mil.): 79
Dividends
Yield: 2.9%
Payout: 26.5%
Market value ($ mil.): 5,104

	STOCK PRICE ($) FY Close	P/E High	P/E Low	PER SHARE ($) Earnings	Dividends	Book Value
12/14	63.81	0	0	6.79	1.91	475.17
12/13	78.00	0	0	16.55	1.77	501.12
12/12	82.15	0	0	29.85	2.09	478.38
12/11	82.10	0	0	40.76	2.16	428.55
12/10	107.69	0	0	48.09	1.97	423.45
Annual Growth	(12.3%)	—	—	(38.7%)	(0.8%)	2.9%

Power Corp. of Canada

Founded in the 1920s to develop hydroelectric power Power Corporation of Canada now generates cash not electricity. Through its majority stake in Power Financial the company controls one of Canada's leading mutual fund firms (IGM Financial) one of its largest life insurers (Great-West Lifeco) and other insurance firms. It also owns Gesca which publishes Montreal's La Presse and six other daily newspapers in Quebec and Ontario and a majority of Pargesa Group which has stakes in large companies involved in energy (TOTAL) utilities (GDF SUEZ) construction (Lafarge) wines and spirits (Pernod Ricard) and other sectors in Europe through a controlling stake in Groupe Bruxelles Lambert.

In addition Power Corporation has investments in hedge funds private equity fund managers in France and the US and companies involved in biotechnology clean tech digital media and television production. Through Great-West Lifeco the company owns US-based mutual fund manager Putnam which it acquired from insurance brokerage Marsh & McLennan in 2007. The nearly $4 billion deal gave Power Corporation a significant presence in the US.

The company proved to be rather resilient during the economic downturn as its portfolio companies for the most part performed relatively well. Earnings were up in 2010 as IGM Financial and Great-West Lifeco reported higher sales. Power Corporation continues to focus on its core asset management and retirement planning operations and build the online presence of its media holdings. In 2011 the company made a move to enter China's fast-growing fund management sector by arranging to buy a 10% state in China Asset Management.

Former chairman Paul Desmarais (whose sons Paul and Andr are co-CEOs) owns more than 60% of Power Corporation of Canada.

EXECUTIVES

SVP Power Corporation, Arnaud Vial, age 63, $475,000 total compensation
EVP, John A. Rae, $497,000 total compensation
Deputy Chairman President and Co-CEO, Andr ©R. Desmarais, age 59, $1,000,000 total compensation
Chairman and Co-CEO, Paul Desmarais, age 61, $1,000,000 total compensation
EVP and CFO, Gregory D. Tretiak
Vice Chairman, Henri-Paul Rousseau, age 66
Vice Chairman, Michel Plessis-B ©air
Auditors: Deloitte LLP

LOCATIONS

HQ: Power Corp. of Canada
751 Victoria Square, Montreal, Quebec H2Y 2J3
Phone: 514 286-7400 **Fax:** 514 286-7484
Web: www.powercorporation.com

2013 Sales

	% of total
Canada	53
Europe	28
US	19
Total	**100**

PRODUCTS/OPERATIONS

2013 Sales

	% of total
Premium income	69
Net investment income	9
Fees & media income	22
Total	**100**

2013 Sales by Segment

	% of total
Great-West Lifeco	88
IGM Financial	9
Other	3
Total	**100**

Selected Investments

Communications
Gesca Ltée (newspaper publisher)
Square Victoria Communications Group Inc.
Square Victoria Digital Properties Inc.
Financial Services
Great-West Lifeco Inc. (68%)
The Canada Life Assurance Company
Great-West Life & Annuity Insurance Company
The Great-West Life Assurance Company
London Life Insurance Company
Putnam Investments LLC
IGM Financial Inc. (57%)
Investment Planning Counsel (91%)
Investors Group
Mackenzie Financial Corporation
Power Financial Corporation (66%)
Victoria Square Ventures Inc.
Other
Pergesa Holding S.A. (Switzerland)

COMPETITORS

AGF Management
Berkshire Hathaway
Brookfield Asset Management
CI Financial
CPP Investment Board
Caisse de d©p´t et placement du Qu©bec
Dundee Corp.
Loews
Manulife Financial
Onex
Ontario Teachers' Pension Plan
Street Capital

HISTORICAL FINANCIALS

Company Type: Public

Income Statement

FYE: December 31

	ASSETS ($ mil.)	NET INCOME ($ mil.)	INCOME AS % OF ASSETS	EMPLOYEES
12/14	326,232	44	0.0%	0
12/13	324,456	48	0.0%	0
12/12	273,127	50	0.0%	30,900
12/11	250,461	40	0.0%	30,700
12/10	248,053	41	0.0%	31,126
Annual Growth	7.1%	2.2%	—	—

2014 Year-End Financials

Return on assets: 0.0%
Return on equity: 0.4%
Long-term debt ($ mil.): —
No. of shares (mil.): 412
Sales ($ mil): 36,997
Dividends
Yield: 0.0%
Payout: 42.1%
Market value ($ mil.): 11,273

	STOCK PRICE ($) FY Close	P/E High/Low		PER SHARE ($) Earnings	Dividends	Book Value
12/14	27.32	10	9	2.37	1.00	25.07
12/13	30.09	15	11	1.96	1.09	25.27
12/12	25.58	15	12	1.80	1.17	24.70
12/11	23.33	12	9	2.27	1.14	23.43
12/10	27.79	20	16	1.57	1.16	23.06
Annual Growth	(0.4%)	—	—	10.8%	(3.7%)	2.1%

Power Financial Corp

Power Financial gets a charge out of insurance and investments. The holding company seeks controlling stakes in financial services companies in the US the UK and Canada. Core investments include 68%-owned Great-West Lifeco (subsidiaries include Great-West Life Assurance Canada Life and London Life Insurance leading providers of insurance in Canada). Lifeco's US subsidiary Great-West Life & Annuity Insurance provides employee benefits and retirement plans. Boston-based fund manager Putnam Investments is also part of the family. Power Financial owns about half of IGM Financial which owns Investors Group and Mackenzie Financial distributors of mutual funds and other investment products and services.

Power Financial also is a 50% partner in Dutch holding company Parjointco with the Fr ¨re-Bourgeois and CNP groups the joint venture that owns a 54% stake in Pargesa which invests in building materials utilities minerals and energy companies (with Groupe Bruxelles Lambert it owns stakes in Imerys and TOTAL).

In 2007 Power Financial surprised many when it purchased the once-venerable but recently disgraced Putnam Investments. Speculation turned to I-told-you-so the following year when Putnam like most money managers was slammed by the subprime mortgage and credit market collapse. In mid-2008 Power Financial brought in long-time Fidelity Investments COO Robert Reynolds as president and CEO of Putnam. The new leader trimmed staff tied pay to performance and started two new funds to attract fresh money.

Power Corporation of Canada the country's fifth largest firm by revenue owns two-thirds of Power Financial. Canada's well-known billionaire Desmarais family controls Power Corporation.

EXECUTIVES

President and CEO, R. Jeffrey Orr, $3,358,665 total compensation
SVP Power Financial and Power Corporation, Arnaud Vial, age 63, $209,000 total compensation
EVP and CFO, Gregory D. Tretiak
Managing Director Power Financial Europe B.V., Jocelyn Lefebvre
Vice Chairman, Raymond L. McFeetors, age 70
Co-Chairman, Andr ©R. Desmarais, age 59
Co-Chairman, Paul Desmarais, age 61
Vice Chairman, Henri-Paul Rousseau, age 66
Vice Chairman, Amaury de Seze
Vice Chairman, Michel Plessis-B ©air
Auditors: Deloitte LLP

LOCATIONS

HQ: Power Financial Corp
751 Victoria Square, Montreal, Quebec H2Y 2J3
Phone: 514 286-7400 **Fax:** 514 286-7484
Web: www.powerfinancial.com

2010 Revenues

	% of total
Canada	52
Europe	28
US	20
Total	**100**

PRODUCTS/OPERATIONS

2010 Revenues

	% of total
Great-West Lifeco	70
IGM	23
Pargesa	7
Total	**100**

Selected Subsidiaries & Affiliates

Great-West Lifeco Inc. (68%)
Great-West Life & Annuity Insurance Company (US)
Great-West Life Assurance Company
Canada Life Financial Corporation
London Insurance Group Inc.
Putnam LLC
IGM Financial Inc. (57%)
Investment Planning Counsel (94%)
Investors Group Inc.
Mackenzie Financial Corporation

COMPETITORS

AXA Financial
Allstate
CIGNA
Industrial Alliance Insurance and Financial Servic

Manulife Financial
Prudential
RBC Financial Group
State Farm
Sun Life

HISTORICAL FINANCIALS

Company Type: Public

Income Statement FYE: December 31

	ASSETS ($ mil.)	NET INCOME ($ mil.)	INCOME AS % OF ASSETS	EMPLOYEES
12/14	322,832	1,844	0.6%	0
12/13	321,358	1,783	0.6%	0
12/12	270,058	1,634	0.6%	17,870
12/11	247,698	1,688	0.7%	29,100
12/10	245,165	1,471	0.6%	0
Annual Growth	7.1%	5.8%	—	—

2014 Year-End Financials

Return on assets: 0.6%
Return on equity: 12.8%
Long-term debt ($ mil.): —
No. of shares (mil.): 711
Sales ($ mil): 36,257
Dividends
Yield: 0.0%
Payout: 46.6%
Market value ($ mil.): 22,256

	STOCK PRICE ($) FY Close	P/E High/Low		PER SHARE ($) Earnings	Dividends	Book Value
12/14	31.27	10	9	2.59	1.21	20.65
12/13	34.02	13	10	2.47	1.32	21.31
12/12	27.29	13	11	2.31	1.41	19.89
12/11	25.07	13	10	2.36	1.37	18.72
12/10	30.84	16	13	2.06	1.37	18.13
Annual Growth	0.3%	—	—	5.8%	(3.1%)	3.3%

Prudential Plc

When it comes to life insurance a little prudence goes a long way. Working through its subsidiaries Prudential is the UK's largest life insurer and the largest European insurer operating in Asia. In addition to insurance Prudential UK's products include pensions annuities investment bonds and fund management. Other businesses include UK fund manager M&G. In Asia the company sells life insurance savings and investment products in about a dozen countries through its Prudential Corporation Asia unit. In the US Prudential owns Jackson National Life Insurance which offers annuities and life insurance. Prudential plc was formed in 1848 to offer life insurance and loans to the middle class.

Operations

Prudential serves more than 24 million policyholders through its global insurance divisions and it has a total of some £405 million in assets under management. About 13 million customers are in Asian markets.

The company's operations are divided into four segments: Jackson National in the US Prudential Corporation Asia and Prudential UK and M&G based in the UK market. Operating subsidiaries within the UK-based divisions include Prudential Assurance Prudential Annuities Prudential Retirement and Prudential Assurance Singapore.

Insurance revenues account for more than 90% of annual earnings while asset management services provided by the M&G division make up the remainder of annual revenue.

Geographic Reach

Through its UK-based businesses Prudential has about 50 branch locations in the UK other European countries and India. Jackson National distributes products in all 50 US states from about 20 regional offices. In Asia Prudential has about 30 businesses that are spread over 14 markets.

Sales and Marketing

Prudential conducts sales through independent brokers and agents institutional product distributors regional brokers captive agents banks and investment advisors.

In addition to joint ventures with banks in China (with CITIC Group) and India (with ICICI Bank) Prudential has bank distribution agreements in other Asian markets. It life accident and health insurance policies are sold in Singapore Indonesia and Thailand through the more than 500 branches of United Overseas Bank.

Financial Performance

Rises in earned premiums and investment returns led to a 54% revenue increase to some £55.5 billion ($89.6 billion) in 2012. The company reported premium growth in all three core markets (the US Asia and the UK).

However sales declined in both 2010 and 2011 after a large jump in 2009. Prudential has seen volatile earnings in recent years due to the fact that the company relies on investment returns for more than 40% of its insurance income (in addition to premiums and fees) which makes it vulnerable to changes in market conditions.

Profits rose 55% to £2.2 billion ($3.6 billion) in 2012 due to higher revenues. Prudential has seen steadily climbing net income over the past five years as revenues outweigh expenses.

Strategy

A key part of Prudential's growth strategy and differentiation from its competitors is its presence in Asia particularly in markets including Southeast Asia Singapore and Hong Kong. The company entered the new Asian market of Cambodia in 2013. It is especially working to increase sales of savings and insurance products to the emerging group of middle class individuals in Asian markets.

Another strategic area of focus is retirement savings products (such as variable annuities) in the US. Its Jackson National Life Insurance takes advantage of the fact that the US has the largest market for retirement-related financial products. Prudential is also focused on strengthening existing life insurance operations in the US. In the UK the company is maximizing its asset management operations and focusing on core insurance markets.

Prudential also looks to diversify its earnings and offerings by making bolt-on acquisitions when opportunities emerge.

Mergers and Acquisitions

In 2013 the company widened its operations in Southeast Asia through the purchase of Thailand-based Thanachart Life Assurance from Thanachart Bank for some £368 million; the transaction also included a deal in which Prudential distributes policies through Thanachart's banking branches. To expand in the US market Prudential acquired SRLC America a US division of Swiss Re for some £370 million ($587 million) in 2012. The purchase diversified Jackson's life insurance underwriting activities in the US market.

Ownership

Capital Group International owns about 10% of the company.

HISTORY

Actually prudence almost killed Prudential before it ever got started. Founded in 1848 as Prudential Mutual Assurance Investment and Loan Association the firm initially insured middle-class customers. The Dickensian conditions of the working poor made them too risky for insurers. Unfortunately the company found few takers of the right sort and by 1852 Prudential was in peril.

Two events saved Prudential: The House of Commons pressed for insurance coverage for all classes and Prudential's own agents pushed for change. The company expanded into industrial insurance a modest coverage for the working poor. In 1864 to quell criticism of the insurance industry Prudential brought in independent auditors to confirm its soundness. This soon became a marketing tool and business took off. The Pru as it came to be known became the leading industrial insurer by the 1880s. It covered half the country's population by 1905. The firm's salesmen were known for making personal visits to customers (the "Man from the Pru" became a ubiquitous icon in the 1940s and was revived in 1997).

During the two world wars Prudential boosted its reputation by honoring the policies of war victims when it could have legally denied them. Between wars the company added fire and accident insurance in Europe.

The 1980s were volatile for insurance companies especially in the wake of Britain's financial deregulation in 1986. Therefore in 1982 under the direction of CEO Brian Corby the Pru reorganized product lines and in 1985 entered the real estate business. In 1986 it entered the US market by buying US-based Jackson National Life Insurance.

Prudential which had considered selling Mercantile and General Reinsurance in the early 1990s (purchased in 1969) sold the reinsurer back to Swiss Re in 1996. It also formed Prudential Bank and created an Asian emerging-market investment fund that year.

Insurance regulators reprimanded the company for mis-selling financial products in 1997. In 1998 Jackson National bought a California savings and loan enabling it to sell investment products in the US. Also that year the Pru sold its Australian and New Zealand businesses and Prudential Bank launched its pioneering Internet bank Egg Banking.

In 1999 Prudential bought investment manager M&G Group. The company then changed its name to Prudential plc and began talks with the Prudential Insurance Company of America to resolve confusion of their similar names as they expanded into new markets. Also in 1999 the Pru joined forces with the Bank of China to offer pension and asset management in Hong Kong.

The company announced plans in 2000 to sell a chunk of its institutional fund management business as well as its traditional balanced pension business to Deutsche Bank. That year the company spun off 20% of Egg (it sold the rest in 2007).

Entering the Japanese life insurance market Prudential bought Orico Life in 2001. Prudential's hopes of capturing the lucrative annuities market by acquiring American General were dashed that year as American General instead embraced American International Group leaving the Pru with a $600 million break-up fee. To consolidate operations the firm sold its general insurance business in 2001 to Swiss insurer Winterthur (a subsidiary of Credit Suisse).

In early 2006 Prudential rejected a takeover offer from larger rival Aviva valued at nearly $30 billion.

After helping oversee the shift in focus that brought the company growth in Asia and stability during the 2008 economic downturn CEO Mark Tucker stepped down at the end of September 2009. The company chose CFO Tidjane Thiam to replace him. Thiam a native of Ivory Coast became the first black CEO of a FTSE 100 company.

In early 2010 the company expanded its operations in Singapore by acquiring United Overseas Bank's life insurance unit for S$428 million ($307 million). Along with becoming owner of UOB Life Assurance Ltd. Prudential entered into an agreement through which UOB sells Prudential's life accident and health insurance policies for 12 years at the bank's more than 400 branches in Singapore Indonesia and Thailand giving Prudential a greater presence in those markets. In 2011 Prudential targeted the business of Singapore's class of "rising rich" individuals as an important area for growth.

Prudential made a splashy bid on AIG's Hong Kong-based American International Assurance (AIA) business in 2010. The $35.5 billion deal ($25 billion in cash $8.5 billion in securities and $2 billion in stock) would have made Prudential the largest life insurer in Hong Kong and allowed AIG to pay off a chunk of its debt to the US government. However Prudential's shareholders were not impressed and raised a ruckus over the deal. To appease them Prudential attempted to reduce its offer to $30 billion –which AIG coolly refused –and then simply withdrew its entire offer.

EXECUTIVES

Executive Director; Chief Executive The M&G Group, Michael G.A. McLintock, age 54, $320,000 total compensation
Group CEO, Mike Wells
Chairman and CEO Prudential North America, Barry L. Stowe, age 58, $646,000 total compensation
Chief Executive Prudential UK & Europe, Jackie Hunt, age 47
CFO, Nic Nicandrou
CEO Prudential Asia, Tony Wilkey
Group Investment Director and Interim Chief Risk Officer, John Foley
Chairman, Paul Manduca, age 63
Auditors: KPMG LLP

LOCATIONS

HQ: Prudential Plc
12 Arthur Street, London EC4R 9AQ
Phone: (44) 20 7220 7588
Web: www.prudential.co.uk

2012 Sales

	% of total
US	27
Asia	15
UK	14
Investment return	44
Total	**100**

PRODUCTS/OPERATIONS

2012 Sales

	% of total
Insurance	96
Asset management	4
Total	**100**

COMPETITORS

AEGON
AIA Group
AIG
AXA
Allianz
Aviva
BlackRock
Canada Life
Cathay Life Insurance
China Life Insurance
China Pacific Insurance
Citigroup
FMR
Great Eastern Holdings
HSBC
ING
Lincoln Financial Group
Lloyds Banking Group
Manulife Financial
MetLife
Mitsui Sumitomo Insurance
Nationwide Financial
New York Life
Nippon Life Insurance
Ping An Insurance
Prudential
RSA Insurance
Samsung Life Insurance
Schroders
Standard Life
State Farm
Invesco Perpetual
Jupiter Fund Management
Legal & General Group
TIAA-CREF
The Hartford
Tokio Marine
Zurich Insurance Group

HISTORICAL FINANCIALS

Company Type: Public

Income Statement FYE: December 31

	ASSETS ($ mil.)	NET INCOME ($ mil.)	INCOME AS % OF ASSETS	EMPLOYEES
12/14	576,335	3,459	0.6%	20,544
12/13	538,628	2,224	0.4%	20,052
12/12	500,086	3,541	0.7%	27,619
12/11	422,641	2,301	0.5%	25,414
12/10	404,937	2,221	0.5%	25,992
Annual Growth	9.2%	11.7%	—	(5.7%)

2014 Year-End Financials

Return on assets: 0.6%
Return on equity: 20.6%
Long-term debt ($ mil.): —
No. of shares (mil.): —
Sales ($ mil): 94,331
Dividends
Yield: 2.5%
Payout: 81.1%
Market value ($ mil.): —

	STOCK PRICE ($) FY Close	P/E High/Low		PER SHARE ($) Earnings	Dividends	Book Value
12/14	46.17	56	43	1.35	1.17	7.18
12/13	45.00	85	55	0.87	0.94	6.23
12/12	28.55	34	24	1.39	0.81	6.53
12/11	19.74	41	28	0.91	0.76	5.53
12/10	20.86	38	27	0.88	0.60	4.90
Annual Growth	22.0%	—	—	11.4%	17.9%	10.0%

PTT Public Co Ltd.

Thailand fills its tanks thanks to integrated oil company PTT the nation's largest company. Its PTT Oil transportation and marketing unit operates more than 1200 gas stations. PTT Gas procures processes transports and distributes natural gas. PTT owns 49% of the nation's largest refiner Thai Oil. Other PTT units engage in oil and gas exploration and production (in Thailand and elsewhere) produce petrochemicals and mine coal. It is also has major oil and gas trading operations. The company is majority-owned by the Government of Thailand.

Operations

PTT's core businesses are Exploration & Production and Gas and Oil.

PTT Exploration and Production Public Company Limited (PTTEP). PTT has also invested in natural gas-related corporations both in Thailand and abroad.

The Gas Business Group engages in natural gas supply procurement pipeline transmission separation and distribution.

The Oil Business Group engages in distribution of refined fuel and lubricating products covering retail marketing run through PTT service stations wholesale marketing and commercial marketing for government agencies industry sector airlines and oil vessels.

The International Trading Business Group covers procurement and import-export trading of crude oil condensate petroleum and petrochemical products .

On the investment side PTT invests in a wide range of its related businesses with an emphasis on petrochemical and oil refining businesses.

Financial Performance

The company's revenues increased by 28% in 2011 with a jump in profits of 25% reflected the success in natural gas procurement to meet growing demand efficiency improvement of gas separation plants (GSPs) and the commercial operation of GSP unit 6 (Rayong) which boosted production capacity.

Other factors include PTTEP's production increase (especially from the oil sands KKD project in Canada); production capacity expansion in the petrochemical group; improved returns from portfolio risk management investment and development programs; and pricing risk management for PTT and PTT group.

Strategy

The company sees its role as being the lead player in Thailand's oil and gas development and revenue production. PTT is relying on the synergy between various downstream businesses to add business value and reduce operating costs.

Ownership

The Government of Thailand owns 51% of PTT.

Company Background

Thailand which created PTT to secure energy supplies during the oil crunch of the late 1970s sold a third of the company in a 2001 IPO.

In 2008 as part of PTT's energy diversification drive the company opened the world's largest NGV (natural gas vehicle) gas station in Thailand to respond to the growing number of NGV vehicles in the country.

EXECUTIVES

CFO, Wirat Uanarumit
President and CEO, Tevin Vongvanich, age 57
COO Infrastructure, Surong Bulakul, age 60
COO Upstream Petroleum and Gas, Nuttachat Charuchinda
COO Downstream Petroleum, Sarun Rungkasiri
SEVP Petrochemicals and Refining, Sarakorn Kulatham
SEVP Human Resources and Organization Excellence, Pitipan Tepartimargorn
SEVP Corporate Strategy, Chansin Treenuchagron
SEVP Gas, Charcrie Buranakanonda
SEVP Oil, Chavalit Punthong
SEVP International Trading, Boobpha Amornkiatkajorn
SEVP Sustainability Management and Project Engineering, Auttapol Rerkpibook
Chairman, Piyasvasti Amranand
Auditors: The Office of the Auditor General of Thailand

LOCATIONS

HQ: PTT Public Co Ltd.
555 Vibhavadi-Rangsit Road, Chatuchak, Bangkok 10900
Phone: (66) 2 537 2000 **Fax:** (66) 2 537 3498 9
Web: www.pttplc.com

PRODUCTS/OPERATIONS

2011 Sales

	% of total
International trading	53
Oil	21
Natural gas	16
Exploration & production	6
Petrochemical	3
Coal	1
Other	-
Total	**100**

Selected Subsidiaries and Affiliates:
PetroAsia (Huizhou) Co. Ltd. (25%)
PTT Exploration and Production Public Co. Ltd. (66%)
PTT Mart Co. Ltd. (49%)
PTT Natural Gas Distribution Co. Ltd. (58%)
Star Petroleum Refining Co. Ltd. (36%)
Thai Lube Blending Co. Ltd. (49%)
Thai Oil Plc. (50%)

COMPETITORS

BP
Chevron
Salamander Energy

HISTORICAL FINANCIALS

Company Type: Public

Income Statement FYE: December 31

	REVENUE ($ mil.)	NET INCOME ($ mil.)	NET PROFIT MARGIN	EMPLOYEES
12/14	86,213	1,696	2.0%	25,986
12/13	86,831	2,891	3.3%	25,251
12/12	91,301	3,420	3.7%	20,816
12/11	77,158	3,345	4.3%	18,240
12/10	63,259	2,766	4.4%	9,015
Annual Growth	8.0%	(11.5%)	—	30.3%

2014 Year-End Financials

Debt ratio: 0.8%
Return on equity: 8.0%
Cash ($ mil.): 6,197
Current ratio: 1.43
Long-term debt ($ mil.): 11,884
No. of shares (mil.): —
Dividends
Yield: —
Payout: —
Market value ($ mil.): —

Public Bank Berhad (Malaysia)

Public Bank stakes its success on providing banking services to the public. The company has about 250 branches throughout Malaysia where it is one of the top lenders and fund operators. Offerings include deposit accounts credit cards home loans and insurance plans. In addition to retail and commercial services it provides corporate banking brokerage investment banking wealth management and Islamic banking. Public Bank has more than 100 overseas branches in countries including Cambodia China Hong Kong Laos Sri Lanka and Vietnam. The company was founded in 1966 by chairman Tan Sri Dato' Sri Dr. Teh Hong Piow.
Auditors: KPMG

LOCATIONS

HQ: Public Bank Berhad (Malaysia)
27th Floor, Menara Public Bank, 146 Jalan Ampang, Kuala Lumpur 50450
Phone: (60) 3 2163 8888 **Fax:** (60) 3 2163 9917
Web: www.publicbank.com.my

COMPETITORS

AmBank Group
Bank Muamalat
Bank Pembangunan
CIMB Group
HSBC
Hong Leong Bank
Lloyds Banking Group
Maybank
RHB Capital

HISTORICAL FINANCIALS

Company Type: Public

Income Statement FYE: December 31

	ASSETS ($ mil.)	NET INCOME ($ mil.)	INCOME AS % OF ASSETS	EMPLOYEES
12/14	98,869	1,292	1.3%	18,198
12/13	93,326	1,240	1.3%	17,924
12/12	89,694	1,263	1.4%	17,625
12/11	78,703	1,099	1.4%	17,511
12/10	73,435	989	1.3%	17,369
Annual Growth	7.7%	6.9%	—	1.2%

2014 Year-End Financials

Return on assets: 1.3%
Return on equity: 18.6%
Long-term debt ($ mil.): —
No. of shares (mil.): —
Sales ($ mil): 4,586
Dividends
Yield: —
Payout: —
Market value ($ mil.): —

	STOCK PRICE ($) FY Close	P/E High/Low	PER SHARE ($) Earnings	Dividends	Book Value
12/14	0.00	— —	0.35	0.00	2.08
12/13	0.00	— —	0.35	0.00	1.78
Annual Growth	—	— —	(0.0%)	—	3.9%

Qatar National Bank

Qatar National Bank (QNB) is a leading financial institution in the State of Qatar one of the wealthiest nations in the world. Boasting 45% of the total assets in Qatar's banking sector QNB offers customers private and commercial deposit accounts and loans investment management credit cards insurance and mutual funds. International branches are located in a dozen other countries across Africa Asia Europe and the Middle East. Through associate and affiliated companies QNB has a presence in about 25 countries. The company has a local network of more than 50 branches (some cater specifically to women) and hundreds of ATMs. QNB was established in 1964.
Auditors: Firas Qoussous (a member of Ernst & Young)

LOCATIONS

HQ: Qatar National Bank
P.O. Box 1000, Doha
Phone: (974) 44425 444 **Fax:** (974) 4441 3753
Web: www.qnb.com.qa

HISTORICAL FINANCIALS

Company Type: Public

Income Statement FYE: December 31

	ASSETS ($ mil.)	NET INCOME ($ mil.)	INCOME AS % OF ASSETS	EMPLOYEES
12/15	147,918	3,093	2.1%	0
12/14	133,632	2,872	2.1%	0
12/13	121,790	2,603	2.1%	0
12/12	100,734	2,289	2.3%	0
12/11	82,910	2,061	2.5%	0
Annual Growth	15.6%	10.7%	—	—

2015 Year-End Financials

Return on assets: 2.2%
Return on equity: 19.0%
Long-term debt ($ mil.): —
No. of shares (mil.): 699
Sales ($ mil): 6,535
Dividends
Yield: —
Payout: —
Market value ($ mil.): —

QBE Insurance Group Ltd.

QBE Insurance Group may be one of Australia's leading insurers but it also has a hefty global reach. The company offers a variety of insurance and reinsurance through offices in about 50 countries. QBE provides general property/casualty policies as well as liability auto marine aviation energy accident workers' compensation and professional indemnity coverage. The company writes both individual and commercial insurance policies and also administers reinsurance coverage. It sells its products through direct and independent representative agencies.

Geographic Reach

QBE Insurance Group earns about three-fourths of its revenue outside of Australia.

Financial Performance

The company's revenue decreased in fiscal 2013 compared to the previous fiscal year. It reported about $16 billion in revenue for fiscal 2013 down from $17 billion in fiscal 2012. The decreased revenue caused the company to suffer a net loss of $251 million in fiscal 2013 after claiming a net income of $760 million in fiscal 2012.

QBE Insurance Group's cash flow also decreased significantly in fiscal 2013 compared to fiscal 2012 levels.

Strategy

After an extremely acquisitive period the company has been working to catch up to itself. Restructuring efforts have been made to cut costs; for example the company established a global processing center in the Philippines in 2013. In late 2014 QBE Insurance Group agreed to sell its operations in the Czech Republic Hungary and Slovakia to Fairfax Financial Holdings.

EXECUTIVES

CEO European Operations, Richard Pryce
CEO, John Neal, age 51
CEO North American Operations, David B. Duclos
CEO Australian and New Zealand Operations, Colin Fagen
CEO Emerging Markets Division, David Fried
Chief Risk Officer, Jason Brown
Group Executive Officer Operations, Mike Emmett
Managing Director Asia Pacific, Mark Lingafelter
CFO, Stuart Brown
Chairman, Marty Becker
Auditors: PricewaterhouseCoopers

LOCATIONS

HQ: QBE Insurance Group Ltd.
Level 27, 8 Chifley Square, Sydney, New South Wales 2000
Phone: (61) 2 9375 4444 **Fax:** (61) 2 9231 6104
Web: www.qbe.com

COMPETITORS

AEGON
AIG
ING
Insurance Australia

AMP Limited
AXA
AXIS Capital Holdings
Allianz
Allstate
Assurances G©n©rales de France
Australia and New Zealand Banking
Aviva
Commonwealth Bank of Australia
GEICO
Generali
Loews
Munich Re Group
National Australia Bank
Nationwide
RSA Insurance
Samsung Fire & Marine
Standard Chartered
State Farm
Suncorp-Metway
Swiss Re
Travelers Companies
Westpac Banking

HISTORICAL FINANCIALS

Company Type: Public

Income Statement FYE: December 31

	ASSETS ($ mil.)	NET INCOME ($ mil.)	INCOME AS % OF ASSETS	EMPLOYEES
12/14	45,000	742	1.6%	19,442
12/13	47,271	(254)	—	17,000
12/12	50,762	761	1.5%	0
12/11	46,737	704	1.5%	0
12/10	42,188	1,278	3.0%	0
Annual Growth	1.6%	(12.7%)	—	—

2014 Year-End Financials

Return on assets: 1.6%
Return on equity: 6.9%
Long-term debt ($ mil.): —
No. of shares (mil.): 1,363
Sales ($ mil): 14,896
Dividends
Yield: 2.4%
Payout: 40.0%
Market value ($ mil.): 12,349

	STOCK PRICE ($) FY Close	P/E High/Low		PER SHARE ($) Earnings	Dividends	Book Value
12/14	9.06	21	15	0.56	0.22	8.09
12/13	10.27	—	—	(0.23)	0.26	8.30
12/12	11.43	23	16	0.62	0.64	9.51
12/11	13.25	32	18	0.61	0.58	9.34
Annual Growth	(11.9%)	—	—	(3.5%)	(2.3%)	(21.2%)

Quanta Computer Inc

Quanta Computer is an original design manufacturer (ODM) serving some of the leading names in computer hardware including Dell Apple and HP. It is one of the world's largest manufacturers of notebook computers and also produces network servers television set-top boxes monitors LCD TVs and smartphones. Quanta Computer's other business units include Quanta Storage (data storage products) and RoyalTek Company (personal navigation devices and other GPS products). While well known for its notebooks and their smaller computer cousins the netbooks Quanta Computer is diversifying into other consumer electronics and IT products.

Geographic Reach The company is based in Taiwan with additional facilities in Asia Europe and North and South America.

Financial Performance Quanta Computer's 2011 revenue fell just over 1% to NT$1.1 trillion (around $37 billion). Its net income however rose by 22% for the same period to NT$23 billion (about $780 million) as a result of strict cost controls it put in place. The company is focused on inventory reductions and yield rate improvements among other measures.

Strategy The company is focusing its R&D efforts on cloud computing connectivity and client devices. All three areas are part of a broader cloud computing initiative that involves the design and manufacture of data storage products and servers (for providing cloud-computing services) next-generation data networking products (for enabling uninterrupted cloud-computing connections and service coverage) and client devices (for accessing cloud networks). Outside of notebooks other areas of focus include mobile devices automotive electronics high-definition video conferencing and satellite technology.

EXECUTIVES

CFO, Elton Yang
Vice Chairman and President, C.C. Leung
Chairman, Barry Lam
Auditors: KPMG

LOCATIONS

HQ: Quanta Computer Inc
No. 188, Wen Hwa 2nd Road, Guishan District, Taoyuan 33377
Phone: (886) 3 327 2345 **Fax:** (886) 3 327 1511
Web: www.quantatw.com

PRODUCTS/OPERATIONS

Products
QCI
Notebook
Server
OLPC
Camera
Industrial computer

COMPETITORS

ASUSTeK
BenQ
Celestica
China Techfaith
Compal Electronics
First International Computer
Flextronics
Foxconn International
Hon Hai
Inventec
MiTAC
Pegatron
Super Micro Computer
Tatung
TriGem
Wistron

HISTORICAL FINANCIALS

Company Type: Public

Income Statement FYE: December 31

	REVENUE ($ mil.)	NET INCOME ($ mil.)	NET PROFIT MARGIN	EMPLOYEES
12/14	29,254	596	2.0%	0
12/13	29,522	624	2.1%	0
12/12	35,317	794	2.2%	121,917
12/11	36,612	775	2.1%	108,872
12/10	38,651	664	1.7%	68,720
Annual Growth	(6.7%)	(2.7%)	—	—

2014 Year-End Financials

Debt ratio: 1.1%
Return on equity: 14.7%
Cash ($ mil.): 7,012
Current ratio: 1.22
Long-term debt ($ mil.): 724
No. of shares (mil.): —
Dividends
Yield: —
Payout: —
Market value ($ mil.): —

Raiffeisen Zentralbank Oesterreich AG (Austria)

Raiffeesen Zentralbank plays a zentral part in Austrian and worldwide banking. Because being among the largest bankers in Austria's mature market only gets you so far Raiffeisen Zentralbank (RZB) has branched out into other countries and now operates across Central and Eastern Europe. It has more than 3000 banking branches in these regions offering commercial and investment banking services for companies. Raiffeisen Zentralbank owns about 60% of Raiffeisen International Bank (RIB) through which it provides central services to its regional banks. The company was founded in 1927 and is owned by its regional banks.

OperationsRZB operates through three main segments: Raiffeisen Bank International Group (RBI) Raiffeisen Banking Group (RBG) and an extra segment for other equity participations. More than 90% of the company's revenue is generated by the RBI segment. As Austria's third largest bank RBI specializes in commercial and investment banking and considers itself to be the corporate finance partner of the country's top 1000 companies. It also is a leading provider of export financing.

The RBG segment contributes another 7% of revenue and is one of the largest banking groups in Central and Eastern Europe covering 15 markets in the region through subsidiary banks leasing companies and financial service providers. The company offers services involved with mergers and acquisitions privatization and consulting fund equity capital events real estate development fund management and project management.Broadly speaking the bank makes 70% of its revenue in the form of interest income from loans while some 25% is generated from fees and commissions from the bank's investment sales and trading income. Geographic ReachWhile Austria is the bank's largest lending market in generating more than 20% of the bank's income another 25% of revenue comes from countries in Central Europe (Poland Czech Republic Slovakia and Hungary). Loans in the European Union countries of Germany France Great Britain and the Netherlands contribute more than 10% of revenues. The bank also has loans in China Singapore the Ukraine Russia and Southeastern countries of Europe.Sales and MarketingRZB spent 123.3 million (about $149.9 million) on advertising PR and promotional expenses in fiscal 2013 or roughly 19% more than in fiscal 2012 as it intensified its advertising campaigns in Russia. Financial PerformanceRevenue steadily rose for its second straight year climbing by less than 1% to about $13.09 billion mostly thanks to higher net interest margins on loans but also because of favorable foreign currency trades and higher fee and commission income that came from increased payment transactions and securities transactions. Higher revenues and lower interest expenses also drove the bank's net income up by 18% to 422.1 million (or $581.1 million).Cash supply on the other hand was less healthy. Unlike in fiscal 2012 when operations provided 706.4 million (about $933.5 million) operations used 2.46 billion (about $3.39 billion) in fiscal 2013.

EXECUTIVES

Chairman Management Board and CEO, Walter Rothensteiner, age 62
Deputy CEO and Chief Risk Officer, Johann Strobl, age 56
Member Management Board, Johannes Schuster, age 45
Chairman of the Supervisory Board, Erwin Hameseder, age 58
Auditors: KPMG Austria AG Wirtschaftspr fungs- und Steuerberatungsgesellschaft

LOCATIONS

HQ: Raiffeisen Zentralbank Oesterreich AG (Austria)
Am Stadtpark 9, Vienna A-1030
Phone: (43) 1 71707 1298 **Fax:** (43) 1 71707 3802
Web: www.rzb.at

COMPETITORS

ABN AMRO Group	Erste Bank
BAWAG	HSBC
BNP Paribas	Investkredit
Bank Austria	Oberbank AG
Cr©dit Agricole	UBS
Deutsche Bank	

HISTORICAL FINANCIALS

Company Type: Public

Income Statement FYE: December 31

	ASSETS ($ mil.)	NET INCOME ($ mil.)	INCOME AS % OF ASSETS	EMPLOYEES
12/14	176,161	(392)	—	56,212
12/13	202,826	581	0.3%	59,372
12/12	192,375	488	0.3%	0
12/10	182,683	955	0.5%	60,356
12/09	213,115	624	0.3%	59,800
Annual Growth	(3.7%)	—	—	(1.2%)

2014 Year-End Financials

Return on assets: (-0.2%)
Return on equity: (-5.2%)
Long-term debt ($ mil.): —
No. of shares (mil.): —
Sales ($ mil): 11,276
Dividends
Yield: —
Payout: —
Market value ($ mil.): —

Randstad Holding N.V.

Randstad Holding has the supply to meet nearly any demand. The company is one of the largest temporary staffing and employment services agencies in the world (behind Adecco). It operates primarily in Europe but also in Asia and North America under the Randstad brand and several others including Sapphire Technologies (IT staffing) Yacht (industrial staffing) and Tempo-Team (general staffing). Through almost 4200 locations in more than 40 countries Randstad supplies temporary workers for small assignments as well as large-scale deployments. It also offers permanent placement and HR project management and consultancy services. Randstad Holding was established in 1960.

Operations

Randstad's operations are divided across four business segments: staffing professionals HR solutions (payroll services HR consulting and vendor management services) and in-house services (works onsite with clients primarily residing in the manufacturing and logistics sectors).

Financial Performance

The company's total annual revenue increased from $22.5 billion in fiscal 2012 up to $22.8 billion in fiscal 2013. Randstad's net income increased from $48.5 million in fiscal 2012 to $317.5 million in fiscal 2013 on the strength of the gross annual revenue.

Strategy

Believing that the Japanese market is one of the largest staffing markets in the world Randstad is looking to the country as an important location for achieving growth.

HISTORY

Frits Goldschmeding founded Randstad Holding as Uitzendbureau Amstelveen near Amsterdam in 1960.

Originally part of a student project the company turned a small profit its first year and was renamed Randstad Uitzendbureau in 1964. ("The Randstad" is the densely populated area including Amsterdam Rotterdam and the Hague.)

It launched its first operation outside the Netherlands the next year establishing Interlabor Interim in Belgium. By 1970 Randstad had 32 branches in four countries including Germany and the UK.

Continuing its expansion across Europe (it entered France in 1973) the company was recast as Randstad Holding in 1978. The next year it opened its 100th branch and launched its Randon security business in the Netherlands in 1980. In 1985 Randstad celebrated its silver anniversary with 250 branches.

The company went public in 1990 listing its shares on the Amsterdam Stock Exchange. That year it moved its headquarters to the Amsterdam suburb of Diemen.

In 1993 Randstad entered the US market when it bought Atlanta-based Temp Force and later acquired Nashville-based Jane Jones Enterprises. It also expanded its staffing business into Spain that year. Randstad's US business later scored a coup when it became a sponsor of the 1996 Olympic Games in Atlanta. The company placed more than 16000 temporary employees to help out during the games. By 1997 the company had more than 1000 branches in Europe and North America.

Founder and CEO Goldschmeding resigned his post in 1998 and was replaced by Hans Zwarts. That year Randstad bought Strategix Solutions the commercial staffing unit of US-based AccuStaff (later MPS Group) for $850 million. The next year the company bought Germany's Time Power Personal-Dienstleistungen and Spain's Tempo Grup. Randstad and Dutch publisher VNU announced plans to create an online employment site covering Europe in 2000 (the site was closed in 2001).

The following year Randstad bought Spanish staffing firm Umano giving the company 150 additional locations throughout Spain. It also sold its security and cleaning businesses in 2001. Zwarts retired in 2002 and was replaced by 30-year company veteran Cleem Farla. In 2003 Ben Noteboom took over as CEO. In 2004 Randstad opened an office in Poland and bought staffing firm Take Air.

In 2007 Randstad almost doubled Randstad Switzerland's revenue through the acquisition of Job One. The Swiss staffing firm operated about two dozen branches and focuses on the technology health care and construction industries. In the biggest acquisition in its company's history Randstad acquired rival staffing agency Vedior in mid-2008. The deal catapulted Randstad ahead of other staffing rivals making it one of the largest in the world.

Striving to improve its position in Canada and the US Randstad purchased rival SFN Group for about $770 million in 2011.

EXECUTIVES

CFO and Vice Chairman Executive Board, Robert-Jan van de Kraats, age 55, $565,000 total compensation
CEO and Chairman of the Executive Board, Jacques van den Broek, age 55, $497,000 total compensation
President Randstad North America, Linda Galipeau, age 52
Managing Director Randstad Netherlands, Chris Heutink, age 53
Group President Randstad US, Traci L. Fiatte
President and CEO Randstad Group France, Fran $ois B ©arel, age 45
CEO Randstad Canada, Marc- tienne Julien
Chairman, Wout Dekker, age 59
Vice Chairman, Jaap Winter
Auditors: PricewaterhouseCoopers Accountants N.V.

LOCATIONS

HQ: Randstad Holding N.V.
Diemermere 25, Diemen 1112 TC
Phone: (31) 20 569 59 11 **Fax:** (31) 20 569 55 20
Web: www.randstad.com

COMPETITORS

Adecco	Robert Half
Allegis Group	Technical Aid Corporation
CDI	Volt Information
Kelly Services	
ManpowerGroup	

HISTORICAL FINANCIALS

Company Type: Public

Income Statement FYE: December 31

	REVENUE ($ mil.)	NET INCOME ($ mil.)	NET PROFIT MARGIN	EMPLOYEES
12/14	20,967	398	1.9%	609,020
12/13	22,810	300	1.3%	595,730
12/12	22,521	39	0.2%	611,020
12/11	20,986	231	1.1%	605,500
12/10	18,977	385	2.0%	546,980
Annual Growth	2.5%	0.8%	—	2.7%

2014 Year-End Financials

Debt ratio: 9.6%
Return on equity: 10.5%
Cash ($ mil.): 142
Current ratio: 1.11
Long-term debt ($ mil.): 382
No. of shares (mil.): 179
Dividends
Yield: 2.1%
Payout: 20.6%
Market value ($ mil.): 4,289

	STOCK PRICE ($) FY Close	P/E High/Low		PER SHARE ($) Earnings	Dividends	Book Value
12/14	23.85	16	11	2.20	0.51	22.39
12/13	32.43	26	15	1.69	0.69	22.60
12/12	18.60	116	84	0.22	0.65	20.87
12/11	14.80	28	13	1.29	0.64	21.93
12/10	26.36	17	11	2.18	0.00	22.44
Annual Growth	(2.5%)	—	—	0.2%	—	(0.0%)

Reliance Industries Ltd

India and Reliance Industries rely on each other. The company is India's largest petrochemical firm and among the country's largest companies (along with Indian Oil and Tata Group) accounting for 14% of India's total exports and 4% of its total market capitalization. Oil refining and the manufacture of polyolefins and related chemicals account for the bulk of Reliance Industries' sales. It also makes textiles and explores for oil and gas. Reliance Industries operates more than a dozen manufacturing plants in India. The company has fully integrated its oil and gas refining subsidiary Reliance Petroleum in an effort to consolidate the company's position as a major player in the global refining business.

Reliance Industries' diverse portfolio includes the exploration and production of oil and gas petroleum refining and marketing and petrochemicals (including the production of polyester fiber intermediates plastics and chemicals) as well as textiles retail telecommunications and special economic zones.

In India the company has manufacturing plants in Allahabad Barabanki Dahej Hazira Hoshiarpur Jamnagar Nagothane Nagpur Naroda Patalganga Silvassa and Vadodara. Relaince Industries has operations around the world including in Kenya the Netherlands Singapore the UAE the US (oil and gas) and the UK (retail).

In Fiscal 2012 the company reported a 35% spike in revenues driven by a jump in oil prices and increased demand from petroleum products in developing countries coupled with an increase in Indian domestic demand for textiles chemicals and petroleum products. However its net income dipped by 1% due to a spike in current taxation charges. Buoyed by a recovering global economy the expansion of its own operations and higher oil prices in 2011 Reliance Industries posted a 30% rise in revenues.

Reliance Industries operates in the retail sector through subsidiary Reliance Retail Limited. That unit has big ideas about starting an Indian retail revolution with supermarket outlets across the country under the name Reliance Fresh. It operates a joint venture with UK retail legend Marks & Spencer that hopes to open 50 retail locations by 2014. Moving into the financial services sector in 2011 the company formed a joint venture with US-based investment firm D. E. Shaw.

Reliant Industries is targeting oil and gas as a key growth segment. Seeking funds and expertise to boost its oil and gas exploration and production operations in India in 2011 the company sold BP a 30% stake in 23 oil and gas blocks for about $7.2 billion.

The company is also growing its oil and gas exploration and production assets outside of India. In 2010 it also got a strong foothold in the North American gas market by forming a $1.7 billion Marcellus Shale joint venture with Atlas Energy. Atlas Energy is the development operator for the Appalachian joint venture. In return Reliance Industries owned 40% of Atlas Energy's core Marcellus Shale acreage. In 2011 Chevron stepped in and paid $4.3 billion to acquire Atlas and take over its joint venture with Reliant.

In 2010 Reliance Industries formed a 60%-owned joint venture with Carrizo Oil & Gas which acquired 104400 additional acres in the Marcellus Shale play. That same year Reliance Industries acquired a 45% share in a Pioneer Natural Resources tract in southern Texas for $1.35 billion.

The company began to further diversify in 2010. Reentering the telecommunications sector the company acquired 95% of Infidel Broadband Services a national broadband provider for about $1.02 billion. Infotel was the only company to secure a nationwide license to offer wireless broadband service across India a market with 600 million cell phone users. The deal marked Reliance Industries' return to the telecom market after a 5-year hiatus.

Following a prolonged dispute among the founding Ambani family after the death of patriarch Dhirubai Ambani the company demerged into separate entities –including Reliance Capital (financial services) Reliance Communications (telecommunications) and Reliance Energy (utilities) –in 2006. Mukesh Ambani took control of Reliance Industries and Indian Petrochemicals while his brother Anil took over Reliance Capital Reliance Communications and Reliance Energy.

Mukesh Ambani controls almost half of Reliance Industries.

Auditors: Deloitte Haskins & Sells LLP

LOCATIONS

HQ: Reliance Industries Ltd
3rd Floor, Maker Chambers IV, 222, Nariman Point, Mumbai 400 021
Phone: (91) 22 2278 5000 **Fax:** (91) 22 2278 5111
Web: www.ril.com

HISTORICAL FINANCIALS

Company Type: Public

Income Statement FYE: March 31

	REVENUE ($ mil.)	NET INCOME ($ mil.)	NET PROFIT MARGIN	EMPLOYEES
03/15	61,404	3,767	6.1%	24,930
03/14	73,854	3,746	5.1%	23,853
03/13	74,592	3,846	5.2%	23,519
03/12	71,684	3,876	5.4%	23,166
03/11	61,189	4,327	7.1%	22,661
Annual Growth	0.1%	(3.4%)	—	2.4%

2015 Year-End Financials

Debt ratio: 0.4%
Return on equity: 11.3%
Cash ($ mil.): 2,005
Current ratio: 0.99
Long-term debt ($ mil.): 19,310

No. of shares (mil.): —
Dividends
Yield: —
Payout: 22.7%
Market value ($ mil.): —

Renault S.A. (France)

In Renault's road race against rival Peugeot Citro «n to be France's dominant automaker second place will have to deux. Renault manufactures and markets small to midsize cars and light trucks under three brands: Renault Dacia and Renault Samsung Motors (Renault holds 80% Samsung 20%). The company owns Automobile Dacia (Romania's leading automaker) and holds just under half of the Renault-Nissan Alliance (and 43% of Nissan). It also participates in an alliance with Russian car maker AvtoVAZ and helps Germany's Daimlerbuild smart cars. Renault which has become an international brand operates nearly 40 manufacturing facilities in more than 15 countries and sells into 118 nations.

The synergies between Renault and Nissan have produced a reciprocal benefit – Renault has adopted a better production system with Nissan's support and Nissan has embraced better cost-control measures practiced by Renault. The Alliance gives both companies a competitive edge over other automotive companies through shared technologies and platforms. For example Nissan can use Renault's research when developing a diesel engine and Renault can benefit from Nissan's battery technology. By sharing production facilities – which the companies do in Mexico South Africa South Korea and Spain –they save on production purchasing and related costs. The Alliance also allows Renault and Nissan to tackle projects such as electric vehicles the cost of which would be prohibitive if each company had to bear it separately. As is both companies have invested E4 billion (almost $5 billion) into research and development and the manufacturing of vehicles and batteries. The Renault-Nissan Alliance is making a tandem expansion into emerging countries such as Russia India and Brazil. In an attempt to get a larger piece of the growing car market in India Renault has made a point of introducing a steady stream of new models there. To get a larger chunk of the rapidly growing Russian car market Renault-Nissan forged an alliance with Russian carmaker AvtoVAZ. Renault holds about 50% of the company and has invested heavily in upgrading its production plants.

Like most other carmakers Renault-Nissan is investing heavily in Asia. In China the Alliance is principally represented by Nissan which has a partnership with local carmaker Dongfeng Motor. The joint venture plans to produce 40000 vehicles annually. The Alliance is also making concerted steps to expand in India where it has a plant in Chennai. Renault-Nissan entered yet another collaborative agreement in early 2010 when it joined up with Daimler to give Toyota and Volkswagen a run for their money. Renault will provide its small-car technology to Daimler for use in some of its models. As part of the deal Renault and Nissan each took a 1.55% share in Daimler while Daimler has a 3.1% stake in each of them. The company expects the partnership to provide a benefit of about E2 billion ($3.6 billion) to Renault-Nissan by 2015.

Going forward Renault is focusing on the mass marketing of electric vehicles with plans to produce 500000 by 2015. Not just content to make electric cars Renault and Nissan together with German power utility RWE set up 1000 charging stations in Germany to help sell its cars.

The French government and Nissan each hold about 15% of Renault though Nissan has agreed not to exercise the voting control associated with its shares.

HISTORY

In the Paris suburb of Billancourt in 1898 21-year-old Louis Renault assembled a motorized vehicle with a transmission box of his own design. Louis and his brothers Marcel and Fernand established Renault Freres and produced the world's first sedan in 1899. Marcel died in a racing accident (1903) and Fernand left the business (1908) leaving Louis in sole possession of the company. He renamed it La Soci ©©Louis Renault in 1908.

In 1914 a fleet of 600 Paris taxis shuttled French troops to fight the Germans in the Battle of the Marne. Renault also built light tanks and airplane engines. Between world wars Renault expanded into trucks tractors and aircraft engines. Renault sustained heavy damage in WWII but Louis Renault operated the remaining Paris facilities for the Germans during their occupation of France. After the liberation of Paris he was accused of collaboration and died in prison while awaiting trial in 1944. The de Gaulle government nationalized Renault in 1945 and gave the company its present name.

Worldwide economic growth aided Renault's postwar comeback. The company achieved its greatest success in high-volume low-cost cars such as the 4 CV in the late 1940s and 1950s the Renault 4 in the 1960s and 1970s and the Renault 5 in the 1970s and 1980s.

In 1979 Renault acquired 46% of American Motors Corporation (AMC). In the early 1980s AMC fared poorly and Renault suffered from a worldwide slump in auto sales an aging product line and stiff competition from Japanese carmakers. Decreasing sales an unwieldy bureaucracy and above-average wages contributed to a $1.5 billion loss in 1984.

Georges Besse took over Renault in 1985 and trimmed employment by 20000. When Besse was assassinated by Red Army Faction terrorists in 1986 Raymond Levy assumed his role and continued his policies laying off 30000 more workers and selling AMC to Chrysler (1987).

Renault and AB Volvo agreed to extensive cross-ownership and cooperation in 1990. In 1994 Renault swapped its 25% stake in Volvo's car division for the latter's 45% stake in Renault's troubled truck unit. (Volvo sold its remaining 11% stake in 1997.)

The French government reduced its share of the firm from 80% to 52% in 1995 and to 44% the following year. In 1997 it shut down a Belgian plant that employed more than 3000 workers and fired a similar number of employees in France. Renault paid a $13 million civil penalty to the EPA in 1998 to settle allegations that its Mack Trucks unit cheated on its diesel engine emissions tests.

Renault and Fiat struck several deals in 1999. They combined their bus-making operations under the name Irisbus and their foundry operations into jointly owned Teksid. Renault sold a 51% stake in Renault Automation to Fiat's Comau robotics unit. Also that year Renault bought a 51% stake in Romanian automaker Automobile Dacia SA and paid $5.4 billion for a 37% stake in Nissan and a 15% (later increased to 23%) stake in truck affiliate Nissan Diesel Motor.

Early in 2000 the company announced that it would spend around $100 million to build an SUV factory in Brazil and announced plans to trim almost $3 billion in costs between 2001 and 2003. The same year Renault agreed to buy a 70% stake in Samsung Motors' automobile business for around $550 million. It also sold its Mack truck unit to Volvo in exchange for a 15% stake in the Swedish truck maker. Renault planned to buy another 5% of Volvo on the open market. Renault and Nissan also announced plans to save about $1 billion by combining their European sales and marketing operations.

Renault sold its Renault V.I. subsidiary and its Mack Trucks unit to Volvo in return for a 20% stake in the Swedish truck maker.

Later in 2001 Renault furthered strengthen ties with Nissan. The plan increased Renault's stake in Nissan to 44% while granting Nissan a 15% stake in Renault. The French Finance Ministry also announced that it would reduce the French government's stake in Renault from 44% to 25% through a public offering. The two deals were completed in 2002. In 2003 the French government further reduced its stake in Renault from 25% to about 15%.

Early in 2005 Renault sold its 18% stake in Nissan Diesel Motor Co. Ltd. to J.P. Morgan Securities Ltd. who in turn sold the shares on the open market.

The following year Renault called an emergency board meeting to ponder a proposal put forth in writing by billionaire General Motors investor Kirk Kerkorian (he owned about a 10% stake in GM at the time). Kerkorian suggested GM Renault and Nissan form a three-way global automotive alliance but the parties decided otherwise and announced at the Paris Auto Show in 2006 that no such alliance would be formed.

In 2005 Carlos Ghosn was appointed as CEO; he also remained as CEO with Nissan. Ghosn had been Renault's chief cost cutter since 1999. Ghosn made public his plans to revamp Renault by slashing the number of suppliers close five plants and cut its workforce by 14%. While not in the same precarious position as its North American counterparts Chrysler Ford and GM Renault's 2005 profits fell by more than 35% from the previous year and its lineup of products is growing stale.

In 2006 Renault formed a car manufacturing joint venture with India's Mahindra & Mahindra which produced the no-frills midsized Logan model sedan. In 2010 Renault sold its 49% interest in the venture to Mahindra but continued to supply key engine and transmission components. Sales of the Logan never reached expected levels and Renault stated it would rather focus on more profitable alliances in the region including its Renault-Nissan alliance.

Auditors: Ernst & Young Audit

LOCATIONS

HQ: Renault S.A. (France)
13-15, quai Le Gallo, Boulogne-Billancourt, Cedex 92513
Phone: (33) 1 76 84 04 04
Web: www.renault.com

HISTORICAL FINANCIALS

Company Type: Public

Income Statement FYE: December 31

	REVENUE ($ mil.)	NET INCOME ($ mil.)	NET PROFIT MARGIN	EMPLOYEES
12/14	49,902	2,297	4.6%	117,395
12/13	56,352	806	1.4%	121,807
12/12	54,395	2,335	4.3%	127,086
12/11	55,137	2,705	4.9%	128,322
12/10	52,157	4,577	8.8%	124,749
Annual Growth	(1.1%)	(15.8%)	—	(1.5%)

2014 Year-End Financials

Debt ratio: 54.5%
Return on equity: 7.9%
Cash ($ mil.): 15,190
Current ratio: 1.05
Long-term debt ($ mil.): 9,161
No. of shares (mil.): 293
Dividends
Yield: —
Payout: —
Market value ($ mil.): 21,410

	STOCK PRICE ($) FY Close	P/E High	P/E Low	PER SHARE ($) Earnings	Dividends	Book Value
12/14	73.03	25	15	8.37	0.00	101.48
12/13	80.25	79	47	2.95	0.00	107.70
12/12	55.45	15	9	8.57	0.00	109.78
12/11	35.27	16	7	9.93	0.00	106.82
12/10	56.82	8	4	17.00	0.00	101.63
Annual Growth	6.5%	—	—	(16.2%)	—	(0.0%)

Repsol S.A.

The sun shines on Repsol (formerly Repsol YPF) Spain's largest oil company. A fully integrated oil and gas company it operates in Latin America the Middle East and North Africa. Repsol operates five refineries in Spain and one in Peru and produces chemicals plastics and polymers. It sells gas under the brands Campsa Petronor and Repsol at 4500 service stations in Europe and Latin America. It is one of Spain's largest sellers of liquefied petroleum gas and liquefied natural gas. Repsol has proved reserves of 2.2 billion barrels of oil equivalent. Affiliate YPF conducts exploration production refining logistics marketing and chemicals in Argentina. Repsol also owns 30% of Gas Natural Fenosa.

Change in Company Type

In 2012 the Argentine government shocked the company when it seized control of subsidiary YPF as part of a nationalization drive.

Repsol had owned YPF Argentina's #1 oil company since 1999. However the Fernandez government took back a 51% stake in YPF. The bid reflects a growing trend towards nationalization of key industries (airlines private pension funds) that have drawn warnings from Argentina's trading partners.

Geographic ReachRepsol operates globally and has major assets primarily in Spain and Argentina. In 2011 Europe accounted for 63% of company's revenues.OperationsRepsol upstream's division is engaged in oil and natural gas exploration and production activities based on key traditional regions located in Latin America (mainly Trinidad and Tobago Peru Venezuela Bolivia Colombia and Ecuador) and in North Africa (Algeria and Libya). Strategic areas for short and medium-term growth include the US Gulf of Mexico and offshore fields in Brazil.The company's LNG activities include the liquefaction transportation marketing and regasification of liquefied natural gas in addition to electricity generation activities in Spain at the Bahía de Bizkaia Electricidad plan and natural gas marketing in North America.Repsol's downstream business includes the supply and trading of crude and other products oil refining marketing of oil products and LPG and the production and marketing of chemicals.

Financial Performance

Higher oil prices and increased demand lifted Repsol's revenues by 6% in 2011. Net income decreased by 53% in 2011 due to the impact on revenues of the depreciation of the dollar against the euro and increase in personnel expense.

Strategy

Repsol plans to invest more than 21 billion (more than $26 billion) over the next few years in its operations particularly in exploration and production including its Spanish refineries which will receive an investment of about 4 billion (more than $4 billion).

To raise cash and to rebalance its global portfolio in 2011 Repsol sold about 4% of its stake in YPF to Lazard Asset Management for $639 million.Repsol created the New Energies Business Unit in 2010 assigned to the Downstream Division to promote and new cleaner energy initiatives to reduce carbon dioxide emissions.Mergers and AcquisitionsGrowing its operations in 2015 Repsol acquired Canada-based Talisman Energy for $8.3 billion plus debt.

HISTORY

Repsol officially created in 1987 is actually the result of efforts that began as early as the 1920s to organize Spain's fragmented energy industry.

Following an era of dependency on foreign investment prior to and during Francisco Franco's dictatorship (1939-75) Spain began reorganizing its energy industry. In 1979 it set up the Instituto Nacional de Hidrocarburos which in 1981 incorporated all public-sector firms involved in gas and oil under one government agency.

Repsol was formed six years later to provide central management to a Spanish oil company that could compete in the unified European market. The government chose the name Repsol after a well-known brand of Spanish lubricant products. The firm was charged with pursuing a global strategy to bring together all levels of the industry.

In 1989 Repsol offered 26% of the firm on the Madrid and New York stock exchanges raising more than $1 billion. That year Repsol increased its marine fleet with the purchase of the Naviera Vizcaina shipping company and bought Carless Refining & Marketing a UK business with a chain of 500 service stations operating mainly under the Anglo brand. Although Spain was opening its doors to foreign investment the Spanish government maintained control over the country's energy industry including a tightly guarded distribution network under state-controlled Campsa. Campsa oversaw a marketing/logistics system of pipelines storage terminals and sales outlets.

The European Community demanded that Spain open its markets to other EC members forcing Campsa in 1991 to divide its 3800 gasoline stations among its four major shareholders: Cepsa (Spain's largest private refiner) Petromed Ertoil and Repsol. Repsol gained 66% of the logistical network and use of the Campsa brand name.

Repsol and Spanish bank La Caixa merged their interests in natural gas in 1992 to create Gas Natural a new gas distributor. That year the Spanish government began reducing its majority holding and by 1996 its stake had dwindled to 10%. (It sold its remaining stock in 1997.)

Expanding its South American operations Repsol acquired control of Argentinian oil company Astra CAPSA and a Peruvian oil refinery in 1996. That year Repsol purchased a 30% stake in the Tin Fouye Tabankort field in Algeria.

In 1999 Repsol paid $2 billion for a 15% stake in giant oil company YPF which was auctioned off by Argentina's government. After acquiring another 83% of YPF for $13.2 billion Repsol changed its name to Repsol YPF. To help pay down debt incurred in the acquisition Repsol YPF sold its UK North Sea oil and gas operations to US independent Kerr-McGee for $555 million in 2000. That year the company (as part of its commitment to Argentina's government after acquiring YPF) agreed to swap some of its Argentine refining and marketing assets for Brazilian oil and gas operations owned by Petrobras.

In 2002 Repsol YPF sold oil and gas assets in Indonesia to CNOOC for about $585 million. Former chairman of Spain's top gas supplier Gas Natural S.A. Antonio Brufau replaced Alfonso Cortina de Alcocer in 2004 as chairman of Repsol.

In 2006 the company acquired BP's 28% stake in the Shenzi field in the Gulf of Mexico. The next year Repsol YPF began selling minority stakes in YPF to generate cash to support the Argentine company's growth.

EXECUTIVES

Executive Director Strategy Control and Resources, Pedro Fern ˜ndez Frial
Executive Director Commercial Chemicals and Gas and Power, Nemesio Fern ˜ndez-Cuesta Luca de Tena
CFO, Miguel Mart nez San Mart n
Executive Director Exploration and Production, Luis Cabra, age 58
CEO; Executive Director; Member Executive Committee, Josu Jon Imaz San Miguel, age 51
Chairman, Antonio Brufau Niubo
First Vice Chairman, Isidro Faine Casas
Second Vice Chairman, Manuel Manrique Cecilia
Auditors: DELOITTE, S.L.

LOCATIONS

HQ: Repsol S.A.
Mendez Alvaro, 44, Madrid 28045
Phone: (34) 91 75 38 100 **Fax:** (34) 902 303 145
Web: www.repsol.com

PRODUCTS/OPERATIONS

2011 Sales

	% of total
Downstream	63
YPF	17
Gas Natural Fenosa	10
Upstream	6
LNG	4
Corporate	
Total	**100**

COMPETITORS

Anadarko Petroleum
BHP Billiton
BP
Devon Energy
Endesa S.A.
Eni
Exxon Mobil
IBERDROLA
Imperial Oil
Koch Industries Inc.
Marathon Oil
Murphy Oil
Noble Energy
Norsk Hydro ASA
Occidental Petroleum
PEMEX
PETROBRAS
Petrobras Argentina
Petrleos de Venezuela
Pioneer Natural Resources
RasGas
Royal Dutch Shell
TOTAL

HISTORICAL FINANCIALS

Company Type: Public

Income Statement FYE: December 31

	REVENUE ($ mil.)	NET INCOME ($ mil.)	NET PROFIT MARGIN	EMPLOYEES
12/14	55,448	1,959	3.5%	24,289
12/13	76,433	268	0.4%	30,296
12/12	77,152	2,715	3.5%	29,985
12/11	80,848	2,836	3.5%	46,575
12/10	75,018	6,280	8.4%	43,298
Annual Growth	(7.3%)	(25.3%)	—	(13.5%)

2014 Year-End Financials

Debt ratio: 27.4%
Return on equity: 5.8%
Cash ($ mil.): 5,637
Current ratio: 1.66
Long-term debt ($ mil.): 9,252
No. of shares (mil.): 1,350
Dividends
Yield: 11.1%
Payout: 339.2%
Market value ($ mil.): 25,088

	STOCK PRICE ($) FY Close	P/E High/Low	PER SHARE ($) Earnings	Dividends	Book Value
12/14	18.58	22 16	1.42	2.07	25.15
12/13	25.29	182138	0.21	1.01	28.79
12/12	20.90	19 9	2.24	1.29	29.51
12/11	30.51	18 13	2.33	1.11	27.71
12/10	27.94	8 5	5.14	0.93	26.46
Annual Growth	(9.7%)	— —	(27.5%)	22.1%	(1.3%)

Resona Holdings Inc Osaka

Resona Holdings resonate in Japan's retail banking market. It's the holding company of Resona Bank and smaller regional banks Kinki Osaka Bank and Saitama Resona Bank which operate nearly 1450 branches across Japan mainly in the greater Tokyo area and the Kansai region. While it focuses on consumer and small business banking services Resona Bank also provides corporate pension management and real estate services corporate and personal trust services personal loans asset management and estate planning services. Altogether Resona Holdings boasts over ¥45 trillion ($375 billion) in total assets and ¥24 trillion ($20 billion) in trust assets.

OperationsResona Holdings operates three core business segments: Consumer Banking which provides consumer loans asset management and asset succession services; Corporate Banking which provides corporate loans trust asset management real estate services corporate pension management and asset succession services; and Market Trading which provides short-term lending borrowing bond purchase and sale and derivatives trading in financial markets.About 54% of its total revenue came from interest income in fiscal 2015 (ended March 31) while 23% came from non-trust fees and commissions and 3% came from trust fees. About 85% of its total loans and bills discounted were loans to small and medium-sized enterprises (SMEs). More than 60% of its deposits were from individuals.Geographic ReachTokyo-based Resona Holdings has more than 1440 branches across Japan including more than 820 in the Kanto region and 579 in the Kansai region. Its Kinki Osaka Bank subsidiary has 128 manned branches mainly in the Kinki region. About 40% of its branches are manned while the majority are unmanned.Financial PerformanceNote: Growth rates may differ after conversion to US dollars.Resona Holdings' revenues and profits have trended lower over the past several years mostly due to shrinking interest margins on loans amidst the low-interest environment.The company had a breakout year in fiscal 2015 (ended March 31) however as its revenue rose by 4% to ¥861.4 billion ($7.2 billion) on higher fee and commission income from sales of its investment trust and insurance products. Its interest income continued to slide downward due to low interest margins.Despite generating higher revenue in FY2015 the group's net income fell by 4% to ¥211.4 billion ($1.77 billion) mostly due to higher income taxes and a ¥23 billion charge related to the reversal of deferred tax assets in line with the reduction of the effective corporate tax rate. Resona's operating cash levels fell in half to ¥1103 billion ($9 billion) for the year mostly as it extended more of its cash toward loans and bills discounted.

Stategy

Resona Holdings in early 2015 launched its "New Mid-term Management Plan" for the next decade which set its sights on becoming the "No. 1 Retail Bank" through more proactive measures toward continued growth. Continuing to focus on its retail banking business and lending to SMEs the bank planned to "maximize customer value by maintaining its fundamental stance that 'Customers' joy and happiness are Resona's.' The company also in 2015 outlined its three "ACL" initiatives which included: "All Resona" which aimed to offer collaboration of companies and services to provide SME customers with management consulting and other services as they grew; "Cross-selling promotion" which aimed to cross sell life insurance to the group's mortgage customers which numbered 560000 borrowers and grew by 40000 new borrowers annually; and "Low-cost operations" which rely on productivity-boosting initiatives such as installed communication terminals that allow tellers to serve customers more securely and efficiently.Resona Holdings has significant market strength in its key markets in the greater Tokyo metro area and the Kansai region (the most populated and economically active parts of Japan). During 2015 it held 40% of the deposit market in the Saitama and Osaka Prefectures and nearly 20% of the loan market in the region as well.

EXECUTIVES

Executive Officer, Kazuhiro Higashi, age 58
President Saitama Resona Bank, Masahito Kamijo
Representative Executive Officer, Toshiki Hara
Representative Executive Officer, Tetsuya Kan
President The Kinki Osaka Bank, Koji Nakamae
Auditors: Deloitte Touche Tohmatsu LLC

LOCATIONS

HQ: Resona Holdings Inc Osaka
1-5-65 Kiba, Koto-ku, Tokyo 135-0042
Phone: (81) 3 6704 3111
Web: www.resona-gr.co.jp

PRODUCTS/OPERATIONS

2014 Sales

	% of total
Interest income	57
Fees and commissions	23
Other operating income	4
Trust fees	3
Other	13
Total	**100**

Selected Subsidiaries

Daiwa Guarantee Co. Ltd. (credit guarantee)
Resona Bank Ltd. (bank)
Resona Guarantee Co. Ltd. (credit guarantee)
Saitama Resona Bank Ltd. (bank)
Kinki Osaka Shinyo Hosho Co. Ltd. (credit guarantee)
The Kinki Osaka Bank Ltd. (bank)
P.T. Bank Resona Perdania (bank)
Resona Kessai Service Co. Ltd. (collections agency)
Resona Card Co. Ltd. (credit cards)
Resona Capital Co. Ltd. (private equity)
Resona Research Institute Co. Ltd. (consulting)
Resona Business Service Co. Ltd. (staffing)

COMPETITORS

Aozora Bank
Bank of Yokohama
Chiba Bank
Chugoku Bank
Fukuoka Financial Group
Gunma Bank
Hachijuni Bank
Hokuhoku Financial Group
Iyo Bank
Joyo Bank
Juroku Bank
Mitsubishi UFJ Financial Group
Mizuho Financial
Nishi-Nippon City Bank
Shinsei Bank
Shizuoka Bank
Sumitomo Mitsui
Sumitomo Mitsui Trust Holdings
Yamaguchi Financial Group

HISTORICAL FINANCIALS

Company Type: Public

Income Statement FYE: March 31

	ASSETS ($ mil.)	NET INCOME ($ mil.)	INCOME AS % OF ASSETS	EMPLOYEES
03/15	388,288	1,762	0.5%	16,436
03/14	433,246	2,137	0.5%	16,536
03/13	458,175	2,924	0.6%	16,826
03/12	526,633	3,092	0.6%	16,881
03/11	515,742	1,933	0.4%	16,941
Annual Growth	(6.9%)	(2.3%)	—	(0.8%)

2015 Year-End Financials

Return on assets: 0.4%
Return on equity: 11.1%
Long-term debt ($ mil.): —
No. of shares (mil.): —
Sales ($ mil): 7,179
Dividends
Yield: —
Payout: —
Market value ($ mil.): —

Rewe-Zentral AG (Germany, Fed. Rep.)

REWE Group sells the fuel that Germans love best –food and drink. REWE is one of the largest food retailers in Germany (along with METRO AG ALDI and Lidl) and one of the largest in Europe overall. REWE operates some 15000 stores in about a dozen European countries (about 10000 in Germany) including Russia and Ukraine. Store formats include supermarkets (REWE) hypermarkets (toom) discount stores (Penny) drugstores (BIPA) DIY stores (toom Baumarkt) and consumer electronics stores (ProMarkt) among others. The company's other businesses include about 2100 travel agencies several tour operators and foodservice. Founded in 1927 REWE is a cooperative owned by its independent retail members.

REWE has expanded mainly through acquisitions and is targeting growth in the Czech Republic Hungary Romania and the Ukraine. REWE's Penny Market chain (with 320-plus stores) jumped into first place in the Czech discount market with the 2008 purchase of Plus stores from rival Tengelmann. Previously REWE acquired about 95 Delvita supermarkets there from Belgium's Delhaize Group in 2007. REWE is also focusing on expanding Penny Market in Romania where it operates about 100 stores. It has also opened about 20 Billa supermarkets in Russia as well as SELGROS Cash & Carry stores. Currently about 30% of the company's annual revenue is derived from international sales; REWE plans to increase this to 60% by 2015.

To better focus on its core food retailing and travel-related businesses REWE sold its 50% stake in its business-to-business cash-and-carry and foodservice activities –which came under the umbrella of transGourmet Group –to its joint venture partner Switzerland's Coop. The deal which closed in early 2011 strengthens Coop's concentration on the wholesaling business.

REWE's core food retail operations provide about 80% of the company's sales but have faced intense competition from discounters including compatriot ALDI. As a result REWE has shuttered more than 400 outlets in Germany in recent years. On the plus side the German grocery chain acquired about 120 supermarkets in southern and eastern Germany from rival METRO and more than 325 Plus locations from Tengelmann.

While food retailing represents most of REWE's revenue other sources include its leisure travel group (tour operators including ITS Reisen Jahr Reisen Tjaereborg Dertour Meier's Weltreisen and ADAC Reisen) and travel agencies (Atlas Der and Derpart).

REWE is an acronym for Revisionsverband der Westkauf-Genossenschaften or the Auditing Association of the Western Purchasing Cooperatives.

HISTORY

In 1927 17 German food wholesale companies joined forces to create the cooperative that would become REWE-Zentral. The cooperative expanded and had 64 members by 1933. In 1935 the group centralized management giving the head office in Cologne more authority over operations.

WWII caused a slowdown in business during the early 1940s. However by 1947 REWE was again in expansion mode and entered the import business. In 1950 the cooperative expanded internal operations including the addition of an advertising department. Importing became a successful venture and in 1956 the group started a freight and cargo business. The cooperative had multiple regional wholesale businesses and more than 100 members by 1960. In 1974 it added retail outlets including miniMAL Penny and Idea.

In the 1980s REWE continued retail and wholesale acquisitions throughout Germany. The group bought the food retail chains Desuma Hill Otto Mess and Supermarket Handels in 1988.

The cooperative bought Germany's Kafu supermarket chain (2500 stores) in 1992. It entered the UK the next year by purchasing a 28% stake in the Budgens convenience store chain. Also in 1993 REWE opened its first store in Poland. A year later it expanded to Slovakia and Italy. In 1995 REWE opened stores in Spain and scaled back its UK business closing 12 Penny stores and selling four others. The company bought Austria's Billa supermarket chain the following year. In 1997 REWE moved into the Czech Republic.

In 1998 REWE bought another Austrian supermarket chain but was forced to sell 20% of its stores by Austrian regulators (REWE had more than 50% of market share). The company opened stores in Romania and Croatia in 1999.

REWE opened a store in Ukraine in January 2000. In August it sold its stake in Budgens leaving the company without any operations in the UK. Also in August REWE bought parts of the LTU travel group giving it 100% of the LTU Touristik travel agency and 40% of the LTU airline. Early in 2001 REWE bought Italian supermarket chain Standa (about 120 stores in northern and central Italy and Sardinia).

In 2002 REWE sold its Billa supermarkets in Hungary to Spar Ungarn the Hungarian subsidiary of Switzerland's Aspiag Management for an undisclosed price.

To fill a gap in its international presence and reduce its exposure to the depressed German economy REWE acquired Swiss rival Bon Apptit in November 2003.

Long-serving Chief Executive Hans Reischl stepped down in April 2004 eight months ahead of schedule. He was replaced by Dieter Berninghaus who had been in charge of REWE's international business.

In May 2007 REWE acquired about 95 Delvita supermarkets in the Czech Republic from Belgium's Delhaize Group for about $128 million. Previously in mid-2005 Delvita sold its 11 stores in Slovakia to Rewe.

In December 2008 the first SELGROS Cash & Carry store opened in Russia near Moscow.

EXECUTIVES

Member Management Board, Manfred Esser, age 53
CEO, Alain Caparros, age 59
Member Management Boards REWE-Zentral AG and REWE - Zentralfinanz eG, Frank Wiemer, age 56
Member Management Board, Jan Kunath, age 50
CFO, Christian Mielsch, age 53
Member Management Board, Lionel Souque, age 44
Auditors: PricewaterhouseCoopers Aktiengesellschaft Wirtschaftpruefungsgesellschaft

LOCATIONS

HQ: Rewe-Zentral AG (Germany, Fed. Rep.)
Domstrasse 20, Cologne D-50668
Phone: (49) 221 149 0 **Fax:** (49) 221 149 9000
Web: www.rewe.de

2014 Sales

	% of total
National Full-Range Stores	40
International Full-Range Stores	20
National Discount Stores	16
International Discount Stores	9
Travel and Tourism	8
National Specialist Stores	5
Other	2
Total	**100**

2014 Stores

	No.of stores
Germany	4,801
Austria	2,095
Czech Republic	552
Italy	317
Romania	256
Hungary	197

Bulgaria	140
Croatia	131
Slovakia	128
Russia	96
Ukraine	39
Total	**8,752**

Selected Countries of Operation

Austria
Bulgaria
Croatia
Czech Republic
Germany
Hungary
Italy
Romania
Russia
Slovakia
Ukraine

COMPETITORS

A.P. Møller - Mærsk
ALDI
American Express
Auchan
Carlson Wagonlit
Carrefour
Casino Guichard
Coop
Edeka Zentrale
Guyenne et Gascogne
Kuoni Travel
Lidl
Lieken
Lufthansa
METRO AG
Maxeda
SPAR Handels
Tengelmann
Thomas Cook

HISTORICAL FINANCIALS

Company Type: Public

Income Statement FYE: December 31

	REVENUE ($ mil.)	NET INCOME ($ mil.)	NET PROFIT MARGIN	EMPLOYEES
12/14	55,024	380	0.7%	216,414
12/13	61,379	270	0.4%	214,584
12/12	57,341	121	0.2%	0
12/01	4,822	58	1.2%	186,834
12/00	4,502	30	0.7%	179,000
Annual Growth	19.6%	19.6%	—	1.4%

2014 Year-End Financials

Debt ratio: 10.1%
Return on equity: 6.4%
Cash ($ mil.): 841
Current ratio: 0.74
Long-term debt ($ mil.): 1,393
No. of shares (mil.): 1
Dividends
Yield: —
Payout: —
Market value ($ mil.): —

RHB Capital Bhd (Malaysia)

RHB Capital is the holding company for RHB Banking Group which offers retail small business and commercial banking services (through RHB Bank) and insurance securities asset management unit trusts derivatives corporate finance and underwriting (through RHB Investment Bank and RHB Insurance). The group's RHB Islamic Bank unit offers retail and commercial banking services that are sensitive to Islamic and regional laws. RHB Capital operates through more than 200 locations mainly in Malaysia but also Brunei Cambodia Hong Kong Indonesia Singapore Thailand and Vietnam. In 2013 RHB Investment Bank bought OSK Investment Bank. RHB Capital acquired and merged Kwong Yik Bank with DCB Bank in 1997.

Auditors: PricewaterhouseCoopers

LOCATIONS

HQ: RHB Capital Bhd (Malaysia)
Level 9, Tower One, RHB Centre, Jalan Tun Razak, Kuala Lumpur 50400
Phone: (60) 3 9285 2233 **Fax:** (60) 3 9281 9314
Web: www.rhb.com.my

COMPETITORS

AmBank Group
Bank of China
Bank of East Asia
CIMB Group
Hang Seng Bank
Malaysian Industrial Development Finance
Maybank

HISTORICAL FINANCIALS

Company Type: Public

Income Statement FYE: December 31

	ASSETS ($ mil.)	NET INCOME ($ mil.)	INCOME AS % OF ASSETS	EMPLOYEES
12/14	62,730	582	0.9%	16,089
12/13	58,332	558	1.0%	16,692
12/12	61,754	582	0.9%	12,154
12/11	48,088	473	1.0%	11,299
12/10	41,961	460	1.1%	11,722
Annual Growth	10.6%	6.0%	—	8.2%

2014 Year-End Financials

Return on assets: 0.9%
Return on equity: 11.4%
Long-term debt ($ mil.): —
No. of shares (mil.): —
Sales ($ mil): 2,978
Dividends
Yield: —
Payout: —
Market value ($ mil.): —

Rio Tinto Ltd

Rio Tinto is on the lookout for pay dirt. Rio Tinto Limited one of the world's largest mining operations (along with BHP Billiton and Vale) is the Australian half of dual-listed sister companies with Rio Tinto plc taking up residence in London. Although each company trades separately the two Rio Tintos operate as one business. Rio Tinto explores for a variety of commodities: bauxite coal copper diamonds gold iron ore minerals (borates and titanium dioxide) nickel and potash. Iron ore makes up about 44% of the group's sales. It also produces aluminum through its Rio Tinto Alcan unit. Most of its businesses are in Australia and North America but it is expanding its operations in China and Mongolia.

By focusing on a strategy of developing large-scale long-term mining operations and businesses Rio Tinto has tried to weather commodity prices that have dipped and risen over several years. The mining industry is affected by both oversupply and rising costs in raw materials. Like its rivals the company continues to seek acquisitions that will grow shareholder value as it cuts costs and improves productivity.

Despite a year of challenges including six fatalities at its mining sites and flooding that disrupted production in Australia Rio Tinto recorded revenues of $60.5 billion in 2011. Net income however fell about 59% –from $15.3 billion in 2010 to $6.8 billion in 2011. The company attributes an $8.9 billion impairment charge related to its aluminum assets as the cause of its precipitous fall in net earnings that year.

The company's iron ore business also contributed 78% of the group's net income in 2011. Rio Tinto is the world's second-largest supplier of iron ore which is used in steelmaking operations. Its key iron ore operations are in the Pilbara region of Western Australia and in Quebec in Canada.

In 2011 the company started trimming its aluminum operations. It placed 13 assets on the chopping block allowing Rio Tinto Alcan to focus on its high-quality tier one assets (mostly in Canada) and improve performance. The company also planned to transfer its stakes in six Australian and New Zealand operations to a new business unit Pacific Aluminium that would be managed and reported separately from Rio Tinto Alcan.

In 2011 to raise cash the company sold its talc business to Imerys for $340 million. That year Rio Tinto also increased its stake to 49% in Canada-based Ivanhoe Mines which manages the Oyu Tolgoi mine in Mongolia one of the world's largest undeveloped copper-gold projects. In 2012 it upped its holding in Ivanhoe Mines to 51% to become the majority owner. Commercial production at the mine may be delayed however because an agreement to supply electricity has not yet been reached between China and Mongolia.

In another strategic move in 2011 Rio Tinto made an all-cash offer for Canada-based uranium producer Hathor Exploration valued at $578 million after rival Cameco Corp. made a takeover bid for the company. In 2012 Rio Tinto was successful in acquiring Hathor which supplies about a fifth of the world's uranium.

In the first half of 2011 the company completed the acquisition of the Riversdale coal mine which has now been renamed Rio Tinto Coal Mozambique.

In 2012 the company began an overview of operations and announced that it may sell its diamond business. The company operates diamond mines in Canada Zimbabwe and Australia. At its Argyle mine in Australia the company unearthed a rare pink diamond in the rough in 2012. The Argyle mine is undergoing a $2.1 billion expansion and is the world's largest producer of pink diamonds. However in 2011 diamond operations made up only 2% of the company's total earnings before interest tax depreciation and amortization. Argyle's lower production also helped lead to an 86% drop in overall earnings for its diamonds unit that year.

Slimming down further in 2012 the company agreed to sell one of its noncore US operations Atlanta-based wire and cable business Alcan Cable to Kentucky-based General Cable for $185 million. General Cable makes and distributes copper aluminum and fiber-optic wire and cable products. Alcan Cable serves the energy and construction markets.

HISTORY

Rio Tinto Limited began life as the Zinc Corporation in 1905 to recover zinc from the tailings of the silver and lead mines around Australia's mineral-rich Broken Hill area. The company expanded steadily extending its operations into a wide range of mining and metallurgical activities primarily in Australia. By 1914 it had changed its name to Consolidated Zinc Corporation. The company discovered the world's largest deposit of bauxite (1955) and formed Hamersley Holdings with Kaiser Steel (1962) to mine iron ore.

Rio Tinto plc (UK) began with mining operations in Spain in 1873. It sold most of its Spanish holdings in 1954 and branched out to Australia Africa and Canada. In 1962 Rio Tinto and Australia's Consolidated Zinc merged to form RTZ. The companies merged their Australian interests as a partially owned subsidiary CRA (from Conzinc Riotinto of Australia).

In 1968 RTZ bought U.S. Borax which was built on one of the earth's few massive boron deposits. (The use of boron in cleansers was widespread in the late 19th century.) A 1927 discovery in the Mojave Desert led to development of a large boron mine. Until its Turkish mine was nationalized RTZ controlled the world's boron supply. It sold U.S. Borax's consumer products operations in 1988.

RTZ opened a large copper mine at Bougainville in Papua New Guinea in 1969. Subsidiary CRA discovered diamonds in Western Australia's Argyle region three years later. CRA then opened Australia's largest thermal-coal development at Blair Athol in 1984.

RTZ bought Kennecott Corporation in 1989 and expanded its copper operations. Kennecott had been formed by Stephen Birch and named for Robert Kennicott (a typo altered the spelling of the company's name); it had begun mining at Bingham Canyon Utah in 1904. Kennicott had died in Alaska while trying to establish an intercontinental telegraph line. Backed by J.P. Morgan and the Guggenheims Birch also built a railroad to haul the ore. Kennecott merged its railroad and mine operations in 1915. Kennecott consolidated its hold on Chile's Braden copper mine (1925) and on the Utah Copper Company (1936) and other US mines. When copper prices slumped British Petroleum's Standard Oil of Ohio subsidiary bought Kennecott (1981). In 1989 RTZ purchased British Petroleum's US mineral operations including Kennecott.

By the 1990s RTZ and CRA (by then 49%-owned by RTZ) were increasingly competing for mining rights to recently opened areas of Asia and Latin America. RTZ sold the last of its nonmining holdings (building products group) in 1993. In 1995 RTZ brought CRA into its operations. Through Kennecott RTZ purchased US coal mine operators Nerco Cordero Mining Company and Colowyo Coal Company. Also in 1995 the company acquired 13% of Freeport-McMoRan Copper & Gold (sold in 2004).

The RTZ and CRA company names were changed to Rio Tinto plc and Rio Tinto Limited respectively in 1997. Rio Tinto bought a Wyoming coal mine from Kerr-McGee for about $400 million in 1998. The next year Rio Tinto bought 80% of Kestrel (coal Australia) increased its ownership of Blair Athol from 57% to 71% and increased its stake in Comalco (aluminum) to 72%.

In 2000 CEO Leon Davis retired; his position passed to energy group executive Leigh Clifford. In a move that sparked an outcry from union officials Davis accepted a position as non-executive deputy chairman (he retired from the board in 2005). Later that year Rio Tinto acquired both North Limited and Ashton Mining. The company also bought Comalco's outstanding shares and the Peabody Group's Australian subsidiaries.

Rio Tinto sold its Norzink Zink Smelter to Outokumpu in 2001. It also increased its holdings in Queensland Alumina Coal & Allied Industries and Palabora Mining and it began developing the Hail Creek Coal Project in Australia which is based on one of the largest coking coal deposits in the world. In 2003 Rio Tinto sold its 25% stake in Minera Alumbrera (Argentina) and Peak Gold Mine (Australia) to Wheaton River Minerals for around $210 million.

Rio Tinto had owned 14% of Lihir Gold but divested its stake in the company. Prior to that decision the company had controlled Lihir and its management. In late 2005 though Rio Tinto reliquished its management rights and decided to sell its entire stake in Lihir.

Tom Albanese succeeded Clifford in 2007.

In 2007 Rio Tinto swooped in and made a successful $38 billion offer to buy Alcan then the world's #3 aluminum producer. That came not long after Alcoa #2 in the world had offered $33 billion. The deal combined Rio Tinto's own aluminum operations with Alcan's to form the new world leader Rio Tinto Alcan based in Canada. Rio Tinto's operations were located in Australia New Zealand and Africa as well as in Italy and the UK. Alcan's geographic strengths were in North America throughout Europe and in the Asia/Pacific region.

After that acquisition Rio Tinto announced a major divestment program saying it wanted to sell off $15 billion worth of assets. In early 2008 it began that program selling stakes in two North American properties to Hecla Mining and Barrick Gold. The properties had been a part of Kennecott Minerals and netted Rio Tinto about $2.5 billion. Later that year the company spun off most of its North American coal operations into a company called Cloud Peak Energy which it spun off through a public offering in 2009 using the almost $750 million it received to help recoup expenses from the purchase of Alcan. A major step in the divestment plan was taken in early 2009 when the company sold its undeveloped potash assets and a Brazilian iron ore mine to Vale for about $1.5 billion.

The company's most significant deals though have been the ones that didn't happen. In 2008 BHP Billiton approached Rio Tinto with an offer to buy its Anglo-Australian rival at a price that valued the company at nearly $150 billion. Rio Tinto's Board rejected the notion but BHP Billiton kept up its pursuit. The combination would have created the world's largest minerals company and one of the largest companies of any sort in terms of market cap. Months later though at the end of a year mired by the global economic meltdown BHP Billiton announced that the deal no longer provided value to its shareholders and called it off.

In an effort to obstruct BHP Billiton's takeover bid for Rio Tinto in 2008 Alcoa and Aluminum Corporation of China (Chinalco) had acquired 14% of Rio Tinto for $14 billion. Early the next year Chinalco stepped in with an offer to assist Rio Tinto out of a portion of its debt which was considerable. The complicated arrangement would have given Rio Tinto $19.5 billion through investments in aluminum copper and iron ore joint ventures as well as through convertible bonds. Chinalco's stake in Rio Tinto would have been raised to 19% and the Chinese company would have had the right to name two members to Rio Tinto's Board.

However the transaction —never popular with domestic investors —fell through by mid-2009. Rio Tinto instead went with a rights issue hoping to raise $15 billion and an agreed-upon joint venture with BHP Billiton that would have combined the two companies' iron ore projects in Western Australia. However that deal fell through also after German authorities ruled in 2010 that it was anti-competitive.

In late 2010 Rio Tinto made a $3.5 billion tender offer for Australian coal producer Riversdale Mining Ltd. but ran into problems convincing two large institutional shareholders to sell their stakes. Rio Tinto upped the offer to about $4 billion in early 2011 but India's Tata Steel and Brazil's CSN —which together held about 47% of Riversdale — were still not willing to part with their shares. A couple of deadline extensions and price bumps later Rio Tinto acquired both the CSN and Tata stakes to control close to 100% of Riversdale's shares.

EXECUTIVES

Chairman, Jan P. du Plessis, age 60
Group executive Organisational Resources, Hugo Bague
Chief executive Rio Tinto Alcan, Alfredo Barrios
Chief executive Diamonds and Minerals, Alan Davies
Chief executive Iron Ore, Andrew Harding
Chief executive Copper, Jean-Sebastien Jacques
Chief executive Energy, Harry Kenyon-Slaney
Group executive Technology and Innovation, Greg Lilleyman
Auditors: PricewaterhouseCoopers

LOCATIONS

HQ: Rio Tinto Ltd
120 Collins Street, Melbourne, Victoria 3000
Phone: (61) 3 9283 3333 **Fax:** (61) 3 9283 3707
Web: www.riotinto.com

2014 Sales

	% of total
Asia Pacific	
China	38
Japan	15
Australia	2
Other Asia	16
North America	
USA	13
Canada	3
Europe	
UK	1
Other Europe	9
Others	3
Total	**100**

PRODUCTS/OPERATIONS

2014 Sales

	% of total
Iron Ore	46
Aluminum	23
Copper	10
Coal	7
Industrial materials	6
Diamonds	2
Gold	2
Other	4
Total	**100**

Selected Holdings

Aluminum
- Bell Bay
- Boyne Island (59% smelting)
- Queensland Alumina Ltd. (80%)
- Tiwai Point (79% New Zealand)
- Weipa (Australia)

Iron Ore
- Hamersley Iron Pty. Ltd.
- Channar (60%)
- Marandoo mine (Pilbara Australia)
- Nammuldi
- Iron Ore Co. of Canada (59%)
- Robe River Iron Associates (53%)

Energy & Minerals
- Coal
- Bengalla (30% Australia)
- Blair Athol Coal (71%)
- Hail Creek Coal (82%)
- Hunter Valley Operations (76%)
- Kestrel (80%)
- Mt Thorley (61%)
- Warkworth (42%)
- Rio Tinto Diamonds & Minerals
- Rio Tinto Diamond (diamonds Australia Canada Zimbabwe)
- Rio Tinto Minerals (borates titanium dioxide Argentina/Australia/US)

Copper Products
- Escondida (30% Chile)
- Grasberg (40% Indonesia)
- Kennecott Utah Copper (US)
- Northparkes (80%)
- Palabora (58% South Africa)

Gold
- Barneys Canyon (US)
- Bingham Canyon (US)
- Escondida (30% Chile)
- Rawhide (51% US)

COMPETITORS

ALROSA	Glencore
ASARCO	Goldcorp
Alcoa	Grupo M©xico
Anglo American	ITOCHU
AngloGold Ashanti	Kaiser Aluminum
BHP Billiton	Marubeni
Barrick Gold	Newmont Mining
CONSOL Energy	Norsk Hydro ASA
Cliffs Natural Resources	RUSAL
	Recylex
Codelco	Southern Copper
Fortescue Metals	Teck
Freeport-McMoRan	Vale

HISTORICAL FINANCIALS

Company Type: Public

Income Statement FYE: December 31

	REVENUE ($ mil.)	NET INCOME ($ mil.)	NET PROFIT MARGIN	EMPLOYEES
12/14	47,664	6,527	13.7%	59,775
12/13	51,171	3,665	7.2%	66,331
12/12	50,967	(2,990)	—	61,305
12/11	60,537	5,826	9.6%	56,965
12/10	56,576	14,324	25.3%	69,002
Annual Growth	(4.2%)	(17.8%)	—	(3.5%)

2014 Year-End Financials

Debt ratio: 23.3%
Return on equity: 14.1%
Cash ($ mil.): 12,423
Current ratio: 1.70
Long-term debt ($ mil.): 22,535
No. of shares (mil.): 1,849
Dividends
Yield: —
Payout: —
Market value ($ mil.): —

Rio Tinto Plc

No you are not seeing double. Rio Tinto plc one of the world's largest mining operations (along with BHP Billiton and Vale) is the British half of a tandem of dual-listed companies. Rio Tinto plc's Australian counterpart is Rio Tinto Limited which has its headquarters in Melbourne. Rio Tinto explores for a variety of commodities: bauxite coal copper diamonds gold iron ore minerals (borates and titanium dioxide) nickel and potash. Iron ore makes up about 46% of the group's sales. The company also produces aluminum through its Rio Tinto Alcan unit.

Geographic Reach

The company operates in Australia and North America with significant businesses in Asia Europe Africa and South America. China is Rio Tinto's largest geographic segment accounting for 38% of 2014 revenues.

Operations

Rio Tinto engages in the exploration and mining and processing of metals and other mineral resources. Its products include aluminum copper diamonds thermal and metallurgical coal uranium gold industrial minerals (borax titanium dioxide and salt) and iron ore.

Financial Performance

In 2014 the company's net revenue decreased by 7% due to lower iron ore and energy sales as a result of lower prices. That year Rio Tinto improved its net loss to $28 million (compared to a net loss of $2.8 billion in 2013) primarily due to lower operating expenses and impairment charges and a decrease in losses on external debt.In 2014 the company's cash flow decreased by 5% due to lower taxes and lower net interest paid.

Strategy

By focusing on a strategy of developing large-scale long-life mining operations Rio Tinto has tried to weather commodity prices that have dipped and risen over several years. Rio Tinto's tight-fisted operating style while providing exceptional margins for its industry has drawn the ire of unions which have been critical of the company's employment and environmental records.

In 2014 it sold Rio Tinto Coal Mozambique to International Coal Ventures Private Limited and 50.1% of its Clermont Joint Venture to GS Coal Pty Ltd a company jointly owned by Glencore and Sumitomo.

That year the company signed an option agreement with LNG Canada (a joint venture owned by Shell Canada Energy Phoenix Energy Holdings Limited Kogas Canada LNG Ltd and Diamond LNG Canada Ltd) to buy or lease a wharf and associated land at its port facility at Kitimat British Columbia.

HISTORY

Following a tough 2009 in which the global recession depressed commodity prices Rio Tinto rebounded strongly in 2010 posting a 35% increase in overall revenues due primarily to increased sales volumes and prices generated by the beginnings of an economic recovery. Leading the pack for Rio Tinto was its Iron Ore segment which saw an increase of 91% over the previous year followed by the Copper segment with a hike of 24% and the Energy unit with 15%. Profitability soared in 2010 as net income jumped more than 184% due to lower operating costs and significant reductions in debt.

Despite its failed effort the previous year to hike its 9% stake in Rio Tinto to 19% Aluminum Corporation of China (Chinalco) formed a joint venture with Rio Tinto in 2010 to operate an iron ore project in Guinea West Africa. A Chinalco subsidiary will hold 47% of Rio Tinto's Simandou project which is expected to begin producing up to 70 million tons of ore per year by 2015.

In 2011 Rio Tinto and Chinalco teamed up again on a new joint venture that will focus on mineral exploration in China. Chinalco is seeking to find and develop domestic sources of copper coal and potash to offset the cost of importing those raw materials. Chinalco will hold a 51% interest in the joint venture Chinalco Rio Tinto Exploration with Rio Tinto holding the remaining 49%.

One of the world's largest producers of copper Rio Tinto operates the Oyu Tolgoi project in Mongolia along with Canada's Ivanhoe Mines and the Mongolian government. Vancouver-based Ivanhoe controlled one of the world's largest untapped copper and gold deposits in Mongolia and Rio Tinto expects the mine to be one of the world's top 10 copper producers as well as one of the top gold producers by 2018. In 2012 Rio Tinto upped its holding in Ivanhoe from 49% to 51% to become the majority owner.

Also in early 2012 Rio Tinto completed its offer for Canada-based uranium producer Hathor Exploration valued at $578 million after rival Cameco Corp. made a takeover bid for the company in 2011. Hathor supplies about a fifth of the world's uranium.

In 2011 the company also started slimming its aluminum operations. It placed 13 assets on the chopping block allowing Rio Tinto Alcan to focus on its high-quality tier one assets (mostly in Canada) and improve performance. The company also planned to transfer its stakes in six Australian and New Zealand operations to a new business unit Pacific Aluminium.The new unit managed and reported separately from Rio Tinto Alcan would include the company's Gove bauxite mine and alumina refinery Boyne Smelters and Gladstone Power Station Tomago smelter and Bell Bay smelter in Australia. In New Zealand it would include the New Zealand Aluminium Smelters.

For at least a while longer the company is holding on to seven noncore assets managed by Rio Tinto Alcan including operations in France Germany the UK and the US. The company is in no hurry to sell and may wait until the economy improves before divesting certain operations. Rio Tinto has tried a similar divestment strategy before. It embarked on a divestment plan in the mid-2000s with the long-term goal of turning out $15 billion from its divestments. By 2010 the company had gained more than $10 billion from the divestment program.

Rio Tinto was formed in 1972.

EXECUTIVES

Chief executive Iron Ore, Andrew Harding, age 48
Group executive Organisational Resources, Hugo Bague, age 54
Chief Executive Energy, Harry Kenyon-Slaney
Chief Executive Diamonds and Minerals, Alan Davies
Chief Executive Rio Tinto Alcan, Alfredo Barrios, age 49
Chief executive Copper, Jean-S ©astien Jacques
Group executive Technology and Innovation, Greg Lilleyman
Auditors: PricewaterhouseCoopers LLP

LOCATIONS

HQ: Rio Tinto Plc
2 Eastbourne Terrace, London W2 6LG
Phone: (44) 20 7781 2000 **Fax:** (44) 20 7781 1800
Web: www.riotinto.com

2014 Sales by Destination

	% of total
Asia	
China	38
Japan	15
Other countries	16
North America	
US	13
Canada	3
Europe	
UK	1
Other countries	9
Australia	2
Other Countries	3
Total	**100**

PRODUCTS/OPERATIONS

2014 Sales

	% of total
Iron ore	46
Aluminum	24
Copper	12
Energy	9
Diamonds & minerals	8
Other	1
Total	**100**

COMPETITORS

ALROSA	Glencore
ASARCO	Goldcorp
Alcoa	Grupo M©xico
Anglo American	ITOCHU
AngloGold Ashanti	Kaiser Aluminum
BHP Billiton	Marubeni
Barrick Gold	Newmont Mining
CONSOL Energy	Norsk Hydro ASA
Cliffs Natural Resources	Phelps Dodge
	Placer Dome
Codelco	RUSAL
DeBeers	Southern Copper
Falconbridge	Teck

Fortescue Metals
Freeport-McMoRan
Vale
WMC Resources

HISTORICAL FINANCIALS

Company Type: Public

Income Statement FYE: December 31

	REVENUE ($ mil.)	NET INCOME ($ mil.)	NET PROFIT MARGIN	EMPLOYEES
12/14	47,664	(28)	—	59,775
12/13	51,171	(2,586)	—	66,331
12/12	50,967	(14)	—	71,219
12/11	60,537	939	1.6%	67,930
12/10	56,576	860	1.5%	76,894
Annual Growth	(4.2%)	—	—	(6.1%)

2014 Year-End Financials

Debt ratio: —
Return on equity: (-0.0%)
Cash ($ mil.): 12,423
Current ratio: 1.70
Long-term debt ($ mil.): —
No. of shares (mil.): 1,414
Dividends
Yield: 4.4%
Payout: 57.6%
Market value ($ mil.): 65,136

	STOCK PRICE ($) FY Close	P/E High/Low		PER SHARE ($) Earnings	Dividends	Book Value
12/14	46.06	17	12	3.51	2.02	32.73
12/13	56.43	30	20	1.97	1.76	32.48
12/12	58.09	—	—	(1.62)	1.66	33.21
12/11	48.92	25	14	3.01	1.17	36.57
12/10	71.66	34	5	7.26	0.88	38.22
Annual Growth	(10.5%)	—	—	(16.6%)	23.0%	(3.8%)

Roche Holding Ltd.

Roche is on a medicinal roll. The company operates two segments pharmaceuticals and diagnostics and sells its products in some 190 countries. Roche's prescription drugs include cancer therapies MabThera/Rituxan and Avastin Perjeta and Kadcyla for HER2-positive breast cancer hepatitis drug Pegasys idiopathic pulmonary fibrosis drug Esbriet macular degeneration therapy Lucentis and Tamiflu which is used to prevent and treat influenza (including pandemic strains). The company markets many of its bestsellers through subsidiary Genentech and affiliate Chugai Pharmaceutical. Roche's diagnostics arm offers clinical lab supplies genetic tests diabetes monitoring supplies and point-of-care diagnostics for health care providers.

Operations

Roche's pharmaceuticals division accounts for more than three-fourths of annual revenues with oncology drugs making the largest sales contribution (77% of revenues in 2014). The smaller yet faster-growing diagnostics segment is a leading maker of in vitro clinical diagnostic tests through its professional diagnostics segment; it is also an established provider of diabetes tests and glucose monitors.

Some of Roche's pipeline products include Anti-PDL1 immunotherapy medicine for bladder cancer Lampalizumab for geographic atrophy of the eye Cobimetinib and Zelboraf for advanced melanoma and ACE910 bispecific antibody for hemophilia A.

The company treated more than 19 million patients in 2014.

Geographic Reach

The largest geographic markets for the pharma segment are the US and Western Europe. Product marketing efforts in the US are conducted through Roche's main US subsidiary Genentech which is one of the world's largest biotech companies. The company also has a solid stance in the Japanese drug market through its 61.5% stake in Chugai Pharmaceutical and it is experiencing growth in Latin America and Asia.

In the Asia/Pacific region Roche's SPHERE (Scientific Partnership for HER2Testing Excellence) program helps to improve awareness and tests and treats breast and gastric cancers. It operates in a dozen markets: Bangladesh China Hong Kong India Indonesia Korea Malaysia Myanmar the Philippines Taiwan Thailand and Vietnam.

North American operations accounted for 40% of Roche's revenues in 2014 followed by Europe (31%) and other regions.

Financial Performance

As one of the top 10 global pharmaceutical companies Roche has steadily grown its revenues and profits over the last decade. Revenue increased by just under 2% in 2014 to CHF 47.5 billion thanks to growth in both the pharmaceutical and diagnostics segments. The pharmaceutical arm grew 4% that year due to growth in its oncology and immunology portfolios particularly increased sales of its Acemtra treatment for rheumatoid arthritis and its Xolair treatment for chronic hives and asthma. The rising sales of Perjeta and Kadcycla helped offset any declines of Xeloda. The diagnostics arm grew 6% driven by growth in the professional diagnostics and molecular diagnostics operations.

Net income fell 16% to CHF 9.5 billion that year though as expenses related to R&D marketing and distribution rose. Cash flow from operations grew a modest 1% to CHF 15.8 billion due to several factors (including an increase in working capital and a decline in cash used in income tax paid).

Strategy

In order to expand its pharmaceutical product offerings and stave off revenue losses from patent expirations and other competitive pressures Roche invests heavily in internal research and development programs to expand its pipeline of small-molecule and biotechnology drug candidates. The company has about 100 drugs in clinical development stages the bulk of which aim to treat oncology cardiovascular metabolic viral inflammatory autoimmune and central nervous system disorders. In 2014 the company invested CHF 9 billion in core R&D (representing 19% of sales).

Roche also pursues acquisitions and site expansions.

The firm has also widened its R&D programs by forming partnerships with other drugmakers such as Biogen Idec and Pharmasset as well as through acquisitions. In addition to new drug formulas Roche conducts R&D programs on existing drugs to gain regulatory approval for new indications which typically helps to extend a drug's patent protection and increase sales volumes. In 2014 the company signed 55 new agreements including three acquisitions four product transactions 37 research and technology collaborations and 11 product out-licensing agreements.

In 2015 the US FDA provided 510(k) clearance for the cobas MRSA/SA test for the early detection of methicillin-resistanct Staphylococcus aureus (MRSA) and methicillin-resistant Staphylococcus aureus (SA) from nasal specimens; it also approved the cobas TaqScreen MPX test v2.0 for the detection of HIV HCV and HBV in blood and plasma donations. The prior year Roche received Breakthrough Therapy designation for three medicines (anti-PDL1 Lucentis and Esbriet). Also in 2014 the company launched a new test to determine fertility levels as well as a test to predict the likelihood of preeclampsia in pregnancy.

Not one to neglect its smaller division Roche has been aggressively adding to its diagnostic testing stable through R&D partnership and acquisition efforts. In addition to clinical and diabetes tests focus areas for the diagnostics division include tissue-based cancer diagnostics (through its Ventana Medical Systems subsidiary) life science (gene sequencing) technologies and molecular diagnostics which include personalized (or companion) tests that are used to determine the best treatment regimen for a specific patient.

In 2014 Roche signed a distribution agreement with Sigma-Aldrich for its biochemical reagents portfolio which includes cellular analysis kits.

Mergers and Acquisitions

Acquisitions are also key elements in Roche's R&D growth strategy and have expanded its pharmaceutical segment in focused therapeutic areas. For example in 2014 it acquired Seragon Pharmaceuticals out of California for $988 million; it gained rights to Seragon's portfolio of selective estrogen receptor degraders to potentially treat hormone receptor-positive cancers. It also bought Santaris Pharma out of Denmark Austria's Dutalys and California's InterMune (for $8.8 billion) adding Esbriet to its portfolio. The following year it purchased Ariosa Diagnostics a molecular diagnostics company.

In 2013 it enhanced its diagnostics business and strengthened its hematology offerings with the $220 million purchase (plus contingent payments) of Constitution Medical Investors which makes tests for blood diseases. Two years later it bought a controlling stake in Foundation Medicine which makes the FoundationOne cancer test for just over $1 billion. It also acquired Genia Technologies (California) which is developing a single-molecule semiconductor-based DNA sequencing platform; IQuum (Massachusetts) developer of the Laboratory-in-a-tube or Liat system; and Bina Technologies (California) which provides Roche with a big data platform for centralized management and processing of next-generation sequencing data.

The company also announced plans to buy private French company Trophos which makes olesoxime (an experimental treatment for spinal muscular atrophy a debilitating genetic neuromuscular disease) for an upfront payment of 120 million ($140 million) plus further payments up to 350 million.

Ownership

Descendants of the founding Hoffmann and Oeri families own about half of Roche. In addition fellow Swiss drugmaker Novartis owns 33% of the company.

HISTORY

Fritz Hoffmann-La Roche backed by family wealth began making pharmaceuticals in a lab in Basel Switzerland in 1894. At the time drug compounds were mixed at pharmacies and lacked uniformity. Hoffmann was not a chemist but saw the potential for mass-produced standardized branded drugs.

By WWI Hoffman had become successful selling Thiocal (cough medicine) Digalen (digitalis extract) and other products on four continents. During the war the Bolsheviks seized the firm's St. Petersburg Russia facility and its Warsaw plant was almost destroyed. Devastated Hoffmann sold company shares outside the family in 1919 and died in 1920.

As WWII loomed Roche divided its holdings between F. Hoffman-La Roche and Sapac which held many of Roche's foreign operations. US operations became more important during the war. Roche synthesized vitamins C A and E (eventually becoming the world's top vitamin maker) and built plants and research centers worldwide.

Roche continued to develop such successful products as tranquilizers Librium (1960) and Valium (1963) –the world's best-selling prescription drug prior to anti-ulcer successors Tagamet (SmithKline Beecham now part of GlaxoSmithKline) and Prilosec (AstraZeneca). Roche made its first fragrance and flavor buy Givaudan in 1963.

In the 1970s after several governments accused it of price-gouging on Librium and Valium Roche agreed to price restraints. The company was fined for vitamin price-fixing in 1976. It was also rapped that year for its slow response to an Italian factory dioxin leak that killed thousands of animals and forced hundreds of families to evacuate.

Roche became one of the first drugmakers to sell another's products when it agreed to sell Glaxo's Zantac ulcer treatment in the US in 1982. The move let Roche maintain its large US sales force at the time when Valium went off patent decimating the company's drug sales.

Roche acquired a product pipeline when it bought a majority stake in genetic engineering firm Genentech in 1990. In 1994 it bought the struggling Syntex solidifying its position in North America. The company gained Aleve and other products in 1996 when it bought out its joint venture with Procter & Gamble and also acquired Cincinnati-based flavors and fragrances firm Tastemaker.

In its biggest acquisition ever Roche bought Corange in 1998 for $10.2 billion; its subsidiary Boehringer Mannheim was renamed Roche Molecular Biochemicals. In 1999 Roche announced it had located the gene that causes osteoarthritis. The company began to market anti-obesity pharmaceutical Xenical in the US that year despite reports of some unpleasant side effects.

EXECUTIVES

Chairman and CEO Chugai, Osamu Nagayama, age 68
Head Genentech Research and Early Development, Richard Scheller, age 62
Chief Financial and IT Officer, Alan Hippe, age 48
Head of Human Resources Roche Diagnostics, Silvia Ayyoubi, age 62, $725,004 total compensation
CEO, Severin Schwan, age 48, $2,875,002 total compensation
COO Pharmaceuticals, Daniel O'Day, age 51
COO Diagnostics, Roland Diggelmann
Head Roche Partnering, Sophie Kornowski-Bonnet
Head Pharma Research and Early Development, John C. Reed
Chairman, Christoph Franz, age 55
Vice Chairman, Andr ©Hoffman, age 57
Auditors: KPMG AG

LOCATIONS

HQ: Roche Holding Ltd.
Grenzacherstrasse 124, Basel CH-4070
Phone: (41) 61 688 1111 **Fax:** (41) 61 691 93 91
Web: www.roche.com

2014 Sales

	% of total
North America	40
Europe	31
Asia	19
Latin America	7
Africa Australia & Oceania	3
Total	**100**

PRODUCTS/OPERATIONS

2014 Sales

	% of total
Pharmaceuticals	
Oncology	48
Immunology	11
Infectious disease	7
Ophthalmology	3
Neuroscience	1
Other	7
Diagnostics	23
Total	**100**

Selected Products

Top 20 Products (listed alphabetically)
- Actemra/RoActemra (rheumatoid arthritis)
- Activase/TNKase (cardiovascular)
- Avastin (colorectal cancer non-small cell lung cancer breast cancer kidney cancer)
- Bonviva/Boniva (osteoporosis)
- CellCept (transplantation)
- Herceptin (HER2-positive breast cancer)
- Lucentis (wet age-related macular degeneration diabetic macular edema)
- MabThera/Rituxan (non-Hodgkin' s lymphoma rheumatoid arthritis chronic lymphocytic leukemia)
- Madopar (Parkinson' s disease restless leg syndrome)
- Mircera (predialysis)
- NeoRecormon/Epogen (anemia oncology)
- Neutrogin/Neupogen (neutropenia associated with chemotherapy)
- Nutropin (growth hormone deficiency)
- Pegasys (hepatitis B and C)
- Pulmozyme (cystic fibrosis)
- Tamiflu (treatment and prevention of influenza)
- Tarceva (advanced non-small cell lung cancer advanced pancreatic cancer)
- Valcyte/Cymevene (cytomegalovirus infection)
- Xeloda (colorectal cancer breast cancer colon cancer)
- Xolair (asthma)

Other Products
- Anaprox (pain fever and inflammation)
- Bactrim (anti-infective)
- Bondronat (bone disease in breast cancer patients)
- Dilatrend (hypertension)
- Dormicum (sedation)
- Erivedge (basal cell carcinoma)
- Fuzeon (HIV)
- Invirase (HIV)
- Kytril (nausea and vomiting induced by chemotherapy or radiation therapy)
- Lariam (malaria)
- Perjeta (breast cancer)
- Roaccutane/Accutane (acne)
- Rocaltrol/Calcitriol (osteoporosis)
- Rocephin (bacterial infections)
- Roferon-A (hepatitis C hairy cell leukemia AIDS-related Kaposi' s sarcoma)
- Toradol (acute pain)
- Valium (anxiety disorders)
- Vesanoid (leukemia)
- Viracept (HIV)
- Xenical (weight loss weight control)
- Zelboraf (metastatic melanoma)
- Zenapax (transplant rejection)

Selected Acquisitions

COMPETITORS

Abbott Labs
Allergan plc
Amgen
Astellas
AstraZeneca
Bayer AG
Becton Dickinson
Biogen
Bristol-Myers Squibb
Eisai
Eli Lilly
Gilead Sciences
GlaxoSmithKline
Johnson & Johnson
Merck
Merck KGaA
Novartis
Pfizer
Ranbaxy Laboratories
Sanofi
Siemens Healthcare Diagnostics
Takeda Pharmaceutical
Teva

HISTORICAL FINANCIALS

Company Type: Public

Income Statement

FYE: December 31

	REVENUE ($ mil.)	NET INCOME ($ mil.)	NET PROFIT MARGIN	EMPLOYEES
12/14	50,411	9,434	18.7%	88,509
12/13	54,555	12,528	23.0%	85,080
12/12	51,755	10,405	20.1%	82,089
12/11	46,889	9,930	21.2%	80,129
12/10	52,540	9,260	17.6%	80,653
Annual Growth	(1.0%)	0.5%	—	2.4%

2014 Year-End Financials

Debt ratio: 34.3%
Return on equity: 48.0%
Cash ($ mil.): 3,782
Current ratio: 1.35
Long-term debt ($ mil.): 19,558
No. of shares (mil.): 160
Dividends
Yield: 3.2%
Payout: 9.1%
Market value ($ mil.): 5,438

	STOCK PRICE ($) FY Close	P/E High	P/E Low	PER SHARE ($) Earnings	Dividends	Book Value
12/14	33.99	6	3	10.93	1.11	123.75
12/13	70.20	5	4	14.51	0.97	135.33
12/12	50.50	5	4	12.17	0.92	98.82
12/11	42.55	4	3	11.67	0.87	80.49
12/10	36.65	5	3	10.80	0.70	63.24
Annual Growth	(1.9%)	—	—	0.3%	12.4%	18.3%

Rolls Royce Holdings Plc

Rolls-Royce Holdings doesn't make cars so luxurious you'll cry (see Motor Cars) but it sure can make an aircraft engine whine. One of the world's largest aircraft engine makers Rolls-Royce through its Civil and Defense Aerospace businesses makes commercial and military engines for a broad customer base including airlines corporate and utility aircraft and helicopter operators and armed forces around the world. Beyond aviation its Energy unit supplies gas turbine power generation to the oil and gas industry while its Marine segment makes propulsion systems that power 70 navies worldwide. Rolls-Royce has operations in North America Europe and Asia with an emerging presence in the Middle East.

The company supports its geographic markets with manufacturing and service facilities in 50 countries and recent expansion includes construction of a manufacturing and assembly facility in the US (Crosspointe Virginia) as well as an assembly and manufacturing plant in Singapore. The company which addresses four global markets –Civil Aerospace Defense Aerospace Marine and Energy (including nuclear) –keeps its business plans long-term. The lifecycle of Rolls-Royce's products and services averages 40 to 50 years so the company bases its investments in technology programs on forecasts of up to 20 years. Its performance is best viewed by decades rather than individual years. With that in mind the company was nonplussed by the lack of sales growth in 2011 and continues to follow a strategy it has had in place for years that includes investing in technology and infrastructure; growing market share and installed product base; and adding value with product related services.

This strategy has resulted in a company that shelters itself through diversity. The company achieves diversity not only in its regional markets but also in its balanced offering of products and services as well as its product portfolio and the diverse end-markets that it serves. The different geographies product selections and customers mitigate for one another in the event of a market swing. After recognizing a marked increase in revenue from its engine aftercare services the company has boosted its offerings to include aftermarket repair and overhaul as well as field maintenance and fleet data management. All these factors along with its cost savings measures and operational improvements allow the company to forecast its revenue as doubling in a decade (by organic growth alone).

Consistent investments in research and development as well as the occasional acquisition represent part of the company's strategy in action. In early 2011 Rolls-Royce together with Daimler announced plans to acquire Tognum a German engine and powertrain supplier for distributed power generation and marine propulsion markets. This follows the company's strategy to increase market share for its marine products. With a 95% stake in Tognum the two companies can further develop the business jointly. The sizeable hold gives the companies rights to Tognum's intellectual property in the form of patents.

In 2010 subsidiary Rolls-Royce Marine bought Norwegian engineering firm ODIM ASA. The purchase added automated handling systems for seismic and offshore drilling vessels that complement Rolls-Royce's ship design and power systems for the offshore drilling industry. Outside of Norway ODIM has operations in Canada Singapore and Vietnam.

The company's Marine business also boasts an extensive range of products and services from ship design to power systems and controls to aftermarket support services. It is benefitting from defense contracts in the US and the UK where its engines power US Marine Corps and Royal Navy ships respectively. Rolls-Royce's merchant marine operations are headquartered in Shanghai taking strategic advantage of its proximity to the shipbuilding centers of China Japan and Korea –these countries when combined account for a majority of the world's commercial shipbuilding.

These actions come as no surprise after the civil aerospace sector took a beating during the economic crisis and with a recovery slow to materialize. Despite the difficult conditions some regions are showing promise. For example: the Middle East signed a long-term services contract with Emirates Airline (part of The Emirates Group) for more than $2 billion. Singapore Airlines made its $1 billion order for Trent 700 engines in mid-2011 around the same time that Brazil's TAM air carrier signed a contract valued at more than $2 billion for Trent XWB engines. Rolls-Royce engines power some 30 types of civil aircraft from small executive jets to large passenger aircraft. Several of the company's customers saw their aircraft take flight in 2009. Those aircraft powered by Rolls-Royce engines included the Boeing 787 Dreamliner Gulfstream G650 Airbus A400M Embraer Legacy 650. The company also signed an exclusive deal to power the Airbus 350-1000 aircraft.

On the defense side Rolls-Royce commands approximately one-quarter of the world's military engine manufacturing market share. Its portfolio covers all major sectors – combat helicopters unmanned and tactical aircraft training and transport. While the defense budgets for the US and UK have called for funding cuts to certain projects the US government approved funding for the F-35 Joint Strike Fighter so that Rolls-Royce can move ahead in collaboration with General Electric to develop the F136 engine for that aircraft.

Rolls-Royce's Energy (including nuclear) business holds a global position as a leading supplier of power and compression equipment such as industrial gas turbines to the oil and gas industry especially to offshore oil rigs and platforms. With a plan to expand its civil nuclear power generation activities the company established a civil nuclear business unit in 2009 and will build a factory in the UK to assemble test systems and components for nuclear power stations. While Rolls-Royce's traditional markets are showing weak demand emerging economies such as India and Venezuela are showing opportunities for long-term growth for the company's gas turbines and reciprocating engines.

Although Rolls-Royce shares its name with the luxury car the two parted ways when the British government split them in 1971. Since 1996 Sir John Rose has been the driving force behind Rolls-Royce's transformation increasing revenues more than three-fold. He retired in spring 2011 and is succeeded by another John –John F. Rishton –former finance director at British Airways and chief executive of Royal Ahold a Dutch retailer. Rishton began in a non-executive director role at Rolls-Royce in 2007.

HISTORY

In 1906 automobile and aviation enthusiast Charles Rolls and engineer Henry Royce unveiled the Silver Ghost an automobile that earned Rolls-Royce a reputation as maker of the best car in the world.

A year after Rolls' 1910 death in a biplane crash Royce suffered a breakdown. From his home Royce continued to design Rolls-Royce engines such as the Eagle its first aircraft engine in 1914 and other engines used to power airplanes during WWI –but management of the company fell to Claude Johnson who remained chief executive until 1926.

Although the company returned primarily to making cars after WWI its engines were used in several history-making flights and in 1931 set world speed records for land sea and air. Rolls-Royce bought the Bentley Motor Company that year. In 1933 it introduced the Merlin engine which powered the Spitfire Hurricane and Mustang fighters of WWII. Rolls-Royce began designing a jet engine in 1938 and over the years it pioneered the turboprop engine turbofan and vertical takeoff engine.

Realizing that it had to break into the lucrative US airliner market to stay alive Rolls-Royce bought its main British competitor Bristol-Siddley Engines in 1966. With Bristol-Siddley came its contract to build the engine for the Anglo-French Concorde in 1976 and a US presence.

Lockheed ordered the company's RB211 engine for its TriStar in 1968 but Rolls-Royce underestimated the project's technical and financial challenges and entered bankruptcy in 1971. The British government stepped in and nationalized the aerospace division and sold the auto group. The RB211 entered service on the TriStar in 1972 and on the Boeing 747 in 1977.

Rolls-Royce was reprivatized in 1987. In a diversification effort two years later the company bought mining marine and power plant specialist Northern Engineering Industries. In the early 1990s the aerospace market was hurt by military spending cutbacks and a recession; the company cut more than 18000 jobs.

A joint venture with BMW launched the BR710 engine for Gulfstream and Canadair's long-range business jets in 1990. The company bought Allison Engine in 1995.

Rolls-Royce sold Parsons Power Generation Systems to Siemens in 1997. Also that year it won a contract to supply Trent 892 engines for Boeing 777 jets being built for American Airlines (a subsidiary of AMR Corporation) in a deal worth $1 billion.

In 1998 the British government approved a repayable investment of about $335 million in the company to develop a new model of Trent aircraft engines. Narrowing its focus the company sold its power transmission and distribution business to Austria-based VA Technologie.

Rolls-Royce pumped up its gas and oil equipment business in 1999 by buying the rotating compression equipment unit of Cooper Cameron (now Cameron International); it became one of the world leaders in marine propulsion by acquiring Vickers. The company then bought the aero and industrial engine repair service of First Aviation Services and took full control of its aircraft-engine joint venture with BMW; in return BMW received a 10% stake in Rolls.

In 2000 subsidiary Rolls-Royce Energy Systems India Private was awarded its first order: producing a Bergen gas engine for Garden Silk Mills for powering a textile plant in India. That year Rolls-Royce won a contract to supply engines for Israel's El Al airline's Boeing 777s. Late in 2000 it was reported that the company would cut about 5000 jobs over three years.

Early in 2001 Rolls-Royce sold most of its Vickers Turbine Components business. In October the company cut about 11% of its workforce in response to the worldwide crisis in the commercial jet business.

In 2002 the company announced that it had inked a 10-year $2 billion deal to supply engines to Gulfstream Aerospace. That year Rolls-Royce sold its Vickers Defence Systems unit which made tanks and armored vehicles to Alvis Plc. In 2003 Sir Ralph Robins who had been executive chairman for more than a decade retired from his post.

Early in 2004 Rolls-Royce and GE Aircraft Engines were picked to supply engines for Boeing's upcoming 787 Dreamliner. Rolls-Royce was also selected to supply engines for Airbus' upcoming behemoth A380.

In late 2007 it scored one of its largest contracts a $42 million project to provide steering gear and deck machinery for Chinese shipbuilder Sinopacific.

In 2008 it entered into a joint venture with Goodrich Corporation called Aero Engine Controls to produce engine controls for Rolls-Royce aircraft. It also partnered with France's AREVA to construct the first new nuclear reactors built in the UK in more than 20 years.

In 2009 the company focused on developing four advanced manufacturing research centers in the US the UK and Singapore. Rolls-Royce invested £300 million (more than $450 million) in its UK factories as part of its almost £2 billion (over $3 billion) capital replacement plan to be carried out over a period of 10 years. That same year Rolls-Royce engines allowed the BAE Systems' Mantis UAV and AgustaWestland's Lynx Wildcat helicopter to take flight.

Rolls-Royce's nuclear market was strengthened in 2009 by its agreement with electric service provider EDF Energy (formerly known as London Electricity Group) to enter into a joint venture with EDF Energy giving support to the UK facility. The following year the company introduced its STOVL (short take-off and vertical landing) Rolls-Royce LiftSystem.

The bell of financial crisis knelled in 2008 causing the company to implement cost-cutting measures which included headcount reductions of almost 10%. The company in partnership with GE Aviation continued development of the F136 engine for the F-35 Joint Strike Fighter and its Trent 1000 engine took its first flight in the Boeing 787 Dreamliner. Also in 2008 Rolls-Royce established its civil nuclear business to tap a growing global market.

EXECUTIVES

CEO, Warren East, age 54
Group President and Director, Colin P. Smith, age 60
President Marine, Mikael Makinen
CEO Rolls-Royce Power Systems, Ulrich Dohle
CFO, David Smith
President Civil Aerospace, Eric Schulz
President Defence, Chris Cholerton
President Nuclear, Harry Holt
Chairman, Ian E. L. Davis, age 64
Auditors: KPMG LLP

LOCATIONS

HQ: Rolls Royce Holdings Plc
62 Buckingham Gate, London SW1E 6AT
Phone: (44) 20 7222 9020 **Fax:** (44) 20 7227 9170
Web: www.rolls-royce.com

2014

	%
UK	12
USA	27
China	9
Germany	5
Rest of the World	46
Total	**100**

PRODUCTS/OPERATIONS

2014 Sales (by market)

	% of total
Civil aerospace	46
Defense	14
Power Systems	18
Marine	12
Nuclear & Energy	10
Total	**100**

Selected Products and Services

Aircraft engines
Automation and control equipment
Bearings and seals
Diesel and gas turbine engines
Electric propulsion systems
Engine support services
Helicopter engines
Fuel cells
Generators
Offshore drilling equipment
Overhaul and repair services
Ship designs
Technical publications
Training

Selected Subsidiaries

Civil aerospace
Optimized Systems and Solutions Limited (OSyS) (advanced controls and predictive data management)
Rolls-Royce Leasing Limited (engine leasing)
Rolls-Royce Total Care Services Limited (aftermarket support services)
Corporate
Rolls-Royce International Limited (international support and commercial information services)
Rolls-Royce Power Engineering plc (power generation and marine systems)
Energy
Rolls-Royce Fuel Cell Systems Limited (fuel cell system development)
Rolls-Royce Power Development Limited (project development)
Tidal Generation Limited (development of tidal generation systems)
Marine
ODIM ASA (offshore drilling naval and power generation equipment)
Rolls-Royce Marine Electrical Systems Limited (marine electrical systems)
Rolls-Royce Power Development Limited (generation of electricity from independent power projects)
Rolls-Royce Marine Power Operations Limited (nuclear submarine propulsion systems)
Rolls-Royce Power Engineering plc (energy and marine systems)
p>#

COMPETITORS

Emerson Electric
GE Aviation
GE Honda Aero Engines
HEICO
Honeywell Aerospace
IHI Corp.
Kawasaki Heavy Industries
McDermott
Pratt & Whitney
SAFRAN
Siemens AG
Volvo

HISTORICAL FINANCIALS

Company Type: Public

Income Statement FYE: December 31

	REVENUE ($ mil.)	NET INCOME ($ mil.)	NET PROFIT MARGIN	EMPLOYEES
12/14	21,442	107	0.5%	54,100
12/13	25,636	2,259	8.8%	55,200
12/12	19,601	3,676	18.8%	42,800
12/11	17,184	1,313	7.6%	40,400
12/10	17,211	836	4.9%	38,900
Annual Growth	5.6%	(40.1%)	—	8.6%

2014 Year-End Financials

Debt ratio: 15.8%
Return on equity: 1.1%
Cash ($ mil.): 4,467
Current ratio: 1.46
Long-term debt ($ mil.): 3,423
No. of shares (mil.): 1,882
Dividends
Yield: 2.6%
Payout: 842.3%
Market value ($ mil.): 126,486

	STOCK PRICE ($) FY Close	P/E High/Low	PER SHARE ($) Earnings	Dividends	Book Value
12/14	67.19	27431662	0.06	0.36	5.29
12/13	106.03	143100	1.20	0.31	4.93
12/12	71.79	59 48	1.96	0.28	5.24
12/11	57.73	126 93	0.70	0.25	3.73
12/10	48.68	174126	0.45	0.23	3.30
Annual Growth	8.4%	— —	(40.1%)	12.0%	12.6%

Rosneft Oil Co OJSC (Moscow)

Integrated oil giant Rosneft conducts oil and gas exploration and production activities in Siberia the Far East the North Caucasus Timan-Pechora the Volga-Urals region the Black Caspian and Azov Seas and in Kamchatka. It also has exploration projects in Algeria Kazakhstan and Turkmenistan. In 2013 the company reported proved reserves of 33 billion barrels of oil equivalent. It has seven refineries with an aggregate production of 4.9 million barrels of oil equivalent a day. Rosneft also operates shipping and pipeline companies as well as a national network of 2630 gasoline stations. The Russian government owns 75% of Rosneft.

Geographic ReachRosneft is widely engaged in exploration and production across all of Russia's major hydrocarbon regions: Western Siberia Southern and Central Russia Timan-Pechora Eastern Siberia and the Far East. In addition the company participates in several exploration projects in Kazakhstan and Algeria. Rosneft's seven major refineries have convenient locations throughout the country from the Black Sea coast to Asia and its retail network covers 41 regions of the Russian Federation. Rosneft also owns 50% of Ruhr Oel which holds stakes in four refineries in Germany.Operations

Rosneft ranks among the world's top publicly traded oil and gas companies. It is primarily engaged in exploration and production of hydrocarbons production of petroleum products and petrochemicals and marketing of refined products. The company's major exploration projects are located in Russia's most promising oil & gas regions such as Eastern Siberia the shelf of Russia's Black Caspian and Azov seas and the Russian Far East. It has a network of gas stations in 44 regions of Russia.

Financial Performance

Increased industrial demand and higher oil prices helped to lift the company's revenues by 53% in 2013. It also saw its net income increase by 51% that year.

Strategy

Rosneft's development strategy includes both increasing shareholder value and attaining the highest corporate governance standards especially in terms of transparency and responsible business management.It also seeks to grow through acquisitions of other oil companies and by partnerships as a way to gain hydrocarbon assets and industry expertise.

In 2014 Rosneft and SANORS Holding Limited (Novokuibyshevsk Petrochemical Company) signed a deal to build anew world-class petrochemical complex in the Samara region of Russia.

Mergers and Acquisitions

In 2014 Rosneft agreed to buy 49% of Petrocas Energy International Limited creating the joint venture for its activities in the South Caucasus region. Through the JV (Petrocas owns and operates high-quality storage assets in one of the main oil and oil products logistics hub in the region) Rosneft will expand its presence in the area and further diversify its supply routes options. In 2014 Rosneft and Lukoil signed deal regarding Rosneft's acquisition of 20% of National Oil Consortium LLC (NOC) boosting it holdings in NOC to 80%. The remaining 20% is owned by Gazprom Neft.

Other 2014 purchases included the Bishkek Oil Company Group a leader in the oil products market in Bishkek eight companies (part of the Weatherford group) involved in drilling operations in Russia and Venezuela and Orenburg Drilling Company (a key to the re-equipment of Rosneft's fleet of drilling units).

In a major expansion in 2013 Rosneft bought BP's 50% stake in TNK-BP (it already held 50%) in a $55 billion deal. Rosneft paid BP $17.1 billion in cash plus shares.

HISTORY

Rosneft was formed in 1993.

In 2004 Rosneft acquired YUKOS' main oil unit –Yugansk –in a controversial $9.4 billion deal. The acquisition of Yugansk (also known as Yuganskneftegaz) has been more complicated than Rosneft may have wished as questions were raised about how the deal was handled and how the transaction was funded. In 2004 the company agreed to merge with Russian energy giant Gazprom. The Yugansk acquisition threw the merger with Gazprom into disarray with Rosneft claiming that terms of the deal should be renegotiated to account for the change in value of Rosneft's assets. In addition Group Menatep (majority owner of YUKOS) called for Rosneft to repay a loan estimated at about $900 million that is secured by Yugansk assets. In response Rosneft filed an $11 billion suit against YUKOS for unpaid taxes related to Yugansk.

In 2005 Rosneft approved the deal with Gazprom though the acquisition would exclude the Yugansk assets acquired from YUKOS. After months of conflicting reports state-controlled Gazprom abandoned the deal.

In 2006 Rosneft and BP teamed up to develop energy projects in Russia's Arctic. Rosneft raised $10.4 billion in a 2006 IPO (during which BP acquired a $1 billion stake).

In a move toward becoming a global oil company in 2011 Rosneft formed a strategic alliance with BP (involving a stock swap of 5% of BP's shares for 9.5% of Rosneft's) to help fund the exploration of three blocks on the Russian Arctic continental shelf. The blocks have a production capacity on a par with the UK North Sea. However rival Russian partners at TNK-BP (BP's established Russian joint venture) objected to the proposed deal saying that have the legal right to have first choice on BP expansion activities in Russia. An arbitration tribunal in the UK supported their position. BP subsequently agreed to pursue the Rosneft deal through TNK BP. This move was unsuccessful and in May 2011 the BP/Rosneft deal fell through.

It followed this by forming a joint venture with Exxon Mobil to explore oil and gas fields in the Arctic. (This plan was stymied by US sanctions imposed in 2014).

Growing its European refinery footprint in 2011 it also acquired a 50% stake in German refinery Ruhr Oel from PDVSA for about $1.6 billion. BP owns the other 50%.

Beefing up its Russian assets in 2012 also bought 51% of NGK ITERA LLC one of the largest independent producers and traders of natural gas in Russia for RUB 7 billion (US $227 million).

EXECUTIVES

President and Director, Eduard Khudainatov, age 55
VP Finance and Economics, Pavel Fyodorov
Auditors: Ernst & Young LLC

LOCATIONS

HQ: Rosneft Oil Co OJSC (Moscow)
26/1, Sofiyskaya Embankment, Moscow 115035
Phone: (7) 499 517 88 99 **Fax:** (7) 499 517 72 35
Web: www.rosneft.com

PRODUCTS/OPERATIONS

2013 Sales

	% of total
Oil & gas	52
Petroleum products & petrochemicals	47
Support services & other revenues	1
Equity share in profits of associates & joint ventures	-
Total	**100**

COMPETITORS

Exillon Energy
Gazprom
LUKOIL
Tatneft

HISTORICAL FINANCIALS

Company Type: Public

Income Statement FYE: December 31

	REVENUE ($ mil.)	NET INCOME ($ mil.)	NET PROFIT MARGIN	EMPLOYEES
12/14	93,493	5,912	6.3%	248,900
12/13	142,824	16,582	11.6%	228,000
12/12	101,114	11,202	11.1%	166,110
12/11	84,202	9,789	11.6%	160,837
12/10	62,888	9,602	15.3%	159,771
Annual Growth	10.4%	(11.4%)	—	11.7%

2014 Year-End Financials

Debt ratio: 0.6%
Return on equity: 11.6%
Cash ($ mil.): 3,669
Current ratio: 1.05
Long-term debt ($ mil.): 37,207
No. of shares (mil.): —
Dividends
Yield: 0.0%
Payout: 37.4%
Market value ($ mil.): —

	STOCK PRICE ($) FY Close	P/E High/Low		PER SHARE ($) Earnings	Dividends	Book Value
12/14	3.60	0	0	0.56	0.21	4.60
12/13	7.85	0	0	1.61	0.31	8.97
12/12	8.85	0	0	1.19	0.10	7.93
Annual Growth	(36.2%)	—	—	(17.2%)	21.1%	(12.7%)

Royal Bank of Canada (Montreal, Quebec)

Royal Bank of Canada is Canada's #1 bank by assets and market capitalization and is a leading North American financial services company. Royal Bank of Canada and its subsidiaries operate under the brand name RBC providing a diversified set of personal and commercial banking wealth management insurance investor and wholesale banking services globally. RBC serves large and small personal business public sector and institutional clients through offices in Canada the US and about 49 other countries including the UK and other select parts of Europe and Asia/Pacific. Its 2015 acquisition of City National Corp added 75 branches to its network in the US.

Operations

The company has realigned its business segments into five units. It eliminated its International Banking segment and created a new Investor & Treasury Services segment which offers advisory custodial and financing services to safeguard assets and manage risk to institutional investors. That segment includes RBC Investor Services the largest custodian in Canada and formerly a joint venture called RBC Dexia. The company also operates a Personal & Commercial Banking segment which includes personal and business banking operations and certain investment businesses in Canada the US and the Caribbean.

Wholesale banking business Capital Markets continues to provide a full suite of products and services —including corporate and investment banking equity and debt origination and structuring and trading –to public and private companies institutional investors governments and central banks. Rounding out RBC's business segments are Wealth Management and Insurance.

Geographic Reach

Canada is RBC's largest market accounting for more than two-thirds of total revenue. The remainder of revenue is balanced between the US and other international markets (which include Europe and Asia).

Financial Performance

The company has seen stable growth in its revenues over the past few years. RNC's revenues increased by 9% in 2013 due to higher interest and non interest income. Net interest income rose due to solid volume growth of 5% across most of its businesses in the Canadian Banking segment and higher trading-related net interest income (and higher lending activity) in Capital Markets. RBC's net income increased by 8% in 2013 due to a decline in the provision for loan losses.

Strategy

With Canada generating more than two-thirds of RBC's revenue it's no surprise that the company's primary strategy in that market is to remain the undisputed leader in financial services. Other initiatives the company is undertaking to achieve its growth strategy are tightly managing costs deepening client relationships increasing price competitiveness and investing in technology.

Outside of Canada in an effort to be a leading provider of capital markets and wealth management services the company is focusing on high-net-worth corporate and institutional clients in the US the UK and key emerging markets like Hong Kong and Singapore. RBC is the sixth-largest global wealth manager by assets under management. Streamlining its operations in 2014 RBC sold RBC Royal Bank (Jamaica) Limited and RBTT Securities Jamaica Limited to Sagicor Group Jamaica Limited.

Mergers and AcquisitionsIn November 2015 RBC purchased City National Corporation along with some 75 City National Bank branches in the US (mostly in California) for a total consideration valued around $5 billion. The acquisition added $33.5 billion in assets and expanded RBC's reach into the US. Planning to make City National Corporation its American retail banking franchise RBC intended to keep the City National name on the acquired branches and promote product and service cross-selling between City National and RBC.In 2013 growing its specialty financing business RBC acquired the Canadian auto finance and deposit business of Ally Financial in a deal valued at $1.4 billion. The deal positions RBC as a leader in the Canadian auto finance business.

Diversifying its portfolio that year the bank acquired the Athena Energy Group a market leading natural gas supplier in Quebec.

Company Background

In 2012 RBC acquired the Latin American Caribbean and African private banking business of Coutts the wealth management division of Royal Bank of Scotland to increase market share with high-net-worth clients.

RBC in 2012 also shed its money-losing US retail bank operations RBC Bank (USA) and a US credit card business selling them to PNC Financial for $3.6 billion. RBC said those operations lacked the scale to accomplish what the company wanted to do in the US. RBC had also been struggling with credit losses in the US following the economic downturn.

RBC was created as Merchants Bank in 1864 and was incorporated in 1869. It changed its name to The Royal Bank of Canada in 1901 and to Royal Bank of Canada in 1990.

HISTORY

Royal Bank of Canada (RBC) has looked south of the border ever since its 1864 creation as Merchants Bank in Halifax Nova Scotia a port city bustling with trade spawned by the US Civil War.

After incorporating in 1869 as Merchants Bank of Halifax the bank added branches in eastern Canada. Merchants opened a branch in Bermuda in 1882. Gold strikes in Canada and Alaska in the late 1890s pushed it into western Canada.

Merchants opened offices in New York and Cuba in 1899 and changed its name to Royal Bank of Canada in 1901. RBC moved into new Montreal headquarters in 1907 and grew by purchasing such banks as Union Bank of Canada (1925). In 1928 it moved into the 42-story Royal Bank Building then the tallest in the British Empire.

The bank faltered during the Depression but recovered during WWII. After the war RBC financed the expanding minerals and oil and gas industries. When Castro took power in Cuba RBC tried to operate its branches under communist rule but sold out to Banco Nacional de Cuba in 1960.

RBC opened offices in the UK in 1979 and in West Germany Puerto Rico and the Bahamas in 1980. As Canada's banking rules relaxed RBC bought Dominion Securities in 1987. The US Federal Reserve approved RBC's brokerage arm for participation in stock underwriting in 1991.

The bank faced a $650 million loss in 1992 after backing the Reichmann family's Olympia & York property development company which failed under the weight of its UK projects. The next year an ever-diversifying RBC bought Royal Trustco Canada's #2 trust company and Voyageur Travel Insurance its largest retail travel insurer. A management shakeup in late 1994 ended with bank president John Cleghorn taking control of the company.

In 1995 RBC listed on the New York Stock Exchange and the next year joined with Heller Financial (an affiliate of Japan's Fuji Bank) to finance trade between Canada and Mexico. It began offering PC home banking in 1996 and Internet banking in 1997. That year RBC became one of the world's largest securities-custody service providers with its acquisition of The Bank of Nova Scotia's institutional and pension custody operations.

The company and Bank of Montreal agreed to merge in 1998 but Canadian regulators fearing the concentration of banking power seen in the US rejected the merger. In response the bank trimmed its workforce and orchestrated a sale-leaseback of its property portfolio (1999).

In the late 1990s RBC grew its online presence by purchasing the Internet banking operations of Security First Network Bank (now Security First Technologies 1998) the online trading division of Bull & Bear Group (1999) and 20% of AOL Canada (1999). It also bought several trust and fiduciary services businesses from Ernst & Young.

It acquired US mortgage bank Prism Financial and the Canadian retail credit card business of BANK ONE in 2000. RBC also sold its commercial credit portfolio to U.S. Bancorp. The company agreed to pay a substantial fine after institutional asset management subsidiary RT Capital Management came under scrutiny from the Ontario Securities Commission for alleged involvement in illegal pension-fund stock manipulation. RBC ended up selling RT Capital to UBS AG the following year.

Also in 2001 RBC made another US purchase: North Carolina's Centura Banks (now RBC Centura Banks). It sold Houston-based home lender RBC Mortgage to New Century Financial in 2005. Also that year it acquired private bank Abacus Financial which adding locations in the UK and Amsterdam.

RBC spent the decade prior to the global recession building up its US operations. The company moved into the US trust business in 2006 when it purchased American Guaranty & Trust a unit of National Life Insurance Company. In 2007 it bought the electronic brokerage business of New York boutique Carlin Financial Group. Other acquisitions made during that period include debt securities investor Access Capital Strategies energy advisory firm Richardson Barr and DC-area investment bank Ferris Baker Watts.

In 2008 RBC acquired community banks in Alabama Georgia and Florida including Alabama National BanCorporation. That same year RBC agreed to buy back some $850 million in auction-rate securities and pay the New York State attorney general's office a nearly $10 million fine. Auction-rate securities were sold to investors as a low-risk investment but as the economy worsened in 2007 and 2008 banks canceled the regular auctions rendering the securities worthless. Customers and regulators claimed that banks continued to sell them the securities even though they knew the investments had become very high risk.

Also in 2008 RBC Bank expanded its finance operations when it bought the Canadian commercial leasing business of ABN AMRO. It renamed the unit RBC Equipment Finance Group.

To cement its place among the world's 10 largest wealth managers RBC bought UK-based fixed income specialist BlueBay Asset Management for some $1.5 billion in 2010. Also that year it bought BNP Paribas Fortis' Hong Kong wealth management business.

In 2010 it also sold Liberty Life its US life insurance subsidiary that had posted losses for two years to Apollo affiliate Athene Holding. To boost brand recognition of another US unit the company changed the name of Voyageur Asset Management to RBC Global Asset Management (US).

EXECUTIVES

President and CEO, Gordon M. Nixon, age 58, $1,400,000 total compensation
Chief Administrative Officer and CFO, Janice R. Fukakusa, $587,500 total compensation
President CEO and Chairman RBC Global Asset Management, M. George Lewis
COO, Barbara G. Stymiest, $700,000 total compensation
Chief Risk Officer, Mark Hughes
Chair and CEO RBC Capital Markets; Group Head Capital Markets and Investor and Treasury Services, A. Douglas McGregor
Group Head Personal and Commercial Banking, Jennifer Tory
Group Head Technology and Operations, Bruce Ross
Chairman, Kathleen P. Taylor
Auditors: Deloitte LLP

LOCATIONS

HQ: Royal Bank of Canada (Montreal, Quebec)
Royal Bank Plaza, 200 Bay Street, Toronto, Ontario M5J 2J5
Phone: 416 974-8393 **Fax:** 416 974-3535
Web: www.rbc.com

2013 Sales

	% of total
Canada	63
US	18
Other international	19
Total	**100**

PRODUCTS/OPERATIONS

2013 Sales

	% of total
Personal & commercial banking	39
Capital markets	22
Wealth management	18
Insurance	15
Investor & treasury services	6
Total	**100**

COMPETITORS

AGF Management
BMO Financial Group
Bank of America
Barclays
CI Financial
CIBC
Caisse de d©p´t et placement du Qu©bec
Caisses centrale Desjardins
Canadian Western Bank
Central 1 Credit Union
Citigroup
Deutsche Bank
Dundee Corp.
Goldman Sachs
Great-West Lifeco
Guardian Capital Group
HSBC Bank Canada
JPMorgan Chase
Laurentian Bank
National Bank of Canada
Nomura Securities
Power Financial
Scotiabank
TD Bank
UBS

HISTORICAL FINANCIALS

Company Type: Public

Income Statement FYE: October 31

	ASSETS ($ mil.)	NET INCOME ($ mil.)	INCOME AS % OF ASSETS	EMPLOYEES
10/15	816,337	7,542	0.9%	0
10/14	840,559	7,962	0.9%	0
10/13	823,013	7,965	1.0%	0
10/12	827,347	7,462	0.9%	80,000
10/11	796,996	6,368	0.8%	74,000
Annual Growth	0.6%	4.3%	—	—

2015 Year-End Financials

Return on assets: 0.9%
Return on equity: 17.2%
Long-term debt ($ mil.): —
No. of shares (mil.): 1,442
Sales ($ mil): 32,889
Dividends
Yield: 0.0%
Payout: 45.7%
Market value ($ mil.): 82,000

	STOCK PRICE ($) FY Close	P/E High/Low		PER SHARE ($) Earnings	Dividends	Book Value
10/15	56.83	9	8	5.11	2.34	32.73
10/14	71.17	12	10	5.36	2.57	32.67
10/13	67.18	12	9	5.30	2.48	32.22
10/12	57.03	12	9	4.94	2.27	30.72
10/11	48.92	14	11	4.21	2.13	27.71
Annual Growth	3.8%	—	—	5.0%	2.3%	4.3%

Royal Bank of Scotland Group Plc

If you have overdraft protection for your checking account you can thank The Royal Bank of Scotland (RBS) which introduced the service in 1728. Today RBS is one of Europe's largest banking groups. Through subsidiaries Royal Bank of Scotland and National Westminster Bank it has the UK's largest bank network of more than 2000 branches. RBS offers private banking and insurance products through Coutts Group and Adam & Company. Other divisions include Ulster Bank which operates in Ireland and Northern Ireland; and US transaction processor RBS Lynk. After a series of bailouts in 2008 and 2009 the UK government owns 73% of RBS. RBS sold its remaining stake in US-based Citizens Financial Group in late 2015.

OperationsRBS operates three franchises and seven operating segments. Personal & Business Banking (PBB) which made up 33% of RBS' revenue in 2014 comprises the UK Personal & Business Banking segment including Williams & Glyn and Ulster Bank. It serves retail mass-affluent and small business customers (with up to £2 million in annual revenues).Commercial & Private Banking (CPB) comprises the Commercial Banking (18% of 2014 revenues) and Private Banking (6% of 2014 revenues) segments and serves commercial and mid-corporate customers and high-net worth individuals with trade and foreign exchange services as well as private banking services to business owners and entrepreneurs.Corporate & Institutional Banking (CIB) which made up 22% of 2014 revenues provides debt financing risk management and trade services for corporate and international clients mostly in the UK and Western Europe or multinational clients in the US and Asia with substantial trade and investment links in the region. The group's US-based Citizens Financial Group (CFG) which it sold in late 2015 generated 16% of its revenue in 2014 and provided retail and corporate banking services through the Citizens and Charter One brands through branches in 11 US states and offices in other states. RBS Capital Resolution (RCR) which became operational in January 2014 manages a £29 billion pool of high credit risk and troubled asset types.Geographic ReachUK-based RBS operates in Europe Asia the Middle East and North America. About 80% of its revenue came from the UK in 2014 while its business in Europe and the US contributed 9% and 7% respectively.Financial PerformanceNote: Growth rates may differ after conversion to US dollars.RBS' annual losses have been deepening over the past several years as low interest margins have been hurting the bank's top line and bad loan debt has led to elevated (and profit-eating) loan impairment provisions. Further the bank has been forced to sell off riskier loan assets to improve its loan portfolio situation which has led to shrinking loan business over the years.The group's revenue fell by 14% to £19.8 million ($30.8 million) in 2014 mostly as the bank continued to de-risk its loan portfolio and trading assets which led to a double-digit decline in interest income and a 50% dive in income from trading activities respectively. Despite lower revenue in 2014 RBS did manage to significantly cut its losses to less than £3 billion ($4.8 billion) compared to £8.5 billion ($14 billion) in 2013 as its impairment provisions on bad loan debt improved considerably thanks to its continued de-risking measures. Its cash levels also improved with operations using £20.4 billion ($31.7 billion) for the year thanks mostly to reduced losses and a smaller decrease in bank and customer deposit cash.

Stategy

RBS has structured its business "around the needs of its customers" in recent years repositioning itself in 2014 into three franchises and seven operating segments to offer a wide variety of services available for cross-sell to its customer base of two million in Scotland. The reorganized bank would "be a UK-focused retail and corporate bank with an international footprint to drive its corporate business."

Keeping its business more focused on core banking operations RBS has exited several business lines and geographic regions over the past several years. In late 2015 for example RBS sold its remaining stake in US-based Citizens Financial Group to exit its retail banking business in the US. That year it also agreed to sell its internationally-managed Private Banking and Wealth Management business to Union Bancaire Privee (UBP) including its client relationships outside the British Isles. The bank would continue serving its UK Private Banking and Wealth Management clients as well as international clients with strong ties to the UK.RBS has also worked to strengthen its balance sheet in recent years selling off riskier loan assets and freeing up resources for surer loan deals. In 2015 it sold a portfolio of US and Canadian loan commitments and certain associated derivatives as well as coverage banking debt capital markets syndicate and associated capabilities related to the loan commitments. Company BackgroundThe group was crippled by both the global financial crisis and its ambitious international expansion primarily its disastrous 2007 investment in Dutch bank ABN AMRO. In late 2008 the UK took a 60% stake in RBS but the bank still ended up reporting an annual loss of some £28 billion ($41 billion) —the largest loss in British corporate history. The government stepped in at least twice more to help RBS manage its debt and interest payments intervening with the contingency that RBS make significant efforts to get back on solid ground.

HISTORY

Company BackgroundRoyal Bank of Scotland was founded in 1727 but its roots go back to the Darien Company a merchant expedition that was established to set up a Scottish trading colony in Panama. The Darien expedition ended disastrously in 1699. In 1707 England voted to compensate Scottish creditors for the colony's failure (in part because England had promised support then reneged contributing to the collapse) and a small industry sprang up around paying creditors and loaning them money. In 1727 the Equivalent Company the combined entity of these organizations was granted a banking charter and became Royal Bank of Scotland.

In 1826 the Parliament voted to take away Scottish banks' right to issue banknotes for less than five pounds which would have required banks to use gold or silver. Few banks had such reserves and the move sparked an outcry. Novelist Sir Walter Scott's The Letters of Malachi Malagrowther which defended the Scottish one-pound note helped shoot down the proposal.

RBS expanded throughout Scotland over the next 50 years. It opened a London branch in 1874; it didn't establish a branch outside London until it bought Williams Deacon's Bank which had a branch network in North England. RBS continued to use the Williams Deacon's name as it did with Glyn Mills & Co. which it purchased in 1939.

In 1968 RBS took on its modern persona as a public company when it merged with National Commercial Bank. The company moved overseas during the 1970s establishing offices in Hong Kong and major US cities.

RBS spent the next 20 years trying to achieve another merger of the same scale as National Commercial. In 1981 the bank was wooed by Standard Chartered Bank and Hongkong and Shanghai Bank (now part of HSBC Holdings) but British regulators denied both suitors.

The bank moved into telephone operations in 1985 when it set up Direct Line for selling car insurance. In 1988 RBS bought New England bank Citizens Financial (but it plans to divest that business). In 1989 the company entered into an alliance with Banco Santander (now Santander Central Hispano) Spain's largest banking group. The alliance created a cross-pollination of ideas and strategies that boosted both banks' operations. The first fruit of the alliance came in 1991 with the launch of Interbank On-line Systems (IBOS) which connected several European banks and allowed for instantaneous money transfers.

In the 1990s RBS was linked with a variety of partners. It even made a bid for the much larger bank Barclays in a move regarded as cheeky but was rebuffed. In 1997 it announced a joint venture with Richard Branson's Virgin Group called Virgin Direct to offer personal banking. The company also bought Angel Trains Contract a rolling stock leasing company and established a transatlantic banking transfer system (similar to IBOS) with US bank CoreStates (now owned by First Union).

In 2000 RBS acquired NatWest after a prolonged takeover battle with rival Bank of Scotland (now part of HBOS plc). The bank sold Gartmore Investment Management its fund management unit to Nationwide Mutual Insurance Company. Royal Bank also sold the assets of NatWest's Equity Partners unit and launched NatWest Private Banking to target wealthy investors.

In 2004 RBS made several acquisitions to boost its US presence: It paid about $360 million for the credit card business of Connecticut-based People's Bank and bought payments processor Lynk Systems (now RBS Lynk) while Citizens Financial bought Cleveland-based bank Charter One Financial. Also that year Ulster Bank bought Ireland-based retail financial services provider First Active.

In 2007 RBS led the consortium that acquired the Dutch bank for 71 billion in a deal that was called the largest ever in the banking industry. The buyers carved ABN AMRO into pieces; RBS took the global wholesale and international retail operations in Asia Eastern Europe and the Middle East. The ambitious takeover preceded the global economic crisis though and RBS was among the hardest hit financial groups.

The troubled company made several moves to try and raise capital. Early in 2008 the company announced a £12 billion rights issue. RBS also tried but failed to find a buyer for its insurance arm. However other assets were divested that year. The company sold rolling stock leasing firm Angel Trains to Babcock & Brown and others and it sold its joint venture Tesco Personal Finance back to supermarket giant Tesco. The efforts proved inadequate though. The government took a controlling stake in the group in 2008 the same year that RBS reported the largest corporate loss in British history.

Also as part of the government rescue RBS went through a management shakeup. Fred Goodwin the architect of the bank's international expansion was removed as CEO. He was replaced by Stephen Hester formerly the CEO of British Land Company. Johnny Cameron chairman of the group's global banking and markets segment (which lost the group's most money in 2008) was also ousted and chairman Tom McKillop retired early.

RBS also shuffled its corporate structure in 2009. It split its UK retail and commercial banking division into three segments (retail commercial and wealth) and made Ulster Bank its own segment. The group folded its operations support division into other arms and established a segment to manage the selling and runoff of noncore operations. RBS retained the Global Banking & Markets Global Transaction Services US Retail & Commercial and RBS Insurance (including Churchill Insurance) segments although several of their components were transferred to the noncore segment.

RBS has scaled back on the international growth that weakened the group during the economic fallout with the ultimate goal of reducing non-UK operations to less than a quarter of its assets. In 2009 the group sold its 4% stake in Bank of China for some £1.6 billion ($2.4 billion); it also sold most of its operations in Southeast Asia to Australia and New Zealand Banking Group for about $550 million. RBS divested units in Argentina Colombia Chile the United Arab Emirates Kazakhstan and Pakistan —all assets gained as part of its ABN AMRO transaction.

With the government having to step in at least twice to bail out the bank by 2011 RBC was forced to cut costs and sell non-core operations to refocus on its core banking business. In 2010 it sold more than 300 branches and offices to Banco Santander for some £1.65 billion ($2.6 billion). RBS sold its factoring and invoice financing unit to GE

Capital and its payment services unit Global Merchant Services to Advent International and Bain Capital. It also sold its interest in RBS Sempra Commodities. In 2012 the company sold the international private banking business of Coutts to Royal Bank of Canada. Other divisions have been simply wound down and closed. RBS was ordered by the Federal Reserve in 2011 to improve its US operations or risk losing permission to do business in America. In October 2012 RBS sold a 30% stake in Direct Line Group part of its insurance group in an IPO valued at £2.6 billion ($4.2 billion).

EXECUTIVES

Chief Executive RBS Citizens Financial Group, Bruce W. Van Saun, age 57, $333,000 total compensation
Global Head Global Restructuring Group, Derek S. Sach, age 60
Chief Executive Personal and Business Banking, Les Matheson
Finance Director, Nathan Bostock, age 54
Chief Executive Retail Direct, Chris Sullivan, age 57
Executive Chairman Corporate and Institutional Banking, Donald Workman
CEO Markets, Peter Nielsen
CEO RBS Insurance, Paul Geddes, age 45
Chief Executive, Ross McEwan
CEO UK Corporate and Institutional Banking, Mark Catton
Chief Executive Commercial and Private Banking, Alison Rose
Managing Director GTS Cash, Stuart Lawson
President Dmitry Medvedev, Igor Yurgens
Co-CEO CIB, Chris Marks
Co-CEO CIB, Mark Bailie
Chief Executive Williams & Glyn, Jim Brown
Chairman RBS Scotland, Malcolm Buchanan
Chairman, Howard J. Davies, age 65
Auditors: Deloitte LLP

LOCATIONS

HQ: Royal Bank of Scotland Group Plc
RBS Gogarburn, P.O. Box 1000, Edinburgh EH12 1HQ
Phone: (44) 131 626 0000 **Fax:** (44) 131 626 3081
Web: www.rbs.com

2014 Sales

	% of total
UK	80
Rest of Europe	9
US	7
Other countries	4
Total	**100**

PRODUCTS/OPERATIONS

2014 Sales by Segment

	% of total
Personal & Business Banking	
UK Personal & Business Banking	33
Ulster Bank	5
Commercial and Private Banking	
Commercial Banking	18
Private Banking	6
Corporate and Institutional Banking	22
Citizen financial group	16
RBS Capital Resolution	—
Total	**100**

Selected Subsidiaries

Citizens Financial Group Inc. (banking US)
Coutts & Co (private banking)
Direct Line Insurance Group plc
National Westminster Bank Plc
The Royal Bank of Scotland plc
Ulster Bank Limited (Northern Ireland)

COMPETITORS

AIB	JPMorgan Chase
Bank of America	Lloyds Banking Group
Bank of Ireland	PNC Financial
Barclays	Santander UK
Citigroup	Standard Chartered
HSBC	Standard Life
ING Direct UK	permanent tsb

HISTORICAL FINANCIALS

Company Type: Public

Income Statement FYE: December 31

	ASSETS ($ mil.)	NET INCOME ($ mil.)	INCOME AS % OF ASSETS	EMPLOYEES
12/14	1,640,265	(4,840)	—	108,700
12/13	1,698,649	(14,783)	—	114,900
12/12	2,115,244	(9,600)	—	137,200
12/11	2,327,889	(3,085)	—	142,600
12/10	2,256,880	(1,717)	—	145,500
Annual Growth	(7.7%)	—	—	(7.0%)

2014 Year-End Financials

Return on assets: (-0.3%)
Return on equity: (-5.3%)
Long-term debt ($ mil.): —
No. of shares (mil.): —
Sales ($ mil): 30,980
Dividends
Yield: —
Payout: —
Market value ($ mil.): —

	STOCK PRICE ($) FY Close	P/E High/Low		PER SHARE ($) Earnings	Dividends	Book Value
12/14	12.11	—	—	(0.47)	0.00	1.56
12/13	11.33	—	—	(1.33)	0.00	1.70
12/12	10.79	—	—	(0.88)	0.00	1.92
12/11	6.37	—	—	(0.28)	0.00	10.49
12/10	12.32	—	—	(0.08)	0.00	10.66
Annual Growth	(0.4%)	—	—	—	—	(38.2%)

Royal Bank of Scotland plc

Auditors: Deloitte LLP

LOCATIONS

HQ: Royal Bank of Scotland plc
36 St Andrew Square, Edinburgh EH2 2YB
Phone: (44) 131 556 8555
Web: www.rbs.co.uk

HISTORICAL FINANCIALS

Company Type: Public

Income Statement FYE: December 31

	REVENUE ($ mil.)	NET INCOME ($ mil.)	NET PROFIT MARGIN	EMPLOYEES
12/14	28,599	(5,048)	—	84,200
12/13	41,180	(12,078)	—	106,100
12/12	40,424	(6,210)	—	111,000
12/11	42,138	(2,541)	—	113,700
12/10	47,931	(1,510)	—	113,600
Annual Growth	(12.1%)	—	—	(7.2%)

2014 Year-End Financials

Debt ratio: —
Return on equity: (-6.7%)
Cash ($ mil.): 115,489
Current ratio: —
Long-term debt ($ mil.): —
No. of shares (mil.): —
Dividends
Yield: —
Payout: —
Market value ($ mil.): —

	STOCK PRICE ($) FY Close	P/E High/Low	PER SHARE ($) Earnings	Dividends	Book Value
12/14	39.71	—	(0.00)	0.00	11.05
12/13	36.24	—	(0.00)	0.00	12.20
12/12	27.70	—	(0.00)	0.00	14.46
12/11	24.06	—	(0.00)	0.00	14.43
12/10	25.82	—	(0.00)	0.00	13.39
Annual Growth	11.4%	—	—	—	(4.7%)

Royal Dutch Shell Plc

Royal Dutch Shell which sits on an oil and gas throne higher than that of #2 oil company Exxon Mobil has worldwide proved reserves of 13.9 billion barrels of oil equivalent. Most of the oil giant's crude is produced in Nigeria Oman the UK and the US. It is also investing in the Athabasca Oil Sands Project which converts Alberta oil sands to synthetic oil. The company operates 44000 gas stations (the world's largest retail fuel network). Royal Dutch Shell also produces refined products and chemicals at more than 30 refineries transports natural gas trades gas and electricity and develops renewable energy. In a major move in 2015 the company agreed to buy BG Group for $70 billion.

Geographic Reach

The company operates around the world in more than 70 countries including in Australia Brazil Brunei Canada China Denmark Germany Malaysia the Netherlands Nigeria Norway Oman Qatar Russia the UK and the US.

Operations

Royal Dutch Shell operates in three segments: Upstream Downstream and the Corporate segment.

Through Upstream International and Upstream Americas the company explores for and produces crude oil natural gas and natural gas liquids; transports oil and gas; and operates the upstream and midstream infrastructure required to deliver oil and gas to market. Upstream International also manages liquefied natural gas (LNG) and gas-to-liquids (GTL) businesses. Upstream Americas also extracts bitumen from oil sands in Canada which is converted into synthetic crude oil.

In 2013 Royal Dutch Shell added 1.6 billion barrels of oil equivalent of gross proved reserves.The Downstream segment is engaged in the manufacturing supply distribution and marketing of oil products and chemicals; alternative energy (excluding wind); and CO2 management.Downstream accounted for about 88% and Upstream accounted for 10% of Royal Dutch Shell's total revenues in 2013.

In 2013 the company produced 3.2 million barrels of oil equivalent a day and sold about 19.6 million tons of LNG.

The segment's Supply and Distribution infrastructure has more than 1500 storage tanks and 150 distribution facilities in 25 countries. It supplies more than 100 grades of lubricants and 20 different types of fuel serving more than 15000 vessels worldwide.Royal Dutch Shell's Corporate segment manages the company's non-operating activities including Shell's holdings and treasury organization its headquarters and central functions as well as its self-insurance activities.

Financial Performance

The company's revenues declined by 5% in fiscal 2013 primarily due to lower Downstream segment sales decreased interest and lower other income received; partially offset by higher Upstream revenues.Upstream revenues rose thanks to an 1.4% increase in global oil demand driven by emerging economies. Synthetic crude oil prices posted a 7% increase while gas prices were 6% higher than in 2012. These gains were partially offset by lower liquids prices.In the Downstream segment oil products sales volumes dipped by 1% in 2012 reflecting lower marketing and trading volumes partly offset by the increased Refinery intake volumes. The drop was also caused by field declines and the impact of the challenging operating environment in Nigeria.Royal Dutch Shell's net income decreased by 38% in 2013 due to lower revenues and high depreciation charges as a result of impairments and a change in financial reporting requirements.

Strategy

The company's key strengths include the development and application of technology the financial and project-management skills to deliver large field development projects and the management of integrated value chains.

Royal Dutch Shell committed about 85% of its capital investment in 2014 to Upstream activities. It's long term strategy includes developing shale oil and gas plays and future opportunities such as heavy oil plays and new fields in the Arctic Iraq Kazakhstan and Nigeria. However plummeting oil prices led the company to exit the Arctic in 2015.

Looking to focus its onshore US drilling program on a few of the more prolific formations in an effort to boost profitability in 2014 Royal Dutch Shell agreed to sell drilling rights in shale formations in Louisiana and Wyoming for $2.1 billion in two transactions. In one of the deals the company will also receive drilling rights to land in Ohio and Pennsylvania.

To free up cash in 2015 the company sold its Norwegian retail assets. In France it sold its Butagaz LPG business to DCC Energy for EUR464 million.

In 2014 Royal Dutch Shell also agreed to sell its Australian downstream businesses to Vitol for A$2.9 billion (US$2.6 billion).

While committed to developing clean energy as a way to reduce carbon emissions Royal Dutch Shell is focusing on clean oil production technology (such as carbon sequestration) and biofuels which are more in line with its core oil and gas competencies rather than on wind power and solar energy.

Boosting its research and development capability in 2013 the company relaunched its Shell Technology Center Houston as the global base for a number of specific technology focus areas across the upstream and downstream segment. Royal Dutch Shell spends more than a billion dollars a year on research and development activities.

Expanding its Canadian oil and gas production activities in 2012 Royal Dutch Shell announced plans to ramp up production at its Athabasca Oil Sands project in Alberta and to develop shale gas and an LNG export terminal in British Columbia.

Mergers and Acquisitions

In 2014 the company acquired Repsol's LNG portfolio outside of North America including supply positions in Peru and Trinidad and Tobago for about $4 billion.

Growing its North America shale portfolio in 2012 Royal Dutch Shell acquired 618000 net acres in the Permian Basin in West Texas (with production of 26000 barrels of oil equivalent per day) from Chesapeake Energy for $2 billion.It also agreed to buy Hess' stake in the North Sea Beryl area fields and the Scottish Area Gas Evacuation System for $525 million.

In a move to expand its position as a provider of shallow water drilling services in Asia Africa and the Middle East in 2012 it formed Shell Drilling Holdings which bought 37 jackup drilling rigs one swamp barge and associated operations from Transocean for $1.05 billion.

HISTORY

In 1870 Marcus Samuel inherited an interest in his father's London trading company which imported seashells from the Far East. He expanded the business and after securing a contract for Russian oil began selling kerosene in the Far East.

Standard Oil underpriced competitors to defend its Asian markets. Samuel secretly prepared his response and in 1892 unveiled the first of a fleet of tankers. Rejecting Standard's acquisition overtures Samuel created "Shell" Transport and Trading in 1897.

Meanwhile a Dutchman Aeilko Zijlker struck oil in Sumatra and formed Royal Dutch Petroleum in 1890 to exploit the oil field. Young Henri Deterding joined the firm in 1896 and established a sales force in the Far East.

Deterding became Royal Dutch's head in 1900 amid the battle for the Asian market. In 1903 Deterding Samuel and the Rothschilds (a French banking family) created Asiatic Petroleum a marketing alliance. With Shell's non-Asian business eroding Deterding engineered a merger between Royal Dutch and Shell in 1907. Royal Dutch shareholders got 60% control; "Shell" Transport and Trading 40%.

After the 1911 Standard Oil breakup Deterding entered the US building refineries and buying producers. Shell products were available in every state by 1929. Royal Dutch/Shell joined the 1928 "As Is" cartel that fixed prices for most of two decades.

The post-WWII Royal Dutch/Shell profited from worldwide growth in oil consumption. It acquired 100% of Shell Oil its US arm in 1985 but shareholders sued maintaining Shell Oil's assets had been undervalued in the deal. They were awarded $110 million in 1990.

Management's slow response to two 1995 controversies —environmentalists' outrage over the planned sinking of an oil platform and human rights activists' criticism of Royal Dutch/Shell's role in Nigeria –spurred a major shakeup. It began moving away from its decentralized structure and adopted a new policy of corporate openness.

In 1996 Royal Dutch/Shell and Exxon (now Exxon Mobil) formed a worldwide petroleum additives venture. Shell Oil joined Texaco (now part of Chevron) in 1998 to form Equilon Enterprises combining US refining and marketing operations in the West and Midwest. Similarly Shell Oil Texaco and Saudi Arabia's Aramco combined downstream operations on the US's East and Gulf coasts as Motiva Enterprises.

In 1999 Royal Dutch/Shell and the UK's BG plc acquired a controlling stake in Comgas a unit of Companhia Energtica de São Paulo and the largest natural gas distributor in Brazil for about $1 billion.

In 2000 the company sold its coal business to UK-based mining giant Anglo American for more than $850 million. To gain a foothold in the US power marketing scene Royal Dutch/Shell formed a joint venture with construction giant Bechtel (called InterGen). The next year the company agreed to combine its German refining and marketing operations with those of RWE-DEA. Royal Dutch/Shell tried to expand its US natural gas reserves in 2001 by making a $2 billion hostile bid for Barrett Resources but the effort was withdrawn after Barrett agreed to be acquired by Williams for $2.5 billion.

In 2002 in connection with Chevron's acquisition of Texaco Royal Dutch/Shell acquired ChevronTexaco's (now Chevron) stakes in the underperforming US marketing joint ventures Equilon and Motiva. That year the company through its US Shell Oil unit acquired Pennzoil-Quaker State for $1.8 billion. Also that year Royal Dutch/Shell acquired Enterprise Oil for $5 billion plus debt. In addition it purchased RWE's 50% stake in German refining and marketing joint venture Shell & DEA Oil (for $1.35 billion).

In 2004 the group signed a $200 million exploration deal with Libya signaling its return to that country after a more than decade-long absence. Also that year the company reported that it had overestimated its reserves by 24%. The bad news resulted in the ouster of the chairman and CFO.

The Anglo-Dutch entity restructured to stay competitive. Revelations of overestimated oil reserves in 2004 prompted a push for greater transparency in the company's organizational structure. This led to the 2005 merger of former publicly traded owners Royal Dutch Petroleum and The "Shell" Transport and Trading Company into Royal Dutch Shell.

Searching for new oil assets in 2006 the company acquired a large swath of oil sands acreage in Alberta Canada. Further boosting its oil sands business in 2007 the company acquired the 22% of Shell Canada that it did not already own. The company also began investing some $12 billion (in addition to the $2.6 billion already spent) in offshore projects near Dubai. In 2008 Royal Dutch Shell expanded its exploration assets in Alaska by acquiring 275 lease blocks in the Chukchi Sea for $2.1 billion.

In 2009 the company made significant oil discoveries in the deepwater eastern Gulf of Mexico at West Boreas Vito and the Cardamom Deep and in 2010 at the Appomattox prospect in the Mississippi Canyon block. The finds expanded Shell Oil's long-term development plans in the area.

Further expanding its unconventional natural gas resources in 2010 the company spent $4.7 billion to acquire East Resources which holds 1 million acres of Marcellus Shale one of the fastest-growing shale plays in the US.

On the conventional side of the oil business the Gulf of Mexico produces 370000 barrels of oil per day or about 15% of Royal Dutch Shell's worldwide production. In 2010 the company claimed an industry record starting production at the deepest floating drilling and production platform in the world. The Perdido Development operates in 8000 ft. of water in the Gulf of Mexico. In response to the BP oil rig disaster in the Gulf of Mexico the company joined forces with Exxon Mobil Chevron and ConocoPhillips to form a $1 billion rapid-response joint venture that will be able to better manage and contain future deepwater spills.

With an eye toward raising cash and focusing on its majority holdings and joint ventures rather than on minority held businesses in 2010 Royal Dutch Shell sold 10% of its 34% in Australian oil and gas enterprise Woodside Petroleum for $3.3 billion. Royal Dutch Shell also announced that it would seek to sell the rest of its stake in Woodside Petroleum over time. (Earlier in the year the company formed a $3.5 billion joint venture with PetroChina which acquired Arrow Energy a company with major natural gas assets in Northern Australia).

As part of its strategy of selling noncore downstream assets to raise cash in 2010 Royal Dutch Shell sold its Finnish and Swedish operations (including a refinery in Gothenburg and 565 gas stations) to Finland-based St1 for $640 million. In

2011 it sold its UK-based Stanlow refinery to India's Essar Group for $350 million.

In 2010 the company formed a $12 billion joint venture with Brazil's Cosan to ramp up ethanol production.

EXECUTIVES

CFO, Simon Henry, age 54, $449,000 total compensation
CEO, Peter R. Voser, age 57, $1,267,000 total compensation
CEO, Ben van Beurden
Director Downstream, John Abbott
Director Projects and Technology, Harry Brekelmans
Director Upstream International, Andrew Brown
Director Upstream Americas, Marvin Odum
Deputy Chairman, Hans Wijers
Auditors: PricewaterhouseCoopers LLP

LOCATIONS

HQ: Royal Dutch Shell Plc
Carel van Bylandtlaan 30, The Hague 2596 HR
Phone: (31) 70 377 9111 **Fax:** (44) 20 7934 5153
Web: www.shell.com

2013 Sales

	$ mil.	% of total
Europe	175,584	38
Africa Asia Australia/Oceania	157,673	34
US	72,552	16
Other Americas	45,426	10
Share of joint ventures & other income	8,364	2
Total	**459,599**	**100**

PRODUCTS/OPERATIONS

2013 Sales

	$ mil.	% of total
Downstream	403,725	88
Upstream	47,357	10
Share from joint ventures & other income	8,364	2
Corporate & other	153	-
Total	**459,599**	**100**

COMPETITORS

7-Eleven
Ashland Inc.
BHP Billiton
BP
Chevron
ConocoPhillips
Dow Chemical
DuPont
Eastman Chemical
Eni
Exxon Mobil
FEC Resources
Hess Corporation
Huntsman International
Imperial Oil
Koch Industries Inc.
Marathon Oil
Norsk Hydro ASA
Occidental Petroleum
PEMEX
PETROBRAS
PetroKazakhstan
Petrleos de Venezuela
Repsol
Sinopec Shanghai Petrochemical
Sunoco
TOTAL

HISTORICAL FINANCIALS

Company Type: Public

Income Statement FYE: December 31

	REVENUE ($ mil.)	NET INCOME ($ mil.)	NET PROFIT MARGIN	EMPLOYEES
12/14	431,344	14,874	3.4%	94,000
12/13	459,599	16,371	3.6%	92,000
12/12	481,700	26,592	5.5%	87,000
12/11	484,489	30,918	6.4%	90,000
12/10	378,152	20,127	5.3%	97,000
Annual Growth	3.3%	(7.3%)	—	(0.8%)

2014 Year-End Financials

Debt ratio: 12.9%
Return on equity: 8.4%
Cash ($ mil.): 21,607
Current ratio: 1.16
Long-term debt ($ mil.): 38,332
No. of shares (mil.): —
Dividends
Yield: 5.5%
Payout: 157.6%
Market value ($ mil.): —

	STOCK PRICE ($) FY Close	P/E High/Low	PER SHARE ($) Earnings	Dividends	Book Value
12/14	66.95	35 26	2.36	3.72	27.25
12/13	71.27	28 24	2.60	3.56	28.50
12/12	68.95	17 14	4.24	3.42	29.77
12/11	73.09	16 12	4.98	3.36	27.10
12/10	66.78	21 15	3.28	3.36	23.93
Annual Growth	0.1%	— —	(7.9%)	2.6%	3.3%

RWE AG

RWE doesn't stand for Runs With Electricity but it could. RWE is one of Germany's top two electricity suppliers (along with E.ON). Through its subsidiaries the energy conglomerate provides electricity and gas to residential and business customers primarily in Central and Western Europe. It also owns major UK-based utilities and German-based electricity and gas supplier RWE npower. RWE owns oil and gas exploration and production unit RWE-DEA; other businesses include companies engaged in gas transportation and storage power generation (including wind) energy trading information technology and coal mining. In 2011 RWE served 17 million electricity customers and 8 million gas customers.

Geographic ReachRWE operates in Germany the Netherlands/Belgium the UK and in Central Eastern and South Eastern Europe. Germany accounted for more than 50% of the company's revenues in 2011.OperationsIn addition to generating power and distributing electricity and gas in its core geographic markets the company also develops renewable power through RWE Innogy; explores for and produces oil and gas through RWE-DEA; and engages in energy trading and gas midstream activities through RWE Supply & Trading.Financial PerformanceThe company's revenues decreased by 3% in 2011 due to a drop in revenues from the Germany power generation Netherlands/Belgium and Trading/Gas Midstream segments. Power generation revenues declined due to the German government's shift in energy policy (exiting nuclear power) following the reactor disaster at Fukushima. Netherlands/Belgium revenues declined due to a drop in Essent's gas midstream business caused by a drop in electricity generation margins. Trading/Gas Midstream revenues declined due to a drop in the realization of successful forward transactions and in some of its gas purchase contracts.The company's net income decreased by 45% in 2011 due to a decrease in revenues and operating income caused by an increase in the costs of material depreciation amortization and impairment losses and other operating expenses.

Stategy

RWE plans its investments in power stations networks and raw material production facilities in terms of decades not in terms of years. It is looking to compete more effectively in the deregulated German power and gas markets order by restructuring its regional energy businesses. The company's former German utility unit RWE Energie lost its regional monopoly status because of deregulation and RWE has responded by splitting its domestic power generation distribution and supply operations into new units. RWE has also responded by acquiring utilities and energy services companies in the Czech Republic Hungary Poland and Slovakia and by targeting expansion in Europe.RWE is also focusing on the expansion of renewable energy in Germany the UK the Netherlands Poland Spain and Italy.In 2011 the company acquired Energy Resources Holding B.V. which has owns 30 % of EPZ a Dutch electricity generator.

To meet antitrust requirements in 2011 RWE sold its 75% stake in the German natural gas transmission grid business (Thyssengas) to Macquarie Group. To pay down debt in 2011 it also sold its German long-distance power grid to a consortium of five pension funds of German and Swiss insurers for $1.4 billion. RWE retained operational control of the grid.

A possible merger between RWE and Spanish power giant IBERDROLA fell through in 2011 due to market and political concerns.

HISTORY

Founded at the end of the 19th century RWE mirrored the industrialization of Germany in its growth. It was formed as Rheinisch-Westfalisches Elektrizitatswerk in 1898 by Erich Zweigert the mayor of Essen and Hugo Stinnes an industrialist from Mulheim to provide electricity to Essen and surrounding areas. The company began supplying power in 1900.

Stinnes persuaded other cities –Gelsenkirchen and Mulheim –to buy shares in RWE in 1905. In 1908 RWE and rival Vereinigte Elektrizitatswerk Westfalen (VEW) agreed to divide up the territories that each would supply.

Germany's coal shortages caused by WWI prompted RWE to expand its coal operations and it bought Rheinische Aktiengesellschaft f r Braunkohlenbergbau a coal producer in 1932. RWE also built a power line network completed in 1930 to connect populous northern Germany with the south. By 1939 as WWII began the company had plants throughout most of western Germany. However the war destroyed much of its infrastructure and RWE had to rebuild.

The company continued to rely on coal for most of its fuel needs in the 1950s but in 1961 RWE and Bayern Atomkraft sponsored the construction of a demonstration nuclear reactor the first of several such projects at Gundremmingen. The Gundremmingen plant was shut down in 1977 and to replace it RWE built two 1300-MW reactors that began operation in 1984.

RWE began to diversify and in 1988 it acquired Texaco's German petroleum and petrochemical unit which became RWE-DEA. By 1990 RWE's operations also included waste management and construction. RWE reorganized creating RWE Aktiengesellschaft as a holding company for group operations.

RWE-DEA acquired the US's Vista Chemical in 1991 and RWE's Rheinbraun mining unit bought a 50% stake in Consolidation Coal from DuPont. (The mining venture went public in 1999 as CONSOL Energy.) RWE led a consortium that acquired major stakes in three Hungarian power companies in 1995.

Hoping to play a role in Germany's telecommunications market RWE teamed with VEBA in 1997 to form the o.tel.o joint venture and RWE and VEBA gained control of large German mobile phone operator E-Plus. The nation's telecom market was deregulated in 1998 but Mannesmann and former monopoly Deutsche Telekom proved to be formidable competitors. In 1999 RWE and VEBA sold o.tel.o's fixed-line business (along with the o.tel.o brand name) and cable-TV unit Tele Columbus. The next year the companies sold their joint stake in E-Plus.

Faced with deregulating German electricity markets RWE Energie had begun restructuring as soon as the market opened up in 1998. It agreed to buy fellow German power company VEW in a $20 billion deal that closed in 2000. RWE also joined with insurance giant Allianz and France's Vivendi in a successful bid for a 49.9% stake in state-owned water distributor Berliner Wasserbetriebe (Vivendi later spurned an RWE offer to buy its energy businesses).

After taking advantage of deregulating markets in Germany RWE moved to pick up other European utilities: It acquired UK-based Thames Water (later renamed RWE Thames Water) in 2000 and bought a majority stake in Dutch gas supplier Intergas the next year. In 2002 the company issued an exchange offer to acquire UK electricity supplier Innogy (later renamed RWE npower) for a total of about $4.4 billion in cash and $3 billion in assumed debt. It also completed a $3.7 billion purchase of Czech Republic gas supplier Transgas.

In a move to further streamline operations RWE sold its 50% stake in refinery and service station subsidiary Shell & DEA Oil to Deutsche Shell and Shell Petroleum. To do battle in an increasingly competitive utility industry RWE is acquiring stakes in other European utilities. In 2003 RWE also acquired North American utility American Water Works which was combined with the US operations of RWE Thames Water for $4.6 billion in cash and $4 billion in assumed debt.

Recognizing that its international acquisitions of water utilities in the early 2000s had left it overextended RWE has been to selling its water assets in order to save cash and streamline its operations around its core power businesses. Overextended in 2006 the company sold its Thames Water unit to Kemble Water Limited a consortium led by Macquarie Bank's European Infrastructure Funds. It spun off its American Water unit in 2008.

The company saw its revenues drop in 2009 as the global recession hammered gas prices. However the same lower gas prices helped RWE to save costs enabling it to post an improved net income that year.

After being outmaneuvered by EDF in its plan to grow its Pan-European power footprint by acquiring British Energy RWE in 2009 acquired top Dutch power utility Essent for $10.7 billion. The deal boost its position as one of the top electricity and gas utilities in Europe.

Growing its energy sources in 2009 it also formed a joint venture with E.ON to develop 6000 MW of nuclear power capacity in the UK. In a move to reduce its dependency on the wholesale gas markets in 2009 RWE acquired 70% of the Breagh North Sea gas field for about $350 million.

The company announced CEO J rgen Gro - mann who fought Germany's decision to phase out nuclear power stepped down in July 2012. Gro - mann was replaced by Peter Terium the CEO of Essent. COO Rolf Martin Schmitz was named Deputy CEO.

EXECUTIVES

CEO, Peter Terium, age 52
Deputy CEO and COO, Rolf Martin Schmitz, age 58
CFO, Bernhard G nther, age 49
CEO and CFO RWE Supply and Trading, Markus Krebber
Chairman, Manfred Schneider, age 77
Deputy Chairman, Frank Bsirske
Auditors: PricewaterhouseCoopers Aktiengesellschaft Wirtschaftspr fungsgesellschaft

LOCATIONS

HQ: RWE AG
Opernplatz 1, Essen 45128
Phone: (49) 201 12 00 **Fax:** (49) 201 12 15199
Web: www.rwe.com

2014 Sales

	% of total
Germany	57
UK	21
Other EU	22
Rest of Europe	0
Other countries	1
Total	**100**

PRODUCTS/OPERATIONS

2014 Sales

	% of total
Supply/ Distribution Networks Germany	52
Supply United Kingdom	19
Supply Netherlands/ Belgium	9
Central Eastern and South Eastern Europe	8
Trading/ Gas Mid-Stream	7
Conventional Power Generation	4
Renewables	1
Other Consolidation	0
Total	**100**

Selected Divisions and Subsidiaries

RWE Energy (German and continental European downstream energy operations)
RWE npower (affiliated with RWE Innogy electricity and gas supply UK)
RWE Supply & Trading (power gas coal and oil trading)
RWE-DEA AG (oil and gas exploration production and storage)
RWE Power (upstream energy operations)

COMPETITORS

BP
Centrica
E.ON
Electricit© de France
Endesa S.A.
Enel
Exxon Mobil
Royal Dutch Shell
Vattenfall

HISTORICAL FINANCIALS

Company Type: Public

Income Statement FYE: December 31

	REVENUE ($ mil.)	NET INCOME ($ mil.)	NET PROFIT MARGIN	EMPLOYEES
12/14	56,094	2,071	3.7%	61,715
12/13	70,754	(3,795)	—	66,341
12/12	66,918	1,721	2.6%	70,208
12/11	63,577	2,335	3.7%	72,068
12/10	68,151	4,427	6.5%	70,856
Annual Growth	(4.8%)	(17.3%)	—	(3.4%)

2014 Year-End Financials

Debt ratio: 26.1%
Return on equity: 16.6%
Cash ($ mil.): 3,854
Current ratio: 1.14
Long-term debt ($ mil.): 18,504
No. of shares (mil.): 575
Dividends
Yield: 3.2%
Payout: 26.2%
Market value ($ mil.): 17,819

	STOCK PRICE ($) FY Close	P/E High/Low	PER SHARE ($) Earnings	Dividends	Book Value
12/14	30.95	14 11	3.37	1.01	21.31
12/13	36.80	— —	(6.18)	1.90	24.96
12/12	41.64	23 16	2.81	1.93	33.94
12/11	34.93	22 8	4.33	3.38	35.37
12/10	66.39	15 10	8.30	3.42	44.20
Annual Growth	(17.4%) (16.7%)	— —	(20.2%)	(26.3%)	

S-Oil Corp

S-Oil aims to become the most S-uccessful refiner in South Korea and beyond. The company is one of its country's leading refiners and a major provider of lubricants and gasoline. S-Oil is capable of producing 669000 barrels per day at its Onsan refinery and its product menu includes gasoline kerosene diesel lube base oil automotive and industrial oils and petrochemical products such as benzene and toluene. S-Oil operates a naphtha reforming plant with a daily capacity of 45000 barrels and a BTX production plant with an annual capacity of 900000 tons. Its joint venture with Saudi Arabia's Aramco –signed in 1991 –ensures a steady supply of crude oil.

OperationsThe company operates the Onsan Refinery and other facilities at that location that can produce petrochemicals and lube base oil. S-Oil produces and supplies high quality oil products based on the world-class Bunker-C Cracking Center and the xylene Center a paraxylene plant with the world's highest production capacity for a single facility.

Geographic Reach

S-Oil exports more than 60% of its annual production to about 30 countries around the world.

Financial Performance

Thanks to high oil prices and the expansion of its refining capacity S-Oil's 2011 revenues increased by 56% and its net income by 69%.

Business Strategy

The company's long-term strategy includes further investment in the refining business integration with the petrochemical business and growing its renewable energy business.

Buoyed by increasing demand for petroleum products from China and other Asian countries in 2011 S-Oil completed its Onsan refinery expansion project. The expansion doubles the plant's production of paraxylene and benzene to 2.4 million tons a year. It also increased its refining capacity from 580000 barrels per day to 669000 barrels per day.

Company Background

S-Oil began commercial operations in 1980. The company broke off from SsangYong Group in 1999 and changed its name to S-Oil a year later.

EXECUTIVES

CEO and Representative Director, Nasser Al-Mahasher
Auditors: Samil Accounting Corporation (A Member Firm of PircewaterhouseCoopers)

LOCATIONS

HQ: S-Oil Corp
192 Baekbeom-ro Mapo-gu, Seoul 121-805
Phone: (82) 2 3772 5151 **Fax:** (82) 2 782 4879
Web: www.s-oil.com

COMPETITORS

GS Caltex
LG International
SK Group

HISTORICAL FINANCIALS

Company Type: Public

Income Statement FYE: December 31

	REVENUE ($ mil.)	NET INCOME ($ mil.)	NET PROFIT MARGIN	EMPLOYEES
12/14	26,101	(263)	—	2,796
12/13	29,628	275	0.9%	2,749
12/12	32,521	548	1.7%	2,671
12/11	27,542	1,027	3.7%	2,622
12/10	18,292	633	3.5%	2,551
Annual Growth	9.3%	—	—	2.3%

2014 Year-End Financials

Debt ratio: 0.0%
Return on equity: (-5.6%)
Cash ($ mil.): 650
Current ratio: 1.44
Long-term debt ($ mil.): 1,200
No. of shares (mil.): 112
Dividends
Yield: 2.2%
Payout: —
Market value ($ mil.): 2,511

	STOCK PRICE ($) FY Close	P/E High/Low	PER SHARE ($) Earnings	Dividends	Book Value
12/14	22.30	— —	(2.26)	0.50	39.85
12/13	37.20	— —	2.36	0.00	45.22
12/12	51.00	— —	4.73	0.00	44.72
12/11	40.75	— —	8.85	0.00	40.06
12/10	29.23	— —	5.46	0.00	(0.00)
Annual Growth	(6.5%)	— —	—	—	—

SABMiller Plc (United Kingdom)

Thanks to this beer maker "It's 5 O'Clock Somewhere." SABMiller is one of the world's largest brewers producing more than 200 international national and local beer brands spanning the globe. Big brands include Grolsch Miller Peroni Nastro and Pilsner Urquell and many local favorites such as Castle Lager the #1 beer in Africa. In Latin America it owns Bavaria and Cervecería Nacional; in the US the company owns 58% of MillerCoors a joint venture with Molson Coors. SABMiller also owns Australian beer maker Foster's. Beyond brewing SABMiller is one of the world's top bottlers of Coca-Cola products. In late 2015 SABMiller agreed to be acquired by rival AB InBev for $104.4 billion.

Geographic Reach

SABMiller has offices and facilities in more than 80 countries dotting Latin America Europe North America Africa the Asia/Pacific region and South Africa. Approximately 90% of its beverages are sold in markets in which it is the #1 or #2 beer maker. Africa led by South Africa accounts for 31% of the company's net sales. Other major markets include Latin America (35%) Europe (19%) and the Asia Pacific (14%). (North America only accounts for 1%.)

Operations

SABMiller owns more than 100 breweries and 40 bottling plants. It also produces at plants owned and operated through several strategic alliances and joint ventures. Production is organized among six regions: Latin America Europe North America Africa Asia/Pacific and South Africa. In addition to bottling products for The Coca-Cola Company it has hotel and gaming interests through Tsogo Sun Holdings South Africa's largest gaming group doing business as Gold Reef Resorts.

Financial Performance

SABMiller's revenues remained flat from 2014 to 2015 primarily due to a 5% drop in Asia Pacific sales and a 3% decline from Europe sales. This was offset by gains in the UK (8%) and the US (2%) throughout 2015.

Strategy

Many global giants are feeling competitive pressure from local craft makers and are considering mergers as a means to dominate additional market share. Feeling the pressure SABMiller agreed in late 2015 to be acquired by primary competitor AB InBev for $104.4 billion. If the transaction is approved the combined company would be responsible for about a third of the global beer supply and could lead other brewers to consider mergers as they try to stay competitive.

Over the years SABMiller's strategy for growth has included targeted acquisitions international partnerships and a stream of brand introductions. SABMiller has boosted its customer base by entering developing regions where bottled beverage consumption notably beer is accelerating and by increasing its share of more mature markets where consumption is already high.

HISTORY

British sailor Frederick Mead purchased the Castle Brewery in Johannesburg in 1892 about 15 years after gold was discovered in South Africa. Mead took his brewing operation public as South African Breweries (SAB) in 1895. The company launched its flagship Castle Lager three years later and survived the Anglo-Boer War (1899-1902) as South Africa's fastest-growing non-industrial firm. Mead died in 1915.

The brewer acquired the Grand Hotel in Cape Town in 1921 and a stake in Schweppes (carbonated drinks) in 1925. In the late 1940s SAB began an extensive expansion program involving its breweries small hotels and pubs. In 1951 it acquired the Hotel Victoria in Johannesburg. An increase in beer taxes during the 1950s led SAB to start producing liquors. With beer demand slackening South Africa's three largest brewers –SAB Ohlsson's and United Breweries –merged in 1956. The new company which took the SAB name controlled about 90% of the beer market.

Beer taxes continued to pressure sales and in 1960 SAB acquired control of Stellenbosch Farmers' Winery to extend its product range. In 1962 the restriction prohibiting alcohol consumption by blacks was lifted opening an enormous market. SAB continued to extend its range of beer brands during the 1960s by adding licenses to brew Amstel and Carling Black Label.

In 2002 SAB gobbled up Miller Brewing from Philip Morris (now Altria Group) for $5.6 billion making it the world's second-largest brewer at the time. SAB then changed its name to SABMiller plc. SABMiller moved into Western Europe in 2003 with the $270 million purchase of Italian brewer Birra Peroni. In 2005 SABMiller acquired almost 97% of Bavaria S.A. the second-largest brewer in South America. Bavaria's brands include Águila Atlas Cristal and Pilsener.

In an attempt to gain market share SABMiller formed MillerCoors with Molson Coors in 2008 adding the popular domestic labels Miller and Coors as well as imports including Molson Canadian and Pilsner Urquell and craft brews such as Leinenkugel's and Blue Moon to its US offerings.

In 2008 it acquired Dutch brewer Royal Grolsch for about $1.2 billion. In its largest acquisition to date SABMiller purchased Australia's oldest and biggest brewer Foster's Group for $12.3 billion in 2011.

EXECUTIVES

CEO, Alan Clark, age 55
Managing Director Plzensky Prazdroj AS, Tony van Kralingen, age 57
Managing Director SABMiller Europe, Sue Clark, age 51
President SABMiller Latin America, Karl Lippert, age 54
Managing Director SABMiller Africa, Mark J. Bowman, age 48
Managing Director SABMiller Asia Pacific and CEO Carlton and United Breweries, Ari Mervis, age 51
CFO, Domenic De Lorenzo, age 51
Chairman, Jan P. du Plessis, age 60
Deputy Chairman, Guy Elliott
Auditors: PricewaterhouseCoopers LLP

LOCATIONS

HQ: SABMiller Plc (United Kingdom)
One Stanhope Gate, London W1K 1AF
Phone: (44) 20 7659 0100
Web: www.sabmiller.com

2015 Sales

	% of total
Latin America	35
Africa	31
Europe	19
Asia Pacific	14
North America	1
Total	**100**

2015 Sales

	% of total
South Africa	20
Colombia	16
Australia	11
UK	2
USA	1
Rest of world	50
Total	**100**

PRODUCTS/OPERATIONS

Selected Brands

Beer
- Africa
- South Africa
- Appletiser
- Brutal Fruit
- Carling Black Label
- Castle Lite
- Castle Milk Stout
- Hansa Pilsener
- Redd' s
- Sarita
- Skelter' s Straight
- Other Africa
- 2M
- Balimi
- Baron' s
- Bohlinger' s
- Castle
- Chairman' s
- Chibuki
- Club Lager
- Eagle
- Fusion
- Impala
- Kilimanjaro
- Laurentina
- Lion Lager
- Maluti
- Manica
- Mosi
- Ndovu
- N' GOLA
- Nile Special
- Raiz
- Rwenzori
- Safari
- Sibebe
- Stone
- St Louis

Trophy
Tusker
Voltic
White Bull
Zambezi
Asia/Pacific
Bluetongue
Bondi Blonde
Carlton Draught
Cascade
Crown Lager
Fat Yak
Foster' s
Haywards 5000
Huadan Dry Beer
Indus Pride
Knock Out
Löwen
New Three Star
Pure Blonde
Royal Challenge
Shengquan
Singo
Snow
Victoria Bitter
Zero
Zorok
Europe
Amsterdam
Arany &#19
Ciucas
Dębowe Mocne
Dorada
Dreher
Essa
Frisco
Gambrinus
Gingers
Gran Riserva
Grolsch
Kőbányai Sör
Kozel
Ksiazece Tyskie
Lech
Moya Kaluga
Peroni
Pilsner
Radegast
Raffo
Šariš
Siroco
St Stefanus
Smädný Mnich
Stejar
Timisoreana
Topvar
Tri Bogatyrya Svetloye
Tropical
Tyskie
Ursus Premium
Velkopopovický Kozel
Wojak
Wührer
Zolotaya Bochka
Żubr
Global Brands
Grolsch
Miller Genuine Draft
Peroni Nastro Azzurro
Pilsner Urquell
Latin America
Aguila
Arequipe?a
Atlas
Balboa
Barena
Club
Conquer
Coste?a
Cristal
Cusque?a
Golden Light
Imperial
Isenbeck
Pilsen
Pilsener
Poker
Pony Malta
Port Royal
Regia Extra
Rhino
Salva Vida
San Juan
Suprema
North America (Miller Brewing Company and MillerCoors LLC joint venture)
Blue Moon
Coors
Hamm' s
Henry Weinhard' s
Icehouse
Keystone Light
Leinenkugel' s
MGD 64
Mickey' s
Miller
Miller Lite
Milwaukee' s Best
Olde English
Steele Reserve
Hotels and
Tsogo Sung
Gold Reef Resorts Ltd.
Soft drinks and juice
Appletiser
Coca-cola (licensed El Salvador Honduras Angola; South Africa and 20 other African markets)
Club (Ghan
Malta Vigo
Maltizz (C
Pepsi (lic
Tropical (
Water
Ambo (Ethi
Rwenzori (
Voltic (Gh

COMPETITORS

AmBev
Andina
Anheuser-Busch InBev
Asahi Breweries
Asia Pacific Breweries
Boston Beer
Brau Union
Carlsberg A/S
Constellation Brands
Cuauht©moc Moctezuma
Danone Water
Diageo
E. & J. Gallo
Fuller' s
Grupo Modelo
Heineken
Kingway Brewery
Kirin Holdings Company
Nestl© Waters
Pabst
PepsiCo
Pernod Ricard
Quinsa
San Miguel Corporation
Sapporo
Suntory Holdings
Tsingtao
UB Group

HISTORICAL FINANCIALS

Company Type: Public

Income Statement

FYE: March 31

	REVENUE ($ mil.)	NET INCOME ($ mil.)	NET PROFIT MARGIN	EMPLOYEES
03/15	22,130	3,299	14.9%	68,808
03/14	22,311	3,381	15.2%	69,947
03/13	23,213	3,274	14.1%	70,486
03/12	21,760	4,221	19.4%	71,144
03/11	19,408	2,408	12.4%	60,212
Annual Growth	3.3%	8.2%	—	3.4%

2015 Year-End Financials

Debt ratio: 27.9%
Return on equity: 13.3%
Cash ($ mil.): 965
Current ratio: 0.59
Long-term debt ($ mil.): 10,583
No. of shares (mil.): 1,616
Dividends
Yield: 1.9%
Payout: 49.0%
Market value ($ mil.): 84,948

	STOCK PRICE ($) FY Close	P/E High/Low	PER SHARE ($) Earnings	Dividends	Book Value
03/15	52.56	29 24	2.04	1.00	14.34
03/14	50.40	27 21	2.09	0.99	16.38
03/13	52.89	26 18	2.04	0.91	16.46
03/12	40.49	16 12	2.64	0.79	15.75
03/11	35.79	23 18	1.52	0.67	13.87
Annual Growth	10.1%	— —	7.6%	10.3%	0.8%

Safran S.A.

SAFRAN strives to keep civilians and military personnel safe in the air and on land. The company has returned to its aerospace roots while building up its defense and security segments. It restructured its operations to three divisions: Aerospace manufactures aircraft/rocket/space engines and propulsion systems for fixed wing as well as rotorcraft; Defense develops and builds navigation systems drones and optronics; and Security offers biometric identification and access control systems. SAFRAN's segments serve both the civilian and military sectors working alone or in partnership with other major companies. SAFRAN is a product of the Sagem and Snecma merger.

Reporting its results in four segments Safran split its Aerospace division into two segments Aerospace Propulsion and Aircraft Equipment. The largest of SAFRAN's segments is Aerospace Propulsion which accounts for more than half of overall sales. The segment's operations include an alliance with General Electric through CFM International a 50/50 joint venture contracted through 2040. CFM develops and markets the CFM56 turbofan engine for single-aisle commercial jets. In the military sector Aerospace Propulsion makes engines for combat training and transport aircraft. The segment also has made more than 50000 helicopter turbine engines for some 2200 customers in about 150 countries.

The Aircraft Equipment segment accounts for 26% of sales. The segment supplies engine nacelles and thrust reversers for the Airbus A380. It also provides landing systems for the A380 and the Airbus Military A400M the Boeing 787 Dreamliner and the Dassault Aviation Rafale. The segment's wheels and carbon brakes have been installed in more than 3500 planes used by some 300 airlines.

Defense 11% of sales provides inertial navigation systems for use on military transport and combat aircraft helicopters warships armored vehicles and other systems. The segment also provides products for digital combat including technology for vehicle digitization and encryption. Security 11% of sales offers multibiometric identification technologies that can identify persons through fingerprints iris face and vein recognition. It also offers explosive detection systems and smart cards. The segment's systems have been implemented in more than 100 countries.

Safran's revenue increased 9% in 2011 compared with 2010 thanks in part to lower costs and more demand from OEM and aftermarket customers in the aerospace market. Adjusted net income was up 27%. By segment revenue for Aerospace Propulsion rose 9% in 2011 compared with 2010 thanks in part to more demand for CFM and high-thrust engines and helicopter turbines from the civilian aftermarket. OEM customers also bought more CFM56 engines. Sales for Aircraft Equipment also went up 9% in 2011 vs. 2010 to meet more demand for nacelles wheels and brakes from OEMs and civil aerospace services.

Defense inched up 2% in 2011 compared with 2010. The segment enjoyed healthy demand for the Felin soldier integrated equipment suites from the French army and long-range infra-red goggles for export. Security surged about 20% over the same period. The segment did well with e-Documents in the Latin American telecommunications and banking markets and identification products in emerging countries.

The company's new Leading Edge Aviation Propulsion (LEAP) engine for single-aisle commercial jets intended as a replacement of the best-selling CFM56 engine received more than 3000 orders from Airbus Boeing and the Commercial Aircraft Corp. of China (Comac) in 2011 that will bring even more revenue down line through maintenance. Also in 2011 CFM International the Safran-GE joint venture received 1500 –a record number –orders for the CFM56 totaling about $52 billion from civilian and military customers. These orders are also expected to bring more revenue in the future through orders for spare parts and other maintenance services. To meet the challenge of fulfilling demand for the LEAP among other goals Safran hired 6000 new employees –half of them in France –in 2011 and stated plans to hire about as many in 2012.

In 2011 SAFRAN wrapped up its acquisition of US-based L-1 Identity Solutions for more than $1 billion and changed the company's name to MorphoTrust USA. The operating and holding company of MorphoTrust which specializes in biometrics and ID management joined SAFRAN's MorphoTrak security business. The deal positioned SAFRAN as the world's leader in providing biometric identity systems and services. (MorphoTrust's intelligence services group was picked up earlier by BAE SYSTEMS plc.) In 2009 SAFRAN acquired Motorola's biometric operations; the deal included Motorola's Printrak fingerprint identification system. Subsequently Printrak and Sagem S ©urit © subsidiary Sagem Morpho were united as MorphoTrak. The business offers biometric and identification management products and services to federal state and local governments and commercial markets.

The Aerospace Propulsion segment expanded in spring 2011 when SAFRAN acquired the propellants and explosives arm of SNPE SNPE Materiaux Energentiques (SME). The deal pockets SME its subsidiaries and a 50% stake in Roxel a maker of solid rocket motors and 40% stake in Regulus a maker of space launcher propellants. In 2012 SME's operations were merged with Snecma Propulsion Solide (a solid propellant rocket engine business of the Aerospace segment) to form a new subsidiary called Herakles one of the world's leading solid rocket propulsion providers.

The French government is SAFRAN's largest shareholder with a 30% stake.

HISTORY

The Soci ©©'Applications G ® ©ale d' lectricit ©t de M ©anique (Sagem) was founded in 1924 to make equipment and parts for the Michelin tire company. After WWII the company developed military electronics including navigation and attack systems for the French navy's Super Etendard fighter plane.

As Sagem expanded its heavy manufacturing offerings including automotive and coal mining equipment the company continued to design military electronics. By the mid-1980s it was one of Europe's top military suppliers. Employees led a leveraged buyout of the company in 1985.

In 1991 the French secret service discovered that Sagem had sold guidance systems to Iraq that were used in Scud missiles fired at coalition troops and Israel during the Persian Gulf War. After the uproar subsided Sagem orchestrated another big military deal in 1995 when it sold 34 unmanned Sparrow Hawk reconnaissance planes to the Netherlands. Three years later the company streamlined its defense operations by reabsorbing its 75%-owned SAT subsidiary which specialized in military communications.

In 1999 Sagem rolled out its wireless Internet mobile phones to rave reviews. In 2000 it won a $330 million contract to develop 750 missile guidance systems for the French Ministry of Defense.

Early in 2001 the company's longtime chairman and CEO Pierre Faurre died unexpectedly forcing Sagem to reorganize its management structure. The board of directors became the supervisory board headed by Sagem CFO Mario Colaiacovo. Alcatel executive Gr ©oire Olivier was named chairman of the executive board and CEO.

However in the years to come the management structure was due to change even further. In late 2004 Sagem acquired France-based aircraft engine maker Snecma (hoping to expand its aerospace product offerings). Shortly after the company rebranded itself as SAFRAN a French word for the rudder blade on a boat; the newly merged company hoped this new moniker would reflect its ambition for movement strategy and direction. After the merger all the group's subsidiaries located in over 30 countries worldwide maintained their names.

The company decided to get out of the communications business. Early in 2008 it sold Sagem Communications which provided broadband services to The Gores Group a US-based private equity firm. Shortly after SAFRAN sold its Sagem Mobiles operation (mobile phone manufacturing) to French venture capital firm Sofinnova. SAFRAN retained a 10% equity stake in the business which was renamed Sagem Wireless.

In 2008 SAFRAN formed a joint venture with GE to build nacelles for single-aisle aircraft. The new company combined SAFRAN's Aircelle subsidiary and GE's Middle River Aircraft Systems subsidiary. Both subsidiaries had complementary operations and focused on thrust reversers fan cowls acoustic treatment and thermal protection products among other aspects of engine nacelles.

Also in 2008 SAFRAN acquired Sdu Identification which developed secure ID documents from investment firms AAC Capital Partners and Advantage Capital Partners.

Addressing defense on a more domestic level SAFRAN has been working to expand the scope of its Security unit's products. In 2009 SAFRAN acquired an 81% majority stake in GE Homeland Protection which makes explosives and narcotics detection equipment for about $580 million; GE retained a 19% share in the unit.

SAFRAN sold its Cinch Connectors business to Bel Fuse in 2010 for about $39 million. Cinch made a wide range of interconnect devices for aerospace communications computing military and transportation applications.

Auditors: ERNST & YOUNG et Autres

LOCATIONS

HQ: Safran S.A.
2, boulevard du General Martial-Valin, Paris, Cedex 15 75724
Phone: (33) 1 40 60 80 80 **Fax:** (33) 1 40 60 81 02
Web: www.safran-group.com

HISTORICAL FINANCIALS

Company Type: Public

Income Statement FYE: December 31

	REVENUE ($ mil.)	NET INCOME ($ mil.)	NET PROFIT MARGIN	EMPLOYEES
12/14	20,217	(153)	—	68,945
12/13	21,522	1,908	8.9%	66,289
12/12	19,515	1,716	8.8%	62,558
12/11	16,000	618	3.9%	59,805
12/10	15,294	277	1.8%	54,256
Annual Growth	7.2%	—	—	6.2%

2014 Year-End Financials

Debt ratio: 14.7%
Return on equity: (-1.9%)
Cash ($ mil.): 1,984
Current ratio: 0.88
Long-term debt ($ mil.): 2,015
No. of shares (mil.): 416
Dividends
Yield: 3.6%
Payout: —
Market value ($ mil.): 6,355

	STOCK PRICE ($) FY Close	P/E High/Low		PER SHARE ($) Earnings	Dividends	Book Value
12/14	15.26	—	—	(0.36)	0.55	18.25
12/13	17.24	20	5	4.58	0.32	21.94
12/12	43.25	14	10	4.13	0.87	19.21
12/11	30.20	33	23	1.53	0.25	15.70
12/10	31.45	62	35	0.68	0.12	15.17
Annual Growth	(16.5%)	—	—	—	45.2%	4.7%

SAIC Motor Corp Ltd

SAIC Motor Corporation is the largest automotive manufacturer listed on the A-Shares market in China. The Shanghai Automotive Industry Corporation subsidiary makes automobiles (including passenger and commercial vehicles) and spare parts (including engines transmissions powertrain chassis interior and exterior trim electronic appliances). It is also engaged in auto financing logistics vehicle information second-hand cars and other car service and trading businesses. Its operations include Shanghai Volkswagen Shanghai GM SAIC-GM-Wuling Nanjing Iveco SAIC-Iveco-Hongyan and Shanghai Sunwin.

Financial Performance

In 2012 SAIC Motors sold 4.5 million cars with a year-on-year growth of 12% maintaining its edge as market leader edge in the Chinese domestic automotive market.The company's revenues increased by 19% in 2011 while its net profit increased by 23%. The increase in net profit was due to the increase in total revenues (due to a strong increase in the sales of cars) partially offset by a 4% increase SG&A mainly due to the increase of sales-related expenses including transportation and logistics expenses and advertising expenses and a 25% increase in administrative expenses mainly due to the increase in research and development expenditure royalty expenses employee salaries and welfare costs.

Stategy

To help address China's smog issues by increasing the adoption of electric vehicles in 2012 SAIC Motors and Shanghai International Automotive City (Group) Co. (SIAC) signed a memorandum of understanding to develop a new energy vehicle demonstration project at Shanghai Automotive Museum with an eye toward wider implementation of the vehicle. In addition SAIC Motor SIAC and Shanghai Gaozhan New Energy Vehicle Sales and Service Co. Ltd. reached an agreement to develop the Roewe E50 pure electric vehicle under which 200 units of Roewe E50 pure electric vehicle will be produced on a test basis.

Company Background

SAIC Motor Corporation was established in 1984 as Shanghai Volkswagen Automotive a 50-50 joint venture with Volkswagen.

EXECUTIVES

President, Chen Zhixin, age 56
CFO, Gu Feng, age 43

VP SAIC Motor; General Manager SAIC Motor Passenger Vehicle Co and Head Technology Center, Wang Xiaoqiu, age 51
VP SAIC Motor; General Manager Shanghai General Motors Wuling, Shen Yang, age 54
VP SAIC Motor; General Manager Commercial Vehicle; General Manager Shanghai Commercial Vehicle Co, Lan Qingsong, age 51
VP SAIC Motor; General Manager and Party Secretary SAIC Group Beijing Co., Zhu Genlin
Chairman, Chen Hong, age 54
Auditors: Deloitte Touche Tohmatsu

LOCATIONS

HQ: SAIC Motor Corp Ltd
No. 489, Weihai Road, Jingan District, Shanghai 200041
Phone: (86) 21 22011138 **Fax:** (86) 21 22011199
Web: www.saicmotor.com

COMPETITORS

BMW	Honda
BYD	Hyundai Motor
Daimler	Kia Motors
Dongfeng Peugeot	Mazda
FCA US	Nissan
Fiat Chrysler	Peugeot
Ford Motor	Suzuki Motor
General Motors	Toyota

HISTORICAL FINANCIALS

Company Type: Public

Income Statement FYE: December 31

	REVENUE ($ mil.)	NET INCOME ($ mil.)	NET PROFIT MARGIN	EMPLOYEES
12/14	101,508	4,507	4.4%	0
12/13	93,461	4,097	4.4%	0
12/12	77,151	3,328	4.3%	0
12/11	69,077	3,212	4.7%	5,379
12/10	47,541	2,082	4.4%	5,536
Annual Growth	20.9%	21.3%	—	—

2014 Year-End Financials

Debt ratio: 0.4%
Return on equity: 18.9%
Cash ($ mil.): 14,170
Current ratio: 1.19
Long-term debt ($ mil.): 765
No. of shares (mil.): —
Dividends
Yield: —
Payout: —
Market value ($ mil.): —

Samba Financial Group

The sound of money is music to Samba Financial Group's ears. The bank offers retail banking corporate banking investment banking asset management credit cards loans and related services through about 70 branches (25 are ladies only) and some 500 ATMs across Saudi Arabia and branches in London Dubai and Qatar. In Pakistan Samba Financial is the majority owner of Samba Bank Limited with about 30 branches. Its financial products are also Shariah-compliant. In 2014 the company launched a new SambaMobile app for smart phones and tablets. Samba Financial was set up in 1980 when it took over the two Saudi branches owned by Citibank; Citibank sold the last of its stake in the company in 2004.
Auditors: Ernst & Young

LOCATIONS

HQ: Samba Financial Group
King Abdul Aziz Road, P.O.Box. 833, Riyadh 11421
Phone: (966) 1 477 4770 **Fax:** (966) 1 477 4770
Web: www.samba.com.sa

COMPETITORS

Al Rajhi Banking	Dallah Albaraka Group
Arab Banking Corp.	Qatar National Bank
Arab National Bank	Riyad Bank
Banque Saudi Fransi	Saudi British Bank

HISTORICAL FINANCIALS

Company Type: Public

Income Statement FYE: December 31

	ASSETS ($ mil.)	NET INCOME ($ mil.)	INCOME AS % OF ASSETS	EMPLOYEES
12/14	57,935	1,333	2.3%	3,404
12/13	54,667	1,202	2.2%	3,306
12/12	53,119	1,154	2.2%	3,329
12/11	51,406	1,147	2.2%	3,057
12/10	49,976	1,182	2.4%	3,135
Annual Growth	3.8%	3.1%	—	2.1%

2014 Year-End Financials

Return on assets: 2.3%
Return on equity: 13.6%
Long-term debt ($ mil.): —
No. of shares (mil.): 1,200
Sales ($ mil): 2,087
Dividends
Yield: —
Payout: —
Market value ($ mil.): —

Samsung C&T Corp

Samsung C&T is the trading investment construction and engineering arm of the Samsung Group the largest "chaebol" (business conglomerate) in South Korea. The unit's trading and investment group is active in a number of sectors including oil and gas electronics heavy machinery and chemicals. Meanwhile the construction and engineering division handles projects including bridges and ports power plants petrochemical facilities and multifamily residential developments. It has helped build such notable projects as the Petronas Twin Towers in Malaysia and the Burj Khalifa in Dubai – both among the world's tallest buildings. Founded in 1938 Samsung C&T has more than 100 offices worldwide.

The group has experienced a decrease in sales in the construction sector as there has been a lag in the housing and architecture markets. Trading and investment has seen an increase in sales due to the success in the natural resources and chemicals market.

Samsung C&T has recently secured or completed such diverse projects as a UK airport renovation and the construction of the Incheon Bridge (one of the world's longest). The company has increasing looked to the Middle East for new construction projects. In 2011 the group won a more than $2 billion deal to build a thermal power plant in Saudi Arabia. That same year the group agreed to build a more than $2.5 billion liquefied natural gas plant also in Saudi Arabia. Early in 2012 Samsung C&T bought 90% of US oil and gas firm Parallel Petroleum from Apollo Global Management for $772 million. The deal was the largest to date of any Samsung company. It was also Samsung's first acquisition of US onshore operations.

The group is focusing more on natural resources and renewable energy sectors. The group's Samsung Renewable Energy subsidiary is developing wind and solar projects around the world. It is leading a consortium that is investing $7 billion wind and solar projects in Ontario Canada. Among the projects is a new manufacturing facility that will produce solar modules and a cluster of wind and solar power farms.

Samsung C&T entered the international housing market for the first time in 2010. The group announced that it will build an apartment complex in China. The company which typically focuses on residential building in its home country plans to expand into the international housing market if the experiment is successful.
Auditors: Samil Accounting Corporation (A Member Firm of PircewaterhouseCoopers)

LOCATIONS

HQ: Samsung C&T Corp
14, Seocho-daero 74-gil Seocho-gu, Seoul 137-956
Phone: (82) 2 2145 2114 **Fax:** (82) 2 2023 2155
Web: www.samsungcnt.co.kr

HISTORICAL FINANCIALS

Company Type: Public

Income Statement FYE: December 31

	REVENUE ($ mil.)	NET INCOME ($ mil.)	NET PROFIT MARGIN	EMPLOYEES
12/14	25,998	247	1.0%	8,663
12/13	27,037	230	0.9%	8,714
12/12	23,720	422	1.8%	7,860
12/11	18,594	346	1.9%	7,233
12/10	15,835	433	2.7%	5,049
Annual Growth	13.2%	(13.0%)	—	14.5%

2014 Year-End Financials

Debt ratio: 0.0%
Return on equity: 2.2%
Cash ($ mil.): 1,920
Current ratio: 1.15
Long-term debt ($ mil.): 2,796
No. of shares (mil.): 147
Dividends
Yield: —
Payout: —
Market value ($ mil.): —

Samsung Electronics Co., Ltd.

Samsung Electronics is an electronics Samson. One of the world's largest semiconductor manufacturers Samsung Electronics is also South Korea's top electronics company. It makes many kinds of consumer devices including DVD players digital TVs and digital still cameras; computers color monitors LCD panels and printers; semiconductors such as DRAMs static RAMs flash memory and display drivers; and communications devices ranging from wireless handsets and smartphones to networking gear. The company which is the flagship member of Samsung Group also makes microwave ovens refrigerators air conditioners and washing machines. Nearly half of sales come from the Asia/Pacific region.

Operations

The company operates through independent business units: Consumer Electronics (about 55% of sales) IT and Mobile Communications (20% of sales) Semiconductors (15% of sales) and Display Products (10% of sales).

A true vertically integrated company Samsung Electronics is a leader in producing many of the chips and software at the heart of its products. The company has been the leader in the worldwide memory market for more than a decade and has a significant share of the global market for CMOS image sensors for mobile phones.

Geographic Reach

Altogether Samsung has offices in 80 countries. Outside South Korea it has regional headquarters in the US (California and New Jersey through Samsung Electronics America); Europe (Germany and the UK through Samsung Electronics UK); Asia (China Japan India and Singapore); as well as in Brazil Russia South Africa and the UAE.

It has some 40 manufacturing plants located in Brazil China Egypt Hungary India Indonesia Malaysia Mexico Poland Russia South Korea Thailand Vietnam and the US (at Samsung Austin).

America is its largest single market accounting for 30% of sales; Europe contributes about 25%; while China makes up another 20% and South Korea 10%. Other countries across Asia and Africa make up the remaining 15%.

Sales and Marketing

Samsung uses a direct sales force that operates from offices located in more than 50 countries. Its products for the consumer market (electronics appliances) are sold through major retailers worldwide. Other products such as the LCD and OLED panels made by Samsung Display are sold to OEMs. The chips made by Samsung Semiconductor are sold directly as well as through distributors.

Financial Performance

As a market leader the company has enjoyed steady growth in both its native currency (the South Korean won) and US dollars. In 2013 Samsung enjoyed strong sales for its core products — smartphones TVs and memory chips. That year it launched the Galaxy S4 smartphone a curved TV and it began mass producing the world's first 20 nanometer 4Gb ultra high-speed mobile DRAM.

Strategy

Its primary growth strategies are to solidify its market leadership by focusing on product differentiation in each business unit; identify businesses that will sustain growth over the next five to 10 years; and prepare management to anticipate and respond to business risks during times of global market uncertainty.

Over the long term Samsung Electronics is looking to grow in key product areas including mobile devices (phones and tablets) LCD panels flat-panel TVs system LSI chips IT products and home appliances. It is also promoting future growth centered around software and service opportunities while continuing to lay the foundation for future businesses particularly the health and medical equipment markets.

R&D is critical to its product development efforts and its research and development network spans six facilities in South Korea and 18 more in nine other countries including China Japan Israel India Russia the UK and the US.

In a case with potentially wide-ranging implications in August 2012 Samsung Electronics lost a patent infringement lawsuit with Apple in an ongoing copyright battle between the two. Samsung was found to have violated several Apple patents including the "bounce back" effect and the physical design of the iPhone but argued that the design similarities were not copying but benchmarking (a practice used by companies to keep up with rivals on details such as battery life screen size and other core features). Apple was awarded $1 billion in damages (the company originally sought $2.75 billion) but Samsung plans to appeal. The verdict is complicated by a decision the same week in a South Korean court that each company had infringed on the others' patents that resulted in bans and fines for both parties. Samsung continues to be nonetheless a major supplier of components for Apple products including the iPhone.

Mergers and Acquisitions

Samsung attempted to take on Apple's iTunes with the 2012 purchase of mSpot a cloud-based music service. Two-and-a-half years later it shuttered the service since renamed Samsung Music Hub in mid-2014 citing a desire to offer services as individual apps over a single bundled storefront.

The company rid itself of other operations considered non-core or poor performing. In 2013 it sold Liquavista to Amazon.com. Samsung originally bought Liquavista in 2011 hoping to increase its share of the e-reader market. In 2011 it sold its hard disk drive (HDD) business to Seagate for about $1.4 billion. As part of the transaction Seagate will supply Samsung with disk drives for its consumer electronics products while Samsung will provide Seagate with flash memory chips for storage devices. Freeing up resources to focus on newer storage technology in late 2012 it bought NVELO a California-based maker of the Dataplex storage software to add to its solid-state drives (SSDs) offerings.

Samsung Electronics is also investing in industries it isn't traditionally known for. In 2013 it bought Massachusetts-based NeuroLogica the maker of the BodyTom and CereTom portable CT scanners as part of its goal to grow as a health-care technology player.

Auditors: Samil Accounting Corporation (A Member Firm of PircewaterhouseCoopers)

LOCATIONS

HQ: Samsung Electronics Co., Ltd.
129, Samseong-ro, Yeongtong-gu, Suwon-si, Gyeonggi-do 443-742
Phone: (82) 31 200 1114 **Fax:** (82) 31 200 7538
Web: www.samsung.com

HISTORICAL FINANCIALS

Company Type: Public

Income Statement FYE: December 31

	REVENUE ($ mil.)	NET INCOME ($ mil.)	NET PROFIT MARGIN	EMPLOYEES
12/14	188,470	21,097	11.2%	99,382
12/13	217,461	28,356	13.0%	95,794
12/12	188,351	21,715	11.5%	90,700
12/11	142,403	11,529	8.1%	101,970
12/10	137,905	14,090	10.2%	95,659
Annual Growth	8.1%	10.6%	—	1.0%

2014 Year-End Financials

Debt ratio: 0.0%
Return on equity: 15.0%
Cash ($ mil.): 15,392
Current ratio: 2.21
Long-term debt ($ mil.): 1,332
No. of shares (mil.): 130
Dividends
Yield: —
Payout: —
Market value ($ mil.): 143,225

	STOCK PRICE ($) FY Close	P/E High/Low	PER SHARE ($) Earnings	Dividends	Book Value
12/14	1,100.00	— —	139.93	0.00	1,138.46
12/13	1,375.00	— —	188.09	0.00	1,049.15
12/12	1,350.00	— —	144.19	0.00	838.14
12/11	835.00	— —	76.80	0.00	646.02
12/10	660.00	— —	94.24	0.00	587.88
Annual Growth	13.6%	— —	10.4%	—	18.0%

Sanofi

Sanofi is out to make all the world's creatures a little healthier. The company formerly known as Sanofi-Aventis develops and manufactures prescription and over-the-counter drugs and vaccines for mankind and man's best friend. Sanofi's pharmaceutical division is its biggest revenue generator with top sellers that include blood thinners Plavix and Lovenox cancer drug Taxotere and insulin brand Lantus. US consumers will recognize at least one of the brands produced by subsidiary Chattem (Gold Bond Icy Hot and Selsun Blue to name a few). Sanofi also operates Merial one of the world's largest animal health firms. Subsidiary Sanofi Pasteur makes vaccines while its Genzyme unit makes biopharmaceuticals.

The company operates worldwide marketing its products through direct sales representatives and through partnering firms. For example Sanofi co-markets cardiovascular drugs Plavix and Aprovel with Bristol-Myers Squibb (BMS). It also has agreements with Warner Chilcott to market osteoporosis drug Actonel and with Teva Pharmaceuticals for Copaxone. Products are distributed via large wholesalers and to retail chains and health care organizations. Europe and North America are the firm's largest markets.

Sanofi has worked hard to diversify its operations in the wake of and ahead of patent expirations for some of its biggest sellers. Its allergy blockbuster Allegra and sleep aid Ambien have both lost their patent protection in recent years (as has Lovenox) clearing the way for generic competition. Another top seller Plavix lost patent protection in the US in 2012 (resulting in reduced royalties from marketing partner BMS) as did blood pressure drug Avapro. Sanofi's diversification strategy hinges mainly upon making strategic acquisitions in its core therapeutic areas as well as in new markets and emerging regions poised for growth.

To boost offering of delicate biopharmaceuticals Sanofi acquired prescription drug firm Genzyme in 2011 for some $20.1 billion after months of negotiation including a lower hostile bid failed. The deal included an additional $3.8 billion that is contingent on the future performance of Genzyme's lead drug candidates (including multiple sclerosis candidate Lemtrada) and its manufacturing facilities. The purchase of Genzyme gives Sanofi a portfolio of products focused on rare inherited disorders kidney disease orthopedics transplant and immune disease cancer and diagnostic testing. Its top product is rare disease treatment Cerezyme for Gaucher's disease. Following the acquisition Genzyme became the headquarters of the parent's rare disease program. Once Genzyme was formally part of its structure the company chose to simplify the collective organization's identity by shortening its name from Sanofi-Aventis to simply Sanofi.

Another area in which the company has been particularly focused on growing is the worldwide OTC market largely through its US Chattem division which converted Allegra to an OTC product in 2011 following its patent expiration. Also in 2011 Sanofi acquired BMP Sunstone a US-based firm that markets vitamins and mineral supplements and cough and cold medicines in China for about $520 million. Through its majority owned India unit Aventis Pharma Sanofi also expanded its portfolio by buying the marketing and distribution business of Universal Medicare which makes more than 40 branded nutraceutical formulations in India.

Not one to miss an opportunity Sanofi decided it too would take advantage of patent expirations by growing its generics business especially in the European generics market where it maintains the Winthrop brand. It has also established a generic presence in emerging markets (another growth area for the company) in the Middle East Latin America and Asia.

In 2010 Sanofi took its plan to reduce its reliance on prescription drugs one step further by entering the market for medical devices. The company joined forces with medical equipment maker Agamatrix to develop blood sugar monitoring devices for diabetes patients. Sanofi already has a solid presence in the diabetes market with its insulin products Apidra and Lantus. The blood glucose monitoring systems designed to work in conjunction with the company's existing diabetes treatments were launched in European markets under the BGStar and iBGStar brands in 2011.

The next year Sanofi agreed to acquire Pluromed a medical device company that developed proprietary polymer technology used in injectable plugs for improving the safety efficacy and costs of medical interventions. The company also makes LeGoo gel a product used in surgery for temporary endovascular occlusion of blood vessels in the US and Europe.

While it has been growing some operations the company has taken a different approach to its research and development business. Beginning in 2009 Sanofi began cutting back on its pipeline of drug candidates in an effort to save on R&D costs narrowing its focus on the most promising candidates in targeted areas including cancer diabetes cardiology neurology vaccines and biologics. As of early 2011 it had about 55 candidates in its drug pipeline with about a dozen of them in late stages of clinical development. In 2009 it successfully launched a new atrial fibrillation (irregular heart beat) medicine Multaq and in 2010 it introduced prostate cancer drug Jevtana.

The company is also increasingly relying on partnerships and licensing agreements with other firms and academic institutions to support its research efforts. For instance in 2010 Sanofi formed a major outsourcing agreement with contract research organization (CRO) Covance. The deal worth up to $2.2 billion included Covance's purchase of two Sanofi R&D facilities in Europe. Covance will provide drug development services to the company through a ten-year contract.

Though it is streamlining its internal development operations the company still pursues acquisitions to bolster its late-stage pipeline in core research areas. In 2010 the company boosted its pipeline with treatments for leukemia and certain blood disorders by buying privately held TargeGen for $75 million (plus up to $485 million in potential future milestone payments).

In the vaccines market Sanofi's biggest sellers include pediatric combination vaccines and the cervical cancer vaccine Gardasil (marketed through an agreement with Merck). Subsidiary Sanofi Pasteur is also a top maker of flu vaccines and has received a boost from growing concerns over the possibility of an influenza pandemic. While its vaccine business only makes up about 10% of the company's sales Sanofi has made small acquisitions to keep its pipeline pumping.

Sanofi's animal health operations are conducted through its Merial subsidiary which was formerly a 50-50 joint venture with Merck. Sanofi acquired Merck's share of Merial (as Merck prepared for its acquisition of drugmaker Schering-Plough) in 2009 for about $4 billion. The two exercised an option to strike a fresh venture early the next year and announced plans to combine Merial with Merck's animal health business Intervet; however after spending a year planning the merger the two companies ended the agreement in 2011 citing complexities arising from anticipated divestitures to satisfy antitrust regulators. Sanofi has stated that it will instead grow its animal health operations through smaller bolt-on acquisitions.

While the company has been aggressively expanding its product offerings and R&D pipeline of potential blockbusters to help ward off the threat of generic competition it has also been pursuing cost-cutting measures as a means of offsetting future patent losses. In 2011 for instance Sanofi announced that it was reviewing options to divest its US dermatology business Dermik and later that year it sold the unit to Valeant Pharmaceuticals for some $425 million. In addition in 2010 the company downsized certain manufacturing and sales operations to reduce inefficiencies and prepare for lower production and sales volumes of selected products going off-patent. It has also conducted some layoffs.

HISTORY

The Sanofi group got its start in 1973 when French oil conglomerate Elf Aquitaine (later part of TOTAL) merged several health care cosmetics and animal nutrition companies into one subsidiary. In 1977 Sanofi set up a Japanese subsidiary through which it developed joint ventures with Japan's Meiji Seika Kaisha and Taisha Pharmaceutical firms. In 1979 Elf spun off Sanofi although it retained ownership of more than half of the company. Almost from its founding Sanofi grew through acquisitions and alliances. During the 1980s it used a massive war chest to buy stakes and set up joint ventures such as one with American Home Products in 1982.

The company bought "couturier et parfumier" Nina Ricci in 1988; such well-known fragrances as L'Air du Temps put it among the industry's top perfume houses. But Sanofi overreached the next two years and was outbid by American Home Products for AH Robins (the drug firm bankrupted by lawsuits over deaths from its Dalkon Shield IUD) and by Rh ´ne-Poulenc (now part of Aventis) for Rorer. A chastened Sanofi and Kodak subsidiary Sterling Drug in 1991 entered into an alliance that didn't involve an exchange of cash.

In 1993 Sanofi made a splash when it bought the perfume business of fashion designer Yves Saint-Laurent. The next year it bought out much of the pharmaceutical joint venture with Kodak. Sanofi began divesting such noncore businesses as veterinarian and biotech operations in 1995. After suffering a loss in its perfume and beauty division in 1996 it sold Nina Ricci. The rest of its beauty division was sold in 1999 in preparation for the Syntheabo merger.

Syntheabo was founded in 1970 when drug firms Laboratoires Dausse and Laboratoires Robert et Carriere merged. In 1973 it became a 53%-owned subsidiary of beauty products maker L'Or ©al. In 1980 drug firm Metabio-Jouillie became a part of Syntheabo making it the #3 drug company in France. In 1983 Syntheabo and US drugmaker Searle created Lorex to market the French firm's products in the UK. (Syntheabo bought Searle's interest 10 years later.)

Throughout the 1980s Syntheabo acquired merged and formed joint ventures including some in Japan with Mitsubishi Chemical Fujisawa Pharmaceutical (1985) and Tanabe Seiyaku (1987). The company continued its acquisitive ways in the 1990s buying several French rivals.

Syntheabo openly admitted its quest for a large international presence in 1996 announcing it wanted 80% of its sales to come from such foreign markets as Asia and the US. That year the company entered an alliance with Genset to research cancer-causing genes; it also signed on with SmithKline Beecham (now GlaxoSmithKline) and Human Genome Sciences to fund genetic research. Syntheabo's Hungarian subsidiary began planning to make drugs for the first time rather than just selling its parent's products as in the past. The next year Syntheabo bought Pharmacia & Upjohn's German generic drug subsidiary Sanorania Pharma.

As Syntheabo and Sanofi merged in 1999 the new company's concentration on pharmaceuticals dictated several changes including the sale of the company's interests in joint venture Pasteur Sanofi Diagnostics as well as its beauty division home to such well-known perfume lines as Yves Saint Laurent. It also sold its veterinary and animal feed division to what is now BNP Paribas.

Sanofi-Synthelabo made good on its plans to target the US in 2000 expanding its sales force there. But the merger wasn't without its problems: Former Syntheabo CEO Herv ©Gu ©n was ousted as vice chairman and COO of Sanofi-Syntheabo after he and chairman Jean-Fran ®is Dehecq butted heads. In 2002 the company boosted its pipeline by entering into an alliance with Immuno-Designed Molecules a biotechnology firm focusing on cancer drugs. Also that year the FDA approved the firm's colorectal cancer drug Eloxatine in record time.

Sanofi-Syntheabo acquired Aventis –and with it the Allegra franchise and Merial joint venture –in 2004. Following the merger the company changed its name to Sanofi-Aventis.

Even though key patents for Plavix weren't scheduled to expire until 2011 generics maker Apotex introduced a generic version in 2006 that flooded the US market. An injunction issued by US courts halted Apotex's manufacturing of the drug (though not sales of already distributed products) but the episode still reduced Sanofi-Aventis' Plavix sales in the US by about 16% compared to the previous year. Both companies pursued litigation.

The company received EU approval in 2006 for the use of its weight-loss drug rimonabant which entered the market under the brand name Acomplia. However in 2008 Sanofi-Aventis suspended marketing efforts for Acomplia due to reports of psychiatric side effects; the company canceled all clinical trials for the drug later that year.

In 2008 the company acquired the Australian vitamin and mineral supplements business of Symbion (now part of Primary Health Care) for $480 million. It also purchased vaccine-maker Acambis which had a history of working with Sanofi Pasteur and brought with it an approved smallpox vaccine and a solid pipeline of vaccines in development.

In late 2009 it shelled out nearly $2 billion to acquire Chattem which not only gave it a hefty line of well-known consumer products but also increased Sanofi's presence in the US (which accounted for about 30% of the company's annual sales in 2009). As part of that deal Sanofi decided to convert Allegra from a prescription to an OTC drug (following its patent expiration) and transfer it to Chattem to market. The company also expanded its presence in Asia by forming a joint venture with Chinese nutritionals firm Minsheng Pharmaceutical in 2009.

In 2009 the company paid some $1.5 billion to acquire the remaining shares of Czech generics maker Zentiva in which it already held a 25% stake. Zentiva brought with it generic operations in emerging markets including Turkey and Russia. Sanofi also expanded its Asian generics operations by forming a joint venture with Japan's Nichi-Iko Pharmaceuticals and it became sizeable in South America when it bought top Brazilian generic drug manufacturer Medley for $663 million in 2009.

In 2009 it acquired US development firm BiPar Sciences in a deal worth up to $500 million adding

potential therapies for breast ovarian and other cancers; it also purchased ophthalmology development firm Fovea Pharmaceuticals for $540 million.
Auditors: ERNST & YOUNG et Autres

LOCATIONS

HQ: Sanofi
54, Rue La Boetie, Paris 75008
Phone: (33) 1 53 77 40 00 **Fax:** (33) 1 53 77 43 03
Web: www.sanofi.com

HISTORICAL FINANCIALS

Company Type: Public

Income Statement FYE: December 31

	REVENUE ($ mil.)	NET INCOME ($ mil.)	NET PROFIT MARGIN	EMPLOYEES
12/14	41,459	5,336	12.9%	113,496
12/13	45,853	5,117	11.2%	112,128
12/12	47,393	6,546	13.8%	111,974
12/11	45,345	7,363	16.2%	113,719
12/10	42,874	7,316	17.1%	101,575
Annual Growth	(0.8%)	(7.6%)	—	2.8%

2014 Year-End Financials

Debt ratio: 18.4%
Return on equity: 7.7%
Cash ($ mil.): 8,923
Current ratio: 1.80
Long-term debt ($ mil.): 16,137
No. of shares (mil.): 1,309
Dividends
Yield: 4.1%
Payout: 84.8%
Market value ($ mil.): 59,745

	STOCK PRICE ($) FY Close	P/E High/Low		PER SHARE ($) Earnings	Dividends	Book Value
12/14	45.61	16	13	4.01	1.91	52.08
12/13	53.63	21	16	3.83	1.79	59.14
12/12	47.38	13	9	4.93	1.69	57.12
12/11	36.54	9	7	5.55	3.23	54.93
12/10	32.23	9	7	5.59	1.47	54.46
Annual Growth	9.1%	—	—	(8.0%)	6.9%	(1.1%)

SAP SE

It can take a lot of processes to run companies and SAP's software aims to keep them operating smoothly. SAP is the leading provider of enterprise resource planning (ERP) software used to integrate back-office functions such as distribution accounting human resources and manufacturing. Its clients are mainly in the service manufacturing and consumer industries but also in public services and financial services. The backbone of SAP's products has been its on-premise offerings spearheaded by its Business Suite which includes ERP and customer relationship management (CRM) software among others. In recent years the company has been shifting its products to the cloud with its SAP HANA platform.Operations

SAP sells its software and services in two segments. Software and software-related services account for 84% of revenue. The segment includes SAP's on-premise software and its cloud-based software products. The biggest chunk of revenue –53% –comes from payment for support of the company's software. Professional services offered by SAP generate the other 16% of revenue.Geographic Reach

Headquartered in Walldorf Germany SAP has facilities in more than 130 countries. In 2014 the US was SAP's biggest single market accounting fort 28% of the company's revenue. Germany was the next biggest market with 15%. Including Germany the EMEA region contributed 48% of revenue. About 15% of revenue came from the Asia Pacific and Japan region. Demonstrating its commitment to cloud computing the company expanded data centers in Germany and the US opened new centers in Australia and Russia in 2014 and planned new centers in Brazil and Russia. It operates 16 data centers around the world.Sales and Marketing

Most of SAP's sales are generated by the direct sales staffs within the organization although it also sells through partners. In 2014 the company moved a number of employees to sales-oriented roles to accelerate revenue growth. Personnel costs rose 4% for the year.

Companies working in energy and natural resources are SAP's biggest market segment accounting for about a quarter of revenue. Consumer companies are next with 23% of revenue followed by manufacturing and services companies combining for about a third of revenue with government agencies and financial services firms accounting for the rest. The company has more than a quarter million customers.Financial Performance

Revenue increased by about 4% from 2013 to 2014. The company's revenue from cloud subscriptions and support jumped 56% for the year. While the cloud is where SAP wants to take the business cloud-related revenue is still just 6% of the total. Revenue generated by support for its big on-premise software –53% of sales –increased 7% in 2014 from 2013. Sales of those big software systems were down about 2.6% in 2014. Net income ticked down 1% in 2014 on higher costs for software development and sales and marketing. SAP also spent about $672 million on litigation. Cash flow from operations was 4% higher in 2014.

Stategy

The S in SAP stands for Systems but might also stand for Simple. In face the title of its 2014 annual report was "Run Simple." The company's goal is to simplify consumption of its products by moving them to the cloud; simplify how they are developed by basing them on its SAP HANA platform; and simplify how its customers deal with complex streams of data. SAP's main new product SAP HANA (High-Performance Analytic Appliance) is an in-memory database management system that helps SAP customers see in real time what's happening in their companies. SAP intends to base all its future applications on SAP HANA including its cloud computing products. The platform is a weapon in SAP's battle with Oracle for dominance in the enterprise software market. The company reported that is has 5800 SAP HANA customers and 1850 customers of it SAP Business Suite powered by SAP HANA.

Unlike the big on-premise software systems on which most of SAP's revenue rests cloud-based software sold by subscription is a more tenuous source of revenue. Customers usually subscribe for one to three years and can move to another vendor with less risk of disrupting their operations. To hold customers SAP continually improves its software adding new features –often through acquisitions and it share its roadmap of improvements with customers.

SAP is one of several big software companies making the transition from on-premise to cloud software. Besides Oracle Microsoft IBM and others face similar challenges. Some competitors such as BMC have gone private in order to shore up their cloud offerings.

Mergers and Acquisitions

SAP has embraced cloud computing and to a large degree has spent about $16 million to buy its way in by acquiring companies that fill out its business networking capabilities.In 2014 SAP acquired Concur a provider of travel and expense management software for companies. SAP will integrate Concur's travel and expense management software with Ariba's transactional applications solutions and aim them toward a market of more than $600 billion annual transactions in 25 industries.SAP also bought Fieldglass whose programs help businesses oversee contract employees and projects. The intent is that Fieldglass would help round out SAP's acquisitions of SuccessFactorsw hich develops personnel management software and Ariba.In 2014 SAP acquired SeeWhy a provider of cloud-based behavioral target marketing software. The SeeWhy product complements the commerce platform of hybris a 2013 SAP acquisition.

HISTORY

Early History

Former IBM software engineers Hasso Plattner Hans-Werner Hector Dietmar Hopp Claus Wellenreuther and Klaus Tschira started SAP in 1972 when the project they were working on for IBM was moved to another unit.

While rival software firms made many products to automate the various parts of a company's operations these engineers decided to make a single system that would tie a corporation together. In 1973 they launched an instantaneous accounting transaction-processing program called R/1. By 1979 they had adapted the program to create R/2 mainframe software that linked external databases and communication systems.

The company went public in 1988. That year Plattner began a project to create software for the computer network market. In 1992 as sales of its R/2 mainframe software lagged SAP introduced its R/3 software which would later become its flagship SAP ERP.

EXECUTIVES

CEO, William R. (Bill) McDermott, age 53, $1,279,900 total compensation
Head of Scale Quality & Support Board, Gerhard Oswald, age 61, $700,000 total compensation
Member of the Executive Board; Chief Financial Officer, Werner Brandt, age 61, $700,000 total compensation
COO Australia and New Zealand, John Ruthven
CTO, Quentin Clark
President Global Customer Operations, Robert (Rob) Enslin
CIO and Head of Cloud Delivery, Ingrid-Helen Arnold
President Latin America and the Caribbean (LAC), Claudio Muruzabal
Chairman, Hasso Plattner, age 71
Deputy Chairperson Supervisory Board, Christiane Kuntz-Mayr
Auditors: KPMG AG Wirtschaftsprufungsgesellschaft

LOCATIONS

HQ: SAP SE
Dietmar-Hopp-Allee 16, Walldorf D-69190
Phone: (49) 0 6227 7 47474 **Fax:** (49) 0 6227 7 57575
Web: www.sap.com

2014 Sales

	% of total
Europe Middle East & Africa	
Germany	15
Other countries	33
Americas	
US	28
Other countries	9
Asia/Pacific	
Japan	3
Other countries	12
Total	**100**

PRODUCTS/OPERATIONS

2014 Sales by Type

	% of total
Software & related service	
Support	53
Software	25
Cloud Subscription & support	6
Professional and other service	16
Total	**100**

2014 Sales by Market

	% of total
Energy & natural resources	24
Discrete Manufacturing	17
Consumer products	23
Public services	10
Financial services	10
Services	16
Total	**100**

Selected Customers

Aigo
City of Cape Town South Africa
Danone
Beaumont Health System
McLaren Group

Selected Software

SAP Business All-in-One
SAP Business ByDesign
SAP Business One
SAP Business Suite
SAP ERP
SAP HANA
SAP NetWeaver

Selected Services

Application hosting
Business consulting
Custom development
Financing
Implementation
Maintenance
Training

Selected Acquisitions

Concur (2014) Travel and expense management software for companiesHybris (2014) Real-time customer engagement and commerce platformSeeWhy (2014) Cloud-based behavioral target marketing softwareTicket-Web (2013) Ticketing software and customer relationshi
Right Hemisphere (2012; enterprise visualization)
TechniData (2010; environmental health and safety)
Sybase (2010 business intelligence and database management)
Clear Standards (2009 environmental)
Highdeal (2009 billing)
Visiprise (2008 manufacturing process management)
Business Objects (2008 business intelligence)
OutlookSoft (2007 business performance management)
Pilot Software (2007 business performance management)

COMPETITORS

BMC Software	IBM
CA Inc.	MicroStrategy
CDC Software	Microsoft
Electronic Data Processing	Oracle
	Software AG
Epicor Software	Workday Inc.
HP	salesforce.com

HISTORICAL FINANCIALS

Company Type: Public

Income Statement FYE: December 31

	REVENUE ($ mil.)	NET INCOME ($ mil.)	NET PROFIT MARGIN	EMPLOYEES
12/14	21,344	3,986	18.7%	74,406
12/13	23,149	4,579	19.8%	66,572
12/12	21,382	3,720	17.4%	64,422
12/11	18,409	4,446	24.2%	55,765
12/10	16,681	2,423	14.5%	53,513
Annual Growth	6.4%	13.2%	—	8.6%

2014 Year-End Financials

Debt ratio: 36.4%
Return on equity: 18.4%
Cash ($ mil.): 4,045
Current ratio: 1.05
Long-term debt ($ mil.): 10,915
No. of shares (mil.): 1,195
Dividends
Yield: 1.4%
Payout: —
Market value ($ mil.): 83,248

	STOCK PRICE ($) FY Close	P/E High/Low		PER SHARE ($) Earnings	Dividends	Book Value
12/14	69.65	28	22	3.33	0.99	19.83
12/13	87.14	32	26	3.83	0.80	18.50
12/12	80.38	34	23	3.12	1.02	15.66
12/11	52.95	21	15	3.74	0.00	13.80
12/10	50.61	34	27	2.03	0.42	11.05
Annual Growth	8.3%	—	—	13.1%	23.8%	15.7%

Saudi British Bank (The)

The Saudi British Bank (SABB) provides personal private and corporate banking services to customers across Saudi Arabia. Founded in 1978 SABB operates a network of about 80 branches (including more than a dozen locations exclusively for women) offering deposits loans and Takaful (cooperative insurance that complies with Islamic law). It also issues VISA and MasterCard credit cards as well as the SABB Amanah card which offers monthly payment plans that adhere to Islamic principles. Corporate services include cash management treasury and investment banking through HSBC Saudi Arabia Limited. British banking giant HSBC owns about 40% of SABB; Saudi nationals own 60%.

Auditors: KPMG Al Fozan & Al Sadhan

LOCATIONS

HQ: Saudi British Bank (The)
P.O. Box 9084, Riyadh 11413
Phone: (966) 1 405 0677 **Fax:** (966) 1 276 4809
Web: www.sabb.com

COMPETITORS

Ahli United Bank	Gulf International Bank
Al Rajhi Banking	Samba Financial
Arab Banking Corp.	
Arab National Bank	
British Arab Commercial Bank	

HISTORICAL FINANCIALS

Company Type: Public

Income Statement FYE: December 31

	ASSETS ($ mil.)	NET INCOME ($ mil.)	INCOME AS % OF ASSETS	EMPLOYEES
12/14	49,997	1,136	2.3%	3,314
12/13	47,273	1,006	2.1%	3,158
12/12	41,768	863	2.1%	3,049
12/11	36,975	770	2.1%	3,123
12/10	33,431	502	1.5%	3,389
Annual Growth	10.6%	22.7%	—	(0.6%)

2014 Year-End Financials

Return on assets: 2.3%
Return on equity: 17.4%
Long-term debt ($ mil.): —
No. of shares (mil.): 1,000
Sales ($ mil): 1,912
Dividends
Yield: —
Payout: —
Market value ($ mil.): —

Sberbank Russia

Whether you do your saving in Siberia or your asset management in Moscow the Savings Bank of the Russian Federation or Sberbank has a branch for you. With a history going back some 170 years Sberbank is one of the largest banking institutions in Russia serving about 70% of nation's population. It has some 17000 branches throughout the country (crossing 11 time zones) offering banking services ranging from savings to private and investment banking and a complete range of lending and credit services to more than 1 million corporate and 135 million retail customers. The Central Bank of the Russian Federation also known as The Bank of Russia controls Sberbank with a 50% ownership stake.

OperationsIn addition to its main retail banking services Sberbank also boasts a trade finance and an investment banking business. It also provides health life third-party liability and other insurance products for both retail and corporate clients. Its insurance business serves more than 8.5 million individuals and 192000 corporate clients. Sberbank makes about three-fourths of its revenues from loan interest. The company generated 46% of its total revenue from interest on loans to corporate customers in 2014 while another 28% of revenue came from interest on loans to individuals. About 16% of its total revenue came from fee and commission income.Geographic ReachWhile 80% of its assets are in Russia Sberbank also has foreign subsidiary banks in 22 countries including the UK Central and Eastern Europe Turkey and others. Its DenizBank AS subsidiary has branches in Austria Russia Northern CyprusGermany and Bahrain. Sberbank Europe AG Austria (SBE) and its subsidiary banks serve the Czech Republic Slovakia Hungary Croatia Slovenia Bosnia Herzegovina and Ukraine.Sales and MarketingSberbank serves individuals institutions and medium to large-sized businesses and corporations.Financial PerformanceNote: Growth rates may differ after conversion to US dollars.Sberbank's revenues and profits have been on the uptrend in recent years thanks to continued growth in its corporate and retail loan businesses. The bank's revenue jumped by 26% to R$2.25 trillion ($39.6 billion) in 2014 mostly as its corporate loan and retail loan businesses grew by 40% and nearly 30% respectively. The group's net fee and commission income also rose by nearly 28% as the bank received more income from cash and settlement transactions with individuals and legal entities and as its investment banking and financial market businesses grew slightly during the year. (Note: In terms of US$ revenue fell sharply due to the decline in the Ruble.) Despite revenue growth in 2014 Sberbank's net income dropped 20% to R$290.3 billion ($5.1 billion) as the cost of funding rose sharply in December (interest expenses increased by 33% for the year) and as loan provision charges particularly with foreign exchange loans grew with the reduced valued of the Ruble and the overall quality deterioration of the bank's loan portfolio amidst political tensions in the Ukraine and Russia. Sberbank's operating cash nearly doubled to R$830 billion ($14.6 billion) despite lower earnings in 2014 mostly as the bank borrowed more cash from other banks.

Stategy

Sberbank continued to dominate the Russian deposit and loan market in 2015. Beyond reporting that a whopping 70% of the population of Russia used its services during the year the bank boasted a 53% market share of the mortgage loan market and kept its firm grip on more than half of the country's deposits. As part of its "Strategy 2018" goal to diversify and expand its revenue streams the bank plans to grow in the insurance and pension markets in future years. To this end in 2014 Sberbank launched its Sberbank Insurance and Sberbank Insurance Broker subsidiaries to start getting a foothold in the insurance business.To grow its existing business with customers Sberbank regularly releases new banking products many of which are tied to government programs as part of a "one-stop-shop" for government and banking services. During 2014 it launched a slew of new products including: government subsidy programs like consumer loans for military personnel and government-supported education loans; its PRO100 bankcards for personal or payroll card use in the Russian Payment system; and a popular Cash Management service (which grew its user base by 60% during the year) that allowed customers to receive cash flow data between their accounts at different commercial banks.Sberbank has also been moving toward digital banking channels that are quickly taking the industry by storm allowing the bank to slow expensive branch-expansion plans and cut operating costs significantly while giving customers faster access to banking services. As of 2015 Sberbank had 90000 self-service machines as well as 72.2 million subscribers to its Mobile Banking SMS-services with more than 20 million active users.Mergers and AcquisitionsIn early 2012 to build its investment banking practice the company bought Moscow-based Troika Dialog from Standard Bank and Troika's management for some $1.25 billion.OwnershipThe Central Bank of the Russian Federation (The Bank of Russia) is the founder and principal shareholder of Sberbank commanding a 50% stake plus one voting share of the Russian bank.

EXECUTIVES

Deputy Chairman, Sergey Gorkov
Deputy Chairman, Stanislav K. Kuznetsov
Deputy Chairman, Alexander Torbakhov, age 43
Deputy Chairman, Bella Zlatkis
Deputy Chairman, Alexander Morozov
First Deputy Chairman, Lev Khasis, age 49
Chairman of the Board and Chief Executive Officer of Sberbank of Russia, Herman Gref, age 51
First Deputy Chairman, Maxim Poletaev
Deputy Chairman, Andrey Donskih
Deputy Chairman, Vadim Kulik
Vice President Director of the Financial Department, Nikolay Tsekhomskiy
Auditors: CJSC Ernst & Young Vneshaudit

LOCATIONS

HQ: Sberbank Russia
19 Vavilova St., Moscow 117997
Phone: (7) 495 500 55 50 **Fax:** (7) 495 957 5731
Web: www.sberbank.ru

PRODUCTS/OPERATIONS

2014 Sales

	% of total
Interest	
Loans	74
Securities	7
Due from other banks	1
Noninterest	
Fee and commission income	16
Net gain on trading in forieng currency	1
Other	1
Total	**100**

Selected Subsidiary

DenizBank A.S.
Sberbank Europe AG
Sberbank Kazakhstan
BPS-Sberbank (Belarus)
Sberbank Ukraine

Selected Group companies

Auction House of the Russian Federation OJSC
Auction LLC
Sberbank Asset Management CJSC
Sberbank Ast CJSC
Sberbank Capital LLC
Sberbank CIB
Sberbank Insurance Company LLC
Sberbank Leasing CJSC
Sberbank Private Pension Fund
Status Registrar Society CJSC
Strategy Partners Group CJSC
United Credit Bureau CJSC

COMPETITORS

Alfa Group
Deutsche Bank (Moscow)
MDM Bank
Sistema
VTB

HISTORICAL FINANCIALS

Company Type: Public

Income Statement FYE: December 31

	REVENUE ($ mil.)	NET INCOME ($ mil.)	NET PROFIT MARGIN	EMPLOYEES
12/14	36,928	4,964	13.4%	0
12/13	53,177	11,069	20.8%	0
12/12	45,370	11,458	25.3%	286,019
12/11	31,876	9,795	30.7%	266,187
12/10	31,689	5,968	18.8%	257,046
Annual Growth	3.9%	(4.5%)	—	—

2014 Year-End Financials

Debt ratio: —
Return on equity: 15.0%
Cash ($ mil.): 39,225
Current ratio: —
Long-term debt ($ mil.): —
No. of shares (mil.): —
Dividends
Yield: 15.8%
Payout: 94.9%
Market value ($ mil.): —

	STOCK PRICE ($) FY Close	P/E High/Low	PER SHARE ($) Earnings	Dividends	Book Value
12/14	3.87	1 0	0.23	0.61	1.59
12/13	12.57	1 1	0.51	0.24	2.64
12/12	12.56	1 1	0.53	0.19	2.35
12/11	9.94	1 1	0.45	0.00	1.82
Annual Growth	(27.0%)	— —	(15.7%)	—	(3.4%)

Schlumberger Ltd.

Measuring and controlling devices nec n

EXECUTIVES

Pr ©sident Directeur G ©n ©ral, Pascal PANETTA
Auditors: PricewaterhouseCoopers LLP

LOCATIONS

HQ: Schlumberger Ltd.
42 Rue Saint-Dominique, Paris 75007
Phone: 713 513-2000
Web: www.slb.com

HISTORICAL FINANCIALS

Company Type: Public

Income Statement FYE: December 31

	REVENUE ($ mil.)	NET INCOME ($ mil.)	NET PROFIT MARGIN	EMPLOYEES
12/15	35,711	2,072	5.8%	95,000
12/14	48,871	5,438	11.1%	120,000
12/13	46,459	6,732	14.5%	123,000
12/12	42,321	5,490	13.0%	118,000
12/11	39,669	4,997	12.6%	113,000
Annual Growth	(2.6%)	(19.8%)		(4.2%)

2015 Year-End Financials

Debt ratio: 27.9%
Return on equity: 5.6%
Cash ($ mil.): 13,034
Current ratio: 1.91
Long-term debt ($ mil.): 14,442
No. of shares (mil.): 1,256
Dividends
Yield: 2.8%
Payout: 74.9%
Market value ($ mil.): 87,632

	STOCK PRICE ($) FY Close	P/E High/Low	PER SHARE ($) Earnings	Dividends	Book Value
12/15	69.75	58 41	1.63	2.00	28.36
12/14	85.41	28 19	4.16	1.60	29.68
12/13	90.11	19 14	5.05	1.25	30.19
12/12	69.30	19 14	4.10	1.10	26.16
12/11	68.31	26 16	3.67	1.00	23.44
Annual Growth	0.5%	— —	(18.4%)	18.9%	4.9%

Schneider Electric SE

If you're hungry for power this company can help. Schneider Electric is a leading global manufacturer of equipment for electrical power distribution and for industrial control and automation. The company helps power generators distribute electricity; designs automation systems for the automobile and water treatment industries; builds electric networks and utility management systems for energy water treatment oil and gas and marine applications; and manages electric power in residential industrial and commercial buildings. It sells its products to the construction electric power industrial and infrastructure markets.

Geographic ReachSchneider has operations in over 100 countries. The Asia Pacific contributes about 28% of net sales. Other major markets include Western Europe (27%) and North America (25%). The remaining stems from the rest of the world.

Operations

Schneider operates through four operating segments: Buildings and Partner (43% of net sales) Industry (22%) Infrastructure (21%) and Information Technology (IT; 14%).

Sales and Marketing

Distributors account for approximately 42% of its total revenues through an extensive network in 190 countries all over the world. Schneider Electric serves 113 global customers including Apple BHP Billiton EDF ExxonMobil Nestl and Veolia Environment.

Financial Performance

Schneider's revenues jumped 7% and its profits increased 45% from 2013 to 2014 due to increased sales from its Buildings and Partner and Industry segments. These segments experienced solid OEM demand growth from all regions especially Western Europe. (Note: the company's 2013 annual statement was restated due to discontinued operations.)

Mergers and Acquisitions

Schneider has been enhancing its product portfolio through the use of acquisitions. In mid-2015 the company announced it was combining its software operations with British engineering IT firm Aveva in a reverse takeover. The deal will see Aveva acquire Schneider's software division on a debt-free cash-free basis and Schneider will then pay Aveva £550m for new Aveva shares which will result in it owning 54% of the enlarged company. Aveva provides design software for the industrial plant power and shipping industries.

HISTORY

Schneider Electric's predecessor was founded in 1782 to make industrial equipment. After the upheavals of the French Revolution and the Napoleonic Wars the company came under the control of brothers Adolphe and Eugene Schneider in 1836. Within two years they had built the first French locomotive (the country's first rail line opened in 1832).

Schneider became one of France's most important heavy industry companies branching into a variety of machinery and steel operations. However the country's industrial development continued to trail that of Britain and Germany due to recurrent political strife including the revolution of 1848 and the Franco-Prussian War. France also possessed fewer coal and iron deposits.

During WWI Schneider was a key part of France's war effort. It entered the electrical contracting business in 1929 and fought off nationalization attempts in the mid-1930s. The blitzkrieg of 1939 brought much of France under Nazi occupation and the Schneider factories that were not destroyed were commandeered by the Germans.

The company rebuilt after the war aided by the French government. It was restructured as a holding company and its operating units were split into three subsidiaries: civil and electrical engineering industrial manufacturing and construction. Charles Schneider the last family member to lead the company died in 1950.

In 1963 Schneider concluded an alliance with the Empain Group of Belgium and by 1969 three years after Schneider went public the two companies merged to become Empain-Schneider. It was a period when the company made numerous noncore acquisitions entering such fields as ski equipment fashion publishing and travel.

Schneider began reorganizing in 1980. The effort entered its final phase in 1993 with a major recapitalization that saw the merger of its former parent company Socit Parisienne d'Entreprises et de Participations with Schneider SA and the issue of new stock to existing stockholders.

EXECUTIVES

EVP Global Supply Chain, Annette K. Clayton, age 52
Deputy CEO Finance and Legal Affairs, Emmanuel Babeau, age 44
Chairman and CEO, Jean-Pascal Tricoire, age 52
Southeast Asia Operations, Hal Grant, age 55
EVP Global Solutions, Daniel Doimo
EVP Strategy and Technology, Michel Crochon, age 64
EVP Global Marketing and Chief Marketing Officer, Chris Leong
President UK and Ireland, Tanuja Randery
EVP Technology and CTO, Prith Banerjee, age 54
EVP North America Operations, Laurent Vernerey, age 55
EVP Buildings and Partner, Philippe Delorme, age 44
EVP Europe Operations, Leonid Mukhamedov
EVP Information Systems and CIO, Herv ©Coureil, age 45
EVP Industry Business, Clemens Blum, age 60
EVP China Operations, Zhu Hai
EVP France Operations and President Schneider Electric France, Luc R ©mont
EVP Infrastructure, Fr © ©c Abbal
EVP Global Human Resources, Olivier Blum
Auditors: ERNST & YOUNG et Autres

LOCATIONS

HQ: Schneider Electric SE
35 rue Joseph Monier, Rueil-Malmaison, Cedex 92500
Phone: (33) 1 41 29 70 00 **Fax:** (33) 1 41 29 71 00
Web: www.schneider-electric.com

2014 Sales

	% of total
Asia/Pacific	28
Western Europe	27
North America	25
Rest of the world	20
Total	**100**

PRODUCTS/OPERATIONS

2014 Sales

	% of total
Buildings & Partner	43
Industry	22
Infrastructure	21
IT	14
Total	**100**

Selected Products

Advanced human-machine interface terminals
Camera sensors
Centralized building management systems
Circuit breakers
Customized sensors
Disconnectors
Electric vehicle charging infrastructure
Electrical panels
Indicator lights
InRow Cooling Systems
Installation & control systems
Medium voltage cells
Network power control
Optimum temperature control
Power supply
Programmable regulators
Renewable energies integration
Security monitoring equipment
Server cabinets
Software for the integrated management of mission critical infrastructure
Supervision Control & Data Acquisition (SCADA) management systems
Transformers
Uninterruptable power supply
  Monophase
  Three-phase

COMPETITORS

ABB
ALSTOM
Alcatel-Lucent
Bechtel
Beghelli
Bharat Heavy Electricals
Checkpoint Systems
Danaher
EMCOR
Electricit© de France
Emerson Electric
Endress + Hauser
Finmeccanica
Fluor
GE
Itron
Johnson Controls
Legrand
Measurement Specialties
Mitsubishi Electric
Nissin Electric
Rockwell Automation
Roper Technologies
Sentry Technology
Siemens AG
Technology Research Corp.
Transtector
Vicon Industries
Woodhead Industries
Yokogawa Electric

HISTORICAL FINANCIALS

Company Type: Public

Income Statement FYE: December 31

	REVENUE ($ mil.)	NET INCOME ($ mil.)	NET PROFIT MARGIN	EMPLOYEES
12/14	30,313	2,359	7.8%	185,965
12/13	32,423	2,599	8.0%	152,784
12/12	31,562	2,425	7.7%	152,384
12/11	28,956	2,354	8.1%	140,491
12/10	26,205	2,302	8.8%	123,482
Annual Growth	3.7%	0.6%	—	10.8%

2014 Year-End Financials

Debt ratio: 22.6%
Return on equity: 10.5%
Cash ($ mil.): 3,221
Current ratio: 1.20
Long-term debt ($ mil.): 6,110
No. of shares (mil.): 571
Dividends
  Yield: 3.4%
  Payout: —
Market value ($ mil.): 8,234

	STOCK PRICE ($) FY Close	P/E High/Low		PER SHARE ($) Earnings	Dividends	Book Value
12/14	14.41	5	4	4.10	0.50	41.98
12/13	17.55	5	4	4.68	0.49	42.77
12/12	14.79	4	3	4.43	0.43	40.11
12/11	10.51	5	3	4.33	0.00	38.10
12/10	15.34	5	3	4.38	0.25	37.00
Annual Growth	(1.6%)	—	—	(1.7%)	19.1%	3.2%

SCOR S.E. (France)

This company knows the score in the global reinsurance market. SCOR provides treaty (groups of risks) and facultative (individual risks) reinsurance covering the risks of insurance underwriters around the globe. The company reinsures property/casualty life accident and health insurance lines. Most of SCOR's business comes from Europe and North America and is divided into two distinct business segments: Global Life (including long-term care and disability products) and Global P&C (including treaty corporate and specialty property/casualty lines). It serves customers in some 170 countries through offices that specialize in the needs of a specific industry or market.

Operations

The company's life insurance unit SCOR Global Life accounts for about 53% of revenue while SCOR Global P&C (property and casualty) brings in about 47%. Outside of its reinsurance operations the company has a third smaller business named SCOR Global Investments which provides asset and investment management services to the other operating SCOR facilities.

Geographic Reach

SCOR has about 40 offices in nearly 25 cities throughout in the Americas Europe and Asia. Europe contributed about 42% of revenue with France Germany Spain and Italy leading the charge. North America brings in about 40% and the rest comes from Asia and other countries (Australia and South Africa mainly).

Sales and Marketing

Reinsurance is written either through brokers or directly. SCOR employs both methods but breaks it down differently depending on the operating unit. Global Life is 90% direct and 10% broker while Global P&C is 63% broker and 37% direct.

Financial Performance

In 2013 the company reported a 7% increase in revenue as its Life unit performed well on the strength of an earlier acquisition of life insurance provider Generali US. Net income shot up 31% based on improved revenue gains made on the Generali purchase and increased investment returns. Cash flow however dropped due to cash used for acquisitions and investments.

Strategy

SCOR is focused on growing organically through new products and new markets and growing through acquisitions. It followed a large 2011 purchase with the acquisition of Generali US a life insurance provider. The company has also realigned its business portfolio to prioritize North America Asia and the rest of the world.

Mergers and Acquisitions

In 2013 SCOR purchased Italian insurer Assicurazioni Generali's US unit Generali US to boost its life insurance business. The $750 million price tag included Generali US' Kansas City office and staff; it created the country's largest life reinsurance company.

In 2011 the company acquired Transamerica Reinsurance from Dutch insurance giant AEGON for $912.5 million. The purchase included all of Transamerica Re's mortality risk reinsurance (pure life reinsurance) operations while AEGON retained the annuity guarantee business. The purchase made SCOR a top player in the US life reinsurance market and was folded in with the SCOR Global Life team.

HISTORY

SCOR was founded in 1970 by the French government to compete against reinsurers like Munich Re and Swiss Reinsurance; the government eventually ceded control to a group of French insurers including AXA UAP Re and Groupe des Assurances Nationales. By 1972 SCOR was expanding internationally.

Growth continued throughout the 1970s and '80s. In 1989 the firm acquired Deutsche Continental Rückversicherungs in Germany. A year later the firm listed on the Paris stock exchange.

In the early 1990s SCOR's owners began setting up their own reinsurance operations and selling off their holdings in the company. In 1995 AXA and Assurances Generales de France were the last to sell their stakes. Also that year SCOR consolidated ownership in its subsidiaries and streamlined its Asian operations.

The year 1996 was a big one in the US for SCOR. It acquired the reinsurance business of Allstate and also listed on the New York Stock Exchange. As worldwide property/casualty markets took a downturn in 1996 and 1997 SCOR began expanding its life accident and health reinsurance.

Numerous natural disasters in 1998 and 1999 hobbled SCOR's already slumping property/casualty unit; losses were offset by increased business in other lines. SCOR acquired full control of its Commercial Risk Partners subsidiary in 1999 bolstering its specialty reinsurance business. In 2000 SCOR reorganized its industrial risk business to further offset recent losses. That year the company bought Partner Re's US subsidiary PartnerRe Life and Switzerland-based Veritas property/casualty reinsurance portfolio.

In 2001 SCOR joined Inreon an online reinsurance exchange set up by industry bigwigs Swiss Re and Munich Re. In 2002 it liquidated and sold off subsidiary Commercial Risk Partners to reduce costs. Expanding internationally the company opened offices in Korea and India in 2004 and 2005.

In 2007 SCOR acquired Swiss reinsurer Converium Holding beginning with a buy-up of about a third of the company's shares. The purchase agreement went through several drafts (one resulting in a lawsuit alleging that SCOR had deliberately undervalued Converium) but was eventually accepted by both boards of directors. The acquisition added customers in Austria Germany Switzerland and the UK and boosted SCOR into a spot among the top five global life reinsurers.

Also in 2007 SCOR transformed itself into a Societas Europaea a legal structure that allows it more financial freedom in its European operations. In addition the company voluntarily delisted from the New York Stock Exchange.

EXECUTIVES

Deputy CEO Global P&C SE; CEOSCOR Switzerland, Benjamin Gentsch, age 55
Chairman and CEO, Denis Kessler, age 63, $500,000 total compensation
COO, Nicolas Tissot, age 49
CEO SCOR Global P&C SE, Victor Peignet, age 58, $203,000 total compensation
CEO SCOR Global Life SE, Paolo De Martin, age 45
CEO SCOR Global Investments SE, Fran $is De Varenne, age 49
CFO, Mark Kociancic, age 44
Chief Risk Officer, Frieder Kn pling, age 45
Deputy CEO SCOR Global Life SE, Simon Pearson, age 49
CEO P&C, Jean-Paul Conoscente
CEO Canada, Joseph El-Sayegh
Acting CEO Americas, Paul Christoff
Auditors: Mazars

LOCATIONS

HQ: SCOR S.E. (France)
5 avenue Kleber, Paris 75016
Phone: (33) 1 58 44 70 00 **Fax:** (33) 1 58 44 85 00
Web: www.scor.com

2013 Gross Written Premiums

	% of total
Europe	42
Americas	39
Asia-Pacific & other regions	19
Total	**100**

PRODUCTS/OPERATIONS

2013 Premiums

	% of total
Global P&C	53
Global Life	47
Total	**100**

COMPETITORS

AXIS Capital Holdings
Endurance Specialty
Everest Re
General Re
Hannover Re
Munich Re America
Munich Re Group
PartnerRe
Reinsurance Group of America
RenaissanceRe
Scottish Re Group
Swiss Re
Transatlantic Holdings
XL Group plc

HISTORICAL FINANCIALS

Company Type: Public

Income Statement FYE: December 31

	ASSETS ($ mil.)	NET INCOME ($ mil.)	INCOME AS % OF ASSETS	EMPLOYEES
12/14	45,175	622	1.4%	2,555
12/13	47,030	755	1.6%	2,450
12/12	42,955	550	1.3%	2,284
12/11	40,509	426	1.1%	2,184
12/10	38,440	559	1.5%	1,822
Annual Growth	4.1%	2.7%	—	8.8%

2014 Year-End Financials

Return on assets: 1.4%
Return on equity: 9.6%
Long-term debt ($ mil.): —
No. of shares (mil.): 186
Sales ($ mil): 14,278
Dividends
Yield: 5.9%
Payout: 4.7%
Market value ($ mil.): 555

	STOCK PRICE ($) FY Close	P/E High	P/E Low	PER SHARE ($) Earnings	Dividends	Book Value
12/14	2.98	1	1	3.31	0.18	37.19
12/13	3.62	1	1	4.01	0.16	36.68
12/12	2.76	2	1	2.95	0.14	34.51
12/11	2.23	2	1	2.29	0.14	30.82
12/10	2.46	1	1	3.04	0.12	32.06
Annual Growth	4.9%	—	—	2.1%	9.7%	3.8%

Seven & i Holdings Co. Ltd.

Japan's biggest retail conglomerate Seven & i Holdings caters to six of the so-called seven deadly sins (saving wrath for its competition). The "seven" of the company's title reflects the seven areas of business that it is involved with: convenience stores general merchandise and department stores restaurants supermarkets banks and IT services. The "holding" part of the firm's name consists of its subsidiaries: Seven-Eleven Japan (parent of 7-Eleven in the US) Ito-Yokado Sogo & Seibu Co. Seven & i Food Systems Seven Bank and York-Benimaru. Created in 2005 after stock-transfer agreements absorbing its subsidiaries into the company took effect Seven & i operates some 41900 stores worldwide.

After two years of decline the holding company's fiscal 2011 (ends February) total sales inched up a bit while net income more than doubled vs. the previous year. Seven & i's convenience stores posted a sales gain while sales at its superstores and department stores were flat. Already the world's #1 convenience store operator Seven & i's worldwide network of c-stores topped 40000 in fiscal 2011. (Convenience stores account for about 40% of the group's total worldwide sales.) By March 2014 the company is planning to open a record 1500 c-stores (for a net gain of more than 900) as it works to cater to "housewives and the elderly."

While Seven & i rings up more than two-thirds of its total sales at home the holding company oversees about 100 operating companies in 15 other countries in Asia North America and Europe. With the Japanese economy in a prolonged slump and reeling from the effects of the massive earthquake in March 2011 it's looking beyond its borders for growth opportunities. China is an important emerging market for Seven & i Holdings: It currently operates more than 4800 stores and restaurants in Taiwan and supermarkets stores and restaurants in Beijing Chengdu and Shanghai. Indeed in early 2009 Seven & i Food Systems formed a joint venture company with a large Chinese corporation to establish the family restaurant chain "AllDay's" there.

Seeking to further expand its retail empire the company and Ain Pharmaciez formed Seven Health Care which plans to open drugstores inside superstores and shopping malls operated by Seven & i Holdings and to develop generic drugs. Seven Health Care is jointly owned by Seven & i Holdings (10%) and its subsidiaries Ito-Yokado (50%) and Seven-Eleven Japan (10%) as well as Ain Pharmaciez (30%). More recently the company also boosted its entertainment holdings by doubling its stake in Tower Records Japan in 2011 to about 45%. The move made Seven & i the largest shareholder in the music retail chain (ahead of NTT DoCoMo with 42%).

While the global appetite for convenience store fare is growing the hunger for department store merchandise is not. As the Japanese department store industry struggles with weak personal consumption the company rearranged its department store holdings when it merged holding company Millennium Retailing with Sogo and Seibu department stores to form Sogo & Seibu Co. in August 2009. The merger was effected to capitalize on the well-known Sogo and Seibu names reduce costs and to foster collaboration with Seven & i.

The "i" of Seven & i Holdings stands for "innovation" as well as for the similar-sounding Japanese word for "love."

EXECUTIVES

President and COO, Noritoshi Murata, age 71
Chairman and CEO, Toshifumi Suzuki, age 83
President and COO Seven-Eleven Japan, Ryuichi Isaka
Chairman Seven Bank, Takashi Anzai
President and COO York-Benimaru, Zenko Ohtaka
Managing Executive Officer and Chief Administrative Officer, Katsuhiro Goto
President and COO Ito-Yokado, Atsushi Kamei
Executive Officer and CFO, Kunio Takahashi
President Sogo & Seibu, Ryu Matsumoto
President Seven & i Food Systems, Tsuneo Okubo
Auditors: KPMG AZSA LLC

LOCATIONS

HQ: Seven & i Holdings Co. Ltd.
8-8 Niban-cho, Chiyoda-ku, Tokyo 102-8452
Phone: (81) 3 6238 3000
Web: www.7andi.com

2014 Sales

	% of total
Japan	65
North America	33
Other regions	2
Total	**100**

PRODUCTS/OPERATIONS

2014 Sales

	% of total
Convenience stores	45
Superstores	35
Department stores	15
Financial services	3
Food services	1
Other	1
Total	**100**

Selected Subsidiaries

Convenience stores
- 7-Eleven Inc.
- Seven-Eleven (Beijing) Co. (65%)
- Seven-Eleven China Co.
- Seven-Eleven (Hawaii) Inc.
- Seven-Eleven Japan Co.

Superstores
- Chengdu Ito-Yokado (74%)
- Hua Tang Yokado (76%)
- Ito-Yokado
- York Mart
- York-Benimaru

Department stores
- Gottsuo Bin Co.
- The Loft Co. (71%)
- Shell Garden Co.
- Sogo & Seibu Co.

Financial services
- K.K. York Insurance
- Seven & i Financial Center
- Seven Bank (49%)
- Seven Card Service (96%)

Food services
- Seven & i Food Systems
- Seven & i Restaurant (Beijing) Co. (75%)

COMPETITORS

A.S. Watson
AEON
Asahi Kasei
Carrefour
Couche-Tard
Daiei
Dairy Farm International
FamilyMart
Fast Retailing
Isetan Mitsukoshi
J. Front
Kirin Holdings Company
Kokubu
LAWSON
McDonald' s
Nisshin Seifun Group
Seiyu
Takashimaya
Uny
Yamazaki Baking

HISTORICAL FINANCIALS

Company Type: Public

Income Statement

FYE: February 28

	REVENUE ($ mil.)	NET INCOME ($ mil.)	NET PROFIT MARGIN	EMPLOYEES
02/15	50,610	1,449	2.9%	54,665
02/14	55,282	1,724	3.1%	55,364
02/13	54,169	1,498	2.8%	55,011
02/12	59,516	1,614	2.7%	51,888
02/11	62,535	1,367	2.2%	50,765
Annual Growth	(5.2%)	1.5%	—	1.9%

2015 Year-End Financials

Debt ratio: 0.1%	No. of shares (mil.): 884
Return on equity: 7.8%	Dividends
Cash ($ mil.): 7,827	Yield: —
Current ratio: 1.17	Payout: —
Long-term debt ($ mil.): 5,761	Market value ($ mil.): 16,823

	STOCK PRICE ($) FY Close	P/E High/Low	PER SHARE ($) Earnings	Dividends	Book Value
02/15	19.03	— —	1.64	0.00	23.05
02/14	74.77	— —	1.95	1.31	24.68
02/13	58.40	— —	1.69	1.59	24.50
02/12	55.21	— —	1.83	1.47	26.19
02/11	55.83	— —	1.54	1.29	24.56
Annual Growth	(23.6%)	— —	1.5%	—	(1.6%)

Sharp Corp (Japan)

Best known for its consumer electronics Sharp is a well-known maker of electronic components and computer hardware and peripherals. The company's flagship products are LCDs which are used in everything from airplane cockpits to PCs to pinball machines. The company also produces flash memory laser diodes and optical sensors. Sharp also makes printers and cell phones; consumer audio and video products such as Blu-ray disc players and LCD TVs; and a variety of appliances such as air purifiers and steam ovens. The 100-year-old company is also one of the world's largest manufacturers of photovoltaic solar cells.

Geographic Reach

Sharp gets more than half of sales from customers located outside of Japan. The company has established regional headquarters in the Americas China and in Europe as it looks to expand internationally.

Financial Performance

Sharp's financial performance dulled in 2015 (ended March) with revenues falling 18% resulting in a net loss for the year. The loss was the third on the past four years. The company reported lower sales in its major product categories including TVs mobile phones and air conditioners. Sales in the company's business solutions segment rose about 7% based on sales of multi-purpose printers overseas. Cash flow from operations also fell in 2015.

Strategy

In mid-2015 Sharp sold its TV business in the US and other markets in the Americas to the Hisense Group based in China. The sale which includes a manufacturing plant in Mexico was for $27 million. The deal is one of several steps Sharp has taken to restructure and refocus its business as it has lost ground to rivals. Sharp has taken outside investment in the past year and is seeking more. The company is cutting about 10% of its work force –about 5000 jobs.

Sharp has taken steps to expand its business in the Asia-Pacific Region. It opened a manufacturing plant in Indonesia and expanded and bolstered sales networks in Myanmar and Sri Lanka. The company also is seeking to expand in emerging markets in the Middle East and Africa.

The company is looking to new technology to revive its display sales. It has developed a manufacturing process that enables it to make displays of various shapes –not just rectangles.

HISTORY

Early History

Tokuji Hayakawa got started in manufacturing in 1912 when he established Hayakawa Electric Industry to make a type of belt buckle he had designed. Three years later he invented the first mechanical pencil named the Ever-Sharp which was a commercial success. After an earthquake leveled much of Tokyo in 1923 including Hayakawa's business he moved to Osaka and sold the rights to his pencil to finance a new factory. He introduced Japan's first crystal radio sets in 1925 and four years later debuted a vacuum tube radio.

Following WWII Hayakawa Electric developed an experimental TV which it began mass-producing in 1953. The company was ready with color TVs when Japan initiated color broadcasts in 1960. Hayakawa Electric grew tremendously during the 1960s introducing microwave ovens (1962) solar cells (1963) the first electronic all-transistor-diode calculator (1964) and the first gallium arsenide LED (1969). The firm opened a US office in 1962.

In 1970 the company began to make its own semiconductor devices and changed its name to Sharp Corporation a nod to the name of its first product. It began mass production of LCDs in 1973. Sharp later introduced the first electronic calculator with an LCD (1973) solar-powered calculators (1976) and a credit card-sized calculator (1979).

EXECUTIVES

President, Kozo Takahashi
Director; Group General Manager AVC Liquid Crystal Display, Shigeaki Mizushima, age 60
Senior Executive Managing Officer, Fujikazu Nakayama
President Sharp Electronics Marketing, Akira Atarashi
Senior Executive Managing Officer, Norikazu Hoshi
Senior Executive Managing Officer, Tetsuo Onishi
Managing Director Sharp Australia, Keiichi (Kasey) Katsuta
Auditors: KPMG AZSA LLC

LOCATIONS

HQ: Sharp Corp (Japan)
22-22 Nagaike-cho, Abeno-ku, Osaka 545-8522
Phone: (81) 6 6621 1221
Web: www.sharp.co.jp

PRODUCTS/OPERATIONS

2015 Sales

	% of total
Products business	54
Device business	46
Total	**100**

Selected Products

Consumer/information products
- Audiovisual and communication equipment
- Audio amplifiers
- Blu-ray disc players
- Digital cameras
- High-definition televisions
- Liquid crystal display DVD televisions
- Liquid crystal display televisions
- Liquid crystal display video projectors
- Mobile phones
- Video cameras
- Information equipment
- Calculators
- Digital copiers
- Fax machines
- Mobile business tools
- Personal computers
- Printers
- Home appliances
- Air cleaning systems
- Superheated steam ovens

Electronic components
- Flash memory
- Integrated circuits
- Laser diodes and other optoelectronic devices
- Radio-frequency components
- Satellite broadcasting components
- Solar cells and other photovoltaic devices

COMPETITORS

AU Optronics
Broadcom
CASIO COMPUTER
Canon
Electrolux
Epson
Ericsson
First Solar
Fujitsu
HP
Hanwha Q Cells
Hisense
Hitachi
IBM
Konica Minolta
Kyocera
LG Electronics
Lexmark
Mitsubishi Electric
NEC
Oki Electric
Panasonic Corp
Philips Electronics
Pioneer Corporation
Ricoh Company
SANYO
Samsung Electronics
SolarWorld
Sony
SunPower
Suntech Power
TCL
TPV Technology
Tatung
Toshiba
Xerox
Yingli

HISTORICAL FINANCIALS

Company Type: Public

Income Statement FYE: March 31

	REVENUE ($ mil.)	NET INCOME ($ mil.)	NET PROFIT MARGIN	EMPLOYEES
03/15	23,222	(1,853)	—	49,096
03/14	28,358	111	0.4%	50,253
03/13	26,342	(5,795)	—	50,647
03/12	29,938	(4,584)	—	56,756
03/11	36,494	234	0.6%	55,580
Annual Growth	(10.7%)	—	—	(3.1%)

2015 Year-End Financials

Debt ratio: 0.4%
Return on equity: (-197.3%)
Cash ($ mil.): 2,154
Current ratio: 0.77
Long-term debt ($ mil.): 945
No. of shares (mil.): 1,690
Dividends
Yield: —
Payout: —
Market value ($ mil.): 3,246

	STOCK PRICE ($) FY Close	P/E High/Low	PER SHARE ($) Earnings	Dividends	Book Value
03/15	1.92	— —	(1.10)	0.00	0.22
03/14	3.01	— —	0.08	0.00	1.19
03/13	2.78	— —	(5.21)	0.00	1.23
03/12	7.38	— —	(4.17)	0.00	7.15
03/11	9.83	— —	0.20	0.23	11.51
Annual Growth	(33.5%)	— —	—	—	(62.8%)

Shiga Bank, Ltd.

Shiga Bank established in 1933 has grown to become the largest bank in the Shiga prefecture. The bank and its 14 subsidiaries provide customers with typical banking products and services credit card leasing and venture capital financing services and accepts negotiable certificates of deposits and installment-deposits fixed-term savings products. Shiga Bank's primary customers are individuals and small and medium-sized businesses. The bank which operates nearly 140 offices and branches in Japan Hong Kong and Thailand (as well as 10 agents) is banking on the region's expanding economy to improve local economies in the Kyoto and Shiga prefectures. Shiga Bank if controlled by Japan Trustee Service Bank.
Auditors: Deloitte Touche Tohmatsu LLC

LOCATIONS

HQ: Shiga Bank, Ltd.
1-38 Hamamachi, Otsu, Shiga 520-8686
Phone: (81) 77 524 2141
Web: www.shigagin.com

COMPETITORS

Nanto Bank
Oita Bank
Toho Bank

HISTORICAL FINANCIALS

Company Type: Public

Income Statement FYE: March 31

	ASSETS ($ mil.)	NET INCOME ($ mil.)	INCOME AS % OF ASSETS	EMPLOYEES
03/15	41,648	113	0.3%	2,479
03/14	46,284	106	0.2%	2,508
03/13	49,547	58	0.1%	2,530
03/12	55,141	100	0.2%	2,602
03/11	53,383	56	0.1%	2,650
Annual Growth	(6.0%)	19.2%	—	(1.7%)

2015 Year-End Financials

Return on assets: 0.2%
Return on equity: 4.3%
Long-term debt ($ mil.): —
No. of shares (mil.): 260
Sales ($ mil): 737
Dividends
Yield: —
Payout: —
Market value ($ mil.): —

Shin Kong Financial Holding Co., Ltd.

Commercial banking securities dealing asset management and insurance all find a home beneath Shin Kong's umbrella. Also known as SKFH the holding company offers an array of banking and financial services through subsidiaries Shin Kong Life Insurance (SKL) Shin Kong Investment Trust (SKIT) Taiwan Shin Kong Insurance Brokers (SKIB) and Taiwan Shin Kong Commercial Bank (SKB). The company has expanded its product offerings and market presence with a focus on mainland China for growth opportunities. SKFH was established in 2002.

EXECUTIVES

Chief Information Officer; Group Head - Technology and Operations, Jan Verplancke
Chief Executive - Consumer Banking; Group Executive Director, Steve Bertamini
Chairman of the Board, John Peace
Auditors: Deloitte & Touche

LOCATIONS

HQ: Shin Kong Financial Holding Co., Ltd.
Level 38, No. 66, Section 1, Chung-Hsiao West Road, Taipei 100
Phone: (886) 2 23895858
Web: www.skfh.com.tw

PRODUCTS/OPERATIONS

2014 Sales

	% of total
Interest income	31
Other income	69
Total	**100**

COMPETITORS

Cathay Financial Holding
Chinatrust Financial
First Financial Holding
Fubon Financial
Hua Nan Financial
SinoPac Holdings
Taiwan Business Bank

HISTORICAL FINANCIALS

Company Type: Public

Income Statement FYE: December 31

	ASSETS ($ mil.)	NET INCOME ($ mil.)	INCOME AS % OF ASSETS	EMPLOYEES
12/14	88,358	217	0.2%	20,820
12/13	85,014	334	0.4%	20,279
12/12	79,583	338	0.4%	20,677
12/11	70,479	181	0.3%	20,653
12/10	70,935	87	0.1%	20,693
Annual Growth	5.6%	25.6%	—	0.2%

2014 Year-End Financials

Return on assets: 0.2%
Return on equity: 6.5%
Long-term debt ($ mil.): —
No. of shares (mil.): —
Sales ($ mil): 6,028
Dividends
Yield: —
Payout: —
Market value ($ mil.): —

Shinhan Financial Group Co. Ltd.

Shinhan Financial Group one of South Korea's largest financial companies in terms of assets provides retail and corporate banking credit cards insurance asset management securities brokerage and credit reporting services to almost 30 million customers. Its primary subsidiary is Shinhan Bank which has one of the largest branch networks in the country with more than 900 locations. It also owns a stake in the 40-branch Jeju Bank. Shinhan Financial Group has international operations in about a half-dozen other countries including Shinhan Bank America in New York. Other units include Shinhan Investment Corp. (about 100 offices) and Shinhan Life Insurance (about 200 offices).

OperationsShinhan Financial which operates mainly through Shinhan Bank centers its business around three core segments: Retail Banking which provides traditional banking products and services to retail and affluent individuals and non-profit organizations; Corporate and Investment Banking services which makes loans to corporations and small to medium-sized businesses; International Banking which counts the business of Shinhan's overseas branch operations and other international businesses along with securities trading and administrative operations. Through its more than 30 direct and indirect subsidiaries the bank also provides insurance brokerage and asset management services as well as credit card products and services. Shinhan Financial generated roughly 75% its 2014 operating income from interest income one-third of which came from its retail loan business one-fifth coming from its credit card business and just over one-tenth coming from its corporate loan business. The majority of the remaining 25% of total revenue came from fee and commission income mostly from its retail banking and credit card businesses.Geographic Reach

Shinhan Financial generated 96% of its operating income from South Korea in 2014. It had three-fourths of its 1250 locations in Korea with more than one-third of the its offices in the Seoul metropolitan market alone and about 20% of offices in the Kyunggi province. The rest of the Korean branches in the cities of Incheon Busan Kwangju Taegu Ulsan and Taejon. Shinhan Bank's international branches are in some 16 countries including Cambodia Canada China Germany Hong Kong India Japan Kazakhstan Myanmar Poland Singapore the UK the US and Vietnam. It has representative offices in Mexico and Uzbekistan.Sales and MarketingThe company serves retail and affluent individuals small and mid-sized businesses non-profit organizations (such as hospitals airports and schools) and corporations. Its Shinhan Card business primarily sells through the banking and credit card branch network sales agents and business partnerships and affiliations with vendors.Altogether the firm spent Wan$229.64 billion ($208.9 million) on advertising in 2014 up from W$211.3 billion ($192.2 million) and W$188.36 billion ($171.4 million) in 2013 and 2012 respectively.Financial PerformanceNote: Growth rates may differ after conversion to US dollars.Shinhan Financial's revenues and profits have been trending lower in recent years due to shrinking interest margins on loans amidst the low-interest environment.The firm's revenue dipped by 2% to W$16135 billion ($15.43 billion) in 2014 mostly as its interest income on loans dipped by 4% due to a continued decline in interest margins on both its retail loans and corporate loans. Shinhan's net fees and commission income however grew by 6% as its credit card fee income increased with higher consumer credit balances.Despite lower revenues in 2014 Shinhan's net income jumped by 10% to W$2.08 billion ($1.89 million) mostly thanks to significant unrealized fair value gains of the firm's available-for-sale financial assets. The firm's cash levels fell sharply despite higher earnings during the year with operations using W$2.08 billion ($1.89 million) after adjusting Shinhan's earnings for non-cash interest expenses net insurance loss and net trading loss items.

StrategyShinhan Financial Group reiterated in 2015 that its long-term strategy (which it's followed since 2001) included: balanced growth among its banking and non-banking businesses; expansion of its service offerings to grow revenues and differentiate the bank from competitors; and strengthening of its management systems and core expertise in effort to become the market leader in Korea and a world-class financial holding company. To that end in 2015 the company planned to introduce more differentiated financial services; and continue its international expansion efforts by localizing its product offerings and operations and bolstering its local marketing expertise and distribution channels. Shinhan Financial is also moving toward digital banking channels that are quickly taking the industry by storm allowing the bank to slow the growth of its costly branch network and cut operating costs significantly. Indeed more than 8.6 million Shinhan customers –about one-third of its customer base –were enrolled in the firm's smart phone banking service in 2014; nearly double the size of its "Smart" customer base in 2012. Additionally about 59% of all Shinhan bank transactions were done over the bank's internet or mobile banking services while just 5% of transactions were at physical branch locations.Mergers and AcquisitionsIn June 2015 Shinhan Bank purchased a 75% stake in Centratama Nasional Bank along with its $81 million in assets and 41 offices in Indonesia. Similarly in April 2015 Shinhan obtained regulatory approval to acquired a 40% equity interest in Jakarta-based Bank Metro Express a small bank in Indonesia and expected to close the transaction in late 2015. The bank planned to merge the two Indonesian banks in 2016 to strengthen its operations in the Southeast Asia region.

EXECUTIVES

Director; CEO Shinhan Bank, Jin Won Suh, age 64
Deputy President, Jae Gwang Soh, age 54
Deputy President and CFO, Jung Kee Min, age 56
Deputy President, Dong Hwan Lee, age 56
Deputy President, Buhmsoo Choi, age 59
Chairman and CEO, Dong Woo Han, age 67
Deputy President, Sung Ho Wi, age 57
Deputy President, Sin Gee Lee, age 59
Auditors: Samjong Accounting Corporation (A Member Firm of KPMG)

LOCATIONS

HQ: Shinhan Financial Group Co. Ltd.
20 Sejong-daero 9-gil Jung-gu, Seoul 100-724
Phone: (82) 2 6360 3071 **Fax:** (82) 2 6263 3098
Web: www.shinhangroup.com

PRODUCTS/OPERATIONS

2014 Sales

	% of total
Interest income	
Loans	57
Available for sale financia assets	3
Held to maturity financial assets	5
Trading assets	3
Cash and due from banks	1
Other interest income	2
Non Interest income	
Fee and commission income	21
Dividend income	1
Net trading income	2
Net gain on sale of available for sale financial assets	1
Net foreign currency transaction gain	4
Total	**100**

2014 Sales

	% of total
Banking	67
Credit card	25
Securities	4
Life insurance	4
Other	
Total	**100**

Selected Subsidiaries

Jeju Bank (68.9%)
SHC Management
Shinhan AITAS (99.8%)
Shinhan Bank
Shinhan BNP Paribas Asset Management (65%)
Shinhan Capital
Shinhan Card
Shinhan Credit Information
Shinhan Data System
Shinhan Investment Corp.
Shinhan Life Insurance
Shinhan Private Equity Investment Management
Shinhan Savings Bank

COMPETITORS

Busan Bank
Daegu Bank
Hana Bank
Industrial Bank of Korea
KB Financial Group
Korea Exchange Bank
Samsung Life Insurance
Woori

HISTORICAL FINANCIALS

Company Type: Public

Income Statement FYE: December 31

	ASSETS ($ mil.)	NET INCOME ($ mil.)	INCOME AS % OF ASSETS	EMPLOYEES
12/14	308,948	1,902	0.6%	155
12/13	296,009	1,809	0.6%	148
12/12	281,771	2,175	0.8%	155
12/11	248,656	2,675	1.1%	158
12/10	239,510	2,394	1.0%	145
Annual Growth	6.6%	(5.6%)	—	1.7%

2014 Year-End Financials

Return on assets: 0.6%
Return on equity: 7.3%
Long-term debt ($ mil.): —
No. of shares (mil.): 474
Sales ($ mil): 14,747

Dividends
Yield: 1.5%
Payout: 15.5%
Market value ($ mil.): 19,153

	STOCK PRICE ($)	P/E		PER SHARE ($)		
	FY Close	High/Low		Earnings	Dividends	Book Value
12/14	40.39	0	0	3.83	0.63	56.25
12/13	45.70	0	0	3.63	0.62	55.23
12/12	36.64	0	0	4.39	0.66	51.97
12/11	68.21	0	0	5.03	0.65	44.40
12/10	93.82	0	0	4.53	0.71	46.52
Annual Growth	(19.0%)	—	—	(4.1%)	(3.1%)	4.9%

Shinsei Bank Ltd. (Japan)

Shinsei Bank provides retail and corporate banking and several other financial services from 35 branches throughout Japan. Shinsei used to focus on financing Japan's large industrial firms but has been cultivating its retail and small business banking operations. It offers retail banking services such as deposits mortgages and investments as well as higher-margin services such as wealth management market services and institutional asset management bond sales and underwriting trust services and specialty financing in the public and real estate sectors. Founded as the Long-Term Credit Bank of Japan in 1952 the company was reborn as Shinsei (Japanese for "new birth") Bank in 2000.

OperationsShinsei Bank group operates three main business segments. The Individual Group segment (which generated 58% of Shinsei Bank's total revenue and 22% of its profit in fiscal 2015 ended March 31) provides retail banking personal loans credit cards mutual funds insurance housing loans and overseas remittance services. The Institutional Group (which contributed 32% to revenue and 65% to profit) provides public sector finance real estate finance specialty finance health care finance private equity and credit trading (through Shinsei PI Group) leasing and property management services (through Showa Leasing Co) and trust services (through Shinsei Trust). The Global Markets Group (7% of revenue 8% of profit) provides market wealth management and asset management services through subsidiaries such as Shinsei Investment Management and Shinsei Securities. Broadly about 53% of the bank's revenue came from interest income (mostly from loans) in FY2015 while 16% came from fee and commission income. Around 4% of its revenue came from net trading income while the remaining 23% of its revenue came from (non-recurring) net gains on sales of certain non-trading assets.While Shinsei Bank lends to a variety of different industries across Japan about 27% of its entire loan portfolio's value was tied to loans to customers in the finance and insurance and real estate industries. About 7% of its portfolio went to customers in the services industries while another 15% was lent to customers in the manufacturing electric power/gas/heat/water and transportation/postal service industries. Geographic ReachShinsei Bank had 35 branch outlets across Japan in fiscal 2015 (ended March 31) with about one-third of them around Tokyo nine in the Kinki region seven in the Konto region (excluding Tokyo) and one each in the Chugoku Tohoku Tokai Shikoku Kyushi Hokkaido and Hokuriku/Koshinetsu regions of Japan. The bank also had over 43960 ATM locations in Japan with nearly 40% of them located in the Kanto/Tokyo region and another 15% in the Kinki region. Additionally it had ATMs in all the other regions where there were branches along with 434 ATM locations in Okinawa.Financial PerformanceNote: Growth rates may differ after conversion to US dollars. This analysis uses financials from the company's annual report. In domestic currency terms Shinsei Bank's annual revenues and profits have been trending higher since fiscal 2013 (ended March 31 2013) thanks to loan business growth and non-interest growth from fees and commissions and sales of investment products. The bank's total revenue (defined by the company as the total of net interest income and non-interest income) grew to ¥235.3 billion in FY2015 thanks to a combination of: higher net interest income as the bank decreased its funding costs and collected higher dividend income from securities investments in the Institutional Group; and non-interest income growth thanks to an improvement in market-related transaction revenues including ALM operations (the company's corporate internal trading division) as well as a rise in revenue from the installment sales finance business of the consumer finance business. Higher revenue and a decline in loan loss provisions in FY2015 boosted Shinsei Bank's net income up 64% to ¥67.8 billion ($567 million) for the year. The bank's operating cash levels declined sharply despite higher earnings with operations using ¥509 billion or $4.25 billion (operations provided ¥524 billion in FY2014) as the bank's deposit levels fell and as its loan balances grew. Company BackgroundDuring the late 2000s Shinsei had been battered by its exposure to toxic assets including loans to failed Lehman Brothers and structured asset-backed securities. It had also taken a hit in the domestic real estate market in which the company had been a significant lender. Record losses reported for 2008 sparked rumors that Shinsei would merge with Aozora Bank another struggling midsized bank that was nationalized in 2001. The two banks reached a merger agreement in 2009 but called those plans off due to strategic differences.

HISTORY

Company BackgroundThe Japanese government nationalized Shinsei Bank's debt-ridden Long-Term Credit Bank in 1998. It sold the bank to an international group led by US-based Ripplewood Holdings in 2000 making it one of the few major Japanese banks to come under foreign control. Ripplewood spun off the bank in 2004 placing it on the Tokyo Stock Exchange.

In 2007 Shinsei acquired a minority stake in global advisory firm Duff & Phelps. In 2008 it acquired GE's consumer finance business in Japan consisting of credit card personal lending and mortgage operations. In 2010 Shinsei Bank sold Shinsei Asset Management its Mumbai-based asset management operation to Daiwa Bank. The company would use the proceeds to pay down its debt.

EXECUTIVES

President and CEO, Shigeki Toma, age 67
Senior Managing Executive Officer, Hitomi Sato, age 67
Senior Managing Executive Officer and Group CIO, Michiyuki Okano, age 55
Senior Managing Executive Officer, Sanjeev Gupta, age 55
Deputy President, Yukio Nakamura, age 61
Senior Managing Executive Officer and CFO, Shigeru Tsukamoto, age 65
Managing Executive Officer, Norio Funayama, age 58
Managing Executive Officer, Toru Myochin, age 50
Managing Executive Officer, Yoshiaki Kozano, age 53
Managing Executive Officer, Hironobu Satou, age 55
Managing Executive Officer, Shinichirou Seto, age 54
Managing Executive Officer, Masashi Yamashita, age 57
Auditors: Deloitte Touche Tohmatsu LLC

LOCATIONS

HQ: Shinsei Bank Ltd. (Japan)
2-4-3 Nihonbashi-Muromachi, Chuo-ku, Tokyo 103-8303
Phone: (81) 3 6880 7000
Web: www.shinseibank.com

PRODUCTS/OPERATIONS

2014 Sales

	% of total
Net interest income	54
Noninterest income	
Net fee and commission	12
Net trading income	7
Others	27
Total	**100**

COMPETITORS

Aozora Bank
Bank of Yokohama
Mitsubishi UFJ Financial Group
Mizuho Financial
Mizuho Trust & Banking Ltd
Resona
Sumitomo Mitsui
Sumitomo Mitsui Trust Holdings

HISTORICAL FINANCIALS

Company Type: Public

Income Statement FYE: March 31

	ASSETS ($ mil.)	NET INCOME ($ mil.)	INCOME AS % OF ASSETS	EMPLOYEES
03/15	74,094	565	0.8%	5,300
03/14	90,303	400	0.4%	5,064
03/13	95,962	542	0.6%	4,863
03/12	104,957	78	0.1%	4,830
03/11	123,559	515	0.4%	5,718
Annual Growth	(12.0%)	2.4%	—	(1.9%)

2015 Year-End Financials

Return on assets: 0.7%
Return on equity: 9.7%
Long-term debt ($ mil.): —
No. of shares (mil.): —
Sales ($ mil): 3,323

Dividends
Yield: —
Payout: —
Market value ($ mil.): —

Shizuoka Bank, Ltd. (Japan)

One of Japan's largest regional banks The Shizuoka Bank has more than 190 branches in and around Shizuoka prefecture a major manufacturing region southwest of Tokyo. The bank spe-

cializes in making commercial and industrial loans to businesses such as manufacturers wholesalers and retailers within Shizuoka. Other offerings include deposit accounts consumer loans asset management and investment banking services. The Shizuoka Bank also boasts about a dozen major subsidiaries that are devoted to leasing credit cards mortgages securities brokerage and management consulting. It has representative offices and branches in Belgium Hong Kong Shanghai China Singapore and the US.
Auditors: Deloitte Touche Tohmatsu LLC

LOCATIONS

HQ: Shizuoka Bank, Ltd. (Japan)
1-10 Gofuku-cho, Aoi-ku, Shizuoka 420-8761
Phone: (81) 54 261 3131
Web: www.shizuokabank.co.jp

HISTORICAL FINANCIALS

Company Type: Public

Income Statement FYE: March 31

	ASSETS ($ mil.)	NET INCOME ($ mil.)	INCOME AS % OF ASSETS	EMPLOYEES
03/15	93,627	416	0.4%	4,211
03/14	103,642	452	0.4%	4,246
03/13	109,624	605	0.6%	4,269
03/12	118,194	453	0.4%	4,257
03/11	114,025	436	0.4%	4,252
Annual Growth	(4.8%)	(1.2%)	—	(0.2%)

2015 Year-End Financials

Return on assets: 0.4%
Return on equity: 5.7%
Long-term debt ($ mil.): —
No. of shares (mil.): 618
Sales ($ mil): 1,784
Dividends
Yield: —
Payout: —
Market value ($ mil.): —

Showa Shell Sekiyu K.K.

Show and tell? When is comes to oil and petroleum products Showa Shell Sekiyu has plenty to show and talk about. Showa Shell 35%-owned by Royal Dutch Shell and 15% by Saudi Aramco is one of Japan's leading oil refiners. The company imports refines and distributes petroleum products. The firm's three local refining affiliates Showa Yokkaichi Toa Oil and Seibu Oil have a collective refining capacity of 395000 barrels a day. Showa Shell markets its products through 3800 gas stations; it also has solar power electricity city gas (liquefied petroleum gas) and property businesses.

OperationsThe company operates the Yokkaichi Refinery of Showa Yokkaichi Sekiyu Co. Ltd. (210000 barrels per day) the Keihin Refinery of Toa Oil Co. Ltd. (65000 barrels per day) and the Yamaguchi Refinery of Seibu Oil Co. Ltd. (120000 barrels per day). These refineries produce fuel oils such as gasoline; diesel oil; kerosene; basic materials for petrochemical products such as mixed xylene benzene and propylene; lubricants; asphalt; and other products.

Showa Shell markets its products through 3800 gas stations;

The company has developed the technology for manufacturing next-generation CIS thin-film solar panels.It also operates Ohgishima Power which has two natural gas-fired power plants as a joint venture with Tokyo Gas. Electricity produced at the plants is sold primarily to customers in or near Tokyo.Sales and Marketing

Showa Shell sells petroleum products in Japan primarily through its gas station network. Products sold include gasolines kerosene and a range of automotive lubricants. The company also directly sells fuel oil gas oil naphtha lubricants bitumen and LP gas to construction firms electric power and gas utilities fishing fleets manufacturers and shipping companies. Showa Shell's international sales include aviation fuel to airlines and marine bunker fuels and lubricants to shipping firms.

Financial Performance

Showa Shell's revenues increased by 18% in 2011 due to a 17% hike in prices on petroleum products which rose in tandem with higher crude oil prices pushing up sales for the oil business. The increase in crude oil prices also had a positive effect on inventory valuation. In addition the sales volume increased for kerosene and other middle distillates; and 128% increase in Energy Solution Businesses due to the greater scale of sales in the solar business stemming from the start of operations at the third Miyazaki Plant.

Net income increased by 45% in 2011 thanks to higher prices on petroleum products and higher net sales. It also benefited from increased demand for heating fuels due to particularly cold weather at the beginning of the year as well as a recovery in petroleum product margins.

Strategy

In addition to growing its core refining and petroleum products businesses the company is expanding its solar energy assets. In 2011 it launched the Kunitomi Plant its Solar Frontier unit's third Miyazaki plant and one of the largest solar plants in the world.

Ownership

Showa Shell is 35%-owned by Royal Dutch Shell and 15% by Saudi Aramco.

Company Background

The company was founded in 1985 through a merger between Japan's Showa Oil and Royal Dutch Shell's Shell Sekiyu.

EXECUTIVES

Senior Executive Officer, Tomonori Okada
Executive Officer, Jun Arai, age 57
Senior Executive Officer, Atsuhiko Hirano
Chairman and CEO, Shigeya Kato
EVP; President Solar Frontier, Hiroto Tamai
EVP, Tsuyoshi Kameoka
CFO, Douglas Wood
Auditors: PricewaterhouseCoopers Aarata

LOCATIONS

HQ: Showa Shell Sekiyu K.K.
2-3-2 Daiba, Minato-ku, Tokyo 135-8074
Phone: (81) 3 5531 5591 **Fax:** (81) 3 5531 5598
Web: www.showa-shell.co.jp

COMPETITORS

Cosmo Oil
Exxon Mobil
Idemitsu Kosan
JX Holdings
JX Nippon Mining & Metals
JX Nippon Oil & Energy
SK Innovation

HISTORICAL FINANCIALS

Company Type: Public

Income Statement FYE: December 31

	REVENUE ($ mil.)	NET INCOME ($ mil.)	NET PROFIT MARGIN	EMPLOYEES
12/14	25,127	(81)	—	6,039
12/13	28,139	574	2.0%	5,829
12/12	30,526	11	0.0%	5,848
12/11	35,812	298	0.8%	5,947
12/10	28,843	196	0.7%	5,761
Annual Growth	(3.4%)	—	—	1.2%

2014 Year-End Financials

Debt ratio: 0.1%
Return on equity: (-3.3%)
Cash ($ mil.): 377
Current ratio: 1.00
Long-term debt ($ mil.): 836
No. of shares (mil.): 376
Dividends
Yield: —
Payout: —
Market value ($ mil.): 3,810

	STOCK PRICE ($) FY Close	P/E High/Low	PER SHARE ($) Earnings	Dividends	Book Value
12/14	10.12	— —	(0.22)	0.00	6.60
12/13	10.40	— —	1.53	0.00	8.23
12/12	5.75	— —	0.03	0.00	8.44
12/11	10.75	— —	0.79	0.00	9.58
12/10	9.56	— —	0.52	0.00	8.59
Annual Growth	1.4%	— —	—	—	(6.4%)

Siam Commercial Bank Public Co., Ltd. (The)

One of Thailand's largest commercial banks by total assets deposits and loans The Siam Commercial Bank (SCB) hails from royal beginnings. It is the country's oldest bank established by King Rama V in 1906 in response to the proliferation of foreign financial institutions in Thailand. It offers a variety of financial services such as corporate and personal lending retail and wholesale banking credit cards life insurance foreign currency trading and investment banking among others. SCB operates through a network of about 1200 branches and 9140 ATMs; it is expanding regionally. In 2014 SCB had Baht 2553 billion in total assets Baht 1781 billion in deposits and Baht 1733 billion in loans.

EXECUTIVES

President, Yol Phokasub
SEVP and CFO; Head Finance Group and Change Program, Deepak Sarup
SEVP and Chief Risk Officer, Yokporn Tantisawetrat
SEVP; Division Head Special Assets Group, Sarunthorn Chutima
Deputy Chairman and CEO, Arthid Nanthawithaya
SEVP; Group Head General Counsel Group, Wallaya Kaewrungruang
Chairman, Vichit Suraphongchai
Auditors: KPMG Phoomchai Audit Ltd.

LOCATIONS

HQ: Siam Commercial Bank Public Co., Ltd. (The)
9 Ratchadapisek Road,, Jatujak, Bangkok 10900
Phone: (66) 2 544 1000 **Fax:** (66) 2 937 7721
Web: www.scb.co.th

PRODUCTS/OPERATIONS

2013 Sales

	% of total
Interest income	56
Net earned insurance premiums	23
Fees & service income	14
Net trading income	4
Dividend income	2
Net gain on investments	1
Total	**100**

Selected Group Companies

SCB Asset Management
SCB Life Assurance
SCB Securities
The Siam Commercial Bank

COMPETITORS

Bangkok Bank
Bank of Ayudhya
KASIKORNBANK
TMB Bank
Thanachart Capital

HISTORICAL FINANCIALS

Company Type: Public

Income Statement FYE: December 31

	ASSETS ($ mil.)	NET INCOME ($ mil.)	INCOME AS % OF ASSETS	EMPLOYEES
12/14	82,107	1,622	2.0%	0
12/13	77,408	1,534	2.0%	0
12/12	74,179	1,314	1.8%	20,994
12/11	59,670	1,152	1.9%	19,566
12/10	49,168	805	1.6%	18,097
Annual Growth	13.7%	19.1%	—	—

2014 Year-End Financials

Return on assets: 2.0%
Return on equity: 20.0%
Long-term debt ($ mil.): —
No. of shares (mil.): —
Sales ($ mil): 6,558
Dividends
Yield: 0.0%
Payout: —
Market value ($ mil.): —

	STOCK PRICE ($) FY Close	P/E High/Low		PER SHARE ($) Earnings	Dividends	Book Value
12/14	21.41	1	1	0.48	0.51	2.56
12/13	17.16	2	1	0.45	0.54	2.22
12/12	23.65	2	2	0.39	0.11	2.10
Annual Growth	(4.9%)	—	—	5.4%	48.3%	5.1%

Siemens AG (Germany)

For Siemens one of the largest electronics and industrial engineering companies in the galaxy everything comes down to seven segments: Power and Gas; Wind Power and Renewables; Energy Management; Building Technologies; Mobility; Digital Factory; and Process Industries and Drives. Siemens makes everything from automation equipment and building technologies for manufacturers and construction companies to diagnostic and imaging systems for hospitals and clinics. Other products include power generation and distribution equipment for the oil and gas and renewable energy sectors. Siemens Energy Siemens Healthcare Siemens Industry and Siemens Infrastructure & Cities are a few of its primary segments.

Geographic Reach

All in all the company operates through more than 290 major production and manufacturing plants in 200 countries worldwide. The EMEA region accounted for 54% of its net sales in 2014. Other major markets include the Americas (26%) and Asia and Australia (20%).

Operations

Siemens in late 2014 restructured its operations from four segments to seven: Power and Gas (PG); Wind Power and Renewables (WP); Energy Management (EM); Building Technologies (BT); Mobility (MO); Digital Factory (DF); and Process Industries and Drives (PD).

PG offers products for generating electricity from fossil and renewable fuels and for transporting oil and natural gas and WP offers products and services for on- and offshore wind power. EM is a supplier of products systems equipment and services for transmission and distribution of electrical energy while BT manufactures and supplies energy-efficient buildings and infrastructure systems. MO is a provider of passenger and freight transportation systems and services; DF offers automation technology industrial switchgear industry software and services primarily to the manufacturing industry; and PD offers process products systems and services to industry sectors.

In addition to its main segments Siemens operates a financial services division that offers corporate financing fund management insurance and risk management services. It also makes hardware and software for the communications industry through its enterprise communications business.

While its operations are diverse Siemens' long-term strategy focuses on developing and producing products that are attuned to global trends. Addressing climate environmental and energy concerns the company makes wind turbines for the renewable energy industry and energy-efficient building technologies for the construction industry. Siemens' products are also used to build transit systems water and wastewater facilities and other systems that in effect facilitate population growth in mature and emerging urban markets.

Financial Performance

After experiencing two straight years of revenue growth Siemens saw its revenue dip 11% from $103 billion in 2013 to $91 billion in 2014. Profits jumped 17% from nearly $5.8 billion in 2013 to $6.8 billion in 2014 driven by a decrease in expenses. (Note the company's 2013 annual revenue was restated due to discontinued operations.)

Siemens' declines for 2014 primarily reflected weaker orders in power generation and fewer orders from power transmission products. Its former health care segment experienced declines due to reduced orders in Asia Australia and the Americas in addition to a decline in the company's diagnostics business.

Strategy

Siemens' focus on urbanization in emerging markets has been growing particularly more intense in recent years especially in China India and Russia where economies and urban populations have been exploding. The company has been bolstering its presence in these markets by entering into joint ventures and partnerships with native companies. The company also has a growing presence in emerging markets in South America through subsidiaries in Brazil Argentina Chile and other countries.

Siemens has been selling various operations in an effort to weather the turbulence in the global economy and refocus its operations on its core business segments. In 2015 it sold its hospital information system business to Cerner for $1.3 billion. The business was focused on administrative hospital IT and electronic patient records not the lab and medical equipment-based IT software that is more aligned with Siemens' business. The divestiture included 6000 employees in the US Europe (particularly Germany) and Asia.

To bolster its railroad operations Siemens in 2013 bought Invensys Rail the rail signaling business of British engineering firm Invensys. Shelling out $2.8 billion for the purchase Siemens enhanced its market share in the rail automation sector and merged Invensys Rail with its Siemens Infrastructure & Cities segment.

HISTORY

In 1847 electrical engineer Werner von Siemens and craftsman Johann Halske formed Siemens & Halske. The firm's first major project linked Berlin and Frankfurt with the first long-distance telegraph system in Europe (1848). In 1870 it completed a 6600-mile telegraph line from London to Calcutta India and in 1874 it made the first transatlantic cable linking Ireland to the US.

The company's history of firsts includes Europe's first electric power transmission system (1876) the world's first electrified railway (1879) and one of the first elevators (1880). In 1896 it patented the world's first X-ray tube and completed the first European subway in Budapest Hungary.

By the next century it had formed light-bulb cartel OSRAM with German rivals AEG and Auer (1919) and created a venture with Furukawa Electric called Fuji Electric (1923). It developed radios and traffic lights in the 1920s and began producing electron microscopes in 1939.

Siemens & Halske played a critical role in Germany's war effort in WWII and suffered heavy losses. During the 1950s it recovered by developing data processing equipment silicates for semiconductors and the first implantable pacemaker. It moved into the nuclear industry in 1959 when its first reactor went into service at Munich-Garching. In 1966 the company reincorporated as Siemens AG.

EXECUTIVES

CEO Power Generation Services, Randy H. Zwirn
President and CEO, Joe Kaeser, age 58, $780,000 total compensation
CEO Financial Services, Roland W. Chalons-Browne, age 59
CEO Mobility, Jochen Eickholt, age 52
EVP CEO Sector Healthcare and Member Managing Board Siemens AG, Hermann Requardt, age 60, $780,000 total compensation
CTO Labor Director and Member of the Managing Board, Siegfried Russwurm, age 52, $780,000 total compensation
Member of the Managing Board and CEO Infrastructure and Cities Sector, Roland Busch, age 51
CFO and Member of the Managing Board, Ralf P. Thomas, age 54
CEO Energy Management, Ralf Christian
CEO Building Technologies Division, Matthias Rebellius
CEO Drive Technologies Division, Klaus Helmrich, age 57
CEO Digital Factory, Anton S. Huber
CEO Energy Management, Jan Mrosik
CEO Power and Gas Division the Wind Power and Renewables Division the Power Generation Services Division the Region North America and the Region South America, Lisa Davis
CEO Wind Power and Renewables, Markus Tacke
CEO Power and Gas Division, Willi Meixner, age 50
CEO Process Industries and Drives Division, Jurgen Brandes, age 54
Second Deputy Chairman, Werner Wenning, age 69
Chairman, Gerhard Cromme, age 73
First Deputy Chairwoman, Birgit Steinborn, age 55
Auditors: Ernst & Young GmbH

LOCATIONS

HQ: Siemens AG (Germany)
Wittelsbacherplatz 2, Munich 80333
Phone: (49) 89 636 33443 **Fax:** (49) 89 636 30085
Web: www.siemens.com

2014 Sales

	% of total
Europe CIS Africa Middle East	
Germany	15
Other countries	39
Americas	
US	18
Other countries	8
Asia Australia	
China	9
Other countries	11
Total	**100**

PRODUCTS/OPERATIONS

2014 Sales

	% of total
Energy	34
Infrastructure & Cities	26
Industry	23
Health care	17
Total	**100**

Selected Operations

Industry
- Building technology (heating and ventilation security fire safety systems)
- Industry automation (manufacturing and process automation)
- Industry solutions (systems integration for industrial plants)
- Mobility (transportation systems)
- Motion control (converters drives motors numerical control systems)
- OSRAM (light-emitting diodes light bulbs)

Energy
- Fossil power generation (gas and steam turbines and generators power plants)
- Oil and gas (extraction conversion and transportation systems)
- Power distribution (powergrid automation switch gear components)
- Power transmission (high-voltage equipment)
- Renewable energy (wind energy)
- Service rotating equipment (power plant services and operation)

Health care
- Diagnostics (immune diagnostics molecular analysis)
- Imaging and IT (imaging systems and networking)
- Workflow and solutions (health care systems and services)

Other
- BSH Bosch und Siemens Hausgeräte (equity investment)
- ELIN GmbH & Co. (equity investment)
- Enterprise Network Holdings (equity investment)
- Financial services (cross-sector)

Krauss-Maffei Wegmann GmbH & Co. (equity investment)
Siemens Corp. (US)
Siemens Energy (Germany and US)
Siemens Enterprise Communications GmbH (Germany)
Siemens Financial Services GmbH (Germany)
Siemens Healthcare (Germany and US)
Siemens Holdings plc (UK)
Siemens Industry Automation (US; subsidiary of Siemens Industry)
Siemens Industry Inc. (US)
Siemens Industry Inc. (US)
Siemens Ltda. (Brazil)
Siemens Osakeyhtiö Group (Finland)
Siemens Product Lifecycle Management Software Inc. (US; subsidiary of Siemens Industry)
Siemens Water Technologies Corp.(US; subsidiary of Siemens Industry)

COMPETITORS

ABB
ALSTOM
AREVA
Abbott Labs
Alcatel-Lucent
Avaya
Beckman Coulter
Bharat Heavy Electricals
Bombardier
Capgemini
Cerner
Computer Sciences Corp.
Danfoss Turbocor
Danieli
Dassault
Dresser-Rand
Emerson Electric
FANUC
GE
GN ReSound
Gamesa
Hitachi
Hologic
Honeywell International
Huawei Technologies
Johnson Controls
MAN
McKesson
Mitsubishi Electric
Mitsubishi Heavy Industries
Nichia
Nortel Networks
OSRAM Licht
Philips Electronics
Philips Healthcare
Roche Diagnostics
Rockwell Automation
Schneider Electric
Senvion
Sonova
Toshiba
Tyco
United Technologies
Varian Medical Systems
Veolia Environnement
Vestas Wind Systems

HISTORICAL FINANCIALS

Company Type: Public

Income Statement FYE: September 30

	REVENUE ($ mil.)	NET INCOME ($ mil.)	NET PROFIT MARGIN	EMPLOYEES
09/15	84,799	8,164	9.6%	348,000
09/14	90,537	6,763	7.5%	343,000
09/13	102,419	5,782	5.6%	366,400
09/12	101,236	5,764	5.7%	370,000
09/11	99,176	8,290	8.4%	350,500
Annual Growth	(3.8%)	(0.4%)	—	(0.2%)

2015 Year-End Financials

Debt ratio: 27.6%
Return on equity: 22.2%
Cash ($ mil.): 11,163
Current ratio: 1.30
Long-term debt ($ mil.): 29,914
No. of shares (mil.): 808
Dividends
Yield: 3.0%
Payout: 28.2%
Market value ($ mil.): 72,210

	STOCK PRICE ($) FY Close	P/E High/Low		PER SHARE ($) Earnings	Dividends	Book Value
09/15	89.30	14	10	9.80	2.76	47.80
09/14	119.07	20	17	7.94	6.02	46.65
09/13	120.51	24	20	6.79	5.95	45.01
09/12	100.15	20	16	6.52	2.85	46.41
09/11	89.79	19	12	9.39	2.70	48.65
Annual Growth	(0.1%)	—	—	1.1%	0.6%	(0.4%)

SinoPac Financial Holdings Co Ltd

SinoPac is packing away financial services in Asia and on the US west coast. The holding company owns Bank SinoPac which has about 130 branches in Taiwan. Bank SinoPac was created in 2006 after the merger of a bank by that name and International Bank of Taipei or IBT. In the US SinoPac Bancorp owns Far East National Bank which serves California's Asian-American community through more than a dozen branches. Other holdings include SinoPac Securities which offers brokerage services corporate financing and underwriting. The company's SinoPac Credit Cards unit has issued more than 1.7 million cards. SinoPac Holdings' subsidiaries also have operations in China Hong Kong Macao the UK and Vietnam.In addition to banking brokerage and credit card issuing SinoPac Holdings' subsidiaries are involved in insurance asset management factoring venture capital call centers and more.

EXECUTIVES

President, Shou Chuan Ho
Auditors: Deloitte & Touche

LOCATIONS

HQ: SinoPac Financial Holdings Co Ltd
3&6-13/F., No. 306, Section 2, Bade Road, Taipei 104
Phone: (886) 2 8161 8888 **Fax:** (886) 2 8161 8485
Web: www.sinopac.com

COMPETITORS

Bank of East Asia
Cathay Financial Holding
Chang Hwa Bank
Chinatrust Financial
E.Sun
East West Bancorp
First Financial Holding
Fubon Financial
HSBC
Hotung Investment Holdings
Hua Nan Financial
Mega Financial
Shin Kong
Taishin
Taiwan Business Bank
Taiwan Cooperative Bank

HISTORICAL FINANCIALS

Company Type: Public

Income Statement FYE: December 31

	ASSETS ($ mil.)	NET INCOME ($ mil.)	INCOME AS % OF ASSETS	EMPLOYEES
12/14	48,941	410	0.8%	8,783
12/13	49,158	361	0.7%	8,781
12/12	46,760	328	0.7%	8,294
12/11	42,888	101	0.2%	8,095
12/10	42,299	175	0.4%	7,740
Annual Growth	3.7%	23.6%	—	3.2%

2014 Year-End Financials

Return on assets: 0.8%
Return on equity: 11.1%
Long-term debt ($ mil.): —
No. of shares (mil.): —
Sales ($ mil): 1,621
Dividends
Yield: —
Payout: —
Market value ($ mil.): —

Sinopharm Group Co., Ltd.

Drugs proprietaries and sundries

EXECUTIVES

Chairman, Yulin Wei
Auditors: PricewaterhouseCoopers

LOCATIONS

HQ: Sinopharm Group Co., Ltd.
Sinopharm Plaza, No. 1001 Zhongshan West Road, Changning District, Shanghai 200051
Phone: (86) 21 2305 2666
Web: www.sinopharmgroup.com.cn

HISTORICAL FINANCIALS

Company Type: Public

Income Statement FYE: December 31

	REVENUE ($ mil.)	NET INCOME ($ mil.)	NET PROFIT MARGIN	EMPLOYEES
12/14	32,246	463	1.4%	50,099
12/13	27,563	371	1.3%	45,415
12/12	21,780	316	1.5%	40,737
12/11	16,240	247	1.5%	35,394
12/10	10,503	183	1.7%	24,117
Annual Growth	32.4%	26.1%	—	20.1%

2014 Year-End Financials

Debt ratio: 3.6%
Return on equity: 11.6%
Cash ($ mil.): 2,454
Current ratio: 1.28
Long-term debt ($ mil.): 680
No. of shares (mil.): —
Dividends
Yield: —
Payout: —
Market value ($ mil.): —

	STOCK PRICE ($) FY Close	P/E High/Low		PER SHARE ($) Earnings	Dividends	Book Value
12/14	3.49	0	0	0.18	0.00	1.59
12/13	2.87	0	0	0.15	0.00	1.40
12/12	3.15	0	0	0.13	0.00	1.14
12/11	2.57	0	0	0.10	0.00	1.04
12/10	3.52	0	0	0.08	0.00	0.78
Annual Growth	(0.2%)	—	—	22.1%	—	19.4%

SK Innovation Co Ltd

SK Innovation (formerly known as SK Energy) is the energy lubricants and chemicals affiliate of South Korea's SK Group. Korea's largest oil refiner SK Innovation controls about 34% of Korea's fuel retailing market. The firm holds stakes in 30 oil exploration and production projects in 16 countries and has proved reserves of more than 500 million barrels of oil equivalent. It imports liquid petroleum gas (LPG) and claims a 44% share of the Korean LPG market. SK Innovation supplies natural gas to Seoul and other cities in Korea. The company also makes lubricants low-pollutant gasoline petrochemicals and batteries for electric vehicles.

In 2011 in order to be a more flexible organization in dealing with a rapidly changing marketplace SK Innovation spun off its refining unit as SK Energy its chemical operations as SK Global Chemicals and its lubricant oil business as SK Lubricants. All the units are wholly-owned subsidiaries. A part of the innovative push the company's new corporate name claims the company is looking to expand in the field of alternative energy including pursuing new battery and carbon capture technologies.

SK Innovation is focusing on strengthening its overseas oil exploration and production operations. It has formed strategic alliances with other global oil concerns such as Nippon Oil and PERTAMINA to in order to expand activities in China Vietnam and Indonesia.

In 2010 it formed a joint venture with KBR to market and license SK Innovation's petrochemical and related process technologies. That same year it agreed to sell its Brazilian oil interests to Denmark's Mærsk Oil for $2.4 billion. SK Innovation plans to use the proceeds either to invest in developing oil and gas fields or to buy other international oil companies. That year the company signed a contract to operate and maintain Vietnam's first petrochemical plant.

On the innovative technology side of the ledger in 2010 Korea launched its first electric car a vehicle powered by an SK Innovation lithium-ion battery.

In 2008 the company merged with subsidiary SK Incheon Oil a major Korean refiner allowing the company to further its plans to be a major oil and fuels exporter to the growing China market.

EXECUTIVES

President, Chul Khil Chung
Auditors: Anjin & Co. (A Member Firm of Deloitte Touche Tohmatsu)

LOCATIONS

HQ: SK Innovation Co Ltd
26, Jong-ro Jongno-gu, Seoul 110-110
Phone: (82) 2 2121 5114 **Fax:** (82) 2 2121 2118
Web: www.skenergy.com

COMPETITORS

BHP Billiton
Daewoo International
Exxon Mobil
GS Caltex
Hyundai Corporation
Idemitsu Kosan
JX Nippon Oil & Energy
Royal Dutch Shell

HISTORICAL FINANCIALS

Company Type: Public

Income Statement FYE: December 31

	REVENUE ($ mil.)	NET INCOME ($ mil.)	NET PROFIT MARGIN	EMPLOYEES
12/14	60,200	(538)	—	1,878
12/13	63,395	694	1.1%	1,892
12/12	68,680	1,110	1.6%	1,881
12/11	59,007	2,734	4.6%	1,642
12/10	47,911	1,015	2.1%	5,457
Annual Growth	5.9%	—	—	(23.4%)

2014 Year-End Financials

Debt ratio: 0.0%
Return on equity: (-3.8%)
Cash ($ mil.): 2,685
Current ratio: 1.31
Long-term debt ($ mil.): 6,228
No. of shares (mil.): 91
Dividends
Yield: —
Payout: —
Market value ($ mil.): —

SK Networks Co Ltd

Auditors: Hanyoung Accounting Corporation (A Member Firm of Ernst & Young International)

LOCATIONS

HQ: SK Networks Co Ltd
90 Namdamemun-ro, Jung-gu, Seoul 440-816
Phone: (82) 2 2221 2114 **Fax:** (82) 2 2221 0097
Web: www.sknetworks.co.kr

HISTORICAL FINANCIALS

Company Type: Public

Income Statement FYE: December 31

	REVENUE ($ mil.)	NET INCOME ($ mil.)	NET PROFIT MARGIN	EMPLOYEES
12/14	20,480	29	0.1%	3,301
12/13	24,699	(540)	—	3,661
12/12	26,164	45	0.2%	3,912
12/11	23,764	125	0.5%	4,085
12/10	21,548	161	0.8%	3,852
Annual Growth	(1.3%)	(34.7%)	—	(3.8%)

2014 Year-End Financials

Debt ratio: 0.0%
Return on equity: 1.2%
Cash ($ mil.): 1,180
Current ratio: 0.94
Long-term debt ($ mil.): 1,157
No. of shares (mil.): 248
Dividends
Yield: —
Payout: —
Market value ($ mil.): —

Skandinaviska Enskilda Banken

Snow banks are a common winter sight in Sweden; SEB banks are easy to spot year-round. Skandinaviska Enskilda Banken (SEB) provides merchant banking retail banking wealth management and life insurance in some 20 nations mostly in Northern Europe. Its merchant banking division provides lending debt capital markets trading finance and custody services to corporate clients and financial institutions. Its retail division provides business services including loans and card services. SEB Wealth Management offers asset management and private banking services to institutional and wealthy clients. Founded in 1856 the bank boasts nearly SK$3 trillion (around $350 billion) in assets.

OperationsThe bank operates five main business segments: Merchant Banking which generated 38% of total revenue in 2014; Retail Banking (27% of revenue); Wealth Management (10% of revenue) which boasts around SK$1.8 billion ($208 million) in assets under management; Life (10% of revenue) which provides life insurance products; and Baltic (8% of revenue) which counts the bank's operations in the Baltic region.More broadly SEB generated 48% of its total revenue from interest income in 2014 while 22% came from fee and commission income and 8% came from life insurance premium income. The remainder of the bank's revenue came from gains on the bank's investment securities.Geographic Reach-SEB generated 60% of its operating income in Sweden in 2014. Its other top markets are in the Nordic countries of Denmark Finland Germany and Norway as well as in Baltic countries such as Estonia Latvia and Lithuania. Sales and MarketingRetail Banking served 1.7 million private customers and 200000 small and medium-sized businesses in 2014. Its Wealth Management division serves institutions life insurance companies and private individuals. SEB's corporate customers come from a broad range of industries and sectors including manufacturing and service companies as well as investment and property companies.Financial PerformanceNote: Growth rates may differ after conversion to US dollars.SEB's revenues and profits have been rising over the past several years mostly thanks to higher net interest income from its growing loan business and cheap borrowing rates as well as increasing fee and commission income from its growing corporate financing business. (Note: In terms of US Dollars the bank's revenue has struggled to grow due to unfavorable foreign exchange rates.)The bank's revenue jumped by 15% to SK$98 billion ($12.4 billion) in 2014 thanks to a combination of higher fee and commission income from higher volumes of Merchant Banking transactions (such as mergers and acquisitions initial public offerings and new issues) and gains on the bank's investment securities and assets and liabilities held for trading. The bank's insurance business also grew thanks to higher fund values and higher premium volumes. Higher revenue and strong staff cost controls in 2014 also pushed the bank's net income up by 30% to SK$19 billion ($2.46 billion). SEB's cash levels declined sharply with operations using SK$148 billion ($19 billion) during the year mostly due to a decrease in borrowing from credit institutions and a decline in short-term security issue funding compared to the prior year.

Stategy

SEB in 2015 continued to focus on growing its Merchant Banking and Retail divisions. Thanks to its heavy promotional investments in 2014 the bank landed 60 new large corporate and institutional customers 12700 new small and mid-sized enterprise (SME) customers and 27000 private customers.In addition to growing on its own SEB also looks to acquire financial firms that complement its offerings and expand its geographic reach. In 2014 SEB acquisitions boosted its card business in two of its top Noridic markets: Finland and Norway. With events in Russia and Ukraine causing political turmoil financial capitalization has also been an important priority for the bank. Fortunately for SEB the European Central Bank's 2014 stress test confirmed the bank's capital strength and asset quality passed muster. Mergers and AcquisitionsIn 2014 SEB bolstered its card businesses in Finland and Norway after acquiring Nets' Business Eurocard operations and DNB's corporate card portfolio respectively.

HISTORY

Company BackgroundSkandinaviska Enskilda Banken (SEB) was incorporated in 1972 as a result of the merger between Stockholm's Enskilda Bank (founded in 1856 by the Wallenberg family) and Skandinaviska Banken (founded in 1864 and a pioneer in commercial lending in Scandinavia). By 1974 SEB had begun expanding its operations forming an investment management subsidiary. It then became one of the first Swedish banks to go international when it took a stake in the German Deutsch-Skandinavische Bank in 1976. By the end of the 1970s SEB had reached halfway around the world establishing a subsidiary in Singapore to handle Southeast Asian operations.

By the early 1980s SEB was leading the nation in industrial as well as private accounts largely due to deregulation and the introduction of new financial instruments including Swedish treasury bills a commercial paper market and market-rate state bonds. The bank continued to expand opening branches in the Cayman Islands Hamburg London and New York; it also began cross-border banking in Scandinavia through a regional alliance with Bergen Bank of Norway Privatbanken of Denmark and Union Bank of Finland.

In another step toward deregulation the Swedish government lifted the ban on foreign banking in 1985. Within a year a dozen international banks had established themselves in Sweden but SEB continued to expand; its investment banking subsidiary Enskilda Securities opened branches in Hong Kong London New York Paris and Singapore in the latter half of the 1980s.

In 1990 the bank acquired an option to buy about a third of Skandia Sweden's largest private insurance company. But facing strong resistance from Skandia's management SEB accepted defeat and sold most of its option to two Scandinavian insurance companies. Winds of change blew through Sweden in the early 1990s as the country suffered a severe economic recession. Deregulation in the mid-1980s followed by excessive lending to the property market led to inflated real estate prices and then a collapse of the market. Banks investing in property experienced huge losses; many banks (including SEB) had to turn to the government for help to strengthen their capital bases. The mid-1990s saw the bank still trying to recover selling several of its subsidiaries including a vehicle finance unit to GE Capital.

1997 saw SEB acquire Trygg-Hansa (now SEB Trygg Liv) one of Sweden's major insurers. The bank remained acquisitive in 1998 expanding aggressively into the Baltic by buying major stakes in banks in Estonia (Eesti Ühlspank) Latvia (Latvija Unibanken) and Lithuania (Vilniaus Bankas).

In 1999 the bank further emphasized its Internet business making it a separate unit. Also that year SEB sold Trygg-Hansa's non-life business to Denmark's Codan Insurance in exchange for Codan's banking subsidiary and other assets. In 2000 the bank acquired Germany's almost 200-branch BfG Bank from Crdit Lyonnais; it then used BfG to create a cross-selling and Internet alliance with German insurer Gerling. Also in 2000 SEB upped its stake in Eesti Ühispank Vilniaus Bankas and Latvijas Unibanka.

The following year SEB announced plans to acquire fellow Swedish bank ForeningsSparbanken to create SEB SwedBank. EU regulators investigated the proposal and demanded significant concession. As a result the two banks dropped plans for the merger later in 2001.

SEB continued to boost its offerings and services —largely through acquisitions —during the early years of the 21st century. Purchases included Europay in Norway (2002) Danish life insurer Codan Pension (2004) Ukraine's Bank Agio (2005) and Russia's PetroEnergoBank (2006). In 2007 it acquired nearly all of Factorial Bank adding 65 branches in Eastern Ukraine. The following year it bought London-based hedge fund Key Asset Management.

EXECUTIVES

EVP and CFO, Jan Erik Back, age 54
President and CEO, Annika Falkengren, age 53
EVP and Head Corporate and Institutions, Magnus Carlsson, age 59
Country Manager SEB Germany, Fredrik Boheman, age 59
EVP and Head of Retail Banking, Mats Torstendahl, age 54
Country Manager SEB Denmark, Peter H ̦ltermand, age 52
Head of Baltic Division, David Teare, age 52
Country Manager SEB Norway, William Paus, age 48
Country Manager and President SEB Latvia, Ieva Tetere
Country Manager and President SEB Estonia, Allan Parik
Chief Risk Officer, Johan Andersson, age 58
Co-Head Merchant Banking Division, Joachim Alpen, age 48
Head of Life Division, Peter Dahlgren, age 43
Head of Wealth Management, Christoffer Malmer, age 40
Co-Head of Merchant Banking Division, Johan Torgeby, age 41
Country Manager SEB Finland, Marcus Nysten, age 55
Deputy Chairman, Urban Jansson, age 70
Vice Chairman, Jesper Ovesen, age 58
Chairman, Marcus Wallenberg, age 59
Auditors: PricewaterhouseCoopers AB

LOCATIONS

HQ: Skandinaviska Enskilda Banken
Kungstradgardsgatan 8, Stockholm SE-106 40
Phone: (46) 771 62 10 00
Web: www.sebgroup.com

2014 Operating Income

	% of total
Scandinavia	
Sweden	60
Norway	8
Denmark	7
Finland	4
Baltics	
Lithuania	3
Estonia	3
Latvia	2
Germany	7
Other	6
Total	**100**

PRODUCTS/OPERATIONS

2014 Sales by Segment

	% of total
Merchant Banking	38
Retail Banking	27
Life	10
Wealth Management	10
Baltic	8
Other	7
Total	**100**

COMPETITORS

Citigroup Global Markets
Danske Bank
Deutsche Bank
DnB NOR
Goldman Sachs
KBC
Morgan Stanley
Nordea Bank
Skandia
Storebrand ASA
Svenska Handelsbanken
Swedbank AB
UBS Investment Bank

HISTORICAL FINANCIALS

Company Type: Public

Income Statement FYE: December 31

	ASSETS ($ mil.)	NET INCOME ($ mil.)	INCOME AS % OF ASSETS	EMPLOYEES
12/14	341,678	2,486	0.7%	16,742
12/13	387,577	2,303	0.6%	17,096
12/12	376,613	1,785	0.5%	18,168
12/11	342,561	1,610	0.5%	18,912
12/10	325,075	1,005	0.3%	20,717
Annual Growth	1.3%	25.4%	—	(5.2%)

2014 Year-End Financials

Return on assets: 0.7%
Return on equity: 14.9%
Long-term debt ($ mil.): —
No. of shares (mil.): —
Sales ($ mil): 12,481
Dividends
Yield: —
Payout: —
Market value ($ mil.): —

	STOCK PRICE ($) FY Close	P/E High/Low		PER SHARE ($) Earnings	Dividends	Book Value
12/14	12.84	0	0	1.13	0.00	7.95
Annual Growth	—	—	—	—	—	—

Societe Generale

Soci ©©G ® ©ale wants to be top brass in the French banking industry. The bank (more familiarly known as SocGen) commands a three-pronged campaign with operations entailing domestic retail banking (including regional bank Cr ©dit du Nord and majority-owned online bank and brokerage Boursorama) international retail banking and corporate and investment banking. Other key activities include specialized finance consumer finance and insurance and investment management private banking and securities services. Altogether SocGen has more than 3200 branches in France and nearly 4000 additional locations in more than 75 countries worldwide.

SocGen has international banking operations in nearly 40 countries. Key markets for the segment are Russia Central and Eastern Europe the Mediterranean basin sub-Saharan Africa and Asia particularly China India and Vietnam. The company's asset management operations include two joint ventures with fellow French banking giant Cr ©dit Agricole: Amundi (25% owned) and brokerage Newedge (50%).

SocGen reported a 3% decline in net banking income for 2011 but a nearly 40% decrease in profits from E3.9 billion to E2.4 billion (approximately $5 billion to $3.1 billion). The company attributed its results in part to a decline in corporate and investment banking earnings amid turbulent markets as well as restructuring changes and the write down of goodwill and Greek sovereign debt.

SocGen's primary strategic initiatives include controlling risk and improving customer service. Some of the ways the bank is achieving its goals include streamlining its loan application process increasing capital reserves and reducing its exposure to sovereign debt of troubled countries such as Ireland Italy Portugal and Spain. To help improve its capital position SocGen announced plans to sell US asset manager TCW Group to The Carlyle Group in 2012. It's also partnering with Tikehau Group to take over French investment company Salvepar.

HISTORY

In 1864 French steel magnate Joseph Schneider along with a group of Parisian bankers incorporated Soci ©© G ® ©ale pour Favoriser le D ©eloppement du Commerce et de l'Industrie en France. The bank which for obvious reasons came to be known as Soci ©©G ® ©ale had the duty "to encourage the development of trade and industry in France." It took deposits from the public and offered lines of credit to companies. The bank also helped organize businesses and invested in them.

By the 1890s Soci ©©G ® ©ale's branches placed shares with the public and issued private unsecured loans in France and Russia.

The bank counted 14000 shareholders in 1895 and 18 years later the number had boomed to 122000. The bank continued its brisk growth through the first decades of the 20th century opening more than 1400 branches by 1933.

Although Soci ©©G ® ©ale managed to move into Africa and America in the 1930s the Depression and WWII forced the bank to reduce its size and close branches at home.

After WWII the bank was nationalized by the French government to help rebuild the war-ravaged country. Soci ©©G ® ©ale (already active in New York) was well-positioned to distribute the US-sponsored postwar reconstruction initiative aka the Marshall Plan. For 30 years the bank grew steadily under state control.

The 1960s were a boom time for French exports. The decade brought the bank greater expansion both geographically (Europe Latin America) and economically thanks to the specialization of credit investment banking finance leasing for companies and home mortgages for retail customers. Soci ©©G ® ©ale also began dealing in Eurocurrencies (money deposited outside the investing company or government's home country).

In 1973 a new law in France allowed the bank to sell up to 25% of its shares to its staff and a limited circle of institutional investors.

A year later amid the oil crisis low-quality Eurocurrency market loans came back to haunt Soci ©©G ® ©ale. In one case the bank had unwisely lent Eurodollars to the United States National Bank of San Diego which failed and cost Soci ©©G ® ©ale $7.5 million.

In 1975 the bank launched Agrifan an export-based food products trading company to great success. Agrifan was followed by two more companies specializing in food-industry equipment and medical supplies.

Conservatives regained power in the French government in 1986. The next year Soci ©© G ® ©ale was officially privatized.

In 1998 the bank extended the reach of its financial services by acquiring Barr Devlin a US-based investment banker and adviser and Yamaichi Capital Management in Japan.

The next year Soci ©©G ® ©ale undertook a friendly merger with fellow French banking gargantuan Paribas only to have Banque Nationale de Paris swoop in and steal the prize to form BNP Paribas.

Soci ©©G ® ©ale had to satisfy itself with a piecemeal expansion. By 2000 it had hammered out an ambitious strategic alliance with Spain-based Santander Central Hispano. The French bank also snapped up 30% of Italian insurer Societ Assicuratrice Industriale's Banca SAI subsidiary giving it access to SAI's 3 million customers. The buying spree continued into 2001 with Soci ©©G ® ©ale acquiring Deutsche Bank's leasing and vehicle-fleet businesses Gefa and ALD. The bank then bought a controlling stake in LA-based fund manager TCW Group.

SocGen sold its South American retail banking unit Banco Soci ©©G ® ©ale Argentina to Argentine banking group Banco Banex in 2005. The following year SocGen spun off US-based investment bank Cowen Group.

In 2008 SocGen uncovered fraud by one of its traders in one of the world's largest-ever instances of trading fraud. Soon after the company began raising funds to help cover the estimated $7.1 billion cost of the fraud and also initiated legal proceedings against the (by then former) employee. The Banking Commission of France fined the company $6.3 billion for breaches in internal controls.

Additionally chairman and then-CEO Daniel Bouton and co-CEO Philippe Citerne each gave up a half-year's salary to compensate for the company's losses. Although Bouton's offers to resign amidst the firestorm were twice rejected by SocGen's board of directors he eventually did step down. CFO Fr © ©ic Oudea succeeded him in both positions. Didier Alix and Severin Cabannes replaced Citerne as deputy CEOs.

The company spent years building up its portfolio in banks in Central and Eastern Europe including majority stakes in Russia's Rosbank in 2008 and in Macedonia's Ohridska Banka and Bauritanian Bank Banque in 2007. SocGen also expanded its private banking operations. In 2008 its SG Private Banking unit acquired a 37% stake in US-based wealth manager Rockefeller Financial Services and in 2007 it bought ABN AMRO's London private banking unit.

In 2008 SocGen merged the brokerage activities of subsidiary Fimat with Cr ©dit Agricole Corporate and Investment Bank (formerly Calyon) creating a joint venture named Newedge. The following year SocGen merged its asset management business with that of Cr ©dit Agricole creating a combined firm called Amundi with more than E690 billion ($1 trillion) of assets under management. SocGen owns 25% of the joint venture while Cr ©dit Agricole holds the other 75%.

Auditors: ERNST & YOUNG et Autres

LOCATIONS

HQ: Societe Generale
29, Bd Haussman, Paris 75009
Phone: (33) 1 42 14 20 00
Web: www.societegenerale.com

HISTORICAL FINANCIALS

Company Type: Public

Income Statement FYE: December 31

	ASSETS ($ mil.)	NET INCOME ($ mil.)	INCOME AS % OF ASSETS	EMPLOYEES
12/14	1,590,086	3,272	0.2%	148,322
12/13	1,700,629	2,994	0.2%	148,324
12/12	1,648,479	1,020	0.1%	154,009
12/11	1,528,048	3,084	0.2%	159,616
12/10	1,515,133	5,242	0.3%	155,617
Annual Growth	1.2%	(11.1%)	—	(1.2%)

2014 Year-End Financials

Return on assets: 0.2%
Return on equity: 5.0%
Long-term debt ($ mil.): —
No. of shares (mil.): 785
Sales ($ mil): 108,728
Dividends
Yield: 3.2%
Payout: 6.8%
Market value ($ mil.): 6,533

	STOCK PRICE ($) FY Close	P/E High	P/E Low	PER SHARE ($) Earnings	Dividends	Book Value
12/14	8.32	4	3	3.54	0.27	85.40
12/13	11.65	5	3	3.30	0.12	90.47
12/12	7.82	12	6	0.84	0.00	87.07
12/11	4.36	4	1	4.11	0.46	81.50
12/10	10.87	3	2	6.61	0.86	85.68
Annual Growth	(6.5%)	—	—	(14.5%)	(24.9%)	(0.1%)

Societe Nationale des Chemins de Fer Francais (SNCF) (France)

France's state-owned railway company Soci ©© Nationale des Chemins de Fer Fran §is (SNCF) is still blazing a trail as one of the world's largest providers of public transport. Overall the SNCF rail network covers some 120 countries more than 30000 km (almost 20000 mile) of track and about 3000 passenger stations. Through numerous subsidiaries it offers local and regional rail transport as well as long-distance high-speed rail transport. It's also a top operator of parking facilities and bicycle rentals in France. Additionally SNCF is a rail station manager and developer and a global multi-modal operator in freight transport and logistics supporting businesses that ship goods and commodities.

With the addition of the Gares & Connexions (SNCF's train station management and development unit) in 2009 SNCF now operates five divisions. SNCF Geodis (freight transport and logistics services) and SNCF Voyages (long-distance high-speed passenger transport) each represent about a quarter of revenues trailed by SNCF Infra (rail infrastructure engineering and maintenance). However with increased commuter demand followed by subsequent development activities in 2009 and 2010 SNCF's Proximit ©division which handles public urban and outer urban commuter travel is now the company's largest division generating roughly one-third of all revenues.

The growth of SNCF's Proximit ©division requires more in-service train cars to handle the increase in commuters. In early 2010 SNCF ordered 80 train cars from Canada-based Bombardier with an option for an additional 50. The contract is valued at as much as 8 billion (almost $12 billion). Bombardier will build the trains in France for a scheduled shipment in mid-2013.

To be a major player in Europe's increasingly deregulated road and rail transport network SNCF is forging cross-border alliances: transnational ventures have included working with Deutsche Bahn to design a European high-speed rail system operating a bus and rail joint venture with UK-based Go-Ahead Group and entering into a joint venture with UK's FirstGroup to operate TransPennine Expressway in northern England.

Along with its primary rail operations SNCF has been upping its stakes in and taking over a number of other passenger and freight transportation companies to cement its market position. It took a majority stake in Keolia a French bus operator that also has operations in Algeria Australia Canada and Germany after Keolia merged with SNCF subsidiary Effia a provider of car sharing electrical car and other non-motorized transport. SNCF Geodis completed its takeover of wagon and container leasing firm Ermewa.

In late 2010 SNCF Voyages acquired a majority stake in Findworks Technologies which operates Liligo.com a travel price comparison site. The addition of Liligo strengthens SNCF's desire to develop its consumer-oriented online services both in France and across Europe. Liligo will operate as a separate entity within the SNCF family of companies.

HISTORY

France's first railway line opened in 1827 was used to haul coal from Saint-Etienne to the port of Andrezieux. Four years later the first steam locomotives and passenger service were introduced between Saint-Etienne and Lyon. Paris opened its first rail line in 1837. Although the early railway companies were under private ownership the state controlled the network of rail lines through licensing. Under Napoleon III's Second Empire (1852-1870) the government encouraged an expansion of railway lines that linked Paris to every major town and city in France. By 1870 the main routes of France's modern railway system had been laid; by 1914 the network system had grown to nearly 40000 km.

After the devastation of WWI railway companies invested heavily in rebuilding. Burdened by debt the rail network was forced to seek government intervention for its survival. In 1938 the government set up Soci ©©Nationale des Chemins de Fer Fran §is to unify the five largest railway systems: Compagnie de l'Est Compagnie du Midi Compagnie du Nord Compagnie du Paris-Lyon-M ©iterran ©and Compagnie du Paris-Orl ©ns.

Although WWII destroyed the French railway system for a second time the massive rebuilding enabled postwar French governments to adopt modern innovations. In 1950 SNCF began a systemwide electrification of its tracks; a decade later 7600 km of its major lines were powered by electricity.

SNCF also pioneered the development of fast trains. Following an overhaul of SNCF in the early 1970s the company continued to develop high-speed trains to stay competitive with airlines. In 1981 the company's TGV ("train grande vitesse") hit a record speed of 380 kph (236 mph). TGVs entered commercial service that year. By 1987 some 43 cities were connected to Paris by TGVs.

To add to its European logistics and freight services SNCF acquired 20% of Spanish trucking firm TRANSFESA in 1993. In 1995 it launched Eurostar a London-Paris service using the newly opened Channel Tunnel. Partners in the joint venture were Belgian National Railroads (Soci ©©Nationale des Chemins de Fer Belges) and European Passenger Services the British Rail unit later spun off as Eurostar (UK). That year SNCF saw its operations disrupted by a nationwide rail strike that lasted three weeks. In 1995 SNCF also created road transport and logistics group G ©dis which it privatized a year later.

Diversifying further SNCF also entered telecommunications in 1996 and set up a communications network to lease spare capacity. That year the company's chairman resigned following charges of corruption related to his tenure at an oil company. SNCF also plagued by debts and strikes decided to get back on track. It began restructuring and appointed former Aerospatiale chief Louis Gallois to head the company. In 1997 it shifted most of its debt load to R ©eau Ferr ©de France which was created to manage France's rail infrastructure.

In 1999 SNCF acquired Via-GTI France's largest privately owned public transport company which was in a joint venture with UK transport group Go-Ahead to operate the Thameslink train franchise. That year SNCF acquired Swiss rolling stock group Ermewa; it also sold its hotel interests to Accor but formed an alliance with the hotelier to offer discount lodging.

SNCF and German railway Deutsche Bahn agreed in 2000 to collaborate on developing a new generation of high-speed trains.

SNCF's rail operations were hampered by labor unrest in 2003 capped by a strike in May and June of that year. The company responded by cutting costs.

After a decade at SNCF Gallois left the company in 2006 to serve as co-CEO of defense group Airbus.

Adding steam to its European expansion in September 2009 SNCF and Channel Tunnel operator Groupe Eurotunnel bought rail freight company Veolia Cargo from Veolia Transportation (itself owned by Veolia Environnement). SNCF will take over Veolia Cargo's operations in Germany Italy and the Netherlands and Eurotunnel will take over Veolia's France operations.

Auditors: PricewaterhouseCoopers Audit

LOCATIONS

HQ: Societe Nationale des Chemins de Fer Francais (SNCF) (France)
1-7 place aux Etoiles, La Plaine ST Denis, Cedex 93212
Phone: (33) 1 42 85 63 13 **Fax:** (33) 1 42 85 63 16
Web: www.sncf.com

HISTORICAL FINANCIALS

Company Type: Public

Income Statement FYE: December 31

	REVENUE ($ mil.)	NET INCOME ($ mil.)	NET PROFIT MARGIN	EMPLOYEES
12/14	33,114	735	2.2%	245,763
12/13	44,374	(247)	—	244,570
12/12	44,576	504	1.1%	249,343
12/11	42,224	161	0.4%	245,090
12/10	40,774	932	2.3%	240,978
Annual Growth	(5.1%)	(5.8%)	—	0.5%

2014 Year-End Financials

Debt ratio: 54.1%
Return on equity: 9.0%
Cash ($ mil.): 6,573
Current ratio: 0.87
Long-term debt ($ mil.): 16,789
No. of shares (mil.): —
Dividends
Yield: —
Payout: —
Market value ($ mil.): —

Sodexo

This company has a lot of mouths to feed. Formerly Sodexho Alliance Sodexo is the world's #2 contract foodservice provider (after Compass Group) with operations in about 80 countries. Its subsidiaries offer corporate foodservice and hospitality services vending services and foodservices for educational institutions and other public-sector clients. Other operations include event concessions health care foodservices and such outsourced on-site service solutions as cleaning groundskeeping and laundry. Its US-based subsidiary Sodexo Inc. is one of the largest contract foodservice providers in North America. The company has some 33900 service sites worldwide.

In addition to its core foodservice and facilities management services Sodexo is a leading provider of voucher cards in Europe and Latin America used to buy groceries clothing and other basic necessities. The company operates voucher systems for both employers that use the cards as a form of employee benefits as well as for government welfare programs. Vouchers include restaurant gift and childcare passes. (Sodexo refers to its voucher operations as motivation solutions.)

Sodexo's business strategy includes the following: to become a world leader in on-site service solutions and motivation solutions and to maintain its leadership in the foodservice sector. It sets forth these basic goals in order to meet challenges such as the recent and on-going worldwide economic turndown and the aging of the population (particularly in North America). It also faces diminishing sources of and rising costs of its raw materials (ex: energy and food). And finally as the world population continues to grow and at the same time societies' wealth grows Sodexo must to deal with quality-of-life issues with regard to the goods and services it provides.

Working to fulfill these strategies the company won the contract for organizing the 2010 Winter Olympics in Vancouver. During 2009 it increased its contract obligations with France's Ministry of Justice to deliver service solutions to 27 additional prisons. It also won the Microsoft Europe contract and renewed its contract with Procter & Gamble for which Sodexo provides a wide range of services at 38 sites in 13 European countries. It also signed a 30-year contract to design construct and manage a military training center for The Defense Training Review in the UK. (Sodexo hopes to realize €30 billion in revenue over the life of the contract.) In addition Sodexo made acquisitions in high-growth markets in 2009 including Zehnacker in Germany RKHS in India and Comfort Keepers in the US. Following that trend into 2011 the company acquired the Brazilian based Puras do Brazil for approximately €525 million mid year.

During 2008 it signed contracts to provide services to GlaxoSmithKline in Canada and Soci ©©G © ©ale in France. The company has also been making targeted acquisitions to expand both its services and geographical reach. It purchased a 90% stake in Zehnacker Group a facilities management services provider in Germany for more than €170 million ($234 million) in 2008. That same year it acquired Score Groupe in France.

The company changed its name in 2008 to Sodexo dropping both the word "Alliance" and the "h" as part of a global rebranding effort. The name change was intended to raise the company's profile and recognition by focusing on the singular name (that it also hopes is easier to spell and pronounce without the extra letter).

Chairman Pierre Bellon and his family own about 38% of the company.

HISTORY

The Bellon family had been luxury ship hospitality specialists since the turn of the century 60 years before Pierre Bellon founded Sodexho in 1966. By 1971 Bellon had his first contract outside France to provide foodservice to a Brussels hospital. Sodexho continued to expand its services into the late 1970s entering remote site management in Africa and the Middle East in 1975 and starting its service vouchers segment in Belgium and Germany in 1978.

Sodexho jumped the pond in 1980 expanding its businesses into North and South America. The company went public on the Paris Bourse exchange in 1983. Two years later it bought Seiler a Boston vending machine company-turned-restaurateur. Sodexho then bought San Francisco's Food Dimensions in 1987. After beefing up its American operations with four other US acquisitions the company merged Food Dimensions and Seiler in 1989. Sodexho's US river cruise company Spirit Cruises –an echo of the Bellon family's original calling –was also included in the merger. The merged US companies were renamed Sodexho USA in 1993.

The 1990s proved an era of growth and acquisitions for Sodexho. The company expanded into Japan Africa Russia and five Eastern European countries in 1993. The company acquired a 20% stake in Corrections Corporation of America the following year and virtually doubled its size with the acquisition of the UK's Gardner Merchant in 1995. The largest catering company in that region Gardner Merchant had holdings that spanned Australia Asia northern Europe the UK and the US – generally markets where Sodexho did not have a strong presence. That year the company also acquired Partena a Swedish security and care company from Volvo's Fortos.

Gardner Merchant's US business was officially merged with Sodexho USA in 1996 to make it the #4 foodservice company in the US. Also that year Sodexho acquired Brazilian service voucher company Cardapio. After a year of legal wrangling Sodexho also lost a fight for control of Accor's Eurest France to rival caterer Compass Group and sold off its minority interest. The next year Sodexho acquired 49% of Universal Ogden Services renamed Universal Services an American remote site manager. To signify its efforts to maintain the individuality of the companies it acquires Sodexho changed its name to Sodexho Alliance in 1997.

Marriott International merged its foodservice branch with Sodexho's North American foodservice operations in 1998. With a 48% stake Sodexho Alliance became the largest shareholder; former Marriott International stockholders took the rest with the Marriott family controlling 9%. Before the merger Sodexho USA was less than one-fourth the size of Marriott International's foodservice division. Sodexho acquired GR Servicios Hoteleros in 1999 thereby becoming the largest caterer in Spain. The following year it agreed to merge its remote site management operations with Universal Services and rename it Universal Sodexho (later Sodexo Remote Sites).

In 2001 its initial $900 million bid to buy the 52% of Sodexho Marriott Services it didn't already own was rebuffed by its subsidiary's shareholders. Sodexho Alliance made a better offer (about $1.1 billion) and finally reached an agreement to purchase the rest of Sodexho Marriott Services. The deal was completed later that year and Sodexho Marriott Services changed its name to Sodexho Inc. Also that year the company agreed to pay some $470 million for French rival Sogeres and US-based food management firm Wood Dining.

In 2002 the company announced it had detected accounting and management errors in its UK operations causing the value of its stock to fall by nearly one-third. In addition the company replaced its UK management team because of poor performance there.

Admitting no wrongdoing Sodexho settled an $80 million race-bias lawsuit just before it was to go to trial in 2005. The suit brought by the African-American employees of its American subsidiary Sodexho Inc. charged that African-Americans were routinely passed over for promotions and were segregated within the company. In addition to paying the monetary award Sodexho agreed to increase company diversity through promotion incentives monitoring and training.

In 2005 Bellon 75 stepped down as company CEO but remained chairman. He was replaced by Sodexho veteran Michel Landel. The company changed its name to Sodexo in 2008 a rebranding effort that eliminated both the word "Alliance" and the "h" from its name.

EXECUTIVES

CEO, Michel Landel, age 64, $843,447 total compensation
CEO Corporate Services Worldwide, Sylvia Metayer
CEO Energy and Resources Worldwide, Nicholas Japy, age 59
CEO Universities Worldwide, Patrick E. (Pat) Connolly
Group Chief Strategy Organization Research and Development and Innovation Officer, Damien Verdier, age 58
EVP and VP Group Executive Committee; CEO Europe On-Site Services, Pierre Henry, age 64
Region Chair North America and CEO Schools Worldwide, Lorna C. Donatone
CEO Benefits and Rewards Services Worldwide, Denis Machuel
CEO Service Operations Worldwide, Satya-Christophe Menard
CEO Government and Agencies and CEO Sports and Leisure Worldwide, Debbie White
CEO Engineering and Construction, Laurent Auzanneau
Group Chief Brand and Communication Officer, Ana Busto
Group CFO, Marc Rolland
Chairwoman, Sophie Bellon
Auditors: PricewaterhouseCoopers Audit

LOCATIONS

HQ: Sodexo
255, quai de la Bataille de Stalingrad, Issy-les-Moulineaux, Cedex 9 92866
Phone: (33) 1 30 85 75 00
Web: www.sodexo.com

COMPETITORS

ARAMARK	Elior
Accor	Healthcare Services
Autogrill	ISS A/S
Berendsen	SSP
Cintas	SSP America
Compass Group	UniFirst
Delaware North	

HISTORICAL FINANCIALS

Company Type: Public

Income Statement FYE: August 31

	REVENUE ($ mil.)	NET INCOME ($ mil.)	NET PROFIT MARGIN	EMPLOYEES
08/15	22,211	784	3.5%	422,844
08/14	23,768	646	2.7%	419,317
08/13	24,357	581	2.4%	427,921
08/12	22,959	660	2.9%	421,391
08/11	23,183	651	2.8%	391,148
Annual Growth	(1.1%)	4.8%	—	2.0%

2015 Year-End Financials

Debt ratio: 24.1%	No. of shares (mil.): 152
Return on equity: 20.2%	Dividends
Cash ($ mil.): 2,250	Yield: 2.3%
Current ratio: 1.00	Payout: —
Long-term debt ($ mil.): 3,099	Market value ($ mil.): 2,678

	STOCK PRICE ($) FY Close	P/E High/Low	PER SHARE ($) Earnings	Dividends	Book Value
08/15	17.59	23 4	5.09	0.41	27.31
08/14	97.97	33 27	4.21	0.00	27.71
08/13	88.10	34 26	3.81	0.00	25.81
08/12	78.85	23 18	4.34	0.38	25.36
08/11	73.55	27 22	4.25	0.00	24.30
Annual Growth	(30.1%)	— —	4.6%	—	3.0%

SoftBank Group Corp

Auditors: Deloitte Touche Tohmatsu LLC

LOCATIONS

HQ: SoftBank Group Corp
1-9-1 Higashi-Shinbashi, Minato-ku, Tokyo 105-7303
Phone: (81) 3 6889 2290
Web: www.softbank.jp

HISTORICAL FINANCIALS

Company Type: Public

Income Statement FYE: March 31

	REVENUE ($ mil.)	NET INCOME ($ mil.)	NET PROFIT MARGIN	EMPLOYEES
03/15	72,264	5,570	7.7%	72,978
03/14	64,587	5,105	7.9%	77,966
03/13	34,036	3,958	11.6%	32,862
03/12	39,039	3,824	9.8%	22,710
03/11	36,285	2,291	6.3%	21,799
Annual Growth	18.8%	24.9%	—	35.3%

2015 Year-End Financials

Debt ratio: 0.4%
Return on equity: 27.8%
Cash ($ mil.): 27,160
Current ratio: 1.28
Long-term debt ($ mil.): 81,595

No. of shares (mil.): 1,189
Dividends
Yield: 0.6%
Payout: —
Market value ($ mil.): 34,576

	STOCK PRICE ($) FY Close	P/E High/Low	PER SHARE ($) Earnings	Dividends	Book Value
03/15	29.08	0 0	4.66	0.18	19.95
03/14	37.91	0 0	4.27	0.20	15.94
03/13	22.80	0 0	3.49	0.00	14.39
03/12	14.87	— —	3.40	0.00	15.93
03/11	19.78	— —	2.04	0.00	9.81
Annual Growth	10.1%	— —	23.0%	—	19.4%

Sompo Japan Nipponkoa Holdings Inc

Sompo Japan Nipponkoa Holdings (formerly NKSJ Holdings) was created to hold two insurance companies: Sompo Japan and Nipponkoa Insurance. While already strong players in Japan's property/casualty (called non-life in Japan) and life insurance markets when merger mania hit the industry they didn't want to be left out and formed the joint holding company in 2010. The two companies merged into one entity Sompo Japan Nipponkoa Insurance in 2014. The holding company's businesses include domestic property/casualty and life insurance as well as overseas insurance asset and risk management services pension plans and some supplemental health insurance products.

Geographic Reach

Sompo Japan Nipponkoa has operations in some 230 cities in 32 countries in Europe the Middle East the Americas Africa Asia and Oceania. It earns the majority of its revenues in the Japanese market.

Sales and Marketing

Sompo Japan Nipponkoa markets its products through insurance agencies while Sonpo 24 and Saison Automobile and Fire sells directly to customers. Sompo Japan Nipponkoa Himawari Life markets through property/casualty insurance agencies promoting life insurance to property/casualty policyholders.

Financial Performance

The company's revenue increased 6% to ¥3008.3 billion in 2014 on an increase in net premiums written and life insurance premiums written. Investment income also rose that year. Predecessors Sompo Japan and Nipponkoa saw continued growth in net premiums written primarily due to the effect of rate revisions in automobile coverage. In South America the acquiring of additional shares of Brazil's Marítima Seguros boosted earnings.

Net income dropped 1% to ¥43.6 billion due to an increase in net commissions and brokerage fees and provisions for reserve for outstanding losses and claims and provisions for underwriting reserves incurred.

Sompo Japan Nipponkoa reported a cash inflow of ¥123 billion (versus a cash outflow in 2013) due to gains on investments and changes in reserves for outstanding losses and claims.

Strategy

Why merge in the first place? The company cites pressures on its industry from several sources including the country's declining birthrate its rapidly aging population and the effects of climate change. While those are real challenges to the industry the Sompo/Nipponkoa merger also took place at the same time as several other large mergers among Japanese insurance companies. When the dust settles there will be fewer but larger companies elbowing each other to claim market share.

To expand its reinsurance operations the company has established outposts in Hong Kong Kuala Lampur and London. It opened a representative office in Johannesburg in 2014. And it acquired UK-based Canopius Group a specialty player that primarily works through insurance exhange Lloyds.

Also in 2014 Sompo Japan Nipponkoa became the first Japanese property/casualty insurer to receive approval to sell compulsory automobile accident coverage in China.

The company is entering new market sectors that complement its insurance operations. In 2015 it struck up a partnership with nursing care company MessageCo to provide nursing care services. It also acquired a majority stake in Japanese home remodeler FRESHHOUSE to build on its fire insurance sales.

Mergers and Acquisitions

Since the initial merger Sompo Japan Nipponkoa has been working to expand its operations outside the saturated Japanese market. To enter the overseas specialty market the company purchased Canopius Group in 2014; Canopius is one of the top 10 insurers in the Lloyds insurance market.

EXECUTIVES

President and Executive Officer (Group CEO) and Representative Director, Kengo Sakurada
Deputy President and Senior Managing Executive Officer (Group CIO) and Director, Keiji Nishizawa
Deputy President Senior Managing Executive Officer and Director, Shinji Tsuji
Managing Executive Officer and General Manager The Americas Regional Headquarters, Masato Fujikura
Executive Officer General Manager Global Business Planning Department and General Manager China & East Asia Regional Headquarters, Junichi Tanaka
Executive Officer and General Manager South Asia and Pacific Regional Headquarters, Nobuhiro Kojima
Executive Officer and General Manager Europe Regional Headquarters, Takashi Yoshino
Chairman, Masaya Futamiya
Auditors: Ernst & Young ShinNihon LLC

LOCATIONS

HQ: Sompo Japan Nipponkoa Holdings Inc
1-26-1 Nishi-Shinjuku, Shinjuku-ku, Tokyo 160-8338
Phone: (81) 3 3349 3000
Web: www.sompo-hd.com

COMPETITORS

Fuji Fire and Marine
MS&AD Holdings
Nippon Life Insurance
Samsung Fire & Marine
Tokio Marine

HISTORICAL FINANCIALS

Company Type: Public

Income Statement FYE: March 31

	REVENUE ($ mil.)	NET INCOME ($ mil.)	NET PROFIT MARGIN	EMPLOYEES
03/15	27,144	452	1.7%	36,086
03/14	29,001	427	1.5%	35,904
03/13	30,071	463	1.5%	35,481
03/12	33,881	(1,124)	—	35,542
03/11	31,517	(156)	—	34,203
Annual Growth	(3.7%)	—	—	1.3%

2015 Year-End Financials

Debt ratio: 0.0%
Return on equity: 3.3%
Cash ($ mil.): 5,290
Current ratio: 0.17
Long-term debt ($ mil.): 1,133

No. of shares (mil.): 408
Dividends
Yield: —
Payout: —
Market value ($ mil.): —

Sony Corp

Sony is synonymous with consumer electronics. It's especially big in TVs and game consoles like the new PlayStation4. Officially named Sony Kabushiki Kaisha the company designs makes and sells a host of electronic equipment instruments and devices for consumer professional and industrial markets. Professional products include semiconductors and components. A top global media conglomerate Sony boasts additional assets in the areas of music (Sony Music Entertainment) film (Sony Pictures Entertainment and Sony Digital Production) smartphones (Sony Mobile) DVDs (Sony Pictures Home Entertainment) and TV (Sony Pictures Television). Sony also has several financial services businesses and an advertising agency in Japan.

Geographic Reach

Sony's primary manufacturing facilities are located in Asia including Japan where it is headquartered. Japan is also its single largest market by sales (32% in fiscal 2012 ends March). The US China and Europe are also key markets.

Operations

Sony realigned its reportable segments in 2012 as part of a reorganization. The operations of the former Consumer Professional & Devices (CPD) and Networked Products & Services (NPS) segments are now part of the Consumer Products & Services (CPS) –the company's largest segment by sales –and Professional Device & Solutions (PDS) segments. CPS includes LCD televisions Blu Ray disc and DVD players digital and video cameras PCs and gaming consoles. Certain PlayStation products are marketed and distributed by Sony Computer Entertainment LLC and Sony Computer Entertainment Europe Ltd. PDS the company's second largest segment includes broadcast and other B2B products as well as semiconductors and components.

A smaller business segment Sony Ericsson was renamed Sony Mobile Communications in 2012. As a result of a reorganization that Sony is undertaking plans to even further realign its business segments are under way.

Sales and Marketing

Sony's products are marketed worldwide by sales subsidiaries and unaffiliated distributors as well as direct online sales.

Financial Performance

Sony's fiscal 2012 (ends March) sales fell 9% vs. the prior year while net income continued its steep decline. Indeed the company marked its fourth consecutive year of unprofitability in 2012 as its losses widened.

Sony's consumer products and services segment CPS remains the company's bread and butter accounting for 45% is its fiscal 2012 sales. But competition is fierce in this industry with Apple paving the way in music players with the iPod and Microsoft (Xbox 360) and Nintendo (Wii) jockeying for dominance in game console sales globally.

The rising Yen decreasing demand for its products pricing pressures and the lingering global economic crisis has sidelined Sony in recent years. After logging a record profit in 2007 the company has seen its business stall as consumers tightened their belts.

Strategy

The most pressing part of Sony's current strategy is turning around its electronics businesses. With a new management team established in April 2012 the company moves forward with a plan to strengthen certain core areas: digital imaging game and mobile. Sony is trying to develop new products expand its hardware and software offerings and integrate the operations of its smartphone business (operated by Sony Mobile) with its tablet and PC businesses. Another aspect of this strategy is to turn around its TV business to improve profitability there; TVs generate a large chunk of sales within the CPS segment.

The company may have a hit on its hands with the new PlayStation4 (PS4) which went on sale in North America in November 2013. Indeed Sony sold more than 1 million PS4s in the first 24 hours of sales. The new games console is the centerpiece of the new management team's turnaround strategy for Sony's consumer electronics and film businesses.

Sony also has been consolidating manufacturing facilities selling off businesses and facilities and reducing headcounts. Divestments include its TV production assets and personal computer division. It's closing 20 retail stores in the US and cutting 1000 jobs as part of a much larger reorganization.

In a very competitive electronics environment Sony is simultaneously trying to innovate and launch products in new markets such as it is doing with medical peripherals like printers monitors cameras and recorders. The company is drawing on its audio and visual expertise to build a 4K technology product lineup. 4K is said to deliver more than four times the resolution of full HD.

On the music side Sony's wholly owned subsidiary Sony Corporation of America (SCA) in 2012 led a group of investors in a high-profile high-dollar deal. Alongside the Estate of Michael Jackson David Geffen and Blackstone Group SCA acquired EMI Music Publishing for $2.2 billion from Citigroup. The company's Sony/ATV Music Publishing which owns more than 750000 copyrights now oversees EMI Music Publishing and its 1.3 million copyrights on behalf of the investor group. (Sony/ATV Music Publishing is co-owned by subsidiaries of SCA and trusts formed by the Estate of Michael Jackson.)

HISTORY

Akio Morita Masaru Ibuka and Tamon Maeda (Ibuka's father-in-law) started Tokyo Telecommunications Engineering in 1946 with funding from Morita's father's sake business. The company produced the first Japanese tape recorder in 1950. Three years later Morita paid Western Electric (US) $25000 for transistor technology licenses which sparked a consumer electronics revolution in Japan. His firm launched one of the first transistor radios in 1955 followed by the first Sony-trademarked product a pocket-sized radio in 1957. The next year the company changed its name to Sony (from "sonus" Latin for "sound" and "sonny" meaning "little man"). It beat the competition to newly emerging markets for transistor TVs (1959) and solid-state videotape recorders (1961).

Sony launched the first home video recorder (1964) and the first solid-state condenser microphone (1965). Its 1968 introduction of the Trinitron color TV tube began another decade of explosive growth. Sony bet wrong on its Betamax VCR (1976) which lost to rival Matsushita's (now Panasonic Corp.) VHS as the industry standard. However 1979 brought another success the Walkman personal stereo.

Pressured by adverse currency rates and competition worldwide Sony used its technology to diversify beyond consumer electronics and began to move production to other countries. In the 1980s it introduced Japan's first 32-bit workstation and became a major producer of computer chips and floppy disk drives. The purchases of CBS Records in 1988 ($2 billion) and Columbia Pictures in 1989 (a $4.9 billion deal which included TriStar Pictures) made Sony a major force in the rapidly growing entertainment industry.

The firm manufactured Apple's PowerBook but its portable CD player Data Discman was successful only in Japan (1991). In the early 1990s Sony joined Nintendo to create a new kind of game console combining Sony's CD-ROM drive with the graphic capabilities of a workstation. Although Nintendo pulled out in 1992 Sony released PlayStation in Japan (1994) and in the US (1995) to great success. Two years later in a joint venture with Intel it developed a line of PC desktop systems.

Rather than support an industry-wide standard in 1997 Sony teamed up with Philips Electronics to make another recording media called Super Audio CD which could replace videotapes and CDs. (Sony and Philips created the CD and continue to receive royalties from it.)

In 1998 Sony shipped its first digital high-definition TV to the US folded TriStar into Columbia Pictures merged its Loews Theatres unit with Cineplex Odeon and launched its Wega flat-screen TV.

Philips Sun Microsystems and Sony formed a joint venture in early 1999 to develop networked entertainment products. Also in 1999 Nobuyuki Idei became CEO and the company introduced a Walkman with the capability to download music from the Internet.

In 2000 Sony formed PlayStation.com Japan to sell game consoles and software online; it also introduced its 128-bit PlayStation 2 which plays DVD movies and connects to the Internet. The company later restructured placing all of its US entertainment holdings under a newly-formed umbrella company called Sony Broadband Entertainment.

In early 2001 Sony started an online bank with Japan's Sakura Bank and JP Morgan Chase. Struggling to coordinate its content units (music movies games etc.) with its manufacturing operations (TVs VCRs radios etc.) Sony announced yet another corporate restructuring plan; that move placed all electronics units under one upper-management group.

Adverse market conditions in 2001 aggravated by the September 11 attacks led Sony Pictures Entertainment to consolidate its two domestic television operations folding Columbia TriStar Network Television into Columbia TriStar Domestic Television (CTDT).

In February 2002 an investment group led by Onex Corporation acquired its Loews Theatres unit (which filed for bankruptcy in February 2001). In the course of the fiscal year ending March 2002 Sony laid off about 13700 employees primarily in its electronics and music businesses.

In an attempt to capitalize on the strength of its own brand Sony Pictures Entertainment renamed its Columbia TriStar Domestic Television (CTDT) and Columbia TriStar International Television (CTIT) divisions in September 2002 designating them as Sony Pictures Television (SPT) and Sony Pictures Television International (SPTI) respectively. In October 2002 Sony transformed its Aiwa unit into a wholly-owned subsidiary and absorbed the struggling firm in December 2002.

In 2003 Sony adopted a US-style corporate governance model (made possible by a revision in Japan's Commercial Code) and acquired CIS Corp. a Japanese information system consulting firm. In an effort to cut costs through manufacturing consolidation Sony closed its audio equipment plant in Indonesia that year.

Sony unveiled the Vaio Pocket in 2004 a portable music player designed to compete with Apple's iPod; Vaio Pocket debuted in the US later that year. Sony also introduced a similar product Network Walkman –its first Walkman with a hard drive –in 2004. In October 2004 the company launched a music download system in Japan dubbed MusicDrop. The system utilizes Microsoft's Windows Media Player.

To manage its financial units (Sony Life Insurance Company Sony Assurance and Sony Bank) it created Sony Financial Holdings in 2004. The company announced in 2005 that Idei would be succeeded by foreigner Howard Stringer who had been in charge of Sony's entertainment unit. In 2005 Sony sold its minority stake in music club Columbia House to BMG Direct a subsidiary of Germany's Bertelsmann. In December 2005 the company spun off Sony Communication Network the subsidiary that operates So-Net Internet service (which has nearly 3 million subscribers) through an IPO.

In June 2006 Sony created a holding company for its Japanese-based retail operations (Sony Plaza Sony Family Club B&C Laboratories CP Cosmetics Maxim's de Paris and Lifeneo) and sold 51% of the holding company to investment firm Nikko Principal Investments Japan.

In late 2008 Sony bought out NEC's 45% stake in joint venture Sony Optiarc.

The company in 2010 sold the measuring equipment business of Sony Manufacturing Systems to Mori Seiki a Japan-based precision tool maker in a deal valued at about ¥6 billion (nearly $70 million). It also sold off its 90% stake in Sony Baja California its main TV factory in North America located in Tijuana Mexico to Taiwanese company Hon Hai Precision Industry. It generated $217 million for its share in HBO Latin America which it sold to Time Warner.

In February 2012 Sony acquired Telefonaktiebolaget LM Ericsson's 50% stake in Sony Ericsson Mobile Communications AB marking the completion of the previously announced transaction. As a result Sony Ericsson became a wholly-owned subsidiary of Sony and was renamed "Sony Mobile Communications."

EXECUTIVES

President and CEO; Chairman Sony Corporation of America, Kazuo (Kaz) Hirai, age 55

Executive Deputy President Device Solutions Business and RDS Platform and President Device Solutions Business Group, Tomoyuki Suzuki

EVP Imaging Products and Solutions Business President Professional Solutions Group and Digital Imaging Business Group, Shigeki Ishizuka

EVP Manufacturing Logistics Procurement Quality and Environmental Platform and Engineering Platform, Masashi Imamura
EVP Legal Compliance Corporate Communications CSR and External Relations, Shiro Kambe
EVP and CFO, Kenichiro Yoshida
Auditors: PricewaterhouseCoopers Aarata

LOCATIONS

HQ: Sony Corp
7-1, KONAN 1-CHOME, MINATO-KU, Tokyo 108-0075
Phone: (81) 3 6748 2111 **Fax:** (81) 3 6748 2244
Web: www.sony.co.jp

2015 Sales

	% of total
Japan	27
Europe	23
US	19
Asia/Pacific (except Japan and China)	13
China	7
Other	11
Total	**100**

PRODUCTS/OPERATIONS

2015 Sales

	% of total
Mobile communications	16
Game & Network services	16
Home entertainment & sound	14
Financial services	13
Devices	11
Pictures	10
Imaging products & solutions	8
Music	6
Other	6
Total	**100**

Selected Products

Consumer Products & Services (CPS)
- Digital imaging
- Game hardware and software
- Home audio and video
- Personal and mobile products
- Televisions

Professional Device & Solutions (PDS)
- Broadcast and professional-use products
- Semiconductors
- Components

COMPETITORS

Apple Inc.
Bertelsmann
Dell
Disney
Eastman Kodak
Fujitsu
HP
IBM
Intel
Kyocera
LG Electronics
Microsoft
Motorola Solutions
Nintendo
Nokia
Panasonic Corp
Philips Electronics
Pioneer Corporation
SANYO
Samsung Group
Sharp Corp.
Technicolor
Universal Studios

HISTORICAL FINANCIALS

Company Type: Public

Income Statement

FYE: March 31

	REVENUE ($ mil.)	NET INCOME ($ mil.)	NET PROFIT MARGIN	EMPLOYEES
03/15	68,477	(1,050)	—	131,700
03/14	75,250	(1,243)	—	140,900
03/13	72,278	457	0.6%	146,300
03/12	79,156	(5,566)	—	162,700
03/11	86,723	(3,134)	—	168,200
Annual Growth	(5.7%)	—	—	(5.9%)

2015 Year-End Financials

Debt ratio: 0.0%
Return on equity: (-5.5%)
Cash ($ mil.): 7,913
Current ratio: 0.88
Long-term debt ($ mil.): 5,935
No. of shares (mil.): 1,168
Dividends
Yield: 0.9%
Payout: —
Market value ($ mil.): 31,299

	STOCK PRICE ($) FY Close	P/E High/Low	PER SHARE ($) Earnings	Dividends	Book Value
03/15	26.78	— —	(0.94)	0.24	16.52
03/14	19.12	— —	(1.21)	0.25	20.96
03/13	17.40	0 0	0.43	0.27	23.11
03/12	20.77	— —	(5.55)	0.30	24.65
03/11	31.83	— —	(3.12)	0.28	30.66
Annual Growth	(4.2%)	— —	—	(3.8%)	(14.3%)

South African Reserve Bank

Auditors: SizweNtsalubaGobodo Inc.

LOCATIONS

HQ: South African Reserve Bank
370 Helen Joseph Street, Pretoria 0002
Phone: (27) 12 313 3911

HISTORICAL FINANCIALS

Company Type: Public

Income Statement

FYE: March 31

	ASSETS ($ mil.)	NET INCOME ($ mil.)	INCOME AS % OF ASSETS	EMPLOYEES
03/14	56,611	(132)	—	2,218
03/13	55,567	(152)	—	2,186
03/12	57,003	(77)	—	2,218
03/11	54,806	(160)	—	2,215
03/10	45,977	(120)	—	2,117
Annual Growth	5.3%	—	—	1.2%

2014 Year-End Financials

Return on assets: (-0.2%)
Return on equity: (-19.4%)
Long-term debt ($ mil.): —
No. of shares (mil.): 2
Sales ($ mil): 654
Dividends
Yield: —
Payout: —
Market value ($ mil.): —

SSE PLC

SSE (formerly Scottish and Southern) sees a powerful future. One of the UK's top energy firms the integrated company distributes power and gas and other services to more than 10 million customers via subsidiaries Southern Electric Scottish Hydro Electric SWALEC and Atlantic Electric and Gas and others. Regulated assets include 79300 miles of power transmission and distribution lines that serve 3.5 million end-users. SSE has more than 11300 MW of generating capacity. It also owns 50% of Scotia Gas Networks which delivers gas to 5.7 million customers. Other operations include gas exploration energy trading wind farms electrical and environmental contracting gas storage and retail appliance sales.

In response to energy deregulation in the UK SSE is looking to increase its generating capacity expand its customer base and diversify its operations. This has included moving into gas storage and fiber-optic cable operations and developing wind farms in Scotland.

In 2010 the company (as Scottish and Southern) changed its corporate name to a less geographically limiting name (SSE). That year the company acquired the ATLAS Connect fiber telecommunications network (7000 miles) which spans six business parks across Scotland. It also bought the 32 MW Calliachar wind farm project (on which construction is due to start in 2012) from I & H Brown.

SSE is also moving to boost its natural gas sources signing a deal with explorer Faroe Petroleum in 2010 to develop oil and gas fields in the North Sea. In 2011 it acquired natural gas assets and infrastructure in three regions of the North Sea from Hess Limited for $324 million.

That same year SSE acquired the Keadby Wind Farm in North Lincolnshire UK from Renewable Energy Systems Group. The 34-turbine project still in the development stage will produce between 68 and 84 MW of non-polluting energy when it is completed in 2014.

To grow its UK nuclear power assets in 2010 the company (with partners GDF SUEZ and IBERDROLA) formed NuGeneration a nuclear joint venture which aims to build up to 3600 MW of new nuclear power plants. However the Japanese nuclear plant accident in 2011 forced the global nuclear power plant industry to hit the pause button while it reviewed the safety and viability of current and future plants. In late 2011 the company announced plans to sell its 25% stake in NuGeneration to GDF SUEZ and IBERDROLA in a move to focus more on renewable energy.

The company reported a strong growth in revenues (40%) in Fiscal 2011 as a result of expanded capacity and services the acquisition of 310000 new retail customers and a generally favorable price environment. Net income also rose by about 30% due to increased demand and higher rates.

In 2012 through its Airtricity Energy Supply (Northern Ireland) unit the company acquired Phoenix Supply a regulated supplier of natural gas to 130000 customers in Northern Ireland from Phoenix Energy Holdings.

HISTORY

SSE (as Scottish and Southern Energy) was formed by the 1998 merger of Scottish Hydro-Electric and Southern Electric both of which had been created by the privatization of the UK electricity industry.

In the 1980s the Thatcherite government opened up state-owned industries to private capital and management. The electricity industry (except for nuclear power) was privatized by the Electricity Act of 1989. The next year the Central Electricity Generating Board (CEGB) the state monopoly was dismantled and CEGB's 12 regional boards transferred their assets to 12 regional electricity companies (RECs). One of these Southern Electric (first incorporated in 1989) went public in 1990.

Because the government planned to fully deregulate the industry Southern Electric expanded beyond its core electricity supply business. In 1992 it formed Southern Electric Power Generation to invest in independent power projects and the firm moved into natural gas marketing through a joint venture with Phillips Petroleum. It also developed Southern Electric Contracting an electrical contractor and formed a retail appliance company E & S Retail in alliance with fellow REC Eastern Electricity (now a unit of TXU Europe); another REC East Midlands Electricity later came onboard. The retail business renamed Powerhouse Retail lost money and was sold to the Hanson conglomerate in 1995.

That year a wave of takeovers began to swamp the privatized RECs especially by US utilities itching to try out a competitive market. Only Southern Electric was left standing after the government blocked a bid by UK power generator National Power in 1996. To avoid being run over by larger rivals in 1997 Southern Electric allied with British Energy in Sabre Power a venture to build small gas-fired plants to supply industrial customers.

Meanwhile to the north of Southern Electric Scottish Hydro-Electric had been founded in 1943 when less than 20% of northern Scotland's homes were electrified. Originally called the North of Scotland Hydro-Electric Board it built eight hydropower plants in the 1950s and by the mid-1960s most of the region had received electricity.

Like Southern Electric Hydro-Electric was incorporated in 1989 and it was taken public in 1991. However unlike its English counterpart Hydro-Electric remained integrated and encompassed power generation distribution and supply. In the 1990s it diversified into combined-cycle gas turbine plants (more efficient than coal-fired units) and cogeneration plants (producing both heat and power) in England through several joint ventures.

To prepare for deregulation of the retail power market (completed in 1999) Southern Electric acquired Hydro-Electric in 1998 in a $4.8 billion deal and formed Scottish and Southern Energy. Hydro-Electric's Lord Wilson took the chairman position and Southern's Jim Forbes became chief executive. The new company began investing in small-scale generating projects. The next year it introduced affordable renewable energy products and Internet-based billing.

In 2000 Scottish and Southern began building fiber-optic networks in southern England and Scotland. Later in 2000 the company bought British Energy's SWALEC a Wales-based electricity and gas supplier for about $315 million.

In 2002 Jim Forbes retired and Ian Marchant took his place as chief executive. The following year Scottish and Southern agreed to purchase fellow UK utility Midlands Electricity from Aquila (which held 80% of Midlands) and FirstEnergy (which held the remaining 20%); however the deal was canceled later that year.

In 2004 Scottish and Southern completed the acquisition of two power plants in the UK (2000 MW of capacity) from American Electric Power for $456 million.

Scottish and Southern considered a merger with Glasgow rival Scottish Power (acquired by IBERDROLA in 2007) to prevent that company's takeover by Germany's utility group E.ON.

Acquisitions in 2008 included Slough Heating and Power (integrated energy business) Aitricity Holdings (renewable energy) and Seeboard Trading (street lighting projects). That year the company also moved into the Irish power supply market with the purchase of CHP Supply.

Auditors: KPMG LLP

LOCATIONS

HQ: SSE PLC
Inveralmond House, 200 Dunkeld Road, Perth PH1 3AQ
Phone: (44) 17 38456000 **Fax:** (44) 17 38457005
Web: www.sse.com

HISTORICAL FINANCIALS

Company Type: Public

Income Statement FYE: March 31

	REVENUE ($ mil.)	NET INCOME ($ mil.)	NET PROFIT MARGIN	EMPLOYEES
03/15	46,783	802	1.7%	19,965
03/14	50,918	537	1.1%	19,894
03/13	43,012	647	1.5%	19,795
03/12	50,835	316	0.6%	19,489
03/11	45,588	2,420	5.3%	20,249
Annual Growth	0.6%	(24.1%)	—	(0.4%)

2015 Year-End Financials

Debt ratio: 38.7%
Return on equity: 9.7%
Cash ($ mil.): 2,235
Current ratio: 1.02
Long-term debt ($ mil.): 7,933
No. of shares (mil.): 993
Dividends
Yield: 6.0%
Payout: 148.6%
Market value ($ mil.): 22,084

	STOCK PRICE ($) FY Close	P/E High/Low	PER SHARE ($) Earnings	Dividends	Book Value
03/15	22.24	45 39	0.82	1.35	9.05
03/14	24.71	84 64	0.55	1.34	8.74
03/13	22.71	51 44	0.68	1.22	8.74
03/12	21.51	110 90	0.34	1.15	7.78
03/11	20.47	13 10	2.61	1.38	8.93
Annual Growth	2.1%	— —	(25.2%)	(0.5%)	0.3%

Standard Bank Group Ltd

Standard Bank Group sets the standard for sub-Saharan banking. Standard Bank South Africa's largest bank offers a variety of retail and commercial banking corporate and investment banking investment management and life insurance services through about 700 locations in its home country. The group also includes 500-plus additional branches more than 15 other African nations where it operates as Stanbic Bank. Beyond Africa the bank has offices in Asia Europe and the Americas including many emerging markets. It serves individuals and business and corporate customers. Standard Bank holds a controlling stake in South African insurance firm Liberty Holdings.

Geographic Reach

Contributing almost 85% of Standard Bank Group's revenue South Africa is its largest market by far. SBG also operates in 17 other African nations (from Angola to Zambia) as well as the UK and the US. Emerging markets include Argentina Brazil China Turkey and Russia.

Operations

In addition to personal commercial and corporate banking services SBG's insurance arm 53%-owned Liberty offers life insurance and investment and wealth management services to individuals and corporations in select African markets.

Financial Performance

Standard Bank Group struggled during the prolonged global recession. Low interest rates weak demand for credit and other financial factors impacted the company's revenues in 2009 and 2010. In 2011 the bank's revenue was essentially flat (up less than 1%) vs. the prior year while net income rose 23% over the same period. The modest uptick in revenue was credited to increase in banking activities partially offset by decreasing revenues at Liberty.

The personal and business banking division (up 8% in 2011 vs. 2010) outperformed the bank's other units. Revenue in South Africa the bank's largest market declined 1% while revenue from the rest of Africa was up 15% year over year. Revenue from outside of Africa fell 6%.

Strategy

Standard Bank Group is one of four full-service South African banks and claims to be the largest by assets and earnings. SBG aspires to be Africa's leading corporate and investment bank with a deep specialization in natural resources. To that end the bank is strengthening its focus on its core market and is looking to expand in Nigeria and Namibia. The company intends to grow its commercial banking operations there by building new branches. It opened more than 70 branches in Nigeria in 2010 alone.

Despite its Afro-centric focus SBG is also active in emerging markets worldwide including Russia. Indeed Standard Bank acquired about a third of Russian investment bank Troika Dialog in 2009. The partnership helped the group establish a presence in Russia where there is an opportunity to create a substantial domestic and cross-border franchise. However in early 2012 the company sold its stake in Troika Dialog to Russia's Sberbank for $372 million plus additional funds if Troika performs well. Standard Bank hopes to utilize its relationship with Troika to establish partnerships with Sberbank in the future. Other key emerging markets for the bank are Argentina Brazil and Turkey.

EXECUTIVES

Group CEO, Simpiwe (Sim) Tshabalala, age 47
CEO CIB SBG and SBSA, David (Dave) Munro, age 44
Group CEO, Ben Kruger, age 55
CEO PBB Group, Peter Schlebusch, age 48
CFO, Jonathan Peake
Chairman, Thulani Gcabashe, age 57
Auditors: KPMG Inc.

LOCATIONS

HQ: Standard Bank Group Ltd
9th Floor, Standard Bank Centre, 5 Simmonds Street, Johannesburg 2001
Phone: (27) 11 636 9111 **Fax:** (27) 11 636 4207
Web: www.standardbank.com

2011 Total Income

	% of total
South Africa	84
Rest of Africa	10
Outside of Africa	5
Central and other	1
Total	100

Selected Markets

Africa
- Angola
- Botswana
- DRC
- Ghana
- Kenya
- Lesotho
- Malawi
- Mauritius
- Mozambique
- Namibia
- Nigeria
- South Africa
- Swaziland
- Tanzania
- Uganda
- Zambia

Americas

Argentina
Brazil
US
Europe/Asia Pacific
China
Hong Kong
Isle of Man
Japan
Jersey
Russia
Singapore
Taiwan
Turkey
United Arab Emirates
United Kingdom

PRODUCTS/OPERATIONS

2011 Revenue

	% of total
Liberty	45
Personal & business banking	34
Corporate & investment banking	21
Central & other	-
Total	**100**

COMPETITORS

Absa
Citigroup
Commerzbank
FirstRand
Nedcor
Old Mutual
Sanlam
Scotiabank
Standard Chartered

HISTORICAL FINANCIALS

Company Type: Public

Income Statement FYE: December 31

	ASSETS ($ mil.)	NET INCOME ($ mil.)	INCOME AS % OF ASSETS	EMPLOYEES
12/14	164,717	1,549	0.9%	49,259
12/13	160,533	1,571	1.0%	48,808
12/12	181,381	1,937	1.1%	49,017
12/11	184,338	1,675	0.9%	52,127
12/10	201,137	1,679	0.8%	53,351
Annual Growth	(4.9%)	(2.0%)	—	(2.0%)

2014 Year-End Financials

Return on assets: 1.0%
Return on equity: 12.9%
Long-term debt ($ mil.): —
No. of shares (mil.): 1,618
Sales ($ mil): 17,912
Dividends
Yield: 3.2%
Payout: 38.2%
Market value ($ mil.): 19,954

	STOCK PRICE ($) FY Close	P/E High/Low	PER SHARE ($) Earnings	Dividends	Book Value
12/14	12.33	1 1	0.96	0.40	7.62
12/13	12.48	1 1	0.96	0.38	7.89
12/12	14.23	1 1	1.21	0.00	8.47
Annual Growth	(6.9%)	— —	(5.6%)	—	(2.6%)

Standard Chartered Plc

While the British Empire isn't as global as it used to be that hasn't stopped Standard Chartered. The UK-based banking group known as Stanchart primarily operates in its target markets of Asia the Middle East and Africa which offer some of the world's fastest-growing economies. It also operates in Europe and the Americas. In all Stanchart has more than 1700 offices in more than 70 countries. The company operates four business segments revolved around retail banking (deposit accounts loans cards and investment products) and corporate and institutional banking (capital markets cash management international trade custody and clearing services). Stanchart traces its roots back more than 150 years.

OperationsBecause the bank's strategy is centered around client relationships it organizes its business around four client segment groups and five product groups. The bank made 26% of its operating income from its retail banking business in 2014 while transaction banking and financial market products and services each generated around 20%. The remainder of operating income comes from Corporate finance (14%) financial markets (19%) and private banking services (9%). Sorted by client Stanchart generates more than 55% of its operating income from corporate & institutional clients more than 30% from retail clients more than 5% from commercial clients (mid-sized companies) and the remainder from private banking clients (affluent individuals). Geographic Reach

The UK-based bank does business in more than 70 markets mostly in Asia Africa and the Middle East but also in Europe and the Americas. Standard generates about 30% of its operating income from China (its largest market) 20% from the ASEAN region and roughly 10% from each of the Africa South Asia North East Asia and MENAP (Middle East North Africa Afghanistan and Pakistan) regions. About 7% comes from Europe and 5% comes from the Americas.

Sales and Marketing

The Corporate & Institutional business serves financial institutions and global and local corporate clients; while the Retail group serves individuals and small businesses. Private Banking clients include high net worth individuals and Commercial Clients include mid-sized companies. The bank serves clients from a variety of sectors: including energy manufacturing commercial real estate consumer durables and construction.Looking to reinforce its commitment to making a positive impact in the communities where it operates Stanchart in 2012 rolled out an international advertising campaign that spanned multiple media such as TV print outdoor and digital.

Financial Performance

Stanchart's revenue in 2014 fell by 4% to $24.8 billion mostly driven by a $329 million decline in income from the Commercial Clients segment as its Private Equity business' investments underperformed compared to the prior year its renminbi (RMB) products received less demand in Financial Markets and because the division made a number of exits from under-performing business lines.The bank's net income also dove by 36% to $2.7 billion over the period mostly from lower revenue but also because of impairment losses on loans and advances and other credit risk provisions as the credit-worthiness of its loan portfolio worsened. Cash from operations spiked by 458% to $52.8 billion primarily as the bank used less cash toward loans and advances to customers and banks and less cash toward buying other operating assets such as derivative financial instruments.

Strategy

Stanchart has been pursuing a new strategy in its consumer banking business shifting to a customer-focused business model and standardizing its processes in early 2014. It has leveraged its 2008 acquisition of American Express's international banking business to not only boost its private banking operations but strengthen its presence in key markets in Asia Africa and the Middle East. Stanchart has also aggressively added more branches and ATMs to its retail network and invested in making improvements to its online and mobile capabilities.Stanchart has also exited several markets that didn't align with its new strategy and broader portfolio to focus more on its target markets in Asia Africa and the Middle East. In late 2014 for example after witnessing disappointing results from the unit Stanchart sold its Hong Kong-based consumer finance business PrimeCredit to an investment consortium worth more than $600 million. Also in 2014 it exited its Consumer Finance businesses in Hong Kong China and Korea; its Retail Clients businesses in Germany and Lebanon; and its third-party sourcing channel for Retail Clients.In addition the bank has been investing heavily in cost-saving measures across all segments while also making improvements to its online and mobile banking platforms. In mid-2015 to strengthen its balance sheet and free up resources Standard announced that it would slash its operating costs by $1.8 billion by 2018. In late 2014 it announced that it would invest more than $400 million toward productivity improvements in 2015 across Retail Clients Corporate & Institutional Clients and products and support functions. In the Retail Clients market for example the company will concentrate more on key cities as well as its digital and affluent segments (i.e. Priority and Business Clients). As part of this plan the company in 2015 closed its underperforming institutional cash equities equity research and equity capital markets activities; a move that was expected to deliver $100 million in cost savings by 2016 and outpace restructuring costs.

Mergers and AcquisitionsHelping to position Stanchart as a top South African custodian the company in 2013 acquired the South African custody and trustee business of Absa Bank which had developed a profitable custody model across more than 20 sub-Saharan African countries.

Company Background

Asia Africa and the Middle East have been among Stanchart's targeted areas for growth. It owns First Africa Group which provides mergers and acquisitions advisory services to companies wanting to invest in Africa. Stanchart bought Barclays Bank's custody business in 2010 adding operations in eight African nations. In late 2011 the company bought the performing segment of Barclays' credit card business in India at a discount. In 2012 to expand its wholesale banking business in Turkey Stanchart purchased Credit Agricole Yatirim Bankasi Turk A.S. (CAYBT) a fully-owned subsidiary of Credit Agricole Corporate and Investment Bank.

HISTORY

Company BackgroundStandard Chartered began in 1853 as the Chartered Bank of India Australia and China to finance trade between the UK and its Asian colonies. It began establishing offices in 1858. Over the next 40 years The Chartered Bank expanded throughout Asia. In the 20th century the bank opened branches in Germany and the US. In 1957 Chartered entered the Middle East by acquiring Eastern Bank. In 1969 it agreed to merge with Standard Bank.

In 1862 schoolmaster John Paterson established the Standard Bank of British South Africa Ltd. to fund trade with mining businesses. Within two years the bank had 15 branches. Like Chartered Standard had moved into Germany and the US by 1905 and operated in central and southern Africa by 1912.

In 1962 the bank was renamed The Standard Bank Ltd. Three years later it expanded into Gambia Ghana Nigeria and Sierra Leone but the end of colonialism meant instability; business was threatened and ruling parties often nationalized Standard's banks. In 1969 the bank agreed to merge with Chartered Bank.

Asian and Middle Eastern business flourished in the early 1970s while South African branches struggled under growing international pressure on the country's apartheid regime. In response the company diversified into metals trading and consumer finance. It also expanded in the US market with the purchase of Union Bancorp of California.

Standard Chartered failed in a 1981 attempt to gain entry to the UK market through purchasing Royal Bank of Scotland. Four years later that bank went public.

In 1986 Lloyds Bank tried to take over Standard Chartered but investors Robert Holmes a Court Yue-Kong Pao and Khoo Teck Puat acquired enough of the company to block the play. Meanwhile overseas financial deregulation brought more competition and Hong Kong Singapore and Malaysia sank into recession.

Hit by trade sanctions against South Africa the bank in 1987 sold its operations there. As the world tumbled deeper into recession Standard Chartered's loan losses climbed. But the bank began to recover the next year as it trimmed its US bank holdings.

Scandal hit the bank in the 1990s. In 1992 Standard Chartered paid $515 million in restitution after a broker in its Mumbai India office embezzled some $1.2 billion from Indian banks. In 1994 executives with Mocatta were convicted of bribery and the Hong Kong government banned Standard Chartered Securities (sold in 1996) from underwriting stock offerings for nine months after it falsified six IPOs.

In 1997 Standard Chartered refocused on retail banking with its 1998 purchase of what is now Banco Standard Chartered in Latin America and its bank/insurance tie-ups with CGU (now CGNU) and Prudential plc. The promotion of Rana Talwar to CEO brought a strategic focus on emerging markets from which other banks were withdrawing.

Standard Chartered in 1999 bought Thailand's Nakornthon Bank and the non-Swiss trade financing operations of UBS AG and expanded into China through a pact with the Bank of China. In 2000 the company bought Australia and New Zealand Banking Group's Grindlays operations in South Asia and the Middle East. The following year Stanchart began cutting 20% of its workforce. It also folded Grindlay's operations into its own while retaining the brand's name.

In 2004 Stanchart bought the majority of Australia and New Zealand Banking Group's project finance business which is headquartered in London. The business which cost Stanchart about $1.5 billion operates in four regions: the UK the US the Middle East and South Asia (especially India).In 2005 the bank acquired Korea First Bank (now SC First Bank); the deal was the biggest foreign investment ever for South Korea's financial sector. The following year Stanchart paid about $1.2 billion for Taiwan's Hsinchu Bank making it the first foreign bank owner in that country. Also in 2006 the bank acquired 20% of China Bohai Bank.

In 2008 the UK government responded to the global financial crisis by investing £50 billion ($87.9 billion) in the nation's top banks including Stanchart. It agreed to guarantee another £250 billion ($438 billion) in bonds and provide additional liquidity of at least £200 billion ($350 billion) to the banks. The bailout plan was initiated to provide capital directly to the banks in order to revitalize lending activities.Also in 2008 the company made some acquisitions for further international expansion. It bought Asia Trust and Investment Corporation which added some 10 branches in the lucrative Taipei market. Stanchart also bought some of the Brazil operations of Lehman Brothers after that company filed for bankruptcy protection.

EXECUTIVES

Group CEO, William T. (Bill) Winters, age 54
Group Executive Director and CEO Asia, Jaspal Singh Bindra, age 55
Deputy Group CEO Wholesale Banking and Consumer Banking, Alun M. G. (Mike) Rees, age 59
Group Chief Risk Officer, Richard F. Goulding, age 55
Chief Executive India Operations, Zarin Daruwala
Regional CEO ASEAN and South Asia, Ajay Kanwal
CEO Taiwan, John Tan
CEO Philippines, Anirvan Ghosh Dastidar
Group CIO, Michael Gorriz, age 55
Group Head Financial Markets, Jonathan Paul
Group Finance Director, Andy Halford
CEO Iraq, Andreas Meletiou
CEO Singapore, Judy Hsu
Chairman, John W. Peace, age 66
Auditors: KPMG Audit Plc

LOCATIONS

HQ: Standard Chartered Plc
32nd Floor, 4-4A Des Voeux Road, Central,
Phone: (44) 20 7885 8888
Web: www.sc.com

2014 Sales

	% of total
China	30
ASEAN	20
South Asia	10
MENAP	10
Africa	10
North East Asia	8
Europe	7
Americas	5
Total	**100**

PRODUCTS/OPERATIONS

2014 Sales

	% of total
Interest	69
Noninterest	
Fees & commissions	18
Net trading income	8
Other	5
Total	**100**

COMPETITORS

Bank of America
Bank of China
Bank of East Asia
Barclays
Citigroup
DBS Group Holdings
Deutsche Bank
Grupo Santander
HSBC
Hang Seng Bank
Lloyds Banking Group
Maybank
OCBC Bank
Royal Bank of Scotland
Standard Bank Group
State Bank of India
United Overseas Bank
Woori

HISTORICAL FINANCIALS

Company Type: Public

Income Statement

FYE: December 31

	ASSETS ($ mil.)	NET INCOME ($ mil.)	INCOME AS % OF ASSETS	EMPLOYEES
12/14	725,914	2,613	0.4%	90,940
12/13	674,380	4,090	0.6%	86,640
12/12	636,518	4,887	0.8%	89,058
12/11	599,070	4,849	0.8%	86,865
12/10	516,542	4,332	0.8%	85,231
Annual Growth	8.9%	(11.9%)	—	1.6%

2014 Year-End Financials

Return on assets: 0.3%
Return on equity: 5.6%
Long-term debt ($ mil.): —
No. of shares (mil.): —
Sales ($ mil): 25,035
Dividends
Yield: —
Payout: —
Market value ($ mil.): —

Standard Life Assurance Co. (United Kingdom)

Life insurance nsk

EXECUTIVES

Director, Paul Matthews
Auditors: PricewaterhouseCoopers LLP

LOCATIONS

HQ: Standard Life Assurance Co. (United Kingdom)
Standard Life House, 30 Lothian Road, Edinburgh EH1 2DH
Phone: (44) 131 225 2552
Web: www.standardlife.com

HISTORICAL FINANCIALS

Company Type: Public

Income Statement

FYE: December 31

	ASSETS ($ mil.)	NET INCOME ($ mil.)	INCOME AS % OF ASSETS	EMPLOYEES
12/14	317,822	785	0.2%	8,335
12/13	305,074	770	0.3%	8,224
12/12	280,627	1,125	0.4%	8,459
12/11	247,366	460	0.2%	8,789
12/10	239,286	670	0.3%	9,254
Annual Growth	7.4%	4.0%	—	(2.6%)

2014 Year-End Financials

Return on assets: 0.2%
Return on equity: 11.3%
Long-term debt ($ mil.): —
No. of shares (mil.): —
Sales ($ mil): 25,950
Dividends
Yield: —
Payout: —
Market value ($ mil.): —

Standard Life Plc

Trying to set the standard for life insurance and financial services both at home and abroad Standard Life plc is a leading UK insurance asset management and pension firm. The holding company does business through subsidiaries including Standard Life Assurance Limited which provides life and pension products to 4 million customers in the UK market. Other divisions include Standard Life Investments (retail and institutional investment management). Standard Life established in 1825 has 6 million customers in the UK and abroad. In Canada its second largest market the company offers insurance pensions and asset management.

Geographic Reach

Standard Life's operations cover markets in North America Europe Asia and the Middle East.

In addition to the UK (65% of sales) and Canada other international operations include subsidiaries and offices in Austria Australia Bermuda Germany Hong Kong Korea Ireland Singapore the United Arab Emirates and the US. It operates joint ventures in China and India. In all of these markets Standard Life offers life insurance and pension products to individuals and corporate clients.

Operations

The company's operating divisions provide investment protection and savings products; benefit and pension plans; and asset management services to corporations and individuals. Its Standard Life Investments division manages some £180 billion in assets around the globe. Altogether Standard Life's subsidiaries administer some £230 billion in assets (as of mid-2013). Due to the nature of the company's businesses investment returns often account for a larger percent of annual revenues than do insurance premiums and product fees and commissions.

Sales and Marketing

Standard Life distributes products directly to customers as well as through partnerships with banks. It formed a new partnership with RBS in 2012 to provide investment solutions to RBS banking customers.

Financial Performance

Revenue increased 111% in 2012 due to higher investment returns premiums and fee and commission income. Investment returns were up on equity security gains while fee and commission income received a boost from reclassified income. Net income rose 134% on higher revenues.

Strategy

The company is focused on maximizing profits to provide dividend growth and to reinvest in business growth. In the Standard Life Investments business the firm is focused on growing geographically and increasing investment capabilities. It opened new offices in Singapore and the Middle East and launched a new savings product in Germany in 2012. The company is also expanding its Standard Life Wealth division in the domestic market. In addition the Standard Life organization aims to increase customer and shareholder value and provide long-term savings and investment propositions.

Standard Life at one time had a few more eggs in its basket but pressures from the global economic downturn induced the company to simplify its holdings and focus more carefully on insurance long-term savings and investment management. The company sold off its Standard Life Bank (mortgages and savings products) subsidiary to Barclays in early 2010 for in £226 million ($369 million); Standard Life and Barclays entered a partnership to offer retail investment offerings following the deal. Also in 2010 the company sold its Standard Life Healthcare (now part of PruHealth) to South African insurance and finance firm Discovery Holdings for £138 million ($205 million).

Mergers and Acquisitions

To enhance its wealth management operations in 2011 the company acquired financial software and consulting firm Focus Solutions. In 2013 the Standard Life Wealth division further widened its operations through the purchase of the Newton Private Clients division of Newton Management.

HISTORY

The Life Insurance Company of Scotland opened in Edinburgh in 1825 as a subsidiary of The Insurance Company of Scotland a fire insurance firm. In 1832 the subsidiary became a separate business received a royal charter and began anew as The Standard Life Assurance Company. In 1833 Standard Life opened its first overseas agency in Canada and continued to grow by acquisitions.

Company executives established Colonial Life Assurance as a sister company in 1846 to insure clients across the far-flung British empire. When Colonial's success became a threat to Standard Life's own business at home Standard bought Colonial.

In 1869 Standard Life moved into India and China (although only to insure Europeans). It moved into Scandinavia Argentina and South Africa in the 1890s.

After the turn of the century however the company began to spin off foreign offices and focus on its domestic business. Standard Life became a customer-owned mutual company in 1925.

The company was expanding again by the 1990s. It bought health insurer Prime Health (now Standard Life Healthcare) in 1994. The next year it formed a joint venture with India-based Housing Development Finance Corporation to sell insurance. In 1998 it expanded its financial services with the opening of Standard Life Bank and Standard Life Investments.

Expanding globally Standard Life was granted a license in 2000 to sell policies in the huge Indian market. The company opened up an office in Hong Kong in 2001. Just like many other companies Standard Life wanted to do business in China so it set up a joint venture and was granted a license to sell there in 2005.

After long resisting the worldwide trend for demutualization Standard Life's board eventually succumbed to the necessity of such an action. Faced with lackluster equity markets and regulatory criticism of its capital-reserves accounting in 2004 the company announced plans to restructure. The firm's transformation from a mutual organization into a holding company was completed through a public offering in mid-2006; the IPO was the London Stock Exchange's biggest in five years. The company's name was changed from The Standard Life Assurance Company to Standard Life plc.

In 2007 the company made a failed attempt to take over fellow UK insurance firm Resolution plc.

To enhance growth back home the company formed a UK wealth management unit in 2008 and launched additional initiatives to strengthen its corporate offerings and online services. To further this goal it acquired employee benefits management software maker Vebnet in 2008.

At the start of 2010 long-time executive Sir Sandy Crombie stepped down from his post as CEO of Standard Life. Crombie led the company through many challenges including its successful demutualization. David Nish who previously held the title of finance director at Standard Life took over the role of CEO.

EXECUTIVES

Chief Executive, Keith Skeoch, age 69
CFO, Luke Savage, age 54
Chief Executive U.K., Paul Matthews
UK Chief Information Officer, Mark Dixon
Chairman, Gerry E. Grimstone, age 65
Auditors: PricewaterhouseCoopers LLP

LOCATIONS

HQ: Standard Life Plc
Standard Life House, 30 Lothian Road, Edinburgh EH1 2DH
Phone: (44) 131 225 2552
Web: www.standardlife.com

2012 Premiums

	% of total
UK	65
Canada	18
International	17
Total	**100**

PRODUCTS/OPERATIONS

2012 Revenues

	% of total
Investment returns	73
Earned premiums	22
Fee & commission income	5
Total	**100**

Selected Products

Life insurance
Pension products
- Active Money Personal Pension (AMPP)
- Self Invested Personal Pension (SIPP)
- Stakeholder pension
- Starting a pension for a child

Retirement products
- Compulsory Purchase Annuity
- Immediate Vesting Personal Pension
- Immediate Vesting Personal Pension Select
- Impaired Life Annuity
- Income Drawdown

Savings and investment products
- International Bond
- Investment funds
- Other Onshore Bonds
- Stocks and Shares ISA
- Tailored Investment Bond

COMPETITORS

AXA UK
Aviva
Canada Life
Equitable Life
Great-West Lifeco
Legal & General Group
Liverpool Victoria
Phoenix Group
Power Financial
Prudential plc
ReAssure
Royal London Mutual
Schroders
Scottish Equitable
Skandia UK
St. James' s Place plc
Sun Life
permanent tsb

HISTORICAL FINANCIALS

Company Type: Public

Income Statement FYE: December 31

	REVENUE ($ mil.)	NET INCOME ($ mil.)	NET PROFIT MARGIN	EMPLOYEES
12/14	25,894	785	3.0%	8,335
12/13	33,952	770	2.3%	8,224
12/12	30,923	1,125	3.6%	8,458
12/11	14,036	460	3.3%	8,789
12/10	28,830	670	2.3%	9,254
Annual Growth	(2.7%)	4.0%	—	(2.6%)

2014 Year-End Financials

Debt ratio: —
Return on equity: 11.3%
Cash ($ mil.): 16,573
Current ratio: —
Long-term debt ($ mil.): —
No. of shares (mil.): —
Dividends
Yield: 0.0%
Payout: 779.0%
Market value ($ mil.): —

	STOCK PRICE ($) FY Close	P/E High/Low	PER SHARE ($) Earnings	Dividends	Book Value
12/14	25.05	338281	0.33	2.55	3.05
12/13	23.24	319264	0.32	4.21	2.94
12/12	18.83	165104	0.48	2.04	2.98
12/11	12.69	314213	0.20	1.97	2.60
12/10	13.73	205126	0.30	1.67	2.65
Annual Growth	16.2%	— —	2.4%	11.2%	3.5%

Statoil ASA

Crude petroleum and natural gas nsk

HISTORY

To exert greater control over exploration and production of the Norwegian continental shelf (NCS) the government of Norway set up Den norske stats oljeselskap (Statoil) in 1972.

A decade earlier three geologists had visited Norway on behalf of Phillips Petroleum (later renamed ConocoPhillips) to apply for sole rights to explore on the NCS. The government initially refused drilling rights to foreign companies and in 1963 Norway claimed sovereignty over the NCS. Two years later the government began allowing exploration. Phillips' major discovery in the Ekofisk field in 1969 prompted Norway to set up its own oil company. After Statoil's formation in 1972 the company garnered funds to expand through taxation of multinationals production limits leasing contracts and other measures.

In 1974 a giant discovery was made in the North Sea's Statfjord field and Statoil was given a 50% stake. A year later Statoil began exploring for oil and gas exporting oil and commissioning its first subsea oil pipeline the Norpipe which extended to the UK. In 1986 Statoil's gas pipeline system the Statpipe began transporting gas from the North Sea to the mainland.

Moving into retailing Statoil acquired Esso's service stations and other downstream operations in Sweden and Denmark in 1985 and 1986. The next year cost overruns stemming from the extension of Statoil's Mongstad oil refinery led to the ousting of the company's first president Arve Johnsen and many of his deputies. Harald Norvik was appointed CEO in 1988.

In 1990 Statoil and BP teamed up to develop international operations and in 1992 Statoil acquired BP's service stations in Ireland. Statoil and Neste Chemicals (later part of Industri Kapital) formed the Borealis petrochemicals group in 1994.

The company in 1995 acquired Aran Energy moving into exploration of offshore Ireland and the UK. Statoil brought its field projects in China and Azerbaijan onstream in 1997. That year Statoil spun off its shipping operations as Navion partly owned by Norway's Rasmussen group. It also contracted with Kvaerner to build a giant offshore gas platform for the Aasgard field in the Norwegian Sea.

The Aasgard field project resulted in cost overruns in 1999 again leading to a Statoil board shakeup and CEO resignation. Norvik who had advocated partial privatization of Statoil was replaced by Olav Fjell former head of Norway's Postbanken (who resigned in 2003). That year Statoil helped Norsk Hydro take over rival Saga in return for some of Saga's assets.

As part of a major restructuring in 2000 Statoil sold most assets of US unit Statoil Energy. Political opposition that year postponed Statoil's plans for partial privatization but the government proceeded with an IPO in 2001 raising about $3 billion.

In 2002 Statoil sold its oil and gas assets in the Danish North Sea to Dong the Danish state oil company for about $120 million. That year the company also acquired the Polish unit of Sweden's Preem Petroleum which owned 79 gas stations in Poland.

In 2003 Statoil sold its Navion unit to shipping group Teekay for about $800 million. That year it also acquired two Algerian natural gas projects from BP for $740 million. A bribery scandal involving an Iranian oil contract forced the resignation of the chairman CEO and another top executive in 2003.

Statoil sold its 50% stake in petrochemicals venture Borealis in 2005.

In 2006 the company acquired three oil prospects in the Gulf of Mexico from Plains Exploration & Production for $700 million. It also acquired offshore assets in the Gulf of Mexico from Anadarko Petroleum for $901 million.

Expanding its upstream midstream and downstream assets in 2007 the company acquired $4.2 billion of subsea equipment from Aver Kvaerner Canada's North American Oil Sands Corporation for $1.96 billion and 274 gas stations in Scandinavia from ConocoPhillips.

In a major expansion that gave it a major international profile (including a strong presence in the deepwater Gulf of Mexico) in 2007 Statoil acquired the oil and gas exploration and production operations of Norsk Hydro in a $30 billion deal and became StatoilHydro.

In 2008 Statoil acquired ConocoPhillips' Jet gas station chain in Norway Sweden and Denmark.

Growing its exploration and production asset base in 2008 paid about $1.8 billion to acquire holdings in heavy-oil and deep-water projects in Brazil and the Gulf of Mexico from Anadarko Petroleum. That year it also teamed up with Chesapeake Energy to jointly explore unconventional gas opportunities around the world including in the Marcellus Shale play in the US.

EXECUTIVES

Chairman Of The Board, Lars Johannes Nordli
Auditors: KPMG AS

LOCATIONS

HQ: Statoil ASA
Forusbeen 50, Stavanger N-4035
Phone: (47) 51 99 00 00 **Fax:** (47) 51 99 00 50
Web: www.statoil.com

HISTORICAL FINANCIALS

Company Type: Public

Income Statement FYE: December 31

	REVENUE ($ mil.)	NET INCOME ($ mil.)	NET PROFIT MARGIN	EMPLOYEES
12/14	83,920	2,951	3.5%	22,516
12/13	104,898	6,566	6.3%	23,413
12/12	129,328	12,317	9.5%	23,028
12/11	111,467	13,103	11.8%	31,715
12/10	90,766	6,526	7.2%	30,344
Annual Growth	(1.9%)	(18.0%)	—	(7.2%)

2014 Year-End Financials

Debt ratio: 3.1%
Return on equity: 5.9%
Cash ($ mil.): 11,199
Current ratio: 1.42
Long-term debt ($ mil.): 27,640
No. of shares (mil.): —
Dividends
Yield: 9.7%
Payout: 152.9%
Market value ($ mil.): —

	STOCK PRICE ($) FY Close	P/E High	P/E Low	PER SHARE ($) Earnings	Dividends	Book Value
12/14	17.61	4	2	0.93	1.72	16.15
12/13	24.13	2	2	2.06	1.15	18.40
12/12	25.04	1	1	3.86	1.07	17.95
12/11	25.61	1	1	4.11	1.05	14.58
12/10	23.77	2	2	2.05	0.92	11.83
Annual Growth	(7.2%)	—	—	(18.0%)	17.0%	8.1%

Storebrand ASA

Life insurance nsk

EXECUTIVES

Chairman Of The Board, Odd Arild Grefstad
Auditors: Deloitte AS

LOCATIONS

HQ: Storebrand ASA
Professor Kohtsvei 9, Lysaker NO-1327
Phone: (47) 22 31 50 50 **Fax:** (47) 22 48 98 90
Web: www.storebrand.no

HISTORICAL FINANCIALS

Company Type: Public

Income Statement FYE: December 31

	ASSETS ($ mil.)	NET INCOME ($ mil.)	INCOME AS % OF ASSETS	EMPLOYEES
12/14	66,344	278	0.4%	2,232
12/13	74,120	324	0.4%	2,138
12/12	75,119	179	0.2%	2,250
12/11	66,767	112	0.2%	2,221
12/10	66,905	252	0.4%	2,206
Annual Growth	(0.2%)	2.5%	—	0.3%

2014 Year-End Financials

Return on assets: 0.4%
Return on equity: 8.8%
Long-term debt ($ mil.): —
No. of shares (mil.): 447
Sales ($ mil): 8,518
Dividends
Yield: —
Payout: —
Market value ($ mil.): —

	STOCK PRICE ($) FY Close	P/E High	P/E Low	PER SHARE ($) Earnings	Dividends	Book Value
12/14	0.00	0	0	0.62	0.00	7.34
12/13	11.75	0	0	0.73	0.00	8.25
12/12	9.50	0	0	0.40	0.00	7.88
12/11	12.05	0	0	0.25	0.01	6.89
Annual Growth	—	—	—	25.4%	—	1.6%

Sumitomo Corp. (Japan)

Sumitomo Corporation specializes in the general. A Japanese "sogo shosha" (general trading company) Sumitomo is active in a wide range of commercial ventures. Through some 800 subsidiaries and affiliates it imports and exports raw materials and goods including metals machinery electronics fuels chemicals and food products. It also participates in finance logistics and real estate development. The group's auto finance and media holdings are among its fastest-growing operations. Sumitomo Corporation is part of the Sumitomo "keiretsu" a group of companies loosely linked by cross-ownership. Other group companies include Sumitomo Mitsui Banking Sumitomo Life Insurance and electronics maker NEC.

Never one to sit still Sumitomo occupies much of its time trading on its own behalf. The company searches for opportunities to take advantage of market trends and secure new lines of revenue. The company in 2014 increased its 20% stake in major Malaysian fertilizer producer Union Harvest to 60%.

It was one of a number of foreign groups to move into Australia's agricultural sector when it bought half of Emerald Group in 2010. (It acquired the remaining 50% in 2014.) Emerald Group is one of Australia's largest grain trading firms; Japan also happens to be a major importer of Australian wheat. Also that year the company increased its stake in Jupiter Telecommunications (J:COM) Japan's largest cable television operator from 27% to 40%. It had tried unsuccessfully to buy out J:COM's largest owner Liberty Media. Instead Liberty sold its 38% stake to KDDI Corporation one of Japan's largest telecommunications companies.

In late 2012 KDDI and Sumitomo agreed to acquire all outstanding shares of J:COM and merge it with Japan's #2 cable operator Japan Cablenet (owned by KDDI); the resulting entity will control half of Japan's cable market.

Sumitomo has been building up its metals and mining business. In 2010 Sumitomo bought a 30% stake in the iron ore unit of Brazilian steelmaker Usiminas. Due to increasing copper demand especially from China Sumitomo has increased its copper mining operations in Indonesia. The company has also invested in a nickel mine in Madagascar with partners Korea Resources Sherritt International and SNC Lavalin. In 2011 Sumitomo and its Sumitomo Metal unit acquired Standard Steel in the US. The deal allowed Sumitomo to expand its railway business by tapping into the growing demand for train wheels in North America.

As part of a consortium Sumitomo purchased an oil and gas operation in the UK North Sea from Paris-based Wendel in 2009. The company Oranje-Nassau Energie owns six oil blocks capable of producing some 7000 barrels worth of oil and gas a day through 2030. The deal was worth about $900 million. Also that year Sumitomo acquired a 42%-stake in a US wind farm from American International Group; the group already had wind farms in Japan and China in its fold.

In 2008 Sumitomo took full control over its 24-hour home shopping network Jupiter Shop Channel when it bought a 30% equity stake from IAC for 46 billion ($493 million). The acquisition provided the company with more flexibility in running the retail business and to implement a multi-channel strategy. Sumitomo also plans to leverage its existing media and lifestyle business portfolio via the channel.

HISTORY

Around 1630 Masatomo Sumitomo a Buddhist priest from the Kyoto area opened a medicine shop/bookstore after the dissolution of his sect. His descendants preserved his writings on business ethics and he is considered the spiritual founder of the Sumitomo Group. The commercial founder of the "keiretsu" however was Riemon Soga Sumitomo's brother-in-law. Soga researched and duplicated a Western copper-smelting technique that enabled him to build a prosperous copper company. After Soga died in 1636 his son Tomomochi married into the Sumitomo family and became its head.

Tomomochi Soga combined the families' businesses and moved to Osaka. By 1693 the family had turned a dilapidated copper mine into one of Japan's top producers. By the mid-1800s however the company's biggest mine was aging and output had dropped. The family mortgaged its assets to modernize the mine imported French technology and bought ships for copper transport. Production soared.

Sumitomo Bank was created from existing family operations in 1895. A copper wire business founded in 1897 evolved into Sumitomo Electric and Sumitomo Metal Industries. The family formed Sumitomo Chemical in 1913 and in 1925 began selling life insurance.

Nippon Electric Company (NEC) was managed by Sumitomo from 1932 until post-WWII occupation forces split the "zaibatsu" (family-run conglomerate) into numerous independent pieces. Employees of the old Sumitomo group migrated to a real estate and trading company today's Sumitomo Corporation. Sumitomo companies began regrouping in the 1950s at the behest of the Japanese government.

Sumitomo companies went on a buying spree during the "bubble economy" of the 1980s and early 1990s. Purchases included Dunlop's tire operations investments in Phelps Dodge's (now Freeport-McMoRan) Candelaria copper and gold mine in Chile and one-third of Satellite Japan. The Sumitomo Bank bought 13% of US investment house Goldman Sachs. In 1990 however bank chairman Ichiro Isoda resigned in an illegal-loan scandal.

Sumitomo Metal Industries invested about $200 million in LTV in 1993 to shore up its US supply of high-quality steel. Ironically LTV was one of several US steel companies that campaigned against Japanese steel imports in 1998.

In its first loss in 50 years Sumitomo Bank took a $2.8 billion hit in 1995 because of bad loans (the legacy of the economy's bubble burst of 1992). The next year Sumitomo Corporation announced that its head copper-trader Yasuo Hamanaka had engaged in unauthorized trading over the previous decade –first attempting to corner the market then trying to cover his own deficit. Hamanaka pleaded guilty and went to jail. Sumitomo Corporation chairman Tomiichi Akiyama resigned in 1997. By 1998 the company had suffered $3 billion in trading losses fines and restitutions. (Sumitomo Corporation sued four investment banks alleging they had aided Hamanaka; separately Merrill Lynch settled a dispute over its role in the scandal by agreeing in 2000 to pay the company $275 million.)

In 1999 Sumitomo Rubber Industries and Goodyear Tire formed an alliance: Sumitomo Rubber got cash and control of Goodyear's Japanese operations and Goodyear gained control of Sumitomo Rubber's business in the US and Europe. Sumitomo Bank in 1999 announced plans to merge with Sakura Bank; the deal was completed in 2001.

That year Sumitomo Corporation agreed to buy Nomura Trading's steel-related operations; the deal was completed in 2002. Adding to one of its core businesses that year Sumitomo bought the steel products businesses of Nichimen (now Sojitz). Also in 2002 Sumitomo Corporation moved to expand its activities in China.

The year 2004 was a big one for the company: Sumitomo purchased US-based life science venture capital firm Oxford Finance embarked upon a joint venture with Australia-based glove manufacturer Ansell and fabric manufacturer Shinwa to make gloves and other products launched a credit-card subsidiary and acquired Nissin Sugar Manufacturing. In other deals it purchased US pet care products maker Hartz Mountain for $364 million; acquired Kiriu Corp a disc and drum brake-maker with operations in Asia and North America; and took controlling stakes of Sumisho Computer Systems Corp and movie theater chain United Cinemas.

Late in 2005 Sumitomo expanded its retailing operations again when its Sumitomo Corporation of America subsidiary acquired tire distributor TBC Corporation in a $1.1 billion deal. TBC's operations included National Tire & Battery Tire Kingdom and Merchant's Tire & Auto. It also owned the Big O Tires franchise business.

In 2008 the company increased its focus on upstream oil development and the trading of crude oil and petroleum products. To that end it sold its shares in domestic oil distribution unit Sumisho Oil to Idemitsu Kosa. The group also acquired 20% of Abu Dhabi-based energy and desalinated water supplier Shuweihat CMS International Power Company. The deal included a 50% stake in the company's operation and maintenance partnership.

Sumitomo exits or sells divisions that are less profitable. In 2008 it dissolved diamond distribution company FB Jewelry and began the dissolution of GeoFocus a developer of communication systems. The group cited poor performances of both units for the closures.

Auditors: KPMG AZSA LLC

LOCATIONS

HQ: Sumitomo Corp. (Japan)
1-8-11 Harumi, Chuo-ku, Tokyo 104-8610
Phone: (81) 3 5166 5000 **Fax:** (81) 3 5166 6203
Web: www.sumitomocorp.co.jp

HISTORICAL FINANCIALS

Company Type: Public

Income Statement FYE: March 31

	REVENUE ($ mil.)	NET INCOME ($ mil.)	NET PROFIT MARGIN	EMPLOYEES
03/15	31,357	(609)	—	96,795
03/14	32,139	2,161	6.7%	95,557
03/13	32,056	2,470	7.7%	97,451
03/12	39,753	3,055	7.7%	99,075
03/11	37,438	2,417	6.5%	87,232
Annual Growth	(4.3%)	—	—	2.6%

2015 Year-End Financials

Debt ratio: 0.4%
Return on equity: (-3.0%)
Cash ($ mil.): 7,466
Current ratio: 1.59
Long-term debt ($ mil.): 28,948
No. of shares (mil.): 1,247
Dividends
Yield: 4.1%
Payout: —
Market value ($ mil.): 13,363

	STOCK PRICE ($) FY Close	P/E High/Low	PER SHARE ($) Earnings	Dividends	Book Value
03/15	10.71	— —	(0.49)	0.44	16.58
03/14	12.80	0 0	1.73	0.44	18.67
03/13	12.61	0 0	1.97	0.54	17.45
03/12	14.52	0 0	2.44	0.54	16.47
03/11	14.33	0 0	1.93	0.36	15.17
Annual Growth	(7.0%)	— —	—	5.7%	2.2%

Sumitomo Electric Industries, Ltd. (Japan)

You might say that Sumitomo Electric Industries (SEI) produces the wide world of wire. The company which has more than 320 subsidiaries and affiliates around the globe is Japan's largest producer of wire and cable. SEI's automotive segment about half of sales makes automotive wiring harnesses wires wheel speed sensors and dash boards. Next in sales is the electric wire and cable division which makes power and industrial cables as well as magnetic and hybrid products. Other units produce optical fiber cables fiber-optic components industrial cables printed circuits ultrafine wire and semiconductors. SEI was formed in 1897 as Sumitomo Copper Rolling Works.

With nearly half the company's sales coming from the automotive segment SEI's 2009 books took a hit when the global recession eroded demand for autos and all the wiring and other components that go into them. A similar drop in demand for cell phones and other consumer electronics compounded the problem. The company also paid high prices for raw copper in 2008 and then saw the price for finished copper products plummet in 2009. Add a strong yen taking a bite out of export profits and it really got ugly. All told net income for fiscal 2009 dropped 84%.

SEI responded by cutting bonuses and other costs and reducing its Japanese workforce. It also acquired Fujitsu's 50% equity stake in Eudyna Devices making Eudyna a wholly owned subsidiary. The company's moves along with a gradual rebound in auto sales increased smart phone sales and growth across all sectors in China lead to improved results for 2010 and 2011 (a 11% sales growth). The improvements were tempered by weakened domestic demand due to The Great East Japan Earthquake and tsunami that hit the country in early 2011 as well as a higher yen that lead to decreased exports. SEI redoubled its overseas expansion (four new Asian plants) and cost cutting efforts to double operating income and improve net income by 250%.

Because of the number of SEI's customers moving to China the company is expanding its presence in that region. In mid-2010 it formed a joint venture with Chinese partner Nanjing Putian Telecommunications to manufacture fiber-optic equipment to connect Chinese consumers to fiber-optic networks. SEI is investing ¥530 million ($5.72 million) in the venture.

HISTORY

Sumitomo Electric Industries as a part of the Sumitomo group business began nearly 400 years ago with the paired talents of spiritual founder Masatomo Sumitomo (who had received training as a Buddhist priest) and his disciple and brother-in-law Riemon Soga. Sumitomo wrote treatises on the conduct of commercial activity and Soga applied his technological skill in extracting silver from copper ore improving upon traditional Western methods and opened a copper business in Kyoto in 1590 that soon transformed the copper refining industry in Japan.

Soga's prosperous copper business became the founding company of the Sumitomo group. After Soga died in 1636 his son Tomomochi married Masatomo's daughter (entering into the Sumitomo family) and became the company's leader.

By the late 1600s the family was one of Japan's top copper producers. The house of Sumitomo entered several other businesses by the mid-1800s in order to insulate itself from waning copper production. The family established the Sumitomo Copper Rolling Works in 1897 to produce bare copper wire.

In 1909 production of cable for Japan's telecommunications industry began and in 1920 the family took their company public renaming it Sumitomo Electric Wire & Cable Works. The next year the company added high-carbon steel wire manufacturing. Its name changed to Sumitomo Electric Industries (SEI) in 1939.

The company began making rubber products for use in aircraft fuel tanks in 1943. The decade drew to a close with the addition of overhead transmission cable engineering operations.

SEI continued to move into new businesses in the 1960s. In 1960 SEI took a 25% stake in Sumitomo 3M a three-way joint venture with NEC (25%) and 3M (50%) to produce industrial cable in Japan. To capitalize on the boom in Japan's automobile and industrial equipment industries SEI introduced disc brakes to its lineup in 1963. Also SEI formally entered into management participation in Japan's Dunlop Tire Company which was then renamed Sumitomo Rubber Industries. (It had initially invested in the tire maker in 1960.)

SEI hit pay dirt with its automotive businesses producing brakes for manufacturers of passenger cars commercial vehicles motorcycles construction and industrial equipment and railcars. In the late 1960s SEI added traffic control systems.

With the introduction of compound semiconductors (used in wireless transmitters and electronic control devices) and cable television systems the 1970s brought SEI into the arena of value-added high-tech products. SEI began producing optical-fiber cable in 1974.

SEI expanded further into fiber optics when it introduced its first LAN in 1981 and set up its US-based Sumitomo Electric Lightwave unit in 1983.

In 1987 the company began producing antilock brakes (ABS) and invested $45 million in an evenly split ABS manufacturing US joint venture (Lucas Sumitomo) with a unit of Lucas Varity. Lucas Varity was later bought by TRW and Sumitomo eventually acquired its remaining 50%. SEI closed out the 1980s by adding satellite navigation systems to its growing automobile product offerings.

The 1990s saw wider global expansion through more alliances and acquisitions. In 1990 SEI teamed up again with Lucas Varity to establish a joint venture in the UK to make automobile wiring harnesses. (SEI together with one of its own affiliates bought Lucas' half share in the company in 1999.) That year SEI through its Sumitomo Electric Wiring Systems unit formed AutoNeural Systems a joint venture with Ford-affiliated Visteon for automobile wiring harnesses.

In 2000 SEI set up ExceLight Communications (spun off from Sumitomo Electric Lightwave) to make optical components and subsystems for telecommunications cable TV and broadband equipment industries. The company restructured its electric power cable operations in early 2001 forming a manufacturing joint venture with Hitachi Cable and shutting one of its plants in Japan. Early the following year SEI acquired the Japan-based Calsonic Kansei Corporation's wiring harness business. SEI closed its electric furnaces in Japan and spun off its Sumitomo Steel Wire Corp. in late 2002. In early 2003 the company joined efforts with Hitachi Cable and Tatsuta Electric Wire & Cable to form Sumiden Hitachi Cable Ltd. a company that specialized in the manufacture of low-voltage power cables.

In 2006 the company acquired the former Volkswagen Bordnetze (now called Sumitomo Electric Bordnetze) a Germany-based manufacturer of wire harnesses from its previous joint owners Volkswagen and VDO Automotive.

Continuing to strengthen its European operations the company along with subsidiary Sumitomo Electric Sintered Alloy acquired Germany-based Cloyes Europe a sintered parts maker in 2007. SEI will use this acquisition to supply Japanese auto parts makers that have manufacturing facilities in Europe.

Also in 2007 as part of a group realignment SEI increased its ownership in Nissin Electric to more than 50% and it acquired affiliate Toyokuni Electric Cable. The acquisitions are part of the company's efforts to position itself as a global player.

EXECUTIVES

Managing Director, Masayoshi Matsumoto
EVP, Hiroyuki Takenaka
Executive Officer, Fumikiyo Uchioke
Senior Managing Director, Shigeru Tanaka
Senior Managing Director, Hideaki Inayama
Senior Managing Director, Mitsuo Nishida
Auditors: KPMG AZSA LLC

LOCATIONS

HQ: Sumitomo Electric Industries, Ltd. (Japan)
Sumitomo Bldg., 4-5-33 Kitahama, Chuo-ku, Osaka 541-0041
Phone: (81) 6 6220 4141
Web: www.sei.co.jp

2015 Sales

	% of total
Asia	
Japan	42
China	16
Others	12
U.S	13
Others	5
Europe & other regions	12
Total	**100**

PRODUCTS/OPERATIONS

2015 Sales

	% of total
Automotive	51
Environment and Energy	22
Industrial materials & other	11
Electronics	10
Information & communications	6
Total	**100**

Products
Automotive
Information and Communication System
Electronics / Consumer Electronics
Semiconduc
Energy
Environment
Infrastructure
Industrial
Bankruptcy
Wiring harnesses
Vibration-proof rubber
Automotive hoses
Car electrical equipment
Electronic wire products
Compound semiconductors
Metallic material for electronic parts
Electric-beam irradiation products
Flexible printed circuits
Fluorine resin products
Electric conductors
Power transmission wires/ cables/equipment
Magnet wires
Air cushions for railroad vehicles
Power systems
Equipment such as substation equipment/control systems
Charged beam equipment and processing
Electrical/power supply work and engineering porous metals

2015

	%
Wiring harnesses	39
Others	61
Total	**100**

COMPETITORS

Alcatel-Lucent
American Superconductor
Amphenol
Asia Pacific Wire & Cable
Belden
CommScope
Corning
DENSO
Delphi Automotive Systems
Finisar
Fujikura Ltd.
Furukawa Electric
General Cable
Hitachi Cable
LEONI
Lear Corp
Magna International
Mitsubishi Electric
Nexans
OFS BrightWave
Robert Bosch
SWCC SHOWA
Southwire
Superior Essex
Tatung
Tokyo Rope Mfg.
Tyco
Valeo

HISTORICAL FINANCIALS

Company Type: Public

Income Statement FYE: March 31

	REVENUE ($ mil.)	NET INCOME ($ mil.)	NET PROFIT MARGIN	EMPLOYEES
03/15	23,527	998	4.2%	240,798
03/14	24,886	646	2.6%	225,484
03/13	22,955	403	1.8%	206,323
03/12	25,104	717	2.9%	194,734
03/11	24,561	852	3.5%	182,773
Annual Growth	(1.1%)	4.0%	—	7.1%

2015 Year-End Financials

Debt ratio: 0.1%
Return on equity: 9.1%
Cash ($ mil.): 1,439
Current ratio: 1.75
Long-term debt ($ mil.): 2,698
No. of shares (mil.): 793
Dividends
Yield: 1.6%
Payout: —
Market value ($ mil.): —

Sumitomo Life Insurance Co. (Japan)

Sumitomo Life is one of Japan's biggest mutual life insurers (along with Nippon Life). The firm sells individual group life and specialized health policies through more than 70 branch offices and about 1500 district offices. Along with its sales force Sumitomo Life sells its products through a network of financial institutions and affiliates. It also administers pension and employee benefit plans and offers brokerage and consulting. The company has a total of some 7 million policyholders. Sumitomo Life which has operations in other Asian and North American countries is part of the Sumitomo Mitsui keiretsu –a group of firms linked by cross-ownership.

Operations

Sumitomo Life has more than $903 billion in individual life insurance in-force and another $309 billion in group insurance plus $103 billion and $26 billion in individual and group annuities respectively.

Geographic Reach

In addition to Japan Sumitomo Life has operations in China and the US. The company has representative offices in New York London Beijing and Hanoi.

In the US it has offices in Atlanta Chicago Kentucky Los Angeles New York and South Carolina. Sumitomo Life is one of the largest Japanese brokers of employee benefits plans in the country.

Sales and Marketing

The company's principal selling channels are its sales force of about 31000 representatives banks and a third party distribution channel formed through sales agreements with Japan Post Group. It also has some online and retail sales operations.

Financial Performance

Sumitomo Life's revenue decreased 17% to ¥3.5 trillion in 2014 due to a decline in premiums and investment gains. However net income rose 14% to ¥1.2 trillion due to factors including a decline in provisions for policy reserves. Cash flow from operations fell 62% to ¥447.6 billion as the company lost money on tangible fixed assets and reported changed in non-investing liabilities.

Strategy

The company's medium-term strategy (through 2016) focuses on improving customer value by enhancing services and improving quality across operations. It is investing in growth areas including expanding its representative sales force its branch network and its international operations (with a focus on Asia).

As part of the company's push into Southeast Asia Sumitomo Life bought a 40% stake in PT BNI Life Insurance the life insurance unit of Bank Negara Indonesia in 2014. The move valued at more than 4 trillion rupiah ($351 million) made Sumitomo Life the second-largest shareholder in BNI Life.

Pursuing further growth in the expanding US market Sumitomo Life acquired Symetra Financial Corporation for $3.7 billion in early 2016. That deal was one of several that Japanese insurers have made in the US to take advantage of that nation's growing population.

EXECUTIVES

President and CEO, Yoshio Sato
Senior Managing Executive Officer, Koichi Suzaki
Senior Managing Executive Officer, Haruo Urata
Senior Managing Executive Officer, Masahiro Hashimoto
Chairman, Shinichi Yokoyama
Auditors: KPMG AZSA LLC

LOCATIONS

HQ: Sumitomo Life Insurance Co. (Japan)
1-4-35 Shiromi, Chuo-ku, Osaka 540-8512
Phone: (81) 6 6937 1435 **Fax:** 212 750-7930
Web: www.sumitomolife.co.jp

COMPETITORS

AXA Life Insurance
American Life Insurance
Asahi Mutual Life
Dai-ichi Life
Daido Life
Fukoku Mutual
Gibraltar Life Insurance
Meiji Yasuda Life
Mitsui Life
Nippon Life Insurance
T&D Holdings
Taiyo Life

HISTORICAL FINANCIALS

Company Type: Public

Income Statement FYE: March 31

	ASSETS ($ mil.)	NET INCOME ($ mil.)	INCOME AS % OF ASSETS	EMPLOYEES
03/14	257,612	1,188	0.5%	42,109
03/13	282,347	1,146	0.4%	42,098
03/12	292,984	1,316	0.4%	42,953
03/11	286,871	1,315	0.5%	42,366
03/10	247,005	1,197	0.5%	45,281
Annual Growth	1.1%	(0.2%)	—	(1.8%)

2014 Year-End Financials

Return on assets: 0.4%
Return on equity: 9.5%
Long-term debt ($ mil.): —
No. of shares (mil.): —
Sales ($ mil): 34,801
Dividends
Yield: —
Payout: —
Market value ($ mil.): —

Sumitomo Mitsui Financial Group Inc Tokyo

Sumitomo Mitsui Financial Group (SMFG) is the holding company for Sumitomo Mitsui Banking which boasts some 440 domestic branches (mostly in the Tokyo and Osaka regions of Japan) and another nearly 40 locations abroad. As one of Japan's largest banks SMFG provides retail corporate and investment banking; asset management; securities trading; and lending. Other units of SMFG include credit card firm Sumitomo Mitsui Card brokerage SMBC Friend Securities management consulting firm Japan Research Institute and Sumitomo Mitsui Finance and Leasing. SMFG also operates the California-based Manufacturers Bank. SMFG bought Citigroup's Japanese consumer-banking business in late 2014.

OperationsSMFG operates four main business segments. SMFG's Commercial Banking segment made up 65% of the group's entire gross profit (net of the segment's expenses) in FY2015 (ended March 31 2015) and mostly includes the operations of Sumitomo Mitsui Banking as well as other domestic bank subsidiaries including KUBC The Minato Bank and SMBC Trust Bank. It also counts SMFG's foreign bank subsidiaries SMBC Europe SMBC (China) and Manufacturers Bank. Nearly one-third (33%) of the segment's gross profit comes from the Wholesale Banking Unit while more than half (56%) of the segment's gross profit is split fairly evenly between the Retail Banking unit the International Banking unit and the Treasury Unit. The group's Consumer Finance segment (20% of gross profit in FY2015) operates through its Sumitomo Mitsui Card Cedyna and SMBC Consumer Finance subsidiaries. The Securities segment (around 10% of gross profit) operates through SMBC Nikko Securities and SMBC Friend Securities. The group's Leasing segment (5% of gross profit) operates through Sumitomo Mitsui Financial Leasing subsidiary.About 30% of the group's domestic loan portfolio consisted of consumer loans (mostly housing loans) while another 27% was tied to loans made to customers in the real estate/goods rental and leasing and the manufacturing sectors. Loans to the transportation/communications/public enterprises wholesale and retail and services sectors split another 30% of the domestic loan portfolio. Broadly speaking about 51% of SMFG's gross profit came from net interest income in FY2015 while 49% came from net non-interest income mostly stemming from fee and commission revenue through its credit card business investment trust sales commissions fees obtained through securities-related business remittance and transfer fees and loan transaction fees. Geographic Reach-About 76% of SMFG's operating income (and 70% of its loan assets) came from its domestic business in Japan in fiscal 2015 (ended March 31 2015) while the rest came from customers in the Europe and Middle East region (11% of operating income) the Asia and Oceania region (8%) and the Americas (5%).Financial PerformanceNote: Growth rates may differ after conversion to US dollars. This analysis uses financials from the company's annual report.While somewhat volatile SMFG's revenues and profits (in domestic currency terms) have been trending higher since 2011 thanks to a combination of fee and commission-income based growth slowly growing loan business higher investment income gains and a substantial decline in impairment charges on its financial assets as the economy tied to those assets has strengthened. The group's total operating income (net revenue excluding impairment charges) rose 3% to ¥3.33 trillion ($27.8 billion) in fiscal 2015 (ended March 31 2015) mostly thanks to higher net investment income from an increase in net gains from bond sales and higher "other income" sources mostly from operating leases and income related to leased-asset sales. Interest income rose by 4% with growth in loan and advances balances. Fee and commission income dipped slightly on lower investment trust sales commissions and securities-related income partially offset by a rise in credit card business fees.Despite higher operating income SMFG's net profit fell 19% to ¥723 billion (over $6 billion) in FY2015 mostly due to a combination of: a 6% rise in general and administrative expenses with increased costs related to overseas business development and increased overseas hiring; and an 18% rise in "other expenses" mostly related to operating lease costs and costs related to leased-asset sales. SMFG's operating cash levels climbed double digits to ¥7.8 trillion ($65.2 billion) for FY2015 despite decreased earnings primarily tied to an increase in deposits.Mergers and Acquisitions

In December 2015 Sumitomo Mitsui Financial Group won its bidding war for General Electric's leasing business in Japan and was expected to enter an acquisition deal worth ¥570 billion ($4.63 billion) for the unit. The deal would add some ¥500 billion in assets and 1000 new employees to SMFG subsidiary Sumitomo Mitsui Finance and Leasing boosting the subsidiary's assets by more than 10% and making it Japan's second-largest leasing company ahead of Mitsubishi UFJ Lease & Finance upon the deal's closing.In late 2014 the SMFG purchased Citigroup's Japanese consumer-banking business for ¥40 billion ($330 million) in a private deal. SMFG completed its integration of Citi's Japanese retail banking operations in late 2015.

EXECUTIVES

Director; President Sumitomo Mitsui Banking, Takeshi Kunibe
President, Koichi Miyata
Director, Ken Kubo
Director, Yujiro Ito
Managing Director, Jun Ohta
Managing Director, Yasuyuki Kawasaki
Managing Director, Fumiaki Kurahara
Chairman, Masayuki Oku, age 71
Auditors: KPMG AZSA LLC

LOCATIONS

HQ: Sumitomo Mitsui Financial Group Inc Tokyo
1-1-2 Marunouchi, Chiyoda-ku, Tokyo 100-0005
Phone: (81) 3 3282 8111
Web: www.smfg.co.jp

PRODUCTS/OPERATIONS

2013 Sales

	% of total
Interest	
Loans & advances	43
Investment securities	2
Other	1
Noninterest	
Fees & commissions	27
investment income	9
Trading profits	4
Other	14
Total	**100**

COMPETITORS

Bank of Yokohama
Credit Saison
Mitsubishi UFJ Financial Group
Mizuho Financial
Norinchukin Bank
Resona
Shinsei Bank
Sumitomo Mitsui Trust Holdings

HISTORICAL FINANCIALS

Company Type: Public

Income Statement FYE: March 31

	ASSETS ($ mil.)	NET INCOME ($ mil.)	INCOME AS % OF ASSETS	EMPLOYEES
03/15	1,528,951	6,281	0.4%	68,739
03/14	1,564,961	8,093	0.5%	66,475
03/13	1,580,333	8,439	0.5%	64,635
03/12	1,743,755	6,321	0.4%	64,225
03/11	1,664,157	5,747	0.3%	61,555
Annual Growth	(2.1%)	2.2%	—	2.8%

2015 Year-End Financials

Return on assets: 0.4%
Return on equity: 9.2%
Long-term debt ($ mil.): —
No. of shares (mil.): 1,367
Sales ($ mil): 40,438
Dividends
Yield: 2.9%
Payout: —
Market value ($ mil.): 10,582

	STOCK PRICE ($) FY Close	P/E High/Low	PER SHARE ($) Earnings	Dividends	Book Value
03/15	7.74	— —	4.59	0.23	65.20
03/14	8.65	— —	5.92	0.25	63.81
03/13	8.16	— —	6.23	0.00	66.28
03/12	6.64	— —	4.56	0.00	65.46
03/11	6.25	— —	4.07	0.00	62.35
Annual Growth	5.5%	— —	3.1%	—	1.1%

Sumitomo Mitsui Trust Holdings Inc

Chuo Mitsui Trust Holdings entailed Chuo Mitsui Trust and Banking (retail trust banking real estate and stock transfer services) and Chuo Mitsui Asset and Banking Company (pension and securities trusts) which also owned investment trust and private equity managers Chuo Mitsui Asset Management and Chuo Mitsui Capital. The group spans the US the UK Singapore the Cayman Islands and China. It offers consulting to individuals and large corporations alike specializing in brokerage securitization and investment advice related to real estate deals. Chuo Mitsui Trust Holdings and Sumitomo Trust and Banking merged in 2012 to form Sumitomo Mitsui Trust Bank one of Japan's largest asset management groups.

HISTORY

Before world markets were rocked by the shock waves of the US real estate and financial markets crash CMHD received about Y430 billion ($4.4 billion) in government support. The company had been making steady payments since 2006 and planned to pay the remaining Y200 before the August 2009 deadline for the conversion of the government's preferred shares into ordinary shares. But mid-year the bank along with several of its Japanese mid-level peers announced it would be unable to meet the goal due to poor earnings.

Once the crisis passes the company's strategy includes a focus on real estate lending long a mainstay of business and improving its position in the investment trust and real estate investing markets.
Auditors: KPMG AZSA LLC

LOCATIONS

HQ: Sumitomo Mitsui Trust Holdings Inc
1-4-1 Marunouchi, Chiyoda-ku, Tokyo 100-6611
Phone: (81) 3 6256 6000
Web: www.smth.jp

HISTORICAL FINANCIALS

Company Type: Public

Income Statement FYE: March 31

	ASSETS ($ mil.)	NET INCOME ($ mil.)	INCOME AS % OF ASSETS	EMPLOYEES
03/15	385,366	1,330	0.3%	20,965
03/14	405,828	1,333	0.3%	20,890
03/13	400,714	1,421	0.4%	20,189
03/12	419,068	2,007	0.5%	20,305
03/11	171,859	570	0.3%	8,846
Annual Growth	22.4%	23.6%	—	24.1%

2015 Year-End Financials

Return on assets: 0.3%
Return on equity: 7.1%
Long-term debt ($ mil.): —
No. of shares (mil.): —
Sales ($ mil): 10,056
Dividends
Yield: 2.2%
Payout: —
Market value ($ mil.): —

	STOCK PRICE ($) FY Close	P/E High/Low	PER SHARE ($) Earnings	Dividends	Book Value
03/15	4.18	— —	0.34	0.10	5.86
03/14	4.50	— —	0.33	0.10	6.06
03/13	4.67	— —	0.33	0.00	6.72
03/12	3.14	— —	0.47	0.00	6.86
Annual Growth	10.0%	— —	(8.0%)	—	(3.9%)

Sun Life Assurance Company of Canada

Accident and health insurance

EXECUTIVES

President & Board Member, Dean Connor
Auditors: Deloitte LLP

LOCATIONS

HQ: Sun Life Assurance Company of Canada
150 King Street West, Toronto, Ontario M5H 1J9
Phone: 416 979-9966 **Fax:** 416 979-3209
Web: www.sunlife.com

HISTORICAL FINANCIALS

Company Type: Public

Income Statement FYE: December 31

	ASSETS ($ mil.)	NET INCOME ($ mil.)	INCOME AS % OF ASSETS	EMPLOYEES
12/14	189,475	7	0.0%	0
12/13	180,494	(4)	—	0
12/12	179,026	7	0.0%	0
12/11	164,808	6	0.0%	0
12/10	95,546	1,583	1.7%	0
Annual Growth	18.7%	(73.5%)	—	—

Sun Life Financial Inc

Sun Life tries to stay on the sunny side of life and life insurance. The company offers insurance and wealth management products to individuals and business entities primarily in Canada and the US. It also has operations in Asia Europe and the UK. Sun Life's products include individual and group life and health insurance individual annuities group pensions mutual funds and asset management services. The US subsidiaries include Massachusetts Financial Services (or MFS Investment Management). Sun Life's products and services are distributed through direct and independent sales agents as well as banks and consultants.

Geographic Reach

In its home market Sun Life is a key player in individual life insurance employee benefits products as well as mutual funds. Its Asian operations are focused on the growing middle class customers in China India and the Philippines.

Strategy

In the wake of the global financial crisis Sun Life has steadily adjusted its goals and worked to "de-risk" its products. It made an effort to build up its sales to individual customers in Canada tightened up its distribution system and expanded direct sales channels in Asia including China and its joint venture in India. To perk up its branding the company purchased the naming rights to the sports stadium in Miami and rolled out fresh ad campaigns in key markets.

Mergers and Acquisitions

In mid-2015 the company bought Washington-based Prime Advisors to broaden its asset management operations. The purchase followed the acquisition of Ryan Labs Asset Management and the planned acquisition of Bentall Kennedy. Together these deals will boost Sun Life Asset Management's third-party assets under management to some C$50 million.

In a move to grow its US group benefits operations Sun Life has agreed to buy Assurant Employee Benefits from Assurant ; the deal is valued at some $975 million. Post-acquisition Sun Life will provide coverage through about 64000 employers in the US.

Company Background

Sun Life demutualized in 2000 and the money it raised as a publicly traded company helped finance growth. During the first 10 years of its public status it grew through a steady pace of acquisitions beginning with its buy of Clarica Life in 2002. Clarica's products were later rebranded with the Sun Life name. International acquisitions have included Genworth's US employee benefits group (2007) and insurance and pension operations in Hong Kong from Commonwealth Bank of Australia (2005).

EXECUTIVES

Senior Managing Director and Head North American Private Fixed Income, Thomas J. Robinson
Chief Investment Officer, Randolph B. (Randy) Brown
President Sun Life Financial Canada, Kevin P. Dougherty, $500,000 total compensation
Chairman and CEO MFS Investment Management, Robert J. (Rob) Manning
EVP and CFO, Colm J. Freyne, $334,346 total compensation
EVP and Chief Risk Officer, Claude A. Accum
Chief Investment Officer and President Sun Life Investment Management, Stephen C. Peacher, $118,592 total compensation
President Sun Life Financial Canada, Dean A. Connor, $538,462 total compensation
Senior Managing Director and Head Global Property Investments Sun Life Investment Management, Thomas V. (Tom) Pedulla
President Sun Life Financial U.S., Daniel R. Fishbein
President Sun Life Investment Management Inc., Carl S. Bang
President Sun Life Financial Asia, Kevin D. Strain
President and CEO Sun Life Canada (Philippines) Inc., Rizalina G. Mantaring
EVP and CIO, Mark S. Saunders
VP Enterprise Infrastructure, Stevan Lewis
Executive Chair Sun Life Financial Quebec, Isabelle Hudon
CEO Sun Life Financial U.K., Katherine Garner
VP and Country Head India, Sandeep Asthana
EVP Public and Corporate Affairs; Chief Marketing Officer, Mary De Paoli
EVP and Chief Human Resources and Communications Officer, Carrie Blair
EVP and Chief Legal Officer and Public Affairs, Melissa J. Kennedy
SVP and Chief Actuary, Larry R. Madge
CEO Sun Life Hong Kong Limited, Wim Hekstra
CEO Sun Life Malaysia, Ooi Say Teng
CEO PVI Sun Life (Vietnam), Michael Elliott
Co-CEO MFS Investment Management Canada Limited, Michael W. Roberge
CEO MFS Investment Management Canada Limited, Peter Kotsopoulos
SVP and Chief Marketing Officer, Lisa Ritchie
Chairman, James H. (Jim) Sutcliffe, age 58
Auditors: Deloitte LLP

LOCATIONS

HQ: Sun Life Financial Inc
150 King Street West, 14th Floor, Toronto, Ontario M5H 1J9
Phone: 416 979-9966 **Fax:** 416 979-3209
Web: www.sunlife.com

COMPETITORS

AGF Management
AIA Group
Aviva
Canada Life
China Life Insurance
Fairfax Financial Holdings
Great-West Life Assurance
Great-West Lifeco
Industrial Alliance Insurance and Financial Servic
Manulife Financial
MetLife
Prudential
Standard Life
The Hartford

HISTORICAL FINANCIALS

Company Type: Public

Income Statement FYE: December 31

	ASSETS ($ mil.)	NET INCOME ($ mil.)	INCOME AS % OF ASSETS	EMPLOYEES
12/14	192,880	4,660	2.4%	16,275
12/13	187,646	3,477	1.9%	0
12/12	227,013	4,627	2.0%	14,880
12/11	213,730	(196)	—	15,000
12/10	210,695	1,502	0.7%	14,755
Annual Growth	(2.2%)	32.7%	—	2.5%

2014 Year-End Financials

Return on assets: 2.5%
Return on equity: 29.8%
Long-term debt ($ mil.): —
No. of shares (mil.): 613
Sales ($ mil): 22,248

Dividends
Yield: 3.9%
Payout: 54.5%
Market value ($ mil.): 22,105

	STOCK PRICE ($) FY Close	P/E High/Low	PER SHARE ($) Earnings	Dividends	Book Value
12/14	36.06	13 11	2.47	1.30	26.59
12/13	35.33	23 16	1.46	1.38	26.80
12/12	26.53	11 7	2.60	1.44	28.65
12/11	18.52	— —	(0.51)	1.41	26.23
12/10	30.10	13 10	2.40	1.39	28.02
Annual Growth	4.6%	— —	0.8%	(1.5%)	(1.3%)

Suncor Energy Inc.

Suncor Energy takes a shine to the cold of Canada. That country's largest energy firm explores for processes and markets oil and natural gas. In 2014 it reported net proved and probable reserves of 1.7 billion barrels of synthetic oil 127 million barrels of bitumen 115 million barrels of oil and 32 billion cu. ft. of natural gas. Suncor Energy was first company to produce commercial crude oil from Canada's Athabasca oil sands. It also holds 12% of Syncrude. Its Sunoco unit refines crude oil and processes and distributes fuels petrochemicals and heating oils invests in renewable energy and operates a network of gas stations. In 2016 Suncor Energy acquired control of rival Canadian Oil Sands.

Geographic Reach

The company has operations in Canada Germany Libya the Netherlands Norway Syria the UK and the US. In 2012 Canada accounted for 79% of Suncor Energy's revenues.

Operations

Suncor Energy is one of Canada's largest oil sands producers. It oil sands assets include a 36% interest in the Joslyn North mine 41% in the Fort Hills mine and 51% of the Voyageur upgrader project as well as a 12% stake in the Syncrude oil sands mining venture.

The company also has conventional natural gas assets as well as international and offshore oil exploration and production holdings. In addition to its production refining and marketing operations across Canada (and in Colorado) the company has exploration assets in Libya Norway Syria and the UK.

The company has four refineries (in Alberta Ontario Quebec and Colorado —460000 barrels of combined capacity per day) and a network of 1460 Petro-Canada retail gas stations.

Its Renewable Energy interests include seven wind facilities across Canada including Adelaide which is the most recent addition to the portfolio and the St. Clair ethanol plant in Ontario. An eighth wind farm Cedar Point is planned to commence commercial operations later in 2015. Suncor's Energy Trading activities primarily involve the marketing supply and trading of crude oil natural gas power and byproducts and the use of midstream infrastructure and financial derivatives to optimize related trading strategies.

Sales and Marketing

The company's primary markets for synthetic oil and bitumen production from Suncor's Oil Sands segment which is sold to and subsequently marketed by Suncor's Energy Trading business include refining operations in Alberta Ontario the US Midwest and the U.S. Rocky Mountain regions and markets in the US Gulf Coast. Diesel production from upgrading operations is sold primarily in Western Canada marketed by Suncor's Refining and Marketing business.

Oil and gas production from East Coast Canada the North Sea and from North America Onshore is either marketed by the company's Energy Trading business acting as a marketing agent or sold to its Energy Trading business which then markets the products to customers under direct sales arrangements. Suncor's retail service station network operates nationally in Canada primarily under the Petro-Canada brand. This network consists of 1465 outlets across Canada excluding Pioneer retail locations. In addition refined products are marketed through independent dealers and joint arrangements. Suncor's Canadian retail network had annual sales of gasoline motor fuels averaging approximately 4.8 million liters per site in 2014 and holds a 17.3% share (2013 – 17.7%) of the national retail urban market.

Financial Performance

In 2014 the company's revenue increased by 1%due to increase revenue from the oil sands business. Oil Sands operations increased production by 8% in 2014 compared to 2013 driven primarily by increased Firebag production. Suncor's net income decreased by 31% in 2014 due to higher operating expenses as a result of higher depreciation and exploration costs.

The company's operating cash inflow decreased by 12% in 2014 primarily due to a decline in net income and a change in working capital items.

Strategy

Oil sands which hold deposits of heavy bitumen make up nearly a third of Canada's oil production and Suncor's long term business focus is developing synthetic oil from its oil sands holdings in Alberta. Suncor plans to produce 1 million barrels per day of oil equivalent from its oil sands holdings by 2020. In 2014 Suncor signed a farm-in agreement with Shell Canada to acquire a 20% interest in a deepwater exploration opportunity in the Shelburne Basin offshore Nova Scotia. In December 2014 Suncor acquired a 30% interest in an exploration licence in the Flemish Pass off the coast of Newfoundland and Labrador and a 50% interest in another exploration licence in the Carson Basin near the Flemish Pass. On the product shipment front that year the rail offloading facilities at Tracy Quebec were used to move crude to new and existing markets. Suncor also started transporting heavy crude on TransCanada's Gulf Coast Pipeline which provided increased access to global-based pricing.In 2014 the Libya National Oil Company declared force majeure on oil exports from two terminals resulting in the shut in of substantially all of the Suncor's production in that country. Consequently Suncor also declared force majeure for all exploration commitments in Libya. To raise cash in 2014 the company agreed to sell the assets of Pioneer Energy to Parkland Fuel Corporation for $378 million. It also agreed to sell its Wilson Creek assets located near Rimbey Alberta to Tamarack Acquisition Corp for $168.5 million. Mergers and Acquisitions In 2015 the company agreed to purchase an additional 10% working interest in the Fort Hills oil sands project from Total E&P Canada Ltd. for $310 million. As part of the transaction Suncor acquires a further proportionate interest in Fort Hills related logistics including pipelines storage terminals and third-party pipeline capacity agreements. The acquisition of the additional working interest also presents an opportunity for Suncor to lower its capital cost per barrel and enhance its projected return on the Fort Hills project

Company Background

To focus on its growth markets and to pay down debt in 2013 the company agreed to sell its conventional natural gas business in Western Canada to a Centrica and Qatar Petroleum partnership for $1 billion.

To further develop its oil sands assets in 2010 the company formed a strategic alliance with TOTAL. As part of the deal France-based TOTAL paid Suncor Energy about $1.7 billion to acquire 19% of Suncor Energy's 60% interest in the Fort Hills mining project and a 49% stake in the Voyageur Upgrader project near Fort McMurray. Suncor Energy acquired about 37% of TOTAL's stake in the Joslyn project.

Boosting its profile as an integrated energy company in 2009 the company acquired Petro-Canada in a $15 billion deal. The acquisition created an energy behemoth with extensive holdings in oil sands solid conventional exploration and production assets and a major refining and retailing network. Following the Petro-Canada deal the company divested about $1.5 billion of non-core assets in Western Canada the US Trinidad and Tobago and the North Sea. In 2010 Suncor Energy sold its North Sea exploration assets (of Petro Canada Netherlands) to Dana Petroleum for $393 million. Later that year it sold a pair of natural gas properties in Alberta to a subsidiary of Abu Dhabi National Energy Company for $285 million. It also sold its Wildcat Hills assets which produce some 80 million cu. ft. of natural gas per day to Direct Energy for about $360 million.

EXECUTIVES

President & Board Member, Steve W Williams
Vice President, Eric Axford
Vice President, Boris Jackman
Vice President, Mark Little
Vice President, Mike MacSween
Vice President, Steve Reynish
Vice President, Paul Gardner
Vice President, Francois Langlois
Vice President, Janice Odegaard
Vice President, Kris Smith
Auditors: PricewaterhouseCoopers LLP

LOCATIONS

HQ: Suncor Energy Inc.
150 - 6th Avenue S.W., Calgary, Alberta T2P 3E3
Phone: 403 296-6616 **Fax:** 403 724-3627
Web: www.suncor.com

2014 Sales

	% of total
Canada	80
United States	14
Other countries	6
Total	**100**

PRODUCTS/OPERATIONS

2014 Sales

	% of total
Refining & marketing	60
Oil sands	31
Exploration & production	9
Total	**10**

COMPETITORS

Anadarko Petroleum
BP NGL
Canadian Natural
Devon Energy
Dominion Resources
Encana
Husky Energy
Imperial Oil
Murphy Oil
Nordex
Shell Canada
Talisman Energy

HISTORICAL FINANCIALS

Company Type: Public

Income Statement FYE: December 31

	REVENUE ($ mil.)	NET INCOME ($ mil.)	NET PROFIT MARGIN	EMPLOYEES
12/14	34,965	2,330	6.7%	13,980
12/13	37,896	3,678	9.7%	13,946
12/12	38,826	2,798	7.2%	13,932
12/11	39,005	4,219	10.8%	13,026
12/10	32,673	3,837	11.7%	12,076
Annual Growth	1.7%	(11.7%)	—	3.7%

2014 Year-End Financials

Debt ratio: 14.4%
Return on equity: 6.5%
Cash ($ mil.): 4,745
Current ratio: 1.67
Long-term debt ($ mil.): 10,784
No. of shares (mil.): 1,444
Dividends
Yield: 3.2%
Payout: 55.1%
Market value ($ mil.): 45,894

	STOCK PRICE ($) FY Close	P/E High/Low	PER SHARE ($) Earnings	Dividends	Book Value
12/14	31.78	22 15	1.59	0.92	24.88
12/13	35.05	14 10	2.45	0.70	26.20
12/12	32.98	21 15	1.80	0.50	25.89
12/11	28.83	17 9	2.62	0.42	24.28
12/10	38.29	16 12	2.44	0.38	22.53
Annual Growth	(4.6%)	— —	(10.1%)	24.4%	2.5%

Suncorp Group Ltd.

Suncorp-Metway (aka Suncorp Group) wants to be a rising star in Australia's insurance and banking sectors. The group owns Suncorp Insurance which operates one of the country's largest general insurance companies as well as a small but growing life insurance and wealth management business. The general insurance business sells personal and commercial property/casualty insurance under its Suncorp AAMI GIO Vero and Shannons brands. In addition to its insurance business Suncorp also runs Suncorp Bank an operator of some 200 branches in eastern Australia. Among other products the bank offers personal and commercial banking accounts financial planning and loans to consumers and small to midsized businesses.

EXECUTIVES

Managing Director and Group CEO, Michael A. Cameron
CEO Suncorp Bank, John Nesbitt
Chief Risk Officer, Clayton Herbert

CFO, Steve Johnston
CEO Commercial Insurance, Anthony Day
CEO Personal Insurance, Gary Dransfield
CEO Suncorp Business Services, Matt Pancino
Acting CEO Suncorp Life, Jeremy Robson
CEO Vero New Zealand, Paul Smeaton
Chairman, Zygmunt Switkowski
Auditors: KPMG

LOCATIONS

HQ: Suncorp Group Ltd.
Level 28, 266 George Street, Brisbane, Queensland 4000
Phone: (61) 7 3362 1222 **Fax:** (61) 7 3135 2940
Web: www.suncorpgroup.com.au

PRODUCTS/OPERATIONS

2013 Sales

	% of total
General Insurance	
Personal	35
Commercial	23
Banking	19
Life and Wealth Management	13
New Zealand General Insurance	10
Total	**100**

Selected Subsidiaries

Asteron Group Ltd. (life insurance)
GIO General Ltd (general insurance products)
Suncorp Life & Superannuation Limited life (insurance products)
Suncorp Metway Insurance Ltd (general insurance products)
Suncorp Metway Investment Management Limited (investment schemes and provides investment management services)
Vero Insurance Ltd. (New Zealand general insurance)

COMPETITORS

AMP Limited
AXA Asia Pacific
Australia and New Zealand Banking
Commonwealth Bank of Australia
Insurance Australia
Macquarie Group
National Australia Bank
Westpac Banking

HISTORICAL FINANCIALS

Company Type: Public

Income Statement FYE: June 30

	ASSETS ($ mil.)	NET INCOME ($ mil.)	INCOME AS % OF ASSETS	EMPLOYEES
06/15	73,504	870	1.2%	0
06/14	88,728	685	0.8%	0
06/13	88,481	452	0.5%	0
06/12	97,829	737	0.8%	0
06/11	102,355	485	0.5%	0
Annual Growth	(7.9%)	15.7%		

2015 Year-End Financials

Return on assets: 1.1%
Return on equity: 8.3%
Long-term debt ($ mil.): —
No. of shares (mil.): 1,286
Sales ($ mil): 12,850
Dividends
Yield: 0.0%
Payout: 111.9%
Market value ($ mil.): 13,419

	STOCK PRICE ($) FY Close	P/E High/Low		PER SHARE ($) Earnings	Dividends	Book Value
06/15	10.43	13	11	0.67	0.75	8.05
06/14	12.79	22	19	0.54	0.30	10.06
Annual Growth	(18.5%)	—	—	5.7%	25.4%	(5.4%)

Suntory Holdings Ltd

Japan-based Suntory Holdings is a 100-year-old company best known for producing Japan's first whiskey under the Kakubin brand name. Today the company comprises approximately 200 group subsidiaries located worldwide that do everything from distill whiskey to grow and sell flowers. Suntory Holdings has three main areas of operation: producing alcoholic beverages (including MIDORI melon-flavored liqueur); producing health food and supplement and non-alcoholic beverages; and running restaurant fitness and floral operations. It is the Japanese distributor of Häagen-Dazs ice cream and runs a number of Pepsi bottling businesses in both Japan and Vietnam.

Geographic Reach

Japan is Suntory's largest market accounting for nearly 80% of sales. The rest of Asia and Oceania accounts for about 10%. The beverage and food company has operations throughout Asia the Pacific Rim the Americas and Europe (Morrison Bowmore Distillers in Scotland for example). Suntory is a big producer of beer in China.

Operations

Suntory Beverage & Food which includes the soft drink brands is the largest operating company in the Suntory Group accounting for more than 50% of sales. Beyond its Beverage & Foods and Beer & Spirits (30% of sales) businesses Suntory owns: Tipness a chain of fitness clubs in Japan; Suntory Flowers Ltd. and ice cream distributor Häagen-Dazs Japan. Suntory Wellness Ltd. is a health-related business.

Financial Performance

Suntory's sales increased 3% in 2012 compared with 2011 to ¥1.85 billion ($18 billion) primarily due to increased beer and spirit sales. Net income decreased by 42% over the same period due to an increase in deferred income tax incurred in 2012. Japan and the rest of Asia fueled sales growth in 2012 while sales in Europe declined by 4%. Sales in the Americas were flat.

Strategy

In late 2013 Suntory announced the formation of a new company to manage its business in Europe which accounts for approximately 10% of the Japan-based company's sales. The new company will be called Suntory Beverage & Food Ltd. and will be based in London. Sales in Europe declined by 4% in 2012 versus 2011 and Suntory is looking to foster growth. Overall the core Beverage & Food business is working to expand its business as a global player by developing brands tailored to consumer tastes and changing in trends in each region where it does business.

The company has also been inking strategic partnerships. In 2012 it formed a joint venture in India and established Sunotry Narang Pte. Ltd. for the food and beverage business. It also formed a joint venture in China and established Tsingtao Brewery. Suntory is a joint venture partner with PepsiCo and Pepsi Bottling Ventures. In 2012 Suntory partnered with PepsiCo to form a 51%-owned stake in PepsiCo's Vietnam beverage business as PepsiCo continues to operate its foods business there. PepsiCo owns 49%. The strategic alliance is part of long-term plans for PepsiCo to strengthen its existing position in Vietnam and for Suntory to expand its business and boost its share in the growing Southeast Asian markets. In 2011 Suntory teamed up with Indonesian packaged food and drink firm Garudafood to form a soft drink joint venture. The companies aim to take a share of Southeast Asia's rising soft drink demand. As part of the companies' agreement Garudafood transferred its soft drink operations to the joint venture which is 51%-owned by Suntory. Additionally Suntory purchased a roughly 35% interest in Garudafood's sales and distribution arm PT Sinar Niaga Sejahtera.

In 2014 Suntory agreed to purchase US spirits company Beam for $13.6 billion or $83.50 per share representing a 25% premium. The pair already has a distribution partnership in Asia.

Mergers & Acquisitions

The acquisitive company has strengthened its nonalcoholic beverage business in Europe through several purchases in recent years. In 2011 Suntory acquired the European operations of US juice maker Sunny Delight Beverages. The acquisition made through Suntory's Orangina unit (acquired in 2009) included Sunny Delight's operations in Spain the UK France and Portugal. Suntory in 2010 gained approval to sell Sunny Delight in Europe and has focused initially on Spain. Ultimately the Japanese company hopes to catch up to US-based Coca-Cola Co. and PepsiCo Inc. in Europe by pursuing synergies between Orangina and Sunny Delight's European business. Previously Suntory acquired the Frucor fruit-flavored drinks business from Groupe Danone Worldwide Water for about $842 million in 2009. That year also saw it purchase European drink maker Orangina for $1.5 billion from investment firms Blackstone and Lion Capital. Both acquisitions were in line with Suntory's strategy to strengthen its fruit and vegetable beverage holdings. As a consequence of the shrinking Japanese market (due to the aging of its population and low birth rate) Suntory is looking to expand overseas. To that end in 2009 it purchased a US Pepsi bottler Conway-Myrtle Beach Inc. from Pepsi Bottling Ventures. Conway-Myrtle Beach operates in South Carolina. The acquisition added to Suntory's Pepsi bottling operations in the US since it already owns Pepsi Bottling Ventures in North Carolina. That year it also added to its overseas footprint with the acquisition of Hong Kong-based wine importer ASC Fine Wines.

EXECUTIVES

Director and President Beverage and Food Ltd., Nobuhiro Torii
President and Director, Takeshi Niinami
President Suntory Wine International Ltd., Ko Sakurai
Managing Executive Officer and President Suntory Wellness, Masuo Kawasaki
Senior Managing Director and President Suntory Beer and Spirits, Yasunori Tanaka
President Suntory Wine International, Toru Yagi
President Suntory Business Expert, Shunichi Naito
President Suntory Liquors Ltd., Atsushi (Windy) Koizumi
President Suntory (China) Holding Co. Ltd., Kazuhiro Saito
President Suntory Beer Ltd., Tetsu Mizutani
President Suntory Global Innovation Center Ltd., Masato Arishiro
Chairman, Nobutada Saji, age 69
Vice Chairman, Shigehiro Aoyama
Auditors: Deloitte Touche Tohmatsu LLC

LOCATIONS

HQ: Suntory Holdings Ltd
2-1-40 Dojimahama, Kita-ku, Osaka, Osaka 530-8203
Phone: (81) 6 6346 1682
Web: www.suntory.co.jp

2014 Sales

	% of total
Japan	64
Europe	13
Americas	9
Asia Oceania and Other	14
Total	**100**

PRODUCTS/OPERATIONS

2014 Sales

	% of total
Beverages & foods	51
Alcoholic Beverage	36
Other	13
Total	**100**

Selected Operations

Suntory Beverage & Food Ltd.
- Suntory Foods Ltd.
- Suntory Products Ltd.
- Orangina Schweppes Group
- Frucor Group
- Suntory Beverage & Food Asia Pte. Ltd.
- Cerebos Pacific Ltd.
- Pepsi Bottling Ventures LLC

Suntory (China) Holding Co. Ltd.
Suntory Liquors Ltd.
- Suntory Beer & Spirits Ltd.

Suntory Wine International Ltd.
Suntory Wellness Ltd.
Restaurants Processed Foods Fitness Flowers & Other Services
- Dynac Corp.
- Häagen-Dazs Japan Inc.
- Tipness Ltd.
- Suntory Flowers Ltd.

COMPETITORS

Anheuser-Busch InBev	LOTTE
Asahi Breweries	Makita
Asia Pacific Breweries	McDonald' s Japan
Beam Suntory	Mercian
Body Shop	Morinaga
Burger King	Nestl© Waters
Coca-Cola	PepsiCo
Danone Water	Pernod Ricard
Diageo	SABMiller
Energy Brands	Sakata Seed
Ezaki Glico	Sapporo
Kikkoman	Seven & i
Kirin Holdings Company	Skylark
Kokubu	Takara
Konami	Tsingtao

HISTORICAL FINANCIALS

Company Type: Public

Income Statement FYE: December 31

	REVENUE ($ mil.)	NET INCOME ($ mil.)	NET PROFIT MARGIN	EMPLOYEES
12/14	20,578	321	1.6%	37,613
12/13	19,435	1,863	9.6%	34,129
12/12	21,497	425	2.0%	28,767
12/11	23,295	809	3.5%	28,532
12/10	21,421	492	2.3%	25,103
Annual Growth	(1.0%)	(10.1%)	—	10.6%

2014 Year-End Financials

Debt ratio: 0.3%	No. of shares (mil.): 683
Return on equity: 4.6%	Dividends
Cash ($ mil.): 1,670	Yield: —
Current ratio: 1.50	Payout: —
Long-term debt ($ mil.): 16,314	Market value ($ mil.): —

Suzuki Motor Corp. (Japan)

Suzuki Motor Corporation is a leading Japanese carmaker and a global motorcycle manufacturer competing head-to-head with rivals Honda and Yamaha. Suzuki's passenger car models include the Alto Grand Vitara Swift Splash and SX4. Its motorcycle products include cruiser motocross offroad scooter street and touring models as well as ATVs. Suzuki Motor's non-vehicle products include outboard motors for boats and motorized wheelchairs. It builds its lineup on its own and through numerous subsidiaries and joint ventures overseas. Japan accounts for nearly 45% of sales. Suzuki entered the US car market in 1985 with the Samurai the country' first compact SUV.

Geographic Reach

The company has man production facilities in 22 countries and serves more than 200 countries. Outside of Japan (around 45% of its total sales) Asian consumers represent nearly 35% of its sales whereas North American and European purchases combined account for nearly 15%. Suzuki subsidiary Maruti Suzuki India is India's largest passenger car company.

Operations

Suzuki divides its operations into four reportable segments. The Automobile segment generated 88% of the company's total sales for 2012 while its motorcycle operations accounted for 10%. The other segments –marine and power products; and financial services —accounted for the remaining 2%.

Financial Performance

Suzuki's balance sheet has been up and down over the years. After posting increases in both revenue and net income in 2011 the company saw its revenues decrease by 4% in 2012. The lower revenue was attributed to a 1% decrease in its motorcycle segment and a 4% dip in its automobile segment. The company however did recognize a 19% increase in its net income for 2012 due to lower expenses related to sales marketing and promotions.

Strategy

Suzuki is expanding its vehicle lineup in China through Suzuki China which imports and sells Japanese-made cars. The company imports and exports Suzuki-brand vehicles through Suzuki Automobile (Thailand) a joint venture with Siam International Corp. Demand in Vietnam the Philippines and Malaysia has continued to grow modestly too.

In 2012 Suzuki began construction of a new motorcycle plant in Rohtak Haryana of India and a second plant through Chongqing Changan Suzuki Automobile Co. Ltd. (Changan Suzuki) an automobile manufacturing and sales joint venture company in China. The Indian motorcycle market in 2011 exceeded 13 million units and Suzuki expects continuous growth in the region. To capitalize on the expanding Chinese automobile market and to establish an annual capacity of 500000 units Suzuki has decided to construct its second plant in the area next to its current plant.

HISTORY

In 1909 Michio Suzuki started Suzuki Loom Works in Hamamatsu Japan. The company went public in 1920 and continued producing weaving equipment until the onset of WWII when it began to make war-related products.

Suzuki began developing inexpensive motor vehicles in 1947 and in 1952 it introduced a 36cc engine to motorize bicycles. The company changed its name to Suzuki Motor and launched its first motorcycle in 1954. Suzuki's entry into the minicar market came in 1955 with the Suzulight followed by the Suzumoped (1958) a delivery van (1959) and the Suzulight Carry FB small truck (1961).

Suzuki's triumph in the 1962 50cc-class Isle of Man TT motorcycle race started a string of racing successes that brought international prominence to the Suzuki name. The company established its first overseas plant in Thailand in 1967.

In the 1970s Suzuki met market demand for motorcycles with large engines. Meanwhile a mid-1970s recession and falling demand for low-powered cars in Japan led the minicar industry there to produce two-thirds fewer minicars in 1974 than in 1970. Suzuki responded by pushing overseas beginning auto exports and expanding foreign distribution. In 1975 it started producing motorcycles in Taiwan Thailand and Indonesia.

Suzuki boosted capacity internationally throughout the 1980s through joint ventures. Motorcycle sales in Japan peaked in 1982 then tapered off but enjoyed a modest rebound in the late 1980s. In 1988 the company agreed to handle distribution of Peugeot cars in Japan.

Suzuki and General Motors began their longstanding relationship in 1981 when GM bought a small stake in Suzuki. The company began producing Swift subcompacts in 1983 and sold them through GM as the Chevy Sprint and later the Geo Metro. In 1986 Suzuki and GM of Canada jointly formed CAMI Automotive to produce vehicles including Sprints Metros and Geo Trackers (Suzuki Sidekicks) in Ontario; production began in 1989.

Although sales via GM increased through 1990 US efforts with the Suzuki nameplate faltered shortly after Suzuki formed its US subsidiary in Brea California in 1986. A 1988 Consumer Reports claim that the company's Samurai SUV was prone to rolling over devastated US sales. The next year Suzuki's top US executives quit apparently questioning the company's commitment to the US market.

Suzuki established Magyar Suzuki a joint venture with Hungarian automaker Autokonszern Rt. C. Itoh & Co. and International Finance Corporation in 1991 to begin producing the Swift sedan in Hungary. The company expanded a licensing agreement with a Chinese government partner in 1993 becoming the first Japanese company to take an equity stake in a Chinese carmaking venture. The next year Suzuki introduced the Alto van Japan's cheapest car at just over $5000 and the Wagon R miniwagon which quickly became one of Japan's top-selling vehicles.

In a case that was later overturned a woman was awarded $90 million from Suzuki after being paralyzed in a Samurai rollover in 1990. The company sued Consumers Union publisher of Consumer Reports in 1996 charging it had intended to fix the results in the 1988 Samurai testing.

GM raised its 3% stake in Suzuki to 10% in 1998. The company teamed up with GM and Fuji Heavy Industries (Subaru) in 2000 to develop compact cars for the European market. It was also announced that GM would spend about $600 million to double its stake in Suzuki to 20%. In 2001 Suzuki announced that it had agreed to cooperate with Kawasaki in the development of new motorcycles scooters and ATVs.

The following year Suzuki agreed to take control of Maruti Udyog Ltd. the state-owned India-based car manufacturer in an $80 million rights issue deal.

GM sold almost all of its 20% stake in Suzuki in early 2006 to raise cash for its own beleaguered operations. GM divested the remaining 3% stake in late 2008 for about $230 million as it endured a dire cash crisis.

EXECUTIVES

Chairman and CEO, Osamu Suzuki
EVP, Toshihiro Suzuki
EVP, Minoru Tamura
EVP, Osamu Honda

EVP, Yasuhito Harayama
Auditors: Seimei Audit Corp.

LOCATIONS

HQ: Suzuki Motor Corp. (Japan)
300 Takatsuka-cho, Hamamatsu, Shizuoka 432-8611
Phone: (81) 53 440 2030
Web: www.suzuki.co.jp

2015 Sales

	% of total
Japan	48
Asia	36
Europe	12
Other regions	4
Total	**100**

PRODUCTS/OPERATIONS

2015 Sales

	% of total
Automobiles	90
Motorcycles	8
Marine and power products	2
Total	**100**

List of Items
Automobiles
Alto/CELERIO
APV
Grand Vitara SUV
Jimny
Kizashi sport sedan
Splash
Swift
SX4 Crossover Sport SportBack
Motorcycles/ATV
Cruiser
Dual purpose
Motocross
Offroad
Scooter
Sport Enduro Tourer
Street
Supersport
Outboard motors
Carburetor
Electronic
Kerosene 0

COMPETITORS

BMW
Bajaj Auto
Brunswick Corp.
Daimler
Ducati
Ek Chor China Motorcycle
FCA US
Ford Motor
General Motors
Harley-Davidson
Honda
Hyundai Motor
Kawasaki Heavy Industries
Mahindra
Mazda
Nissan
Piaggio & Co.
Polaris Industries
Renault
Tata Motors
Toyota
Triumph Motorcycles
Volkswagen
Yamaha Motor

HISTORICAL FINANCIALS

Company Type: Public

Income Statement FYE: March 31

	REVENUE ($ mil.)	NET INCOME ($ mil.)	NET PROFIT MARGIN	EMPLOYEES
03/15	25,133	807	3.2%	57,409
03/14	28,466	1,041	3.7%	57,749
03/13	27,402	854	3.1%	55,948
03/12	30,625	656	2.1%	54,484
03/11	31,497	545	1.7%	52,731
Annual Growth	(5.5%)	10.3%	—	2.1%

2015 Year-End Financials

Debt ratio: 0.1%
Return on equity: 6.9%
Cash ($ mil.): 3,813
Current ratio: 1.74
Long-term debt ($ mil.): 2,273
No. of shares (mil.): 560
Dividends
Yield: —
Payout: —
Market value ($ mil.): 70,112

	STOCK PRICE ($) FY Close	P/E High/Low	PER SHARE ($) Earnings	Dividends	Book Value
03/15	125.00	— —	1.44	0.00	25.28
03/14	109.45	— —	1.86	0.00	25.81
03/13	90.52	— —	1.40	0.00	24.61
03/12	96.10	— —	1.08	0.00	24.16
03/11	85.50	— —	0.89	0.00	23.83
Annual Growth	10.0%	— —	12.6%	—	1.5%

Svenska Handelsbanken

Svenska Handelsbanken is Swedish for universal banking. The group provides corporate and individual clients with deposit products loans credit cards and other banking services. Subsidiaries operate in several related areas including life insurance mortgages pensions fund management and Internet banking. The bank boasts more than 830 branches in 25 countries with most in Sweden the UK Denmark Finland Norway and the Netherlands. Subsidiaries include corporate financing unit Handelsbanken Finans Handelsbanken Asset Management and Handelsbanken Liv. Founded in 1871 the bank's assets now exceed $360 billion.

OperationsThe bank operates in seven business segments mostly based on geography. These include branch operation segments in Sweden the UK Denmark Finland Norway and the Netherlands as well as a Capital Markets segment.

The bank made more than 80% of its total revenue in 2014 from interest income mostly from corporate loans and mortgage loans but also from consumer loans. The majority of the remaining revenues came from fee and commission income from its investment banking and other corporate finance services with a small portion (3% of revenues) coming from its insurance and pensions operations.Geographic ReachSvenska Handelsbanken generates more than 60% of its revenue in Sweden while its operations in Norway and the UK each bring in 10% of total revenue. The banks other top markets include Denmark Finland and the Netherlands. It also has a presence in countries including Austria China Hong Kong Russia and the US. Financial PerformanceThe bank's net revenues and profits have been on the rise in recent years thanks to a combination of low borrowing rates on deposits growing investment banking and loan business from aggressive branch expansion rising investment gains and strong controls on staffing costs.Svenska's revenue dipped by 5% to SK$63.5 billion ($8.14 billion) in 2014 despite higher loan volumes mostly as interest margins on loans and securities shrank amidst the low-interest environment. Despite lower revenues the bank's net income rose by 6% to SK$15 billion ($1.9 billion) thanks to a decline in interest expenses on deposits and a slower rise in staff costs.The bank's operating cash fell by more than 50% to SK$52.8 billion ($6.76 billion) despite higher earnings in 2014 mostly as it used more cash toward loans to the public and other credit institutions.

Stategy

With its focus on being as local to its customer as possible Svenska Handelsbanken continues to grow its digital banking and its physical branch network in new markets around the world. During 2014 the bank opened 24 new branches across several countries including 17 in the UK two in each Norway and the Netherlands and one branch in each of Denmark and Finland.

HISTORY

Company BackgroundSvenska Handelsbanken (roughly translated as The Swedish Commercial Bank) was founded as Stockholms Handelsbank in 1871 by former directors of Stockholms Enskilda Bank who lost an internal power struggle. Industrialization in the latter stages of the 19th century saw Stockholms Handelsbank expand nationwide with the bank pursuing an aggressive lending policy. Larger companies required larger financing resulting in smaller local banks running into trouble and forcing them to merge with bigger ones. Through a series of mergers of this kind Stockholms Handelsbank exploded in size and branches increased from seven (all Stockholm-based) to 250 nationwide by 1919. To reflect this growth the company changed its name to Svenska Handelsbanken the same year.

Sweden remained neutral during WWI allowing business to prosper but the depression hit hard. The bank had to write off millions in bad loans and additions to its reserves. During the 1930s Handelsbanken regained stability largely thanks to its geographical diversity; operations in areas with high economic activity made up for struggling regions.

Sweden once again remained neutral during WWII but political uncertainty kept deposits high and it became difficult to maintain profitable loan volumes. In the 1940s Svenska Handelsbanken divested many of its industrial holdings and began to rededicate itself to small- and medium-scale lending.

Through a string of purchases in the 1950s and 1960s the bank became the largest bank in Scandinavia and began looking to expand internationally. Joint ventures and acquisitions saw the company move into other parts of Europe and the US in the 1970s. Nordic American Banking a US subsidiary was set up to handle import and export financing for North and South American clients doing business with Scandinavian countries. The 1980s saw the company establish a merchant-banking subsidiary in London and enter the Asian market forming Svenska Handelsbanken Asia (based in Singapore).

The bank remained acquisitive during the first half of the 1990s including a purchase of life insurance company RKA (later renamed Handelsbanken Liv) and parts of the Finnish Skopbank. In 1996 Handelsbanken acquired Swedish mortgage company Stadshypotek.

During the latter half of the 1990s it ventured into e-business and increased its presence in the Nordic countries and the UK. In 1999 the company acquired the Norwegian Bergensbanken after having been beaten by MeritaNordbanken in the chase for Christiania Bank (which was Norway's second-largest at the time). The next year Handelsbanken acquired Spartacus a Danish consumer finance company. In 2001 it made another Danish purchase Midtbank making it one of Denmark's largest bankers. That year it also acquired Swedish life insurance company SPP.

In 2004 Handelsbanken bought Swedish fund manager XACT Fonder from OMHEX (now OMX).

The company bought Lokallbanken in Denmark in 2008. The deal added about 15 branches to Handelsbanken's network.

EXECUTIVES

CFO, Ulf Riese, age 57
Group Functions Executive Central Headquarter, Anders Ohlner, age 61
Group Business Executive UK, Anders Bouvin, age 58
Group Business Executive Norway, Dag Tjernsmo
Group Functions Executive Central Headquarter, Olle Lindstrand, age 67
Head Investor Relations, Mikael Hall ker
President and Group Chief Executive, Frank Vang-Jensen
Group Business Executive Stockholm Sweden, Carina .kerstr ¶n
President and CEO, Par Boman
Chief Risk Officer, Maria Hedin
Group Functions Executive IT, Anders H Johansson
Group Business Executive Merchant Banking International, Jan Amethier
Group Business Executive Finland, Nina Arkilahti
Group Business Executive South West Great Britain, Michael Broom
Group Business Executive Northern Sweden, Magnus Ericson
Group Business Executive Southern Great Britain, John Hodson
Group Business Executive Western Sweden, Katarina Ljungqvist
Group Business Executive North East Great Britain, Simon Lodge
Group Business Executive North East Great Britain, Nick Lowe
Group Business Executive Denmark, Lars Moesgaard
Group Business Executive Eastern Sweden, Stefan Nilsson
Group Business Executive Northern Great Britain, John Parker
Group Business Executive Southern Sweden, G ¶an Stille
Group Business Executive Netherlands, Mikael S ¶ensen
Group Business Executive Stadshypotek, Ulrika Stolt Kirkegaard
Group Business Executive Central Sweden, Pontus .hlund
Head Central Personnel, Anders Ohman
Auditors: KPMG AB

LOCATIONS

HQ: Svenska Handelsbanken
Kungstradgardsgatan 2, Stockholm SE-106 70
Phone: (46) 8 701 10 00
Web: www.handelsbanken.se

2014 Sales

	% of total
Sweden	63
Norway	10
UK	10
Denmark	6
Finland	6
Netherlands	4
Other countries	1
Total	**100**

PRODUCTS/OPERATIONS

2014 Sales by Segment

	% of total
Branch operations	
Sweden	52
Other countries	33
Capital markets	15
Total	**100**

COMPETITORS

BNP Paribas
Citigroup
Cr©dit Agricole
Danske Bank
Deutsche Bank
Nordea Bank
SEB AB
Soci©t© G©n©rale

HISTORICAL FINANCIALS

Company Type: Public

Income Statement FYE: December 31

	ASSETS ($ mil.)	NET INCOME ($ mil.)	INCOME AS % OF ASSETS	EMPLOYEES
12/14	364,372	1,964	0.5%	11,692
12/13	388,352	2,229	0.6%	11,503
12/12	366,543	2,233	0.6%	11,192
12/11	355,859	1,786	0.5%	11,184
12/10	321,154	1,644	0.5%	10,850
Annual Growth	3.2%	4.5%	—	1.9%

2014 Year-End Financials

Return on assets: 0.5%
Return on equity: 12.7%
Long-term debt ($ mil.): —
No. of shares (mil.): 1,907
Sales ($ mil): 8,222
Dividends
Yield: 11.2%
Payout: 2.4%
Market value ($ mil.): 44,624

	STOCK PRICE ($) FY Close	P/E High/Low		PER SHARE ($) Earnings	Dividends	Book Value
12/14	23.40	0	0	1.01	1.26	8.60
12/13	24.68	0	0	1.16	0.82	9.11
12/12	18.03	0	0	1.16	0.72	8.64
12/11	13.43	0	0	0.94	0.02	7.32
12/10	16.30	0	0	0.87	0.01	7.05
Annual Growth	9.5%	—	—	4.0%	228.5%	5.1%

Sveriges Riksbank (Sweden)

Federal reserve banks nsk

EXECUTIVES

Controller, Pether Burvall
Auditors: Swedish National Audit Office

LOCATIONS

HQ: Sveriges Riksbank (Sweden)
Brunkebergstorg 11, Stockholm SE-103 37
Phone: (46) 8 787 00 00 **Fax:** (46) 8 21 05 31
Web: www.riksbank.se

HISTORICAL FINANCIALS

Company Type: Public

Income Statement FYE: December 31

	ASSETS ($ mil.)	NET INCOME ($ mil.)	INCOME AS % OF ASSETS	EMPLOYEES
12/14	64,991	422	0.7%	330
12/13	67,323	(313)	—	341
12/12	53,071	296	0.6%	351
12/11	50,444	569	1.1%	332
12/10	48,754	81	0.2%	339
Annual Growth	7.5%	50.8%	—	(0.7%)

Swedbank A B

From Scandinavia to the Baltics one common denominator might be the institution with which people entrust their money. Swedbank serves more than 10 million private and corporate customers through 315 branches in Sweden and more than 200 branches in the Baltic countries. The bank also has an international presence in countries such as China Russia and Ukraine. Swedbank offers the usual banking staples –checking savings accounts credit cards electronic banking and loans –but also runs the gamut from investment business in the commodity stock and money markets to real estate brokerage and life insurance. The bank was formed by the 1997 merger of F ¶reningsbanken and Sparbanken Sverige.

After enduring some rather big losses as a result of the global economic crisis and (more specifically) bad loans in the Baltics Swedbank is trying to pick up the pieces and move forward. The company was able to recover in 2010 and reported a profit. The improvement was due to economic growth in Sweden and improving financial conditions in the Baltics. Swedbank also received backing from the Swedish government and moved to reduce costs. Conditions continued to improve (along with higher interest rates) in 2011 and net interest income rose by 17%. However profit dipped drastically in the final quarter of 2011 (down 65%) prompting the company to continue cutting costs.

Despite the stumbling block created by the global crash Swedbank maintains its vision to become an international banking group with a Swedish base. The bank is looking to build its business in Estonia Latvia and Lithuania. Estonia entered the eurozone at the end of 2010 which will help reduce business risk and boost the country's economy.

However the European debt crisis which struck in 2011 impacted growth prospects. Swedbank is scaling back some of its international ambitions and is focusing more on its home markets. The company had positioned itself for growth in Russia and Ukraine. However in 2010 Swedbank chose to shift its focus in Russia and Ukraine away from private customers and to target only corporate customers in the bank's home markets. The private customer offering will be gradually phased out and the number of branches reduced.

Swedbank is placing more emphasis on its corporate customers. Large corporates and institutions is a major contributor to Swedbank's income and the company's goal is to be the primary provider of financial advice and capital market products in its core markets. The company is working to broaden customer relations and attract new corporate and institutional clients. One way it is doing this is by growing its Norwegian brokerage First Securities which offers equity trading and research corporate finance and fixed-income trading. In 2010 Swedbank bought the half of First Securities it already didn't own.

Swedbank's smallest business segment is also its newest. Born out of the global economic meltdown Ektornet manages and develops Swedbank's repossessed assets and tries to recover as much value as possible. The real estate segment seeks to reduce costs and minimize impairment losses for the company.
Auditors: Deloitte AB

LOCATIONS

HQ: Swedbank A B
LandsvA$?gen 40, Stockholm SE-105 34
Phone: (46) 8 585 900 00 **Fax:** (46) 8 796 80 92
Web: www.swedbank.com

HISTORICAL FINANCIALS

Company Type: Public

Income Statement FYE: December 31

	ASSETS ($ mil.)	NET INCOME ($ mil.)	INCOME AS % OF ASSETS	EMPLOYEES
12/14	274,416	2,127	0.8%	14,624
12/13	284,004	2,012	0.7%	14,265
12/12	283,511	2,216	0.8%	16,088
12/11	269,256	1,702	0.6%	18,716
12/10	255,858	1,110	0.4%	20,639
Annual Growth	1.8%	17.7%	—	(8.3%)

2014 Year-End Financials

Return on assets: 0.8%
Return on equity: 14.5%
Long-term debt ($ mil.): —
No. of shares (mil.): 1,102
Sales ($ mil): 8,288
Dividends
Yield: 6.2%
Payout: 67.7%
Market value ($ mil.): 27,450

	STOCK PRICE ($) FY Close	P/E High	P/E Low	PER SHARE ($) Earnings	Dividends	Book Value
12/14	24.91	2	1	1.92	1.56	13.76
12/13	28.31	3	2	1.58	1.52	15.57
12/12	19.80	2	1	1.87	0.78	17.75
12/11	12.85	2	1	1.38	0.31	15.66
12/10	14.06	2	1	0.96	1.99	14.87
Annual Growth	15.4%	—	—	18.9%	(5.8%)	(1.9%)

Swiss Life (UK) plc (United Kingdom)

Auditors: PricewaterhouseCoopers AG

LOCATIONS

HQ: Swiss Life (UK) plc (United Kingdom)
General-Guisan-Quai 40, P.O. Box 2831, Zurich CH-8022
Phone: (41) 43 284 33 11
Web: www.swisslife.com

HISTORICAL FINANCIALS

Company Type: Public

Income Statement FYE: December 31

	ASSETS ($ mil.)	NET INCOME ($ mil.)	INCOME AS % OF ASSETS	EMPLOYEES
12/14	194,962	822	0.4%	7,492
12/13	191,380	876	0.5%	6,992
12/12*	179,406	106	0.1%	7,046
01/12	161,771	0	—	0
12/01	2,814	(6)	—	0
Annual Growth	38.5%	—	—	—

*Fiscal year change

2014 Year-End Financials

Return on assets: 0.4%
Return on equity: 7.5%
Long-term debt ($ mil.): —
No. of shares (mil.): 31
Sales ($ mil): 15,190
Dividends
Yield: —
Payout: —
Market value ($ mil.): —

Swiss Life Holding AG

Auditors: PricewaterhouseCoopers AG

LOCATIONS

HQ: Swiss Life Holding AG
General-Guisan-Quai 40, P.O. Box 2831, Zurich CH-8022
Phone: (41) 43 284 33 11 **Fax:** (41) 43 284 63 11
Web: www.swisslife.com; www.swisslife.com

HISTORICAL FINANCIALS

Company Type: Public

Income Statement FYE: December 31

	REVENUE ($ mil.)	NET INCOME ($ mil.)	NET PROFIT MARGIN	EMPLOYEES
12/14	20,697	822	4.0%	7,492
12/13	21,841	876	4.0%	6,992
12/12	20,808	100	0.5%	7,046
12/11	18,379	643	3.5%	7,168
12/10	19,068	595	3.1%	7,483
Annual Growth	2.1%	8.4%	—	0.0%

2014 Year-End Financials

Debt ratio: —
Return on equity: 7.5%
Cash ($ mil.): 6,128
Current ratio: —
Long-term debt ($ mil.): —
No. of shares (mil.): 31
Dividends
Yield: 0.0%
Payout: 1.3%
Market value ($ mil.): 376

	STOCK PRICE ($) FY Close	P/E High	P/E Low	PER SHARE ($) Earnings	Dividends	Book Value
12/14	11.80	1	0	24.37	0.32	404.36
12/13	10.45	1	0	27.18	0.26	314.77
12/12	5.80	—	—	3.12	0.27	350.28
12/11	5.80	1	0	20.06	0.33	304.53
12/10	6.88	0	0	18.56	0.10	247.93
Annual Growth	14.4%	—	—	7.0%	32.5%	13.0%

Swiss Life Insurance & Pension Co. (Switzerland)

Auditors: PricewaterhouseCoopers AG

LOCATIONS

HQ: Swiss Life Insurance & Pension Co. (Switzerland)
General Guisan-Quai 40, P.O. Box 2831, Zurich CH-8022
Phone: (41) 43 284 33 11
Web: www.swisslife.com

HISTORICAL FINANCIALS

Company Type: Public

Income Statement FYE: December 31

	REVENUE ($ mil.)	NET INCOME ($ mil.)	NET PROFIT MARGIN	EMPLOYEES
12/14	20,697	822	4.0%	7,492
12/13	21,841	876	4.0%	6,992
12/12	20,808	100	0.5%	7,046
12/11	18,379	643	3.5%	7,168
12/10	19,068	595	3.1%	7,483
Annual Growth	2.1%	8.4%	—	0.0%

2014 Year-End Financials

Debt ratio: —
Return on equity: 7.5%
Cash ($ mil.): 6,128
Current ratio: —
Long-term debt ($ mil.): —
No. of shares (mil.): 31
Dividends
Yield: —
Payout: —
Market value ($ mil.): —

Swiss Re Ltd

Auditors: PricewaterhouseCoopers AG

LOCATIONS

HQ: Swiss Re Ltd.
Mythenquai 50/60, PO Box, Zurich 8022
Phone: (41) 43 285 2121 **Fax:** (41) 43 285 2999
Web: www.swissre.com

HISTORICAL FINANCIALS

Company Type: Public

Income Statement FYE: December 31

	REVENUE ($ mil.)	NET INCOME ($ mil.)	NET PROFIT MARGIN	EMPLOYEES
12/14	37,347	3,569	9.6%	12,224
12/13	36,902	4,511	12.2%	11,574
12/12	33,624	4,257	12.7%	11,193
12/11	28,083	2,626	9.4%	10,788
12/10	28,835	1,980	6.9%	10,362
Annual Growth	6.7%	15.9%	—	4.2%

2014 Year-End Financials

Debt ratio: 7.0%
Return on equity: 10.3%
Cash ($ mil.): 7,471
Current ratio: 11.02
Long-term debt ($ mil.): 12,615
No. of shares (mil.): 342
Dividends
Yield: 20.4%
Payout: 95.8%
Market value ($ mil.): 28,940

	STOCK PRICE ($) FY Close	P/E High	P/E Low	PER SHARE ($) Earnings	Dividends	Book Value
12/14	84.57	9	7	9.39	9.00	105.00
12/13	92.38	7	6	11.89	8.03	96.30
12/12	72.30	6	4	11.06	3.29	99.08
12/11	50.55	8	5	7.49	0.00	86.33
Annual Growth	18.7%	—	—	5.8%	—	5.0%

T&D Holdings Inc

No mystery in a name here: T&D Holdings serves as the holding company for Japanese insurance companies Taiyo Life and Daido Life. Combined the companies constitute one of Japan's top life insurers. Taiyo Life gears its products to individuals while Daido Life's products are targeted toward small businesses. Another subsidiary T&D Financial Life sells whole life policies through financial institutions the likes of banks securities firms and insurance shop agents. Other businesses under the T&D umbrella include T&D Asset Management T&D Customer Services (administrative services) and Pet & Family (pet insurance) and T&D Information Systems (computer processing).

Operations

T&D Holdings' Taiyo Life division which accounts for 40% of the holding company's annual revenues serves households with comprehensive life products including death benefits and medical or nursing care coverage. Meanwhile the Daido Life unit (another 40% of sales) focuses on the sale of term life insurance and illness policies through business accounts. The third-largest business unit T&D Financial Life sells whole life policies.

Geographic Reach

The company operates in Japan.

Sales and Marketing

The operating units of T&D Holdings use targeted sales techniques. With a focus on selling to housewives and middle-aged women Taiyo Life employs a sales force made up of some 8600 women (similar in age to their target market base) who visit homes to present tailor-made coverage options. Daido Life gears its marketing efforts towards small and midsized businesses by partnering with enterprise associations (such as the National Federation of Corporate Taxpayers Association); it has some 3800 in-house sales representatives. The company's T&D Financial Life unit markets through a network of some 120 agencies including financial institutions.

Financial Performance

In fiscal 2014 (ended March) revenue decreased 14% to ¥2085 billion as new policy sales in the Taiyo Life and Daido Life units declined. The decline in new policies primarily reflected the impact of an increase in insurance premiums in 2013. It was partially offset by an increase in revenue from T&D Financial Life.

Net income rose 24% to ¥78.9 billion in fiscal 2014 as provisions for policy and other reserves declined and operating expenses decreased. Cash flow from operations fell 75% to ¥159 billion.

Strategy

T&D Holdings is seeking to grow by branching out beyond its traditional market segments. Its Taiyo Life unit is working to expand policy sales by marketing policies geared at men and children. Daido Life is adding products for business owners such as living protection coverage while T&D Financial Life is introducing new products for bereaved families and retirees. The group is also seeking to expand its international operations.

T&D Holdings is also growing its operations into the provision of short-term small-amount policies for pet shops. The company seeks to expand in new and existing business fields through alliances and acquisitions as well.

In 2014 Daido Life launched a new whole life product Life Gift which meets the growing demand for inheritance planning as Japan's population ages.

Company Background

T&D Holdings was formed through the merger of Taiyo Life and Daido Life in 2004. The companies first began working together through an alliance formed in 1999.

EXECUTIVES

President and Representative Director, Kenji Nakagome, age 62
Senior Executive Officer and Director Finance and Accounting Department, Tamiji Matsumoto, age 61
EVP and Representative Director Group Planning Department, Sonosuke Usui
Senior Executive Officer and Director, Terunori Yokoyama, age 62
Senior Managing Executive Officer and Director Daido Life, Masahiro Ueda
Managing Executive Officer and Director Taiyo Life, Kouichi Seike
Auditors: Ernst & Young ShinNihon LLC

LOCATIONS

HQ: T&D Holdings Inc
1-2-3 Kaigan, Minato-ku, Tokyo 105-0022
Phone: (81) 3 3434 9151 **Fax:** (81) 3 3434 9055
Web: www.td-holdings.co.jp

PRODUCTS/OPERATIONS

2014 Sales

	% of total
Daido Life	40
Taiyo Life	37
T&D Financial Life	20
Other	3
Total	**100**

Selected Subsidiaries and Affiliates

AIC Private Equity Fund General Partner Ltd
Alternative Investment Capital Ltd.
Daido Life Insurance Company
Daido Management Service Co. Ltd.
Nihon System Shuno Inc.
Pet & Family Small-amount Short-term Insurance Company
T&D Asset Management Cayman Inc.
T&D Asset Management Co. Ltd.
T&D Confirm Ltd.
T&D Customer Services Co. Ltd.
T&D Financial Life Insurance Company
T&D Information System Ltd.
T&D Lease Co. Ltd.
Taiyo Credit Guarantee Co. Ltd.
Taiyo Life Insurance Company
Toyo Insurance Agency Co. Ltd.
Zenkoku Business Center Co. Ltd.

COMPETITORS

Aflac
American Life Insurance
Asahi Mutual Life
Dai-ichi Life
Fukoku Mutual
Gibraltar Life Insurance
Meiji Yasuda Life
Mitsui Life
Nippon Life Insurance
Sumitomo Life

HISTORICAL FINANCIALS

Company Type: Public

Income Statement FYE: March 31

	ASSETS ($ mil.)	NET INCOME ($ mil.)	INCOME AS % OF ASSETS	EMPLOYEES
03/15	122,226	785	0.6%	19,418
03/14	133,736	765	0.6%	19,868
03/13	145,269	677	0.5%	20,497
03/12	156,784	326	0.2%	20,982
03/11	153,861	288	0.2%	21,732
Annual Growth	(5.6%)	28.5%	—	(2.8%)

2015 Year-End Financials

Return on assets: 0.6%
Return on equity: 7.9%
Long-term debt ($ mil.): —
No. of shares (mil.): 664
Sales ($ mil): 20,106
Dividends
Yield: 1.7%
Payout: —
Market value ($ mil.): 4,621

	STOCK PRICE ($) FY Close	P/E High/Low		PER SHARE ($) Earnings	Dividends	Book Value
03/15	6.95	—	—	1.18	0.12	16.86
03/14	6.21	—	—	1.14	0.00	14.70
03/13	5.90	—	—	1.00	0.00	14.50
03/12	5.43	—	—	0.48	0.00	12.39
03/11	12.21	—	—	0.42	0.00	11.03
Annual Growth	(13.1%)	—	—	29.1%	—	11.2%

Taiwan Cooperative Bank

Taiwan Cooperative Bank is Taking Care of Business. Known as TCB for short the bank was founded in 1946 during the Japanese occupation of Taiwan to foster the country's burgeoning cooperative system. Today the bank still provides financing for economic development particularly for cooperative enterprises and small and middle-market businesses with a focus on the fishing and farming sectors. It also provides standard banking services such as deposits and financial management to businesses and consumers. TCB has more than 300 branches in its home country plus six offices in the US China Belgium and Philippines. The Taiwanese government owns nearly 40% of the bank.

In late 2009 TCB formed a life insurance joint venture with BNP Paribas. The program strengthened the bank's foothold in the insurance market by taking advantage of its branch network. The deal expanded TCB's offerings to include savings-linked insurance products and mortgage insurance. Shortly afterwards TCB and BNP announced plans for another joint venture –this time focused on asset management services. TCB's stake in both ventures is 51% to BNP's 49%.

EXECUTIVES

President, Tsan Chang Liao
Auditors: Deloitte & Touche

LOCATIONS

HQ: Taiwan Cooperative Bank
No. 77, Guan Qian Road, Jhongjheng District, Taipei 100
Phone: (886) 2 2311 8811 **Fax:** (886) 2 2375 2954
Web: www.tcb-bank.com.tw

COMPETITORS

Chang Hwa Bank
Fubon Financial
Hua Nan Financial
SinoPac Holdings
Taiwan Business Bank

HISTORICAL FINANCIALS

Company Type: Public

Income Statement

FYE: December 31

	ASSETS ($ mil.)	NET INCOME ($ mil.)	INCOME AS % OF ASSETS	EMPLOYEES
12/14	91,920	319	0.3%	8,437
12/13	97,967	269	0.3%	8,476
12/12*	98,462	254	0.3%	8,563
01/12	90,991	0	—	0
12/11	90,932	250	0.3%	8,697
Annual Growth	0.4%	8.5%	—	(1.0%)

*Fiscal year change

2014 Year-End Financials

Return on assets: 0.3%
Return on equity: 6.9%
Long-term debt ($ mil.): —
No. of shares (mil.): —
Sales ($ mil): 1,980
Dividends
Yield: —
Payout: —
Market value ($ mil.): —

Taiwan Power Co.

Taiwan Power (Taipower) is looking to get by with a little help from its friends. With a generating capacity of more than 38080 MW the state-owned utility serves nearly 12 million industrial commercial and residential customers. Thermal sources (coal oil and liquefied natural gas) fuel most of Taipower's plants; nuclear energy and hydroelectric sources make up the balance. Unable to meet Taiwan's power needs on its own the utility has opened its market to independent power producers allowing companies to build power plants and sell to Taipower. Taipower has resumed construction on the nation's fourth nuclear plant. The Taiwan government has announced plans to privatize Taipower (it owned 97% in 2009).

To reduce carbon emissions Taipower is mulling the benefits of wind. The company is planning wind-generated electricity projects that could cost TWD 120 billion. Taipower already operates 30 wind turbines and is planning another 200 on Taiwan and the island of Penghu in the Taiwan Strait.

It is also experimenting with the commercial use of solar power systems and hydrogen fuel cells.

EXECUTIVES

President, Chun Chiu Huang
Auditors: KPMG

LOCATIONS

HQ: Taiwan Power Co.
242 Roosevelt Road, Section 3, Taipei 100
Phone: (886) 2 2365 1234 **Fax:** (886) 2 2365 0037
Web: www.taipower.com.tw

HISTORICAL FINANCIALS

Company Type: Public

Income Statement

FYE: December 31

	REVENUE ($ mil.)	NET INCOME ($ mil.)	NET PROFIT MARGIN	EMPLOYEES
12/14	20,298	441	2.2%	26,533
12/13	19,878	(571)	—	26,629
12/12	18,855	(2,761)	—	27,082
12/11	17,270	(1,430)	—	27,261
12/10	17,566	(1,232)	—	26,828
Annual Growth	3.7%	—	—	(0.3%)

2014 Year-End Financials

Debt ratio: 1.8%
Return on equity: 7.4%
Cash ($ mil.): 70
Current ratio: 0.18
Long-term debt ($ mil.): 24,346
No. of shares (mil.): —
Dividends
Yield: —
Payout: —
Market value ($ mil.): —

Taiwan Semiconductor Manufacturing Co., Ltd.

If you're absolutely fabless this company is for you. Taiwan Semiconductor Manufacturing Company (TSMC) is the first and largest dedicated silicon foundry (contract semiconductor manufacturer) in the world with nine plants in Asia and one in the US. Logic semiconductors make up about 75% of sales while mixed-signal products are most of the rest. Largely a wafer fabricator TSMC makes chips for semiconductor and systems companies who don't have their own manufacturing facilities (accounting for about 85% of sales). Those companies include AMD Broadcom NVIDIA and QUALCOMM. Remaining sales come from integrated device manufacturers including STMicroelectronics and Texas Instruments. The company gets about 69% of its sales from customers in the US.

Operations

While wafer manufacturing makes up about 90% of sales TSMC's remaining sales come mainly from fabricating masks –a kind of silkscreen used to expose silicon wafers to a certain light pattern –and it also provides services such as design probing and testing and assembly. Constituting its largest-selling product logic semiconductors are standard logic devices such as microprocessors microcontrollers digital signal processors graphic chips and chip sets. The bulk of its remaining business mixed-signal semiconductors is used in systems for data storage and program instructions such as SRAM DRAM and flash memory.

Financial Performance

The company's revenue and net income enjoyed robust year-over-year growth. Revenue increased more than 20% in 2014 from 2013 on increased demand for computer and memory devices from customers –wafer shipments were 18% higher. Its net income jumped more than 30% bolstered by the revenue increase. Cash flow from operations also had a healthy gain up 21% in 2014 from 2013.

Strategy

TSMC continues to increase the capacity and improve the efficiency of its wafer fabrication processes but it is also seeking long-term growth opportunities outside the traditional foundry business model.

But as semiconductor fabrication plants (factories) become more expensive to build more chip companies are concentrating on design and contracting manufacturing to TSMC and rivals like United Microelectronics Corp. Intel still makes its own chips and companies such as NXP make most of their own. But as a leading contractor TSMC must keep pace with the changing technologies for making chips.

In 2014 about 9% of revenue came from the company's newer 20-nanometer wafers which are more complex and carry a higher price. The older more established 28-nanometer wafer were 33% of revenue in 2014 up from 30% in 2013. The company is working on smaller sizes including a 7-nanometer wafer. In 2015 TSMC development for the 7-nanometer technology is to focus on selection of transistor architecture baseline manufacturing process setup for both transistors and interconnects and reliability evaluations.

TSMC hit the off switch on its LED lighting business in early 2015 when it sold TSMC Solid State Lighting to Epistar the largest manufacturer of LED epitaxial wafers and dies. The deal was structured so that no employee of TSMC SSL will lose employment.

HISTORY

Early History

The big foundries –including TSMC's Taiwanese archrival United Microelectronics Corporation (UMC) –played a major role in the growth of the worldwide fabless semiconductor industry in the 21st century. Foundries aim to save clients the costs and time associated with building expensive wafer fabrication plants (fabs) of their own. Their services are especially vital for fabless companies whose entire business model is predicated on outsourcing all manufacturing.

Morris Chang learned early to adapt to rapid change. The future founder and chairman of Taiwan Semiconductor Manufacturing Company (TSMC) lived in six cities before age 18 as his family fled the ravages of the Sino-Japanese War and WWII in China. Chang immigrated to the US to attend MIT and Stanford where he ultimately earned a Ph.D. in electrical engineering.

In 25 years at Texas Instruments (TI) Chang worked his way up from the ranks of technical management into the executive suite. In 1983 he resigned from TI to become CEO of General Instrument but in 1985 the Taiwanese government recruited him to head its Industrial Technology Research Institute (ITRI). He remained chairman of ITRI from 1988 to 1994.

Working from his position at ITRI Chang became chairman of contract electronics manufacturer United Microelectronics Corporation (UMC) in 1987. Also that year he founded TSMC as the world's first dedicated contract semiconductor manufacturer –the first silicon foundry. Chang's pioneering role in the foundry industry has earned him many accolades including the first-ever Robert N. Noyce Medal of the Institute of Electrical and Electronics Engineers and the first-ever Exemplary Leadership award (subsequently named in his honor) of the Fabless Semiconductor Association (now the Global Semiconductor Alliance). Known for his analytical mind Chang was once ranked among the top 1000 players of contract bridge in the world.

TSMC became profitable within 15 months of its founding. Throughout the 1990s it continued to be among industry leaders both in production capacity and in deployment of cutting-edge technology.

EXECUTIVES

President TSMC Japan, Makoto Onodera

President and Co-CEO, Mark Liu
SVP and CIO, Stephen T. (Steve) Tso
SVP and CFO, Lora Ho
President TSMC Europe, Maria Marced
President TSMC China, L.C. Tu
SVP and President TSMC North America, Rick Cassidy, age 64
VP Research and Development; CTO, Jack Sun
President and Co-CEO, C.C. Wei
VP Operations Mainstream Fabs, J.K. Lin
VP Operations 300mm Fabs, J.K. Wang
Vice Chairman, F. C. Tseng
Chairman, Morris Chang, age 84
Auditors: Deloitte & Touche

LOCATIONS

HQ: Taiwan Semiconductor Manufacturing Co., Ltd.
No. 8, Li-Hsin Road 6, Hsinchu Science Park, Hsinchu 300
Phone: (886) 3 563 6688 Fax: (886) 3 563 7000
Web: www.tsmc.com

PRODUCTS/OPERATIONS

Selected Services

Semiconductor photomasks (circuit pattern guides)
- Design
- Manufacturing

Semiconductor wafers (integrated circuits and other semiconductor devices)
- Computer-aided design
- Manufacturing
- Packaging

2014 Sales

	% of Total
Fabless semiconductor companies/Systems companies	85
Integrated Device	15
Others	0
Total	100

2014 Sales

	% of Total
North America	69
Asia Pacific	13
China	7
EMEA	6
Japan	5
Total	100

2014 Sales

	% of Total
Logic	75
Mixed-Signal	24
Others	1
Total	100

Fabless semiconductor companies
- Advanced Micro Devices
- Altera
- Broadcom
- Marvell
- MediaTek
- NVIDIA
- QUALCOMM

Integrated device manufacturers
- LSI Corp.
- STMicroelectronics
- Texas Instruments

COMPETITORS

Advanced Semiconductor Engineering
Advanced Semiconductor Manufacturing
ChipMOS
Dai Nippon Printing
Dongbu HiTek
GLOBALFOUNDRIES
Grace Semiconductor
MagnaChip
Photronics
SK Hynix
SMIC
Samsung Electronics
Shanghai Hua Hong NEC
Silterra
Toppan Photomasks
Tower Semiconductor
UMC
Winbond Electronics
X-FAB Silicon Foundries

HISTORICAL FINANCIALS

Company Type: Public

Income Statement

FYE: December 31

	REVENUE ($ mil.)	NET INCOME ($ mil.)	NET PROFIT MARGIN	EMPLOYEES
12/14	24,090	8,031	33.3%	43,591
12/13	20,020	6,169	30.8%	40,483
12/12	17,443	5,725	32.8%	39,267
12/11	14,090	4,427	31.4%	35,457
12/10	14,417	5,553	38.5%	33,232
Annual Growth	13.7%	9.7%	—	7.0%

2014 Year-End Financials

Debt ratio: 0.5%
Return on equity: 27.4%
Cash ($ mil.): 11,320
Current ratio: 2.79
Long-term debt ($ mil.): 6,774
No. of shares (mil.): —
Dividends
Yield: 1.7%
Payout: 122.0%
Market value ($ mil.): —

	STOCK PRICE ($) FY Close	P/E High/Low	PER SHARE ($) Earnings	Dividends	Book Value
12/14	22.38	2 2	0.31	0.40	1.25
12/13	17.44	3 2	0.24	0.40	1.08
12/12	17.16	3 2	0.22	0.40	0.96
12/11	12.91	3 2	0.17	0.40	0.80
12/10	12.54	2 2	0.21	0.37	0.76
Annual Growth	15.6%	—	9.7%	1.8%	13.1%

Talanx AG

Talanx Group offers its customers an army of protection. The Germany-based insurance group is the third-largest in the country. Talanx operates in property/casualty insurance life insurance and financial services as well as reinsurance in both the property/casualty and life categories. Brands include HDI and HDI Direkt which provides insurance policies to both private and industrial customers; Aspecta a provider of individual insurance and investment products; Hannover Re one of the world's largest reinsurers; and fund guarantor and asset manager AmpegaGirling among others. Talanx has operations in 150 countries worldwide. Talanx is part of HDI Haftpflichtverband der Deutschen Industrie.

Operations

The company reports its business in five segments: industrial lines retail Germany retail international non-life reinsurance and life/health reinsurance. Non-life reinsurance leads the pack with 28% of revenue; retail Germany (24% of sales) and life/health reinsurance (22% of sales) follow.

The non-life reinsurance division is primarily handled by subsidiary Hannover Re. Retail Germany (Talanx Deutschland) concentrates on serving the retail and commercial sectors with property/casualty life and bancassurance while retail international does the same in 14 countries abroad (and has more than 8 million clients). The industrial lines division is led by HDI-Gerling Industrie Versicherung which offers individual customer support services from about a dozen locations across the nation.

The group also provides asset management services.

Geographic Reach

Europe accounts for about 65% of premiums written with Germany holding the majority across the board. The US is the company's largest non-European region.

Major operations outside of Germany are located in Austria Hungary Italy Spain Poland Russia and Turkey. The company also has operations in the Americas Africa and the Asia/Pacific region. Talanx prefers to operate semi-independent businesses in local markets and expands by acquiring or opening divisions in new territories. It operates in 150 countries.

Japanese insurer Meiji Yasuda Life Insurance has been expanding into Europe using Talanx as a springboard; it took a 7% stake in Talanx during the company's 2012 IPO. The two companies use a joint venture with a Talanx subsidiary as the framework to grow in Central and Eastern European markets.

Sales and Marketing

Talanx uses both its own sales agents and offices and brokers and independent agents as well as specialized cooperatives in its various markets. Its primary insurance units also advertise via television ads sponsorships and through other channels.

Financial Performance

Revenue grew 3% to 23.8 billion in 2014 as most segments reported increased earnings (with the exception of corporate operations). Leading the growth was industrial lines which rose 12% and retail international which rose 6% on the success of Italian subsidiary HDI Assicurazioni.

Net income rose 5% to 769 million due to the higher revenue and investment income which improved partly as a result of the sale of the remaining shares in Swiss Life.

Strategy

Growth is the name of the game at Talanx and the company plans to accomplish by organic and acquisitive means. The company has a goal of generating half of its primary insurance premiums from outside of Germany by 2018. Key target areas include Central and Eastern Europe (CEE) and Latin America. In 2015 it acquired Chilean insurer Inversiones Magallenes and in 2014 its industrial lines division added a new unit in Brazil. Streamlining its Eastern European retail operations Talanx sold subsidiaries in Bulgaria and Ukraine in early 2015.

The company also focuses on improving profitability and customer relations especially in its retail divisions.

In the financial services arena Talanx entered into a joint venture with NORD/LB Norddeutsche Landesbank and Bankhaus Lampe in 2015; Talanx holds a 45% stake in the venture which is named Caplantic Atlernative Assets.

Mergers and Acquisitions

In 2014 the company acquired Inversiones Magallenes in Chile for approximately 180 million.

Background

The company traces its roots back over a century but began operating as a holding company under the name HDI Beteilgung AG in 1996. In 1998 it was renamed Talanx which is a blend of the words "talent" and "phalanx" (a Greek word referring to a battle formation).

In 2012 the company completed its IPO and began trading on Germany's Frankfurt Stock Exchange. The company raised about 817 million which it used to grow its business. Post-IPO HDI Haftpflichtverband der Deutschen Industrie maintained a 79% stake in Talanx.

EXECUTIVES

Chairman Management Board, Herbert K. Haas, age 61
Member Management Board, Immo Querner
Member Management Board Reinsurance, Ulrich Wallin, age 54

Member Management Board, Thomas Noth
Member Management Group Retail Germany, Heinz-Peter Ro
Chairman Supervisory Board, Wolf-Dieter Baumgartl, age 72
Deputy Chairman Supervisory Board, Eckhard Rohkamm
Deputy Chairman Supervisory Board, Ralf Rieger
Auditors: KPMG Deutsche Treuhand Gesellschaft

LOCATIONS

HQ: Talanx AG
Riethorst 2, Hannover 30659
Phone: (49) 511 3747 0 **Fax:** (49) 511 3747 2525
Web: www.talanx.com

2014 Sales

	% of total
Europe	
Germany	32
UK	9
Central and Eastern Europe including Turkey	8
Rest of Europe	15
North America	
US	12
Rest of North America	3
Asia & Australia	12
Latin America	7
Africa	2
Total	100

PRODUCTS/OPERATIONS

2014 Sales

	% of total
Non-life reinsurance	28
Life/health reinsurance	22
Retail Germany	24
Retail international	16
Industrial lines	10
Total	100

COMPETITORS

AEGON
AXA
Allianz
ERGO
General Re
Generali
ING
Munich Re Group
Swiss Re
Zurich Insurance Group

HISTORICAL FINANCIALS

Company Type: Public

Income Statement FYE: December 31

	REVENUE ($ mil.)	NET INCOME ($ mil.)	NET PROFIT MARGIN	EMPLOYEES
12/14	36,000	934	2.6%	21,371
12/13	38,938	1,049	2.7%	21,529
12/12	35,397	830	2.3%	20,887
12/11	31,411	672	2.1%	17,061
12/10	31,363	294	0.9%	16,874
Annual Growth	3.5%	33.5%	—	6.1%

2014 Year-End Financials

Debt ratio: —
Return on equity: 10.1%
Cash ($ mil.): 2,607
Current ratio: —
Long-term debt ($ mil.): —
No. of shares (mil.): 252
Dividends
Yield: —
Payout: —
Market value ($ mil.): —

Tata Motors Ltd

Tata Motors enjoys giant-sized growth thanks to its Nano cars. The company –India's largest automobile maker by sales –makes buses trucks tractor-trailers passenger cars (Indica Indigo Jaguar Land Rover Safari Sumo and the popular micro car Nano) light commercial vehicles and utility vehicles. It also makes construction equipment and provides IT services. Tata Motors sells through more than 1000 dealers in India as well as exports vehicles to countries in Africa Asia Europe the Middle East and South America. In addition the company distributes Fiat-brand cars in India through its Tata-Fiat dealer network.

Geographic Reach

Through subsidiaries and affiliated companies Tata Motors has operations in India the UK South Korea Thailand Spain and South Africa. China is its largest market representing 28% of its total sales. India the UK and the US follow with 16% 12% and 11% of total sales respectively. Other European countries account for 13% of total sales while the rest of the world contributes roughly 20%.

Operations

Tata Motors' business segments are primarily its automotive operations which develop design manufacture assemble and sell vehicles and provide financing. The automotive segment is divided into Tata and other brand vehicles as well as Jaguar Land Rover. Other operations include information technology or IT services and machine tools and factory automation products and services.

Tata Motors also has franchisee and joint venture assembly operations in Bangladesh Ukraine and Senegal.

Sales and Marketing

Tata Motors' vehicles are sold through a network of authorized dealers and service centers across the Indian market and a network of distributors and local dealers in international markets.

Financial Performance

Tata Motors has seen significant growth over the last five years with 2014 representing its best year to date. From 2013 to 2014 its total revenues in rupees increased by 24% (or 13% when converted into US dollar) and its net income surged by 46% (34% in US dollar).

The historic growth for 2014 was fueled by a spike in sales from its Range Rover and Jaguar vehicles. The increase was also attributable to an indirect tax incentive by Jaguar Land Rover.

Strategy

Tata Motors is a leader in the only growth area for the automotive market in recent years –India –which gives it a slight edge over competitors in the region. It is also extending its commercial vehicles penetration into countries like Bangladesh Nepal Sri Lanka and Bhutan.

In 2015 Tata Motors launched four new next-generation PRIMA heavy commercial vehicles for the very first time in Bangladesh with partner Nitol Motors Limited. The next-generation Tata PRIMA is a combination of power fuel efficiency superior technology and safety. Also in 2015 Tata Motors launched the GenX Nano range its new compact hatch. The new GenX Nano comes with advanced technological features which strengthens its value as a city car.

Company Background

In 2008 Tata Motors bought the Jaguar and Land Rover brands from Ford for about $2.3 billion. It took over the two struggling businesses in an effort to diversify its customer base by expanding its product portfolio from commercial and small passenger vehicles to premium cars.

EXECUTIVES

CEO and Managing Director Jaguar Land Rover, Ralf Speth, age 60
President and Head Engineering Research Centre, Tim Leverton
President and CFO, C. Ramakrishnan, $14,178,000 total compensation
Executive Director and Head Commercial Vehicles Business Unit, Ravindra Pisharody, $8,085,002 total compensation
Executive Director and Head Quality, Satish B. Borwankar
Head of Business International Passenger and Commercial Vehicles, Ranjit Yadav
SVP and Head Purchasing and Supply Chain, Venkatram Mamillapalle
SVP and Head Commercial Passenger Vehicle Business Unit, Ankush Arora
President Passenger Vehicle Business Unit, Mayank Pareek
CEO and Managing Director, Guenter Butschek, age 55
Chairman, Cyrus P. Mistry, age 47
Auditors: Deloitte Haskins & Sells

LOCATIONS

HQ: Tata Motors Ltd
Bombay House, 24, Homi Mody Street, Mumbai, Maharashtra 400 001
Phone: (91) 22 6665 8282 **Fax:** (91) 22 6665 7799
Web: www.tatamotors.com

2014 Sales

	% of total
China	28
India	16
Europe	
UK	12
Other countries	13
US	11
Other regions	20
Total	100

Selected Subsidiaries

Concorde Motors (India) Limited
Jaguar Land Rover PLC-UK
PT Tata Indonesia
Sheba Properties Ltd-India
TAL Manufacturing Solutions Ltd-India
Tata Daewoo Commercial Vehicle Co Ltd- South Korea
Tata Hispano Motors Carrocera SA- Spain
Tata Marcopolo Motors Ltd-India.
Tata Motors (SA) Proprietary Ltd -South Africa.
Tata Motors European Technical center PLC -UK
Tata Motors Finance Ltd -India
Tata Motors Insurance Broking and Advisory Services Ltd-India
Tata Motors(Thailand) Ltd
Tata Precision Industries Pts Ltd-Singapore
Tata Technologies Ltd-India
TML Distribution Company Ltd-India
TML Drivelines Ltd-India
TML Holdings Pte Ltd- Singapore

PRODUCTS/OPERATIONS

2014 Sales

	% of total
Jaguar Land Rover	80
Tata and other brand vehicles including financing	19
Others	1
Total	100

Selected Products and Services

Light commercial vehicles
- Ace
- Magic
- Winger

Medium and heavy commercial vehicles
- Paradiso
- Prima

Passenger cars
- Indica
- Indica Vista

Indigo eCS
Indigo Manza
Jaguar
Nano

Utility vehicles
Aria
Land Rover
Range Rover
Sumo
Safari
Venture
Xenon XT

COMPETITORS

BMW
Bajaj Auto
Caterpillar
Daimler
FCA US
Fiat Chrysler
Ford Motor
Fuji Heavy Industries
General Motors
Hindustan Motors
Honda
Hyundai Motor
Isuzu
Kia Motors
Komatsu
Mahindra
Mazda
Nissan
Renault
Suzuki Motor
Toyota
Volkswagen
Volvo

HISTORICAL FINANCIALS

Company Type: Public

Income Statement FYE: March 31

	REVENUE ($ mil.)	NET INCOME ($ mil.)	NET PROFIT MARGIN	EMPLOYEES
03/15	41,974	2,051	4.9%	73,485
03/14	39,000	2,176	5.6%	68,889
03/13	34,813	1,633	4.7%	62,716
03/12	32,724	2,273	6.9%	58,618
03/11	27,635	1,646	6.0%	26,214
Annual Growth	11.0%	5.7%	—	29.4%

2015 Year-End Financials

Debt ratio: 0.4%
Return on equity: 22.0%
Cash ($ mil.): 4,825
Current ratio: 1.00
Long-term debt ($ mil.): 8,711
No. of shares (mil.): —
Dividends
Yield: 0.3%
Payout: 21.8%
Market value ($ mil.): —

	STOCK PRICE ($) FY Close	P/E High/Low		PER SHARE ($) Earnings	Dividends	Book Value
03/15	45.06	1	1	0.63	0.14	2.66
03/14	35.41	1	1	0.68	0.13	3.25
03/13	24.41	1	1	0.51	0.34	2.14
03/12	26.97	1	0	0.71	0.37	2.03
03/11	27.79	8	3	0.11	0.30	1.48
Annual Growth	12.8%	—	—	54.7%	(17.1%)	15.8%

Tata Steel Ltd.

Tata Steel is India's largest private sector steel company. The company's steel-making and finishing facilities have the capacity to produce nearly 30 million tons of crude steel a year. Tata Steel's products include hot and cold rolled coils and sheets galvanized sheets tubes wire rods rings and bearings. Its domestic facilities are located in Jamshedpur in eastern India and Tata Steel's international operations include UK-based subsidiary Tata Steel Europe Singapore's NatSteel and Tata Steel Thailand. The company also owns interests in coal and iron projects that supply the steel maker with raw materials.

Geographic Reach

Tata Steel has operations in 26 countries and a commercial presence in more than 50. About 32% of its net sales come from India. Other markets include Europe (52%) Asia (11%) and other regions (5%).

Operations

Tata Steel is one of the largest steel makers in the world. Products include hot and cold rolled coils and sheets galvanized sheets tubes wire rods rings and bearings. Steel sales primarily in India account for the bulk of the company's business although it also owns interests in coal and iron projects.

Financial Performance

Total Steel's revenues from 2014 to 2015 decreased due to fewer sales from China Europe and Thailand. Throughout 2015 the company's bottom line was negatively affected by slow growth in China low global steel prices and higher pension payments at Tata Steel UK.

Its Indian operations in 2015 were adversely impacted by the regulatory uncertainties in the mining sector. For the first time in its history Tata Steel closed several of its critical mines for varying periods. This led to supply and production disruptions that significantly impacted its cost structure.

Strategy

To combat stagnant growth in Europe and China Tata Steel is entering new segment markets restructuring its operations and cutting costs and introducing new products to diversified markets. The company's bright spot remains India: that country's government is aiming to triple its steel capacity to 300 million metric tons by 2025 in response to surging growth in the manufacturing sector.

Company Background

Tat Steel was founded in 1907 as Asia's first private sector integrated steel company.

EXECUTIVES

Group CFO, Koushik Chatterjee, age 48
Managing Director Tata Steel India and South East Asia, T. V. Narendran, age 50
Chief Group Information Services, Shreekant Mokashi
Managing Director and CEO Tata Steel Europe, Karl-Ulrich Koehler
CTO, Ashok Kumar
Chairman, Cyrus P. Mistry, age 47
Auditors: Messrs Deloitte Haskins & Sells

LOCATIONS

HQ: Tata Steel Ltd.
Bombay House, 24 Homi Mody Street, Mumbai 400 001
Phone: (91) 22 6665 8282 **Fax:** (91) 22 6665 7724
Web: www.tatasteel.com

2015 Sales

	% of total
Outside India	68
Within India	32
Total	100

PRODUCTS/OPERATIONS

2015 Sales

	% of total
Steel	91
Others	7
Unallocable	1
Other income	1
Total	100

Selected Operations

Steel
Ferroalloys & Minerals (chrome mines & manufacturing ferro chrome & ferro manganese)
Bearings (ball bearings clutch release bearings & double row self-aligning bearings)
Tubes
Wire

COMPETITORS

ArcelorMittal
Baosteel
Essar Group
JFE Holdings
Kobe Steel
Mitsubishi Materials
Nippon Steel & Sumitomo Metal Corporation
POSCO
Steel Authority of India
United States Steel

HISTORICAL FINANCIALS

Company Type: Public

Income Statement FYE: March 31

	REVENUE ($ mil.)	NET INCOME ($ mil.)	NET PROFIT MARGIN	EMPLOYEES
03/15	22,432	(627)	—	79,647
03/14	24,836	598	2.4%	80,391
03/13	24,903	(1,300)	—	80,534
03/12	26,431	1,059	4.0%	81,622
03/11	26,787	2,014	7.5%	81,251
Annual Growth	(4.3%)	—	—	(0.5%)

2015 Year-End Financials

Debt ratio: 0.7%
Return on equity: (-10.2%)
Cash ($ mil.): 1,399
Current ratio: 1.17
Long-term debt ($ mil.): 10,500
No. of shares (mil.): 971
Dividends
Yield: —
Payout: —
Market value ($ mil.): —

Telecom Italia SPA

Telecom Italia's wireline unit is Italy's #1 telephone operator with some 4.1 million fixed access lines. It serves Italian customers through millions of broadband and wireless connections. While Telecom Italia does most of its business in Italy Latin America is a key international market. The company provides wholesale network access in South America as well as Italy. Its TIM Brasil subsidiary is a leader in the Brazilian wireless market with more than 64.1 million subscribers; its Argentina subsidiaries cater to 1.6 million broadband subscribers and 18.2 million mobile subscribers.

Geographic Reach

Telecom Italia has a presence in Italy Latin America North America Europe Africa and Asia. It generates about 64% of its revenue from its domestic market (Italy) and the remaining 36% derive from Brazil and Argentina.

Operations

The operating segments of Telecom Italia are organized according to the relative geographical location for the telecommunications business and relative to the specific businesses for the other segments. The market of its main business unit is focused mainly in serving customers in Europe Asia and South America.

In addition subsidiary Telecom Italia Media produces and distributes TV and Web content and Olivetti provides office equipment such as ink-jet printer heads mostly for the banking industry.

Financial Performance

Thanks to growth in foreign markets the company's revenues increased by 9% from 2010 to 2011. Revenues from Brazil were up by 18% as a result of a 26% increase in the market share of mobile lines. Revenue from Argentina increased by 27% in 2011 due to the growth of customers in the fixed and broadband businesses as well as mobile businesses.

Despite this growth Telecom Italia recorded a net loss for 2011 due to the acquisition of goods and services and net impairment losses on non-current assets.

Strategy

Over the last few years the company has been selling off interests not related to its businesses in Italy or Brazil. These deals were also part of Telecom Italia's ongoing effort to sell non-core businesses in order to reduce debt.

Outside Italy the company is focused on bolstering its operations only in Brazil an emerging market that now accounts for almost 20% of revenue. In 2011 it bought AES Atimus a Brazilian subsidiary of US power company AES. AES Atimus operates a 3400-mile fiber optic network in Rio de Janeiro and Sao Paulo. The deal 700 million ($1 billion) was Telecom Italia's largest acquisition in a decade.

In another 2011 acquisition that boosted its Latin American holdings Telecom Italia paid about $145 million to raise its ownership stake in Sofora Telecomunicaciones the holding company which owns Telecom Argentina from 58% to 68%. Closer to home Telecom Italia bought 71% of Italian mobile phone retailer 4G Holding from GIR Srl a company controlled by 4G's CEO 2011. The deal boosted the company's domestic retail presence by 200 shops as it works to get its brand out in front of more wireless customers in a saturated market. GIR retained 29% of 4G Holding.

Ownership

The former state-owned monopoly has one major institutional shareholder. An investment group made up primarily of Italian financial backers known as Telco SpA owns a 22% stake. Telco is made up of Telefónica (46%) Italian insurance giant Generali (31%) investment bank Mediobanca (12%) and commercial bank Intesa Sanpaolo (11%).

HISTORY

After gaining political power in Italy Benito Mussolini began a program of nationalization focusing first on three major banks and their equity portfolios. Included were three local phone companies that became the core of Società Finanziaria Telefonica (STET) created in 1933 to handle Italy's phone services under the state's industrial holding company Istituto per La Ricostruzione Industriale (IRI).

Germany and Italy grew closer in the years leading up to WWII and Italian equipment makers entered a venture with Siemens to make phone equipment. STET came through the war with most of its infrastructure intact and a monopoly on phone service in Italy. Siemens' properties along with those of other equipment makers were taken over by another company TETI which was nationalized and put under STET's control in 1958. This expanded STET's monopoly to include equipment manufacturing.

Italy's industries were increasingly nationalized under IRI. Companies within the IRI family forged alliances with each other and with independent companies which frequently were absorbed into STET.

STET's scope expanded during the 1960s and 1970s to include satellite and data communications but its monopoly was undermined by new technologies such as faxes PCs and teleconferencing. In the technology race among equipment makers STET fell behind. And in a satellite communications era STET's status as a necessary long-distance carrier was threatened. Despite these pressures change did not come easily to STET. State monopolies maintained popular support not only on nationalistic grounds but also because of labor's strong anticompetitive stance.

Anticipating privatization however IRI reorganized STET in 1994 and poured new capital into the company. STET's five telecom companies —SIP (domestic phone operator) Italcable (intercontinental) Telespazio (satellite) SIRM (maritime) and Iritel (domestic long distance) —were merged into one Telecom Italia. Its mobile phone business was spun off as Telecom Italia Mobile (TIM) in 1995.

To end political feuding the government abruptly replaced the heads of STET and Telecom Italia in 1997. Telecom Italia was merged with STET which took the Telecom Italia name and was privatized that year. Berardino Libonati became chairman and Franco Bernabe formerly CEO of oil company ENI took the helm as CEO. The company began taking stakes in foreign telecom companies including mobilkom austria Spanish broadcaster Retevision and —as European Union competition began in 1998 —Telekom Austria.

Erstwhile rival Olivetti launched a hostile takeover bid for Telecom Italia in 1999. Though Telecom Italia tried to fend off the smaller firm with various maneuvers including a proposed merger with Deutsche Telekom Olivetti gained 55% of Telecom Italia. Olivetti CEO Roberto Colaninno took over as chairman and CEO.

That year Telecom Italia sold 50% of Stream its pay TV unit to an investor group led by News Corp. The company also announced plans to spin off and sell a stake in its ISP Tin.it. In 2000 however Telecom Italia instead combined Tin.it with SEAT Pagine Gialle a yellow pages directory publisher and Internet portal operator (spun off from the parent company and sold in 2003). Also that year the company sold off 81% of its telecom equipment unit Italtel and its 49% stake in installations firm Sirti.

In 2001 Colaninno and several other Telecom Italia officials were named as suspects in an investigation of whether the company had violated accounting conflict of interest and share manipulation laws. Colaninno was replaced when tire maker Pirelli and Edizione Holding the parent company of the Benetton Group acquired a 23% stake in Olivetti.

Telecom Italia teamed up with News Corp. to develop the Stream pay TV joint venture renamed Sky Italia. The venture gained a kick-start when the two companies teamed to buy Italian pay-TV business Telepiu from Vivendi Universal in a cash and debt assumption deal that was valued at $871 million. The deal included agreements to drop disputes between Telepiu and Stream. Telecom Italia then sold a 30% stake in the venture to News Corp. It retained a 20% share with News Corp. controlling 80%.

In 2003 the company abandoned plans to acquire phone directories group Pagine Utili from Fininvest in a deal that would have been worth more than $130 million because of protests by Italian regulators who claimed the deal would breach competition laws. It also spun off its international services division starting in 2003 into a separate company Telecom Italia Sparkle which concentrated on services to other fixed-line operators ISPs and international corporations and sold its nearly 62% stake in SEAT Pagine Gialle to an investor group for $3.55 billion.

Once the subsidiary Telecom Italia became the parent company after the 2003 merger with former parent Olivetti. The reorganization simplified a corporate structure that was at best confusing: Olivetti through its Tecnost unit had acquired a controlling 55% stake in Telecom Italia in 1999. Two years later tire maker Pirelli and the Benetton family teamed up to take control of Olivetti. Olivetti's largest shareholder was Olimpia a company owned by Pirelli and the Benetton Group among others.

Because Telecom Italia accounted for more than 95% of the revenues of Olivetti the reorganization also kept the focus on the core business. The merger was met with favor among market watchers and some shareholders although a group of international investors opposed the restructuring.

Reorganization continued at the company and it began selling some international fixed-line assets and putting some wireless operations outside Italy on the market. Disposals included Digitel the Venezuelan wireless carrier to Oswaldo Cisneros' Telvenco in a deal valued at about $425 million. It also sold its 81% stake in Greek wireless carrier Hellas Telecommunications to US-based private equity firms Texas Pacific Group and Apax Partners in a deal valued at $1.4 billion; stakes in Spanish joint venture Auna and satellite unit Telespazio (to Finmeccanica); and in 2005 it sold its holdings in IT services and consulting company Finsiel to Italian outsourcing firm Gruppo COS.

After spurning an offer from AT&T to buy the company Telecom Italia named Pasquale Pistorio chairman in 2007 replacing Guido Rossi who had held the position for only seven months. Telefonica subsequently won control of the company. Later that year Pistorio was replaced by Gabriele Galateri as chairman; Galateri was nominated by another top shareholder Mediobanca.

In 2010 the company began selling off interests not related to its businesses in Italy or Brazil. It sold its 70% stake in Elettra which specialized in laying submarine cables to France Telecom (later renamed Orange) for 20 million ($27 million); its Netherlands fixed-line provider BBNed to Tele2 for 50 million ($64 million); and its German broadband unit HanseNet to Telefónica for the tidy sum of 900 million ($1.2 billion) in cash. The following year Telecom Italia sold its 27% stake in the state-run Cuban phone company ETECSA for $706 million to Rafin SA a financial services firm in that country. Also in 2011 the company sold subsidiary Loquendo to US-based Nuance Communications. The sales were part of Telecom Italia's ongoing effort to sell non-core businesses in order to reduce debt.

EXECUTIVES

CEO, Marco Patuano, age 51
Chairman, Giuseppe Recchi, age 51
Auditors: PricewaterhouseCoopers S.p.A.

LOCATIONS

HQ: Telecom Italia SPA
Corso d' Italia, 41, Rome 00198
Phone: (39) 06 36 88 1
Web: www.telecomitalia.com

2011 Sales

	% of total
Italy	64
Other regions	36
Total	**100**

PRODUCTS/OPERATIONS

2011 Sales

	% of total
Services	93
Equipment sales	7
Total	**100**

COMPETITORS

Am©rica Mvil
BT
Cable & Wireless
Canon
Deutsche Telekom
FastWeb
HP
IBM
KPN
Millicom
Orange
Ricoh Company
Swisscom
Telefnica
Tiscali
Vivo Participa§ıes
Vodafone Omnitel
Wind Telecomunicazioni
Xerox

HISTORICAL FINANCIALS

Company Type: Public

Income Statement

FYE: December 31

	REVENUE ($ mil.)	NET INCOME ($ mil.)	NET PROFIT MARGIN	EMPLOYEES
12/14	27,424	1,640	6.0%	66,025
12/13	33,418	(927)	—	65,623
12/12	40,044	(2,144)	—	83,184
12/11	39,870	(6,112)	—	84,154
12/10	37,973	4,177	11.0%	84,200
Annual Growth	(7.8%)	(20.8%)	—	(5.9%)

2014 Year-End Financials

Debt ratio: 62.8%
Return on equity: 7.6%
Cash ($ mil.): 5,849
Current ratio: 1.11
Long-term debt ($ mil.): 39,291
No. of shares (mil.): —
Dividends
Yield: —
Payout: —
Market value ($ mil.): —

	STOCK PRICE ($) FY Close	P/E High/Low	PER SHARE ($) Earnings	Dividends	Book Value
12/14	10.54	172121	0.09	0.00	1.66
12/13	9.96	— —	(0.04)	0.22	1.77
12/12	9.05	— —	(0.11)	0.45	1.93
12/11	10.65	— —	(0.31)	0.56	2.22
12/10	12.94	96 73	0.21	0.48	2.91
Annual Growth	(5.0%)	— —	(20.6%)	—	(13.1%)

Telefonaktiebolaget LM Ericsson (Sweden)

Ericsson opens all lines of communication. The world's leading maker of mobile broadband infrastructure gear provides the equipment that telecom carriers use to build and expand their networks. The company also provides wireline broadband metro area Ethernet LTE modems and optical transport equipment. Its services unit handles operations ranging from systems integration to network deployment and management. Ericsson's multimedia arm provides content-related products including Internet television systems. The company traces its roots back to 1876 when Lars Magnus Ericsson opened up a telegraph repair shop in Stockholm.

Operations

Ericsson's core business comprises three segments: networks global services and support solutions. The networks segment which accounts for just more than half of the company's sales develops and deploys the latest generation of mobile broadband networks (LTE) and maintains and refines older networks (GSM WCDMA etc.) for its network operator customers. The segment also provides equipment for Internet protocol (IP) microwave transport and core networks including IP routers core routers and switches cables and interconnect products microwave radio links optical transport components radio base stations and wireline network access equipment.

Serving network operators Ericsson's professional services segment supports its customers network operations through its consulting customer support network design and integration and training services. The segment also offers managed services like application hosting and network operations. The growing professional services unit is supported by four global service centers in India China Mexico and Romania. The services segment accounts for about 43% of the company's net sales.

The company's multimedia support solutions segment offers software for consumer-facing applications including mobile and Internet television messaging and music as well as billing support systems for telecommunications network operators. About 6% of sales come through solutions.

Financial Performance

For 2014 Ericsson's revenue was flat and profit dropped 8% from 2013 levels. Sales growth in China the Middle East and India was offset by lower sales in North America (the company's biggest market) and Japan where several larger mobile broadband coverage projects were completed. Reported sales for segments Networks and Global Services were flat compared with 2013 while Support Solutions reported sales grew by 3%. Net income fell as operating costs and finance expenses rose.

Strategy

Ericsson has focused on building its broadband network equipment and services businesses and expanding geographically. The company strengthened its operations in India in a deal with Tata Sky the leading direct-to-the-home (DTH) telecom in India. Ericsson's AVP 4000 System Encoder will deliver Sky Tata content to homes through its video compression platform. Tata Sky will be able to increase the number of channels it offers and the viewing quality. In Africa Ericsson will manage Smile Communications' LTE operations in Nigeria Tanzania Uganda and the Democratic Republic of Congo (DRC). Ericsson will provide localization and customization of Volvo ITS4Mobility intelligent transportation system in Latin America.

In 2013 semiconductor manufacturer STMicroelectronics (ST) sold its stake in ST-Ericsson a now-dissolved joint venture with Ericsson. The two companies split the joint venture's assets with Ericsson taking over the development and sales of the newer LTE multimedia thin modems (which complement its mobile broadband business) and ST taking a portion of the existing ST-Ericsson modem product line. Other assets including a global navigation satellite system were sold to third parties.

As the top company in its industry Ericsson is the target of its competitors. The proposed union of Lucent-Alcatel and Nokia could strengthen their operations. Huawei based in China is another formidable competitor.

In 4Q 2015 Ericsson entered into a strategic partnership with Cisco Systems the leading maker of networking equipment. The companies intend to cooperate to develop products and services in areas such as 5G cloud computing Internet protocol and the Internet of Things. Their goal is to add $1 billion in revenue for each company by 2018. The companies will cooperate on developing networks through reference architectures and joint development systems-based management and control a broad reseller agreement and collaboration in key emerging market segments. Cisco's networking capabilities and increasing development of networking software should complement Ericsson's telecom strengths. It should also strengthen Ericsson in its competition with Lucent-Alcatel-Nokia and Huawei.

Mergers and Acquisitions

Ericsson has been making acquisitions to shore up some areas of its technology offerings and to expand further into areas where it already has strength.

In 2014 Ericsson bought a majority stake in Apcera the US-based developer of the Continuum platform as-a-service (PaaS) product. The acquisition was designed to strengthen Ericsson in the cloud market by extending the company's network approach into operator and enterprise cloud.

With the acquisition of another US company Azuki Systems a provider of TV Anywhere delivery platforms Ericsson adds to its TV and media portfolio. The acquisition should help Ericsson add functions and quality to its video-related services.

Fabrix Systems a provider of cloud storage computing and network delivery for video applications that Ericsson acquired in 2014 adds a cloud-based and computing platform to optimize media storage processing and delivery applications such as cloud DVR and video-on-demand expansion.

The acquisition of MetraTech Corp. a provider of metadata-based billing commerce and settlement software builds on Ericsson's expertise in billing and expands its presence in the US.

HISTORY

Lars Magnus Ericsson opened a telegraph repair shop in Stockholm in 1876 the same year Alexander Graham Bell applied for a US patent on the telephone. Within two years Ericsson was making telephones. His company grew rapidly supplying equipment first to Swedish phone companies and later to other European companies. In 1885 Ericsson crafted a combination receiver-speaker in one handset.

In 1911 Ericsson and SAT the Stockholm telephone company merged under the Ericsson banner. The company adopted its present name in 1926. In 1930 international financier Ivar "The Match King" Kreuger owner of the Swedish Match Co. won control of Ericsson. His triumph was short-lived. Krueger committed suicide in 1932 and one of his creditors Sosthenes Behn's ITT took over.

ITT in 1960 sold its interest in Ericsson to the top Swedish industrialist family the Wallenbergs. In 1975 Ericsson introduced its computer-controlled exchange called AXE. Buoyed by AXE's success the company unveiled the "office of the future" in the early 1980s diversifying into computers and office furniture.

However Ericsson's timing was off: The demand for office automation never materialized and profits plunged. Electrolux chairman Hans Werthen was recruited to split his time between the two companies and rescue Ericsson. The company sold its computer business to Nokia in 1988 and refocused on telephone equipment. It dusted off its aging AXE system for the burgeoning cellular market and quickly won key contracts.

The company and aircraft maker Saab merged their military aviation electronics operations as Ericsson Saab Avionics in 1996. (It was dissolved in 1998.) In 1998 manager Sven-Christer Nilsson was appointed CEO. He reorganized the company and laid off 14000 workers.

After Ericsson fought bitterly with rival QUALCOMM over wireless standards and patents the companies settled in 1999 agreeing to push for the standardization of third-generation technology based on QUALCOMM's code-division multiple access (CDMA) technology. As a part of the deal Ericsson purchased QUALCOMM's infrastructure business. To expand its Internet offerings Ericsson bought Internet router maker Torrent and Internet telephony company Touchwave.

By 1999 Nilsson was pushed out for moving too slowly on restructuring plans and was replaced as CEO by chairman Lars Ramqvist who put many of the duties on president Kurt Hellstrom. Hellstrom immediately set out to simplify the company's managerial and accounting structure trim its workforce and slow-growth businesses and push new phone models to market.

The next year Ericsson sold noncore businesses including its private radio systems power supply and equipment shelter operations. The company also agreed to develop a standard for secure wireless transactions with Nokia and Motorola and formed a joint venture with Web router maker Juniper Networks to sell routers for mobile Internet applications.

Fierce competition an industrywide slowdown in handset sales and manufacturing glitches led Ericsson to outsource the manufacture of its phones to Flextronics and form a joint venture (Sony Ericsson Mobile Communications) with Sony to link the development and marketing of their handsets in 2001. Ericsson also sold its direct enterprise sales and service unit outsourced IT operations in Europe to Electronic Data Systems (which later became HP Enterprise Services) and cut more than 20000 jobs that year. Hellstrom became CEO in 2001.

Chairman Ramqvist became honorary chairman in 2002; Electrolux CEO Michael Treschow was named as the acting chairman. Ericsson announced 20000 more layoffs in 2002. That year the company sold its semiconductor unit to Infineon for about $380 million.

Ericsson sold its optoelectronic components business in 2003. Hellstrom retired later that year and Carl-Henric Svanberg former CEO of Assa Abloy was appointed as company president and CEO. In 2005 Ericsson acquired certain telecom hardware assets from troubled Marconi (later renamed telent) for about $2.1 billion.

The company acquired seven companies in 2007 the largest of which were Redback Networks ($1.9 billion) and TANDBERG Television ($1.4 billion). The Redback buy gained Ericsson broadband IP routers while the TANDBERG Television purchase brought software and services for the cable television market. It also picked up fiber-access technology company Entrisphere in an effort to expand its broadband access offerings in North America.

Looking to broaden its multimedia offerings the company purchased Mobeon a Swedish provider of IP-based voice and video mail. Other 2007 acquisitions included German customer care software provider LHS Swedish mobile service deliver platform developer Drutt and Spanish IPTV specialist HyC. In an effort to refocus its multimedia operations on key areas such as service delivery and provisioning Ericsson sold its enterprise PBX products business to Aastra Technologies for about $100 million in 2008.

To expand its North American business Ericsson bought bankrupt Nortel Network's CDMA and LTE-based wireless business there in 2009 for $1.1 billion. The deal significantly boosted its profile as a provider of mobile networking gear to wireless carriers on the continent. The company's other acquisitions that year complemented its manufacturing and services activities. These purchases included the manufacturing operations of Estonian electronics maker Elcoteq as well as Turkish systems integrator Bizitek.

In 2010 EVP/CFO Hans Vestberg took over as president and CEO of Ericsson succeeding Carl-Henric Svanberg who resigned to become chairman of BP.

EXECUTIVES

EVP and Head Global Services, Magnus Mandersson, age 53
President and CEO; Head of Segment Networks, Hans Vestberg, age 50, $15,750,000 total compensation
Head of Region North America, Angel Ruiz, age 60
EVP and CFO, Jan Frykhammar, age 50
SVP; Head of Business Unit Support Solutions, Per G. Borgklint, age 40
SVP and Head of Asia-Pacific, Mats H. Olsson, age 61
SVP CTO and Head Technology and Portfolio Management, Ulf Ewaldsson
SVP CIO and Head of Group Function Business Excellence and Common Functions, Anders Thulin, age 53
President and Country Manager Singapore and Brunei, Martin Wiktorin
SVP Chief Marketing and Communications Officer and Head of Group Function Marketing and Communications, Helena Norrman, age 46
Chairman, Leif Johansson, age 64
Deputy Chairman, Jacob Wallenberg, age 59
Deputy Chairman, Anders Nyr ©, age 61
Auditors: PricewaterhouseCoopers AB

LOCATIONS

HQ: Telefonaktiebolaget LM Ericsson (Sweden)
Torshamnsgatan 23, Stockholm SE-164 83
Phone: (46) 10 719 0000
Web: www.ericsson.com

2014 Sales

	% of total
North America	24
China & North East Asia	12
Mediterranean	10
Latin America	10
Western & Central Europe	9
Middle East	9
South East Asia & Pacific	7
Northern Europe & Central Asia	6
Sub-Saharan Africa	4
India	3
Other	6
Total	100

PRODUCTS/OPERATIONS

2014 Sales

	% of total
Networks	51
Services	43
Support	6
Total	100

COMPETITORS

Accenture
Alcatel-Lucent
Amdocs
Cisco Systems
HP Enterprise Services
HTC Corporation
Harmonic
Huawei Technologies
IBM
Juniper Networks
LG Electronics
Motorola Mobility
Nokia Siemens Networks
Oracle
QUALCOMM
Samsung Electronics
Sharp Corp.
Tata Consultancy
Tech Mahindra
Technicolor
ZTE

HISTORICAL FINANCIALS

Company Type: Public

Income Statement

FYE: December 31

	REVENUE ($ mil.)	NET INCOME ($ mil.)	NET PROFIT MARGIN	EMPLOYEES
12/14	29,492	1,496	5.1%	118,055
12/13	35,465	1,872	5.3%	114,340
12/12	34,964	886	2.5%	110,255
12/11	32,901	1,768	5.4%	104,525
12/10	30,325	1,662	5.5%	90,261
Annual Growth	(0.7%)	(2.6%)	—	6.9%

2014 Year-End Financials

Debt ratio: 1.0%
Return on equity: 8.1%
Cash ($ mil.): 5,302
Current ratio: 2.00
Long-term debt ($ mil.): 2,828
No. of shares (mil.): —
Dividends
Yield: —
Payout: —
Market value ($ mil.): —

Telefonica SA

Auditors: Ernst & Young, S.L.

LOCATIONS

HQ: Telefonica SA
Distrito Telefonica, Ronda de la Comunicacion, s/n, Madrid 28050
Phone: (34) 91 482 8700 **Fax:** (34) 91 482 8600
Web: www.telefonica.com

HISTORICAL FINANCIALS

Company Type: Public

Income Statement

FYE: December 31

	REVENUE ($ mil.)	NET INCOME ($ mil.)	NET PROFIT MARGIN	EMPLOYEES
12/14	61,233	3,647	6.0%	123,700
12/13	78,557	6,323	8.0%	291,027
12/12	82,188	5,177	6.3%	133,186
12/11	81,276	6,988	8.6%	291,027
12/10	81,288	13,607	16.7%	285,106
Annual Growth	(6.8%)	(28.0%)	—	(18.8%)

2014 Year-End Financials

Debt ratio: 59.4%
Return on equity: 14.1%
Cash ($ mil.): 7,936
Current ratio: 0.77
Long-term debt ($ mil.): 61,611
No. of shares (mil.): —
Dividends
Yield: 6.7%
Payout: 119.1%
Market value ($ mil.): —

	STOCK PRICE ($) FY Close	P/E High/Low	PER SHARE ($) Earnings	Dividends	Book Value
12/14	14.21	26 22	0.74	0.96	5.51
12/13	16.34	18 13	1.39	0.47	6.45
12/12	13.49	21 13	1.15	2.08	5.99
12/11	17.19	59 14	1.53	1.93	6.25
12/10	68.42	36 27	2.96	1.72	7.26
Annual Growth	(32.5%)	— —	(29.2%)	(13.5%)	(6.7%)

Tesco PLC (United Kingdom)

Tesco is the #1 retailer in the UK and one of the top retailers in the world by annual sales behind Wal-Mart and Carrefour. Tesco and its subsidiaries have more than 6200 stores in 14 countries in Europe Asia and North America with about half located in the UK. Although built on the "pile it high sell it cheap" creed of founder Sir Jack Cohen Tesco abandoned its discount format to become a multi-format retailer in stores and online. Among its banners are Tesco Extra superstores; Tesco Express Tesco Metro and One Stop convenience stores; Homeplus hypermarket small express and virtual stores in South Korea; and Dobbies gardening stores in the UK Scotland and northern Ireland.

Geographic Reach

Tesco's presence spans about a dozen countries worldwide. Outside of the UK which is its largest market the company's other European-based stores are located in the Czech Republic Hungary Ireland Poland Slovakia and Turkey. In Asia it operates in China India Malaysia South Korea and Thailand. It is exiting the US market with the sale of its Fresh & Easy banner.

Operations

As a multi-format multi-channel retailer Tesco's various physical retail store operations are complemented by its online retailing operations including tesco.com (the world's largest online grocery retailer) and Tesco Direct. As a provider of financial services Tesco is the UK's largest supermarket bank through Tesco Personal Finance (which does business as Tesco Bank). Through wholly owned dunnhumby Tesco offers data analytics and customer insight to such clients as Coca-Cola Kroger and Procter & Gamble. The dunnhumby group includes marketing expert BzzAgent and price optimization company KSS Retail.

Tesco boasts an impressive presence in Asia. Homeplus in South Korea is the company's largest international business with some 475 stores consisting of large hypermarkets and small Tesco Express stores an online business and virtual stores in subway and bus stops where customers can buy products via their mobile devices and get them delivered to their homes. In Southeast Asia Tesco is a market leader in Thailand where it operates locally as Tesco Lotus. It operates in Malaysia with conglomerate partner Sime Darby while in India the company has an exclusive franchise agreement with the retail arm of Tata Group to develop Star Bazaar hypermarkets there.

In China Tesco is playing catch up to global rivals Wal-Mart and Carrefour which entered that market nearly a decade before Tesco. There it has more than 100 stores along the eastern seaboard provinces and it is developing shopping malls under the Lifespace brand that are anchored by Tesco hypermarkets. China is also a major sourcing market for Tesco; it has international sourcing headquarters in Hong Kong and a hub in Singapore.

Financial Performance

Tesco is under pressure to reverse a slide in its core UK business after 20 years of solid growth and profitability. In early 2012 the company issued its first earnings warning in two decades. While group sales rose about 5% in fiscal 2012 (ends February) compared to the previous year and group profit rose modestly Tesco lost money at home. The UK lagged Asia Europe and the US in sales growth and profitability.

Strategy

After being criticized for allowing its UK business to deteriorate while it focused on expansion abroad Tesco is refocusing its strategy on core UK growth which is still a key driver of sales and profit. In fiscal 2013 it is investing 1 billion (roughly $1.6 billion) to improve the shopping experience for its UK customers in stores and online. The retailer will overhaul its existing UK stores by adding more staff and improving in-store service accelerating its remodeling schedule and offering better prices and more personalized promotions. It will also add about 38% less retail space in Britain this year than last as it moves away from big stores in favor of smaller shops and the Internet. To that end Tesco will ramp up investment in its online operations and accelerate the roll out of its Click and Collect program which allows shoppers to pick up orders placed online.

Tesco has seen its market share decline in recent years as rival Wal-Mart-owned ASDA and deep discounters such as ALDI and Lidl increase their share of the fiercely competitive UK grocery market. To win the hearts of cash-strapped consumers and keep them in its stores Tesco has expanded its own Tesco Value line of discount products and its Tesco Finest brand –both of which exceed 1 billion in annual sales. Also Tesco is facing even stronger competition from its chief UK rival ASDA which recently acquired the Netto chain of discount stores in the UK. To bolster its One Stope Stores convenience chain Tesco acquired more than 75 stores from privately owned Mills Group (boosting its store count to more than 600 across England and Wales) in 2011.

Outside of the UK Tesco is strategically reviewing certain underperforming international operations including its US-based Fresh & Easy business a chain of 200 unprofitable stores launched in 2007. Indeed Tesco has struck a deal to exit the US with the sale of about 150 Fresh & Easy stores to The Yucaipa Cos. (It will close the remaining 50 stores). Across the Pacific in a two-stage process Tesco is selling its 50% stake in its loss-making Tesco Japan business to AEON for a nominal sum after after nine years of struggling in that market.

HISTORY

With WWI behind him in 1919 Jack Cohen invested his serviceman's gratuity in a grocery stall in London's East End. He introduced his first private-label product Tesco Tea in 1924 –the name was the combination of the initials of his tea supplier (T. E. Stockwell) and the first two letters of Cohen's last name. By the late 1920s Cohen had several stalls and in 1929 he opened his first store under the Tesco name in Edgeware London.

Cohen founded Tesco Stores Limited in 1932. During the rest of the decade the company added more than 100 stores mainly in London. Cohen visited the US in 1935 studying its self-service supermarkets and returned to England with a plan of using a similar "pile it high and sell it cheap" format. Delayed by WWII Tesco opened its first American-styled store in 1947 and went public that year as Tesco Stores Holdings. By 1950 the company ran 20 self-service stores.

Tesco grew primarily through acquisitions during the 1950s and 1960s adding about 600 stores. By the early 1970s however competition and a recession battered Tesco. Managing director Ian MacLaurin initiated radical changes including abandoning trading stamps and to shed its down-market image refurbishing stores with a more upscale decor. A price-slashing initiative in 1977 dramatically increased Tesco's market share within a year. Because cheap brands were best-sellers Tesco began creating its own private-label brands. The company also started closing unprofitable stores while opening superstores some with gas stations.

In 1979 the year Sir Jack Cohen died Tesco entered Ireland by buying Three Guys (abandoning the effort in 1986). In 1983 the company became Tesco and two years later it named MacLaurin as chairman. By 1991 Tesco was the UK's largest independent gasoline retailer.

Looking for new opportunities in 1992 Tesco introduced small urban stores called Tesco Metro and the next year began expanding outside England acquiring stores in France and Scotland. In 1994 it acquired an initial 51% stake in Global a 43-store grocery chain in Hungary. That year it also opened Tesco Express (combination convenience stores and gas stations).

Tesco acquired 31 Stavia stores in Poland in 1995; a year later it added 13 Kmart stores in the Czech Republic and Slovakia. Tesco returned to Ireland in 1997 by acquiring 109 Associated British Food stores. It also launched its financial services division –Tesco Personal Finance –that year and named John Gardiner as chairman (replacing the retiring MacLaurin) and Terry Leahy as CEO. In 1998 the retailer purchased 75% of food retailer Lotus with 13 stores in Thailand. The following year Tesco partnered with Samsung to develop Homeplus hypermarkets in South Korea.

By 2000 Tesco's profitable online shopping business was one of the world's most successful and the company made it a separate subsidiary Tesco.com. To build on that success Tesco bought a 35% stake in GroceryWorks a subsidiary of the US Safeway grocery chain in June 2001.

Tesco acquired the travel company First Class Leisure in March 2002 and renamed the business Tesco Freetime. The acquisition was yet another move by the supermarket chain to expand beyond groceries. Tesco became the market leader in the fragmented Polish food retailing arena by acquiring German hypermarket operator HIT in July 2002. In January 2003 Tesco completed the acquisition of the British convenience store chain T&S Stores for 519 million. In July it acquired a 95% stake in Japanese convenience store operator C Two-Network for about 139 million. In November Tesco acquired Kipa a small hypermarket operator in Turkey for 96 million.

To strengthen its presence in the convenience market Tesco bought T&S Stores (now One Stop Stores) in 2003 and has converted many of its 800-plus shops to its Express banner.

In April 2004 David Reid became non-executive chairman replacing Gardiner who retired from Tesco. In August Tesco sold the Dillons chain of newsstands to TM Retail for an undisclosed amount. Tesco had acquired Dillons when it purchased T&S Stores.

Tesco transferred some 770 back office jobs in January 2005 from the UK to Bangalore India where it opened a software development and accounting office. In mid-year Tesco opened its first Kipa store in Turkey since it acquired the Turkish chain in 2003. The 50000-sq.-ft. store brought Tesco's store count in Turkey to six.

In 2006 the company bought 27 small stores from Edeka in the Czech Republic. In the fall it launched a higher-end 30-piece apparel line for men and women called F&F Collection by Lee Rees-Oliviere (Tesco's head designer recruited in 2005 from Marks and Spencer). In October Tesco sold its 38% stake in Internet grocer GroceryWorks to Safeway its partner in the venture. In December Tesco increased its stake in China's Ting Hsin Holding Corp. to 90% from 50% in a deal valued at about $352 million. (Tesco entered China in 2004 paying approximately $275 million for 50% in Ting Hsin's subsidiary Ting Cao.)

Tesco increased its international selling space by 25% in the fiscal year ending in February 2007. In early November the British retailer opened its first US store: a Fresh & Easy Neighborhood Market in Hemet California (outside Los Angeles). Also in 2007 Tesco acquired nearly a two-thirds ownership stake in the Scottish garden center operator Dobbies Garden Centers PLC. (It increased its ownership to 100% in July 2008).

In August 2008 Tesco bought the UK operation of Handleman a leading UK-based distributor and store merchandiser of books music computer games and other products for about 9.4 million (about $16 million). Tesco retained a substantial portion of Handleman's UK workforce. Also that year Tesco made a major acquisition of a chain of hypermarkets in South Korea from E-Land Group for about $2 billion.

Tesco bought out its joint venture partner – Royal Bank of Scotland –in Tesco Personal Finance (TPF) for about $1.9 billion in 2008. TPF which was formed in 1997 has grown to serve more than 6 million customer accounts and offers insurance credit cards loans mortgages and savings products. The purchase is part of Tesco's strategy to expand into the service sector which is outpacing food in terms of growth. The timing of its push into retail banking –just ahead of the banking crisis in the UK –was auspicious. Tesco is enjoying increased demand for its banking services as distrust of traditional banks has grown in the aftermath of big bank bailouts in the UK during the financial crisis. TPF is also getting into the auto and home insurance markets via a partnership with the UK arm of Fortis Insurance.

In early 2011 international executive Philip Clarke replaced retiring longtime chief executive Terry Leahy.

Also that year Tesco acquired an 80% stake in the British video-on-demand (VoD) service Blinkbox which competes with Amazon.com's LoveFilm. Tesco entered the VoD market to position itself for the next phase of Internet-driven home entertainment even though the retailer is a huge seller of DVDs.

Auditors: PricewaterhouseCoopers LLP

LOCATIONS

HQ: Tesco PLC (United Kingdom)
Tesco House, Delamare Road, Cheshunt, Hertfordshire EN8 9SL
Phone: (44) 1992 632222 **Fax:** (44) 1992 630794
Web: www.tescoplc.com

HISTORICAL FINANCIALS

Company Type: Public

Income Statement FYE: February 28

	REVENUE ($ mil.)	NET INCOME ($ mil.)	NET PROFIT MARGIN	EMPLOYEES
02/15	96,065	(8,854)	—	506,984
02/14	105,931	1,623	1.5%	510,444
02/13	98,950	189	0.2%	537,784
02/12	101,973	4,433	4.3%	519,671
02/11	98,061	4,272	4.4%	492,714
Annual Growth	(0.5%)	—	—	0.7%

2015 Year-End Financials

Debt ratio: 44.1%
Return on equity: (-51.8%)
Cash ($ mil.): 3,339
Current ratio: 0.60
Long-term debt ($ mil.): 16,427
No. of shares (mil.): —
Dividends
Yield: 0.0%
Payout: —
Market value ($ mil.): —

	STOCK PRICE ($) FY Close	P/E High/Low	PER SHARE ($) Earnings	Dividends	Book Value
02/15	11.38	— —	(1.09)	0.50	1.34
02/14	16.76	162131	0.20	0.68	3.03
02/13	17.14	1121884	0.02	0.62	3.21
02/12	15.24	57 43	0.55	0.64	3.51
02/11	20.03	66 55	0.53	0.60	3.31
Annual Growth	(13.2%)	— —	—	(4.6%)	(20.2%)

Teva Pharmaceutical Industries Ltd

Teva Pharmaceutical Industries is the biggest name in the no-name world of generic pharmaceuticals. The company makes hundreds of generic versions of brand-name antibiotics heart drugs heartburn medications and more. Headquartered in Israel Teva is the world's largest generic medicines maker using its portfolio of more than 1000 molecules to produce generics in nearly every therapeutic area. In specialty medicines Teva is a leader in making innovative treatments for disorders of the central nervous system (CNS) as well as respiratory products. The company operates in two segments: generics (which accounts for about half of sales) and specialty medicines.

Operations

Generic medicines produced by Teva include chemical and therapeutic versions of a tablets capsules injectables inhalants liquids ointments and creams. Specialty medicines include Copaxone Azilect Nuvigil ProAir HFA and QVAR. In addition to focusing on CNR and respiratory therapies Teva also provides specialty medicines in the areas of oncology women's health and others.

Teva also participates in a joint venture with Procter & Gamble. It owns 49% of the venture named PGT Healthcare which makes over-the-counter drugs. P&G brought big consumer health brand names to the venture (including Pepto Bismol and Vicks) while Teva brought international manufacturing and regulatory expertise. The company also has a collaboration with Takeda Pharmaceutical through which Takeda can commercialize Teva's treatments for Parkinson's disease (Copaxone) and multiple sclerosis (Azilect) in Japan.

The company also supplies active pharmaceutical ingredients (APIs) the essential raw materials used in drug manufacturing.

Teva holds a portfolio of more than 1000 molecules; it produces some 64 billion tablets and capsules annually at its 66 manufacturing facilities. Its pipeline includes about 20 products in phase II or III.

Geographic Reach

While Teva has research and manufacturing operations in more than 60 countries in the Americas Europe Asia and the Middle East more than half of the company's sales come from its US operations.

In 2014 the US accounted for 45% of Teva's generic revenues while Europe accounted for 32%.

Sales and Marketing

Teva's finished product are sold directly to retailers and medical providers as well as through wholesale distribution firms.

Advertising expenses for 2014 totaled $302 million down from $321 million in 2013 and $337 million in 2012.

Financial Performance

Teva's revenue has been relatively flat at around $20.3 billion since fiscal 2012. In 2014 revenue decreased by less than one percent to $20.3 billion as declines in generics occurred. In Europe regulatory measures such as price reductions impacted earnings. However US operations saw growth due to the release of new generics.

Net income had been on a decline until 2014 when it more than doubled to $3.1 billion thanks to income from legal settlements (related to the settlement of pantoprazole patent litigation) as well as a reduction in selling and marketing expenses. Cash flow from operations rose 58% to $5.1 billion due to lower payments for legal settlements and Israeli tax settlements among other factors.

Strategy

Continuing growth strategies include expansion efforts in emerging markets and increasing its portfolio in over-the-counter medicines. Teva continues with its historical strategy of filing patent challenges on branded products thus attempting to gain a "first-to-market" advantage with its generic equivalents; however in recent years these patent challenges have grown more expensive and less exclusive which has eroded their usefulness.

Lingering impacts from acquisition expenses as well as the patent expiration of top-selling branded drug Copaxone prompted Teva to launch a cost control program in 2013 to cut $2 billion in annual expenses by 2017. The program includes a 10% workforce reduction; the first such downsizing program in the company's history. In 2015 it agreed to sell its facility in Sellersville Pennsylvania to G&W Laboratories to cut excess manufacturing capacity and cut costs.

Perhaps in response to losing exclusivity of its Copaxone Teva made an unsolicited $40 billion bid for generics rival Mylan in mid-2015. Mylan had just made its own unsolicited offer to purchase Perrigo for some $29 billion; either deal would be among the largest of the year. However Teva subsequently dropped its plans to buy Mylan; instead it agreed to buy the generics business of Allergan for some $40.5 billion. In another deal to build its portfolio Teva agreed to form a joint venture with top Japanese firm Takeda Pharmaceutical. Takeda will gradually transfer its generics business to the venture (which will be 51%-owned by Teva) as it focuses more heavily on developing new drugs.

After regulatory compliance expenses pinched the company's animal health business in 2011 Teva sold off those operations to Bayer HealthCare in early 2013 in a deal worth up to $145 million. The business included dermatology and food products for companion animals.

In 2015 Teva plans to launch inhalation powder ProAir RespiClick in the US. It did launch a generic version of Exforge tablets which treat high blood pressure as well as Lovenox both in the US. In 2014 the company introduced psychiatric drug Adasuve.

Mergers and Acquisitions

Acquisitions around the globe have helped the company enter new markets and secure market dominance in others. In 2014 Teva acquired biotech company Labrys Biologics which is focused on migraine treatments for $207 million.

The company now plans to buy California-based Auspex Pharmaceuticals which is developing drugs for central nervous system disorders including Huntington's disease and Tourette's syndrome for some $3.2 billion. It is also buying US-based private software firm Gecko Health Innovations which makes products that alert respiratory patients when it's time to take their medicine. And in yet another deal aimed at growing its emerging market operations Teva is buying Mexico-based drugmaker Representaciones e Investigaciones Mdicas SA (more simply known as Rimsa) for $2.3 billion.

HISTORY

Teva traces its origins to Salomon Levin and Elstein Ltd. a drug distribution firm based in Jerusalem which at the time was a Jewish section of British-controlled Palestine.

Ironically in the 1930s the company benefited from the emigration of Jewish people many of whom were scientists seeking to escape the Nazi regime in Germany which at the time was the global leader in drug development. The company went public in 1951.

In 1968 Eli Hurvitz was appointed to Teva's board of directors and scripted much of the company's growth. In 1970 Teva merged with Assia Chemical Laboratories (Hurvitz's old employer) and another company to form Teva Pharmaceutical Industries.

Ten years later Teva sold a 20% stake of itself to Koor Industries in exchange for Koor subsidiary Ikapharm Teva's closest competitor. (Koor later launched a takeover bid but the Founders Group Teva's controlling shareholders foiled the attempt.)

In 1985 Teva moved into the US. It formed a joint venture with W. R. Grace called TAG Pharmaceuticals (Teva bought out W. R. Grace's portion in 1991). In 1985 TAG bought Lemmon Co. famous —or infamous —for its tranquilizer Quaalude which had gained notoriety as the recreational drug of choice for many young people. Lemmon which ceased production of Quaalude prior to Teva's purchase became the acquirer's generic manufacturing division.

Teva bought Abic Israel's #2 drugmaker in a complex 1988 transaction that gave Canadian investor and Seagram's heir Charles Bronfman a stake in the company. British publisher Robert Maxwell also bought a substantial stake in Teva. (Following Maxwell's mysterious death in 1993 his estate sold his stake.)

In the 1990s Teva turned its attention to Europe buying companies in France Hungary Italy and the UK. In 1996 the company bought US firm Biocraft Laboratories merging it with Lemmon and forming Teva Pharmaceuticals USA.

In 1998 the company reorganized after officials realized that it had to evolve from being a collection of disparate operating entities to a more centralized operation. It also divested several operations –including its Russian joint venture its yeast and alcohol fermentation business and some of its German operations –in order to concentrate on pharmaceuticals.

EXECUTIVES

President and CEO, Erez Vigodman, age 56
EVP and CFO, Eyal Desheh, age 62
President and CEO Global Operations, Carlo de Notaristefani, age 57
President of Global R&D and Chief Scientific Officer, Michael Hayden
President and CEO Teva Europe, Robert Koremans
Chairman, Yitzhak Peterburg
Auditors: Kesselman & Kesselman

LOCATIONS

HQ: Teva Pharmaceutical Industries Ltd
5 Basel Street, P.O. Box 3190, Petach Tikva 49131
Phone: (972) 3 926 7267
Web: www.tevapharm.com

2014 Sales

	% of total
US	52
Europe	29
Rest of the world	19
Total	**100**

PRODUCTS/OPERATIONS

2014 Sales

	$ mil.	% of total
Generic products	9,814	48
Specialty products		
Central nervous system	5,575	28
Oncology	1,180	6
Respiratory	957	5
Women's health	504	2
Other	344	2
Other revenues	1,898	9
Total	**20,272**	**100**

Selected Products

Branded products
- Central nervous system
- Azilect (Parkinson' s)
- Copaxone (multiple sclerosis)
- Provigil (narcolepsy)
- Specialty respiratory
- ProAir (bronchial spasms)
- Qvar (chronic asthma)
- Women' s health
- Seasonique

Biosimilar products
- Eporatio (erythopoietin treatment for chemotherapy-induced anemia)
- Granulocyte Colony Stimulating Factor (anti-infective for oncology patients)
- Tev-Tropin (human growth hormone)

Generic products
- Amoxicillin (Amoxil)
- Atorvastatin (Lipitor)
- Bromatapp (Dimetapp)
- Candesartan (Atacand)
- Cimetidine (Tagamet)
- Ciprofloxacin (Cipro)
- Clemastine fumarate (Tavist)
- Clotrimazole (Lotrimin)
- Diclofenac extended release (Voltaren XR)
- Diltiazem HCl (Cardizem)
- Donepezil (Aricept)
- Fluconazole Injection (Diflucan)
- Fluoxetine (Prozac)
- Galantamine (Reminyl)
- Ketoconazole cream (Nizoral Cream)
- Lamivudine (Epivir)
- Lovastatin (Mevacor)
- Metronidazole (Flagyl)
- Quetiapine (Seroquel)
- Sotalol hydrochloride (Betapace)
- Sulfamethoxazole and Trimethoprim (Bactrim)
- Tizanidine (Zanaflex)
- Tramadol hydrochloride (Ultram/Ultracet)

Selected Acquisitions

COMPETITORS

Abbott Labs
Allergan plc
AstraZeneca
Bayer HealthCare Pharmaceuticals Inc.
Bio-Rad Labs
Biogen
Boehringer Ingelheim
Bristol-Myers Squibb
Dr. Reddy' s
GlaxoSmithKline
Johnson & Johnson
Merck
Mylan
Novartis
Perrigo
Pfizer
Ranbaxy Laboratories
Sandoz International GmbH
Sanofi
Taro
Wockhardt

HISTORICAL FINANCIALS

Company Type: Public

Income Statement

FYE: December 31

	REVENUE ($ mil.)	NET INCOME ($ mil.)	NET PROFIT MARGIN	EMPLOYEES
12/14	20,272	3,055	15.1%	43,009
12/13	20,314	1,269	6.2%	44,945
12/12	20,317	1,963	9.7%	45,948
12/11	18,312	2,759	15.1%	45,754
12/10	16,121	3,331	20.7%	39,660
Annual Growth	5.9%	(2.1%)	—	2.0%

2014 Year-End Financials

Debt ratio: 22.2%
Return on equity: 13.3%
Cash ($ mil.): 2,226
Current ratio: 1.17
Long-term debt ($ mil.): 8,566
No. of shares (mil.): 852
Dividends
Yield: 2.0%
Payout: 32.3%
Market value ($ mil.): 48,999

	STOCK PRICE ($) FY Close	P/E High/Low	PER SHARE ($) Earnings	Dividends	Book Value
12/14	57.51	16 11	3.56	1.15	27.36
12/13	40.08	28 25	1.49	1.09	26.61
12/12	37.34	20 16	2.25	0.80	26.57
12/11	40.36	18 11	3.09	0.78	25.14
12/10	52.13	17 13	3.67	0.67	24.47
Annual Growth	2.5%	— —	(0.8%)	14.6%	2.8%

ThyssenKrupp AG

How do you say "giant engineering and steel company" in German? Try ThyssenKrupp and pronounce it "TISS-in kroop." The company is one of the world's largest steel producers and operates worldwide in two business areas: Materials and Technologies. The first comprises the company's steel (carbon and stainless steel) and materials services businesses. ThyssenKrupp's Technologies group consists of its elevators unit marine systems components technology (for the auto and engineering markets) and plant technology (construction and environmental services) segments. Although its combined interests range from elevators to shipbuilding the company has historically relied upon the steel market.

Geographic Reach

Led by regional headquarters ThyssenKrupp serves customers in North and South America China India and the Asia-Pacific region. It has operations in 78 countries and has 546 subsidiaries.

Operations

The company's business operations are organized into two divisions and seven operating business areas. The Materials division consists of the Steel Europe Steel Americas and Materials Services units. The Technologies division comprises the company's Elevator Technology Plant Technology Components Technology and Marine Systems units.

Financial Performance

In fiscal 2014 (ended September) ThyssenKrupp's revenues grew by 7% due to strong growth in its capital goods business and sales from the recent acquisitions of Acciai Speciali Terni (AST) and VDM.That year the company posted net income of 195 million (compared to net loss of 1.58 billion in 2013) thanks to higher revenues and lower operating expenses.

ThyssenKrupp's operating cash inflow increased to 887 million in 2014 (up from 786 million in the previous year) as the result of improved net income and a change in working capital.

Strategy

In 2014 ThyssenKrupp Metallurgical Products expanded its operations in South America opening its first location in Bolivia extending its global network of sales offices. As well as marketing nonferrous metal tin ThyssenKrupp Metallurgical Products will focus on trading copper and tungsten from that country. That year it also began construction of a new automotive supply plant in Brazil.To raise cash to reinvest in core operations in 2014 ThyssenKrupp sold ThyssenKrupp Steel USA's rolling and coating plant in Calvert Alabama to a consortium of ArcelorMittal and Nippon Steel & Sumitomo Metal for $1.55 billion. (The deal is expected to deliver $60 million in annual savings). That year the company also arranged for a long-term slab supply contract with the ThyssenKrupp CSA steel mill in Brazil. The consortium will purchase 2 million tons of slabs per year from ThyssenKrupp CSA up to 2019.In 2014 ThyssenKrupp Metallurgical Products expanded its product portfolio signing an 10-year offtake agreement with NioCorp Developments for ferroniobium a rare heavy metal. This offtake agreement makes the ThyssenKrupp Metallurgical Products the exclusive European distribution partner to NioCorp which is developing the only primary niobium deposits in the US at its Elk Creek project in Nebraska.

Mergers and Acquisitions

As part of the 2014 acquisitions of the AST and VDM service centers from Outokumpu ThyssenKrupp sold its 29.9% holdings in that company. (The deal stems from the sale of ThyssenKrupp's stainless steel company Inoxumto to Outokumpu in 2012).

In 2013 ThyssenKrupp Aerospace acquired UK-based The Waterjet Group. With its equipment ThyssenKrupp is able to process a wide range of materials and sizes for its European and international customer base.

HISTORY

Formed separately in the 1800s both Thyssen and Krupp flourished in their early years under family control. Friedrich Krupp opened his steel factory in 1811. He died in 1826 and left the nearly bankrupt factory in the hands of his 14-year-old son Alfred who turned the business around. At the first World's Fair in 1851 Alfred unveiled a steel cannon far superior to earlier bronze models.

Twenty years later August Thyssen founded a puddling and rolling mill near Mulheim. He bought small factories and mines and by WWI he ran Germany's largest iron and steel company. During the world wars the resources of both companies were turned toward military efforts.

Post-WWII years were tough for both companies. Thyssen was split up by the Allies and when it began production again in 1953 it consisted of one steel plant. In the Krupp camp Alfred's great-grandson Alfried was convicted in 1948 of using slave labor during WWII. Released from prison in 1951 Alfried rebuilt Krupp. After near ruin following WWII both companies emerged and enjoyed a resurgence along with the German economy in which they prospered and expanded during the 1950s.

By the 1980s Thyssen's businesses included ships locomotives offshore oil rigs specialty steel and metals trading and distribution. Krupp continued to grow and in 1992 it took over engineering and steelmaking concern Hoesch AG. (Eberhard Hoesch had begun making railroad tracks in the 1820s. The company grew and expanded into infrastructure and building products.)

The new Fried. Krupp AG Hoesch-Krupp bought Italian specialty steelmaker Acciai Speciali Terni chemical-plant builder Uhde and South African shipper J.H. Bachmann. Its automotive division formed a joint venture in Brazil and added production sites in China Mexico Romania and the US.

In 1997 Thyssen expanded in North America with its $675 million acquisition of Giddings & Lewis (machine tools US) and the purchase of Copper & Brass Sales (metals processing and distributing).

Krupp attempted a hostile takeover of Thyssen in 1997. The takeover failed but the companies soon agreed to merge their steel operations to form Thyssen Krupp Stahl. Bigger plans were in the works and in 1998 the two companies agreed to merge. That year Thyssen sold its Plusnet fixed-line phone business to Esprit Telecom Group.

In 1999 Krupp's automotive division (Krupp Hoesch Automotive) bought Cummins' Atlas Crankshaft subsidiary. Thyssen also bought US-based Dover's elevator business for $1.1 billion. Krupp and Thyssen completed their merger in 1999. The company planned to spin off its steel operations but held off due to its success in 2000. ThyssenKrupp did however sell its Krupp Kunststofftechnik unit (plastic molding machines) for about $183 million. To speed corporate decision-making the company made plans to scrap its dual-management structure in 2001.

Early in 2001 ThyssenKrupp agreed to buy 51% of Fiat unit Magneti Marelli's suspension-systems and shock-absorbers business. It also had the option of buying the remainder after 2004. In 2002 the company formed alliances with NKK and Kawasaki Steel to share its steel sheet making technologies while expanding its business with Japanese automotive makers in Europe. ThyssenKrupp's joint venture with Chinese steelmaker ANSC Angang New Steel known as TAGAL began producing galvanized coil of which about 80% will be used in China's burgeoning automotive industry.

In 2004 ThyssenKrupp sold its residential real estate unit for around $2.8 billion to a consortium of real estate funds operated by Morgan Stanley and Corpus-Immobiliengruppe. It divested the automotive segment of the capital goods unit in 2006 selling it off in pieces.

ThyssenKrupp opened three major new steel facilities in the Americas in 2010. A new integrated steel mill in Santa Cruz Brazil started production in mid-year. The $7 billion plant the company's biggest project ever is a partnership with South American giant Vale SA which owns a 25% stake in the venture. The company also began production at two plants in Calvert Alabama: a $3.6 billion carbon steel plant and a $1.4 billion stainless steel rolling plant. The company also constructed —and consolidated its corporate staff in —a new headquarters building in Essen Germany in 2010.

EXECUTIVES

CEO ThyssenKrupp Industrial Solutions, Hans Christoph Atzpodien, age 60
Chairman Executive Board, Heinrich Hiesinger, age 55
CEO ThyssenKrupp Materials Services, Joachim Limberg, age 61
CEO Components Technology Business, Karsten Kroos, age 56
CEO ThyssenKrupp Steel Europe, Andreas J. Goss, age 51
CEO ThyssenKrupp Elevator, Andreas Schierenbeck
CFO, Guido Kerkhoff, age 48
CEO ThyssenKrupp North America, Patrick Bass
Chairman Industrial Solutions, Jens Michael Wegmann, age 50
Chairman Supervisory Board, Ulrich Lehner, age 69
Vice Chairwoman Supervisory Board, Sabine Maa en, age 49
Auditors: PricewaterhouseCoopers

LOCATIONS

HQ: ThyssenKrupp AG
ThyssenKrupp Allee 1, Essen D-45143
Phone: (49) 201 844 0 **Fax:** (49) 201 844 53600
Web: www.thyssenkrupp.com

COMPETITORS

Acerinox
ArcelorMittal
Bechtel
Descours & Cabaud
GEA Group
ITOCHU
Ingersoll-Rand
JFE Holdings
Kobe Steel
MAN
Magna International
Marubeni
Nippon Steel & Sumitomo Metal Corporation
POSCO
Qingdao Iron and Steel
Schindler Holding
Tata Europe
United States Steel
United Technologies

HISTORICAL FINANCIALS

Company Type: Public

Income Statement FYE: September 30

	REVENUE ($ mil.)	NET INCOME ($ mil.)	NET PROFIT MARGIN	EMPLOYEES
09/15	47,960	346	0.7%	154,906
09/14	51,996	264	0.5%	160,745
09/13	52,044	(1,884)	—	156,856
09/12	51,880	(6,035)	—	167,961
09/11	58,490	(1,741)	—	180,050
Annual Growth	(4.8%)	—	—	(3.7%)

2015 Year-End Financials

Debt ratio: 24.9%
Return on equity: 10.0%
Cash ($ mil.): 5,084
Current ratio: 1.14
Long-term debt ($ mil.): 7,158
No. of shares (mil.): 565
Dividends
Yield: —
Payout: 20.0%
Market value ($ mil.): —

Toho Bank, Ltd. (The)

The Toho Bank is a regional bank serving the Fukushima Prefecture in Japan. Armed with more than 115 branches and ATMs installed at more than 230 locations the bank offers local customers businesses and public institutions the traditional array of banking services including savings lending real estate venture firm support and financing and foreign and domestic exchange products. Toho Bank was established in 1941 and owns subsidiaries and affiliated companies such as The Toho Real Estate Service Co. The Toho Card Co. and The Toho Staff Service Co.

EXECUTIVES

President, Seishi Kitamura
Auditors: Ernst & Young ShinNihon LLC

LOCATIONS

HQ: Toho Bank, Ltd. (The)
3-25 Ohmachi, Fukushima 960-8633
Phone: (81) 24 523 3131 **Fax:** (81) 24 524 1583
Web: www.tohobank.co.jp

COMPETITORS

Aozora Bank
Iyo Bank
Mitsubishi UFJ Financial Group
Miyazaki Bank
Shizuoka Bank
Towa Bank

HISTORICAL FINANCIALS

Company Type: Public

Income Statement FYE: March 31

	ASSETS ($ mil.)	NET INCOME ($ mil.)	INCOME AS % OF ASSETS	EMPLOYEES
03/15	48,952	82	0.2%	1,895
03/14	52,170	88	0.2%	1,923
03/13	49,604	67	0.1%	1,925
03/12	51,716	57	0.1%	1,934
03/11	39,387	54	0.1%	1,963
Annual Growth	5.6%	10.7%	—	(0.9%)

2015 Year-End Financials

Return on assets: 0.1%
Return on equity: 5.6%
Long-term debt ($ mil.): —
No. of shares (mil.): 252
Sales ($ mil): 537

Dividends
Yield: —
Payout: —
Market value ($ mil.): —

Tokio Marine Holdings Inc

Tokio Marine Holdings might have old roots but it still knows how to learn new tricks. Japan's oldest property/casualty insurance company the firm has one of the largest insurance sales networks in Japan and has expanded its insurance operations to about 40 additional countries in Asia Oceania Europe Africa the Middle East and the Americas. Through Tokio Marine & Nichido Fire (TMNF) Nisshin Fire Philadelphia Insurance Companies Kiln HCC Insurance and other subsidiaries Tokio Marine Holdings provides marine property/casualty personal accident fire auto and life insurance as well as reinsurance. It also offers asset management pension plans and other services.

Operations

Tokio Marine operates in four segments: domestic property/casualty insurance domestic life insurance overseas insurance and finance and others (investment advisory staffing business etc.). Domestic property/casualty insurance accounts for some 60% of sales.

Geographic Reach

The firm has insurance operations in about 40 countries throughout Asia and Oceania Europe the Middle East and the Americas. The majority of Tokio Marine's revenue comes from Japan (about 70% in fiscal 2014).

Sales and Marketing

Tokio Marine markets its products through a network of agents. Property/casualty subsidiary Tokio Marine & Nichido Life sells its products through banks property/casualty insurance agencies and an in-house sales staff.

Financial Performance

Tokio Marine's revenue has been trending upward during recent fiscal years. In fiscal 2014 (ended March) revenue increased 8% to ¥4166 billion largely due to an increase in overseas business. Domestic sales of automobile and fire policies also boosted earnings. Net income rose 42% to ¥184 billion in fiscal 2014 as fewer claims were paid and impairment losses on securities declined. Meanwhile operating cash flow increased 26% to ¥424 billion.

Strategy

The company is looking to expand both by offering new products and through acquisitions. It has increasingly built up its international operations lowering its dependence on the saturated Japanese market. In 2015 it opened its fifth branch in China. Tokio Marine Management opened a branch in Dallas that year as well.

In early 2014 Tokio Marine & Nichido Life launched a new medical insurance product –Medical Kit Love R –which is easier for customers with pre-existing medical conditions to purchase.

Mergers and Acquisitions

In 2015 Tokio Marine bought US-based HCC Insurance Holdings in a $7.5 billion transaction. The purchase significantly expands the company's presence in the US particularly in the specialty property/casualty market and will boost its international earnings. HCC sells coverage including directors' and officers' liability medical stop-loss insurance and policies for the marine aviation and energy industries.

Other countries targeted for growth efforts include China and India.

HISTORY

After the US forced Japan to open to trade in 1854 Western marine insurers began operating there. In 1878 Japan's government organized backers for a Japanese marine insurance firm. Tokio Marine and Fire Insurance was founded the next year.

Tokio grew quickly insuring trading companies like Mitsubishi and Mitsui; it soon had offices in London Paris and New York. Increased competition in the 1890s forced it to curtail its foreign operations and begin using brokers in most other countries.

Victory in the Russo-Japanese War of 1904-05 buoyed the country but the economy slowed as it demobilized. Businesses responded by forming cooperative groups known as zaibatsu. Tokio Marine and Fire was allied with the Mitsubishi group.

Before WWI Tokio expanded by adding fire personal accident theft and auto insurance and it continued to buy foreign sales brokers. Japan's insurance industry consolidated in the 1920s and the company bought up smaller competitors. The 1923 Tokyo earthquake hit the industry hard but Tokio's new fire insurance operations had little exposure.

Most of Tokio's foreign operations were seized during WWII. In 1944 Tokio merged with Mitsubishi Marine Insurance and Meiji Fire Insurance. Business grew in WWII but wartime destruction left Tokio with nothing to insure and no money to pay claims.

After the war Tokio slowly recovered and resumed overseas operations. Although the US had dismantled the zaibatsu during occupation Tokio allied once again with Mitsubishi when Japan's government rebuilt most of the old groups as keiretsu.

During the 1950s and 1960s the company grew its personal lines adding homeowners coverage. Domestic business slowed during the 1970s and 1980s and Tokio boosted operations overseas. It added commercial property/casualty insurer Houston General Insurance (a US company sold in 1997) Tokio Reinsurance and interests in insurance and investment management firms.

In the 1980s the firm invested heavily in real estate through jusen (mortgage companies). Japan's overheated real estate market collapsed in the early 1990s dumping masses of nonperforming assets on jusen and their investors (the country's major banks and insurers including Tokio).

Deregulation began in 1996 and economic recession soon followed. In 1998 Tokio joined other members of the Mitsubishi group including Bank of Tokyo-Mitsubishi and Meiji Life Insurance to form investment banking pension and trust joint ventures. The firm also formed its own investment trust and allied with such foreign financial companies as BANK ONE and United Asset Management to develop new investment products. Brokerage firm Charles Schwab Tokio Marine Securities a joint venture was launched in 1999. That year Tokio consolidated its foreign reinsurance operations into Tokio Marine Global Re in Dublin Ireland and kicked off a business push that included reorganizing its agent force and planning for online sales.

Millea Holdings was created in 2002 as the holding company for the merger between Tokio Marine and Fire and Nichido Fire and Marine. The two were combined and renamed Tokio Marine & Nichido Fire Insurance a subsidiary of Millea Holdings.

The company's 2005 acquisition of Real Seguros allowed the company to bring its life insurance products to Brazil (renamed Tokio Marine Seguradora). In 2006 Millea acquired Nisshin Fire and Marine Insurance Company as a separately operated subsidiary. In 2007 the firm purchased Asia General Holdings and its life insurance subsidiaries which operated in Singapore and Malaysia. It also purchased Japanese fire insurance provider Nihon Kousei Kyousaikai.

In 2008 Millea Holdings changed its name to Tokio Marine Holdings to reflect the positive brand recognition associated with the Tokio Marine name.

EXECUTIVES

EVP, Takaaki Tamai, age 65
President and CEO, Tsuyoshi Nagano
Managing Executive Officer, Masashi Oba
President Tokio Marine & Nichido Life, Toshifumi Kitazawa
EVP, Kazuo Kouduki
Chairman, Shuzo Sumi
Auditors: PricewaterhouseCoopers Aarata

LOCATIONS

HQ: Tokio Marine Holdings Inc
1-2-1 Marunouchi, Chiyoda-ku, Tokyo 100-0005
Phone: (81) 3 6212 3333
Web: www.tokiomarinehd.com/en/

2014 Sales

	% of total
Japan	71
US	16
Other regions	13
Total	100

PRODUCTS/OPERATIONS

2014 Sales

	% of total
Domestic property/casualty insurance	58
Overseas insurance	27
Domestic life & insurance	13
Finance & others	2
Total	**100**

Selected Mergers and Acquisitions

FY2012
Delphi Financial Group ($2.7 billion; Wilmington DE; specialty life insurer)

COMPETITORS

AIG
Allianz
Aviva
Brit Insurance
Dai-ichi Life
Daido Life
Equity Insurance
Fuji Fire and Marine
HCC Insurance
Hiscox
ING
MS&AD Holdings
Markel
Nippon Life Insurance
Prudential plc
Sompo Holdings
Sumitomo Life
Travelers Companies
Zurich Insurance Group

HISTORICAL FINANCIALS

Company Type: Public

Income Statement

FYE: March 31

	ASSETS ($ mil.)	NET INCOME ($ mil.)	INCOME AS % OF ASSETS	EMPLOYEES
03/15	174,110	2,062	1.2%	33,786
03/14	183,570	1,783	1.0%	33,310
03/13	191,614	1,377	0.7%	33,006
03/12	199,176	73	0.0%	30,831
03/11	199,605	868	0.4%	29,758
Annual Growth	(3.4%)	24.1%	—	3.2%

2015 Year-End Financials

Return on assets: 1.2%
Return on equity: 7.8%
Long-term debt ($ mil.): —
No. of shares (mil.): 754
Sales ($ mil): 36,087
Dividends
Yield: 1.9%
Payout: —
Market value ($ mil.): 28,505

	STOCK PRICE ($) FY Close	P/E High/Low	PER SHARE ($) Earnings	Dividends	Book Value
03/15	37.78	— —	2.70	0.73	39.87
03/14	30.16	— —	2.32	0.96	34.59
03/13	28.72	— —	1.79	0.00	32.74
03/12	27.66	— —	0.10	0.00	29.53
03/11	26.78	— —	1.12	0.59	29.99
Annual Growth	9.0%	— —	24.7%	5.3%	7.4%

Tokyo Electric Power Co. Inc. (The) (Japan)

Japan Inc. would grind to a halt without Tokyo Electric Power Company (TEPCO) which supplies power to 28.8 million customers in Tokyo Yokohama and the rest of the Kanto region. As one of the world's largest electric utilities TEPCO's 190 power plants have the generating capacity of approximately 64500 MW primarily produced by thermal nuclear and hydroelectric power sources. In 2011 it faced a major crisis when its Fukushima Dai-ichi nuclear plant complex experienced a partial meltdown at three reactors and radioactive material was released in the wake of a major earthquake and tsunami. The disaster could lead to multi-billion dollar losses which it has been selling assets to cover.

Public confidence had already been shaken by a rash of accidents within Japan's nuclear industry. The company had struggled to restore its credibility after the Japanese government shut down TEPCO's 17 nuclear reactors due to safety concerns prompted by the company's admittance of falsifying safety data to cover up faults at several of its nuclear facilities in 2002. In 2009 it reopened the Kashiwazaki-Kariwa Nuclear Power Station which was closed in 2007 due to a major earthquake in the region.

Through affiliates TEPCO also offers cable TV and Internet services international consulting and investing in non-Japan-based independent power producers. Other businesses include construction real estate and transportation companies.

The company is developing new green energy sources such as wind and solar in order to meet carbon emission reduction targets. In 2009 the company agreed to build a major solar project in Kawasaki Kanagawa to serve about 5900 households. In 2010 it teamed up with Toyota Tsusho to fund wind power company Eurus Energy Holdings which acquired solar power company Jindosun Park in 2011. Jindosun oversees the generation of 2974KW of electricity mostly in South Korea and will activate a 45000KW plant in the US in mid-2011.

Broadening its international power assets in 2011 the company agreed to buy 12% of Thailand-based independent power producer Electricity Generating PCL for about $274 million. However the daunting financial impact of the Fukushima disaster has cast a pall over the company's international expansion plans.

The company is selling assets to pay off its massive debt. In 2012 it agreed to sell its 67.5% stake in Australian power station Loy Yang A to the plant's minority owner AGL Resources for $1.6 billion.

HISTORY

The Tokyo Electric Power Company (TEPCO) descended from Tokyo Electric Light which was formed in 1883. In 1887 the company switched on Japan's first power plant a 25-KW fossil fuel generator. Fossil fuels were the main source of electricity in Japan until 1912 when long-distance transmission techniques became more efficient making hydroelectric power cheaper.

In 1938 Japan nationalized electric utilities despite strong objections from Yasuzaemon Matsunaga a leader in Japan's utility industry and former president of the Japan Electric Association. After WWII Matsunaga championed public ownership of Japan's power companies which helped in 1951 to establish the current system of 10 regional companies each with a service monopoly. Tokyo Electric Power was the largest. That year it was listed on the Tokyo Stock Exchange and was regulated by the Ministry of International Trade and Industry. (The ministry has regulated electric utilities since 1965.)

Fossil fuel plants made a comeback in Japan in the postwar era because they could be built more economically than hydroelectric plants. When the OPEC oil embargo of the 1970s demonstrated Japan's dependence on foreign oil TEPCO increased its use of liquefied natural gas (LNG) and nuclear energy sources. (It brought its first nuke online in 1971.) In 1977 it formed the Energy Conservation Center to promote conservation and related legislation.

To further reduce its oil dependence TEPCO joined other US and Japanese firms in building a coal gasification plant in California's Mojave Desert in 1982. Two years later TEPCO announced it would begin building its first coal-burning generator since the oil crisis. It established Tokyo Telecommunication Network (TTNet) a partnership to provide telecommunications services in 1986 and TEPCO Cable TV in 1989.

As part of its interest in alternative energy systems TEPCO established a global environment department in 1990 to conduct R&D on energy and the environment. Its environmental program has included reforestation and fuel cell research.

Liberalization in 1995 allowed Japan's electric utilities to buy power from independent power producers; TEPCO quickly lined up 10 suppliers. The company proceeded with energy experimentation in 1996 trying a 6000-KW sodium-sulfur battery at a Yokohama transformer station. The next year the company announced that it would become the first electric utility to sell liquefied natural gas as part of its energy mix and finished building the world's largest nuclear plant.

To gain experience in deregulating markets TEPCO invested in US power generating company Orion Power in 1999. (It agreed to sell its 5% stake to Reliant Energy in 2001.) At home the firm joined Microsoft and SOFTBANK to form SpeedNet which provides Internet access over TTNet's network. In 2000 TEPCO got its first taste of deregulation when large customers (accounting for about a third of the market) began choosing their electricity suppliers. Also in 2000 TEPCO joined a group of nine Japanese electric companies to create POWEREDCOM. (In 2005 TEPCO sold its stake in POWEREDCOM to KDDI in order to focus on its core power business).

In 2001 TEPCO joined up with Sumitomo and Electricit de France to build Vietnam's first independent power plant.

To raise cash in 2006 Mirant (now GenOn Energy) sold its power plants in the Philippines to TEPCO and Marubeni for $3.4 billion.

EXECUTIVES

EVP, Hiroshi Yamaguchi
EVP, Zengo Aizawa
President, Naomi Hirose
EVP, Yoshiyuki Ishizaki
Chairman, Kazuhiko Shimokobe
Auditors: Ernst & Young ShinNihon LLC

LOCATIONS

HQ: Tokyo Electric Power Co. Inc. (The) (Japan)
1-1-3 Uchisaiwai-cho, Chiyoda-Ku, Tokyo 100-8560
Phone: (81) 3 6373 1111
Web: www.tepco.co.jp

PRODUCTS/OPERATIONS

2014 Sales

	% of total
Customer service	95
Fuel & Power	2
Power Grid	2
Corporate	1
Total	**100**

Selected Subsidiaries

TEPCO CABLE TELEVISION Inc. (85% cable television)
TEPCO SYSTEMS CORPORATION (information software and services)
Toden Kogyo Co. Ltd. (facilities construction and maintenance)
Toden Real Estate Co. Inc. (property management)
Tokyo Densetsu Service Co. Ltd. (facilities construction and maintenance)

Tokyo Electric Power Environmental Engineering Company Incorporated (facilities construction and maintenance)
Tokyo Electric Power Services Company Limited (facilities construction and maintenance)

COMPETITORS

Chubu Electric Power	KDDI
Chugoku Electric Power	KEPCO
Hokkaido Electric Power	Korea Electric Power
Hokuriku Electric Power	Kyushu Electric Power
Internet Initiative Japan	NTT
Jinpan International	Osaka Gas
	Shikoku Electric
	Tohoku Electric Power
	Tokyo Gas

HISTORICAL FINANCIALS

Company Type: Public

Income Statement FYE: March 31

	REVENUE ($ mil.)	NET INCOME ($ mil.)	NET PROFIT MARGIN	EMPLOYEES
03/15	56,696	3,763	6.6%	43,330
03/14	64,245	4,249	6.6%	45,744
03/13	63,514	(7,283)	—	48,757
03/12	65,213	(9,528)	—	52,046
03/11	64,832	(15,063)	—	52,970
Annual Growth	(3.3%)	—	—	(4.9%)

2015 Year-End Financials

Debt ratio: 0.4%
Return on equity: 24.9%
Cash ($ mil.): 11,621
Current ratio: 1.21
Long-term debt ($ mil.): 50,545
No. of shares (mil.): 1,599
Dividends
Yield: —
Payout: —
Market value ($ mil.): —

TonenGeneral Sekiyu K.K.

TonenGeneral Sekiyu is a leading Japanese refiner that came into being in 2000 as the result of the merger of Japanese refiners Tonen and General Sekiyu both affiliates of global oil and gas behemoth Exxon Mobil. TonenGeneral Sekiyu (50.02%-owned by Exxon Mobil) combines Tonen's 505000 barrels a day of refining capacity in Kawasaki and Wakayama with General Sekiyu's 156000 barrels a day of capacity at Sakai. It also operates a 100000 barrels-a-day refinery at Nishihara (in Okinawa) through its 87.5%-owned Nansei Sekiyu subsidiary. TonenGeneral Sekiyu operates gas stations across Japan under the Esso General and Mobil brands. In 2015 JX Holdings agreed to merge with TonenGeneral Sekiyu.

The company is trying to diversify its sources of crude oil supply (about 70% comes from the Middle East) and upgrade its refineries in order to reduce costs.

Auditors: PricewaterhouseCoopers Aarata

LOCATIONS

HQ: TonenGeneral Sekiyu K.K.
1-8-15 Kohnan, Minato-ku, Tokyo 108-8005
Phone: (81) 3 6713 4400
Web: www.tonengeneral.co.jp

COMPETITORS

Idemitsu Kosan	JX Nippon Oil & Energy
JX Nippon Mining & Metals	Showa Shell Sekiyu

HISTORICAL FINANCIALS

Company Type: Public

Income Statement FYE: December 31

	REVENUE ($ mil.)	NET INCOME ($ mil.)	NET PROFIT MARGIN	EMPLOYEES
12/14	28,924	(117)	—	3,512
12/13	30,876	218	0.7%	2,921
12/12	32,566	635	2.0%	2,805
12/11	34,594	1,715	5.0%	2,171
12/10	29,490	527	1.8%	2,178
Annual Growth	(0.5%)	—	—	12.7%

2014 Year-End Financials

Debt ratio: 0.2%
Return on equity: (-5.0%)
Cash ($ mil.): 293
Current ratio: 0.90
Long-term debt ($ mil.): 1,821
No. of shares (mil.): 364
Dividends
Yield: —
Payout: —
Market value ($ mil.): —

Toronto Dominion Bank

The Toronto-Dominion Bank wants to score financial TDs at home and abroad. Also known as TD Bank or TD Financial the company ranks among the world's top online financial services firms and is one of the largest banks in Canada where it operates more than 1100 branches under the TD Trust banner. US subsidiary TD Bank N.A. has another 1300 branches in about 15 eastern states. TD also offers commercial financial and advisory services. Other units include TD Insurance TD Asset Management (mutual funds) and TD Securities (investment banking equities and foreign exchange). Its TD Waterhouse is the largest online brokerage in the UK and Canada; TD Bank also owns 45% of US discount brokerage TD Ameritrade.

OperationsTD Bank operates three main business segments: Canadian Retail U.S. Retail and Wholesale Banking.Canadian Retail which generates nearly 65% of the bank's revenue provides a full range of traditional banking products and other financial services to customers in the Canadian personal and commercial banking businesses including wealth and insurance services. Within this segment under its TD Canada Trust brand the bank offers personal and small business banking products and services to nearly 15 million customers through its network of 1165 branches.U.S. Retail which brings in another roughly 25% of revenue operates under the brand TD Bank and comprises the bank's US-based retail commercial and wealth management services. Retail provides a full suite of financial products and services through its network of 1300-plus branches located along the east coast of the US.Wholesale Banking which contributes just under 10% of bank revenue provides a variety of capital market investment banking and corporate banking products and services. Operating under the TD Securities brand this segment also provides services including underwriting and distribution of new debt and equity issues offering advice on strategic acquisitions and divestitures and meeting the investment brokerage needs of clients. Geographic ReachTD Bank mainly operates through its more than 1165 branches spread across Canada. Its US subsidiary TD Bank N.A. operates another 1300 branches in 15 eastern states from Maine to Florida.Sales and MarketingUnder the TD Securities brand the bank targets highly-rated companies governments and institutions in key financial markets around the world.Interested in building its brand across the US the bank boosted its marketing and business development spending by 9% to C$750 million in fiscal 2014. By comparison in 2012 the bank spent C$668 million or 12% less than in fiscal 2014. Financial PerformanceNote: Growth rates may differ after conversion to US dollars.TD Bank enjoyed its seventh straight year of revenue growth in fiscal 2014 (ended October) thanks to an improving economy domestically and in the US. Revenue jumped by 8% to C$36.65 billion ($32.7 billion) thanks to higher interest income from strong loan and deposit volume growth from the US Retail and Canadian Retail and from higher trading-related interest income from the Wholesale Banking segment. The bank also reported higher non-interest income mostly as its Canadian Retail segment collected more trading and management fees from wealth asset growth. The bank's net income also spiked by 20% to C$7.63 billion ($6.82 billion) in 2014 mostly thanks to higher revenues a decline in loan loss provisions and because the bank paid less interest on its deposits.Operations provided C$25.97 billion ($23.2 billion) or 6% less cash than in 2013 mostly as the bank paid back more of its securitization liabilities as their terms expired.

Stategy

To expand its consumer base TD has made its services more convenient to customers through a series of actions. In 2015 it launched its new SMS-based customer service for mobile phones in Canada via "TDHELP" making it the first major bank in Canada to offer such a service. In 2014 it opened a new branch in the fast-growing town of Milton in Ontario Canada. It's also been growing its credit accounts through smart acquisitions in recent years. In 2013 the bank acquired a controlling stake of Aimia's Aeroplan credit card portfolio gaining new business from non-TD customers and new revenue streams from their lines of credit. Similarly in late 2012 TD Bank and Target Corporation inked a deal for the purchase of the retailer's existing US Visa and private label credit card portfolio (with a gross outstanding balance of $5.9 billion). As part of an associated seven-year program agreement TD was granted exclusive rights as the issuer of the Target-branded Visa and private label credit cards to Target's US customers. Both deals have been paying off as the bank reported its eighth year of revenue growth in fiscal 2014 largely thanks to these relatively-new revenue sources. To raise capital and better focus on its core operations TD Bank has also divested some of its businesses in recent years. In 2013 for example bank subsidiary TD Waterhouse Canada sold its TD Waterhouse Institutional Services business to a subsidiary of National Bank of Canada for $250 million in cash.Mergers and AcquisitionsIn 2014 TD Bank acquired the remaining stake in NatWest Stockbrokers Limited from National Westminster Bank (NatWest). UK-subisidiary TD Direct Investing Limited had been partnering with NatWest for the past dozen years to provide stockbroking services to NatWest and Royal Bank of Scotland (RBS) customers under the NatWest Stockbrokers and RBS Direct Trader brands.

HISTORY

The Bank of Toronto was established in 1855 by flour traders who wanted their own banking facilities. Its growth encouraged another group of businessmen to found the Dominion Bank in 1869. Dominion emphasized commercial banking and invested heavily in railways and construction.

As the new nation expanded westward both banks established branch networks. They helped fund Canada's primary industries –dairy mining oil pulp and textiles. True to its pioneering spirit a Bank of Toronto official claimed to be the first to have set up a branch office with the help of aviation (in Manitoba in the 1920s).

The demand for agricultural products and commodities dropped after WWI but production continued full throttle creating a world grain glut that helped trigger the stock market crash of 1929. Both the Bank of Toronto and Dominion Bank contracted during the 1930s. After growing during and subsequent to WWII The Bank of Toronto and Dominion Bank decided to increase their capital base merging into a 450-branch bank in 1955.

In the 1970s TD Bank opened offices in Bangkok Beirut and Frankfurt among other cities abroad. During the 1980s it was active in making loans to less-developed countries. After the deregulation of the Canadian securities industry in 1987 then-CEO Richard Thomson reduced international lending and began focusing on brokerage activities. The strategy paid off when several Latin American countries fell behind on their loans in the late 1980s.

As the North American economy slowed in the early 1990s TD Bank's nonperforming loans increased and with it its loan loss reserves. The bank still made acquisitions including Central Guaranty Trust (1993) and Lancaster Financial Holdings (1995 investment banking). It worked to build its financial services expanding its range of service offerings and geographic coverage and buying New York-based Waterhouse Investor Services (1996); 97% of Australia-based Pont Securities (1997); and California-based Kennedy Cabot & Co. (1997). In 1998 the bank sold its payroll services to Ceridian and its Waterhouse Securities unit bought US discount brokerage Jack White & Co.

That year the government nixed TD Bank's merger with Canadian Imperial on the same day it voided the Royal Bank of Canada/Bank of Montreal deal. The banks believed the consolidation was necessary to stave off foreign banks' encroachment into Canada but the government had domestic antitrust concerns: Though Canada has one-tenth the population of the US its five top banks all ranked in the top 15 in North America.

In 1999 TD Bank bought Trimark Financial's retail trust banking business and spun off part of Waterhouse Investor Services which would become part of TD Waterhouse Group. That year the bank ramped up its focus on Internet banking.

Not giving up on acquisition-fueled growth in 2000 the company bought CT Financial Services (now TD Canada Trust) from British American Tobacco. As a condition for government approval TD Bank had to sell its MasterCard credit portfolio (sold to Citibank Canada) and a dozen southern Ontario branches (to Bank of Montreal).

The company's plans to hitch a ride on the Wal-Mart gravy train derailed in 2001. Arrangements to open bank branches in some US-based Wal-Mart stores were squelched by regulators enforcing the banking and commerce barrier. TD Bank later closed all of its existing branches (more than 100 in all) inside Canadian Wal-Marts as part of a broader restructuring.

TD Bank suffered its first-ever annual loss during fiscal year 2002. Write-downs on loans to telecommunications technology and energy firms contributed mightily to the dismal results.

Frustrated by limited growth opportunities at home in 2005 TD Bank ventured south of the border with its purchase of a stake in Banknorth. TD Bank paid about $4.8 billion in cash and stock for its original 51% stake (it bought the rest in 2007). Additionally in 2006 the company assumed about a 40% ownership in TD AMERITRADE as part of the sale of TD Waterhouse.

In 2008 the company acquired New Jersey-based Commerce Bancorp. The $8.5 billion acquisition deal added some 450 branches along the eastern seaboard to TD Bank's US network and exemplified the company's plans to expand abroad. TD merged Commerce with its TD Banknorth unit to create TD Bank.

EXECUTIVES

Group Head US Banking; President and CEO TD Bank, Mike Pedersen
SVP Corporate Development, Riaz E. Ahmed
Group Head Wholesale Banking TD Bank Group and Chairman President and CEO TD Securities, Robert E. (Bob) Dorrance, age 59, $500,000 total compensation
Group Head Canadian Banking Auto Finance and Wealth Management; President and CEO TD Canada Trust, Timothy D. (Tim) Hockey, age 52, $500,000 total compensation
President and CEO, Bharat B. Masrani, age 59, $584,650 total compensation
Group Head Risk Management and Chief Risk Officer, Mark R. Chauvin
EVP Finance, Colleen M. Johnston, $490,274 total compensation
Group Head Direct Channels Technology Marketing and People Strategies TD Bank Group, Theresa L. (Teri) Currie
Group Head Legal Compliance and Anti-Money Laundering Financial Crimes and Fraud Management Enterprise Projects and General Counsel, Norie C. Campbell
Chairman, Brian M. Levitt, age 68
Deputy Chair, Frank J. McKenna, age 67
Auditors: Ernst & Young LLP

LOCATIONS

HQ: Toronto Dominion Bank
Toronto-Dominion Centre, King Street West & Bay Street, Toronto, Ontario M5K 1A2
Phone: 416 944-6367 **Fax:** 416 982-6166
Web: www.td.com

PRODUCTS/OPERATIONS

2013 Sales

	% of total
Interest	
Loans	55
Securities	11
Noninterest	
Insurance revenue	11
Investments & securities services	9
Serice charges	6
Others	8
Total	**100**

Selected Canadian Subsidiaries

CT Financial Assurance Company (99.9%)
Meloche Monnex Inc.
  Security National Insurance Company
  Primmum Insurance Company
  TD Direct Insurance Inc.
  TD General Insurance Company
  TD Home and Auto Insurance Company
TD Asset Finance Corp.
TD Asset Management Inc.
  TD Waterhouse Private Investment Counsel Inc.
TD Investment Services Inc.
TD Life Insurance Company
TD Mortgage Corporation
  The Canada Trust Company
  TD Pacific Mortgage Corporation
TD Mortgage Investment Corporation
TD Nordique Investments Limited
TD Parellel Private Equity Investors Ltd.
TD Securities Inc.
TD Timberlane Investments Limited
  TD McMurray Investments Limited
  TD Redpath Investments Limited
  TD Riverside Investments Limited
TD Vermillion Holdings ULC
  TD Financial International Ltd. (Bermuda)
  Canada Trustco International Limited (Barbados)
  TD Reinsurance (Barbados) Inc.
  Toronto Dominion International Inc. (Barbados)
TD Waterhouse Canada Inc.
  thinkorswim Canada
Truscan Property Corporation

Selected US Subsidiaries

TDAM USA Inc.
Toronto Dominion Holdings (U.S.A.) Inc.
  TD Holdings II Inc.
  TD Securities (USA) LLC
  Toronto Dominion (Texas) LLC
  Toronto Dominion Capital (U.S.A.) Inc.
  Toronto Dominion Investments Inc.

Selected Other International Subsidiaries

Internaxx Bank S.A. (Luxembourg)
NatWest Personal Financial Management Limited (50% UK)
  NatWest Stockbrokers Limited
TD Ireland
  TD Global Finance
TD Waterhouse Bank N.V. (The Netherlands)
TD Waterhouse Investor Services (UK) Limited
  TD Waterhouse Investor Services (Europe) Limited (UK)
Toronto Dominion (South East Asia) Limited (Singapore)

COMPETITORS

BMO Financial Group
Bank of America
Berkshire Hills Bancorp
CI Financial
CIBC
Caisses centrale Desjardins
Charles Schwab
E*TRADE Financial
Edward Jones
FMR
KeyCorp
Laurentian Bank
Morgan Stanley
National Bank of Canada
RBC Financial Group
Scotiabank
Sovereign Bank

HISTORICAL FINANCIALS

Company Type: Public

Income Statement

FYE: October 31

	ASSETS ($ mil.)	NET INCOME ($ mil.)	INCOME AS % OF ASSETS	EMPLOYEES
10/15	839,261	5,937	0.7%	81,483
10/14	844,306	6,821	0.8%	81,137
10/13	824,651	6,092	0.7%	78,748
10/12	813,315	6,187	0.8%	78,397
10/11	738,424	5,783	0.8%	75,631
Annual Growth	3.3%	0.7%	—	1.9%

2015 Year-End Financials

Return on assets: 0.7%
Return on equity: 13.0%
Long-term debt ($ mil.): —
No. of shares (mil.): 1,855
Sales ($ mil): 28,808
Dividends
  Yield: 0.0%
  Payout: 47.5%
Market value ($ mil.): 76,096

	STOCK PRICE ($) FY Close	P/E High/Low		PER SHARE ($) Earnings	Dividends	Book Value
10/15	41.02	10	9	3.20	1.52	26.80
10/14	49.26	22	10	3.70	1.69	26.49
10/13	91.72	26	22	3.30	1.59	26.29
10/12	81.34	25	20	3.39	1.44	26.01
10/11	75.28	27	22	3.23	1.32	23.69
Annual Growth	(14.1%)	—	—	(0.2%)	3.7%	3.1%

Toshiba Corp

Toshiba products play an active role be it in computing controlling powering or communicating —transporting playing or even just chillin'. The company's portfolio includes personal and professional computers (PCs point-of-sale systems) telecommunications and medical equipment (LCDs for mobile devices X-ray machines) industrial machinery (power plant reactors elevators) consumer appliances (air conditioners Blu-ray Disc recorders) electronic components (electron tubes batteries) and semiconductors. Its portfolio also includes air traffic control and railway transportation systems. Customers outside Japan account for 55% of Toshiba's revenues.

In 2009 the company announced its biggest ever annual loss. The global recession took its toll across all of Toshiba's primary product groups — digital products social infrastructure electronic devices and home appliances —with each experiencing a drop in revenues and only social infrastructure reporting positive operating income.

As the global recession eased in 2009 and 2010 Toshiba saw strengthening sales and better financial results in some segments such as digital products electronic devices and home appliances. Revenue rose 1% year-over-year in the fiscal year that ended in March 2011. The company also recorded net income in 2010 and 2011.

By segment sales of digital products (about 33% of sales) decreased by 3% in fiscal 2011. Social infrastructure (also 33%) was down 2%. Electronic devices (20%) rose 6%. Home appliances (9%) increased 3%.

By 2013 the company plans to increase sales of digital products by 10% electronic devices by 13% social infrastructure by 10% and home appliances by 4%. Geographically Toshiba wants to increase its proportion of international sales from 55% to more than 65% during the same time period. While increasing sales and improving profitability remain top strategic goals Toshiba also aspires to becoming a greener company reducing its CO2 emissions and promoting more environmentally friendly products and technologies.

Digital products includes personal computers visual products hard disk drives (HDDs) and multifunction peripherals. Social infrastructure consists of energy-related equipment medical equipment IT products and elevators. Under electronic devices are semiconductors and liquid crystal displays. The home appliance segment comprises refrigerators washing/drying machines light fixtures and air conditioners. Included in the other segment is logistics services.

In 2012 Toshiba made a move to increase the scope of its storage device portfolio specifically HDDs when it bought certain of Western Digital's 3.5 inch HDD assets. The deal gives Toshiba the ability to provide products covering all aspects of the HDD market and increase its capacity to supply nearline HDDs. Demand for nearline HDDs is growing along with continued expansion in the server market. As part of the sale Western Digital acquired Toshiba Storage Device (Thailand) a disk drive manufacturer that has not resumed operations since the Thailand flooding in 2011. The sale of the HDD assets were required for Western Digital to get regulatory approval for its purchase of Hitachi Global Storage Technologies.

In 2010 the company combined its wireless handset business with that of archrival Fujitsu to create Fujitsu Toshiba Mobile Communications Limited the largest cell phone maker in Japan. The companies hope to better compete with market leader Nokia and a number of key players from Asia and North America; Fujitsu owns an 80% stake in the new company while Toshiba owns around 20%. Fujitsu is now looking to acquire Toshiba's interest in the JV in an effort to boost its smartphone operations.

In 2011 the company announced a deal that would both increase its overseas sales and provide entry into the smart grid market. Toshiba bought Swiss smart meter hardware and communications module maker Landis+Gyr for $2.3 billion including debt. Founded in 1896 Landis+Gyr boasted more than 8000 utility customers worldwide and operations in more than 30 countries; it was selected to supply 10000 smart meters to the State Grid Corporation of China as that country constructs the world's largest smart grid. Toshiba is eager to enter the burgeoning smart grid market especially as concerns about the safety of nuclear power overshadow growth plans for its nuclear power division.

Toshiba which holds a 67% stake in Westinghouse Electric shares ownership with The Shaw Group (20%) and IHI (3%). The remaining 10% is held by Kazatomprom a state-owned uranium supplier based in Kazakhstan which acquired the stake from Toshiba for $540 million in 2007. In 2011 Toshiba announced that it would acquire Shaw's stake.

In 2011 Toshiba Medical Systems bought longtime partner Vital Images a developer of visualization and analysis software used in computed tomography (CT) scanners and magnetic resonance imaging (MRI) equipment. Toshiba Medical Systems paid about $273 million in cash for the company in an effort to further expand its global imaging business.

Toshiba has used partnerships (often with competitors) to fuel product development and reduce costs. The company has worked with rivals such as Fujitsu and NEC on semiconductor development. It has a strategic relationship with SanDisk for the production of NAND flash memories.

Toshiba bought out Panasonic's stake in another joint venture Toshiba Matsushita Display Technology in 2009. Toshiba took full ownership of the unit so it can more quickly implement restructuring measures. Renamed Toshiba Mobile Display the company is a leading provider of LCDs used in mobile phones in-vehicle displays and portable computers.

In 2012 Toshiba became part of a joint venture named Japan Display Inc. (JDI) that combined its small- and medium-sized LCD panel business with those of Hitachi and Sony along with investment by a Japanese government-backed fund. The government owns 70% of JDI while the three companies each hold 10%. Also that year subsidiary Toshiba TEC which offers point-of-sale systems for retailers bought IBM's retail store solutions business for about $850 million. The initial stage of the deal will be a joint venture Toshiba Global Commerce Solutions Holdings Corporation with IBM owning just shy of 20% and Toshiba TEC owning the rest and then buying out IBM three years later. The joint venture began operations in the US Canada Mexico and Australia. Late in 2011 Toshiba and OJSC Power Machines announced a joint venture for electrical power transformer manufacturing slated for a 2013 start. The plant is to be built in St. Petersburg with Toshiba holding a nearly 50/50 ownership with OJSC Power Machines.

HISTORY

Two Japanese electrical equipment manufacturers came together in 1939 to create Toshiba. Tanaka Seizo-sha Japan's first telegraph equipment manufacturer was founded in 1875 by Hisashige Tanaka the so-called Edison of Japan. In the 1890s the company started making heavier electrical equipment such as transformers and electric motors adopting the name Shibaura Seisakusho Works in 1893. Seisakusho went on to pioneer the production of hydroelectric generators (1894) and X-ray tubes (1915) in Japan.

The other half of Toshiba Hakunetsusha & Company was founded by Ichisuke Fujioka and Shoichi Miyoshi as Japan's first incandescent lamp maker (1890). Renamed Tokyo Electric Company (1899) the company developed the coiled filament lightbulb (1921) Japan's first radio receiver and cathode-ray tube (1924) and the internally frosted glass lightbulb (1925). In 1939 it merged with Shibaura Seisakusho to form Tokyo Shibaura Electric Company (Toshiba).

Toshiba was the first company in Japan to make fluorescent lamps (1940) radar systems (1942) broadcasting equipment (1952) and digital computers (1954). Production of black-and-white televisions began in 1949. Even so through the 1970s the company was considered an also-ran trailing other Japanese business groups known as keiretsu partly because of its bureaucratic management style.

Electrical engineer Shoichi Saba became president in 1980. Saba invested heavily in Toshiba's information and communications segments. The company became the first in the world to produce the powerful one-megabit DRAM chip (1985). That year it unveiled its first laptop PC. In the meantime Saba (named chairman 1986) pushed Toshiba into joint ventures to exchange technology with companies such as Siemens and Motorola.

But in 1987 Toshiba incurred the wrath of the US government. A subsidiary sold submarine sound-deadening equipment to the USSR resulting in threats of US sanctions and a precipitous decline in its stock price and in US sales. Chairman Saba and president Sugichiro Watari resigned in shame.

Toshiba in 1992 bought a $500 million stake in Time Warner (the stake was reduced in 1998). In 1996 the company appointed marketing and multimedia specialist Taizo Nishimuro as president breaking its tradition of filling the position with an engineer from its heavy electrical operations.

In 1997 Toshiba and IBM formed joint venture Dominion Semiconductor to develop memory chips. (IBM sold its stake to Toshiba in 1999.) The next year the company looked to boost earnings by cutting its workforce and allying with other manufacturers such as Fujitsu and General Electric in development deals. But continued semiconductor price declines and sluggish demand in Japan caused the company to record its first annual loss in more than two decades.

Nishimuro made plans to cut 5000 jobs and streamlined Toshiba's 15 divisions to eight inhouse companies. Toshiba in 1999 agreed to take a $1 billion charge to settle a class-action lawsuit alleging some manufacturers supplied potentially corrupt disk drives in its portable computers —even though no Toshiba customer complaints were filed.

In 2000 Nishimuro stepped down as CEO. SVP and Information and Industrial Systems and Services subsidiary president Tadashi Okamura assumed the post. Nishimuro filled the vacant chairman's seat. Toshiba announced another restructuring effort in 2001 which included plans to reduce its workforce shift manufacturing to overseas plants and withdraw from unprofitable businesses. The following year it sold its DRAM manufacturing plant Dominion Semiconductor to Micron Technology.

In 2004 Toshiba partnered with Canon to develop surface conduction electron emitter display (SED) panels an alternative technology to LCD televisions. In 2005 Atsutoshi Nishida an executive that led the company's PC operations succeeded Okamura as CEO.

In 2006 Toshiba acquired nuclear power plant equipment and service provider Westinghouse Electric for $5.4 billion. Canon purchased Toshiba's stake in the SED joint venture in 2007.

The company acknowledged a setback for its consumer electronics business in 2008 when it announced the discontinuation of HD-DVD development. Toshiba was the primary backer of the HD-DVD format for high-definition DVD players and recorders –a market where it battled with Sony the primary backer of the competing Blu-ray format for support among manufacturers media companies and consumers.

In 2009 Norio Sasaki became CEO of Toshiba; Nishida was named chairman.

Toshiba acquired the hard-disk drive business of Fujitsu in 2009. In addition to augmenting Toshiba's consumer product-oriented disk drive line the purchase moved the company into the enterprise disk drive business. Toshiba formed three new subsidiaries with the purchase including Toshiba Storage Device Corp. The company also bought the Advanced Visual Imaging Systems division of imaging and graphics systems maker Barco that year. The purchase augmented its Toshiba Medical Systems unit which develops diagnostic medical imaging systems.

Auditors: Ernst & Young ShinNihon LLC

LOCATIONS

HQ: Toshiba Corp
1-1-1 Shibaura, Minato-ku, Tokyo 105-8001
Phone: (81) 3 3457 4511 **Fax:** (81) 3 3456 1631
Web: www.toshiba.co.jp

HISTORICAL FINANCIALS

Company Type: Public

Income Statement FYE: March 31

	REVENUE ($ mil.)	NET INCOME ($ mil.)	NET PROFIT MARGIN	EMPLOYEES
03/15	56,723	(315)	—	198,741
03/14	63,811	492	0.8%	200,260
03/13	63,079	824	1.3%	206,087
03/12	75,639	898	1.2%	209,784
03/11	78,417	1,664	2.1%	202,638
Annual Growth	(7.8%)	—	—	(0.5%)

2015 Year-End Financials

Debt ratio: 0.1%
Return on equity: (-3.2%)
Cash ($ mil.): 1,661
Current ratio: 1.15
Long-term debt ($ mil.): 8,709
No. of shares (mil.): —
Dividends
Yield: 1.7%
Payout: —
Market value ($ mil.): —

	STOCK PRICE ($) FY Close	P/E High/Low		PER SHARE ($) Earnings	Dividends	Book Value
03/15	25.17	—	—	(0.07)	0.44	2.13
03/14	25.41	3	2	0.12	0.47	2.81
03/13	30.40	2	1	0.19	0.52	2.60
03/12	26.57	2	1	0.21	0.51	2.50
03/11	29.60	1	1	0.38	0.14	2.48
Annual Growth	(4.0%)	—	—	—	32.2%	(3.6%)

Total S.A.

With operations in more than 130 countries TOTAL engages in all aspects of the petroleum industry including Upstream operations (oil and gas exploration development and production LNG) and Marketing and Services operations (refining marketing and the trading and shipping of crude oil and petroleum products). The company also produces base chemicals (petrochemicals and fertilizers) and specialty chemicals for the industrial and consumer markets (rubber processing adhesives resins and electroplating). In addition TOTAL has interests in power generation.

Geographic Reach

TOTAL has operations in 130 countries. France accounts for nearly a quarter of sales with the rest of Europe generating about 48%.

Operations

The company's business is divided into three main segments: Upstream Marketing and Services and Refining and Chemicals.

TOTAL has a refining capacity of 2.2 million barrels a day and explores for and produces oil and gas in 50 countries and had reserves of 11.5 billion barrels of oil equivalent (50% of which were proved developed reserves) in 2014. Liquids (crude oil condensates natural gas liquids and bitumen) represented 46% of these reserves; natural gas the remaining 54%. With more than 60 years of experience in the field its expertise covers natural gas as well as liquid natural gas (LNG) and liquefied petroleum gas (LPG).

The company's Marketing and Services segment has more than 15500 service stations.

TOTAL is also one of the world's largest integrated chemical producers and a leader in each of its markets –Petrochemicals and Fertilizers and Specialties.

Financial Performance

In 2014 the company's net revenues decreased by 10% due to an 11% drop in Upstream sales 7% in Refining & Chemicals and 4% in Marketing & Services .TOTAL's net income dropped by 62% in 2014 due to lower revenues the impact of purchases and an increase in depreciation depletion and amortization of tangible assets and mineral interests.In 2014 the company's cash flow decreased by 10% due to a drop in net income and changes in working capital as a result of higher inventories and accounts receivable.

Strategy

In 2014 TOTAL teamed up with Denmark's DONG Energy to develop the Edradour gas field in the West of Shetland area and to acquire a 60% stake in the neighboring Glenlivet discovery. The fields are expected to yield more than 65 million barrels of oil equivalent of reserves. That year it also signed an LNG (liquefied natural gas) Cooperation Agreement strengthening the partnership between TOTAL and CNOOC. Under the terms of an existing 15-year contract TOTAL has been supplying China with up to 1 million tons per year of LNG since 2010. The new deal sets a framework for an additional supply of 1 million tons per year of LNG as well as further cooperation throughout the LNG value chainTo raise cash and to focus on its core businesses in 2015 Total agreed to sell its gas station network and commercial sales supply and logistics assets in Turkey to Demiroren for 325 million (around $356 million). It also agreed to sell all of its interests in the FUKA and SIRGE gas pipelines and the St. Fergus Gas Terminal to North Sea Midstream Partners for £585 million ($905 million).

In 2014 TOTAL sold Total Coal South Africa its coal-producing affiliate to Exxaro Resources for $472 million. The deal is part of the company's 2012-14 asset sale program designed to help it more actively manage its portfolio. In 2014 the company also entered into a definitive agreement for the acquisition by Temasek of TOTAL's entire remaining 10.4% stake in GTT (Gaztransport & Technigaz). To raise cash in 2014 affiliate Total E&P USA signed an agreement to sell its 25% interest in Cardinal Gas Services LLC a midstream company in Ohio's Utica shale play to E1 Corporation and a consortium led by Samchully both from Korea for about $450 million.

Over the long term the company is committed to building its leading position in all three segments of its business through acquisitions divestitures and investments. It is investing heavily in refinery expansion in Jubail Saudi Arabia and in Port Arthur Texas. Other long-term growth initiatives include teaming up with Gazprom and Statoil to develop the vast Shtokman gas field in the Barents Sea.

In 2014 the company signed an agreement with Pavilion Gas a subsidiary of Pavilion Energy for the supply of 0.7 million tonnes per year of liquefied natural gas to Asia including Singapore starting in 2018.

In 2013 the Upstream segment launched major projects in Canada Congo Nigeria and Russia and acquired 20% of the high-potential Libra field in Brazil. TOTAL continued to extend its oil and gas acreage that year by obtaining licenses in promising exploration areas particularly in Bolivia Brazil Iraq and South Africa. It made large discoveries in Iraq and Argentina in 2013.

Mergers and Acquisitions

As part of its strategy of developing higher-value-added polymers and differentiating itself in markets away from commodity plastics in 2015 the company acquired 68% of Germany's Polyblend which makes polymer plastics intended primarily for the automotive industry.

HISTORY

A French consortium formed the Compagnie Française des Ptroles (CFP) in 1924 to develop an oil industry for the country. Lacking reserves within its borders France had a 24% stake in the Turkish Petroleum Company (TPC) acquired from Germany in 1920 as part of the spoils from WWI. When oil was discovered in Iraq in 1927 the TPC partners (CFP; Anglo-Persian Oil later BP; Royal Dutch Shell; and a consortium of five US oil companies) became major players in the oil game.

After WWII CFP diversified its sources for crude opening a supply in 1947 from the Venezuelan company Pantepec and making several major discoveries in colonial Algeria in 1956. It also began supplying crude to Japan South Korea and Taiwan in the 1950s. To market its products in North Africa and France and other European areas it introduced the brand name TOTAL in 1954. It began making petrochemicals in 1956. Decades later in 1985 the company adopted its brand name as part of its new name TOTAL Compagnie Française des Ptroles shortened in 1991 to TOTAL.

EXECUTIVES

SVP Human Resources and Corporate Communications, Jean-Jacques Guilbaud, age 63
President Exploration and Production, Yves-Louis Darricarr ©e, age 64
President Marketing and Services and New Energies, Philippe Boisseau, age 53
President Exploration and Production, Arnaud Breuillac
CEO Total E&P Nigeria, Elisabeth Proust
CFO, Patrick de La Chevardi "re
Chairman and CEO, Patrick Pouyann ©age 52
CEO Total E&P Canada, Laurent Maurel
President Refining and Chemicals, Philippe Sauquet
CIO, Patrick Hereng
President Gas Division, Laurent Vivier
President of the Executive Committee, Patrick Pouyann
Auditors: KPMG Audit

LOCATIONS

HQ: Total S.A.
2, place Jean Millier, La Defense 6, Courbevoie 92400
Phone: (33) 1 47 44 45 46 **Fax:** (33) 1 47 44 49 44
Web: www.total.com

2014 Sales

	% of total
Europe	
France	22
Other countries	48
Africa	10
North America	10
Other regions	10
Total	**100**

PRODUCTS/OPERATIONS

2014 Sales

	% of total
Refining & Chemicals	45
Marketing & Services	45
Upstream	10
Total	**100**

COMPETITORS

Akzo Nobel
Ashland Inc.
BASF SE
BHP Billiton
BP
Chevron
ConocoPhillips
DuPont
Eni
Exxon Mobil
Imperial Oil
MOL
Norsk Hydro ASA
Occidental Petroleum
PEMEX
PETROBRAS
Pakistan State Oil
Petrleos de Venezuela
Royal Dutch Shell
Statoil
ZaZa Energy

HISTORICAL FINANCIALS

Company Type: Public

Income Statement

FYE: December 31

	REVENUE ($ mil.)	NET INCOME ($ mil.)	NET PROFIT MARGIN	EMPLOYEES
12/14	212,018	4,244	2.0%	100,307
12/13	236,323	11,619	4.9%	98,799
12/12	240,279	14,095	5.9%	97,126
12/11	215,424	15,878	7.4%	96,104
12/10	188,009	14,147	7.5%	92,855
Annual Growth	3.1%	(26.0%)	—	1.9%

2014 Year-End Financials

Debt ratio: 24.5%
Return on equity: 5.2%
Cash ($ mil.): 25,181
Current ratio: 1.45
Long-term debt ($ mil.): 45,481
No. of shares (mil.): —
Dividends
Yield: 6.1%
Payout: —
Market value ($ mil.): —

	STOCK PRICE ($) FY Close	P/E High/Low	PER SHARE ($) Earnings	Dividends	Book Value
12/14	51.20	40 26	1.86	3.16	39.69
12/13	61.27	17 13	5.12	3.11	44.08
12/12	52.01	12 9	6.22	2.86	42.57
12/11	51.11	11 7	7.04	0.00	39.04
12/10	53.48	13 10	6.30	2.93	36.14
Annual Growth	(1.1%)	— —	(26.3%)	1.9%	2.4%

Toyota Motor Corp

Toyota Motor among the world's largest automotive manufacturers by auto sales (running a tight race with GM) designs and manufactures a diverse product line-up that ranges from subcompacts to luxury and sports vehicles to SUVs trucks minivans and buses. Its vehicles are produced either with combustion or hybrid engines as with the Prius. Toyota's subsidiaries also manufacture vehicles: Daihatsu Motor produces mini-vehicles while Hino Motors produces trucks and buses. Additionally Toyota makes automotive parts for its own use and for sale to others. Popular models include the Camry Corolla Land Cruiser and luxury Lexus line as well as the Tundra truck.

Major Toyota subsidiaries include Toyota Auto Body Co. Ltd. Toyota Motor Sales U.S.A. Toyota Motor North America Toyota Motor Engineering & Manufacturing North America Toyota Financial Services Corporation and Toyota Motor Credit Corporation.

Toyota divides its operations into the three segments of automotive (91% of total sales) financial services (6%) and other (3%). Automotive is obviously Toyota's bread and butter; the segment makes passenger and commercial vehicles minivans trucks and related parts. Its less known financial services segment provides financing to dealers and their customers for the lease or purchase of Toyota vehicles.

Toyota maintains a vast geographical reach selling to 170 countries and regions through more than 500 consolidated subsidiaries and some 210 affiliated companies. Almost 60% of its sales come from Asia (Japan counts for 48%) while North America generates around 20% of total sales. Countries in Europe Africa the Middle East Oceania and Latin America account for the remainder.

Toyota has been focused on regaining its financial footing after suffering through several economic disasters. From 2010 to 2011 its overall net revenue decreased by 2% due to the March 2011 Great East Japan Earthquake flood in Thailand and a shortage of parts supplies stemming from those disasters. Its geographical segments were also stung by volatile exchange rates. However despite these challenges the total number of overall vehicles sold in 2012 for Toyota was roughly 7.3 million vehicles up 0.6% compared to 2011.

Like its competitors Toyota is beefing up its Chinese operations by joining forces with local automotive players. With its partner China FAW Group Corporation Toyota builds nine models including Land Cruisers and Corollas in the country. The third factory operated by the JV began producing Corollas in May 2012.

Along with China India is generating a lot of interest in the automotive industry. Toyota in late 2010 opened a manufacturing plant near Bangalore through its Toyota Kirloskar Motor (TKM) joint venture with partner Kirloskar Group. The move established Toyota's presence in India's heartland by launching its compact Etios to the Indian market.

While Toyota shared the pain of its global competitors during the Great Recession it was spared the government-supervised bankruptcy reorganizations that Chrysler and GM endured. During the hard times Toyota focused on consolidating its North American operations shifting its resources and closing underperforming operations. In early 2010 it sold off Toyota Financial Services Securities Corp. (the brokerage unit of its financial arm Toyota Financial Services Corp.) to Tokai Tokyo Financial Holdings.

Toyota was met with massive recalls beginning in 2010 in regard to defective gas pedals faulty floor mats and problems with braking software. It recalled more than 8 million vehicles worldwide and halted production of the subject models including the top-selling Camry at US and Canadian plants. The recalls were the largest for Toyota in the US and the suspension of sales and production resulting from vehicle defects topped the industry's charts.

HISTORY

In 1926 Sakichi Toyoda founded Toyoda Automatic Loom Works. In 1930 he sold the rights to the loom he invented and gave the proceeds to his son Kiichiro Toyoda to begin an automotive business. Kiichiro opened an auto shop within the loom works in 1933. When protectionist legislation (1936) improved prospects for Japanese automakers Kiichiro split off the car department took it public (1937) and changed its name to Toyota.

During WWII the company made military trucks but financial problems after the war caused Toyota to reorganize in 1950. Its postwar commitment to R&D paid off with the launch of the four-wheel-drive Land Cruiser (1951); full-sized Crown (1955); and the small Corona (1957).

Toyota Motor Sales U.S.A. debuted the Toyopet Crown in the US in 1957 but it proved underpowered for the US market. Toyota had better luck with the Corona in 1965 and with the Corolla (which became the best-selling car of all time) in 1968. By 1970 Toyota was the world's fourth largest carmaker.

Toyota expanded rapidly in the US. During the 1970s the oil crisis caused demand for fuel-efficient cars and Toyota was there to grab market share from US makers. In 1975 Toyota displaced Volkswagen as the US's #1 auto importer. Toyota began auto production in the US in 1984 through NUMMI its joint venture with General Motors. The Lexus line was launched in the US in 1989.

Because of European restrictions on Japanese auto imports until 2000 Toyota's European expansion slowed. Toyota responded in 1992 by agreeing to distribute cars in Japan for Volkswagen and also by establishing an engine plant (later moved to full auto production) in the UK.

The SUV mania of the 1990s spurred Toyota's introduction of luxury minivans and light trucks. Hiroshi Okuda a 40-year veteran with Toyota and the first person from outside the Toyoda family to run the firm succeeded Tatsuro Toyoda as president in 1995. The next year Toyota consolidated its North American production units into Cincinnati-based Toyota Motor Manufacturing North America.

In 1997 Toyota introduced the Prius a hybrid electric- and gas-powered car. The next year Toyota boosted its stake in affiliate Daihatsu Motor (mini-vehicles) to about 51% and started Toyota Mapmaster (51% owned) to make map databases for car navigation systems. Okuda became chairman in 1999 replacing Shoichiro Toyoda and Fujio Cho became president (later chairman). Also that year Toyota agreed to form a joint venture with Isuzu Motors to manufacture buses.

In 2000 Toyota launched the WiLL Vi a sedan aimed at young people. It announced that it was building an online replacement parts marketplace with i2 Technologies and formed a financial services company (Toyota Financial Service) and a brokerage firm (Toyota Financial Services Securities Corp.). Toyota also bought a 5% stake in Yamaha Motor (the world's #2 motorcycle maker) and raised its stake in truck maker Hino Motors from about 20% to around 34%.

International developments included Toyota's agreement with the Chinese government to produce passenger cars for sale in China built by Tianjin Toyota Motor Corp. a joint venture between Chinese carmaker Tianjin Automobile Xiali and Toyota. In 2001 Toyota opened a plant in France. Later that year Toyota also increased its stake in Hino Motors to 50%. With partners Toyoda Gosei and Horie Metal Co. Ltd. Toyota formed a joint venture in 2002 to manufacture resin fuel tank systems. In 2004 Toyota forged a joint venture agreement with Guangzhou Automobile Group to build engines in China. The following year Toyota established 14 Lexus dealerships in China. The company began joint car production in Europe with Peugeot S.A. in 2005. Also in 2005 Toyota bought just under 9% of Fuji Heavy Industries —the Japanese maker of Subaru passenger vehicles. The two companies began production of Toyota Camrys at Fuji Heavy Industries' underutilized Subaru of Indiana plant in 2007.

After suffering through the Great Recession from 2008 to 2010 Toyota faced another unforeseen crisis. In March 2011 its business suffered unexpectedly from the Great East Japan Earthquake which triggered a deadly tsunami and subsequent nuclear crisis that forced Tokyo Electric Power (Tepco) to shut down reactors at two nuclear power plants and five other conventional power plants. The events forced manufacturers to reduce their output or move production to other regions. Toyota along with its rivals (Nissan Honda and Mazda) were forced to close their factories days after the devastation.

EXECUTIVES

Senior Managing Director Asia and China Operations Group, Akio Toyoda, age 59
EVP and Board Member, Masamoto Maekawa
EVP and Representative Director, Satoshi Ozawa, age 66
EVP and Board Member, Seiichi Sudo
EVP and Board Member, Yasumori Ihara, age 64
Senior Managing Officer, Mitsuhisa Kato
EVP and Board Member, Nobuyori Kodaira, age 66
CEO Tecno Art Research, Hiroshi Kawahara
Chairman, Takeshi Uchiyamada, age 69
Auditors: PricewaterhouseCoopers Aarata

LOCATIONS

HQ: Toyota Motor Corp
1 Toyota-cho, Toyota, Aichi 471-8571
Phone: (81) 565 28 2121 **Fax:** (81) 565 23 5800
Web: www.toyota.co.jp

2015 Sales

	% of total
Japan	42
North America	28
Asia	15
Europe	8
Other	7
Total	**100**

PRODUCTS/OPERATIONS

2015 Sales

	% of total
Automotive	90
Financial services	6
Other	4
Total	**100**

Selected Products

Vehicles
- 4Runner
- Allion (sold in Japan)
- Alphard (minivan sold in Japan)
- Aurus (hybrid)
- Avalon
- Camry (also hybrid)
- Corolla
- Corolla Rumion
- Crown
- FJ Cruiser
- Highlander (also hybrid)
- Land Cruiser
- Lexus
- GX
- LS600h (hybrid)
- LX (SUV)
- RX
- SC
- Mark X (sold in Japan)
- Matrix
- Premio (sold in Japan)
- Prius (hybrid)
- RAV4
- Scion
- Sequoia
- Sienna (minivan)
- Tacoma (truck)
- Tundra (truck)
- Vanguard
- Vellfire (minivan)
- Venza
- Wish (minivan sold in Japan)
- Yaris (marketed in Japan as the Vitz)

Other products
- Factory automation equipment
- Forklifts and other industrial vehicles
- Housing products

COMPETITORS

BMW	Isuzu
Brilliance China	Kia Motors
Caterpillar	Komatsu
Chery Automobile	Kubota
Daimler	Land Rover
Deere	Mazda
FCA US	Mitsubishi Motors
Fiat Chrysler	Nissan
Ford Motor	Peugeot
Fuji Heavy Industries	Renault
General Motors	Shanghai Automotive
Global Diversified Industries	Suzuki Motor
	Tata Motors
Honda	Volkswagen
Hyundai Motor	Volvo

HISTORICAL FINANCIALS

Company Type: Public

Income Statement

FYE: March 31

	REVENUE ($ mil.)	NET INCOME ($ mil.)	NET PROFIT MARGIN	EMPLOYEES
03/15	226,993	18,114	8.0%	344,109
03/14	248,905	17,662	7.1%	338,875
03/13	234,495	10,225	4.4%	333,498
03/12	226,546	3,456	1.5%	325,905
03/11	229,374	4,929	2.1%	317,716
Annual Growth	(0.3%)	38.5%	—	2.0%

2015 Year-End Financials

Debt ratio: 0.3%
Return on equity: 13.9%
Cash ($ mil.): 43,473
Current ratio: 1.09
Long-term debt ($ mil.): 83,467
No. of shares (mil.): —
Dividends
Yield: 2.3%
Payout: 51.0%
Market value ($ mil.): —

	STOCK PRICE ($) FY Close	P/E High	P/E Low	PER SHARE ($) Earnings	Dividends	Book Value
03/15	139.89	0	0	5.73	3.22	44.47
03/14	112.90	0	0	5.57	2.54	44.22
03/13	102.64	0	0	3.23	1.28	40.76
03/12	86.82	1	1	1.10	1.22	40.61
03/11	80.25	1	1	1.57	1.03	39.79
Annual Growth	14.9%	—	—	38.2%	32.9%	2.8%

Toyota Tsusho Corp

Toyota Tsusho is the trading unit for the Toyota Group which includes Toyota Motor and auto parts maker DENSO. The company brokers a wide array of goods including metals such as steel and aluminum (comprising its largest division) machinery and electronics energy and chemicals and various consumer products. As its family relationship would imply Toyota Tsusho exports Toyota vehicles around the world but plenty of non-automotive consumer products also contribute to its business. Those other products include foodstuffs like produce and wine as well as personal nursing care equipment. Toyota Motor Corporation owns 22% of the company while Toyota Industries owns 11%.

With the global recession as a background Toyota Tusho's revenues fell almost 19% in 2010. The downturn was precipitated by an across-the-board drop in the company's sales led by a 28% dip in its Automotive division and 21% in its Metals unit. Correspondingly net income was off 32% over 2009.

In 2010 parent company Toyota Motor introduced a new low-carbon plastic material to be used in a number of its 2011 model vehicles. The "Ecological Plastic" developed by Toyota Tusho marks the world's first use of bio-polyethylene terephthalate derived from sugar cane. The new material is a second-generation bio-plastic that is more durable than earlier substances.

Also that year Eurus Energy Holdings a joint venture between Tokyo Electric Power and Toyota Tsusho acquired South Korean solar power company Jindosun Park Inc. Jindosun oversees the generation of 2974KW of electricity mostly in South Korea and will activate a 45000KW plant in the US in mid-2011.

In 2010 Toyota Tsusho acquired UK-based CalEnergy Gas's 5% stake in the Otway Gas Project and exploration rights in the Bass Straits in Australia. Toyota Tsusho considers Australia an important country for upstream investments in the gas value chain.

The company agreed in 2009 to separate its automotive fabrics business and join the unit with similar businesses of Toyota Boshoku and Kawashima Selkon. Toyota Tsusho own 30% of the resulting company. The move away from sole ownership of that business fits within Tsusho's general strategic plan to earn half of its revenue from the automotive sector by 2015.

The acquisition of TOMEN Corporation made Toyota Tsusho the sixth-largest trading company in Japan and it expanded the company's operations in the non-auto sector. Products under Tomen's purview include chemicals and plastics foodstuffs IT telecommunications and power supply equipment and textiles.
Auditors: PricewaterhouseCoopers Aarata

LOCATIONS

HQ: Toyota Tsusho Corp
Century Toyota Bldg., 4-9-8 Meieki, Nakamura-ku, Nagoya, Aichi 450-8575
Phone: (81) 52 584 5482 **Fax:** 502 868 3355
Web: www.toyota-tsusho.com

HISTORICAL FINANCIALS

Company Type: Public

Income Statement FYE: March 31

	REVENUE ($ mil.)	NET INCOME ($ mil.)	NET PROFIT MARGIN	EMPLOYEES
03/15	72,207	563	0.8%	53,241
03/14	75,017	707	0.9%	50,423
03/13	67,001	716	1.1%	48,336
03/12	72,129	807	1.1%	33,845
03/11	69,362	569	0.8%	31,081
Annual Growth	1.0%	(0.3%)	—	14.4%

2015 Year-End Financials

Debt ratio: 0.3%
Return on equity: 6.4%
Cash ($ mil.): 4,160
Current ratio: 1.34
Long-term debt ($ mil.): 8,120
No. of shares (mil.): 351
Dividends
Yield: —
Payout: —
Market value ($ mil.): —

TUI AG

TUI has the European travel business cornered. One of the world's largest integrated tourism companies TUI sells leisure travel packages and provides other travel services under some 200 brands in some 20 countries. Its hotel portfolio counts around 250 hotels in about 30 countries (brands include Riu Grecotel and Dorfhotel) and its cruise segment includes subsidiary Hapag-Lloyd Cruises a leading provider of discovery and luxury cruises to the German market and TUI Cruises a joint venture with Royal Caribbean Cruises. The travel company also owns a stake in container ship operator Hapag-Lloyd AG.

HISTORY

What became TUI was founded in Berlin in 1923 as Preussische Bergwerks-und Hutten-Aktiengesellschaft (Prussian Mine and Foundry Company) to operate former state-owned mining companies saltworks and smelters. Despite outmoded equipment and a war-shattered economy the company prospered. So in 1929 the Prussian parliament combined Preussag with Hibernia and Preussischen Elektrizitats to form the state-run VEBA group hoping to stimulate foreign investment.

Operating as part of VEBA didn't work out as well as Preussag had hoped and WWII left the company a shell of its former self. In 1952 as restrictions on steel production were lifted and industry rebounded Preussag relocated to Hanover. After taking steps to reestablish itself Preussag made a public offering in 1959; VEBA kept about 22%.

A worldwide steel glut that lasted through the 1960s forced Preussag to diversify. Acquisitions included railroad tank car and transport agent VTG and shipbuilding and chemical companies. The company also formed oil exploration unit Preussag Energie in 1968. In 1969 VEBA sold its remaining stake in Preussag to Westdeusche Landesbank (WestLB).

When the 1970s oil crisis drove up steel costs Preussag began international ventures to counter falling revenues at home. But the 1980s brought PR disasters. The European Commission fined Preussag and five other zinc producers for antitrust violations in 1984.

In 1989 Preussag reorganized into a holding company with four independent units: coal oil natural gas and plant construction. But it was about to take a sharp business turn. Michael Frenzel who had managed WestLB's industry holdings became CEO in 1994 in the midst of another steel recession. Frenzel was determined to shift Preussag away from its rusting past and toward services and technology. In 1997 it acquired container shipping and travel firm Hapag-Lloyd which had a 30% stake in Touristik Union International (TUI). By the end of 1998 the acquisitions of the rest of TUI First Reisebuero Management and a 25% stake in the UK's Thomas Cook (raised to 50.1% in 1999) had made Preussag Europe's top tourism group.

As part of its restructuring Preussag traded its plant engineering units and half of its shipbuilding unit (HDW) to Babcock Borsig for a 33% stake in that company in 1999. Preussag then made plans to transfer another 25% of HDW to Sweden's Celsius in a deal (along with Babcock Borsig) to merge Celsius' Kockums submarine shipyards with HDW. That year Hapag-Lloyd and TUI were merged into Hapag Touristik Union (renamed TUI Group in 2000); VTG merged with Lehnkering a 126-year-old freight forwarding group becoming VTG-Lehnkering.

Preussag also acquired a stake in French package tour leader Nouvelles Frontires and sold a metals trading unit W. & O. Bergmann to Enron. By 2002 the company had sold off most of its non-tourism operations changed its name to TUI and restructured its business to concentrate on travel-related businesses.

In 2004 TUI sold a division of its VTG-Lehnkering logistics operation to investors for an undisclosed amount. Also that year TUI Travel Solutions GmbH sold 50% of its stake in TQ3 Travel Solutions to Navigant International. (It sold the rest of TQ3 to Navigant two years later.)

WestLB surrendered its majority shareholding of TUI in 2004 freeing up 90% of the company's shares for free float.

In 2005 the company purchased Canada-based CP Ships for almost $2 billion making Hapag-Lloyd one of the world's largest container carriers.

Two years later TUI expanded its travel business by buying First Choice Holidays and combining the UK-based company with its existing tourism operations to form TUI Travel a publicly traded company in which TUI held a controlling stake. Around the same time the company decided to shed its container shipping operations and focus solely on its tourism and travel services businesses. To this end in March 2009 TUI sold Hapag-Lloyd to a German consortium but retained a 43% stake in the company. (TUI's stake in Hapag-Lloyd increased to about 50% as loans to the company were converted to equity.)

EXECUTIVES

Chief HR and Legal Affairs, Peter Engelen, age 59
Chief Tourism; CEO First Choice Holidays and TUI Travel, Peter Long, age 63
CFO, Mikhail Noskov
Chairman, Michael Frenzel, age 68
Deputy Chairman, Petra Gerstenkorn, age 61
Auditors: PricewaterhouseCoopers Aktiengesellschaft Wirtschaftspruefungsgesellschaft

LOCATIONS

HQ: TUI AG
Karl-Wiechert-Allee 4, Hanover D-30625
Phone: (49) 511 566 00 **Fax:** (49) 511 56 1901
Web: www.tui-group.com

PRODUCTS/OPERATIONS

2015 Sales

	% of total
Tourism	
Northern Region	35
Central Region	28
Western Region	15
Hotels & Resorts	3
Cruise	
Other Tourism	2
Specialist Group	9
Hotelbeds Group	6
All other segments	1
Total	**100**

COMPETITORS

Accor
American Express
Carlson Wagonlit
Carnival Corporation
Club Med
Kuoni Travel
REWE
Royal Caribbean Cruises
Thomas Cook
Travelport

HISTORICAL FINANCIALS

Company Type: Public

Income Statement FYE: September 30

	REVENUE ($ mil.)	NET INCOME ($ mil.)	NET PROFIT MARGIN	EMPLOYEES
09/15	22,436	381	1.7%	76,036
09/14	23,559	131	0.6%	77,309
09/13	24,939	5	0.0%	74,445
09/12	23,701	(19)	—	73,812
09/11	23,582	32	0.1%	73,707
Annual Growth	(1.2%)	85.5%	—	0.8%

2015 Year-End Financials

Debt ratio: 15.0%
Return on equity: 15.7%
Cash ($ mil.): 1,875
Current ratio: 0.58
Long-term debt ($ mil.): 1,853
No. of shares (mil.): 586
Dividends
Yield: 1.3%
Payout: 16.7%
Market value ($ mil.): 5,338

	STOCK PRICE ($) FY Close	P/E High/Low	PER SHARE ($) Earnings	Dividends	Book Value
09/15	9.10	15 12	0.71	0.12	3.66
09/14	6.97	28 21	0.39	0.00	10.57
09/13	6.05	— —	(0.11)	0.00	10.96
09/12	6.04	— —	(0.21)	0.00	10.67
09/11	6.04	— —	(0.01)	0.00	13.24
Annual Growth	10.8%	—	—	—	(27.5%)

Turkiye Garanti Bankasi A.S.

Türkiye Garanti Bankasi (Garanti Bank Turkey) provides banking services from about 1000 domestic branches and more than 4000 ATMs across Turkey though subsidiaries and branches can also be found in China Cyprus Germany Luxembourg Malta Russia and the UK. In addition to traditional deposit products Garanti Bank provides brokerage factoring insurance leasing personal pension plans portfolio management and other services. As Turkey's second-largest private bank Garanti serves more than 13 million customers and boasts assets of more than $100 billion. The bank is jointly owned by Dogus Holding Co. and Spain's second-largest lender Banco Bilbao Vizcaya Argentaria which owns a 39% stake.

OperationsBroadly speaking Garanti Bank Turkey generates more than 80% of its revenue in the form of interest income (mostly from retail and corporate loans) while the remainder of its revenue comes from fee and commission income. Its three main segments include Retail Banking (which generates 30% of revenue); Corporate Banking (which brings in more than 30% of revenue) and Investment Banking (making up nearly 15% of revenue). The bank's subsidiaries include Garantibank International N.V. Garantibank Moscow and Garanti Romania.Geographic ReachIn addition to its nearly 1000 domestic branches across Turkey Garanti has six foreign branches in Cyprus and one branch in Luxembourg and Malta each. It also has three representative offices in London Dusseldorf and Shanghai.Sales and MarketingGaranti's 19000 employees provide banking services to more than 13 million customers through its branch network and call center as well as through digital banking platforms (social banking mobile and internet).Financial PerformanceNote: Growth rates may differ after conversion to US dollars.Garanti's revenue has hovered between $8 billion and $10 billion over the past few years. Revenue in 2014 jumped by double digits to T$17.89 billion ($9.43 billion) mostly thanks to 12% growth in net fees and commissions income but also thanks to a 20% jump in interest income (loan business grew by 16%) as interest rates remained high while the country's central bank battled 9.5% inflation.Higher revenue in 2014 drove the bank's net income up by double digits to T$3.68 billion. Cash levels also improved along with the higher cash earnings.

Stategy

To achieve its long-term sustainable growth strategy Garanti Bank Turkey has been focusing on growing its domestic loan business with an eye toward making safer loans with strong risk-adjusted returns. Indeed to its credit the bank's non-performing loans made up just 3% of its total loan portfolio in 2014. For 2015 the bank's CEO remained fairly certain that its domestic loan business would be driven by new business loans and grow by 15% to 20% for the year right in line with industry-wide forecasts in the country. The bank also provides a "one-stop-shop" experience for its clients with its wide array of other financial products and services giving the bank cross-selling leverage to grow existing business relationships with its more than 13 million customers. In 2014 the bank was the market leader in consumer loans mortgages and auto loans in Turkey and the second largest market player in the assets loans and customer deposits categories.

EXECUTIVES

President CEO and Director, Ergun - zen
Executive Vice President Financial Institutions and Corporate Banking, Ali Fuat Erbil
Executive Vice President Technology Operational Services and Central Marketing, H sn Erel
Executive Vice President Domestic & Overseas Subsidiaries Coordination, Turgay G ¶hensin
Executive Vice President Support Services, Adnan Memis
Executive Vice President Strategic and Financial Planning, Murat Mergin
EVP Human Resources Training Treasury & Investment Banking, G ¶khan Er n
Executive Vice President - Loans, Erhan Adali
Executive Vice President Delivery Channels Social Platforms Management Customer Satisfaction, Didem Din §r Baser
Executive Vice President General Accounting & Financial Reporting, brahim Aydinli
Executive Vice President Commercial Banking, Recep Bastug
Executive Vice President Legal Services and Retail Risk Monitoring, Aydin D ren
Executive Vice President Project and Acquisition Finance Sustainability, Ebru Dildar Edin
EVP Retail and Private Banking Call Center Garanti Payment Systems CEO, Onur Gen §
Executive Vice President SME Banking Corporate Brand Management and Marketing Communication, Nafiz Karadere
Executive Vice President Purchasing & Tax Management, Aydin Senel
Executive Vice President Delivery Channels, Didem Bas
Chairman, Ferit Faik Sahenk
Vice Chairman, S leyman S ¶zen
Auditors: Deloitte-DRT Bagimsiz Denetim ve Serbest Muhasebeci Mali Musavirlik AS

LOCATIONS

HQ: Turkiye Garanti Bankasi A.S.
Levent, Nispetiye Mahallesi, Aytar Caddesi, No. 2, Besiktas, Istanbul, Istanbul Province 34340
Phone: (90) 212 318 18 18 **Fax:** (90) 212 318 18 88
Web: www.garantibank.com

PRODUCTS/OPERATIONS

2014 Sales

	% of total
Interest income	80
Net fee and commission income	15
Other operting income	5
Total	**100**

2014 Sales

	% of total
Corporate Banking	33
Retail Banking	31
Investment Banking	13
Others	23
Total	**100**

COMPETITORS

Akbank
Finansbank
Isbank
Ko§
Sabanci
Sekerbank
Trk Ekonomi Bankasi
Yapi Kredi

HISTORICAL FINANCIALS

Company Type: Public

Income Statement FYE: December 31

	ASSETS ($ mil.)	NET INCOME ($ mil.)	INCOME AS % OF ASSETS	EMPLOYEES
12/15	94,086	1,291	1.4%	23,191
12/14	104,782	1,638	1.6%	19,036
12/13	101,791	1,669	1.6%	21,853
12/12	99,102	1,878	1.9%	20,287
12/11	85,900	1,789	2.1%	16,775
Annual Growth	2.3%	(7.8%)	—	8.4%

2015 Year-End Financials

Return on assets: 1.4%
Return on equity: 12.8%
Long-term debt ($ mil.): —
No. of shares (mil.): —
Sales ($ mil): 8,344
Dividends
Yield: 1.5%
Payout: 11.4%
Market value ($ mil.): —

	STOCK PRICE ($) FY Close	P/E High	P/E Low	PER SHARE ($) Earnings	Dividends	Book Value
12/15	2.38	4	2	0.31	0.04	0.03
12/14	3.97	5	3	0.39	0.09	0.03
12/13	3.21	6	4	0.40	0.06	0.03
12/12	5.20	7	4	0.45	0.06	0.03
12/11	3.11	5	4	0.43	0.05	0.02
Annual Growth	(6.5%)	—	—	(7.8%)	(7.8%)	3.3%

Turkiye Is Bankasi A.S.

Türkiye İş Bankasι or Isbank is banking in Turkey. Serving some 15 million customers the institution known as Isbank is the country's largest publicly-traded bank and provides corporate banking commercial lending treasury banking private banking and traditional retail banking products and services through more than 1300 branches and 6300-plus ATMs across Turkey. It also boasts insurance investment advisory and real estate investment businesses. Founded in 1924 by mandate of the Turkish Republic's founding father Mustafa Kemal Atatürk employees now own a roughly 40% stake in the bank while the Republican People's Party owns a 28% stake in the name of the founder.

OperationsThe bank operates through five main banking businesses. Its Commercial Banking and Corporate Banking businesses which made up 36% and 18% of the bank's total revenue in 2014 respectively provides large corporations SMEs and other trading companies with project financing traditional account and card products operating and investment loans foreign trade transactions and financing letters of guarantee and credit and other corporate banking services.Isbank's Retail Banking (20% of revenue) provides traditional banking services to individuals while its Treasury Banking business (20% of revenue) provides medium and long-term funding tools including securities and foreign currency trading money market transactions swaps futures and other complex financial transactions. The bank's small Private Banking business (less than 1% of revenue) serves high-net worth individuals with cash management and wealth management services.Its non-banking operations (5% of revenue) include: insurance; 'investment and finance' which provides leasing factoring brokerage corporate finance investment advisory private portfolio management and real estate investments; and the 'manufacturing and trading' business which involves glass production and complementary industrial and commercial operations and food production. In 2015 the bank also had equity investments in 25 companies operating mainly in the industry and financial sector.The bank generated more than 80% of its total revenue in 2014 from interest income (mostly from loans) while about 12% came from fee and commission based income. The rest of revenue mostly came from non-banking business (mostly manufacturing and insurance) and securities trading income. Geographic ReachIsbank boasts more than 1330 branches across Turkey (it's home country) but also has foreign branches in London The Turkish Republic of Northern Cyprus Baghdad Batumi Tbilisi Pristine and Prizren. It also has banking subsidiaries in Germany and Russia.Financial Performance Note: Growth rates may differ after conversion to US dollars.Isbank has struggled to consistently grow its revenue profit in recent years though its financials have been relatively stable in the years following the financial crisis. Isbank enjoyed a breakout year in 2014 however with revenue growing by double digits to 33.37 billion Turkish Lira (about $14.4 billion) as the bank grew its loan business across its Corporate Commercial and Retail Banking businesses. Commercial banking led most of the growth with its revenue spiking by more than 50% during the year while income from Commercial and Retail banking swelled by 31% and 23% respectively. The bank also saw 30%-plus growth in its Investment and Finance and Manufacturing and Trading divisions during the year as well.Higher revenue in 2014 drove Isbank's net income up by 4% to TL$4.57 billion (roughly $1.96 billion) while the bank's operations used more cash than in the prior year as it took in fewer deposits and used more cash toward repurchase agreements.

Stategy

Isbank stated in 2015 that its top three objectives were to: provide fast and efficient services that meet its customers needs; consistently enhance its shareholder value; and motivate its employees to maximize their performance.The bank has been expanding its branch and ATM network in recent years to grow its loan business focusing mostly on growing relationships with large corporate as well as small-to-midsize enterprise (SME) customers. In 2014 alone the bank added 44 new branches to its network and more than 600 new ATMs growing its total network by more than 3%.OwnershipThe Isbank Pension Fund representing active and retired bank employees owned about 40% of Isbank through the Private Pension Fund of Employees in early 2015. Some 28% of the bank was owned in the name of Atatürk by the Republican People's Party.

EXECUTIVES

CEO and Director, Adnan Bali, age 54

Auditors: Akis Bagimsiz Denetim ve Serbest Muhasebeci Mali Musavirlik A.S.

LOCATIONS

HQ: Turkiye Is Bankasi A.S.
Is Kuleleri, Istanbul, Levent 34330
Phone: (90) 212 316 00 00 **Fax:** (90) 212 316 09 00
Web: www.isbank.com.tr

PRODUCTS/OPERATIONS

2014 Sales

	% of total
Interest income	52
Non-interest income	
Income from manufacturing operations	21
Income from insurance operations	11
Fee and commission income	7
Securities trading income	3
Income from other operations	2
Foreign exchange gains	2
Others	2
Total	**100**

2014 Sales

	% of total
Banking business	
Commercial	35
Retail	20
Treasury investment	19
Corporate	18
others	2
Non-banking business	
Investment and finance	3
Insurance	2
Manufacturingtrading and service	1
Total	**100**

COMPETITORS

Akbank
Bank of Cyprus
Development Bank of Turkey
Finansbank
GarantiBank
Sekerbank
Trk Ekonomi Bankasi
Yapi Kredi

HISTORICAL FINANCIALS

Company Type: Public

Income Statement FYE: December 31

	ASSETS ($ mil.)	NET INCOME ($ mil.)	INCOME AS % OF ASSETS	EMPLOYEES
12/14	116,528	1,615	1.4%	24,308
12/13	112,508	1,724	1.5%	24,129
12/12	111,088	2,330	2.1%	24,411
12/11	96,960	1,303	1.3%	24,887
12/10	97,346	1,716	1.8%	23,944
Annual Growth	4.6%	(1.5%)	—	0.4%

2014 Year-End Financials

Return on assets: 1.4%
Return on equity: 14.5%
Long-term debt ($ mil.): —
No. of shares (mil.): —
Sales ($ mil): 13,815
Dividends
Yield: —
Payout: 272.9%
Market value ($ mil.): —

	STOCK PRICE ($) FY Close	P/E High/Low	PER SHARE ($) Earnings	Dividends	Book Value
12/14	0.00	— —	0.01	0.04	(0.00)
12/13	2.02	59 43	0.02	0.05	(0.00)
12/12	3.20	86 63	0.02	0.05	(0.00)
12/11	2.76	147109	0.01	0.06	(0.00)
Annual Growth	—	— —	5.5%	(10.2%)	—

UBS Group AG

Auditors: Ernst & Young Ltd.

LOCATIONS

HQ: UBS Group AG
Bahnhofstrasse 45, Zurich CH-8001
Phone: (41) 44 234 11 11
Web: www.ubs.com

HISTORICAL FINANCIALS

Company Type: Public

Income Statement FYE: December 31

	REVENUE ($ mil.)	NET INCOME ($ mil.)	NET PROFIT MARGIN	EMPLOYEES
12/14	35,123	3,503	10.0%	60,155
12/13	39,429	3,559	9.0%	60,205
12/12	38,759	(2,705)	—	62,628
Annual Growth	(4.8%)	—	—	(2.0%)

2014 Year-End Financials

Debt ratio: —
Return on equity: 6.9%
Cash ($ mil.): 105,210
Current ratio: —
Long-term debt ($ mil.): —
No. of shares (mil.): —
Dividends
Yield: —
Payout: —
Market value ($ mil.): —

	STOCK PRICE ($) FY Close	P/E High/Low	PER SHARE ($) Earnings	Dividends	Book Value
12/14	0.00	— —	0.92	0.00	14.10
12/13	0.00	— —	0.93	0.00	14.86
Annual Growth	—	— —	(0.6%)	—	(2.6%)

Ultrapar Participacoes S.A.

Ultrapar's strategy goes well beyond breaking even in Brazil. Holding company Ultrapar Participções' subsidiaries distribute liquefied petroleum gas (LPG) through subsidiary Ultragaz refine and market petroleum products (through Companhia Brasileira de Petróleo Ipiranga) produce chemicals and petrochemicals and provide storage- and transportation-related products. Its Oxiteno unit oversees chemical and petrochemical activities while Ultracargo handles transportation and storage. Ultrapar also operates a petroleum refining business through its investment in Refinaria de Petróleo Riograndense S.A. Ultra S.A holds a 66% stake in Ultrapar.

Operations

The company operates five main business segments: gas distribution fuel distribution chemicals storage and drugstores. The gas distribution segment (Ultragaz) distributes LPG to residential commercial and industrial consumers especially in the South Southeast and Northeast regions of Brazil. The fuel distribution segment (Ipiranga) operates the distribution and marketing of gasoline ethanol diesel fuel oil kerosene natural gas for vehicles and lubricants and related activities throughout all the Brazilian territory. Ipiranga contributed 86% of the company's total revenues in 2014. The chemicals segment (Oxiteno) produces ethylene oxide and its main derivatives and fatty alcohols which are raw materials used in the home and personal care agrochemical paints varnishes and other industries. The storage segment (Ultracargo) operates liquid bulk terminals especially in the Southeast and Northeast regions of Brazil. The drugstores segment (Extrafarma) trades pharmaceutical hygiene and beauty products through its own drugstore chain in the states of Pará Amapá Maranhão Piauí Ceará and Rio Grande do Norte. Ultragaz (the LPG distribution subsidiary of Ultrapar and one of the largest distributors in Brazil) introduced LPG for home cooking in that country and helped pioneer the development of the petrochemical industry there. It delivers LPG to 11 million households and to 48000 customers in the bulk segment. The company also manufactures 1500 products used in various industrial sectors such as cosmetics detergents crop protection chemicals packaging textiles and coatings.

Geographic Reach

Ultragaz operates in all regions of Brazil through a distribution network comprised of 17 filling plants. Ipiranga has presence in Brazilian territory. Extrafarma operates in six states in the North and Northeast regions of Brazil and distribution centers one in Belm and another one in Aquiraz. Oxiteno has eleven industrial units in Brazil Mexico the US Uruguay and Venezuela and commercial offices in Argentina Belgium China and Colombia.

Ultrapar through Oxiteno operates three plants in Mexico. Oxiteno's six international plants produce specialty chemicals. It also has commercial offices in the US Argentina Belgium China and Colombia.

Sales and Marketing

Ultragaz distributes LPG to residential commercial and industrial market segments. Ipiranga distributes gasoline ethanol diesel NGV fuel oil kerosene and lubricants through a network of 7056 service stations and directly to large customers. Extrafarma has distribution centers and has 223 drugstores. It has a vehicle fleet and a network of 4900 independent retailers in the bottled segment.

Financial Performance

In 2014 Ultrapar's net revenues from sales and services increased 11% (in local currency) mainly as a result of the increased sales volumes in all businesses. Ultrapar's net revenues from sales and services includes revenues from fuel and gas sales by Ultragaz and Ipiranga respectively pharmaceutical products sales by Extrafarma specialty chemicals sales by Oxiteno and liquid bulk storage services provided by Ultracargo reduced by sales taxes such as ICMS PIS and Cofins and by discounts and sales returns.

Ipiranga's net revenues from sales and services increased by 10% due to higher sales volume and diesel refinery prices and an increase in gasoline refinery prices coupled with an increase in ethanol costs and an improved sales mix resulting from investments in the expansion of the service station network. Sales volume of gasoline ethanol and natural gas for vehicles increased mainly as a result of growth in the light vehicles fleet and strong investments made in new service stations and in the conversion of unbranded service stations. Diesel volumes remained stable with an increase in the reseller segment (the result of investments for the expansion of the network) offset by the weak performance of the economy.

Ultragaz Oxiteno Ultracargo and Extrafarma also reported higher revenues.Ultrapar's net income increased by 2% (in local currency) thanks to higher net sales.In 2014 Ultrapar's cash from operating activities grew by 25%.

Strategy

Ultrapar's strategy is to grow via organic expansion and investment in research and development and innovation. The company is focusing in on the Midwest Northeast and North regions of Brazil to open new service stations geographically. Ultragaz aims at expanding the use of LPG for localized heating such as pre-heating of industrial furnaces especially in steel and metallurgical plants and in new applications in agribusiness such as drying grains and plague control with greater operational and economic efficiency. Ultrapar's focus on R&D has resulted in the introduction of 57 new products. The company's strategy based on the growth and improvement of its reseller network on differentiating its services with the support of innovation and also on creating new marketing channels. The Ultragaz Connect application was created in 2014 to allow the purchase of LPG bottles through smartphones and to generate greater speed and safety for the consumer as well as cost reduction for resellers.

Mergers and Acquisitions

Moving into the retail pharmacy business in 2014 Ultrapar acquired Extrafarma one of Brazil's top ten drugstore chains. This acquisition allows Ultrapar to accelerate Extrafarma's expansion plans through drugstore openings in the company's Ipiranga service stations and Ultragaz resellers. The deal is valued at $419 million.

Company Background

In 2008 Ultrapar acquired Chevron's Texaco-branded fuel distribution business (2000 gas stations) in Brazil for $720 million.

In 2010 it bought fuel distributor Distribuidora Nacional de Petroleo (DNP) for about $50 million. DNP has a network of 110 gas stations in the northern Brazilian states of Acre Amazonas Mato Grosso Para Rondonia and Roraima.

EXECUTIVES

CEO, Thilo Mannhardt, age 60
CEO Ultragaz, Pedro Jorge Filho, age 62
CEO Oxiteno, Jo o Benjamin Parolin, age 56
CEO Extrafarma, Andr ©Covre, age 44
CEO Ipiranga, Leocadio Antunes de Almeida Filho, age 64
CEO Ultracargo, Ricardo Isaac Catran, age 60
Chief Financial and Investor Relations Officer, Andr ©Pires de Oliveira Dias, age 48
Vice Chairman, Lucio de Castro Andrade Filho, age 71
Chairman, Paulo Guliherme Aguiar Cunha, age 76
Auditors: KPMG Auditores Independentes

LOCATIONS

HQ: Ultrapar Participacoes S.A.
Av. Brigadeiro Luiz Antonio 1343, 9 Andar, Sao Paulo, SP 01317-910
Phone: (55) 11 3177 6695 **Fax:** (55) 11 3177 6107
Web: www.ultra.com.br

PRODUCTS/OPERATIONS

2013 Sales

	% of total
Fuels/lubricants	88
Gas	6
Chemicals	5
Logistics	1
Total	**100**

Selected Subsidiaries

Ipiranga (fuels & lubricants)
Oxiteno (petrochemicals)
Ultracargo (transportation logistics)
Ultragaz (LPG distribution)

COMPETITORS

Eni

HISTORICAL FINANCIALS

Company Type: Public

Income Statement FYE: December 31

	REVENUE ($ mil.)	NET INCOME ($ mil.)	NET PROFIT MARGIN	EMPLOYEES
12/14	25,490	467	1.8%	13,973
12/13	25,798	518	2.0%	9,235
12/12	26,372	494	1.9%	9,282
12/11	26,091	455	1.7%	9,055
12/10	25,591	461	1.8%	8,883
Annual Growth	(0.1%)	0.3%	—	12.0%

2014 Year-End Financials

Debt ratio: 16.1%	No. of shares (mil.): 556
Return on equity: 17.4%	Dividends
Cash ($ mil.): 1,064	Yield: 3.2%
Current ratio: 1.67	Payout: 62.6%
Long-term debt ($ mil.): 1,856	Market value ($ mil.): 10,611

	STOCK PRICE ($) FY Close	P/E High/Low		PER SHARE ($) Earnings	Dividends	Book Value
12/14	19.07	10	8	0.85	0.61	5.21
12/13	23.65	11	8	0.97	0.61	5.07
12/12	22.28	13	8	0.92	0.55	5.38
12/11	17.20	37	8	0.85	0.50	5.47
12/10	64.62	47	32	0.86	0.36	5.70
Annual Growth	(26.3%)	—	—	(0.3%)	14.5%	(2.2%)

Unicredito S.p.A. Roma

Let's give credit where credit is due: UniCredit (formerly UniCredito Italiano) is a giant in Europe and is Italy's largest bank. The financial services group and its units operate in nearly 20 European countries with more than 8500 branches in about 50 markets. UniCredit is also the largest foreign bank in Central and Eastern Europe (CEE) with 4295 branches and units. It is organized into several divisions including retail banking (targeting families and small- to mid-sized businesses) corporate and investment banking private banking and CEE. UniCredit's retail banking operations are led by its bank of the same name in Italy UniCredit Bank in Germany UniCredit Bank Austria and Bank Pekao in Poland.

OperationsUniCredit operates eight main business segments. Its Commercial Banking Italy segment makes up more than 35% of the bank's overall revenue while the Central and Eastern Europe (CEE) division and the Corporate & Investment Banking segments each make up more than 15% of revenue. The Commercial Banking Germany (10%) Poland (8%) and Commercial Banking Austria (7%) segments each make up the next largest segments while Asset Management and Asset Gathering make up the remainder of revenue.Geographic ReachThe bank operates through more than 8500 branches across 17 European countries and 50 markets. Nearly 50% of its revenue is generated in Italy while another 20% of revenue is generated in Germany. The company's other largest markets include the Central and Eastern Europe region (roughly 15% of revenue) Austria (nearly 10%) and Poland (more than 5%). Financial PerformanceNote: Growth rates may differ after conversion to US dollars.UniCredit has struggled with declining revenue and profit in recent years as its relatively risky loan portfolio has been plagued with goodwill impairment charges and loan loss provisions. Revenue in 2014 fell by 4% to 22.51 billion ($27.36 billion) mostly as net trading income fell by nearly 38% as it collected less in gains on its financial assets and liabilities held for trading. Dividend and other income from equity investments also fell by 18% during the year hurting the top line further. The bank did see 4% growth however in its fee and commission income thanks to more investment service fees as its assets under management grew by 29.2 billion ($35.49 billion) over the year. Profit on the other hand rebounded sharply to 2.01 billion ($2.44 billion) in 2014 (compared to a 13.97 billion loss in 2013) mostly as the bank paid 68% less toward its loan loss provision expenses as it continued to de-risk its loan portfolio.Cash levels declined considerably in 2014 with operations using 5.57 billion ($6.77 billion) mostly as the bank used more of its cash toward financial assets held for trading.

Stategy

Struggling with an unfavorable loan portfolio UniCredit has been following its 2013-2018 Strategic Plan targets with the goal of increasing its loan coverage levels and decrease its impairment charges and risk. Meanwhile it's been collecting more of its revenue from non-interest income sources and fee income; indeed in 2014 fee and commission income (which made up 34% of total revenue) was the bright spot for growth during the year adding 211 million ($256.47 million) to the company's top line.With the goal of establishing itself as the premier bank in Europe for quality of service UniCredit strives to differentiate itself from competitors by looking at and participating in digital upgrades such as mobile-banking mobile payment and other customer-oriented banking channels that are quickly taking the industry by storm. A digital channel focus will allow the bank to decrease its branch network and cut operating costs significantly while giving customers faster access to banking services at the same time over digital devices.

HISTORY

Company BackgroundUniCredito Italiano's ancestor Banca di Genova was formed in 1870 just after Italy unified. Within a year the bank was in a South American banking venture Banco de Italia y Rio de la Plata. A banking crisis beginning in the late 1880s threatened the company which was saved and reorganized with the aid of German banking interests. The changes gave the bank – which was renamed Credito Italiano –an advantage over home-grown rivals and pointed it in the direction of German-style universal banking including making direct investments in Italy's late-blooming industrial sector.

In the early 20th century Credito Italiano joined other banks in foreign ventures in Albania Brazil and China and opened offices in London and New York.

After the 1929 crash Credito Italiano acquired several failed banks. But Credito Italiano itself was none too healthy: Government attempts in the 1920s to peg the lira to the pound led to industrial stagnation leaving the bank holding highly illiquid industrial investments and by the early 1930s it was essentially an industrial holding company.

Credito Italiano's existence was threatened when the Depression hit in earnest. To save the bank and its peers Mussolini established the Istituto per la Ricostruzione Industriale (IRI) in 1933 as a "temporary" Resolution Trust-style holding company (IRI was finally liquidated in 2000) to take over the industrial assets of Credito Italiano and several other banks. IRI was instantly a major shareholder in Credito Italiano. IRI-held banks were designated "banks of national interest" three years later and were allowed to provide only short-term commercial banking services a limit that remained in effect for more than 50 years.

In 1946 to fill the need for long-term industrial credit to rebuild war-torn Italy Credito Italiano joined with Banca Commerciale Italiana (now part of IntesaBci) and Banco di Roma to form Mediobanca.

Credito Italiano went public in 1969 (IRI sold its interest in the bank in 1993). As a bank of national interest Credito Italiano was called upon to help bail out several of the country's industrial groups in 1979 (it did so reluctantly).

Changing laws allowed the company to expand its branch network in 1980 and in 1982 IRI allowed Credito Italiano to raise capital (although it was still obliged to prop up struggling state industries). But the 1987 US stock market crash caused Credito Italiano's earnings to plunge 33%. Two years later it bought a stake in Banca Nazionale dell'Agricoltura then Italy's largest private bank.

In 1995 the company joined forces with Rolo Banca 1473 (named for the year its progenitor was founded) to form Credito Italiano Group. Two years later Alessandro Profumo became CEO. He would usher in more than a decade of rapid and agressive expansion.

Credito Italiano merged in 1998 with UniCredito a collection of several northern Italian banks. One Cassa di Risparmio di Verona Vicenza Belluno e Ancona (Cariverona) began in 1501 as a pawnshop operated by monks.

Foreshadowing the bank's shift to an Internet growth strategy (announced after talks with Spain's Banco Bilbao Vizcaya Argentaria fell through) UniCredito in 1999 announced plans for an electronic stock market to include after-hours trading. It also continued to boost holdings in Eastern European banks. In 2000 the company entered into securities brokerage and mutual fund administration with its purchase of US-based Pioneer Investment Management.

In 2001 UniCredito bought 10% of the Pirelli/Benetton-owned holding company formed to control Italian telecommunications company Olivetti. The following year the company partnered with Koç Holding to take a majority stake in Yapi Kredi.

The bank acquired HVB and Bank Austria in 2005 in an $18 billion cross-border deal one of the largest such deals ever seen in Europe. The bank strengthened its hold at home in 2007 with the nearly $30 billion purchase of Italian bank Capitalia. Antitrust authorities ordered UniCredit to sell its stake in Assicurazioni Generali following the Capitalia transaction.

EXECUTIVES

Deputy General Manager; Head Global Banking Services, Paolo Fiorentino, age 60
Deputy General Manager; Manager Retail, Roberto Nicastro, age 51
CEO, Federico Ghizzoni, age 60
Deputy General Manager and Head of Strategy and Finance, Marina Natale, age 53
Country Manager Italy, Gabriele Piccini, age 59
Country Chairman Germany, Theodor Weimer, age 56
Chief Risk Officer, Alessandro Maria Decio, age 50
Group CFO, Bernardo Mingrone
Country Chairman Poland, Luigi Lovaglio, age 60
Country Chairman Austria, Willibald Cernko, age 59
Deputy General Manager and Head CIB Division, Gianni Franco Papa, age 59
Head Asset Gathering and CEO and General Manager FinecoBank, Alessandro Foti, age 55
Head Central and Eastern Europe Division, Carlo Vivaldi, age 50
Chairman, Giuseppe Vita, age 80
Deputy Vice Chairman, Candido Fois, age 74
Auditors: Deloitte & Touche S.p.A.

LOCATIONS

HQ: Unicredito S.p.A. Roma
Piazza Gae Aulenti 3 - Tower A, Milano 20154
Phone: (39) 2 88 621 **Fax:** (39) 2 8862 3463
Web: www.unicreditgroup.eu

2014 Sales

	% of total
Italy	48
Germany	20
Austria	9
Poland	7
Other countries	16
Total	**100**

PRODUCTS/OPERATIONS

2014 Sales

	% of total
Commercial banking Italy	36
Corporate & investment banking	16
Central & Eastern Europe	16
Commercial Banking Germany	11
Poland	8
Commercial Banking Austria	7
Asset management	4
Asset gathering	2
Total	**100**

COMPETITORS

ABN AMRO Group
Antonveneta
BNL bc
Banco Popolare
Credit Suisse
Deutsche Bank
BNP Paribas
Banca Popolare di Milano
Intesa Sanpaolo
UBS

HISTORICAL FINANCIALS

Company Type: Public

Income Statement FYE: December 31

	ASSETS ($ mil.)	NET INCOME ($ mil.)	INCOME AS % OF ASSETS	EMPLOYEES
12/14	1,026,150	2,440	0.2%	143,520
12/13	1,164,495	(19,225)	—	153,449
12/12	1,221,604	1,139	0.1%	162,864
12/11	1,198,730	(11,908)	—	167,014
12/10	1,244,000	1,771	0.1%	167,914
Annual Growth	(4.7%)	8.3%	—	(3.8%)

2014 Year-End Financials

Return on assets: 0.2%
Return on equity: 4.1%
Long-term debt ($ mil.): —
No. of shares (mil.): —
Sales ($ mil): 41,925
Dividends
Yield: 1.5%
Payout: —
Market value ($ mil.): —

	STOCK PRICE ($) FY Close	P/E High/Low	PER SHARE ($) Earnings	Dividends	Book Value
12/14	6.50	46 28	0.42	0.14	10.24
12/13	7.46	— —	(3.39)	0.12	11.14
12/12	4.89	71 30	0.20	0.00	14.30
Annual Growth	15.4%	— —	20.5%	—	(8.0%)

Unilever N.V.

From Dove soap to Ben & Jerry's ice cream Unilever N.V. manufactures more than 400 different food and wellness product brands that are used by two billion people worldwide every day. Along with its UK-based counterpart Unilever PLC the Netherlands-based Unilever N.V. operates jointly as the Unilever Group which has a single board of directors and one set of financial statements. Unilever is one of the top manufacturers of dressings savory and spreads with brand names Hellmann's Knorr and Ragú. Its other top products include ice cream (Breyers Ben & Jerry's) tea (Lipton) and soaps (Dove Lux). Unilever traces its roots back to 1872.OperationsThe company boasts a vast products portfolio consisting of 400 health and wellness brands which include: Knorr Hellmann's Lipton Becel/Flora (Healthy Heart) Rama/Blue Band (Family Goodness) Wall's/Algida (Heartbrand) Omo Dove Lux Rexona (including Sure and Degree) and Axe/Lynx among others.Unilever group is organized based on its four main product groups. Roughly 35% of its revenue is generated by personal care products which include skin and hair care products deodorants and oral care products. Another nearly 30% comes from the food product segment which consist of snacks soups bouillons sauces margarines mayonnaise salad dressings and spreads. Refreshment products bring in nearly 20% of sales and include ice cream tea beverages weight-management products and nutritionally enhanced staples for sale in developing markets. The home care product division brings in the remainder of revenue and consists of a variety of cleaning products powders liquids and capsules and soap bars.Financial PerformanceFollowing five years of sales growth Unilever Group's revenue in 2014 fell by 14% to

$58.9 billion with sales declines from all product segments. Two-thirds of the drop was driven by a 7% decline food product sales mostly from lagging spread sales in the European and North American markets. The group's refreshment product sales also fell by 4% further hurting the top line. The company's Personal Care segment fell the least as its Dove brand remained strong.Declining revenue caused the group's net income to drop by 6% to $6.29 billion after two years of profit growth in 2012 and 2013. Operations provided $6.74 billion or 22% less cash than in 2013 partly from lower earnings but mostly due to a combination of negative cash flows from working capital and from an elimination of profits from discontinued brand operations.

Stategy

To free up resources and focus them on growing divisions and product lines Unilever Group has made a series of brand divestitures in recent years. In In 2013 as part of its strategy of making Foods fit for growth the company sold off its flailing Wish-Bone Skippy and Unipro brands. Between 2011 and 2013 the company made a series of brand acquisitions to strategically expand its product portfolio buying Alberto Culver Sara Lee Kalina and Toni & Guy.

EXECUTIVES

CEO, Paul Polman, age 58, $1,033,000 total compensation
CEO Unilever Indonesia, Hemant Bakshi
President Personal Care, Alan Jope
President Foods, Antoine de Saint Affrique
President Europe, Jan Zijderveld
CFO, Jean Marc Hu ‹t
President Refreshment, Kevin Havelock
President Home Care, Nitin Paranjpe
President Russia Ukraine and Belarus, J.V. Raman
Chairman, Michael Treschow, age 72
Auditors: PricewaterhouseCoopers Accountants N.V.

LOCATIONS

HQ: Unilever N.V.
Weena 455, Rotterdam 3013 AL
Phone: (31) 10 217 4000 **Fax:** (31) 10 217 4798
Web: www.unilever.com

2014 Sales

	% of total
United States	14
Netherlands/ United Kingdom	8
Others	78
Total	**100**

PRODUCTS/OPERATIONS

2014 Sales

	% of total
Personal Care	37
Foods	25
Refreshment	19
Home Care	19
Total	**100**

Selected Brands

Axe
Becel
Bertolli
Biotex
Blue Band
Cif
Conimex
Domestos
Dove
Duke
Hellmann' s
Knorr
Lipton
Neutral
OLA
OMO
Prodent
Unox
Zendium
zwitsal

COMPETITORS

Alticor
Atkins Nutritionals
Avon
Beiersdorf
Big Heart Pet Brands
Boulder Brands
Campbell Soup
Church & Dwight
Clorox
Coca-Cola
Colgate-Palmolive
ConAgra
Dairy Farmers of America
Danone
Est©e Lauder
General Mills
Henkel
Johnson & Johnson
Kao
L' Or©al
LVMH
Mars Incorporated
McBride plc
Meda Pharmaceuticals
Mondelez International
Nestl©
Procter & Gamble
R.C. Bigelow
Reckitt Benckiser
Republic of Tea
Revlon
S.C. Johnson
Shiseido
Tata Global Beverages
The Dial Corporation

HISTORICAL FINANCIALS

Company Type: Public

Income Statement FYE: December 31

	REVENUE ($ mil.)	NET INCOME ($ mil.)	NET PROFIT MARGIN	EMPLOYEES
12/14	58,874	6,285	10.7%	173,000
12/13	68,557	6,666	9.7%	174,000
12/12	67,647	5,904	8.7%	172,000
12/11	60,102	5,499	9.2%	169,000
12/10	59,239	5,680	9.6%	165,000
Annual Growth	(0.2%)	2.6%	—	1.2%

2014 Year-End Financials

Debt ratio: 32.2%
Return on equity: 36.9%
Cash ($ mil.): 2,614
Current ratio: 0.63
Long-term debt ($ mil.): 8,734
No. of shares (mil.): 1,573
Dividends
Yield: 3.8%
Payout: 63.2%
Market value ($ mil.): 61,416

	STOCK PRICE ($) FY Close	P/E High/Low	PER SHARE ($) Earnings	Dividends	Book Value
12/14	39.04	22 18	2.18	1.51	10.55
12/13	40.23	27 22	2.29	1.40	12.55
12/12	38.30	25 20	2.03	1.23	11.71
12/11	34.37	23 18	1.89	1.14	10.78
12/10	31.40	21 18	1.95	1.11	11.31
Annual Growth	5.6%	— —	2.7%	7.8%	(1.7%)

Unilever Plc (United Kingdom)

It takes two parents –one Dutch and one British –to make one Unilever. Unilever N.V. and Unilever PLC together with their group companies constitute a global food personal care and household products powerhouse. The group's vast portfolio of consumer products includes a dozen global brands including Hellmann's (mayonnaise) Knorr (soups) Lipton (tea) and Dove and Lux (soaps) that each ring up more than 1 billion ($1.4 billion) in sales. Unilever's consumer goods are sold in more than 190 countries. The company was the world's #1 consumer products maker until Procter & Gamble purchased Gillette in 2005. Based in England Unilever PLC trades on the London and New York stock exchanges.

Geographic Reach

Unilever's business is organized across three geographic areas: the Americas; Europe; and Other markets (Asia Australasia Africa the Middle East Turkey Russia Ukraine and Belarus).

Operations

The company operates in four segments: Personal Care (36% of Unilever's 2014 revenues); Foods 27%; Refreshment 19%; and Home Care 18%.

Sales and Marketing

Unilever's products are generally sold through its own sales force as well as through independent brokers agents and distributors to chain wholesale co-operative and independent grocery accounts food service distributors and institutions. Products are physically distributed through a network of distribution centers satellite warehouses company-operated and public storage facilities depots and other facilities.E-commerceis an increasingly significant distribution channel. In the retail market e-commerce sales account for 1.2% of total sales and it is expected to double to 2.4% by 2020 due to growth in emerging markets where mobile phones one of the most effective ways of delivering advertising to individuals.

Global digital advertising is estimated at $137.5 billion or about 25% of Unilever's total advertising spend.

Financial Performance

In 2014 the company's revenues decreased by 14% due the following factors:Revenues from personal care dropped as the result of lower volume growth driven by a slowdown in global markets and strong competition;

Food sales declined due to exchange rate movements and business disposals (including the Ragu and Bertolli pasta sauces business) while savory and dressings both grew (but spreads declined due to lower consumer demand for margarine in Europe and North America);Refreshment revenues dropped due to exchange rate movements and business disposals (primarily SlimŸFast) offset by acquisitions (Talenti Gelato & Sorbetto); Revenues from Home Care showed strong growth supported by the impact of the Qinyuan acquisition partially offset by exchange rate movements. Unilever's net income declined by 5.7% in 2014 due to lower revenues.In 2014 cash from operating activities increased by 12% due to the net inflow of acquisitions and disposals.

Strategy

Unilever aims to double its business with innovative brands backed by marketing and a best-in-class supply chain. The strategic choices across four categories (personal care home care foods refreshment emerging markets) focus on growing brands in emerging markets which retain good long-term growth prospects.

Unilever points to several countries for steady growth. These include Africa the Americas (including Brazil and Mexico) China Europe India and Russia. China Russia and Brazil are three of the company's biggest hair care markets in the world.In 2015 Unilever launched a crowdsourcing initiative to drive sustainable growth by serving as a hub to centrally organize all crowdsourcing briefs.

To raise cash to pay down debt a reinvest in growth areas in 2014 company sold its global Ragu and Bertolli pasta sauce business to Mizkan Group for $2.15 billion and its SlimŸFast brand to Kainos Capital for an undisclosed amount. Ot also sold its global Skippy business to Hormel Foods for $700 million.

Other 2014 disposals included its Royal pasta brand in the Philippines to RFM Corporation for $48 million and the sale of its meat snacks business including the Bifi and Peperami brands to Jack Link's for an undisclosed amount.

Mergers and Acquisitions

Growing its portfolio in emerging markets in 2014 Unilever acquired 55% of the Qinyuan Group a leading Chinese water purification business for an undisclosed amount. It also acquired US-based Talenti Gelato & Sorbetto for an undisclosed amount.

Company Background

Unilever acquired salon hair care products maker TIGI in 2009. The more than $410 million purchase which includes the firm's hair styling academies adds the Bed Head Catwalk and S-factor brands among others to Unilever's hair care products offering. TIGI remains headquartered in Dallas and operates as a stand-alone global business unit within Unilever.

CEO Patrick Cescau retired at the end of 2008 and was replaced by Paul Polman an executive at Nestl USA who has some 25 years of experience at P&G.

EXECUTIVES

CFO, Graeme Pitkethly
Chairman Unilever Arabia, Kevin Havelock, age 58
CEO and Director, Paul Polman, age 58
Chief Research and Development Officer, David Blanchard
President Unilever Home Care Division, Nitin Paranjpe, age 51
Chief Supply Chain Officer, Pier Luigi Sigismondi, age 49
General Manager UK and Ireland, Gina R. Boswell, age 52
President Personal Care, Alan Jope
President Unilever Foods Division, Antoine Saint-Affrique
President Unilever Europe, Jan Zijderveld
President North America, Kees Kruythoff
Chairman, Michael Treschow, age 72
Auditors: KPMG Accountants N.V.

LOCATIONS

HQ: Unilever Plc (United Kingdom)
Unilever House, Blackfriars, London EC4Y 0DY
Phone: (44) 20 7822 5252 **Fax:** (44) 20 7822 6108
Web: www.unilever.com

PRODUCTS/OPERATIONS

Selected Global Brands

Axe/Lynx (
Blue Band
Dove (pers
Heartbrand ice creams
Hellmann's
Knorr (sou
Lipton (te
Lux (soap
Omo (deter
Rexona (de
Sunsilk (h

2014 Sales

	% in total
Personal	36
Foods	27
Refreshment	19
Home Care	18
Total	**100**

COMPETITORS

Church & Dwight Canada
Henkel
Mondelez International
Nestl©
Premier Foods
Procter & Gamble
R&R Ice Cream
Reckitt Benckiser

HISTORICAL FINANCIALS

Company Type: Public

Income Statement

FYE: December 31

	REVENUE ($ mil.)	NET INCOME ($ mil.)	NET PROFIT MARGIN	EMPLOYEES
12/14	58,874	6,285	10.7%	173,000
12/13	68,557	6,666	9.7%	174,000
12/12	67,647	5,904	8.7%	172,000
12/11	60,102	5,499	9.2%	169,000
12/10	59,239	5,680	9.6%	165,000
Annual Growth	(0.2%)	2.6%	—	1.2%

2014 Year-End Financials

Debt ratio: 32.2%
Return on equity: 36.9%
Cash ($ mil.): 2,614
Current ratio: 0.63
Long-term debt ($ mil.): 8,734
No. of shares (mil.): 1,283
Dividends
Yield: 3.6%
Payout: 62.6%
Market value ($ mil.): 51,954

	STOCK PRICE ($) FY Close	P/E High/Low	PER SHARE ($) Earnings	Dividends	Book Value
12/14	40.48	23 19	2.18	1.49	12.93
12/13	41.20	27 22	2.29	1.40	15.39
12/12	38.72	25 20	2.03	1.23	15.57
12/11	33.52	22 18	1.89	1.14	14.11
12/10	30.88	21 18	1.95	1.11	14.80
Annual Growth	7.0%	— —	2.7%	7.6%	(3.3%)

Unione Di Banche Italiane SpA

Unione di Banche Italiane known as UBI Banca serves individuals and businesses through nine subsidiary banks with some 1560 branches in Italy (concentrated in the Lombardy region). It also operates offices in about a dozen other countries across Europe Asia and South America and boasts some 3.6 million customers worldwide. Beyond standard retail banking deposit and checking accounts the banking group also provides asset management leasing operations private banking insurance corporate banking mortgages and other types of loans. The group was formed in 2007 when Banche Popolari Unite acquired rival Banca Lombarda e Piemontese and changed its name to UBI Banca.

OperationsBroadly speaking about 53% of UBI Banca's operating income (net of expenses) came from net interest income (mostly from loans) in 2014. Another 36% of its operating income came from net fee and commission income with half of that coming from management trading and advisory services (mostly portfolio management services) and another one-third of that coming from collection and payment services and management of multilateral trading systems. Nearly 61% of UBI Banca's loan portfolio was split fairly evenly between mortgage loans and other medium to long-term financing in 2014. An additional 12% of the loan portfolio was made up of current account overdrafts while 8% was from finance leases. The rest of the portfolio was split among credit card debt personal loans and salary-backed loans (4% of the portfolio) factoring (2%) reverse repurchase agreements (1%) and other debt instruments (less than 1%). By sector about 14% of its loan portfolio was tied to funds lent to various types of manufacturing companies. Another 27% of the portfolio was tied to loans to the real estate construction and wholesale/retail/auto repair sectors.Geographic ReachThe banking group boasted 1560 branches in Italy; six international branches in France Germany and Spain; and eight offices in Poland Luxembourg Shanghai Sao Paolo Moscow Mumbai and Hong Kong in 2014. About half of UBI Banca's branches and (68% of its loan portfolio assets) were located in the Lombardy region of Italy. About 82% of the group's loans were held by branches in the North West region of Italy while about 10% were held by branches in Central Italy.Sales and MarketingUBI Banca served some 3.3 million private individuals and families 270 thousand businesses (mostly small businesses and small-to-midsize enterprises or SMEs) and 29 thousand authorities and associations in 2014.

Stategy

UBI Banca has been moving toward digital banking channels that are quickly taking the industry by storm allowing the bank to slow expensive branch-expansion plans and cut operating costs significantly while giving customers faster access to banking services. During 2014 the company's mobile banking customer base grew by 51% while its internet banking customer base increased nearly 15% to 1.12 million users. All told the group's "multi-channel" customers grew 11% to 1.35 million during 2014 an amount equal to one-third of the bank's total customer base. The banking group has taken a number of cost-cutting and growth initiative measures in recent years to boost profits amidst an increasingly regulated industry. From April 2007 through the January 2015 the banking group reduced its branch count by more than 20% (from 1970 branches to 1560) while reducing its staff count by 16% over the same time period. As a result the group has slashed its total operating costs by a staggering 19% since 2007. Additionally the group reduced its cost-to-income ratio (a measure of efficiency) from a high of 70% in 2010 to 61.8% at the end of 2014.UBI Banca is better capitalized than many of its Italian peers. In a late 2014 stress test among European banks nine out of 15 failing banks were Italian but UBI Banca reported that it passed with capital levels "well above the minimum thresholds required." Strong financial capitalization could help quell risk-averse customer concerns and could keep its financial condition more stable than peers' in market downturns and recessions.

EXECUTIVES

Vice Presidente, MARIO CERA
Vice Presidente, GIORGIO FRIGERI
Vice Presidente, ALBERTO FOLONARI
Vice Presidente, ARMANDO SANTUS
Auditors: Deloitte & Touche S.p.A.

LOCATIONS

HQ: Unione Di Banche Italiane SpA
Piazza Vittorio Veneto 8, Bergamo 24122
Phone: (39) 035 392111
Web: www.ubibanca.it

PRODUCTS/OPERATIONS

2013 Branch Offices

	Total
Banca Popolare di Bergamo Spa	357
Banco di Brescia spa	322
Banca Regionale Europea Spa	256
Banca Carime Spa	255
Banca Popolare di Ancona Spa	219
Banca Popolare Commerceio e industria Spa	219
Banca di valle Camonica Spa	66
UBI Banca Private Investment Spa	25
IW Bank Spa	2
UBI Banca Scpa	4
Total	**1,725**

2013 Sales

	% of total
Retail	
Private	37
Small Business	31
Corporate	26
Private	6
Total	**100**

Selected Subsidiaries

Aviva Assicurazioni Vita Spa (49.9%)
Banco di San Giorgio Spa (93%)
Banca Populare Commercio e Industria Spa (84%)
Banca Populare di Bergamo Spa
Banca Regionale Europea Spa (60%)
Capitalgest Alternative Investments SGR Spa
Centrobanca Spa (98%)
FinanzAttiva Servizi Srl
IW Bank Spa (80%)
Mercato Impresa Spa (99%)
Prestitalia Spa (23%)
S.B.I.M. Spa
UBI Assicurazioni Spa
UBI Banca Private Investment Spa
UBI Gestioni Fiduciarie Sim Spa
UBI Leasing Spa (99%)
UBI Pramerica SGR Spa (65%)

COMPETITORS

Antonveneta	Banco Popolare
BNL bc	HSBC
BPER-Emilia Romagna	Intesa Sanpaolo
Banca Carige	Monte dei Paschi di Siena
Banca Popolare di Milano	UniCredit

HISTORICAL FINANCIALS

Company Type: Public

Income Statement FYE: December 31

	ASSETS ($ mil.)	NET INCOME ($ mil.)	INCOME AS % OF ASSETS	EMPLOYEES
12/14	148,032	(882)	—	18,132
12/13	171,048	345	0.2%	18,337
12/12	174,554	109	0.1%	19,114
12/11	167,894	(2,381)	—	19,405
12/10	174,735	230	0.1%	19,699
Annual Growth	(4.1%)	—	—	(2.1%)

2014 Year-End Financials

Return on assets: (-0.5%)
Return on equity: (-7.2%)
Long-term debt ($ mil.): —
No. of shares (mil.): 900
Sales ($ mil): 5,784
Dividends
Yield: —
Payout: —
Market value ($ mil.): —

	STOCK PRICE ($) FY Close	P/E High/Low		PER SHARE ($) Earnings	Dividends	Book Value
12/14	0.00	—	—	(0.98)	0.00	13.24
12/13	3.05	—	—	0.37	0.00	15.82
12/12	3.05	54	44	0.12	0.00	14.25
12/11	3.80	—	—	(3.06)	0.00	12.84
Annual Growth	—	—	—	—	—	0.8%

Unipol Gruppo Finanziaro SPA Bologna

Unipol Gruppo Finanziario (better known simply as Unipol) serves the insurance and banking sectors and other markets such as supplementary pensions and health. It operates primarily through its subsidiary UnipolSai Assicurazioni SpA established in 2014 when three companies merged. While its main focus is on offering life auto property/casualty health and other general insurance Unipol provides merchant banking and consumer banking services. The firm has 5 billion in assets under management. Its Unipol Banca boasts about 300 branches. The acquisitive company targets insurance firms and banks. Holding company Holmo SpA controls Unipol through its Finanziaria dell'Economia Sociale (Finsoe) unit.

EXECUTIVES

General Manager; CEO UGF Assicurazioni, Carlo Cimbri, age 50
Director, Pierluigi Stefanini, age 62
Vice Chairman, Giovanni Antonelli
Auditors: PricewaterhouseCoopers SpA

LOCATIONS

HQ: Unipol Gruppo Finanziaro SPA Bologna
Via Stalingrado, 45, Bologna 40128
Phone: (39) 051 507 61 11 **Fax:** (39) 051 507 66 66
Web: www.unipol.it

COMPETITORS

Allianz S.p.A.	Milano Assicurazioni
BNL bc	Monte dei Paschi di Siena
Banco Popolare	UniCredit
Cattolica Assicurazioni	UnipolSai
ERGO Previdenza	Vittoria Assicurazioni
Generali	alleanza toro
Intesa Sanpaolo	

HISTORICAL FINANCIALS

Company Type: Public

Income Statement FYE: December 31

	REVENUE ($ mil.)	NET INCOME ($ mil.)	NET PROFIT MARGIN	EMPLOYEES
12/14	25,862	233	0.9%	14,223
12/13	27,056	(108)	—	15,230
12/12	18,905	393	2.1%	15,212
12/11	12,895	(140)	—	7,638
12/10	14,020	42	0.3%	7,529
Annual Growth	16.5%	53.1%	—	17.2%

2014 Year-End Financials

Debt ratio: —
Return on equity: 3.4%
Cash ($ mil.): 819
Current ratio: —
Long-term debt ($ mil.): —
No. of shares (mil.): 437
Dividends
Yield: —
Payout: 21.8%
Market value ($ mil.): —

	STOCK PRICE ($) FY Close	P/E High/Low		PER SHARE ($) Earnings	Dividends	Book Value
12/14	0.00			0.32	0.07	15.81
12/13	0.11	—	—	(0.15)	0.07	17.05
12/12	10.77	10	0	1.67	1.21	16.59
12/11	0.08	—	—	(0.04)	0.00	1.88
Annual Growth	—	—	—	—	—	70.2%

UnipolSai Assicurazioni SpA

Auditors: PricewaterhouseCoopers S.p.A.

LOCATIONS

HQ: UnipolSai Assicurazioni SpA
Via Stalingrado 45, Bologna 40128
Phone: (39) 051 5077111 **Fax:** (39) 051 375349
Web: www.unipolsai.com

HISTORICAL FINANCIALS

Company Type: Public

Income Statement FYE: December 31

	REVENUE ($ mil.)	NET INCOME ($ mil.)	NET PROFIT MARGIN	EMPLOYEES
12/14	23,185	898	3.9%	7,376
12/13	15,660	454	2.9%	7,389
12/12	14,992	(988)	—	7,377
12/11	15,178	(1,102)	—	7,591
12/10	18,892	(960)	—	7,917
Annual Growth	5.3%	—	—	(1.8%)

2014 Year-End Financials

Debt ratio: —
Return on equity: 16.8%
Cash ($ mil.): 831
Current ratio: —
Long-term debt ($ mil.): —
No. of shares (mil.): —
Dividends
Yield: —
Payout: —
Market value ($ mil.): —

UNIQA Versicherungen AG (Austria)

UNIQA Insurance Group a leading insurance provider in Central and Eastern Europe operates about 40 companies in nearly 20 countries that serve more than 9 million customers. The group offers property/casualty life and health insurance and related financial services. Subsidiaries include UNIQA Sachversicherung (property and casualty insurance lines) UNIQA Personenversicherung (personal insurance) and Raiffeisen Versicherung which covers accident and life insurance lines and distributes through affiliated Raiffeisen bank branches. Its Salzburger Landes-Versicherung subsidiary which offers property and and casualty insurance serves regional insurance companies and is Austria's oldest fire insurer.
Auditors: PwC Wirtschaftspruefung GmbH

LOCATIONS

HQ: UNIQA Versicherungen AG (Austria)
Untere Donaustrasse 21, Vienna 1029
Phone: (43) 1 211 75 3773 **Fax:** (43) 1 211 75 793773
Web: www.uniqagroup.com

HISTORICAL FINANCIALS

Company Type: Public

Income Statement FYE: December 31

	ASSETS ($ mil.)	NET INCOME ($ mil.)	INCOME AS % OF ASSETS	EMPLOYEES
12/14	40,158	352	0.9%	14,336
12/13	42,773	390	0.9%	14,277
12/12	39,590	171	0.4%	14,795
12/11	36,950	(317)	—	15,081
12/10	38,404	62	0.2%	15,066
Annual Growth	1.1%	54.3%	—	(1.2%)

2014 Year-End Financials

Return on assets: 0.9%
Return on equity: 9.9%
Long-term debt ($ mil.): —
No. of shares (mil.): 308
Sales ($ mil): 7,657
Dividends
Yield: —
Payout: —
Market value ($ mil.): —

United Arab Emirates (United Arab Emirates)

Auditors: PricewaterhouseCoopers

LOCATIONS

HQ: United Arab Emirates (United Arab Emirates)
PO Box 686, Dubai
Phone:
Web: www.emirates.com

HISTORICAL FINANCIALS

Company Type: Public

Income Statement FYE: March 31

	REVENUE ($ mil.)	NET INCOME ($ mil.)	NET PROFIT MARGIN	EMPLOYEES
03/15	23,613	1,240	5.3%	84,153
03/14	21,976	885	4.0%	75,496
03/13	19,373	621	3.2%	69,707
Annual Growth	10.4%	41.3%	—	9.9%

2015 Year-End Financials

Debt ratio: 11.6%
Return on equity: 17.1%
Cash ($ mil.): 4,597
Current ratio: 0.80
Long-term debt ($ mil.): 11,551
No. of shares (mil.): —
Dividends
Yield: —
Payout: —
Market value ($ mil.): —

	STOCK PRICE ($) FY Close	P/E High/Low		PER SHARE ($) Earnings	Dividends	Book Value
03/15	0.00	—	—	(0.00)	0.00	(0.00)
03/14	0.00	—	—	(0.00)	0.00	(0.00)
Annual Growth	—	—	—	—	—	—

United Overseas Bank Ltd. (Singapore)

One of Singapore's top financial institutions United Overseas Bank (UOB) provides a range of commercial banking and personal financial services. Offerings include checking and savings accounts private banking loans investment banking commodities trading and asset management. It is also one of the largest issuers of credit cards in the Asia-Pacific region. Altogether the bank has about 500 branches and 1300 ATMs across Asia (its largest markets are in Singapore Thailand and Indonesia) and a handful of representative offices in Europe and North America.

Operations

UOB is organized into three businesses – Retail Wholesale and Global Markets and Investment Management. Its retail business covers personal accounts private banking and small businesses. It accounts for about 35% of revenue. The wholesale division serves large corporations and financial institutions; it also accounts for about 35% of revenue. Global markets and investment management which provides asset management foreign exchange money market funds derivatives and other capital market activities accounts for 20% of revenue.

Geographic Reach

Altogether the bank has operations in about 15 Asian countries. While it's headquartered in Singapore it only has about 75 branches in that country of 5 million people. The more populated countries of Indonesia (246 million people) has some 215 branches while Thailand with 67 million people has more than 160 branches. Outside Asia UOB has branches in London Los Angeles New York City Paris and Vancouver.

Company Background

UOB was founded in 1935 as the United Chinese Bank and catered mainly to the Fujian community in Singapore. The bank changed its name to United Overseas Bank in 1965.

EXECUTIVES

Head Group Retail, Francis C. Y. Lee
Head Global Markets and Investment Management, Terence S. E. Ong
Chief Risk Officer, Chan Seong
CFO, Lee Wai Fai
Deputy Chairman and CEO, Wee Ee Cheong, age 61
Head Group Wholesale Banking, Frederick V. F. Chin
Head Group Technology and Operations, Susan W. C. Hwee
President and Director PT Bank UOB Indonesia, Armand B. Arief
President and CEO United Overseas Bank (Thai) Public Company Limited, Peter M. T. Foo
President and CEO United Overseas Bank (China) Limited, Eric V. F. Lian
CEO United Overseas Bank (Malaysia) Bhd, Wong Kim Choong
Chairman, Hsieh Fu Hua, age 63
Auditors: Ernst & Young LLP

LOCATIONS

HQ: United Overseas Bank Ltd. (Singapore)
80 Raffles Place, UOB Plaza, 048624
Phone: (65) 6533 9898 **Fax:** (65) 6534 2334
Web: www.uobgroup.com

2012 Sales

	% of sales
Singapore	58
Malaysia	15
Thailand	8
Indonesia	7
China	6
Other	6
Total	100

Selected Subsidiaries

Far Eastern Bank Limited (Singapore)
PT Bank UOB Indonesia
United Overseas Bank (China)
United Overseas Bank (Malaysia)
United Overseas Bank (Philippines)
United Overseas Bank (Thailand)
United Overseas Insurance Limited Singapore
UOB Australia Limited
UOB Capital Investments Pte Ltd Singapore
UOB Capital Management Pte Ltd Singapore
UOB Holdings Private Limited Singapore
UOB Insurance (H.K.) Limited Hong Kong
UOB International Investment Private Limited

PRODUCTS/OPERATIONS

2012 Sales

	% of total
Interest income	61
Fees & commission	23
Other non-interest income	16
Total	100

2012 Sales

	% of total
Retail	36
Wholesale	36
Global markets & investment mgmt.	19
Other	9
Total	100

COMPETITORS

Astra International
Bangkok Bank
Bank Central Asia
Bank Danamon Indonesia
Bank Mandiri
Bank Rakyat
Bank of China
DBS Group Holdings
Edaran Otomobil
HSBC
Hang Seng Bank
Hong Leong Finance
Maybank
OCBC Bank
Standard Chartered

HISTORICAL FINANCIALS

Company Type: Public

Income Statement FYE: December 31

	ASSETS ($ mil.)	NET INCOME ($ mil.)	INCOME AS % OF ASSETS	EMPLOYEES
12/14	232,170	2,459	1.1%	0
12/13	224,984	2,380	1.1%	0
12/12	206,769	2,291	1.1%	0
12/11	182,320	1,790	1.0%	0
12/10	166,717	2,102	1.3%	0
Annual Growth	8.6%	4.0%	—	—

2014 Year-End Financials

Return on assets: 1.1%
Return on equity: 11.6%
Long-term debt ($ mil.): —
No. of shares (mil.): 1,602
Sales ($ mil): 7,749
Dividends
Yield: 3.2%
Payout: 76.1%
Market value ($ mil.): 59,251

	STOCK PRICE ($) FY Close	P/E High/Low	PER SHARE ($) Earnings	Dividends	Book Value
12/14	36.97	19 15	1.49	1.20	13.96
12/13	33.62	19 16	1.46	1.11	13.25
12/12	32.85	19 14	1.40	0.95	13.02
12/11	23.56	22 16	1.09	1.06	11.23
12/10	28.36	19 16	1.32	0.84	10.86
Annual Growth	6.9%	—'—	3.1%	9.1%	6.5%

Vale S.A.

Vale has more than just one iron in the fire. Iron ore and pellets account for more than two-thirds of Vale's sales and the company accounts for a third of the world's ocean-shipped iron ore. Vale also mines for bauxite nickel kaolin and potash. Other products include steel copper and aluminum. It has holdings in hydroelectric power generation and in the rail and shipping businesses mainly to support its mining activities in Brazil. The company is the world's second-largest iron ore miner having grown dramatically with the 2006 acquisition of Vale Limited (formerly Vale Inco). To keep all of its materials coming out of the ground Vale maintains its exploration efforts in 24 countries around the world.

Vale's revenues almost doubled in 2010 growing more than 94% as a result of increased production and higher prices for its major products particularly metals including iron ore nickel and copper. Net income grew 223% for the year on the strength of higher sales volumes and profit on the sale of assets.

In early 2012 the company declared force majeure on a number of its iron ore sales contract after high rainfall in three Brazilian states curtailed Vale's operations. The company estimated a loss of 2 million metric tons in iron ore shipments.

In 2011 Vale agreed to buy out minority shareholders of its Vale Fertilizantes SA subsidiary in a $1.4 billion move to consolidate its fertilizer business. Vale sought to buy the 16% of Fertilizantes it did not already own. The subsidiary is a small part of Vale's overall fertilizer business which the company had planned to spin off in 2011 but canceled those plans when it proved to be more profitable than Vale had projected.

Vale spent much of 2010 acquiring fertilizer companies and forming ventures. Mitsui teamed up with US fertilizer company Mosaic in 2010 for a joint venture investing in a Vale phosphorus ore development project in Peru. Mitsui spent $275 million to acquire a 25% stake and voting rights in a Vale subsidiary while Mosaic holds a 24% stake. The project is located in northwestern Peru's Piura province. Vale also completed a $4.7 billion deal for Brazil's Fosfertil and US-based agribusiness Bunge Co. to create Vale Fertilizantes.

Also in 2011 Vale announced plans to acquire South Africa-based copper and cobalt miner Metorex Ltd. for about $1.1 billion. However prior to the deal's close China's Jinchuan Group countered Vale's bid for Metrorex with a $1.34 billion offer. Vale subsequently dropped its offer refusing to engage in a bidding war.

In 2010 Vale sold its Brazilian aluminum operations to Norwegian aluminum producer Norsk Hydro for $5.7 billion. Norsk Hydro paid Vale a combination of cash and a 22% stake in Norsk Hydro. Vale said it divested Paragominas one of the world's largest bauxite mines because it did not see enough growth potential in the operation.

Remaining active in the mining sector Vale is developing a copper mine in Zambia in a $400 million joint venture with African Rainbow Minerals. The Konkola North project is expected to begin production in 2013. In 2010 Vale acquired a 51% stake in Guinea iron-ore mining firm BSG Resources for $2.5 billion. The acquisition expands Vale's presence in Africa where it is also developing the Moatize coal deposit in Mozambique in a $6 billion joint venture with South Korean steelmaker POSCO.

In 2011 Vale resumed work on a $6.2 billion steelworks operation in Espirito Santo in southeast Brazil. The project part of a network of five mills planned around the country was dropped in 2009 after local authorities refused to issue an environmental permit. Now with permit in hand Vale is going forward with the redesigned project which is expected to produce about 5 million tons of slab steel a year beginning in 2014. Vale which had originally partnered with China's Baosteel Group is seeking another partner for the project.

To complement its rail port and shipping facilities Vale created a new logistics company for cargo transport in 2011. Vale Logistics Integrada will handle the company's general cargo assets including its operations for moving iron ore and other minerals from its mines to its customers. The company received $1.5 billion in sales from logistics services in 2010 primarily from the shipping of agricultural and steel products fuel and construction materials.

Murilo Pinto de Oliveira Ferreira was named president and CEO of Vale in 2011. He succeeds Roger Agnelli who completed his 10-year term in the position. Ferreira was previously the CEO of Vale Canada and Executive Director of Vale's Nickel and Base Metals Sales.

Investment group Valepar controls a third of Vale. The Brazilian government holds limited veto power on any permanent company changes.

HISTORY

During the 1890s as land reforms opened the way for foreign investments in Brazil the mineral-rich state of Minas Gerais caught the attention of mining companies from Europe and the US. British engineers founded the Itabira Iron Ore Company and took over the Doce River Valley's Vit ria-Minas Railroad. After Brazil's revolution (1930) Itabira was split up. One of the new companies Itabira Minera § o began shipping iron ore in 1940.

A 1942 agreement prompted by the outbreak of WWII established iron export regulations from Brazil to the US and the UK. Later that year the Companhia Vale do Rio Doce (CVRD) was formed with the Brazilian government owning 80%. The new company received the assets of Itabira including Brazil's "iron mountain" Cau ©Peak. By the end of the 1940s 80% of Brazil's iron ore exports were mined by CVRD. During the 1950s CVRD invested in land holdings and shipping operations. The company set up a shipping and logistics subsidiary in 1962.

CVRD teamed up with US Steel in 1970 to mine iron ore at Caraj ˜s in Amazonian Brazil; two years later the site was found to hold the world's largest iron ore reserves (18 billion tons). By 1975 CVRD had become the world's largest iron ore exporter. A year later the company finished doubling the tracks of the Vit ria-Minas Railroad. It also set up a manganese mining company (Urucum Minera § o) and an alumina production facility (Alumina do Norte do Brasil or Alunorte).

To support its Caraj ˜s mining operations CVRD added the Estrada de Ferro de Caraj ˜s railway (finished 1985) and a hydroelectric project. In all the giant Caraj ˜s project involved investments from the US Japan France the European Economic Community and the World Bank. (The Caraj ˜s area like many mining sites in Brazil has been the site of intense controversy because it attracts subsistence miners including children who work under dangerous circumstances.) By the late 1980s the company had become a major supplier of pelletized iron used as feed for steel mill blast furnaces.

In 1992 CVRD expanded into the production of chemicals (Rio Capim Qu mica now Par ˜ Pigmentos SA). The company acquired stakes in two steel mills —Sider rgica de Tubar o and A § Minas Gerais SA —in 1993. In 1996 it invested in gold finds in Par ˜ state. CVRD was privatized in 1997 and the next year set the sales record for a private Brazilian company.

The company listed ADR shares on the NYSE in 2000. Acquisitions that year included Brazilian iron ore companies SOCOIMEX and SAMITRI (73%). CVRD sold its 50% stake in pulp and paper group Bahia Sul to Suzano for $320 million in 2001. It also sold its 51% share of pulp maker Cenibra and its share of steelmaker Companhia Sider rgica Nacional (CSN).

In 2002 the Brazilian Treasury and the National Social and Economic Bank (BNDES) sold 33% of CVRD's shares further privatizing the company. CVRD disposed of its last gold mine (Fazenda Brasileiro) in 2003. It also exited the dry bulk-shipping business that year.

Under pressure from increasing globalization Vale had been forced to trim some of its operations (including its stake in CSN) to focus on mining and bulk transport. Those asset sales helped fund Vale's win over Australian mining giant BHP Billiton the world's #2 iron ore producer in a battle for Brazil's iron miner Caemi Minera § o e Metalurgia #4 worldwide. (From 2001 through 2006 the company picked up stakes in Caemi until it owned it fully.) The deal for Inco trumped offers from Canadian miner Teck and US copper producer Phelps Dodge.

Toward the end of 2007 the company —then called Companhia Vale do Rio Doce —decided that it wanted a new brand identity and so ditched its longtime nickname CVRD in favor of Vale. Two years later it changed its name legally dropping the more formal Companhia Vale do Rio Doce.

EXECUTIVES

CEO, Murilo Pinto de Oliveira Ferreira
Executive Director Capital Projects, Galib Chaim
Executive Director Fertilizers and Coal, Roger Downey
CFO, Luciano Siani
Executive Director Logistics and Mineral Research, Humberto Freitas
Executive Director Ferrous Minerals, Peter Poppinga
Executive Director Base Metals; CEO Vale Canada, Jennifer Maki
Vice Chairman, M ˜rio da Silveira Teixeira, age 70
Chairman, Dan Conrado
Auditors: KPMG Auditores Independentes

LOCATIONS

HQ: Vale S.A.
Av. Graca Aranha 26, 18 Andar, Centro, Rio de Janeiro, RJ 20030-900
Phone: (55) 21 3814 4477 **Fax:** (55) 21 3814 9935
Web: www.cvrd.com.br

2013 Sales

	$ mil.	% of total
China	18,921	40
Europe	8,763	19
Brazil	6,190	13

Japan	4,035	9
Asia except Japan and China	3,600	8
America except United States	1,848	4
Middle East/ Africa/Oceania	2,098	4
United States of America	1,312	3
Total	**46,767**	**100**

PRODUCTS/OPERATIONS

2013 Sales chart

	$ mil.	% of total
Bulk Materials	35,802	76
Basic Metals	7,286	16
Fertilizers	2,814	6
Others	865	2
Total	**46,767**	**100**

COMPETITORS

AHMSA
Alcoa
Anglo American
BHP Billiton
BHP Billiton Plc
Cliffs Natural Resources
Exxaro
Freeport-McMoRan
Kumba Iron Ore
Norilsk Nickel
Rio Tinto Limited
Rio Tinto plc
Teck

HISTORICAL FINANCIALS

Company Type: Public

Income Statement FYE: December 31

	REVENUE ($ mil.)	NET INCOME ($ mil.)	NET PROFIT MARGIN	EMPLOYEES
12/14	37,539	1,010	2.7%	0
12/13	46,767	990	2.1%	83,286
12/12	47,694	5,511	11.6%	70,785
12/11	58,990	22,885	38.8%	79,646
12/10	45,293	17,264	38.1%	70,785
Annual Growth	(4.6%)	(50.8%)	—	—

2014 Year-End Financials

Debt ratio: 26.2%
Return on equity: 1.7%
Cash ($ mil.): 3,974
Current ratio: 1.55
Long-term debt ($ mil.): 29,114
No. of shares (mil.): —
Dividends
Yield: 8.2%
Payout: 518.7%
Market value ($ mil.): —

	STOCK PRICE ($) FY Close	P/E High/Low	PER SHARE ($) Earnings	Dividends	Book Value
12/14	8.18	117 53	0.13	0.67	17.30
12/13	15.25	195115	0.11	0.72	19.88
12/12	20.96	25 15	1.07	0.99	14.41
12/11	21.45	9 5	4.33	1.56	15.25
12/10	34.57	11 7	3.23	0.45	13.24
Annual Growth	(30.3%)	— —	(55.2%)	10.8%	6.9%

Vattenfall AB

Auditors: Ernst & Young AB

LOCATIONS

HQ: Vattenfall AB
Birger Jarlsgatan 33, Stockholm SE-169 92
Phone: (46) 8 739 50 00 **Fax:** (46) 8 37 01 70
Web: www.vattenfall.com

HISTORICAL FINANCIALS

Company Type: Public

Income Statement FYE: December 31

	REVENUE ($ mil.)	NET INCOME ($ mil.)	NET PROFIT MARGIN	EMPLOYEES
12/14	21,467	(1,057)	—	30,181
12/13	26,778	(2,131)	—	31,819
12/12	25,683	2,599	10.1%	32,794
12/11	26,249	1,606	6.1%	34,685
12/10	31,849	1,938	6.1%	38,179
Annual Growth	(9.4%)	—	—	(5.7%)

2014 Year-End Financials

Debt ratio: 3.1%
Return on equity: (-6.9%)
Cash ($ mil.): 1,588
Current ratio: 1.14
Long-term debt ($ mil.): 10,939
No. of shares (mil.): 131
Dividends
Yield: —
Payout: —
Market value ($ mil.): —

Veolia Environnement

Voila! Veolia Environnement holds water —as well as wastewater waste management energy and passenger transportation —operations. The company provides more than 90 million people with drinking water. One of the world's leading wastewater companies it serves more than 62 million people a year. It also provides waste management services managing some 54 million metric tons of waste and provides energy at 120000 facilities. Energy unit Dalkia (Veolia Energy Services) operates global cogeneration facilities and heating and cooling systems. Joint venture Veolia Transdev (up for sale) is a top European provider of bus light-rail and rail transport and operates in about 30 countries.

Geographic Reach

The company has a strong presence in the European Union North America and northern Asia.

Operations

Veolia Environnement offers a broad range of utility services: supplying water and recycling wastewater; collecting and treating waste; supplying heat and cooled air; and optimizing industrial processes. It provides technical services to its municipal and industrial customers in the water services market. The company's operations are conducted through three divisions each specializing in a single business sector: Veolia Eau (Water) Veolia Energie (Dalkia Energy Services) and Veolia Propret @Environmental Services). The Group designs and provides water waste and energy management solutions that contribute to the sustainable development of communities and industries.

Veolia Environnement's expertise includes securing water and wastewater management contracts from large cities and industrial companies. In waste management it focuses on treating and recycling hazardous waste and on large concession contracts in the UK. Through its Dalkia unit it manages large public networks and local energy cycles. It plans to concentrate on high added-value services and technologies to attain more profitable growth.

Sales and Marketing

The company provides more than 100 million people with drinking water. One of the world's leading wastewater companies it serves more than 70 million people a year. It also provides waste management services managing some 60 million metric tons of waste and provides energy at 120000 facilities.

Financial Performance

Veolia Environnement's revenues decreased by 4% in 2013 due to changes in the Environmental Services division primarily related to the divestiture of activities in Switzerland the Baltic States the disposal of Energonut in Italy and Pinellas in 2012 as well as the divestiture of Marine Services Offshore in the US in 2013. This was partially offset by the acquisition of the 50% stake held by the Fomento de Construcciones y Contratas (FCC) Group in Proactiva Medio Ambiente in 2013.In 2013 the company posted a net loss of $186.3 million (compared to net income of $530.4 million in 2012) due to lower revenues reduced operating income and decreased income from the discontinued operations.Operating cash inflow decreased by 11% in 2013 due to a decrease in the working capital as the result of measures to manage customer receivables and Days Sales Outstanding despite an extension in certain businesses/countries of days sales outstanding for customer receivables due from public authorities; and Advances received at the end of December 2013 for new major projects in the Technologies and Networks activity.

Strategy

The company's strategy is refocusing the Group geographically and concentrating on areas where it can seize less capital intensive opportunities. To reduce debt in 2014 Veolia Environnement sold its 65% stake in Marius Pedersen Group which provides solid waste management services in Denmark the Czech Republic and Slovakia to Entrepren ˛r Marius Pedersens Fond (Marius Pedersen Foundation) for 240 million ($325.3 million). It also agreed to sell its water waste and energy activities in Israel in a deal that will contribute to Veolia's debt reduction by around 250 million ($338.8 million).

In addition in 2013 Veolia was looking to sell its 50% stake in Veolia Transdev its transportation joint venture with French state bank Caisse des D ℗´ts et Consignations (CDC) in order to focus on its core businesses.In 2014 Masdar (Abu Dhabi Future Energy Company) selected Veolia Environnement to collaborate on the ambitious Renewable Energy Water Desalination Program in Abu Dhabi.

Mergers and Acquisitions

In 2014 the company signed an agreement to acquire EDF's interest in the international activities of Dalkia and to transfer to EDF Veolia Environnement's interest in Dalkia's French activities.In 2013 Veolia Environnement acquired the 50% stake it did not own (held by the Fomento de Construcciones y Contratas) in Proactiva Medio Ambiente. The deal allow the company to consolidate its positions in Latin America in waste management and water treatment and support its development strategy in this high-growth region.

Company Background

Veolia Environnement was formed from the water waste energy and transport businesses of the former Vivendi group. (The name Veolia is derived from Aeolus the keeper of the winds in Greek mythology). The group spun off Veolia Environnement (then called Vivendi Environnement) sold a minority stake to the public and renamed itself Vivendi Universal in 2000 (and Vivendi in 2006).

HISTORY

What is now Veolia Environnement originated in 1853 as Compagnie G ® ©ale des Eaux in Paris. The company irrigated farmlands and subsequently supplied water. By 1860 Paris had granted the company a 50-year contract to provide the city's water. In 1880 it moved beyond France to provide water in Venice Italy. Operations in Turkey (Istanbul) and Portugal (Oporto) followed.

Compagnie G © ©ale des Eaux extended its water network in 1924 and by WWII it supplied half of all urban households in France. After the war the company expanded into household waste collection (1953) and operation of household waste incineration and compost plants (1967). Wastewater treatment activities began in 1972.

In the next decade Compagnie G © ©ale des Eaux dove into diversification. It increased its holding in energy-conversion systems operator Compagnie G © ©ale de Chauffe to 100% (making it France's leading energy company) in 1980. That year it merged its wastewater treatment subsidiaries to create Omnium de Traitement et de Valorisation (OTV). Its waste operations were further augmented through the takeover of Compagnie G © ©ale d'Entreprises Automobiles (CGEA) a transport and waste management firm. The company also ventured into telecommunications pay-TV and construction (it gained a controlling stake in builder SGE in 1988 but disposed of its interest in the firm later known as VINCI in 2000).

CGEA bid for and won control of several former British Rail lines in 1996 when the UK's railway system was privatized. Operating under the name Connex the company began to run trains throughout southeastern England the UK's largest commuting area.

In 1998 CGEA changed its name to Vivendi. The group (which came to include mobile phone provider Cegetel and a stake in the Havas media company) transferred the Compagnie G © ©ale des Eaux name to its water business. Vivendi also organized its Compagnie G © ©ale de Chauffe and Sithe Energies (now a part of Dynergy) subsidiaries into a single energy division named Dalkia. In 1999 Sithe Energies bought 23 thermal power plants from US utility GPU (later FirstEnergy) and became the leading independent power producer in the northeastern US.

Vivendi continued its charge into the US that year. The group acquired waste services company Superior Services (then the US's fourth-biggest solid waste company). Its purchase of USFilter transformed Vivendi into the world's largest water company and marked the biggest acquisition of a US firm by a French company.

The ever-evolving Vivendi transformed into a global media company and renamed itself Vivendi Universal in 2000. It bought Seagram and French pay-TV provider CANAL+ and spun off its water waste management transportation and energy operations (Vivendi Environnement) after turning down German utility RWE's $28 million offer to buy the business.

Vivendi Environnement's waste operations grew after snapping up operations in Brazil Hong Kong and Mexico from Waste Management. In 2001 the company merged its Dalkia energy operations with the energy services operations of Electricit ©de France (EDF).

In 2002 Vivendi Universal reduced its stake in Vivendi Environnement from 63% to about 20%; the following year Vivendi Environnement changed its name to Veolia Environnement. Vivendi finally divested all of its interest in Veolia in the middle of 2006.

In 2007 the company acquired Thermal North America Inc. the largest portfolio of district heating and cooling networks in the US.

Late in 2009 the company named Antoine Fr ©ot as CEO. He had been in charge of Veolia's water division previously.

To generate cash in 2010 Veolia Environnement sold US waste-to-energy contractor Montenay International (which held its North American waste-to-energy assets) to Covanta Holding for $450 million. Marking a push for more green energy projects in Europe that year the company opened France's largest biomass-fueled boiler plant serving a district heating system in Val d'Oise.

In 2011 Veolia Transport merged with Transdev to create the world's largest private-sector transportation business jointly owned by Veolia Environnement and Caisse des D ©´ts. Although the joint venture announced plans to seek a public listing when market conditions permitted by the end of 2011 Veolia Environnement had decided to sell its half of the venture.

After binging on acquisitions from 2006 to 2008 Veolia started slimming down its operations in 2012 to combat worsening economic conditions. In late 2011 it presented a strategy to restructure its portfolio and cut debt streamline its organization and reduce costs. Its plan for 2012-2013 called for generating $6.6 billion (5 billion) from asset sales. As part of that plan in 2012 the company sold its US solid waste operations part of its Veolia Environmental Services North America unit to US investment firm Highstar Capital for $1.9 billion (1.5 billion).

The company also sold a majority stake in its UK regulated water businesses –Veolia Water Central Veolia Water East and Veolia Water Southeast – for $1.9 billion (1.5 billion) to Infracapital Partners an investment fund managed by the European investment arm of Prudential plc (M&G) and Morgan Stanley Infrastructure Partners.

Auditors: ERNST & YOUNG et Autres

LOCATIONS

HQ: Veolia Environnement
36/38, avenue Kleber, Paris, Cedex 75116
Phone: (33) 1 71 75 00 00
Web: www.veolia.com

HISTORICAL FINANCIALS

Company Type: Public

Income Statement

FYE: December 31

	REVENUE ($ mil.)	NET INCOME ($ mil.)	NET PROFIT MARGIN	EMPLOYEES
12/14	29,025	299	1.0%	179,508
12/13	30,721	(186)	—	202,800
12/12	38,801	519	1.3%	318,376
12/11	38,347	(633)	—	331,266
12/10	46,557	777	1.7%	317,034
Annual Growth	(11.1%)	(21.2%)	—	(13.3%)

2014 Year-End Financials

Debt ratio: 40.4%
Return on equity: 2.9%
Cash ($ mil.): 3,827
Current ratio: 0.97
Long-term debt ($ mil.): 10,118
No. of shares (mil.): 548
Dividends
Yield: 5.4%
Payout: 208.6%
Market value ($ mil.): 9,643

	STOCK PRICE ($) FY Close	P/E High/Low	PER SHARE ($) Earnings	Dividends	Book Value
12/14	17.58	55 42	0.40	0.95	18.38
12/13	16.36	— —	(0.40)	0.93	21.13
12/12	12.24	22 12	1.03	0.89	18.56
12/11	11.05	— —	(1.28)	1.58	18.09
12/10	29.36	29 20	1.62	1.45	21.99
Annual Growth	(12.0%)	— —	(29.5%)	(9.9%)	(4.4%)

Vinci SA

Veni vidi vici ...VINCI. Through its VINCI Construction division this company conquers the world as one of the largest building civil engineering and maintenance contractors. VINCI operates in two divisions: concessions and contracting. Its concessions business which builds and operates motorways parking garages rail infrastructure stadiums and airports includes motorway operator VINCI Autoroutes and airport manager VINCI Airports. Under the contracting umbrella VINCI provides electrical engineering maintenance and facilities management. Roadworks and transportation infrastructure is handled by Eurovia. VINCI is active in some 100 countries with France accounting for more than 60% of its sales.

Operations

VINCI divides its business into two segments: Contracting and Concessions.The Contracting segment which generated 84% of the company's total revenue in 2014 consists of VINCI Construction (39% of revenue); VINCI Energies (24% of revenues); and its Eurovia subsidiary (21% of revenues) which builds roads motorways airports rail and light rail infrastructure and operates a network of more than 400 quarries that produce 82 million tons of aggregates per year. Concessions which accounted for 15% of total revenue in 2014 consists of VINCI Autoroutes VINCI Airports VINCI Railways and VINCI Park. VINCI Park (and subsidiaries such as LAZ Parking in the US) which the firm sold the bulk of its stakes in 2014 managed more than a million on-street and off-street parking spaces in Europe North America and Asia. VINCI Immobilier the group's real estate unit accounted for about 1% of sales in 2014.

Geographic Reach

VINCI is Europe's biggest construction and concessions company. France is the company's largest market accounting for more than 60% of its annual revenue. Other important markets for the firm include Germany and the UK. Beyond Europe the group is active in Asia Africa the Americas and the Middle East.

Financial Performance

VINCI's revenues and profits have been growing at a steady pace over the past few years thanks to a strengthening global construction market and growth across its various Concessions businesses.The firm's revenue reversed course in 2014 however falling by 4% to 38.7 billion ($47.04 billion) mostly as its main contracting business shrank by 5% as construction demand declined in the telecom manufacturing and infrastructure sectors in France. The VINCI Construction business in France shrank by nearly 5% due to a combination of reduced share holdings on the Belgian group CFE (from 47% to 12% at the end of 2013) the advancement of the LGV Tours-Brodeaux project and lower market demand in the building and public infrastructure sectors. The Eurovia subsidiary's revenue also declined after a slowdown in public sector orders after budget cuts followed the local elections in France. The company's concessions businesses however grew by nearly 4% thanks to growth in VINCI Autoroutes and double-digit growth at VINCI Airports.Despite revenue declines in 2014 VINCI's net income jumped by 27% to 2.5 billion ($3.04 billion) thanks to several non-recurring income items mostly stemming from the sale of the company's investment securities and the capital gain on the sale of the bulk of its investment stake in VINCI Park. Not counting these non-recurring items profits inched up by less than 1% thanks to tight controls on operating costs. The firm's operating cash remained mostly flat at 3.6 billion ($4.38 billion) in 2014.

Strategy

VINCI continued to pursue its global expansion and diversification strategy in 2015 seeking to grow organically and through acquisitions. It also looked to bolster the expertise of its international specialized civil engineering networks especially in Latin America and continued developing major projects in emerging markets in central and eastern Europe the Middle East and India. In 2014 to free up cash for more international expansion in the Americas and Asia VINCI sold the bulk of its parking lot business to Ardian and Credit Agricole Assurances.

The company also sees opportunities in North America where aging infrastructure needs to be replaced. Indeed VINCI in 2014 won major contracts to expand or upgrade roads and transportation infrastructure in California Indiana and Georgia.VINCI has an ongoing strategy to acquire specialty companies that have a global reach. Specific target areas include ground technologies oil and gas infrastructure and nuclear engineering. VINCI is aligning its growth areas with marketplace trends such as urban development mobility needs and growing demand for new energy infrastructure.

Mergers and Acquisitions

In 2015 to extend its reach into Asia's oil and gas industry and diversify its revenue VINCI purchased Indonesia-based PT Istana Karang Laut which had expertise in onshore and offshore activities. The deal opened up markets in Central and South-East Asia where energy demand remained strong and where resources had not yet been exploited.Also in 2015 to strengthen its position in the Brazilian market the company acquired Orteng Engenharia e Sistemas S.A. which is based in Belo Horizonte Minas Gerais and designs builds and maintains electrical equipment PLCs and turnkey solutions in the energy manufacturing and infrastructure sectors.

In 2014 the company added to its holdings in Confiroute taking 100% ownership. The deal was priced in the range of 780 million to 800 million. It also acquired Imtech ICT the information and communication technologies division of Imtech as well as the Electrix company from McConnell Dowell a subsidiary of South African group Aveng.

In 2013 the company acquired ANA the company holding the 50-year concession for Portugal's 10 airports in a transaction valued at about 3.1 billion ($4.3 billion). The purchase furthered VINCI's strategy of making VINCI Airports a leading international players in airport concessions. With the addition of ANA'S airports VINCI now manages concessions at 23 airports in Portugal France and Cambodia. The French firm in July 2013 acquired an additional 5% stake in Arports de Paris in July for 365 million ($504.5 million) bringing its holding to 8%. Also in 2013 VINCI purchased London-based Mentor IMC Group Ltd. a global oil and gas project resource specialist thereby broadening the customer base of its Energies' oil and gas business.

Company Background

In 2009 in Qatar the French firm partnered with Qatari Diar which holds shares in VINCI to design and build a new motorway on the outskirts of Doha. The project was an outgrowth of an effort by VINCI to establish local roots in Qatar through the formation of subsidiary QDVC which had positioned itself in seven years as a major player in the Qatari construction market. Previously VINCI and Quatri Diar announced plans for a parking lot joint venture which would run lots in Qatar. The two entities also worked together on a 2.2 billion ($3 billion) bridge linking Qatar and Bahrain.

HISTORY

Company BackgroundVINCI's origins lie with French conglomerate Vivendi (now Vivendi Universal) which was founded in 1853 as Compagnie Gnrale des Eaux. Its mission was to irrigate French farmland and supply water to towns. The company won contracts to serve Lyons (1853) Nantes (1854) Paris (1860) and Venice (1880). Gnrale des Eaux moved into construction in 1972 building an office tower (and later hotels and houses) in Paris. The company also entered communications in the 1980s.

In 1988 Gnrale des Eaux acquired control of construction and civil engineering giant Socit Gnrale d'Entreprises. SGE subsidiaries included Campenon Bernard SGE (part of Gnrale des Eaux since 1981) Sogea Freyssinet Cochery Bourdin Chauss Saunier Duval Tunzini Lefort Francheteau and Wanner. SGE traces its construction roots to 1910. It became a subsidiary of Gnrale d'Electricit in 1966. Glassmaker Saint-Gobain acquired control of SGE in 1984. Under Gnrale des Eaux SGE enhanced its European profile through acquisitions including British builder Norwest Holst (1989) German road builder VBU (1991) and German pipe and duct maker MLTU (1992).

Gnrale des Eaux acquired publisher Havas in 1998 and took the name Vivendi –representing vivacity and mobility. Its purchase of USFilter in 1999 made Vivendi the world's largest water company. Vivendi's SGE unit (renamed VINCI) agreed to acquire the construction arm of rival conglomerate Suez's GTM unit in 2000.

Groupe GTM traces its roots to Socit Lyonnaise des Eaux et de L'Eclairage a leading French water utility. Formed in 1880 Lyonnaise des Eaux built up its French and international operations to include water distribution as well as gas and electricity production and distribution. A century later the company had diversified into such businesses as heating (Cofreth) waste management (Sita) and communications acquiring a stake in Lyonnaise Communications (now Lyonnaise Câble) in 1986.

In 1990 Lyonnaise des Eaux acquired construction firm Dumez whose subsidiary GTM-Entrepose was France's largest car park manager. Four years later Dumez-GTM was formed to consolidate the construction and civil engineering businesses of Dumez and GTM-Entrepose. In 1997 Lyonnaise des Eaux and Compagnie de Suez merged to create a leading provider of private infrastructure services Suez Lyonnaise des Eaux (which shortened its name to SUEZ in 2001). Compagnie Universal du Canal Maritime de Suez the builder of the Suez Canal was founded in 1858 and became Financire de Suez in 1958. In 1967 Financire de Suez acquired control of Lyonnaise des Eaux.

SGE changed its name to VINCI in 2000. That year as part of their strategy to rationalize operations and focus on core businesses Vivendi and SUEZ agreed to a friendly takeover of GTM by VINCI. SUEZ emerged as the combined company's largest shareholder but by the following year both SUEZ and Vivendi Universal had exited most of VINCI's capital leaving no core stockholder.

To better control its car park management operations the company in 2001 created VINCI Park to operate as an umbrella of its VINCI Concessions unit. It expanded its concessions holdings even more in 2002 by hooking up with construction group Eiffage to grab a 17% stake in Europe's second-largest toll road operator ASF which was floated that year by the French government.

In 2003 the group won the contract to manage the restoration of the historic Hall of Mirrors. It also won the concession contract to operate along with joint venture partner Keolis the International Airport of Grenoble.

VINCI completed its acquisition of ASF in 2005. The deal was part of a government program to privatize motorway companies.

The company has had volatile internal struggles. There was unrest in the board room during 2006 as chairman Antoine Zacharias reportedly wanted to oust CEO Xavier Vuillard in favor of Nexity CEO Alain Dinin. Zacharias was the one who ended up resigning and at the end of 2006 Dinin resigned from VINCI's board.

In 2007 VINCI's top French construction businesses Sogea Construction and GTM Construction merged to create VINCI Construction France its domestic construction giant.

The company strengthened its position in the UK in 2008 when it bought British construction and facilities management firm Taylor Woodrow from Taylor Wimpey. The deal consolidated VINCI's position in UK facilities management and public-private partnership projects such as rail airports and energy infrastructure. In 2009 VINCI Construction acquired the troubled UK builder Haymills Group as that company teetered on the brink of collapse.

In 2008 Eurovia branched out from the road to the rails when it acquired rail infrastructure firm Vossloh Infrastructure Services (now ETF-Eurovia Travaux Ferroviaires) from Vossloh. The division specializes in rail track maintenance and installation.

EXECUTIVES

COO Energy Business Line, Yves Meigni ©age 59
Chairman VINCI Autoroutes, Pierre Coppey, age 52
Executive Vice-President and Chief Financial Officer, Christian Labeyrie, age 59
Chairman and Chief Executive Officer, Xavier Huillard, age 61
Chairman VINCI Construction, Jean Rossi, age 66
Executive Vice-President Contracting, Richard Francioli, age 56
Chairman and Chief Executive Officer Eurovia, Jacques Tavernier, age 65
CEO VINCI Concessions, Louis-Roch Burgard, age 47
Auditors: Deloitte & Associ ©

LOCATIONS

HQ: Vinci SA
1, cours Ferdinand-de-Lesseps, Rueil-Malmaison, Cedex 92851
Phone: (33) 1 47 16 35 00 **Fax:** (33) 1 47 51 91 02
Web: www.vinci.com

2014 Sales

	% of total
France	62
United Kingdom	7
Germany	6
Central and Eastern Europe	5
Benelux	2
Rest of Europe	4
Americas	5
Asia Middle East and other	5
Africa	4
Total	**100**

PRODUCTS/OPERATIONS

2014 Sales

	% of total
Contracting	84
Concessions	15
VINCI immobilier	1
Total	**100**

Selected Subsidiaries

VINCI Construction
- CFE (12.11%; Benelux)
- VINCI Construction France
- VINCI PLC (UK)
- VINCI Construction Filiales Internationales (Germany Central Europe overseas France Africa)
- VINCI Construction Grands Projets
- Freyssinet (specialized civil engineering)

VINCI Concessions
VINCI Park
Eurovia
VINCI Energies

Actemium (industry solutions)
Axians (voice-data-image communication)
Citéos (urban lighting)
Graniou (telecommunications infrastructure)
Omexom (high-voltage power transmission)
Opteor (maintenance)

COMPETITORS

Atlantia	HOCHTIEF
Bechtel	Louis Berger
Bilfinger	Parsons Corporation
Bouygues	Schneider Electric
EIFFAGE	Skanska
FCC Barcelona	WS Atkins

HISTORICAL FINANCIALS

Company Type: Public

Income Statement FYE: December 31

	REVENUE ($ mil.)	NET INCOME ($ mil.)	NET PROFIT MARGIN	EMPLOYEES
12/14	47,720	3,021	6.3%	185,293
12/13	56,568	2,701	4.8%	190,704
12/12	52,062	2,526	4.9%	192,701
12/11	49,023	2,463	5.0%	183,320
12/10	45,821	2,376	5.2%	179,527
Annual Growth	1.0%	6.2%	—	0.8%

2014 Year-End Financials

Debt ratio: 40.8%	No. of shares (mil.): 554
Return on equity: 17.2%	Dividends
Cash ($ mil.): 7,792	Yield: 5.4%
Current ratio: 0.89	Payout: 12.4%
Long-term debt ($ mil.): 20,826	Market value ($ mil.): 7,510

	STOCK PRICE ($) FY Close	P/E High/Low		PER SHARE ($) Earnings	Dividends	Book Value
12/14	13.55	4	3	5.38	0.73	32.32
12/13	16.46	5	3	4.87	0.58	34.96
12/12	12.00	4	3	4.67	0.73	32.77
12/11	10.86	4	3	4.50	0.55	30.86
12/10	13.65	5	3	4.42	0.51	30.42
Annual Growth	(0.2%)	—	—	5.1%	9.5%	1.5%

Vodafone Group Plc

Customers have voted with their phones to make Vodafone one of the world's top wireless phone carriers with more than 444 million customers in nearly 30 countries. (It has partnerships with other mobile networks in another 50 countries.) In terms of subscribers Vodafone trails only China Mobile. The company does around 70% of its business in Europe where it is a leader in the wireless markets in the UK and Germany. It also provides data broadband Internet and fixed-line phone services; in Germany its largest market those services are overseen by subsidiary Arcor. Vodafone increasingly serves callers in Africa the Middle East and Asia through subsidiaries and joint ventures.

Geographic Reach

Altogether Vodafone has direct operations in 26 countries: Albania Australia Congo the Czech Republic Egypt Germany Ghana Greece Hungary India Ireland Italy Kenya Lesotho Malta Mozambique the Netherlands New Zealand Portugal Qatar Romania South Africa Spain Tanzania Turkey and the UK.

Germany is its largest single market accounting for 20% of overall revenues followed by the UK with 15%. Operations in Italy jumped to account for 11% of revenue. Vodafone's Vodacom brand in southern Africa makes up another 12% of sales.

The company has retail stores in all of its markets as well as offshore operations in finance administration IT customer service and human resources across Egypt India and Europe.

Sales and Marketing

Vodafone counts 444 million customers. More than 90% of its mobile customers are individuals and the rest are enterprise customers ranging from large multinational firms to small- and mid-sized businesses. It also has 11.8 million fixed broadband customers mainly in Germany Italy and Spain making it the fourth-largest provider of fixed broadband services in Western Europe.

Financial Performance

Revenue for 2015 (ended March) increased 10% fueled by acquisitions. The company's organic growth slowed nearly 5% in Europe in the face of intense competition. Net income plummeted 90% lower in 2015 on rising costs. Capital spending in 2015 reduced cash flow from operations.

Strategy

In 2014 Vodafone sold its 45% stake in US-based Verizon Wireless to Verizon Communications and entered the Canadian market in a partnership deal with Rogers Communications the top mobile provider in the market. In 2015 Vodafone boosted its presence in Italy and Spain through acquisitions.

Besides spending on acquisitions Vodafone through its Project Spring is investing £19 billion over two years to build up and extend its infrastructure in its markets. In Europe the company increased 4G coverage to 72% with a goal of 90%. It has upgraded its network to improve voice and data quality with high capacity backhaul and Single Radio Access Network. The company reaches 28 million European homes with cable and fiber infrastructure. In Africa Middle East and Asia Pacific Vodafone increased 3G and 4G coverage. The company should cover 95% of the population in India with 3G by the end of 2015.

Mergers and Acquisitions

Vodafone has become a global telecom primarily through partnerships and acquisitions. In 2014 it bought Spanish wireless carrier Ono for almost $10 billion. Ono serves almost 2 million customers and is the market leader in high-speed broadband services. Vodafone sees a significant opportunity to accelerate growth in the mature Spanish market by leveraging its distribution and marketing capabilities and through cross-selling to each company's customer base.

HISTORY

Early History

Vodafone was formed in 1983 as a joint venture between Racal Electronics (a UK electronics firm) and Millicom (a US telecom company) and was granted one of two mobile phone licenses in the UK. It launched service in 1985 as a Racal subsidiary. Vodafone and Cellnet the other licensee were swamped with demand. In 1988 Racal offered 20% of Vodafone to the public; three years later the rest of the firm was spun off to become Vodafone Group.

Vodafone moved beyond the UK in the 1990s. By 1993 it had interests in mobile phone networks in Australia Greece Hong Kong Malta and Scandinavia.

EXECUTIVES

CEO, Vittorio A. Colao, age 52, $1,110,000 total compensation
CEO India, Marten Pieters, age 62
CFO, Nicholas J. (Nick) Read, age 49
Group Chief Commercial and Operations Officer, Paolo Bertoluzzo, age 49
CEO UK Business, Jeroen Hoencamp
CEO Ghana, Haris Broumidis
CEO Australia, I ±aki Berroeta
CEO New Zealand, Russell Stanners
CEO Egypt, Hatem Dowidar
CEO Germany, Jens Schulte-Bockum
Regional CEO Africa Middle East and Asia/Pacific, Serpil Timuray, age 46
Regional CEO Europe, Philipp Humm, age 56
EVP Managed Network and Services, Nick Lambert
CEO Vodafone Fiji, Pradeep Lal
CEO Vodafone Uganda, Allan Richardson
Chairman, Gerard J. Kleisterlee, age 67
Auditors: PricewaterhouseCoopers LLP

LOCATIONS

HQ: Vodafone Group Plc
Vodafone House, The Connection, Newbury, Berkshire RG14 2FN
Phone: (44) 1635 33251 **Fax:** (44) 1635 238080
Web: www.vodafone.com

2015 Sales

	% of total
Europe	
Germany	20
UK	15
Spain	9
Italy	11
Other	12
Africa Middle East & Asia/Pacific	
Vodacom (southern Africa)	10
India	10
Other	11
Non-controlled interests & common functions	2
Total	**100**

PRODUCTS/OPERATIONS

Countries of Operation (controlled interests)

Africa/the Middle East/Asia-Pacific
- Australia
- Democratic Republic of Congo
- Egypt
- Fiji
- Ghana
- India
- Lesotho
- Mozambique
- New Zealand
- Qatar
- South Africa
- Tanzania

Europe
- Albania
- Czech Republic
- Germany
- Greece
- Hungary
- Ireland
- Italy
- Malta
- The Netherlands
- Portugal
- Romania
- Spain
- Turkey
- UK

COMPETITORS

AT&T Mobility	Proximus
BT	Swisscom
China Mobile	Telefnica Europe
Deutsche Telekom	Telekom Austria
KPN	Telstra
NTT DoCoMo	Virgin Mobile Telecoms
Orange	

HISTORICAL FINANCIALS

Company Type: Public

Income Statement FYE: March 31

	REVENUE ($ mil.)	NET INCOME ($ mil.)	NET PROFIT MARGIN	EMPLOYEES
03/15	62,408	8,514	13.6%	105,300
03/14	63,838	98,646	154.5%	89,146
03/13	67,539	651	1.0%	91,272
03/12	74,379	11,148	15.0%	86,373
03/11	73,826	12,820	17.4%	83,862
Annual Growth	(4.1%)	(9.7%)	—	5.9%

2015 Year-End Financials

Debt ratio: 42.2%
Return on equity: 8.4%
Cash ($ mil.): 10,171
Current ratio: 0.69
Long-term debt ($ mil.): 33,157

No. of shares (mil.): —
Dividends
Yield: 5.4%
Payout: 501.1%
Market value ($ mil.): —

	STOCK PRICE ($) FY Close	P/E High/Low	PER SHARE ($) Earnings	Dividends	Book Value
03/15	32.68	163126	0.32	1.78	3.69
03/14	36.81	19 13	3.70	0.00	4.46
03/13	28.40	18371479	0.02	0.00	4.07
03/12	27.67	116 98	0.40	0.00	4.55
03/11	28.75	106 75	0.45	0.00	5.01
Annual Growth	3.3%	— —	(8.0%)	—	(7.4%)

Volkswagen A.G. (Germany, Fed. Rep.)

With cars named for climate patterns insects and small mammals Volkswagen (VW) leads the Continent as Europe's #1 carmaker. Along with Golf (Gulf Stream reference) and the New Beetle VW's annual production of more than 10 million cars trucks and vans includes such models as Passat (trade wind) Jetta (jet stream) Rabbit and Fox. VW owns a garage full of luxury carmakers –AUDI Lamborghini Bentley and Bugatti. Other brands include SEAT (family cars Spain) and Škoda (family cars the Czech Republic). VW also owns 49.9% stake in Porsche. In late 2015 the company made headlines announcing that 11 million of its diesel cars contained software allegedly used to cheat emission tests.

Geographic Reach

VW sells its cars worldwide with operations in 153 countries across Europe North America South America Africa and Asia. The company holds a global market share of more than 11%. Sales outside of Germany account for almost 81% of the company's revenue although the rest of Europe accounted for more than 40% of revenue in 2014.

Operations

VW's makes more than 10 million cars trucks and vans annually. VW AG is the holding company for VW Group that comprises segments including Automotive and Financial Services which provides customer financing leasing banking insurance and fleet management.

VW manufactures 12 brands (Volkswagen Passenger Cars Audi SEAT ŠKODA Bentley Bugatti Lamborghini Porsche Ducati Volkswagen Commercial Vehicles Scania and MAN) and almost 335 models in 120 production plants.

For its commercial vehicles segment VW holds 99.6% of the voting rights in Swedish truck maker Scania. It holds more than 30% of MAN which is considered a majority stake.

Financial Performance

VW has achieved steady growth over the last few years as its revenue increased 3% from 2013 to 2014 due to higher sales volumes and improvements in its price mix. The company recognized major increases in sales from passenger cars and financial services in 2014 mainly due to higher business volumes.

Its profits jumped 20% from 2013 to 2014 due to the higher revenue coupled with optimized product costs and lower administrative expenses. VW's operating cash flows decreased by 14% in 2014 due to increased outflows of inventories along with financial receivables and leased assets.

Strategy

VW has preserved Porsche's brand autonomy. VW sees the combined group –which includes 11 distinct and separate brands along with the Porsche Holding auto trading business currently held by the Porsche and Piëch families –as a way to become an industry leader in terms of global market presence innovation purchasing and manufacturing.

Causing shockwaves around the entire industry VW in late 2015 admitted that 11 million of its diesel cars were equipped with software allegedly used to trick emission tests. Detecting when a vehicle was undergoing emissions testing the device would allow the car's emissions control to work properly. However when the car was operating under normal driving conditions the emissions control systems would not work properly spewing allegedly 10 to 40 times more nitrogen oxide (NOx) into the air than is allowed by EPA regulations. As part of its strategy to rectify the issue VW is earmarking $7.27 billion to cover the service corrections and win back public support with its customers. In addition VW could pay up to $18 billion in fines in the US alone and VW executives could be criminally charged.

HISTORY

Since the early 1920s auto engineer Ferdinand Porsche (whose son later founded the Porsche car company) had wanted to make a small car for the masses. He found no backers until he met Adolf Hitler in 1934. Hitler formed the Gesellschaft zur Vorbereitung des deutschen Volkswagen (Company for the Development of the German People's Car) in 1937 and built a factory in Wolfsburg Germany. No cars were delivered during WWII as the company produced military vehicles using the slave labor of Jews and Russian prisoners of war.

Following WWII British occupation forces oversaw the rebuilding of the bomb-damaged plant and initial production of the odd-looking "people's car" (1945). The British appointed Heinz Nordhoff to manage Volkswagen (1948) and then turned the company over to the German government (1949).

In the 1950s VW launched the Microbus and built foreign plants. Although US sales began slowly by the end of the decade acceptance of the little car had increased. Advertising that coined the name "Beetle" helped carve VW's niche in the US.

VW sold stock to the German public in 1960. In 1966 it purchased Auto Union (AUDI) from Daimler-Benz. The Beetle became a counterculture symbol in the 1960s and US sales took off. By the time of Nordhoff's death in 1968 the Beetle had become the best-selling car in history.

EXECUTIVES

Member Management Board Group Production, Michael Macht, age 54
Member Management Board China, Jochem Heizmann, age 64
Member Management Board; Chairman Board of Management Audi AG, Rupert Stadler, age 52
Chairman and CFO, Hans D. P ¶sch, age 64
Member Management Board Human Resources and Organization, Horst G. Neumann, age 66
Member Management Board Sales and Marketing, Christian Klingler, age 47
Member Management Board Procurement, Francisco J. Garc a Sanz, age 59
Member Management Board Group Commercial Vehicles, Leif –stling
CEO Bentley Bugatti Brands, Wolfgang Duerheimer
Chairman Vokswagen Passenger Cars, Herbert Diess
CEO, Matthias Mueller, age 62
CEO Saudi Arabia, Naif Bin Faisal Al-Sudairy
Auditors: PricewaterhouseCoopers Aktiengesellschaft

LOCATIONS

HQ: Volkswagen A.G. (Germany, Fed. Rep.)
Letterbox 1848-2, Wolfsburg D-38436
Phone: (49) 5361 9 0 **Fax:** (49) 5361 928282
Web: www.volkswagen.com

PRODUCTS/OPERATIONS

Selected Brands

Audi
Bentley
Bugatti
Lamborghini
Scania
SEAT
Škoda
Volkswagen
Volkswagen Commercial Vehicles

Selected Makes and Models

AUDI
A1
A3
A3 Cabriolet
A3 Sportback
A4
A4 allroad quattro
A4 Avant
A5 Cabriolet
A5 Coupé
A5 Sportback
A6
A6 allroad quattro
A6 Avant
A7 Sportback
A8
A8L
A8L W12
Q5
Q7
Q7 V12 TDI
R8
R8 Spyder
R8 Spyder FSI quattro
RS5 Coupé
RS6
S3
S3 Sportback
S4
S4 Avant
S5 Cabriolet
S5 Coupé
S5 Sportback
TT Coupé
TT Roadster
TT RS Coupé
TT RS Roadster
TTS Coupé
TTS Roadster
Bentley
Continental Flying Spur
Continental Flying Spur Speed

- Continental GT
- Continental GTC
- Continental GTC Speed
- Continental SuperSports
- Continental SuperSports Convertible
- Mulsanne

Bugatti
- Veyron
- Veyron Grand Sport
- Veyron Super Sport

Lamborghini
- Gallardo LP
- Gallardo LP Spyder
- Gallardo LP Spyder Performante
- Gallardo LP Superleggera
- Murciélago LP Coupé
- Murciélago LP Roadster

Scania
- Buses
- Engines
- Trucks

SEAT
- Alhambra
- Alhambra ECOMOTIVE
- Altea
- Altea ECOMOTIVE
- Altea Freetrack
- Altea XL
- Altea XL ECOMOTIVE
- Cordoba
- Exeo
- Exeo ST
- Ibiza
- Ibiza Cupra
- Ibiza ECOMOTIVE
- Ibiza FR
- Ibiza SC
- Ibiza SC Bocanegra
- Ibiza ST
- León
- León Cupra
- León ECOMOTIVE
- León FR

Škoda
- Fabia
- Fabia Combi
- Fabia Combi GreenLine
- Fabia Combi RS
- Fabia Combi Scout
- Fabia GreenLine
- Fabia RS
- Fabia Scout
- Octavia
- Octavia Combi
- Octavia Combi GreenLine
- Octavia Combi GreenLine
- Octavia Combi LPG
- Octavia GreenLine
- Octavia LPG
- Octavia RS
- Octavia Scout
- Octavia Tour
- Octavia Tour Combi
- Roomster
- Roomster GreenLine
- Roomster Scout
- Praktik
- Superb
- Superb Combi
- Superb Combi GreenLine
- Superb GreenLine
- Yeti
- Yeti GreenLine

Volkswagen Commercial Vehicles
- Caddy
- California
- Caravelle
- Crafter
- Multivan
- Saveiro
- Transporter shuttle

Volkswagen Passenger Vehicles
- CrossPolo
- CrossTouran
- Eos
- Fox
- Golf
- Golf Estate
- New Beetle
- New Beetle Cabriolet
- Jetta
- Passat
- Phaeton
- Polo
- Routan
- Scirocco
- Sharan
- Tiguan
- Touareg
- Touran
- Voyage

COMPETITORS

BMW	Isuzu
Daimler	Mazda
FCA US	Nissan
Ford Motor	Peugeot
Fuji Heavy Industries	Renault
General Motors	Suzuki Motor
Honda	Toyota

HISTORICAL FINANCIALS

Company Type: Public

Income Statement FYE: December 31

	REVENUE ($ mil.)	NET INCOME ($ mil.)	NET PROFIT MARGIN	EMPLOYEES
12/14	246,088	13,184	5.4%	592,586
12/13	271,226	12,481	4.6%	578,171
12/12	253,956	28,624	11.3%	549,763
12/11	206,094	19,930	9.7%	501,956
12/10	169,805	9,147	5.4%	399,381
Annual Growth	9.7%	9.6%	—	10.4%

2014 Year-End Financials

Debt ratio: 46.3%	No. of shares (mil.): 295
Return on equity: 12.2%	Dividends
Cash ($ mil.): 23,244	Yield: 1.8%
Current ratio: 1.00	Payout: 2.6%
Long-term debt ($ mil.): 83,159	Market value ($ mil.): 12,707

	STOCK PRICE ($) FY Close	P/E High	P/E Low	PER SHARE ($) Earnings	Dividends	Book Value
12/14	43.06	2	2	26.55	0.81	370.68
12/13	54.70	3	2	25.65	0.67	409.31
12/12	43.47	1	1	61.18	0.58	346.23
12/11	26.69	1	1	42.81	0.42	252.20
12/10	28.55	2	1	20.30	0.53	208.56
Annual Growth	10.8%	—	—	6.9%	11.3%	15.5%

Volvo AB

Despite the fact that the name "Volvo" still conjures up visions of soccer moms Volvo should really only inspire images of burly truck drivers. The company is one of the world's largest makers of trucks buses and construction equipment. In North America the company makes big rigs through its Volvo Trucks North America unit; Volvo also owns controlling interests in the well-known Mack Trucks brand in North America and Renault Trucks in Europe. Other products include marine (Volvo Penta) and industrial engines. Overall Volvo has production facilities in nearly 20 countries.

Geographic Reach

Volvo's main business segments (Trucks Construction Equipment Buses Financial Services and Penta) sell their products and services in 190 markets worldwide. It has production facilities in nearly 20 countries. Europe accounts for 37% of sales. Other major markets include North America (27%) Asia (18%) South America (10%) and other markets (8%).

Strategy

Part of the company's response to continued economic uncertainty is building smaller less expensive trucks particularly under its Renault label. It positions them for developing markets but lower price appeals to all. Volvo is also working to meet strict EU environmental requirements for trucks buses construction equipment and its Penta vehicles.

Speaking of developing markets Volvo positioned itself to take part in the world's largest economy when in 2013 it signed an agreement with China's Dongfeng Motor Group to produce heavy-duty trucks. The Swedish company in 2015 obtained a 45% stake in Dongfeng Commercial Vehicles a subsidiary of the Chinese firm that will make big trucks for China and other countries.

Company Background

Swedish ball bearing maker SKF formed Volvo (Latin for "I roll") as a subsidiary in 1915. Volvo began building cars in 1926 trucks in 1928 and bus chassis in 1932 in Gothenburg. Sweden's winters and icy roads made the company keenly attentive to engineering and safety. Volvo bought an engine maker in 1931. In 1935 Volvo became an independent company led by Assar Gabrielsson and Gustaf Larson.

Sweden's neutrality during WWII allowed Volvo to grow and move into component manufacturing and tractor production. Output in 1949 exceeded 100000 units 80% of which were sold in Sweden. The purchase of Bolinder-Munktell (farm machinery diesel engines; Sweden; 1950) enhanced Volvo's position in the Swedish tractor market. Volvo introduced turbocharged diesel truck engines and windshield defrosters and washers in the 1950s. By 1956 car production had outstripped truck and bus output.

HISTORY

Swedish ball bearing maker SKF formed Volvo (Latin for "I roll") as a subsidiary in 1915. Volvo began building cars in 1926 trucks in 1928 and bus chassis in 1932 in Gothenburg. Sweden's winters and icy roads made the company keenly attentive to engineering and safety. Volvo bought an engine maker in 1931. In 1935 Volvo became an independent company led by Assar Gabrielsson and Gustaf Larson.

Sweden's neutrality during WWII allowed Volvo to grow and move into component manufacturing and tractor production. Output in 1949 exceeded 100000 units 80% of which were sold in Sweden. The purchase of Bolinder-Munktell (farm machinery diesel engines; Sweden; 1950) enhanced Volvo's position in the Swedish tractor market. Volvo introduced turbocharged diesel truck engines and windshield defrosters and washers in the 1950s. By 1956 car production had outstripped truck and bus output.

Aware that it was too small to compete in global markets Volvo diversified (energy industrial products food finance and trading). Volvo increased its market share by purchasing several trucking and construction equipment companies that included White Motors' truck unit (US 1981) and Leyland Bus (UK 1986). In the 1980s Volvo acquired drug and biotechnology concern Pharmacia (now Pfizer) and Custos (investments Sweden). The company consolidated its food and drug units with state-controlled holding company Procordia in 1990.

At that time however Volvo was facing stagnant sales. It embarked on the largest industrial undertaking in Swedish history spending more than $2 billion to modernize plants and develop a series of high-performance family sedans which it introduced in 1991. Still high costs and persistent recession in Europe kept the company in the red during the early 1990s.

Adding to its troubles there was public outcry against a planned merger with French automaker Renault. The plan was abandoned in 1993 and the company sold its drug and consumer product interests (which had landed back in Volvo's lap when the government divested Procordia in 1993). These sales brought Volvo back into the black.

In 1997 Volvo sold its 11% stake in Renault left over from the abandoned merger. The next year the company strengthened its line of excavators and its Far Eastern presence by buying Samsung Heavy Industries' construction equipment unit. Volvo also bought Mexico's bus maker Mexicana de Autobuses and GM's share in Volvo GM Heavy Truck (now Volvo Trucks North America).

Anticipating a lower demand for cars Volvo closed an assembly plant in Canada in 1998 and in 1999 Volvo acquired a 13% stake (later upped to 25%) in rival truck maker Scania. To pay for its new focus on making heavy trucks Volvo sold its auto brand and manufacturing operations in Sweden Belgium and the Netherlands to Ford Motor Company for $6.45 billion in 1999. Volvo then agreed to take a 20% stake in the truck and construction equipment operations of Japan's Mitsubishi Motors.

In 2000 Volvo boosted its stake in Scania to 46% but its hope of acquiring a majority interest died when the EU rejected the $7.53 billion deal. Volvo then turned to France's Renault and bought the company's Mack truck unit in exchange for a 15% stake in Volvo.

Volvo's Renault Trucks subsidiary inked a technology transfer deal in 2002 with Chinese truckmaker Dongfeng Motors. The agreement cleared the road for Dongfeng to equip its heavy- and medium-duty trucks with Renault engines. In 2003 Volvo became the first Western truck manufacturer to produce vehicles under its own name in Russia. The following year Volvo opened a new truck factory in China with its partner China National Heavy Truck Corporation. Also in 2004 Volvo Construction Equipment (Volvo CE) sold its line of compact motor graders to Champion LLC a company headed up by Gary Abernathy a former manager at Volvo CE. Volvo acquired the remaining 50% of bus manufacturer Pr ©ost Car from Henlys Group in late 2004.

To boost its presence in Asia in early 2006 Volvo acquired a 13% stake in Nissan Diesel Motor (now named UD Trucks Corporation) for a reported $195 million. Later that year Volvo bought another 6% of Nissan Diesel Motor from Nissan Motor with the intention of acquiring the remaining outstanding shares (which it did in 2007). Also in 2006 the company negotiated with Nissan and the Chinese government to purchase Nissan's 50% stake in Dongfeng Motor Co. Ltd. –China's largest maker of commercial trucks.

In response to new emissions standards that went into effect in late 2006 in Europe and the beginning of 2007 in North America Volvo has been sprucing up the operations of its Mack and Renault brands. The move is in step with Volvo's other truck operations which also have been revamped to comply with the new standards.

Asia has also been the focus of group's development efforts. The 2007 acquisitions of Japanese truck manufacturer Nissan Diesel and Chinese wheel loader maker Lingong gave Volvo increased manufacturing capacity in the region. Part of its Asian expansion included buying for $1.3 billion. Though its manufacturing facilities are based in the US the target of the acquisition was the heavy compactors pavers and asphalt millers demanded by the growing number of infrastructure projects in China and India.

Scaling back on other operations the company sold its Volvo Material Handling Equipment business in mid-2008 to Linamar's Skyjack division. Volvo's Material Handling unit which had been part of Volvo's acquisition of Ingersoll Rand's road construction equipment business was considered to be peripheral to Volvo's operations.

Beginning in fall 2008 the company responded to the difficult business environment by scaling back production to reduce costs and match demand. Volvo also edged up new product pricing to offset lower sales volumes. Its simultaneous effort to slash inventories resulted in a robust rise cash flow in 2009 that has helped to sustain operations. A 20% reduction in headcount in 2008 through 2009 accompanied the resizing. Nonetheless Volvo suffered more than a SEK 14 million ($2 billion) loss in 2009.

EXECUTIVES

CFO, Jan Gurander, age 54
EVP Corporate Strategy, Karin Falk, age 50
EVP Group Trucks Technology and Volvo Group; CTO, Torbj ¶n Holmstr ¶n, age 60
President Volvo Trucks North America, Peter Karlsten, age 58
President Volvo Construction Equipment North America, Dennis R. (Denny) Slagle, age 62
EVP Corporate Communications, M rten Wikforss, age 51
EVP Business Areas, H kan Karlsson, age 54
President and CEO, Olof Persson, age 50
EVP Group Trucks Operations, Mikael Bratt, age 48
EVP Corporate Human Resources, Kerstin Renard, age 55
EVP Corporate Process IT and CIO, Magnus Carlander, age 61
EVP Group Truck Sales and Marketing and JVs APAC, Joachim Rosenberg, age 45
EVP Volvo Construction Equipment, Martin Weissburg, age 53
EVP Corporate Legal and Compliance and General Counsel, Sofia Fr ¤ndberg, age 51
EVP Corporate Sustainability and Public Affairs, Niklas Gustavsson, age 44
EVP Volvo Financial Services, Scott Rafkin, age 46
Chairman, Carl-Henric Svanberg, age 63
Auditors: PricewaterhouseCoopers AB

LOCATIONS

HQ: Volvo AB
Volvo Bergegaards v., Goeteborg SE-405 08
Phone: (46) 31 66 00 00 **Fax:** (46) 31 53 72 96
Web: www.volvogroup.com

2014 Sales

	% of total
Europe	37
North America	27
Asia	18
South America	10
Other regions	8
Total	**100**

PRODUCTS/OPERATIONS

2014 Sales

	% of total
Trucks	66
Construction equipment	18
Buses	6
Customer finance	4
Volvo Penta	3
Corporate functions Group functions and Other	3
Total	**100**

Selected Products & Brand Names

Buses
- Chassis
- City & intercity buses
- Coaches

Construction equipment
- Articulated haulers
- Asphalt milling machines
- Backhoe loaders
- Compaction equipment
- Crawler excavators
- Motor graders
- Pavers
- Skid steer loaders
- Wheel loaders
- Wheeled excavators

Financial services
- Customer & dealer financing

Trucks
- Mack
- Renault
- UD Trucks
- VE Commercial Vehicles (46% India)
- Volvo

Volvo Penta
- Industrial engines & drive systems (gensets & materials handling)
- Marine engines & drive systems (leisure & commercial boats)

COMPETITORS

Cummins Westport
Daimler
Daimler Trucks North America
Deere
Fiat Chrysler
Fuji Heavy Industries
General Motors
Hino Motors
Honda
Isuzu
MAN
Mitsubishi Motors
Navistar
Navistar International
Nissan
Oshkosh Truck
PACCAR
Penske
Scania
Suzuki Motor
Terex
Toyota

HISTORICAL FINANCIALS

Company Type: Public

Income Statement

FYE: December 31

	REVENUE ($ mil.)	NET INCOME ($ mil.)	NET PROFIT MARGIN	EMPLOYEES
12/14	36,602	271	0.7%	92,822
12/13	42,522	558	1.3%	95,533
12/12	46,610	1,694	3.6%	102,082
12/11	45,000	2,573	5.7%	102,248
12/10	39,481	1,620	4.1%	94,250
Annual Growth	(1.9%)	(36.0%)	—	(0.4%)

2014 Year-End Financials

Debt ratio: 5.0%
Return on equity: 2.7%
Cash ($ mil.): 3,394
Current ratio: 1.30
Long-term debt ($ mil.): 13,975
No. of shares (mil.): 2,029
Dividends
Yield: 0.0%
Payout: 290.0%
Market value ($ mil.): 21,876

	STOCK PRICE ($) FY Close	P/E High	P/E Low	PER SHARE ($) Earnings	Dividends	Book Value
12/14	10.78	13	9	0.13	0.39	4.99
12/13	13.14	9	7	0.27	0.48	5.85
12/12	13.67	3	2	0.84	0.46	6.48
12/11	10.84	2	1	1.27	0.38	6.05
12/10	17.61	3	2	0.80	0.00	5.38
Annual Growth	(11.5%)	—	—	(36.1%)	—	(1.8%)

Wal-Mart de Mexico S.A.B. de C.V.

Wal-Mart de Mxico y Centroamrica is the numero uno retailer in Mexico Costa Rica El Salvador Guatemala Honduras and Nicaragua with nearly 2900 stores. These include Bodega food and general merchandise stores and Superama supermarkets Suburbia apparel shops as well as half a dozen Ragazzi Italian restaurants. It also runs Wal-Mart Supercenters SAM'S CLUB and ClubCo warehouse stores and Banco Wal-Mart. Its stores are located in 555 cities throughout the region. Wal-Mart Stores formed a joint venture with Mexico's Cifra in 1991 and in 2000 acquired it and renamed the business Wal-Mart de Mxico. Wal-Mex then added Wal-Mart's operations in Central America and the business became Wal-Mart de Mxico y Centroamrica.

Financial Performance

Wal-Mart de Mxico y Centroamrica reported 432.9 billion pesos ($32.8 billion) in sales for the the 12 months ended June 2014.

Strategy

Walmex discontinued its Vips restaurant business in early 2014 with an agreement to sell the 360 restaurants to Alsea S.A.B. de C.V. for about $625 million. The Vips sale is subject to approval by Mexican regulatory authorities and is expected to close in 2014. The move leaves Walmex with just six Italian eateries under the Ragazzi name.

Banco Wal-Mart (launched in 2007) operates more than 260 branches located inside Bodega Aurrerá Wal-Mart and SAM'S CLUB stores in some 30 cities and cater to a clientele that for the most part is new to banking. The bank has been losing money for its parent though. To cut its losses in late 2014 Wal-Mart de Mxico y Centroamrica agreed to sell the banking unit to a group of buyers that includes Grupo Financiero Inbursa the financial services operations of billionaire Carlos Slim Helú. The deal is valued at MXN 3.6 billion ($247 million).

HISTORY

Spanish-born Jerónimo Arango Arias studied art and literature at several American universities without graduating. In his twenties he wandered around Spain Mexico and the US. He struck upon an idea after seeing a crowd waiting in line at the E. J. Korvette discount department store in New York City. Jerónimo called his two brothers Plácido and Manuel and convinced them to join him in a new business venture.

Borrowing about $250000 from their father a Spanish immigrant to Mexico successful in textiles the three brothers opened their first Aurrerá Bolivar discount store in downtown Mexico City in 1958. Offering goods and clothing well below manufacturers' list prices the store was an immediate hit with consumers but encountered hostility from competing Mexico City retailers. When local retailers threatened to boycott the Arangos' suppliers the company turned to suppliers in Guadalajara and Monterrey.

In 1965 the Arango brothers formed a joint venture with Jewel Cos. of Chicago to open new Aurrerá stores. Jewel bought a 49% interest in the business a year later. Plácido and Manuel left the business with their portion of the money but Jerónimo stayed as head of the company taking it public in 1976.

By 1981 almost a third of Jewel's earnings came from its operations in Mexico. But the next year the peso crashed obliterating its earnings there. American Stores took over Jewel in 1984 and Jerónimo bought back Jewel's stake in the company (which was renamed Cifra that year).

With the Mexican economy staggering from the peso devaluation weak oil markets and a huge debt crisis Jerónimo was taking a major risk. Although no new stores were opened none were closed. Employees were expected to work longer and those who left were not replaced. With Mexico's middle class hit hard Jerónimo emphasized the Bodega Aurrerá; no-frills warehouses which discounted all kinds of nonperishable merchandise from canned chili to VCRs.

Cifra and Wal-Mart Stores formed a joint venture in 1991 to open Club Aurrerá membership clubs similar to Sam's Club outlets. The two companies expanded the venture the next year to include the development of Sam's Club and Wal-Mart Supercenters in Mexico.

Remodeling began on Cifra's stores in 1992. The work was completed two years later and the company was poised to take advantage of Mexico's much-improved economy.

However devaluation struck again late in 1994. The resulting contraction of credit and rise in prices hit Mexican consumers hard and Cifra's 1995 sales declined 15%. But again it kept on as many employees as possible transferring them to new stores that had been in development. Despite the hard times Cifra opened 27 new stores (including 15 restaurants). The company was able to withstand the difficulties in part because it stayed debt-free.

Wal-Mart consolidated its joint venture into Cifra in 1997 in exchange for about 34% of that company; Wal-Mart later raised its stake to 51%. The cost-conscious companies combined the joint venture stores and Cifra's separate stores under one umbrella. Cifra opened 11 stores and eight restaurants that year.

Cifra opened nine stores and 17 restaurants in 1998; the next year it opened about 20 stores and nearly 25 restaurants. In early 2000 Cifra was renamed Wal-Mart de Mxico. Shortly thereafter Wal-Mart upped its stake in Wal-Mart de Mxico to about 61%.

In 2001 all the Aurrerá stores were converted to either Wal-Mart Supercenters or Bodega stores.

Eduardo Castro-Wright was promoted in 2002 from COO to CEO of Wal-Mart de Mxico succeeding Cesareo Fernandez who retained the chairman's title. The retailer opened 50 new outlets that year.

In March 2003 Mexico's Federal Competition Commission closed an investigation of Wal-Mex's purchasing practices citing a lack of evidence that the retailer violated competition laws. Overall that year Wal-Mex entered nine new cities in Mexico and added 46 new outlets. In 2004 Mexico's largest retailer grew bigger adding 17 restaurants 23 Aurrerá stores eight SAM'S CLUBS six supercenters and four Superama stores.

In January 2005 Fernandez stepped down as chairman and was succeeded by Ernesto Vega. A month later Castro-Wright left Wal-Mex to become EVP and COO of the Wal-Mart Stores Division in the US. He was succeeded by Eduardo Solorzano formerly COO of Wal-Mex. Also that year Wal-Mex acquired the Mexican assets of French retailer Carrefour. Carrefour which operated 29 hypermarkets in Mexico restructured its operations and left the Mexican market.

In November 2006 Wal-Mex received a license from Mexico's Finance Ministry to organize and operate a bank there. Overall in 2006 the retailer opened 120 new locations including stores in Monterrey the country's most affluent city and throughout northern Mexico where its Texas rival H. E. Butt Grocery is well established. In November 2007 Wal-Mart Bank began operations with 16 branches in five Mexican states.

Wal-Mex inked a deal with Tobacco One in August 2008 to distribute the tobacco firm's Rojo cigarette line in about 140 supercenters and some 60 Superarma stores throughout Mexico.

In December 2009 Wal-Mex announced the acquisition of Walmart's operations in Central America from Walmart Stores and two minority partners. The transaction was completed in early 2010 and Wal-Mex became Walmart Mxico and Central America. In January 2010 Eduardo Solorzano Morales resigned as CEO of the company but became chairman. He was succeeded by Scot Rank Crawford.

Auditors: Mancera, S.C. (member of Ernst & Young Global)

LOCATIONS

HQ: Wal-Mart de Mexico S.A.B. de C.V.
Blvd. Manuel Avila Camacho # 647, Delegacion Miguel Hidalgo, Mexico, Distrito Federal 11220

Phone: (52) 55 5283 0100 **Fax:** (52) 55 5328 3557

Web: www.walmartmexico.com.mx

2014 Stores

	No.
Mexico	2,210
Costa Rica	216
Guatemala	213
El Salvador	85
Nicaragua	84
Honduras	79
Total	**2,887**

PRODUCTS/OPERATIONS

2014 Mexico Stores

	% of total
Bodega Aurrera Express	863
Bodega Aurrera	439
Mi Bodega Aurrera	296
Walmart Supercenter	243
Sam's Club	158
Suburbia	109
Superama	92
Farmacia Walmart	10
Total	**2,210**

Selected Operations

Bodegas & discount stores
- Bodega Aurrera
- Dispensa Familiar
- MAXI Bodega
- PALI

Hypermarkets
- Hiper Paiz
- Hiper Mas
- Walmart

Warehouse clubs
- Sam' s Club
- ClubCo

Supermarkets
- La Union
- Mas por Menos
- Paiz
- Superama

Apparel Stores
- Suburbia

Restaurants
- El Porton
- VIPS

COMPETITORS

Banamex
Banorte
Chedraui
Comerci
Costco Wholesale
El Puerto de Liverpool
Gigante
Grupo Carso
H-E-B
Safeway
Sanborns
Santander Mexico
Soriana

HISTORICAL FINANCIALS

Company Type: Public

Income Statement FYE: December 31

	REVENUE ($ mil.)	NET INCOME ($ mil.)	NET PROFIT MARGIN	EMPLOYEES
12/14	30,003	2,070	6.9%	228,063
12/13	32,467	1,734	5.3%	226,289
12/12	32,172	1,791	5.6%	248,246
12/11	27,120	1,580	5.8%	238,128
12/10	27,091	1,577	5.8%	219,767
Annual Growth	2.6%	7.0%	—	0.9%

2014 Year-End Financials

Debt ratio: 1.4%
Return on equity: 20.7%
Cash ($ mil.): 1,908
Current ratio: 1.20
Long-term debt ($ mil.): —
No. of shares (mil.): —
Dividends
Yield: 4.4%
Payout: 719.6%
Market value ($ mil.): —

	STOCK PRICE ($) FY Close	P/E High/Low		PER SHARE ($) Earnings	Dividends	Book Value
12/14	21.44	14	11	0.12	0.95	0.58
12/13	26.12	25	19	0.10	0.75	0.62
12/12	32.78	26	20	0.10	0.40	0.61
12/11	27.39	23	16	0.09	0.40	0.52
12/10	28.58	—	—	0.09	0.57	0.55
Annual Growth	(6.9%)	—	—	7.2%	13.4%	1.3%

Wesfarmers Ltd.

Wesfarmers got its start as a farmers' cooperative in Western Australia a century ago. Today it's one of the country's most diverse companies and largest retailers following its acquisition of food and liquor retailer Coles Group. Wesfarmers has interests in far-ranging businesses including general merchandise (Kmart and Target) home-improvement (Bunnings) and office products retailing; coal mining; gas processing and distribution; chemical and fertilizer production; building materials sales; distribution of maintenance repair and operating products and industrial and safety products; and insurance. True to its heritage Wesfarmers still provides agricultural merchandise and services.

Geographic Reach

Perth-based Wesfarmers rings up 98% of its sales in Australia. New Zealand accounts for the rest. The company also has operations in Bangladesh and the UK.

Operations

The Coles division (formed in 2007) is Wesfarmers' largest business (accounting for 60% of the group's sales and 41% of its EBIT). It is one of Australia's leading food liquor and convenience retailers with a national presence. Wesfarmers has more than 2200 outlets under the Coles and BiLO supermarkets banners First Choice Liquor Liquorland and Vintage Cellars names and Coles Express banner. Other retail operations include Kmart and Target stores home improvement and office supplies stores. Wesfarmers is also engaged in coal production and export insurance (commercial and consumer) chemicals energy and fertilizers as well as industrial and safety products.

Financial Performance

Since buying Australian supermarket and liquor store operator Coles (in 2007) Wesfarmers has seen its sales increase more than 500%. In fiscal 2013 (ended June) Wesfarmers' sales grew 3% (before the impact of currency translation) versus the prior year. Operating income rose 3% over the same period. Driving the annual sales increase was improved performance of Coles and Wesfarmers' other retail operations (with the exception of Target) as well as the insurance and chemicals energy and fertilizers divisions. The company's Resources and Industrial and Safety businesses posted declines.

Strategy

The $18-billion purchase of Cole Group was transformational for Wesfarmers. Indeed the acquisition –at the time ranked as the largest takeover in Australia's history –gave Wesfarmers the designation as the country's top retailer. A five-year turnaround focused on the Coles supermarket chain began soon after the acquisition. As part of the reorganization Coles Group sold its online pharmacy business –Pharmacy Direct –and also shed some supermarket and liquor stores in an effort to improve its overall store network. The grocer also improved its fresh food and produce offerings and remodeled stores. While Coles has made progress and is beginning to regain market share (after years of losses) the 740-store chain continues to trail archrival Woolworths. Together Woolworths and Coles account for almost 80% of supermarket sales in Australia.

Beyond the retail arena recent acquisitions include the purchase of the New Zealand-based packaging firm Expresspak. To strengthen its position in the food service industry Wesfarmers Industrial acquired Expresspak which specializes in paper and plastic food and beverage packaging to add to its Packaging House business. As part of the deal the firm operates independently under the Expresspak name but shares its resources with Wesfarmers' subsidiary Packaging House whose offerings are largely of the industrial sort (steel strapping tape film). The acquisition put Packaging House which provides hygiene food service cleaning and chemicals and industrial packaging in a market-leading position in the food service packaging sector.

In April 2010 the company merged its Wesfarmers Chemicals & Fertilizers and Wesfarmers Energy divisions to form Wesfarmers Chemicals Energy & Fertilisers and also made other organizational and management changes in the industrial divisions. More recently Westfarmers began mulling a bid for ammonia producer Burrup Fertilisers but is meeting resistance from Australia's competition regulator. As part of its reorganization the company in late 2011 sold its Premier Coal (exploration production and processing) businesses to China-based Yanzhou Coal Mining for roughly $296 million.

A series of recent catastrophic events including the 2010 Christchurch New Zealand earthquake brushfires in Western Australia and sereve weather events have led to higher reinsurance costs and claims activity for Wesfarmers' insurance division a tiny part of its overall business.

Auditors: Ernst & Young

LOCATIONS

HQ: Wesfarmers Ltd.
Level 11, Wesfarmers House, 40 The Esplanade, Perth, Western Australia 6000
Phone: (61) 8 9327 4211 **Fax:** (61) 8 9327 4216
Web: www.wesfarmers.com.au

HISTORICAL FINANCIALS

Company Type: Public

Income Statement FYE: June 30

	REVENUE ($ mil.)	NET INCOME ($ mil.)	NET PROFIT MARGIN	EMPLOYEES
06/15	47,988	1,875	3.9%	205,000
06/14	56,547	2,526	4.5%	99,000
06/13	55,187	2,085	3.8%	200,000
06/12	59,148	2,165	3.7%	0
06/11	58,821	2,060	3.5%	200,000
Annual Growth	(5.0%)	(2.3%)	—	0.6%

2015 Year-End Financials

Debt ratio: 12.4%
Return on equity: 9.6%
Cash ($ mil.): 546
Current ratio: 0.93
Long-term debt ($ mil.): 3,546
No. of shares (mil.): 1,123
Dividends
Yield: 1.9%
Payout: 17.3%
Market value ($ mil.): 16,823

	STOCK PRICE ($) FY Close	P/E High/Low		PER SHARE ($) Earnings	Dividends	Book Value
06/15	14.97	8	0	1.66	0.23	16.95
06/14	19.69	10	8	2.20	178.53	21.36
06/13	18.16	10	7	1.80	0.00	20.74
06/12	15.30	9	7	1.87	0.00	22.56
06/11	17.17	11	9	1.78	0.00	23.46
Annual Growth	(3.4%)	—	—	(1.8%)	—	(7.8%)

Weston (George) Limited

George Weston Limited fuels Canadians through those long winters. About 95% of the company's sales come from its 63%-owned Loblaw Companies Limited Canada's largest supermarket operator (with more than 1000 stores under some 20 banners including Loblaws Extra Foods T&T and Zehrs Markets) and the country's largest wholesale food distributor. The rest comes from Weston Foods with operations in Canada and the US that focus on freshly baked goods frozen dough biscuits and other bakery products. (Its Interbake Foods division is a major supplier of Girl Scout cookies in the US.) Chairman Galen Weston owns about 63% of the company which was founded by his grandfather in 1882.

Both Loblaw and Weston Foods are facing challenges resulting from changing consumer preferences concerning what to eat and where to shop. In response George Weston has been restructuring both businesses to better match changing tastes. The weak economy on both sides of the US and Canadian border have put a damper on sales. Total sales rose less than 1% in 2010 vs. 2009 and were slightly below 2008 levels. The Loblaw segment outperformed Weston Foods with sales up about 1% vs. a nearly 4% decline for Weston Foods. Loblaw's 2010 sales got a boost from the acquisition of T&T Supermarket in late 2009. (T&T is Canada's largest retailer of Asian foods.)

Looking to position itself on a more profitable path to growth George Weston purged a couple of its businesses. In early 2009 the company sold its US-based fresh baked and baked goods business Dunedin Holdings to Mexico's Grupo Bimbo for about $2.5 billion. The sale included the Arnold Brownberry Entemann's Freihofer Stroehmann and Thomas' brand names. (The company's Interbake Foods and Maplehurst Bakeries businesses in the US were not included in the transaction.) Previously George Weston had sold its Neilson Dairy business to Saputo.

Cash from the divestitures was used to introduce new higher-margin products that customers want to eat and to fund acquisitions. To this end George Weston acquired Keystone Bakery Holdings a US provider of frozen cupcakes doughnuts and cookies for in-store bakeries and foodservice firms. The $185-million deal expanded the frozen baked goods division of its Maplehurst Bakeries unit. Aside from sweet treats George Weston is looking to shift its product mix to include more whole grains as an increased focus on healthier breads has hurt sales of white-flour-based products. In late 2010 the company acquired artisan and European-style bread manufacturer ACE Bakery for C$110 million (US$108 million). Based in Toronto ACE was made a subsidiary of Weston Foods (Canada). Its breads are distributed in Canada and the US.

Loblaw which is in the last year of a five-year restructuring plan is facing increased competition from non-traditional rivals such as Wal-Mart Canada and Costco Wholesale Canada which are claiming a growing share of the retail grocery market. In response the company is cutting prices and sprucing up its retail stores. It's also aggressively expanding its low-price Real Canadian Superstore format which numbers more than 100 stores and its No Frill chain of discount supermarkets to better compete with foreign superstore operators. In recent years Loblaw has been shuttering struggling Provigo stores.

HISTORY

A baker's apprentice George Weston began delivering bread in Toronto with a single horse in 1882. He added the Model Bakery in 1896 and began making cookies and biscuits in 1908.

Upon George's death in 1924 his son Garfield gained control of the company and took it public as George Weston Limited in 1928. Having popularized the premium English biscuit in Canada Garfield acquired bakeries in the UK to make cheap biscuits (uncommon at the time). He grouped the bakeries as a separate public company called Allied Bakeries in 1935 (it later became Associated British Foods and is still controlled by the Weston family).

Expansion-minded Garfield led the company into the US with the purchase of Associated Biscuit in 1939. By the late 1930s George Weston was making cakes breads and almost 500 kinds of candy and biscuits.

During the 1940s the company made a number of acquisitions including papermaker E.B. Eddy (1943; sold 1998 to papermaker Domtar giving it a 20% stake in Domtar) Southern Biscuit (1944) Western Grocers (1944 its first distribution company) and William Neilson (1948 chocolate and dairy products).

In 1953 it acquired a controlling interest in Loblaw Groceterias Canada's largest grocery chain. George Weston continued its acquisitions during the 1950s and 1960s adding grocer National Tea and diversifying into packaging (Somerville Industries 1957) and fisheries (British Columbia Packers 1962; Conners Bros. 1967).

By 1970 when Garfield's son Galen became president the company's holdings were in disarray. Galen brought in new managers consolidated the food distribution and sales operations under Loblaw Companies Limited and cut back on National Tea (which shrank from over 900 stores in 1972 to 82 in 1993). When Garfield died in 1978 Galen became chairman.

Ever since Galen a polo-playing chum of Prince Charles was the target of a failed kidnapping attempt by the Irish Republican Army in 1983 the family has kept a low public profile.

George Weston became the #1 chocolate maker in Canada with its purchase of Cadbury Schweppes' Canadian assets in 1987. The 1980s concluded with a five-year price war in St. Louis among its National Tea stores Kroger and a local grocer. This ultimately proved fruitless and Loblaw sold its US supermarkets in 1995 ending its US retail presence. As part of its divestiture of underachieving subsidiaries the company sold its Neilson confectionery business back to Cadbury Schweppes in 1996 and sold its chocolate products company in 1998.

In early 1998 Loblaw set its sights on Quebec buying Montreal-based Provigo. Other George Weston acquisitions in the late 1990s included Oshawa Foods' 80-store Agora Foods franchise supermarket unit in eastern Canada and its Fieldfresh Farms dairy business the frozen-bagel business of Quaker Oats Pennsylvania-based Maier's Bakery and Bunge International's Australian meat processor Don Smallgoods. It also sold its British Columbia Packers fisheries unit.

Early in 2001 George Weston surprised analysts when it won Unilever's Bestfoods Baking Company (Entenmann's Oroweat) with a bid of $1.8 billion. The company reduced its stake in Loblaw by 2% and sold its Connors canned seafood business to fund the purchase which was completed in July 2001. To help pay down debt in early 2002 the company sold its Orowheat business in the western US to Mexican bread giant Grupo Bimbo for $610 million.

In 2003 Weston's food distribution business introduced about 1500 private label products. It sold its fisheries operations in Chile at a loss in 2004 for about $20 million. That September the company purchased Quebec-based Boulangerie Gadoua Lte a family-owned baking business.

In 2005 the company sold its Heritage Salmon subsidiary thus exiting the unprofitable fisheries business entirely. The company also restructured its US biscuit operations and opened a new fresh bakery plant in Orlando Florida in 2005 as part of its push to increase its business in the southeastern US. A new bakery in the midwestern US began production of bread and English muffins in late 2006.

In early 2007 Weston's Loblaw subsidiary announced it was writing down its operations in Quebec to the tune of $768 million tied to its struggling Provigo grocery stores.

In December 2008 the company sold the Neilson dairy division of Weston Foods Canada to Saputo for some C$465 million in cash (about $373 million). It will use the money to pay down debt. In January 2009 it completed the sale of its fresh bread and baked goods business in the US. Later in the year Loblaw acquired T&T Supermarket Canada's largest retailer of Asian food.

In September 2010 George Weston through its Maplehurst Bakeries subsidiary acquired Keystone Bakery Holdings for approximately $185 million. Keystone is comprised of three operating companies: Freed's Bakery of Manchester New Hampshire a leading supplier of frozen thaw and sell iced cupcakes; Granny's Kitchens of Frankfort New York a leading supplier of both frozen pre-fried and frozen thaw and sell donuts; and Heartland Baking of DuQuoin Illinois a specialty supplier of frozen thaw and sell cookies. In November Weston Foods acquired artisan and European-style bread manufacturer ACE Bakery for C$110 million (US$108 million). Based in Toronto ACE was made a subsidiary of Weston Foods (Canada). Its breads are distributed in Canada and the US.

Chairman and president Galen Weston stepped down as the company's president in late 2011 but remained chairman.

EXECUTIVES

EVP Corporate Development, Robert G. (Bob) Vaux, age 67, $650,000 total compensation
President, Paviter S. (Pavi) Binning, age 55
EVP and CFO, Richard Dufresne
EVP and Chief Legal Officer, Gordon A.M. Currie
Chairman, W. Galen G. Weston, age 42
Auditors: KPMG LLP

LOCATIONS

HQ: Weston (George) Limited
22 St. Clair Avenue East, Toronto, Ontario M4T 2S7
Phone: 416 922-2500 **Fax:** 416 922-8508
Web: www.weston.ca

2014 Sales

	% of total
Canada	98
US	2
Total	**100**

PRODUCTS/OPERATIONS

2014 Sales

	% of total
Loblaw	96
Weston Foods	4
Total	**100**

Selected Operating Divisions

Food Distribution (selected Loblaw banners)
- Atlantic SaveEasy
- Dominion
- Extra Foods
- Fortinos
- Loblaws
- Maxi
- Maxi & Co.
- No frills
- The Real Canadian Superstore
- The Real Canadian Wholesale Club
- SuperValu
- T&T Supermarkets
- Your Independent Grocer
- Zehrs Markets

Food Processing (selected units)
- ACE Bakery (artisan breads)
- Interbake Foods Inc. (cookies and crackers US)
- Maplehurst Bakeries Inc. (frozen bakery products US)
- Weston Bakeries Limited (fresh baked goods)

COMPETITORS

7-Eleven
Bridgford Foods
Campbell Canada
Canadian Tire
Costco Wholesale Canada
Couche-Tard
Flowers Foods
Grupo Bimbo
H and M Construction
IGA
Jean Coutu
Jim Pattison Group
Katz Group
Kellogg U.S. Snacks
METRO
Maple Leaf Foods
Otis Spunkmeyer
Shoppers Drug Mart
Sobeys
Urban Outfitters
Wal-Mart Canada
Zara

HISTORICAL FINANCIALS

Company Type: Public

Income Statement FYE: December 31

	REVENUE ($ mil.)	NET INCOME ($ mil.)	NET PROFIT MARGIN	EMPLOYEES
12/14	37,925	108	0.3%	0
12/13	31,581	852	2.7%	138,000
12/12	32,920	488	1.5%	140,000
12/11	31,738	622	2.0%	142,000
12/10	31,914	452	1.4%	142,000
Annual Growth	4.4%	(30.0%)	—	—

2014 Year-End Financials

Debt ratio: 32.5%
Return on equity: 1.8%
Cash ($ mil.): 1,151
Current ratio: 1.57
Long-term debt ($ mil.): 10,626
No. of shares (mil.): 127
Dividends
Yield: 0.0%
Payout: 261.7%
Market value ($ mil.): 11,023

	STOCK PRICE ($) FY Close	P/E High/Low	PER SHARE ($) Earnings	Dividends	Book Value
12/14	86.18	139101	0.55	1.45	49.21
12/13	73.07	17 13	4.62	1.53	46.51
12/12	71.20	21 17	3.40	1.47	44.63
12/11	65.49	18 14	4.46	9.01	41.75
12/10	83.08	27 22	2.93	1.44	40.56
Annual Growth	0.9%	— —	(34.1%)	0.1%	5.0%

Westpac Banking Corp

Westpac Banking keeps its pact to serve customers in Australia New Zealand and the neighboring Pacific Islands. The company serves some 12 million customers through more than 1500 branches and is one of the largest banks in Australia. Retail banking division Australian Financial Services (AFS) group includes Westpac St. George Bank of Melbourne and BankSA branded banking locations. AFS also offers wealth management insurance and consulting through BT Financial Group. Meanwhile Westpac Institutional Bank offers corporate financial services and Westpac New Zealand provides retail wealth and institutional services.

Operations

Between its six operating divisions Westpac has a total of some $770 billion in assets. The company's Australian Financial Services (AFS) division is the largest segment generating 40% of the bank's revenue. It includes the Westpac Retail and Business Banking unit (consumer and small to midsized banking customers) the St. George Banking group and the BT Financial Group as well as the banking products and risk management segments. The Westpac Retail & Business Banking (RBB) segment is the next largest making up more than 20% of the bank's revenue and provides sales and services for consumers small-to-medium enterprises (SME) commercial and agribusiness customers in Australia.The remaining segments split the remaining revenue and include: St. George Banking Group Westpac Institutional Bank BT Financial Group and Westpac New Zealand. St. George Banking Group offers similar services to the RBB segment but operates under the St. George BankSA Bank of Melbourne and RAMS brands in Australia. Westpac Institutional Bank serves corporations institutions and government entities across Australia and New Zealand as well as overseas. BT Financial operates under brands including Ascalon Asgard Advance Asset Management Magnitude and Securitor. Westpac New Zealand which makes up just over 5% of revenue primarily serves small to midsized businesses and consumers in New Zealand.

Geographic Reach

Australia accounts for 85% of Westpac's annual revenues while New Zealand accounts for another 12%. In addition to branches and subsidiaries located across Australia New Zealand and neighboring islands Westpac's institutional division has offices in London New York City Hong Kong and Singapore.

Sales and Marketing

Westpac's retail services are promoted through its retail banking locations as well as through relationship managers wealth specialists business banking centers customer service channels and online. The institutional segment conducts sales through dedicated industry relationship and specialist product teams. The bank spent roughly A$159 million (about $138.7 million) on advertising in fiscal 2014 about 3% less than in 2013 but 8% more than it spent in 2012.

Financial Performance

(Note: Growth rates may differ after conversion to US dollars.)Westpac's revenue fell for a second year to A$38.6 billion (In US dollars a 6% revenue decline to $33.75 billion) in fiscal 2014 as it collected less interest income from treasury investments and as net interest margins were squeezed. The bank's non-interest income however grew by 11% thanks to growth in wealth management insurance and banking fees.Despite falling revenue the bank was able to boost net income by 12% to A$7.6 million (In US dollars a 4% revenue increase to $6.6 billion) as it collected more from fee-based income and incurred less interest expense in paying lower rates on customer deposits. Operations provided A$25.6 million (about $24.8 billion) in fiscal 2014 or 11% more cash than it did in 2013 as the bank collected more from deposits and other financial liabilities at fair value.Broadly speaking the bank's assets have been consistently growing for the past several years. From fiscal 2013 to fiscal 2014 total assets grew by 10% to A$770.8 billion (about $672.5 billion) with loan assets growing by 8% to A$580.3 billion (about $506.3 billion) and deposits growing by 9% to A$460.8 billion (about $402.1 billion).

Strategy

Westpac's primary operating vision is to become the largest financial services firm in Australia. The company also aims to build strong customer relationships and provide superior shareholder returns. Though it occasionally makes acquisitions Westpac is currently focused on organic growth measures to increase customer numbers. To those ends Westpac is beginning to expand its operations and relations in Asia. In 2014 the bank opened its first sub-branch in the Shangahai Free Trade Zone (FTZ) which it intends to use as a testing ground for a number of economic reforms and to be a strategic zone for the bank's customers to increase their presence in China. The bank hopes to take advantage of future opportunities in the region as China continues to liberate its economic and financial markets. Also in 2014 in a move designed to increase its brand awareness and please business travelers and tourists from China the bank also announced that it would accept China UnionPay cards —one of the fastest growing card networks in the world –at its more than 150000 ATMs branches and other acceptance points in Australia and New Zealand.In addition the firm is working to increase products-per-customer numbers through deposit wealth and insurance cross-selling programs. In late 2013 it acquired motor vehicle finance business Capital Finance Australia Ltd. and BOS International Australia Ltd. to add a new customer base that it can cross-sell all of its other banking products to. The acquisition also effectively broadened the bank's geographic reach and product line and added $7.9 billion more in motor vehicle finance equipment finance and corporate loans to Westpac's portfolio.Mergers and AcquisitionsIn late 2013 Westpac acquired Lloyds Banking Group's Australian asset finance business Capital Finance Australia Limited and its corporate loan portfolio BOS International (Australia) Ltd. for $1.45 billion which was funded from internal resources.

HISTORY

Westpac proudly calls itself Australia's "First Bank." But when predecessor Bank of New South Wales was founded in 1817 some 90% of the eponymous colony's inhabitants were convicts or their relatives. (The penal colony was established just 30 years before the bank.) The British challenged the bank's charter forcing it to become a joint-stock company.

New South Wales' parliament rechartered the company as a bank in 1850 amidst the country's first gold rushes. (Some bank branches consisted of tents in mining camps.) Heavy British investment and an influx of colonists kept the country growing. The bank's future partner Commercial Bank of Australia was founded in 1866 in Melbourne in the neighboring colony of Victoria. More than half of the country's banks disappeared in a panic at the end of the century when land speculation and a collapse in wool prices caused a depression.

Australia became a country with the onset of the 20th century and its government formed Commonwealth Bank a central bank. The Bank of New South Wales now known as "The Wales" helped finance Australia's WWI efforts. Along with the rest of the world the country and the bank rode up the Roaring '20s and down the Great Depression.

About 65% of the bank's male staff enlisted during WWII. Its New Guinea branches closed; others were hit by air raids. In 1947 the government moved to nationalize the prospering country's banks within the Commonwealth Bank but the courts helped the banks fend off the attack on their independence.

The Bank of New South Wales moved into the newly opened savings banking market in 1956. The next year it bought into Australian Guarantee Corporation (it bought the rest in 1988).

The bank expanded abroad and diversified operations in the 1970s. Battered by a lagging protectionist economy Australia moved to deregulate banking in the 1980s. As foreign banks hustled in Bank of New South Wales and Commercial Bank of Australia in 1982 made what was then the largest merger in Australia's history.

The new bank known as Westpac (for its Western Pacific market area) began building its non-teller-based banking networks in the early 1980s. The company developed an extensive ATM network and established telephone and computerized banking. Later that decade it bought a stake in London gold dealer Johnson Matthey (1986) and all of William E. Pollock Government Securities (1987).

In 1992 Australia's wealthiest man Kerry Packer took a 10% share in troubled Westpac gaining board seats for himself and friend "Chainsaw" Al Dunlap. Packer's power grab failed and he sold the stake in 1993.

After buying itself into the equities market in the mid-1980s Westpac sold its Ord Minnett brokerage division in 1993. The bank withdrew from Asia and expanded closer to home in the mid

1990s buying Western Australia's Challenge Bank in 1995 Trust Bank of New Zealand in 1996 and Victoria's Bank of Melbourne in 1997.

In 1998 the bank agreed to merge its back-office operations with those of ANZ Banking Group providing economies of scale while avoiding antitrust issues. The next year Westpac announced 3000 job cuts mainly through attrition to ready itself for increased competition from changes in Australian law. Pacific operations caused waves in 2000: Westpac said it would pull out of Kiribati in response to government action and a coup in Fiji prompted the bank to reduce employees' hours (a move that was criticized by the Fiji government). The next year however Westpac was strengthening ties to the Pacific market. It doubled its holdings in the Bank of Tonga (on the island of Tonga) and its share of Pacific Commercial Bank (on the island of Samoa).

In 2007 subsidiary Westpac Essential Services Trust formed a joint venture with another Australian firm to operate the Airport Link Company a rail-to-airport passenger service in Sydney. The trust was established so investors could invest in public-private partnership (PPP) assets.

Westpac's acquisition of St.George Bank in 2008 catapulted Westpac from fourth to second among Australia's leading banks. The combination set Westpac and its St.George subsidiary behind only the National Australia Bank in terms of assets.

EXECUTIVES

CEO, Brian C. Hartzer, age 48
COO, John Arthur
Deputy CEO, Philip (Phil) Coffey, age 56, $752,226 total compensation
CEO St.George Banking Group, George Frazis, age 51
Group Executive Westpac Institutional Bank, Rob Whitfield, age 48, $439,250 total compensation
CEO BT Financial Group, Brad Cooper, age 52, $403,670 total compensation
Group Executive Westpac Retail and Business Banking, Jason Yetton
CIO, David Curran
Chief Risk Officer, Alexandra Holcomb
CFO, Peter King
Acting CEO Westpac New Zealand Limited, David McLean
Chairman, Lindsay P. Maxsted
Auditors: PricewaterhouseCoopers

LOCATIONS

HQ: Westpac Banking Corp
275 Kent Street, Sydney, New South Wales 2000
Phone: (61) 2 9293 9270 **Fax:** (61) 2 8253 4128
Web: www.westpac.com.au

2014 Sales

	% of total
Australia	85
New Zealand	12
Other countries	3
Total	**100**

PRODUCTS/OPERATIONS

2014 Sales by Segment

	% of total
Australian Financial Services	41
Westpac Retail and Business Banking	22
St.George Bank	12
Westpac Institutional Bank	9
BT Financial Group (Australia)	8
Westpac New Zealand	6
Other	2
Total	**100**

COMPETITORS

Australia and New Zealand Banking
Barclays
Commonwealth Bank of Australia
HBOS Australia
HSBC
Hang Seng Bank
Macquarie Group
National Australia Bank

HISTORICAL FINANCIALS

Company Type: Public

Income Statement FYE: September 30

	ASSETS ($ mil.)	NET INCOME ($ mil.)	INCOME AS % OF ASSETS	EMPLOYEES
09/15	570,798	5,630	1.0%	35,241
09/14	671,697	6,588	1.0%	36,373
09/13	648,927	6,349	1.0%	35,597
09/12	704,404	6,230	0.9%	35,675
09/11	651,105	6,791	1.0%	37,806
Annual Growth	(3.2%)	(4.6%)	—	(1.7%)

2015 Year-End Financials

Return on assets: 1.0%
Return on equity: 15.7%
Long-term debt ($ mil.): —
No. of shares (mil.): —
Sales ($ mil): 27,880
Dividends
Yield: 6.8%
Payout: 69.8%
Market value ($ mil.): —

	STOCK PRICE ($) FY Close	P/E High	P/E Low	PER SHARE ($) Earnings	PER SHARE ($) Dividends	PER SHARE ($) Book Value
09/15	21.06	11	8	1.75	1.44	11.76
09/14	28.11	13	11	2.08	1.71	13.63
09/13	30.67	72	13	2.01	8.75	14.03
09/12	128.33	67	51	1.99	1.69	15.06
09/11	96.06	54	38	2.17	7.73	13.47
Annual Growth	(31.6%)	—	—	(5.2%)	(34.3%)	(3.3%)

Wilmar International Ltd

Founded in 1991 Wilmar International is among Asia's largest agribusiness groups. The company grows refines and sells palm soy and other edible oils and grains. It is divided into three units: plantations for growing palm and rubber trees; processing plants for refining the oil and grains; and a consumer division which sells the oils in China India and Indonesia. Wilmar International also makes and sells fertilizer and palm-based biodiesel sold in Europe and the US. The company has operations in 15-plus countries on four continents and owns more than 450 processing plants across Southeast Asia. It sells its products in 50-plus countries worldwide. Beyond agribusiness it is acquiring property in China.

EXECUTIVES

Chairman and CEO, Kuok Khoon Hong, age 64
Country Head Indonesia, Hendri Saksti
Country Head Malaysia, Yee Chek Toong
Head Technical Division, Matthew J. Morgenroth
Head Plantations Division, Goh Ing Sing
Vice Chairman China, Mu Yankui
Chief Scientific Advisor, Chua Nam-Hai
Head Oleochemicals and Biofuels, Rahul Kale
Head Sugar Division, Bohbot Jean-Luc
Head Shipping Division, Kenny B. H. Chwee
CFO, Ho Kiam Kong
COO, Pua Seck Guan
Executive Deputy Chairman, Martua Sitorus, age 54
Auditors: Ernst & Young LLP

LOCATIONS

HQ: Wilmar International Ltd
56 Neil Road, 088830
Phone: (65) 6216 0244 **Fax:** (65) 6536 2192
Web: www.wilmar-international.com

2013 Sales

	% of total
China	37
Southeast Asia	23
Australia/New Zealand	9
Europe	7
India	5
Africa	3
Others	16
Total	**100**

PRODUCTS/OPERATIONS

2013 Sales

	% of total
Palm & laurics	49
Oilseeds & grains	25
Consumer products	7
Plantation & palm oil mills	1
Sugar	12
Others	6
Total	**100**

Selected Operations

Palm oil cultivation
Oilseed crushing
Edible oil refining
Sugar milling & refining
Grain processing
Fertilizer manufacturing

COMPETITORS

Amsteel
Anglo-Eastern Plantations
Asia Food & Properties
Bunge Limited
Genting Malaysia
Golden Agri-Resources
Hong Leong Malaysia
IOI Corporation
Inch Kenneth Kajang Rubber
Kuala Lumpur Kepong
Narborough Plantations
New Britain Palm
Sime Darby

HISTORICAL FINANCIALS

Company Type: Public

Income Statement FYE: December 31

	REVENUE ($ mil.)	NET INCOME ($ mil.)	NET PROFIT MARGIN	EMPLOYEES
12/14	43,084	1,156	2.7%	92,000
12/13	44,085	1,318	3.0%	90,000
12/12	45,463	1,255	2.8%	93,000
12/11	44,710	1,600	3.6%	90,000
12/10	30,377	1,323	4.4%	88,000
Annual Growth	9.1%	(3.3%)	—	1.1%

2014 Year-End Financials

Debt ratio: 51.3%
Return on equity: 7.5%
Cash ($ mil.): 1,947
Current ratio: 1.28
Long-term debt ($ mil.): 7,158
No. of shares (mil.): —
Dividends
Yield: 2.2%
Payout: 296.6%
Market value ($ mil.): —

	STOCK PRICE ($) FY Close	P/E High/Low	PER SHARE ($) Earnings	Dividends	Book Value
12/14	24.41	156129	0.18	0.54	2.42
12/13	26.84	152116	0.21	0.40	2.34
12/12	27.35	240126	0.20	0.37	2.24
12/11	38.48	197138	0.25	0.38	2.09
12/10	43.94	257188	0.21	0.55	1.85
Annual Growth	(13.7%)	— —	(3.3%)	(0.6%)	6.9%

Wolseley Plc Jersey

HISTORY

In the late 1800s Irishman Frederick Wolseley immigrated to Australia where he developed the world's first mechanical sheep shearer. In 1889 he formed Wolseley Sheep Shearing Machine Company. Herbert Austin a young engineer who perfected Wolseley's machine moved back to England and became manager of the company's Birmingham factory when the company relocated there in 1893.

In 1895 Austin amazed by an automobile exhibition he attended in Paris obtained an advance from the company to develop an automobile; it went into production in 1901. The car manufacturing operations were separated from the company's other machinery operations and soon were bought by Vickers. (Austin went out on his own in 1905 and began producing cars under his own name –the venerable Austin line.)

By the middle of the century Wolseley Sheep Shearing had grown to include central heating and plumbing products distribution. In 1958 it joined with Geo. H. Hughes to form Wolseley-Hughes. At the time the company was a small manufacturer with 11 distribution depots.

The company's watershed transition began in 1976 when Jeremy Lancaster took over the chairmanship from his father. (In the 20 years that Lancaster was chairman profits rose from about $6 million in 1976 to more than $350 million in 1996.) In the late 1970s the company began expanding rapidly through acquisitions. In 1982 it went public and acquired Ferguson Enterprises a leading distributor of plumbing supplies on the US's East Coast. The acquisition marked the company's first substantial US purchase. Three years later the company formed Wolseley Centers which distributed building products under the names Plumb Center Controls Center and Pipeline Center. In 1986 the company changed its name to Wolseley plc. Acquisitions that year included Carolina Builders Corporation and M.P. Harris & Co. Late 1980s acquisitions included Familian (1987) the largest plumbing supplier on the US's West Coast and Familian Northwest (1988).

Wolseley then looked across the English Channel. In 1992 it bought Brossette France's largest specialist distributor of plumbing supplies. The company moved further eastward in 1994 acquiring – AG Group (now Wolseley Austria) Austria's largest wholesale plumbing supply business. In addition to 40 Austrian branches – AG also had five branches in both Hungary and Germany and four in the Czech Republic. The – AG deal solidified Wolseley's position as the world's #1 plumbing and heating merchant.

Wolseley turned its attention back to the US in the mid-1990s buying a half-dozen companies including Building Material Supply. John Young became CEO that year when Jeremy Lancaster retired from the company.

In 1998 the company began integrating California-based Familian and Virginia-based Ferguson Enterprises –together responsible for more than half of Wolseley's US distribution revenues –under Ferguson's management. The company continued making acquisitions that year and the next including its first Italian company (Manzardo plumbing and heating supplies); it also grew by opening new outlets. Wolseley sold some of its burner and boiler manufacturing operations in 1999.

Chairman Richard Ireland became acting chief executive in June 2000 with the retirement of Young for health reasons. That year the company sold most of its manufacturing businesses. It sold its remaining boiler and burner manufacturing businesses in early 2001. In May 2001 Ferguson Enterprises CEO Charles Banks was named group chief executive.

Also in 2001 Wolseley bought the heating and plumbing operations of Westburne Group (from France-based Rexel a distributor of electrical equipment) for $356 million to further expand in the US. In 2002 Wolseley bought Clayton Acquisition a Florida-based wholesale distributor of waterworks for $110 million. Additionally in 2002 the company bought Wasco a Dutch heating-equipment supplier for $58 million to expand in Europe. In December of that year Ireland was replaced as chairman by deputy chairman John Whybrow.

In July 2003 Wolseley bought Pinault Bois & Materiaux (now PB & M) which distributes lumber and building supplies in France from Pinault-Printemps-Redoute. Wolseley acquired three North American businesses JM Lumber Liberty Equipment & Supply and Nuroc Plumbing and Heating Supplies in September 2003.

The company acquired Tobler Management [now Wolseley (Schweiz)] a Swiss HVAC wholesaler from CapVis in December 2003. PB & M acquired Groupe Simoni a French building materials distributor in January 2004. Wolseley expanded its Irish business through the August 2004 acquisition of Brooks Group an Irish building supply company from UPM-Kymmene. Capping an acquisitive year Wolseley also acquired Parnell-Martin Management and Record Supply Company in the US and TAPS Wholesale Bath Centre in Canada in December 2004.

Overall in the fiscal year ended July 2005 the company spent 431 million on 26 acquisitions.

In April 2006 Wolseley acquired Brandon Hire for 72 million. The acquisition of DT Group in September brought Wolseley into new markets in Denmark Finland Norway and Sweden. In October the company purchased Woodcote - stavebni materialy a.s. a general builders merchant with operations in the Czech Republic the Slovak Republic Hungary Poland Romania and Croatia. Overall in fiscal 2006 the company added 279 new locations.

In August 2007 Wolseley purchased Davidson Pipe Company in the US thereby gaining access to the New York metropolitan market.

In 2008 the company acquired Gama Myjava in Slovakia.

In May 2009 Wolseley sold a 51% stake in Stock Building Supply to The Gores Group LLC a US private equity firm. In June Ian Meakins joined Wolseley as CEO. He succeeded Claude "Chip" Hornsby who resigned from the position after three years.

In July 2011 the company sold its Electric Center business to Edmundson Electrical. In November Wolseley sold its remaining 49% stake in Stock Building Supply to Gores Group.

EXECUTIVES

Chairman, Gareth Davis
Auditors: PricewaterhouseCoopers LLP

LOCATIONS

HQ: Wolseley Plc Jersey
26 New Street, St Helier, Jersey JE2 3RA
Phone: (44) 118 929 8700 **Fax:** (44) 118 929 8701
Web: www.wolseley.com

HISTORICAL FINANCIALS

Company Type: Public

Income Statement FYE: July 31

	REVENUE ($ mil.)	NET INCOME ($ mil.)	NET PROFIT MARGIN	EMPLOYEES
07/15	20,761	331	1.6%	40,375
07/14	22,162	850	3.8%	39,454
07/13	20,003	463	2.3%	39,995
07/12	21,038	89	0.4%	43,170
07/11	22,095	441	2.0%	46,246
Annual Growth	(1.5%)	(6.9%)	—	(3.3%)

2015 Year-End Financials

Debt ratio: 40.4%
Return on equity: 7.7%
Cash ($ mil.): 1,720
Current ratio: 1.38
Long-term debt ($ mil.): 1,460
No. of shares (mil.): 266
Dividends
Yield: 1.7%
Payout: 9.2%
Market value ($ mil.): 1,789

	STOCK PRICE ($) FY Close	P/E High/Low	PER SHARE ($) Earnings	Dividends	Book Value
07/15	6.71	8 6	1.28	0.12	15.19
07/14	5.20	3 3	3.19	0.04	18.28
07/13	4.81	5 3	1.67	0.00	16.92
07/12	3.58	19 10	0.32	0.00	17.73
07/11	2.96	4 3	1.67	0.00	20.86
Annual Growth	22.7%	— —	(6.6%)	—	(7.6%)

Woolworths Ltd.

Chow Down Under with Australia's #1 food retailer (ahead of Coles) – Woolworths (aka "Woolies"). The diversified retailer operates about 3200 stores in Australia and New Zealand including more than 1000 supermarkets under the Woolworths Foodtown Countdown and Thomas Dux banners. It also operates BWS and Dan Murphy's liquor stores. In addition Woolworths sells gasoline and leverages its distribution network to provide wholesale merchandise for third-party supermarkets. Woolworths' 165-odd general merchandise discount stores operate under the Big W name. It also runs about 395 consumer electronics shops under the Dick Smith and Tandy brand names. Woolworths also operates nearly 300 hotels.

Woolworths' total fiscal 2011 (ends June) sales rose nearly 5% vs. the previous year. The retailer's supermarket Australian supermarkets outperformed their counterparts in New Zealand. Indeed sales at the New Zealand markets declined slightly in 2011 vs. 2010 while the Australian markets rose more than 4%. Sales at the company's Big W general merchandise stores dipped while the consumer electronics category rose 4%. Online sales increased 63% with Woolworths onlne now available to 85% of Australia's population.

Woolworths along with other Australian retailers has been hit by weak consumer demand and competition from online retailers. Looking to streamline its operations the company in early 2012 announced plans to sell its Dick Smith consumer electronics business but will continue to participate in the category through its Big W stores and an expanded online offering. Stung by competition from Internet retailers the company is focused on expanding its online operations. (The company's pending exit from the Dick Smith business will not impact the its partnership with India's Tata Group for a chain of consumer electronics stores in India. Woolworths is supplying Tata's chain of 50 Croma stores there.)

The decision to sell Dick Smith followed the purchase by the firm's Australian Leisure and Hospitality Group (ALH) of about 30 hotels in New South Wales in late 2011. ALH operates sports bars and pubs restaurants retail liquor stores gaming outlets and nightclubs and hotels across Australia. To stock its liquor cabinet Woolworths in 2011 acquired The Cellarmasters Group from Archer Capital for A$340 million ($346 million). Cellarmasters is a leading direct-to-home wine retailer with operations in Australia and New Zealand. It also has a winemaking operation. The purchase complemented the company's existing liquor brands which include Dan Murphy's BWS Woolworth's Liquor and Langton's.

On the home front Woolworths is taking on the big-box home improvement market in partnership with the #2 home improvement chain in the US — Lowe's Companies. The Danks joint venture which is two-thirds owned by Woolworths has begun opening Lowe's-style home improvement stores in Australia under the Danks and Masters banners. Plans are for more than 150 such sites over the next five years. The stores will compete with market leader Bunnings owned by rival Wesfarmers which also owns Coles.

HISTORY

Harold Percival Christmas first tried a mail-order dress business before opening the popular Frock Salon retail store. Christmas and his partners opened a branch store in the Imperial Arcade in Sydney in 1924 renaming it "Woolworths Stupendous Bargain Basement" and luring customers with advertisements calling it "a handy place where good things are cheap ... you'll want to live at Woolworths." The company borrowed the name from Frank Woolworth's successful US chain after determining that chain had no plans to open stores in Australia. Woolworths was listed on the Australian stock exchange in 1924.

Food sales came more than 30 years later. Woolworths opened its first freestanding full-line supermarket in 1960 then diversified into specialty retail buying the Rockmans women's clothing store chain the next year (sold in 2000). It expanded into discounting with the Big W chain in 1976 and further diversified when it bought 60% of the Dick Smith Electronics store chain in 1981 (buying the remainder in 1983).

The purchase of the Safeway grocery chain (the Australian operations of the US-based chain) put Woolworths on the top of the supermarket heap in 1985. But the company was hurting (it lost $13 million in 1985-86) because of a restructuring in the early 1980s that had weakened management by bulking up the front offices and dividing responsibilities. Woolworths got a shot in the arm from Paul Simons who returned to the company in 1987 after running competitor Franklins. Simons cleaned house in the front offices closed unprofitable stores and began the successful "Fresh Food People" marketing strategy.

Industrial Equity Limited (IEL) bought the company in 1989; IEL then became part of the Adelaide Steamship group which spun off Woolworths as a public company in 1993. Career Woolworths manager Reg Clairs took over as CEO the following year following the untimely death (on a golf course) in 1993 of Harry Watts who was being groomed for the job. As a result the company has an unwritten rule of avoiding CEOs older than 60.

Clairs took the company in a variety of new directions. Woolworths began supplying fresh food to neighbor Asia in 1995. The company added Plus Petrol outlets adjacent to Woolworths Supermarkets in 1996. It also started a superstore concept for its Dick Smith Electronics chain (Power House) that year. In 1997 the company launched its Woolworths Metro store chain which targets commuters and other on-the-run shoppers in urban areas and it aggressively jumped into wholesaling to independent grocers.

Clairs (who was turning 60 in 1999) stepped down in late 1998 and Roger Corbett took over as CEO. Woolworths also began offering banking services to its customers and bought Dan Murphy a Victoria-based liquor chain in 1998. It divested its Chisholm Manufacturing meat plants in 2000.

In 2001 Woolworths acquired two liquor store chains (Liberty Liquor Booze Bros) more than 200 Tandy Electronics stores and 72 Franklins supermarkets from Hong Kong-based Dairy Farm International Holdings (most of which were later converted to the Woolworths and Food for Less banners). It sold its Crazy Prices general merchandise stores and began restructuring its liquor operations into four distinctive formats.

Woolworths exited the New Zealand market in 2002 when it sold its supermarkets group there to Foodland Associated for $690 million.

Supermarket division chief Bill Wavish resigned in May 2003 and was replaced by former chief general manager of supermarket operations Tom Flood. Wavish was considered one of the top candidates to replace CEO Corbett. Also in 2003 the company discontinued its Australian Independent Wholesalers (AIW) operations. Flood who like Wavish was considered a likely successor to Corbett resigned abruptly in August 2004.

The company acquired Australia's biggest pub owner Australian Leisure & Hospitality (ALH) in 2005. Woolworths operates ALH's retailing activities leaving the pubs and gaming operations to its partner in the purchase The Bruce Mathieson Group. (Previously the duo had acquired a 16% stake in ALH.) In mid-2005 the company acquired the New Zealand supermarkets of Foodland Associated and 22 Action stores in Western Australia Queensland and New South Wales for about $1.8 billion.

In September 2006 the company announced it had purchased a 10% stake in New Zealand's The Warehouse retail chain. Corbett retired as CEO in October. He was succeeded by Michael Luscombe the company's long-serving director of supermarkets.

Woolworths offered about $1.7 billion in 2008 to buy all of New Zealand's leading general merchandise retailer Warehouse Group. The purchase however which would have allowed Woolworths to expand from food into general merchandise in New Zealand was blocked by that country's competition regulator in mid-2008. An attempt to take over Australia's JB Hi-Fi an independent chain of home entertainment products also failed.

In February 2011 Woolworths acquired The Cellarmasters Group from Archer Capital for A$340 million ($346 million). In October Grant O'Brien was named CEO of the company.

EXECUTIVES

Managing Director and CEO, Grant O'Brien, age 54
CIO, Clive Whincup
Managing Director of Australian Supermarkets and Petrol, Tjeerd Jegen
Director Liquor, Bradford (Brad) Banducci
CFO, David Marr
CEO BIG W, Sally Macdonald
Chairman, Gordon M. Cairns, age 58
Auditors: Deloitte Touche Tohmatsu

LOCATIONS

HQ: Woolworths Ltd.
1 Woolworths Way, Bella Vista, Sydney, New South Wales 2153
Phone: (61) 2 8885 0000
Web: www.woolworthslimited.com.au

2015 Sales

	% of total
Australia	91
New Zealand	9
Total	100

PRODUCTS/OPERATIONS

2015 Sales

	% of total
Australia Food Liquor and Petrol	79
New Zealand Supermarkets	9
General merchandise	7
Hotels	2
Home Improvement	3
Total	100

COMPETITORS

ALDI
BP
Harvey Norman Holdings
Metcash
Royal Dutch Shell
Wesfarmers

HISTORICAL FINANCIALS

Company Type: Public

Income Statement FYE: June 30

	REVENUE ($ mil.)	NET INCOME ($ mil.)	NET PROFIT MARGIN	EMPLOYEES
06/15	46,775	1,649	3.5%	190,000
06/14	57,272	2,303	4.0%	198,000
06/13	54,119	2,084	3.9%	197,637
06/12	55,514	1,824	3.3%	190,000
06/11	57,313	2,242	3.9%	190,000
Annual Growth	(5.0%)	(7.4%)	—	0.0%

2015 Year-End Financials

Debt ratio: 14.3%
Return on equity: 20.3%
Cash ($ mil.): 1,024
Current ratio: 0.84
Long-term debt ($ mil.): 2,366
No. of shares (mil.): 1,266
Dividends
Yield: —
Payout: 244.1%
Market value ($ mil.): —

XL Group Plc

Auditors: PricewaterhouseCoopers LLP

LOCATIONS

HQ: XL Group Plc
XL House, 8 St. Stephen' s Green, Dublin 2
Phone: (353) 1 400 5500
Web: www.xlgroup.com

HISTORICAL FINANCIALS

Company Type: Public

Income Statement FYE: December 31

	ASSETS ($ mil.)	NET INCOME ($ mil.)	INCOME AS % OF ASSETS	EMPLOYEES
12/14	45,046	188	0.4%	4,663
12/13	45,652	1,059	2.3%	4,291
12/12	45,387	651	1.4%	4,007
12/11	44,626	(403)	—	3,818
12/10	45,023	643	1.4%	3,576
Annual Growth	0.0%	(26.4%)	—	6.9%

2014 Year-End Financials

Return on assets: 0.4%	Dividends
Return on equity: 1.8%	Yield: 1.8%
Long-term debt ($ mil.): —	Payout: 92.7%
No. of shares (mil.): 255	Market value ($ mil.): —
Sales ($ mil): 6,602	

Yapi Ve Kredi Bankasi A.S.

Yapi ve Kredi Bankasi (Yapi Kredi for short) boasts over $80 billion in assets making it Turkey's fourth-largest private bank. Yapi Kredi provides financial services –including retail corporate and private banking services –in Turkey through more than 1000 branches and about 4025 ATMs. It also operates in Bahrain and has subsidiary banks in Azerbaijan Germany the Netherlands and Russia. Yapi Kredi which launched Turkey's first credit card in 1988 now has 6 million cardholders. The bank also provides leasing factoring mutual funds insurance investment banking and brokerage services. Koç Financial Services (KFS) jointly owned by UniCredit and Koç Holding owns 82% of Yapi Kredi.

OperationsYapi Kredi's operates three major business segments. Its Retail Banking segment serves individuals and small- to medium- enterprises (SMEs) with consumer loans (auto mortgage and general purpose) and commercial installment loans respectively. About 59% of its loans were corporate and commercial loans in 2014 while retail loans and credit card receivables made up 27% and 14% of its total portfolio. The Retail Banking segment also provides card payment systems investment accounts insurance products and payroll services. Its Corporate & Commercial Banking segment has three subgroups: Corporate Banking for large-scale companies Commercial Banking for medium-sized companies and Multinational Companies Banking. Yapi Kredi's Private Banking and Wealth Management segment provides investment products to high net worth customers. About 80% of Yapi Kredi's total revenue came from interest income (mostly from loans) in 2014 while another 14% came from fees and commissions income. The rest of its revenue came from trading gains (2%) and other miscellaneous income sources (4%). Geographic ReachBeyond its 1000 branches in Turkey Yapi Kredi has subsidiary-owned branches in Amsterdam Moscow Baku (in Azerbaijan) and an offshore branch in Bahrain.Sales and MarketingYapi Kredi's retail banking arm serves individuals with up to T$500000 (roughly $170000) in financial assets and SMEs with annual turnovers of less than $10 million. Its commercial banking customers typically have annual turnover of more than $10 million while its corporate banking customers are businesses with turnover of more than $100 million. The bank served more than 10 million customers in 2014.Financial PerformanceNote: Growth rates may differ after conversion to US dollars. This analysis uses financials from the company's annual report.Yapi Kredi's revenue jumped 21% to T$15.9 billion ($6.8 billion) in 2014 mostly from higher interest income as its loan assets swelled by 26% (compared to sector growth of 18%) with growth in TL company general purpose and SME loans during the year. Its fee and commission income grew by 10% despite new regulations while deposits rose by 22%.Even with revenue growth the bank's net income fell 44% to T$2.06 billion ($887 million) mostly as its discontinued operations had generated some T$1.6 billion in 2013 but also because the bank incurred higher provisions for loan and other receivable impairments. Yapi Kredi's operating cash levels jumped 72% with operations using T$1.13 billion ($486 million) –compared to T$3.97 billion ($1.86 billion) in 2013 –mostly thanks to favorable working capital changes and higher cash earnings.

Stategy

Yapi Kredi has been moving toward digital banking channels that are quickly taking the industry by storm allowing the bank to slow expensive branch-expansion plans and cut operating costs significantly while giving customers faster access to banking services. To this end the bank in 2015 planned to continue boosting its mobile and internet banking customer base (which reached 1.2 million and 4.2 million users at the end of 2014 respectively). It also would continue to expand its ATM network and self-service banking corners implement video channel for digital banking customers increase IVR self service usage for its call center and divert more of its calls away from branches into a central location. Though its brick-and-mortar expansion plans have slowed compared to prior years Yapi Kredi still added 54 physical branches to its network in 2014 to grow its business. Yapi Kredi's aggressive expansion over the years has been effective at growing its customer base and overall business. Indeed during 2014 the bank added 600000 new customers to its business growing its base about 2.7 times faster than in previous years and bringing its total customer count to 10.6 million.The bank has been the market leader in credit card market share since 1988 and controlled nearly a 22% market share of the outstanding volume nearly 20% of the issuing volume and an 18% market share on the number of credit cards outstanding during 2014. Yapi Kredi was also the market leader in leasing and factoring and was number two in mutual funds and brokerage categories. Company BackgroundYapi Kredi was previously controlled by Çukurova one of Turkey's largest business congomerates. Çukurova fell to near-collapse in the aftermath of Turkey's economic crisis in 2001 and the group sold Yapi Kredi to Koçbank owner Koç Financial Services (KFS) in 2005. The following year KFS merged Yapi Kredi and Koçbank in what was the largest bank merger Turkey had seen. The combined group took the Yapi Kredi name.Koç Financial Services (KFS) which is jointly owned by UniCredit and Koç Holding owns 82% of Yapi Kredi which was founded in 1944.

EXECUTIVES

Vice Chairman and COO, Federico Ghizzoni, age 60
CEO General Manager and Director, Tayfun Bayazit, age 59
Executive Director and COO, Allessandro M. Decio, age 49
EVP Credit Cards and Consumer Lending, Nazan Somer, age 53
CFO Financial Planning Administration and Control, Marco Cravario
Head Operations, Y ksel Rizeli, age 63
Vice Chairman and COO, Federico Ghizzoni, age 60
CEO General Manager and Director, Tayfun Bayazit, age 59
Auditors: Guney Bagimsiz Denetim ve Serbest Muhasebeci Mali Musavirlik Anonim Sirketi

LOCATIONS

HQ: Yapi Ve Kredi Bankasi A.S.
Yapi Kredi Plaza D Blok, Istanbul, Levent 34330
Phone: (90) 212 339 70 00 **Fax:** (90) 212 339 60 00
Web: www.yapikredi.com.tr

COMPETITORS

Akbank
Citigroup
Deutsche Bank
Finansbank
GarantiBank
HSBC
Isbank
Trk Ekonomi Bankasi

HISTORICAL FINANCIALS

Company Type: Public

Income Statement FYE: December 31

	ASSETS ($ mil.)	NET INCOME ($ mil.)	INCOME AS % OF ASSETS	EMPLOYEES
12/14	83,754	883	1.1%	18,534
12/13	74,944	1,710	2.3%	16,680
12/12	73,418	1,165	1.6%	17,459
12/11	62,224	1,210	1.9%	17,306
12/10	59,478	1,444	2.4%	16,780
Annual Growth	8.9%	(11.6%)	—	2.5%

2014 Year-End Financials

Return on assets: 1.1%	Dividends
Return on equity: 10.6%	Yield: 0.0%
Long-term debt ($ mil.): —	Payout: 1,402.4%
No. of shares (mil.): —	Market value ($ mil.): —
Sales ($ mil): 6,887	

Yorkshire Building Society

Yorkshire Building Society (YBS) provides mortgages savings personal loans and brokerage services. One of the UK's largest mutually owned financial institutions the group also offers insurance coverage including mortgage-payment policies and home and auto insurance. YBS' brands include Barnsley Building Society the Barnsley Chelsea Building Society the Chelsea Norwich & Peterborough Building Society N&P and Egg and its subsidiary companies. All together YBS operates more than 200 branches and agency offices in the UK and Northern Ireland. It has 3.4 million members and assets of more than £34.5 billion.

OperationsYBS is one of the largest building societies in the UK and as a mutual organization is owned by and run for the benefit of members. It has no external shareholders. Its YBS Share Plans unit has been administering share plans for more than 30 years.

Company Background

The society merged with Chelsea Building Society in 2010 and with Norwich & Peterborough Building Society the following year; the two institutions continue to operate under their own brands.

The company was established in 1864 as the Huddersfield Equitable Permanent Benefit Building Society.

EXECUTIVES

CEO, Chris Pilling
COO and Finance Director, Robin Churchouse, age 49
Chief Information and Change Officer, David Henderson, age 54
Chief Commercial Officer and Executive Director, Mike Regnier
Chairman, John Heaps
Auditors: Deloitte LLP

LOCATIONS

HQ: Yorkshire Building Society
Yorkshire House, Yorkshire Drive, Bradford BD5 8LJ
Phone:
Web: www.ybs.co.uk

COMPETITORS

The Newcastle
The Principality
West Bromwich Building Society

HISTORICAL FINANCIALS

Company Type: Public

Income Statement FYE: December 31

	ASSETS ($ mil.)	NET INCOME ($ mil.)	INCOME AS % OF ASSETS	EMPLOYEES
12/14	58,650	230	0.4%	4,516
12/13	56,936	244	0.4%	4,218
12/12	53,992	198	0.4%	4,088
12/11	50,434	164	0.3%	3,266
12/10	46,713	142	0.3%	2,922
Annual Growth	5.9%	12.7%	—	11.5%

2014 Year-End Financials

Return on assets: 0.4%
Return on equity: 0.5%
Long-term debt ($ mil.): —
No. of shares (mil.): —
Sales ($ mil): 2,091
Dividends
Yield: —
Payout: —
Market value ($ mil.): —

ZF Friedrichshafen AG (Germany)

ZF Friedrichshafen (ZF) shifts easily from land to air to sea. The company makes automatic and manual transmissions for commercial vehicles cars aircraft and marine vessels. ZF also makes rail transmissions and industrial drives such as servo gearboxes. Its off-road division makes transmissions for construction equipment and farm machinery. ZF's chassis unit makes automotive rear-axle systems and suspension modules. Through ZF Lenksysteme (a joint venture with Robert Bosch) the company makes steering systems. ZF was founded in 1915 by Ferdinand von Zeppelin (the Zeppelin inventor). The Zeppelin Stiftung Foundation which is largely controlled by the town of Friedrichshafen owns more than 90% of the company.

Geography continues to be an important subject for the company. As with most of its competitiors ZF has turned its attention toward the East. Automobile production in China is expected to increase by about 50% in 2010 compared to 2005. For continued growth the company is beefing up its sales activities in the emerging region. ZF is also keeping an eye out for partnerships and potential joint ventures that will help it strengthen its global footprint while complementing its product mix.

ZF has not forgotten about Western Europe the source of 60% of the company sales. In late 2010 ZF acquired Fonderie Lorraine a France-based supplier of light-alloy internal transmission parts and housings from fellow German manufacturer HONSEL. The deal strengthens the supply chain for ZF's automatic transmissions in the region and will allow the company to take advantage of the light-alloy foundry operations to facilitate the manufacture of the the company's new 8-speed automatic transmissions.

The company opened a new production plant for powertrain and suspension components at its Slovakian site in Levice and a production facility in Europe for the industrial manufacture of hybrid modules for passenger cars. It signed an agreement with Continental in May 2009 to develop and produce commercial vehicle hybrid drives; ZF will produce the drive system and Continental will supply the electronics. The company signed a supply agreement to produce 35000 dual-mass flywheels and clutches for Subaru's first diesel boxer engine and together with Porsche it developed the seven-speed dual clutch transmission which began volume production. ZF opened its new Development Center in Friedrichshafen for its Commercial Vehicle and Special Driveline Technology division.

Weakened by the ripple effects of Detroit's problems the beleaguered North American auto component industry is a target-rich environment for acquisitions. In North America ZF is restructuring its operations while keeping an eye out for potential acquisitions particularly for companies involved in gear technology as evidenced by its November 2008 acquisition of Cherry Corporation which it has renamed as ZF Electronics. The acquisition strengthened its technology position in the electronics sector. ZF is going forward with a joint venture with Chrysler to make axles for Chrysler and other customers beginning in 2010.

The company has expanded its after-sales business by merging key organizations to form the new Services business unit. This segment will be involved in logistics and infrastructure with an eye on building its range of products and services available to customers. ZF operates more than 100 production companies six main development locations over 40 after-market trading companies and sales and service centers over 10 marketing offices and has 650 service partners worldwide.

HISTORY

After the 1908 fiery demonstration of an early airship Count Ferdinand Graf von Zeppelin thought he was ruined. However despite its unfortunate fate the airship's brief flight managed to captivate the interest of the citizens of Friedrichshafen Germany. The townspeople donated funds to Count Zeppelin raising more than 6 million German marks. He used the money to found Luftschiffbau Zeppelin GmbH in 1908. The company was controlled by the Zeppelin Stiftung (founded by the count) for the town of Friedrichshafen.

In 1915 Zahnradfabrik Friedrichshafen GmbH (ZF) was created by Luftschiffbau Zeppelin for the development and manufacture of special gears for airships and other aircraft. Count Zeppelin died two years later.

ZF was converted from a private firm to a stock corporation in 1921. To reflect the change the company's name was changed to Zahnradfabrik Friedrichshafen AG. ZF AG developed the first helical-gear transmission in 1929. The company began producing automotive steering systems in 1932.

Like much of Germany's industrial production capacity Zahnradfabrik Friedrichshafen's operations were out of commission by the end of WWII. Reconstruction of the company's factories was completed in 1946 when production resumed with 1000 workers.

In accordance with the count's will complete ownership of the Zeppelin Stiftung foundation was transferred to the city of Friedrichshafen in 1947. Three years later most of ZF's ownership (90%) was assigned to the Zeppelin Stiftung.

ZF expanded into South America in 1959 with the establishment of ZF do Brasil SA. The company developed its first automatic transmission in 1961. A little over a decade later (1973) the company reached 1 billion German marks in sales and employed 18000 workers. ZF entered the US in 1979 with the founding of ZF of North America in Chicago. In 1986 the company expanded its US operations to include a factory for the production of pickup truck transmissions in Gainesville Georgia.

The company changed its name from Zahnradfabrik Friedrichshafen AG to the relatively less-cumbersome ZF Friedrichshafen AG in 1992. By 1997 ZF had established four joint ventures in China. The following year was busy for the company. It formed ZF Lenksysteme a joint venture with Robert Bosch for the manufacture of automotive steering systems. By mid-1998 ZF had also founded ZF Batavia LLC with Ford Motor Company in the US for the production of automatic transmissions for passenger cars and ZF Meritor with Meritor (now ArvinMeritor) for the production and distribution of commercial vehicle transmissions in North America.

In 2000 ZF and Sauer AG formed ZF Graziano Materials Handling Components GmbH a joint venture that combined their respective forklift transmission operations.

The following year ZF agreed to acquire Mannesmann Sachs AG (transmission and driveline components). The deal was completed in 2002 and the division was renamed ZF Sachs AG.

In 2008 to stay lean the company shed some noncore operations including its ZF Meritor joint venture with ArvinMeritor.

EXECUTIVES

EVP and Member Management Board, Michael Paul, age 64
CEO, Stefan Sommer, age 53
EVP and Member Management Board, Reinhard Buhl, age 63
EVP and Member Management Board, Peter Ottenbruch, age 58
Member Management Board, Rolf Lutz, age 63
EVP and Member Management Board, Gerhard Wagner, age 62
EVP and Financial Director, Konstantin Sauer, age 56
President Asia/Pacific, Rudi von Meister
EVP and Member Management Board, J rgen Holeksa, age 50
EVP and Member Board Management, Wilhelm Rehm
CEO ZF Marine Propulsion Systems, Daniel H □rter

Chairman Supervisory Board, Dr. Giorgio Behr, age 68
Auditors: Ernst & Young GmbH Wirtschaftsprufungsgesellschaft

LOCATIONS

HQ: ZF Friedrichshafen AG (Germany)
Graf-von-Soden-Platz 1, Friedrichshafen D-88046
Phone: (49) 7541 77 0 **Fax:** (49) 7541 77 90 80 00
Web: www.zf.com

2009 Sales

	% of total
Europe	
Western	60
Eastern	5
Asia/Pacific	18
North America	10
South America	5
Africa	2
Total	**100**

PRODUCTS/OPERATIONS

2009 Sales

	% of total
Powertrain & suspension components	21
Car driveline technology	19
Commercial vehicle & special driveline technology	19
Off-road driveline technology & axle systems	14
Car chassis technology	13
Steering technology	13
Services	11
Rubber-metal technology	5
Electronic components	2
Marine propulsion systems	2
Aviation technology	1
Corporate R&D corporate headquarters & service companies	1
Total	**100**

2009 Sales by Market

	% of total
Cars & light commercial vehicles	65
Commercial vehicles	21
Construction & agricultural machinery marine craft aircraft special & rail vehicles	14
Total	**100**

Selected Divisions and Products

Aftermarket
- Spare parts

Aviation technology
- Aircraft transmissions

Car chassis technology
- Airbag housings
- Axle systems
- Gearshift systems
- Rubber-metal components
- Suspension joints
- Tie rods
- Wheel suspension modules

Car driveline technology
- Automatic transmissions
- Continuously variable transmissions
- Manual transmissions

Commercial vehicle and special driveline technology
- Automatic transmissions
- Electromagnetic clutches
- Hydrodynamic retarders
- Manual transmissions
- Torque converter units
- Transfer gearboxes

Marine propulsion systems
- Marine transmissions

Off-road driveline technology and axle systems
- Agricultural machinery axles
- Agricultural machinery transmissions
- Axles for fork-lift trucks
- Axle systems for commercial vehicles
- Construction machinery axles
- Construction machinery transmissions
- Transmissions for elevators
- Transmissions for fork-lift trucks
- Transmissions for mobile mixers

Powertrain and suspension components
- Axle modules
- Cab dampers
- Clutch systems
- Electric propulsion systems
- Powertrain automation
- Ride-height control systems
- Shock absorbers
- Torque converters

Rubber-metal technology
- Bumper impact dampers
- Chassis suspension
- Plastic components
- Powertrain suspension
- Vibration and noise control products

Steering technology
- Ball and nut power steerings for cars and commercial vehicles
- Electro-hydraulic steering systems
- Limited-slip differentials
- Rack and pinion power steerings
- Rear axle steering systems for commercial vehicles
- Steer by wire systems (electric steerings)
- Steering accessories
- Steering columns
- Steering pumps
- Steering shafts
- Steering valves

COMPETITORS

Aisin Seiki
American Axle & Manufacturing
Carraro
Continental AG
DENSO
Dana Holding
Delphi Automotive Systems
GKN
Magna International
Meritor
Metaldyne
Robert Bosch LLC
Visteon
ZF TRW Automotive

HISTORICAL FINANCIALS

Company Type: Public

Income Statement FYE: December 31

	REVENUE ($ mil.)	NET INCOME ($ mil.)	NET PROFIT MARGIN	EMPLOYEES
12/14	22,383	787	3.5%	71,402
12/13	23,180	601	2.6%	72,643
12/12	22,889	402	1.8%	74,775
12/11	20,060	649	3.2%	71,488
12/10	17,274	546	3.2%	64,600
Annual Growth	6.7%	9.6%	—	2.5%

2014 Year-End Financials

Debt ratio: 7.0%
Return on equity: 15.4%
Cash ($ mil.): 1,354
Current ratio: 1.59
Long-term debt ($ mil.): 339
No. of shares (mil.): 500
Dividends
Yield: —
Payout: —
Market value ($ mil.): —

Zurich Insurance Group Ltd

The operations of Zurich Insurance Group have crossed over the Alps and spread around the globe. Serving approximately 170 countries worldwide the company is a major global provider of property/casualty and life insurance. Focused on markets in Europe and North America the company's general insurance segment offers commercial and personal property/casualty and specialty coverage while its global life segment offers life insurance annuities and other investment policies. Zurich's Farmers Group division offers personal property/casualty insurance policies in the US. The company was founded in 1872.

Operations

Zurich's general insurance segment which accounts for about half of the company's annual premiums and fees provides property/casualty and specialty insurance to a variety of clients. Its global corporate unit focuses on risk management for large international and domestic clients while the Europe general insurance division provides property/casualty and specialty lines for businesses and individuals. In the US Zurich provides commercial and specialty property/casualty policies for small to midsized business customers through its North America commercial unit which includes Zurich American Insurance Company and its subsidiaries.

Zurich's global life segment (40% of premiums and fees) offers life investment pension and savings plans for individuals and groups. Global life operates through regional subsidiaries to provide localized services to its clients. Its businesses include Farmers New World Life in the US Openwork in the UK and other subsidiaries and partnerships in Europe. The division is growing in emerging markets as well.

The company's third major division Farmers Group provides personal auto and homeowners' coverage in the US as well as small business life and specialty insurance policies. Its operating divisions include 21st Century Insurance and Bristol West Holdings.

Geographic Reach

With operations spread around the globe Zurich's general insurance division's core markets include Germany Italy Spain Switzerland the UK and the US in addition to the domestic Swiss market. Other international business units are focused in Latin America the Asia/Pacific region South Africa and other emerging markets.

In 2015 Zurich established a new Global Life Europe Middle East and Africa region which includes it existing Global Life operations in Europe and the Middle East its International Life business on the Isle of Man and the EuroLife Luxembourg business.

Marketing and Sales

All of the Zurich operating segments use a mixture of distribution channels to promote their products. The company has affiliated agents and it also uses independent brokers employee benefits consultants financial advisors and bank representatives to promote its policies. Zurich markets its products to individual commercial and corporate customers.

Financial Performance

Zurich reported a revenue increase of just under 1% to $72.5 billion in 2014 due to growth in net premiums driven by sales of individual savings products in the markets of Spain and Germany; investment gains also contributed to the rise. Net income decreased 3% that year to $3.9 billion due to higher insurance benefits and losses gross of reinsurance.

Cash flow from operations spiked 194% to $5.8 billion in 2014 due to a change in reserves for insurance contracts and movements in receivables and payables.

Strategy

The company's strategy for growth includes targeting corporate mid-market commercial and select retail markets increasing operational efficiency cutting costs and investing for improved returns. At the same time as it is focused on tightening its organization and improving returns in existing markets Zurich is also looking to expand in high-growth emerging markets such as Brazil China Russia Spain Turkey and Taiwan. Zurich has also benefited from its efforts to expand into markets deemed "under-represented." One strategy is to provide niche product offerings to reach targeted customer segments such as expatriates and minority groups. In the US market the Farmers division is working to expand its operations in the eastern states.

While investing in promising markets the group also intends to turn underperforming units around or exit those markets completely. For example in 2014 Zurich sold its general insurance retail business in Russia to OLMA Group for some $23 million.

Mergers and Acquisitions

In 2014 the company acquired a 50% stake in Mediterráneo Seguros Diversos in Spain boosting its general insurance operations even further. It also acquired the rest of Deutscher Herold it didn't already own.

HISTORY

The roots of Zurich Financial Services stretch back to the 1872 founding of a reinsurer for Switzerland Transport Insurance. The company soon branched out into accident travel and workers' compensation insurance and in 1875 it changed its name to Transport and Accident Insurance plc Zurich to reflect the changes. It then expanded into Berlin (the jumping-off point for its expansion into Scandinavia and Russia) and Stuttgart Germany. The company exited marine lines in 1880; it later left the reinsurance business and expanded into liability insurance; in 1894 it changed its name to Zurich General Accident and Liability Insurance.

In 1912 Zurich crossed the Atlantic expanding operations into the US. It agreed in 1925 to provide insurance for Ford cars at favorable terms. Zurich's business was hard hit during the war years of the late 1930s and 1940s. In 1955 the company changed its name to Zurich Insurance.

Starting in the 1960s Zurich began buying other insurers including Alpina (1965 Switzerland) Agrippina (1969 Germany) and Maryland Casualty Group (1989 US). It also bought the property liability operations of American General.

The company shifted its strategy in the early 1990s expanding into what it deemed underrepresented markets in the UK and the US. Being big wasn't enough; Zurich needed to find a focus. It also jettisoned such marginal or unprofitable business lines as commercial fire insurance in Germany.

In 1995 Zurich bought struggling Chicago-based asset manager Kemper and in 1997 bought lackluster mutual fund manager Scudder Stevens & Clark forming Scudder Kemper. That year it also bought failed Hong Kong investment bank Peregrine Investment Holdings.

Zurich merged in 1998 with the financial services businesses of B.A.T Industries formerly known as the British-American Tobacco Co. created in 1902 as a joint venture between UK-based Imperial Tobacco and American Tobacco. As public disapproval of smoking grew in the 1970s British-American Tobacco began diversifying; it changed its name to B.A.T Industries in 1976 and moved into insurance. In 1984 it rescued UK insurer Eagle Star from a hostile offer by German insurance giant Allianz. The next year it bought Hambro Life Assurance renaming it Allied Dunbar. Moving into the large US market in 1988 B.A.T bought Farmers Insurance Group.

While B.A.T battled the antismoking army of the 1990s the insurance industry struggled with stagnant growth. In 1997 Europe's largest insurance firms were named as defendants in class action lawsuits that sought recovery for unpaid claims on Holocaust-era insurance policies. In 1998 Zurich became a founding member of the International Commission on Holocaust Era Insurance Claims (ICHEIC).

Also in 1998 Zurich and B.A.T's insurance units merged to create Zurich Financial Services. The firm reshuffled some of its holdings and sold Eagle Star Reinsurance. In 1999 Zurich spun off its real estate holdings into PSP Swiss Property and at the turn of the century it focused on expansion buying the new business of insurer Abbey Life which it merged into Allied Dunbar. In 2000 the holding companies formed to own Zurich (Zurich Allied and Allied Zurich) were merged into the firm.

EXECUTIVES

Chairman and Interim CEO, Tom de Swaan, age 70
Regional Chairman Europe Middle East and Africa, Axel P. Lehmann, age 56
COO and CTO, Robert Dickie, age 55
CEO Farmer's Group, Jeffrey J. (Jeff) Dailey, age 58
CEO North American Commercial, Mike Foley, age 54
CEO General Insurance and Global Life, Kristof Terryn, age 49
CFO, George Quinn
CEO Global Corporate in North America (GCiNA), Paul Horgan
Chief Risk Officer and Regional Chairman Asia Pacific, Cecilia Reyes, age 57
Chief Investment Officer, Urban Angehrn, age 51
Group General Counsel, Yannick Hausmann
CEO Zurich Insurance Malaysia, Philip Smith
CEO UK Life and Interim CEO Global Life Europe the Middle East and Asia (EMEA), Gary Shaughnessy, age 49
Auditors: PricewaterhouseCoopers AG

LOCATIONS

HQ: Zurich Insurance Group Ltd
Mythenquai 2, Zurich 8002
Phone: (41) 0 625 25 25 **Fax:** (41) 0 625 35 55
Web: www.zurich.com

PRODUCTS/OPERATIONS

2014 Premiums and Fees

	% of total
General Insurance	45
Global Life	42
Farmers	9
Other operations	4
Total	**100**

Selected Subsidiaries

Farmers Group Inc. (property/casualty US)
- 21st Century Insurance Company (property/casualty US)
- Farmers New World Life Insurance Company (life insurance US)
- Foremost Insurance Company (specialty insurance US)
- Bristol West Holdings Inc. (specialty insurance US)
- Zurich American Insurance Company (general insurance US)

Zurich Insurance plc (general insurance UK)
Zurich International Life Limited (life insurance UK)

Selected Acquisitions

COMPETITORS

AEGON
AIG
AXA
Allianz
Aviva
CNA Financial
GEICO
Generali
ING
MetLife
Mitsui Sumitomo Insurance
Prudential
Prudential plc
State Farm
The Hartford
Travelers Companies

HISTORICAL FINANCIALS

Company Type: Public

Income Statement FYE: December 31

	ASSETS ($ mil.)	NET INCOME ($ mil.)	INCOME AS % OF ASSETS	EMPLOYEES
12/14	406,529	3,895	1.0%	54,551
12/13	415,053	4,028	1.0%	55,102
12/12	409,267	3,878	0.9%	52,722
12/11	385,869	3,766	1.0%	52,648
12/10	375,661	3,434	0.9%	54,934
Annual Growth	2.0%	3.2%	—	(0.2%)

2014 Year-End Financials

Return on assets: 0.9%
Return on equity: 11.5%
Long-term debt ($ mil.): —
No. of shares (mil.): 148
Sales ($ mil): 72,569

Dividends
Yield: 6.1%
Payout: 7.3%
Market value ($ mil.): 4,628

	STOCK PRICE ($) FY Close	P/E High	P/E Low	PER SHARE ($) Earnings	Dividends	Book Value
12/14	31.20	1	1	26.08	1.90	234.14
12/13	29.17	1	1	27.22	1.80	220.24
12/12	26.80	1	1	26.31	1.82	234.73
12/11	22.68	1	1	25.61	1.83	216.67
12/10	25.89	1	1	23.44	1.47	220.29
Annual Growth	4.8%	—	—	2.7%	6.6%	1.5%

Hoover's Handbook of

World Business

Executive index

Index of Executives

A

B

C

D

E

F

G

H

I

J

K

L

M

N

U

V

W

X

Y

Z